PUBLICATIONS

OF THE

NAVY RECORDS SOCIETY

VOL. 160

ELIZABETHAN NAVAL ADMINISTRATION

The Navy Records Society was established in 1893 for the purpose of printing unpublished manuscripts and rare works of naval interest. The Society is open to all who are interested in naval history, and any person wishing to become a member should either complete the online application form on the Society's website, www.navyrecords.org.uk, or apply to the Hon. Secretary, The Mill, Stanford Dingley, Reading, RG7 6LS, United Kingdom, email address robinbrodhurst@gmail.com. The annual subscription is £40, which entitles the member to receive one free copy of each work issued by the Society in that year, and to buy earlier issues at much reduced prices.

Subscriptions and orders for back volumes should be sent to the Membership Secretary, 8 Hawthorn Way, Lindford, Hants GU35 0RB.

ELIZABETHAN NAVAL ADMINISTRATION

Edited by

C.S. KNIGHTON
M.A., Ph.D., D.Phil., F.S.A., F.R.Hist.S.

and

DAVID LOADES
M.A., Ph.D., Litt.D., F.S.A., F.R.Hist.S.

PUBLISHED BY ASHGATE
FOR THE NAVY RECORDS SOCIETY
2013

. by
ɛ Publishing Limited
Court East
ıon Road
Farnham, Surrey
GU9 7PT
England

Ashgate Publishing Company
110 Cherry Street
Suite 3–1
Burlington, VT 05401–3818
USA

Ashgate website: http://www.ashgate.com

British Library Cataloguing in Publication Data

Elizabethan naval administration. – (Navy Records
Society publications)
1. Great Britain – History, Naval – Tudors, 1485–1603 – Sources.
2. Great Britain – History – Elizabeth, 1558–1603 – Sources.
3. Great Britain. Royal Navy – History – 16th century – Sources.
I. Series II. Knighton, C. S. III. Loades, D. M.
359'.00941'09031-dc23

Library of Congress Cataloging-in-Publication Data

Elizabethan naval administration / edited by C.S. Knighton and David Loades.
p. cm. – (Navy Records Society publications)
Includes index.
ISBN 978–1–4094–6341–2 (hbk. : alk. paper) – ISBN 978–1–4094–6342–9 (ebook)
1. Great Britain. Royal Navy – History – 16th century – Sources.
2. Great Britain. Royal Navy – Management – History – 16th century.
3. Great Britain – History, Naval – Tudors, 1485–1603.
4. Great Britain – History – Elizabeth, 1558–1603.
I. Knighton, C. S. II. Loades, D. M.
DA86.E42 2013
359.00941'09031–dc23

ISBN 9781409463412 (hbk)
ISBN 9781409463429 (ebk – PDF)
ISBN 9781472406965 (ebk – ePUB)

Printed on acid-free paper

Typeset in Times by Manton Typesetters, Louth, Lincolnshire, UK.

Printed and bound in Great Britain by
TJ International Ltd, Padstow, Cornwall.

CONTENTS

PREFACE

This volume has been designed to stand alongside *The Navy of Edward VI and Mary I* (NRS, Vol. 157, 2011), with which it shares much common apparatus. Two substantial appendices containing details of all RN ships and most senior naval personnel mentioned in both volumes were printed in the first; and certain parts of the technical introduction printed there is repeated here.

Crown copyright material is used by permission of the Controller of Her Majesty's Stationery Office, and the original State Papers were made available to us by the kind assistance of Mr A. H. Lawes. Papers at Hatfield House are printed by permission of the Most Honourable the Marquess of Salisbury. We are grateful to His Lordship's Librarian and Archivist, Mr R. H. Harcourt Williams, for aiding our research. Documents from the British Library, the Bodleian Library, Oxford, and the Pepys Library at Magdalene College, Cambridge, are included by permission of their several custodians, to whom we are indebted for access and guidance in our work. To the British Library, and to the Head of Modern Historical Manuscripts Dr F. Harris, we are in particular grateful for allowing us to print extracts from the Library's online catalogue as an appendix to our own work. Dr R. Luckett helpfully advised us about the provenance of items formerly in his care as Pepys Librarian. We are also appreciative of the research facilities provided by Cambridge University Library and the Suffolk Record Office, Bury St Edmunds. This volume has been produced alongside the Society's edition of the Pepys Library MS 'Fragments of Ancient English Shipwrightry', and we have tried to ensure that these two publications are mutually consistent and supportive. To this end we have been much assisted by Mr R. A. Barker, co-editor of 'Fragments', and by Dr S. L. Adams and Dr S. P. Rose, who have contributed essays respectively on Hawkins's 'Bargains' and nautical terminology for that volume. Dr J. D. Davies has kindly responded to our enquiries. We are obliged to Dr M. Hayward, Director of the AHRC Research Centre for Textile Conservation and Textile Studies, University of Southampton, for advice on fabrics. Miss A. Morgan, Archivist of the City of Plymouth, kindly helped us to identify some civic officials. We also thank Mr M. Birch of Castell Publishing, Miss J. Briody of Goole

Local Studies Library, Miss P. J. Martin, Senior Public Services Officer of the East Riding Archives and Local Studies Service, Miss J. Brookes at Selby Library, and Mrs A. J. L. Meadley for responding to our queries about Suffolk, Yorkshire and Dorset place-names.

Professor Loades is much obliged to the Trustees of the Leverhulme Foundation for the award of an Emeritus Fellowship, which assisted with the research expenses of this volume and our previous one.

ABBREVIATIONS

Books cited here and in the footnotes are published in London or by the issuing societies unless otherwise stated; where London is specified this is to distinguish the edition cited from an American issue with different pagination. Some briefer forms are used in the appendices, as specified in their respective head-notes.

Adams, 'Hawkins bargains'	S. Adams, 'The Hawkins bargains', forthcoming in *FAES*
Anderson	R. C. Anderson (comp.), *List of English Men-of-War, 1509–1649* (SNR Occasional Publication no. 7, 1959) [*entry numbers used for identifying vessels not covered by* Glasgow, 'List']
Andrews, *Last Voyage*	K. R. Andrews (ed.), *The Last Voyage of Drake and Hawkins* (Hakluyt Soc., 2nd ser. Vol. 142, 1972)
APC	J. R. Dasent (ed.) *Acts of the Privy Council of England*, new ser. (1890–1907)
Beaven, *Aldermen*	A. B. Beaven, *The Aldermen of the City of London: from Henry III – 1908* (1908–13)
BIHR	*Bulletin of the Institute of Historical Research* [continued as *Historical Research*]
BL	British Library
BND	J. B. Hattendorf et al. (eds), *British Naval Documents, 1204–1960* (NRS, Vol. 131, 1993)
Bodl.	Bodleian Library, Oxford
Cal. Scot.	*Calendar of the State Papers relating to Scotland and Mary Queen of Scots 1547–1603*
Cat. PL	C. S. Knighton (comp.). *Catalogue of the Pepys Library at Magdalene College, Cambridge*, V, *Manuscripts*, ii, *Modern* (Woodbridge, 1981)
Cat. Rawl.	G. D. Macray (comp.), *Catalogi Codicum Manuscriptorum Bibliothecæ Bodleianæ*, V, i, *Viri Munificentissimi Ricardi Rawlinson … complectens* (Oxford, 1862)

Coleman, 'Artifice or Accident?'	C. Coleman, 'Artifice or accident? The reorganization of the Exchequer of Receipt, *c.* 1554–1572', in C. Coleman and D. R. Starkey (eds), *Revolution Reassessed: Revisions in the History of Tudor Government and Administration* (Oxford, 1986), pp. 163–98
Corbett, *Spanish War*	J. S. Corbett (ed.), *Papers Relating to the Navy during the Spanish War, 1585–1587* (NRS, Vol. II, 1898)
CPR	*Calendar of the Patent Rolls* [including continuation published by List & Index Soc. of which first vols were styled *Draft Calendar*]
CSPD	*Calendar of State Papers, Domestic Series*
CSPDE	*Calendar of State Papers, Domestic Series, Edward VI*, revised edn (1992)
CSPDM	*Calendar of State Papers, Domestic Series, Mary I*, revised edn (1998)
CSPF	*Calendar of State Papers, Foreign Series* [continued as *List and Analysis of State Papers, Foreign Series*]
Dickin, *Brightlingsea*	E. P. Dickin, *A History of Brightlingsea: A Member of the Cinque Ports*, 2nd edn (Brightlingsea, 1939)
Dietz, *Engl. Pub. Finance*	F. C. Dietz, *English Public Finance 1558–1641* (American Historical Association, New York and London, 1932) [repr. as pt 2 of *English Public Finance 1485–1641* (1964)]
Drake, *Hasted's Kent*	H. F. Drake (ed.), *Hasted's History of Kent*, pt 1, *The Hundred of Blackheath* (1886) [only part of revised edn of E. Hasted, *A History and Topographical Survey of the County of Kent* (orig. Canterbury, 1778–99); with (pp 40–43) extracts from Deptford parish registers]
EcHR	*Economic History Review*
EHR	*English Historical Review*
Elton, *Tudor Revolution*	G. R. Elton, *The Tudor Revolution in Government: A Study of Administrative Changes in the Reign of Henry VIII* (Cambridge, 1953)
Elton, 'War in the Receipt'	G. R. Elton, 'The Elizabethan Exchequer: war in the Receipt', originally in S. T. Bindoff, J. Hurstfield and C. H. Williams (eds), *Elizabethan Government and Society: Essays Presented to Sir*

	John Neale (1961), pp. 213–48; repr. Elton, *Studies in Tudor and Stuart Politics and Government* (Cambridge, 1974–92), i, pp. 355–88
EPNS	English Place-Name Society
EPNS, *Essex*	P. H. Reaney, *The Place-Names of Essex* (EPNS, XII, 1935)
EPNS, *Glos.*	A. H. Smith, *The Place-Names of Gloucestershire* (EPNS, XXXVIII–XLI, 1964–65)
EPNS, *Surrey*	J. E. B. Glover, A. Mawer and F. M. Stenton, with A. Bonner, *The Place-Names of Surrey* (EPNS, XI, 1934)
EPNS, *Sussex*	A. Mawer and F. M. Stenton, with J. E. B. Glover, *The Place-Names of Sussex* (EPNS, VII, 1930)
EPNS, *Yorkshire WR*	A. H. Smith, *The Place-Names of the West Riding of Yorkshire* (EPNS, XXX–XXXVII, 1961–63)
FAES	R. A. Barker and C. S. Knighton (eds), *Fragments of Ancient English Shipwrightry* (NRS, forthcoming) [edition of PL 2820]
GEC, *Baronetage*	G. E. Cokayne, *The Complete Baronetage* (Exeter, 1900–9)
GEC, *Peerage*	G. E. Cokayne, *The Complete Peerage*, ed. V. Gibbs, H. A. Doubleday, Lord Howard de Walden and P. W. Hammond (London and Stroud, 1910–98)
Glasgow, 'List'	T. Glasgow, jnr, 'List of ships in the Royal Navy from 1539 to 1588 – the Navy from its infancy to the defeat of the Spanish Armada', *MM*, LVI (1970), pp. 299–307
Glasgow, 'Maturing'	T. Glasgow, jnr, 'Maturing of naval administration, 1556–1564', *MM*, LVI (1970), pp. 3–23
Glasgow, 'Royal Navy'	T. Glasgow, jnr, 'The Royal Navy at the start of the reign of Elizabeth', *MM*, LI (1965), pp. 73–6
Gunson, 'Family of Gunson'	W. N. Gunson, 'The family of Gunson or Gonson of London and Essex', *Family History*, VIII, nos 46/47, new ser. nos 22/23 (1974), pp. 133–45
Hakluyt	R. Hakluyt, *The Principal Navigations Voyages Traffiques & Discoveries of the English Nation*, ed. Sir W. Raleigh (Glasgow, 1903–5)

Hammer, *Elizabeth's Wars*	P. E. J. Hammer, *Elizabeth's Wars: War, Government and Society in Tudor England, 1544–1604* (Basingstoke, 2003)
HBC	F. M. Powicke and E. B. Fryde (eds), *Handbook of British Chronology* (RHS Guides and Handbooks no. 2; 2nd edn, 1961)
Heal, *Goldsmiths*	A. Heal, *The London Goldsmiths, 1200–1800: A Record of the Names and Addresses of the Craftsmen, their Shop-signs and Trade-cards* (Cambridge, 1935; repr. Newton Abbot, 1972)
Hist. Parl.	*The History of Parliament.* S. T. Bindoff, *The House of Commons, 1509–1558* (1982); P. W. Hasler, *The House of Commons, 1558–1603* (1981)
HJ	*The Historical Journal*
HMC	Historical Manuscripts Commission
HMC, *Bath*, v	G. Dyfnallt Owen (ed.), *Calendar of the Manuscripts of the Most Honourable the Marquess of Bath, preserved at Longleat, Wiltshire,* v, *Talbot, Dudley and Devereux Papers, 1533–1659* (HMC 58, 1980)
HMC, *Pepys*	E. K. Purnell (ed.), *Report on the Pepys Manuscripts, preserved at Magdalene College, Cambridge* (HMC, 1911)
HMC, *Salisbury*	*Calendar of the Manuscripts of the Most Hon. the Marquis of Salisbury, K.G., etc., preserved at Hatfield House, Hertfordshire* (HMC, 1883–1976)
Inv. Hen. VIII	D. R. Starkey (ed.), *The Inventory of King Henry VIII: Society of Antiquaries MS 129 and British Library MS Harley 149. The Transcript* (1998)
Kelsey, *Hawkins*	H. Kelsey, *Sir John Hawkins: Queen Elizabeth's Slave Trader* (2003)
Kenny, *Elizabeth's Admiral*	K. R. Kenny, *Elizabeth's Admiral: The Political Career of Charles Howard, Earl of Nottingham 1536–1624* (Baltimore and London, 1970)
L&ASPF	*List and Analysis of State Papers Foreign Series* (1964–) [continuation of *Calendar of State Papers, Foreign Series*]
Laughton, *Armada*	J. K. Laughton (ed.), *State Papers relating to the Defeat of the Spanish Armada*, anno *1588* (NRS, Vols 1–2, 1894)

Lewis, 'Armada Guns II'	M. Lewis, 'Armada guns: a comparative study of English and Spanish armaments. Section II. The guns of the Queen's ships, 1569–99', *MM*, XXVIII (1942), pp. 104–7
Loades, *Conspiracies*	D. M. Loades, *Two Tudor Conspiracies* (Cambridge, 1965)
Loades, *Tudor Navy*	D. M. Loades, *The Tudor Navy: An Administrative, Political and Military History* (Aldershot, 1992)
'Lord Admiral Lisle'	C. S. Knighton and D. M. Loades, 'Lord Admiral Lisle and the invasion of Scotland 1544', in S. P. Rose (ed.), *The Naval Miscellany VII* (NRS, Vol. 153, 2008), pp. 56–96
LP	J. S. Brewer, J. Gairdner and R. H. Brodie (eds), *Letters and Papers, Foreign and Domestic, of the Reign of Henry VIII* (1862–1932) [cited by entry number]
McDermott, *Frobisher*	J. McDermott, *Martin Frobisher: Elizabethan Privateer* (2001)
Machyn, *Diary*	J. G. Nichols (ed.), *The Diary of Henry Machyn, Citizen and Merchant-Taylor of London, from A.D. 1550 to A.D. 1563* (Camden Soc. [1st ser.], XLII, 1848)
MM	*The Mariner's Mirror*
Monson, *Tracts*	M. Oppenheim (ed.), *The Naval Tracts of Sir William Monson* (NRS, Vols 22–3, 43, 45, 47, 1902–14)
NEM	C. S. Knighton and D. Loades (eds), *The Navy of Edward VI and Mary I* (NRS, Vol. 157, 2011) [companion to the present volume]
NRS	Navy Records Society
ODNB	H. C. G. Matthew and B. Harrison (eds), *Oxford Dictionary of National Biography* (Oxford, 2004) [print edn periodically updated online]
OED	*The Oxford English Dictionary*
Oppenheim, *History*	M. Oppenheim, *A History of the Administration of the Royal Navy and of Merchant Shipping in relation to the Navy from 1509 to 1660 with an Introduction treating of the preceding Period* (1896; repr. Aldershot, 1988)
Oppenheim, *Naval Accounts Hen. VII*	M. Oppenheim (ed.), *Naval Accounts and Inventories of the Reign of Henry VII, 1485–8 and 1495–7* (NRS, Vol. 8, 1896)

Part. Friends	G. de la Bédoyère (ed.), *Particular Friends: The Correspondence of Samuel Pepys and John Evelyn* (Woodbridge, 1997)
Pepys, *Diary*	R. C. Latham and W. Matthews (eds), *The Diary of Samuel Pepys* (1970–83)
Pepys, *Navy White Book*	R. C. Latham (ed.), *Samuel Pepys and the Second Dutch War: Pepys's Navy White Book and Brooke House Papers* (NRS, Vol. 133, 1995)
Pett, *Autobiography*	W. G. Perrin (ed.), *The Autobiography of Phineas Pett* (NRS, Vol. 51, 1918)
PL	Pepys Library, Magdalene College, Cambridge
Pollitt, 'Rationality and expedience'	R. Pollitt, 'Rationality and expedience in the growth of Elizabethan naval administration', in R. W. Love, jnr (ed.), *Changing Interpretations and New Sources in Naval History: Papers from the Third United States Naval Academy Symposium* (New York and London, 1980), pp. 68–79
RHS	Royal Historical Society
Rodger, *Safeguard*	N. A. M. Rodger, *The Safeguard of the Sea: A Naval History of Britain 660–1649* (1997)
Sainty, *Exchequer Officers*	J. C. Sainty (comp.), *Officers of the Exchequer* (List & Index Soc., special series, no. 18, 1983)
SNR	Society for Nautical Research
TCBS	*Transactions of the Cambridge Bibliographical Society*
TRP	P. L. Hughes and J. F. Larkin (eds), *Tudor Royal Proclamations* (1969)
TRHS	*Transactions of the Royal Historical Society*
Wallenberg, *Place-Names of Kent*	J. K. Wallenberg, *The Place-Names of Kent* (Uppsala, 1934)
Williamson, *Hawkins* (1927)	J.A. Williamson, *Sir John Hawkins: The Time and the Man* (Oxford, 1927)

Manuscript Sources

All documents printed in this volume or cited in the footnotes are, except where otherwise stated, in the National Archives (formerly and now incorporating the Public Record Office); they are identified by the following departmental abbreviations:

AO 1	Auditors of the Imprest and Commissioners of Audit, Declared Accounts (in Rolls)
C 66	Chancery, Patent Rolls
E 351	Exchequer, Pipe Office, Declared Accounts (in Rolls)
E 404	Exchequer of Receipt, Warrants for Issues
PROB 11	Prerogative Court of Canterbury, Registered Wills
PSO 2	Privy Seal Office, Signet and other Warrants
SP 1	State Papers, Domestic, Henry VIII
SP 12	State Papers, Domestic, Elizabeth I
SP 15	State Papers, Domestic, Addenda, Edward VI to James I

Other Repositories Cited by Abbreviation

Bodl.	Bodleian Library, Oxford
PL	Pepys Library, Magdalene College, Cambridge

Other Abbreviations and Symbols

d.	died
wef	with effect from

* Indicates MS annotations to the original documents, as more specifically explained in the head-notes of the items concerned.

\# Used before cross-reference between certain entries in **4** and **5**.

Some further abbreviations are applied locally.

INTRODUCTION

Although Elizabeth's Navy has been a subject of enduring interest to scholars and the general public over the years, no general selection from the large body of surviving documents has previously been published. The Navy Records Society devoted its first two and another of its earliest volumes to the Armada and subsequent events of the Spanish war,[1] but the nearest to a comprehensive view of Elizabethan naval administration and finance came in the Society's centenary volume.[2] It is therefore appropriate to return to this field, particularly (but not exclusively) in the earlier years of the reign when there was no formal war. Between 1558 and 1585 the Navy was deployed variously in small-scale campaigns (such as those in Scotland in 1560, at Le Havre in 1563, and Smerwick in 1580), in the pursuit of pirates and in making occasional shows of force. Although the present work relates to such operations, its emphasis is primarily on the financial and administrative processes which supported them, covering such aspects as mustering, victualling and demobilisation as well as the repair and maintenance of the ships themselves. The general content is therefore closer to that of another of the Society's pioneering volumes, which presented similar though less detailed evidence from the reign of Henry VII.[3]

This collection is the second of two dealing with Tudor naval administration, the first of which was concerned with the Navy of Edward VI and Mary I, encompassing the first phase under the management instituted by Henry VIII at the end of his reign. The present volume opens with two foundation documents for the Elizabethan Navy – the first ship list, and the first ordinances for the Admiralty officers. The centrepiece is Benjamin Gonson's massive Quarter Book for 1562–63, which covers (among much else) the preparations for the Le Havre campaign. Although we have deliberately chosen not to make any additions to the Society's

[1]J. K. Laughton (ed.), *State Papers Relating to the Defeat of the Spanish Armada,* anno *1588* (NRS, Vols 1–2, 1894). J. S. Corbett (ed.), *Papers Relating to the Navy during the Spanish War, 1585–1587* (NRS, Vol. 11, 1898).

[2]J. B. Hattendorf et al. (eds), *British Naval Documents, 1204–1960* (NRS, Vol. 131, 1993) [hereafter *BND*], Part II: 1485–1603, ed. N. A. M. Rodger and D. Loades.

[3]M. Oppenheim (ed.), *Naval Accounts and Inventories of the Reign of Henry VII, 1485–8 and 1495–7* (NRS, Vol. 8, 1896).

substantial dossier on the Armada,[1] the discovery of one hitherto unnoticed item from 1590–91 became the basis for a final section illustrating the organisation behind one of the post-Armada operations. The documents are drawn primarily from the Public Record Office, the Pepys Library at Magdalene College, Cambridge, and those parts of Pepys's collection which eventually found their way into the Rawlinson MSS at the Bodleian Library in Oxford. We have also been able to reconstruct some of documents from the Cotton MSS in the British Library by using copies made for Pepys before the fire which wrecked the originals.[2]

Elizabeth inherited a war with France into which England had been drawn through Mary's marriage to Philip of Spain. The end of the Anglo-Spanish monarchy allowed the country to disengage from a conflict in which it had no independent aims, and which had gone badly. The consequences of Mary's French war nevertheless shaped the military and naval strategy of Elizabeth's early years, and in the longer term impacted even more significantly on English defence policy. The loss of Calais in January 1558 had removed the last English possession on the European mainland. It completed the long process by which the frontiers of the Crown's dominion withdrew from the middle of France to the English Channel. That seaway was thereafter a moat rather than a highway, and the Navy, which to the medieval kings had been primarily an agency for transporting themselves and their troops to the Continent, became a front-line defence force in its own right. It had been partly in recognition of this strategic evolution that Henry VIII had created his standing Navy and the infrastructure to sustain it: from the building of the Thames storehouses, so prominently featured below (1512–13), to the setting up of the independent naval department with whose records we are chiefly concerned, the Council for Marine Causes (1546).[3] Over the same period

[1]Laughton's collection has now been supplemented by S. Adams, 'The Armada correspondence in Cotton MSS Otho E VII and E IX', in M. Duffy (ed.), *The Naval Miscellany, Volume VI* (NRS, Vol. 146, 2003), pp. 37–92.

[2]The Cotton library was badly damaged by a fire at Ashburnham House, Westminster, on 23 October 1731. Many volumes lost the edges of each page, and further cropping was inevitable during conservation. Dr Adams's contribution to *Miscellany VI* drew attention to the value of the Pepysian copies in supplying the lost sections of Cotton texts.

[3]For the development of naval administration, see generally M. Oppenheim, *A History of the Administration of the Royal Navy and of Merchant Shipping in relation to the Navy from 1509 to 1660 with an Introduction treating of the preceding Period* (1896; repr. Aldershot, 1988); C. F. Richmond, 'English naval power in the fifteenth century', *History*, LII (1967), pp. 1–15; C. S. L. Davies, 'The administration of the Navy under Henry VIII: the origins of the Navy Board', *EHR*, LIII (1965), pp. 268–83; T. Glasgow, jnr, 'Maturing of naval administration, 1556–1564', *MM*, LVI, (1970), pp. 3–23; D. Loades, *The Tudor Navy: An Administrative, Political and Naval History* (Aldershot, 1992) and *The Making of the Elizabethan Navy: From the Solent to the Armada* (Woodbridge, 2009); N. A. M. Rodger, *The Safeguard of the Sea: A Naval History of Great Britain*, i, *660–1649* (1997).

the old pattern of dynastic warfare, characterised by complex treaties of brief duration and the chivalric overtones of aristocratic sport, was being replaced by ideological conflict focused on acceptance or rejection of papal authority over the church.[1] This had involved England as soon as Henry himself broke with Rome in the 1530s, and for the first time in centuries the country faced a real threat of assault on its shores. That moment arrived with the action which saw the loss of Henry's *Mary Rose* in July 1545. The prospect of invasion masquerading as crusade became more enduring when a specifically Protestant settlement was established in 1549 and, although the country was only briefly at war during Edward's reign, the Navy had been kept in repair and in commission. Although the invasion scare subsided with the accession of a Catholic ruler in 1553, Mary had done nothing to alter the priorities of the Marine Council established by her father. Her husband regarded the English Navy as a potential asset for his own wars, and had no desire to see it reduced or mothballed.[2] Eventually, in 1557, he managed to involve England in his own quarrel with France and the papacy. Meanwhile, at the start of that year, the Privy Council made important changes in the procedures of the Marine Council: overall responsibility was placed in the hands of the Lord Treasurer, with an ordinary or budget set at £14,000 a year, and the Surveyor-General of Victualling instructed to account separately.[3] The ordinary was, however, put on hold for the duration of the war. Although peace negotiations were already under way when Mary died in November 1558, the Navy was in good condition and at full strength. About forty ships were in commission and several of them were still at sea on 17 November as the new reign began. Elizabeth was no more interested in ships than her sister had been, but she had very different priorities for ensuring her country's security. Mary had rested it on the Habsburg alliance, but Elizabeth was set on restoring England's independence. By reintroducing a Protestant church she exposed it to the same dangers which had existed before Mary's accession. This meant maintaining a strong Navy, and that was the advice given to the Queen unanimously by her Privy Council and her powerful secretary Sir William Cecil.

In March 1559, with the war obviously coming to an end (peace was signed at Cateau-Cambrésis in April) and all campaigning suspended, the

[1]Cf. G. R. Elton, 'War and the English in the reign of Henry VIII', in L. Freedman et al. (eds), *War, Strategy and International Politics: Essays in Honour of Sir Michael Howard* (Oxford, 1992), p. 1 and sources cited in nn. 2–4.

[2]*CSPDM*, nos 230, 447. D. Loades, 'Philip II and the Government of England', in C. Cross et al. (eds), *Law and Government under the Tudors: Essays Presented to Sir Geoffrey Elton, Regius Professor of Modern History in the University of Cambridge, on the Occasion of his Retirement* (Cambridge, 1988), pp. 191–2.

[3]*APC 1556–8*, p. 39. *BND*, pp. 70–71. *NEM*, pp. 309–10.

Privy Council decided to take stock of the Navy, and to formulate some kind of a long-term policy for what was obviously going to be England's principal military arm for the foreseeable future. The result was 'The Book of Sea Causes', dated 24 March, which has been printed in the Society's centenary volume *British Naval Documents*.[1] The survey began by listing of 22[2] of the Queen's own ships 'meet to be kept and preserved' and a further 10 'very much worn' which could not continue in service without extensive repair. It was recommended that the latter should be sold as soon as peace was established; but for the present 'doubtful time' they remained on the active list. Several smaller royal vessels also existed though not named here. It was estimated that in time of war the Queen's ships could be supplemented by 45 hired merchantmen, and served by 20 small vessels as victuallers. Various policy statements then follow. In peacetime, Gillingham Water was 'the meetest harbour' for the Queen's ships; in time of war, after being 'perfectly grounded and rigged' in the Thames, the fleet should be sent to Portsmouth. Finally the shape of the future Navy is laid out. A total of 30 vessels was thought sufficient for the Queen to have of her own, and could be 'brought to this perfection'[3] within five years. This notional fleet was rated by burthen (24 ships, from one of 800 tuns down to six of 200 tuns, with four barks of 60/80 tuns and two pinnaces of 40). The policy was never strictly adhered to, and seems not to have been formally adopted, but it provided basic guidance for the next 20 years. Between 1559 and 1580 over 20 ships of 100 tuns and more were either built, rebuilt or purchased, and a similar number of smaller vessels.[4] Over the same time some fourteen large ships were taken out of service, and two were lost, the smaller ships showing a slightly higher turnover. The advent of Elizabeth therefore showed no sharp break with the past.

Although England did not officially go to war until 1585, there was no longer any such thing as complete peace – at least as far as the Navy was concerned. During the Scottish intervention of 1560 a squadron commanded by William Winter blockaded the Firth of Forth, and the Navy was heavily involved in the Le Havre campaign of 1562–63. In the first undertaking the

[1]As no. 38 (pp. 62–70), from SP 12/3, no. 44 (*CSPD 1547–80*, p. 126).

[2]*BND* omits *Tiger* 160 tuns 120 men (after *Bull*). The total tonnage stated is 5,510 (not 1,510 as printed); the MS figures actually add to 5,470 because *Brigantine*'s tonnage is given as '*nulla*' in the tonnage column, but this is known from other sources to be 40, and with it included the MS total is correct. The total of men is correctly stated as 3,890 (not 3,880 as printed).

[3]Not 'their perfection' as *BND* (p. 69).

[4]T. Glasgow, Jnr, 'List of ships in the Royal Navy from 1539 to 1588 – the Navy from its infancy to the defeat of the Spanish Armada', *MM*, LVI (1970), pp. 299–307 and (for ships mentioned in this volume) fuller details in *NEM*, Appendix 1 (pp. 455–523).

Navy played a vital role thwarting a French takeover in Scotland, an achievement well recognised by contemporaries and later commentators.[1] The operation is featured only in passing here [**13**]. Rather more will be found about the Le Havre expedition [**4** *passim*];[2] indeed the Declared Account here printed [**5**] was subject to special scrutiny as part of a general examination of military spending in the aftermath of what had proved a disastrous undertaking. Ironically the success of the Scottish campaign had encouraged Elizabeth's government to a second adventure, directed this time at the mainland of France. Many English Protestants were keen to take the side of their Huguenot co-religionists in the civil war which was now beginning in France. Elizabeth and Cecil were at first unwilling to become involved, but when the Huguenots seized Le Havre and offered it to England in return for support, a new prospect emerged. England did not envisage permanent occupation of the port, but saw it as a pledge which might be exchanged for Calais if the Huguenots won the war outright or forced the French government to make concessions. The ensuing campaign involved virtually the whole of Elizabeth's fleet, though its role was essentially that of troop-carrier and purveyor. Such naval fighting as there was did not go well. Two ships were lost in action and two others by accident on active service, though the Navy's ranks were temporarily swelled by fifteen small vessels seized just before the evacuation. As with the attempt to relieve Calais in 1558, the operation was bedevilled by foul weather. Still more devastating was an outbreak of bubonic plague which spread rapidly through the fleet, and was then carried back home by those who had not died aboard. Even without these complications it is unlikely that the English could have secured their position against superior French firepower. These factors rather than any deficiency in the ships or their command adequately explain the decision to withdraw. The only useful outcome was to make of Elizabeth very wary of repeating the mistake, and it would be two decades before she again sent troops into a European theatre.

There were always still ships at sea; sometimes endeavouring (officially at least) to catch pirates: sometimes escorting fishing or merchant fleets, sometimes carrying diplomatic missions, and sometimes simply patrolling.

[1]See T. Glasgow jnr, 'The Navy in the first Elizabethan undeclared war, 1559–1560', *MM*, LIV (1968), esp. p. 36: 'during the long reign of Elizabeth I, her ships saw more spectacular service … but never was the royal navy more competent or effective than in this affair'.

[2]The English called Le Havre 'Newhaven', and the name is often still used in historical writing. We have retained it as such where it occurs in the texts, but use the modern French name elsewhere. The naval events of the campaign are most fully described in T. Glasgow, jnr, 'The Navy in the French wars of Mary and Elizabeth I. Part III. The Navy in the Le Havre expedition, 1562–1564', *MM*, LIV (1968), pp. 281–96. The political and diplomatic background is discussed in W. T. MacCaffrey, 'The Newhaven expedition, 1562–1563', *HJ*, XL (1997), pp. 1–21.

Royal ships were occasionally provided for trading expeditions as the Queen's investment in the enterprise; the Quarter Book reflects these ventures only incidentally, mentioning repairs for ships which met misfortune on the way to Guinea [**4** (p. 213)]. Other ventures were more directly aggressive (and even piratical). It was while engaged in such a mission that the veteran *Jesus of Lübeck*, rebuilt in 1563 [**4** (p. 85)], was eventually lost at San Juan d'Ulloa in 1568. At times of high political tension, the Navy was put on alert; operational costs and victualling costs were estimated, and supplies collected.[1] The estimates from 1574 [**30**] and 1579 [**19**] have to be seen in this context, although no major operation was mounted in either year.

The direction of naval policy owed much to continuity of personnel in the Marine Council. Here also there had been no sharp break with the past. At Elizabeth's accession William Winter, Benjamin Gonson and Edward Baeshe remained in post as, respectively, Surveyor of the Navy, Treasurer, and Surveyor-General of naval victualling, though Baeshe's function was soon to be redefined. Richard Howlett, the Clerk of the Ships, stood down in 1560, and was replaced by Winter's brother, George. William Broke, the Clerk Comptroller, died in 1561 and William Holstock, hitherto Keeper of the Storehouses, was appointed in his place. Sir William Woodhouse remained as Vice-Admiral (*alias* Lieutenant of the Admiralty), though when he died in 1565 his office was discontinued for the rest of the Tudor period.[2] Thereafter the Council turnover was slow. Gonson served until his death in 1577, when he was succeeded by his son-in-law John Hawkins. George Winter was replaced by William Borough in 1580. Both Baeshe and William Winter died in office, the former in 1587 and the latter in 1589, by which time he was the last surviving link between the Pinkie campaign of 1547 and the Armada. Shortly before the 'Book of Sea Causes' was drawn up, Elizabeth reactivated the Privy Council's decision of 1557, and on 11 March 1559 she issued a warrant dormant fixing the naval ordinary at £12,000;[3] this

[1]Cf. *BND*, pp. 103–8, in addition to documents reproduced here.

[2]For Woodhouse's functions in this capacity, see T. Glasgow, jnr, 'Vice-Admiral Woodhouse and shipkeeping in the Tudor Navy', *MM*, LXIII, (1977), pp. 253–63. The office was revived in 1604, and survives today as the purely ceremonial appointment of Vice-Admiral of the United Kingdom, in the Royal Household: M. Lewis, *England's Sea Officers: The Story of the Naval Profession* (1939), pp. 161–4. For Cecil's purpose in abolishing the post at this point, see R. Pollitt, 'Rationality and expedience in the growth of Elizabethan Naval Administration', in R. W. Love, jnr (ed.), *Changing Interpretations and New Sources in Naval History* (New York, 1980), pp. 68–79, and S. Adams, 'The Hawkins bargains and naval shipbuilding', forthcoming in R. A. Barker and C. S. Knighton (eds), *Fragments of Ancient English Shipwrightry* (NRS, forthcoming) [hereafter *FAES*].

[3]The original warrant is not extant, but it is repeatedly cited in the accounts, e.g. **4** (p. 23), and **5** (p. 526).

was £2,000 short of the figure sought by the Admiralty [**1**]. The Lord Treasurer's supervisory role seems to have been abandoned, because the ordinances of *c.* 1560, which specify exact procedures for the conduct of every office, mention him only in a limited capacity.[1] Every officer is accountable, directly or indirectly, to the Lord Admiral. In 1565 the Surveyor-General's victualling operations were put on a contract basis [**28**] and a standard allowance was made to him for every man at sea or in harbour – 5d a day for the former, 4½d for the latter. A victualling schedule current in 1568, setting out the daily rations for each man, had been drawn up a quarter of a century earlier,[2] but prices had moved on since then and Baeshe was always struggling to provide within the allowances. Nevertheless he contrived both to retain a reputation for honesty and to die a fairly rich man. His success can be measured from the crescendo of complaint provoked by his successor, James Quarles.

Placing the victualling upon a contract basis had a number of consequences. Purveyance as a prerogative right was abandoned, although not at once, and thereafter Baeshe's local deputies and commissioners had to buy in the open market; hence his plea for extra allowances in the 'dear year' of 1574. Cecil's intention was to establish a quota system which would enable counties to calculate their liability in advance. He began to do this after 1572 when, as Lord Burghley and Lord Treasurer, he assumed overall responsibility for the Navy. However, it was an uphill task against much local resistance and was not finally accomplished until about 1590.[3] What this meant (in theory at least) was that every time a victualling commission was issued, each county was due to provide so many bushels of wheat, so many cheese, so many beeves, and so on. Both the quantities and the particular commodities varied from county to county, but it was the responsibility of the Justices of the Peace in each shire or city to make sure that the quotas were met, and delivered to Baeshe's deputies at a given time and place. Needless to say, the practice often fell far short of the theory.[4] Elizabeth liked contracts, because they were ways of making expenditure more predictable, and also of cushioning the effects of random price rises. She also disliked the ordinary and reduced it, first to

[1]That is, as Treasurer of the Exchequer, as below, p. 3 n. 5. But cf. **4** (p. 451), for an instance of the Lord Treasurer acting along with the Navy administrators.

[2]PL 1266, p. 251 (copy made 1568 and dated 34 Henry VIII [1542/3]). Printed from a 17th-cent. copy (Bodl. MS Rawlinson C. 846, pp. 132–3) in *BND*, pp. 102–3.

[3]Shortly before he retired, in January 1587, Baeshe had drawn up a schedule 'declaring out of what shire the wheat, malt, oxen, butter and cheese is to be had': *BND*, pp. 109–11. See also A. Woodworth, 'Purveyance for the Royal Household in the reign of Queen Elizabeth', *Transactions of the American Philosophical Society*, new ser. XXXV, i (Philadelphia, 1945).

[4]Loades, *Tudor Navy*, pp. 205–7.

£10,000 a year and then to £5,714. This did not mean that the Navy was getting cheaper, but simply that more money was being provided by occasional warrants. The great advantage of this from the Queen's point of view was that it meant that warrants could be drawn on whatever revenue source happened to be available, whereas the ordinary was always paid out of the Exchequer.[1] Elizabeth was not exactly mean when it came to the Navy – she could not afford to be – but she was always looking for economies, and perhaps the most controversial of these were Hawkins's 'bargains' which were introduced in 1579. These were modelled on Baeshe's contract of 1565, and specified that each contracted officer should perform specified duties in return for a fixed payment.

This was rather like the system used for farming the customs revenues. Hawkins himself, for example, contracted to maintain (but not repair) 25 ships for £1,200 a year. The master shipwrights Peter Pett and Matthew Baker at the same time contracted to ground and grave the ships at regular intervals, and to carry out specified repairs, in return for £1,000 a year.[2] Inevitably disputes arose almost at once, as contracted officers endeavoured to shift work to their uncontracted colleagues, or on to each other. The shipwrights in particular accused Hawkins of every kind of fraud and malfeasance, and it is likely that the itemised savings of £8,100 a year [**19**] were always more notional than real. A subsequent enquiry exonerated Hawkins, but as pressure built on the Admiralty after 1582, with the threat of war looming the system was abandoned [**20–23**]. The friction and bad feeling which it must have generated in any case heavily outweighed any slight financial advantage.[3] The intention was that each contractor should make a profit, and save the Exchequer money at the same time, but, like most such schemes, it was overambitious. In 1575 there were 28 ships recorded in service. Between 1580 and 1592 a further 18 ships of over 100 tuns were added, and in 1589 the total number listed was 44 [**37**]. The Armada had proved the supreme test. Each side assembled, armed and victualled about 140 ships. It took Philip two years to mobilise and equip his fleet, at a cost of over 2 million ducats (about £700,000), while Elizabeth mobilised her response in six months, at not much more than a quarter of the cost. Whatever may be said about the fighting, the advantages of home waters, or the fact that the English twice ran out of ammunition, the contrast is very striking. In spite of all its failings, the Admiralty vindicated itself triumphantly on that occasion.

[1]See below, Introduction to Section V, p. 564.

[2]SP 12/132, no. 42 (*CSPD 1547–80*, p. 634); to be printed in *FAES*.

[3]Loades, *Tudor Navy*, pp. 184–5. S. Adams, 'New light on the "Reformation" of John Hawkins: the Ellesmere naval survey of January 1584', *EHR*, CV (1990), pp. 96–111, and 'Hawkins bargains'.

That exceptional achievement was built upon the settled practices of calmer times. When ships were out of commission their guns and rigging had to be stored, and the ships themselves looked after on a care and maintenance basis. They had to be regularly surveyed, careened and repaired, whether they were in service or not. This in turn meant employing a great variety of clerks, craftsmen and workmen, who had to be paid, fed and sometimes housed. It also meant procuring all manner of supplies, either through the Crown's own agencies or by contracting with merchants. There were always some ships under repair, and any new building made exceptional demands for all these requirements. The maintenance and extension of store installations required further men and material, albeit on a much smaller scale. When ships were required for action, they had to be rigged and armed, and crews had to be recruited, mustered, paid and brought to the points of embarkation. Masters, mariners, gunners, soldiers, shipwrights, caulkers and labourers had to be found all over southern England and Wales, using a network of commissioners and other agents, and local officers had to be persuaded, or bribed, to co-operate. The crew of a large ship was a complex community, because under the captain and master served a variety of under-officers, from the master gunner to the cook, as well as experienced and inexperienced seamen, gromets (youths under 18) and boys (under 14).[1] When a ship returned from active service its crew was paid off, and provided with money to 'conduct' them to their places of origin. Every mariner needed a certificate of discharge, and ships which had been requisitioned had to be similarly paid off and discharged. Skeleton crews were used to move warships from one anchorage to another, and some masters and seamen specialised in this kind of work. When a ship was laid up, shipkeepers had to be appointed, and properly supervised. It had been the lack of such supervision which had caused the loss of the *Edward* (ex *Great Harry*) in 1553.[2]

Deptford was by this time the main store and dockyard, with similar facilities at Woolwich and Portsmouth. Gillingham was the principal anchorage, and there were minor outposts at Rye and Harwich, and at Brightlingsea on the River Colne. Occasionally royal ships were serviced at Newcastle, Bristol or Dover, but there were no permanent facilities there. The naval dockyards were the largest industrial organisation in the land, and needed a huge and relentless intake of materials. Cordage and

[1]These were the notional age brackets, though the accounts show some individuals variously occurring as 'boy', gromet' and 'mariner' outside the natural progression, suggesting that the grades were not always strictly applied, or that payment sometimes reflected function rather than age. Cf. Index *s.a.* Butler, Thomas; Fletcher, Francis.

[2]See below [**1**] and *NEM*, p. 487.

canvas was generally bought in large quantities from City merchants such as Alderman Christopher Draper, and ferried down to Deptford for distribution. The royal forests in Kent and Sussex provided some of the timber required, and the Navy had only to pay for it to be felled and carted to the yards where it was needed. But these local supplies were not enough, and wood was also brought down from as far away as Yorkshire. Specialist timber such as masts and deals came mostly from the Baltic, and had to be bought from the shippers. Ironwork was mainly to be had from regular suppliers close to the yards, though a Staffordshire man was also used. The yards consumed a prodigious quantity of nails and bolts of all sorts, as well as more complex fittings. Lead, glass, wickerwork and leather were also constantly needed, as well as animal hair (for caulking) and burning reed (for cleansing hulls of weed and encrustacea). Many tradesmen must have been kept in business by these requirements; the dockyard industry thereby sustained employment well beyond the direct workforce. One of the Navy's more unlikely agents was the supplier of spades and shovels, John Benbow, who doubled as a singer in Elizabeth's chapel. There was as yet no cat on the Admiralty establishment,[1] so an essential purchase was the rat poison provided by Roger Cratway (who was also the cook of the *Mary Rose*).

The Keeper of the 'Great Storehouse' at Deptford was a senior officer only just below the level of the Principal Officers; like them he held office by patent and was paid directly from the Exchequer. Each dockyard had a small regular staff of clerks, subordinate storekeepers, clerks and purveyors paid quarterly by the Navy Treasurer. The much larger numbers of craftsmen and labourers and shipkeepers were hired as they were needed. Payment was reckoned by day, night or tide, and graded according to status. Many of the men were employed from time to time in different capacities, and might be moved from yard to yard, or even to serve aboard ship.[2] If ship repairs had to be undertaken at one of the outports, such as Bristol or Plymouth, then shipwrights travelled from Portsmouth or Deptford to oversee it. But men appearing in one place as dockyard carpenters or shipwrights might serve another time as ship's carpenters, or as caulkers or mere labourers. All those listed as watchmen had other jobs. Many of the yard workers also feature as suppliers, and some of the local men (or their wives) are paid for lodging their itinerant colleagues. In consequence the overall number on the payroll was a good deal smaller than appears from a casual glance at the Quarter Book. The movement and multiple functioning of men known only from these entries can never

[1]Cf. Admiralty minutes of April–June 1921 in *BND*, pp. 887–9.
[2]See the instances noted below at **4** (p. 433).

be traced exhaustively. Widely variant spellings and a limited range of forenames complicate the issue (and even a distinctive combination of forename and surname might belong to more than one member of a family). Even so it is possible to find a good many connections, and the cumulative impression is of a close-knit, mobile and multi-skilled (or at least multi-tasked) workforce.

The Principal Officers also employed their own clerks, in addition to those based in the yards. Most of these men are known to us only by name, if at all; one of them, however, has left us a comprehensive memorandum of his routine business. This was James Humphrey, who worked for the Clerk Comptroller (William Holstock at the time), and who compiled a book of model letters and forms for use on various occasions, which passed eventually into the hands of Samuel Pepys [**6–15**]. The Officers, who were based on Tower Hill in London, kept up a constant correspondence with their agents in the ports, with the Lord Admiral, wherever he happened to be, with the Privy Council and with the commanders of individual ships. Letters and instructions were mostly carried by the Admiralty's own messengers such as John Elmer, or by ships' officers; but sometimes post riders were engaged. When ships were keeping close to shore, as they commonly did, messengers would usually travel overland, because in a straight race a horse could easily outrun the average warship.[1] Contact between ship and shore would be by the ship's own boats, and so does not feature in the accounts. In some circumstances a fast-sailing pinnace might be sent to overhaul a fleet, but the sources we print mention only one rather different kind of hot pursuit.[2]

Ordnance required another complex of administrative procedures. When a ship was prepared for active service, she had to be armed, and this was normally done at Deptford, so that the guns could be brought down river from the Tower where they were stored. Similarly when a ship was being laid up, the first thing that happened was that she returned to Deptford. The guns were taken out of her and returned to store, while the ship herself proceeded to Gillingham to join the others at anchor.[3] Small arms, such as arquebuses, bills and body armour seem to have been

[1]See, for example, the engagement of a local man to ride up through Suffolk to alert the officers at Yarmouth to ships approaching from Harwich: below, **4** (p. 460). An Elizabethan pinnace might be capable, in favourable conditions, of 8 or 9 knots, but a likely average is around 4.5 knots: cf. speeds for merchantmen discussed in I. Friel, *The Good Ship: Ships, Shipbuilding and Technology in England, 1200–1500* (1995), pp. 84–6. Ships could travel at night when a horse could not, but in daylight a post rider averaging 7½ m.p.h. (see Pepys, *Diary*, X, p. 452) could be expected to arrive ahead of a fleet moving along a parallel course.

[2]The bizarre instance of a Thames passenger-boat commandeered to chase a barge which was evading the press officers: below, **4** (p. 463).

[3]See payments in relation to *Hart*, *New Bark*, *Phoenix* and *Swallow* **4** (pp. 408–9).

handled in the same way, unless the soldiers had already been armed by the counties from which they were drawn. This may have happened late in the reign, at the time of the Armada for instance, but county armourie did not even begin to come into existence until the 1570s, and the metho used to provide ships with such weapons is not clear.

What is clear is that the Elizabethan Admiralty was a sizeabl organisation, with a permanent staff of two or three dozen, and a regula workforce numbering many hundreds, operating in five main locations When the fleet was deployed in strength many thousands of seamen wer needed. How willingly these men served can only be guessed. Sometime rewards were given to local officers for bringing men to the musters, an there are notes of absentees, suggesting reluctance, but no record says tha ships were seriously undermanned, or that missions ever had to be aborte for lack of crews. Contrary to what is sometimes said, the welfare of thes men was not callously neglected. Each was paid conduct money at a fixe rate per mile, both going and coming, and although he was normall expected to bring his own clothes, the rations provided in transit wer generous.[1] Once men were embarked, victuals were normally only problem if a ship had to remain at sea for an exceptionally long period and even then she could be resupplied from 'victuallers' (tenders) provided she was in home waters. Baeshe had been generally efficien and serious complaints only began after Quarles had took over in 158 and then had to cope with the exceptional circumstances of the Armad campaign, when the number of ships was unprecedented, with many o them constrained to spend weeks at Plymouth, far from the main suppl bases. The sixteenth century was unfamiliar with the modern notion of balanced diet, and the staple items of bread, beef, beer and cheese lacke vitamin C. This did not matter greatly if the service was no more than month or two, but it wrought havoc with long-distance voyages. Althoug by the end of the century the value of scorbutics was known, most master and pursers (to say nothing of seamen) were too conservative to use them. The sicknesses which beset the Navy regularly in its normal duties wa not scurvy but typhoid, intermittently compounded by plague. Althoug every ship of any size carried a surgeon, his main duty was to deal wit the (infrequent) battle casualties, or the results of accidents rather tha illness. If typhoid or plague appeared, the only immediate remedy was t set the sufferer ashore with whatever part of his pay the purser coul provide. If this did not check the infection, the ship had to be taken ou

[1]Every man was supposed to receive a wheaten loaf of 20 oz, 2 lbs of fresh beef, and gallon of ale every day: *BND*, pp. 102–3.

[2]D. W. Waters, 'Limes, lemons and scurvy in Elizabethan and early Stuart times', *MM* XLI, (1955), pp. 209–21.

of commission and 'cleansed'. If that could not be done, the effects could be devastating, as happened at the end of the Armada campaign.[1] The system could cope with the normal discharge of two or three ships at a time, and a handful of sick mariners, but in the face of the mass discharge of over a hundred ships, and literally thousands of invalids in twenty different locations, it broke down completely. Neither was the money available, nor the medical services able to cope. This, however, was an extreme case, and it is probably safe to say that no early modern administration could have done any better. The spiritual aspect of welfare is mentioned, rather surprisingly, only once in the documents here printed [**22**]. This was not because it was usually ignored but because chaplains, when they were carried, were seldom on the normal payroll. Only the larger ships carried a full-time minister, and he was allocated by the social status of the captain rather than the needs of the men. Sometimes a preacher was paid at the specified rate, but more often he was either supported by a benefice from which he had taken some form of leave, or paid privately by the captain or admiral.[2] Noblemen or wealthy gentlemen serving with the fleet were often accompanied by their 'retinues', which might include a personal chaplain. In those circumstances, and if no official minister was appointed, he would provide services for the whole ship. When no chaplain was available, the captain or the master would usually conduct public prayers on a daily basis, but of course none of this left any record in the accounts.[3]

Wage rates were not generous. Before 1585 a seaman was paid a mere 3d a day, and even the captain of a Great Ship received only 16d, unless he was also an Admiral. At the same time a labourer working ashore might be paid anything from 2d to 6d a day, depending on skill and circumstances, while a master craftsman would receive 10d or 12d. However, it must be remembered that sea rates did not include the victuals which were also provided, and were costed at the same rate. So that a seaman at 6s 8d a month actually cost the Exchequer 13s 4d, and a captain at 40s, £4. Likewise a mariner at sea cost £8 a year and a captain £48. Ashore victuals were provided for some, but not all, of the workforce, and the basis for the distinction is not clear. It is probable that the different rates of pay for the same job reflect the provision (or otherwise) of food. In 1585, in response to inflation, and at the suggestion of John Hawkins [**20**] wages at sea were raised by 33 per cent, so that an ordinary seaman received 10s a month, plus his victuals, 'and so every officer will be increased after that rate'. As inflation during the reign was approximately 100 per cent

[1]G. Parker and C. Martin, *The Spanish Armada* (1988), pp. 253–4.
[2]Rodger, *Safeguard*, pp. 306–8.
[3]Ibid., pp. 311–12.

this could be regarded as too little and too late, but wage rates ashore were similarly lagging, and there is no reason to suppose that naval rates were considered particularly inadequate. There were, however, two problems. In the first place privateers were paid on a quite different basis, by a share of the plunder rather than a wage. Although this meant that if there was no plunder there was no pay, most privateers were doing well enough to make this an attractive option, and a few men made their fortunes at it.[1] The attraction of serving in a privateer was such that experienced mariners often tried to avoid naval service if possible and inexperienced men had to be recruited in their place. The second problem with naval pay was the actual availability of the money. The Queen had a great reputation for parsimony, but that was not the real issue. The difficulty lay in getting sufficient specie to the places where it was needed when the ships actually arrived. Individual ships on routine missions seldom caused a problem, but if a fleet had to be discharged – and particularly if weather conditions scattered the ships – the crews might well find no money awaiting them when they came ashore. Either they had to wait, and run up debts, or to take notes of credit (which might never be honoured) and beg their way home.[2] In the case of the Armada fleet there were problems of scale, of dispersal and also of sickness, and unpaid mariners not only rioted, but attempted to lay siege to the court.[3] This was a unique reaction, and emergency steps had to be taken, but it was not typical of the way in which the Admiralty functioned. The payment of crews was not always as efficient as it was for dockyard workers, but it should not be thought that seamen were constantly cheated of their wages by a cash-strapped government. Usually the system worked.

In the documents which follow, politics feature relatively little, but some things emerge clearly. Hawkins was a much more innovative and controversial Treasurer than Gonson, and upset his colleagues considerably. Baeshe was extraordinarily efficient, and in spite of his protests did his difficult job well. It was only after his death that it become clear just how well he had done. Wooden ships deteriorate rapidly, whether they are in use or not, and England could not afford to have any significant

[1]K. R. Andrews, *Elizabethan Privateering* (Cambridge, 1964) and *Trade, Plunder and Settlement: Maritime Enterprises and the Genesis of the British Empire, 1480–1630* (Cambridge, 1984), pp. 222–38. H. Kelsey, *Sir Francis Drake: the Queen's Pirate* (1998), pp. 207–40.

[2]From about 1600, these notes of credit were known as 'tickets', and by Pepys's time they were a form of currency all too familiar to seamen: *OED*.

[3]In July 1589 a mob of discharged seamen and soldiers, many of them plague-stricken and all very angry, advanced on the court, then at Westminster. The government issued a proclamation, denying them access: *TRP*, iii. 39–40 (no. 712). On this occasion there was an additional concern to prevent the spread of plague from the ports.

proportion of its fleet out of action for long. The whole reign was politically and militarily tense, and about a third of it was spent at war. English soldiers were not the maladroits of historical mythology, but it was upon the Navy that the country depended.[1] The fleet varied in size from about 30 to about 45 ships, and the amount of maintenance and repair work required is astonishing. The dockyards not only performed the largest and most complex industrial operation in Elizabethan England, but by the standards of any age they were demonstrably well-run. Only at the very end of Elizabeth's reign, and well expressed in the reports of the Jacobean Commissions,[2] did the efficiency begin to falter and significant corruption to undermine what had been one of the great mid-Tudor and early Elizabethan achievements.

Editorial Procedures

In keeping with NRS convention, the texts are printed in modern spelling; the language, however, is not modernised, and that requires the retention of some archaisms. Common forms such as 'hath' and 'cometh' have been retained because they are not precisely equivalent to the modern 'has' and 'comes'. On the other hand, 'Her Highness ships' has been understood as an obsolete spelling of the possessive, and is rendered as 'Her Highness's ships'. The scribal use of singular and plural is followed: so 'succours' and 'groundings' where we would say 'succour' and 'grounding', but (in most instances) so many 'nail' and 'last' rather than 'nails' and 'lasts'.

Technical terms not in current usage have generally been given in the first form recognised by the *OED*, though if another spelling is established in maritime usage, that has been preferred.

Capitalisation and punctuation are editorial.

Layout is based on the form of the originals, and therefore varies from piece to piece, but is a reinterpretation for the printed page. Therefore in the Quarter Book, by far the largest entry, the repeated headings of the original are omitted and replaced by editorial running-heads which serve the same purpose in the new format. The original headings are retained only when new sections begin.

Corrections to text by the original scribes are shown roman within square brackets, with *inserted*, *deleted* or *repl.* (for 'replacing'). Auditor's

[1]On the army, see M. C. Fissell, *English Warfare, 1511–1642* (2001), pp. 137–54, which presents an unconventional view of English soldiers. On the Navy in its general military context, see P. E. J. Hammer, *Elizabeth's Wars: War, Government and Society in Tudor England, 1544–1604* (Basingstoke, 2003), esp. pp. 161–9, 254–6.

[2]A. P. McGowan (ed.), *The Jacobean Commissions of Enquiry, 1608 and 1618* (NRS, Vol. 116, 1971).

markings and other addenda are italic within square brackets, prefaced by *, as more particularly explained at the head of each relevant entry. Correspondences between certain entries in **4** and **5** are marked by codes in bold within square brackets, prefaced by # (as detailed in the Introduction to Section II). Editorial explanations and other interpolations are italic (sometimes bold italic) within square brackets, without any symbol.

Proper Names

All identifiable place-names are modernised, and the MS spellings are given in the index. Unidentified place-names are in the MS forms, within inverted commas. Surnames of those identified in the footnotes or the Biographical Notes (*NEM*, Appendix 2) are standardised, and the variant spellings given after the headword for each surname in the index. All other surnames are left in their MS forms; in consequence many individuals appear in a variety of spellings; much further regimentation could have been imposed on the minor characters, but many uncertainties would still have remained, so it was felt best to apply a definable distinction. Forenames are standardised except where unusual or uncertain; in a few cases the original spelling is appended (within square brackets) to the standard form. The names of royal ships are always in the spellings shown in *NEM* Appendix 1, with MS variants given in the index. Other ship names are retained in the forms in which they occur, including any locational suffix, which may indicate origin rather than current deployment; the modern forms of these place-names are supplied editorially where it has been thought this might be useful.

Numerals

Because the volume contains elements from many sources, which use a variety of forms for money sums and other figures, no attempt is made to follow the original usages precisely. The treatment of money sums is explained more particularly below. Except within Latin phrases, all Roman numerals are rendered Arabic. Numerals have generally been printed for numbers above one, whether the MS uses them or writes the number in words or a mixture of numerals and words. Numbers below 10 have, however, commonly been given in words when attached to persons, ships and buildings, or elsewhere when Arabic numerals would appear ungainly to the modern eye. Numbers expressed in scores (whether in writing or by the use of the suprascript, as *vij*^{xx} for 140) have been rendered as simple numerals. But where calculation by standard hundred of 5 score or long hundred of 6 score is stipulated, the words 'score' and 'hundred' are left in words. In all these respects the concern has been to represent the original texts in modern typography rather than to replicate the occurrence of Roman numerals or written-out numbers in the MSS.

Straightforward corrections to figures are inset within square brackets preceded by *recte*. More complex corrections are shown in footnotes. This editorial function has not been comprehensive; but all figures involving hundredweights and long hundreds have been checked and aberrations noted.

Dates, Weights and Measures

Dating Style and the Year of Grace

Dates are given throughout in the old style (Julian Calendar), except in a few cases in editorial matter where the double dating old/new (Julian/Gregorian) is supplied for clarity. In the documents the year of grace for dates up to 24 March is given in the MS forms, with editorial explanation of the modern reckoning, as '21 March 1562 [*1563*]'. In the editorial matter the calendar year is always dated from 1 January. Within English phrasing Roman numerals for the days of the month have been converted to Arabic numerals.

Regnal Years

Elizabeth I's regnal year began on 17 November. In the Quarter Book [**4**] the regular dating formula is *Anno Domini* 1562. *Anno regni regine Elizabethe quarto* ('In the year of Our Lord 1562. In the fourth year of the reign of Queen Elizabeth'), with the Arabic numerals as printed. In the Declared Account [**5**] various Latin forms occur such as '*viij die Novembris dicto anno quarto domine regine* ('the 8th day of November in the said fourth year of the Lady Queen'). In all these cases the Roman numerals have been retained with the rest of the original format. The usual variants are *eiusdem mensis* ('of the same month') and *dicto anno* ('in the said year') or, where the scribe remembers to refer both to the regnal year and the year of Grace, *dictis annis* ('in the said years').

The regnal years most frequently encountered here are:

1 Eliz. *anno primo*	17 November 1558 – 16 November 1559
2 Eliz. *anno secundo*	17 November 1559 – 16 November 1560
3 Eliz. *anno tertio*	17 November 1560 – 16 November 1561
4 Eliz. *anno quarto*	17 November 1561 – 16 November 1562
5 Eliz. *anno quinto*	17 November 1562 – 16 November 1563
6 Eliz. *anno sexto*	17 November 1563 – 16 November 1564
7 Eliz. *anno septimo*	17 November 1564 – 16 November 1565

Abbreviations for Certain Days of the Month
The contemporary usages 'one and twentieth' etc. for the day of the month resulted in the abbreviations '21th', '22th', '23th' and '31th'. These have been retained in preference to '21st', '22nd', '23rd' and '31st', representing the modern expression of dates with the larger element first.

Duodecimal Currency

2 × 1 farthing (¼d) – 1 halfpenny (½d)
2 halfpence – 1 penny (1d)
12 pence – 1 shilling (1s)
20 shillings – 1 pound (£1)

The mark (13s 4d) was an accounting unit, never an actual coin.

Sums of money, however represented in the MSS, are here rendered in standard £sd forms. 'Top heavy' pence or shillings (as 20d, 45s) are retained as such within blocks of text, but in displayed totals they are converted to £sd (as 1s 8d, £2 5s). In the *recepta* of the Quarter Book where each sum is duplicated, the version within the text is printed in words and the displayed total in figures, whatever the format of the original.

Linear Measure

12 inches – 1 foot
36 inches/3 feet – 1 yard
45 inches – 1 ell (of cloth)
1,760 yards – 1 mile

Quantities of Cut Paper

24 sheets – 1 quire
20 quires/480 sheets – 1 ream
(commonly rounded to 500 sheets)

Capacity

2 pints – 1 quart
4 quarts – 1 gallon
8 gallons – 1 bushel
8 bushels – 1 quarter (qr)

Avoirdupois Weight

16 ounces (oz) – 1 pound (lb)
14 pounds – 1 stone

2 stone/28 pounds – 1 quarter (qr)
4 quarters/112 pounds – 1 hundredweight (cwt)
20 hundredweight/2,240 pounds – 1 ton

Although the modern hundredweight of 112 lbs was generally adopted by the mid-sixteenth century, some use was still made of the hundredweight of 100 pounds from which the measure had taken its name. A quantity of sye is computed by simple hundreds of pounds [**4** (p. 266)], and rosin may sometimes have been reckoned in the same way [**4** (p. 325)]. This could apply to other commodities which cannot be checked; doubtless variations also reflect the practices of individual suppliers.[1]

Commonly the Quarter Book runs together modern hundredweights and pounds into a single figure, as:

ccl pounds weight

This normally means not 250 lbs but 274 lbs, that is [(2 × 112) + 50]

Wherever this reckoning is known or assumed to apply, the modern hundredweight is indicated by the word 'hundred' written out, and the actual quantity is inset in italic figures within square brackets. So in this example the quantity would be shown as:

2 hundred 50 pounds weight [*274 lbs*]

Sometimes where there are no loose pounds, the complete hundredweights are still expressed as so many hundreds of pounds, as:

v^{c} pound weight

In such cases the meaning cannot be checked by calculating the price per lb, but has been taken as a variant form of the usual measure of 112 lbs (see p. 104 n. 2 for a demonstration of this).

Where there are no pounds and the word 'weight' is not in the MS, it is supplied editorially, as:

2 hundred[*weight*]

Where (as at p. 200) the hundredweight is specifically said to be of '5 score', or if that usage is clear from the calculation, the figures are as expressed in the MS, without an inset interpolation:

340½ pounds weight

[1]For some comparative detail, see *NEM*, p. xxxv n. 1 and p. xxxvi n. 1.

The thousandweight is normally 10 cwt of 112 lbs. Sometimes the thousands are separated by *mille* and sometimes the figure is expressed in top-heavy hundreds; these variant usages have been retained, so:

xxj^{c}l pounds *is printed as* 21 hundred 50 pounds

ij^{ml}cl pounds *is printed as* 2 thousand [*one*] hundred 50 pounds

In both cases the ostensible 2,150 is 2,402 (21 × 112 + 50), and is identified as such in the usual editorial insert.

All the calculation of hundredweights has been investigated. The quantity in pounds has been inset in all cases involving loose pounds, and occasionally (for regularity within entries) for complete hundredweights. Errors which seem likely to derive from mistranscription by the Quarter Book scribes have been corrected within the text and further explained in the footnotes. The notes give a modern recalculation of all the questionable figures. Where (as in most cases) the price per cwt does not break down to complete pence or even farthings per lb, the modern calculation applies a precision far beyond the means and requirements of the original accountants. Almost all the 'imprecision' can in fact readily be explained by the necessary rounding up or down of fractions of pence, which doubtless varied from one supplier to another. Indeed because the margin of error is usually so minute, the recalculations demonstrate the preponderating accuracy of the original accounting, not its weakness.[1]

Long Hundreds

Certain commodities (such as rafters) are reckoned by the long hundred of 120, and this usage is usually specified by the accountant. In these cases the actual quantity as well as the rate is expressed in the long hundred. Thus:

200 rafters at £12 10s every 100 after 6 score to the 100

This means not 200 items at so much for every 120, but 240 items.

Likewise 293 rafters means 333, i.e. [2 × 120 + 93]

[1]See especially the largest single computation in the Quarter Book [**4** (p. 321)], for a sum in excess of £2.5k which is within 0.02d of the notional figure achieved by decimal calculation, and so correct to the halfpenny stated. It will be found, unsurprisingly, that substantial merchants generally price their goods with precision, and that mistakes more commonly occur with small-time operators and casual suppliers.

For clarity in these cases the word ‘hundred’ is written out wherever the long hundred is clearly meant, however represented in the MS, and the actual quantity is added editorially:

2 hundred [*240*] rafters at £12 19s every hundred after 6 score to the hundred
2 hundred 93 rafters [*333*]

Obsolete Measures
Measures which were obsolete by the twentieth century are explained in the Glossary (Appendix 2).

Note on Terms: Admiralty, Navy, Marine Causes

In the sixteenth century, Admiralty was used to denote the whole range of maritime administration: the Council for Marine Causes, its officers and dependent structure, as well as the Admiralty Courts which exercised the Lord Admiral’s jurisdiction over marine causes, both centrally and locally. After the Restoration the meaning changed, because there was then an Admiralty which was distinct from the Navy Office or Navy Board, as by then the sixteenth-century Council for Marine Causes was known. The principal officials established in 1546 (Treasurer, Comptroller, Surveyor, Clerk) are already sometimes jointly called the Navy Officers or the Officers of the Navy (in distinction to the ships’ officers). They have their continuance in the subordinate post-Restoration department, and their headquarters remained in the City. The separate and superior Admiralty existing between the reigns of Charles II and William IV was essentially a political and policy-making body, with its offices in Whitehall. In the Elizabethan period, those higher functions remained chiefly with the central agencies of government, the Principal Secretaries and the Privy Council. Almost all the concerns of the present volume are those which by the later arrangement would be the responsibility of the Navy Board rather than the Admiralty.

I

FIRST NAVAL BUSINESS IN THE STATE PAPERS

The first specifically naval paper found in the Elizabethan State Papers [**1**] is a ship list drawn up four months after the Queen's accession, and a month before the more substantial 'Book of Sea Causes'. Since the latter is printed in *British Naval Documents*,[1] it is not repeated here. Both documents were part of the general stocktaking at the start of the new reign. The first list also includes incidental information, affirming that operational costs should not be charged against the ordinary, and listing the seven merchant ships at that time in royal service. Cecil's marginalia show an attention to maritime affairs proper in an old ship-lord,[2] and are the only evidence for *Minion* being given away to Lord Admiral Seymour. In the case of *Trinity Henry* the verdict 'decayed utterly' seems a little premature, since the Quarter Book shows this vessel was still maintained afloat, albeit relentlessly leaky, four years later. But although it is instructive, the February 1559 list is no more than a memorandum.

From about a year later come the first ordinances for the Admiralty officers [**2**],[3] which are mainly a systematic record of the changes which had been introduced after the 1557 review.[4] They are important because they mark a stage in the bureaucratisation of naval administration, and because they emphasise the interdependence of the marine officers, particularly the extent by which they were required to check up on each other. The most notable omission is any reference to the Lord Treasurer, who by terms of the earlier reforms was supposed to be in overall charge.[5] Perhaps the Marquess of Winchester, though retained in office by

[1]See above, p. xxii & n. 1.

[2]He had been part-owner of a merchantman in Edward's reign: *CSPDE*, no. 474.

[3]They are among undated papers in an artificial collection bound together and calendared in the 1850s as 'probably … 1560' (*CSPD 1547–80*, pp. 165–70). The ordinances could well have been written even earlier in Elizabeth's reign, or conceivably as late as 1564 (when the office of Vice-Admiral, to which they refer, was discontinued). For convenience they have been called 'of *c*. 1560' here.

[4]See Introduction above, p. xxi.

[5]Except (in the instructions for the Master of the Ordnance) for reference to the Lord Treasurer in his technical and departmental *alter ego* as Treasurer of the Exchequer; but clearly the 1557 regulations involved the Lord Treasurer in his larger political role as a Privy Councillor and Great Officer of State.

Elizabeth, had no desire to continue his involvement as established under Mary; or perhaps his role in the formation of policy was simply taken for granted in an administrative directive. However, every officer is described as being responsible to the Lord Admiral, or the Vice-Admiral in his absence, for the discharge of his regular duties, and policy decisions are to be taken by the whole council, reporting to the Lord Admiral. There is no mention of the Lord Treasurer in that context either.

The ordinances, however, do not present a complete picture. The Treasurer (of the Navy), in addition to the detailed procedures described here, was also required to render an annual account to specially appointed commissioners. Similarly the accountability of the Surveyor-General of the Victuals is incomplete. It is declared that he should receive his money 'in prest' from the Treasurer, but not that he should account to him, or as part of his own account. In practice he was required to account separately to the Admiral, and that was done until the contract system was introduced in 1565 [**28**].

It is clear also that a great deal of paperwork was generated which has now disappeared. The council was presumably required to keep a record of its decisions, and every officer was required to report and account in writing, but all that has been discovered are the annual accounts of the Treasurer and the Surveyor-General, plus a few of the Quarter Books which happened to find their way into the hands of Samuel Pepys. Of the accounts of the Surveyor and Rigger, Comptroller, Clerk of the Ships and Clerk of the Store, or indeed of the minute book of the council, no trace has been found. This is perhaps because (unlike accounts to commissioners) these were 'in-house' documents, and were not subject to outside scrutiny or audit. The Lord Admiral, like the Lord Treasurer, was a Privy Councillor *ex officio*, and the Privy Council's overall control was probably exercised through him. It would not have been thought necessary to say so in a document of this kind.

Brief though it is, this paper is of great significance as the first version of regulations which were revised and extended by successive Lord Admirals in the seventeenth century. They reached their most enduring form as the Duke of York's General Instructions to the Navy Board of 1662, which were printed in 1717 as *The Œconomy of His Majesty's Navy Office*. This lineal connection has at least been noted from the other end.[1] Only one previous writer appears to have discussed the regulations in their original context.[2] This is not the place to follow the process by which the Elizabethan ordinances evolved into the instruction manual of Pepys's

[1]C. S. Knighton, *Pepys and the Navy* (Stroud, 2003), pp. 14–15, and sources cited on p. 179 n. 19.

[2]Pollitt, 'Rationality and expedience', pp. 71–3.

day and beyond. But it serves as a further reminder that most of the work of the Tudor Admiralty would descend to the Stuart and Georgian Navy Board.[1]

[1] An additional point of interest appeared when this volume was in the press. It had been presumed that [**1**] contained the last reference to *Peter Pomegranate*, and that the intended rebuild was cancelled: *NEM*, p. 501. However it is now suggested that *Peter* was rebuilt as *Elizabeth Jonas*: R. Hutchinson, *The Spanish Armada* (2013), p. 256. This would mean that the sister ship of Henry VIII's *Mary Rose* survived through successive rebuilds until 1618: see *NEM*, p. 477.

1 *List of the Queen's ships; with annotations by Sir William Cecil*

[SP 12/2, no. 30 (*CSPD 1547–80*, p. 121)][1] *20 February 1559*

The 20th day of February 1558 [1559] *anno primo Elizabethe primo.*

The names of all Her Highness's ships and where at this present they do remain, with remembrances concerning the same.

	ships	*tuns*	*men*
At Gillingham	The *Mary Rose*	600	350
	The *Lion*	500	330
	The *Philip and Mary*	450	300
In the River of Thames	The *Great Bark*	600	330
	The *Jesus*	600	330
	The *Tiger*	160	120
	The *Bull*	160	120
	The *Red Galley*	–	300
	The *Black Galley*	–	300
	The *Brigantine*	–	100
	The *Flower de luce*	40	30
	The *Sun*	60	60
At Portsmouth	The *New Bark*	160	120
	The *Mary Willoughby*	160	120
	The *Jerfalcon*	140	100
	The *Sacret*	160	120
	The *Salamander*	300	200
	The *Anne Gallant*	300	200
	The *Double Rose*	40	30
	The *Hare*	40	30

[1] A stock-taking exercise three months after Elizabeth's accession. A summary (omitting the latter part, and supplying construction dates from elsewhere) was given by T. Glasgow jnr, 'The Royal Navy at the start of the reign of Elizabeth', *MM*, LI (1965) pp. 73–6. This contains some errors in transcription, especially from Cecil's notoriously difficult hand, of which only the most striking instance is specifically corrected here. See also Glasgow 'Maturing', pp. 11–12. Cecil was Principal Secretary 1550–53, 1558–72; Lord Treasurer 1572 to death, 1598. Created Baron Burghley 1571, KG 1572. The Queen's first minister GEC, *Peerage*, ii, pp. 429–30. *ODNB*. *Hist. Parl. 1509–58*, i, pp. 603–6; *1558–1603*, i, pp 582–8. C. Read, *Mr Secretary Cecil and Queen Elizabeth* (1955) and *Lord Burghley and Queen Elizabeth* (1958). B. W. Beckingsale, *Burghley: Tudor Statesman, 1520–1598* (1967) S. Alford, *The Early Elizabethan Polity: William Cecil and the British Succession Crisis 1558–1569* (Cambridge, 1998), and *Burghley: William Cecil at the Court of Elizabeth I* (2008).

The Narrow Seas	The *Saker*	70	60
	The *Bark of Boulogne*	60	60
	The *Bright Falcon*	60	60
	The *Sprite*	40	30
Presently to be sent northward	The *Greyhound*	160	120
	The *Falcon*	100	80
	The *Phoenix*	70	60

Ships presently dry-docked, in new making, and to be repaired:

At Woolwich in new making	The *Peter*	800	600
At Portsmouth in new making	The *Jennet*	200	160
At Portsmouth to be repaired	The *Sweepstake*	300	200
At Deptford to be repaired	The *Hart*	300	200
	The *Antelope*	300	200
	The *Swallow*	200	160
	The *George*	120	100

Number of Her Majesty's ships, barks and galleys: 34

Toward the maintenance of all the said ships, the Queen's Highness's pleasure is to be known for the continuance of the ordinary of £14,000 by the year from Christmas last, as well for the new building and repairing of the same ships and provisions for the same, and for wages and victuals of shipwrights, caulkers and other artificers, as also shipkeepers in harbour for their like wages and victuals.

It is to be remembered that if Her Highness's pleasure be to have the said ships or any of them put to the seas in fashion of war, the charge thereof is extraordinary, and not to be accounted within the aforesaid ordinary of £14,000 by the year.

Merchants' ships and barks presently in Her Highness's service[1]	The *Prymerose of London*	300	200
	The *Hart of Dover*	–	–
	The *Peter of Dover*	–	–
	The *Jhesus of Dover*	–	–

[1]Cf. the *Prymeros*, *Swallow* of Dover and *Grayhond* of Dover serving with the fleet in the Narrow Seas at the start of the French war in May 1557: *CSPDM*, no. 766.

The *Grayhounde of Dartmowth*	–	40
The *Swallow of Dover*	40	40
The *Grayhounde of Dover*	40	40

[*Minuted by Cecil (against the Deptford section but not referring specifically to it)*]

800 [*tuns*]	*Henry Grace à Dieu* burned 1553[1]
120	The *Minion* given to Sir Thomas Seymour[2]
121	The *Primrose* sold for £1,800, *unde* £1,000 paid[3]
122	*Trinity Henry* decayed utterly[4]
123	The *Dragon* } decayed
120	The *Lion* } decayed

2 *Ordinances for the Admiralty officers*

[SP 12/15, no. 4 (*CSPD 1547–80*, p. 165)][5] [*Undated;* c. *1560*]

For the office of our Admiralty and Marine Affairs.

Forasmuch as since the erection of the said office by our late dearest father King Henry the eight there hath been no certain ordinances established so as every officer in his degree is appointed to his charge; and considering that in these our days our Navy is one of the chiefest defence for the preservation of us and our realm against the malice of any

[1]On 25 Aug. while docked at Woolwich: Machyn, *Diary*, p. 43. The ship, which the diarist called the 'the grettest … in the world', had been rechristened *Edward* on Edward VI's accession, but is remembered (as here) by the older name. See *NEM*, p. 487.

[2]Maternal uncle of Edward VI, and younger brother of Lord Protector Somerset; himself created Baron Seymour of Sudeley 16 Feb. 1547 and appointed Lord Admiral the following day; deprived of office 18 Jan. 1549 and executed for treason on 20 March: *ODNB*. *Hist. Parl. 1509–58*, iii, pp. 297–301. Glasgow ('Royal Navy', p. 75) saw this entry as 'Given to London for trading', a misreading which has complicated understanding of the ship's history. She must have been given to Seymour by 10 Jan. 1548, because she is not in the RN list of that date which forms part of the great posthumous inventory of Henry VIII's goods: *Inv. Hen. VIII*, pp. 144–6. Her ordnance is listed there (pp. 149–50) along with that of other ships, all delivered into the Tower 1 Jan. 1548.

[3]One of several redundant royal ships sold by Queen Mary. The Navy Treasurer's account for 1554/5 confirms the sale of *Primrose* to a consortium of London merchants (Sir George Barne, Sir John Yorke, William Garrard and Francis Lambart) for £1,000, by authority of a warrant to the Lord Admiral and Navy Officers dated 10 Dec. 1554: *NEM*, p. 416.

[4]Still being maintained at the Colne yard in 1562/3 though the attempts to keep her afloat would soon thereafter be abandoned: cf. **4** (pp. 176–9, 386–9).

[5]A 17th-cent. copy in the British Library (Add. MS 9295, ff. 17–18v) assigns the piece to the reign of Edward VI. A synopsis with some extracts from the SP text was printed in H. B. Wheatley (ed.), *The Diary of Samuel Pepys*, Supplementary Volume, *Pepysiana* (1899), pp. 155–7.

foreign potentate, we have therefore thought good by great advice and deliberation to make certain ordinances and decrees, which our pleasure and express commandment is that all our officers shall on their parties execute and follow as they tender our pleasure, and will answer to the contrary.

The several offices as they are established:

The Vice-Admiral.
The Master of the Ordnance and Surveyor of the Marine Causes: one officer.
The Treasurer.
The Comptroller.
The General Surveyor of our Victuals.
The Clerk of our Ships.
The Clerk of our Store.

First, the said officers once in the week or as more as the case shall require, to assemble themselves together at our house at Tower Hill and consult upon such our causes as shall be meetest for the good order of our Navy, and once every month to make report to our High Admiral of their doings, or to the Vice-Admiral in his absence.

It is agreed that our ships shall be safely kept in harbour with as little charge as may be, and that the captain of our blockhouse of Upnor at Gillingham with his gunners shall be at the muster and under the charge of our Lord Admiral.

The Master of our Ordnance once a quarter or oftener shall make declaration to our Lord Admiral, or to the Vice-Admiral in his absence, of the state of his office and of such wants as shall be needful for his office, so as in time it may be supplied, and the books of his accounts and reckonings shall be quarterly signed by the hands of three or two of our said officers, whereof our Vice-Admiral to be one. And also he shall yearly by the books so subscribed account for his office before our Treasurer, Barons and other officers of our Exchequer. And the said office of the Ordnance shall be surveyed, considered and viewed once a quarter or oftener by our Vice-Admiral or others of our officers to be called by him.

The Treasurer to make declaration weekly to our Vice-Admiral of his receipts and payments [*inserted* and he to make no payments but] by warrants of three or two of our said officers, whereof our Vice-Admiral, Surveyor of our Ships and Comptroller to be always one. And at every quarter to make up his books, so as our charge may appear, and to have to his quarter books the subscription of three or two of our said officers, whereof our Vice-Admiral, Surveyor and Comptroller to be one. And once a month or oftener if need be, to signify to our Lord Admiral the state of his office, or to our Vice-Admiral in his absence. Provided always that for all provisions, emptions and victuals, money may be so paid out by our Treasurer that where there is most need, the same may be first despatched by order of our officers as is aforesaid, and not otherwise.

The Surveyor General of our Victuals to make no victualling but such as shall be warranted unto him by the hands of three or two of our said officers, and at every quarter's end to have the hands of three or two of our officers to his quarter book, whereof our Vice-Admiral, Surveyor of our Ships and Comptroller to be one, and to receive the prests for his victualling at the hands of our said Treasurer. And once a month or oftener if need shall be, to make declaration to our Lord Admiral or to our Vice-Admiral in his absence of the state of his office. Provided always that there be a sufficient store of victuals always in readiness so as upon fourteen days' warning he may deliver victuals for 2,000 men to the seas for a month; and he is to account as the Treasurer does for his office.

The Surveyor of our Ships, Comptroller and Clerk of our Ships and Clerk of our Store to see our ships from time to time grounded and trimmed, and to keep them in that good order and readiness, that always upon fourteen days' warning we may set to the seas at the least twelve or sixteen sail, and the rest in short time after. And they to make and to bring in monthly a report to our Vice-Admiral and to the rest of our said officers of the state of our said ships, so as the same as occasion shall command may be declared to our Lord Admiral.

The Clerk of our Ships to make provision of timber and other necessaries for the building and repairing of our ships from time to time; albeit to enter the felling of no timber without the consent and agreement of three of our said officers, whereof the Vice-Admiral, Surveyor and Comptroller to be always one. And for money for his office to have it by prest at the hands of the Treasurer. And his accounts to be seen and perused by three or two of the officers, whereof the Vice-Admiral, Surveyor and Comptroller to be one, and the account to be subscribed by the hands of three or two of our said officers, and to be delivered over to the Treasurer to pass in his accounts.

The Clerk of the Store to keep perfect books of all such provisions as shall come to his hands, with the prices to be entered. And the same provisions to be delivered out of his office by warrants of three or two of our officers. And the same Clerk of the Store once a quarter or oftener as occasion shall command shall bring and deliver to our Lord Admiral, or in his absence to our Vice-Admiral, a note of all provisions in his charge, and he to account once a year before our Vice-Admiral, Surveyor and Comptroller and other our officers. And it is to be considered that once a quarter or oftener the store to be perused with the remainder a-shipboard, and the waste and expenses of every ship for the whole year to be seen. And that there be such a special care had that for all sudden service there may be a sufficient furniture of provisions.

Item, our pleasure and commandment is that all our said officers do agree in one consultation, and all such necessary orders as shall be taken amongst them from time to time to be entered in a ledger book for the whole year, to remain of record.

The Assistants not to be accounted any of our head officers, but yet to travail in our causes when they shall be thereunto commanded or appointed by our Lord Admiral or Vice-Admiral or other officers.

Item, our mind and pleasure is that every of our said officers shall see into their fellows' offices, to the intent that when God shall dispose his will upon any of them, they living may be able, if we shall prefer any of them, to receive the same.

These ordinances to be read once a quarter amongst our officers, so as thereby every of them may the better understand his duty, and to be safely kept in our consultation house at Tower Hill.

II

THE NAVY TREASURER'S QUARTER BOOK FOR 1562–1563

The main item here [4] is the first of the five Quarter Books surviving from the reign of Elizabeth,[1] and is reproduced in full because of the unique insight which it provides into the detailed working of the Admiralty and its various agencies at that time.[2] The regular income of £12,000 a year provided by the warrant of 1559 is recorded in its successive tranches under 'Ordinary: Receipts'. Most of this revenue is absorbed by the wages and other charges itemised in the quarterly sections for the several royal dockyards, as 'Ordinary: Deptford' or 'Ordinary: Portsmouth'. Further charges against the same income are listed under 'Ordinary: Conduct' (recruitment of shipwrights, caulkers and other craftsmen), 'Ordinary: Prests' (money advanced to Edward Baeshe for the victualling of shipkeepers and workmen in the harbours), and 'Ordinary: Charges', which relate to the collection of the money from the Exchequer. Extraordinary income is listed separately. This was obtained under a number of ad hoc warrants from different sources, and was so called not because it was exceptional, but simply because it was not issued under the ordinary warrant. Extraordinary expenditure relates to the actual 'setting forth' of the ships to the seas, and apart from that incurred at Portsmouth, is mostly under one or other of the general categories. 'Extraordinary: Conduct' relates to the recruitment of seamen, gunners and soldiers to serve in the ships; 'Extraordinary: Prests' to money advanced to Baeshe for victualling the ships for active service, and 'Extraordinary: Charges' to a variety of miscellaneous costs, most of them relating to communications. The 'Extraordinary: Sea Charges' cover the diets and wages of captains, masters and mariners on active service. It should be noted that at this stage Gonson is still passing substantial sums of money to Baeshe, who accounted separately in accordance with the Privy Council order of 1557.[3] This was to change with the introduction of the victualling contract in 1565.

[1]The others are listed and related to the corresponding Declared Accounts in Appendix I below.
[2]A tabular synopsis is given below (pp. 16–18).
[3]*APC 1556–8*, p. 40.

The overall composition is uniform, as the following table shows. The most significant variations are in the entries for Portsmouth, much fuller as the yard became the centre of operations during the Le Havre campaign, and in the sections on conduct money and sea charges, which increase for the same reason.

Synopsis of the Quarter Book for 1562–63

[*In this table the sectional headings have been amplified for clarity*]

Folios of MS	*Contents*	*Pages of this edition*
Cover	Title	22
	Year 1 January – 31 December 1562	
1–2v	Ordinary receipts	23–6
3–7	Extraordinary receipts	26–31
8–57	Ordinary expenses: Deptford	
8–14v	*1 January – 31 March*	31–41
15–25	*1 April – 30 June*	41–56
26–41	*1 July – 30 September*	56–79
42–57	*1 October – 31 December*	79–104
58–67	Ordinary expenses: Woolwich	
58–60	*1 January – 31 March*	107–10
61–3	*1 April – 30 June*	110–13
64–5	*1 July – 30 September*	113–14
66–7	*1 October – 31 December*	114–16
68–112	Ordinary expenses: Gillingham	
68–77v	*1 January – 31 March*	116–28
78–88v	*1 April – 30 June*	128–42
89–101	*1 July – 30 September*	142–59
102–12	*1 October – 31 December*	159–75
113–116v	Ordinary expenses: Colne	
113r–v	*1 January – 31 March*	175–7
114r–v	*1 April – 30 June*	177
115r–v	*1 July – 30 September*	177–8
116r–v	*1 October – 31 December*	179–80
117–134v	Ordinary expenses: Portsmouth	
117r–v	*1 January – 31 March*	179–80
118r–v	*1 April – 30 June*	180–1
119–122v	*1 July – 30 September*	181–5

308–309v	Ordinary expenses: conduct money	432–4
310–310v	Ordinary expenses: prests	435
311	Ordinary expenses: Exchequer charges	436
312–320	Extraordinary expenses: conduct money	436–49
321v	[Extraordinary expenses]: coat money	449–50
322–341v	Extraordinary expenses: miscellaneous charges	450–84
342–344v	Extraordinary expenses: prests	484–7
345–55	Extraordinary expenses: sea charges	487–500
356–61	Extraordinary expenses: conduct (homeward)	501–9

This volume corresponds exactly with the period covered by Gonson's Declared or summary account, rendered in this instance to special commissioners [**5**]. The book 'signed with the hands of the officers' referred to in the latter document is this same Quarter Book. However, the data from the Quarter Book is comprehensively re-assembled in the Declared Account, which had a different purpose, and the correspondences are not always easily seen. To assist cross-reference throughout this volume an algebraic key has been supplied, introduced by the # symbol:

A1–A4	ordinary 1562
B1–B18	extraordinary 1562
X1–X4	ordinary 1563
Y1–Y28	extraordinary 1563

The Quarter Book treats the years separately, and so has a second *recepta* for 1563 beginning at f. 167. Within each of these there are first the ordinary receipts from the four several tellers, then the extraordinary receipts from all the various sources in a single chronological order. The totals for 1562 (**A1–4**) and 1563 (**X1–4**) have been inserted editorially at the appropriate points.

The Declared Account, covering both years, structures the revenue more precisely. It first runs together the ordinary receipts from each teller for the combined years, and totals them, i.e. (**A1–4**) + (**X1–4**). It then lists receipts via the tellers on extraordinary warrants (**B3, 6, 8, 9, 11, 13–18, Y2, 6, 10–12, 14–20, 22–8**), and gives a combined total from the tellers for ordinary and extraordinary. Then follow the receipts from all the other sources: the sales (**B1, 2**), the court of Wards (**B7, 10, 12**), the privy seal loan (**Y1, 3–5, 7–9, 13, 21**), the privy purse (**B5**), and finally the sale of the *Jerfalcon* (**B4**).

The Quarter Book does not provide cumulative totals of receipt and expenditure; its interest lies in the mass of particular detail it records. Fortuitously it also enables us to supply some *lacunae* in the Declared Account. As noted in the Introduction to Section III, the Exchequer scribe telescoped some of the lists of warrants; but since his sub-totals are the same as those of the Quarter Book, the missing data can readily be recovered. With this reconstruction in place, it will be found that *recepta* or charge sides of both accounts match one another perfectly, and are internally correct. The Quarter Book has also been used to correct some other slips in the Declared Account. The Quarter Books and Declared Accounts do not cover fees and allowances of the Lord Admiral and the senior officials (Vice-Admiral or Lieutenant, Surveyor/Master of Ordnance, Treasurer, Comptroller, Clerk of the Ships, Keeper of the Storehouses), who were paid directly from the Exchequer under the terms of their respective patents. In 1562/3 this amounted to over £767 in main salaries, extended to a notional £1,357 including travel allowances and clerks' wages; discontinuance of the Vice-Admiral's post after 1564 reduced this outlay by £100+ *per annum.*[1]

A few of the original privy seal warrants survive in the Exchequer files, and those which have been located are noted.[2] The signet warrants which authorised the application of the higher seal were often retained by the individual Lords Privy Seal; a good many others would have perished in the fire which destroyed the departmental archive in 1619. Just two relevant survivors have been found and noted against the entries in the Quarter Book.[3] One warrant has been printed in full at the head of this section [**3**] as an example of the instruments to which the Quarter Book so often refers.

Some fragmentary drafts and other papers used in the preparation of this Quarter Book also survive in the Evelyn MSS now in the British Library. These shed interesting light on the compositional process, and supply some details omitted or compressed in the final version.[4] There are complete fair copy versions of the Deptford and ordinary accounts for

[1]See *NEM*, pp. 525–6.

[2]No warrants of any kind survive in the Exchequer files for 4 Eliz. (1561–62). Those which do for years 5 and 6 (1562–64) are in E 404/115. The individual warrants in this file are not separately numbered, and reference is made to the year bundles.

[3]Both from PSO 2/13, bundle May 1563 (those marked **#Y6, #Y10** on pp. 244–5); the PSO warrants are gathered into monthly bundles, but are not individually numbered.

[4]BL, Add. MSS 78169–78171 (formerly Christ Church, Oxford, MSS 68, 69, 283). Evelyn's archive, along with his library, passed to descendants who in 1949 deposited them at Christ Church. The library was sold and dispersed in the 1970s, though a nucleus of some 00 volumes was preserved through purchase by the British Library. When the archive was sold by the Evelyn Trustees in 1995, the whole collection was acquired for the BL, with substantial assistance from the National Heritage Memorial Fund: T. Hoffmann et al., 'John Evelyn's Archive at the British Library', in *John Evelyn in the British Library* (BL Publication, 1995), pp. 11–73, with (p. 59) a brief list of the Elizabethan naval MSS inherited from the Gonson family. Much fuller descriptions are given in the BL provisional catalogue, and in Appendix 4 below, which is developed from the BL catalogue by courtesy of the Library authorities.

the Christmas quarters[1] of 1562 and 1563 and fragments of the like for Deptford, Woolwich and Portsmouth in the Michaelmas, Lady Day and Christmas quarters of 1563. Some of these carry auditor's markings, while others are signed on each page by Holstock and George Winter. These survivals demonstrate that the Quarter Book went through at least two complete draft stages before the final version (which is also signed by William Winter). The draft versions include some marginal notes for rearrangement of material (as 'enter among the labourers'), a few separate bills attached by pin, and memoranda of settlements to individuals. The three files also contain some shorter deleted drafts, and original accounts which the Quarter Book summarises. The annotations and supporting papers show that the *expense* of the Quarter Book itself cannot be taken as a sure record of payments discharged. Some bills ostensibly settled in 1563 were still being paid off by instalments into the second half of 1565

The penultimate rescensions are of particular importance in interpreting the suffix '*sr*'' appended to many names in all categories of the listed workforce. The abbreviation itself stands for the Latin *servus*, as '*mr*' more obviously does for *magister*, though these terms would have been spoken and read in the English forms 'master' and 'server'. The latter was a general term for an artisan's assistant.[2] Some of the surviving drafts for the Quarter Book are marginated with brackets linking servers to a preceding name (usually but not always identified as master), and occasionally that name is added to the bracket, indicating that the servers' pay was delivered to him along with his own. In these cases at least it is clear that the groupings identify a settled sub-section of the workforce under a particular leader, perhaps in some cases his apprentices. Other margination seems merely to show that occasionally an individual's pay was entrusted to one of the dockyard officers, to a spouse or colleague, or even to a colleague's spouse. In many cases the qualification 'server' is not carried over from the drafts which explains some of the seemingly random pay scales in the final account. The edition notes the lost 'server' identifications in the few places where this is possible,[3] and indicates where the drafts supply other details.

The Quarter Book itself consists of 370 paper folios bound in parchment. The paper itself was supplied by the London stationer William Prestwood

[1]Even though accounting was by quarters of the calendar year reckoned from 1 January (i.e. determining 31 March, 30 June, 30 September and 31 December), the quarters were loosely referred to by the names derived from the conventional terminal dates of Lady Day (25 March), Midsummer (24 June), Michaelmas (29 Sept.) and Christmas (25 Dec.). The names of the quarters do not appear in the finished book, but are often used in the papers from which this was compiled.

[2]*OED*, 'server', 1.c.; cf. 'serve' *v*[1]. 36.

[3]See particularly the example of Matthew Baker's servers noted in full on p. 87, where the draft supplies one 'server' identification which the final version gives in every other instance

p. 325]. The text occupies the first 361 folios (with occasional blanks), and is written in two fine clear examples of secretary hand, the second rather more flourished. The first 158 folios were evidently written by the Comptroller's clerk, Thomas Baker, who is paid for engrossing the books to 31 December 1562 [p. 451]. The second scribe (ff. 159–361) was Stephen Alexander, clerk at Deptford, who is paid for 'making perfect' the reckonings in the Quarter Books for the whole calendar year 1563 [p. 477].[1] In fact the last two sections for 1562 (159–163v) are in the second hand, though the division of labour accords broadly with the payments to Baker and Alexander. The modernised text reflects some slight variation in the respective scribal practices (for example, Baker generally wrote 'dock' and 'plank' but Alexander preferred 'docks' and 'planks'). The manuscript also contains auditing marks (such as '*ex*'' for *examinatur*), some additional calculations, and the occasional supply of missing section heads. The only foliation is by modern pencil, applied on every fifth leaf.

Although these books were public records, they must have been retained personally by Gonson (a common enough practice at the time), because they were inherited by his daughter, Thomasine. She married Christopher Browne, the son of Sir Richard Browne, a senior servant of the Earl of Leicester; through this connection the Gonson archive, together with many of Leicester's own papers, came eventually into the hands of Sir Richard's great-grand-daughter, Mary, who married John Evelyn.[2] From Evelyn much of this material, especially items of naval interest, passed to Samuel Pepys.[3] After his death, the papers which had been bound and incorporated into his main library passed by bequest to Magdalene College, Cambridge, where they still remain. Other parts of Pepys's archive were acquired by Richard Rawlinson, and came in time to the Bodleian Library in Oxford; the surviving Quarter Books are preserved by that descent.

[1] Alexander is identified as the second scribe by the record that he had entered up the Colne section for Michaelmas quarter 1563: BL, Add. MS 78171 [item 1(g)], f. 40, as detailed in Appendix 4 below. He had assisted the composition of the previous year's account, principally by supplying details from the pay-books: below, p. 225.

[2] The archival descent is fully set out in S. Adams, 'The papers of Robert Dudley, Earl of Leicester. I. The Browne-Evelyn collection', *Archives*, XX (1992), pp. 63–85.

[3] Evelyn showed one of the volumes ('a Lieger of the Treasurer of the Navy … just 100 years old') to Pepys on 24 Nov. 1665, which Pepys liked so much that Evelyn immediately made him a present of it, and promised to find others, yet older: Pepys, *Diary*, vi, pp. 307–8 and n. 1. Pepys eventually acquired eleven volumes of such accounts though only five survive, and it is the earliest of them (Rawlinson MS A. 200, for 1562–63) which is printed here. For the others, and their correspondence with the Exchequer Declared Accounts, see Appendix 1.

3 *Privy Seal warrant to the Exchequer for payment of ships at sea*

[E 404/115, bundle 5 Eliz. I][1] *28 October 156*

Elizabeth, by the Grace of God, Queen of England, France and Ireland, Defender of the Faith, &c., to the Treasurer and Chamberlains of our Exchequer, greeting; and will and command you that, of such our treasure as is presently or hereafter shall come into the receipt of our said Exchequer, you do content and pay to our servant Benjamin Gonson, Treasurer of our Admiralty,[2] the sum of two hundred fifty-three pounds six shillings eight pence, to be by him paid over in prest to our servant Edward Baeshe, General Surveyor of our Victuals for the Seas, for the victualling of 380 men serving us on the Narrow Seas in the *Aid*, the *Falcon*, the *Phoenix*, the *Bark of Boulogne* and the *Hare*, under the charge of Sir Thomas Cotton, knight, for one month beginning the 29th day of October and to end the 25th of November next. And these our letters shall be your warrant and discharge in this behalf. Given under our privy seal at our castle of Windsor the 28th day of October the fifth year of our reign.

[*Countersigned*] Richard Oseley, [Clerk of the Privy Seal].

4 *Navy Treasurer's Quarter Book*

[Bodl. MS Rawlinson A. 200 (*Cat. Rawl.*, col. 260)][4] *1562–6*

[*Cover*] The accounts as well ordinary as extraordinary of Benjamin Gonson, Treasurer of the Queen's Majesty's Marine Causes, for two whole years begun the first day of January 1561 [*1562*] and ended the last day of December 1563.

[1]Printed here as a sample of the type of warrant frequently cited in the next document. The issues it authorised are recorded in the Quarter Book as received 20 December: p. 25 entry **#Y28**.

[2]Appointed 8 July 1549: *CPR 1549–51*, p. 164; for further career details, see *NEM*, pp. 545–6.

[3]Appointed 18 June 1550: *CPR 1549–51*, p. 309; for further career details, see *NEM*, pp. 526–8.

[4]The MS has been annotated by an auditor. Where his marginalia supplement the sub-headings provided by the original scribe they are used here for the same purpose; when they make some further computation they are printed at the end of the paragraphs to which they relate. The frequent simple check mark '*ex*' (for '*examinatur*') is not printed. Otherwise the auditor's insertions are given here within square brackets preceded by *. The page headings are printed only where the formula changes, and the officers' signatures at the foot are printed only in the first and last instances.

[*Part I: for the year 1 January – 31 December 1562*]

[f. 1] **Ordinary. Receipts**:

Anno Domini 1561 [*1562*]. *Anno regni regine Elizabethe quarto*

Money received by Benjamin Gonson, Treasurer of Her Highness's Marine Causes, upon Her Grace's warrants, as hereafter more plainly appeareth.

Received of the Treasurer and Chamberlains of the Exchequer by virtue of Her Grace's warrant of privy seal to them directed dated at Her Highness's palace of Westminster the 11th day of March 1558 [*1559*] and in the first year of Her Highness's reign, containing the sum of £12,000 by the year;[1] as well toward payment of wages and victuals of shipwrights, caulkers, sawyers, smiths and other artificers and workmen for new building and repairing of Her Grace's ships and provisions for the same; and for wages and victuals of masters, mariners and gunners keeping Her Highness's ships afloat in harbour; as also for provision of cordage, canvas and divers other needful things for the rigging and tackling of the said ships to the seas: of Richard Stoneley one of the four tellers there,[2] *viz.* the 24th day of March 1561 [*1562*] – £500; the 19th day of September 1562 – £500; the 5th day of November 1562 – £100; the 10th day of December 1562 *anno quinto dicti Elizabethe regine*[3] – £500; the 18th day of the same month – £500; the 25th day of the same – £1,000; the 28th day of the same – £700; and the last day of the same month – £600. In the whole –

[1]See Introduction above, p. xxiv.

[2]The tellers received and recorded all sums payable into the Exchequer. For the office and the general administrative background see W. H. Bryson (ed.), 'A book of all the several officers of the court of Exchequer … by Lawrence Squibb', in *Camden Miscellany vol. XXVI* (RHS Camden 4th ser. XIV, 1975), pp. 133–4; G. R. Elton, *The Tudor Revolution in Government: Administrative Changes in the Reign of Henry VIII* (Cambridge, 1953), pp. 20–21 and *passim*; Elton, 'The Elizabethan Exchequer: war in the Receipt', repr. in his *Studies in Tudor and Stuart Politics and Government* (Cambridge, 1974–92), i, pp. 358–9 and *passim*; C. Coleman, 'Accident or artifice? The reorganization of the Exchequer of Receipt, *c.* 1554–1572', in Coleman and D. R. Starkey (eds), *Revolution Reassessed: Revisions in the History of Tudor Government and Administration* (Oxford, 1986), pp. 168–9 and *passim*. Stoneley was appointed by patent 10 Feb. 1554: *CPR 1553–4*, p. 84. In post until surrender by 6 Feb. 1598, despite substantial defaults on his account revealed in the 1570s; died 1600: *Hist. Parl. 1558–1603*, iii, pp. 450–1. J. C. Sainty (comp.), *Officers of the Exchequer* (List & Index Soc., special ser. 18, 1983), p. 232. Coleman, *loc. cit.*, p. 191 & n. 101, and *passim*. As noted below, three of the four tellers featured in the present document met similar trouble.

[3]Elizabeth's fifth regnal year had begun on 17 Nov.

£4,400 **[#A1]**.[1] *[*Examinatur per certificatorium Thome Felton clerici pellium*]*[2]

[f. 1v] Received of the Treasurer and Chamberlains of the Exchequer by virtue of Her Grace's warrant of privy seal to them directed dated at her palace of Westminster the 11th day of March 1558 [*1559*] and in the first year of Her Highness's reign, containing the sum of £12,000 by the year; as well toward payment of wages and victuals of shipwrights, caulkers, sawyers, smiths and other artificers and workmen for new building and repairing of Her Grace's ships and provisions for the same and for wages and victuals of masters, mariners and gunners keeping Her Highness's ships afloat in harbour; as also for provisions of cordage, canvas and divers other needful things for the rigging and tackling of the said ships to the seas: of Thomas Gardener, esquire, one of the four tellers there,[3] *viz.* the 8th day of May 1562 – £500; the 3rd day of June 1562 – £300; the 21th day of July 1562 – £100; the 20th day of August 1562 – £1,000; the 27th day of September 1562 – £500; the 27th day of November 1562 *anno quinto dicti Elizabethe regine* – £400; the 4th day of December 1562 – £100; the 12th day of the same month – £1,000; the 17th day of the same month – £150; the 28th day of the same month –

[1]Inset references preceded by # relate the *recepta* of the Quarter Book to the equivalent entries in the Declared Account **5**; see synopsis in Introduction above, p. 18.

[2]The clerk of the pells oversaw the work of the tellers and made further record of their receipts. The title, deriving from the pells or skins on which accounts were written, was originally and sometimes still phrased in the singular (*clericus pellis*), but the abbreviation *pell'* always used in this MS is extended to the plural form which gained currency. Felton's post was actually writer of the tallies (from appointment by Lord Treasurer Wiltshire 1[illegible] May 1550 to his death on 4 Sept. 1566), while the clerk of the pells was Robert Hare (from appointment by Lord Treasurer Winchester [as Wiltshire had become] 30 May 1560 until vacated by 1 April 1570); but these two officials were engaged in a prolonged contest for each other's responsibilities. Hare had been brought in as Winchester's personal deputy with wider remit and a more elaborate title ('clerk to the Lord Treasurer and writer and keeper of the pells of receipt and issue') which seemingly allowed Felton to poach the inferior but more ancient style 'clerk of the pell(s)'. Cf. Squibb, 'Officers of the Exchequer', p. 132; Sainty, *Exchequer Officers*, pp. 207, 215; Elton, *Tudor Revolution*, pp. 188, 252–3; *idem* 'War in the Receipt', pp. 359–61, 365 and *passim*; J. D. Alsop, 'The Exchequer of Receipt in the reign of Edward VI' (Cambridge PhD dissertation, 1978), esp. pp. 58–9, 60–1, 334– (biographical notes on Felton), 308–13 (transcribing Felton's treatise on the procedures of the Receipt); Coleman, 'Artifice or accident?', pp. 168–9, 183–4 and *passim* (making use of further unpublished work by Prof. Alsop). The John Felton who assassinated Lord Admiral Buckingham in 1628 appears to have come from another branch of this family: A. Hervey, 'Playford and the Feltons', *Proceedings of the Suffolk Institute of Archaeology and Natural History*, IV (1874), pp. 21, 23, 39–40, 54. *ODNB* 'Felton, John'.

[3]Appointed by patent 19 Feb. 1560: *CPR 1558–60*, p. 281. Deprived 4 May 1569 and subsequently imprisoned for defrauding the Crown of almost £30,000 by speculation with public moneys held on account (not in itself illegal, but he had been unable to make restitution): *Hist. Parl. 1509–58*, ii, p. 187. Sainty, *Exchequer Officers*, p. 232. Coleman, 'Accident or artifice?', pp. 191, 192 & n. 107, 193 & n. 109.

£500; and the 30th day of the same month of December – £470. In all – £5,020 **[#A2]**. *[*Examinatur per certificatorium clerici pellium predicti*]

[f. 2] Received of the Treasurer and Chamberlains of the Exchequer by virtue of Her Grace's warrant of privy seal to them directed dated at Her Highness palace of Westminster the 11th day of March 1558 [*1559*] and in the first year of Her Grace's reign, containing the sum of £12,000 by the year as well toward payment of wages and victuals of shipwrights, caulkers, sawyers, smiths and other artificers and workmen for new building and repairing of Her Highness's ships and provisions for the same, and for wages and victuals of masters, mariners and gunners keeping Her Grace's ships afloat in harbour; as also for provisions of cordage, canvas and divers other needful things for the rigging and tackling of the said ships to the seas: of William Patten, esquire, one of the four tellers there,[1] *viz*. the 9th day of November 1562 – £500; the 28th day of December 1562 *anno quinto dicti Elizabethe regine* – £540; the 29th day of the same month – £1,140. In all – £2,180 **[#A3]**. *[*Examinatur per certificatorium predicti*]

[f. 2v] Received of the Treasurer and Chamberlains of the Exchequer by virtue of Her Grace's warrant of privy seal to them directed dated at her palace of Westminster the 11th day of March 1558 [*1559*] and in the first year of Her Highness's reign, containing the sum of £12,000 by the year, as well towards payment of wages and victuals of shipwrights, caulkers, sawyers, smiths and other artificers and workmen for new building and repairing of Her Grace's ships and provisions for the same and for wages and victuals of masters, mariners and gunners keeping Her Highness's ships afloat in harbour; as also for provision of cordage, canvas and diverse other needful things for the rigging and tackling of the said ships to the seas: of Henry Killigrew, esquire, one of the four tellers there,[2] the 24th day of December 1562 *anno quinto dicti*

[1]Appointed by patent 23 June 1562: *CPR 1560–3*, p. 340. Suspended 17 Jan. 1568 on being being found to have lost £7,900 of the Crown's money, and deprived 13 July. On loss of this and other public employments he turned to scholarship, though best remembered for his original publication *The expedicion into Scotlāde of the most woothely fortunate prince Edward* (1548), the account of the 1547 invasion which he accompanied as a military judge: *ODNB*. Sainty, *Exchequer Officials*, p. 232. Coleman, 'Artifice or accident?', p. 191 & n. 101. B. O'Kill, 'The printed works of William Patten (*c*. 1510–*c*. 1600)', *TCBS*, VII (1977), pp. 28–45. For his ancestry, cf. V. Davis, *William Waynflete: Bishop and Educationalist* (Studies in the History of Medieval Religion, VI: Woodbridge, 1993), pp. 6–7.

[2]Appointed by patent 23 June 1561: *CPR 1560–3*, p. 127. Probably in reward for his service in Scotland the previous year, and in office until a year before his death in 1603, though his extensive political, military and diplomatic career meant his Exchequer duties were usually delegated. Knighted 1591: *ODNB*. *Hist. Parl. 1509–58*, ii, pp. 466–7; *1558–1603*, ii, pp. 374–5. Sainty, *Exchequer Officers*, p. 232. A. C. Miller, *Sir Henry Killigrew: Elizabethan Soldier and Diplomat* (Leicester, 1963), esp. pp. 66–7, 228–30.

Elizabethe regine – £400. *Summa* – £400 **[#A4]**. *[*Examinatur per certificatorium predicti*]

[#A1–4: *total ordinary receipts 1562 – £12,000***]**

[f. 3] **Extraordinary. Receipts**:

Anno Domini 1561 [*1562*]. *Anno regni regine Elizabethe quarto*

*[*Sale money*]. Received the 22th day of January *anno supradicto* of Thomas Gardener, esquire, one of the tellers of the receipt at Westminster and keeper of Her Grace's money growing upon the sales by virtue of Her Highness's warrant to him directed given under Her Grace's signet at her palace of Westminster the 21th day of this present, containing the sum of £8,000 appointed to be paid to divers persons by the High Treasurer or Under-treasurer of the Exchequer toward the satisfaction and payment of the marine causes or affairs within my charge, determinable upon mine account at Christmas last, as by the said appointment with the said Thomas Gardener remaining more plainly appeareth: the sum of three thousand pounds – £3,000 **[#B1]**. *[*Examinatur per certificatorium Thome Gardener*]

*[*Sale money*]. Received the 24th day of January *anno supradicto* of the aforesaid Thomas Gardener, esquire, one of the tellers of the receipt at Westminster and keeper of Her Grace's money growing upon the sales by virtue of Her Highness's warrant to him directed given under Her Grace's signet at Her Highness's palace of Westminster the 23th day of this present, containing the sum of £5,000 appointed to be paid to divers persons by the High Treasurer or Under-treasurer of the Exchequer towards the satisfaction and payment of the marine causes or affairs within my charge determinable upon mine account at Christmas last, as by the said appointment with the said Thomas Gardener remaining more plainly appeareth: the sum of three thousand pounds – £3,000 **[#B2]**. *[*Examinatur per certificatorium Thome Gardener*]

[f. 3v] Received the 8th day of March *anno supradicto* of the Treasurer and Chamberlains of the Exchequer by virtue of Her Grace's warrant of privy seal to them directed dated at Her Highness's palace of Westminster the 6th day of this present at the hands of Richard Stoneley, esquire, one of the tellers there, in full satisfaction and payment of Her Grace's marine affairs within my charge determinable upon mine account at the feast of Christmas last past: the sum of one thousand five hundred twenty-four pounds seven shillings – £1,524 7 **[#B3]**. *[*Examinatur per certificatorium predicti*]

Received the last day of September *anno supradicto* of Francis Lee of Rotherhithe, gunpowder maker, for a ship of Her Majesty's called the *Jerfalcon*, sold by virtue of Her Grace's warrant given under her signet at her manor of Greenwich the 29 day of June last, to the right trusty and well beloved the Lord Clinton and Saye, High Admiral of England,[1] &c. directed, the sum of four score pounds – £80 **[#B4]**.

Received the 28th day of September *anno supradicto* of the Queen's most excellent Majesty by the hands of the Right Honourable Sir William Cecil, knight, Her Highness's Principal Secretary, to Her Grace's use towards the charges and maintenance of Her Majesty's Navy,[2] the sum of one thousand pounds current money – £1,000 **[#B5]**.

[f. 4] *Anno Domini 1562. Anno regni regine Elizabethe quarto*

Received the 7th day of July *anno supradicto* of the Treasurer and Chamberlains of the Exchequer by virtue of Her Grace's warrant of privy seal to them directed dated at Her Grace's manor of Greenwich the 3rd day of this present of Richard Stoneley, one of the tellers there, by way of prest for the setting forth of the *Saker* and the *Phoenix* furnished for one month with 60 men appointed to transport Her Highness's provisions into the north parts:[3] the sum of threescore six pounds thirteen shillings four pence – £66 13s 4d **[#B6]**. *[*Examinatur per certificatorium Thome Felton predicti*]

[1]Edward, Baron Clinton and Saye (Earl of Lincoln 1572), Lord Admiral 1550–54; reappointed 10 Feb. 1558 and in office till his death (1585): *CPR 1557–8*, p. 2. *HBC*, p. 133; see fuller career details in *NEM*, pp. 542–3.

[2]A loan made available immediately out of the privy purse on the Queen's authority, for which a privy seal warrant was issued retrospectively on 17 July 1563 (cf. **18** below). Large reserves of cash were still kept in the royal palaces; from an early point in Elizabeth's reign Cecil had taken effective control of their disbursement, over the head of the Household official (First Gentleman of the Privy Chamber) formally in charge: P. Wright, 'A change in direction: the ramifications of a female household, 1558–1603', in D. Starkey (ed.), *The English Court: from the Wars of the Roses to the Civil War* (1987), pp. 152–3 & n. 25, drawing attention to a note of miscellaneous payments by Cecil on the Queen's authority, May–Aug. 1561: HMC, *Salisbury*, i, pp. 261–2. The present detail usefully corroborates the evidence noted by Wright and the inference drawn from it.

[3]Extra provisions were required in the north in anticipation of the passage of the Queen of Scots and a train of 1,000 en route to an interview with Elizabeth. Articles for the meeting, at York or as far south as Nottingham, were concluded at Greenwich on 6 July. On 8 July the Privy Council ordered 200 quarters of wheat and the like of malt to be bought in Buckinghamshire and sent to Berwick. Arrangements were still being made on 12 July, but the meeting was cancelled three days later: *APC 1558–70*, p. 113. *Cal. Scot. 1547–63*, no. 1126 (pp. 640–1). SP 12/23, no. 53 (*CSPD 1547–80*, p. 202). This entry suggests that the provisioning mission was set in hand three days before the terms of the interview were formally agreed; no evidence has been found that the ships actually sailed, so this charge may simply cover aborted preparations.

Received the 23th day of July *anno supradicto* of Sir William Damsell, knight, Receiver-general of Her Grace's court of Wards and Liveries,[1] by virtue of Her Highness's warrant to him directed given under Her Grace's signet at her manor of Greenwich this present 23th day of July: the sum of eight hundred three score twelve pounds ten shillings; as well to be immediately delivered over to Edward Baeshe, General Surveyor of Her Grace's victuals for the seas, for the victualling of four ships and one bark with 990 men, as also for the conduct money of 850 men appointed to be called to serve Her Grace in her said ships – £872 10s **[#B7]**. *[*Examinatur per certificatorium Willielmi Dansell militis*]

[f. 4v] Received the 4th day of September *anno supradicto* of the Treasurer and Chamberlains of the Exchequer by virtue of Her Grace's warrant of privy seal to them directed dated at her manor of Greenwich the 4th day of August last by the hands of Richard Stoneley, esquire, one of the tellers there: the sum of one hundred forty pounds, to be delivered over to Edward Baeshe, General Surveyor of Her Grace's victuals for the seas, for the victualling of 140 men for 6 weeks appointed to serve Her Highness in one of her ships and a bark called the *Willoughby* and the *Phoenix*, as well for the waftage of certain Her Highness's munitions presently shipped for Her Grace's realm of Ireland, as for the apprehension of certain pirates at the seas[2] – £140 **[#B8]**. *[*Examinatur per certificatorium Thome Felton clerici pellium*]

Received the 15th day of September *anno supradicto* of the Treasurer and Chamberlains of the Exchequer by virtue of Her Grace's warrant of privy seal to them directed dated at her manor of Greenwich the 4th day of this present, by the hands of Richard Stoneley, one of the tellers there: the sum of one hundred thirteen pounds six shillings eight pence, to be paid over in prest to Edward Baeshe, General Surveyor of Her Grace's sea victuals, for one month of 28 days for 170 men appointed to serve Her Highness at the seas in the *New Bark* and the *Saker* – £113 6s 8d **[#B9]**. *[*Examinatur per certificatorium predicti*]

[f. 5] Received the 9th day of September *anno supradicto* of Sir William Damsell, knight, Receiver-general of Her Grace's court of Wards and

[1]Appointed 27 Dec. 1550; reappointed 17 Jan. 1554 with special proviso preserving his function and revenues in event of the court's reorganisation or dissolution: *CPR 1549–51* p. 311; *1553–4*, p. 49. A Merchant Adventurer who had entered public service as the Crown's factor in the Netherlands (1546–52), and knighted 1553. Retained his appointment in Wards to his death in 1582: *Hist. Parl. 1509–58*, ii, pp. 9–10; *1558–1603*, ii, p. 11. J. Hurstfield *The Queen's Wards: Wardship and Marriage under Elizabeth I* (1958), pp. 212, 226–7 and *passim*.

[2]In June the Privy Council had been informed of piracies in the Irish Sea and elsewhere and on 30 July the Queen ordered Clinton to send four ships (evidently including *Swallow*) under Sir William Woodhouse to clear pirates from the English Channel: *APC 1558–70*, pp. 107–8, 129–30; SP 12/23, no. 64 (*CSPD 1547–80*, p. 203).

Liveries, by virtue of Her Highness's warrant under her signet at her manor of Greenwich the 7th day of this present: the sum of three hundred twenty-six pounds thirteen shillings four pence, for the wages and conduct money home of 400 mariners presently to be discharged out of two of Her Grace's ships the *Hope* and the *Lion* – £326 13s 4d **[#B10]**. *[*Examinatur per certificatorium Willielmi Dansell militis*]

Received the 19th day of September *anno supradicto* of the Treasurer and Chamberlains of the Exchequer by virtue of Her Grace's warrant of privy seal to them directed dated at her manor of Greenwich the 15th day of this present, at the hands of Richard Stoneley, one of the four tellers there: the sum of one hundred and thirty pounds, to be immediately paid over to Edward Baeshe, General Surveyor of Her Grace's victuals, for the victualling of 390 men for 14 days appointed to serve Her Highness at the seas in the *Hart*, the *Swallow* and the *Hare* – £130 **[#B11]**. *[*Examinatur per certificatorium Thome Felton predicti*]

[f. 5v] Received the 5th day of October *anno supradicto* of Sir William Damsell, knight, Receiver-general of Her Grace's court of Wards and Liveries, by virtue of Her Highness's warrant to him directed, given under her signet at Her Grace's honor of Hampton Court the second day of this present: the sum of one hundred fourescore six pounds thirteen shillings four pence, to be delivered over in prest to Edward Baeshe, General Surveyor of Her Grace's victuals for the seas, for the victualling of 560 men for 14 days appointed to serve Her Highness at the seas in the *Swallow*, the *Hart*, the *New Bark*, The *Saker* and the *Hare* – £186 13s 4d **[#B12]**. *[*Examinatur per certificatorium Willielmi Dansell*]

Received of the Treasurer and Chamberlains of the Exchequer by virtue of Her Grace's warrant of privy seal to them directed dated at Her Highness's honor of Hampton Court the 14th day of October: the sum of seven hundred twenty-seven pounds six shillings eight pence, for the payment of masters and men of three Her Grace's ships now discharged, *viz.* of Richard Stoneley, one of the tellers, there the 16th day of this present month of October at the hands of Burde and Smythe – £519; and of Thomas Gardener, one of the tellers, there the same day – £208 6s 8d **[#B13]**. *Summa* – £727 6s 8d. *[*Examinatur per certificatorium Willielimi Dansell*].

[f. 6] Received the 6th day of November *anno supradicto* of the Treasurer and Chamberlains of the Exchequer by virtue of Her Grace's warrant of privy seal to them directed dated at her manor of Hampton Court the third day of this present at, the hands of Richard Stoneley, one of the tellers, there: the sum of one hundred twenty pounds, to be delivered over in prest to Edward Baeshe, General Surveyor of Her Grace's victuals for the seas; as well for a provision of victuals for three weeks for 200 men serving Her Highness at the seas in the *New Bark*, the *Saker* and the *Hare*, to begin the first of this present month of November; as also for one month's victuals for 30 men likewise appointed to serve Her Highness at the seas in the *Double Rose* to begin the 13th day of October last – £120 **[#B14]**. *[*Examinatur per certificatorium Thome Felton predicti*]

Received the 11th day of November *anno supradicto* of the Treasurer and Chamberlains of the Exchequer by virtue of Her Grace's warrant of privy seal to them directed dated at her honor of Hampton Court the 8th day of this present, at the hands of Richard Stoneley esquire one of the tellers there: the sum of threescore four pounds, for the prest and conduct of 320 mariners for the conduction of five Her Grace's ships to Portsmouth for Her Highness's service, *viz.* the *Antelope*, the *Jennet*, the *Greyhound*, the new ship[1] and the *Bark of Boulogne* – £64 **[#B15]**. *[*Examinatur per certificatorium Thomas Felton predicti*]

[f. 6v] Received of the Treasurer and Chamberlains of the Exchequer by virtue of Her Grace's warrant of privy seal to them directed dated at Her Highness's honor of Strand[2] the 15th day of November: the sum of three hundred fourscore-six pounds thirteen shillings four pence, to be delivered over in prest to Edward Baeshe, General Surveyor of Her Grace's victuals for the seas, as well for three weeks' victuals for the *Phoenix* for 40 men begun the first of this month of November, and for one month's victuals for the *New Bark*, the *Saker*, the *Hare* and the *Phoenix* with 240 men serving Her Highness at the seas to begin the 22th day of this present month of November;[3] as also for the like victualling of 310 men for one month appointed to carry and transport certain Her Grace's ships from Gillingham to Portsmouth, *viz.* the *Jennet*, the *Antelope*, the *Greyhound*, the new ship and the *Bark of Boulogne*; *viz.* of Richard Stoneley the 18th day of November *anno quinto supradicto regine Elizabethe* – £100; of Henry Killigrew the 19th day of the same month and year – £246 13s 4d; and of William Patten the 20th day of the same month and year – £40. *Summa* – £386 13s 4d **[#B16]**. *[*Examinatur per certificatorium Thome Felton predicti*]

Received of the Treasurer and Chamberlains of the Exchequer by virtue of Her Grace's warrant of privy seal to them directed dated at her manor of Strand the 7th day of December *anno supradicto*: the sum of five

[1]The *Aid*, which had been launched at Deptford on 6 October. As explained in the victualling schedule [**25**], on arrival at Portsmouth she took the place originally designated for *New Bark*, with the same complement; *New Bark*'s captain transferred to the new ship *wef* 1 Dec.: below, pp. 228, 235, 236.

[2]Somerset Place, which had been Elizabeth's town house before her accession, and was occasionally used by her as Queen.

[3]Cf. Baeshe's application for a warrant of £160 to victual these four ships for the month beginning 22 Nov. [**24**].

hundred twenty-one pounds six shillings and eight pence, to be employed as well for the diets of William Driver, captain of the *New Bark*, and wages of 119 persons serving there as masters, mariners and gunners for four months one week beginning the 4th day of August last and ending the last of November following, and for Thomas Hare, captain of the *Phoenix*, and [*Robert*][1] Marsh, captain of the *Hare*, each of them having 39 persons serving in them, for like time and rate, and to John Henshaw, captain of the *Saker*, and 49 persons serving under him for like time and rate, and to Thomas Elye, master of the *Double Rose* and 29 persons serving there by the space of 7 weeks 2 days begun the 11th day of October last and ending the last day of November last for like time and rate; *viz.* of Richard Stoneley, one of the tellers there, the 16th day of December *anno supradicto* – £200; of Henry Killigrew, one other of the tellers there, the 26th day of the same month of December *anno supradicto* – £221 6s 8d; and of Thomas Gardener, another of the tellers there, the 27th day of the same month of December – £100. *Summa* – £521 6s 8d **[#B17]**.

[f. 7] Received the 24th day of December *anno supradicto* of the Treasurer and Chamberlains of the Exchequer by virtue of Her Grace's warrant of privy seal to them directed dated at Her Highness's manor of Strand the 8th day of this present, at the hands of Henry Killigrew, one of the tellers there: the sum of two hundred pounds, to be delivered over in prest to Edward Baeshe, General Surveyor of Her Grace's victuals for the seas, for the victualling of six Her Highness's ships, *viz.* the *New Bark*, the *Saker*, the *Phoenix*, the *Hare*, the *Bark of Boulogne* and the *Double Rose* for one month of 28 days to begin the 20th day of this present month of December and to end the 16th day of [*January*][2] next – £200 **[#B18]**.
*[*Examinatur per certificatorium predicti*] [f. 7v *blank*]

[**#B1–18:** *total extraordinary receipts 1562 – £12,459 10s 4d*]

[f. 8] **Ordinary. Deptford**:

Anno Domini 1562. *Anno regni regine Elizabethe quarto*

A payment made the last day of March as well to keepers of storehouses, dock and timber-yards, as also to shipwrights, caulkers, sawyers, smiths, carpenters, labourers and others working upon the new building of Her Grace's ships there and provisions for the same, and to sundry persons

[1]MS 'Thomas', doubtless by confusion with the preceding Thomas, and perhaps also with the Thomas Marshe occurring a little below (p. 32); *Hare*'s captain and Captain Hare are correctly distinguished at pp. 235–6. 161. Cf. also *NEM*, pp. 549–50, 559.

[2]MS 'Februarij', in obvious error. Cf. Baeshe's application for this warrant [**25**].

for divers provisions of them had and delivered into Her Highness's storehouse for the use of Her Grace's ships; begun the first day of January last and this day ended, as followeth:

*[*Timber-yard keeper*]. To Thomas Marshe, mariner,[1] the last day of March for his wages daily attending and serving Her Highness in safe-keeping of Her Grace's timber-yards wherein lieth her timber, plank and board for the use of her ships, as also for the rigging, grounding and tackling of Her Grace's ships to the seas, by the space of 12 weeks 6 days begun the first day of January last and this day ended, at 20s every month – £3 4s 3d.

*[< deleted *Labourers'*> *Mariners' wages – 42s 10d; victuals – 42s 10d*]. To Robert Tasse and William Olyve, mariners, the same day for their wages daily attending and serving Her Highness in labouring about the coiling and tarring of cables, cablets, hawsers and other provisions brought into the storehouses and the same delivered out again for the use of Her Grace's ships, by the space of 12 weeks 6 days begun and ended as aforesaid, at 6s 8d every month the man – 42s 10d; and more to them for their victuals for the like time as abovesaid, at 20d every week the man – 42s 10d. *Summa* – £4 5s 8d.

[*Signed*] W. Winter. William Holstock. G. Winter.[2]

Summa – £7 9s 11d.[3]

[f. 8v] *[*Labourer in coiling of cables*]. To Richard Harwood mariner, the last day of March for his wages and victuals daily attending and serving Her Highness in labouring about the carriage of provisions and coiling up of cables in Her Grace's storehouse for the use of her ships, by the space of 12 weeks 6 days begun the first day of January last and ended as aforesaid, at 13s 4d every month. *Summa* – £2 2s 10d.

*[*Shipkeeper*]. To William Partricke, mariner, the same day for his wages daily attending and serving Her Highness in safe-keeping of one

[1]Here and in similar entries in the Deptford sections the abbreviation 'mr' is taken to stand for 'mariner' rather than (as it normally does) 'master'. Marshe the timber-yard keeper is 'mr' in every quarterly entry, while most other names are invariably followed by 'mariner'. But for two of the labourers the style varies in successive quarters: John Benwell is 'mr' ×3, 'mariner' ×3, then 'mr' again; Richard Harwood is 'mariner' ×2, 'mr', 'mariner' ×3, 'mr' ×2. Nothing can be deduced from the scribal variations, and it is safest to extend the abbreviation to the word by which these officials are elsewhere described.

[2]William Winter, Surveyor and Rigger (1549–89), William Holstock, Comptroller (1561–89) and William's brother George Winter, Clerk of the Ships (1560–80); for full career details see *NEM*, pp. 551–2, 571–2. The signatures of these officers appear at the foot of each succeeding page (except the blanks); they are printed only in this instance and the last.

[3]The sum of the page, occasionally written '*Summa pagine*', hereafter signalled '[*Page total*]'.

of Her Grace's new ships lying in the dry dock[1] there by like time of 3 months 6 days begun and ended as aforesaid, at 6s 8d every month. *Summa* – £1 1s 5d.

*[*Labourer*]. To John Benwell, mariner, the same day for his wages daily attending and serving Her Highness in labouring about the carriage of provisions and coiling up of cables by like 12 weeks 6 days begun and ended as abovesaid, at 13s 4d *per mensem* – £2 2s 10d.

*[*Shipkeeper*]. To Giles Hall, mariner, the same day for his wages serving Her Highness in safe-keeping of one of Her Grace's ships at Deptford lying in the dry dock there,[2] by like time of one quarter of a year begun and ended as abovesaid, at 13s 4d *per mensem* – £2 2s 10d.

*[*Labourer in coiling of cables*]. To Thomas Larke and Christopher Brayfot, mariners, the same day for their wages and victuals daily attending and serving Her Highness in labouring about the carriage of provisions and coiling up of cables as aforesaid, by like time of 12 weeks 6 days begun and ended as aforesaid, at 13s 4d every man the month. *Summa* – £4 5s 8d.

[*Page total*] – £11 15s 7d.

[f . 9] *[*Shipkeeper*]. To Paul Saunders, boatswain, the last day of March for his wages daily attending and serving Her Highness in safe-keeping of her ship named the *Jerfalcon* there by the space of 12 weeks 6 days begun the first day of January last and ended as abovesaid, at 6s 8d the month. *Summa* – £1 1s 5d.

*[*Keeper of prick and cheque book*].[3] To James Jentill the same day for his wages daily serving Her Highness for the keeping of the prick and

[1] Dry docks were originally, and still at this time, excavated basins sealed off with walls of earth and rubble before being pumped dry, to enable the undersides of ships to be inspected and repaired. Such docks existed at all the main bases, although ships were still frequently beached outside of a dock, for routine maintenance (cf. below, p. 35. 10). It appears to have been at Deptford in 1578 that closable timber gates were first introduced, a major technical innovation which significantly assisted English maritime development: Oppenheim, *History*, p. 150. Rodger, *Safeguard*, pp. 335–6. B. Dietz, 'Dikes, dockheads and gates: English docks and sea power in the sixteenth and seventeenth centuries', *MM*, LXXXVIII (2002), pp. 145, 153 n. 12.

[2] The *George* hoy; cf. below, p. 57 and other entries.

[3] The officer later known as clerk of the cheque, keeping the muster-book of the dockyard workforce, recording payments and absences; for his functions (and abuses of them), see R. C. Latham (ed.), *Samuel Pepys and the Second Dutch War: Pepys's Navy White Book and Brooke House Papers* (NRS, Vol. 133, 1995), pp. 64–5 and *passim*. A pin-prick marked each man's attendance: cf. the nineteenth-century 'prick-bill' at Christ Church, Oxford [*OED*]. This form of the word 'check', a usage distinct from that in banking, survives in the titles of officers of the Honourable Corps of Gentlemen at Arms and The Queen's Bodyguard of the Yeoman of the Guard. Cf. E. F. Rimbault (ed.), *The Old Cheque-Book, or Book of Remembrance, of the Chapel Royal, from 1561 to 1744* (Camden Soc. new ser. III, 1872), pp. xii–xiii.

cheque book of masters, mariners and gunners serving in Her Grace's ships within the river of Thames, by the space of 90 days begun and ended as aforesaid, at 8d *per diem. Summa* – £3.

*[*Keeper of storehouse*]. To Henry Abraham the same day for his wages daily attending and serving Her Highness for the safe-keeping of Her Grace's storehouses there wherein lieth divers and sundry kinds of provisions as cables, hawsers, small cordage, oakum and other sorts of stuffs for the use of Her Grace's ships, by like 90 days begun and ended as aforesaid, at 8d *per diem* – £3.

*[*Purveyor*]. To Edward Gotley the same day for his wages daily attending and serving Her Highness in providing of all kinds of provisions and necessaries for the building and repairing of Her Grace's ships, by like time of 90 days begun and ended as aforesaid, at 8d *per diem. Summa* – £3.

*[*Surveying of provisions*]. To Thomas Thomas the same day for his wages daily serving Her Highness for the taking of the survey of all manner of necessary provisions had of divers persons for the furniture of Her Grace's ships, as well at their setting forth to the seas as also at their coming home again into harbour, by like time of 90 days begun the first day of January last and ended as abovesaid, at 8d *per diem* – £3.

[*Page total*] – £13 1s 4d.

[f. 9v] *[*Keeper of timber-yard*]. To John Kinge, mariner, the last day of March for his wages daily attending and serving Her Highness in safe-keeping of her timber-yards wherein lieth Her Grace's timber for the use of her ships, by the space of 3 months 6 days begun and ended as aforesaid, at 6s 8d *per mensem* – £1 1s 5d.

*[<*Labourer* deleted> *Plug keeper*]. To William Ally, labourer, the same day for his wages daily serving Her Highness about the keeping of the plug and letting out of the water for the dry keeping of the same dock wherein lieth Her Grace's two new ships,[1] by like time of 90 days begun and ended as abovesaid, at 8d *per diem. Summa* – £3.

*[*Keeper of timber-yard*]. To Thomas Woodde, porter, the same day for his wages daily serving Her Highness in safe-keeping of the timber-yards there wherein lieth Her Grace's timber, plank, masts, reed and other necessaries for the use of her ships, by like 90 days begun and ended as aforesaid, at 8d *per diem* – £3.

*[*Riding charges*]. To John Elmer, messenger, the same day for his wages daily serving Her Highness for the carrying of the officers' letters

[1] That is, breaching and closing up the wall of the dock as required; the temporary nature of this 'plug' involved frequent maintenance. Cf. Oppenheim, *Naval Accounts Hen. VII,* pp 170–1. The ships are identified below (p. 61) as *Triumph* and *Victory.*

in post to divers and sundry places along the sea coasts for the marine causes, by like time of 90 days begun and ended as abovesaid, at 12d *per diem* – £4 10s.

*[*Shipwright*]. To Augustino Levello, Venetian shipwright, the same day for his wages daily attending and serving Her Highness for the repairing and mending of Her Grace's two galleys,[1] by the like 90 days begun and ended as aforesaid, at 16d *per diem*. *Summa* – £6.

[*Page total*] – £17 11s 5d.

[f. 10] *[*Clerk*]. To Stephen Alexander the last day of March for his wages daily attending and serving Her Highness for the writing making and keeping of the book of report of all such provisions and necessaries had and taken of sundry persons for the use of Her Grace's ships, for one quarter of a year due as aforesaid. *Summa* – £6 13s 4d.

*[*Caulker*]. To Robert Hart the same day for his wages daily serving Her Highness in giving attendance for the caulking of Her Grace's ships by like time of 90 days begun and ended as abovesaid, at 8d *per diem* – £3.

*[*Caulker*]. To Thomas Bolton, caulker, the same day for his wages daily attending and serving Her Highness for the caulking of her ships at their groundings, by 90 days begun the first day of January last and ended the 26 day of March, at 8d *per diem* – £2 16s 8d.

*[*Shipwright*]. To Matthew Baker, shipwright,[2] the same day for his wages daily attending and serving Her Highness in her ships by the space of 90 days begun the first day of January last and ended as abovesaid, at 8d every day. *Summa* – £3.

*[*Shipwright*]. To Edward Bright, master shipwright,[3] the same day for his wages daily attending and serving Her Highness for the working upon Her Grace's ships there by the space of 78 days within this time begun the first day of January last and ended the 19th day of this present, at 12d *per diem* – £3 18s.

[*Page total*] – £19 8s.

[1] In fact the Navy had three galleys in service at this time: *Mermaid* (or *Black Galley*), *Speedwell* and *Tryright*, each originally a French prize. Henry VIII's *Galley Subtle* (or *Red Galley*) had gone out of service in 1559, and was to be replaced in 1563 with *Eleanor* (p. 419 below), also of French origin. Because English shipwrights had no skill with galleys, this Italian was retained at a special wage to look after them. In fact three are mentioned next time (p. 44), but the entry reverts to two (pp. 61, 85), before becoming unspecific (p. 254), so must refer only to the numbers under repair in any particular quarter.

[2] Later the Queen's master shipwright by patent 23 June 1572: *CPR 1569–72*, no. 3303; for full career details see *NEM*, pp. 529–30.

[3] Co-builder of *Elizabeth Jonas*; for career details see *NEM*, pp. 533–4.

[f. 10v] *Shipwrights* *[*Artificers*]

Peter Pett, master,[1] 7 days at 12d	7s
Christopher Sweteman, server,[2] 6 days at 6d	3s
George Kingstun, 6 days at 4d	2s
Edward Bright, master, 12 days at 12d	12s
Davy Baker, server, 12 days at 6d	6s
Thomas Jewell, 12 days at 6d	6s
Daniel Bright, 12 days at 6d	6s
Caulkers *[*Artificers*]	
Thomas Bolton, master, 5 days at 8d	3s 4d
William Bolton, server, 5 days at 6d	2s 6d
Walter Claye, 5 days at 6d	2s 6d
Richard Bartun, 5 days at 7d	2s 11d
John Graye, server, 5 days at 5d	2s 1d
Robert Brigges, 5 days at 7d	2s 11d
John Dowell, 4 days at 6d	2s
James Dowell, 4 days at 5d	20d
Smiths *[*Artificers*]	
Richard Welles, 45 days at 8d	30s
Thomas Welles, server, 45 days at 4d	15s
Richard Atkinson, 45 days at 4d	15s
Thomas Wattes, 42 days at 6d	21s
Thomas Davy, 42 days at 6d	21s
Thomas Jonson, 45 days at 6d	32s 6d

[*Page total*] – £9 6s 5d.

[f. 11] *Victualling.* To Peter Pett, master shipwright, the 21th day o January for the victualling of himself and 20 other shipwrights, caulkers and smiths working upon Her Highness's ships there by the space of 43 days among them all, Sundays and holy days in the same accounted begun the first day of January and ended as abovesaid, which maketh 6 weeks 3 days, at 4s every week the man. *Summa* – £12 5s 9d.

Lodging. To Thomas Bolton and Neme Welles the 24th day o February for the lodging of 13 of the aforenamed shipwrights, caulkers smiths and other[*s*] working upon Her Grace's two new ships there, i seven featherbeds by the space of 53 weeks among all, begun the first da of January last and ended as abovesaid, at 2d every week the man. *Summ* – 8s 10d.

[*Page total*] – £12 14s 7d.

[1]Royal master shipwright by patent 29 April 1558, granting this daily fee: *CPR 1557–8* p. 100; for full career details see *NEM*, p. 562.

[2]Assistant: see Introduction, p. 20, for the significance of this commonly occurring term.

[f. 11v] *House-carpenters*

John Leache, 31 days at 12d	31s
Thomas Hill, 39 days at 10d	32s 6d
John Thrall, 38 days at 9d	28s 6d
Robert Thorrelley, 38 days at 7d	22s
	[£5 14s 2d*]*

Labourers

Willam Ally, master, 30 nights at 4d	10s
Richard Raynsforth, 12 days at 7d	7s
John Hurlestone, 94 days and tides[1] at 6d	47s
Nicholas Gest, 94 days and tides at 6d	47s
Thomas Thisstellton, 94 days and tides at 6d	47s
George Mathew, 94 days and tides at 6d	47s
John Lowman, 94 days and tides at 6d	47s
James Howper, 94 days and tides at 6d	47s
John Gibson, 5 days at 6d	2s 6d
Henry Stevenson, 4 days at 6d	2s
George Bell, 2 days at 6d	12d
John Twyford, 2 days at 6d	12d
Robert Scot, 1 day at 6d	6d
John Jennyns, 1 day at 6d	6d
Robert Marshall, 3 days at 6d	18d
John Bastian, 2 days at 6d	12d
William Kelley, 4 days at 6d	2s
Edward Plumer, 4 days at 6d	2s
Richard Shafte, 1 day at 6d	6d
Edward Lamtun, 1 day at 6d	6d
Henry Courtland, 1 day at 6d	6d
	[£15 14s 6d*]*

[*Page total*] – £21 8s 8d.

[f. 12] *Watchmen*

Nicholas Gest, 36 nights at 6d	18s

[1] A tide was originally the term applied to the interval between tides (i.e. slack water) when certain work could be undertaken on ships which had been beached. It then became a standard unit of overtime or bonus payment for difficult or urgent work, irrespective of the actual state of the water. These entries therefore mean that the man concerned did so much time at the standard rate and then so much overtime, bringing his total earnings to the equivalent of (in this first instance) 94 days at the standard rate. The implication is that the six men listed here were a gang employed on a specific job. 'Night' could also mean a fixed unit of 5 hours' overtime, and is probably so used here. By the Restoration a 'tide' had become a fixed unit of 1½ hours' overtime; for these later usages see R. V. Saville (ed.), 'The management of the royal dockyards, 1672–1678', in N. A. M. Rodger (ed.), *The Naval Miscellany, Volume V* (NRS, Vol. 125, 1984), pp. 97–8; Pepys, *Navy White Book*, pp. 45, 46 & n. 1.

John Hurleston, 36 nights at 6d	18s
Thomas Thissellton, 36 nights at 6d	18s
George Mathew, 36 nights at 6d	18s
James Howper, 36 nights at 6d	18s
John Loweman, 36 nights at 6d	18s
Thomas Smythe, 32 nights at 6d	16s
William Partrick, 25 nights at 6d	12s 6d
Paul Saunders, 26 nights at 6d	13s
John Twyford, 22 nights at 6d	11s
Edward Plumer, 20 nights at 6d	10s
Henry Stevenson, 19 nights at 6d	9s 6d

[*Page total*] – £9.

[f. 12v] *Emptions*

Timber, plank, shores and trenails. To James Davyson of London the last day of March for price of 23 loads 8 foot of timber oak of him had and delivered at Deptford for the use of Her Highness's ships, at 10s every load after 50 foot to the load. *Summa* – £11 11s 8d.

To Richard Dyngle of Chislet the same day for price of 6 loads and a half of elm timber of him had and delivered as aforesaid for the use of Her Grace's ships, at 5s every load – 32s 6d; and more to him for 5 loads of oaken shores after talwood mark,[1] at 5s every load – 25s. *Summa* – £2 17s 6d.

To Henry Fyllyan of Yalding in Kent the last day of March for price of 1,740 foot of 4-inch plank oak of him had and delivered at Deptford Strand for the new building and making of Her Highness's two ships there, at 11s every 100 foot – £9 11s 10d; more for 2,924 foot of 3-inch plank oak, at 11s every 100 foot – £16 1s 9d; more for 832 foot of 2-inch plank oak, at 10s every 100 foot – £4 3s 1½d; more for 5 loads 30 foot of timber oak, at 11s every load after 50 foot to the load – £3 3s 3d; and more to him for 13,000 of trenails of 24 inches long, at 2s every 100 – £13. *Summa* – £45 19s 11½d.

To the said Henry Fyllyan the same day for price of 4,349 foot of 4-inch plank of him had and delivered as aforesaid for the use of Her Highness's ships, at 11s every 100 – £23 18s 4½d; more for 2,379 foot of 3-inch plank oak, at 11s every 100 – £13 1s 8d; more for 1,606 foot of 2-inch plank oak, at 10s every 100 – £8 0s 7½d; more for 29 foot of inch ½ board oak, price – 10d; more for 600 of trenails of 30 inches long, at 2s 6d every 100 – 15s; and more for 44 foot of timber oak, price – 8s 9d. *Summa* – £46 5s.

[*Page total*] – £106 14s 1½d.

[1] I.e. as sized for firewood.

[f. 13] *Timber oak.* To William Greves of Deptford the last day of March for price of 29 foot of timber oak of him had and delivered at Deptford for the new making of Her Highness's ship boats there, at 4½d every foot. *Summa* – £8 0s 5½d.

A pump. To William Bexley of Foots Cray in Kent the same day for price of one elm pump of him had and delivered at Deptford for the use of Her Highness's ships, containing in length 16 foot at 20d every foot, by agreement – 26s 8d; and more to him for ironwork for the same pump, price – 6s. *Summa* – £1 12s 8d.

Ironwork. To Thomas Willson of Ratcliff, smith, the same day for price of 3 hundred 2 quarters 26 pounds weight [*418 lbs*] of his own new iron of him had and by him made into spikes and overlop nails, and the same delivered at Deptford for the use of Her Grace's ships, at 24s 6d every hundredweight – £4 11s 5d;[1] more for 8,100 of 10d nail, at 8s 4d every 1,000 – £3 7s 6d; more for 8,200 of 6d nail, at 5s every 1,000 – 41s; more for 1,100 of 4d nail, price – 3s 8d; and more to him for 1,000 of 3d nail, price – 2s 6d.[2] *Summa* – £10 6s 1d.[3]

To Richard Welles of Greenwich, smith, the same day for the working of 2 hundred 2 quarters weight [*280 lbs*] of Her Highness's old iron by him made and wrought into spikes and overlop nails for the use of Her Grace's ships, at 13s 4d every hundredweight working. *Summa* – £1 13s 4d.

Hire of smith's tools. To the said Richard Welles the same day for hire of his smith's tools occupied in Her Highness's forge at Deptford for the use of Her Highness's ships, by one quarter of a year ended as abovesaid. *Summa* by agreement – 10s.

[*Page total*] – £14 10s 6½d.

[f. 13v] *Shivers of Brass.* To Robert Hunt of London, founder, the last day of March for price of 6 great brass shivers of him had and by him delivered at Deptford for the use of Her Highness's ships, which was of Her Grace's old brass, weighing 9 hundred [*one*] quarter 14 pounds weight [*1,050 lbs*], at 4d every pound casting and working. *Summa* – £17 10s.

Anchors. To Butolph Moungey[4] of Gillingham in Kent the same day for price of 3 great anchors of him had and delivered at Deptford for the use of Her Highness's ships, weighing 3 thousand 7 hundred 2 quarters weight [*4,200 lbs*], at 18s 8d every hundredweight. *Summa* – £35.

[1]The calculation yields a futher ¼d: [(3 × 112) + (2 × 56) + 26] × (294 ÷ 112) = 1097.25d.

[2]As these figures readily show, nails were classified by the price per measure of (approximately) 100.

[3]The first of several items in a summary of this man's bills for 1562: BL, Add. MS 78171 [item 1(e)], f. 38, as detailed in Appendix 4 below.

[4]Admiralty official: for career details see *NEM*, p. 560.

Burning reed. To John Rawllyns of Paris Garden, reedman, the same day for price of 2,000 of burning reed[1] by him delivered at Deptford for the use of Her Highness's ships, at 12d every 100. *Summa* – £1.

To James Gybbes of Rainham, reedman, the same day for price of 2,000 of burning reed by him delivered as aforesaid for the use of Her Grace's ships, at 12d every 100. *Summa* – £1.

To John Maze of Plumstead, reedman, the same day for price of 1,800 of burning reed by him delivered as abovesaid for the use of Her Highness's ships, at 12d every 100 of reed. *Summa* – 18s.

Pitch, tar and rosin. To Thomas Clay of London the same day for price of 4 thousand pound weight[2] of yellow rosin of him had and delivered at Deptford for the use of Her Highness's ships, at 7s every hundredweight – £14; more for 2 last of hard stone pitch of the oaken band, at £3 12s every last – £7 4s; more for one last 3 barrels of Riga tar of the great band,[3] at 8s every barrel – £6; and more to him for the hire of a lighter for the bringing down of the same from London to Deptford, by agreement – 3s 6d. *Summa* – £27 7s 6d.

[*Page total*] – £82 15s 6d.

[f. 14] *Oil* *[*£17 16s 8d*] *and Spanish iron* *[*£12 6s 8d*]. To William Megges of London, merchant, the last day of March for price of one hogshead of oil for the use of Her Grace's ships, price by agreement. *Summa* – £2 16s 8d.

To William Merryck of London, merchant, the same day for price of one tun and one hogshead of train oil by him delivered at Deptford for the use of Her Grace's ships, at £3 every hogshead – £15; and more to him for one ton of Spanish iron,[4] price – £12 6s 8d. *Summa* – £27 6s 8d.

Ink. To William Kirby of London the same day for price of one gallon and one pottle of ink by him delivered as aforesaid for the writing of sundry pay books for Her Highness's marine causes, at 5s 8d the gallon. *Summa* – 8s.

Oakum. To William Collins, John Hawkins, Richard Harwood and eight other persons of Deptford, Greenwich, Lewisham and thereabouts the same day for the working and picking of one thousand 7 hundred [*one*] quarter 20 pounds weight [*1,952 lbs*] of Her Highness's old ropes and

[1]Used for breaming.

[2]Uncertain if meaning 4,000 lbs at 7s per 100 lbs, or 40 cwt (4,480 lbs) at 7s per cwt, because the sum is the same.

[3]MS 'Ryze'. Here and elsewhere 'band' is a form of 'bond', i.e. thickness or binding consistency.

[4]A century later Pepys was assured by a merchant that Spanish iron, mostly coming from Bilbao, was 'for all uses the best in the world, especially for ships, it being able to bear the blows of the greatest sledges'; it was therefore commonly specified in contracts: Pepys, *Navy White Book*, pp. 36, 356 n. 2.

junks into oakum for the needful caulking of Her Grace's ships, at 3s 8d every hundredweight working. *Summa* – £3 3s 11½d.

Hair or sye and white lockram. To Peter Pett, master shipwright, the same day for price of 47 stone of sye or hair by him delivered for the use of Her Highness's ships,[1] at 13d every stone. *Summa* – £2 10s 11d.

To Edward Hall of London the same day for price of nine ells of white lockram of him had and by him delivered at Deptford, at 12d every ell. *Summa* – 9s.

[*Page total*] – £36 15s 2½d.

[f. 14v] *Claps and scupper-leathers.* To John Harryson of Tower Hill, shoemaker, the last day of March for price of 5 dozen of scupper-leathers of him had and by him delivered there for the use of Her Highness's ships, at 16d the piece – £4; more for 5 dozen [*and*] 9 great pump-hose, at 2s 8d the piece – £9 4s; more for 3 dozen and one claps, at 16d the piece – 49s 4d; more for 16 small claps, at 8d the piece – 10s 8d; and more to him for 18 pump-hoses, at 16d the piece – 24s. *Summa* – £17 8s.

Scoops, bowls, pulleys and steel shovels. To John Childerlay of London, turner, the same day for price of 6 steel shovels by him delivered at Deptford for the use of Her Highness's ships, at 12d the piece – 6s; more for 6 spades, at 7d the piece – 3s 6d; more for 2 dozen of great bowls, at 8d the piece – 16s; more [*for*] 2 dozen of steel shovels, at 7d the piece – 14s; more for 2 dozen of scoops, at 4d the piece – 8s; more for 12 polancre pulleys, at 10d the piece – 10s; more for 2 dozen of pulleys, at 6d the piece – 12s; more for 12 pulleys, at 4d the piece – 4s; and more to him for 2 dozen and 2 pulleys, at 3d the piece – 6s 6d. *Summa* – £4.

Compasses and running glasses. To Richard Stevens of Tower Hill, compass-maker, the last day of March for price of 6 dozen compasses by him delivered at Deptford for the use of Her Highness's ships, at 2s 8d the piece – £9 12s; and more to him for 6 dozen of running glasses, at 10d the piece – £3. *Summa* – £12 12s.

Baskets. To Thomas Edes of London, basket maker, the same day for price of 4 dozen of baskets by him delivered at Deptford for the use of Her Highness's ships, at 18d the dozen. *Summa* – 6s.

[*Page total*] – £34 6s.

[f. 15] A payment made the last day of June as well to masters, mariners, keepers of timber-yards, storehouses, labourers and others daily attending and serving Her Highness about the taking in of cables, hawsers and divers other kinds of stuffs brought into Her Grace's great storehouse at Deptford

[1]Used for caulking; 'sye' probably here in the original sense of cowhair, though it came to mean tow generally: *OED* 'sye' *sb.*[1].

Strand and delivered out of the same again; as also to shipwrights, caulkers, sawyers and other artificers and workmen working upon the new making of three of Her Highness's new ships there,[1] with divers kinds of provisions had of sundry persons towards the repairing of the same, for one quarter of a year begun the first day of April last and this day ended, as followeth:

*[*Keeper of timber-yard*]. To Thomas Marshe, mariner, the last day of June for his wages daily attending and serving Her Highness for the safe-keeping of Her Grace's provisions of divers kinds of stuffs lying in her timber-yards there, as also for the rigging, tackling and grounding of Her Highness's ships, by the space of 13 weeks begun the first day of April last and ended the last day of June then next, at 20s every month – £3 5s.

*[*Labourer in coiling up cables*]. To John Benwell, mariner, the same day for his wages daily attending and serving Her Highness in labouring about the carriage of provisions and coiling up of cables by like time of 13 weeks begun and ended as abovesaid, at 13s 4d every month. *Summa* – £2 3s 4d.

[*Page total*] – £5 8s 4d.

[f. 15v] *[*Labourer in coiling up cables*]. To Robert Tasse and Adam Dickenson, mariners, the last day of June for their wages daily attending and serving Her Highness in labouring about the coiling, carriage and delivering of cables, hawsers, and divers other provisions brought into the storehouses there and the same delivered out again for the use of Her Grace's ships, by the space of 13 weeks begun the first day of April last and ended as abovesaid, at 6s 8d every man *per mensem* – 43s 4d; more to them for their victuals for like time as aforesaid, at 20d every man the week – 43s 4d. *Summa* – £4 6s 8d.

*[*Labourer in coiling up cables*]. To Richard Harwood, mariner, the same day for his wages and victuals daily attending and serving Her Highness in labouring about the carriage of provisions and coiling up of cables as aforesaid, by like time of 13 weeks begun and ended as abovesaid, at 13s 4d *per mensem* – £2 3s 4d.

*[*Shipkeeper*]. To William Pattricke, mariner, the same day for his wages daily attending and serving Her Highness in safe-keeping of one of Her Grace's new ships in her timber-yard there, as also other service there to be done, by like 13 weeks begun and ended as abovesaid, at 6s 8d *per mensem* – £1 1s 8d.

*[*Clerk*]. To James Gentill the same day for his wages daily attending and serving Her Highness for the keeping of the prick and cheque book

[1]These are identified below (pp. 61, 67 etc.) as the *Triumph*, the *Victory* and the *Aid*.

of masters, mariners and gunners serving in Her Grace's ships within the river of Thames, by the space of 91 days begun the first day of April last and ended as aforesaid, at 8d *per diem* – £3 0s 8d.

*[*Storehouse keeper*]. To Henry Abraham the same day for his wages daily attending and serving Her Highness for the safe-keeping of Her Grace's storehouses there wherein lieth divers and sundry kinds of provisions for the use of Her Grace's ships, by like 91 days begun and ended as aforesaid, at 8d *per diem. Summa* – £3 0s 8d.

[*Page total*] – £13 13s.

[f. 16] *[*Purveyor*]. To Edward Gotelye the last day of June for his wages daily attending and serving Her Highness in providing of all kinds of provisions and necessaries for the building and repairing of Her Grace's ships, by the like 91 days begun and ended as is aforesaid, at 8d *per diem* – £3 0s 8d.

*[*Surveyor*]. To Thomas Thomas the same day for his wages daily attending and serving Her Highness for the taking of the surveys of all manner of necessary provisions had and taken of divers persons for the furniture of Her Grace's ships, as well at their setting forth to the seas as also at their coming home again into harbour, by like time of 91 days begun and ended as aforesaid, at 8d *per diem* – £3 0s 8d.

*[*Dock keeper*]. To William Ally, labourer, the same day for his wages daily attending and serving Her Highness in keeping of the plug for the letting out of the water out of the dock wherein lieth Her Grace's two new ships for the drier keeping of the same, by like time of 91 days begun and ended as aforesaid, at 8d *per diem* – £3 0s 8d.

*[*Keeper of timber-yards*]. To Thomas Woode, porter, the same day for his wages daily attending and serving Her Highness in safe-keeping of her timber-yards there wherein lieth her timber, plank and other necessaries for the use of Her Grace's ships, by 91 days begun and ended as aforesaid, at 8d *per diem* – £3 0s 8d.

*[*Riding charges*]. To John Ellmer, messenger, the same day for his wages daily attending and serving Her Highness for the carrying of the officers' letters in post to divers and sundry places along the sea coast for Her Grace's marine causes, by 91 days begun and ended as abovesaid, at 12d *per diem. Summa* – £4 11s 0d.

[*Page total*] – £16 13s 8d.

[f. 16v] *[*Shipkeeper*]. To Giles Hall, master, the last day of June for his wages daily attending and serving Her Highness in keeping of Her Grace's hoy named the *George* by the space of 11 weeks 3 days begun the first day of April last and ended the 19 day of this present then next, at 13s 4d *per mensem* – £1 18s 1d

*[*Shipkeeper*]. To Paul Saunders, mariner, the same day for his wages daily attending and serving Her Highness in safe-keeping of Her Grace's ship named the *Jerfalcon* by 13 weeks begun and ended as aforesaid, at 6s 8d *per mensem* – £1 1s 8d.

*[*Labourer in coiling up cables*]. To John Kinge, mariner, the same day for his wages daily attending and serving Her Highness in labouring about the carriage of provisions and coiling up of cables as is aforesaid, by 13 weeks begun the first day of April last and this day ended, at 6s 8d *per mensem* – £1 1s 8d.

*[*Shipwright*]. To Augustino Levello, Venetian shipwright, the same day for his wages daily attending and serving Her Highness for the repairing and mending of Her Grace's three galleys, by 91 days begun and ended as aforesaid at 16d *per diem* – £6 1s 4d.

*[*Shipwright*]. To Robert Hart the same day for his wages daily attending and serving Her Highness for the mending and repairing of Her Grace's ships, by the space of 13 weeks begun and ended as abovesaid, at 8d *per diem* – £3 0s 8d.

*[*Caulker*]. To Thomas Bolton, master caulker, the same day for his wages daily attending and serving Her Highness for the mending and repairing of Her Grace's ships, by the space of 74 days within the quarter, at 8d *per diem. Summa* – £2 9s 4d.

[*Page total*] – £15 12s 9d.

[f. 17] *[*Shipwright*]. To Matthew Baker, master shipwright, the last day of June for his wages daily attending and serving Her Highness in working upon Her Grace's ships there, by the space of 54 days begun the first day of April last and ended the 24th day of May then next, at 8d *per diem.*

*[*Clerk*]. To Stephen Alexander the same day for his wages daily attending and serving Her Highness for the writing, making and keeping of the book of report of all such provisions and necessaries had of divers and sundry persons for the use of Her Grace's ships, for one quarter of a year, due as aforesaid – £6 13s 4d.

*[*Labourer in coiling up of cables*]. To Henry Webb and William Pears, mariners, the same day for their wages and victuals daily attending and serving Her Highness in labouring about the carriage of provisions and coiling up of cables and hawsers as aforesaid, by like 13 weeks begun and ended as abovesaid, at 13s 4d every month the man – £4 6s 8d.

*[*Shipwright*]. To Peter Pett, master shipwright, the same day for his wages daily attending and serving Her Highness upon Her Grace's ships there, by 91 days begun the first day of April last and ended as abovesaid, at 12d *per diem* – £4 11s.

*[*Shipwright*]. To Edward Bright, master shipwright, the same day for his wages daily attending and serving Her Highness upon her ships at Deptford, by 61 days begun the first day of April last and ended the last day of May then next, at 12d *per diem* – £3 1s.

[*Page total*] – £20 8s.

[f. 17v] *Shipwrights*

Matthew Baker, master, 37 days at 12d	37s
Matthew Norton, server, 32 days at 5d	13s 4d
John Hoole, server, 32 days at 5d	13s 4d
Philip Garret, 32 days at 6d	16s
John Rande, 32 days at 8d	21s 4d
James Cootes, 32 days at 6d	16s
George Flower, 32 days at 6d	16s
John Ellysonne, 5 days at 7d	2s 11d
John Hall, server, 31 days at 6d	15s 6d
Lewis Richardes, 32 days at 6d	16s
Thomas Brayne, 32 days at 6d	16s
John Diggons, 32 days at 6d	16s
James Diggons, 32 days at 3d	8s
Robert Vize, 32 days at 6d	16s
John Wellsheman, 32 days at 8d	21s 4d
John Hubbard, 32 days at 6d	16s
John Daultonn, 30 days at 6d	15s
Daniel Bright, 31 days at 6d	15s 6d
Ralph Browne, 30 days at 6d	15s
Michael Towe, 26 days at 8d	15s 2d
John Towe, 23 days at 5d	9s 8d
Edward Holborne, 22 days at 8d	14s 8d
Henry New, 26 days at 5d	10s 10d
Walter Holbourne, 16 days at 7d	9s 4d
John Langtun, 15 days at 7d	8s 9d
William Wheller, 26 days at 5d	10s 10d
John Addams, 17 days at 8d	11s 4d
William Sybbley, 16 days at 4d	5s 4d.

[*Page total*] – £20 2s 1d.

[f. 18] John Tylling, server, 13 days at 6d	6s 6d
Anthony Holdernes, 14 days at 7d	8s 2d
John Jewell, 14 days at 6d	7s
John Jonnes, 4 days at 3d	3s 6d
James Jacobb, 7 days at 6d	3s 6d
Edward Bright, master, 30 days at 12d	30s

Thomas Juell, 26 days at 6d	13s
Davy Baker, 26 days at 6d	13s
John Lestow, 26 days at 6d	13s
John Hayward, 15 days at 8d	10s
Michael Gamond, 15 days at 5d	6s 3d
Henry Symond, 15 days at 4d	5s
William Spicer, 7 days at 7d	4s 1d
Stephen Bevis, 17 days at 6d	8s 6d
Thomas Robynson, 13 days at 6d	6s 6d
Stephen Robynson, 13 days at 4d	4s 4d
Edward Clarke, 5 days at 6d	2s 6d
Thomas Raynoldes, 5 days at 8d	3s 4d
William Clarke, 21 days at 8d	14s
Thomas Bolltun, 5 days at 10d	4s 2d
William Boltun, 5 days at 6d	2s 6d
Walter Clay, 5 days at 6d	2s 6d
John Eastwood, 1 day at 6d	6d
Richard Collyns, 1 day at 6d	6d
Henry Greves, 4 days at 7d	2s 4d
Thomas Jackson, 3 days at 4d	12d
William Grene, 2 days at 9d	18d
Thomas Hewes, 2 days at [*blank*]	[*blank*]
Edward Wall, 2 days at 6d	12d
Robert Willys, 2 days at 3d	6d
Richard Myddletun, 1 day at 6d	6d
Robert Asshetun, 1 day at 6d	6d
Thomas Willson, 37 days at 12d	37s
Henry Rowse, server, 37 days at 3d	9s 3d

[*Page total*] – £11 5s 11d.

[f. 18v] *Sawyers*

Thomas Myller, 40 days at 6d	20s
Gilbert Davys, 40 days at 6d	20s
John Ricardes, 13 days at 6d	6s 6d
John Bastyan, 13 days at 6d	6s 6d
	[£2 13s*]

Victualling. To Thomas Willson of Ratcliff the last day of June for victualling of 61 shipwrights, sawyers and others working upon the new building of Her Highness's new ship there, as also for making of new masts for Her Grace's two new ships, by 1,527 days among them, the Sundays and holy days in the same accounted, begun the 25th day of May last and this day ended, which maketh 218 weeks 1 day, at 4½d every week the man. *Summa* – £44 0s 1½d.

Lodging. To Alice Bory, Jonne [*Joan*] Juell and six other persons of Deptford the same day for the lodging of 44 of the aforenamed shipwrights, sawyers and others working upon Her Highness's said new ships there, in 22 featherbeds by the space of 172 weeks begun the 25th day of May last and this day ended, at 2d every week the man. *Summa* – £1 8s 8d.

[*Page total*] – £48 1s 9½d.

[f. 19] Wages and victuals of shipwrights working upon the hewing and squaring of 9 great elms at Beddington[1] for keels for Her Highness's ships, *viz.*

Shipwrights

Matthew Baker, master, 14 days at 12d	14s
Henry Layne, 14 days at 8d	9s 4d
Robert Wright, 14 days at 5d	5s 10d
	[£1 9s 2d*]*

Victualling. To the said Matthew Baker and two other shipwrights the last day of June for the victualling of themselves working upon the hewing and squaring of the said keels by the space of 42 days among them within this same time, at 6d every day the man – £1 1s.

[*Page total*] – £2 10s 2d.

[f. 19v] Wages of house-carpenters working upon the said keels in hewing and squaring as aforesaid.

House-carpenters

John Woorman, 8½ days at 10d	7s 1d
Thomas Worman, 10½ days at 10d	8s 9d
John Worman, junior, 8½ days at 10d	4s 3d [*sic*]
Richard Worman, 8½ days at 10d	7s 1d
Richard Fittell, 8½ days at 4d	2s 10d
William Drew, server, 9 days at 10d	7s 6d
Walter Drew, server, 7½ days at 4d	2s 6d
Richard Bett, 8½ days at 10d	7s 1d
Richard Norris, server, 8½ days at 8d	5s 8d
Richard Houmfray, server, 9½ days at 5d	3s 11½d
John Baker, 8 days at 10d	6s 8d
Robert Addeson, 10½ days at 8d	7s

[1]See below, p. 54.

Thomas Symondes, 10 days at 10d	8s 4d
Thomas Rounde, 2 days at 10d	20d
William Rounde, 2 days at 6d	12d
Martin Rawlinge, 4 days at 10d	3s 4d
Thomas Beamounde, 3 days at 6d	18d

[*Page total*] – £4 6s 2½d.

[f. 20] Wages of house-carpenters working upon a new crane at Deptford, with other needful service there to be done within this time.

John Leache, 40 days at 12d	40s
Thomas Hill, server, 23 days at 10d	19s 2d
John Throlley, server, 16 days at 9d	12s
Robert Throlley, server, 39 days at 7d	22s 9d
Robert Aunstome, 24 days at 10d	20s
Thomas Woodde, 11 days at 10d	9s 2d
Richard Stampe, 8 days at 10d	6s 8d
	[£6 9s 9d*]

Labourers

John Hurllstone, 87 days at 6d	43s 6d
Nicholas Archedall, 80 days at 6d	40s
Thomas Thisselltonn, 80 days at 6d	40s
George Mathew, 66 days at 6d	33s
John Lowman, 56 days at 6d	28s
James Howper, 80 days at 6d	40s
John Gybbsone, 56 days at 6d	28s
Henry Stevenson, 30 days at 6d	15s
Thomas Loweman, 28 days at 6d	14s
John Pytthe, 30 days at 6d	15s
John Brodehurst, 30 days at 6d	15s
William Twayttes, 30 days at 6d	15s
John Bastyan, 26 days at 6d	13s
John Addams, 21 days at 6d	10s 6d
Thomas Clarke, 19 days at 6d	9s 6d
	[£17 19s 6d*]

[*Page total*] – £24 9s 3d.

[f. 20v] John Wallys, 19 days at 6d	9s 6d
Edward Plumer, 38 days at 6d	19s
John Raynsforth, 5 days at 7d	2s 11d
James Teall, 4 days at 6d	2s
William Gunby, 4 days at 6d	2s
Philip Deakeon, 1 day at 8d	8d

Thomas Pears, 1 day at 8d	8d
Peter Preswyke, 1 day at 8d	8d
William Jonnes, 1 day at 8d	8d
John Browne, 1 day at 8d	8d
Nicholas Waters, 1 day at 8d	8d
Howell Sommer, 11 days at 6d	5s 6d
Owen Williams, 1 day at 8d	8d
John Robenson, 1 day at 8d	8d
William Dawby, 1 day at 8d	8d
Thomas Morrys, 1 day at 8d	8d
	[£2 7s 7d*]
Watchmen	
William Ally, 34 nights at 4d	11s 4d
John Hurllestone, 34 nights at 4d	11s 4d
Nicholas Archedaill, 33 nights at 4d	11s
Thomas Thysselltun, 33 nights at 4d	11s
George Mathew, 25 nights at 4d	8s 4d
Thomas Lowman, 34 nights at 4d	11s 4d
James Howper, 34 nights at 4d	11s 4d
Thomas Smyth, 34 nights at 4d	11s 4d
Paul Saunders, 34 nights at 4d	11s 4d
William Patrycke, 34 nights at 4d	11s 4d
Edward Plumer, 34 nights at 4d	11s 4d
John Twyford, 6 nights at 4d	2s
Henry Stevensonne, 6 nights at 4d	2s
John Gybbsonne, 14 nights at 4d	4s 8d
Giles Hall, 20 nights at 4d	6s 8d
	[£6 16s 4d*]

[*Page total*] – £9 3s 11d.

[f. 21] *Emptions*

Ironwork. To Thomas Ive of Limehouse, smith, the last day of June for price of 21 hundred 20 pounds weight [*2,372 lbs*] of his own new iron by him made and wrought into bolts, spikes, rings and keys of all sorts and the same delivered at Deptford for the use of Her Highness's ships, at 23s 4d every hundredweight – £24 14s 2d; more for 1,000 of 10d nail, price – 8s 4d; more for 1,000 of 6d nail, price – 5s; more for 1,000 of 4d nail, price – 3s 4d; and more to him for 1,000 of 3d nail, price – 2s 6d. *Summa* – £25 13s 4d.

To Richard Wells, smith, the same day for price of 26 hundred one quarter and 4 pounds weight [*2,944 lbs*] of his own new iron by him made and wrought into bolts, rings, keys, hasps, staples, hoops and dogs of iron, setting bolts, ring-bolts, and spikes of all sorts, and the same delivered as aforesaid for the use of Her Highness's ships, at 23s 4d every hundredweight – £30 13s 4d; and more to him for new working of 2 hundred 2 quarters 16 pounds weight [*296 lbs*] of Her Highness's old iron by him made and wrought into divers bolts for the use of Her Grace's ships, at 9s 4d every hundredweight – 24s 8d. *Summa* – £31 18s.

To Thomas Willson of Ratcliff, smith, the same day for price of one hundred 8 pounds weight [*120 lbs*] of his own new iron by him made and wrought into spikes and bolts for the use of Her Highness's ships as aforesaid, at 23s 4d every hundredweight – 25s; more for 1,000 of 10d nail, price – 8s 4d; more for 1,000 of 6d nail, price – 5s; more for 1,000 of 4d nail, price – 3s 4d; and more to him for 1,000 of 3d nail, price – 2s 6d. *Summa* – £2 4s 2d.

Iron pots. To Henry Abraham the same day for price of 6 iron pots by him delivered at Deptford for the use of Her Highness's ships, at 6s the piece – 36s; and more to him for the hire of a wherry for bringing of certain scoops and shovels from London to Deptford, to be sent to Chatham for service there to be done – 3s. *Summa* – £1 19s. *[*Carriage by water – 3s*]

[*Page total*] – £61 14s 6d.

[f. 21v] *Locks and keys.* To Gilbert Pollstedd of Greenwich, locksmith, the last day of June for the making of new locks and keys as well for the great gates and doors of the storehouses within the timber-yards there, as also for Her [*Highness's*] clerk's office, *viz.* for one pipe-key[1] for a stock lock – 6d; more for a new lock for a cupboard door, price – 18d; more for a key and mending a lock, price – 8d; more for mending of 2 locks, price – 6d; more for a hasp for a lock – 4d; more for a plate-lock and a key – 12d; more for a new casement for a window, price – 18d; and more to him for 6 new locks and keys, price – 8s 4d. *Summa* – 14s 4d.

Shivers and caps of brass. To Robert Hunt of London the same day for price of 5 new shivers and 2 caps of brass of his own stuff, by him delivered there into Her Highness's storehouses for the use of Her Grace's ships, weighing [*one*] hundred [*one*] quarter 17 pounds weight, at 6½d every pound weight. *Summa* – £4 5s 0½d.

Glazing of windows. To Robert Rogers of St Katherine's, glazier, the same day for price of 6 foot of new glass by him delivered and set up in Her Highness's house at Deptford, at 5d every foot – 2s 6d; more for setting of 20 foot of Her [*Grace's*] old glass, at 2¼d the foot – 4s 2d; and

[1]Key with hollow barrel fitting over pintle in lock.

more to him for setting in of 54 quarrels of glass, at 1d the piece – 4s 6d. [*Summa*] – 11s 2d.

Bowls, shovels and scoops. To John Benbow of London[1] the same day for price of 4 dozen of steel shovels by him delivered there for the use of Her Grace's ships, at 7s every dozen – 28s; more for 2 dozen of scoops, at 4s 6d the dozen – 9s; and more to him for 2 dozen of great bowls for pitch and rosin, at 8d the piece – 16s. *Summa* – £2 13s.

[*Page total*] – £8 3s 6½d.

[f. 22] *Cables, hawsers, pitch, tar, thrums, sail needles, latchet lines and caulking oil.* To Christopher Draper of London, alderman,[2] the last day of June for price of 23 thousand 4 hundred 2 quarters 21 pounds weight [*26,285 lbs*] of Dansk[3] cordage by him delivered into Her Grace's great storehouse at Deptford for use of Her Highness's ships, *viz.* 4 tarred cables of 11 and 12 inches compass, 5 cablets tarred of 5, 6, and 7 inches compass, 14 hawsers of 4, 5, and 6 inches compass, at 17s every hundredweight – £199 9s 8d;[4] more for 3 lasts 6 barrels of tar, at £5 every last – £17 10s; more for one last of pitch, price – £4 6s 8d; more for 2 white hawsers weighing 6 hundred 2 quarters 18 pounds [*746 lbs*], at 28s the hundredweight – £9 6s 6d; more for 2 hundredweight of thrums, at 28s every hundred[*weight*] – 56s; more for 100 pounds weight of white twine, at 7d every pound weight – 58s 4d; more for 500 of round sail needles, price – 16s 8d; more for one last of tar of the great band, price – £5; more for 6 barrels of tar, price – 50s; more for 3 last of pitch of the great band, at £4 5s every last – £12 15s; more for one tun of caulking oil, price £10 10s; more for 200 coils of latchet and oillet lines tarred, weighing 4 thousand [*one*] hundred [*one*] quarter 22 pounds weight [*4,642 lbs*], at 23s 4d every hundredweight – £48 7s 1d; and more to him for 40 dozen of round sail needles, at 5d every dozen – 16s 8d. *Summa* – £317 2s 7d. *[*Cordage and tackling – £261 14s 11d*; *pitch and tar – £42 0s 22d*; *thrums – 56s*; *caulking oil – £10 10s*]

*[*Thrums*]. To George Jackson of London the same day for price of 2 hundred 2 quarters weight [*280 lbs*] of thrums by him delivered at Deptford for the use of Her Grace's ships, at 2½d every pound – 58s 4d;

[1]Turner to the Navy since 1553: for career details see *NEM*, pp. 531–2.

[2]Ironmonger and alderman of Cordwainer Ward; Sheriff 1560–61, Lord Mayor 1566–67, knighted 1567, died 1581: Beaven, *Aldermen*, i, p. 115 and *passim*. He was first cousin of Benjamin Gonson, and godfather of his fourth daughter, Elizabeth (born Feb. 1556); Draper's wife was godmother of Gonson's sixth daughter, Mary (born Nov. 1559): BL, Add. MS 15857, f. 153. W. N. Gunson, 'The family of Gunson or Gonson of London and Essex', *Family History*, VIII, nos 46/47, new ser. nos 22/23 (1974), p. 134.

[3]In ordinary usage meaning Danish, but in this context standing for Danzig, and by extension Baltic or 'Eastland' goods generally.

[4]The calculation gives 47876.248, and so is within ¼d of the sum stated (47876d).

and more to him for 16 gallons of oil, at 16d the gallon – 21s 4d. *Summa* – £3 19s 8d.

*[*Caulking oil*]. To William Padge of London the same day for price of 34 gallons of oil by him delivered at Deptford for the needful caulking of Her Highness's ships, at 14d every gallon. *Summa* – £1 19s 8d.

[*Page total*] – £323 1s 11d.

[f. 22v]. *Cables, anchors, pulleys, shivers and cocks of brass and a rudder.* To Butolph Moungey the last day of June for price of one shot of cables by him delivered at Deptford into Her Highness's storehouse there for the use of Her Grace's ships, which was taken out of a certain hulk that was lost by tempest of weather near Portsmouth weighing 5 thousand 7 hundred [*one*] quarter weight [*6,412 lbs*] of 15 inches compass, at 13s 4d every hundredweight – £38 3s 4d; more for one shot of cables worn of 13 inches compass, weighing 4 thousand 5 hundred [*one*] quarter weight [*5,068 lbs*], at 6s 8d every hundredweight – £15 1s 8d; more for one shot of new cables weighing 5 thousand 2 hundred 50 pounds weight [*5,874 lbs*], at 15s every hundred[*weight*] – £39 7s;[1] more for 4 great anchors weighing 5 thousand [*one*] hundred [*one*] quarter weight [*5,740 lbs*], at 18s 8d every hundredweight – £47 16s 8d; more for great blocks and pulleys of all sorts with shivers and cocks of brass, by agreement – 40s; more for a foresail, mainsail, mizzen and topsail, price – £5; and more to him for a great rudder with the ironwork, by agreement – £3. *Summa* – £150 8s 8d. *[*Cables – £92 12s 8d*; *anchors – £47 16s*; *pulleys – 40s*; *sails – 100s*; *a rudder – 60s*]

Sounding leads *[*2s 11½d*] *and new lead* *[*£8 1s 4½d*]. To Julian Richardes of London, widow, the same day for the price of 2 sounding leads by her delivered at Deptford for the use of Her Grace's ships, weighing 17½ pounds weight, at 2d every pound – 2s 11½d; and more to her for 10 hundred 3 quarters one pound weight [*1,205 lbs*] of new lead, at 15s every hundredweight – £8 1s 4½d. *Summa* – £8 4s 4d.

Sail canvas. To John Collins of London the same day for price of 5 pieces of sail canvas of medrinacks of English making by him delivered there for the use of Her Grace's ships, at 35s every piece – £8 15s; and more to him for 4 other pieces of medrinacks, at 30s the piece – £6. *Summa* – £14 15s.

[*Page total*] – £173 8s.

[f. 23] *Old junks and ropes made into wrain-ropes and oakum.* To William Brooke of Deptford, ropemaker, the last day of June for workmanship of 16 hundred [*one*] quarter 16 pounds weight [*1,836 lbs*]

[1]The calculation gives 9440.3568d, and so is about 3½d below the stated sum (9444d).

of Her Highness's old junks and ropes by him made and wrought into netting- and wrain-ropes for the use of Her Highness's ships, at 3s 8d every hundredweight. *Summa* – £3 0s 0½d.[1]

To Robert Awger, Amy Pouell, Annes Bartelet and 10 other persons of Deptford, Greenwich, Lewisham and thereabouts the same day for the working and picking of 2 thousand 3 hundred 19 pounds weight [*2,595 lbs*] of Her Highness's old ropes and junks into oakum for the needful caulking of Her Grace's ships, at 3s 8d every hundredweight working. *Summa* – £4 5s 3d.[2]

Provision of timber. To Edward Gotley, purveyor, the same day for price of 244 loads of timber oak by him provided out of Her Highness's woods called Strudgwick Wood and Farneyfield in Sussex[3] and by him delivered at Deptford for the use of Her Highness's ships, at 10s every load after 50 foot to the load – £122; more for 11,200 foot of 4-inch plank oak, at 12s every 100 foot – £67 4s; more for 19,400 foot of 3-inch plank oak, at 10s every 100 foot – £97; more for 23,300 [*foot*] of 2-inch plank oak, at 8s every 100 [*foot*] – £93 4s; more for 7,200 foot of inch ½ board oak, at 7s every 100 foot – £25 4s; more for 2,500 [*foot*] of cloveboard oak, at 46s 8d every 100 [*foot*] – £58 6s 8d; and more to him for 9,400 [*foot*] of inch board oak, at 5s every 100 foot – £23 10s. *Summa* – £486 8s 8d.

To William Hardwicke of London the same day for price of 22 loads of elm timber of him had and delivered at Deptford for the use of Her Highness's ships, at 5s the load – £5 10s.

[*Page total*] – £499 3s 11½d.

[f. 23v]. *Provision of timber.* To Henry Bamford, purveyor, the last day of June for price of 66½ loads 16 foot of compass timber and knees by him provided and the same delivered at Deptford Strand for the use of Her Highness's ships, at 13s 4d every load after 50 foot to the load – £44 10s 10d; and more to him for 4 loads of compass timber oak out of Hertfordshire and delivered as aforesaid, at 13s 4d every load – 53s 4d. *Summa* – £47 4s 2d.[4]

Timber oak and plank. To John Coldwell of London the same day for price of 5½ loads of squared timber oak by him delivered at Deptford for

[1]The calculation gives 721.28563d, and so is about ¾d above the stated sum (720.5d).

[2]The calculation gives 1019.4641d, and would be 1020.36 if a simple total of 2,319 lbs was intended, and so by either system is about 3d short of the stated sum (1023d).

[3]Strudgwick Wood is in the Sussex parish of Kirdford; Farneyfield Copse is in Capel, just north of the Surrey/Sussex border: EPNS, *Surrey*, p. 268.

[4]Some part of Bamford's charges for this quarter is recorded in the loose papers from Gonson's archive: BL, Add MS. 78171 [item 1(a)], ff. 3–10, as further described in Appendix 4 below.

the use of Her Highness's ships, at 10s every load after 50 foot to the load – £2 15s.

To Christopher Baker of Deptford[1] the same day for price of 50 loads of compass timber oak of him had and delivered at Deptford for the use of Her Highness's ships, at 10s every load after 50 foot to the load – £25; and more to him for 1,000 foot of 3-inch plank oak at 10s every 100 foot, £5. *Summa* – £30.

Elms. To Francis Carew of Beddington[2] the same day for price of 9 great elms of him had and delivered for the new making of keels for Her Highness's ships; by agreement – £3 6s 8d.

Carriage of shores. To Richard Mylles, John Brockehowse, Henry Ollyff, William Clerk, George Cane and 15 other persons of Lewisham, Peckham, Eltham, Camberwell and Dulwich[3] the same day for carriage of 40 loads of shores out of Her Highness's wood called West Wood[4] to Deptford Strand for the use of Her Grace's ships, at 14d every load after 50 foot to the load. *Summa* – £2 6s 8d.

[*Page total*] – £85 12s 6d.

[f. 24] *Sawing of timber.* To Nicholas West and Thomas Gunes, sawyers, the last day of June for sawing and breaking of timber for Her Highness at Fickleshole in Kent[5] by 6 days within this time, at 10d every day the man – 10s; and more to them for making of a sawpit – 8d. *Summa* – 10s 8d.[6]

Carriage of timber. To John Woodden, Nicholas Richebell, William Wood, John Ive, Richard Hayward, Edward Wood, John Paullmer and 36 other persons of Tatsfield, Warlingham, Caterham, Tandridge Court and

[1]Subsequently Keeper of the Storehouses and sometime naval commander; for career details see *NEM*, pp. 528–9.

[2]Son of Sir Nicholas Carew, Master of the Horse to Henry VIII, executed 1539. Although Francis never obtained a court appointment, he frequently entertained Elizabeth I at his family seat at Beddington. He was already famous as an arborator, albeit in growing fruit trees rather than providing timber for shipbuilding: *Hist. Parl. 1558–1603*, i, pp. 537–8. Cf. SP 12/22, no. 22 (*CSPD 1547–80*, p. 197). The MS spellings 'Bedingfeld' here and 'Benningfould' (p. 97) are not likely to be true forms of the Surrey place-name, but perhaps occur by confusion with Bedingfield in Suffolk (f. 183). Cf. next note.

[3]MS 'Donnwich' cannot be an authentic form of Dulwich (the place in Surrey clearly intended) but is presumably a mistake from familiarity with the Suffolk port of Dunwich.

[4]Probably the one of this name in the manor of Bexley: J. K. Wallenberg, *The Place Names of Kent* (Uppsala, 1934), p. 15. J. Glover, *the Place Names of Kent* (2nd edn Rainham, 1976), p. 204. The 200-acre wood had belonged to Sheen Priory, and had latterly been granted to Cardinal Pole: *CPR 1557–8*, p. 148; *1560–3*, p. 126. The location is marked by modern West-Wood Lane between Welling and Blackfen. Cf. *NEM*, p. 551. But another West Wood is in Tatsfield.

[5]*recte* Surrey, though on the border with Kent.

[6]For this and related charges see BL, Add. MS 78171 [item 1(a)], ff. 1–2, as further described in Appendix 4 below.

Godstone the same day for carriage of 14½ loads of Her Highness's timber out of Fickleshole to Deptford Strand for the use of Her Grace's ships, at 3s every load after 50 foot to the load. *Summa* – £6 10s 6d.

Cutting of elms. To Nicholas Margery the same day for his pains taken in cutting and hewing of elm timber into 3 cross carves; by agreement – 6s 8d.

Loading of carts *[*Labourers*]. To Richard Golden the same day for his wages in giving attendance at West Wood for the loading of divers carts with shores for the use of Her [*Highness's*] ships, by the space of 8 days within this time, at 6d *per diem* – 4s.

To Thomas Byrd the same day for his wages in giving attendance at 'Prebell Hill' for the loading of divers wains and carts with timber for the use of Her Grace's ships, by the space of 9 days within this time, at 6d *per diem* – 4s 6d.[1]

House rent. To Peter Pett of Deptford the same day for the rent of two cellars of him hired wherein lieth Her Highness's store of rosin for the use of her ships, by one quarter of a year begun the first day of April last and this day ended – 20s.

[*Page total*] – £8 16s 4d.

[f. 24v] *Pulleys, parrels, bowls, steel shovels.* To John Childerley of London, turner, the same day for price of 3 dozen of pulleys of him had and by him delivered at Deptford for the use of Her Highness's ships, at 4s every dozen – 12s; more for 2 dozen of pulleys, at 8d the piece – 16s; more for 24 small parrels of 2 set apiece, at 12d every parrel – 24s; more for one dozen of pulleys, at 16d the piece – 16s; more for 2 dozen of great bowls for pitch and rosin, at 8d the piece – 16s; and more to him for 2½ dozen of steel shovels, at 7s every dozen – 17s 6d. *Summa* – £5 1s 6d.

Ballast baskets. To Thomas Edes of London, basket maker, the same day for price of 6 dozen of baskets for ballast by him delivered at Deptford for the use of Her Highness's ships, at 18d every dozen. *Summa* – 9s.

Water buckets. To John Williamson of London, cooper, the same day for price of 9 dozen of water buckets by him delivered at Deptford for the use of Her Grace's ships, at 5s every dozen. *Summa* – £2 5s.

English nails and padlocks. To Peter Whalley of London the same day for price of one some of 2d English nail by him delivered at Deptford Strand for use of Her Highness's ships, price – 14s; and more to him for 12 padlocks with keys, at 8d the piece – 8s. *Summa* – £1 2s.

Carriage of rubbish. To John Elmer of Deptford the same day for the hire of his cart and 5 horse serving Her Highness in carrying 352 loads of rubbish out of Her Grace's yard at Deptford, at 1d every load – 29s 4d;

[1]Cf. BL, Add. MS 78171 [item 1(a)], where the place is identified as Cudham.

and more to him for the wages of his man going with the same cart by 16 days within this time, at 6d *per diem* – 8s. [*Summa*] – £1 17s 4d.

[*Page total*] – £10 14s 10d.

[f. 25] *Hair* *[*40s*] *and burning reed* *[*43s 4d*]. To Peter Pett of Deptford the last day of June for price of 30 stone of hair by him delivered at Deptford for the use of Her Highness's ships, at 16d every stone – 40s; and more to him for 3,328 sheaves of burning reed, at 10s every 1,000 – 33s 4d. *Summa* – £3 13s 4d.

To James Gybbes of Rainham, reedman, the same day for price of 1,000 [*sheaves*] of burning reed of him had and delivered at Deptford for use of Her Highness's ships, at 12d every 100 of reed – 10s.

Hire of a lighter. To John Wattes of London the same day for the hire of his lighter in carrying of the officers of the Admiralty for the execution of certain prisoners at Wapping; by agreement – 6s.

[*Page total*] – £4 9s 4d. [f. 25v *blank*]

[f. 26] A payment made the last day of September to masters, mariners and gunners, keepers of storehouses and timber-yards serving Her Highness in keeping afloat of certain Her Grace's ships within the river of Thames, as labouring about the taking up of cables, hawsers and divers other kinds of stuff received into Her Highness's storehouses and delivered out the same to her ships; as also to shipwrights, caulkers, sawyers, smiths, topmakers, boatmakers, labourers, marshmen and others working upon the making of three new ships and opening of the dockhead for the launching of the same; with divers kinds of provisions had of sundry persons for the use of the said ships for one whole quarter of a year begun the first day of July last and this day ended, as followeth:

The Great Bark

Mariners

Thomas Goldstone, boatswain, 8 weeks, 5 days	36s 3d
Richard Connard, purser, 7 weeks	17s 6d
Thomas Gattes, steward, 5 days	2s 1d
John Newball, 8 weeks, 5 days	14s 6d
Richard Diamonde, 8 weeks, 5 days	14s 6d
Mark Bullyn, 8 weeks, 5 days	14s 6d
Peter Trewe, 8 weeks, 5 days	14s 6d
William Brigges, 8 weeks, 5 days	14s 6d
Thomas Tybball, 8 weeks, 5 days	14s 6d
Robert Key, 8 weeks, 5 days	14s 6d
Thomas Ratcliff, gromet, 8 weeks, 5 days	10s 10d
Edward Wickes, boy, 8 weeks, 5 days	7s 3d

John Johnson, 8 weeks, 5 days — 14s 6d
[*Page total*] – £10 14s 5d.

[f. 26v] John Bazell, cook, 8 weeks — 18s 4d
Miles Robinson, 8 weeks 5 days — 14s 6d
Lawrence Mewse, master gunner, 8 weeks 5 days — 21s 8d

The George Hoy
Mariners

Giles Hall, master, 13 weeks 1 day	53s 10d
Richard Abraham, 13 weeks 1 day	21s 11d
Henry Raynsforthe, 13 weeks 1 day	21s 11d
John Kinge, 13 weeks 1 day	21s 11d
William Collins, 2 weeks 3 days	4s
John Roche, 13 weeks 1 day	21s 11d
Thomas Raynolds, 13 weeks 1 day	21s 11d
Richard Lettman, 13 weeks 1 day	21s 11d
Nicholas Arney, 8 weeks 2 days	13s 10d
John Dalamore, cook, 10 weeks 5 days	24s 6d
John Hawnse, 3 weeks	5s

The Mary Grace Hoy
Mariners

William Pearsone, master, 13 weeks 1 day	£3 5s
John Yonge, 13 weeks 1 day	21s 11d
Fabian Bullyn, 13 weeks 1 day	21s 11d
John Bennet, 13 weeks 1 day	21s 11d
Thomas Harringtonn, 13 weeks 1 day	21s 11d
William Warde, 13 weeks 1 day	21s 11d
Henry Harrysonne, 13 weeks 1 day	21s 11d
Thomas Draves, 13 weeks 1 day	21s 11d

[*Page total*] – £25 5s 7d.

[f. 27] *The Triumph*
Mariners

Henry Cooke, purser, 2 weeks 6 days	6s 8d
Davy Burre, 2 weeks 5 days	4s 6d
Thomas Hilliarde, 2 weeks 5 days	4s 6d
Jarmyn Huggyns, 1 week 3 days	2s 4d
Henry Bull, 1 week 3 days	2s 4d
Richard Bennet, 1 week 3 days	2s 4d
John Raggate, 1 week 3 days	2s 4d
John Williams, 1 week	20d
John Penneall, 1 week 1 day	23d

Thomas Russell, 1 week 1 day	23d
Robert Fowler, 1 week 4 days	2s 8d
Allbrighte Fries, 1 week 1 day	23d
Bartholomew Gromer, 1 week 1 day	23d
Robert Wintertonn, 1 week 1 day	23d
Nicholas Carrowe, 4 days	12d
Robert Loyst, 1 week 1 day	23d
William May, 1 week 1 day	23d
Peter Morgan, 1 week 1 day	23d
John Robinson, 1 week 1 day	23d
William Saben, 4 days	12d
William Clerke, [*blank*]	[*blank*]
Richard Smythe, 4 days	12d
William Mayor, 1 week 1 day	23d
John Hayes, 1 week	20d
Thomas Burrell, 1 week	20d
Richard Jonnes, 1 week	20d
Nicholas Worteley, 1 week	20d
Richard Burrell, 4 days	12d
Thomas Holland, 5 days	14d
George Mylles, 1 week	20d

[*Page total*] – £3 2s.

[f. 27v] *The Victory*

Mariners

John Light, boatswain, 5 weeks 5 days	16s 8d
Thomas Gattes, cook, 2 weeks 6 days	6s 3d
Hugh Pope, purser, 2 weeks 5 days	6s 8d
John Sillvester, 2 weeks 5 days	4s 6d
Thomas Dandye, 1 week	20d
Richard Curle, 2 weeks	3s 4d
William Lewys, 2 weeks	3s 4d
Edward Pille, 5 days	14d
James Tailler, 5 days	14d
Edward Storry, 5 days	14d
Robert Marshe, 5 days	14d
Robert Awboro, 5 days	14d
Harry Tayllor, 5 days	14d
John Tompson, 5 days	14d
Richard Clarke, 5 days	14d
John Grene, 5 days	14d
Richard Allyn, 5 days	14d

William Pearcevall, 2 weeks 5 days	4s 6d
John Freman, 5 days	14d
Andrew Dawson, 5 days	14d
John Phillippes, 5 days	14d
Richard Coxe, 5 days	14d
John Daynes, 1 week 2 days	14d
Peter Saunders, 1 week 2 days	14d
Abel Smythe, 1 week	20d
Thomas Ally, 3 days	8d

[*Page total*] – £3 9s 11d.

[f. 28] *[*Keeper of timber-yards*]. To Thomas Marshe, mariner, the last day of September for his wages daily attending and serving Her Highness for the safe-keeping of Her Grace's provisions of divers kinds of stuffs lying in her timber-yards there for the use of her ships, as also for the grounding, rigging, tallowing and tackling of Her Highness's ships, by the space of 3 months one week one day, at 20s every month. *Summa* – £3 5s 8d.

*[*Labourer in coiling up of cables*]. To John Benwell, mariner, the same day for his wages daily attending and serving Her Highness in labouring about the carriage of provisions, of cables, cablets, hawsers and other kinds of stuffs brought into the storehouses there and the same delivered out again for the use of Her Grace's ships, by the space of 3 months one week one day begun the first day of July last and this day ended, at 13s 4d *per mensem* – £2 3s 10d.

*[*Labourer in coiling up of cables*]. To Richard Harwoode, mariner, the same day for his wages and victuals daily attending and serving Her Highness in labouring about the carriage of provisions and coiling up of cables and hawsers by like time of 3 months one week one day begun and ended as abovesaid, at 13s 4d *per mensem* – £2 3s 10d.

*[*Labourer in coiling up cables*]. To Adam Dickenson and Robert Woode, mariners, the same day for their wages daily attending and serving Her Highness in labouring about the coiling, carrying and delivering of provisions as aforesaid brought into the storehouse and delivered out the same again to the use of Her Grace's ships, by 3 months one week one day begun and ended as aforesaid, at 6s 8d every man the month – 43s 10d; and more to them for their victuals for like time as abovesaid, at 20d every man the week – 43s 10d. *Summa* – £4 7s 8d.

*[*Labourer in coiling up of cables*]. To Christopher Brethet and William Smythe, mariners, the same day for their wages and victuals daily attending and serving Her Highness in labouring about the carriage of provisions and coiling up of cables as aforesaid, by like time of 3 months

one week one day begun and ended as abovesaid, at 13s 4d *per mensem* the man – £4 7s 8d.

[*Page total*] – £16 8s 8d.

[f. 28v] *[*Labourer in coiling up of cables*]. To William Patricke, mariner, the last day of September for his wages daily attending and serving Her Highness in labouring about the carriage of provisions and coiling up of cables and hawsers as aforesaid, by 3 months one week one day begun the first day of July last and this day ended, at 6s 8d *per mensem* – £1 1s 11d.

*[*Labourer in coiling up of cables*]. To Paul Saunders, mariner, the same day for his wages daily attending and serving Her Highness in labouring about the carriage of provisions and coiling up of cables and hawsers as abovesaid, by like time of 3 months one week one day begun and ended as aforesaid, at 6s 8d every month. *Summa* – £1 1s 11d.

*[*Carpenter*]. To Robert Harte, master sawyer, the same day for his wages daily attending and serving Her Highness in sawing and slitting of timber and plank for the use of Her Grace's ships, by 92 days begun and ended as aforesaid, at 8d *per diem* – £3 1s 4d.

*[*Clerk*]. To James Jentill the same day for his wages daily attending and serving Her Highness for the keeping of the prick and cheque book of masters, mariners and gunners serving in Her Grace's ships within the river of Thames, by like time of 92 days begun and ended as aforesaid, at 8d *per diem* – £3 1s 4d.

*[*Keeper of storehouse*]. To Henry Abraham the same day for his wages daily attending and serving Her Highness for the safe-keeping of Her Grace's storehouses there wherin lieth divers and sundry provisions, as cables, hawsers, small cordage and divers other sorts of stuffs for the use of Her Highness's ships, by like 92 days begun and ended as abovesaid, at 8d *per diem* – £3 1s 4d.

*[*Purveyor*]. To Edward Gotely the same day for his wages daily attending and serving Her Highness in providing of all kinds of provisions and necessaries for the building and repairing of Her Grace's ships, by 92 days begun and ended as abovesaid, at 8d *per diem* – £3 1s 4d.

[*Page total*] – £14 9s 2d.

[f. 29] *[*Surveyor*]. To Thomas Thomas the last day of September for his wages daily attending and serving Her Highness for the taking of the surveys of all manner of necessaries [*and*] provisions had of divers persons for the furniture of Her Grace's ships as well at their setting forth to the seas as also at their coming home again from thence into harbour, by the space of 92 days begun the first day of July last and this day ended, at 8d *per diem* – £3 1s 4d.

*[*Keeper of the plug*]. To William Ally, labourer, the same day for his wages daily attending and serving Her Highness in safe-keeping of the plug for the letting out of the water for the dry keeping of the dock where was made the *Triumph* and the *Victory*,[1] by like 92 days begun and ended as abovesaid, at 8d *per diem* – £3 1s 4d.

*[*Keeper of timber-yard*]. To Thomas Woode, porter, the same day for his wages daily attending and serving Her Highness in safe-keeping of the timber-yards wherein lieth Her Grace's timber, plank and divers other kinds of stuffs for the use of her ships, by like space of 92 days begun and ended as abovesaid, at 8d *per diem* – £3 1s 4d.

*[*Riding charges*]. To John Ellmer, messenger, the same day for his wages daily attending and serving Her Highness in carrying of the officers' letters in post to divers and sundry places along the sea coast for the marine affairs, by the space of 92 days begun and ended as abovesaid, at 12d *per diem* – £4 12s.

*[*Shipwright*]. To Augustino Levello, Venetian shipwright, the same day for his wages daily attending and serving Her Highness for the repairing of her two galleys, by the like 92 days begun and ended as abovesaid, at 16d *per diem* – £6 2s 8d.

[*Page total*] – £19 18s 8d.

[f. 29v] *[*Clerk*]. To Stephen Alexander the last day of September for his wages daily attending and serving Her Highness for the writing, making, and keeping of the book of report of all such provisions and necessaries had of divers and sundry persons for the use of Her Grace's ships, by one quarter of a year begun the first day of July last and this day ended, as aforesaid – £6 13s 4d.

*[*Labourer in coiling up of cables*]. To Robert Tasse, mariner, the same day for his wages and victuals daily attending and serving Her Highness in labouring about the carriage of divers kinds of provisions and coiling up of cables and hawsers as aforesaid, by the space of 3 months one week one day, begun and ended as aforesaid, at 13s 4d every month. *Summa* – £2 3s 10d.

*[*Labourer in coiling up of cables*]. To John Kinge, mariner, the same day for his wages daily attending and serving Her Highness in labouring about the carriage of provisions and coiling up of cables and hawsers as aforesaid, by like time of 3 months one week one day begun and ended as abovesaid, at 6s 8d *per mensem* – £1 1s 11d.

[*Page total*] – £9 19s 1d.

[1]These two ships were launched in Sept. 1562: Glasgow, 'List', p. 305.

[f. 30] *Shipwrights*

Peter Pett, master, 100 days and nights at 12d	£5
Richard Chapman, 83 days and nights at 6d	41s 6d
Roger Runer, server, 83 days and nights at 6d	41s 6d
George Kingestonn, server, 21 days at 4d	7s
John Bunche, 18 days at 8d	12s
John Pulter, server, 13 days at 5d	5s 5d
William Harberd, 17 days at 4d	5s 8d
Henry Shearewoode, 18 days at 8d	12s
Godfrey Smythe, server, 1 day at 6d	6d
John Runynge, 70 days at 7d	40s 10d
John Wilkinson, server, 69 days at 2d	11s 6d
William Marshall, 7 days at 6d	3s 6d
Lancelot Burtun, 8 days at 6d	4s
John Griffithe, server, 16 days at 4d	5s 4d
Henry Layne, 43 days at 8d	28s 8d
Robert Wright, server, 62 days at 4d	20s 8d
John Peaze, 2 days at 10d	20d
Thomas Waltun, server, 2 days at 6d	12d
Robert Baker, 49½ days at 6d	24s 9d
John Usherwood, 37 days at 7d	21s 7d
Oliver Water, server, 49 days at 6d	24s 6d
James Dixson, 37 days at 10d	30s 10d
Richard Rice, server, 27 days at 8d	18s
Edward Bright, master, 102 days and nights at 12d	£5 2s
Thomas Jenell, server, 86 days and nights at 6d	43s
Davy Baker, server, 86 days and nights at 6d	43s
John Laystowe, server, 23 days at 6d	11s 6d
Matthew Baker, master, 96 days and nights at 12d	£4 16s

[*Page total*] – £37 17s 11d.

[f. 30v] Matthew Nortůn, server, 83 days and nights at 5d	34s 7d
John Hoole, server, 83 days and nights at 5d	34s 7d
Philip Garret, 73 days and nights at 6d	36s 6d
John Rande, 82 days and nights at 9d	£3 1s 6d
James Cotes, server, 82 days and nights at 6d	41s
George Flowre, server, 82 days and nights at 6d	41s
John Ellysonne, 70 days at 8d	47s 4d
John Halle, server, 83 days and nights at 6d	41s 6d
Lewis Richardes, 82 days and nights at 6d	41s
Thomas Bryan, 73 days and nights at 6d	36s 6d

John Hutchins, server, 26 days at 6d	13s 6d
John Diggons, 82 days and nights at 6d	41s
James Diggons, 82 days and nights at 5d	34s 2d
Robert Vyze, 82 days and nights at 6d	41s
John Welsheman, 74 days at 8d	49s 4d
John Hubbert, server, 78 days at 6d	39s
John Daltun, 83 days and nights at 5d	48s 5d
Davy Horne, server, 64 days and nights at 3d	16s
Daniel Bright, 86 days and nights at 6d	43s
Ralph Broune, 81 days and nights at 6d	40s 6d
Michael Toow, 82 days and nights at 7d	47s 10d
John Toowe, server, 82 days and nights at 5d	34s 2d
Edward Hollborne, 82 days and nights at 8d	54s 8d
Henry Newe, server, 82 days and nights at 5d	34s 2d
Walter Holborne, 66 days at 8d	44s
John Haywarde, 62 days at 8d	41s 4d
Michael Gammon, server, 67½ days at 5d	28s 1½d
Henry Symon, server, 61 days at 4d	20s 4d
William Wheller, server, 79 days at 5d	32s 11d
John Clarke, 82 days and nights at 8d	54s 8d
John Langtun, 10 days at 7d	5s 10d
John Addams, 15 days at 8d	10s
William Sibley, server, 16 days at 4d	5s 4d
Anthony Houldernes, 72 days at 7d	42s
John Jewell, server, 83 days and nights at 6d	41s 6d
John Jonnes, server, 25 days at 3d	6s 3d
William Spicer, 81 days and nights at 7d	47s 3d
Thomas Osborne, 54 days and nights at 3d	13s 6d

[*Page total*] – £67 5s 3½d.

[f. 31] James Jacobe, 19 days at 6d	9s 6d
Stephen Bevis, 83 days at 6d	41s 6d
Thomas Robinson, 74 days and nights at 6d	37s
Stephen Robinson, server, 79 days and nights at 4d	26s 4d
John Tyllinge, 9 days at 6d	4s 6d
Edward Clarke, 41 days at 6d	20s 6d
Thomas Raynoldes, 24 days at 8d	16s
Henry Raynoldes, server, 24½ days at 2d	4s 1d
Edward Farmyer, 10 days at 6d	5s
John Mayor, server, 5 days at 6d	2s 6d
John Younge, 10 days at 6d	5s
Davy Roche, server, 5 days at 6d	2s 1d [*recte* 6d]

Richard Farrar, 41 days at 6d	20s 6d
Thomas Deakon, server, 53 days at 6d	26s 6d
Henry Greves, 65 days at 7d	37s 11d
Thomas Jackson, server, 1 day at 4d	4d
William Greves, 48 days and nights at 9d	36s
Thomas Lewes, server, 48 days and nights at 6d	24s
Edward Wooller, 65 days and nights at 6d	32s 6d
Robert Wyllis, 81 days and nights at 3d	20s 3d
Richard Mydelltun, 26 days at 6d	13s
Robert Ashetun, 77½ days and nights at 6d	38s 9d
Thomas Barnarde, 38 days at 6d	19s
Michael Chamber, 3 days at 7d	21d
Thomas Hodge, 71 days and nights at 6d	35s 6d
William Hodge, 78 days and nights at 4d	26s
Mark Hodge, 79 days and nights at 6d	39s 6d
Thomas Bonnam, server, 65 days and nights at 4d	21s 8d
Raynolde Woode, 60 days and nights at 6d	30s
John Hurley, 58 days and nights at 6d	29s
Thomas Hewes, 59½ days and nights at 6d	29s 9d
Nicholas Foxe, 55½ days and nights at 6d	27s 9d
William Larde, 10 days at 6d	5s
James Joyce, 6 days at 6d	3s
George Harrison, 11 days at 6d	5s 6d
Henry Cleaue, 11 days at 6d	5s 6d
Richard Eastun, 2 days at 8d	16d

[*Page total*] – £35 4s.

[f. 31v] Cuthbert Lawes, 2 days at 6d	12d
John Eastun, 7 days at 6d	3s 6d
Richard Uppney, 10 days at 6d	5s
Richard Johnson, 53½ days and nights at 6d	26s 9d
John Lawson, 15 days at 6d	7s 6d
Robert Davy, 45 days and nights at 6d	22s 6d
William Eastridge, server, 6 days at 4d	2s
John Mylles, 9 days at 7d	5s 3d
Robert Arther, server, 9 days at 5d	3s 9d
George Chester, 3 days at 6d	18d
Robert Hodgkinson, 54½ days and nights at 8d	36s 4d
Thomas Hely, server, 35 days and nights at 3d	8s 9d
Nicholas Clay, 54 days at 7d	31s 6d
John Claye, server, 50½ days and nights at 5d	21s 3d
John Sager, 50½ days and nights at 5d	21s 3d

Thomas Blosse, 52 days and nights at 8d	34s 8d
Henry Nellet, 56 days and nights at 5d	23s 4d
John Winney, 56½ days and nights at 7d	32s 11½d
John Weathers, 54 days and nights at 5d	22s 6d
Richard Claye, 54 days and nights at 8d	36s
John Brome, 53½ days and nights at 8d	35s 8d
Gregory Turner, 51½ days and nights at 4d	17s 2d
John Hopper, 45½ days and nights at 6d	22s 9d
Henry Barnes, 9 days at 12d	9s
Robert Carre, server, 5 days at 4d	20d
William Bennet, server, 8 days at 5d	3s 4d
William Welshe, 8 days at 8d	5s 4d
Thomas Freman, server, 8 days at 5d	3s 4d
William Carter, server, 8 days at 5d	3s 4d
Richard Parris, 24 days at 10d	20s
John Parris, server, 24 days at 6d	12s
Roger Oldam, 24 days at 8d	16s
Thomas Wilson, 92 days at 12d	£4 12s
John Hurlestone, 98 days and nights at 6d	49s
Henry Rowse, server, 98 days and nights at 3d	24s 6d

[*Page total*] – £33 2s 3½d.

[f. 32] *Caulkers*

Thomas Bolltun, master, 97½ days & nights at 10d	£4 1s 3d
John Atkinson, server, 35 days at 6d	17s 6d
William Boultun, server, 87½ days and nights at 6d	43s 9d
John Pinocke, 35 days at 7d	20s 5d
Philip Payne, 84½ days and nights at 7d	49s 3½d
John Paullmer, 83½ days and nights at 6d	41s 9d
John Hillard, 83½ days and nights at 6d	41s 9d
Walter Johnson, 84½ days and nights at 6d	42s 3d
John Hassell, server, 11 days at 2d	22d
John Smythe, 53 days at 8d	35s 4d
Robert Grigge, server, 89½ days and nights at 6d	44s 9d
Richard Bartun, 46 days at 7d	26s 10d
John Graye, server, 20 days at 5d	8s 4d
Roger Laken, 53 days at 7d	30s 11d
Henry Adee, server, 52 days at 3d	13s
Henry Pouder, server, 43 days and nights at 5d	18s 4d
Richard Cowller, 64½ days and nights at 6d	32s 3d
William Fourde, 40½ days at 7d	23s 7½d
William Mundes, 79½ days and nights at 8d	53s

Oliver Davy, server, 7 days at 2d	14d
John Mozer, 53½ days and nights at 6d	26s 9d
John Hearsse, 80½ days and nights at 6d	40s 3d
Thomas Clarke, 76½ days and nights at 7d	44s 7½d
John Webbe, 66½ days and nights at 7d	38s 9½d
William Raget, server, 78 days and nights at 4d	26s
Thomas Norcot, 37½ days at 7d	21s 10½d
John Bende, 78½ days and nights at 3d	19s 7½d
Gregory Knyghte, 71½ days and nights at 7d	41s 8½d
Richard Mylles, server, 4 days at 3d	12d
John Clerke, 51 days at 7d	29s 9d
William Johnson, server, 19 days at 3d	4s 9d
Richard Whight, 68 days at 7d	39s 8d

[*Page total*] – £48 2s 1½d.

[f. 32v] Henry Reede, 77 days at 4d	25s 8d
Nicholas Foster, 7 days at 6d	3s 6d
Walter Deane, 59 days at 7d	34s 5d
Robert Smart, server, 65 days and nights at 3d	16s 3d
Ambrose Adye, 2 days at 6d	12d
Christopher Clarke, 2 days at 4d	8d
Robert Brigges, 48 days and nights at 7d	28s
Humphrey Deall, 62 days and nights at 4d	20s 8d
Humphrey Lewys, 2 days at 6d	12d
John Dowell, 2 days at 6d	12d
John Stockedaille, 59½ days and nights at 6d	29s 9d
Michael Rowse, 50½ days and nights at 6d	25s 3d
Edmund Barret, 4 days at 7d	2s 4d
John Maryboat, 4 days at 6d	2s
John Mathew, 3 days at 10d	2s 6d
Richard Frythe, 69 days at 3d	17s 3d
Sawyers	
Thomas Miller, 82½ days and nights at 6d	41s 3d
Robert Davys, 82½ days and nights at 6d	41s 3d
John Richardes, 80½ days and nights at 6d	40s 3d
Robert Grene, 80½ days and nights at 6d	40s 3d
Thomas Phillipp, 6 days at 6d	3s
Henry Harvy, 24 days at 6d	12s
John Punche, 18 days at 6d	9s
Smiths	
Thomas Ive, master, 8 days at 12d	8s
William Suddrede, 21 days at 6d	10s 6d

John Oliver, 21 days at 6d	10s 6d
Jeffrey Tatam, 11 days at 6d	5s 6d
Thomas Bridges, 4 days at 8d	2s 8d

[*Page total*] – £21 15s 5d.

[f. 33] *Topmakers*

William Beckesley, 34 days at 8d	22s 8d
William Kakete, 34 days at 6d	17s
Abraham Harman, server, 34 days at 5d	14s 2d
John Smarte, 24 days at 6d	12s

Boatmakers

Richard Skarlett, master, 7 days at 10d	5s 10d
Robert Myddellwoode, server, 7 days at 6d	3s 6d
Francis Tythe, 4 days at 8d	2s 8d
Richard Dode, server, 4 days at 6d	2s
Robert Felltun, 7 days at 8d	4s 8d
Henry Hebbdun, 7 days at 5d	2s 11d
Rowland Sheapparde, 7 days at 8d	4s 8d
Thomas Norwell, 7 days at 8d	4s 8d
William Ornxe, server, 7 days at 4d	2s 4d
Edward Sore, server, 7 days at 4d	2s 4d
John Webbe, 1 day at 8d	8d
John Vickars, server, 7 days at 6d	3s 6d
Thomas Porter, 7 days at 8d	4s 8d

Victualling. To Thomas Willson of Ratcliff the last day of September for the victualling of 214 shipwrights, caulkers, sawyers, smiths, topmakers, boatmakers and others working upon the new making of two Her Grace's ships and one bark named the *Triumph*, the *Victory* and the *Aid* there by the space of 10,135 days among them all, the Sundays and holy days within the same accounted, which maketh 1,447 weeks 6 days begun the first day of July last and this day ended, at 4s 1d every week the man. *Summa* – £295 12s 1d.

[*Page total*] – £301 2s 4d. *[*Artificers – £5 10s 3d*; *victualling – £295 12s 1d*]

[f. 33v] *Lodging.* To Joan King, Alice Bory, Elizabeth Fraunces, Joan Rocke and 18 other persons of Deptford, Greenwich, Lewisham, and thereabouts the last day of September for the lodging of 170 of the aforenamed shipwrights, caulkers, sawyers, smiths, topmakers, boatmakers and others, working upon Her Grace's said new ships, in 98 featherbeds by the space of 1,917 weeks among them all, begun the first day of July last and this day ended, at 2d every week the man. *Summa* – £15 19s 6d.

House-carpenters

John Leche, master, 87 days and nights at 12d	£4 7s
Robert Throwley, server, 87 days and nights at 7d	50s 9d
Thomas Hill, 30 days at 10d	25s
Thomas Awood, 60 days and nights at 10d	50s
Richard Stampe, 19 days at 10d	15s 10d
Robert Awnstemn, 22 days at 10d	18s 4d
Henry Weste, server, 24 days at 10d	20s
Thomas Hillary, 16½ days at 10d	13s 9d
Thomas Hilltun, server, 16½ days at 8d	11s
Thomas Phillippe, 16 days at 10d	13s 4d

[*Page total*] – £31 4s 6d. *[*Lodging – £15 19s 6d*; *artificers – £15 5s*]

[f. 34] *Bricklayers*

Edmund Esgarre, 4 days at 10d	3s 4d
Thomas Esgarre, 4 days at 9d	3s
Robert Nelle, 14 days at 10d	11s 8d
George Parker, 5 days at 10d	4s 2d
Philip John, 3 days at 8d	2s
Thomas Cole, 10 days at 10d	8s 4d
William Ardington, 3 days at 8d	2s
John Kindesley, 3 days at 8d	2s
John Flowre, 10 days at 8d	6s 8d
John Callaway, 9 days at 11d	8s 3d
John Mylles, 7 days at 9d	5s 3d
Stephen Hudgens, 8 days at 8d	5s 4d
James Hudgens, 7 days at 10d	5s 10d
Robert Gardener, 7 days at 9d	5s 3d
Robert Kelley, 3 days at 7d	21d
Christopher White, 3 days at 8d	2s

Labourers

William Alley, master, 30 nights at 4d	10s
Nicholas Archedall, 92 days and nights at 6d	46s
George Mathew, 89 days and nights at 6d	44s 6d
John Loweman, 83½ days and nights at 6d	41s 9d
John Gibson, 102 days and nights at 6d	51s
Edward Plumer, 97 days and nights at 6d	48s 6d
Henry Stevenson, 98 days and nights at 6d	49s
Thomas Loweman, 84 days at 6d	42s
James Howper, 102 days at nights at 6d	51s
John Pythen, senior, 117 days and nights at 6d	58s 6d

John Brodehurste, 117½ days and nights at 6d 58s 9d

[*Page total*] – £28 17s 10d. *[*Artificers – 56s 10d*; *labourers – £26 1s*]

[f. 34v] William Twayttes, 117½ days and nights at 6d 58s 9d

John Bastian, 117 days and nights at 6d 58s 6d

John Addams, 98 days and nights at 6d 49s

Thomas Clarke, 86½ days and nights at 6d 43s 3d

John Wallis, 86 days and nights at 6d 43s

Richard Raynsforthe, 98½ days and nights at 7d 57s 5½d

James Tealle, 116 days and nights at 6d 58s

William Gonnby, 109½ days and nights at 6d 54s 9d

John Jans, 83 days and nights at 6d 41s 6d

Robert Watson, 107 days and nights at 6d 53s 6d

Thomas Lingarde, 104 days and nights at 6d 52s

John Brace, 108½ days and nights at 6d 54s 3d

Thomas Thisselton, 102 days and nights at 6d 51s

Robert Scote, 29 days at 6d 14s 6d

Robert Stevens, 27½ days at 6d 13s 9d

George Newtun, 28½ days at 6d 14s 3d

Morgan ap Price, 106 days and nights at 6d 53s

Richard Coxe, 79½ days and nights at 6d 39s 9d

Lawrence Langcaster, 102½ days and nights at 6d 51s 3d

John ap Price, 75½ days and nights at 6d 37s 9d

Davy Deane, 17 days at 6d 8s 6d

John Goodgam, 48½ days and 5 nights at 6d 26s 9d

James Hodgson, 28½ days at 6d 14s 3d

Edward Grene, 16½ days at 6d 8s 3d

Ralph Courteland, 42 days and nights at 6d 21s

John Waynsfourth, 52 days and nights at 6d 26s 3d

John Mansfilde, 57½ days and nights at 6d 28s 9d

William ap Price, 42½ days and nights at 6d 21s 3d

John Jonnes, 10 days at 6d 5s

John Marshall, 42½ days and nights at 6d 21s 3d

William Tasse, 84 days at 6d 42s

John Dawne, 28½ days at 6d 14s 3d

George Bell, 11½ days at 6d 5s 9d

Richard Williams, 11 days at 6d 5s 6d

Bartholomew Bavon, 34 days at 6d 17s

William Pithen, 114½ days and nights at 6d 57s 3d

[*Page total*] – £61 2s 2½d.

[f. 35] *Marshmen*[1]

John Hilltun, master, 50 days and tides at 8d	33s 4d
Jeffrey Hayward, 48 days and tides at 7d	28s
John Sharpe, 48½ days and tides at 7d	28s 3½d
Egene Pennett, 48½ days and tides at 7d	28s 3½d
Leonard Tailler, 47 days and tides at 7d	27s 5d
William Jakes, 48 days and tides at 7d	28s
John Sturgeon, 48 days and tides at 7d	28s
Richard Williams, 31½ days and tides at 7d	18s 4½d
Davy Deane, 48 days and tides at 7d	28s
Bartholomew Jennyns, 32 days and tides at 7d	18s 8d
Richard Hawkins, 45½ days and tides at 7d	26s 6½d
George Hardewicke, 45½ days and tides at 7d	26s 6½d
John Coke, 31 days and tides at 7d	18s 1d
John Stafforde, 25 days and tides at 7d	14s 7d
John Mosse, 24½ days at 7d	14s 3½d
Thomas Morris, 48 days and tides at 7d	28s
William Kelley, 47 days and tides at 7d	27s 5d
John Haynes, 1 day at 7d	7d
George Fraunces, 1 day at 7d	7d
William Hedd, 1 day at 7d	7d
William Straine, 2 days at 7d	14d
Ewryan Dode, 2 days at 7d	14d
Starling Druman, 27½ days and tides at 7d	16s 0½d
Griffiths Jonnes, 24 days and tides at 7d	14s
Ralph Willde, 2 days at 7d	14d
John Mylles, 38 days and tides at 7d	22s 2d
Richard Crayne, 41 days and tides at 7d	23s 11d
Richard Smythe, 43½ days and tides at 7d	25s 4½d
Thomas Draper, 42½ days and tides at 7d	24s 9½d
John Browne, 44 days and tides at 7d	25s 8d
William Goghe, 45 days and tides at 7d	26s 3d

[*Page total*] – £30 5s 1½d.

[f. 35v] Lawrence Heede, 48 days and tides at 7d	28s
William Awgers, 31½ days and tides at 7d	18s 11½d
James More, 27 days and tides at 7d	15s 9d
John Chapman, 22 days and tides at 7d	12s 10d
John Carpenter, 21 days and tides at 7d	12s 3d

[1]Those who dug out the dockhead when a ship was launched; they disappear from the accounts in the early 1580s, following the introduction of dock gates: Rodger, *Safeguard*, p. 335.

Martin Kingeslonde, 4 days at 7d	2s 4d
Henry Harrrison, 21 days and tides at 7d	12s 3d
John Wadeslay, 26 days and tides at 7d	15s 2d
Ralph Thornnetonn, 24 days and tides at 7d	14s
John Tompson, 20½ days and tides at 7d	11s 11½d
Sallaman Tye, 18½ days and tides at 7d	10s 9½d
John Blake, 19½ days and tides at 7d	11s 4½d
William Baily, 20½ days and tides at 7d	11s 11½d
Thomas Saill, 27½ days and tides at 7d	16s 0½d
John Bakon, 25 days and tides at 7d	14s 7d
Francis Howell, 21 days and tides at 7d	12s 3d
Thomas Cant, 24½ days and tides at 7d	14s 3½d
Rowland Bell, 25½ days and tides at 7d	14s 10½d
Edward Hearsley, 16½ days and tides at 7d	9s 7½d
Robert Lacke, 25 days and tides at 7d	14s 7d
Thomas Brokesam, 18½ days and tides at 7d	10s 9½d
Robert Fourde, 40 days and tides at 7d	23s 4d
George Bell, 22½ days and tides at 7d	13s 1½d
John Twyforde, 43½ days and tides at 7d	25s 4½d
John Johnson, 44½ days and tides at 7d	25s 11½d
Thomas Johnson, 19 days and tides at 7d	11s 1d
John Wallis, 23 days and tides at 7d	13s 5d
William Northe, 25 days at 6d	12s 6d

[*Page total*] – £20 9s 5d.

[f. 36] *Watchmen*

William Ally, 36 days and nights at 4d	12s
John Hurllestonn, 36 days and nights at 4d	12s
Nicholas Archedaille, 36 days and nights at 4d	12s
Thomas Smythe, 36 days and nights at 4d	12s
Thomas Thisselltun, 34 days and nights at 4d	11s 4d
George Mathew, 34 days and nights at 4d	11s 4d
William Partricke, 34 days and nights at 4d	11s 4d
Edward Plumer, 34 days and nights at 4d	11s 4d
Paul Saunders, 34 days and nights at 4d	11s 4d
John Addams, 34 days and nights at 4d	11s 4d
John Loweman, 34 days and nights at 4d	11s 4d
James Howper, 34 days and nights at 4d	11s 4d
	[£6 18s 8d*]

Storehouse rent. To Peter Pett of Deptford the last day of September for one quarter of a year's rent of two cellars of him hired wherein lieth

Her Highness's store of rosin for the use of Her Grace's ships, due at this present – £1.

[*Page total*] – £7 18s 8d.

[f. 36v]. *Emptions*

Ironwork. *[*Anchors*]. To Gilbert Mattyse of St Katherine's, smith, the last day of September for price of 2 new anchors of him had for the use of Her Highness's ship named the *Hare*, weighing 5 hundred 3 quarters one pound weight [*645 lbs*], at 23s 4d every hundredweight. *Summa* – £6 14s 2d.[1]

To John Preston, smith, the same day for price of 2 new anchors of him had for the use of Her Highness's ship named the *Saker* ('Sacaker'), weighing 9 hundred 3 quarters 15 pounds weight [*1,107 lbs*], at 23s 4d every hundredweight. *Summa* – £11 10s 7½d.

*[*Nails*]. To William Pennyfather of London the same day for price of one some of Flemish 2d nail of him had for the use of Her Highness's ships, price – 11s; more for half a some of English 2d nail, price – 7s; and more for 3,000 of 2d nails, price – 3s 6d. *Summa* – £1 1s 6d.

*[*Ironwork – £51 8s 1d; nails – £39 12s 7d* <recte *6d*>]. To Thomas Willson of Ratcliff, smith, the same day for price of 4 thousand 4 hundred 6½ pounds weight [*4,934½ lbs*] of his own new iron by him made into bolts, spikes, clench, rove and overlop nail for the use of Her Highness's three new ships there, at 23s 4d every hundredweight – £51 8s 1d;[2] more for 36,650 of 10d nail, at 8s 4d every 1,000 – £15 5s 5d; more for 43,750 of 6d nail, at 5s every 1,000 – £10 18s 9d; more for 39,300 of 4d nail, at 3s 4d the 1,000 – £6 11s; more for 31,200 of 3d nail, at 2s 6d every 1,000 – £3 18s; and more to him for 13,700 of scupper nails, at 3s 4d every 1,000 – 59s 4d. *Summa* – £91 0s 7d.

*[*Nails*]. To Thomas Downynge of Paris Garden, smith, the same day for price of 10,400 of 10d nail of him had for the use of Her Highness's ships, at 8s 4d every 1,000 – £4 6s 8d; more for 7,500 of 6d nail, at 5s every 1,000 – 37s 6d; and more to him for 4,000 of 4d nail, at 3s 4d every 1,000 – 13s 4d. *Summa* – £6 17s 6d.

[*Page total*] – £117 4s 4½d.

[f. 37] *[*Locks, keys, hooks, hinges and such other*]. To Gilbert Pollstonne of Greenwich, locksmith, the last day of September for the workmanship and making of certain locks, keys and hinges as well for two new cabins there in Her Grace's ships the *Triumph* and the *Victory*, as also for port-hinges, stocklocks, and divers other necessaries for the

[1]The calculation gives 1612.5d and so is 2½d above the sum stated (1610d).
[2]The calculation gives 12336.25d and so is ¾d below the sum stated (12337d).

use of the said ships, *viz*. for 16 long rivets with counter rivets, at 2d the piece – 2s 8d; more for 11 pair of hinges, at 2s the piece – 22s; more for 12 pair of dovetails, at 8d the pair – 8s; more for 12 locks, at 2s the lock – 24s; more for 4 dozen of hooks with staples and nails, at 2s the dozen – 8s; more for 40 hooks with eyes and staples, at 12d the piece – 40s; more for 4 iron pins for folding trestles, price – 4d; more for 10 pair of great dovetails, at 12d the pair – 10s; more for 50 rivets nails, price – 2s; more for 6 pair of vices for the beasts to stand on,[1] at 12d the piece – 6s; more for 4 pair of square-hinges with 4 casements for windows, at 12d the pair – 4s; more for 8 small squares, at 2d the piece – 16d; more for 4 bars, at 2d the piece – 8d; more for 4 shuttings with rings, at 6d the piece – 2s; more for 7 pair of hinges, at 8d the pair – 4s 8d; more for a stock lock, price 20d; more for 4 keys, price – 2s; and more to him for 4 hooks with staples for folding trestles, with nails for the same, price – 2s 8d. *Summa* – £7 2s.

*[*Iron – £90 14s 2d; nails – £13 19s 4d*]. To Thomas Ive of Limehouse, smith, the same day for price of 7 thousand 7 hundred and 3 quarters weight [*8,708 lbs*] of his own new iron of him had and made into bolts, rings, keys, spikes, clench, rove and overlop nails for the use of Her Highness's three new ships there, at 23s 4d every hundredweight – £90 14s 2d; more for 13,200 of 10d nail, at 8s 4d every 1,000 – £5 10s; more for 15,000 of 6d nail, at 5s every 1,000 – £3 15s; more for 10,000 of 4d nail, at 3s 4d every 1,000 – 33s 4d; more for 10,000 of 3d nail, at 2s 6d every 1,000 – 25s; and more to him for 6,000 of scupper nails, at 4s 4d every 1,000 – 26s. *Summa* – £104 3s 6d.

[*Page total*] – £111 5s 6d.

[f. 37v] To Richard Welles of Greenwich, smith, the last day of September for price of 6 new running irons of him had for the use of Her Highness's ships, at 6d the piece – 3s; and more to him for 8 great gimlets, at 5d the piece – 3s 4d. *Summa* – 6s 4d.

To Robert Brodelay of Southwark, smith, the same day for price of 12,000 of brods of him had for the use of Her [*Highness's*] ships, of inch long, at 6d every 100 – £3; more for 6,700 of brods of inch ½ long, at 8d every 100 – 44s 8d; more for 7,400 brods of 2 inches long, at 10d every 100 – £3 1s 8d; more for 2,100 brods of 2½ inches long, at 12d every 100 – 21s; more for 3,800 brods of 3 inches long, at 14d every 100 – 44s 4d; more for 700 of brods of 3½ inches long, at 16d every 100 – 9s 4d; more for 3,000 of brods of 4 inches, at 18d every 100 – 45s; and more to him for 2,700 of brods of 4½ inches long, at 20d every 100 – 45s. *Summa* – £16 11s.

[1]Perhaps capstans used for winding ships aground, as described in a purchase of 1530: *LP*, iv, III, no. 6138(2).

Copper nails. To Ollyff Burre of Southwark, coppersmith, the same day for price of 30½ pounds weight of his great copper nails by him delivered there for the mending of Her [*Highness's*] great copper pans for Her Grace's ships, at 16d every pound weight. *Summa* – £2 0s 8d.

To John Colleman of Southwark, tinker, the same day for price of 9 pounds weight of his great copper nails of him had for the new mending of Her Highness's pitch kettles there, at 16d every pound – 12s; more to him for his wages working upon the same kettles, by 5 days at 10d the day – 4s 2d; and more to him for two of his men[*'s*] wages, by the space of 10 days between them at 8d every day – 6s 8d. *Summa*. £1 2s 10d.

[*Page total*] – £20 0s 10d.

[f. 38] *Cablets, hawsers, cordage, pitch, tar and masts*. *[*Cables – £406 12s*; *masts – £876*; *pitch and tar – £90*]. To Thomas Allen of London, merchant,[1] the last day of September for price of 46 thousand 4 hundred 2 quarters 21 pounds weight [*52,045 lbs*] of Dansk ropes by him provided and delivered into Her Majesty's great storehouse at Deptford for the furniture of Her Grace's ships, *viz*. 49 cables of 9, 8, 7, 6, 5 and 5½ inches compass, 74 hawsers and warps of 4, 3, and 2 inches compass, price by agreement 17s 6d every hundredweight – £406 12s; more for 30 great masts of Lettish[2] trees, of 33, 34, 35 yards long, at £24 every mast – £720; more for 13 spruce masts of 23, 24, 25 and 26 yards long, at £12 every mast – £156; more [*for*] 10 last of pitch of the great band, at £4 10s every last – £45; and more to him for 10 last of tar, at £4 10s every last – £45. *Summa* – £1,372 12s.

*[*Hawsers – £9 8s 6d*; *pitch and tar – £31 3s 4d*; *needles – 10s 10d*; *sail twine – 32s 6d*]. To Christopher Draper of London, alderman, the same day for 2 white hawsers of him had for the use of Her Highness's ships, weighing 6 hundred 2 quarters 26 pounds weight [*754 lbs*], at 28s every hundredweight – £9 8s 6d; more for 4 last of tar of the great band, at £4 13s 4d every last – £18 13s 4d; more for 2 last and 6 barrels of pitch, at 8s 4d the barrel – £12 10s; more for 26 dozen of iron needles, at 5d every dozen – 10s 10d; and more to him for 60 pounds of sail twine, at 6½d the pound – 22s 6d. *Summa* – £42 15s 2d.

[1]Leading Baltic merchant and Crown agent ('the Queen's merchant') at Danzig. Later a vociferous opponent of Hawkins's administration, and likely author of one or more defamatory papers submitted to the government: Corbett, *Spanish War*, pp. 213–24; including allegation of embezzlement by Hawkins in association with work in Chapman's yard (p. 214). The animosity may have developed when Hawkins stopped Allen and Sir William Winter running a racket in Baltic supplies: J. A.Williamson, *Sir John Hawkins: The Time and the Man* (Oxford, 1927), pp. 334 n. 3, 372–5.

[2]MS 'Lettus', i.e. of the country of the Letts, here used as an equivalent of 'Baltic' or 'Eastland'.

*[*Masts*]. To Richard Cragge of London, merchant, the same day for price of 6 great masts of Lettish trees of him had and delivered at Deptford Strand for the use of Her Highness's ships, of 33, 34 and 35 yards long, at £24 every mast. *Summa* – £144.

Cocks and shivers of brass. To Robert Hunte of London, founder, the same day for price of 6 shivers and 3 cocks of brass of him had for the use of Her Highness's ships, weighing 97½ pounds, at 6½d every pound weight. *Summa* – £2 12s 9¾d.

[*Page total*] – £1,561 19s 9¾d.

[f. 38v] *Old junks and ropes made into netting- and wrain-ropes.* To William Brooke of Deptford the last day of September for the workmanship of 21 hundred one quarter weight [*2,380 lbs*] of Her Highness's old junks and ropes by him made into netting- and wrain-ropes for the use of Her Grace's ships, at 3s 8d every hundredweight working. *Summa* – £3 17s 11d.

To William Coxe of Ratcliff, ropemaker, the same day for 13 hundred 2 quarters weight [*1,512 lbs*] of Her Highness's old junks and ropes by him made and wrought into netting- and wrain-ropes for the use of Her Grace's ships, at 3s 8d every hundredweight working. *Summa* – £2 9s 6d.

To Thomas Russell of Ratcliff, ropemaker, the same day for the workmanship of 13 hundred 3 quarters weight [*1,540 lbs*] of Her Highness's old junks and ropes by him made as aforesaid into netting- and wrain-ropes for the use of Her Grace's ships, at 3s 8d every hundredweight working. *Summa* – £2 10s 5d.

Old oakum. To Nicholas Archedall, John Lowman, John Hurlestone and 11 other persons of Deptford, Greenwich, Lewisham and thereabout the same day for the working and picking of 3 thousand 2 hundred 7 pounds weight [*3,591 lbs*] of Her Highness's old junks and ropes by them made and wrought into oakum for the needful caulking of Her Grace's ships, at 3s 8d every hundredweight. *Summa* – £5 17s 7d.[1]

Canvas. To Edward Hall of London, merchant, the same day for price of one piece of white dowlas canvas of him had for the new making of flags for the use of Her Grace's ships, price – £5 6s 8d; more for 8 ells of canvas, at 14d every ell – 9s 4d; more for 12¼ yards of coarse canvas, at 8d every ell [*recte* yard] – 8s 2d; and more to him for 24 bolts of oleron canvas, at 17s 6d every bolt – £21. *Summa* – £27 4s 2d.

[*Page total*] – £41 19s 7d. *[*Old junks – £14 15s 5d*; *canvas – £27 4s 2d*]

[f. 39] *Canvas.* To Francis Allvey, merchant, the last day of September for price of 14 pieces of medrinacks canvas of him had and delivered at

[1]The calculation gives 1410.7498d, and so is ¼d below the sum stated (1411d).

Deptford for the use of Her Highness's ships, at 35s every piece – £24 10s.

Canvas and say. To Thomas Tomplinson the same day for price of 3 pieces of red say of him had for the new making of flags for [*word repeated*] the use of Her Highness's ships; by agreement – £5 1s 8d.

Making of flags. To Stephen Andros of London, tailor, the same day for the making of 9 great flags of white canvas and red say with the cross of St George for the use of Her Highness's ships, at 2s every flag – 18s; more for the like making of 4 small flags, at 16d the piece – 5s 4d; and more to him for thread for the same flags, price – 16d. *Summa* – £1 4s 8d.

Sye, deal-boards, flags, cloveboards and grindstones. *[*Sye or hair – 43s; deal-boards – 30s*]. To Peter Pett of Deptford, master shipwright, the same day for price of 32 stone and 2 pounds of sye or hair of him had for the use of Her Highness's ships, at 16d every stone – 43s; and more to him for 30 narrow deal-boards, at 12d the piece – 30s. *Summa* – £3 13s.

*[*Thrums – 11s 8d*; *making of flags – 34s 8d*; *nails 13s*; *grindstones 8s*; *boards 70s*]. To Edward Gotelay of Deptford the same day for price of 2 quarters weight of thrums by him delivered there for the use of Her Highness's ships, at 2½d every pound – 11s 8d; more for making two new flags with the cross of St George for the *Saker* and the *Phoenix*, at 13s 4d the flag – 26s 8d; more for one some of English 2d nail, price – 13s; more for 2 grindstones of 3 foot over, price – 8s; more for painting and colouring of 2 top armours for the same ships, price – 8s; and more to him for 150 of cloveboards oak, price – £3 10s. *Summa* – £6 17s 4d.

[*Page total*] – £41 6s 8d.

[f. 39v] *Masts, fir poles, thrums and oil.* To William Paidge of London, merchant, the last day of September for price of 22 small masts by him delivered at Deptford for the use of Her Highness's ships, at 10s every mast – £11; more for one shock of Dansk deal containing 60 boards, at 3s 4d the piece – £10; more for one grindstone of 4 foot broad, price – 3s 4d; more for 50 fir poles, at 6d the piece – 25s; more for 50 long fir poles, at 20d the piece – £4 3s 4d; more for 91 pounds of thrums, at 2½d the pound – 18s 11½d; more for one hogshead of caulking oil, price – £3 6s 8d; more for 51½ gallons of oil, at 14d the gallon – £3 0s 1d; and more to him for 26 gallons of oil, at 16d every gallon – 34s 8d. *Summa* – £35 12s 0½d. *[*Masts and fir poles – £16 8s 4d*; *boards – £10*; *a grindstone – 3s 4d*; *thrums – 18s 11½d; caulking oil – £8 1s 1d*]

Timber oak. To Christopher Nayller of London the same day for price of 346 loads of timber oak by him provided in Sussex and the same delivered at Deptford for the new building, making and repairing of Her Highness's ships there, at 10s every load after 50 foot the load – £173;

more for 27,225 foot of 3- and 4-inch plank oak, at 10s every 100 foot – £136 2s 6d; more for 14,600 foot of 2-inch ½ plank oak, at 8s every 100 foot – £58 8s; and more to him for 60,230 foot of inch ½ board [*word repeated*] oak, at 5s every 100 foot – £150 11s 6d. *Summa* – £518 2s.

Paper and ink. To William Prestwood of London the same day for price of 3 reams of paper royal of him had for the making of paybooks for shipwrights, caulkers and others as also for the engrossing of the same, at 20s 4d every ream – £3 1s; more for 11 reams 9 quires of small paper, at 6s the ream – £3 9s; more for 3 gallons and 2 quarts of ink, at 5s 4d the gallon – 18s 8d; more for binding of 5 great ledger books and for other books of paper for the office of Her [*Highness's*] marine affairs – 42s; more for 2 pounds weight of casting counters, price – 4s 8d; and more to him for one ream ½ of demi-paper, at 13s 4d the ream – 20s. *Summa* – £10 15s 4d.

[*Page total*] – £564 9s 4½d.

[f. 40] *Pulleys, steel shovels, scoops, shivers and cocks of brass.* To John Benbow of London the last day of September for price of 45 pulleys of him had for the use of Her Highness's ships, at 16d the piece – £3; more for 12 pulleys, at 20d the piece – 20s; more for 27 pulleys, at 12d the piece – 27s; more for 34 pulleys, at 8d the piece – 22s 8d; more for 38 pulleys, at 4d the piece – 12s 8d; more for 6 pulleys, at 6d the piece – 3s; more for one parrel of 3 sets, price – 5s; more for one parrel of 5 sets, price – 15s; more for 36 pulleys, at 2d the piece – 6s; more for one shiver with a cock of brass, price – 8d; more for 8 dozen [*and*] 8 scoops, at 4s 6d the dozen – 39s; more for 21 dozen of steel shovels, at 7s the dozen – £7 7s; and more to him for 5 dozen and 8 great bowls, at 8d the piece – 45s 4d. *Summa* – £20 3s 4d.

To Joan Childerlaye of London, widow, the same day for price of 11 dozen of shod shovels of him [*recte* her] had for the use of Her Highness's ships, at 7s every dozen – £3 17s; more for 4 dozen of scoops, at 4s 6d every dozen – 18s; more for 3 dozen of great bowls for pitch and rosin, at 8s the dozen – 24s; more for 12 great pulleys, at 12d the piece – 12s; more to her for 12 pulleys, at 6d the piece – 6s. *Summa* – £6 17s.

Turned posts. To William Frithe of Southwark, turner, the same day for workmanship and turning of 10 great posts for Her [*Highness's*] new ships there, at 12d the piece – 10s; more for the turning of 60 balusters for the use of the same ships, at 4d the piece – 20s; more for 60 small balusters of oak, at 1d the piece – 5s; and more for 12 other balusters, at 2d the piece – 2s. *Summa* – £1 17s.

Water buckets. To John Williamson of London, cooper the same day for price of 18 dozen of water buckets of wood by him delivered at

Deptford for the use of Her Highness's ships, at 5s every dozen. *Summa* – £4 10s.

[*Page total*] – £33 7s 4d. *[*Turner's stuff – £28 17s 4d*; *buckets – £4 10s*]

[f. 40v] *Sounding leads.* To Julian Richardes of London, widow, the last day of September for price of 25 hundred 2 quarters 4 pounds weight [*2,860 lbs*] of her own new lead by her delivered at Deptford for the use of Her Highness's ships, at 15s every hundred[*weight*] – £19 3s 1d;[1] more for [*one*] hundred 2 quarters 13½[2] pounds weight [*181½ lbs*] of sounding leads, at 15s 2d every hundred[*weight*] – 24s 7¼d; more for 46 pounds weight of tin solder, at 8d every pound – 30s 8d; more for wages of her three men working upon Her Grace's two new ships by the space of 35 days between them, at 10d *per diem* – 29s 2d; and more to her for the bringing down of the same lead by water – 4s. *Summa* – £23 11s 6¼d. *[*Lead new – £19 3s 1d*; *solder – 30s 8d*; *wages of a plumber – 29s 2d*; *carriage – 4s*]

*[*Baskets*]. To Anne Edes of London, widow, the same day for price of 27 dozen of ballast baskets of her had and delivered at Deptford for the use of Her Highness's ships, at 18d every dozen – 40s 6d; more for 12 dozen of middle baskets, at 4d the piece – 48s; more for 12 great baskets, at 8d the piece – 8s; more for 2 dozen and 3 baskets, at 6d the piece – 13s 6d; and more to her for 4 dozen of baskets, at 5d the piece – 20s. *Summa* – £6 10s.

Carriage of rubbish and gravel. To John Elmer of Deptford the same day for the hire of his 2 carts 5 horses and 3 men serving Her Highness in carrying away of 200 loads of rubbish out of her working yard there for the better working of Her Grace's shipwrights, as also for the carrying of 200 loads of gravel for the ballasting of Her Highness's said ship, at 1d every load carrying – 33s 4d; and more for the wages of the aforesaid three men for filling of the same carts by 27 days among them all, at 6d *per diem* – 13s 6d. *Summa* – £2 6s 10d.

To Thomas Inrette of Deptford the same day for the hire of his cart and horses serving Her Highness in carrying 29 loads of gravel for the ballasting of Her Highness's new ships there, at 1d every load – 2s 5d; and more to him for the wages of his man, by 4 days at 6d *per diem* – 2s. [*Summa*] – 4s 5d.

[*Page total*] – £32 12s 9d.

[1]The calculation gives 4596.4284d, and so is over ½d above the stated sum (4597d). In this instance calculation by hundredweight of 100 lbs works minutely better (giving 4597.2d).

[2]MS '*c ij quarters di' xiij li.*': the *dimidium* and the *xiij li.* have been accidentally transposed; as recomposed the figure fits the calculation adequately: [112 + (2 × 28) + 13.5)] × (182d ÷112) = 294.9375d (the stated sum being 295.25d).

[f. 41] *Carriage of gravel.* To William Tewsone the last day of September for the hire of his cart and 5 horses serving Her Highness in carrying 91 loads of gravel for ballast for the said two new ships, at 1d every load – 7s 7d; and more to him for wages of his man for the filling of the same cart by the space of 4 days, at 6d *per diem* – 2s. *Summa* – 9s 7d.

Pump-hose, claps and scupper-leathers. To John Harryson of Tower Hill, shoemaker, the same day for price of 6 dozen and 5 great pump-hose of the largest sort of him had for the use of Her Highness's ships, at 2s 8d the piece – £10 5s 4d; more for 7 dozen and 10 great claps, at 16d the piece – £6 5s 4d; more for 16 dozen and 7 scupper-leathers, at 16d the piece – £13 5s 4d; more for 7 small claps, at 8d the piece – 4s 8d; more for 8 pump-hose, at 16d the piece – 10s 8d; more for 22 great pump-hose, at 2s 8d the piece – 58s 8d; more for 8 great claps, at 16d the piece – 10s 8d; and more to him for 4 dozen and 8 scupper-leathers, at 16d the piece – £3 14s 8d. *Summa* – £37 15s 4d.

[*Page total*] – £38 4s 11d. [f. 41v *blank*]

[f. 42] *Anno Domini 1562. Anno regni regine Elizabethe quinto*

A payment made the last day of December as well to masters, mariners and gunners keeping Her Highness's ships afloat in harbour and to keepers of storehouses, docks and timber-yards there wherein lieth Her Grace's provisions for the use of her ships, as also to shipwrights, caulkers, sawyers, smiths, labourers and other artificers and workmen for new building and repairing of Her Majesty's ships, and to divers persons for sundry kinds of provisions and necessaries had towards the same; by one quarter of a year begun the first day of October last, and this day ended, as followeth:[1]

[1] A corrected draft for this Deptford quarter survives as BL, Add. MS 78169. Significant details not carried through to the final account are noted here; a conspectus of the draft is given in Appendix 4 below. The draft begins (f. 1) with this more fulsome heading: 'A payment made the last day of December *anno predicto* to masters, mariners, gunners, keepers of timber-yards [*and*] storehouses daily attending and serving the Queen's Highness, as well for safe-keeping of Her Grace's ships within the river of Thames, as labouring about in taking down, unrigging, masting and having of the sails from the yards, and tackling, with the cables, hawsers, anchors, pulleys, shivers, with divers other kinds of stuffs out of the same ships, and for the laying up of the same into Her Grace's great storehouses at Deptford Strand for the use of her ships; as also to shipwrights, caulkers, sawyers, smiths, boatmakers, topmakers, marshmen, labourers and others working upon the new making of her three new ships and boats called the *Victory*, the *Triumph* and the *Aid*, and for the new making and repairing of the *Jesus of Lübeck* and the *Great Bark* now; as also to sundry persons for divers kinds of stuffs, provisions had for the necessary use of Her Highness's ships, begun there the first day of October last 1562 and ended the day abovesaid.'

The Sun	
Mariners	
Thomas Mathewe, master, 4 weeks 2 days	21s 6d
Nicholas Starkey, boatswain, 13 weeks 1 day	30s 0½d
Ralph Bucklond, 13 weeks 1 day	21s 11d
John Coke, 8 weeks 1 day	13s 7d
John Canne, 2 weeks 2 days	3s 10d
Thomas Blakers, server, 3 weeks,	5s
William Elles, master gunner, 13 weeks 1 day	32s 10d
The Double Rose	
Mariners	
Thomas Elye, master, 1 week 6 days	9s 4d
William Wilkinson, boatswain, 1 week 6 days	4s 3d
John Hunt, 1 week 6 days	3s 1d
Thomas Marychurche, purser, 1 week 6 days	4s 8d
Thomas Painter, cook, 1 week 6 days	4s 3d
Thomas Basterde, boy, 1 week 6 days	18½d

[*Page total*] – £7 15s 10d.

[f. 42v] *The Mary Grace Hoy*	
Mariners	
William Peerson, master, 13 weeks 1 day	£3 5s 8½d
John Younge, 13 weeks 1 day	21s 11d
Fabian Bullin, 13 weeks 1 day	21s 11d
John Bennet, 13 weeks 1 day	21s 11d
Thomas Harrington, 13 weeks 1 day	21s 11d
William Warde, 13 weeks 1 day	21s 11d
Thomas Draves, 9 weeks 5 days	16s 2d
John Woodcote, 13 weeks 1 day	21s 11d
George Parpoint, 9 weeks 4 days	16s
Nicholas Tracy, 9 weeks 4 days	16s
Richard Bigges, 3 weeks 2 days	5s 6d
The George Hoy	
Mariners	
Giles Hall, master, 13 weeks 1 day	£3 5s 8½d
Richard Abraham,[1] 13 weeks 1 day	21s 11d
Henry Raynsforthe, 13 weeks 1 day	21s 11d
John Kinge, cook,[2] 13 weeks 1 day	30s
John Roche, 13 weeks 1 day	21s 11d

[1]Draft notes payment made to John Roche: ibid., f. 1v.
[2]Draft notes payment made to W. Kent: ibid.

Thomas Raynoldes,[1] 13 weeks 1 day	21s 11d
Richard Letteman, 13 weeks 1 day	21s 11d
Thomas Ally, 12 weeks 3 days	20s 8d
John Goode, 12 weeks 3 days	20s 8d
Thomas Stonne, 9 weeks 4 days	16s
William Batthurst, master's mate, 9 weeks 4 days	27s 11d
Thomas Ollyver, boy, 12 weeks 3 days	10s 4d
Giles Hall junior, 3 weeks	5s

[*Page total*] – £27 16s 9d.

[f. 43] *The Aid*

Mariners

William Hollande, master [*blank*]	[*blank*]
Paul Saunder, boatswain,[2] 4 weeks 2 days	12s 6d
Edward Coxe, purser, 4 weeks 2 days	10s 8d
John Lowman, cook, 1 week I day	3s 4d
Richard Stonne,[3] 4 weeks 2 days	7s 2d
William Collison, steward, 4 weeks 2 days	8s
Even John Hewes, 4 weeks 1 day	6s 11d
George Clarke, 3 weeks	5s
William Burton, 2 weeks 4 days	4s 4d
Thomas Mott, 1 week	20d
John Thurstonne, 3 weeks	5s
Nicholas Bailly, 1 day	3d
Richard Dickenson, 1 week	20d
Robert Gilles, 3 weeks	5s
John Young, 3 weeks	5s
Andrew Sampson, 2 weeks 4 days	4s 4d
Roger Willford, 2 weeks 4 days	4s 4d
Thomas Panton, 2 weeks 4 days	4s 4d
Percival Whiteley, 2 weeks 4 days	4s 4d
Anthony Howldernes, carpenter,[4] 2 weeks 2 days	6s 8d
John Juell, 2 weeks 2 days	3s 10d
William Gray, boy, 2 weeks 2 days	23d
Edward Pepwell, 2 weeks 1 day	3s 7d
Richard Pereman, 1 week	20d
John Harris, 1 week 6 days	3s 1d
John Smythe, 1 week	20d

[1]Draft notes payment made to John Jentell: ibid.
[2]Draft notes payment made to E. Broede: ibid., f. 2.
[3]Draft notes payment made to boatswain: ibid.
[4]Draft brackets this man with next, identifies the latter as server, and notes both sums paid to their respective wives, or perhaps the wife of one of them ('*ux*''): ibid.

Thomas Wilson, 1 week 6 days	3s 1d
Cuthbert Wune, 1 week 4 days	2s 8d
Thomas Martin, 1 week 4 days	2s 8d
Saunder Lawraunce, 1 week 3 days	2s 5d
John Ellet, 1 week 3 days	2s 5d
Peter Stonne, 1 week 4 days	2s 8d
Peter Vanpommer, 1 week 4 days	2s 8d
Lance Pysson, 1 week 4 days	2s 8d
John Allyn, steward,[1] 1 week 4 days	2s 8d
Walter Gimlyn, 1 week 1 day	23d
Thomas Rocke, surgeon, 2 weeks	4s 4d

[*Page total*] – £7 5s 5d.

[f. 43v] Thomas Colle, 1 week 1 day	23d
John Willing, gromet, 1 week 1 day	17d
Richard Martyn, 5 days	14d
Richard Laughan, 4 days	12d
Anthony Walter, 4 days	12d
Bernard Harryson, 4 days	12d
John Gardner, 4 days	12d
John Payne, 4 days	12d
Thomas Loweman, 4 days	12d
John Gyll, 4 days	12d
William Kelley, 4 days	12d
Henry Ward, 3 days	8d
Stephen Rochester, 3 days	8d
Thomas Mathew, master, 3 days	2s
John Penneal, 4 days	12d
John Browne, 4 days	12d
Peter Amerson, 3 days	8d
Ralph Warde,[2] 3 days	8d
Robert White, 3 days	8d
Philip Williams, 2 days	6d
William Dood, 3 days	8d
John Morgayne, 1 day	3d
Thomas Wastell, 1 day	3d
Gunners	
Thomas List, master, 4 weeks 2 days	10s 8d
Matthew Quickerrell,[3] 6 days	17d

[1]Draft notes payment made to wife ('*ux*''): ibid., f. 2v.
[2]*Idem*.
[3]Draft notes payment made to master gunner: ibid., f. 3.

Jeffrey Rudde, 6 days	17d
Richard Pinson, 6 days	17d
John Arnold,[1] 6 days	17d
William Lymmyng, 6 days	17d
Ranulph Kirbye, 6 days	17d
John Linsey, 6 days	17d
Robert Harvy, 6 days	17d
Lancelot Degre, 6 days	17d
John Coxe, 6 days	17d
William Woode, boy, 6 days	8½d

[*Page total*] – £2 7s 0½d.

[f. 44] *[*Keeper of timber-yard*]. To Thomas Marshe, mariner, the last day of December for his wages daily attending and serving Her Highness for the safe-keeping of Her Grace's timber-yards there wherein lieth her timber, plank and divers other things pertaining to Her Majesty's ships, as also for the rigging and tackling of Her Highness's ships to the seas, by one quarter of a year containing 13 weeks one day, begun the first day of October last and this day ended, at 20s every month. *Summa* – £3 5s 8d.

*[*Coiling up of cables*]. To Robert Woode and Richard Token, mariners, the same day for [his *corrected to*] their wages daily attending and serving Her Highness in labouring about the coiling and carrying of cables, hawsers and other provisions into Her Grace's great storehouse at Deptford, and delivering out of the same again for the use of her ships, by like 13 weeks one day begun and ended as abovesaid [*at*] 20d every week the man – 43s 10d; and more for their victuals for like time, at 20d every week the man – 43s 10d. *Summa* – £4 7s 8d.[2]

*[*Coiling up of cables*]. To Christopher Braythete and William Smythe, mariners, the same day for their wages and victuals daily attending and serving Her Highness in labouring about the carriage of provisions and coiling up of cables as aforesaid, by the space of 13 weeks one day begun and ended as abovesaid, at 13s 4d *per mensem* the man – £4 7s 8d.

*[*Coiling up of cables*]. To Robert Tasse, mariner, the same day for his wages and victuals daily attending and serving Her Highness in labouring about the carriage of provisions and coiling up of cables and hawsers, by like time of 13 weeks one day, begun and ended as aforesaid, at 13s 4d *per mensem* – £2 3s 10d.[3]

[1]Draft notes payment made to wife ('*ux*''): ibid.
[2]Draft notes 10s paid to wife of ('*ux*'') Adams: ibid., f. 4.
[3]Draft notes payment to wife ('*ux*''): ibid., f. 4v.

*[*Coiling up of cables*]. To Richard Harwood, mariner, the same day for his wages and victuals dailing attending and serving Her Highness in labouring about the carriage of provisions and coiling up of cables and hawsers as is aforesaid, by like 13 weeks one day begun and ended as abovesaid, at 13s 4d *per mensem* – £2 3s 10d.

[*Page total*] – £16 8s 8d. *[*Keeper of yards – 65s 8d*; *coiling up of cables – £13 3s*]

[f. 44v] *[*Mariners' wages for carrying of provisions and coiling up of cables*]. To John Benwell, mariner, the last day of December for his wages daily attending and serving Her Highness in labouring about the carrying of provisions and coiling up of cables and hawsers in Her Grace's great storehouse there, by the space of 13 weeks one day begun the first day of October last and this day ended, at 13s 4d *per mensem* – £2 3s 10d.

To William Patricke, mariner, the same day for his wages daily attending and serving Her Highness in labouring about the carriage of provisions and coiling up of cables and hawsers in Her Grace's great storehouse there, by like 13 weeks one day, begun and ended as abovesaid, at 6s 8d *per mensem* – £1 1s 11d.

To John Kinge, mariner, the same day for his wages daily attending and serving Her Highness in labouring about the carriage of provisions and coiling up of cables and hawsers as aforesaid, by like 13 weeks one day begun the first day of October last and this day ended, at 6s 8d *per mensem* – £1 1s 11d.

*[*Clerk*]. To James Jentill the same day for his wages daily attending and serving Her Highness for the keeping of the prick and cheque book of masters, mariners and gunners keeping Her Grace's ships afloat within the river of Thames, by 92 days begun and ended as aforesaid, at 8d *per diem* – £3 1s 4d.

*[*Keeper of storehouse*]. To Henry Abraham the same day for his wages daily attending and serving Her Highness for the safe-keeping of Her Grace's storehouses there, wherein lieth her provisions of cables, hawsers, small cordage, canvas and divers other kinds of stuffs for the use of Her Majesty's ships, by the like time of 92 days begun and ended as aforesaid, at 8d *per diem* – £3 1s 4d.

[*Page total*] – £10 10s 4d.

[f. 45] *[*Surveyor*]. To Thomas Thomas the last day of December for his wages daily attending and serving Her Highness for the taking of surveys of all manner of necessaries [*and*] provisions had of divers persons for the furniture of Her Grace's ships, as well at their setting forth to the seas as also at their coming home again from thence into harbour, by one quarter of a year containing 92 days begun the first day of October last and this day ended, at 8d *per diem* – £3 1s 4d.[1]

*[*Purveyor*]. To James Humfray the same day for his wages daily attending and serving Her Highness in providing all kinds of provisions and necessaries for the building and repairing of Her Grace's ships, by like 92 days begun and ended as abovesaid at 8d *per diem* – £3 1s 4d.

*[*Plug keeper*]. To William Alye, labourer, the same day for his wages daily attending and serving Her Highness in keeping of the plug and letting out of the water in the dock there for the dry keeping of the same, wherein lieth the *Jesus of Lübeck* and the *Great Bark* to be new made,[2] by 92 days begun and ended as abovesaid, at 8d *per diem*. £3 1s 4d.

*[*Keeper of timber-yard*]. To Thomas Awoode, porter, the same day for his wages daily attending and serving Her Highness in safe-keeping of Her Grace's timber-yards there, wherein lieth her timber, plank and board for the use of Her Majesty's ships aforesaid, [*by like 92 days*] begun and ended [*as abovesaid*], at 8d *per diem* – £3 1s 4d.

*[*Riding charges*]. To John Elmer, messenger, the same day for his wages daily attending and serving Her Highness for the carrying of the officers' letters in post to divers and sundry places along the sea coast for Her Majesty's marine causes, by like 92 days begun and ended as abovesaid, at 12d *per diem* – £4 12s.

[*Page total*] – £16 17s 4d.

[f. 45v] *[*Carpenter*]. To Robert Harte, sawyer, the last day of December for his wages daily attending and serving Her Highness in sawing and cutting of timber and plank for the use of Her Grace's ships, by like 92 days begun and ended as aforesaid, at 8d *per diem* – £3 1s 4d.

*[*Shipwright*]. To Augustino Levello, Venetian shipwright, the same day for his wages daily attending and serving Her Highness for the repairing and mending of Her Grace's two galleys, by 92 days begun the first day of October last and this day ended, at 16d *per diem* – £6 2s 8d.[3]

*[*Clerk*]. To Stephen Alexander the same day for his wages daily attending and serving Her Highness for the writing and keeping of the book of report of all manner of provisions and necessaries had for the use of Her Majesty's ships, by one quarter of a year due at this present – £6 13s 4d.

*[*Mariner in carriage of provisions and coiling up of cables*]. To Paul Saunder, mariner, the same day for his wages daily attending and serving

[1]Draft notes payment to Baker: ibid., f. 5.

[2]The *Great Bark* would be renamed *White Bear* on relaunch. For *Jesus* this was a reprieve, but despite her refit she remained something of a museum piece. See further below, pp. 86 n. 1, 210, and *NEM*, pp. 483–4, 489.

[3]Draft notes payment of 40s to Jeffrey Vaughan 26 Oct. 1563: BL, Add. MS 78169, f. 6.

Her Highness in labouring about the carriage of provisions and coiling up of cables and hawsers in Her Grace's great storehouse there, by the space of one month 3 days begun the first day of October last and ended the last day of the same, at 6s 8d *per mensem* – 7s 4d.

[*Page total*] – £16 4s 8d.

[f. 46] *Shipwrights*[1]

Peter Pett, master,[2] 8 days at 12d	8s
Richard Chapman, 7 days at 6d	3s 6d
Roger Raynner, server, 27 days at 6d	3s 6d
George Kingstun, 27 days at 4d	9s
John Brunet, 27 days at 7d	15s 9d
John Wilkinson,[3] 35 days at 3d	8s 9d
Robert Baker, 27 days at 6d	13s 6d
Oliver Water, 27 days at 6d	13s 6d
William Welshe,[4] 27 days at 8d	18s
Thomas Freman, server, 27 days at 5d	11s 3d
William Carter, server, 27 days at 5d	11s 3d
Robert Hodgkinson, 68 days at 8d	45s 4d
Thomas Ellee, server, 72 days at 3d	18s
Nicholas Claye, server,[5] 30½ days at 7d	17s 9½d
John Claye, server 30½ days at 5d	12s 8½d
Thomas Sager, 30½ days at 5d	12s 8½d
Thomas Bllosse, 28 days at 8d	18s 8d
Henry Nellet, server, 28 days at 5d	11s 8d
John Winny, 30½ days at 7d	17s 9½d
John Weathers,[6] 30½ days at 5d	12s 8½d
Richard Clay, 27 days at 8d	18s
John Broome, 27 days at 8d	18s
Gregory Turner, server, 27 days at 4d	9s

[1]Prefaced in draft by a new heading: 'A payment made the last day of December to shipwrights, caulkers, sawyers, smiths, boatmakers, topmakers, marshmen, labourers and others working at Deptford Strand upon the finishing of the Queen's Highness's three new ships there, *viz.* the *Victory*, the *Triumph* and the *Aid*, as also upon the new making and mending of the *Jesus of Lübeck* and the *Great Bark* and three new ship boats begun there the first day of October last and ended as abovesaid': ibid., f. 7.

[2]Draft brackets Pett with the three men following, each of whom is identified as server: ibid. This indicates all sums paid to Pett (as next and further examples).

[3]Draft identifies as server: ibid.

[4]Draft brackets Welshe with the two servers following, and notes all sums as paid to Welshe: ibid.

[5]Identification as server is a copying error by anticipation of next name; draft gives the designation to John Claye not Nicholas, which is consistent with their respective pay rates: ibid.

[6]Draft identifies as server: ibid., f. 7v.

Matthew Baker, master,[1] 92 days at 12d	£4 12s
Matthew Nortun, server, 77 days at 5d	32s 1d
John Hoolle, 77 days at 5d	32s 1d
John Rande,[2] 77½ days at 9d	58s 1½d
James Cotes, server, 77½ days at 6d	38s 9d
George Flowre, server, 77½ days at 6d	38s 9d
John Ellison, 77½ days at 8d	51s 8d
John Hawll, server, 77½ days at 6d	38s 9d
Edward Bright, master,[3] 92 days at 12d	£4 12s

[*Page total*] – £40 12s 7d.

[f. 46v] Thomas Juell, server, 77 days at 6d	38s 6d
Davy Baker, 73 days at 6d	36s 6d
John Leestow, server, 49 days at 6d	24s 6d
Daniel Bright, 77 days at 6d	38s 6d
Ralph Browne, 27 days at 6d	13s 6d
John Daultun, 68 days at 7d	39s 8d
Davy Horne, server, 77 days at 4d	25s 8d
Thomas Bryan, 27 days at 7d	15s 9½d
John Hutchins, server, 27 days at 6d	13s 6d
Lewis Richardes, server, 27 days at 6d	13s 6d
James Diggons, server, 27 days at 5d	11s 3d
John Diggons, server, 27 days at 6d	13s 6d
Robert Veze, 27 days at 6d	13s 6d
Michael Tow,[4] 77 days at 7d	44s 11d
John Tow, 77 days at 5d	32s 1d
Edward Holborne,[5] 73 days at 8d	48s 8d
Henry Newe, 77½ days at 5d	32s 3½d
Walter Holborne, 71 days at 8d	47s 4d
John Haywarde,[6] 69 days at 8d	46s
Michael Gamound, 68 days at 5d	28s 4d
Henry Symondes, server, 61 days at 4d	20s 4d

[1]Draft brackets Baker with the two men following, identifies Hoolle as server, and notes all sums paid to Baker: ibid.

[2]Draft brackets Rande with two servers following, and notes all sums paid to Rande's wife ('*ux*''): ibid.

[3]Draft brackets E. Bright with four men following, identifies Baker and D. Bright as servers, and notes all sums paid to [E.] Bright's wife: ibid.

[4]Draft brackets M. Tow with J. Tow, identifies latter as server, and notes both sums paid to former: ibid., f. 8.

[5]Draft brackets Holborne with man following and identifies latter as server: ibid.

[6]Draft brackets Haywarde with three men following, identifies Gamound and Symondes (as 'Samond' evidently begun by accidental repetition) as servers, and notes all sums paid to Walter Holborne: ibid.

William Wheller, 77½ days at 5d	32s 3½d
John Bylles, 1 day at 6d	6d
Richard Keyser,[1] 3 days at 4d	12d
Anthony Houldernes, 39 days at 7d	22s 9d
John Juell, server, 39 days at 6d	19s 6d
William Gray,[2] 39 days at 4d	13s
William Spicer, 72 days at 7d	42s
Thomas Osborne, server, 79½ days at 3d	19s 10½d
Stephen Bevis, 9 days at 6d	4s 6d
Thomas Robinsonne, 75 days at 6d	37s 6d
Stephen Robinsonne, server, 62 days at 5d	25s 10d
Edward Clarke, 60½ days at 6d	30s 3d
Thomas Raynoldes, 56½ days at 8d	37s 8d
Henry Raynoldes, server, 60½ days at 2d	10s 3d
Richard Farrar, 52 days at 6d	26s
Thomas Deakon,[3] 77 days at 6d	38s 6d
Philip Garret, server,[4] 77 days at 6d	38s 6d
Henry Greves,[5] 60 days at 7d	35s
Thomas Bonnam, server, 77½ days at 4d	25s 10d

[*Page total*] – £52 18 6½d.

[f. 47] William Greves,[6] 77½ days at 9d	58s 1½d
Thomas Hewes, server, 77½ days at 6d	38s 9d
Edmund Waller,[7] 28 days at 6d	14s
Robert Willis, server, 28 days at 3d	7s
Robert Asshetun, 27 days at 6d	13s 6d
Thomas Hodge,[8] 24 days at 6d	12s
William Hodge, server, 27 days at 4d	9s
Mark Hodge, 27 days at 6d	13s 6d
Randall Wood, 75½ days at 6d	37s 9d
John Hurley, 27 days at 6d	13s 6d
Thomas Hewes, server, 27 days at 6d	13s 6d
Nicholas Foxe, 27 days at 6d	13s 6d
Richard Johnson, 77 days at 6d	38s 6d
Robert Davy, 70½ days at 6d	35s 3d

[1]Draft identifies as server: ibid.
[2]*Idem.*
[3]*Idem.*
[4]Draft notes payment made to wife of Christopher Baker ('*ux' Xpofer Ba.*'): ibid.
[5]Draft brackets this man with next: ibid., f. 8v.
[6]*Idem.*
[7]*Idem.*
[8]*Idem:* ibid., f. 8v.

John Howper, 27 days at 6d	13s 6d
James Dixson, 49 days at 10d	40s 10d
Richard Rice,[1] 49 days at 8d	32s 8d
John Mathew, 39 days at 10d	32s 6d
William Manby, 26 days at 4d	8s 8d
John Clarke,[2] 77½ days at 8d	51s 8d
George Graye, server, 42 days at 4d	14s
Robert Wright, server,[3] 71 days at 5d	29s 7d
Raynold Newe, server, 74 days at 5d	30s 10d
Henry Freeman, 23 days at 6d	11s 6d
Caulkers	
Thomas Bolltun, master, 28 days at 10d	23s 4d
William Boltun, server, 23 days at 6d	11s 6d
John Atkinson, server, 16 days at 6d	8s
Richard Barton, 17 days at 7d	9s 11d
Henry Powder,[4] 22 days at 5d	9s 2d
William Mundes, 22½ days at 8d	15s
John Moyzer, 21 days at 6d	10s 6d
William Ragget, server,[5] 22½ days at 4d	7s 6d
Thomas Northcot, 1 day at 7d	7d
John Bende, server,[6] 9 days at 3d	2s 3d
Gregory Knightley, 23 days at 7d	13s 5d

[*Page total*] – £34 14s 8½d.

[f. 47v] John Cleareke, 4 days at 7d	2s 4d
Thomas Horseley, server, 1 day at 4d	4d
Robert Brigges, 15 days at 7d	8s 9d
Humphrey Daill, server, 15 days at 4d	5s
John Stockedaill, 17 days at 6d	8s 6d
Michael Rowse, 23 days at 6d	11s 6d
Philip Payne, 22½ days at 7d	13s 1½d
John Palmer, 22½ days at 6d	11s 3d
John Hilliarde, 23 days at 6d	11s 6d
Walter Johnson, 22½ days at 6d	11s 3d
John Hasell, server, 4 days at 2d	8d

[1]Draft identifies as server: ibid., f. 8v.

[2]Draft brackets this man with next and notes payment made to Clarke ('Clerk'): ibid.

[3]Draft brackets this man with next, and notes payment made to Henry Lane: ibid.

[4]Draft notes payment made to [T.] Bolltun ('Bolton'): ibid., f. 9.

[5]Draft notes payment made to 'Web': ibid. This must be John Webbe, caulker; above, p. 66.

[6]Draft notes payment made to 'Marshall': ibid.. The only Marshall in this quarter's pay is John, labourer and watchman: below, pp. 95, 96; but the recipient might be William Marshall, shipwright: above, p. 62.

Robert Crigge, 22½ days at 6d	11s 3d
John Hearse, 22½ days at 6d	11s 3d
William Elleson, 18½ days at 6d	9s 3d
Samuel Clarke, server, 18½ days at 2d	3s 1d
Gabriel Wright, 10 days at 7d	5s 10d
Sawyers	
Thomas Myller,[1] 77 days at 6d	38s 6d
Robert Davis, 77 days at 6d	38s 6d
John Ricardes, 45 days at 6d	22s 6d
Robert Grene, 45 days at 6d	22s 6d
Henry Harvy, 27 days at 6d	13s 6d
John Punche, 27 days at 6d	13s 6d
Topmakers[2]	
William Bexley, master,[3] 43 days at 8d	28s 8d
William Kakete, server, 43 days at 6d	21s 6d
Abraham Harman, server, 43 days at 5d	17s 11d
John Smarte, 43 days at 6d	21s 6d
John White, server, 43 days at 6d	21s 6d
James Reweman, server, 43 days at 6d	21s 6d
Thomas Curtas, 12 days at 6d	6s
John Pickover,[4] 29 days at 6d	19s 6d
John White, senior, 12 days at 7d	7s
John Fyssher, server, 12 days at 4d	4s

[*Page total*] – £22 3s 11½d.

[f. 48] *Boatmakers*

Richard Skarlett, master, 21 days at 10d	17s 4d
Robert Meddelwoode, server, 21 days at 6d	10s 6d
John Vicars, server, 21 days at 5d	8s 9d
Francis Tythe, 21 days at 8d	14s
Richard Dodde, server, 21 days at 6d	10s 6d
Robert Felltun, 21 days at 8d	14s
Henry Hebbdun, server, 21 days at 5d	8s 9d
Rowland Sheapparde, 21 days at 8d	14s
Thomas Norwell, 21 days at 8d	14s
William Cruxe, server, 21 days at 4d	7s

[1] Draft brackets this man with next and notes payment made to [Robert] Hart: BL, Add. MS 78169, f. 9v.

[2] Draft heading 'and oarmakers': ibid.

[3] Draft brackets Bexley with five men following, identifies Smarte as server, and notes al[l] sums paid to Bexley: ibid.

[4] Draft identifies as server, and notes payment made to Curtas ('Curtes'): ibid.

Edward Stoore,[1] 21 days at 4d	7s
Thomas Porter, 21 days at 8d	14s
Robert Paddye, 27 days at 7d	15s 9d
William Wetheredge, server, 35 days at 4d	11s 8d
John Lawson, 27 days at 6d	13s 6d
William Knight, 20 days at 8d	13s 4d
John Cossin, server, 20 days at 4d	6s 8d
Thomas Richardbye, 20 days at 7d	11s 8d
William Symondes, 18 days at 7d	10s 6d
Thomas Russell, 18 days at 6d	9s
George Rumbolde, 18 days at 6d	9s
Smiths	
Thomas Ive, master,[2] 3 days at 12d	3s
John Wright, server, 28 days at 6d	14s
John Teailler, 28 days at 6d	14s
Richard Duff, server, 28 days at 6d	14s
Thomas Willson, 92 days at 12d	£4 12s
John Hurlestone, 92 days at 6d	46s
Henry Rowse, 92 days at 3d	23s

[*Page total*] – £22 6s 11d.

[f. 48v] *Victualling.* To Thomas Willson of Ratcliff the last day of December for the victualling of 168 of the aforenamed shipwrights, caulkers, sawyers, smiths, boatmakers and others working upon the new making, repairing and mending of five Her Highness's ships called the *Triumph*, the *Victory*, the *Aid*, the *Jesus of Lübeck*, the *Great Bark*, and two new ship boats, by the space of 7,870 days among them all, Sundays and holy days within the same accounted, begun the first day of October last and this day ended, which maketh 1,124 weeks 2 days, at 4s 1d every week the man. *Summa* – £229 10s 4d.[3]

[1]Draft identifies as server: ibid., f. 10.

[2]Draft brackets Ive with three men following, identifies Teailler as server, and notes all sums paid to Ive ('Ivey'): ibid., f. 10v.

[3]Draft has an additional breakdown of the supplies, here summarised: For 1,176 dozen loaves of bread, at 12d the dozen – £58 16s. For 29 tuns of beer, at 19s the tun – £27 11s. For 19,524 lbs of beef, at 12s every 100 [lbs] – £117 2s 6d [*recte* 10½d]. For 200 qtrs of Holland ling, at £4 3s 4d every hundred – £9 7s 6d. For 2 barrels and 2 firkins of butter, at 54s 4d the barrel – £6 13s 4d. For 3½ weys 21 lbs of Suffolk cheese, at 37s 4d the wey – £6 13s 7d. Fresh butter and other necessaries – 12s 1d. For 20 bushels of biscuit, at 11d the bushel – 18s 4d. Carriage of the said victuals by water – 33s. One peck of mustard seed – 10d. For 12 drinking cups and 12 platters – 2s 4d. *Sum* – £229 10s 6d, at 4s 1d a man every week: ibid., f. 24v. The sum in this version is correct; the pence total has been mis-copied as 4d in the summary in the draft (f. 10v) and so to the equivalent in the final version (as here).

Lodging. To Eme Symson, Annes James, Avis Waters, Annes Hurllestone, Elizabeth Alley, Joan Larke and 17 other persons of Deptford, Greenwich and thereabouts the same day for the lodging of 189 of the aforesaid shipwrights, caulkers and others in 95 featherbeds, [*working*] upon the new making and repairing of Her Highness's said ships and ship boats there, by the space of 1,590½ weeks among them all begun the first day of October last and this day ended, at 2d every week the man. *Summa* – £13 5s 1d.[1]

[*Page total*] – £242 15s 5d.

[f. 49] *House-carpenters*

John Leache,[2] 85 days and tides at 12d	£4 5s
Robert Throuley, server, 85 days and tides at 7d	49s 7d
Thomas Awoode, 23 days at 10d	19s 2d
Robert Aunstume, 16½ days at 10d	13s 9d
Henry West, server, 16½ days at 10d	13s 9d
Richard Stampe, 16½ days at 10d	13s 9d
Thomas Phillippe, 16½ days at 10d	13s 9d
Thomas Hilliarde,[3] 38 days at 10d	31s 8d
Hugh Jonnes, server, 38 days at 10d	31s 8d
Bricklayers	
John Callaway, 27 days at 11d	24s 9d
John Mylles, server, 27 days at 9d	20s 3d
Stephen Huggens, server, 27 days at 10d	22s 6d
James Huggans, 22 days at 10d	18s 4d
Robert Gardener, 9 days at 9d	6s 9d
Christopher White,[4] 27 days at 10d	22s 6d
Robert Neell, 5 days at 10d	4s 2d
Thomas Colle, 9 days at 10d	7s 6d
John Flowre, 20 days at 10d	16s 8d
Richard Freman, 9 days at 8d	6s
Anthony Hill, 9 days at 8d	6s

[1]Draft (BL, Add. MS 78169, f. 11) lists all lodging keepers, with respective numbers of men, beds, and days. Symson's money is noted as paid to Juell's wife ('*ux*''), presumably the Jone Juell subsequently named, and James is identified as Symson's server ('*serviente*' here in full). The 17 other names are Maud Fellon (whose payment is made to Fox's wife), Joan Kyng, Joan Juell, Amye Poell, Ellyn Baker, Mary Trew (payment to William Greves), Joan Bright, Anne Awgers, Maud Foxe, Alice Addams (payment to her daughter), Elizabeth Symonds, Alice Bory, Alice Newbery, Joan Rock, Annes Backler, Elizabeth Fraunces and Joan Archedaill.

[2]Draft brackets Leache with server following, and notes both sums paid to Leache ('Jo. Leche'): ibid., f. 11v.

[3]Draft brackets this man with next, and notes both sums paid to J. Leche: ibid.

[4]Draft identifies as server: ibid.

William Allforde, server, 8 days at 4d 2s 8d

[*Page total*] – £21 10s 2d.

[f. 49v] *Marshmen*[1]

John Hilltun, master, 18½ days and tides at 8d 12s 4d
Jeffrey Heayward, 23½ days and tides at 7d 13s 8½d
John Sharppe, 23½ days and tides at 7d 13s 8½d
Egenet Punett, 23½ days and tides at 7d 13s 8½d
Leonard Teayller, 12½ days at 7d 7s 3½d
William Jakes, 23½ days and tides at 7d 13s 8½d
John Sturgeon, 12½ days at 7d 7s 3½d
Davy Deane, 12½ days at 7d 7s 3½d
Bartholomew Jennyns, 12½ days at 7d 7s 3½d
Richard Hawkins, 18½ days and tides at 7d 10s 9½d
George Hardwicke, 18½ days and tides at 7d 10s 9½d
Thomas Morris, 12½ days at 7d 7s 3½d
William Kelley, 18½ days and tides at 7d 10s 9½d
John Mylles, 12½ days at 7d 7s 3½d
Richard Crayne, 18½ days and tides at 7d 10s 9½d
Richard Smythe, 18½ days and tides at 7d 10s 9½d
Thomas Draper, 12½ days at 7d 7s 3½d
John Browne, 12½ days at 7d 7s 3½d
William Gothe, 23½ days at 7d 13s 8½d
Lawrence Headd, 29½ days and tides at 7d 17s 2½d
William Awgers, 12½ days at 7d 7s 3½d
Thomas Cant, 12½ days at 7d 7s 3½d
Rowland Bell, 12½ days at 7d 7s 3½d
John Twyforde, 12½ days at 7d 7s 3½d
John Wallis, 18½ days and tides at 7d 10s 9½d
Starling Drewman, 10 days at 7d 5s 10d
Griffin Jonnes, 12½ days at 7d 7s 3½d
Richard Williams, 12½ day at 7d 7s 3½d
Thomas Saill, 12½ days at 7d 7s 3½d
John Bakon, 12½ days at 7d 7s 3½d
Francis Howell, 9½ days at 7d 5s 6½d
Edward Horseley, 7½ days at 7d 4s 4½d
Robert Lake, 12½ days at 7d 7s 3½d

[1]Prefaced in draft by this heading: 'Marshmen and labourers working at Deptford Strand, as well for the opening and taking up of the dockhead for the new scouring and casting of the same dock against the launching and having out of Her Highness's two new great ships there called the *Victory* and the *Triumph*, as also for the dry docking of the *Great Bark* and the *Jesus of Lübeck* there to be new made and a-mended, as also shutting up again of the same, with other needful service there to be done': ibid., f. 12.

Robert Forde, 12 days at 7d	7s 3½d
John Cooke, 7½ days at 7d	4s 4½d
[*Page total*] – £15 14s 2½d.	
[f. 50] Ralph Thornetun, 12½ days at 7d	7s 3½d
John Waddesley, 12½ days at 7d	7s 3½d
James More, 18½ days and tides at 7d	10s 9½d
George Bell, 12½ days at 7d	7s 3½d
William Alley, 30 nights at 4d	10s
Nicholas Archedaill, 29 days at 6d	14s 6d
Thomas Thissellwoode, 94 days and tides at 6d	47s
George Mathew, 10 days at 6d	5s
John Lowman, 53 days at 6d	26s 6d
John Gibbeson, 88 days and tides at 6d	44s
Edward Plumer, 74½ days and tides at 6d	37s 3d
Thomas Loweman, 29½ days at 6d	14s 9d
John Pithen, 5½ days at 6d	2s 9d
John Johnson, 18½ days at 7d	10s 9½d
Labourers	
John Brodehurst, 28½ days at 6d	14s 3d
William Twayttes, 84½ days and tides at 6d	42s 3d
John Bastian, 83 days and tides at 6d	41s 6d
John Adams, 89 days and tides at 6d	44s 6d
Thomas Clarke, 5½ days at 6d	2s 9d
Richard Rainsfoorth, 83 days at tides at 7d	48s 5d
James Teall, 81 days and tides at 6d	40s 6d
William Gonnbye, 91 days at 6d	45s 6d
William Pitthen, 5½ days at 6d	2s 9d
John Janes, 83 days and tides at 6d	41s 6d
Robert Watson, 5½ days at 6d	2s 9d
Thomas Lingard, 5½ days at 6d	2s 9d
John Brace, 86½ days and tides at 6d	43s 3d
Morgan Apprice,[1] 82 days and tides at 6d	41s
Richard Coxe, 27½ days at 6d	13s 9d
Henry Stephenson, 92 days at 6d	46s
Lawrence Langcaster, 82 days at 6d	41s
John Apprice, 28½ days at 6d	14s 3d
John Goodgam, 5½ days at 6d	2s 9d
James Hodgeson,[2] 5½ days at 6d	2s 9d
Ralph Courtelande, 84½ days and tides at 6d	42s 3d

[1]Draft notes payment made to 'Fox': ibid., f. 13.
[2]*Idem.*

John Waynesfourthe, 5½ days at 6d	2s 9d
[*Page total*] – £41 4s 4½d.	
[f. 50v] John Mannsfellde, 57 days at 6d	28s 6d
William Apprice, 85½ days and tides at 6d	42s 9d
John Marshall, 76 days at 6d	38s
Robert Scott, 5½ days at 6d	2s 9d
George Newton, 76 days at 6d	38s
Robert Stevens, 30½ days at 6d	15s 3d
Philip Deakon,[1] 10 days at 8d	6s 8d
William Tasse,[2] 84 days and tides at 6d	42s
John Dawne, 5½ days at 6d	2s 9d
George Bell, 79½ days and tides at 6d	39s 9d
William Wallis, 61 days at 6d	30s 6d
Edmund Burman,[3] 93 days and tides at 6d	46s 6d
Anthony Hyll, 39 days at 6d	19s 6d
Robert Harris,[4] 32 days at 6d	16s
John Twiforde, 32 days at 6d	16s
John Raby, 27½ days at 6d	13s 9d
John Barry,[5] 30½ days at 6d	15s 3d
John Sturgeon, 31 days at 6d	15s 6d
Richard Ottee, 31 days at 6d	15s 6d
John Parker, 28 days at 6d	14s
William Barnarde, 40 days at 6d	20s
Anthony Weslonde, 32½ days at 6d	16s 3d
	[£25 0s 2d*]
Watchmen	
William Allye, 37 nights at 6d	18s 6d
John Hurlestone, 37 nights at 6d	18s 6d
Nicholas Archedaill, 37 nights at 6d	18s 6d
Thomas Smythe, 37 nights at 6d	18s 6d
John Adams, 38 nights at 6d	19s
Thomas Thisseltun, 38 nights at 6d	19s
William Apprice, 38 nights at 6d	19s
Edward Burnam,[6] 38 nights at 6d	19s
Ralph Courtelande, 37 nights at 6d	18s 6d

[1]Draft notes payment made to H. Abraham: ibid.
[2]Draft notes payment made to James Jentell: ibid.
[3]Draft notes payment made to Stephen Alexander ('S.A.'): ibid., f. 13v.
[4]Draft notes payment made to [William] Allye: ibid.
[5]Draft notes payment made to 'Fox': ibid.
[6]Draft notes payment made to Stephen Alexander ('S.A.'): ibid.

John Marshall,[1] 37 nights at 6d	18s 6d
William Twayttes, 37 nights at 6d	18s 6d
John Wallis, 37 nights at 6d	18s 6d
Morgan Apprice,[2] 8 nights at 6d	4s
Thomas Clerke, 2 days at 6d	12d
	[£11 4s*]

[*Page total*] – £36 4s 2d.

[f. 51] *Emptions*[3]

Timber oak *[*£31 6s 8d*], *a bark* *[*£14*] *and Bilbao iron* *[*£4 14s 1d*]. To Francis Rainboro of London, merchant,[4] the last day of December for price [*of*] 62½ loads and 15 foot of compass timber oak of him had and delivered at Deptford Strand for the use of Her Highness's ships there, at 10s every load after 50 foot to the load – £31 6s 8d; more to him for a bark, being of the portage of 15 tuns, of him had for the use of Her Highness for the sounding of the sands at the Thames mouth, by agreement – £14; more for 5 trivets, 8 ring-bolts, 19 setting bolts, and spikes of all sorts, weighing 19 hundred 3 quarters 18 pounds, at 23s 4d every hundredweight – £23 4s 7d; and more to him for 7 tons 8 hundred 14 pounds weight of Bilbao iron, at £11 the ton – £81 9s 6d. *Summa* – £150 0s 9d.[5]

Deal-boards *[*£23 4s*] *and masts* *[*£7 10s*]. To John Warner of London, merchant, the same day for price of 116 deal-boards of him had and delivered at Deptford for the use of Her Highness's ships, at 4s the piece – £23 4s; and more to him for 3 masts of 8 and 9 hands about, at 50s the mast – £7 10s. *Summa* – £30 14s.

Wainscot boards *[*£18*] *and 2 grinding stones* *[*14s*]. To William Girddeler of London the same day for price of 150 of wainscot boards by him delivered there for the use of Her Grace's ships, at £12 the 100 – £18; and more to him for 2 great grinding stones of 5 foot over, price – 14s 8d. *Summa* – £18 14s 8d.[6]

[1]Draft notes payment made to 'Gest': ibid. Probably Nicholas Gest: above, p. 37.

[2]Draft notes payment made to 'Fox': BL, Add. MS 78169, f. 13v.

[3]In the draft (ibid., ff. 15, 19v) two entries in this section are deleted because they were transferred to the Extraordinary Charges section of the final account: see below, p. 225 (Alexander), 226 (Myndge).

[4]The Rainboroughs became one of the leading shipowners on the River: cf. W. R. Chaplin, 'William Rainsborough (1587–1642) and his associates of the Trinity House', *MM*, XXXI (1945), pp. 178–97; K. R. Andrews, *Ships, Money and Politics: Seafaring and Naval Enterprise in the Reign of Charles I* (Cambridge, 1991), p. 173 and *passim*; W. D. Jones, *Thomas Rainborowe (c. 1610–1648), Civil War Seaman, Siegemaster and Radical* (Woodbridge, 2005).

[5]Draft notes payment made to Vincent Gonson ('Vinsent'): BL, Add. MS 78169, f. 15.

[6]Draft notes payment made to the merchant's wife ('*uxor*'') by two bills: ibid., f. 16.

Elm timber *[*£9 18s*] *and trenails* *[*44s 11d. Carriage – 19s 2d*]. To Henry Laine of Bexley, purveyor, the same day for price of 19½ loads, 15½ foot of elm timber of him had and delivered for the use of Her Majesty's ships there, at 10s every load after 50 foot to the load – £9 18s; more paid by him to divers persons of Welling, Erith, Bexley, Dartford and thereabouts in Kent for the carrying of 11½ loads of elm timber from Beddington[1] to Deptford Strand for the use as aforesaid, at 20d every load carrying – 19s 2d; more for 1,100 of trenails of 30 inches long, at 2s 6d every 100 – 25s; more for 925 trenails of 26 inches long, at 2s 2d the 100 – 19s 11d [*recte* 21s]. *Summa* – £13 2s 1d.

[*Page total*] – £212 11s 6d.

[f. 51v] *Trenails.* To John Cowper of Kent the last day of December for price of 40,250 of trenails by him delivered at Deptford for the use of Her Highness's ships, *viz.* 2,000 trenails of 18 inches long after 5 score to the hundred, at 18d every 100 – 30s; more for 8,000 of trenails of 30 inch long, at 2s 6d every 100 – £10; more for 15,000 of trenails of 24 inches long, at 2s every 100 – £15; more for 1,000 of trenails of 28 inches long, at 2s 4d the 100 – 23s 4d; more for 1,000 of trenails of 26 inches long, at 2s 2d every 100 – 21s 8d; more for 1,500 of trenails of 25 inches long, at 2s 1d every 100 – 30s 3d; and more to him for 11,750 of trenails of 20 inches long, at 20d every 100 – £9 15s. *Summa* – £40 2s 1d.

Timber, plank, board and lath. To Christopher Nailler of London the same day for price of 2,337 foot of 5-inch plank oak by him provided and delivered at Deptford for the use of Her Highness's ships there, at 15s every 100 foot – £17 10s 8d; more for 18,999 foot of 4-inch plank oak, at 12s every 100 [*foot*] – £114; more for 13,753 foot of 3-inch plank oak, at 10s every 100 [*foot*] – £68 15s 4d; more for 6,379 foot of 2-inch plank oak, at 8s every 100 [*foot*] – £25 10s 6d; more for 31,819 foot of inch ½ board oak and featheredge board, at 5s every 100 [*foot*] – £79 11s; more for 214 loads 34 foot of timber oak squared, at 10s every load – £107 6s 10d; more for 200 of cloveboard, at 46s 8d every 100 – £4 13s 4d; more for 5½ loads of heart lath oak,[2] at 20s the load – £5 10s. *Summa* – £422 17s 8d.

Timber and plank. To George Bridger of Hever in Kent the same day for price of 86 loads 16 foot of timber oak of him had and by him delivered at Deptford for the use of Her Majesty's ships there, after 50 foot the load at 11s every load – £47 9s 5¼d; and more to him for 100 foot of 3-inch plank oak, price – 10s. *Summa* – £47 19s 5¼d.

[*Page total*] – £510 19s 2¼d.

[1] MS 'Benningfould. Cf. above, p. 54.

[2] A lath made from the heartwood of the oak.

[f. 52] *Timber, plank, board, oak, spokes and deal-boards.* To John Leache of Deptford Strand the last day of December for price of 25 loads of timber oak of him had for the use of Her Highness's ships and delivered the same at Deptford, at 12s every load after 50 foot to the load – £15; and more to him for 26 spokes[1] of oak for long trenails of 26 inches long, at 1d the piece – 2s 2d. *Summa* – £15 2s 2d.

To William James of London the same day for price of 36 loads of oaken timber of him had and by him delivered at Deptford for the use of Her Grace's ships as aforesaid, at 10s every load after 50 foot to the load – £18; more to him for 1,400 foot of 3- and 4-inch plank oak, at 10s every 100 foot – £7; and more to him for 950 [*foot*] of inch board oak – price – 47s 6d. *Summa* – £27 7s 6d.

Deal-boards, wooden buckets and hoops. To Matthew Baker of Blackwall the same day for price of 30 spruce deal-boards of him had for the use of Her Grace's ships there, at 4s the piece – £6; and more to him for 10 small Norway deal-boards, at 8d the piece – 6s 8d. *Summa* – £6 6s 8d.

To Thomas Johnson of London the same day for price of 16 deal-boards of him had and delivered at Deptford for the use of Her Highness's ships, at 4s 4d the piece – £3 9s 4d; and more to him for 2 long broad deal-boards, at 6s the piece – 12s. *Summa* – £4 1s 4d.

To John Williamson of London, cooper, the same day for price of 15 dozen of wood buckets of him had for the use of Her Highness's ships, at 5s every dozen. *Summa* – £3 15s.

To John Lowe of London, cooper, the same day for price of 12 broad hoops of him had and delivered there, of 4, 5, 6 and 8 foot over, for the use as aforesaid, price – £1.[2]

[*Page total*] – £57 12s 8d *[*Timber and boards – £52 17s 8d*; *buckets and hoops – £4 15s*]

[f. 52v] *Pulleys, baskets and axes.* To John Benbow of London the last day of December for price of 2 great pulleys of him had and by him delivered for the use of Her Highness's ships, at 18d the piece – 3s; more for 30 pulleys, at 6d the piece – 15s; more for 24 pulleys, at 4d the piece – 8s; more for 16 pulleys, at 2d the piece – 2s 8d; more for 20 pulleys, at 2s the piece – 40s; more for 2 dozen of pulleys, at 16d the piece – 32s; more for 12 pulleys, at 12d the piece – 12s; more for 12 pulleys, at 8d the piece – 8s; more for 7 dozen of great bowls, at 10d the piece – £3 10s;

[1]Perhaps simply poles or stakes, though *OED* (*sb*. 2) gives only Scottish examples for such general usage in the 16th century. More likely the meaning is the specific and long-established one, and indicates a form of recycling.

[2]In the draft this entry is deleted: BL, Add. MS 78169, f. 16.

more for 24 dozen of shod shovels, at 8s the dozen – £9 12s; and more to him for 8 dozen of scoops, at 5s the dozen – 40s. *Summa* – £21 2s 8d.

To Christian Edes of London, widow, the same day for price of 25 dozen of ballast baskets of her had and delivered at Deptford for the use of Her Highness's ships, at 18d the dozen – 37 6d; more for 9 baskets, at 6d the piece – 4s 6d; more for 8 dozen of middle baskets, at 6s the dozen – 48s; more for 8 great maunds, at 14d the piece – 9s 4d; more for 2 dozen of great baskets, at 8d the piece – 16s; and more to her for 2 great baskets, at 6d the piece – 12d. *Summa* – £5 16s 4d.

To Peter Pett, master shipwright, the same day for price of 12 new axes by him provided and spent in and upon Her Highness's works at Deptford Strand, at 16d the piece – 16s; more for 8 ginnets, at 18d the piece – 12s; more for 12 augers, at 10d the piece – 10s; and more to him for 2 handsaws, at 12d the piece – 2s. *Summa* – £2.

Compasses and running glasses. To Richard Stevens of Tower Hill, compass-maker, the same day for the price of 2 dozen of compasses by him delivered at Deptford for the use of Her Highness's ships, at 2s 8d the piece – £3 4s; and more to him for 6 dozen of running glasses, at 10s every dozen – £3. *Summa* – £6 4s.

[*Page total*] – £35 3s.

[f. 53] *Carving and painting*. To Richard Rowlande of Southwark, carver, the last day of December, for the workmanship, carving and setting up of the Queen's Majesty's arms of wood in Her Highness's ship the *Aid*, price – £5; more for carving of 3 great heads of wood,[1] at 10s the piece – 30s; and more to him for carving of 2 terms[2] of wood for the garnishing and setting out of the same ship, price – 20s. *Summa* – £7 10s.

To James Coke of London, painter, the same day for the workmanship in painting and colouring of Her Highness's new ship called the *Aid* at Deptford in timber colour, as also in painting of Her Highness's said arms of England in colours and gold, now set in the same ship stern for the garnishing thereof; by agreement – £18.

Land carriage of provisions. To Thomas Jewry, Simon Bedill, Thomas Jackson, Bryan Mylles, John Wooden, John Haynes, John Ratlyn, Nicholas Rachedaill and 44 other persons of Bromley, Addington, Limpsfield, Tatsfield, Caterham, Tandridge, Oxted, Warlingham, Titsey,

[1]For the carved beak-heads carried by some of the warships shown in the second (BL) section of the Anthony Roll, see H. S. Vaughan, 'Figure-heads and beak-heads of the ships of Henry VIII', *MM*, IV (1914), pp. 37–43, a pioneering study we regrettably failed to cite in our edition of the Roll.

[2]Probably in the original meaning of pillar or pedestal bust (from representations of the god Terminus: *OED* 'term' *sb*. V. 15) rather than in the much later more general application (V. 16) of carving below the taffrail.

Farleigh, Bletchingley, Lewisham, Godstone and thereabouts in Kent and Surrey the same day for the carriage of 52 loads 49½ foot of timber oak by them brought from Fickleshole in Kent[1] aforesaid to Deptford for the use of Her Highness's ships there, at 3s every load. *Summa* – £7 18s 11½d.[2]

To Walter Duff, Ralph Pett, Henry Pyke, Thomas Hamonde, Robert Lewin, Nicholas Lingcolne, Henry Ollyff, Jeffrey Price, William Mylles [*and*] John Frenche the same day, and 30 other persons of Bromley, Camberwell, Peckham, Beckenham, Eltham, Lewisham and thereabouts in Kent [*and Surrey*] for the carrying of 94½ loads and 15 shide of shores oak out of Her Highness's wood called West Wood in the county of Kent aforesaid to Deptford for the use of Her Majesty's ships there, at 14d the load. *Summa* – £5 10s 7d.[3]

[*Page total*] – £38 19s 6½d.

[f. 53v] *Land carriage of provisions.* To Henry Allen, Robert Holden, Thomas Kikell [*and*] Thomas Walker the last day of December, and six other persons of Bexley, Orpington, and St Mary Cray and thereabouts in Kent for the carrying of 10 loads 12½ foot of timber oak out of Her Highness's park at Eltham to Deptford for the use of Her Grace's ships, at 12d every load. *Summa* – 10s 3d.[4]

Ironwork. To Thomas Willson of Ratcliff, smith, the same day for price of 11 thousand [*one*] hundred 3 quarters 22½ pounds weight [*12,538½ lbs*] of his own new iron by him made into bolts and spikes of all sorts, rings, keys, clench, rove and overlop nails, and the same delivered at Deptford for the use of Her Highness's ships there, at 23s 4d every hundredweight – £130 12s;[5] more for 57,650 of 10d nail, at 8s 4d every 1,000 – £24 0s 5d; more for 72,750 of 6d nail, at 5s every 1,000 – £18 13s 9d; more for 41,750 of 4d nail, at 3s 4d every 1,000 – £6 19s

[1] *recte* Surrey; cf. above, p. 54 n. 5.

[2] Draft notes payment made to John Leche: BL, Add. MS 78169, f. 21v. Leche's original bill also survives, in which all the carriers are named: Add. MS 78171 [item 1(a)]. See further Appendix 4 below.

[3] Draft notes payment made to Leche: BL, Add. MS 78169, f. 21v. Leche's original bill names all the carriers, and distinguishes one consignment for Deptford (£2 6s 5d) and another to the 'slawter house' at Deptford, for Woolwich: Add. MS 78171 [item 1(a)]. Leche's bills are also noted as entered in Christmas quarter 1562. These bills show that the Quarter Book's common formula of A, B, C and so many other persons of X, W and Z does not necessarily mean any correlation between the persons and places mentioned: in the second list the 10 men named (Duff … Frenche) are the first 10 in the list of 40, but they are described respectively as of Camberwell, Peckham, Camberwell, Battersea, Beckenham, Peckham, Peckham, Camberwell, Beckenham, Lewisham.

[4] Draft notes payment made to Leche: BL, Add. MS 78169, f. 21v. In Leche's bills this is described as Henry Awstyn's timber, and the sum is noted as entered in this Deptford quarter: Add. MS 78181, item (a).

[5] The calculation gives 31346.25d, which is 2¼d above the stated sum (31344d).

2d; and more to him for 29,000 of 3d nail, at 2s 6d every 1,000 – £3 12 6d. *Summa* – £183 7s 10d. *[*<ironwork> £130 12s*; *nails – £52 15s 10d*][1]

To Thomas Ive of Limehouse, smith, the same day for price of 9 thousand 8 hundred [*one*] quarter weight [*11,004 lbs*] of his own new iron, by him made into bolts, rings, keys, spikes of all sorts, rove, clench and overlop nails, and the same delivered at Deptford for the use of Her Highness's ships, at 23s 4d every hundredweight – £114 12s 6d; more for 22,200 of 10d nail, at 8s 4d the 1,000 – £9 5s; more for 22,800 of 6d nail, at 5s every 1,000 – £5 14s; more for 29,250 of 4d nail, at 3s 4d every 1,000 – £4 17s 8d; and more to him for 26,500 of 3d nail, at 2s 6d every 1,000 – £3 6s 3d. *Summa* – £137 15s 5d.[2] *[*Ironwork – £114 12s 6d*; *nails – £22 12s 1d*]

Anchors. To Gilbert Mattyce of St Katherine's, smith, the same day for price of 2 new anchors of him had for the use of Her Majesty's ships, weighing 8 hundredweight, at 23s 4d every hundred[*weight*]. *Summa* – £9 6s 8d.

[*Page total*] *Summa* – £331 0s 2d. *[*Ironwork with £75 8s 9d for nails – £330 9s 11d*; *land carriage – 10s 3d*]

[f. 54] *Ironwork*. To William Hodges of Paris Garden, smith, the last day of December for price of 7,000 of great scupper nails of him had and delivered at Deptford for the use of Her Highness's ships, at 5s 4d every 1,000 – 37s 4d; and more to him for 2,500 of small scupper nails, at 4s the 1,000 – 10s. *Summa* – £2 7s 4d.

To Thomas Downing of Paris Garden, smith, the same day for the price of 10,000 of long scupper nails of him had for the use of Her Majesty's ships, at 5s 4d every 1,000 – 53s 4d; and more to him for bringing down of the same nails by water from London to Deptford – 8d. *Summa* – £2 14s.

To William Pennefather of London, ironmonger, the same day for price of 4 somes of English 2d nails by him delivered as aforesaid for the use of Her Highness's ships, at 13s 4d the some – £2 13s 4d; more for 3 great iron pots, at 6s 8d the piece – 20s; more for 2 some of pump nails, at 11s 8d the some – 23s 4d; and more to him for 2 great padlocks and keys, price – 2s 4d. *Summa* – £4 19s.

Brass kettles and iron pots. To Richard Hutton of London the same day for price of 4 great brass kettles by him delivered there for the use of

[1]The auditor has used the original subheading 'ironwork' (which applies to this paragraph and the next) in making his summary of the payments to Willson.

[2]Draft notes payments in prest of £37 15s, and in full of £100 to James Bakon: BL, Add. MS 78169, f. 19.

Her Highness's ships, weighing 2 hundred [*one*] quarter 10 pounds weight [*262 lbs*], at 11d every pound – £12 0s 2d; and more to him for 4 great broad kettle bands of iron, weighing 2 hundred 11 pounds [*235 lbs*], at 3d every pound weight – 58s 9d. *Summa* – £14 18s 11d.

To Thomas Poll of London the same day for price of 3 pitch pots of iron by him delivered for the use of Her Highness's ships, at 7s the pot – 21s; more for 2 great iron pots, at 6s the piece – 12s; more for one large iron pot, price – 8s; and more to him for bringing down the same pots by water – 6d. *Summa* – £2 1s 6d.[1]

[*Page total*] £27 0s 9d. *[*Iron and brass with £7 8s for nails – £26 16s 3d; carriage – 14d; locks – 2s 4d*]

[f. 54v] *Anchors.* To Thomas Ive of Limehouse, smith, the last day of December for price of 3 new anchors by him delivered for the use of Her Highness's ships the *Flower* [*de Luce*], the *Mary Grace Hoy* and the *Aid*, weighing 16 hundred 3 quarters 3 pounds weight [*1,879 lbs*], at 23s 4d every hundredweight. *Summa* – £19 11s 5½d.

New iron. To William Webb of London, merchant, the same day for price of [*one*] thousand 5 hundred 2 quarters 10 pounds weight [*1,746 lbs*] of English iron by him delivered at Deptford for the use of Her Majesty's ships, at 12s 6d every hundredweight – £9 14s 10d;[2] more for 15 hundredweight [*1,680 lbs*] of Bilbao iron, at 11s 8d every hundredweight – £8 15s; and more to him for 9 hundred [*one*] quarter 18 pounds [*weight*] [*1,054 lbs*] of Spanish iron, at 13s every hundredweight – £6 2s 4d. *Summa* – £24 12s 2d.[3]

Shivers and cocks of brass. To Robert Hunt of London, founder, the same day for price of 8 shivers of brass by him delivered at Deptford for the use of Her Grace's ships, weighing [*one*] hundred one pound weight [*113 lbs*], at 6½d the pound – £3 1s 2½d; and more to him for 72 cocks and 11 shivers of brass weighing 2 hundred 13 pounds weight [*237 lbs*], at 7d every pound – £6 18s 3d. *Summa* – £9 19s 6d.

New lead. To Julian Richardes of London, widow, the same day for price of [*one*] thousand 9 hundred 25 pounds weight [*2,153 lbs*] of her new lead by her delivered for the use of Her Highness's ships, at 15s every hundredweight – £14 8s 3¼d;[4] more for [*one*] hundred 6 pounds weight [*118 lbs*] of tin solder, at 8d the pound – £3 18s 8d; more for 3 hundred 10 pounds weight [*346 lbs*] of sounding leads, at 2d the pound – 57s 8d; more for the wages of two of her servants working on three of Her Grace's

[1]Draft notes payment made to Hew Doxseye: ibid., f. 14.

[2]The calculation gives 2338.3928d, which is less than ½d above the sum stated (2338d).

[3]Draft notes payment made to James Bakon: BL, Add. MS 78169, f. 15v.

[4]The calculation gives 3460.1784d, which is less than ½d above the sum stated (3459.25d).

ships the *Triumph*, the *Victory* and the *Aid*, by 42 days at 10d the day – 35s; and more to her for bringing down of the same lead from London to Deptford at sundry times – 4s. *Summa* – £23 3s 7¼d.

Sea coal. To Robert Anderson of London the same day for price of 18½ chalder of seacoal by him delivered there for the use of Her Highness's ships, at 11s every chaldron. *Summa* – £10 3s 6d.

[*Page total*] £87 10s 2¾d. *[*Iron and brass* <corrected to> *£54 3s 1d; lead – £21 4s 7¼d; plumbers' wages – 35s; sea coal – £10 3s 6d; carriage – 4s*]

[f. 55] *Meting*[1] *and carriage of sea coal.* To Thomas Pope of London the last day of December for the meting of 18½ chaldron of sea coal there for the use of Her Highness's smith's forge, at 4d every chaldron meting. *Summa* – 6s 2d.

To Thomas Hiller, Thomas White, and two other porters of London the same day for their pains and labour in carrying a-land 8½ chaldron of sea coal into Her Highness's working yard there for the use of Her Highness's forge, at 12d every chaldron. *Summa* – 8s 6d.

Pitch, tar and all kind of cordage. To Christopher Draper of London, alderman, the same day for price of 50 white 'callis'[2] lines of him had and delivered into Her Highness's great storehouse there for the use of Her Majesty's ships, at 2s the piece – £5; more for 6 thousand 2 hundred 2 quarters 10½ pounds [*weight*] [*7,010½ lbs*] of tarred latchet and oillet lines, at 23s 4d every hundredweight – £73 0s 6¼d; more for 133 tarred hawsers and warps of 2, 3, 4, and 5 inches about, weighing 41 thousand 5 hundred 2 quarters 23½ pounds weight [*46,559½ lbs*], at 17s 6d every hundredweight – £363 15s 0¾d;[3] more for 2,250 small needles, at 3s 4d every 100 – £3 18s 4d; more for 45 dozen of white twine, at 6s the dozen – £14 10s; more for half a tun of train oil, price – £6; more for 20 spruce deal-boards, at 4s 4d the piece – £4 6s 8d; more for 5 last of pitch, at £4 13s 4d the last – £23 6s 8d; more for 4 last of tar, at £4 13s 4d the last – £18 13s 4d; more for [*one*] hundredweight of tarred marline, price – 37s 4d; more for 64½ pounds weight of white marline, at 4d the pound – 31s 6d; more for 2 hundredweight [*224 lbs*] of tarred twine, at 6d the pound – £5 12s; and more to him for bringing down of the same provisons by water from London to Deptford; by agreement – £3 6s 8d. *Summa* – £523

[1]Weighing.

[2]Occurring elsewhere (*ex inform.* Dr M. Hayward) but the meaning has not been established. Possibly it is a derivation from 'Calais', though that place was not known for manufacture of cordage. Cf. the white (untarred) rope supplied by Draper for hinges: below, p. 262.

[3]The calculation gives 87299.062d, which is about ¾d below the sum stated (879300.75d).

8s 1d.[1] *[*Cordage – £482 10s 2d*; *needles – £3 18s 4d*; *pitch and tar – £29 6s 8d*; *carriage – £3 6s 8d*; *deal-boards – £4 6s 8d*]

Thrums. To Thomas Eve of London the same day for price of 37 pounds weight of thrums by him delivered there for the use of Her Highness's ships, at 2¼d every pound. *Summa* – 6s 11¼d.

[*Page total*] – £524 9s 8¼d.

[f. 55v] *Hawsers, marline, small cordage, train oil and thrums.* To Richard Hewson of London, merchant, the last day of December for price of 52 tarred hawsers of 3, 6 and 7 inches compass by him delivered into Her Highness's great storehouse there for the use of Her Grace's ships, weighing 11 thousand 7 hundred 21 pounds weight [*13,125 lbs*], at 17s 6d every hundredweight – £102 10s 9¼d.

To Richard Cragge of London, merchant, the same day for price of 5 hundred pound weight[2] [*560 lbs*] of small tarred marline by him delivered into Her Highness's great storehouse there for the use of Her Grace's ships, at 37s 4d every hundredweight – £9 6s 8d; more for 6 hundred 3 quarters 3 pounds weight [*759 lbs*] of tarred ratline and latchet line, at 23s 4d every hundredweight – £7 18s 1½d; and more to him for 9 hundred 12 pounds weight [*1,020 lbs*] of small sounding lines tarred, at 23s 4d every hundred[*weight*] – £10 12s 6d. *Summa* – £27 17s 3½d.

To William Padge of London, merchant, the same day for price of one tun of train oil by him delivered at Deptford for the use of Her Highness's ships, price – £12; more for 40 pounds weight of thrums, at 3d the pound – 10s; and more to him for 30 deal-boards, at 4s the piece – £6. *Summa* – £18 10s. *[*Oil – £12*; *thrums – 10s*; *boards – £6*].

Old oakum. To Joan King, Annes Bartelet, Edward Coxe, Nicholas Starkey, and seven other persons[3] of Deptford, Greenwich, Lewisham and thereabouts the same day for the working and picking [*of*] 2 thousand 3 hundred 2 quarters 16 pounds weight [*2,648 lbs*] of Her Highness's old junks and ropes by them made into oakum for the needful caulking of Her Grace's ships, at 3s 8d every hundredweight picking – £4 6s 8d.[4]

Making of flags. To Stephen Andros of London the same day for the making of 12 great flags with the cross of St George for the use of Her

[1]Draft notes payments of £600 and £83 5s 10d: BL, Add. MS 78169, f. 17v. This must include settlement of an earlier account.

[2]So expressed. This particular calculation would naturally be the same for 5 × 100 lbs; but the other entries in the paragraph express the regular usage perfectly: ([6.75 × 112] + 3) × (280 ÷ 112) = 1897.5d (the exact sum stated); ([9 × 112] + 12) × (280d ÷ 112) = 2550d (likewise). So the first entry can confidently be taken as 560 lbs, not 500.

[3]Draft identifies these as Thomas Rock, Thomas Newbery, Richard Harwood, Joan Juell, Elizabeth Jarvis, Thomas Chapman and Thomas Harryson: BL, Add. MS 78169, f. 20v.

[4]The calculation gives 1040.2856d, which is ¼d above the sum stated (1040d).

Grace's ships, at 2s every flag making – 24s; more for 8 other flags, at 16d the piece – 10s 8d; and more to him for thread for the sewing of the same flags – 2s 6d. *Summa* – £1 17s 2d.[1]

[*Page total*] – £155 1s 10¾d.

[f. 56] *Red say.* To John Sleade of London, mercer, the last day of December for price of 4 pieces of red say by him delivered for the making of the foresaid flags with the cross of St George for the use of Her Highness's ships, at 36s the piece – £7 4s; and more to him for one other piece of red say, price – 20s. *Summa* – £8 4s.[2]

Canvas. To Edward Hawll of London the same day for price of 2 pieces of dowlas canvas by him delivered for the new making of flags for use of Her Grace's ships, at £5 10s the piece – £11; more for 180 yards of vitry canvas, at 10d the yard – £7 10s; and more to him for 3½ ells of soutage,[3] price 2s. *Summa* – £18 12s.

Netting- and wrain-ropes. To William Brooke of Deptford, ropemaker, the same day for the workmanship of 18 hundred 3 quarters 7 pounds weight [*2,107 lbs*] of Her Highness's old junks and ropes by him made into netting- and wrain-ropes for the use of Her Highness's ships, at 3s 8d every hundredweight – £3 8s 11¾d.

To Thomas Russell of Ratcliff, ropemaker the same day for workmanship of 13 hundred 3 quarters 14 pounds weight [*1,554 lbs*] of Her [*Highness's*] old junks and ropes by him made into netting- and wrain-ropes for the use of Her Highness's ships, at 3s 8d every hundredweight – £2 10s 10½d.

To William Coxe of Ratcliff, ropemaker, the same day for workmanship of 7 hundred 3 quarters 14 pounds weight [*882 lbs*] of Her Highness's old junks and ropes by him made into netting- and wrain-ropes for the like use as aforesaid, at 3s 8d every hundredweight – £1 8s 10½d.[4]

[*Page total*] – £34 4s 8½d.

[f. 56v] *Scupper-leathers, claps, pump-hose and pump-boxes.* To John Harryson of Tower Hill, shoemaker, the last day of December for price of 18 dozen of scupper-leathers by him delivered there for the use of Her Highness's ships, at 16d the piece – £14 8s; more for 8 dozen of claps, at 16d the piece – £6 8s; more for 24 small pump-hose, at 16d the piece – 32s; more for making and trimming of 9 great pump-boxes, at 2s the piece – 18s; more for 24 small claps, at 8d the piece – 16s; and more to him for

[1]Draft notes payment made to 'Lylly': BL, Add. MS 78169, f. 22.

[2]Draft notes payment made to James Humphrey ('Humfreye'): ibid., f. 14.

[3]MS 'souttwiche'. Another type of canvas; no provenance for the name is suggested in *OED*.

[4]Draft notes payment made to Vincent Gonson: BL, Add. MS 78169, f. 19v.

8 dozen of large pump-hose, at 2s 8d the piece – £12 16s. *Summa* – £36 18s.[1]

Brick, lime and sand. To Stephen Parret of Deptford the same day for price of 32,000 of brick by him delivered for the new making of hearths and furnaces in Her Highness's three new ships there called the *Triumph*, the *Victory* and the *Aid*, at 11s every 1,000 – £17 12s; more for 34 hundred[*weight*] of lime, at 7s the hundred[*weight*] – £11 18s; more for 25 loads of sand, at 8d the load – 16s 8d; and more to him for carriage of 26 loads of brick from the kiln to Deptford Strand, at 4d the load after 500 bricks to the load – 8s 8d. *Summa* – £30 15s 4d.

Tile. To James Brockhowse of Lewisham the same day for price of 9,000 of house tile by him delivered for the new mending, repairing and tiling of Her Highness's storehouses there, wherein lieth all kinds of stuffs pertaining to Her Grace's ships, at 11s every 1,000 – £4 19s; and more to him for 50 long roof tile, at 1d the piece – 4s 2d. *Summa* – £5 3s 2d.

Ink and counters. To William Kirbye of London the same day for the price of 3 quarts of ink by him delivered unto Her Highness's officers [*the*] clerks of Her Majesty's marine causes for the writing and making up of books concerning the same, at 16d every quart – 4s; and more to him for 4 pounds weight of casting counters, at 2s the pound – 8s. *Summa* – 12s.[2]

[*Page total*] – £74 8s 6d.

[f. 57] *Carriage of brick.* To William Tewson of Deptford the last day of December for the carrying of 9 loads of brick from the kiln to Deptford Strand for the use of Her Highness's ships, at 4d every load after 500 of brick to the load – 3s.

House rent. To Peter Pett of Deptford the same day for one quarter of a year's rent for two cellars of him hired wherein lieth Her Highness's store of rosin for the use of Her Majesty's ships, due at this present – £1.

Ballast. To Richard Pope of Erith the same day for price of 178 ton of gravel for the ballasting of two Her Highness's ships called the *Triumph* and the *Victory*, at 4d every ton – £2 19s 4d.

Reed. To James Gibbes of Rainham, reedman, the same day for price of 2,000 of reed by him delivered at Deptford for the needful breaming of Her Highness's ships at their groundings, at 10s every 1,000 – £1.

[*Page total*] – £5 2s 4d. [f. 57v *blank*]

[1]Draft notes payments of £12 in prest, another of £12 in prest to the merchant's wife, and of £12 18s in full payment: ibid., f. 16.

[2]Draft notes payment to John Brown: ibid., f. 18.

[f. 58] **Ordinary. Woolwich**:

Anno domini 1562. *Anno regni regine Elizabethe quarto*

A payment made the last day of March as well to keepers of storehouses, dock and timber-yards, and to labourers for unloading and discharge of divers hoys laden with timber and plank, as also to sundry persons for divers kinds of provisions of them had and delivered for the use of Her Grace's ships there; begun the first day of January last, and this day ended, as followeth:

Labourers.

John Hilltun, master, 5 days at 7d	2s 11d
John Marshe, 14 days at 6d	7s
Raynold Kent, 20 days at 6d	10s
Matthew Martyn, 16 days at 6d	8s
John Wallis, 6 days at 6d	3s
William Corby, 6 days at 6d	3s
Thomas Morres, 6 days at 6d	3s
John Powell, 8 days at 6d	4s
Thomas Phillippes, 20 days at 6d	10s
John Kent, 14 days at 6d	7s
Charles Deane, 11 days at 6d	5s 6d
John Blacke, 8 days at 6d	4s
Henry Harvy, 6 days at 6d	3s
William Goodeshipp, 6 days at 6d	3s
Gilbert Chappman, 6 days at 6d	3s
John Chappman, 9 days at 6d	4s 6d
William Allam, 5 days at 6d	2s 6d
John Robartes, 9 days at 6d	4s 6d
John Wittinge, 12 days at 6d	6s
Robert Ollyf, 30 days at 6d	15s

[*Page total*] – £5 8s 11d.

[f. 58v] Robert Body, 17 days at 6d	8s 6d
Thomas Snow, 10 days at 6d	5s
Humphrey Bailly, 12 days at 6d	6s
Thomas Harringham, 12 days at 6d	6s
John Cammocke, 12 days at 6d	6s
Roger Bysshopp, 20 days at 6d	10s
James Ryvell, 8 days at 6d	4s
William Littellwood, 16 days at 6d	8s
Henry Moreman, 16 days at 6d	8s
John Tompson, 16 days at 6d	8s

Edmund Lamson, 26 days at 6d	13s
Richard Raynsefourth, 42 days and tides at 7d	24s 6d
Henry Stevenson, 34 days and tides at 6d	17s
George Bell, 34 days and tides at 6d	17s
Ralph Courtland, 34 days and tides at 6d	17s
John Gybson, 37 days and tides at 6d	18s 6d
John Twyford, 33 days and tides at 6d	16s 6d
John Bastian, 34 days and tides at 6d	17s
Henry Courteland, 35 days and tides at 6d	17s 6d
Richard Shaffte, 31 days and tides at 6d	15s 6d
Reynolde Kent, 27 days and tides at 6d	13s 6d
Martin Mathew, 27 days and tides at 6d	13s 6d
Thomas Harringam, 27 days and tides at 6d	13s 6d
James Rivell, 27 days and tides at 6d	13s 6d
John Cammocke, 27 days and tides at 6d	13s 6d
John Willsman, 28 days and tides at 6d	14s
Henry Moreman, 27 days and tides at 6d	13s 6d
John Carpenter, 29 days and tides at 6d	14s 6d
Edmund Lamson, 29 days and tides at 6d	14s 6d
John Kent, 27 days and tides at 6d	13s 6d
Edward Plumer, 33 days and tides at 6d	16s 6d
Edmund Base, 20 days at 6d	10s
Richard Blaicke, 5 days at 6d	2s 6d
William Kelly, 6 days at 6d	3s
Richard Falsam, 6 days at 6d	3s
Richard Thornefall, 10 days at 6d	5s
Thomas Richardes, 20 days at 6d	10s
Richard Burwood, 27 days at 6d	13s 6d
Henry Florett, 33 days at 6d	16s 6d
Ralph Brocke, 26 days at 6d	13s

[*Page total*] – £23 13s 6d.

[f. 59] William Pye, 26 days at 6d	13s
Roger Wayre, 20 days at 6d	10s
George Veasee, 35 days at 6d	17s 6d
House-carpenters	
John Leeche, 23 days at 12d	23s
Thomas Hill, 23 days at 10d	19s 2d
John Throwley, 23 days at 9d	17s 3d
Richard Throwley, 23 days at 7d	13s 5d

*[*Storehouse keepers*]. To Jerome Hewster the last day of March for his wages daily attending and serving Her Highness in safe-keeping of

Her Grace's storehouses there wherein lieth divers kinds of stuffs for the use of her ships, by one quarter of a year begun the first day of January last and this day ended, at 6d *per diem* – £2 5s.

To John Jicket, porter, the same day for his wages daily attending and serving Her Highness in safe-keeping of her dock and timber-yards there wherein lieth Her Grace's timber, plank and board for the use of her ships, by one quarter of a year begun and ended as aforesaid, at 6d *per diem* – £2 5s.

[*Page total*] – £10 3s 3d.

[f. 59v] *Emptions.*

Ironwork. To Anthony Smyth of Woolwich the last day of March for price of 200 of 20d nail by him delivered there for the new mending of the crane and wharf at Woolwich, at 20d every 100 – 3s 4d; more for 500 of 6d nail, price – 2s 6d; more for 400 of 10d nail, price 3s 4d; more for 500 of 4d nail, price 20d; and more for mending of bolts for the same use – 20d. *Summa* – 12s 6d.

To Richard Welles of Greenwich, smith, the same day for the working of 5 hundredweight of Her Highness's old iron by him made and wrought into bolts, hoops and small spikes for the use of the crane and wharf there as aforesaid, at 13s 4d every hundredweight. *Summa* – £3 6s 8d.

Marsh earth. To Joan Bouchtun of Plumstead, widow, the same day for price of 12 lighterful of marsh earth of her had and taken for the new mending and repairing of Her Highness's wharf there, at 2s 6d every lighterful – £1 10s 0d.

To John Taster of London, lighterman, the same day for service of his lighter serving Her Highness in carrying of marsh earth for the mending of the wharf there, by 4 weeks at 6s 8d every week – £1 6s 8d.

Burning reed. To John Rawlins of Paris Garden the same day for price of 4,500 of burning reed by him delivered at Woolwich for the use of Her Highness's ships, at 10s every 1,000 – £2 5s.

Steel shovels. To John Benbow of London, turner, the same day for price of 2 dozen of steel shovels by him delivered at Woolwich for the needful use of the wharf there, at 7s every dozen – 14s.

[*Page total*] – £9 14s 2d.

[f. 60] *Timber, plank and trenails.* To Henry Fillian of Yalding in Kent the last day of March for price of 2,715 foot of 2-inch plank oak of him had and delivered at Woolwich for the use of Her Grace's ships, at 10s every 100 foot – £13 11s 3d; more for 600 foot of inch ½ board oak, at 5s every 100 [*foot*] – 36s; more for 4,975 foot of 3-inch plank, at 11s every 100 [*foot*] – £27 7s 3d; more for 4,679 foot of 4-inch plank, at 11s every 100 [*foot*] – £25 14s 6d; more for 29 loads of timber oak, at 11s every load after 50 foot to the load – £15 19s; and more to him for 6,000 of trenails of 30 inches long, at 2s 6d every 100 – £7 10s. *Summa* – £91 18s.

To John Dethicke of Colchester, purveyor, the same day for price of 72½ loads 6 foot of compass and long timber oak by him delivered there for the use of Her Highness's ships, at 10s every load after 50 foot to the load – £36 6s 3d; more for 3,500 foot of 3-inch plank oak, at 10s every 100 [*foot*] – £17 10s; more for 3,880 foot of 4-inch plank oak, at 10s every 100 [*foot*] – £19 8s; more for 300 foot of 2-inch plank oak, at 8s every 100 [*foot*] – 24s; and more to him for 21,000 of trenails, *viz.* 10,000 of 36 inches long, at 3s every 100 – £15; more for 6,000 of 24 inches long, at 2s every 100 – £6; more for 3,000 of 20 inches long, at 20d every 100 – 50s; and more for 2,000 of 30 inches long, at 2s 6d every 100 – 50s. *Summa* – £100 8s 3d.

To Henry Danes of Inworth in Essex, purveyor, the same day for price of 144 loads of compass and long timber oak by him delivered there for the use of Her Grace's ships, at 10s every load after 50 foot to the load – £72; more for 1,290 foot of 2-inch plank oak, at 8s every 100 foot – £5 3s 2d; and more to him for 1,090 foot of 3-inch plank oak, at 10s every 100 foot – £5 8s 11½d. *Summa* – £82 12s 1½d.

[*Page total*] – £274 18s 4½d. [f. 60v *blank*]

[f. 61] A payment made the last day of June as well to keepers of storehouses, dock and timber-yards and to divers labourers for unloading and discharging of divers hoys with timber and plank, as also to sundry persons for divers kinds of provisions of them had and delivered for the use of Her Grace's ships there; begun the first day of April last, and this day ended, as followeth:

Labourers

Richard Raynsforthe, master, 35 days at 8d	23s 4d
Matthew Martyn, 33 days at 7d	19s 3d
John Cammocke, 34 days at 7d	19s 10d
Ralph Courtland, 33 days at 7d	19s 3d
William Gonnbye, 33 days at 7d	19s 3d
James Teall, 33 days at 7d	19s 3d
John Bastian, 33 days at 6d	16s 6d
Stephen Longockom, 33 days at 6d	16s 6d
Thomas Snowe, 33 days at 6d	16s 6d
William Clowder, 16 days at 7d	9s 4d
Edward Lamson, 78 days at 6d	39s
Richard Raynsfourthe, 4 days at 7d	2s 4d
John Cammocke, 20 days at 6d	10s

Matthew Martyn, 4 days at 6d	2s
John Carpenter, 4 days at 6d	2s
John Marshe, 5 days at 7d	2s 11d
Robert Wingros, 4 days at 6d	2s

[*Page total*] – £11 19s 3d.

[f. 61v] John Powell, 4 days at 6d	2s
Thomas Harringham, 3 days at 6d	18d
John Wattes, 2 days at 6d	12d
John Thomas, 6 days at 6d	3s
John Pattynson, 6 days at 6d	3s
John Carter, 4 days at 6d	2s
Stephen Longockom, 6 days at 6d	3s
James Ryddswell, 3 days at 6d	18d
John Kyent, 4 days at 6d	2s
Tilers	
John Callaway, master, 28 days at 10d	23s 4d
Stephen Hugons, 28 days at 10d	23s 3d
Henry Saye, 16 days at 7d	9s 4d

*[*Keepers of storehouses*]. To Jerome Hewster the last day of June for his wages daily attending and serving Her Highness in safe-keeping of her storehouses there wherein lieth Her Grace's store for the use of her ships, by the space of 91 days begun the first day of April last and this day ended, at 6d *per diem* – £2 5s 6d.

To John Jickett, porter, the same day for his wages daily attending and serving Her Highness in safe-keeping of her timber-yard wherein lieth her timber and plank for the use of Her Highness's ships, by like 91 days begun and ended as aforesaid, at 6d *per diem* – £2 5s 6d.

[*Page total*] – £8 6s.

[f. 62] *Emptions*

Timber, plank, board, joists and shores. To Edward Goteley, purveyor, the last day of June for price of 87 loads of compass and long timber oak of him had and provided out of Her Highness's woods called Strudgwick Wood and Farneyfold in Sussex and by him delivered at Woolwich for the use of Her Grace's ships, at 10s every load after 50 foot to the load – £43 10s; more [*for*] 13,250 foot of 4-inch plank oak, at 12s every 100 foot – £79 10s; more for 500 foot of 3-inch plank oak, at 10s every 100 foot – 50s; more for 950 foot of 2-inch plank oak, at 8s every 100 foot – £3 16s; more for 6 loads of timber oak in joists, at 16s every load – £4 16s; and more to him for 125 foot of inch board oak, at 5s every 100 foot – 6s 3d. *Summa* – £134 8s 3d.

To Henry Layne, purveyor, the same day for price of 41½ loads 17 foot of compass timber oak and knees of him had and provided in Cheshunt Park in Hertfordshire and the same delivered at Woolwich for the use of Her Grace's ships, at 13s 4d every load after 50 foot to the load. *Summa* – £27 18s 1d.

To Thomas Smyth of Deptford the same day for price of 1,000 foot of inch board oak of him had and delivered for the use of Her Highness's ships, at 6s every load – £3; more for 200 foot of 2-inch plank, at 8s 4d the 100 – 16s 8d; and more to him for 1,400 foot of 3-inch plank, at 10s every 100 [*foot*] – £7. *Summa* – £10 16s 8d.

To Sir William Garrard, knight,[1] the same day for price of 20 loads of shores of him taken and delivered at Woolwich for the use of Her Highness's ships, at 3s 8d every load. *Summa* – £3 13s 4d.

[*Page total*] – £176 16s 4d.

[f. 62v] *Steel shovels.* To John Benbow of London the last day of June for price of one dozen of steel shovels of him had and by him delivered at Woolwich for the use of Her Highness's ships; price by agreement – 7s.

Carriage of rubbish. To Jerome Hewster the same day for service of his cart with three horses and one man serving Her Highness in carrying of 340 loads of rubbish out of Her Grace's yard there, at 1d every load – 28s 4d; and more to him for 100 loads of gravel for making plain the dock there, at 4d every load – 33s 4d. *Summa* – £3 1s 8d.

Carriage of shores. To Richard Mylles, John Brokhowse, Henry Ollyff, William Clerke, George Cane and 12 other persons of Lewisham, Peckham, Eltham and Dulwich the same day for carrying of 54 loads of shores out of Her Highness's wood called West Wood to Woolwich for the use of Her Grace's ships, at 14d every load after 50 shide to every load. *Summa* – £3 3s.

Burning reed. To John Marsheall the same day for price of 2,000 of burning reed of him had and delivered there for the use of Her Highness's ships, at 10s every 1,000. *Summa* – £1.

Tile pins. To John Callaway the same day for price of 2½ bushels of tile pins of him had and taken for the needful tiling of Her Highness's storehouses there, price – 2s 6d.

[*Page total*] – £7 14s 2d.

[f. 63] *Tile.* To James Brookehowse of Lewisham the last day of June for price of 25 roof tile of him had and delivered for the new tiling and

[1]Alderman of Lime St Ward, Sheriff 1552–53, Lord Mayor 1555–56, knighted in his mayoral year, Governor of the Russia Company, Assistant of the Merchant Adventurers 1564; d. 1571. His son Sir John was Lord Mayor 1601–2: Beaven, *Aldermen*, ii, p. 32 and *passim*. GEC, *Baronetage*, i, p. 188. *Hist. Parl. 1558–1603*, i, pp. 191–2.

mending of Her Highness's storehouses there, at 1d the piece – 2s 1d; and more to him for 5,000 of house tile, at 12s every 1000 – £3. *Summa* – £3 2s 1d.

To William Anderson, limeman, the same day for price of 1,500 of tile by him delivered at Woolwich for the repairing and tiling of Her Highness's storehouses there as aforesaid, at 12s the 1,000 – 18s; and more to him for 5 hundred[*weight*] of lime, at 6s every 100 [*weight*] – 30s. *Summa* – £2 8s.

[*Page total*] – £5 10s 1d. [f. 63v *blank*]

[f. 64] A payment made the last day of September as well to keepers of storehouses, dock and timber-yards and to labourers for unloading and discharging of divers hoys laden with timber and plank, as also to sundry persons for divers kinds of provisions of them had and delivered there for the use of Her Grace's ships; begun the first day of July last and this day ended, as followeth:

Labourers

John Marshe, master, 12 days at 8d	8s
John Hiltonn, 10 days at 8d	6s 8d
Richard Rainsfourth, 4 days at 7d	2s 4d
Martin Matthew, 6 days at 6d	3s
Thomas Phillippes, 10 days at 6d	5s
William Brone, 8 days at 6d	4s
John Cartar, 8 days at 6d	4s
John Powell, 10 days at 6d	5s
John Cammocke, 20 days at 6d	10s
John Claytonn, 8 days at 6d	4s
Thomas Harringham, 8 days at 6d	4s
John Tompson, 8 days at 6d	4s
William Allam, 6 days at 6d	3s
Thomas Snowe, 12 days at 6d	6s
Richard Blayke, 6 days at 6d	3s
William Littellwoode, 20 days at 6d	10s
Henry ap John, 10 days at 6d	5s

[*Page total*] – £4. 7s.

[f. 64v] John Blacke, 6 days at 6d	3s
Richard Lennerde, 6 days at 6d	3s
John Robart, 8 days at 6d	4s
John James, 10 days at 6d	5s
Robert Wingrows, 6 days at 6d	3s
Gilbert Chappman, 6 days at 6d	3s

Stephen Longercom, 20 days at 6d	10s
John Carpenter, 8 days at 6d	4s
John Pattynson, 8 days at 6d	4s
Hugh Jonnes, 10 days at 6d	5s
William Frynde, 10 days at 6d	5s
William Tailler, 6 days at 6d	3s
John Byfelde, 6 days at 6d	3s
John Lyans, 10 days at 6d	5s
Edmund Lamson, 78 days at nights at 6d	39s

*[*Keepers of storehouses*]. To Jerome Hewster the last day of September for his wages daily attending and serving Her Highness in safe-keeping of Her Grace's storehouses there wherein lieth divers kinds of provisions for the use of Her Highness's ships, by one quarter of a year begun the first day of July last and this day ended, at 6d *per diem* – £2 6s.

To John Jecket, porter, the same day for his wages daily attending and serving Her Highness in keeping of the dock and timber-yards there, wherein lieth Her Grace's timber and plank for the use of Her Highness's ships, by 92 days begun and ended as abovesaid, at 6d *per diem* – £2 6s.

[*Page total*] – £9 11s.

[f. 65] *Emptions*

Gravel. To John Abartun and John Asbye of Woolwich the last day of September for price of 100 loads of gravel by them provided and delivered there for the flooring of Her Highness's dock there, at 2d every load. *Summa* – 16s 8d.

Timber. To John Dethicke of Colchester, purveyor, the same day for price of 203 loads of compass and long timber oak by him provided of divers persons of Ipswich in Suffolk and thereabouts, and the same delivered at Woolwich for the use of Her Grace's ships, at 10s every load after 50 foot to the load – £101 10s; more for 6,061 foot of 3-inch plank oak, at 10s every 100 foot – £30 6s 1d; more for 3,215½ foot of 4-inch plank oak, at 10s every 100 foot – £16 1s 6¾d; and more to him for 2,096 foot of 2-inch plank oak, at 8s every 100 foot – £8 7s 6d. *Summa* – £156 5s 1¾d.

[*Page total*] – £157 1s 9¾d. [f. 65v *blank*]

[f. 66] *Anno Domini 1562. Anno regni regine Elizabethe quinto*

A payment made the last day of December as well to keepers of storehouses, dock and timber-yards and to labourers for unloading and discharging of certain hoys loaded with timber and plank, as also to sundry persons for divers kinds of provisions of them had and delivered there for the use of Her Grace's ships; begun the first day of October last and this day ended, as followeth:

Labourers

John Marshe, master, 6 days at 8d	4s
John Hillton, 16 days at 7d	9s 4d
Thomas Cowdell, 6 days at 6d	3s
Henry Moreman, 8 days at 6d	4s
Robert Wingrose, 8 days at 6d	4s
William Corby, 8 days at 6d	4s
Reginald Kent, 8 days at 6d	4s
John Daby, 8 days at 6d	4s
John Grene, 8 days at 6d	4s
John Chapman, 7 days at 6d	3s 6d
John Clayttun, 10 days at 6d	5s
James Rigwell, 8 days at 6d	4s
John Carpenter, 14 days at 6d	7s
Henry Harris, 10 days at 6d	5s
Richard Lennarde, 8 days at 6d	4s
Philip Robartes, 8 days at 6d	4s
Gilbert Chapman, 8 days at 6d	4s
John Tailler, 10 days at 6d	5s
John Robartes, 8 days at 6d	4s
William Tailler, 8 days at 6d	4s
Robert Tailler, 8 days at 6d	4s
John Cammocke, 8 days at 6d	4s
Charles Deane, 8 days at 6d	4s
Richard Blayke, 8 days at 6d	4s
William Allam, 10 days at 6d	5s

[*Page total*] – £5 10s 10d.

[f. 66v] William Littellwod, 16 days at 6d	8s
John Roodes, 16 days at 6d	8s
John Paine, 12 days at 6d	6s
William Broune, 16 days at 6d	8s
John Kent, 8 days at 6d	4s
John Cooke, 4 days at 6d	2s
John Wadworthe, 4 days at 6d	2s
Lawrence Chapman, 8 days at 6d	4s
Ralph Thornetonn, 10 days at 6d	5s
William Bonner, 10 days at 6d	5s
Matthew Martin, 8 days at 6d	4s
John Ortun, 12 days at 6d	6s

Thomas Sknow, 12 days at 6d	6s
John James, 12 days at 6d	6s
Stephen Longokam, 40 days at 6d	20s

*[*Keepers of storehouses*]. To Jerome Hewster the last day of December for his wages daily attending and serving Her Highness in safe-keeping of Her Grace's storehouses there wherein lieth divers kinds of provisions for the use of her ships, by one quarter of a year begun the first day of October last and this day ended, at 6d *per diem* – £2 6s.

To John Jicket, porter, the same day for his wages daily attending and serving Her Highness in safe-keeping of Her Grace's timber-yards at Woolwich wherein lieth her timber and plank for the use of Her Highness's ships, by like time of 92 days begun and ended as aforesaid, at 6d *per diem* – £2 6s.

[*Page total*] – £9 6s.

[f. 67] *Emptions*

*[*Timber and boards – £25 6s 8d*; *thrums – £5 15s*].[1] To Henry Bamforde of Cheshunt in Hertfordshire, purveyor, the last day of December for price of 35 loads of compass timber oak and knees by him provided and delivered at Woolwich for the use of Her Grace's ships, at 13s 4d every load after 50 foot to the load – £23 6s 8d; more for 3,000 of trenails of 36 inches long, at 3s every 100 – £4 10s; and more to him for 1,000 of trenails of 30 inches long, at 2s 6d every 100 – 25s. *Summa* – £29 1s 8d.

To Richard Kradge the same day for price of 10 spruce deal-boards of him had and delivered at Woolwich for the use of Her Highness's ships, at 4s the piece. *Summa* – £2.

[*Page total*] – £31 1s 8d. [f. 67v *blank*]

[f. 68] **Ordinary. Gillingham**:

Anno Domini 1562. *Anno regni regine Elizabethe quarto*

A payment made the last day of March as well to masters, mariners, gunners and others daily attending and serving Her Highness in safe-keeping of Her Grace's ships afloat in harbour, and to divers persons for rent of storehouses wherein lieth Her Highness's store for the use of Her Grace's ships, as also for divers other things needful for Her Majesty's said ships; begun the first day of January last, and this day ended, as followeth:

[1] Auditor's calculation covers both entries on this page.

The Elizabeth Jonas

Mariners

William Wood, master, 12 weeks 6 days	£6 8s 7d
John Teyge, boatswain, 12 weeks 6 days	53s 7d
Lancelot Trystram, purser, 12 weeks 6 days	45s
Thomas Waller, cook & steward, 12 weeks 6 days	29s 5½d
John Collens, 12 weeks 6 days	21s 5d
Peter Padden, 12 weeks 6 days	21s 5d
Richard Brisholde, 12 weeks 6 days	21s 5d
Edward Branden, 12 weeks 6 days	21s 5d
Nicholas Cossyn, 1 week 5 days	2s 10d
Edward Crocker, 4 weeks 2 days	7s 2d
Edmund Joyll, 12 weeks 6 days	21s 5d
William Kisshan, 12 weeks 6 days	21s 5d
John Donnyng, 7 weeks 3 days	12s 4d
Patrick Morrow, 12 weeks 6 days	21s 5d
Harry Baker, 12 weeks 6 days	21s 5d
Robert Healling, gromet, 12 weeks 6 days	16s 1d
Robert Chamber, boy, 12 weeks 6 days	10s 8½d
Henry Morrys, gromet, 12 weeks 6 days	16s 1d

[*Page total*] – £24 14s 2d.

[f. 68v] Nicholas Johnson, carpenter, 12 weeks 6 days	53s 7d
Richard Crippes, server, 2 weeks 4 days	4s 4d
John Hichecocke, server, 12 weeks 6 days	21s 5d
Isaac Ashley, gromet, 12 weeks 6 days	16s 1d
Thomas Johnson, boy, 10 weeks 2 days	8s 7d
Robert Browne, 8 weeks 3 days	14s
James Morter, 8 weeks 3 days	14s
[*Gunners*]	
Lawrence Dilke, master gunner, 8 weeks 3 days	21s
Richard Elles, server, 2 weeks	3s 4d

The Hope

Mariners

John Hurlocke, master, 12 weeks 6 days	£6 8s 7d
Robert West, boatswain, 12 weeks 6 days	53s 7d
Michael Gonson, purser, 12 weeks 6 days	32s 2d
John Mathew, cook and steward, 12 weeks 6 days	29s 5½d
Thomas Coxe, 2 weeks	3s 4d
Richard Abethell, 12 weeks 6 days	21s 5d
Thomas Starke, 12 weeks 6 days	21s 5d
Richard Letman, 12 weeks 6 days	21s 5d

Thomas Laine, 12 weeks 6 days	21s 5d
Roger Awsten, 12 weeks 6 days	21s 5d
Richard Gayter, 12 weeks 6 days	21s 5d
Gregory Steward, 12 weeks 6 days	21s 5d
Robert Cowdall, 7 weeks 3 days	12s 4d
Andrew Streke, 12 weeks 6 days	21s 5d
John Yonge, 12 weeks 6 days	21s 5d
Thomas Drakes, 12 weeks 6 days	21s 5d
William Bateman, gromet, 12 weeks 6 days	16s 1d
John Appulton, boy, 12 weeks 6 days	10s 8½d
Thomas Morrys, 3 weeks 6 days	6s 5d
[*Gunners*]	
Thomas Dyxson, master gunner, 12 weeks 6 days	32s 2d
James Robartes, server, 12 weeks 6 days	21s 5d

[*Page total*] – £35 16s 9d.

[f. 69] *The Mary Rose*

Mariners	
William Hollande, master, 6 weeks 2 days	52s 5d
William Robinson, boatswain, 12 weeks 6 days	53s 7d
Christopher Davy, purser, 12 weeks 6 days	32s 2d
Roger Cratway, cook & steward, 12 weeks 6 days	29s 5½d
Peter Inglish, 4 weeks 2 days	7s 2d
John Yonge, 12 weeks 6 days	21s 5d
John Davy, 9 weeks 3 days	15s 8d
John Cosyn, 12 weeks 6 days	21s 5d
Robert Aungell, 12 weeks 6 days	21s 5d
John Baswell, 12 weeks 6 days	21s 5d
William Richard, boy, 6 weeks 2 days	5s 3d
John Bunche, carpenter, 12 weeks 6 days	53s 7d
John Pulter, server, 12 weeks 6 days	21s 5d
William Harber, gromet, 12 weeks 6 days	16s 1d
Humphrey Stevenson, 8 weeks 5 days	14s 6d
Rowland Derawe, 6 weeks 5 days	11s 2d
Edward Pynnar, boy, 6 weeks 5 days	5s 7d
Robert Spencer, 2 weeks	3s 4d
Gunner	
John Butler, master, 12 weeks 6 days	32s 2d

[*Page total*] – £21 19s 2½d.

[f. 69v] *The Great Bark*

Mariners	
Thomas Goldstone, boatswain, 12 weeks 6 days	53s 7d

Richard Connard, purser, 12 weeks 6 days	32s 2d
Thomas Gayttes, steward, 12 weeks 6 days	29s 5½d
John Newball, 12 weeks 6 days	21s 5d
William Richard, 6 weeks 3 days	[*blank*]
Richard Dyamound, 12 weeks 6 days	21s 5d
John Key, 6 weeks 3 days	[*blank*]
Mark Bullyn, 12 weeks 6 days	21s 5d
Robert Whight, 12 weeks 6 days	21s 5d
William Harrwoode, 12 weeks 6 days	21s 5d
Peter Trewe,12 weeks 6 days	21s 5d
William Brigges, 12 weeks 6 days	21s 5d
Thomas Tybball, 12 weeks 6 days	21s 5d
William Sharppe, 12 weeks 6 days	21s 5d
Edward Wickes, boy, 12 weeks 6 days	10s 8½d
William Welshe, carpenter, 12 weeks 6 days	53s 7d
Thomas Freman, gromet, 12 weeks 6 days	16s 1d
William Charttram, gromet, 12 weeks 6 days	16s 1d
Robert Keye, 4 weeks 6 days	8s 1d
Gunners	
Lawrence Mewis, master, 12 weeks 6 days	32s 2d
Miles Sparke, server, 12 weeks 6 days	21s 5d

[*Page total*] – £23 6s 1d.

[f. 70] *The Lion*

Mariners	
William Keys, boatswain, 12 weeks 6 days	53s 7d
John Butler, purser, 12 weeks 6 days	32s 2d
John Corle, steward, 12 weeks 6 days	29s 5½d
John Russell, 12 weeks 6 days	21s 5d
Christopher Chaundeller, 12 weeks 6 days	21s 5d
Richard Reade, 12 weeks 6 days	21s 5d
Davy Griffyn, 12 weeks 6 days	21s 5d
William Wilkins, 12 weeks 6 days	21s 5d
Leonard Barret, 12 weeks 6 days	21s 5d
John Kennet, boy, 12 weeks 6 days	10s 8½d
Richard Hamond, boy, 5 days	7½d
Nicholas Arney, 3 weeks 6 days	6s 5d
Griffin Davythe, 3 weeks 4 days	6s
Robert Todde, 1 week 6 days	3s 1d
Gunner	
Edward Tompson, master, 12 weeks 6 days	32s 2d

[*Page total*] – £15 2s 8½d.

[f. 70v] *The Philip and Mary*

Mariners

John Jonnes, boatswain, 12 weeks 6 days	53s 7d
John Pursell, purser, 12 weeks 6 days	32s 2d
John Geffrey, steward, 12 weeks 6 days	29s 5½d
Francis Williams, 12 weeks 6 days	21s 5d
Philip John, 3 weeks 3 days	[*blank*]
Gregory Wickes, 12 weeks 6 days	21s 5d
Seache [*Zach*] Swetteman, 12 weeks 6 days	21s 5d
Richard Neell, 12 weeks 6 days	21s 5d
Arthur Lyversuche, 12 weeks 6 days	21s 5d
Edward Collson, 12 weeks 6 days	21s 5d
Thomas Sharpplye, 12 weeks 6 days	21s 5d
Bartholomew Gates, gromet, 12 weeks 6 days	16s 1d
Richard West, 6 weeks 5 days	11s 2d
Gunner	
Matthew Sharppe, master, 12 weeks 6 days	32s 2d

[*Page total*] – £16 4s 6½d.

[f. 71] *The Christopher*

Mariners

William Rogers, master, 12 weeks 6 days	£4 5s 9d
Richard Pereman, boatswain, 12 weeks 6 days	53s 7d
Rowland Mocklow, purser, 12 weeks 6 days	32s 2d
John Blythe, steward, 12 weeks 6 days	29s 5½d
Walter Hewes, 4 weeks 2 days	7s 2d
Fabian Bullin, 12 weeks 6 days	21s 5d
Thomas Linge, 12 weeks 6 days	21s 5d
Robert Gosling, 12 weeks 6 days	21s 5d
William Romney, 12 weeks 6 days	21s 5d
Thomas James, 12 weeks 6 days	21s 5d
James Bull, 12 weeks 6 days	21s 5d
Roger Read, 12 weeks 6 days	21s 5d
Thomas Sybley, 2 weeks	3s 4d
John William, boy, 12 weeks 6 days	10s 8½d
John Jaxson, 7 weeks 2 days	12s 2d
John Bull, 12 weeks 6 days	21s 5d
Gunner	
Jobe Bushe, master, 12 weeks 6 days	32s 2d

[*Page total*] – £21 17s 10d.

[f. 71v] *The Jesus*

Mariners

Thomas Elye, boatswain, 12 weeks 6 days	53s 7d
John Croxton, purser, 12 weeks 6 days	32s 2d
Thomas Purden, steward, 12 weeks 6 days	29s 5½d
Robert Chopp, 4 weeks 3 days	[*blank*]
Edward Bray, 12 weeks 6 days	21s 5d
Richard Lavars, 3 weeks 3 days	[*blank*]
John Bull, 12 weeks 6 days	21s 5d
William John, 3 weeks 3 days	[*blank*]
John Bennet, 12 weeks 6 days	21s 5d
John Roo, 12 weeks 6 days	21s 5d
Thomas Baster, boy, 12 weeks 6 days	10s 8½d
Henry Shearwood, carpenter, 12 weeks 6 days	53s 7d
Godfrey Smyth, 12 weeks 6 days	21s 5d
William Stace, 9 weeks 6 days	16s 5d
Richard Smythe, 7 weeks 6 days	13s 1d
John Lardge, 7 weeks 6 days	13s 1d
William Hilles, 3 weeks 3 days	5s 8d
Gunners	
Giles Delanoy, master, 12 weeks 6 days	32s 2d
Walter Symond, 4 weeks 6 days	8s 1d

[*Page total*] – £18 15s 1d.

[f. 72] *The Hart*

Mariners

Henry Willoby, master, 3 weeks 3 days	22s 9d
Richard Browne, boatswain, 12 weeks 6 days	37s 6d
Thomas Wilkes, purser, 12 weeks 6 days	32s 2d
John Tompson, steward, 12 weeks 6 days	29s 5½d
John Kennet, 12 weeks 6 days	21s 5d
Thomas Northway, 12 weeks 6 days	21s 5d
John Mapp, 12 weeks 6 days	21s 5d
John Rothe, 12 weeks 6 days	21s 5d
William Martin, 12 weeks 6 days	21s 5d
John Twyman, 12 weeks 6 days	21s 5d
Tytcher Foster, boy, 12 weeks 6 days	10s 8½d
[*Gunners*]	
Robert Tompson, master gunner, 12 weeks 6 days	32s 2d
Francis John, 12 weeks 6 days	21s 5d

The Antelope

Mariners

Richard Wright, boatswain, 12 weeks 6 days	37s 6d
Thomas Austen, purser, 12 weeks 6 days	32s 2d
John Paulmer, steward, 12 weeks 6 days	29s 5½d
William Wilkins, 12 weeks 6 days	21s 5d
William Molle, 12 weeks 6 days	21s 5d
Richard Tratton, 12 weeks 6 days	21s 5d
George Lyell, 12 weeks 6 days	21s 5d
John Wakom, 12 weeks 6 days	21s 5d
William Collins, 12 weeks 6 days	21s 5d
Davy Short, gromet, 12 weeks 6 days	16s 1d
William Manyng, 11 weeks	18s 4d
[*Gunner*]	
Roger Bothe, master gunner, 12 weeks 6 days	32s 2d

[*Page total*] – £30 8s 10½d.

[f. 72v] *The Swallow*

Mariners

William Barnes, master, 12 weeks 6 days	£6 8s 6d
William Saunders, boatswain, 12 weeks 6 days	36s 6d
John Robartes, purser, 12 weeks 6 days	32s 2d
John Bore, steward, 12 weeks 6 days	29s 5½d
Walter Gymlyn, 12 weeks 6 days	21s 5d
Richard Fyshebill, 12 weeks 6 days	21s 5d
John Badder, 12 weeks 6 days	21s 5d
Matthew Fysher, 12 weeks 6 days	21s 5d
Robert Usher, boy, 12 weeks 6 days	10s 8½d
[*Gunner*]	
Jacob Myller, master gunner, 12 weeks 6 days	32s 2d

The Jennet

Richard Trew, boatswain, 12 weeks 6 days	37s 6d
Henry Cooke, purser, 12 weeks 6 days	32s 2d
John Adams, steward, 12 weeks 6 days	29s 5½d
John Phillippes, 12 weeks 6 days	21s 5d
Henry Stapull, 12 weeks 6 days	21s 5d
John Bucklar, 12 weeks 6 days	21s 5d
Elizander [*Alexander*] Golde, boy, 12 weeks 6 days	10s 8½d
Morgan Emyn, 9 weeks 4 days	16s
William Walker, gromet, 12 weeks 6 days	16s 1d
[*Gunner*]	
Richard Haynes, master gunner, 12 weeks 6 days	32s 2d

[*Page total*] – £29 14s 6d.

[f. 73] *The New Bark*

George Braunche, boatswain, 12 weeks 6 days	37s 6d
Richard Dennes, steward, 12 weeks 6 days	29s 5½d
Thomas Vaghan, 12 weeks 6 days	21s 5d
Richard Abraham, 12 weeks 6 days	21s 5d
William Bull, 12 weeks 6 days	21s 5d
Thomas Whittell, 12 weeks 6 days	21s 5d
Gabriel Kyrby, boy, 12 weeks 6 days	10s 8½d
[*Gunner*]	
John Phillippes, master gunner, 12 weeks 6 days	32s 2d

The Willoughby

Mariners

Robert Flynnt, boatswain, 12 weeks 6 days	37s 6d
Roger Davy, steward, 12 weeks 6 days	29s 5½d
Henry Raynsforthe, 12 weeks 6 days	21s 5d
William Warwicke, 12 weeks 6 days	21s 5d
George Browne, 12 weeks 6 days	21s 5d
John Tor, 12 weeks 6 days	21s 5d
Thomas Myddelton, boy, 12 weeks 6 days	10s 8½d
[*Gunner*]	
John Mallpas, master gunner, 12 weeks 6 days	32s 2d

[*Page total*] – £19 11s.

[f. 73v] *The Greyhound*

Mariners

Robert Harwood, boatswain, 12 weeks 6 days	37s 6d
Edmund Dawson, purser, 12 weeks 6 days	29s 5½d
Miles Sparke, 12 weeks 6 days	21s 5d
Thomas Harrington, 12 weeks 6 days	21s 5d
Thomas Jonnes, 12 weeks 6 days	21s 5d
Roger Browne, boy, 12 weeks 6 days	10s 8½d
Richard Tyller, 6 weeks 4 days	11s
[*Gunner*]	
John Bannkes, master gunner, 12 weeks 6 days	32s 2d

The Tiger

Mariners

John Aboen, boatswain, 12 weeks 6 days	37s 6d
John Hawkins, purser, 12 weeks 6 days	29s 5½d
John Bowye, 12 weeks 6 days	21s 5d
William Ward, 12 weeks 6 days	21s 5d
Thomas Butteller, 12 weeks 6 days	21s 5d
John Nycolas, 3 weeks 3 days	[*blank*]

John Newton, boy, 12 weeks 6 days	10s 8½d
John Arnold, gromet, 3 weeks 3 days	4s 4d
[*Gunner*]	
John More, master gunner, 12 weeks 6 days	32s 2d
The Bull	
Mariners	
Andrew Walker, boatswain, 12 weeks 6 days	37s 6d
John Willy, purser, 12 weeks 6 days	29s 5½d
Richard Gillet, 12 weeks	20s
William Loo, 5 weeks 3 days	[*blank*]
Richard Crannolde, 12 weeks 6 days	21s 5d
William Collyson, 12 weeks 6 days	21s 5d
Edward Thomas, boy, 8 weeks 5 days	7s 3d
[*Gunner*]	
Robert Buttler, master gunner, 12 weeks 6 days	32s 2d

[*Page total*] – £26 12s 8½d.

[f. 74] *The Falcon*	
Mariners	
Lawrence Cleare, boatswain, 12 weeks 6 days	37s 6d
George Haull, purser, 12 weeks 6 days	29s 5½d
John Hodge, 12 weeks 6 days	21s 5d
[*Gunner*]	
John Comynge, master gunner, 12 weeks 6 days	32s 2d
The Phoenix	
Mariners	
John Wynyard, boatswain, 12 weeks 6 days	37s 6d
Griffin Hewson, steward, 12 weeks 6 days	29s 5½d
Jenkyn Ryce, 12 weeks 6 days	21s 5d
[*Gunner*]	
John Harrys, master gunner, 12 weeks 6 days	32s 2d
The Bright Falcon	
Mariners	
Richard Blacke, boatswain, 12 weeks 6 days	37s 6d
Edward Tayller, 12 weeks 6 days	21s 5d
Richard Jonnes, 12 weeks 6 days	21s 5d
[*Gunner*]	
John Walker, master gunner, 12 weeks 6 days	32s 6d
The Sun	
Mariners	
Nicholas Starkey, boatswain, 12 weeks 6 days	37s 6d
Ralph Buckland, 12 weeks 6 days	21s 5d

[*Gunner*]	
William Ellis, master gunner, 12 weeks 6 days	32s 2d
[*Page total*] – £22 4s 8d.	
[f. 74v] *The Saker*	
Mariners	
John Burnam, boatswain, 12 weeks, 6 days	37s 6d
Thomas Thorney, steward, 12 weeks 6 days	29s 5½d
Thomas King, gromet, 10 weeks 4 days	13s 2d
[*Gunner*]	
John Hunt, master gunner, 12 weeks 6 days	32s 2d
The Bark of Boulogne	
Mariners	
John Lambe, boatswain, 12 weeks 6 days	37s 6d
Edward Coxe, steward, 12 weeks 6 days	29s 5½d
William Peache, 12 weeks 6 days	21s 5d
[*Gunner*]	
John Williams, master gunner, 12 weeks 6 days	32s 2d
The Hare	
Mariners	
John Aman, boatswain, 12 weeks 6 days	29s 5½d
Anthony Reade, gromet, 10 weeks 4 days	13s 2d
[*Gunner*]	
Nicholas Hardey, master gunner 12 weeks 6 days	32s 2d
The Double Rose	
Mariners	
John Hunt, 12 weeks 6 days	21s 5d
Richard Harman, 12 weeks 6 days	21s 5d
[*Page total*] – £17 10s 5½d.	
[f. 75] *The Galley Speedwell*	
Mariners	
Cuthbert Clarke, boatswain, 12 weeks 6 days	53s 7d
Anthony Darnatho, 12 weeks 6 days	21s 5d
Thomas Raynolde, 12 weeks 6 days	21s 5d
Thomas Foster, boy, 12 weeks 6 days	10s 8½d
[*Gunner*]	
Maurice Aboen, master gunner, 12 weeks 6 days	32s 2d
The Galley Tryright	
Mariners	
Simon Barnesley, boatswain, 12 weeks 6 days	37s 6d
John Godden, purser, 12 weeks 6 days	32s 2d
William Kent, steward, 12 weeks 6 days	29s 5½d

John King, 8 weeks 3 days	14s
[*Gunner*]	
John Farley, master gunner, 12 weeks 6 days	32s 2d
The Galley Mermaid	
Mariners	
William Prynce, 9 weeks	15s
Henry Fouller, 12 weeks 6 days	21s 5d
Henry Pendley, 12 weeks 6 days	21s 5d
John Davy, boatswain, 3 weeks 3 days	10s
The Mary Grace Hoy	
Mariner	
William Pearson, master, 12 weeks 6 days	53s 7d

[*Page total*] – £20 6s.

[f. 75v] Wages of gunners daily attendant in Her Highness's fort at Upnor for the safe-keeping of Her Grace's ships in Gillingham Water, begun the first day of January last and this day ended, as followeth:

Thomas Sergent, master, 90 days at 16d	£6
Anthony Phenrutter, 90 days at 12d	£4 10s
Richard Abesede, 80 days at 12d	£4
Prince Holmes, 90 days at 12d	£4 10s
Robert Woullgrove, 90 days at 12d	£4 10s
William Bowyll, 90 days at 12d	£4 10s
Randall Stevenson, 90 days at 12d	£4 10s
William Chisyllton, 90 days at 12d	£4 10s

*[*Clerk*]. To Thomas Heynes the last day of March for his wages daily attending and serving Her Highness for the keeping of the book of cheque of masters, mariners and gunners in keeping Her Highness's ships afloat in harbour, as also the prick book of shipwrights and caulkers, by one quarter of a year begun the first day of January last and ended as abovesaid – £5.

[*Page total*] – £42.

[f. 76] *[*Purveyor*]. To Butolph Moungey the last day of March for his wages and victuals daily attending and serving Her Highness in making of provisions of cables, cablets and ropes of all sorts, by one quarter of a year begun the first day of January and this day ended, at 8d *per diem* – £3.

To Thomas Baker the same day for his wages daily attending and serving Her Highness in delivering of cables, cablets, ropes of all sorts, canvas, twine, needles and divers other kinds of stuffs out of her storehouses there to the use of Her Grace's ships, by one quarter of a year begun and ended as abovesaid – £2.

[*Page total*] – £5.

[f. 76v] *Emptions*

Ironwork. To George Hoppe of Chatham, smith, the last day of March for price of 20 pounds weight of new iron by him wrought into bolts for the use of Her Grace's ships, at 2½d every pound weight – 4s 2d; more for 400 of 10d nail, price – 3s 4d; more for 300 of 6d nail, at 6d the 100 – 18d; and more to him for 300 of 4d nail – 12d. *Summa* – 10s

To John Startup of Gillingham, smith, the same day for price of 11 pounds weight of new iron by him wrought for the use of Her Grace's ships into bolts, rings and keys, at 2½d every pound weight – 2s 3½d; more for 100 of 6d nail – 6d; and more for 100 of 10d nail – 10d. *Summa* – 3s 7½d.

Inch board. To John Nebbe of Hollingbourne the same day for price of 1,600 foot of oaken inch board by him delivered for the use of Her Highness's ships there, at 4s every 100 foot. *Summa* – £3 4s.

To John Pendelltun the same day for price of 200 foot of inch board oak of him had and delivered for the use of Her Highness's ships there, at 5s every 100 foot. *Summa* – 10s.

*[*Artificers*]. To William Phedam, bricklayer, the same day for working about the tiling of Her Highness's victualling house there, by the space of 6 days at 10d the day – 5s; more to his man for like time, at 6d – 3s; more to Edmund Bell and George Warbuckell, sawyers, for sawing of certain timber for the use of the same, by the space of 2 days at 12d the man *per diem* – 4s; more to Thomas Morton, carpenter, for making of a new door – 2s; more to Thomas Long and William Mylls for price of 6 loads of bushes and stakes for the use of the hedges thereunto belonging – 14s;. and more to Christopher Collyer and Robert Colt for the mending and repairing of the same hedges; by agreement – 12s 6d. *Summa* – £2 0s 6d.

[*Page total*] – £6 8s 1½d.

[f. 77] *A boat.* To John Hurlocke, master, the last day of March for price of one small boat of him had and delivered to Thomas Sergeaunt for the use of Her Highness's fort at Upnor; price by agreement – £2.

Oakum. To John Butler, Lawrence Clear and 8 other persons of Gillingham, Chatham, Rochester and thereabouts the same day for the working and picking of 6 thousand 8 hundred 2 quarters weight [*7,672 lbs*] of Her Highness's old ropes and junks into oakum for the needful use of Her Grace's ships, at 3s 4d every hundredweight – £11 8s 1½d;[1] and more to Thomas Hunt for the like working and picking of 4 hundred 5 pounds weight [*453 lbs*] of oakum for the like use as aforesaid, at 3s 8d every hundredweight – 14s 9d.[2] *Summa* – £12 2s 10½d.

[1]The calculation gives 2739.9995d, which is 1½d above the sum stated (2737.5d).
[2]The calculation gives 177.96426d, which is about 1d above the sum stated (177d).

Netting-ropes. To Thomas Hunt, ropemaker, the same day for price of 18 coil of netting-ropes weighing 7 hundred 1 quarter 15 pounds [*weight*] [*827 lbs*], at 3s 8d every hundredweight – £1 7s 1d.

House rent. To Adam Keller of Chatham the same day for rent of a certain storehouse and ground thereunto belonging wherein lieth Her Grace's store of provisions, as cables, hawsers, ropes of all sorts, canvas, twine, needles and divers other kinds of stuffs, by one quarter of a year begun the first day of January last and this day ended as abovesaid – 10s.

To Thomas Wynnall the same day for the rent of a certain storehouse wherein lieth Her Highness's store of pitch, tar, oakum, rosin, and divers other things for the use of Her Grace's ships, by one quarter of a year begun and ended as aforesaid – 3s 4d.

[*Page total*] – £16 3s 3½d.

[f. 77v] To Richard Mylles of Chatham the same day for rent of a certain storehouse wherein lieth Her Highness's reed for the breaming of Her Grace's ships at their groundings, by one quarter of a year begun the first day of January last and this day ended – 1s 3d.

Water carriage of provisions. To Richard Barker, master, the last day of March for service of his hoy named the *John of Myllale* [Millhall] in carrying of divers kinds of stuffs, as pitch, tar, shovels, scoops, bowls, spikes, overlop nails, baskets, thrums, twine, sail needles, cloveboards, pulleys, rosin, pump-hoses, clench nails, roves, timber, plank, quarters and divers other things from London to Gillingham, and there delivered the same for the use of Her Grace's ships; by agreement – £1 10s.

[*Page total*] – £1 11s 3d.

[f. 78] A payment made the last day of June as well to masters, mariners, gunners and others daily attending and serving Her Highness in safe-keeping of Her Grace's ships afloat in harbour, and to divers persons for rent of storehouses wherein lieth Her Highness's store for the use of Her Grace's ships, as to shipwrights and caulkers for repairing and mending of Her Majesty's said ships, and provisions for the same; begun the first day of April last and this day ended, as followeth:

The Elizabeth Jonas

Mariners

William Woode, master, 13 weeks	£6 10s
John Teygge, boatswain, 13 weeks	54s 2d
Lancelot Trystram, purser, 13 weeks	45s 6d
Thomas Waller, steward, 13 weeks	29s 9½d
John Collyns, 13 weeks	21s 8d
Peter Padden, 13 weeks	21s 8d

Richard Brishold, 13 weeks	21s 8d
Edward Brenden, 13 weeks	21s 8d
Edmund Joyll, 13 weeks	21s 8d
William Kyshan, 13 weeks	21s 8d
Patrick Morow, 7 weeks 2 days	12s 2d
Henry Baker, 13 weeks	21s 8d
Robert Browne, 13 weeks	21s 8d
Robert Healling, gromet, 13 weeks	16s 3d
Robert Chamber, boy, 7 weeks 1 day	5s 11½d
Henry Morris, gromet, 13 weeks	16s 3d
Nicholas Johnson, carpenter, 10 weeks 5 days	44s 7d
John Hichecock, server, 10 weeks 5 days	17s 10d

[*Page total*] – £27 5s 10d.

[f. 78v] Isaac Asheley, 10 weeks 5 days	17s 10d
Thomas Johnson, boy, 10 weeks 5 days	8s 11d
William Andros, boy, 8 weeks 5 days	7s 3d
John Pyrton, 5 weeks 6 days	9s 9d
Robert Cooke, 5 weeks	8s 4d
Henry Wood, 4 weeks 2 days	7s 2d
[*Gunners*]	
Lawrence Dilk, master gunner, 13 weeks	32s 6d
Richard Elles, server, 13 weeks	21s 8d

The Hope

Mariners

John Hurlocke, master, 13 weeks	£6 10s
Robert West, boatswain, 13 weeks	54s 2d
Michael Gonson, purser, 13 weeks	32s 6d
John Mathew, steward, 13 weeks	29s 9½d
Thomas Starke, 13 weeks	21s 8d
Richard Abethell, 13 weeks	21s 8d
Richard Letman, 13 weeks	21s 8d
Thomas Lane, 13 weeks	21s 8d
Roger Austen, 13 weeks	21s 8d
Richard Gayter, 13 weeks	21s 8d
Gregory Steward, 13 weeks	21s 8d
Andrew Streke, 13 weeks	21s 8d
John Yonge, 5 weeks	8s 4d
Thomas Draykes, 13 weeks	21s 8d
Thomas Morrys, 13 weeks	21s 8d
William Bateman, gromet, 13 weeks	16s 3d
John Appulton, boy, 13 weeks	10s 10d

Andrew Bren, 13 weeks	21s 8d
Gunners	
Thomas Dickson, master, 13 weeks	32s 6d
James Robartes, 13 weeks	21s 8d

[*Page total*] – £34 7s 9½d.

[f. 79] *The Mary Rose*

Mariners	
William Robinson, boatswain, 13 weeks	44s 2d
Christopher Davy, purser, 13 weeks	32s 6d
Roger Cratway, steward, 13 weeks	29s 9½d
Robert Spencer, 13 weeks	21s 8d
John Younge, 13 weeks	21s 8d
John Baswell, 13 weeks	21s 8d
John Cossyn, 13 weeks	21s 8d
Robert Angell, 13 weeks	21s 8d
Humphrey Stevinson, 13 weeks	21s 8d
Rowland Derawe, 13 weeks	21s 8d
Edward Laughan, boy, 13 weeks	10s 10d
John Bunch, carpenter, 10 weeks 5 days	44s 7d
John Pulter, server, 10 weeks 5 days	17s 10d
William Harber, gromet, 10 weeks 5 days	13s 4d
Thomas Leonarde, gromet, 10 weeks 5 days	13s 4d
Gunner	
John Buttler, master, 13 weeks	32s 6d

[*Page total*] – £20 0s 6½d.

[f. 79v] *The Great Bark*

Mariners	
Thomas Goldestone, boatswain, 13 weeks	54s 2d
Richard Conard, purser, 13 weeks	32s 6d
Thomas Gayttes, steward, 13 weeks	29s 9½d
John Newball, 13 weeks	21s 8d
Richard Dyamounde, 13 weeks	21s 8d
Mark Bullyn, 13 weeks	21s 8d
Robert White, 13 weeks	21s 8d
William Harwood, 13 weeks	21s 8d
Peter Trewe, 13 weeks	21s 8d
William Brigges, 13 weeks	21s 8d
Thomas Tybball, 13 weeks	21s 8d
William Sharpe, 13 weeks	21s 8d
John Kennet, 2 weeks 4 days	4s 4d
Robert Key, 13 weeks	21s 8d

Edward Wickes, boy, 13 weeks	10s 10d
William Welshe, carpenter, 10 weeks 5 days	44s 7d
Thomas Freman, gromet, 10 weeks 5 days	13s 4d
William Chartram, gromet, 10 weeks 5 days	13s 4d
Thomas Phillippes, 6 weeks	10s
Thomas Ratley, gromet, 9 weeks 6 days	12s 3d
Peter Cade, 3 weeks 2 days	5s 6d
Gunners	
Lawrence Mewis, master, 13 weeks	32s 6d
Miles Robenson, 13 weeks	21s 8d

[*Page total*] – £25 1s 5½d.

[f. 80] *The Lion*

William Keys, boatswain, 13 weeks	54s 2d
John Butteler, purser, 13 weeks	32s 6d
John Corle, steward, 13 weeks	29s 9½d
John Russell, 13 weeks	21s 8d
Christopher Chaundeler, 13 weeks	21s 8d
Richard Reade, 13 weeks	21s 8d
Davy Gryffyn, 13 weeks	21s 8d
William Wilkins, 13 weeks	21s 8d
Leonard Barret, 4 weeks	6s 8d
Nicholas Arney, 13 weeks	21s 8d
Gryffyth Davyth, 13 weeks	21s 8d
Robert Tode, 2 weeks 4 days	4s 4d
Thomas Tayllor, gromet, 13 weeks	16s 3d
William Gryffyn, 6 weeks 4 days	11s
Cornelius Brayan, 5 weeks 6 days	9s 9d
Jarvis Hutton, 4 weeks 2 days	7s 2d
Gunner	
Edward Tompson, master, 13 weeks	32s 6d

[*Page total*] – £17 15s 9½d.

[f. 80v] *The Philip and Mary*

Mariners	
John Jonnes, boatswain, 13 weeks	54s 2d
John Pursell, purser, 13 weeks	32s 6d
John Jeffray, steward, 13 weeks	29s 9½d
Francis Williams, 13 weeks	21s 8d
Gregory Wickes, 13 weeks	21s 8d
Seache Sweteman, 13 weeks	21s 8d
Richard Neel, 13 weeks	21s 8d
Arthur Lyversuch, 13 weeks	21s 8d

Thomas Sharpley, 13 weeks	21s 8d
Edward Colloson, 13 weeks	21s 8d
Richard West, 13 weeks	21s 8d
Bartholomew Gattes, gromet, 13 weeks	16s 3d
Thomas Barbar, 13 weeks	21s 8d
Gunner	
Matthew Sharppe, master, 13 weeks	32s 6d

[*Page total*] – £18 0s 2½d.

[f. 81] *The Christopher*

Mariners	
William Rogers, master, 13 weeks	£4 6s 8d
Richard Pereman, boatswain, 13 weeks	54s 2d
Rowland Mocklow, purser, 13 weeks	32s 6d
John Blythe, steward, 13 weeks	29s 9½d
Francis Bullyn, 13 weeks	21s 8d
Thomas Linge, 13 weeks	21s 8d
Robert Gosling, 13 weeks	21s 8d
William Romney, 13 weeks	21s 8d
Thomas James, 13 weeks	21s 8d
James Bull, 13 weeks	21s 8d
John Bull, 8 weeks 5 days	14s 6d
Roger Read, 13 weeks	21s 8d
John Jaxson, gromet, 13 weeks	16s 3d
Thomas Sybley, [*blank*]	[*blank*]
John Willyam, boy, 13 weeks	10s 10d
John Waderef, 4 weeks 1 day	6s 11d
Gunner	
Jobe Bushe, master, 13 weeks	32s 6d

[*Page total*] – £21 15s 9½d.

[f. 81v] *The Jesus*

Mariners	
Thomas Elye, boatswain, 13 weeks	54s 2d
John Croxston, purser, 13 weeks	32s 6d
Thomas Purden, steward, 13 weeks	29s 9½d
Edward Bray, 13 weeks	21s 8d
John Bull, 13 weeks	21s 8d
John Bennet, 13 weeks	21s 8d
John Roo, 13 weeks	21s 8d
John Lardge, 13 weeks	21s 8d
William Stacey, 13 weeks	21s 8d
Walter Symond, 13 weeks	21s 8d

Henry Shearewood, carpenter, 10 weeks 5 days	47s 7d
Godfrey Smyth, server, 10 weeks 5 days	17s 10d
Thomas Baster, boy, 13 weeks	10s 10d
George Vallet, boy, [*blank*]	[*blank*]
Robert Willis, 9 weeks 6 days	16s 5d
Gunner	
Giles Delanoy, master, 13 weeks	32s 6d

[*Page total*] – £19 10s 3½d.

[f. 82] *The Hart*

Mariners	
Henry Willobye, master, 13 weeks	£4 6s 8d
Richard Browne, boatswain, 13 weeks	37s 11d
Thomas Wilkes, purser, 13 weeks	32s 6d
John Tompson, steward, 13 weeks	29s 9½d
Thomas Northway, 13 weeks	21s 8d
Francis John, 7 weeks 3 days	12s 4d
John Mapp, 13 weeks	21s 8d
John Roche, 13 weeks	21s 8d
William Martyn, 13 weeks	21s 8d
John Twynnam, 13 weeks	21s 8d
Tyther Foster, boy, 13 weeks	10s 10d
Anthony Adderton, gromet, 5 weeks 4 days	6s 11d
[*Gunner*]	
Robert Tompson, master gunner, 13 weeks	32s 6d

The Antelope

Mariners	
Richard Wright, boatswain, 13 weeks	37s 11d
Thomas Awsten, purser, 13 weeks	32s 6d
John Pallmer, steward, 13 weeks	29s 9½d
William Wilkinson, 13 weeks	21s 8d
William Moyll, 13 weeks	21s 8d
Richard Tratton, 13 weeks	21s 8d
George Lyell, 13 weeks	21s 8d
John Wakom, 13 weeks	21s 8d
William Collens, 13 weeks	21s 8d
Davy Short, gromet, 13 weeks	16s 3d
William Mannynge, 13 weeks	21s 8d
[*Gunner*]	
Roger Both, master gunner, 13 weeks,	32s 6d

[*Page total*] – £32 18s 5d.

[f. 82v] *The Swallow*

Mariners

William Barnes, master, 13 weeks	£6 10s
William Saunders, boatswain, 13 weeks	37s 11d
John Robartes, purser, 13 weeks	32s 6d
John Bore, steward, 13 weeks	29s 9½d
Richard Fyshebell, 13 weeks	21s 8d
John Badder, 13 weeks	21s 8d
Matthew Fysher, 13 weeks	21s 8d
Robert Ussher, boy, 13 weeks	10s 10d
Walter Gymlyn, 13 weeks	21s 8d
[*Gunner*]	
Jacob Myller, master gunner, 13 weeks	32s 6d

The Jennet

Mariners

Richard Trewe, boatswain,13 weeks	37s 11d
Henry Cooke, purser, 13 weeks	32s 6d
John Adams, steward, 13 weeks	29s 9½d
John Phillippes, 13 weeks	21s 8d
John Buckler, 13 weeks	21s 8d
Henry Stapull, 13 weeks	21s 8d
Morgan Emen, 4 weeks 3 days	7s 4d
William Walker, gromet, 13 weeks	16s 3d
Alexander Golde, boy, 13 weeks	10s 10d
William Sampson, 10 weeks 2 days	17s 2d
[*Gunner*]	
Richard Haynes, master gunner, 13 weeks,	32s 6d

[*Page total*] – £30 9s 6d.

[f. 83] *The New Bark*

Mariners

George Braunche, boatswain, 13 weeks	37s 11d
Richard Dennes, steward, 13 weeks	29s 9½d
Thomas Vaughan, 13 weeks	21s 8d
Richard Abraham, 13 weeks	21s 8d
William Bull, 13 weeks	21s 8d
Thomas Whitell, 13 weeks	21s 8d
Gabriel Kirbye, boy, 13 weeks	10s 10d
[*Gunner*]	
John Phillippes, master gunner, 13 weeks	32s 6d

The Willoughby

Mariners

Robert Flinte, boatswain, 13 weeks	37s 11d

John Davy, steward, 13 weeks	29s 9½d
Henry Rainsforthe, 13 weeks	21s 8d
William Warwicke, 13 weeks	21s 8d
George Browne, 13 weeks	21s 8d
John Turner, 13 weeks	21s 8d
Thomas Mydellton, boy, 13 weeks	10s 10d
[*Gunner*]	
John Malpas, master gunner, 13 weeks	32s 6d
The Greyhound	
Mariners	
Robert Harwood, boatswain, 13 weeks	37s 11d
Edmund Dawson, steward, 13 weeks	29s 9½d
Miles Sparke, 13 weeks	21s 8d
Thomas Harrington, 13 weeks	21s 8d
Thomas Jonnes, 13 weeks	21s 8d
Richard Tyller, 13 weeks	21s 8d
Roger Browne, boy, 13 weeks	10s 10d
[*Gunner*]	
John Bankes, master gunner, 13 weeks	32s 6d

[*Page total*] – £29 13s 1½d.

[f. 83v] *The Tiger*	
Mariners	
John Abowen, boatswain, 13 weeks	37s 11d
John Hawkins, steward, 13 weeks	29s 9½d
John Bowe, 13 weeks	21s 8d
William Warde, 13 weeks	21s 8d
Thomas Buttler, 13 weeks	21s 8d
John Newton, boy, 13 weeks	10s 10d
John Arnolde, gromet, 10 weeks	13s 9d
[*Gunner*]	
John Morowe, master gunner, 13 weeks	32s 6d
The Bull	
Mariners	
Andrew Walker, boatswain, 13 weeks	37s 11d
John Willy, steward, 13 weeks	29s 9½d
Richard Crannolde, 13 weeks	21s 8d
William Collyson, 13 weeks	21s 8d
Edward Thomas, boy, 13 weeks	10s 10d
William Hilles, 8 weeks 5 days	14s 6d
Henry Harryson, 4 weeks 2 days	7s 2d
[*Gunner*]	
Robert Butler, master gunner, 13 weeks	32s 6d

The Falcon	
Mariners	
Lawrence Cleare, boatswain, 13 weeks	37s 11d
George Haull, steward, 13 weeks	29s 9½d
Richard Langley, boy, 4 weeks 2 days	3s 7d
John Hodge, 13 weeks	21s 8d
[*Gunner*]	
John Commen, master gunner, 13 weeks	32s 6d

[*Page total*] – £24 11s 3½d.

[f. 84] *The Phoenix*	
Mariners	
John Winyard, boatswain, 13 weeks	37s 11d
Griffin Hewson, steward, 13 weeks	29s 9½d
Thomas Howlton, gromet, 13 weeks	16s 3d
[*Gunner*]	
John Harrys, master gunner, 13 weeks	32s 6d
The Bright Falcon	
Mariners	
Robert Blaike, boatswain, 13 weeks	37s 11d
Edward Tayllor, 13 weeks	21s 8d
Richard Jonnes, 13 weeks	21s 8d
[*Gunner*]	
John Walker, master gunner, 13 weeks	32s 6d
The Sun	
Mariners	
Nicholas Starke, boatswain, 13 weeks	37s 11d
Ralph Bucklond, 13 weeks	21s 8d
[*Gunner*]	
William Elles, master gunner, 13 weeks	32s 6d
The Saker	
Mariners	
John Burnham, boatswain, 13 weeks	37s 11d
Thomas Thorney, steward, 13 weeks	29s 9½d
Thomas Kinge, gromet, 13 weeks	16s 3d
[*Gunner*]	
John Hunt, master gunner, 13 weeks	32s 6d

[*Page total*] – £21 18s 9d.

[f. 84v] *The Bark of Boulogne*	
Mariners	
Richard Lamb, boatswain, 13 weeks,	37s 11d
Edward Cox, steward, 13 weeks,	29s 9½d

William Peache, 13 weeks,	21s 8d
[Gunner]	
John Williams, master gunner, 13 weeks	32s 6d
The Hare	
Mariners	
John Aman, boatswain, 13 weeks	29s 9½d
Richard Woodman, gromet, 13 weeks	16s 3d
[Gunner]	
Nicholas Hardye, master gunner, 13 weeks	32s 6d
The Double Rose	
Mariners	
John Hunt, 13 weeks	21s 8d
Richard Harman, 13 weeks	21s 8d
The Galley Speedwell	
Mariners	
Cuthbert Clarke, boatswain, 13 weeks	54s 2d
Anthony Darnatho, 13 weeks	21s 8d
Thomas Raynold, 13 weeks	21s 8d
Thomas Foster, boy, 13 weeks	10s 10d
William Prince, 13 weeks	21s 8d
[Gunner]	
Morris Abowen, master gunner, 13 weeks	32s 6d

[*Page total*] – £20 6s 3d.

[f. 85] *The Galley Tryright*	
Mariners	
Simon Barnesley boatswain, 13 weeks	37s 11d
John Godden, purser, 13 weeks	32s 6d
William Kent, steward, 13 weeks	29s 9½d
John Kinge, 13 weeks	21s 8d
John Warryn, 13 weeks	21s 8d
[Gunner]	
John Farley, master gunner, 13 weeks	32s 6d
The Galley Mermaid	
Mariners	
John Davy, boatswain, 13 weeks	37s 11d
Henry Pendley, 13 weeks	21s 8d
Henry Fuller, 13 weeks	21s 8d
Sylvester Bewell, 13 weeks	21s 8d
The Mary Grace Hoy	
Mariner	
William Poarson, master, 13 weeks	54s 2d

[*Page total*] – £16 13s 1½d.

[f. 85v] Wages of gunners daily attending in Her Highness's fort at Upnor for the safe-keeping of Her Grace's ships in Gillingham Water, begun the first day of April last and this day ended, as followeth:

Thomas Sergent, master, 91 days at 16d	£6 1s 4d
Anthony Venrutter, 91 days at 12d	£4 11s
Richard Abecede, 91 days at 12d	£4 11s
Prince Holmes, 91 days at 12d	£4 11s
Robert Woulgrave, 91 days at 12d	£4 11s
William Bowyll, 91 days at 12d	£4 11s
William Chisellton, 91 days at 12d	£4 11s
Randall Stevinson, 91 days at 12d	£4 11s
	[£37 18s 4d*]

*[*Purveyor*]. To Butolph Moungey the last day of June for his wages and victuals daily attending and serving Her Highness in making of provision for Her Grace's ships, *viz.* as cables, ropes and other cordage, [*by one quarter of a year*] begun the first day of April and this day ended as aforesaid, at 8d *per diem* – £3 0s 8d.

*[*Clerk*]. To Thomas Heynes the same day for his wages daily attending and serving Her Highness in keeping of the book of cheque of masters, mariners, gunners and others keeping of Her Grace's ships afloat in harbour, as also of the prick book of shipwrights and caulkers, by one quarter of a year begun and ended as abovesaid – £5.

*[*Purveyor*]. To Thomas Baker the same day for his wages daily serving Her Highness in delivering of cables, cablets, ropes of all sorts, canvas, twine, needles and divers other kinds of stuffs out of the storehouses there to the use of Her Grace's ships, by the space of one quarter of a year begun and ended as abovesaid – £2.

[*Page total*] – £47 19s.

[f. 86] *Shipwrights*

Nicholas Johnson, 22½ days and tides at 10d	18s 9d
John Hichecocke, 22½ days and tides at 4d	7s 6d
Isaac Ashelley, 22½ days and tides at 5d	9s 6½d
Thomas Johnson, 22½ days and tides at 2d	3s 9d
John Bunche, 22½ days and tides at 8d	15s
John Pulter, server, 22½ days and tides at 5d	9s 4½d
William Harber, 22½ days and tides at 4d	7s 6d
William Welshe, 22½ days and tides at 8d	15s
Thomas Freman, server, 22½ days and tides at 4d	7s 6d
William Chartram, server, 22½ days and tides at 3d	5s 7½d
Henry Shearwood, 22½ days and tides at 7d	13s 1½d

Godfrey Smyth, server, 22½ days and tides at 6d	11s 3d
Thomas Purden, 20 days and tides at 2d	3s 4d
William Mannynge, 21 days and tides at 3d	5s 3d
Thomas Willson, 18 days at 12d	18s
George Mathew, 18 days at 6d	9s
Henry Rowse, 18 days at 4d	6s
William Phedam, 11 days at 10d	9s 2d
Robert Mytchell, 8 days at 7d	4s 8d
Edmund Bell, 3 days at 12d	3s
George Warbuckell, 3 days at 12d	3s
Thomas Mortone, 1 day at 12d	12d
William Phedam, 8 days at 10d	6s 8d

[*Page total*] – £9 13s.

[f. 86v] *Caulkers*

Thomas Boltun, master, 24½ days and tides at 10d	20s 5d
William Bolton, server, 24½ days and tides at 6d	12s 3d
Walter Cley, 24½ days at tides at 6d	12s 3d
Roger Redye, 24½ day and tides at 5d	10s 2½d
Thomas Clarke, 19 days and tides at 6d	9s 6d
John Mullet, 19 days and tides at 6d	9s 6d
John White, 10 days and tides at 6d	5s
George Harryson, 24½ days and tides at 7d	14s 3½d
Leonard Cowper, 24½ days and tides at 6d	12s 3d
Richard Cowler, 24½ days and tides at 6d	12s 3d
Roger Browne, 24½ days and tides at 6d	12s 3d
John Stockdaill, 24½ days and tides at 6d	12s 3d
John Haywood, 24½ days and tides at 6d	12s 3d
Richard Clappam, 24½ days and tides at 6d	12s 3d
John Clarke, 23½ days at tides at 6d	11s 9d
Rowland Martyn, 23½ days and tides at 6d	11s 9d
William Eleson, 23½ days and tides at 6d	11s 9d
Samuel Clarke, server, 23½ days and tides at 2d	3s 11d
William Bastian, 23½ days and tides at 6d	11s 9d
John Estewood, 23½ days and tides at 6d	11s 9d
Roger Collins, 23½ days and tides at 6d	11s 9d
Gregory Aldrige, 20 days and tides at 7d	11s 8d.
	[£12 13s*]

Victualling. To Thomas Willson the last day of June for the victualling of 39 shipwrights, caulkers and others working upon the repairing, mending ransacking and caulking of Her Highness's ships there, by the space of 627 days among them all, Sundays and holy days in the same accounted, which maketh 89 weeks 4 days, begun the 29th day of April last and ended the 16th day of May next, at 4s 1d every week the man. *Summa* – £18 5s 4d.

[*Page total*] – £30 18s 4d.

[f. 87] *Lodging*. To mother Evye, Margaret Smyth and Alice Hills of Chatham the last day of June for the lodging of 39 of the aforesaid shipwrights and caulkers in 20 featherbeds by 92 weeks begun the 29th day of April last and ended the 16th day of May next, at 2d every week the man – 15s 4d.

Emptions

House rent. To Adam Keler of Chatham the last day of June for one quarter of a year's rent for a certain storehouse and ground of him hired wherein lieth Her Grace's store, as cables, cablets, hawsers and ropes of all sorts, as also twine, needles and pump-hoses for the use of Her Highness's ships, begun the first day of April last and ended as abovesaid – 10s.

To Thomas Winnall the same day for rent of a certain storehouse and ground thereunto belonging wherein lieth Her Grace's store, as pitch, tar, rosin, oakum, sails, and divers other needful things for the use of Her Highness's ships, by one quarter of a year begun and ended as aforesaid – 3s 4d.

To Richard Mylls of Chatham the same day for the rent of a certain storehouse of him hired wherein lieth Her Grace's store of reed for the breaming of Her Highness's ships at their groundings, by one quarter of a year begun and ended as abovesaid – 1s 3d.

[*Page total*] – £1 9s 11d.

[f. 87v] *Burning reed*. To Richard Myllеs of New Hythe the last day of June for price of 1,500 of reed of him had and by him delivered at Chatham for the use of Her Highness's ships, at 13s 4d every 1,000 – 20s; more to him for the hire of a lighter and three men to bring down the said reed from New Hythe to Chatham – 5s. *Summa* – £1 5s.

To Robert Gayttes of Burham Court the same day for price of 2,900 of burning reed by him delivered for the use of Her Grace's ships, at 13s 4d every 1,000 – £1 18s 8d.

To William Hamond of Snodland the same day for price of 1,500 of burning reed by him delivered for the needful breaming of Her Grace's ships at their groundings, at 13s 4d every 1,000 – £1.

To John Fenner and Richard Fenner of New Hythe the same day for the price of 1,850 of burning reed by them delivered for the use aforesaid, at 13s 4d every 1,000 – 24s 8d. *Summa* – £1 4s 8d.

Mapstaves and breaming staves. To Thomas Tyrre of Gillingham the same day for price of one load of mapstaves and breaming staves for the needful use of Her Grace's ships – 3s.

Billet. To William Larkyn of Chatham the same day for price of 2,500 of billet by him delivered for the heating of rosin and pitch for the use of Her Highness's ships at their groundings, at 9s every 1,000 of billet. *Summa* – £1 2s 6d.

[*Page total*] – £6 13s 10d.

[f. 88] *Plank oak, inch board and featheredge board.* To Thomas Smyth of Deptford the last day of June for price of 493 foot of 4-inch plank oak of him had and delivered at Chatham, for the use of Her Highness's ships, at 12s every 100 [*foot*] – £2 19s 3d; and more to him for 16½ loads of timber oak, at 13s 4d every load after 50 foot to the load – £11. *Summa* – £13 19s 3d.

To Thomas Tayllor the same day for price of 800 foot of inch board oak by him delivered for the use of Her Grace's ships, at 5s every 100 foot – 40s; and more to him for price of 1,201 foot of featheredge board, at 3s every 100 [*foot*] – 36s. *Summa* – £3 16s.

To John Francklyn the same day for price of 1,538 foot of inch board oak of him had and by him delivered for the use of Her Grace's ships, at 5s every 100 foot – £3 16s 8d; and more to him for price of 1,048 foot of featheredge board for use as aforesaid, at 4s every 100 foot – 40s 6d. [*Summa*] – £5 17s 2d.

Ironwork. To George Hoppe of Chatham, smith, the same day for price of 3 hundred 2 quarters 21 pounds weight [*413 lbs*] of his own new iron by him made and wrought into bolts, rings, keys, clench, roves, grommets and staples for the use of Her Highness's ships, at 23s 4d every hundredweight – £4 6s;[1] more for the working of one hundredweight of Her Grace's old iron, at 9s 4d the hundredweight – 9s 4d; more to him for 2,350 of 20d nail, at 20d every 100 – 39s 2d; more for 500 of 3d nail – 15d; more for 300 of 2s nail – 6s; more for 100 of 10d nail – 10d; more for a lock, price – 2s. *Summa* – £7 4s 7d.

Brick. To Thomas Gayton of Snodland[2] the same day for price of 2,700 of brick had of him for the repairing and mending of Her Highness's furnaces and backs in Her Highness's ships, at 9s every 1,000. *Summa* – £1 4s 4d.

[*Page total*] – £32 1s 4d.

[1]The calculation gives 1032.5d, which is ½d above the sum stated (1032d).

[2]MS 'South Land'. Not an authentic variant (the first element neither related to nor commonly corrupted to 'south') but a transcription error, surprising because the place had been given correctly on the preceding verso. Cf. also below, p. 346, and Wallenberg, *Place-Names of Kent*, p. 150.

[f. 88v] *Ironwork.* To John Startupp of Gillingham, smith, the same day for price of 2 hundred 6½ pounds [*weight*] [*230½ lbs*] of new iron by him made and wrought into bolts, rings, keys, hinges for ports, shackles, links for chains and divers other things for the use of Her Highness's ships, at 23s 4d every hundredweight – 47s 6¼d;[1] more for 20 pounds weight of iron by him wrought as aforesaid, at 1d the pound – 20d; more for 100 of 6d nail – 6d; more for 100 of 10d nails, price – 10d; more for 200 of 20d nail, at 20d the 100 – 3s 4d; and more to him for 200 of small roves and clench, at 2s every 100 – 4s. *Summa* – £2 17s 10d.

Water carriage of provisions. To Thomas Allyn, master of a hoy called the *Martyn of Maidston* the same day for service of his hoy in carrying of 3 thousandweight of rosin, one hundredweight of thrums, 4 dozen of shovels, 2 dozen of scoops, 4 dozen of bowls, 5 dozen and 10 pulleys, 2 dozen of ships' parrels, 12 sheets of lead, one tun of oil, 3 last of pitch, one last of tar, one dozen of baskets, 3 hundredweight of carvel spikes and overlop nails, as also 64 lings, 22 cheeses, 2 firkins of butter, 2 pounds of candles and 2 tuns of beer, with divers other kinds of stuffs sent from Her Highness's storehouse at Deptford to Gillingham and there delivered the same for the use of Her Grace's ships there; by agreement – 13s 4d.

Oakum. To William Browne, Roger Cratway, William Walker, John Newball, Richard Browne and eight other persons of Gillingham, Chatham, Rochester and thereabouts for the working and picking of 71 hundred 3 quarters 22 pounds weight of Her Highness's old ropes and junks into oakum for the needful caulking of Her Grace's ships, at 3s 4d every hundredweight working – £11 19s 9½d.

[*Page total*] – £15 10s 11½d.

[f. 89] A payment made the last day of September as well to masters, mariners and gunners serving Her Highness in keeping of Her Grace's ships afloat there, as also to shipwrights, caulkers, sawyers, house-carpenters and others working upon the mending, repairing and caulking of Her Highness's said ships there, with provisions had of divers persons towards the same, for one whole quarter of a year begun the first day of July last and this day ended, as followeth:

The Elizabeth Jonas

Mariners

William Wood, master, 13 weeks 1 day	£6 11s 5d
John Teygge, boatswain, 13 weeks 1 day	54s 9d
Lancelot Tristram, purser, 13 weeks 1 day	46s

[1]The calculation gives 576.25d, which is 6d above the sum stated (570.25d).

Thomas Waller, cook and steward, 13 weeks 1 day 30s 1½d
John Collins, 13 weeks 1 day 21s 11d
Peter Padden, 13 weeks 1 day 21s 11d
Richard Brisholde, 13 weeks 1 day 21s 11d
Edward Branden, 13 weeks 1 day 21s 11d
Edmund Joyell, 13 weeks 1 day 21s 11d
William Kisshan, 13 weeks 1 day 21s 11d
Henry Baker, 13 weeks 1 day 21s 11d
John Pyrton, 13 weeks 1 day 21s 11d
Robert Cooke, 13 weeks 1 day 21s 11d
Henry Wood, 13 weeks 1 day 21s 11d
William Martyn, 13 weeks 1 day 21s 11d
Robert Hellinge, gromet, 13 weeks 1 day 16s 5d
Henry Morris, gromet, 13 weeks 1 day 16s 5d
William Andros, boy, 13 weeks 1 day 10s 11½d
Nicholas Johnson, carpenter, 11 weeks 5 days 48s 9d

[*Page total*] – £29 2s 7d.

[f. 89v] John Hichecok, server, 11 weeks 5 days 19s 6d
Isaac Asheley, 9 weeks 3 days 15s 9d
Thomas Johnson, boy, 11 weeks 5 days 9s 9d
John Burnet, gromet, 13 weeks 1 day 16s 5d
Peter Cade, 1 week 20d
Thomas Baker, 2 weeks 6 days 4s 9d
William Parris, 2 weeks 6 days 4s 9d
John Reade, 2 weeks 6 days 4s 9d
John Barnarde, 2 days 6d

[*Gunners*]

Lawrence Dilke, master gunner, 13 weeks 1 day 32s 10d
Richard Ellis, gunner 11 weeks 18s 4d

The Hope

Mariners

John Hurlocke, master, 8 weeks £4
Robert West, boatswain, 8 weeks 33s 4d
Michael Gonson, purser, 8 weeks 20s
John Mathew, steward, 8 weeks 18s 4d
Thomas Starkey, 8 weeks 13s 4d
Richard Abethell, 8 weeks 13s 4d
James Robarttes, 8 weeks 13s 4d
Roger Austen, 8 weeks 13s 4d
Richard Gaiter, 5 weeks 1 day 8s 7d
Gregory Steward, 8 weeks 13s 4d

Andrew Streke, 8 weeks	13s 4d
John Younge, 5 weeks 1 day	8s 7d
Thomas Draikes, 8 weeks	13s 4d
Thomas Morris, 5 weeks 1 day	8s 7d
Andrew Brene, 8 weeks	13s 4d
William Bateman, gromet, 8 weeks	10s
John Appulton, boy, 8 weeks	6s 8d
Thomas Marychurche, 2 weeks 6 days	4s 9d
Hugh Bowye, 2 weeks 6 days	4s 9d
Henry Burges, 2 weeks 6 days	4s 9d
John Sustian, 2 weeks 6 days	4s 9d
William Trevet, 2 weeks 6 days	4s 9d
Henry Shearwood, carpenter, 2 weeks 6 days	11s 10d
Thomas Platterrer, boy, 2 weeks 6 days	2s 4½d
John Meret, 2 weeks 6 days	4s 9d
[*Gunner*]	
Thomas Dixson, master gunner, 8 weeks	20s

[*Page total*] – £24 12s 5½d.

[f. 90] *The Mary Rose*

Mariners	
William Robinson, boatswain, 13 weeks 1 day	54s 9d
Christopher Davy, purser, 13 weeks 1 day	32s 10d
Roger Cratway, steward, 13 weeks 1 day	30s 1½d
Robert Spencer, 7 days	20d
John Baswell, 5 weeks 1 day	8s 7d
John Cosyne, 13 weeks 1 day	21s 11d
Robert Angell, 13 weeks 1 day	21s 11d
Humphrey Stevenson, 13 weeks 1 day	21s 11d
Rowland Drawe, 13 weeks 1 day	21s 11d
Thomas Leonarde, gromet, 13 weeks 1 day	16s 5d
John Welles, gromet, 13 weeks 1 day	16s 5d
Edward Lawghen, boy, 13 weeks 1 day	10s 11½d
John Bunche, carpenter, 8 weeks 3 days	35s 1d
John Pulter, server, 5 days	14d
William Harber, 8 weeks 5 days	10s 6d
Thomas Frannlyn, 2 weeks 6 days	4s 9d
John Ketche, 2 weeks 6 days	4s 9d
Gunner	
John Buttler, master, 13 weeks 1 day	32s 10d

[*Page total*] – £17 8s 6d.

[f. 90v] *The Great Bark*

Mariners

Thomas Goldestone, boatswain, 4 weeks 3 days	18s 5d
Richard Conarde, purser, 4 weeks 3 days	11s
Thomas Gaittes, steward, 4 weeks 3 days	10s 2d
John Neweball, 4 weeks 3 days	7s 4d
Richard Dyamounde, 4 weeks 3 days	7s 4d
Mark Bullyn, 4 weeks 3 days	7s 4d
Robert Whight, 4 weeks 3 days	7s 4d
William Harrode, 7 days	1s 8d
Peter Trewe, 4 weeks 3 days	7s 4d
William Brigges, 4 weeks 3 days	7s 4d
Thomas Tyball, 4 weeks 3 days	7s 4d
Robert Key, 4 weeks 3 days	7s 4d
Peter Cade, 4 weeks 3 days	7s 4d
Thomas Rattley, gromet, 4 weeks 3 days	5s 6d
Edward Wekes, boy, 4 weeks 3 days	3s 8d
William Welshe, carpenter, 4 weeks 3 days	18s 5d
Thomas Freman, gromet, 4 weeks 3 days	5s 6d
William Chartram, gromet, 4 weeks 3 days	5s 6d
Gunners	
Lawrence Mewse, master, 4 weeks 3 days	11s
Miles Robinson, server, 4 weeks 3 days	7s 4d

[*Page total*] – £8 4s 2d.

[f. 91] *The Lion*

Mariners

William Hollande, master, 2 weeks 6 days	23s 10d
William Keyes, boatswain, 8 weeks	33s 4d
John Buttler, purser, 8 weeks	20s
John Curle, steward, 8 weeks	18s 4d
John Rusell, 8 weeks	13s 4d
Christopher Chaundeller, 5 weeks 1 day	8s 7d
Richard Reade, 5 weeks 1 day	8s 7d
Davy Griffin, 5 weeks 1 day	8s 7d
William Wilkins, 8 weeks	13s 4d
Gryfith Davyth, 5 weeks 1 day	8s 7d
William Griffin, 5 weeks 1 day	8s 7d
Cornelius Brian, 5 weeks 1 day	8s 7d
Jervis Huton, 5 weeks 1 day	8s 7d
John Kennet, boy, 8 weeks	6s 8d
Nicholas Waller, 2 weeks 6 days	4s 9d

Thomas Tayllor, gromet, 2 weeks 6 days	3s 7d
Thomas King, 2 weeks 6 days	4s 9d
William Jonson, 2 weeks 6 days	4s 9d
John Hewes, 2 weeks 6 days	4s 9d
William Samonde, 2 weeks 6 days	4s 9d
William Rice, boy, 2 weeks 6 days	2s 4½d
Francis Fletcher, 2 weeks 6 days	4s 9d
William Welshe, carpenter, 2 weeks 6 days	11s 10d
Thomas Freman, gromet, 2 weeks 6 days	3s 6d
William Chattram, gromet, 2 weeks 6 days	3s 6d
Thomas Godfray, 2 weeks	3s 4d
Gunners	
Edward Tompson, master, 8 weeks	20s
Peter Arney, 2 weeks 6 days	4s 9d

[*Page total*] – £13 10s 3½d.

[f. 91v] *The Philip and Mary*

Mariners	
William Barnes, master, 8 weeks	£4
John Jonnes, boatswain, 13 weeks 1 day	54s 9d
John Pursell, purser, 13 weeks 1 day	32s 10d
John Jeffray, steward, 13 weeks 1 day	30s 1½d
Francis Williams, 13 weeks 1 day	21s 11d
Gregory Wickes, 13 weeks 1 day	21s 11d
Zeache Sweteman, 13 weeks 1 day	2s 11d
Richard Neall, 7 days	20d
Arthur Leversuche, 13 weeks 1 day	21s 11d
Thomas Sharpley, 13 weeks 1 day	21s 11d
Edward Collson, 13 weeks 1 day	21s 11d
Richard West, 13 weeks 1 day	21s 11d
Bartholomew Gaittes, gromet, 13 weeks 1 day	16s 5d
Thomas Barber, 13 weeks 1 day	21s 11d
Richard Baskom, gromet, 13 weeks 1 day	16s 5d
Germain Gallwey, 8 weeks 6 days	14s 9d
Robert Ussher, boy, 8 weeks	6s 8d
William Petche, 2 days	6d
Gunner	
Matthew Sharpe, master, 13 weeks 1 day	32s 10d

[*Page total*] – £23 2s 3½d.

[f. 92] *The Christopher*

William Rogers, master, 13 weeks 1 day	£4 7s 7d
Richard Pereman, boatswain, 13 weeks 1 day	54s 9d

Rowland Mocklowe, purser, 13 weeks 1 day	32s 10d
John Blithe, steward, 13 weeks 1 day	30s 1½d
Thomas Linge, 13 weeks 1 day	21s 11d
Robert Goslinge, 13 weeks 1 day	21s 11d
William Romney, 13 weeks 1 day	21s 11d
Thomas James, 13 weeks 1 day	21s 11d
James Bull, 13 weeks 1 day	21s 11d
Roger Reade, 13 weeks 1 day	21s 11d
John Woddreff, 13 weeks 1 day	21s 11d
John Jaxson, 4 weeks	6s 8d
John William, boy, 13 weeks 1 day	10s 11½d
Paul Lambart, 5 weeks 2 days	8s 10d
George Tompson, 5 weeks 1 day	8s 7d
John Baker, 4 weeks 2 days	7s 2d
Robert Headley, 4 weeks 2 days	7s 2d
Robert Batersbye, 5 weeks	8s 4d
Thomas Sibbley, 2 weeks 6 days	4s 9d
Trigg Williams, 2 weeks 3 days	4s
Andrew Everington, 4 weeks 2 days	7s 2d
Gunner	
Jobe Bushe, master, 13 weeks 1 day	32s 10d

[*Page total*] – £23 5s 1d.

[f. 92v] *The Jesus*

Mariners	
Thomas Elle, boatswain, 13 weeks 1 day	54s 9d
John Croxstone, purser, 13 weeks 1 day	32s 10d
Thomas Purton, steward, 13 weeks 1 day	30s 1½d
Edward Bray, 7 days	20d
John Bull, 13 weeks 1 day	21s 11d
John Roo, 13 weeks 1 day	21s 11d
John Lardge, 13 weeks 1 day	21s 11d
William Stacey, 5 weeks 1 day	8s 7d
Robert Willes, 13 weeks 1 day	21s 11d
Thomas Baster, boy, 13 weeks 1 day	10s 11½d
George Vallet, boy, [*blank*]	[*blank*]
Henry Shearewood, carpenter, 5 days	2s 11d
Godfrey Smyth, 5 days	14d
John Elexaunder, 7 weeks 5 days	12s 10d
John Holydaie, 7 weeks 5 days	12s 10d
Henry Cowper, 7 weeks 5 days	12s 10d
John Mytchell, 2 weeks 2 days	3s 10d

Edmund Bolland, 2 weeks 2 days	3s 10d
John Sellond, 2 weeks 2 days	3s 10d
Gunners	
Giles Delanoye, master, 13 weeks 1 day	32s 10d
Walter Symonndes, 13 weeks 1 day	21s 11d

[*Page total*] – £16 5s 5d.

[f. 93] *The Hart*

Mariners	
Henry Willobie, master, 5 weeks 1 day	34s 3d
Richard Browne, boatswain, 5 weeks 1 day	15s
Thomas Wilkes, purser, 5 weeks 1 day	12s 10d
John Tompson, steward, 5 weeks 1 day	11s 9d
Thomas Northway, 5 weeks 1 day	8s 7d
John Mappe, 5 weeks 1 day	8s 7d
John Twinam, 5 weeks 1 day	8s 7d
Anthony Addertonn, gromet, 5 weeks 1 day	6s 8d
Thomas Mappe, gromet, 5 weeks 1 day	6s 8d
Ticher Foster, boy, 5 weeks 1 day	4s 3½d
John Harte, boy, 5 weeks 1 day	4s 3½d
John Vallet, 2 weeks 3 days	4s
[*Gunner*]	
Robert Tompson, master gunner, 5 weeks 1 day	12s 10d

The Antelope

Mariners	
Richard Wright, boatswain, 13 weeks 1 day	38s 4d
Thomas Awsten, purser, 13 weeks 1 day	32s 10d
John Paulmer, steward, 13 weeks 1 day	30s 1½d
William Wilkinson, 13 weeks 1 day	21s 11d
William Moll, 13 weeks 1 day	21s 11d
Richard Tratton, 1 week	20d
George Lyell, 13 weeks 1 day	21s 11d
John Wakom, 13 weeks 1 day	21s 11d
William Collens, 2 weeks 4 days	4s 4d
William Mannynge, 13 weeks 1 day	21s 11d
Davy Short, gromet, 13 weeks 1 day	16s 5d
Thomas Evans, 2 days	6d
Thomas Webb, 2 weeks 6 days	4s 9d
[*Gunner*]	
Roger Bowthe, master gunner, 13 weeks 1 day	32s 10d

[*Page total*] – £20 9s 8½d.

[f. 93v] *The Swallow*

Mariners

William Barnes, master, 5 weeks 1 day	51s 5d
William Saunders, boatswain, 5 weeks 1 day	15s
John Robarttes, purser, 5 weeks 1 day	12s 10d
John Bore, steward, 3 weeks	6s 10½d
Richard Fishebill, 5 weeks 1 day	8s 7d
John Baddar, 5 weeks 1 day	8s 7d
Walter Gimlyn, 5 weeks 1 day	8s 7d
Matthew Fisher, 5 weeks 1 day	8s 7d
Robert Ussher, boy, 5 weeks 1 day	4s 3½d
[*Gunner*]	
Jacob Myller, master gunner, 5 weeks 1 day	12s 10d

The Jennet

Mariners

Richard Trewe, boatswain, 13 weeks 1 day	38s 4d
Henry Cooke, purser, 13 weeks 1 day	32s 10d
John Addams, steward, 13 weeks 1 day	30s 1½d
William Sampson, 10 weeks 1 day	16s 11d
John Phillippes, 13 weeks 1 day	21s 11d
John Buckler, 7 days	20d
Henry Stapull, 13 weeks 1 day	21s 11d
William Walker, 13 weeks 1 day	21s 11d
Alexander Golde, boy, 13 weeks 1 day	10s 11½d
John Brene, 2 weeks 6 days	4s 9d
[*Gunner*]	
Richard Haynes, master gunner, 13 weeks 1 day	32s 10d

[*Page total*] – £18 11s 9d.

[f. 94] *The New Bark*

Mariners

George Braunche, boatswain, 10 weeks 1 day	29s 7d
Richard Dennes, steward, 5 weeks 1 day	11s 9½d
Thomas Vaughan, 10 weeks 1 day	16s 11d
William Bull, 10 weeks 1 day	16s 11d
Thomas Whitell, 1 week	20d
Gabriel Kirbie, boy, 10 weeks 1 day	8s 5½d
John Grant, 4 weeks 4 days	7s 8d
John Fisher, 3 weeks 6 days	6s 5d
Roger Davy, purser, 5 weeks 5 days	13s 1½d
[*Gunner*]	
John Phillippes, master gunner, 10 weeks 1 day	25s 4d

The Willoughby

Mariners

Robert Flinte, boatswain, 5 weeks 1 day	14s 11d
George Browne, 5 weeks 1 day	8s 7d
William Warwicke, 7 days	20d
John Turner, 5 weeks 1 day	8s 7d
Benjamin Flint, gromet, 5 weeks 1 day	6s 5d
Roger Davie, steward, 4 weeks 1 day	11s 2d
George Haulle, purser, 5 days	20d
[*Gunner*]	
John Malpas, master gunner, 5 weeks 1 day	12s 10d

The Greyhound

Mariners

Robert Harwood, boatswain, 13 weeks 1 day	38s 4d
Edmund Dawson, steward, 13 weeks 1 day	30s 1½d
Miles Sparke, 10 weeks 1 day	16s 11d
Thomas Jonnes, 5 weeks 1 day	8s 7d
Richard Tyller, 13 weeks 1 day	21s 11d
Roger Browne, boy, 13 weeks 1 day	10s 11½d
Andrew Malin, 7 weeks 5 days	12s 10d
Edward Thoms, 4 weeks 2 days	7s 2d
Henry Roose, 2 days	6d
Walter Tawbote, 2 weeks 6 days	4s 9d
[*Gunner*]	
John Bankes, master gunner, 13 weeks 1 day	32s 10d

[*Page total*] – £19 7s 7½d.

[f. 94v] *The Tiger*

Mariners

John Abowen, boatswain, 13 weeks 1 day	38s 4d
John Hawkins, steward, 13 weeks 1 day	30s 1½d
John Bowye, 13 weeks 1 day	21s 11d
Thomas Buttler, 13 weeks 1 day	21s 11d
Thomas Wacey, gromet, 13 weeks 1 day	16s 5d
John Newton, boy, 13 weeks 1 day	10s 11½d
Thomas Haull, 10 weeks	16s 8d
[*Gunner*]	
John More, master gunner, 13 weeks 1 day	32s 10d

The Bull

Mariners

Andrew Walker, boatswain, 13 weeks 1 day	38s 4d
John Willy, steward, 13 weeks 1 day	30s 1½d
Richard Crannolde, 13 weeks 1 day	21s 11d

William Colleson, 13 weeks 1 day	21s 11d
Edward Thomas, boy, 13 weeks 1 day	10s 11½d
Christopher Cowper, gromet, 7 weeks	7s 9d
Robert Hartley, 2 weeks 6 days	3s 9d
[*Gunner*]	
Robert Butteler, master gunner, 13 weeks 1 day	32s 10d
The Falcon	
Mariners	
Lawrence Cleare, boatswain, 13 weeks 1 day	38s 4d
George Haulle, steward, 4 weeks 3 days	10s 2d
John Hodge, 10 weeks 1 day	16s 11d
Richard Langley, gromet, 10 weeks 2 days	12s 10d
William Brooke, steward, 8 weeks 5 days	20s
Michael Adrian, 2 days	6d
[*Gunner*]	
John Comyn, master gunner, 13 weeks 1 day	32s 10d

[*Page total*] – £24 8s 4d.

[f. 95] *The Phoenix*	
Mariners	
John Winward, boatswain, 7 days	2s 10d
Griffin Hewson, steward, 7 days	2s 4½d
Thomas Holton, gromet, 7 days	15d
[*Gunner*]	
John Harris master gunner, 7 days	2s 6d
The Bright Falcon	
Mariners	
Robert Blaike, boatswain, 13 weeks 1 day	38s 4d
Edward Teayllour, 13 weeks 1 day	21s 11d
Henry Williams, 13 weeks 1 day	21s 11d
[*Gunner*]	
John Walker, master gunner, 13 weeks 1 day	32s 10d
The Sun	
Mariners	
Nicholas Starkey, boatswain, 13 weeks 1 day	38s 4d
Ralph Buckeland, 13 weeks 1 day	21s 11d
John Cooke, 2 weeks 1 day	4s 9d
[*Gunner*]	
William Ellis, master gunner 13 weeks 1 day	32s 10d
The Saker	
Mariners	
John Burnam, boatswain, 10 weeks 1 day	29s 7d
Thomas Thorney, steward, 10 weeks 1 day	23s 3d

[Gunner]	
John Hunt, master gunner, 10 weeks 1 day	25s 4d
The Bark of Boulogne	
Mariners	
Richard Lambe, boatswain, 13 weeks 1 day	38s 4d
Edward Coxe, steward, 13 weeks 1 day	30s 1½d
William Peache, 13 weeks 1 day	21s 11d
[Gunner]	
John Williames, master gunner, 13 weeks 1 day	32s 10d

[*Page total*] – £21 3s 2d.

[f. 95v] *The Hare*	
Mariners	
John Aman, boatswain, 5 weeks 1 day	11s 9d
Thomas Lane, steward, 5 weeks 1 day	8s 7d
Richard Woodman, gromet, 5 weeks 1 day	6s 5d
[Gunner]	
Nicholas Hardy, master gunner, 5 weeks 1 day	12s 10d
The Double Rose	
Mariners	
John Hunt, 13 weeks 1 day	21s 11d
Richard Harman, 13 weeks 1 day	21s 11d
The Galley Speedwell	
Mariners	
Cuthbert Clarke, boatswain, 13 weeks 1 day	54s 9d
Anthony Darnatho, 13 weeks 1 day	21s 11d
William Prince, 13 weeks 1 day	21s 11d
Thomas Foster, boy, 13 weeks 1 day	10s 11½d
[Gunner]	
Maurice Abowen, master gunner, 13 weeks 1 day	32s 10d
The Galley Tryright	
Mariners	
Simon Barnsley, boatswain, 13 weeks 1 day	38s 4d
John Goden, purser, 13 weeks 1 day	32s 10d
William Kent, steward, 13 weeks 1 day	30s 1½d
John Teayllor, 13 weeks 1 day	21s 11d
John Marynnar, server, 5 weeks 3 days	9s
[Gunner]	
John Farley, master gunner, 13 weeks 1 day	32s 10d
The Galley Mermaid	
Mariners	
John Davy, boatswain, 8 weeks	23s 4d

Henry Penlley, 13 weeks 1 day	21s 11d
Henry Fowller, 13 weeks 1 day	21s 11d
Sylvester Bewell, 10 weeks 5 days	17s 10d

[*Page total*] – £23 15s 10d.

[f. 96] Wages of gunners daily attending in Her Highness's fort at Upnor for the safe-keeping of Her Grace's ships in Gillingham Water, begun the first day of July last and this day ended, as followeth:

Thomas Sergent, master, 92 days at 16d	£6 2s 8d
Anthony Venruter, 72 days at 12d	£3 12s
Richard Abesede, 92 days at 12d	£4 12s
Prince Homes, 62 days at 12d	£3 2s
Robert Woullgrowe, 92 days at 12d	£4 12s
William Bowell, 92 days at 12d	£4 12s
William Cheselton, 92 days at 12d	£4 12s
Randall Stevenson, 92 days at 12d	£4 12s
	[£35 16s 8d*]

*[*Purveyor*]. To Butolph Moungey the last day of September for his wages daily attending and serving Her Highness in making of provisions for Her Grace's ships, *viz.* cables, ropes and other cordage by him provided and delivered into her storehouses there, by one quarter of a year begun the first day of July last and this day ended, at 8d *per diem* – £3 1s 4d.

*[*Clerk*]. To Thomas Henos the same day for his wages daily attending and serving Her Highness in keeping of the book of cheque of masters, mariners and gunners serving Her Grace for the safe-keeping of Her Highness's ships afloat in harbour, as also the prick book of shipwrights, caulkers and others, by one quarter of a year begun and ended as abovesaid – £5.

*[*Purveyor*]. To Thomas Baker the same day for his wages daily serving Her Highness in delivering of cables, cablets, ropes of all sorts, canvas, twine, needles and divers other kinds of stuffs out of her storehouses there to the use of Her Grace's ships, by one quarter of a year begun and ended as abovesaid – £2.

[*Page total*] – £45 18s.

[f. 96v] *Shipwrights*

Nicholas Johnson, 10½ days at 10d	8s 9d
John Hichecoke, server, 10½ days at 4d	3s 6d
Thomas Johnson, server, 10½ days at 2d	21d
Richard Crippes, 10½ days at 6d	5s 3d

Robert Packeman, 8½ days at 6d	4s 3d
William Hartrope, 10 days at 6d	5s
Nicholas Foster, 10½ days at 6d	5s 3d
William Welshe, 5 days at 8d	3s 4d
Thomas Freman, 5 days at 4d	20d
William Chattram, server, 5 days at 3d	15d
Caulkers	
John Bunche, 11½ days at 8d	7s 8d
William Harber, 11½ days at 4d	3s 10d
Henry Shearewoode, 10½ days at 7d	6s 1½d
Henry Whight, 7½ days at 7d	4s 4½d
Gabriel Wright, 7½ days at 7d	4s 4½d
Roger Collins, 7½ days at 6d	3s 9d
Robert Welshe, 10½ days at 6d	5s 3d
Robert Tapsher, 7½ days at 6d	3s 9d
William Bulbecke, 6 days at 10d	5s
John Barellegg, 6 days at 4d	2s
Richard Wheller, server, 6 days at 2d	12d
John Moisher, 6 days at 6d	3s
John Belles, 6 days at 6d	3s
William Bastian, 6 days at 6d	3s
Walter Clay, 6 days at 6d	3s
Thomas Pavey, 6 days at 6d	3s
Edward Hiller, server, 6 days at 3d	18d
John Pulter, 3 days at 5d	15d

[*Page total*] – £5 4s 10½d.

[f. 97] Godfrey Smyth, 3 days at 6d	18d
Richard Clappam, 4½ days at 6d	2s 3d
Robert Hartropp, 4½ days at 6d	2s 3d
George Mathew, 11 days at 6d	5s 6d
Thomas Purton, 7½ days at 2d	15d
William Mannyng, 7½ days at 3d	22½d
Giles Bevyson, 10 days at 6d	5s
	[£19s 7½d*]
Topmakers	
William Bexley, 17 days at 8d	11s 4d
William Kaket, 17 days at 6d	8s 6d
Abraham Harmounde, server, 17 days at 5d	7s 1d
	*[*26s 11d*]

Victualling. To Thomas Willson the 6th day of August for the victualling of 36 shipwrights, caulkers, topmakers and others serving Her Highness in repairing, mending and caulking of Her Grace's ships there, by the space of 266 days among them all, Sundays and holy days accounted, which maketh 38 weeks, begun the 27th day of July and this day ended, at 4s 1d every week the man – £7 15s 2d.

Lodging. To Joan Smyth, Alice Hills, Annes Hunt and divers other persons of Chatham, Rochester and thereabouts the 6th day of August for the lodging of 38 of the aforementioned shipwrights, caulkers, topmakers and others working upon the repairing of Her Grace's ships there by the space of 40 weeks in 18 featherbeds, begun the 27th day of July and this day ended, at 2d every week the man – 6s 8d.

[*Page total*] – £10 8s 4½d.

[f. 97v] Wages of house-carpenters and sawyers working upon the making of two sheds for the safe-keeping of Her Highness's store of galley oars, ship tops, pitch, tar and divers other kinds of provisions for the use of Her Grace's ships, as followeth:

House-carpenters	
John Tottey, 57 days at 8d	38s
Alexander Gibbons, 38 days at 6d	19s
Thomas Thorneton, 56 days at 6d	28s
William Chappman, 47 days at 6d	23s 6d
Richard Danniell, server, 53 days at 4d	17s 8d
Sawyers	
Edmund Bell, 38 days at 6d	19s
Humphrey Marshall, 6 days at 6d	3s
Thomas Blackborne, 48 days at 6d	24s
Richard Garret, 16 days at 6d	8s

Victualling. To John Hurlocke the 12th day of September for the victualling of the said 9 house-carpenters and sawyers working upon the making of the sheds aforesaid, by the space of 352 days among them, which maketh 50 weeks 2 days, begun the 7th day of July last and ended as abovesaid, at 4s every week the man – £10 1s 4d.

[*Page total*] – £19 1s 6d.

[f. 98] *Lodging.* To Anne Hurlocke the last day of September for the lodging of three of the aforenamed topmakers in two featherbeds by the space of 8 weeks among them, working upon the new making of two sheds and ship tops there, begun the first day of July last and ended the 17th day of the same, at 2d every week the man – 1s 4d.

House-carpenters	
John Tottye, 5 days at 12d	5s
Alexander Gibbans, 5 days at 10d	4s 2d
Thomas Thorneton, 5 days at 10d	4s 2d
Bricklayer	
William Phedam, 5 days at 10d	4s 2d

[*Page total*] – 18s 10d.

[f. 98v] *Emptions*

Ironwork *[*£19 11s 5d*; *nails £10 0s 2d*; *locks 6s*]. To George Hoppe of Chatham, smith, the last day of September for price of 8 hundred 2 quarters 15 pounds weight [*967 lbs*] of his own new iron by him made and wrought into bolts, keys, rings, port-hinges and spikes for the use of Her Grace's ships, at 23s 4d every hundredweight – £10 1s 7½d;[1] more for the working of 2 quarters 17 pounds [*weight*] [*73 lbs*] of Her Grace's old iron by him made as aforesaid, at 1d the pound – 6s 1d; more for 3,500 of 20d nail, at 16s 8d the 1,000 – 58s 4d; more for 4,100 of 10d nail – 34s 2d; more for 1,500 of 6d nail – 7s 6d; more for 1,000 of 2d nail – 20d; more for 300 of 5d nail – 15d; more for 3,000 of 4d nail – 10s; more for 3,000 of 3d nail – 7s 6d; more for 6,000 of sprigs – 7s; and more to him for a lock and a key with certain hasps and staples for the use aforesaid – 6d. *Summa* – £17 1s 1½d.

To John Startupp of Gillingham, smith, the same day for the price of 2 hundred 31 pounds weight [*255 lbs*] of new iron of him had and wrought into bolts, rings, keys and port-hinges for the use of Her Highness's ships as aforesaid, at 23s 4d the hundredweight. *Summa* – £2 13s 1½d.

To Thomas Willson of Ratcliff, smith, the same day for the price of 5 hundredweight of his own new iron by him made and wrought into spikes, clenches, rove and overlop nails for the use of Her Highness's ships, at 23s 4d every hundredweight – £5 16s 8d; more for 6 mattocks of iron weighing 56 pounds, at 2½d every pound weight – 11s 8d; more for 3,000 of 10d nail, at 8s 4d every 1,000 – 25s;. more for 6,000 of 6d nail, at 5s every 1,000 – 30s; and more to him for 6,000 of 4d nail, at 3s 4d every 1,000 – 20s. *Summa* – £10 3s 4d.

A grindstone. To Butolph Moungey the same day for price of one great grindstone of him had and delivered for the use of Her Highness's ships at Chatham; price by agreement – 6s 8d.

[*Page total*] – £30 4s 3d.

[f. 99] *Water carriage of provisions*. To Nicholas Crages, master of a hoy called the *Mary and Jonne of Myllale* [Millhall] the last day of

[1]The calculation gives 2417.5d, which is 2d below the sum stated (2419.5d).

September for service of his hoy for the bringing of 3 ton of timber and 5 masts from Deptford to Chatham for the use of Her Highness's ships; price by agreement – £1.

To Andrew Bullding, master of a hoy called the *John of Newhede* [New Hythe], the same day for the bringing down of 2 new cables and 2 dozen of pump-hoses for the use of Her Grace's ships there, from Deptford Strand to Chatham; by agreement – 10s.

To John Godfray, master of a hoy called the *Samuell of Mylton*, the same day for service of his hoy serving Her Highness in carrying of one anchor, 10 cables and cablets, 8 tarred hawsers, 3½ dozen of boat oars, 5 compasses, 7 running glasses, 3 barrels of pitch, 3 barrels of tar, 6 sounding leads, and divers other necessaries received at Her Grace's storehouse at Deptford and delivered the same at Chatham; by agreement – 13s 4d.

To Andrew Markes, master of a hoy called the *Seyhound of London*, the same day for the bringing down of certain of Her Highness's store, as timber, plank, ironwork, pump-hoses and divers other kinds of stuffs received out of Her Grace's great storehouse at Deptford and delivered the same at Chatham for the use of Her Highness's ships there; sum by agreement – £3 12s.

To Thomas Woodall, master of a hoy called the *Sonne of Maidestone* the same day for the bringing down of 20 spruce deals [*and*] 20 masts for the use of Her Highness's ships from London and delivered the same at Chatham; by agreement – £1 6s 8d.

[*Page total*] – £7 2s.

[f. 99v] *Bright rosin.* To Robert Borrough of Rochester the last day of September for price of 4 hundredweight of bright rosin of him had for the use of Her Highness's ships at their groundings, at 9s every hundredweight – £1 16s.

Water carriage. To Nicholas Hilles of Chatham the same day for the hire of his crayer to and fro for the carrying of 60 mariners and gunners prested out of divers places to serve in Her Majesty's ships riding then without Nore Head. *Summa* by agreement – £1.

House rent. To Adam Keller of Chatham the same day for the hire of a certain house and ground thereunto belonging wherein lieth Her Grace's store of all kinds of provisions, as cables, cablets, ropes of all sorts, twine, needles and divers other kinds of stuffs, by one quarter of a year begun the first day of July last and this day ended – 10s.

To Thomas Winnall of Chatham the same day for the hire of a certain storehouse wherein lieth Her Highness's store of rosin, oakum, sails for galleys [*and*] boards of all sorts, by one quarter of a year begun the first day of July last and ended as abovesaid – 3s 4d.

To Richard Mylles of Chatham the same day for rent of a certain storehouse wherein lieth Her Grace's store of reed for the breaming of Her Grace's ships at their groundings, by one quarter of a year begun and ended as abovesaid – 1s 3d.

To William Phedam of Rochester, bricklayer, the same day for the underpinning of the house upon the wharf near Chatham; by agreement – 8s.

[*Page total*] – £3 18s 7d.

[f. 100] *Carriage of stone and sand.* To William Larking of Chatham the last day of September for the hire of his cart and 10 horses for the carriage of certain stone and sand for the underpinning of a new shed and house there for the laying in of Her Highness's boat oars, by the space of 2 days at 20d *per diem*. *Summa* – 3s 4d.

Laying of stone and reed. To Thomas Smyth of Rochester, freemason, the same day as well for the underpinning of Her Highness's long house and shed there, as also for the tiling of the house upon the wharf near Chatham; by agreement – £3 13s 4d.

To Richard Fenner, John Fenner, and two others of New Hythe, reedmen, the same day for price of 6,600 of reed by them laid upon the new shed there, at 12d every 100 laying – £3 6s; more for 1,600 of lath nailing upon the same – 2s 8d; and more to them for 1,600 bends[1] by them provided, at 5d the 100 – 6s 8d. *Summa* – £3 15s 4d.

Rods. To Richard Rogers of Chatham the same day for price of one load of hazel rods by him delivered as aforesaid for the use of the said shed. *Summa* – 3s 4d.

Tile. To William Wood the same day for price of 8,000 of tile of him had and by him delivered at Chatham for the use of Her [*Highness's*] storehouses there, at 10s every 1,000 – £4.

To Thomas Ayres of Rochester the same day for price of 120 of corner tile of him had for the said new house upon the wharf, at 1½d the couple. *Summa* – 7s 6d.

To Robert Harwoode the same day for price of 20 roof tile had of him for the use as aforesaid, at 1½d the piece. *Summa* – 2s 6d.

[*Page total*] – £12 5s 4d.

[f. 100v] *Hoops.* To John West of Maidstone the last day of September for price of 20 hoops by him delivered for the use of Her Highness's ships' tops there; by agreement – 6s 8d.

Oakum. To Thomas Hunt of Chatham, ropemaker, the same day for price of 3 thousand 2 hundred 2 quarters 21 pounds weight [*3,661 lbs*] of

[1]In this instance the metal loops used by thatchers to hold sections of reed in place.

Her Highness's old junks and ropes by him made and wrought into netting- and wrain-ropes for the use of Her Grace's ships, at 3s 8d every hundredweight – £5 19s 10¾d;[1] and more to him for the picking of 7 hundred 2 quarters 14 pounds weight [*854 lbs*] of Her Highness's said junks into oakum for the needful caulking of Her Grace's ships, at 3s 8d every hundredweight picking – 27s 11d.[2] [*Summa*] – £7 7s 9¾d.

To Peter Hilles, Michael Gonson, Henry Cooke and 13 other persons of Gillingham, Chatham, Rochester and thereabouts the same day for the working and picking of 8 thousand 8 hundred 2 quarters 18 pounds weight [*9,930 lbs*] of Her Highness's old junks and ropes by them made and wrought into oakum for the needful caulking of Her Grace's ships, at 3s 4d every hundredweight picking. *Summa* – £14 15s 6d.[3]

*[*Labourers*]. To William Manynge, William Prince, Henry Pendley and Henry Fuller labourers the same day for their pains taken in the repairing and mending of the grounding place and wharf there wherein is set a new frame, as also all kinds of labour to be done about the storehouse, by one whole quarter of a year to end this day, at 5s the man – £1.

*[*Water carriage*]. To Howell Somer, owner of a hoy called the *John of London*, the same day for service of his hoy, of the portage of 60 tuns, serving Her Highness with four men and one boy in the same for the carrying cables, hawsers, small cordage, oakum, pitch, tar, shovels, scoops, with divers other kinds of stuffs, from Deptford and delivered the same at Chatham for the use of Her Grace's ships, by the space of 14[4] days begun the first day of August last and ended the 14th day of the same, at 3s 4d every tun *per mensem* – £5.

[*Page total*] – £28 9s 11¾d.

[f. 101] *Timber*. To John Startupe of Chatham, miller, the last day of September for price of 2 elms of him had for windlasses for ships' boats there, and for carriage down of the same elms to the waterside; by agreement – 4s 8d.

Summa predicta. [f. 101v *blank*]

[f. 102] *Anno Domino 1562. Anno regni regine Elizabethe quinto*

A payment made the last day of December as well to masters, mariners and gunners keeping Her Highness's ships afloat in harbour and to keepers

[1]The calculation gives 1438.2498d, which is ½d below the sum stated (1438.75d).
[2]The calculation gives 335.49996d, which is ½d above the sum stated (335d).
[3]The calculation gives 3546.428d, which is about ½d above the sum stated (3546d).
[4]MS 14th ('*xivth*') by faulty anticipation of next usage.

of storehouses and timber-yards there wherein lieth Her Majesty's provisions for the use of her ships, and rent of the same, as also to divers persons for sundry kinds of stuffs of them had for the use of Her Grace's ships aforesaid; by one quarter of a year begun the first day of October last, and this day ended, as followeth:

The Elizabeth Jonas

Mariners

John Teygge, boatswain, 13 weeks 1 day	54s 9d
Lancelot Tristram, purser, 13 weeks 1 day	46s
Thomas Waller, steward, 13 weeks 1 day	30s 1½d
John Collens, 13 weeks 1 day	21s 11d
Peter Padden, 7 weeks	11s 8d
Richard Brisholde, 13 weeks 1 day	21s 11d
Edward Brenden, 13 weeks 1 day	21s 11d
William Kisshan, 13 weeks 1 day	21s 11d
John Pyrton, 13 weeks 1 day	21s 11d
Robert Cooke, 6 weeks 3 days	10s 8d
Henry Woode, 13 weeks 1 day	21s 11d
William Martin, 6 weeks 5 days	11s 2d
Thomas Baker, 11 weeks	18s 4d
William Parris, 11 weeks	18s 4d
Robert Hellinge, gromet, 13 weeks 1 day	16s 5d
John Burnet, gromet, 13 weeks 1 day	16s 5d
John Blyethe, 13 weeks 1 day	21s 11d
William Runey, 13 weeks 1 day	21s 11d
John Wooddriff, 13 weeks 1 day	21s 11d
Roger Reade, 13 weeks 1 day	21s 11d
George Voise, 13 weeks 1 day	21s 11d
Roger Cobiam, 13 weeks 1 day	21s 11d
Nicholas Lovet, 4 weeks 5 days	7s 10d
Thomas Searle, 4 weeks 5 days	7s 10d
James Robartson, 4 weeks 5 days	7s 10d

[*Page total*] – £26 0s 4½d.

[f. 102v] John Twickbyrde, 4 weeks 5 days	7s 10d
Nicholas Johnson, carpenter, 13 weeks 1 day	54s 9d
John Hitchekoke, server, 13 weeks 1 day	21s 11d
Isaac Asheley, server, 13 weeks 1 day	21s 11d
Thomas Johnson, boy, 4 weeks 3 days	3s 8d
[*Gunner*]	
Lawrence Dylke, master gunner, 13 weeks 1 day	32s 10d

The Hope

Mariners

John Hurlocke, master, 13 weeks 1 day	£6 11s 5d
Robert West, boatswain, 13 weeks 1 day	54s 9d
Michael Gonson, purser, 13 weeks 1 day	32s 10d
John Mathew, steward, 13 weeks 1 day	30s 1½d
Thomas Starke, 13 weeks 1 day	21s 11d
[*Roger*][1] Awsten, 13 weeks 1 day	21s 11d
Gregory Stewarde, 13 weeks 1 day	21s 11d
Andrew Streke, 13 weeks 1 day	21s 11d
Thomas Dreaikes, 13 weeks 1 day	21s 11d
Andrew Brenn, 13 weeks 1 day	21s 11d
Hugh Bewye, 13 weeks 1 day	21s 11d
Henry Burdges, 13 weeks 1 day	21s 11d
John Sustian, 13 weeks 1 day	21s 11d
William Trevet, 2 weeks 3 days	4s
John Merete, 13 weeks 1 day	21s 11d
William Bateman, gromet, 13 weeks 1 day	16s 5d
John Appulton, boy, 13 weeks 1 day	10s 11½d
Peter Harryson, server, 13 weeks 1 day	21s 11d
Richard Abethell, 13 weeks 1 day	21s 11d
John Beache, 5 weeks 1 day	8s 7d
Henry Shearewood, carpenter, 13 weeks 1 day	54s 9d
Thomas Platterrer, boy, 13 weeks 1 day	10s 11½d
[*Gunners*]	
Thomas Dyxson, master gunner, 13 weeks 1 day	32s 10d
James Robartes, server, 13 weeks 1 day	21s 11d

[*Page total*] – £40 8s 0½d.

[f. 103] *The Mary Rose*

Mariners

William Robinson, boatswain, 13 weeks 1 day	54s 9d
Christopher Davy, purser, 13 weeks 1 day	32s 10d
Roger Cratway, steward, 13 weeks 1 day	30s 1½d
John Cossyn, 13 weeks 1 day	21s 11d
Robert Aungell, 4 weeks 3 days	7s 4d
Humphrey Stevinson, 13 weeks 1 day	21s 11d
Rowland Deraw, 13 weeks 1 day	21s 11d
John Welles, 13 weeks 1 day	21s 11d
Edward Laughan, boy, 13 weeks 1 day	10s 11½d
Thomas Francklyn, 1 week 3 days	2s 4d

[1]MS here 'Robart', but always Roger elsewhere; cf. above, p. 118 and other entries.

John Keatche, 6 weeks 4 days	11s
Thomas Leonard, gromet, 13 weeks 1 day	16s 5d
Thomas Kingdowne, 7 weeks 6 days	13s 1d
Thomas Buttler, gromet, 7 weeks 6 days	9s 10d
John Drewe, 4 weeks 5 days	7s 10d
William Runey, 4 weeks 4 days	7s 4d
William Cocke, 4 weeks 4 days	7s 4d
John Gilbart, 4 weeks 4 days	7s 4d
John Bunche, carpenter, 13 weeks 1 day	54s 9d
William Harbarde, gromet, 13 weeks 1 day	16s 5d
John Poulter, server, 1 week 3 days	2s 4d
Gunner	
John Buttler, master, 13 weeks 1 day	32s 10d

[*Page total*] – £20 12s 6d.

[f. 103v] *The Lion*

Mariners	
William Hollande, master, 13 weeks 1 day	£5 9s 6d
William Keyes, boatswain, 13 weeks 1 day	54s 9d
John Buttler, purser, 13 weeks 1 day	32s 10d
John Corle, steward, 13 weeks 1 day	30s 1½d
John Russell, 13 weeks 1 day	21s 11d
William Wilkins, 13 weeks 1 day	21s 11d
Thomas Tayllor, gromet, 13 weeks 1 day	21s 11d
John Symonndes, 13 weeks 1 day	21s 11d
William Richardes, boy, 13 weeks 1 day	10s 11d
John Bennet, boy, 13 weeks 1 day	10s 11d
Thomas Linge, 13 weeks 1 day	21s 11d
Robert Goslinge, 13 weeks 1 day	21s 11d
Nicholas Waller, 13 weeks 1 day	21s 11d
Thomas Kinge, 8 weeks 5 days	14s 6d
William Johnson, 13 weeks 1 day	21s 11d
John Hewes, 6 weeks 5 days	11s 2d
Francis Fletcher, gromet, 13 weeks 1 day	16s 5d
John Barber, trumpeter, 3 weeks 3 days	5s 8d
Sylvester Bewell, 4 weeks 4 days	7s 8d
Nicholas Hewes, 4 weeks 4 days	7s 8d
William Charles, 4 weeks 4 days	7s 8d
Thomas Dayll, 4 weeks 4 days	7s 8d
Thomas Browne, 3 weeks	5s
Gunners	
Edward Tompson, master, 13 weeks 1 day	32s 10d

Peter Arney, server, 13 weeks 1 day 21s 11d
[*Page total*] – £27 17s 0½d.

[f. 104] *The Philip and Mary*
Mariners
John Homes, boatswain, 13 weeks 1 day 54s 9d
John Pursell, purser, 13 weeks 1 day 32s 10d
John Jeffrey, steward, 13 weeks 1 day 30s 1½d
Francis Williams, 13 weeks 1 day 21s 11d
Thomas Sharpley, 13 weeks 1 day 21s 11d
Zeache Sweteman, 13 weeks 1 day 21s 11d
Arthur Leversuche, 13 weeks 1 day 21s 11d
Edward Collson, 13 weeks 1 day 21s 11d
Richard Weste, 13 weeks 1 day 21s 11d
Thomas Barber, 7 weeks 11s 8d
Bartholomew Gaittes, gromet, 13 weeks 1 day 16s 5d
Richard Baskom, gromet, 4 weeks 5s
Jermyn Galway, server, 8 weeks 8 days 14s 6d
Gregory Wickes, 13 weeks 1 day 21s 11d
Thomas James, 13 weeks 1 day 21s 11d
Edward Hurllstone, gromet, 13 weeks 1 day 16s 5d
John West, 5 weeks 8s 4d
John Morris, 5 weeks 8s 4d
John Smythe, 5 weeks 8s 4d
John Clarke, 3 days 8d
Richard Hutchins, 4 days 12d
Gunner
Matthew Sharppe, master, 13 weeks 1 day 32s 10d
[*Page total*] – £20 16s 6½d.

[f. 104v] *The Christopher*
Mariners
Richard Pereman, boatswain, 5 weeks 4 days 23s 2d
Andrew Everingtun, 13 weeks 1 day 21s 11d
John William, boy, 5 weeks 4 days 4s 8d
The Antelope
Mariners
Richard Wrighte, boatswain, 8 weeks 5 days 25s 5d
Thomas Awsten, purser, 8 weeks 5 days 21s 8d
John Pallmer, cook, 8 weeks 5 days 20s
William Moll, 8 weeks 5 days 14s 6d
George Lyelle, 8 weeks 5 days 14s 6d
William Mannynge, 8 weeks 5 days 14s 6d

Davy Shorte, gromet, 8 weeks 5 days	10s 10d
James Bull, 8 weeks 5 days	14s 6d
John Wakom, 7 weeks 5 days	12s 10d
Thomas Webb, 8 weeks 5 days	14s 6d
George Brodehed, gromet, 8 weeks 5 days	10s 10d
[*Gunner*]	
Roger Bowth, master gunner, 8 weeks 5 days	21s 8d
The Jennet	
Mariners	
Richard Trewe, boatswain, 8 weeks 5 days	25s 5d
William Broke, purser, 8 weeks 5 days	21s 8d
John Adams, steward, 8 weeks 5 days	20s
Henry Stappull, 8 weeks 5 days	14s 8d
Alexander Goulde, boy, 8 weeks 5 days	7s 3d
John Phillippes, 8 weeks 5 days	14s 6d
John Bryan, 8 weeks 5 days	14s 6d
[*Gunners*]	
Richard Haynes, master gunner, 8 weeks 5 days	21s 8d
Davy Evens, server, 8 weeks 5 days	14s 6d

[*Page total*] – £19 19s 8d.

[f. 105] *The Greyhound*

Mariners	
Robert Harrode, boatswain, 8 weeks 5 days	25s 5d
Edmund Dawson, purser, 8 weeks 5 days	20s
Richard Tyller, 7 weeks 5 days	12s 10d
Roger Browne, boy, 8 weeks 5 days	7s 3d
Andrew Mallin, 8 weeks 5 days	14s 6d
Walter Tawlbot, 8 weeks 5 days	14s 6d
[*Gunner*]	
John Banckes, master gunner, 8 weeks 5 days	21s 8d
The Tiger	
Mariners	
John Abowen, boatswain, 13 weeks 1 day	38s 4d
John Hawkins, purser, 13 weeks 1 day	30s 1½d
John Bowye, 13 weeks 1 day	21s 11d
Thomas Buttler, 13 weeks 1 day	21s 11d
John Newtonn, boy, 13 weeks 1 day	10s 11½d
Thomas Wacey, gromet, 8 weeks 5 days	10s 10d
Thomas Hawll, 13 weeks 1 day	21s 11d
John Johnson, 4 weeks 3 days	7s 4d
Walter Whearewoode, 4 weeks 3 days	7s 4d

[*Gunner*]
John More, master gunner, 13 weeks 1 day 32s 10d
[*Page total*] – £15 19s 8d.

[f. 105v] *The Bull*
Mariners
Andrew Walker, boatswain, 13 weeks 1 day 38s 4d
John Willy, purser, 13 weeks 1 day 30s 1½d
Christopher Cowper, 13 weeks 1 day 21s 11d
Edward Thomas, gromet, 13 weeks 1 day 16s 5d
Richard Cronell, 13 weeks 1 day 21s 11d
Robert Harteley, 13 weeks 1 day 21s 11d
Henry Tanner, 4 weeks 3 days 7s 4d
Richard Pittman, 4 weeks 3 days 7s 4d
[*Gunner*]
Robert Buttler, master gunner, 13 weeks 1 day 32s 10d
The Falcon
Mariners
Lawrence Cleare, boatswain, 13 weeks 1 day 38s 4d
Henry Baker, purser, 13 weeks 1 day 30s 1½d
Richard Laughan, boy, 13 weeks 1 day 10s 11½d
[*Gunner*]
John Comyn, master gunner, 13 weeks 1 day 32s 10d
The Bright Falcon
Mariners
Robert Blacke, boatswain, 13 weeks 1 day 38s 4d
Edward Teayllor, 13 weeks 1 day 21s 11d
Henry Williams, 13 weeks 1 day 21s 11d
John Worroll, 4 weeks 3 days 7s 4d
[*Gunner*]
John Walker, master gunner, 13 weeks 1 day 32s 10d
[*Page total*] – £21 12s 9½d.

[f. 106] *The Bark of Boulogne*
Mariners
Richard Lamb, boatswain, 8 weeks 5 days 25s 5d
Edward Coxe, purser, 4 weeks 3 days 10s 2d
William Peatche, 8 weeks 5 days 14s 6d
Robert Aungell, purser, 4 weeks 2 days 9s 10d
[*Gunner*]
John Williams, master gunner, 8 weeks 5 days 21s 8d

The Galley Speedwell	
Mariners	
Cuthbert Clarke, boatswain, 13 weeks 1 day	54s 9d
Anthony Dearnatho, 13 weeks 1 day	21s 11d
William Prince, 13 weeks 1 day	21s 11d
Thomas Foster, boy, 13 weeks 1 day	10s 11½d
Thomas Purden, 4 weeks 6 days	8s 1d
[*Gunner*]	
Morris Abowen, master gunner, 13 weeks 1 day	32s 10d
The Galley Tryright	
Mariners	
Simon Barnesley, boatswain, 13 weeks 1 day	38s 4d
John Godden, purser, 13 weeks 1 day	32s 10d
William Kent, steward, 13 weeks 1 day	30s 1½d
John Teayllor, 13 weeks 1 day	21s 11d
Thomas Bucklond, 4 weeks 3 days	7s 4d
[*Gunners*]	
John Farley, master gunner, 8 weeks 5 days	21s 8d
Thomas Neell, master gunner, 4 weeks 3 days	11s 2d

[*Page total*] – £19 15s 5d.

[f. 106v] *The Galley Mermaid*	
Mariners	
John Davy, boatswain, 8 weeks	23s 4d
Henry Pendeley, 13 weeks 1 day	21s 11d
Henry Fuller, 13 weeks 1 day	21s 11d
Simon Marden, 4 weeks 4 days	7s 4d
John Harris, 2 weeks	3s 4d
George Porter, 4 weeks 4 days	7s 4d
Richard Harman, 13 weeks 1 day	21s 11d
The Willoughby	
Mariners	
Robert Flinte, boatswain, 10 weeks 5 days	31s 3d
George Hawll, purser, 10 weeks 5 days	24s 7d
Richard Deones, 10 weeks 5 days	17s 10d
Thomas Durrant, 10 weeks 5 days	17s 10d
Benjamin Flint, gromet, 10 weeks 5 days	13s 4d
Thomas Woodebridge, 10 weeks 5 days	17s 10d
Richard Babbe, 1 week 1 day	23d
[*Gunners*]	
John Mallpas, master gunner, 10 weeks 5 days	26s 8d
John Turner, server, 10 weeks 5 days	17s 10d

[*Page total*] – £13 16s 2d.

[f. 107] *The Triumph*

Mariners

William Wood, master, 7 weeks 5 days	£3 17s 2d
Thomas Goldeston, boatswain, 7 weeks 5 days	37s 1d
Henry Cooke, purser, 7 weeks 5 days	19s 7d
John Bassewell, steward, 7 weeks 5 days	17s 8½d
John Neweball, 7 weeks 5 days	12s 10d
Mark Bullen, 7 weeks 5 days	12s 10d
Robert White, 7 weeks 5 days	12s 10d
Peter Trewe, 7 weeks 5 days	12s 10d
Thomas Tybball, 7 weeks 5 days	12s 10d
Robert Key, 7 weeks 5 days	12s 10d
Thomas Ratcliff, 7 weeks 5 days	12s 10d
Edward Wekes, 7 weeks 5 days	12s 10d
Henry Morris, gromet, 7 weeks 5 days	9s 8d
Davy Barre, 7 weeks 5 days	12s 10d
Peter Morgyn, 7 weeks 5 days	12s 10d
John Robson, 7 weeks 5 days	12s 10d
George Myelles, 7 weeks 5 days	12s 10d
William Sowman, 1 week 5 days	2s 10d
John Wekes, 3 weeks 2 days	5s 6d
Thomas Jolly, 6 weeks 4 days	10s
Richard Pulter, 3 weeks 2 days	5s 6d
Henry Magat, 7 weeks 5 days	12s 10d
Robert Gylles, 7 weeks 5 days	12s 10d
John Gybbson, 1 week 5 days	2s 10d
Richard Dyamounde, 2 weeks	3s 4d
William Brigges, 2 weeks 2 days	3s 10d
John Raggat, 7 weeks 5 days	12s 10d
John Bowye, 7 weeks 5 days	12s 10d
Peter Edwardes, 7 weeks 5 days	12s 10d
Henry Bull, 3 weeks 2 days	5s 6d
Richard Bennet, 3 weeks 2 days	5s 6d
Robert Loist, 3 weeks 2 days	5s 6d
Nicholas Workeley, 3 weeks 2 days	5s 6d
Richard Jonnes, 6 days	17d
Nicholas Moone, quartermaster, 3 weeks 2 days	5s 6d
John Maister, 3 weeks 2 days	5s 6d
John Clarke, 3 weeks 2 days	5s 6d
John Horneby, 2 weeks	3s 4d

[*Page total*] – £22 6s 0½d.

[f. 107v] Stephen Huggyn, 1 week 5 days	2s 10d
Matthew Maister, 3 weeks 2 days	5s 6d
Richard Stokes, 3 weeks 2 days	5s 6d
Edward Rose, surgeon, 3 weeks 2 days	12s 3d
John Novyn, 1 week	20d
Richard Houlte, 3 weeks 2 days	5s 6d
William Porter, 6 days	17d
Anthony Dibdaill, 1 week 5 days	2s 10d
John Chappline, 3 weeks 2 days	5s 6d
George Maister, 1 week 5 days	2s 10d
Edmund Carter, 3 weeks 2 days	5s 6d
William Tucker, 1 week 5 days	2s 10d
Richard Pearse, 3 weeks 2 days	5s 6d
Nicholas Gilbart, 3 weeks 2 days	5s 6d
Henry Billington, server, 1 week 5 days	2s 10d
Hugh Gilbart, boy, 3 weeks 2 days	2s 9d
John White, 3 weeks 2 days	5s 6d
John Coxe, 1 week 5 days	2s 10d
William Thomas, 5 days	14d
Richard Lovet, 3 weeks 2 days	5s 6d
John Phillippes, 5 days	14d
William Beare, 5 days	14d
Robert Merse, 5 days	14d
Edward Pyll, 5 days	14d
Richard Clark, 5 days	14d
Nicholas Becke, 5 days	14d
Thomas Etell, 3 weeks 2 days	5s 6d
Thomas Skill, 5 days	14d
William Hamonde, 5 days	14d
Robert Atkins, 3 weeks 2 days	5s 6d
Garret Johnson, 1 week 5 days	2s 10d
Lawrence Gillam, 5 days	14d
Walter Griffin, 3 weeks 2 days	5s 6d
Richard Holmes, 5 days	14d
John Archer, quartermaster, 5 days	2s 1d
William Spender, 5 days	14d
John Safforne, boy, 5 days	7d

[*Page total*] – £6 7s.

[f. 108] Vincent Godfrey, 5 days	14d
Martin Fraunce, 5 days	14d
Thomas Jonnes, 3 weeks 2 days	5s 6d

William Blanden, 3 weeks 2 days	5s 6d
William White, 1 week 5 days	2s 10d
Robert Willson, 5 days	14d
William Harwood, 3 weeks 2 days	5s 6d
William Clegge, 3 weeks 2 days	5s 6d
Robert Myller, 5 days	14d
William Crostone, 5 days	14d
Thomas Clarke, 5 days	14d
James Commen, 5 days	14d
Richard Thomas, 3 weeks 2 days	5s 6d
Roger Kempe, 5 days	14d
William Patche, 5 days	14d
Jasper Willson, 1 week 4 days	2s 7d
Roger Chappman, 3 weeks 2 days	5s 6d
Thomas Mowlton, 5 days	14d
Ralph Chamberlain, 1 week 5 days	2s 10d
William Wellshe, carpenter, 7 weeks 5 days	32s 1d
Thomas Freman, gromet, 7 weeks 5 days	9s 7d
William Chartram, gromet, 7 weeks 5 days	9s 7d
Ralph Browne, 7 weeks 5 days	27s 6d
[*Edmund*][1] Waller, 7 weeks 5 days	22s 6d
Robert Willis, gromet, 7 weeks 5 days	9s 7d
John Hurlocke, 8 weeks	13s 4d
[*Gunner*]	
Stephen Bull, master, 7 weeks 5 days	19s 7d

[*Page total*] – £9 11s 8d.

[f. 108v] *The Victory*

Mariners

William Barnes, master, 7 weeks 5 days	£3 17s 2d
John Light, boatswain, 7 weeks 5 days	32s 1d
Hugh Pope, purser, 7 weeks 5 days	19s 7d
Thomas Gaittes, steward, 7 weeks 5 days	17s 8½d
Robert Ussher, boy, 7 weeks 5 days	6s 5d
William Pearcevall, 7 weeks 5 days	12s 10d
Abel Smythe, 7 weeks 5 days	12s 10d
George Steward, 7 weeks 5 days	12s 10d
Peter Hanson, 7 weeks 5 days	12s 10d
Adam Puckewell, quartermaster, 7 weeks 5 days	22s 6d
Thomas Cossyn, 7 weeks 5 days	12s 10d
Richard Blacke, 7 weeks 5 days	12s 10d

[1]MS here 'Edwarde', but always Edmund elsewhere; cf. below, p. 335 and other entries.

Leonard Houlte, boy, 7 weeks 5 days	6s 5d
Richard Smythe, 4 weeks 5 days	7s 10d
Stephen Justis, 4 weeks 5 days	7s 10d
Raulphe Ducke, 4 weeks 5 days	7s 10d
John Greane, 4 weeks 5 days	7s 10d
Arnold Harte, 4 weeks 5 days	7s 10d
Thomas Cocke, 2 weeks 2 days	3s 10d
John Whitaker, 2 weeks 2 days	3s 10d
Peter Patyson, 2 days	6d
John Stacye, 2 weeks 2 days	3s 10d
William Clarke, 5 weeks 6 days	9s 9d
Peter Sawders, 3 weeks 2 days	5s 6d
Richard Curle, 3 weeks 2 days	5s 6d
Peter Powill, 3 weeks 2 days	5s 6d
John Bigges, 1 week 4 days	2s 8d
Oliver Gaskon, 3 weeks 2 days	5s 6d
Nicholas Smythe, 5 days	14d
William Dogget, 1 week 4 days	2s 8d
William Conrede, 3 weèks 2 days	5s 6d
Thomas Andros, 5 days	14d
John Grene, 5 days	14d
John Ball, 3 weeks 2 days	5s 6d
John Maideston, 1 week 4 days	2s 8d
Thomas Jonnes, 3 weeks 2 days	5s 6d
Ellis Knight, 3 weeks 2 days	5s 6d

[*Page total*] – £18 15s 3½d.

[f. 109] Nicholas Cley, carpenter, 7 weeks 5 days	32s 1d
John Clay, gromet, 7 weeks 5 days	9s 7d
John Sager, 7 weeks 5 days	12s 10d
Thomas Hodge, 7 weeks 5 days	12s 10d
Mark Hodge, 7 weeks 5 days	12s 10d
William Hodge, gromet, 7 weeks 5 days	9s 7d
Roger Rayner, server, 7 weeks 5 days	[*blank*]
George Kingston, 7 weeks 5 days	[*blank*]
[*Gunner*]	
William Thomas, master gunner, 7 weeks 5 days	19s 7d

Wages of gunners daily attending in Her Highness's fort at Upnor for the safe-keeping of Her Grace's ships in Gillingham Water, begun the first day of October past and this day ended, as followeth:

Thomas Sergent, master, 92 days at 16d	£6 2s 8d
Richard Absede, 92 days at 12d	£4 12s

Robert Wullgrow, 92 days at 12d	£4 12s
William Bowell, 92 days at 12d	£4 12s
William Cheselton, 92 days at 12d	£4 12s
Randall Stevinson, 92 days at [*12d*]	£4 12s
William Tawnton, 87 days at 12d	£4 7s

[*Page total*] – £38 19s.

[f. 109v] *[*Purveyor*]. To Butolph Moungey the last day of December for his wages daily attending and serving Her Highness in making of provision for Her Grace's ships, *viz.* cables, ropes and other cordage by him provided and delivered into Her Grace's storehouses there, by one quarter of a year begun the first day of October last and this day ended, at 8d *per diem* – £3 1s 4d.

*[*Clerk*]. To Thomas Hennos the same day for his wages daily attending and serving Her Highness in keeping of the book of cheque of masters, mariners and gunners serving Her Grace for the keeping of Her Highness's ships afloat in harbour, as also the prick book of shipwrights, sawyers and others, by one quarter of a year begun and ended as abovesaid – £5.

*[*Keeper of storehouse or purveyor*]. To Thomas Baker the same day for his wages daily serving Her Highness in delivering of cables, cablets, ropes of all sorts, canvas, twine, needles and divers other kinds of stuffs out of her storehouses there to the use of Her Graces's ships, by one quarter of a year begun the first day of October last and this day ended as abovesaid – £2.

Watchmen	
Andrew Everington, 83 nights at 3d	20s 9d
Henry Penley, 83 nights at 3d	20s 9d

[*Page total*] – £12 2s 10d.

[f. 110] *Shipwrights*	
Michael Chamber, 33 days at 6d	16s 6d
Richard Crippes, 32 days at 6d	16s
Thomas Poulter, 27 days at 8d	18s
John Clarke, 29 days at 4d	9s 8d
Richard Dennes, 60 days at 3d	15s
Thomas Smythe, 2 days at 12d	2s
Sawyers	
Edmund Bell, 47 days at 6d	23s 6d
William Pette,[1] 47 days at 6d	23s 6d

[1]Perhaps Peter Pett's eldest son and designated successor, who predeceased him in 1587. The patent by which William became master shipwright in survivorship with his father (1582) referred to his previous service in building royal ships and assistance in marine affairs: *CPR 1580–2*, no. 1032. Pett, *Autobiography*, pp. xxiii–xxxiv, xlvii–xlviii, l.

William Symonde, 38 days at 6d	19s
William Bereman, 38 days at 6d	19s
Edmund Bell, 8 days at 12d	8s
William Norwoode, 4 days at 12d	4s
Thomas Murton, 4 days at 12d	4s
Roger Rayner, 50 days at 6d	25s
George Kingston, 50 days at 4d	16s 8d

Lodging. To Ellin Guye, Margaret Smythe and divers other persons of Chatham, Gillingham, Rochester and thereabouts the last day of December for the lodging of 30 shipwrights and sawyers in 15 featherbeds by 1,678 days among them all, which maketh 230 weeks, begun the 12th[1] day of November last and this day ended, at 2d every man the week – £1 18s 4d.

[*Page total*] – £12 18s 2d.

[f. 110v] *Emptions*

Timber oak. To William Truslo of Aylesford the last day of December for price of 1½ tons of timber oak of him had for the use of Her Highness's ships, price – 15s.

To Robert Pallmer of Millhall the same day for price of one piece of oaken timber containing one ton for the use as beforesaid. *Summa* – 10s.

To Thomas Parker of Gillingham the same day for price of one piece of oaken timber of him had for the use of Her Highness's ships there, containing 35 foot – 8s 9d.

Shores. To John Hurlocke, master of one of Her Highness's ships, the same day for price of one load of shores of him had for the use of Her Grace's ships as aforesaid, price – 4s.

Land carriage. To Thomas Hewet of St Margaret's the same day, and 20 other persons of Cobham and thereabouts, for the carriage of 21 loads of timber from Cobham aforesaid to Chatham, being distance 4 miles, at 3d every mile the load – £1 1s.

Water carriage. To William Wystin, master of a hoy called the *William of Aylsforde*, the same day for the service of his hoy in carrying of 7 cables of 11 inches compass, 4 cables of 12 inches, 3 cablets of 8 inches, 3 dozen of boat oars, 10 small masts for tops and divers other needful things taken in at Deptford Strand and the same delivered at Chatham for the use of Her Grace's ships there; by agreement – £1 13s 4d.

[1]MS '*ijth*', an error for 12th ('*xijth*') rather than 2nd ('*ijnd*') because the computation allows for just over seven weeks, fitting the 50 days inclusive from 12 November to 31 December.

Board. To Henry Shorte of Gillingham the same day for price of 400 foot of inch board of him had for the use of Her Grace's ships, at 5s every 100 foot – £1.

[*Page total*] – £5 12s 1d.

[f. 111] *Water carriage of provisions.* To Vincent Powell, Dutchman, the last day of December for service of his hoy serving Her Highness in carrying of provisions, *viz.* overlop nails, 2 hogsheads of train oil, 6 sheets of flat lead, 6 thousandweight of rosin, 8 loads of timber oak, 26 planks, with divers other necessaries taken out of Her Grace's great storehouse at Deptford Strand and the same delivered at Chatham for the use of Her Majesty's ships there. *Summa* – £1 13s 4d.

To Robert Haull, master of a hoy called the *Powill of Ypswiche* [i.e. *Paul of Ipswich*] the same day for service of his hoy, serving Her Highness in carrying of certain Her Majesty's store, *viz.* 3 great flags of St George and one small flag, 102 bolts of British [*Breton*] medrinacks, 37 bolts of English medrinacks, 2 hundredweight of carvel spikes, 3,000 of 10d nail, 7,200 of 6d nail, and divers other kinds of ironwork and necessaries taken up at Deptford Strand and delivered the same at Chatham as aforesaid; by agreement – £1 10s.

To Robert Raunger, master of a hoy called the *Edwarde of Newhiff* [i.e. *New Hythe*], the same day for carrying of 19 cables and cablets of 15 and 16 inches compass, 5 ton of timber and other stuffs received at Her Highness's great storehouse at Deptford and delivered at Chatham for the use of Her Majesty's ships as aforesaid – £1 10s.

To John Griges, master of a hoy called the *Elizabethe of Manytre* [i.e. *Manningtree*], the same day for the carriage of certain provisions, as 20 bolts of poldavy, 20 bolts of medrinacks, 9½ dozen of twine, 200 of marline, 10 dozen of boat oars, 6 mattocks, 12 hair tilts, 12 ring-bolts, 12 setting bolts, 6 hundredweight of spikes and overlop nails, with divers other kinds of provisions taken up at Deptford and delivered the same at Chatham as aforesaid for the use of Her Majesty's ships; by agreement – £1 16s 8d.

To John Gaittes, master of a hoy called the *Jullyon of Maydestone*, the same day for the carriage of 2,000 [*foot*] of inch board oak and delivered the same at Chatham for the use of Her Grace's ships – 10s.

[*Page total*] – £7.

[f. 111v] *Ironwork *[£17 16s 8d; nails – £10 17s 2d; locks – 3s 4d*]. To George Hoppe of Chatham, smith, the last day of December for price of 11½ hundred 13 pounds weight [*1,301 lbs*] of his own new iron by him made and wrought into bolts, rings and keys, great spikes, overlop nails, rove, clench nail and port-hinges for the use of Her Highness's ships there, at 23s 4d every hundredweight – £13 10s 11d;[1] more to him for the working of 6 hundred 13 [*repl.* 12] pounds [*weight*] [*685 lbs*] of Her Highness's old iron by him made into bolts for the use as aforesaid, at 8s 4d every hundredweight – 51s 1d;[2] more for grommets and staples, 274 pair at 1½d the pair – 34s 3d; more for 1,000 of nails, at 2s 6d every 100 – 25s; more for 100 of 3s nail – 3s; more for 5,600 of 20d nail, at 20d every 100 – £4 13s 4d; more for 7,000 of 10d nail, at 10d every 100 – 58s 4d; more for 7,500 of 6d nail – 37s 6d; and more to him for 2 locks and 2 keys for the storehouse there – 3s 4d. *Summa* – £28 16s 9d.

Oakum. To Joan Browne, Elin Harwoode, Anes Gaittes, Elizabeth Goldeston, Joan Newball, Eme Cooke and 17 other persons of Gillingham, Chatham, Rochester and thereabouts the same day for the working and picking of 9 thousand 1½ hundred 20 pounds weight [*10,268 lbs*] of Her Highness's old junks and ropes by them made and wrought into oakum for the needful use of Her Majesty's ships there, at 3s 4d every hundredweight working – £15 5s 7d.

Netting-ropes and oakum. To Thomas Hunt of Chatham, ropemaker, the same day for workmanship of 33 coil of netting-ropes by him made of Her Highness's old junks, weighing 14 hundredweight [*1,568 lbs*], at 3s 8d every hundredweight 51s 4d; and more to him for the picking of 9 hundred 2 quarters weight [*1,064 lbs*] of Her Grace's said junks into oakum for the use of Her Majesty's ships, at 3s 8d the hundred[*weight*] – 34s 10d. *Summa* – £4 6s 2d.

Ox tallow. To Thomas Goldston of Ratcliff the same day for price of 2 hundredweight of hard tallow of him had for the use of Her Grace's ships there, at 10s every hundredweight – £1.

[*Page total*] – £49 8s 6d.

[f. 112] *[*Labourer*]. To Henry Pendley, William Prince and William Mannyng [*and*] one other, labourers, the last day of December for their pains taken in daily labouring about the mending and repairing of the wharfs and grounding place there, with other kind of labour done about the same, by one quarter of a year at 5 shillings every man – £1.

To John Hurlocke the same day for price of 3 bushels of hair of him had for the use of Her Highness's ships there, at 4d every bushel – 1s.

House rent. To Adam Keller of Chatham the same day for rent of a certain storehouse and ground of him hired wherein lieth Her Highness's store of provisions, as cables, cablets, ropes, canvas and divers kinds of stuffs pertaining to Her Highness's ships, by one quarter of a year begun the first day of October and this day ended – 10s.

[1]The calculation gives 3252.5d, which is 1½d above the sum stated (3251d).

[2]The calculation gives 611.60711d, which is about 1½d below the sum stated (613d).

To Thomas Winnall of Chatham the same day for hire of a certain storehouse and ground thereunto belonging, wherein lieth Her Highness's pitch, tar, rosin, oakum and divers other kinds of provisions for the use of Her Grace's ships, by one quarter of a year begun and ended as aforesaid – 3s 4d.

To Richard Mylles of Chatham the same day for rent of a certain storehouse wherein lieth Her Highness's reed for the breaming of Her Grace's ships at their groundings, by one quarter of a year begun and ended as abovesaid – 1s 3d.

To Roger Cratway of Frindsbury[1] the same day for certain stuffs by him bought and consumed in the destroying of rats and mice for the safeguard of Her Highness's sails, canvas and flags within the whole fleet for one whole year; by agreement – £2.

[*Page total*] – £3 15s 7d. [f. 112v *blank*]

[f. 113] **Ordinary. Colne**:[2]

Anno Domini 1562. Anno regni regine Elizabethe quarto

A payment made the last day of March as well to keepers of storehouses, dock and timber-yards there wherein lieth Her Highness's store of all kinds of provisions for the use of Her Grace's ships, and for provisions had toward the repairing of the said storehouses, as also for rent of the same; by one quarter of a year begun the first day of January last and this day ended, as followeth:

[1]MS 'Fansbury'. Although later variants ('Fynnesburye' at ff. 243, 254v, 'Fynesbury' at ff. 262v, 263) suggest Finsbury (Middlesex), Frindsbury near Rochester is more probable in the context, and is confirmed by the entry at f. 88v which mentions Cratway among others from the Medway towns; cf. Thomas Sergaunt of the same place (f. 263), who is undoubtedly the man named elsewhere as captain of the adjacent fort of Upnor.

[2]Royal ships had been stationed in the Colne estuary since Henry VIII's time, and probably earlier in view of Brightlingsea's unique status as the only limb of the Cinque Ports north of the Thames. The facility developed following the recommendation of the King in 1543: 'Lord Admiral Lisle', p. 70; *NEM*, p. 107 & n. 1), but its usage remained intermittent. The shore installation was little more than a timber-yard and a few storehouses. By the time of this account the only activity appears to have been pumping water out of the elderly *Trinity Henry*. Even this must have been abandoned soon afterwards, since the hull, 'long since' laid by the shore, was sold, together with an old storehouse and forge, to the storekeeper Edward Lambart for £38 10s, by virtue of an indenture of 25 June 1566 which effectively wound up the whole operation: E 351/2202, m. 1d. Cf. E. P. Dickin, *A History of Brightlingsea: A Member of the Cinque Ports* (2nd edn, Brightlingsea, 1939), pp. 136–42, which gives extensive extracts from the present MS and other sources. The precise location of the yard has not been discovered, but it was perhaps where Colne Road runs from the town centre to the area still known as the Shipyard: cf. Appendix 4 below, p. 567.

*[*Keeper of storehouses*]. To Edward Lambart[1] the last day of March for his wages daily attending and serving Her Highness in safe-keeping of Her Grace's storehouses and timber-yard there wherein lieth divers kinds of stuffs pertaining to Her Highness's ships, for one quarter of a year containing 90 days begun the first day of January last and this day ended, at 12d *per diem* – £4 10s.

*[*Shipkeeper*]. To Thomas Richardsone, mariner, the same day for his wages daily attending and serving Her Highness in safe-keeping of Her Grace's ship named the *Trinity Henry* by the space of 90 days begun and ended as aforesaid, at 6d *per diem* – £2 5s.

[*Page total*] – £6 15s.

[f. 113v] *Emptions*

*[*Artificers*]. To William Abraham, tiler, the last day of March for wages of himself and his man in new mending and repairing of Her Highness's storehouses there by the space of 8 days between them, at 12d every day – 8s; more to him for 2 stone of lime, at 3s the stone – 6s; more for 4 loads [*inserted* of clay] at 6d the load – 2s; more for 2 loads of sand, price – 12d; more for splints for mending of the walls there, price – 6d. *Summa* – 17s 6d.

*[*Iron*]. To Jasper Smyth the same day for 4 small dogs of iron by him delivered for the new mending of Her Highness's storehouses there, weighing 28½ pounds weight at 4d every pound weight. *Summa* – 8s 2d.

*[*Labourer*]. To Robert Consent and three other labourers the same day for labouring in lading out of water out of the *Trinity Henry*, with other service there to be done within this time; by agreement – 9s 4d.

House rent. To William Bereff[2] the same day for rent of a certain storehouse and ground of him hired wherein lieth Her Grace's store of provisions of all kinds for the use of her ships, by one quarter of a year due at this present – 13s 4d.

To Thomas Bereff the same day for one quarter of a year's rent of a certain storehouse and ground of him hired wherein lieth divers kinds of stuffs for Her Grace's ships, due at this present – 6s 8d.

[*Page total*] – £2 15s.

[1]In 1561 a candidate for the post of Deputy (chief officer) of Brightlingsea, when Thomas Beriffe was elected. In the same year he bought a crane for the dockyard from the churchwardens for £3 6s 8d: Dickin, *Brightlingsea*, pp. 109, 142.

[2]The Beriffe family were from 1460 to 1660 occupants of Jacobe's Hall, a substantial 13th-century building in the centre of Brightlingsea, the town's principal residence and still inhabited. Thomas Beriffe, who died in 1563, had been Deputy four times; along with much other property in the town he owned half of the *Mary Fortune*. William Beriffe held the same post for 12 years before his death in 1578: PROB 11/46, ff. 312v–314 (Thomas's will, dated 4 Sept., proved 16 Dec. 1563). Dickin, *Brightlingsea*, pp. 78, 82, 118, 208 and *passim*. *Brightlingsea Official Guide* (Macclesfield, 1991), pp. 13–14.

[f. 114] A payment made the last day of June as well to keepers of storehouses, dock and timber-yards there wherein lieth Her Highness's store of all kinds of provisions for the use of Her Grace's ships, as also for rent of the said storehouses, by one quarter of a year begun the first day of April last and this day ended, as followeth:

*[*Storehouse keeper*]. To Edward Lambarte the last day of June for his wages daily attending and serving Her Highness in safe-keeping of Her Grace's storehouses and timber-yards there wherein lieth divers kinds of stuffs pertaining to her ships, by the space of 91 days begun the first day of April last and this day ended, at 12d *per diem*. *Summa* – £4 11s.

*[*Shipkeeper*]. To Thomas Richardson, mariner, the same day for his wages daily attending and serving Her Highness in safe-keeping of Her Grace's ship there named the *Trinity Henry* by like time begun and ended as abovesaid, at 6d *per diem* – £2 5s 6d.

[*Page total*] – £6 16s 6d.

[f. 114v] *Emptions*

*[*Labourers*]. To Robert Concent and three other labourers the last day of June for their wages in labouring about the cleansing, scouring and having out of the water in the dock there wherein lieth Her Highness's ship named the *Trinity Henry*; by agreement – 8s.

To John Paige and divers other mariners the same day for their pains taken with their boat at sundry times in searching for one Her Grace's great anchors which was let fall in Borefleet Water[1] between a hoy and the *Great Bark*'s boat at the *Great Bark*'s last being there, as yet not found. *Summa* – 12s 6d.

House rent. To William Bereff the same day for one quarter's rent of a certain storehouse and ground of him hired wherein lieth Her Grace's store of all kinds of stuffs for the use of Her Highness's ships, due at this present – 13s 4d.

To Thomas Bereff the same day for one quarter of a year's house rent of a certain house and ground of him hired wherein lieth divers kinds of stuffs for the use of Her Grace's ships, due at this present – 6s 8d.

[*Page total*] – £2 0s 6d.

[f. 115] A payment made the last day of September as well to keepers of storehouses, dock and timber-yards there wherein lieth Her Highness's store of all kinds of provisions for the use of Her Grace's ships, as also for rent of the said storehouses, by one quarter of a year begun the first day of July last and this day ended, as followeth:

[1]Brightlingsea Creek, formerly known as Borefleet, separating Brightlingsea from St Osyth: cf. EPNS, *Essex*, pp. 13–14.

*[*Storehouse keeper*]. To Edward Lambert the last day of September for his wages daily attending and serving Her Highness in safe-keeping of Her Grace's storehouses and timber-yards there wherein lieth divers kinds of stuffs pertaining to her ships, by 92 days begun the first day of July last and this day ended, at 12d *per diem* – £4 12s.

*[*Shipkeeper*]. To Thomas Richardson, mariner, the same day for his wages daily attending and serving Her Highness in safe-keeping of Her Grace's ship named the *Trinity Henry* by the space of 92 days begun and ended as abovesaid, at 6d *per diem* – £2 6s.

[*Page total*] – £6 18s.

[f. 115v] *Emptions*

House rent. To William Bereff the same day for rent of a certain storehouse and ground of him hired wherein lieth Her Grace's store of all kinds of necessaries for the use of Her Highness's ships, due at this present – 13s 4d.

To Thomas Berryff the same day for rent of a certain storehouse and ground of him hired wherein lieth divers kinds of stuff pertaining to Her Grace's ships, by one quarter of a year, due at this present – 6s 8d.

*[*Labourers*]. To Robert Concent and three other labourers the same day for their wages in labouring about the scouring and having of the water out of the dock there wherein Her Highness's ship lieth, the *Trinity Henry*; by agreement. *Summa* – 7s 4d.

[*Page total*] – £1 7s 4d.

[f. 116] *Anno Domini 1562. Anno regni regine Elizabethe quinto*

A payment made the last day of December as well to keepers of storehouses, dock and timber-yards there wherein lieth Her Highness's store of all kinds of provisions for the use of Her Grace's ships, as also for the rent of the said storehouses; by one quarter of a year begun the first day of October last and this day ended, as followeth:

*[*Storehousekeeper*]. To Edward Lambard the last day of December for his [*wages*] daily attending and serving Her Highness in safe-keeping of Her Grace's storehouses and timber-yards there wherin lieth divers kinds of stuffs pertaining to her ships, by one quarter of a year containing 92 days begun the first day of October and this day ended, at 12d *per diem* – £4 12s.

*[*Shipkeeper*]. To Thomas Richardson, mariner, the same day for his wages daily attending and serving Her Highness in safe-keeping of Her Grace's ship named the *Trinity Henry* by the space of 92 days begun and ended as aforesaid, at 6d *per diem* – £2 6s.

[*Page total*] – £6 18s.

[f. 116v] *Emptions*

*[*Labourers*]. To Robert Consent and three other labourers the last day of December for their wages in labouring about the scouring and having out of the water in the dock there wherein lieth Her Highness's ship called the *Trinity Henry* at divers times within this quarter – 8s.

House rent. To William Beryff the same day for the rent of a certain storehouse and ground of him hired wherein lieth Her Highness's store of provisions and necessaries for the use of Her Grace's ships, due at this present – 13s 4d.

To Thomas Beryff the same day for rent of a certain storehouse and ground of him hired wherein lieth divers kinds of stuffs pertaining to Her Grace's ships, by one quarter of a year due at this present – 6s 8d.

[*Page total*] – £1 8s.

[f. 117] **Ordinary. Portsmouth**:

Anno Domini 1562. Anno regni regine Elizabethe quarto

A payment made the last day of March as well to keepers of storehouses, dock and timber-yards there wherein lieth Her Highness's store of all kinds of provision for the use of Her Grace's ships, as also for provisions had of divers persons for the repairing of the same; begun the first day of January last and this day ended, as followeth:

*[*Storehouse keepers*]. To John Thomas the last day of March for his wages daily attending and serving Her Highness in safe-keeping of her storehouses there wherein lieth Her Grace's store of provision for the use of her ships, for one quarter of a year due at this present – £5.

To John Powell the same day for his wages daily attending and serving Her Highness in safe-keeping of the dock and timber-yard there wherein lieth Her Grace's timber and plank for the use aforesaid, by the space of 90 days begun and ended as abovesaid, at 6d *per diem* – £2 5s.

To Edward Prestman, labourer, the same day for his wages daily attending and serving Her Highness in keeping of the plug for the letting out of the water for the dry keeping of the dock there, by one quarter of a year begun and ended as aforesaid, at 4d *per diem* – £1 10s.

[*Page total*] – £8 15s.

[f. 117v] *Emptions*

*[*Timber*]. To Peter Porter the last day of March for price of 22 loads of compass and long timber oak by him delivered there for the use of Her Highness's ships, at 10s every load after 50 foot to the load – £11; more for 1,200 foot of 4-inch plank oak, at 10s every 100 [*foot*] – £6; and more

to him for 1,014 foot of 3-inch plank oak, at 10s every 100 foot – £5 14s. *Summa* – £22 14s.

*[*Carpenters*]. To William Wraye and William Dyamond of Portsmouth, carpenters, the same day for hewing and squaring of 21 loads of timber oak for the new mending and making of gates about Her Highness's timber-yards, as also for weatherboarding of Her Grace's storehouse there, at 14d every load squaring. *Summa* – £1 4s 6d.

*[*Shipkeepers*]. To John Homley, boatswain, the same day for his wages daily attending and serving Her Highness in safe-keeping of the *Brigantine* there, by the space of 9 weeks 3 days begun the 25th day of January last and this day ended, at 9s 2d *per mensem* – 21s 6d; and more to Thomas Brewton, master gunner, for his wages serving Her Highness in the same ship by like time of 9 weeks 3 days begun and ended as aforesaid, at 10s *per mensem* – 23s 6d. *Summa* – £2 5s.

[*Page total*] – £25 10s 8d.

[f. 118] A payment made the last day of June to keepers of storehouses, dock and timber-yards there wherein lieth Her Highness's timber, plank and board, and divers other necessaries for the use of her ships, begun the first day of April last and this day ended, as followeth:

*[*Storehouse keepers*]. To John Thomas the last day of June for his wages daily attending and serving Her Highness in safe-keeping of her storehouses wherein lieth Her Grace's store of provisions for the use of her ships, by one quarter of a year begun the first day of April last and ended as abovesaid – £5.

To John Powell the same day for his wages daily attending and serving Her Highness in safe-keeping of her timber-yards there wherein lieth her timber and plank for the use of Her Grace's ships, by 91 days begun and ended as abovesaid, at 6d *per diem* – £2 5s 6d.

To Edmund Prestman, labourer. the same day for his wages daily attending and serving Her Highness in safe-keeping of the plug for the letting out of the water for the dry keeping of the dock there, by like 91 days begun and ended as aforesaid, at 4d *per diem* – £1 10s 4d.

[*Page total*] – £8 15s 10d.

[f. 118v] *[*Shipkeepers*]. To John Homley, boatswain, the last day of June for his wages daily attending and serving Her Highness in safe-keeping of the *Brigantine* there by the space of 13 weeks one day begun the first day of April last and this day ended, at 9s 2d *per mensem* – 30s 1½d; and more to Thomas Brewton, master gunner for his wages serving Her Highness in the same ship by like time of 13 weeks one day begun and ended as aforesaid, at 10s *per mensem* – 32s 10d. *Summa* – £3 2s 11½d.

To Henry Clarke, boatswain, the same day for his wages daily attending and serving Her Highness in safe-keeping of the *Flower de Luce* there by the space of one week begun the 25th day of this present month of June and ended the last day of the same, at 9s 2d *per mensem* – 2s 3½d; and more to George Pearce for his wages serving in the same ship by like time of one week begun and ended as aforesaid, at 6s 8d *per mensem* – 20d. *Summa* – 3s 11½d.

[*Page total*] – £3 6s 11d.

[f. 119] A payment made the last day of September as well to masters, mariners and gunners serving Her Highness in keeping Her Majesty's ships afloat in harbour, as also to keepers of storehouses, dock and timber-yards there wherein lieth Her Highness's provisions for the use of Her Grace's said ships, by one quarter of a year begun the first day of July last and this day ended, as followeth:

The Brigantine	
Mariner	
John Homley, boatswain, 12 weeks 4 days	28s 10d
[*Gunner*]	
Thomas Brewton, master gunner, 12 weeks 4 days	31s 4d
The Flower de Luce	
Mariners	
Henry Clarke, boatswain, 12 weeks 4 days	28s 10d
George Perce, 12 weeks 4 days	21s

[*Page total*] – £5 10s.

[f. 119v] *The Minion*	
Mariners	
Robert Root, boatswain, 4 weeks 2 days	12s 6d
George Hollys, purser, 4 weeks 2 days	10s 9d
James Smythe, cook, 4 weeks 2 days	9s 10d
Richard Wellshe, 4 weeks 2 days	7s 2d
William Smythe, 4 weeks 2 days	7s 2d
Nicholas Mashipp, 4 weeks 2 days	7s 2d
Thomas Rogers, 4 weeks 4 days	7s 8d
Richard Tepp, 4 weeks 4 days	7s 8d
William Seman, 4 weeks 4 days	7s 8d
Christopher Clerke, 4 weeks 4 days	7s 8d
Walter Frauncke, 4 weeks 4 days	7s 8d
John Bowden, 4 weeks 4 days	7s 8d

Richard Gell, 2 weeks 4 days	4s 4d
Stephen Laurence, 2 weeks 4 days	4s 4d
[*Gunner*]	
Robert Stanton, master gunner, 2 weeks	5s
The Primrose	
Mariners	
John Harry, boatswain, 4 weeks 2 days	12s 6d
John Pett, purser, 4 weeks 2 days	10s 9d
George Broune, cook, 4 weeks 2 days	9s 10d
John Townnesende, 4 weeks 2 days	7s 2d
Nicholas Doulling, 4 weeks 2 days	7s 2d
John Gabriell, gromet, 4 weeks 2 days	5s 4d
John Gray, 4 weeks 2 days	7s 2d
Thomas Loraunce, 4 weeks 4 days	7s 8d
James Myllet, 4 weeks 4 days	7s 8d
Robert Jollyf, 4 weeks 4 days	7s 8d
William Godfray, 4 weeks 4 days	7s 8d
Thomas Ryce, 4 weeks 4 days	7s 8d
William Ermett, gromet, 4 weeks 4 days	5s 4d
William Kede, 1 week 5 days	2s 10d
Edward Penner, 1 week 5 days	2s 10d
[*Gunner*]	
Henry Macklande, master gunner, 2 weeks	5s

[*Page total*] – £11 8s 6d.

[f. 120] A payment made the last day of September to shipwrights, caulkers, sawyers, smiths and labourers working in and upon the new making and repairing of three Her Grace's ships there, *viz*. the *Phoenix*, the *Flower de Luce* and the *Brigantine*, begun as aforesaid and this day ended, as followeth:

Shipwrights	
John Pease, master, 2 days at 10d	20d
Raynold Vesey, server, 1 day at 6d	6d
William Dalopley, 10½ days at 8d	7s
Edmund Forte, server, 10½ days at 3d	2s 7½d
John Worwoode, 10½ days at 6d	5s 3d
John Small, 10½ days at 6d	5s 3d
Stephen Browne, 9½ days at 8d	6s 4d
Thomas Browne, 10½ days at 6d	5s 3d
Thomas Lawraunce, server, 9½ days at 2d	19d
Christopher Stevens, 10½ days at 6d	5s 3d

Nicholas Godden, 9½ days 6d	4s 9d
Ralph Tutway, 7½ days at 6d	3s 9d
George Upson, 3 days at 7d	21d
James Frederick, 3 days at 6d	18d
William Pennet, 3 days at 6d	18d
Robert Adams, 2 days at 7d	14d
Thomas Newberie, 2 days at 7d	14d
Richard Bull, 2 days at 6d	12d
Osmund Edmoundes, server, 3 days at 3d	9d

Sawyers

John Leonarde, 4½ days at 6d	2s 3d
John Rumbridge, 4½ days at 6d	2s 3d

[*Page total*] – £3 2s 6½d.

[f. 120v] *Smiths*

Robert Raynolde, 8½ days at 6d	4s 3d
John Realme, 8½ days at 3d	2s 1½d
John Payne, 7½ days at 4d	2s 6d

Victualling. To John Thomas of Portsmouth the last day of September for the victualling of 24 of the aforenamed shipwrights, caulkers, sawyers and smiths working upon the new mending and repairing of three Her Grace's ships there, the *Phoenix*, the *Flower de Luce* and the *Brigantine* by the space of 186 days among them all, Sundays and holy days in the same accounted, begun the 16th day of this present month of September and ended the 26th day of the same, which maketh 26 weeks 4 days, at 4s every week the man. *Summa* – £5 7s 6½d.

Labourers

Giles Bevyson, 9½ days at 6d	4s 9d
Edward Prestman, 9½ days at 6d	4s 9d
John Thomas, 9½ days at 6d	4s 9d

[*Page total*] – £6 10s 8d.

[f. 121] *Emptions*

Furzes and straw. To Richard Foster of Portsea the last day of September for price of 2 loads of furzes of him had for the use of Her Highnesss's ships, at 14d every load – 2s 4d; more for one load of straw for the like use as aforesaid, price – 2s 8d. *Summa* – 5s.

Rosin. To James Wright of Southampton, merchant, the same day for price of 10 hundredweight of yellow rosin of him had for the use of Her Highness's ships there, at 8s every hundredweight – £4; and more to him for bringing of the same rosin from Hampton to Portsmouth, price – 5s. *Summa* – £4 5s.

Rosin, hawsers, sail twine, needles, scupper-leathers *[*£8 13s 6d*], *pump-hoses* *[*23s*] *and a copper kettle* *[*18s*].[1] To William James of Southampton, merchant, the same day for price of 6 hundred 2 quarters weight of small hawsers tarred of 2 and 4 inches compass of him had for the use of Her Highness's ships, at 21s 8d every hundredweight – £7 0s 10d; and more to him for one copper kettle weighing 18 pounds weight, at 12d every pound – 18s. *Summa* – £7 18s 10d.

To William Fyllder of Portsmouth the same day for price of 22 pounds weight of sail twine of him had for the use of Her Highness's ships, at 8d every pound – 14s 8d; more for 12 dozen of sail needles, at 6d every dozen – 6s; more for 18 scupper-leathers, at 8d the piece – 12s; more for 12 pump-hoses, at 15d the piece – 15s;. and more to him for 12 claps of leather, at 8d the piece – 8s. *Summa* – £2 15s 8d.

[*Page total*] – £15 4s 6d.

[f. 121v] *Oleron canvas.* To John Gillam of Southampton the last day of September for price of 3 bolts of oleron canvas of him had for the use of Her Highness's ships, at 26s 8d every bolt. *Summa* – £4.

Timber and fir poles. To John Powell of Portsmouth the same day for price of 4 loads of compass timber oak of him had for the use of Her Highness's ships, at 10s every load – 40s; and more to him for 7 fir poles, at 4d the piece – 2s 4d. *Summa* – £2 2s 4d.

Ironwork. To John Robinson of Fareham, smith the same day for price of 1,200 of 20d nail of him had for the use of Her Highness's ships there, price – 20s; more for 2,000 of 10d nail, at 8s 4d every 1,000 – 16s 8d; more for 2,000 of 8d nail, at 6s 8d every 1,000 – 13s 4d; and more to him for 3,000 of 6d nail, at 5s every 1,000 – 15s. *Summa* – £3 5s.

To William Jackson, smith, the same day for price of 4,000 of 10d nail of him had for the use of Her Highness's ships, at 8s 4d every 1,000 – 33s 4d; more for 4,000 of 6d nail, at 5s every 1,000 – 20s; more for 4,000 of 8d nail, at 6s 8d every 1,000 – 26s 8d; more for 4,000 of 4d nail, at 3s 4d every 1,000 – 13s 4d; and more to him for 2,000 of 20d nail, at 16s 8d every 1,000 – 33s 4d. *Summa* – £6 6s 8d.

[*Page total*] – £15 14s.

[f. 122] *[*Keepers of storehouses and yards*]. To John Thomas the last day of September for his wages daily attending and serving Her Highness in safe-keeping of her storehouses there wherein lieth Her

[1]Original heading and auditor's summaries apply to this paragraph and the next; the auditor has counted Fyllder's scupper-leathers (12s) in with the cordage and needles from both suppliers (£8 1s 6d) to produce the first sub-total, and combined the pump-hoses and claps to produce the second.

Grace's store of provisions for the use of her ships, by one quarter of a year begun the first day of July last and this day ended – £5.

To John Powell the same day for his wages daily attending and serving Her Highness in safe-keeping of Her Grace's timber-yard there wherein lieth her timber, plank and board for the use of Her Highness's ships, by the space of 92 days begun and ended as abovesaid, at 6d *per diem* – £2 6s.

To Edward Prestman, labourer the same day for his wages daily attending and serving Her Highness in keeping of the plug and letting out of the water for the drier keeping of the dock there, by like 92 days begun and ended as aforesaid, at 4d *per diem* – £1 10s 8d.

Tilers

John Lay, 6 days at 12d	6s
Thomas Williamson, 6 days at 6d	3s

[*Page total*] – £9 5s 8d.

[f. 122v] *Emptions*

*[*Carriage*]. To John Playfote the last day of September for the hire of his 4 horse and his man serving Her Highness for the bringing of certain timber out of the field near Portsmouth and into Her Grace's timber-yard, by the space of 8 days within this time at 16d every day. *Summa* – 10s 8d.

*[*Loam*]. To John Graye the same day for price of 4 loads of loam by him delivered there for the mending of the walls about Her Highness's storehouses, at 8d every load. *Summa* – 2s 8d.

*[*Glazier*]. To John Connrycke, glazier of Southampton, the same day for the mending and setting in of 46 new quarrels of glass into the windows of Her Highness's storehouse there, at 1d the piece. *Summa* – 3s 10d.

[*Page total*] – 17s 2d.

[f. 123] *Anno Domini 1562. Anno regni regine Elizabethe quinto*

A payment made the last day of December as well to masters, mariners and gunners serving Her Highness in safe-keeping of Her Grace's ships afloat in harbour, and to keepers of storehouses, dock and timber-yards there wherein lieth divers kinds of stuffs pertaining to her ships, as also to shipwrights, caulkers, sawyers, smiths, labourers and other artificers and workmen for the new mending and repairing of Her Grace's said ships, and to divers persons for sundry provisions of them had towards the same; by one quarter of a year begun the first day of October last and this day ended, as followeth:

The Hart	
Mariners	
William Murraunt, master, 10 weeks 2 days	£3 8s 6d
Richard Broune, boatswain, 10 weeks 2 days	29s
Thomas Wilkes, purser, 10 weeks 2 days	25s 9d
John Tompson, steward, 10 weeks 2 day	23s 7d
Thomas Northway, 10 weeks 2 days	17s 2d
John Twinam, 10 weeks 2 days	17s 2d
John Mappe, 10 weeks 2 days	17s 2d
Thomas Mappe, 10 weeks 2 days	17s 2d
Anthony Atherton, 10 weeks 2 days	17s 2d
Nicholas Waters, 10 weeks 2 days	17s 2d
Morgan Bennet, 6 weeks 5 days	11s 2d
William Buttricke, 6 weeks 6 days	11s 5d
John Cane, 10 weeks 2 days	17s 2d
John Nycholas, 10 weeks 2 days	17s 2d
Jeffrey Preston, 10 weeks 2 days	17s 2d
William Catlin, 10 weeks 2 days	17s 2d
William Kneell, 10 weeks 2 days	17s 2d
William Foster, 10 weeks 2 days	17s 2d
John Patten, 10 weeks 2 days	17s 2d
Edward Gladyn, 10 weeks 2 days	17s 2d
[*Page total*] – £20 9s 9d.	
[f. 123v] Lawrence Broune, 10 weeks 2 days	17s 2d
Richard Broune, 10 weeks 2 days	17s 2d
Arthur Allred, 10 weeks 2 days	17s 2d
Richard Broke, 10 weeks 2 days	17s 2d
Tytcher Foster, gromet, 10 weeks 2 days	12s 10d
John Linche, 10 weeks 2 days	17s 2d
Richard Ragat, 10 weeks 2 days	17s 2d
[*Gunner*]	
Robert Tompson, master gunner, 10 weeks 2 days	25s 9d
The Swallow	
Mariners	
Thomas Fuller, master, 10 weeks 2 days	£3 8s 6d
William Saunders, boatswain, 10 weeks 2 days	29s
John Robertes, purser, 10 weeks 2 days	25s 9d
Davy Gryffin, steward, 10 weeks 2 days	23s 7d
Richard Fishebell, 10 weeks 2 days	17s 2d
Matthew Fisher, 10 weeks 2 days	17s 2d
John Bull, 10 weeks 2 days	17s 2d

William Barthillmewe, [*blank*]	[*blank*]
William Harwoode, 10 weeks 2 days	17s 2d
Robert Hindyf, 10 weeks 2 days	17s 2d
Thomas Richarde, 10 weeks 2 days	17s 2d
Nicholas Edwardes, 10 weeks 2 days	17s 2d
Richard Basset, [*blank*]	[*blank*]
Humphrey Cnokes, [*blank*]	[*blank*]
Richard Myller, 10 weeks 2 days	17s 2d
Richard Tompson, 10 weeks 2 days	17s 2d
Walter Newestube, 10 weeks 2 days	17s 2d
Thomas Wilkins, 10 weeks 2 days	17s 2d
Thomas Hilles, 6 weeks 5 days	11s 2d
Edward Even, 10 weeks 2 days	17s 2d
William Francke, 10 weeks 2 days	17s 2d

[*Page total*] – £26 2s 9d

[f. 124] Thomas Burtonne, 10 weeks 2 days	17s 2d
John Brooke, boy, 10 weeks 2 days	8s 7d
John Patricke, 1 week	20d
John Haynnes, 9 weeks 3 days	15s 9d
John Cooke, 9 weeks 3 days	15s 9d
William Baker, boy, [*blank*]	[*blank*]
Thomas Brokes, 5 weeks 3 days	9s
Thomas Brime, 4 weeks 2 days	7s 2d
Gunner	
Jacob Myller, master, 10 weeks 2 days	25s 9d
The Minion	
Mariners	
George Irelande, master, 11 weeks 4 days	58s
Robert Rote, boatswain, 11 weeks 4 days	33s 9d
George Hollyns, purser, 11 weeks 4 days	28s 11½d
James Smythe, cook, 8 weeks 5 days	20s
Nicholas Manshippe, 4 weeks 5 days	7s 10d
Richard Wellshe, 11 weeks 4 days	19s 4d
John Bowden, 11 weeks 4 days	19s 4d
William Rutler, 4 weeks 5 days	7s 10d
John Hocket, 11 weeks 4 days	19s 4d
Charles Phillippes, 11 weeks 4 days	19s 4d
John Phillippes, 4 weeks 5 days	7s 10d

[*Page total*] – £17 2s 4½d.

[f. 124v] Stephen Laver, [*blank*]	[*blank*]
John Teage, 4 weeks 5 days	7s 10d

John Tompson, 4 weeks 5 days	7s 10d
Robert Fowller, 4 weeks 5 days	7s 10d
James Laget, 5 weeks 5 days	9s 6d
Patrick Clarke, 4 weeks	6s 8d
Edward Barker, 4 weeks	6s 8d
Robert Bennet, 4 weeks	6s 8d
Raynold George, 4 weeks	6s 8d
Richard Saterlay, 4 weeks	6s 8d
John Orrey, 4 weeks	6s 8d
John Hopper, 3 weeks	5s
John Tytus, 3 weeks	5s
Robert Roche, 3 weeks	5s
Davy Hollande, 3 weeks	5s
John Grant, 2 weeks 6 days	4s 9d
William Galte, 1 week 5 days	2s 11d
John Houlton, 1 week 5 days	2s 11d
Thomas Hilles, 2 weeks 3 days	4s 1d
John Griffin, 2 weeks 3 days	4s 1d
Richard Davy, 2 weeks 3 days	4s 1d
Cornelius Layne, 2 weeks 3 days	4s 1d
John Morrell, 2 weeks 3 days	4s 1d
Nicholas Smythe, 2 weeks 3 days	4s 1d
Thomas Mone, 2 weeks 3 days	4s 1d
Morgan Bennet, 2 weeks 3 days	4s 1d
Davy Vyvyon, 2 weeks 3 days	4s 1d
William Flinte, 10 days	2s 8d
Roger Harwoode, 5 days	14½d
Henry Heys, 5 days	14½d
John Andros, 5 days	14½d
William Dearinge, 3 days	9d

[*Page total*] – £7 7s 4½d.

[f. 125] *The Primrose*

Mariners

Ralph Cockes, master, 11 weeks 4 days	58s
John Harris, boatswain, 11 weeks 4 days	31s 2d
John Peatt, purser, 11 weeks 4 days	28s 11½d
George Broune, cook, 10 weeks 6 days	24s 11d
William Kide, 7 weeks 6 days	13s 1d
Thomas Ryce, 6 weeks 1 day	10s 3d
Edward Pinner, 10 weeks 6 days	18s 1d
Davy Lovet, 4 weeks	6s 8d
John Cray, 8 weeks 5 days	14s 6½d

William Powgles, 4 weeks 5 days 7s 10½d
Robert Jeollyf, 7 weeks 6 days 13s 1d
Nicholas Dowlley, 11 weeks 4 days 19s 4d
William Armete, 11 weeks 4 days 19s 4d
Robert Motte, 5 weeks 4 days 9s 4d
John Young, 4 weeks 3 days 7s 5d
William Thomas, 4 weeks 6s 8d
John Hewes, 4 weeks 6s 8d
Henry Richarde, 4 weeks 6s 8d
John Leche, 4 weeks 6s 8d
John Powell, 4 weeks 6s 8d
William Martyn, 3 weeks 5s
Peter Paddon, 3 weeks 5s
Thomas Barbar, 3 weeks 5s
Richard Frende, 3 weeks 5s
William White, 3 weeks 5s
Richard Younge, 3 weeks 5s
Peter Cade, 3 weeks 5s
John Aman, 3 weeks 5s
Richard Diamounde, 3 weeks 5s
William Brigges, 3 weeks 5s
William Doget, 3 weeks 5s
Thomas Stanley, 3 weeks 5s
William Arden, 2 weeks 4 days 4s 4d
Thomas Willson, 2 weeks 4 days 4s 4d
Roger Morris, 2 weeks 4 days 4s 4d
John Davis, boatswain, 2 weeks 3 days 7s 1d
[*Page total*] – £19 15s 5½d.

[f. 125v] Andrew Allyn, 1 week 5 days 7s 10½d
Walter Thompson, 3 weeks 1 day 5s 3d
John Cockes, 3 weeks 1 day 5s 3d
Roger Tourner, 1 week 4 days 2s 8d
John Coxe, 1 week 4 days 2s 8d
John Allen junior, 1 week 4 days 2s 8d
Gregory Broune, 1 week 4 days 2s 8d
William Westley, 1 week 4 days 2s 8d
Thomas Peareson, 1 week 4 days 2s 8d
Charles Butcher, 1 week 4 days 2s 8d
Raynold Dowell, 6 days 17d
Raynold Tompson, 6 days 17d
John Empson, 6 days 17d
Henry Bassington, 6 days 17d

John Pardye, 6 days	17d
John White, 6 days	17d
Philip Williams, 6 days	17d
Christeostum Owen, 6 days	17d
Richard Tyller, 6 days	17d
Richard Smythe, 6 days	17d
William Stapulltun, 6 days	17d
Stephen Harris, 6 days	17d
Richard Vadyns, 6 days	17d
Francis Snyer, 6 days	17d
Roger Skite, 6 days	17d
Thomas Harwood, 6 days	17d
John Wakom, 6 days	17d
Simon Low, 6 days	17d
Robert Farley, 6 days	17d
Peter Saunderson, 6 days	17d
John Langham, 5 days	15d
Jerome Gallaway, 5 days	15d
Robert Bramston, 5 days	15d
John Hillyard, 5 days	15d
Walter Gymlyn, 5 days	15d

[*Page total*] – £3 6s 7½d.

[f. 126] *The New Bark*

Mariners

Willam Sampson, master, 4 weeks 3 days	29s 4d
George Braunche, boatswain, 4 weeks 3 days	12s 11d
Roger Davy, purser, 4 weeks 3 days	11s
Thomas Willson, cook, 4 weeks 3 days	10s 1d
Cornelius Brian, 4 weeks 3 days	7s 5d
Thomas Jonnes, 4 weeks 3 days	7s 5d
Richard Edwardes, 4 weeks 3 days	7s 5d
Clement Jestlyn, 4 weeks 3 days	7s 5d
Robert Marche, 4 weeks 3 days	7s 5d
Humphrey Dennes, 4 weeks 3 days	7s 5d
William Dawson, 4 weeks 3 days	7s 5d
Edmund Proude, carpenter, 4 weeks 3 days	12s 11d
Gabriel Kyrbye, gromet, 4 weeks 3 days	5s 6d
Robert Sampson, boy, 4 weeks 3 days	3s 8½d

Gunner

John Phillippes, master, 4 weeks 3 days	11s

[*Page total*] – £7 8s 4½d.

[f. 126v] *[*Keepers of storehouses and yards*]. To John Thomas the last day of December for his wages daily attending and serving Her Highness in safe-keeping of her storehouses there wherein lieth Her Grace's store of all kinds of necessaries for the use of Her Highness's ships, by one quarter of a year due at this present – £5.

To John Powell, porter, the same day for his wages daily attending and serving Her Highness in safe-keeping of her timber-yard there wherein lieth Her Grace's timber, plank, boards and other necessaries for the use of Her Highness's ships, by 92 days begun the first day of October last and this day ended, at 6d *per diem* – £2 6s.

To Edward Prestman, labourer, the same day for his wages daily serving Her Highness in safe-keeping of the plug and letting out of the water in the dock there for the drier keeping of the same, by the space of 6 days within this time, at 4d *per diem* – 2s.

[*Page total*] – £7 8s.

[f. 127] *Shipwrights*

Peter Pett, master, 80 days and tides at 12d	£4
Richard Chapman, server, 69 days and tides at 6d	34s 6d
John Carpenter, 68½ days and tides at 8d	45s 8d
Thomas Chartram, server, 68½ days and tides at 6d	34s 3d
Stephen Rogers, 25 days at 8d	16s 8d
Thomas Goode, server, 63 days at 4d	21s
Vincent Newstubbe, 68½ days at 7d	39s 11½d
Robert Cotten, 68½ days at 5d	28s 4½d
John Trenayll, 68½ days at 2d	11s 5d
Nicholas Godden, 58 days at 6d	29s
John Pease, 73 days and tides at 12d	£3 13s
William Dalloplye, 72 days and tides at 7d	42s
Edmund Forte, 71 days and tides at 4d	23s 8d
Stephen Broune, 62 days at 7d	36s 3d
Richard Gilbye, server, 68 days at 5d	28s 4d
John Stokes, 61 days at 8d	40s 8d
William Harley, server, 61 days at 6d	30s 6d
George Upson, 62 days at 7d	36s 2d
John Poulter, 59½ days at 6d	29s 9d
James Federicke, 48 days at 6d	24s
William Pinnell, 48 days at 6d	24s
Hugh Goasse, 57 days at 7d	33s 8d
Morris Gosse, boy, 56½ days at 3d	14s 1½d
John Pynnoke, 70 days and tides at 7d	40s 10d

Nicholas Pownter, 19 days at 6d	9s 6d
Thomas Wyse, 62½ days at 7d	36s 5½d
Philip Bartram, 49½ days at 7d	28s 10½d
Colin Morris, 49½ days at 2d	8s 3d
John Burgis, 2 days at 6d	12d
Thomas Darby, 48 days at 6d	24s

[*Page total*] – £46 4s 10½d.

[f. 127v] Davy Bigges, 56½ days at 8d	37s 8d
John Barry, server, 70 days at 6d	35s
William Hurlocke, 57½ days at 4d	19s 2d
Richard Flight, 62½ days at 8d	41s 4d
John Samborow, 61½ days at 6d	30s 9d
John Androwe, server, 61½ days at 4d	20s 6d
John Worwoode, 42 days at 6d	21s
Davy Rogers, 61½ days at 7d	35s 10d
Nicholas Gater, 68 days at 6d	34s
John Savaige, 49 days at 6d	24s 6d
John Bell, server, 46 days at 3d	11s 6d
Richard Bull, 44 days at 6d	22s
Osmund Edmoundes, server, 44 days at 4d	14s 8d
Christopher Sweteman, 69 days at 6d	34s 6d
James Wright, 1 day at 6d	6d
Raynold Veayzei, 66 days at 6d	33s
James Holcrofte, server, 54½ days at 5d	22s 7½d
Charles Butcher, 59 days at 6d	29s 6d
George Hart, 54½ days at 4d	18s 2½d
Davy Rogers junior, 57 days at 2d	9s 6d
Robert Tayller, 47 days at 6d	23s 6d
William Hewet, server, 54 days at 4d	18s
Robert Harris, 32 days at 7d	18s 8d
John West, 45½ days at 7d	26s 3d
Christopher Stevens, 37 days at 6d	18s 6d
John Richardson, server, 47½ days at 4d	15s 10d
Robert Roman, server, 47½ days at 2d	7s 11d
Thomas Hacker junior, 64½ days at 6d	32s 3d
John Pett, 51½ days at 8d	34s 4d
Robert Pett, 51½ days at 6d	25s 9d
Richard Coxe, 42 days at 6d	21s
Edmund Bevis, 48 days at 7d	28s
John Hearse, 57½ days at 6d	28s 9d
John Turnam, 40 days at 8d	26s 8d

Thomas Samborow, 42½ days at 6d	21s 3d
Thomas Greneleaff, 42½ days at 6d	21s 3d
John Browning, 41½ days at 7d	24s 2½d
John Wilkin, server, 40½ days at 4d	13s 6d

[*Page total*] – £45 1s 4d.

[f. 128] John Winny, 32½ days at 7d	18s 11½d
John Wehethers, 32½ days at 5d	13s 6½d
Richard Claye, 38½ days at 8d	25s 8d
John Brome, 30½ days at 8d	20s 4d
George Tourner, 32½ days at 4d	10s 10d
Thomas Bryan, 38½ days at 7d	22s 5½d
John Hutchens, server, 38½ days at 6d	19s 3d
John Diggons, 38½ days at 6d	19s 3d
Robert Veze, 38½ days at 6d	19s 3d
Robert Askon, 38½ days at 6d	19s 3d
Nicholas Foxe, 39 days at 6d	19s 6d
Robert Paddye, 38½ days at 7d	22s 5½d
William Weatherhead, 38½ days at 4d	12s 10d
John Lawson, 39 days at 6d	19s 6d
John Hurley, 22½ days at 6d	11s 3d
Thomas Hewes, 24½ days at 4d	8s 2d
Robert Baker, 38 days at 6d	19s
Richard Bartonn, 35½ days at 7d	20s 8½d
George Harris, 35 days at 6d	17s 6d
Roger Laken, 33½ days at 7d	19s 6½d
Henry Pounder, 33½ days at 5d	13s 11d
Henry Adye, 33½ days at 3d	8s 4½d
John Smythe, 18 days at 7d	10s 6d
John Johnson, 28 days at 4d	9s 4d
John Wright, 12 days at 6d	6s
Thomas Walton, 28 days at 4d	9s 4d
John Pryer, 8 days at [*blank*]	[*blank*]

[*Page total*] – £20 16 8½d.

[f. 128v] *Caulkers*

Thomas Boltonn, master, 50 days at 10d	41s 8d
William Boltun, server, 46½ days at 6d	23s 3d
John Atkinson, server, 58½ days at 6d	29s 3d
William Fourde, 38 days at 7d	22s 2d
William Mune, 58½ days at 8d	39s
John Mosier, 37 days at 6d	18s 6d
Thomas Clerke, 44 days at 7d	25s 8d

John Myllet, server, 45 days at 6d	22s 6d
John Webbe, 28½ days at 7d	16s 7½d
William Ragete, 31½ days at 4d	10s 6d
Thomas Northecot, 46½ days at 7d	27s 1½d
John Arodes, 46½ days at 3d	11s 7½d
Gregory Knightley, 20½ days at 7d	11s 11½d
John Clarke, 46½ days at 7d	27s 1½d
William Jonnes, server, 40½ days at 3d	11s 7½d
Walter Deane, 58½ days at 7d	34s 1½d
Robert Brigges, 45½ days at 7d	26s 6½d
Humphrey Daill, 42½ days at 4d	14s 2d
John Stockdaill, 41 days at 6d	20s 6d
Michael Rowse, 46½ days at 6d	23s 3d
Robert Dymmocke, 58½ days at 7d	34s 1½d
Richard Clappam, 37½ days at 6d	18s 9d
Thomas Pavy, 40 days at 7d	23s 4d
Edward Hilliar, server, 40 days at 4d	13s 4d
John Haywarde, 47 days at 6d	23s 6d
Robert Richarde, 55 days at 7d	32s 1d
Philip Payne, 35½ days at 7d	20s 8½d
John Hillar, 47½ days at 6d	23s 9d
Walter Johnson, 50½ days at 6d	25s 3d
Robert Grige, 40½ days at 6d	20s 3d
William Broune, 44½ days at 6d	22s 3d
John Castellman, 55½ days at 3d	18s 6d
John Bowden, 7½ days at 6d	3s 9d
Richard Holte, server, 5½ days at 5d	2s 2½d
John Thomas, 75 days at 6d	37s 6d
George Watson, 81 days at 6d	40s 6d
William Averey, 75 days at 4d	25s
Nicholas Archedaill, 55 days at 6d	27s 6d
Davy Lovet, server, 49 days at 4d	16s 4d
John Paullmer, 51½ days at 6d	25s 9d

[*Page total*] – £45 11s 6½d.

[f. 129] *Sawyers*

Thomas Berde, 57½ days at 6d	28s 9d
Thomas Smythe, 57½ days at 5d	24s 4½d
Richard Wilkins, 19 days at 6d	9s 6d
John Bigbroke, 19 days at 4d	6s 4d
Henry Richbye, 52 days at 6d	26s
Thomas Marshall, 52 days at 5d	21s 8d
William Gonnshot, 36 days at 6d	18s

John Tearmes, 11½ days at 6d	5s 9d
John Anokes, 11½ days at 5d	4s 10½d
William Cowycke, 36 days at 5d	15s
Topmakers	
William Bexley, 23 days at 8d	15s 4d
William Kaket, server, 23 days at 6d	11s 6d
John Romen, 23 days at 6d	11s 6d
John Whyte, 23 days at 6d	11s 6d
Abraham Harwoode, 23 days at 5d	9s 7d
House-carpenters	
Thomas Spencer, 32 days at 8d	21s 4d
John Foster, 34 days at 4d	11s 4d
John Yoman, 26 days at 7d	15s 2d
John Gibbes, 12 days at 6d	6s
John Modye, 12 days at 4d	4s
John Pendyn, 5 days at 8d	3s 4d
Robert Jellyf, 2 days at 4d	8d
William Foster, 7 days at 6d	3s 6d

[*Page total*] – £14 5s.

[f. 129v] *Joiners*

George Joyner, 20 days at 8d	13s 4d
Lewis Inglysh, 16 days at 7d	9s 4d
James Joyner, 20 days at 6d	10s
John Pimpon, 20 days at 4d	6s 8d
Smiths	
Robert Raynolde, 68 days at 6d	34s
John Paine, 48 days at 4d	16s
William Masse, 62 days at 4d	20s 8d
Richard Welles, master, 59 days at 8d	39s 4d
Thomas Davy, 59 days at 6d	29s 6d
Thomas Johnson, 49 days at 4d	16s 4d
Thomas Welles, 59 days at 4d	19s 8d
Knight Marshall, 2 days at 4d	8d
Hugh Goking, 20 days at 4d	6s 8d
Edward Hopper, 4 days at 4d	16d
Bricklayers	
John Bowley, 5 days at 6d	2s 6d
Gryffith Lawraunce, 5 days at 4d	20d
Simon Wood, 7 days at 6d	3s 6d
John Pereman, 7 days at 4d	2s 4d
Nicholas Lawraunce, 7 days at 2d	14d

[*Page total*] – £11 14s 8d.

[f. 130] *Victualling.* To John Thomas of Portsmouth the last day of December for the victualling of 176 of the aforenamed shipwrights, caulkers, smiths, topmakers, joiners, house-carpenters and others working upon the new mending and repairing of Her Highness's ships there, by the space of 7,826 days, the Sundays and holy days in the same accounted, begun the first day of October last and this day ended, which maketh 1,118 weeks at 4s 3¾d every week the man. *Summa* – £241 0s 7½d.

Lodging. To Jullyan Thomas, George Browne, John Pease, and 23 other persons of Portsmouth, Fareham, Kingston, Gosport and thereabouts the same day for the lodging of 100 shipwrights and caulkers in 50 featherbeds by the space of 453½ weeks among them all, working upon Her Highness's ships there, begun and ended as aforesaid, at 2d every week the man. *Summa* – £3 15s 7d.

To Eme Presteman of Kingston the same day for her pains and labour taken in washing of 190 pair of sheets of Her Highness's store for the use of her shipwrights, caulkers and others being occupied upon Her Highness's ships there as aforesaid, at 1d every pair. *Summa* – 15s 10d.

[*Page total*] – £245 12s 0½d.

[f. 130v] *Labourers*

Edward Prestman, master, 80 days and tides at 8d	53s 4d
John Shamler, 7 days at 6d	3s 6d
John Costen, 7 days at 6d	3s 6d
John Coxe senior, 7 days at 6d	3s 6d
John Coxe junior, 3 days at 6d	18d
Davy Grene, 7 days at 6d	3s 6d
John Mylles, 7 days at 6d	3s 6d
Thomas Warner, 7 days at 6d	3s 6d
Griffin Lawraunce, 6 days at 6d	3s
Henry Paddocke, 5 days at 6d	2s 6d
John Martemonth, 7 days at 6d	3s 6d
Richard Baker, 7 days at 6d	3s 6d
John Churche, 7 days at 6d	3s 6d
John Noker, 5 days at 6d	2s 6d
John Forder, 7 days at 6d	3s 6d
John Sligan, 11 days at 6d	5s 6d
John Paidge, 11 days at 6d	5s 6d
William Spencer, 9 days at 6d	4s 6d
William Shamler, 9 days at 6d	4s 6d
John Woode, 11 days at 6d	5s 6d
Richard Fawkener, 16 days at 6d	8s
William Bredam, 5 days at 6d	2s 6d

Robert Anderson, 4 days at 6d	2s
John Joynnannce, 50 days at 6d	25s
William Haull, 41½ days at 6d	20s 9d
John Sparkes, 57½ days at 6d	28s 9d
Hugh Deane, 26 days at 5d	10s 10d
John Abraham, 24 days at 6d	12s
Nicholas Harwoode, 34 days at 6d	17s
Thomas Baulche, 62 days at 6d	31s
Thomas Pirryn, 26 days at 6d	13s
John Fayremanners, 53½ days at 6d	26s 9d

[*Page total*] – £16 0s 11d.

[f. 131] Richard Holte, 59 days at 6d	29s 6d
Philip Greay, 53 days at 6d	26s 6d
Thomas Willshier, 60 days at 6d	30s
John Morris, 62 days at 6d	31s
Richard Hurte, 53 days at 6d	26s 6d
Knight Marshall, 59 days at 6d	29s 6d
John Saunder, 35 days at 6d	17s 6d
Robert Willseman, 41 days at 6d	20s 6d
William Mylles, 54 days at 4d	18s
Giles Bevyson, 44 days at 6d	22s
Anthony Tristram, 74 days at 6d	37s
John Bawdewen, 3 days at 6d	18d
William Pope, 38½ days at 6d	19s 3d
William Ripper, 23 days at 6d	11s 6d
John Myrry, 31½ days at 6d	15s 9d
Thomas Lewes, 19½ days at 6d	9s 9d
Robert Percevall, 42½ days at 6d	21s 3d
Thomas Foxe, 11½ days at 6d	5s 9d
John Vinsente, 13 days at 6d	6s 6d
William Morris, 23 days at 6d	11s 6d
William Canvay, 11½ days at 6d	5s 9d
William Avery, 4 days at 6d	2s
	[£19 18s*]

Watchmen

Thomas Williams, 8 nights at 4d	2s 8d
John Abraham, 17 nights at 4d	5s 8d
Richard Fawconer, 17 nights at 4d	5s 8d
John Sparkes, 17 nights at 4d	5s 8d
Philip Gay, 17 nights at 4d	5s 8d
Thomas Pyrren, 17 nights at 4d	5s 8d

Thomas Baulche, 17 nights at 4d	5s 8d
John Morrys, 17 nights at 4d	5s 8d
John Paidge, 17 nights at 4d	5s 8d
	*[*48s*]

[*Page total*] – £22 6s 6d.

[f. 131v] *Emptions*

Timber and shores. To John Poundes of Portsmouth the last day of December for price of 4 loads of elm timber of him had for the use of Her Highness's ships, at 4s every load 16s; and more to him for carrying of the same 4 loads of elm timber from Farlington to the dock at Portsmouth – 5s. *Summa* – £1 1s.

To Ralph Love of Portsmouth the same day for price of 25 great shores oak of him had for the use of Her Highness's ships, at 4d every shore – 8s 4d; more for carriage of the same shores from Fareham to Gosport, at 12d the load – 8s; more for 50 shide of dry seasoned shores oak, price – 3s 4d; and more to him for felling of the same 8 loads of shores – 4s. *Summa* – £1 3s 4d.

Deal-boards, inch board, quarters and planks. To Thomas Wakom of London the same day for price of 11 Norway deal-boards of him had for the use of Her Highness's ships, at 18d every board. *Summa* – 16s 6d.

To William Holland of Havant the same day for price of 450 foot of inch board oak of him had for the use of Her Grace's ships, at 4s every 100 foot – 18s; and more to him for 10 quarters oak, at 4d the piece – 3s 4d. *Summa* – £1 1s 4d.

To Nicholas Okes of Beaulieu the same day for price of 870 foot of 2-inch plank oak of him had for the use of Her Highness's ships, at 8s every 100 [*foot*] – £3 9s 6d; and more to him for 12 fir spars, at 4d the piece – 4s. *Summa* – £3 13s 6d.

To John Turnam of Eling the same day for price of 322½ foot of inch ½ board oak of him had for the use of Her Highness's ships, at 7s 6d every 100 [*foot*] – 23s 11d; and more to him for one spruce deal-board, price – 4s. *Summa* – £1 7s 11d.

Straw. To Richard Foster of Fareham the same day for price of 2 loads of straw of him had for the use of Her Highness's ships, at 4s every load; by agreement. *Summa* – 8s.

[*Page total*] – £9 11s 6d.

[f. 132] *Inch board oak, plank, quarrels and fir poles.* To John Searlle of Botley the last day of December for price of 550 foot of inch board oak of him had for the use of Her Grace's ships, at 4s every 100 [*foot*] – 22s; more to him for 200 [*foot*] of inch ½ board oak, at 5s every 100 [*foot*] –

10s; and more to him for price of 15 small quarters oak, at 2d the piece – 2s 6d. *Summa* – £1 14s 6d.

To John Turnam of Southampton the same day for price of 975 foot of 2-inch plank oak of him had for the use of Her Highness's ships, at 9s every 100 [*foot*] – £4 7s 9d; and more to him for 500 foot of inch board oak, at 5s every 100 [*foot*] – 25s. *Summa* – £5 12s 9d.

To John Powell of Portsmouth the same day for price of 300 foot of dry seasoned inch board oak of him had for the use of Her Grace's ships, at 5s every 100 [*foot*] – 15s; and more to him for 10 fir poles, at 4d the piece – 3s 4d. *Summa* – 18s 4d.

Trenails. To Thomas Hacker, carpenter the same day for the price of 600 of trenails oak of him had for the use of Her Highness's ships, of 24 inches long, at 2s every 100. *Summa* – 12s.

Deal-boards. To Luke Grysson of Newhaven[1] the same day for price of 4 spruce deal-boards of him had for the use of Her Highness's ships, at 4s the piece – 16s; and more to him for one broad Norway deal-board, price – 16d. *Summa* – 17s 4d.

Hoops. To Henry James of Southampton the same day for price of 42 great broad hoops of him had for the use of Her Highness's ships, at 7d the piece – 24s 6d; and more to him for bringing down of the same hoops from Hampton to Portsmouth; by agreement – 16d. *Summa* – £1 5s 10d.

Sawing. To William Berde and Thomas Smythe, sawyers, the same day for sawing and cutting of 400 foot of 2-inch plank oak for the use of Her Highness's ships as aforesaid, at 20d every 100 foot sawing; by agreement – 6s 8d.

[*Page total*] – £11 7s 5d.

[f. 132v] *Service of lighters.* To Owen Symonndes of Fareham the last day of December for service of his lighter serving Her Highness in carrying of timber oak from Redbridge to the dock near Portsmouth for the use of Her Grace's ships there; by agreement – 8s.

To Robert Harssellet of Eling the same day for service of his lighter serving Her Highness in carrying of 20 tons and 28 foot of timber oak from Redbridge to Portsmouth; by agreement – £1 15s 2d.

To Jeffrey Wayde of Eling the same day for service of his lighter serving Her Highness in carrying of timber from Redbridge to Portsmouth; by agreement – 7s.

Service of hoys. To Adam Harssenote of Colchester the same day for service of his hoy serving Her Highness for the carrying of pitch, tar,

[1]Here 'Mycheyng' and at f. 140v 'Mychen', forms of the older name of the Sussex place, to which the name Newhaven was given from the 16th cent., though in 1587 the village was still 'Michin' and 'Newhaven' was simply the port: EPNS, *Sussex*, p. 324.

rosin, oakum, lead, kettles and divers other necessaries received at Her Grace's great storehouse at Deptford and the same delivered at Portsmouth for the use of her ships there; by agreement – £3.

To Roger Waller of Harwich the same day for service of his hoy serving Her Highness in bringing of 60 wainscot boards from London to Portsmouth for the use as aforesaid; by agreement – £1.

To Thomas Ussher of Rochester the same day for service of his hoy serving Her Highness in bringing of one shock of deal-boards, timber and iron from London to the dock near Portsmouth for the use of Her Grace's ships there; by agreement – £1 6s 8d.

To John Mardall of Millhall, master, the same day for service of his hoy serving Her Highness in bringing of ropes, canvas, compasses, running glasses, with divers other kinds of stuffs received at Deptford and delivered the same at Portsmouth for the use of Her Grace's ships; by agreement – £2.

[*Page total*] – £9 16s 10d.

[f. 133] *Ironwork.* To John Sheldun of the Forest of Dean, smith, the last day of December for price of 12,800 of 2s nail of him had for the use of Her Highness's ships, at 20s every 1,000 – £12 16s; more for 2,200 of 22d nail, at 22d every 100 – 40s 4d; more 9,600 of 20d nail, at 16s 8d every 1,000 – £8;. more to him for 7,300 of 10d nail, at 8s 4d every 1,000 – £3 0s 10d; more for 22,500 of 6d nail, at 5s every 1,000 – £5 12s 6d; more for 14,000 of 4d nail, at 3s 4d every 1,000 – 46s 8d; and more to him for 11,000 of 3d nail, at 2s 6d every 1,000 – 27s 6d. *Summa* – £35 3s 10d.

To John Holloway of Portsmouth the same day, smith, for price of 1,200 of 10d nail of him had for the use of Her Grace's ships, at 8s 4d every 1,000 – 10s; and more to him for 100 of 6d nail, price 6d – *Summa* – 10s 6d.

To Robert Arnold of Fareham the same day for price of 1,120 pounds weight of his own new iron by him made into spikes of all sorts and overlop nails for the use of Her Highness's ships there, after 5 score pounds to the hundred[*weight*] at 3d every pound weight – £14.

To Nicholas Hunte of Southampton, smith, the same day for price of 340½ pounds weight of his own new iron by him made into spikes and overlop nails of all sorts, and the same delivered for the use of Her Grace's ships, after 5 score pounds to the hundred[*weight*] at 3d every pound weight – £4 5s 1d;[1] more for 4,475 of 2s nail, at 20s every 1,000 – £4 9s

[1]Note the explanation here and in the previous entry that the hundredweights are simple multiples of 100 lbs; but the second calculation is defective, giving 1021.5d, which is ½d below the sum stated (1021d).

6d; and more to him for 650 of 'Cally'[1] varnish nails, at 1s 10d every 100 – 11s 11d. *Summa* – £9 6s 6d.

Gads of steel. To Robert Raynold, smith, the same day for price of 32 gads of steel of him had for the needful mending of certain smith's tools working there upon Her Grace's iron for the use of her ships; by agreement – 1s 4d.

[*Page total*] – £59 2s 2d.

[f. 133v] *Furzes.* To Thomas Pirryn of Kingston the last day of December for price of 57 loads of furzes of him had for the use of Her [*Highness's*] ships there, at 16d every load with the carriage – £3 17s 4d.

Broom. To Nicholas Locke of Gosport the same day for price of 17 loads of dry broom of him had for the needful breaming of Her Highness's ships there, at 2s every load – 34s; and more to him for bringing of the same by water from Gosport to Portsmouth; by agreement – 2s 11d. *Summa* – £1 16s 11d.

Hair. To John Halloway of Southampton the same day for price of 79 bushels of hair of him had for the use of Her Grace's ships, at 4d every bushel – 26s 4d; and more to him for bringing of the same hair by water to Portsmouth; by agreement – 2s 9d. *Summa* – £1 9s 1d.

Brick. To the Lady Cotton, widow,[2] the same day for the price of 2,200 of brick of her had for the new making and mending of certain hearths in Her Highness's ships there, price – 10s; and more to her for the carriage of the same brick from Bedhampton to Portsmouth, containing 6 cartloads, at 16d every load – 8s. *Summa* – 18s.

Pitch. To Anthony Tristram the same day for price of 4 barrels of pitch of him had for the use of Her Highness's ships, at 6s every barrel – £1 4s

Slate stone. To John Tredle of Gosport the same day for price of 2,000 of slate of him had for the new covering and mending of Her Highness's storehouse there, at [*word repeated*] 6s 2d every 1,000 delivered at Portsmouth – 12s 4d.

To James Wright, tiler, the same day for wages and victuals of himself and his man working in laying and covering of Her Highness's storehouses with slate, by the space of 4 days at 19d every day – 6s 4d.

[*Page total*] – £10 4s.

[f. 134] *Old Oakum.* To Anne Payne, Joan Homeley, Joan Rice, Joan Gibbons, Anne Griffin and 12 other persons of Gosport, Portsmouth,

[1]Meaning unknown, but cf. above, p. 103 n. 2.

[2]Jane, widow of Sir Richard Cotton of Bedhampton (d. 1556), one of the leading gentlemen in Hampshire and a Privy Councillor under Edward VI: *Hist. Parl. 1509–58*, i, p. 711.

Kingston, Fareham and thereabouts the last day of December for working and picking of 3 thousand 6 hundred 2 quarters 2 pounds weight [*4,090 lbs*] of Her Highness's old junks and ropes into oakum for the use of Her Grace's ships, at 3s 4d every hundredweight working. *Summa* – £5 9s 3½d.[1]

Ballast. To Roger Hastlet of Fareham, ballastman, the same day for price of 155 tons of gravel of him had for the needful lasting and ballasting of Her Highness's two ships the *Minion* and the *Primrose*, at 4d every ton of ballast. *Summa* – £2 11s 8d.

Ox tallow. To Jeffrey Vaughan the same day for price of 4 hundredweight of white ox tallow of him had for the use of Her Highness's ships there, at 18s every hundredweight – £3 12s.

Compasses and running glasses. To Richard Stevens, compass-maker, the same day for price of 4 great compasses of him had for the use of Her Highness's ships, at 6s the piece – 24s; and more to him for 4 great running glasses of the largest sort, at 3s the glass – 12s. *Summa* – £1 16s.

Timber, plank, board and quarters. To Christopher Nayller of London the same day for price of 2,944 foot of 3-inch plank oak by him delivered there for the use of Her Highness's ships, at 10s every 100 foot – £14 14s; more for 9,639 foot of 2-inch plank oak, at 8s every 100 foot – £38 11s 2d; more for 26,169 foot of inch ½ board oak, at 5s every 100 foot – £65 8s 5d; more for 7 loads 21 foot of sawn quarters, at 16s every load – £5 18s 9d; more for 500 of cloveboard, at 46s 8d every 100 – £11 13s 4d; and more to him for 6 loads of squared timber oak, at 10s every load after 50 foot to the load – £3. *Summa* – £139 5s 8d

[*Page total*] – £152 14s 7½d.

[f. 134v] *Cloveboards.* To Thomas Welles of Arundel the last day of December for price of 200 of great cloveboard oak by him delivered there for the use of Her Highness's ships, at £3 6s 8d every 100 of cloveboard – £6 13s 4d; and more to him for 250 of smaller cloveboard oak, at 53s 4d every 100 – £6 13s 4d. *Summa* – £13 6s 8d.

Water carriage. To John Tottam, master, the same day for service of his hoy serving Her Highness in bringing of cloveboards, train oil and other stuffs from Arundel to the dock near Portsmouth for the use of Her Grace's ships there; by agreement – £1 4s 4½d.

[*Page total*] – £14 10s 0½d.

[1]The calculation gives £6 1s 8½d to the nearest ½d (1460.714d), which is clearly wide of the sum stated (1311.5d). By cwt of 5 score the calculation is minimally variant (1460.8d) because the loose lbs are so small a component of the weight. The measure should probably be 32 cwt 3 qrs 3 lbs [*3,671 lbs*], which would yield 1311.0712d at the rate stated. Expressed as xxx^{ml} ij^{c} iij^{qr} iij^{li} this could easily have been miscopied as xxx^{ml} vj^{c} ij^{qr} ij^{li}, and there is a likely confusion with the 3,600+ lbs actually involved.

[f. 135] **Ordinary. Conduct**:

Anno Domini 1562. Anno regni regine Elizabethe quarto

Conduct in calling to service of shipwrights, caulkers and others, as followeth:

To Nicholas Johnson the 28th day of April for the conduct of himself and two other shipwrights from London to Her Highness's works at Gillingham, distant 24 miles, at 12d every man – 3s.

To Thomas Bolton, master caulker, the same day for the conduct of himself, William Bolton, Walter Claye, Roger Redey, Thomas Clarke and 16 other caulkers from London to Gillingham to Her Highness's works there, at 12d every man – £1 1s.

To Jerome Hewster the 26th day of July for the conduct of Henry Whight, Gabriel Wright, William Bulbacke, Randall Woode and 17 other caulkers by him prested from London to Gillingham to Her Highness's works there, at 12d every man – £1 1s.

To George Upson, George Chester and four other shipwrights the 4th day of August for their conduct from London to Gillingham as aforesaid, at 12d every man – 6s.

To Robert Boddy the 23th day of September for the conduct of himself, William Watson and Richard Jonnes, oarmakers, from London to Portsmouth, distant 60 miles, at 2s 6d every man – 7s 6d.

To John Wellsheman the last day of September for the conduct of himself and John Hubbarde, shipwrights, from Bristol to Deptford, at 4s every man – 8s.

To Robert Grigge, shipwright, the same day for his conduct from Portsmouth to Her Grace's works aforesaid – 2s 6d.

[*Page total*] – £3 9s.

[f. 135v] To George Savy the 11th day of October for the conduct of himself, George Mathew and two other shipwrights from London to Her Highness's works at Portsmouth, distance 60 miles, at 2s 6d every man – 10s.

To Richard Welles the 14th day of October for the conduct of himself, Thomas Davy and two other smiths from London to Her Highness's works at Portsmouth as aforesaid, at 2s 6d every man – 10s.

To Thomas Bolton the last day of October for the conduct of himself, William Bolton, John Atkinson, Richard Barton, Roger Lakin, Richard Cowler and 27 other caulkers from London to Her Highness's works at Portsmouth, at 2s 6d every man – £4 2s 6d.

To John Brumett the same day for the conduct of himself, Robert Baker, John Winney, Richard Claye, John Browne and 15 other shipwrights from London to Her Grace's works at Portsmouth, at 2s 6d every man – £2 10s.

Anno regni regine Elizabethe quinto

To William Bexley the 30th day of November for the conduct of himself, William Kakette, James Robinson and two other oarmakers from London to Portsmouth as aforesaid, at 2s 6d every man – 12s 6d.

To Thomas Bolton the last day of December for the conduct of himself, William Bolton, Thomas Northcot, Robert Whight, Thomas Coxe and 14 other caulkers by him prested from London to Portsmouth, at 2s 6d every man – £2 7s 6d.

To Richard Welles the same day for the conduct of himself, Thomas Davy and two other smiths from London to Portsmouth, at 2s 6d every man – 10s.

[*Page total*] – £11 2s 6d.

[f. 136] To Peter Pett the last day of December for the conduct of John Pett, John Browninge, Robert Paddy, Robert Pette, Richard Chapman and Christopher Sweteman, shipwrights, by him prested from London to Portsmouth, at 2s 6d every man – 15s.

To Roger Porter the same day for the conduct of Nicholas Godwin, Vincent Newestube, John Herseye, Thomas Smythe, Philip Payne and four other caulkers from Fareham, Hayling, Langstone, Eling and thereabouts to Deptford to Her Grace's works there, at 2s 6d every of them – £1 2s 6d.

[*Page total*] – £1 17s 6d. [f. 136v *blank*]

[f. 137] *Anno Domini 1562. Anno regni regine Elizabethe quarto*

Conduct in discharge from service of shipwrights, caulkers and others; as followeth:

To Thomas Bolton the 16th day of May for the conduct of himself, William Bolton, Walter Claye, Roger Ready, Thomas Clarke and 16 other caulkers discharged from Her Highness's works at Gillingham to London, from whence they were prested to the said service, at 12d every man – £1 1s.

To Henry Whight the 6th day of August for the conduct of himself, Gabriel Wright, Roger Collins and nine other caulkers discharged from Her Highness's works as aforesaid, at 12d every man – 12s.

Anno regni regine Elizabethe quinto

To George Upson the 23th day of December for the conduct of himself, John Pulter, James Federicke, George Savydge, John Bell, Richard Bull and 19 other shipwrights discharged from Her Highness's works at Portsmouth to London, from whence they were prested, at 2s 6d every man – £3 2s 6d.

To Thomas Wise the same day for the conduct of himself, Philip Bartram, Thomas Darby, Richard Flight, John Samborow, John Worwoode, Davy Rogers and 10 other shipwrights discharged from the said works to Poole, from whence they were prested, being distant 36 miles, at 18d every man – £1 5s 6d.

To Thomas Bolton the same day for the conduct of himself, William Bolton, John Atkinson, William Forde, William Mun, John Mosyer, Thomas Clarke, John Myllete, John Web and 15 other caulkers discharged from Her Grace's said works to London, from whence they were prested to the said service, at 2s 6d every man – £3.

[*Page total*] – £9 1s.

[f. 137v] To Richard Welles the 23th day of December for the conduct of himself, Thomas Davy and two other smiths discharged from the said works as aforesaid to London, at 2s 6d every man – 10s.

To Richard Chapman the same day for the conduct of himself, Christopher Sweteman and two other shipwrights discharged from the said works to London, at 2s 6d every man – 10s.

To John Northe the same day for the conduct of himself, Robert Harris, John Turner, Thomas Samborrowe, Hugh Goase, Walter Jonson, Nicholas Painter and 20 other shipwrights discharged from Her Highness's works at Portsmouth to Christchurch and thereabouts, at 12d every man – £1 7s.

[*Page total*] – £2 7s.

[f. 138] **Ordinary. Prests**:

Anno Domini 1561 [1562]. *Anno regni regine Elizabethe quarto*

Money delivered in prest to Edward Baeshe, General Surveyor of Her Grace's victuals for the seas, for the victualling of Her Highness's ships in harbour, as followeth:

To Edward Baeshe, General Surveyor of Her Grace's victuals for the seas, the 2nd day of March *anno supradicto* in prest upon the ordinary victualling of masters, mariners and gunners keeping Her Highness's ships afloat in harbour, five hundred pounds – £500.

Anno Domini 1562

To the said Edward Baeshe, General Surveyor of Her Grace's victuals for the seas, the 14th day of April *anno supradicto* in prest upon the ordinary victualling of masters, mariners and gunners keeping Her Majesty's ships afloat in harbour, two hundred pounds – £200.

To the foresaid Edward Baeshe, General Surveyor of Her Majesty's said victuals for the seas, the first day of June *anno supradicto* in prest upon the ordinary victualling of masters, mariners and gunners keeping Her Highness's ships afloat in harbour, three hundred pounds – £300.

To the foresaid Edward Baeshe, General Surveyor of Her Grace's said victuals for the seas, the 20th day of September *anno supradicto* in prest upon the ordinary victualling of masters mariners and gunners keeping Her Highness's ships afloat in harbour, five hundred pounds – £500.

To the said Edward Baeshe, General Surveyor of Her Grace's victuals for the seas, the tenth day of November *anno supradicto* in prest upon the ordinary victualling of masters, mariners and gunners keeping Her Grace's ships afloat in harbour, five hundred pounds – £500.

[*Page total*] – £2,000.

[f. 138v] *Anno Domini 1562. Anno regni regine Elizabethe quinto*

To the foresaid Edward Baeshe, General Surveyor of Her Grace's victuals for the seas, the 27th day of November *anno supradicto* in prest upon the ordinary victualling of masters, mariners and gunners keeping Her Majesty's ships afloat in harbour, four hundred pounds – £400.

[*Page total*] – £400.

[f. 139] **Ordinary. Charges**:

Anno Domini 1562. Anno regni regine Elizabethe quinto

To John Browne the last day of December *anno supradicto* for charges by him sustained in receiving of £12,000 at the Receipt of the Exchequer at the hands of the tellers there at divers times within the time of this account by virtue of Her Grace's warrant of £12,000 by the year for the reparation and maintenance of Her Highness's ships and provisions for the same, at 30s every £1,000, bags, wax, paper, parchment, carriage and suchlike within the same charge accounted – £18.

[*Page total*] – £18. [f. 139v *blank*]

[f. 140] **Extraordinary. Conduct**:

Anno Domini 1562. Anno regni regine Elizabethe quarto

Conduct as well of mariners, soldiers and gunners fet[1] from divers places by virtue of Her Highness's commission to serve in Her Grace's ships from time to time.

To Edward Lambarde of Brightlingsea and Henry Paskall of Colchester the first day of August for the conduct of George Maister, Edmund Carter, John Maister, Robert Freman, William Newman, Matthew Maister and 22[2] other mariners by them prested from Harwich, Thorpe, Walton on the Naze, Ramsey, Bradfield and thereabouts in Essex to serve in certain Her Grace's ships at Gillingham appointed to the seas, being distant 36 miles, at 18d every man – 42s; more for the conduct of John Tattell, Thomas Underwoode, Robert Harrys, William Harris and 54 other mariners by them prested from Rowhedge, Old Heath, Alresford, Fingringhoe, Salcott and thereabouts in Essex to Gillingham, distant 24 miles, at 12d every man – 58s; and more to him for the conduct of Thomas Richeman, James Johnson and 24 other mariners from Maldon, Bradwell, Burnham, Paglesham and thereabouts in Essex to Gillingham, distant 12 miles, at 6d every man – 12s 6d. *Summa* – £5 12s 6d.

To Thomas Wodcote and Rowland Mocklowe the same day for the conduct of Philip Williams, Richard Lewette, Thomas Morris, William Mayre, John Watters and 160 other mariners by them prested from Limehouse, Blackwall, Ratcliff, Rotherhithe, St Katherine's, as also out of divers merchants' ships within the river of Thames, to serve in certain Her Grace's ships at Gillingham appointed to the seas, being distant 24 miles, at 12d every man – £8 5s.

[*Page total*] – £13 17s 6d.

[f. 140v] To Butolph Moungey the first day of August for the conduct of John Egar, George Foxe, George Richardson, Bartholomew Harte, John Baker and 217 other mariners by him prested from Folkestone, Hythe, Margate, Lydd, Rye, Winchelsea, Hastings, Newhaven, Brighton, Kingston, Heene, Worthing, Lancing, Old Shoreham, New Shoreham, and in divers places thereabouts in Kent and Sussex to Gillingham as aforesaid, distant 36 miles, at 18d every man – £16 13s.

To Thomas Jonnes of Lynn the same day for the conduct of Thomas Alam, John Fuller, John Tayllor, Richard Dalle, William Davye, William Scalles, Andrew Clarke, James Williams, William Davie junior, William Adams, Robert Adams and 80 other mariners by him prested from Lynn

[1] MS 'fete', i.e. past participle of the obsolete verb *fet* synonymous with *fetch.*

[2] MS 'xxij.th' in error suggested by the familiar dating formula.

and thereabouts in Norfolk to serve in Her Highness's ships at Gillingham appointed to the seas, being distant 96 miles, at 4s 4d every man – £19 14s 4d.

To John Malyn of Dover the same day for the conduct of John Jonson, John Lasshe, Thomas Robins, Jarman Doves and 12 other mariners by him prested from Dover and thereabouts to Gillingham distant 36 miles, at 18d every man – 24s; and more to him for the conduct of John Woulredge, Walter Hewes and two other mariners by him prested from Canterbury and thereabouts to Gillingham, distant 24 miles, at 12d every man – 4s. *Summa* – £1 8s.

To Richard Brissell, Robert Cooke, Henry Woode, William Martin[1] and 18 other mariners the same day called from Gillingham for the transportation of the *Great Bark* to Deptford, there to be new made, and for their conduct from Deptford to Gillingham again, at 12d every man – £1 2s.

[*Page total*] – £38 17s 4d.

[f. 141] To Edward Gotley the first day of August for the conduct of John Howper, John Mowar, Thomas Baker, Thomas Trewe, Richard Browne and 30 other mariners by him prested from West Purbeck, East Purbeck, Wareham and thereabouts in Dorsetshire to serve in Her Grace's ships at Gillingham appointed to the seas, being distant 120 miles, at 5s every man – £8 15s; more for the conduct of Nicholas Androw, Cuthbert Watson, John Edwardes, Peter Harvy and 41 other mariners for their conduct from Poole, Lytchett and thereabouts in Dorsetshire to Gillingham, distant 112 miles, at 4s 6d every man – £10 2s 6d; more for the conduct of Thomas Dove, Richard Hike, John Turner, Richard Jubber and 11 other mariners for their conduct from Christchurch, Milford, Lymington and thereabouts in Hampshire to Gillingham, distant 100 miles, at 4s every man – £3; and more to him for the conduct of John Lorence, John Ruddam, John Totton, John Castell, William Skipper, William Baker, John Somer and 30 other mariners by him prested from Fawley, Hythe, Lepe, Southampton, Titchfield, Fareham, Portchester, Stoke and thereabouts in Hampshire to Gillingham, distant 86 miles, at 3s 6d every man – £6 9s 6d. *Summa* – £28 7s.

To James Humphrey the same day for the conduct of Edmund Sheareman, Morris Bentley, Jeffrey Barnesaye, Thomas Stanley, John Warde and 35 other mariners by him prested from Ipswich, Woodbridge, Sutton, Melton, Butley and thereabouts in Essex and Suffolk to Gillingham, distant 60 miles, at 2s 6d every man – £5; and more to him

[1]The four named were seconded from *Elizabeth Jonas* (cf. above, p. 143); the coincidence of the three later names makes certain the identification of 'Brissell' here with 'Brisholde' named above.

for the conduct of William Moone, John Crosby, John Browne, Richard Brooke, Thomas Myddow, John Catchepoll, Thomas Westerby and 86 other mariners from Orford, Aldeburgh, Thorpe, Sizewell, Dunwich, Westleton, 'Wyntarton',[1] Theberton, Southwold, Easton, Reydon, Covehithe, Lowestoft and thereabouts in Essex and Suffolk to Gillingham, being distant 72 miles, at 3s every man – £13 19s. *Summa* – £18 19s.

[*Page total*] – £47 6s.

[f. 141v] To Edward Tompson, master gunner, the first day of August for the conduct of Thomas Marshall, Morgan Appowell, Anthony Amys and 27 other gunners by him prested to serve in Her Grace's ship the *Lion*, appointed to the seas, from London to Gillingham, distant 24 miles, at 12d every man – £1 10s.

To Thomas Dixson, master gunner, the same day for the conduct of Thomas Rishe, William Sharpe, Walter Powell and 27 other gunners by him prested to serve in Her Highness's ship the *Hope*, from London to Gillingham, distant 24 miles, at 12d every man – £1 10s.

To Robert Tompson, master gunner, the same day for the conduct of Jeffrey Rudde, William Shepparde, Lancelot Degree, William Kney and 20 other gunners by him prested to serve in Her Grace's ship the *Hart*, from London to Gillingham, distant 24 miles, at 12d every man – £1 4s.

To Jacob Myller, master gunner, the same day for the conduct of John Parker, Hugh Williams, William Robinson, Edward Hudson, William Jenkinson and 15 other gunners by him prested to serve in Her Grace's ship the *Swallow*, from London to Gillingham, distant 24 miles, at 12d every man – £1.

To John Malpas, master gunner, the same day for the conduct of Jeffrey Cooke, Christopher Rasynns and eight other gunners by him prested from London to Gillingham to serve in Her Highness's ship the *Mary Willoughby*, being distant 24 miles, at 12d every man – 10s.

To Nicholas Harde, master gunner, the same day for the conduct of John Boateman, Symound Kirke and four other gunners by him prested from London to Gillingham to serve in Her Highness's ship the *Hare*, distant 24 miles, at 12d every man – 6s.

[*Page total*] – £6.

[f. 142] To Alexander Harryson, John Merecke, Richard Wilson and seven other surgeons the first day of August for their conduct from London

[1] *Winterton* lies 5 miles north of Great Yarmouth, in Norfolk, and is therefore out of position in this otherwise close sequence of places south to north along the Suffolk coast. Possibly *Wenhaston* is meant; cf. a 14th-cent. form *Wenhavestun*, which is taken to suggest the Blyth was still then navigable at that point: M. Birch, *Origins of Suffolk Place-Names* (Mendlesham, 2003), p. 71.

to Gillingham appointed to serve in Her Highness's ships there, being distant 24 miles, at 12d every man – 10s.

To James Robartes, Richard Gater, Andrew Starke and five other mariners the same day for their conduct from London to Gillingham to serve in Her Grace's ships there, at 12d every man – 8s.

To Thomas Goldston, boatswain, John Neweball, Richard Diamounde, Peter Paddon, William Kisshan, Henry Woode, William Robinson[1] and 37 other mariners the same day for their conduct called for the transporting of the *Great Bark* from Gillingham to Deptford, at 12d every man – £2 4s.

To Hugh Bowye, Henry Burgis, John Sustian[2] and 33 other mariners the 30th day of September for their conduct serving Her Highness in transporting of Her Grace's ship the *Jesus* from Gillingham to Deptford, there to be new made, at 12d every man – £1 16s.

To Richard Brisholde, William Martyn, Robert West, Thomas Starke and 46 other mariners the 25th day of October for their conduct being called from Gillingham to Deptford for the launching of Her Highness's two new ships there, at 12d every man, £2 10s.

Anno regni regine Elizabethe quinto

To John Malyn of Dover the 25th day of November for the conduct of Nicholas Lovet, Thomas Searls, James Robinson, John Twickeberde, Richard Smythe, Stephen Justis, Ralph Ducke, John Greame, Arnold Hocrofte and 54 other mariners by him prested from Folkestone, Dover, Kingsdown, Walmer, Deal, Sandwich and thereabouts in Kent to serve in Her Highness's ships at Gillingham, being distant 36 miles, at 18d every man – £4 14s 6d.

[*Page total*] – £12 2s 6d.

[f. 142v] To Edward Lambarde of Brightlingsea the 25th day of November for the conduct of Thomas Mathew, William Gilles, Richard Fraunche, John Hincharde, and 15 other mariners by him prested from Harwich, Manningtree and thereabouts to serve in Her Grace's ships at Gillingham, being distant 36 miles, at 18d every man – 28s 6d; more to him for the conduct of John West, John Morris, George Cato, John Smythe and 18 other mariners by him prested from St Osyth, Wivenhoe, Bradwell, and thereabouts to Gillingham, distant 24 miles, at 12d every man – 22s;

[1]The first three named were from *Great Bark*'s regular crew, and transferred to *Triumph* when their ship was docked; Paddon, Kisshan and Wood were seconded from *Elizabeth Jonas*, and Robinson was boatswain of *Mary Rose* (cf. above, pp. 143, 144, 145, 167).

[2]The three named were seconded from *Hope* (cf. above, p. 161).

and more to him for the conduct of Michael Parry, William Scote, William Rigges, John Saunder and nine other mariners by him prested from Paglesham, Burnham, Milton, and thereabouts, distant 12 miles, at 6d every man – 6s 6d. [*Summa*] – £2 17s.

To Henry Dannes of Inworth in Essex and James Humphrey of Ipswich the same day for the conduct of Robert Wright, Oliver Pette and three other mariners by them prested from Holbrook in Suffolk to serve in Her Highness's ships at Gillingham, distant 48 miles, at 2s every man – 10s; more for the conduct of John Dearemore, John Lawraunce, Richard Poope, Richard Saunders, Robert Farley, William Brewes, Lawrence Smyth, Thomas Brewton, Robert Smythe, Peter Johnson and 29 other mariners by them prested from Ipswich, Walton, Woodbridge, Eyke and thereabouts in Suffolk to Gillingham, distant 60 miles, at 2s 6d every man – £4 17s 6d; and more to them for the conduct of William Falkoner, Oliver Johnson, Thomas Morecoke, Thomas Shaw, Thomas Roose, Ralph Thompson, Edward Howper, Edward Stevenson, George Busshell, William Draper, Thomas Shrubb, Richard Parker and 63 other mariners by them prested from Orford, Thorpe, Aldeburgh, Sizewell, Eastbridge, Dunwich, Walberswick, Southwold and thereabouts to Gillingham, distant 80 miles, at 3s every man – £11 5s. *Summa* – £16 12s 6d.

To William Burgis, William Mathew, Edmund West, Roger Starke and 46 other mariners the same day for their conduct from Gillingham to London for the launching of Her Grace's new ship called the *Aid*,[1] at 12d every man – £2 10s.

[*Page total*] – £21 19s 6d.

[f. 143] To Fabian Bulyn, John Bennet, Thomas Harrington, William Warde and 11 other mariners the 26th day of December for their conduct from Gillingham to London, discharged out of Her Grace's two hoys[2] and being commanded back again, at 12d every man – 15s.

To Roger Bowth, Richard Haynes, John Banckes and John Williams, master gunners, the same day for the conduct of William Thomas, Richard Williams and 26[3] other gunners by them prested from London to Gillingham, at 12d every man – £1 8s.

To Jeffrey Vaughan the same day for the conduct of Thomas Browne, Robert Taillor Robert Harris, Christopher Stevens, John Wourwood, John West and 14 other mariners by him prested from Poole, Lymington and thereabouts to Portsmouth, at 18d every man – 30s; and more to him for the conduct of Nicholas Punton, Nicholas Diggons, Thomas Bryan and

[1]On 6 Oct.: *NEM*, p. 466.
[2]The four named were from *Mary Grace*; the other hoy was *George* (cf. above, p. 57).
[3]MS 'xxvjth' by faulty association with date in previous entry.

four other mariners by him prested from Rye and thereabouts to Portsmouth aforesaid, at 3s every man – 21s. *Summa* – £2 11s.

To William Sampson, master, the same day for the conduct of himself and eight other mariners from Gillingham to Dover, being distant 36 miles, at 18d every man – 13s 6d.

[*Page total*] – £5 7s 6d. [f. 143v *blank*]

[f. 144] **Extraordinary. Charges:**

Anno Domini 1561 [1562]. *Anno regni regine Elizabethe quarto*

To divers persons sustained about the necessary causes belonging to Her Highness's ships:

To John Browne, John Elmer and two others the first day of January for their charges in boat-hire and horse-hire in carrying of Her Highness's treasure from London to Gillingham for the payment and discharge of captains, masters, mariners and gunners having served in Her Grace's ships, galleys [*and*] ship boats at Harwich, Her Highness being there – £2 3s.

To John Elmer, messenger, the 3rd day of January for his charges riding with letters from London to Portsmouth, to Thomas Morley, one of the officers of the Queen's ships[1] – 20s; more for the charges of himself and his horse attending there the coming of Mr Morley from Plymouth, by the space of 4 days at 2s 6d *per diem* – 10s; more the 19th day of the same for one other journey to Portsmouth to Thomas Morley with letters – 20s; more the 26th day of this present for one journey to Chatham with John Browne for the carriage of money to make a pay there – 6s 8d; more the 12th day of February for one other journey to Chatham with letters to Butolph Moungey and Thomas Henos – 6s 8d; more the 20th day of February for one journey with letters to Gillingham to Mr Holstock – 6s 8d; more the 12th day of March for one journey to Farningham in Kent with letters from William Winter to Bexley the topmaker – 5s; more the 17th day of May 1562 for one journey with letters to Cobham Hall to my Lord Cobham there – 5s; more the 19th day of the same for one other journey with letters from my Lord Admiral to my Lord Cobham – 5s; more the 22th day of the same month of May for one journey to Rochester and from thence to Rye and so alongst the sea coast attending upon my Lord Admiral [*at*] his Lordship's commandment, by the space of 8 days at 2s 6d *per diem* – 20s; more for one journey the 12th day of June with

[1]Clerk and Keeper of the Storehouses since Dec. 1561: for career details see *NEM*, pp. 559–60.

letters to Potter Row from William Holstock, Comptroller of Her Highness's Marine Affairs, to Henry Daynes – 10s; and more to him for one other journey made by him with letters to Weybridge, to William Latymer for the sending away of certain Her Grace's timber from thence – 5s. *Summa* – £6.

To James Gentell the same day for certain charges by him sustained in boat-hire and other ways at divers and sundry times in going to Rotherhithe, London, Woolwich and Blackwall aboard the Queen's Majesty's ships for the mustering of mariners and gunners appointed to Her Grace's ships, being occupied about the same by the space of 7 days, at 8d *per diem* – 4s 8d.

[*Page total*] – £8 7s 8d.

[f. 144v] To Thomas Morley the 3rd day of February for the charges of himself, his man and their two horses riding from London to Portsmouth, Plymouth and back again for the surveying of the *Primrose*, the *Flower de Luce* and the *Brigantine*, spoiled by foul weather, and for repairing and mending of them of the said spoils to proceed on their voyage,[1] by the space of 50 days begun the 16th day of December last and ended as abovesaid, at 4s every of them *per diem* – £20; more to him for the charges of William Prestman and his horse sent from Portsmouth to Plymouth with a letter from Bristol by George Winter, Clerk of Her Highness's Ships, by the space of 12 days within the said time, at 4s *per diem* – 48s; more to him for the charge of guides in the same jouney – 20s; and more to him for his passage by water at divers ferries – 6s. *Summa* – £23 14s.

*[*Repairing of the* Minion]. To Peter Pett and Butolph Moungey for the charges of themselves, their one man and three horses travelling from London to Bristol for the repairing and mending of the *Minion*, being spoiled at the seas with foul weather – 59s; more for their own charges remaining there by the space of 26 days, at 12d every man *per diem* – £3 18s; more for their horsemeat by like time – 52s; and more to them for their charges from Bristol to London and back again – 25s. *Summa* – £10 14s 4d.

[1]These ships, along with *Minion*, were chartered to the Guinea merchants, whose trade had been newly regulated by the Queen in May 1561. After sailing from the Thames on 1 Sept., the expedition met with a succession of accidents (including a collision in the Straits of Dover between *Primrose* and *Minion*) which necessitated the repairs mentioned here. *Minion*, taken into Bristol, was originally thought beyond Pett's capacity to repair: Hakluyt, vi, pp. 255–7 (John Lok's report to the company, 11 Dec.). Nevertheless, in the new year the voyage was resumed and eventually returned the Queen £1,000 as her third of the profits: see generally Williamson, *Hawkins* (1927), pp. 55–6; also *CSPF 1562*, no. 461 (report of detention of *Flower de Luce* in the Canaries, March 1562) and below, p. 225.

To William Holstock the 27th day of February for so much paid by him for the hire of a ketch and three men that was sent from against Hadleigh castle to Sheerness to cause the *Phoenix* and the *Hare* to meet the *Bark of Boulogne* at the east end of the North Sand – 5s

To the same William Holstock the 28th day of February for so much given to a through post at Dover to bring letters from thence to Mr Secretary Cecil to the court at Westminster to give advertisement of the ships being there – £1 6s 8d.

To the said William Holstock the 7th day of March for so much paid by him to a through post at Queenborough to carry letters from thence to Mr Secretary Cecil to the court at Westminster of advertisement of the return of the *Bark of Boulogne* and the *Hare* – 16s 6d.

[*Page total*] – £36 16s 6d.

[f. 145] To Butolph Moungey the 21th day of March for the charges of himself, his man and their two horses by the space of 11 days begun the 21 day of January and ended the last day of the same month, both days included, being occupied in Kent about the presting of mariners for the *Primrose*, and sent the same to Portsmouth, at 6s 8d every day, the which ship was then sent to the seas. *Summa* – £3 13s 4d.

Anno Domini 1562

To John Elmer, messenger, the 20th day of July for the charges of himself and his horse, riding with letters from London to Waxham in Norfolk, to Sir Thomas Woodhouse – 40s; more the 21th day of the same for one journey with letters to Butolph Moungey at Gillingham – 6s 8d; more for his pains attending at London and also at the court by the commandment of Sir William Woodhouse by the space of 2 days, being appointed to have ridden to Lynn about Her Highness's affairs – 2s 6d; more for one other journey with letters to Mr Malyn at Dover the 31th day of the same – 20s; more the 5th day of August for one journey with letters to Queenborough. to Sir William Woodhouse from my Lord Admiral – 13s 4d; more the 6th day of August for one journey to Her Highness's ships riding by north the minster[1] with letters from my Lord Admiral to Sir William Woodhouse – 13s 4d; more for one journey the 8th day of the same to Margate and from thence to Dover to enquire of Her Grace's ships then being at the seas, being commanded by my Lord Admiral to see in what state they were after the tempest – 26s 8d; more the 11th day of the same for one journey with letters to Dover from my Lord Admiral to Sir William Woodhouse – 20s; more the 16th day of the

[1]The church from which Minster (in Sheppey) takes its name.

same for one journey with letters from my Lord Admiral to Sir William Woodhouse, then being at the Downs – 20s;. more the 28th day of the same for one journey with letters to Benjamin Gonson, Treasurer of Her Grace's Marine Causes, then being at Moulsham Hall in Essex[1] – 6s 8d; more the 30th day of the same for one journey with letters to Dover from my Lord Admiral to Sir William Woodhouse – 20s; more the 6th day of September for one journey with letters to Sir William Damsell at Beckenham[2] – 2s 6d; more the 11th day of the same for one journey to Queenborough with letters to William Driver, captain of the *New Bark* – 13s 4d; and more to him the 25th day of the same for one journey to Portsmouth with letters to Thomas Morley there[3] – 20s. *Summa* – £11 5s.

[*Page total*] – £14 18s 4d.

[f. 145v] To Thomas Baker the 20th day of July for his charges in horse-hire and boat-hire travelling from London to Gillingham for the taking of survey of 16 Her Grace's ships, as well of all such tackle and apparel as presently remaineth aboard them, as also to understand and know the wants of the same ships for their settings forth to the seas; remaining there about the same by the space of 8 days, at 2s 6d *per diem* – £1.

To Edward Gotley the 24th day of July for the charges of himself, one man and their two horses riding about the presting of 132 mariners out of Dorsetshire and Hampshire to serve in Her Grace's ships at Gillingham appointed to the seas, travailing about the same by the space of 12 days, at 3s 4d every man *per diem* – £4; more for so much paid by him to sundry persons for the carrying of precepts to the constables and tithingmen in divers parishes for the mustering of the foresaid mariners at the places appointed, as also money given to the mayors' officers at Poole and Southampton – 7s; more for the passage of himself and his horses at divers passages – 2s 6d; more for a horse that died in the same journey – 40s;. and more to him for his charges going to Gillingham for the mustering of the said men by the space of three days, at 3s 4d *per diem* – 10s. *Summa* – £6 19s 6d.

To Henry Dannes the same day for charges of himself, his man and their two horses appointed by the officers of Her Grace's Marine Affairs to carry Her Highness's treasure into Essex and Suffolk to Edward Lambart and James Humphrey for the presting of mariners to serve in Her Grace's ships appointed to the seas; by agreement – £1 13s 4d.

[1]The grandiose seat of Thomas Mildmay, a prominent financial official since the 1530s and still Auditor of the Duchy of Cornwall, who was married to Gonson's sister Avis: *Hist. Parl. 1509–58*, ii, p. 601.

[2]The site of Damsell's original property in Kent: ibid., ii, p. 10.

[3]Presumably answering Morley's report of 26 Sept. concerning victualling of ships for Le Havre: SP 12/24, no. 51 (*CSPD 1547–80*, p. 207).

To Thomas Jonns of Lynn the first day of August for the charges of himself his man and their two horses travelling from London to Lynn in Norfolk about the presting of 91 mariners to serve in Her Grace's ships at Gillingham appointed to the seas, travailing about the same by the space of 8 days, at 2s 6d the man *per diem* – £2.

To William Garton of Yarmouth the same day for the hire of his crayer called the *Ellin of Yarmouth* and for the wages and victuals of five men serving in the same in carrying of letters from the Queen's Majesty's most honourable Privy Council to William Holstock, captain of Her Grace's ship the *Swallow*, and delivered the same at the sea thwart of Hull; by agreement – £3 15s 10d.

[*Page total*] – £15 8s 8d.

[f. 146] To Edward Lambard of Brightlingsea the first day of August for the charges of himself, his man and their two horses riding about the presting of 109 mariners out of divers places in Essex to serve in Her Grace's ships at Gillingham appointed to the seas, travailing about the same by the space of 6 days, at 3s 4d the man *per diem* – 40s; more for so much paid by him to sundry persons for the carrying of precepts to the constables of divers parishes for the mustering of the foresaid mariners at the places appointed – 13s 8d; more to Miles Woodles for the charges of himself and his horse riding to St Osyth, Clacton, Thorpe, Kirby, Walton on the Naze and divers other towns thereabouts in Essex for the like presting of mariners by the space of 2 days, at 2s 6d *per diem* – 5s; and more to the said Lambard for the charges of himself, his man and their two horses riding from Brightlingsea to Gillingham for the mustering of the said men there by the space of 4 days, at 2s 6d every man *per diem* – 20s. *Summa* – £3 18s 8d.

To James Humphrey and Thomas Fuller the same day for the charges of themselves and their horses riding about the presting of 133 mariners out of divers places in Suffolk to serve Her Grace's ships at Gillingham appointed to the seas, by the space of 10 days at 2s 6d the man *per diem* – 50s; and more for so much paid by them as well for horse-hire, as also to sundry persons for the finding out of mariners which absented themselves from the prest, and for the passage of them and their horses over divers passages, with other charges incident to the same – £2 9s 4d. *Summa* – £4 19s 4d.

To Rowland Mocklow and Thomas Woodcote the same day for their charges as well in boat-hire as in other ways in travailing about the presting of 165 mariners and watermen from Blackwall, Limehouse, Ratcliff and St Katherine's, also out of divers merchants' ships in the river of Thames, to serve in Her Highness's ships at Gillingham appointed to the seas, by the space of 7 days at 3s every man *per diem* – 42s; and more to the Bailly of St Katherine's for his pains in watching 2 nights about the sending away of the said men – 2s. *Summa* – £2 4s.

[*Page total*] – £11 2s.

[f. 146v] To Butolph Moungey the first day of August for the charges of himself, his man and their two horses riding from Gillingham to London by the space of three days for the receiving of money and certain instructions delivered to him by the officers of Her Grace's Marine Causes for the presting of 222 mariners out of sundry places in Kent and Sussex, at 3s 4d the man *per diem* – 20s; more paid by him for three letters of attendance, at 3s the letter – 9s; more for the charge of himself, two men and three horses travailing about the presting of the said men by the space of 9 days, at 4s every man the day – £5 8s; more to him for the charges of himself travailing about the presting of 30 mariners from Hoo, Milton, Maidstone and thereabouts in Kent, by the space of 2 days at 3s 4d *per diem* – 6s 8d; more paid for ferryage of his horses over certain rivers in Kent and Sussex – 3s; and more to him for so much given to the sergeants in sundry towns for the more expedition of the said service there to be done – 2s 8d. *Summa* – £7 9s 4d.

To John Malyn of Dover the same day for the charges of himself and his horse riding about the presting of 55 mariners from Dover and thereabouts to serve in Her Highness's ships at Gillingham appointed to the seas, travailing about the same by the space of 5 days, at 2s 4d *per diem* – 11s 8d.

*[*Lanterns. Locks*]. To William Keys, boatswain of one Her Grace's ships called the *Lion* the 4th day of August for certain charges by him laid out for the new mending and repairing of the glass lantern belonging to the same ship, *viz.* as ironwork, painting and glazing of the same, being spoiled and broken at the seas in foul weather – 20s; and more to him for a lock for the captain's cabin, and for mending of 2 other locks for the cupboards within the same cabin – 3s. *Summa* – £1 3s.

To Jerome Hewster the 6th day of August for his pains travailing about the presting of 21 caulkers appointed for the caulking of Her Highness's ships at Gillingham, by the space of 4 days at 12d *per diem* – 4s.

[*Page total*] – £9 8s.

[f. 147] To Thomas Baker the 6th day of August for his charges as well boat-hire as horse-hire, travailing by several journeys from London to Gillingham for the taking of survey of Her Majesty's ships then appointed to the seas, and for his charges remaining there by the space of 11 days about the delivering to them such wants as was necessary about the same business, at 2s 6d *per diem* – £1 7s 6d.

To Michael Gonson, purser, for so much laid out by him for candle spent in Her Majesty's ship the *Hope*, Sir William Woodhouse being Admiral in the same ship, for the giving of light in the night time at her being at the seas – 4s.

To William Unthanke of Dover for the charge and hire of his crayer named the *William of Dover* with eight men and one boy for the conveying of letters from Her Majesty's most honourable Council to Sir William Woodhouse being at the seas,[1] which crayer went from Dover to Dieppe and back again; by agreement – £1 10s.

To Edward Thompson, Thomas Dyxson, Robert Thompson, Jacob Myller, Nicholas Harde and John Malpas, master gunners, the same day for their costs and charges sustained about the presting of gunners to serve Her Highness at the sea, and for their travel between London and Gillingham, to and fro – £1 16s 8d.

To James Jentill the same day for his charges of boat-hire and horse-hire travelling from London to Gillingham, attending there by the space of 8 days for the mustering of mariners, gunners and others prested by divers persons to serve in Her Highness ships at the seas, at 2s 6d *per diem* – £1.

To Rowland Mocklow the same day for the charges of himself and Richard Powll as well in boat-hire as in other ways travailing about the presting of 76 watermen from divers places within the river of Thames to serve in the *Brigantine* at Portsmouth, traviling about the same by the space of 4 days, at 4s the man *per diem* – £1 12s.

[*Page total*] – £7 10s 2d.

[f. 147v] To Thomas Baker the 4th day of September for his charges riding from London to Portsmouth for the taking of survey of two Her Majesty's ships called the *Minion* and the *Primrose* at their coming from the seas, as also for his charges back again – £1 10s 8d.

To Sir William Woodhouse, knight, Vice-Admiral of England, the same day for charges by him laid out in sending of letters at sundry times to Her Majesty's most honourable Privy Council in time that he had charge in the Narrow Seas as Admiral in the *Hope*[2] – £3.

To William Holstock the 8th day of September for charges by him laid out to divers persons in sending of letters from the Downs to London to the officers of Her Grace's Marine Affairs in the time of his being captain in the *Lion* there[3] – £2 9s 8d.

[1]On 29 Aug. the Council ordered Woodhouse to detach *Swallow* to escort Sir Hugh Paulet to his charge as Captain of Jersey, and to search for pirates in the Channel: *APC 1558–70* pp. 129–30.

[2]6 Aug.–8 Sept.: below, p. 233.

[3]6 Aug.–12 Sept.: below, ibid.

To John Browne, Jasper Hemmyngway, John Elmer and one other the 10th day of September for their charges as well in horse-hire as boat-hire travelling from London to Gillingham with Her Highness's treasure for the payment of captains' diets and wages of masters, mariners and gunners serving in two of Her Grace's ships called the *Hope* and the *Lion*, discharged from the seas; remaining there for the payment of the same by the space of three days – £2.

*[*Victualling of mariners*]. To Thomas Mariechurche the same day for charges by him sustained for the victualling of 10 mariners which were by Sir William Woodhouse commanded to remain at Dover in a pinnace called the *Flight*,[1] attending there by the space of six days to receive such letters as the Queen's Majesty's most honourable Privy Council did send to the said Sir William Woodhouse, he then lying upon the coast of France; by agreement – £1 1s 6d.

[*Page total*] – £10 1s 10d.

[f. 148] To Thomas Woodcot the 11th day of September for his charges, as well boat-hire as other ways, travailing about the presting of 42 mariners within the river of Thames for the launching and rigging of Her Highness's two new ships at Deptford Strand, by the space of 8 days at 3s 4d *per diem* – 26s 8d; and more for his pains in presting of 100 mariners for the transporting of the said ships from Deptford to Gillingham, travailing about the same by the space of 7 days, at 2s 4d *per diem* – 16s 4d. *Summa* – £2 3s.

To William Fallyot of Southampton the 15th day of September for the charges of himself and his horse riding in post from Thomas Morley at Hampton aforesaid to Sir William Woodhouse, knight, Vice-Admiral of England, being at the court at Greenwich; by agreement – 13s 4d.

To John Vivyan of Portsmouth the 18th day of September for his charges and horse-hire riding in post with letters from Thomas Morley aforesaid to the officers of Her Grace's Marine Afairs at London, and being sent back again with answer of the same; by agreement – £1 6s 8d.

To Thomas James, gentleman,[2] the same day for certain charges by him sustained in sending of letters at sundry times to Her Majesty's Privy Council for intelligence out of France – £1.

To George Beeston, gentleman, the same day for charges by him laid out in sending of letters at sundry times to Her Majesty's honourable Council in the time that he had the charge in the Narrow Seas as Admiral in the *Hart*[3] – £2.

[1]The only royal ship of this name occ. 1592 (no other detail given): Anderson 204. Mariechurche was serving aboad the Admiral's ship *Hope*: cf. above, p. 144.

[2]Possibly the London merchant of this name later suspected as a Spanish agent: A. Haynes, *The Elizabethan Secret Services* (Stroud, 1992), p. 99.

[3]9 Sept.–19 Oct.: below, pp. 233–4.

To Henry Bamford the same day for the charges of himself and his horse, travelling with the Queen's Highness's commission into Kent and Hertfordshire for the providing of timber for the use of Her Grace's ships, by 70 days at 20d *per diem* – £5 16s 8d.

[*Page total*] – £12 19s 8d.

[f. 148v] To George Hall, purser, the 18th day of September for certain charges by him laid out for the use of Her Grace's ship the *Willoughby* at her going into Ireland last, *viz.* first for his charges by the space of 4 days being sent to Portsmouth to prepare a main yard and topsail yard with with boards and quarters for the use of the same ship – 3s 4d; more for the hire of a horse and for his own charges commanded to Poole from Weymouth to provide victuals for the *Willoughby* and the *Phoenix*, being occupied about the same by the space of 6 days – 11s 8d; more given to a boy for his pains in carrying of a letter to Captain Malyn of the same ship, from Poole to Weymouth – 12d; more for the hooping of 7 tun of beer – 16d; more for so much laid out by him to a pilot to carry the ship with victuals from Poole to St Alban's foreland [*St Aldhelm's Head*], being 4 leagues – 2s 6d; more for 2 pipes of cask at Poole – 2s 4d; and more for the charges of six mariners being occupied about the lading of the said victuals at Poole – 3s 4d; more to him for his charges travelling overland from the Cow[1] after he had delivered victuals to the *Phoenix* to Weymouth to the *Willoughby* again by 6 days – 10s; more for his charges by one day travailing at Dublin in Ireland about the victualling of the same ship – 12d; more for his charges travelling from Milford to Pembroke, Carew Castle and Haverfordwest, being occupied there by 8 days for the preparing of victuals for the *Willoughby* – 10s; and more to him for his charges with horse-hire from Dover to the court with letters to the Lord Admiral to give his lordship intelligence of the arrival of the same ship there, by the space of 6 days – 13s 4d. *Summa* – £2 19s 10d.

To Richard Darby of Portsmouth the same day for price of 100 foot of inch board oak of him had for the use of Her Grace's ship the *Willoughby* at her going into Ireland – 5s 4d; and more to him for 60 foot of quarters, price – 3s 4d. *Summa* – 8s 8d.

[*Page total*] – £3 8s 6d.

[f. 149] To John Elmer, messenger, the 29th day of September for one journey by him made with letters to Sir William Woodhouse at Hampton

[1]The terms East and West Cow originally applied to two sandbanks of bovine suggestion off the mouth of the Medina; then to the blockhouses built either side the river by Henry VIII, and to the adjacent anchorage ('*the roads called the Esturly or the Westerly Cowe*'), which is the likely sense here. The settlements only became East and West Cowes in the 18th cent.: A. D. Mills, *The Place-Names of the Isle of Wight: Their Origins and Meanings* (Donington [Lincs], 2001), pp. 42, 43.

Court – 5s; more the 12th day of October for one other journey to Dover with letters to Captain Malyn – 20s; more the 13th day of the same for one other journey with letters to Hampton Court to my Lord Admiral – 5s; more the 23th day of the same month for one other journey with letters to my Lord Admiral at Hampton Court aforesaid – 5s; more the 28th day of the same for one other journey with letters to his lordship and Sir William Woodhouse, and being commanded to attend there by the space of 2 days for answer of a warrant – 6s 8d; more the first day of November for one journey with letters to the said Malyn at Dover – 20s; more the 5th day of the same for one other journey with letters to Gillingham to Butolph Moungey from my Lord Admiral, and from thence to Malling in Kent, to him there – 10s; more for one journey with letters the 8th day of the same to Dover to the masters of Her Grace's two hoys the *George* and the *Mary Grace*[1] – 20s; more the 28th day of the same for one journey with letters to Chatham to John Hurlocke, master of one of Her Grace's ships[2] – 6s 8d; more to him for the hire of two horses and his own charges by the space of three days from London to Chatham with Her Highness's treasure – 13s. *Summa* – £5 11s 4d.

To James Alday the last day of September for his charges as well horse-hire as other ways in bringing of letters to the court at two several times with intelligence out of France from Sir William Woodhouse and George Beeston, Admirals for the time being – £4 19s 9d.

To John Powell the same day for his charges in bringing of letters in post from Portsmouth to London to the officers of Her Grace's Marine Causes – 13s 4d.

To Thomas Syble the same day for his charges with letters from London to Dover; by agreement – 10s.

[*Page total*] – [*deleted* £3 8s 6d] £11 14s 5d.

[f. 149v] To John Hawkins[3] the last day of September for his pains and travail with letters to the West Swale, to the *George* and the *Mary Grace*, to haste them to Dover – 7s 8d.

To Thomas Clay the 6th day of October for charges by him laid out for William Holstock, Comptroller of Her Majesty's Ships, being commanded by Her Majesty's most honourable Privy Council[4] to travel to Portsmouth for the more speedier embarking of Sir Adrian Poynings, Cuthbert Vaughan and other captains with 1,800 soldiers to pass from Portsmouth to Newhaven [*Le Havre*] in Normandy having post horses for himself, his

[1]Giles Hall and William Pearson: above, p. 80.

[2]The *Hope*: above, p. 117 and *passim*.

[3]The steward/purser of *Tiger*: above, p. 123 and *passim*.

[4]There is a gap in the Privy Council register from Sept. 1562 to Jan. 1563 (cf. *APC 1558–70*, p. 133), and therefore in information about orders for the Le Havre operation.

man and his guide, from London aforesaid to Portsmouth being distant 60 miles, at 5s every horse – 15s; more for the hire of his post horses back again from Portsmouth to London, at 5s the horse – 15s; more for the hire of guides from town to town, in and out – 5s; and more to him for other charges sustained in the said journey, by the space of 5 days at 6s 8d the day – £1 13s 4d. *Summa* – £3 8s 4d.

*[*Mariner's reward*]. To William Pointell, mariner, the same day in consideration of hurts happened to him at the launching of the *Aid* by the breaking of a cable, and towards his healing; paid to his hostess, Joan Pointell – £1.

*[*Sea charges*]. To John Borley the same day for his charges and pains taken in the *New Bark* in giving his [*inserted* attendance] for the conveying over of the Lord of Warwick from Dover to Newhaven in France,[1] by the space of 14 days – £1.

To John Browne, Jasper Hemmyngway, Thomas Baker, John Elmer and one other the 18th day of October for their charges with the hire of five horses travelling from London to Portsmouth and back again, being sent thither with Her Highness's treasure for the payment of captains' diets [*and*] wages of masters, mariners and gunners serving in two of Her Grace's ships at the seas, called the *Hart* and the *Swallow*, then being discharged from the said service – £6 13 4d.

[*Page total*] – £12 9s 4d.

[f. 150] *[*A skiff*]. To John Kelbe of Erith the 18th day of October for price of a skiff of him bought and delivered at Deptford for the needful use of Her Highness's pinnace called the *Double Rose* at her going to the seas; by agreement – £1 18s.

To Rowland Mocklow the 25th day of October for charges by him sustained travelling from London to Gillingham for the fetching of mariners out of Her Grace's ships there for the transporting of Her Highness's new ships from Deptford to Gillingham aforesaid – 3s.

*[*Wood and candles*]. To Henry Cooke and Hugh Poppe, pursers of two Her Grace's ships called the *Triumph* and the *Victory* the 13th day of November for and in recompense of wood, candles and certain other necessaries consumed in the transporting of the said ships from London [*recte* Deptford][2] to Gillingham; by agreement – £1.

[1]Ambrose, Earl of Warwick, elder surviving son of John Dudley, Duke of Northumberland; he was appointed Captain-General of the Le Havre expedition on 1 Oct. 1562: GEC, *Peerage*, xii, II, pp. 400–404. *ODNB*. The main force sailed from Portsmouth on 3 Oct., though Warwick's arrival in Le Havre is not confirmed until a report (from Portsmouth) on the 31st: SP 12/25, nos 3, 27 (*CSPD 1547–80*, pp. 208, 209).

[2]Scribal error by following the first 'to Gillingham' in the previous entry instead of the second.

Anno regni regine Elizabethe quinto

To Edward Lambarde the 25th day of November for the charges of himself and his man with their two horses, travailing about the presting of 62 mariners out of sundry places in Essex to Gillingham to serve in Her Grace's ships there, by the space of 7 days, at 3s 4d every of them *per diem* – £2 6s 8d; and more for so much paid by him to Henry Paskall and Thomas Lambard for their charges as well in horse-hire as other ways travelling with precepts to divers towns alongst the sea coast for the mustering of the said mariners at the places appointed; by agreement – 17s; *Summa* – £3 3s 8d

To Henry Daynes the same day for the charges of himself his man and their two horses travelling from London to Southwold in Suffolk for the presting of 119 mariners to serve in Her Highness's ships at Gillingham appointed to the seas, by the space of 12 days at 3s every man *per diem* – £3 12s; and more to James Humphrey for the charges of himself and his horse by the space of 10 days travailing about the like presting of mariners out of divers places in Suffolk to serve as aforesaid, at 3s *per diem* – 30s. *Summa* – £5 2s.

[*Page total*] – £11 6s 8d.

[f. 150v] To Thomas Baker the 26th day of November for his boat-hire, horse-hire and other charges by him sustained travailing in and about the survey of 15 Her Highness ships and galleys remaining at Chatham, being occupied in the said business by the space of 11 days, at 2s 6d *per diem* – £1 7s 6d.

To Thomas Woodcot the same day for his charges as well in boat-hire as other ways, travailing about the presting of mariners out of divers vessels within the river of Thames to serve in Her Grace's new ship called the *Aid*,[1] by the space of three days at 2s 4d *per diem* – 7s; and more for so much paid by him for a box for the commission – 4d. *Summa* – 7s 4d.

To Roger Benstead of Hinton in Hampshire the 4th day of December for the hire of his cart with horses from London to Portsmouth for the carrying of oillet lines, latchet lines and divers other provisions for the use of Her Grace's ships there; by agreement – £1 13s 4d.

To Thomas Bolton the same day for his charges as well in presting of certain caulkers sent down from London to Portsmouth. as also for the hire of a horse thither – 8s.

To Butolph Moungey, John Love and two other the same day for the charges of themselves and their horses from London to Portsmouth, and

[1]Mariners and others to the number of 300 were embarked in *Aid* at 5 o'clock on the afternoon of 16 Dec.: SP 12/26, no. 16 (*CSPD 1547–80*, p. 213).

from thence to Newhaven in Normandy by sea at the commandment of my Lord Admiral for service there to be done, by the space of 13 days at 3s every man *per diem* – £7 16s.

To John Henshaw, Captain of the Queen's Majesty's ship the *Saker*, the same day for his horse-hire and other charges travelling from Newhaven in Normandy to Hampton Court and back again with letters of importance from the Earl of Warwick to the Queen's Majesty's most honourable Privy Council – £2.[1]

[*Page total*] – £13 12s 2d.

[f. 151] To Peter Pett, master shipwright, the 4th day of December for the charges of himself his man and their two horses travelling from London to Portsmouth by four several journeys for the repairing of Her Grace's ships – £3 10s; and more to him for his charges attending at Deptford and Portsmouth by the space of 18 days, at 12d *per diem* – 18s. *Summa* – £4 8s.

To John Browne the 20th day of December for the charges of himself, Thomas Claye, Hugh Powell, John Elmer, William Curre and one other and for the hire of six horses as well from London to Gillingham for the safe carrying of Her Highness's treasure as also from thence back again, by the space of 5 days, in making of a pay to the shipwrights and shipkeepers for one half year ended the last day of June last – £4 12s 8d.

To John Browne the 24th day of December for the charges of himself, Davy Langforde, John Elmer, William Currey and two others, and for the hire of six horses as well from London to Portsmouth as from thence back again, for the safe conducting of Her Highness's treasure for the payment of captains, wages of masters, mariners and gunners till the last day of November last serving in the *New Bark*, the *Saker*, the *Phoenix* and the *Flower de Luce*,[2] by the space of 14 days tarrying for the coming of the same ships from Newhaven – £8 10s 4d.

*[*Timber*]. To William Hollande the same day for 2 pieces of elm timber to make capstans' bars for Her Highness's ship the *Lion*, by him bought at Deal town and delivered the same aboard; price by agreement – 4s 8d.

*[*Land carriage*]. To Thomas Spencer of London, carman, the same day for the hire of his cart and horses from London to Portsmouth for the carrying of a great chest filled with provisions for the *Minion* and the *Primrose*, *viz.* flags of St George, great compasses and great running

[1]In December a dispatch to Warwick was delayed when *Phoenix* was forced back to port: SP 12/26, no. 21 (*CSPD 1547–80*, p. 213).

[2]Such payments for *New Bark*, *Saker*, *Phoenix*, *Hare* and *Double Rose* to 30 November are itemised in **17** below. Movements of *New Bark*, *Saker* and *Phoenix* in October/November are reported in SP 12/25, nos 27, 28, 34 (*CSPD 1547–80*, pp. 209, 210).

glasses, and shivers and cocks of brass, with divers other kinds of things for the furnishing of the same ships for Ethiopia;[1] by agreement – £1 6s 8d.

[*Page total*] – £19 2s 4d.

[f. 151v] *[*Water carriage – 20s*; *Sea charges – 60s*; *Boards – 27s 2d*]. To William Driver[2] the 24th day of December for the hire of a small crayer of Gillingham to carry from thence into the Downs certain cordage to the Queen's Majesty's ships there – 20s; more to him for so much paid to a French lodesman by the space of one month serving in the *New Bark* upon the coast of France – £3; more to him for sending of three letters from Dover to Portsmouth to the Lord Admiral before the posts were laid – 47s 8d; and more to him for certain deal-boards, three casements, 13 foot of glass and 2 pounds of glue for the mending of the cabin in the *Aid* – 27s 2d. *Summa* – £7 14s 10d.

To Edward Goteley the same day for charges by him laid out as well for boat-hire as other ways in providing of divers necessaries for the use of Her Highness's ships by the space of 2 whole years begun at the feast of St Michael the Archangel in *anno Domini* 1560 and ended as abovesaid, at £4 the year – £8.

To Stephen Alexander for certain charges by him sustained in boat-hire and other ways at divers times in going and coming to London for the making perfect of Her Highness's reckonings in the Quarter Books concerning the general paybooks pertaining to Her Grace's Marine Causes, for one half year begun the first day of January last and ended the last day of June next – £2 3s 4d.[3]

To the said Edward Gooteley the same day for charges of himself and his horse travelling by two several journeys into divers woods in Kent for the survey of the remain of Her Grace's timber there, by the space of 16 days; by agreement – £2 3s 4d.

[1]The second venture of the re-formed Guinea company, which sailed from Dartmouth in February 1563. A draft of the charter party between the Queen and Lord Mayor and other citizens of London envisaged that these two ships would undertake a 'voiage for traffique and trade of merchandizes unto the parties of Aphrica and Ethiopia' though in fact they went no further than the Gold Coast. The agreement is undated but follows the inauguration of Sir Thomas Lodge's mayoralty on 8 Nov. 1562; the draft, and memoranda comparing this exedition with the previous one (above, p. 213 n. 1), are in SP 12/26, nos 43–5 (quotation from no. 43; *CSPD 1547–80*, p. 215). Another undated paper (SP 15/17, no. 115; *CSPD Addenda 1566–79*, pp. 246–8) appears to be related to the same business. The voyage itself is narrated in Hakluyt, vi, pp. 258–61. Cf. Williamson, *Hawkins* (1927), pp. 56–7.

[2]Captain of *New Bark*.

[3]An equivalent entry of 40s for the second half of the year (to 31 Dec. 1562), is deleted in the section of the draft Deptford ordinary which survives (for Christmas quarter): BL, Add. MS 78169, f. 19v. Likewise in 1563 this item was evidently first entered as a quarterly charge of 20s on the ordinary, but transferred to the Extraordinary Charges of the final account as a composite sum of £4: see below, p. 477 & n. 1.

To Peter Pett, one of the Queen's master shipwrights, the same day for charge of himself and his horse travelling into divers places in Kent and Hertfordshire for the surveying of certain woods there for the use of Her Grace's ships, being occupied about the same by the space of 10 days, at 3s 4d *per diem* – £1 13s 4d.

To Lancelot Tristram the same day for the charges of himself and his horse travelling into sundry places in Kent for the presting of certain shipwrights sent to Her Highness's works at Deptford; as also in making of provisions of divers kinds of stuffs for the use of Her Grace's ships at Chatham, *viz.* timber board, reed, lime and sand, being occupied about the same by the space of 15 days, at 2s 6d *per diem* – £1 17s 6d.

[*Page total*] – £23 12s 4d.

[f. 152] *[*A mast. Boards and spars*]. To Alexander Myndge of Dover the 24th day of December for price of a main mast by him delivered for the use of Her Highness's bark the *Hare*, who by foul weather had spent her mast at the sea; by agreement – 50s; more for price of 495 foot of seasoned inch board oak for the use of Her Highness's ships the *Hart* and the *Swallow*, being then at the seas, at 5s 8d every 100 foot – 32s 11d; and more to him for 10 double spars for the use of the same ships, at 6d every spar – 5s. *Summa* – £4 7s 11d.[1]

To William Wood, master, the same day for charges by him sustained at divers and sundry times as well for boat-hire as other ways, in coming from Chatham to London by the commandment of the officers of Her Grace's Marine Causes for the launching of Her Highness's ships at Deptford, as also for other needful service by him done; by agreement – £2.

*[*Portage of money out of the Receipt*]. To John Browne the last day of December *anno supradicto* for charges by him sustained in receiving of £9,346 17s as well in the Receipt[2] at Westminster at the hands of the tellers there, as also at the hands of others by several Her Grace's warrants to them directed at divers times within the time of this account for Her Grace's charges by sea, at 30s every £1,000; bags, wax, paper, parchment, carriages and suchlike within the said charges accounted – £14.

To Jeffrey Vaughan the same day for the charges of himself with two horses travelling from London to Portsmouth and there continuing the

[1]In the draft a form of this entry had originally been entered in the ordinary in the Deptford ordinary: 'To Alexander Mynge of Dover, the same day for price of 495 foot of inch board oak of him had for the repairing and mending of Her Highness's ship named the *Hart* at her last being at Dover, at 6s 8d every 100 foot – 31s 11d [*sic*]; more for 10 double quarters oak, at 6d the piece – 5s; and more to him for one mast for the use of the *Hare* – 50s. *Summa* – £4 7s 11d': BL, Add. MS 78169, f. 15. The figure of 32s 11d in the final version is correct.

[2]The Receipt of the Exchequer.

space of 86 days, not only in setting to the seas Her Highness's ships the *Minion* and the *Primrose*, but also furthering divers Her Grace's other affairs there, as mustering of men serving in the *Aid*, the *Phoenix*, the *Saker* and other Her Grace's ships presently at the seas, his said travail beginning the 7th day of October and ended as abovesaid, at 3s 4d *per diem* – £14 6s 8d; and more to him for charges of his man for like time, at 8d *per diem* – £2 17s 4d. *Summa* – £17 4s.

[*Page total*] – £37 11s 11d. [f. 152v *blank*]

[f. 153] **Extraordinary. Prests**:

Anno Domini 1562. Anno regni regine Elizabethe quinto

Money delivered in prest to Edward Baeshe, General Surveyor of Her Grace's victuals for the seas, as followeth:

To Edward Baeshe, General Surveyor of Her Grace's victuals for the seas, the eighth day of July *anno supradicto* in prest for the victualling of 60 men in the *Saker* and the *Phoenix*, appointed to transport Her Highness's provisions into the north parts – thirty six pounds – £36.

To the said Edward Baeshe the 24th day of July *anno supradicto* in prest for the victualling of 990 men appointed to serve in four Her Highness's ships and one bark at the seas for one month, six hundred threescore pounds – £660.

To the said Edward Baeshe the first day of September *anno supradicto* in prest for the setting forth of one Her Highness's ships and a bark called the *Willoughby* and the *Phoenix* with 140 men for 6 weeks, appointed as well for the waftage of certain Her Grace's munitions presently shipped for Ireland, as also for the apprehension of certain pirates now at the seas,[1] one hundred and forty pounds – £140.

To the foresaid Edward Baeshe the 16th day of September *anno supradicto* in prest for the victualling of 170 men for one month of 28 days appointed to serve Her Highness at the seas in two Her Grace's ships called the *New Bark* and the *Saker*, one hundred and thirteen pounds, six shillings and eight pence – £113 6s 8d.[2]

[*Page total*] – £949 6s 8d.

[f. 153v] To the forenamed Edward Baeshe the 20th day of September *anno supradicto* in prest for the victualling of 390 men for 14 days

[1]On 20 July the Lord Admiral was ordered to prepare two ships for this purpose: SP 12/23, no. 57 (*CSPD 1547–80*, p. 203). The operation was commanded from *Willoughby* by Capt. Malyn: below, p. 234.

[2]On 9 Sept. the Lord Admiral was ordered to send these ships under Capt. Beeston to patrol the Channel: SP 12/24, no. 26 (*CSPD 1547–80*, p. 205).

appointed to serve Her Highness at the seas in two Her Grace's ships and one bark, named the *Hart*, the *Swallow* and the *Hare*, one hundred and thirty pounds – £130.

To the said Edward Baeshe the 6th day of October *anno supradicto* in prest for the victualling of 560 men for 14 days appointed to serve Her Highness at the seas in the *Swallow*, the *Hart*, the *New Bark*, the *Saker* and the *Hare*, one hundred fourscore six pounds, thirteen shillings and four pence – £186 13s 4d.

To the same Edward Baeshe the 16th day of October *anno supradicto* in prest for the victualling of one hundred men serving in the *Mary Willoughby* for one month, three score pounds – £60.[1]

To the said Edward Baeshe the 7th day of November *anno supradicto* in prest as well for a provision of victuals for three weeks for 200 men serving Her Highness at the seas in the *New Bark*, the *Saker* and the *Hare*, to begin the first day of this present month of November; as also for one month's victuals for 30 men likeways appointed to serve Her Grace at the seas in the *Double Rose*, to begin the 13th day of October last, one hundred twenty pounds – £120.

[*Page total*] – £496 13s 4d.

[f. 154] To the foresaid Edward Baeshe the 21th day of November *anno supradicto* in prest as well for three weeks' victuals for the *Phoenix* for 40 men, begun the first day of this present month of November, and for one month's victuals for the *New Bark*, the *Saker*, the *Hare* and the *Phoenix* with 240 men serving Her [*Highness*] at the seas, to begin the 22th day of this present month of November; as also for the victualling of 310 men for one month appointed to carry and transport certain Her Majesty's ships from Gillingham to Portsmouth, *viz.* the *Jennet*, the *Antelope*, the *Greyhound*, the new ship and the *Bark of Boulogne* – three hundred fourscore six pounds, thirteen shillings and four pence – £386 13s 4d.[2]

To the said Edward Baeshe the 25th day of December *anno supradicto* in prest for the victualling of six Her Majesty's ships, *viz.* the *New Bark*, the *Saker*, the *Phoenix*, the *Hare*, the *Bark of Boulogne* and the *Double Rose* for one month of 28 days to begin the 20th day of this present month of December and to end the 16th day of January next, two hundred pounds – £200.[3]

[*Page total*] – £586 13s 4d. [f. 154v *blank*]

[1]Cf. estimate of 14 Oct. for sea wages [**16**], which includes this £60.

[2]Charges itemised in Baeshe's estimate of 11 Nov. [**24**]. The operation was commanded from *Greyhound* by Capt. Malyn: below, p. 237.

[3]Charges itemised in Baeshe's estimate of 5 Dec. [**25**].

[f. 155] **Extraordinary. Portsmouth**:

Anno Domini 1561 [1562]. *Anno regni regine Elizabethe quarto*

A payment made the 24th day of January as well to shipwrights, sawyers, smiths and other artificers and workmen for new mending and repairing of the *Primrose* and the *Flower de Luce*, being spoiled at the seas by foul weather, as also to sundry persons for divers provisions had toward the same; begun the first day of January last, and this day ended, as followeth:

Shipwrights

John Peaze, master, 24 days at 10d	20s
Nicholas Gater, 24 days at 6d	12s
Thomas Chartam, 24 days at 6d	12s
Raynold Veze, server, 24 days at 4d	8s
John Herse, 24 days at 6d	12s
Stephen Rogers, 16 days at 8d	10s 8d
Thomas Good, server, 16 days at 4d	5s 4d
Davy Bygges, 16 days at 8d	10s 8d
John Barrey, 17 days at 6d	8s 6d
William Hurllocke, 16 days at 3d	4s
Stephen Browne, 16 days at 8d	10s 8d
William Dalloply, 16 days at 8d	10s 8d
Edmund Forde, 16 days at 3d	4s
Thomas Greneleff, 17 days at 7d	9s 11d
Thomas Cappe, server, 17 days at 4d	5s 8d
John Smythe, 15 days at 8d	10s
Robert Grigge, 15 days at 6d	7s 6d
John Northe, 14 days at 6d	7s
Robert Harrys, 12 days at 6d	6s

[*Page total*] – £8 13s 7d.

[f. 155v] John Turner, 14 days at 8d	9s 4d
Thomas Sambro, 14 days at 5d	6s 2d
Hugh Gosse, 14 days at 7d	8s 2d
Philip Payne, 14 days at 6d	7s
Walter Johnson, 12 days at 6d	6s
Nicholas Poyter, 14 days at 6d	7s
Christopher Stevens, 14 days at 6d	7s
Robert Blacke, 14 days at 6d	7s
John Heller, 14 days at 6d	7s
John Paullmer, 14 days at 6d	7s
Robert Tayller, 3 days at 6d	18d
Edmund Bevys, 12 days at 8d	8s

Richard Flight, 12 days at 8d	8s
John Samboro, 12 days at 6d	6s
John Androw, 12 days at 7d	7s
John Androw, server, 12 days at 3d	3s
John Thomas, 24 days at 6d	12s
Smiths	
Peter Browne, 22 days at 6d	11s
John Owllet, 22 days at 4d	7s 4d
John Payne, 24 days at 4d	8s
Robert Raynolde, 18 days at 7d	10s 6d
William Pope, 18 days at 4d	6s
Clement Rede, 15 days at 3d	3s 9d
George Jackson, 13 days at 2d	2s 2d

[*Page total*] – [£28 13s 10d *deleted*] £8 5s 11d.

[f. 156] *Sawyers*	
Thomas Berde, 14 days at 6d	7s
Thomas Smythe, 14 days at 5d	5s 2d
John Comes, 2 days at 6d	12d
John Legat, 5½ days at 5d	2s 3½d
John Bowden, 24 days at 4d	8s
Thomas Foster, 24 days at 4d	8s
Edward Prestman, 22 days at 6d	11s
	*[*43s 1d*]

Victualling. To John Thomas of Portsmouth the 24th day of January for victualling of 50 of the aforenamed shipwrights, sawyers and smiths working upon the new mending and repairing of Her Highness's ships there named the *Primrose* and the *Flower de Luce*, being spoiled at the seas by foul weather, by the space of 844 days among them all, the Sundays and holy days in the same accounted, begun the first day of January last and ended as is aforesaid, which maketh 120 weeks one day – £21 10s 9d.

[*Page total*] – £23 13s 10½d.

[f. 156v] *Emptions*

Ironwork. To John Pope of Portsmouth, smith, the 24th day of January for the working of 56 pounds weight of Her Highness's old iron by him made and wrought into a swivel for the use of Her Highness's said ships, at 1d every pound weight, *Summa* – 4s 8d.

To John Hallaway of Portsmouth the same day for price of 600 of 6d nail by him delivered for the use of the same ships, at 6d every 100 – 3s; more for 600 of 4d nail, at 4d every 100 – 2s; more for 400 [*of*] 10d nail, at 10d every 100 – 3s 4d; more for 400 of 8d nail, at 8d every 100 – 2s 8d. *Summa* – 11s.

To John Robenson of Fareham the same day for price of 3,000 of 10d nail of him taken and delivered to the use of the same ships, at 8s [*inserted* 4d] every 1,000 – 25s; more for 3,000 of 8d nail, at 6s 8d every 1,000 – 20s; more for 4,000 of 6d nail, at 5s every 1,000 – 20s; more to him for 4,000 of 4d nail, at 3s 4d every 1,000 – 13s 4d. *Summa* – £3 18s 4d.

Anchors, warps, a flag and a copper kettle. To William Howse of Southampton the same day for price of one new flag with the cross of St George by him delivered for the use of the same ships; by agreement – 16s; more for one small anchor weighing 2 hundred 3 quarters weight [*308 lbs*], at 14s 10d every hundredweight – 41s;[1] more for 3 small warps tarred of 2½ inches compass, weighing 2 hundred one quarter weight [*252 lbs*], at 18s every hundred[*weight*] – 40s 6d; and more to him for one copper kettle weighing 12 pounds weight, at 11d every pound weight – 11s. *Summa* – £5 8s 6d.

To Humphrey Mosley the same day for price of one great anchor of him had and taken for the use of the *Primrose*, weighing 9 hundred 7 pounds weight [*1,015 lbs*], at 23s 4d every hundredweight. *Summa* – £10 11s 6d.[2]

[*Page total*] – £20 14s.

[f. 157] *Anchors and cables.* To William Jonson of Fareham the 24th day of January for price of one anchor of him had and taken for the use of the *Flower de Luce*, weighing 4 hundred one quarter 6 pounds [*482 lbs*], at 15s every hundredweight – £3 3s 10d;[3] and more to him for one cable tarred of 5 inches compass, weighing 4 hundred 6 pounds weight [*454 lbs*], at 18s every hundred[*weight*] – £3 13s.[4] *Summa* – £6 16s 10d.

To Thomas Whomes of Southampton the same day for price of one tarred cable by him delivered for the use of the same ships, weighing 3 hundred 3 quarters 18 pounds [*438 lbs*], at 18s every hundredweight – £3 10s 6d;[5] and more to him for one small anchor weighing 2 hundred 14 pounds [*238 lbs*], at 23s 4d every hundredweight – £2 9s 6d.[6] *Summa* – £6.

[1]The calculation (irrespective of how cwt is reckoned) gives 489.5d, which is 2½d below the sum stated (492d). It will be noted that calculation of quite small quantities involving cwts is markedly less accurate in this section than elsewhere, indicating that the Quarter Books were compiled from a variety of sources, not all of them audited to the same specifications.

[2]The calculation gives 2537.5d, which is ½d below the sum stated (2538d).

[3]The calculation gives 774.64282d, which is about 8½d above the sum stated (766d). The measure should probably be approximately 481 lbs (i.e. 4½ cwt 5 lbs), making 7730d at the rate stated.

[4]The calculation gives 875.57141d, which is less than ½d below the sum stated (876d).

[5]The calculation gives 844.71427d, which is about 1¼d below the sum stated (846d).

[6]The calculation gives 595d, which is 1d above the sum stated.

Timber oak, inch board and knees. To William Prestman the same day for price of 100 foot of inch board oak of him had and taken for the use of the same ships. *Summa* – 5s

To Robert Spuddell of Dartmouth the same day for price of 11 loads 6 foot of timber oak of him had and taken for the use of the same ships, at 10s every load after 50 foot to the load. *Summa* – £5 11s.

To Thomas Hacker of Southampton the same day for price of 3 loads of timber oak in knees by him delivered for the use of the same ships, at 13s 4d every load. *Summa* – £2.

To Peter Rogers of Southampton the same day for price of 100 foot of inch ½ board oak of him taken for the same use as aforesaid – 6s.

[f. 157v] *Inch board, plank oak, elms and claps of leather.* To John Mower the 24th day of January for price of 200 foot of inch board oak of him had and taken and by him delivered for the use of the said ships, at 4s every 100 foot – 8s; and more to him for 6 small claps of leather for the use of the *Flower de Luce*, at 6d the piece – 3s. *Summa* – 11s.

To Henry Slater of Portsmouth the same day for the price of 300 foot of 4-inch plank oak by him delivered for the use of the same ships, at 11s every 100 foot. *Summa* – £1 13s.

To Andrew Poynninges the same day for price of 2 elms of him had and delivered for the use of the same ships; by agreement – [*blank*].

Cordage and sail canvas. To William Smythe the same day for price of 3 coil of small ropes tarred, of him had for the use of the same ship, weighing one hundred 2 quarters 24 pounds [*192 lbs*], at 20s every hundredweight. *Summa* – £1 14s 6d.[1]

To Stephen Wender the same day for price of 30 pounds weight of sail twine of him had and delivered the same for the use of the said ships, at 8d every pound – 20s; and more to him for 200 [*recte* 2 dozen] of sail needles, at 18d every dozen – 3s *Summa* – £1 13s.

To John Favor of Southampton, merchant, the same day for price of 21 bolts of oleron [of *otiose*] canvas by him delivered to the same ships for the needful mending of their sails, at 25s 7d every bolt. *Summa* – £26 17s 3d.

[*Page total*] – £31 18s 9d.

[f. 158] *[*Water carriage*]. To John Skypper the 24th day of January for the hire of his boat serving Her Highness carrying of 10 bolts of oleron aboard the bark laden with provisions appointed to meet the same ships at Plymouth, and there to deliver the same; by agreement – 3s 4d.

To Thomas Poppynaie of Portsmouth the same day for hire of his lighter serving Her Highness in taking out of ordnance and other things out of

[1]The calculation gives 411.42856d, which is about 2½d below the sum stated (414d).

the *Flower de Luce*, and for wages and victuals of his two men serving in the same, by like 24 days; by agreement – £2

To John Peaze of Portsmouth the same day for the hire of his bark and for wages and victuals serving Her Highness in the same for the carrying of certain provisions, as also for the towing down of a main mast for the same ship at Plymouth and there delivered the same, by the space of 18 days within this time; by agreement – £3 7s.

[*Page total*] – £5 10s 4d. [f. 158v *blank*]

[f. 159] **Extraordinary. Sea charges**:

Anno Domini 1562. Anno regni regine Elizabethe quarto

The Hope. To Sir William Woodhouse, knight, Vice-Admiral of England, the 8th day of September for the diets of himself serving the Queen's Majesty on the seas as captain in the said ship, and Admiral of Her Grace's fleet then on the seas, by the space of 34 days begun the 6th day of August last past and ended the day abovesaid, at 20s every day – £34; more for the wages of a master and 299 other mariners and gunners serving under him in the said ship, by the space of one month one week and one day begun the 6th of August and ended the 10th day of September abovesaid, at 6s 8d every man the month – £128 15s; more for 26 deadshares divided amongst the master and other officers of the said ship, at 6s 5d every share – £8 6s 10d; more in reward to four gunners – 4s; more in reward to four trumpeters, at 10s 9d the man – £2 3s; more in reward to a drum – 4s 2d; more in reward to a lodesman – 10s 9d; and more in reward to a surgeon – 10s 9d. *Summa* – £174 14s 6d.

The Lion. To William Holstock, captain, the 12th day of the same for his diets serving Her Highness as captain of the said ship and Vice-Admiral of the same fleet by the space of 38 days begun the 6th day of August aforesaid and ended the 12th day of September next, at 6s 8d every day – £12 13s 4d; more for the wages of a master and 291 other mariners and gunners serving under him in the said ship, by the space of one month one week and one day begun the 6th day of August and ended as aforesaid, at 6s 8d every man the month – £125 6s 4d; more for 26 deadshares, at 6s 5d the share – £8 6s 10d; more in reward to four gunners – 4s; more in reward to four trumpeters, at 10s 9d the man – 43s; more in reward to a drum – 4s 2d; and more in reward to a surgeon – 10s 9d. *Summa* – £149 8s 5d.

[*Page total*] – £324 2s 11d.

[f. 159v] *The Hart.* To George Beeston, captain, the 19th day of October for his diets serving in the said ship as Admiral for the time of all the Queen's Majesty's ships then on the seas by the space of 41 days begun the 9th day of September and ended the day abovesaid, at 8s every day – £16 8s; more to him for his diets in the same ship by 35 days begun the 5th day of August and ended the 8th day of September following before he was appointed Admiral,[1] at 18d *per diem* – 52s 6d; more for the wages of a master and 197 other mariners and gunners serving under him in the said ship, by the space of 2 months 2 weeks 4 days begun the 6th of August and ended the 18th day of October, at 6s 8d every man the month – £174 18s; more for 20 deadshares, at 13s 2d the share – £13 3s 4d; more in reward to four gunners, at 2s 2d the man – 8s 8d; more in reward to two trumpeters, at 22s 2d the man – 44s 4d; more in reward to a drummer – 9s; and more in reward to a surgeon – 22s 2d. *Summa* – £211 6s.

The Swallow. To Thomas Jones, captain, the 18th day of October for his diets serving in the said ship by the space of 74 days begun the 6th day of August and ended the day abovesaid, at 18d *per diem* – £5 11s; more for the wages of a master and 159 other mariners and gunners serving under him in the said ship by the space of 2 months 2 weeks and 4 days begun and ended as aforeesaid, at 6s 8d every man the month – £141 6s 8d; more for 20 deadshares, at 13s 2d the share – £13 3s 4d; more in reward to four gunners, at 2s 2d the man – 8s 8d; more in reward to a trumpeter – 22s 2d; more in reward to a drum – 9s; and more in reward to a surgeon – 22s 2d. *Summa* – £163 3s.

[*Page total*] – £374 9s.

[f. 160] *The Willoughby.* To John Malyn, captain, the 17th day of October for his diets serving in the same ship as Admiral of two of the Queen's Majesty's ships appointed to waft certain Her Grace's munitions, artillery and ordnance into Ireland, as also to apprehend divers pirates and rovers haunting the same coast,[2] by the space of 73 days begun the 6th of August and ended the day abovesaid, at 3s 4d *per diem* – £12 3s 4d; more for the wages of a master and 117 other mariners and gunners serving under him in the same ship, by the space of 2 months 2 weeks 3 days begun and ended as abovesaid, at 17s 8d the man – £104 4s 8d; more for 20 deadshares, at 13s the share – £13; more in reward to four gunners, at 2s 2d the man – 8s 8d; more in reward to a trumpeter – 21s 10d; more in reward to a drum – 9s; more in reward to a surgeon – 21s 10d; and more in reward to a pilot – 21s 10d. *Summa* – £133 11s 2d.

The Triumph. To William Wood, master, the 7th day of November for the wages of himself and 79 other mariners and gunners serving with him

[1]It was on 9 Sept. that the Queen ordered the Lord Admiral to depute the Channel patrol to Beeston: above, p. 227 n. 2.

[2]Cf. above, p. 227 & n. 1.

in the said ship, by the space of one month one week 3 days begun the first of October last and ended the day abovesaid, at 9s every man – £36; and more for 17 deadshares, at 6s 9d every share – £5 14s 9d. *Summa* – £41 14s 9d.

The Victory. To William Barnes, master, the said 7th of November for the wages of himself and 49 other mariners and gunners serving with him in the said ship by the space of one month one week 3 days begun the first day of October and ended as is aforesaid, at 9s every man – £22 10s; and more for 12 deadshares, at 6s 9d every share – £14 1s. *Summa* – £26 11s.

[*Page total*] – £201 16s 11d.

[f. 160v] *Anno regni regine Elizabethe quinto*

The New Bark. To William Driver, captain, the last day of November for his diets serving in the same ship as Admiral of all Her Grace's ships then on the seas, by the space of 50 days begun the 12th of October and ended as abovesaid, at 6s 8d *per diem* – £16 13s 4d; more to him for his diets in the same ship by 32 days begun the 10th of September and ended the 12th day of October next, before he was appointed Admiral, at 18d *per diem* – 48s 6d; more for the wages of a master and 119 other mariners and gunners serving under him in the same ship by the space of 2 months 3 weeks 5 days begun the 10th of September and ended the last day of November above-written, at 19s 6d every man – £117; more for 20 deadshares, at 14s 8d the share – £14 13s 4d; more in reward to four gunners, at 2s 5d the man – 9s 8d; more in reward to two trumpeters, at 24s 2d the man – 48s 4d; and more in reward to a surgeon – 24s 2d. *Summa* – £154 17s 4d.

The Saker. To John Henshaw, captain, the last day of December for his diets serving in the same ship by the space of 113 days begun the 10th day of September last and ended as is aforesaid, at 18d *per diem* – £8 9s 6d; more for the wages of a master and 49 other mariners and gunners serving under him in the same ship by the space of 4 months one day begun and ended as abovesaid, at 26s 10d every man – £67 1s 8d; more for 14 deadshares, at 20s 2d the share – £14 2s 4d; more in reward to four gunners – 13s 4d; more in reward to a surgeon – 24s 2d; and more in reward to a trumpeter – 23s. *Summa* – £93 4s.

[*Page total*] – £248 1s 4d.

[f. 161] *The Phoenix*. To Thomas Hare, captain, the last day of December for his diets serving in the same ship by the space of 164 days begun the 21th of July and ended as aforesaid, at 18d *per diem* – £12 6s;

more for the wages of 45 mariners and gunners serving under him in the same ship by the space of 6 months one week 2 days begun the 8th day of July and ended the day above-specified, at 42s 1d the man – £94 13s 9d; more for 14 deadshares, at 31s 6d the share – £22 1s; more in reward to four gunners, at 5s 1d the man – 20s 4d; and more in reward to a trumpeter – 52s 6d. *Summa* – £132 13s 7d.

The Hare. To Robert Marsh,[1] captain, the said last day of December for his diets serving in the same ship by the space of 149 days begun the 5th of August and ended the day abovesaid, at 18d *per diem* – £11 3s 6d; more for the wages of a master and 29 other mariners and gunners serving under him in the said ship by the space of 5 months one week one day begun the 6th of August and ended the day above-written, at 35s 2d every man – £52 15s; more for 14 deadshares, at 26s 4d the share – £18 8s 10d; more in reward to four gunners, at 4s 4d the man – 17s 8d; and more in reward to a trumpeter – 44s. *Summa* – £85 9s.

The Double Rose. To Thomas Elye, master of the same pinnace, the last day of December for the wages of himself and 28 other mariners and gunners serving with him in the said ship by the space of 3 months one week and one day begun the first of October last and ended as abovesaid, at 21s 10d every man – £31 13s 10d; and more for 8 deadshares divided amongst the said master and his company, at 16s 4d the share – £6 10s 8d. *Summa* – £38 4s 6d.

[*Page total*] – £256 7s 1d.

[f. 161v] *The Aid*. To William Driver, captain, the last day of December for his diets serving in the same ship as Admiral of all Her Highness's ships then on the seas by the space of 31 days begun the first day of December and ended as abovesaid, at 6s 8d *per diem* – £10 6s 8d; more for the wages of a master and 119 other mariners and gunners serving under him in the said ship[2] by the space of one month 3 days begun and ended as afore is mentioned, at 7s 4d every man – £44; more for 20 deadshares, at 5s 6d every share – £5 10s; more in reward to four gunners – 3s 8d; more in reward to two trumpeters – 17s 8d; and more in reward to a surgeon – 8s 10d. *Summa* – £61 6s 10d.

The Bark of Boulogne. To Thomas Gourlay, captain, the said last day of December for his diets serving in the same ship by the space of 31 days begun the first day of this present month of December and ended as aforesaid, at 18d *per diem* – 46s 6d; more for the wages of a master and 39 other mariners and gunners serving under him in the said ship,

[1]See *NEM*, p. 559.

[2]These were the men who had served under Driver in *New Bark*, for which the newly-launched *Aid* was substituted as soon as she joined the fleet: cf. **25** below.

by the space of one month 3 days begun and ended as above-written, at 7s 4d the man – £14 13s 4d; more for 14 deadshares, at 5s 6d the share – £3 17s; and more in reward to four gunners – 3s 8d. *Summa* – £21 0s 6d.

The Antelope. To William Barnes, master, the same last day of December for the wages of himself and 59 other mariners and gunners serving with him in the same ship by the space of one month 3 days begun the first day of December and ended as abovesaid, at 7s 4d the man – £22; more for 16 deadshares, at 5s 6d the share – £4 8s; and more in reward to four gunners – 3s 8d. *Summa* – £26 11s 8d.

[*Page total*] – £108 19s.

[f. 162] *The Jennet*. To John Vallett, master, the last day of December for the wages of himself and 63 other mariners and gunners serving with him in the same ship by the space of one month 3 days begun the first day of December and ended as abovesaid, at 7s 4d the man – £23 9s 4d; more for 16 deadshares, at 5s 6d the share – £4 8s; and more in reward to four gunners – 3s 8d; *Summa* – £28 1s.

The Greyhound. To John Malyn, captain, the said last day of December for his diets serving in the same ship as Admiral for the transporting of five Her Majesty's ships from Gillingham to Portsmouth,[1] and from thence to continue in the Narrow Seas, by the space of 31 days begun and ended as afore is mentioned, at 5s *per diem* – £7 15s; more for the wages of a master and 59 other mariners and gunners serving under him in the said ship by the like time of 31 days, at 7s 4d the man – £22; more for 17 deadshares, at 5s 6d the share – £4 13s 6d; more in reward to four gunners – 4s 8d; more in reward to a surgeon – 9s 1d; and more in reward to a trumpeter – 9s 1d. *Summa* – £35 10s 4d.

[*Page total*] – £63 11s 4d. [f. 162v *blank*]

[f. 163] **Extraordinary. Conduct**:

Anno Domini 1562. Anno regni regine Elizabethe quarto

Conduct to masters, mariners, gunners, soldiers and others discharged from Her Highness's service to the places from whence they were prested:

The Hope. To Thomas Goodwyn, John Dowes, Richard Heellar, William Nobell, John Sympson, Thomas Adams, Davy Coxson, George Maister and Richard Sawyer the 10th day of September for the conduct of them and 163 other mariners, gunners and soldiers late serving Her

[1]These ships are specified above, p. 228.

Highness in the same ship and now discharged to the places from whence they were prested, according to the distance of miles – £20 5s.

The Lion. To George Hyer, John Barnarde, William Gyelles, Thomas Mathew, Thomas Hayron, Edward Alle, Thomas Stoore, John Cave, William Flemynge, William Paulmer, [*and*] John Gylles the 12th day of the same for the conduct of them and 117 other mariners, gunners and soldiers, late serving Her Majesty in the said ship and now discharged to the places from whence they were prested, according to the distance of miles – £11 15s 6d.

The Hart. To John Pylgrym, John Tattell, Thomas Underwoode, Robert Harrys, Richard Lavender, Richard Barker, John Barker, Robert Freman, William Newman [*and*] Thomas Burtton for the conduct of them and 125 other mariners, gunners and soldiers late serving Her Highness in the same ship and now discharged to the places from whence they were prested, according to the distance of miles – £25 10s.

The Swallow. To John Ogar, George Foxe, George Richardson, Thomas Chester, Thomas Searlle, John Pecock, William Everington, William Topley, John Blythe [*and*] Henry Foote for the conduct of them and 115 other mariners, gunners and soldiers late serving Her Majesty in the same ship and now discharged to the places from whence they were prested, according to the distance of miles – £20 17s 6d.

[*Page total*] – £78 8s.

[f. 163v] *The Willoughby.* To William Fewman, Nicholas Moone, John Maister, John Clarke, John Horneby, Stephen Huggin, Matthew Maister, Richard Stookes,[1] Richard Dennys [*and*] Richard Masse the 18th day of October for the conduct of them and 52 other mariners, gunners and soldiers late serving Her Highness in the same ship and now discharged to the places from whence they were prested, according to the distance of miles – £5 7s.

The Triumph. To Richard Dyamonde [*and*] William Brigges for the conduct of them and five other mariners late serving Her Majesty in the same ship and now discharged to the places from whence they were prested, according to the distance of miles – 15s.

The Victory. To Henry Cowper and William Doggett for their conduct late serving Her Highness in the same ship and now discharged to the places from whence they were prested, according to the distance of miles – 5s 6d.

The New Bark. To John Fyssher, John Godfrey, John Howsey, Edward Bushe, John Pearse, Thomas Wayeman, William Jennynges, William

[1]But cf. above, p. 168, where most of these names (Moone to Stookes) are listed aboard *Triumph*.

Tyverton, Thomas Ayllarde [*and*] Robert Richardson for the conduct of them and 44 other mariners and gunners late serving Her Majesty in the same ship, and now discharged to the places from whence they were prested, according to the distance of miles – £7 12s 6d.

The Saker. To Henry Bridges [*and*] Thomas Streame for the conduct of them and nine other mariners and gunners late serving Her Highness in the same ship and now discharged to the places from whence they were prested, according to the distance of miles – £1 14s 6d.

The Phoenix. To Thomas Raynolde, James Sherla [*and*] Richard Ramer for the conduct of them and three other mariners late serving Her Majesty in the same ship and now discharged to the places from whence they were prested, according to the distance of miles – 18s 6d.

[*Page total*] – £16 13s.

Anno regni regine Elizabethe quinto

[f. 164] *The Hare*. To Henry Brooke, Clement Spencer and Rowland Downe the last day of December for the conduct of them and five other mariners and gunners late serving Her Highness in the same ship and now discharged to the places from whence they were prested, according to the distance of miles – £1 9s.

The Double Rose. To Thomas Ellye, Richard Cloughe, John Awstyn [*and*] Edward Graundger for the conduct of them and nine other mariners and gunners late serving Her Highness in the same ship and now discharged to the places from whence they were prested, according to the distance of miles – £1 2s 6d.

The Aid. To Bernard Harryson and Thomas Gryffyn, mariners, for their conduct [*ellipse*] late serving Her Highness in the same ship and now discharged to the places from whence they were prested, according to the distance of miles – 6s 6d.

The Antelope. To John Garnner, Lawrence Smythe, Christopher Brewton, Thomas Shawe, John Tyllison [*and*] Thomas Morecocke for the conduct of them and 12 other mariners and gunners late serving Her Majesty in the same ship and now discharged to the places from whence they were prested, according to the distance of miles – £3 9s 6d.

The Jennet. To William Bryce, William Cotterell, William Saunderson, John Gybson [*and*] John Campen for the conduct of them and 10 other mariners and gunners late serving Her Highness in the same ship, and now discharged to the places from whence they were prested, according to the distance of miles – £3 15s.

The Greyhound. To Robert Marckes and Thomas Evans for the conduct of them and one other mariner late serving Her Majesty in the same ship and now discharged to the places from whence they were prested, according to the distance of miles – 7s.

[*Page total*] – £10 9s 6d. [f. 164v *blank*]

[***Part II: for the year 1 January – 31 December 1563***]

[f. 165] **Ordinary. Receipts**:

Anno Domini 1562 [1563]. *Anno regni regine Elizabethe quinto*

Received of the Treasurer and Chamberlains of the Exchequer by virtue of Her Grace's warrant of privy seal to them directed dated at Her Highness's palace of Westminster the 11th day of March 1558 [*1559*] and in the first year of Her Majesty's reign, containing the sum of twelve thousand pounds by the year, as well toward the payment of wages and victuals of shipwrights, caulkers, sawyers, smiths and other artificers and workmen for new building and repairing of Her Highness's ships and provisions for the same, and for wages and victuals of masters, mariners and gunners keeping Her Grace's ships afloat in harbour; as also for provision of cordage, canvas and divers other needful things for the rigging and tackling of the said ships to the seas: of Thomas Gardener, esquire, one of the four tellers there, *viz.* the first day of February 1562 [*1563*] – £300; the 10th day of March 1562 [*1563*] – £400; the 20th day of the same month of March 1562 [*1563*] – £1,000; the 24th day of May 1563 – £230; the 25th day of August 1563 – £1,000; the 4th day of November 1563 – £500; and the 8th day of December 1563 and *anno regni regine Elizabethe sexto* – £300. In the whole – £3,730 **[#X1]**.[1] *[*Examinatur per certificatorium Thome Felton, clerici pellium*]

[*Page total*] – *Summa predicta.*

[f. 165v] *Anno Domini 1563. Anno regni regine Elizabethe quinto*

Received of the Treasurer and Chamberlains of the Exchequer by virtue of Her Grace's warrant of privy seal to them directed dated at Her Majesty's palace of Westminster the 11th day of March 1558 [*1559*] in the first year of Her Highness's reign containing the sum of twelve thousand pounds by the year, as well towards payment of wages and victuals of shipwrights, caulkers, sawyers, smiths and other artificers and

[1]Inset references preceded by # relate the *recepta* of Quarter Book to the equivalent entries in the Declared Account [**5**]; see synopsis in Sectional Introduction II, above, p. 18.

workmen for new building and repairing of Her Grace's ships and provisions for the same, and for wages and victuals of masters, mariners and gunners keeping Her Highness's ships afloat in harbour; as also for provisions of cordage, canvas and divers other needful things for the rigging and tackling of the said ships to the seas: of Henry Killigrew, esquire, one of the four tellers there, *viz.* the 4th day of November 1563 – £500; and the 10th day of December 1563 *et anno regni regine Elizabethe sexto* – £700. In the whole – £1,200 **[#X2]**. *[*Examinatur per certificatorium predicti*].

[*Page total*] – *Summa predicta.*

[f. 166] Received of the Treasurer and Chamberlains of the Exchequer by virtue of Her Grace's warrant of privy seal to them directed, dated at Her Highness's palace of Westminster the 11th day of March 1558 [*1559*] in the first year of Her Majesty's reign containing the sum of twelve thousand pounds by the year, as well toward payment of wages and victuals of shipwrights, caulkers, sawyers, smiths and other artificers and workmen for new building and repairing of Her Grace's ships and provisions for the same, and for wages and victuals of masters, mariners and gunners keeping Her Highness's ships afloat in harbour; as also for provisions of cordage, canvas and divers other needful things for the rigging and tackling of the said ships to the seas: of William Patten, esquire, one of the four tellers there, *viz.* the 4th day of November 1563 – £400; and the 13th day of December 1563 *et anno regni regine Elizabethe sexto* – £800. In the whole – £1,200 **[#X3]**. *[*Examinatur per certificatorium predicti*]

[*Page total*] – *Summa predicta.*

[f. 166v] Received of the Treasurer and Chamberlains of the Exchequer by virtue of Her Grace's warrant of privy seal to them directed dated at her palace of Westminster the 11th day of March 1558 [*1559*] in the first year of Her Majesty's reign containing the sum of twelve thousand pounds by the year, as well towards payment of wages and victuals of shipwrights, caulkers, sawyers, smiths and other artificers and workmen for new building and repairing of Her Highness's ships and provisions for the same, and for wages and victuals of masters, mariners and gunners keeping Her Grace's ships afloat in harbour; as also for provision of cordage, canvas and divers other needful things for the rigging and tackling of the said ships to the seas: of Richard Stoneley, esquire, one of the four tellers there, *viz.* the 24th day of February 1562 [*1563*] – £500; the 25th day of May 1563 – £500; the 28th day of the same month of May – £500; the 4th day of November 1563 – £200; the 10th day of December *anno regni regine Elizabethe sexto* – £800; and the 20th day of December 1563

– £1,000. In the whole – £3,500 **[#X4]**. *[*Examinatur per certificatorium predicti*]

[*Page total*] – *Summa predicta.*

[#X1–4: *total ordinary receipts 1563 – £9,630*]

[f. 167] **Extraordinary. Receipts:**

Anno Domini 1562 [1563]. *Anno regni regine Elizabethe quinto*

Received the 21th day of January *annis supradictis*[1] of the right honourable Sir Edward Rogers, knight, Comptroller of Her Grace's most honourable Household,[2] by virtue of Her Highness's warrant to him directed given under her signet at her palace of Westminster the 18th day of this present: the sum of threescore pounds six shillings eight pence, as well to be delivered to Edward Baeshe, General Surveyor of Her Grace's victuals for the seas, for victuals for 100 men appointed to pass to Newhaven in two brigantines, and to be employed for the presting of the said 100 men, as also for tilts to cover the same two brigantines – £60 6s 8d **[#Y1]**. *[*Examinatur per computum Edwardi Rogers militis factum de denariis domine regine prestitis*]

Received the 5th day of February *annis supradictis* of the Treasurer and Chamberlains of the Exchequer by virtue of Her Grace's warrant of privy seal to them directed dated at her palace of Westminster the 6th day of January last[3] at the hands of Henry Killigrew, one of the tellers, there: the sum of three hundred threescore six pounds thirteen shillings four pence to be delivered over in prest to Edward Baeshe, General Surveyor of Her Highness's victuals for the seas, as well for one month's victuals of 28 days delivered to Her Grace's ship the *Greyhound* for 120 men begun the 20th day of December last, as also for one other month's victuals for 430 men serving in several Her Highness's ships, *viz.* the *Aid*, the *Greyhound*, the *Saker*, the *Phoenix*, the *Bark of Boulogne,* the *Hare* and the *Double Rose*, begun the 17th day of January last and to end the

[1]The first scribe Thomas Baker (ff. 1–158) generally abbreviated this formula ambiguously as *ann' supradict'*, but it is evident from his occasional extension of one or both words in the singular (ff. 6v, 138, 153v) that he intended *anno supradicto* throughout. Stephen Alexander (ff. 165–361) in this first instance and frequently hereafter extends it in the plural, indicating his more precise reference to the preceding combination of year of grace and regnal year.

[2]Privy Councillor and Vice-Chamberlain of the Household soon after Elizabeth's accession, becoming Comptroller by January 1559: *ODNB. Hist. Parl. 1509–58*, iii, pp. 206–7; *1558–1603*, iii, pp. 300–1.

[3]E 404/115, bundle 5 Eliz.

13th day of this present month of February – £366 13s 4d **[#Y2]**. *[*Examinatur per certificatorium predicti*][1]

[*Page total*] – *Summa predicta.*

[f. 167v] Received the 14th day of February *annis supradictis* of the right honourable Sir Edward Rogers, knight, Comptroller of Her Majesty's most honourable Household, and collector general of Her Highness's loan,[2] by virtue of Her Grace's warrant to him directed given under her signet at her palace of Westminster the 5th day of this present: the sum of two hundred threescore thirteen pounds six shillings and eight pence to be employed about the provision of victuals for one month of 28 days for 410 men serving in six Her Grace's ships and barks at the seas, begun the 13th day of this present month of February – £273 6s 8d **[#Y3]**. *[*Examinatur per computum dicti Edwardi Rogers militis*]

Received the 12th day of March *annis supradictis* of the right honourable Sir Edward Rogers, knight, Comptroller of Her Grace's most honourable Household, by virtue of Her Highness warrant to him directed given under her signet at Her Majesty's palace of Westminster the 8th day of this present: the sum of three hundred six pounds thirteen shillings four pence, to be immediately paid over in prest to Edward Baeshe, General Surveyor of Her Grace's victuals for the seas, as well for one month's victuals of 28 days for 410 men serving in six Her Highness's ships and barks on the seas, to begin the 13th day of this present month of March and to end the 10th day of April following, as also for 14 days' victuals delivered at Dover for 100 men serving in two Her Majesty's brigantines, begun the 11th day of February last – £306 13s 4d **[#Y4]**. *[*Examinatur per computum predicti*]

[*Page total*] *Summa* [blank].[3]

[1] In this section this formula (or just *per certificatorium*) always refers back to the first source cited by the auditor (above, p. 240), i.e. standing for *per certificatorium predicti* [*Thome Felton clerici pellium*].

[2] During 1562 and 1563, following successful precedent in Mary's reign, the government solicited loans from private individuals, guaranteeing repayment with privy seal warrants. Rogers's account, examined by commission appointed in April 1564, show that almost £45,000 was raised: *CPR 1563–6*, no. 494 (p. 122). F. C. Dietz, *English Public Finance 1558–1641* (American Historical Association, New York and London, 1932), p. 17. Rogers also stood chief surety, along with the Lord Treasurer and Under-treasurer, for a loan of £10,000 by which the City of London underwrote the Le Havre operation: SP 12/27, no. 61 (*CSPD 1547–80*, p. 219). But references here and in the Declared Account [**5**] to the loan money refer to the proceeds of the privy seal loan – of which, it will be seen, the Navy received less than a twentieth part.

[3] Alexander clearly followed the latter usage of Baker in giving page totals, but from this point realised they were scarcely necessary in the *recepta*, where Baker did not in fact provide them. The blank *Summa* for the remainder of the section (to f. 173v) is not reproduced here.

[f. 168] *Anno Domini 1563. Anno regni regine Elizabethe quinto*

Received the 3rd day of April *annis supradictis* of the right honourable Sir Edward Rogers, knight, Comptroller of Her Highness's most honourable Household, by virtue of Her Grace's warrant to him directed given under her signet at her palace of Westminster the 30th day of March last: the sum of one hundred fourscore thirteen pounds six shillings and eight pence, to be paid over in prest to Edward Baeshe, Surveyor General of Her Majesty's victuals for the seas, for one month's victuals of 28 days provided for 290 men serving Her Highness in five Her Grace's ships and barks at the seas, to begin the 11th day of this present month of April and to end the 8th day of May next – £193 6s 8d **[#Y5]**. *[*Examinatur per computum dicti Edwardi Rogers militis*]

Received the 11th day of May *annis supradictis* of the Treasurer and Chamberlains of the Exchequer by virtue of Her Grace's warrant of privy seal to them directed dated at Her Highness's palace of Westminster the 10th day of this present[1] at the hands of Richard Stoneley, one of the tellers there, the sum of two hundred pounds, to be employed upon certain mariners appointed to fetch certain ships from Newhaven – £200 **[#Y6]**. *[*Examinatur per certificatorium predicti*]

[f. 168v] Received the 14th day of May *annis supradictis* of the right honourable Sir Edward Rogers, knight, Comptroller of Her Majesty's most honourable Household, by virtue of Her Grace's warrant to him directed given under her signet at Her Highness's palace of Westminster the 8th day of this present: the sum of one hundred fourscore thirteen pounds six shillings eight pence, to be paid over in prest to Edward Baeshe, General Surveyor of Her Grace's victuals for the seas, for one month's victuals of 28 days for 190 men serving Her Highness in five Her Majesty's ships and barks at the seas, begun the 9th day of this present month of May and to end on the 5th day of June next – £193 6s 8d **[#Y7]**. *[*Examinatur per computum dicti Edwardi Rogers*]

Received the 23th day of May *annis supradictis* of the right honourable Sir Edward Rogers, knight, Comptroller of Her Grace's most honourable Household, by virtue of Her Majesty's warrant to him directed given under her signet at her palace of Westminster the said 23th day of May: the sum of one hundred fourscore fifteen pounds, as well for the prest and conduct of 180 mariners and gunners appointed to serve in Her Highness's ship the *Swallow* to be equipped from Portsmouth to the seas, as also to be delivered over to Edward Baeshe for one month's victuals for the said ship – £195 **[#Y8]**. *[*Examinatur per computum dicti Edwardi Rogers*]

[1] PSO 2/13, bundle May 1563.

[f. 169] Received the 23th day of May *annis supradictis* of the right honourable Sir Edward Rogers, knight, Comptroller of Her Highness's most honourable Household, by virtue of Her Grace's warrant given under her signet at her palace of Westminster the said 23th day of May to him directed: the sum of threescore seven pounds six shillings eight pence, as well for the prest and conduct of 80 men appointed to serve in Her Majesty's ship the *Falcon*, as also to be delivered over in prest to Edward Baeshe, General Surveyor of Her Highness's victuals for the seas, for the victualling of the said 80 men for one month of 28 days – £67 6s 8d **[#Y9]**. *[*Examinatur per computum dicti Edwardi Rogers militis*]

Received of the Treasurer and Chamberlains of the Exchequer by virtue of Her Grace's warrant of privy seal to them directed dated at Her Highness's palace of Westminster the 10th day of May *annis supradictis*:[1] the sum of one thousand three hundred thirty-seven pounds sixteen shillings eight pence, to be paid as well for the diets of captains and wages of masters, mariners and gunners serving on the seas in the *Aid* and other Her Grace's ships and barks by the space of 5 months begun the first day of December last and to end the last day of May following, as also for certain extraordinary charges sustained within the said time for Her Majesty's affairs, *viz.* of William Patten, one of the tellers there, the 24th day of May 1563 – £800; of Richard Stoneley, one other of the tellers there, the same 24th day of May 1563 – £337 16s 8d; and of Thomas Gardener, one other of the tellers there, the said 24th day of May *annis supradictis* – £200. *Summa* – £1,337 16s 8d **[#Y10]**. *[*Examinatur per certificatorium predicti*]

[f. 169v] Received the first day of June *annis supradictis* of the Treasurer and Chamberlains of the Exchequer by virtue of Her Highness's warrant of privy seal to them directed dated at Her Grace's palace of Westminster the 30th day of May last by the hands of Thomas Gardener, one of the tellers there: the sum of two hundred fourscore and ten pounds, to be employed upon the setting forth to the seas for Her Highness's service three Her Majesty's ships, that is to say the *Antelope*, the *Jennet* and the *Double Rose* – £290 **[#Y11]**. *[*Ex certificatorium predicti*]

Received of the Treasurer and Chamberlains of the Exchequer by virtue of Her Grace's warrant of privy seal to them directed dated at her palace of Westminster the 8th day of June *annis supradictis*: the sum of nine hundred threescore fourteen pounds, to be delivered over in prest to Edward Baeshe, General Surveyor of Her Highness's victuals for the seas, as well for victualling of certain Her Grace's ships at the seas for the month of June, as also for like victualling of 980 men serving in 10 Her

[1] Ibid.

Majesty's ships for the month of July next, *viz*. of Richard Stoneley, one of the tellers there, the 25th day of June 1563 – £500; and more of the said Stoneley the 13th day of July following – £474. [*Summa*] – £974 **[#Y12]**. *[*Examinatur per certificatorium predicti*]

[f. 170] Received the 27th day of June *annis supradictis* of the right honourable Sir Edward Rogers, knight, Comptroller of Her Grace's most honourable Household, by virtue of Her Highness's warrant to him directed given under her signet at her manor of Greenwich the 26th day of this present: the sum of six hundred nineteen pounds in prest, as well to be delivered over to Edward Baeshe, General Surveyor of Her Grace's victuals for the seas, for the victualling of certain ships appointed for Her Majesty's service northwards, as also to be employed about the presting and conducting of mariners and others to serve in Her Highness's said ships – £619 **[#Y13]**. *[*Examinatur per computum Edwardi Rogers predicti*]

Received of the Treasurer and Chamberlains of the Exchequer by virtue of Her Grace's warrant of privy seal to them directed, dated at her manor of Greenwich the 4th day of July *annis supradictis*:[1] the sum of two hundred fourscore ten pounds, by way of prest to be employed as well for wages and victuals of shipwrights, caulkers, sawyers, smiths and other artificers and workmen for making of four brigantines, as also for divers kinds of stuffs to be provided for the perfecting of the same brigantines, *viz*. of Henry Killigrew, one of the tellers there, the 8th day of July 1563 – £100; and more of the said Killigrew the 13th day of the same month of July *annis supradictis* – £190. *Summa* – £290 **[#Y14]**. *[*Examinatur per certificatorium predicti*]

[f. 170v] Received of the Treasurer and Chamberlains of the Exchequer by virtue of Her Highness's warrant of privy seal to them directed dated at Her Grace's manor of Greenwich the 5th day of July *annis supradictis* the sum of eight hundred sixteen pounds eleven shillings eight pence, to be immediately paid over to Edward Baeshe, General Surveyor of Her Highness's victuals for the seas, for the victualling of 1,020 men serving Her Majesty at the seas in 11 Her Grace's ships and barks, as well for part of this present month of July as for the whole month of August next, *viz*. of Thomas Gardener, one of the tellers there, the 13th day of July 1563 – £400; and of Richard Stoneley, one other of the tellers there, the 19th day of the said month of July – £416 11s 8d. *Summa* – £816 11s 8d **[#Y15]**. *[*Examinatur per certificatorium predicti*]

Received of the Treasurer and Chamberlains of the Exchequer by virtue of Her Majesty's warrant of privy seal to them directed, dated at Her

[1] E 404/115, bundle 5 Eliz.

Highness's manor of Greenwich the 7th day of July *annis supradictis*: the sum of two thousand pounds in prest, to be employed about the charges in conveying out of the river of Gillingham four Her Grace's ships and three Her Highness's galleys to Portsmouth, *viz.* of William Patten, one of the tellers there, the 8th day of July 1563 – £500; and of Thomas Gardener, one other of the tellers there, the said 8th day of July 1563 – £1,500. *Summa* – £2,000 **[#Y16]**. *[*Examinatur per certificatorium predicti*]

[f. 171] Received the 13th day of July *annis supradictis* of the Treasurer and Chamberlains of the Exchequer by virtue of Her Grace's warrant of privy seal to them directed dated at her manor of Greenwich the 11th day of this present, by the hands of Henry Killigrew one of the tellers there: the sum of two hundred nine pounds twelve shillings eight pence, as well for the prest and conduct money of 240 men for the manning of four new galliots and for the rigging wages and victuals of 34 persons for 7 days to sew their sails and other necessary business, as also to be delivered over to Edward Baeshe, General Surveyor of Her Highness's victuals for the seas, for the provision of victuals for the said 240 men for one month of 28 days – £209 12s 8d **[#Y17]**. *[*Examinatur per certificatorium predicti*]

Received the 15th day of July *annis supradictis* of the Treasurer and Chamberlains of the Exchequer by virtue of Her Highness's warrant of privy seal to them directed dated at her manor of Greenwich the 14th day of this present, by the hands of Richard Stoneley, one of the tellers there: the sum of three hundred threescore eighteen pounds six shillings eight pence, to be employed for coats and conduct of certain numbers of men appointed to be set forth out of sundry shires for Her Majesty's service under the conduction of the Lord High Admiral of England[1] – £378 6s 8d **[#Y18]**. *[*Examinatur per certificatorium predicti*]

[f. 171v] Received of the Treasurer and Chamberlains of the Exchequer by virtue of Her Grace's warrant of privy seal to them directed dated at Her Highness's manor of Greenwich the 16th day of July *annis supradictis*: the sum of four thousand seven hundred fifty one pounds, as well for the victualling of Her Highness's Navy appointed for Her Grace's service under the conduction of her High Admiral of England, as also for the diets of captains and wages of masters, gunners, mariners, rowers and soldiers serving Her Majesty, as well under William Winter as in the Navy set forth under the said High Admiral, *viz.* of Thomas Gardener, one of the tellers there, the 18th day of July 1563 – £1,743 1s 8d; of the said Gardener the 19th day of the same month of July – £1,264 16s 8d; more

[1] An early usage here (also pp. 248, 452, 463, 476, 486, 491, and 556 below) of the full title, which only became firmly established in the 17th century.

of the same Gardener the 25th day of August 1563 – £500; more of the said Gardener the 24th day of October following – £243 1s 8d; and more of him the said 24th day of October – £100; of William Patten, one other of the tellers there, the same 24th day of October *annis supradictis* – £200; of Richard Stoneley, one other of the tellers there, the said 24th day of October – £300; and of Henry Killigrew, one other of the tellers there, the same 24th day of October – £400. *Summa* – £4,751 **[#Y19]**. *[*Examinatur per certificatorium Thome Felton predicti*]

[f. 172] Received of the Treasurer and Chamberlains of the Exchequer by virtue of Her Grace's warrant of privy seal to them directed dated at her manor of Greenwich the 17th day of July *annis supradictis*: the sum of three thousand six hundred forty pounds, to be delivered over to Edward Baeshe, General Surveyor of Her Highness's victuals for the seas, for the victualling of 5,200 men serving Her Majesty on the seas under the conduction of the Lord High Admiral of England, *viz*. of Thomas Gardener, one of the tellers there, the 19th day of July 1563 – £2,735 3s 4d; and more of the said Gardener the 30th day of the same month of July – £904 16s 8d. *Summa* – £3,640 **[#Y20]**. *[*Examinatur per certificatorium predicti*]

Received the 2nd day of September *annis supradictis* of the right honourable Sir Edward Rogers, knight, Comptroller of Her Highness's most honourable Household, by virtue of Her Grace's warrant to him directed given under her signet at her castle of Windsor the first day of this present: the sum of one hundred pounds, for the prest and conduct of 400 mariners employed presently for the bringing about of six Her Majesty's ships into Gillingham Water, *viz*. the *Elizabeth Jonas*, the *Victory*, the *Philip and Mary*, the *Jennet*, the *Minion* and the *Primrose* – £100 **[#Y21]**. *[*Examinatur per computum predicti*]

[f. 172v] Received of the Treasurer and Chamberlains of the Exchequer by virtue of Her Majesty's warrant of privy seal to them directed dated at Her Grace's castle of Windsor the second day of September *annis supradictis*: the sum of four hundred fourscore one pounds five shillings, to be defrayed for the wages and victuals of 400 mariners employed presently for the bringing about of six Her Highness's ships into Gillingham Water, the *Elizabeth Jonas*, the *Victory*, the *Philip and Mary*, the *Jennet*, the *Minion* and the *Primrose*, *viz*. of Richard Stoneley, one of the tellers there, the 5th day of September 1563 – £240 12s 6d; and of Thomas Gardener, one other of the tellers there, the 27th day of the same month – £240 12s 6d. *Summa* – £481 5s **[#Y22]**. *[*Examinatur per certificatorium*]

Received the 5th day of October *annis supradictis* of the Treasurer and Chamberlains of the Exchequer by virtue of Her Grace's warrant of privy seal to them directed dated at her castle of Windsor the 2nd day of this present,[1] at the hands of Richard Stoneley, one of the tellers there: the sum of one hundred threescore ten pounds, to be paid to 950 mariners and gunners discharged out of certain Her Highness's ships brought about from Portsmouth to Gillingham Water – £170 **[#Y23]**. *[*Examinatur per certificatorium*]

Received the 13th day of October *annis supradictis* of the Treasurer and Chamberlains of the Exchequer by virtue of Her Grace's warrant of privy seal to them directed dated at her castle of Windsor the 12th day of this present,[2] by the hands of Richard Stoneley, one of the tellers there: the sum of three hundred fourscore nineteen pounds seven shillings, to be paid over in prest to Edward Baeshe, General Surveyor of Her Highness's victuals for the seas, towards the victualling of Her Majesty's ships the *Willoughby* with 120 men for 10 weeks 4 days and the *Swallow* with 180 men for 5 weeks to end the 28th day of the said month of October, which ships were victualled by Sir Thomas Woodhouse, knight,[3] upon the coast of Norfolk – £399 7s **[#Y24]**.[4] *[*Examinatur per certificatorium*]

[f. 173] *Anno regni regine Elizabethe sexto*

Received the 23th day of November *annis supradictis* of the Treasurer and Chamberlains of the Exchequer by virtue of Her Grace's warrant of privy seal to them directed dated at her castle of Windsor the 17th day of this present,[5] at the hands of Henry Killigrew, one of the tellers there; the sum of four hundred threescore eight pounds two shillings, to be paid as well for the diets of two captains and wages of 318 mariners and gunners serving under them in two Her Grace's ships in the North Seas, the *Swallow* and the *Willoughby*, by the space of 2 months and 3 weeks begun the first day of September last and ended the 16th day of November aforesaid, after 28 days to the month; as also for the conduct money of 300 of the said men to be discharged out of the abovesaid ships to the places from whence they were prested – £468 2s **[#Y25]**. *[*Examinatur per certificatorium predicti*]

[1]E 404/115, bundle 5 Eliz. The same warrant authorises payments to John White of Southwick for the works at Portsmouth (£400), and to John Revell, Surveyor of the Queen's works, for repairs of the Queen's houses at Hatfield (£100) and elsewhere (£300).

[2]Ibid.

[3]Elder brother of Sir William, with whom he had been joint-Vice-Admiral of Norfolk and Suffolk since 1543, and seated at Waxham. Knighted for his services during Kett's rebellion. Although MP for Yarmouth in 1559, he was decreasingly active in public affairs after Elizabeth's accession: *Hist. Parl. 1509–58*, iii, pp. 652–3; *1558–1603*, iii, p. 648; for further career details see *NEM*, p. 573.

[4]See Baeshe's report of 24 Oct. [**26**].

[5]E 404/115, bundle 6 Eliz.

Received the 20th day of December *annis supradictis* of the Treasurer and Chamberlains of the Exchequer by virtue of Her Highness's warrant of privy seal to them directed dated at her castle of Windsor the 12th day of October last,[1] at the hands of Richard Stoneley, one of the tellers there, the sum of two hundred fifty-three pounds six shillings eight pence, to be paid over in prest to Edward Baeshe, General Surveyor of Her Grace's victuals for the seas, for the victualling of 380 men serving Her Majesty in the Narrow Seas in the *Aid*, the *Falcon*, the *Phoenix*, the *Bark of Boulogne* and the *Hare*, under the charge of Sir Thomas Cotton, knight, for one month ended the 28th day of October aforesaid. – £253 6s 8d **[#Y26]**.[2] *[*Examinatur per certificatorium predicti*]

[f. 173v] Received the 20th day of December *annis supradictis* of the Treasurer and Chamberlains of the Exchequer by virtue of Her Grace's warrant of privy seal to them directed dated at her castle of Windsor the 28th day of October last,[3] at the hands of William Patten, one of the tellers there: the sum of two hundred fifty-three pounds six shillings eight pence to be paid over in prest to Edward Baeshe, General Surveyor of Her Highness's victuals for the seas, for the victualling of 380 men serving Her Majesty on the Narrow Seas in the *Aid*, the *Falcon*, the *Phoenix*, the *Bark of Boulogne* and the *Hare* under the charge of Sir Thomas Cotton knight, for one month begun the 29th day of October aforesaid and ended the 25th day of November next – £253 6s 8d **[#Y27]**. *[*Examinatur per certificatorium*]

Received the 20th day of December *annis supradictis* of the Treasurer and Chamberlains of the Exchequer by virtue of Her Majesty's warrant of privy seal to them directed dated at her castle of Windsor the 24th day of November last,[4] at the hands of Richard Stoneley, one of the tellers there: the sum of two hundred fifty-three pounds six shillings eight pence to be paid over in prest to Edward Baeshe, General Surveyor of Her Grace's victuals for the seas, for the victualling of 380 men serving Her Highness on the Narrow Seas in the *Aid*, the *Falcon*, the *Phoenix*, the *Bark of Boulogne* and the *Hare* under the charge of Sir Thomas Cotton, knight for one month of 28 days begun the 26th day of November aforesaid and to end the 23th day of this present month of December following – £253 6s 8d **[#Y28]**.[5] *[*Examinatur per certificatorium*]

[1] E 404/115, bundle 5 Eliz.

[2] See Baeshe's reports of 24 Oct. and 17 Dec. [**26–7**].

[3] E 404/115, bundle 5 Eliz. This is the warrant printed by way of sample as **3** above. Also referred to in **26** and **27** below.

[4] E 404/115, bundle 6 Eliz.

[5] Also referred to in **27** below.

[#Y1–28: ***total extraordinary receipts 1563 – £19,541 1s 8d*****]**

[f. 174] **Ordinary. Deptford**:

Anno Domini 1563. Anno regni regine Elizabethe quinto

A payment made the last day of March as well to masters, mariners, keepers of storehouses docks and timber-yards there wherein lieth Her Grace's provisions for the use of her ships, and to shipwrights, caulkers, sawyers, labourers and other artificers and workmen for new building and repairing of two Her Highness's ships, the *Great Bark* and the *Jesus*; as also to divers persons for sundry kinds of provisions and necessaries by them delivered into Her Majesty's storehouses at Deptford for the use of her ships; by one quarter of a year begun the first day of January last and this day ended, as followeth:

The Sun

Mariners

Nicholas Starkey, boatswain, 7 weeks	16s 0½d
Ralph Bucklande, 3 weeks 6 days	6s 5d
Francis Byrchall, boy, 7 weeks	5s 10d
John Lardge, 1 week 2 days	2s 2d
[*Gunner*]	
William Ellys, master gunner, 7 weeks	17s 6d

[*Page total*] – £1 7s 11½d [*recte* £2 16s 11½].

[f. 174v] *The George Hoy*

Mariners

Giles Hall, master, 12 weeks 6 days	£3 4s 3d
Richard Abraham, 12 weeks 6 days	21s 5d
Henry Raynesforth, 1 week	20d
John Kynge, steward, 12 weeks 6 days	29s 6d
Thomas Raynolde, 1 week 1 day	23d
Richard Letman, 12 weeks 6 days	21s 5d
Thomas Olyver, boy, 12 weeks 6 days	10s 8½d
John Bennet, 12 weeks 6 days	21s 5d
John Leatche, 12 weeks 6 days	21s 5d
Andrew Everington, 12 weeks 6 days	21s 5d
Thomas Lyee, 6 weeks 1 day	10s 3d
John Quayde, 11 weeks 5 days	19s 6d

[*Page total*] – £12 4s 10½d.

[f. 175] *[*Keeper of timber-yards*]. To Thomas Marshe, mariner, the last day of March for his wages daily attending and serving Her Highness for the safe-keeping of Her Grace's provisions of divers kinds of stuffs lying in her timber-yards there, and for the rigging and tackling of Her Majesty's ships to the seas, by one quarter of a year containing 12 weeks 6 days begun the first day of January last and ended as abovesaid, at 20s every month. *Summa* – £3 4s.

*[*Mariners' wages for carrying of provisions and coiling up of cables*]. To Robert Woode and Richard Token, mariners, the same day for their wages daily attending and serving Her Highness in labouring about the coiling and carrying of cables, hawsers and other provisions into Her Grace's great storehouse at Deptford and delivering out of the same again for the use of Her Grace's ships, by like 12 weeks 6 days begun and ended as aforesaid, at 6s 8d every man the month – 42s 10d; and more to them for their victuals for like time, at 20d every week the man – 42s 10d. *Summa* – £4 5s 8d.

To William Currea and Christopher Brethet, mariners, the same day for their wages and victuals daily attending and serving Her Highness in labouring about the carriage of provisions and coiling up of cables and hawsers as is aforesaid, by 12 weeks 6 days begun and ended as abovesaid, at 13s 4d the man *per mensem* – £4 5s 8d.

To Robert Tasse, mariner, the same day for his wages and victuals daily attending and serving Her Highness in labouring about the carriage of provisions and coiling up of cables and hawsers as aforesaid, by like time of 12 weeks 6 days begun and ended as aforesaid, at 13s 4d *per mensem* – £2 2s 10d.

[*Page total*] – £13 18s 2d.

[f. 175v] To Robert Harwood, mariner, the last day of March for his wages and victuals daily attending and serving Her Highness in labouring about the carriage of provisions and coiling up of cables and hawsers in Her Grace's great storehouse there, by the space of 12 weeks 6 days begun the first day of January last and ended as abovesaid, at 13s 4d *per mensem* – £2 2s 10d.

To John Benwell, mariner, the same day for his wages daily attending and serving Her Highness about the carriage of provisions and coiling up of cables and hawsers as aforesaid, by like 12 weeks 6 days begun and ended as abovesaid, at 13s 4d *per mensem* – £2 2s 10d.

To William Pattricke, mariner, the same day for his wages daily attending and serving Her Highness in labouring about the carriage of provisions and coiling up of cables and hawsers in Her Grace's storehouse there, by like 12 weeks 6 days begun and ended as aforesaid, at 6s 8d *per mensem* – £1 1s 5d.

To John Kynge, mariner, the same day for his wages daily attending and serving Her Highness in labouring about the carriage of provisions and coiling up of cables and hawsers as aforesaid, by like 12 weeks 6 days begun and ended as abovesaid, at 6s 8d *per mensem* – £1 1s 5d.

*[*Carpenter*]. To Robert Hartt, master sawyer, the same day for his wages daily attending and serving Her Highness in sawing and cutting of timber and plank for the use of Her Majesty's ships, by 90 days begun and ended as abovesaid, at 8d *per diem* – £3.

[*Page total*] – £9 8s 6d.

[f. 176] *[*Clerk*]. To James Gentyll the last day of March for his wages daily attending and serving Her Highness for the keeping of the prick and cheque book of masters, mariners and gunners keeping Her Grace's ships afloat within the river of Thames, by 90 days begun the first day of January last and this day ended, at 8d *per diem* – £3.

*[*Keeper of storehouse*]. To Henry Abraham the same day for his wages daily attending and serving Her Highness for the safe-keeping of Her Grace's storehouses there wherein lieth Her Majesty's store of all kind of provisions for the use of her ships, by the like time of 90 days begun and ended as aforesaid, at 8d *per diem* – £3.

*[*Purveyor*]. To James Humphrey the same day for his wages daily attending and serving Her Highness in providing all manner of provisions and necessaries for the building and repairing of Her Majesty's ships, by 90 days begun and ended as abovesaid, at 8d *per diem* – £3.

*[*Plug keeper*]. To William Allie, labourer, the same day for his wages daily attending and serving Her Highness in keeping of the plug and letting out of the water in the dock there for the drier keeping of the same, wherein lieth two Her Grace's ships the *Great Bark* and the *Jesus* to be new made, by like 90 days begun and ended as abovesaid, at 8d *per diem* – £3.

*[*Keeper of timber-yards*]. To Thomas Wood, porter, the same day for his wages daily attending and serving Her Highness in safe-keeping of Her Grace's timber-yards there wherein lieth her timber, planks, boards, masts and divers other things for the use of Her Majesty's ships, by 90 days begun and ended as is aforesaid, at 8d *per diem* – £3.

[*Page total*] – £15.

[f. 176v] *[*Surveyor*]. To George Wourrall the last day of March for his wages daily attending and serving Her Highness for the taking surveys of all manner of necessaries had of divers persons for the furniture of Her Grace's ships as well at their setting forth to the seas as also at their coming home again into harbour, by 90 days begun the first day of January last and ended as abovesaid, at 8d *per diem* – £3.

*[*Riding charges*]. To John Elmer, messenger, the same day for his wages daily attending and serving Her Highness for carrying of the

officers' letters in post to divers and sundry places alongst the sea coast for Her Majesty's marine causes, by like 90 days begun and ended as aforesaid, at 12d *per diem* – £4 10s.

*[*Shipwright*]. To Augustino Levello, Venetian shipwright, the same day for his wages daily attending and serving Her Highness for the repairing and mending of Her Grace's galleys, by 90 days begun and ended as abovesaid, at 16d *per diem* – £6.

*[*Clerk*]. To Stephen Alexander the same day for his wages daily attending and serving Her Highness for the writing, making and keeping of the books of report of all such provisions and necessaries as are taken of divers and sundry persons for the use of Her Majesty's ships, by one quarter of a year, due at this present – £6 13s 4d.

[*Page total*] – £20 3s 4d.

[f. 177] *Shipwrights*

Edward Bright, master, 90 days at 12d	£4 10s
Thomas Juell, server, 77 days at 6d	38s 6d
John Lestoo, server, 77 days at 6d	38s 6d
Daniel Bright, server, 77 days at 6d	38s 6d
William Foster, server, 74 days at 6d	37s
Robert Hodgekynson, 67 days at 8d	44s 8d
Thomas Hely, server, 77 days at 3d	19s 3d
Matthew Baker, master, 90 days at 12d	£4 10s
Matthew Norton, server, 77 days at 5d	32s 1d
John Hoole, server, 77 days at 5d	32s 1d
Philip Garrett, 77 days at 6d	38s 6d
John Rande, 77 days at 10d	£3 4s 2d
James Cootes, server, 77 days at 6d	38s 6d
George Flower, server, 77 days at 6d	38s 6d
John Ellysson, 74 days at 8d	49s 4d
John Halle, server, 77 days at 6d	38s 6d
John Daulton, 72 days at 7d	42s
Davy Horne, server, 77 days at 4d	25s 8d
Michael Too, server, 77 days at 7d	44s 11d
John Too, server, 74 days at 6d	37s
Edward Holborne, 72 days at 8d	48s
Henry Newe, server, 76 days at 5d	31s 8d
Peter Pett, master, 59 days at 12d	59s
Walter Holborne, 69 days at 8d	46s
William Wheller, server, 75 days at 5d	31s 3d
John Haywarde, 57 days at 8d	38s
Michael Gamond, server, 67 days at 6d	33s 6d

Henry Samon, server, 27 days at 4d	9s
John Brunet, 69 days at 8d	46s
John Wilkynson, server, 77 days at 4d	25s 8d
Robert Baker, 54 days at 6d	27s
Richard Claye, 69 days at 8d	46s

[*Page total*] – £65 18s 9d.

[f. 177v] Robert Paddye, 69 days at 7d	40s 3d
William Wethered, server, 77 days at 4d	25s 8d
William Spycer, 72 days at 7d	42s
Thomas Osborne, server, 76 days at 4d	25s 4d
Thomas Robynson, 68 days at 7d	39s 8d
Stephen Robynson, server, 76 days at 5d	31s 8d
Edward Clarke, 70 days at 7d	40s 10d
Edward Davye, server, 33 days at 3d	8s 3d
Thomas Raynoldes, 8 days at 8d	5s 4d
Henry Raynoldes, server, 20 days at 2d	3s 4d
Richard Farrer, 51½ days at 7d	30s 0½d
Thomas Deacon, server, 76 days at 6d	38s
Henry Greaves, 60 days at 7d	35s
Thomas Bonnam, server, 76 days at 5d	31s 8d
William Greaves, 77 days at 9d	57s 9d
Thomas Hewes, server, 77 days at 6d	38s 6d
Ralph Wright, server, 63 days at 5d	26s 3d
Randall Wood, 74½ days at 7d	43s 5½d
Richard Johnson, 77 days at 6d	38s 6d
Robert Davye, 65 days at 6d	32s 6d
Henry Freman, 77 days at 6d	38s 6d
Robert Assheton, 76 days at 6d	38s
Davy Baker, 77 days at 6d	38s 6d
John Bygges, 9 days at 6d	4s 6d
John Mysselton, 73 days at 7d	42s 7d
James Dyggons, server, 75 days at 5d	31s 3d
William Picklington, 37 days at 6d	18s 6d
Stephen Bedlo, server, 47 days at 2d	7s 10d
Thomas Tyrrie, 49 days at 7d	28s 7d
John Pett, 67 days at 8d	44s 8d
Robert Pett, server, 69 days at 5d	28s 9d
Thomas Harman, 68 days at 7d	39s 8d
Nicholas Adams, server, 69 days at 3d	17s 3d
George Upsone, 67 days at 6d	33s 6d
Henry Upsone, server, 59 days at 4d	19s 8d

William Pymbill, 3 days at 6d	18d
[*Page total*] – £53 7s 3d.	
[f. 178] Christopher Yngle, 3 days at 6d	18d
Richard Payne, 51 days at 6d	25s 6d
Thomas Moore, server, 51 days at 4d	17s
Thomas Bryan, 47 days at 7d	27s 5d
Richard Cooke, server, 50 days at 4d	16s 8d
John Dyggons, 50 days at 6d	25s
Lewis Rychardes, 50 days at 6d	25s
Roger Rayner, 31 days at 6d	15s 6d
Anthony Holdernes, 21 days at 7d	12s 3d
William Graye, server, 27 days at 2d	4s 6d
John Clarke, 70 days at 8d	46s 8d
George Graye, server, 77 days at 4d	25s 8d
Thomas Northcott, 35 days at 7d	20s 5d
John Arodes, server, 37 days at 5d	15s 5d
Walter Claye, 20 days at 6d	10s
William Larde, 63 days at 6d	31s 6d
Thomas Hewes, server, 10 days at 6d	5s
Robert Waller, server, 27 days at 2d	4s 6d
Thomas Whomes, 10 days at 6d	5s
Richard Rooke, 10 days at 6d	5s
William Evered, server, 10 days at 4d	3s 4d
William Carro, 10 days at 6d	5s
Richard Adams, 3 days at 8d	2s
John Tyllie, server, 3 days at 6d	18d
Thomas White, server, 3 days at 5d	15d
William Sybley, 3 days at 4d	12d
Caulkers	
Thomas Bolton, master, 24 days at 10d	20s
William Bolton , server, 21 days at 6d	10s 6d
John Fuller, server, 21 days at 6d	10s 6d
Robert Brydges, 12 days at 7d	7s
Humphrey Dayll, server, 18 days at 6d	9s
Edward Bridges, server, 21 days at 2d	3s 6d
[*Page total*] – £20 14s 1d.	
[f. 178v] Robert White, 16 days at 7d	9s 4d
Henry Reade, server, 18½ days at 4d	6s 2d
Michael Rowse, 21 days at 6d	10s 6d
John Stockdayll, 18 days at 6d	9s
John Eastun, 20 days at 6d	10s

Thomas Wynchester, server, 21 days at 2d	3s 6d
Thomas Coxe, 20 days at 6d	10s
William Forde, 21 days at 7d	12s 3d
Robert Richardes, 18½ days at 7d	10s 9½d
John Castellman, server, 20 days at 4d	6s 8d
Thomas Pavy, 20 days at 7d	11s 8d
Edward Hylliarde, server, 20 days at 4d	6s 8d
John Hayewarde, 20 days at 7d	11s 8d
Nicholas Hayewarde, server, 16 days at 5d	6s 8d
William Wood, server, 20 days at 2d	3s 4d
Gregory Knightly, 20 days at 7d	11s 8d
William Bastiane, 12 days at 6d	6s
Arthur Charlles, server, 14 days at 4d	4s 8d
Thomas Willson, 90 days at 12d	£4 10s
John Hurlestone, 90 days at 6d	45s
Thomas Heele, 80 days at 6d	40s
Henry Rowse, server, 90 days at 3d	22s 6d
Nicholas Archedayll, 63 days at 6d	31s 6d
John Juell, server, 17 days at 6d	8s 6d
Robert Wright, server, 50 days at 6d	25s
Raynold Newe, 71 days at 6d	35s 6d
William Byrde, 80 days at 6d	40s
Sawyers	
Thomas Myller, 77 days at 6d	38s 6d
Robert Davyes, 77 days at 6d	38s 6d
John Richardes, 77 days at 6d	38s 6d
Robert Grene, 72 days at 6d	36s
Bennet Over, 9 days at 6d	4s 6d
Robert Turnbull, 9 days at 6d	4s 6d

[*Page total*] – £32 6s 6½d.

[f. 179] *Victualling.* To Thomas Willson of Ratcliff the last day of March for the victualling of 131 of the aforenamed shipwrights, caulkers and sawyers working as well upon the new making and building of Her Highness's ship called the *Great Bark*, as also upon the redubbing and mending of Her Grace's ship the *Jesus* there, by the space of 7,710 days among them all, Sundays and holy days within the same accounted, begun the first day of January last and this day ended, which maketh 1,101 weeks 3 days, at 4s 2¼d every week the man. *Summa* – £230 12s 5d.

Lodging. To Maude Fellon, Anne Batler, Alice Addams, Joan Bright, Elizabeth Fraunces and 14 other persons of Deptford, Greenwich, Lewisham and thereabouts the same day for the lodging of 131 of the aforesaid shipwrights, caulkers and sawyers in 67 featherbeds, working upon the new making and redubbing of Her Majesty's said ships there, by the space of 1,288 weeks among them all, begun the first day of January last and ended as aforesaid, at 2d every week the man – £10 14s 8d.

[*Page total*] – £241 7s 1d.

[f. 179v] *House-carpenters*

John Leache, 68 days at 12d	£3 8s
Robert Throulley, server, 68 days at 10d	56s 8d
Thomas Biggyn, 68 days at 10d	56s 8d
	[£8 19s 4d*]
Bricklayers	
John Callawaye, master, 12 days at 12d	12s
Stephen Huggins, 12 days at 10d	10s
Richard Savage, 12 days at 10d	10s
Michael Hutchyns, 12 days at 8d	8s
Labourers	
William Allye, master, 30 nights at 4d	10s
Richard Raynsforth, 92 days and nights at 7d	53s 8d
Henry Stephenson, 86 days and nights at 6d	43s
Thomas Thisseletun, 92 days and nights at 6d	46s
John Gybson, 79 days and nights at 6d	39s 6d
Edward Plumer, 70 days and nights at 6d	35s
John Brodehurst, 20 days at 6d	10s
William Twayttes, 89 days and nights at 6d	44s 6d
John Bastyane, 91 days and nights at 6d	45s 6d
John Addams, 82 days and nights at 6d	41s
James Tealle, 77 days at 6d	38s 6d
William Gunbye, 26 days at 6d	13s
John Janns, 75½ days and nights at 6d	37s 9d
John Brace, 23 days at 6d	11s 6d
Morgan Apprice, 92 days and nights at 6d	46s
Richard Coxe, 80½ days and nights at 6d	40s 3d
Lawrence Langcaster, 69½ days and nights at 6d	34s 9d
	[£30 11s 11d*]

[*Page total*] – £40 11s 3d.

[f. 180] John Apprice, 20 days at 6d	10s
Ralph Courtland, 90½ days and nights at 6d	45s 3d
John Mansfelde, 18½ days at 6d	9s 3d
William Apprice, 92 days and nights at 6d	46s
John Marshall, 66 days at 6d	33s

Robert Stephens, 23 days at 6d	11s 6d
George Newtun, 14 days at 6d	7s
George Bell, 88 days and nights at 6d	44s
William Wallys, 18 days at 6d	9s
Anthony Hyll, 21 days at 6d	10s 6d
Anthony Westlonde, 89 days and nights at 6d	44s 6d
Robert Harrys, 7 days at 6d	3s 6d
George Twyforde, 56 days at 6d	28s
John Raby, 26 days at 6d	13s
John Sturgeon, 81 days and nights at 6d	40s 4d
Richard Otte, 86 days and nights at 6d	43s
Edward Burnam, 92 days and nights at 6d	46s
John Heye, 92 days and nights at 6d	46s
John Bradley, 77 days at 6d	38s 6d
William Searlle, 63 days at 6d	31s 6d
Michael Hutchins, 15 days at 6d	7s 6d
George Mathew, 16 days at 6d	8s
Barnaby Nackell, 31 days at 6d	15s 6d
Thomas Clarke, 31 days at 6d	15s 6d
William Brock, 19 days at 6d	9s 6d
John Watson, 18½ days at 6d	9s 3d
William Pythen, 18½ days at 6d	9s 3d
Thomas Tressam, 5 days at 6d	2s 6d
John Parker, 20½ days at 6d	10s 3d
Robert Baltropp, 84 days and nights at 6d	42s

[*Page total*] – £34 9s 3d.

[f. 180v] *Watchmen*

John Brodehurst, 6 nights at 6d	3s
William Currar, 30 nights at 6d	15s
Nicholas Archedayll, 30 nights at 6d	15s
John Hurlstone, 30 nights at 6d	15s
John Addams, 33 nights at 6d	16s 6d
Thomas Thisseletun, 33 nights at 6d	16s 6d
William Apprice, 33 nights at 6d	16s 6d
Edward Burnam, 33 nights at 6d	16s 6d
Ralph Courtlande, 7 nights at 6d	3s 6d
John Marshall, 7 nights at 6d	3s 6d
William Twayttes, 30 nights at 6d	15s
John Wallys, 7 nights at 6d	3s 6d
John Gybson, 6 nights at 6d	3s
John Brace, 6 nights at 6d	3s

John Twyforde, 24 nights at 6d	12s
Robert Harrys, 2 nights at 6d	12d
Anthony Hyll, 5 nights at 6d	2s 6d
Anthony Westlond, 31 nights at 6d	15s 6d
George Bell, 31 nights at 6d	15s 6d
Henry Stevenson, 5 nights at 6d	2s 6d
John Raby, 4 nights at 6d	2s
John Hayen, 28 nights at 6d	14s
William Brock, 7 nights at 6d	3s 6d

[*Page total*] – £10 14s.

[f. 181] *Emptions*

Ironwork. To Thomas Ivye of Limehouse, smith, the last day of March for price of 9 thousand 6 hundred 2 quarters 5 pounds weight [*10,813 lbs*] of his own new iron by him made and wrought into ring-bolts, setting bolts, spikes, clench, rove, overlop nails, rudder irons and crows of iron, and the same delivered at Deptford into Her Highness's storehouse there for the use of Her Grace's ships, at 23s 4d every hundredweight – £112 12s 8½d; more for 8,000 of 10d nail, at 8s 4d every 1,000 – £3 6s 8d; more for 8,000 of 6d nail, at 5s every 1,000 – 40s; more for 7,000 of 4d nail, at 3s 4d every 1,000 – 24s 4d; and more to him for 7,000 of 3d nail, at 2s 6d every 1,000 – 17s 6d. *Summa* – £120 0s 2½d.

To Thomas Willson of Ratcliff, smith, the same day for price of 46 hundred 3 quarters 8 pounds weight [*5,244 lbs*] of his own new iron by him made and wrought into bolts, spikes, clench, rove, overlop nails, and rudder irons, and the same delivered as aforesaid for the use of Her Majesty's ships, at 23s 4d every hundredweight – £54 12s 6d; more for 15,550 of 10d nail, at 8s 4d every 1,000 – £6 9s 7d; more for 23,600 of 6d nail, at 5s every 1,000 – £5 18s; more for 41,800 of 4d nail, at 3s 4d every 1,000 – £6 19s; and more to him for 26,000 of 3d nail, at 2s 6d every 1,000 – £3 5s. *Summa* – £77 4s 1d.

To Richard Welles of Greenwich, smith, the same day for price of 11 hundred 3 quarters 24 pounds weight [*1,340 lbs*] of his own new iron by him made and wrought into bolts, spikes and overlop nails for the use of Her Highness ships as aforesaid, at 23s 4d every hundredweight – £13 19s 2d; and more to him for the working of one hundred 2 quarters 9 pounds weight [*177 lbs*] of Her Grace's old iron into bolts and spikes for use of Her Majesty's said ships, at 8s 4d every hundredweight working – 13s 3d.[1] *Summa* – £14 12s 5d.

[*Page total*] – £211 16 8½d. *[*With £30 0s 1d for nails*]

[1]The calculation gives 158.0357d, which is about ½d below the sum stated (159d).

[f. 181v] *Poldavis and oleron canvas.* To Edward Haull of London, merchant, the last day of March for price of 20 bolts of oleron canvas by him delivered into Her Grace's great storehouse at Deptford for the use of Her Highness's ships, at 17s 6d every bolt – £17 10s; more for [*one*] hundred 96¾ [*216¾*] ells of vitry canvas, after 6 score ells to every hundred[1] at 11½d the ell – £10 7s 8½d; more for 18 ells of white lockram, at 12d the ell – 18s; and more to him for 2 ells of canvas, at 9d the ell – 18d. *Summa* – £28 17s 2½d.

To John Browne of London the same day for price of 100 bolts of poldavis canvas of him taken and the same delivered into Her Majesty's storehouse there for the use of Her Highness's ships, at 36s 8d every bolt. *Summa* – £183 6s 8d.

To John Collens of London the same day for price of 20 bolts of poldavis canvas of English making of him had and the same delivered as is aforesaid for the use of Her Grace's ships, at 35s every bolt – £35.

Pulleys, shovels and scoops. To John Benbow of London the same day for price of 18 pulleys of ash by him delivered there for the use of Her Highness's ships, at 8d the piece – 12s; more for 30 pulleys, at 4d the piece – 10s; more for one shiver with a cock of brass – 10d; more for one load of ash, price 2s 6d; more for 2 dozen of steel shovels, at 8s the dozen – 16s; and more to him for 2 dozen of scoops, at 5s every dozen – 10s. *Summa* – £2 11s 4d.

[*Page total*] – £249 15s 2½d.

[f. 182] *Cables, cablets, hawsers, warps, pitch and oakum, &c.* To Christopher Draper of London, alderman, the last day of March for price of 2 hogsheads of train oil by him delivered into Her Grace's great storehouse at Deptford for the use of Her Highness's ships, at 55s the hogshead – £5 10s; more for [*one*] hundredweight of twine, at 7d every pound – £3 5s 4d; more for [*one*] hundred 6 pounds weight [*118 lbs*] of latchet lines, at 3d every pound – 29s 6d; more for 36 pieces of tarred cablets, hawsers and warps, weighing 5 thousand 5 hundred 14 pounds weight [*6,174 lbs*], at 18s 8d every hundredweight – £51 9s; more for 4 sacks of poppet oakum weighing 2 thousand 8 hundred [*one*] quarter 14 pounds weight [*3,178 lbs*], at 20s every hundredweight – £28 7s 6d; more for 2 bolts of canvas, at 10s the piece – 20s; more for 5 tarred cablets and hawsers weighing 3 thousand 2 quarters 6 pounds weight [*3,422 lbs*], at

[1] A lingering use of the old *great* or *long hundred* of 120: cf. *OED* 'hundred' *sb.* and *a.* 3. The calibration applies to the quantity stated as well as the charge, and therefore the clerk's *c.iiij*^{xx}*.xvj elles iij quarters* here represents not for 196¾ but (120 + 96¾) = 216¾. This figure multiplied by the unit cost comes to ⅛d above the stated total, which is therefore correctly rounded down to the nearest farthing.

18s every hundredweight – £27 10s;[1] more for 200 coil of white rope for gimmer ropes[2] weighing 4 hundred 3 quarters 3 [*recte* 10] pounds weight [*535* recte *542 lbs*], at 28s every hundredweight – £6 15s 6d;[3] more for 6 barrels of pitch, after £4 13s 4d the last – 46s 8d; and more to him for the hire of a lighter for the bringing of the same provisions from London to Deptford Strand; by agreement – 6s 8d. *Summa* – £128 0s 2d.

To William Merricke of London, merchant, the same day for price of 98 thousand 8 hundred 3 quarters weight [*110,740 lbs*] of Russian cordage by him delivered into Her Majesty's great storehouse there for the use of Her Highness's ships, *viz.* 7 tarred cables and cablets of 7, 10, 11, 12 and 13 inches compass, 130 tarred hawsers of 4, 5, 6, and 7 inches compass about, at 15s every hundredweight – £741 11s 3d.

Deal-boards. To John Warner of London, merchant, the same day for the price of 60 deal-boards of him taken and the same delivered as aforesaid for the use of Her Highness's ships, at 4s every deal-board – £12.

[*Page total*] – £881 11s 5d. *[*Cordage and tackling – £860 7s 1d*; *pitch and tar – £7 16s 8d*; *boards – £12*; *water carriage – 6s 8d*]

[f. 182v] *Thrums, spars, masts and tilt hair.* To William Page of London, merchant, the same day for price of 56 pounds weight of thrums of him had for the use of Her Grace's ships, at 2½d every pound – 11s 8d; more for 12 fir spars, at 4d the piece – 4s; more for 6 Norway masts of 6, 7 and 5 hands about, at 10s the piece – £3; more for 20 fir poles, at 4d the piece – 6s 8d; and more to him for 16 bolts of tilt hair, at 10s the piece – £8. *Summa* – £12 2s 4d.

To Thomas Claye of London the same day for price of 19½ bolts of tilt hair by him delivered into Her Majesty's great storehouse there for the use of Her Highness's ships, at 10s every bolt – £9 15s.

Ballast baskets, maunds and wicker lattice. To Christian Edes of London, widow, the same day for price of 27½ dozen of middle baskets of her had and delivered at Deptford for the use of Her Grace's ships, at 4s every dozen – £5 10s; more for 30 dozen of ballast baskets, at 22d every dozen – £2 15s; more for 30 great maunds, at 16d the piece – 40s; and more to her for 46 yards of double wicker lattice for the windows about Her Highness's great storehouse there, at 18d every yard of lattice – £3 9s. *Summa* – £13 14s.

[1] The calculation gives 6599.5713d, which is within ½d of the sum stated (6600d).

[2] MS 'jym[er] roopes'. A gimmer was any kind of hinge (*OED* 'gimmer' [1]. 2.).

[3] The MS calculation gives £6 13s 9d (1605d), which is 21d below the sum stated (1626d). In view of the precision in Draper's other reckonings such a discrepancy is likely to be a transcription error, especially because the price per pound (3d) is easily computed. The sum would be correct for 4 cwt 3 qrs 10 lbs, so it is likely that the Quarter Book scribe repeated *iij* from the qrs instead of *x* as the figure for lbs.

New flags. To Stephen Androwes of London the same day for price of 5 new flags with the cross of St George of red say, of him taken and delivered into Her Majesty's storehouse there for the use of Her Highness's ships, at 16s 8d every flag. *Summa* – £4 3s 4d.

[*Page total*] – £39 14s 8d.

[f. 183] *Timber and plank oak.* To Christopher Nayller of London the last day of March for price of 91 loads 20 foot of compass and long timber oak by him delivered at Deptford for the use of Her Highness's ships, at 10s every load after 50 foot to the load – £45 12s 3d; more for 5,768½ foot of 4-inch plank oak, at 12s every 100 foot – £33 13s 4d; and more to him for 2,502 foot of 3-inch plank oak, at 10s every 100 foot – £12 10s 2d. *Summa* – £91 16s 8d.

To Roger Porter of London the same day for price of 242 loads of hooks, knees and other compass timber oak of him taken and the same delivered as aforesaid for the use of Her Majesty's ships, at 10s 8d every load after 50 foot to the load – £129 1s 4d.

To Henry Seckford, esquire,[1] the same day for price of 786 loads 12 foot of timber oak of him had for the use of Her Grace's ships out of the woods of Bedingfield and Redlingfield in Suffolk, at 20d every load at the stub[2] – £65 11s 1d.

Broad hoops. To John Lowe of London, cooper, the same day for price of 15 great broad hoops of 11 foot over, of him had and the same delivered as aforesaid for the use of Her Highness's ships, at 2s 4d every hoop – 35s; and more to him for 15 smaller hoops of 9 and 8 foot over, at 20d every hoop – 25s. *Summa* – £3.

[*Page total*] – £289 9s 1d.

[f. 183v] *Old junks wrought into netting-, wrain-, eye-ropes and oakum.* To William Brooke of Deptford, ropemaker, the last day of March for the workmanship of 4 thousand 2 hundredweight [*4,704 lbs*] of Her Highness's old junks and ropes by him wrought into wrain-, netting- and eye-ropes for the use of Her Majesty's ships, at 3s 8d every hundredweight working – £7 14s.

To William Cockes of Stepney, ropemaker, the same day for the like working of [*one*] thousand 7 hundred 2 quarters weight [*1,960 lbs*] of Her

[1]Brother of Thomas Seckford (Master of Requests and a leading agent of his county's interest at court); Henry was a Gentleman of the Privy Chamber, appointed Master of the Queen's Tents and Pavilions (1560) and victualler for the Irish garrisons (1574), knighted 1603: *CPR 1558–60*, p. 325. *APC 1571–5*, p. 259. Shaw, ii, p. 106. *Hist. Parl. 1558–1603*, iii, pp. 362–4 (for Thomas). D. N. J. MacCulloch, *Suffolk and the Tudors: Politics and Religion in an English County, 1500–1600* (Oxford, 1986), p. 242. S. Maxwell, 'Henry Seckford: sixteenth-century merchant, courtier and privateer', *MM*, LXXXII (1996), pp. 387–97.

[2]Meaning bought on the ground, as growing wood: *OED*, 'stub', *sb.* 1. b.

Grace's old junks and ropes into netting-, wrain- and eye-ropes for the use as aforesaid, at 3s 8d every hundredweight working – £3 4s 2d.

To Thomas Russell of Ratcliff, ropemaker, the same day for the working of 2 thousand 8 hundred one quarter weight [*3,164 lbs*] of the like old junks and ropes into eye-, netting- and wrain-ropes for the use of Her Highness's said ships, at 3s 8d every hundredweight working – £5 3s 7d.

To Nicholas Archedayll, Henry Saylle, Thomas Rocke and six other persons of Deptford, Greenwich and thereabouts the same day for the working and picking of [*one*] thousand 7 hundred one quarter weight [*1,932 lbs*] of Her Grace's old junks and ropes into oakum for the needful caulking of Her Majesty's ships, at 3s 8d every hundredweight working – £3 3s 4d [*recte* 3d].[1]

Casting of shivers. To Robert Hunt of London, founder, the same day for the new working and casting of [*one*] hundred [*one*] quarter 15 pounds weight [*155 lbs*] of Her Highness's old brass by him made and wrought into 13 shivers for the use of Her Grace's ships, at 4d every pound weight working – £2 1s 8d.

[*Page total*] – £21 16s 9d.

[f. 184] *Cabins.* To Lewis Stocket of London, joiner, the last day of March for a certain bargain by him made with the officers of Her Grace's Marine Causes as well for the workmanship, sealing and finishing of the two cabins set up in Her Highness's two great new ships named the *Triumph* and the *Victory* there, as also for making of new cupboards, settles, bedsteads, forms, stools, trestles, tables and aumbries, all of joined work, in the same two ships; by him taken in great, by agreement – £70.

Ships' tops. To Peter Pett of Deptford, master shipwright, the same day for the workmanship and making of 13 new tops, great and small, for the use of Her Highness's two great new ships called the *Triumph* and the *Victory*, for the main tops, foretops, mizzen tops and topgallants of the same two ships there; by agreement – £23 0s 6d.

Painting and colouring. To James Cooke of London, painter, the same day for the workmanship, painting and colouring of two Her Majesty's brigantines, named the *Wolf* and the *Fox*,[2] with their oars, in red done with oil; by agreement – £5 10s.

Making of oars. To John Cartter of Wapping, oarmaker, the same day for workmanship and making of 60 long oars for the use of Her Grace's two brigantines called the *Wolf* and the *Fox*, at 12d the piece – £3; and

[1]The calculation gives 759d, which is 1d below the sum stated; the Quarter Book scribe probably mis-copied the correct final *iijs iijd* as the more commonly occurring *iijs iiijd*.

[2]These two vessels are not otherwise known.

more to him for price of 300 of long nails, at 2s every 100 – 6s. *Summa* – £3 6s.

[*Page total*] – £101 16s 6d.

[f. 184v] *Burning reed.* To William Latham of Rainham, reedman, the last day of March for price of 1,000 of burning reed by him delivered at Deptford for the needful breaming of Her Highness's ships at their groundings, at 12d every 100 – 10s.

To Agnes Allexaunder of Deptford the same day for price of 3,000 of dry burning reed of her had and the same delivered as aforesaid for the use of the Queen's Majesty's ships, at 10s every 1,000 – £1 10s.

Lead and solder. To Julian Richardes of London, widow, the same day for price of 18 pounds weight of new lead made into pipes for scuppers for the use of Her Grace's ships, after 15s the hundreweight – 2s 5d; more for 2 pounds weight of tin solder, at 8d the pound – 16d; and more to her for the wages of two her men by 2 days working upon Her Grace's brigantines named the *Wolf* and the *Fox* – 20d. *Summa* – 5s 5d.

Water buckets. To John Williamson of London, cooper, the same day for price of 12 wooden buckets of him had and the same delivered at Deptford for the use of Her Grace's ships, at 5d the piece – 5s.

House rent. To Peter Pett of Deptford the same day for one quarter of a year's rent of two cellars of him hired wherein lieth Her Highness's store of rosin for the use of Her Grace's ships; due at this present – £1.

[*Page total*] – £3 10s 5d.

[f. 185] *Water carriage.* To Vincent Poulle of St Katherine's the last day of March for service of his hoy of the portage of 40 tuns serving Her Highness in carrying of Her Grace's timber and plank from Woolwich to Deptford and there delivered the same for the use of Her Majesty's ships, by the space of one month begun the first day of March last and ended as is abovesaid, at 3s 4d every tun *per mensem. Summa* – £6 13s 4d.

To Raynold Barnes, master, the same day for service of his hoy serving Her Highness in fetching of certain cables, cablets, hawsers, warps, sails and other tackle pertaining to Her Grace's ship the *Jesus* from Chatham to Deptford and there delivered the same; by agreement – £1 10s.

Ox tallow. To Hugh Bennet of London the same day for price of 3 hundredweight of hard ox tallow of him had and the same delivered at Deptford for the use of Her Grace's ships, at 20s every hundredweight – £3.

To Simon Burtun of London, chandler, the same day for price of 3 hundred 10 pounds weight [*346 lbs*] of hard ox tallow of him taken and the same delivered as aforesaid for the use of Her Highness's ships, at 18s 8d every hundredweight – £2 17s 8d.

Wainscot. To William Gyrdeler of London, merchant, the same day for price of 6 wainscot boards of him had and the same delivered at Deptford for the use of Her Grace's ships, at 2s every board – 12s.

[*Page total*] – £14 13s.

[f. 185v] *Running glasses*. To Richard Stevens of Tower Hill, compass-maker, the last day of March for price of 2½ dozen of running glasses of him had and the same delivered into Her Highness's great storehouse at Deptford for the use of Her Grace's ships, at 10d the piece. *Summa* – £1 5s.

Cart wheels. To John Stanbrydge of Lewisham the same day for price of one pair of wheels of ash of him had for the use of Her Highness's timber cart for the needful drawing of Her Grace's timber to the ships' sides for the unloading of hoys there, price – 12s.

Sye. To John Stampp of Colchester the same day for price of 336 pounds weight of sye of him had for the use of Her Majesty's ships, at 2d every pound – 56s; and more to Thomas Mitche for bringing the same sye from Colchester to Deptford – 3s 4d. *Summa* – £3 0s 4d.

Hire of a lighter. To Robert Cockes of London, lighterman, the same day for service of his lighter serving Her Highness in carrying of cables, cablets, hawsers, warps and other small cordage taken of divers persons for the use of Her Grace's ships from London to Deptford; by agreement – 7s 6d.

[*Page total*] – £5 4s 10d.

[f. 186] *Anno Domini 1563. Anno regni regine Elizabethe quinto*

A payment made the last day of June as well to masters, mariners, keepers of storehouses, docks and timber-yards there wherein lieth Her Grace's provisions for the use of her ships, and to shipwrights, caulkers, sawyers, smiths, oarmakers, joiners, labourers and other artificers and workmen for new making and repairing of Her Highness's two ships the *Great Bark* and the *Jesus*; as also to sundry persons for divers kinds of provisions and necessaries by them delivered into Her Majesty's storehouses at Deptford for the use of Her Grace's ships; by one quarter of a year begun the first day of April last and this day ended, as followeth:

Timber-yard keeper. To Thomas Marshe, mariner, the last day of June for his wages daily attending and serving Her Highness for the safe-keeping of Her Grace's provisions of divers kinds of stuffs lying in her timber-yards there, and for the rigging and tackling of Her Majesty's ships to the seas; by one quarter of a year containing 13 weeks begun the first day of April last and ended as is abovesaid, at 20s every month. *Summa* – £3 5s.

[*Page total*] – £3 5s.

[f. 186v] *[*Mariners' wages for carrying of provisions and coiling up of cables*]. To Robert Woode and Richard Tooken, mariners, the last day of June for their wages and victuals daily attending and serving Her Highness in labouring about the carrying and coiling up of cables, hawsers, warps and other provisions into Her Grace's great storehouse at Deptford, and delivering out of the same again to the use of Her Majesty's ships, by the space of 13 weeks begun the first day of April last and this day ended, at 13s 4d every month the man. *Summa* – £4 6s 8d.

To Christopher Barefoote and William Davy, mariners, the same day for their wages and victuals daily attending and serving Her Highness in labouring about the carriage of provisions and coiling up of cables, cablets, hawsers and warps as aforesaid, by like 13 weeks begun and ended as is aforesaid, at 13s 4d either of them *per mensem* – £4 6s 8d.

To Robert Tasse, mariner, the same day for his wages and victuals daily attending and serving Her Highness in labouring about the carriage of provisions and coiling up of cables and hawsers as aforesaid, by like 13 weeks begun and ended as abovesaid, at 13s 4d *per mensem* – £2 3s 4d.

To Richard Harwood, mariner, the same day for his wages daily attending and serving Her Highness in labouring about the carriage of provisions and coiling up of cables and hawsers as is abovesaid, by like time of 13 weeks begun and ended as aforesaid, at 13s 4d *per mensem* – £2 3s 4d.

To John Benwell, mariner, the same day for his wages daily attending and serving Her Highness about the carrying of provisions and coiling up of cables as aforesaid, by like 13 weeks begun and ended as abovesaid, at 13s 4d *per mensem* – £2 3s 4d.

[*Page total*] – £15 3s 4d.

[f. 187] *[*Mariners' wages for coiling up of cables*]. To William Pattricke, mariner, the last day of June for his wages daily attending and serving Her Highness in labouring about the carriage of provisions and coiling up of cables and hawsers in Her Grace's great storehouse there, by the space of 13 weeks begun the first day of April last and ended as abovesaid, at 6s 8d *per mensem* – £1 1s 8d.

To John Kynge, mariner, the same day for his wages daily attending and serving Her Highness in labouring about the carrying of provisions and coiling up of cables and hawsers as abovesaid, by like 13 weeks begun and ended as aforesaid, at 6s 8d every month – £1 1s 8d.

*[*Clerk*]. To James Gentyll the same day for his wages daily attending and serving Her Highness in keeping of the prick and cheque book of masters, mariners and gunners serving in Her Grace's ships upon the river of Thames, by one quarter of a year containing 91 days begun and ended as aforesaid, at 8d *per diem* – £3 0s 8d.

*[*Keeper of storehouse*]. To Henry Abraham the same day for his wages daily attending and serving Her Highness for the safe-keeping of Her Grace's storehouses there wherein lieth Her Majesty's store of all kinds of provisions for the use of her ships, by like time of 91 days begun and ended as abovesaid, at 8d *per diem* – £3 0s 8d.

*[*Purveyor*]. To James Humphrey the same day for his wages daily attending and serving Her Highness for providing all manner of necessaries for the building and repairing of Her Grace's ships, by the space of 91 days begun and ended as is aforesaid, at 8d *per diem* – £3 0s 8d.

[*Page total*] – £11 5s 4d.

[f. 187v] *[*Surveyor*]. To George Worrall the last day of June for his wages daily attending and serving Her Highness for the taking surveys of all manner of necessaries taken of divers persons for the furniture of Her Grace's ships as well at their setting forth to the seas as also at their coming home again into harbour, by 91 days begun the first day of April last and ended as abovesaid, at 8d *per diem* – £3 0s 8d.

*[*Plug keeper*]. To William Ally, labourer, the same day for his wages daily attending and serving Her Highness in keeping of the plug and letting out of the water in the dock their for the drier keeping of the same, wherein lieth two Her Grace's ships the *Great Bark* and the *Jesus* to be new made, by the like time of 91 days begun and ended as is abovesaid, at 8d *per diem* – £3 0s 8d.

*[*Keeper of timber-yard*]. To Thomas Woode, porter, the same day for his wages daily attending and serving Her Highness in safe-keeping of her timber-yards there, wherein lieth her timber, plank and other necessaries for the use of Her Grace's ships, by 91 days begun and ended as is aforesaid, at 8d *per diem* – £3 0s 8d.

*[*Purveyor*]. To Roger Porter the same day for his wages daily attending and serving Her Highness in providing of timber and plank for the use of Her Majesty's ships, by like 91 days begun and ended as abovesaid, at 8d *per diem* – £3 0s 8d.

Riding charges. To John Elmer, messenger, the same day for his wages daily attending and serving Her Highness for carrying of the officers' letters in post to divers and sundry places alongst the sea coast for Her Grace's marine causes, by like time of 91 days begun and ended as aforesaid, at 12d *per diem* – £4 11s.

[*Page total*] – £16 13s 8d.

[f. 188] *[*Shipwright*]. To Augustino Levello, Venetian shipwright, the last day of June for his wages daily attending and serving Her Highness for the repairing and mending of Her Grace's galleys, by the space of 91 days begun the first day of April last and this day ended, at 16d *per diem* – £6 1s 4d.

*[*Clerk*]. To Stephen Alexander the same day for his wages daily attending and serving Her Highness for the writing, making and keeping of the books of report of all such provisions and necessaries as are taken of divers and sundry persons for the use of Her Majesty's ships, by one quarter of a year due at this present – £6 13s 4d.

*[*Shipkeeper*]. To Thomas Elye, boatswain, the same day for his wages daily attending and serving Her Highness in safe-keeping of Her Grace's ship named the *Jesus* there by the space of 10 weeks 1 day, begun the 21th day of April last and this day ended, at 6s 8d *per mensem* – 16s 11d.

Mariners

The George Hoy

Giles Hall, master, 4 weeks 2 days	21s 6d
Richard Abraham, 3 weeks 6 days	6s 5d
John Kynge, cook, 3 weeks 3 days	7s 10½d
John Bennett, 4 weeks 2 days	7s 2d
John Leache, 4 weeks 2 days	7s 2d
Andrew Everington, 3 weeks 5 days	6s 2d
John Quade, 4 weeks 2 days	7s 2d
John Halle, boy, 4 weeks 2 days	3s 7d
Thomas Elkyn, 3 days	12d
Thomas Newlande, 3 days	12d

[*Page total*] – £17 0s 7½d.

[f. 188v] *Shipwrights*

Edward Bright, master, 91 days at 12d	£4 11s
Thomas Juell, server, 75 days at 6d	37s 6d
John Lestowe, server, 53 days at 6d	26s 6d
Daniel Bright, server, 75 days at 6d	37s 6d
William Foster, server, 75 days at 6d	37s 6d
Matthew Baker, master, 91 days at 12d	£4 11s
Matthew Norton, server, 75 days at 6d	37s 6d
John Hoole, server, 75 days at 5d	31s 3d
Hugh Blande, server, 17 days at 6d	8s 6d
Philip Garret, 75 days at 6d	37s 6d
John Rande, 71½ days at 10d	59s 7d
James Cotes, server, 74½ days at 6d	37s 3d
George Flower, server, 74 days at 6d	37s
John Ellyson, 39 days at 8d	26s
John Halle, server, 49 days at 6d	24s 6d

John Dalton, 68 days at 7d	39s 8d
Davy Horne, server, 75 days at 4d	25s
Roger Rayner, 22 days at 6d	11s
Michael Too, 71 days at 7d	41s 5d
John Too, server, 74 days at 6d	37s
Edward Holborne, 74 days at 8d	49s 4d
Henry New, server, 74½ days at 5d	31s 0½d
Walter Holborne, 72 days at 8d	48s
William Wheler, server, 71 days at 5d	29s 7d
John Hayewarde, 50 days at 8d	33s 4d
Michael Gamon, server, 55 days at 6d	27s 6d
Henry Samon, server, 6 days at 4d	2s
Edward Briges, server, 54½ days at 3d	13s 7½d
John Brunett, 63½ days at 8d	42s 4d
John Wilkynson, server, 74½ days at 4d	24s 8d
Robert Baker, 73½ days at 6d	36s 9d

[*Page total*] – £55 12s 4d.

[f. 189] Richard Claye, 63 days at 8d	42s 8d
Robert Paddye, 46½ days at 7d	27s 1½d
William Wythered, server, 74½ days at 4d	24s 10d
William Spycer, 73 days at 7d	42s 7d
Thomas Osborne, server, 73½ days at 4d	24s 6d
Robert Waller, server, 74½ days at 2d	12s 5d
Thomas Robynson, 25½ days at 7d	14s 10½d
Stephen Robynson, server, 49½ days at 5d	20s 7½d
Edward Clarke, 74½ days at 7d	43s 5½d
Edward Davye, server, 73½ days at 3d	18s 4½d
Richard Farrer, 6 days at 7d	3s 6d
Thomas Deakon, server, 6 days at 6d	3s
Henry Greaves, 64 days at 7d	37s 4d
Thomas Bonnam, server, 74½ days at 5d	31s 0½d
William Greaves, 73½ days at 9d	55s 1½d
Thomas Hewes, server, 73½ days at 6d	36s 9d
Edward Tutmarshe, server, 74½ days at 6d	37s 3d
William Larde, server, 46½ days at 6d	23s 3d
Richard Johnson, server, 73½ days at 6d	36s 9d
Randall Wood, 55½ days at 7d	32s 4½d
Robert Davye, 70½ days at 6d	35s 3d
Henry Freman, 68 days at 6d	34s
Robert Ashetun, 67 days at 6d	33s 6d
Davy Baker, 67½ days at 6d	33s 9d

John Myssontun, 62½ days at 7d	36s 5½d
James Dyggons, server, 71 days at 5d	29s 7d
Thomas Tyrrye, 66½ days at 7d	38s 9½d
William Grenewaye, server, 59 days at 6d	29s 6d
John Segg, server, 60 days at 4d	20s
Thomas Harman, 66 days at 7d	38s 6d
Nicholas Addams, server, 74½ days at 3d	18s 7½d
John Pett, server, 46½ days at 8d	31s
Robert Pett, server, 71½ days at 5d	21s 8d
George Upson, 71½ days at 6d	35s 9d
Henry Upson, server, 74½ days at 4d	24s 10d
Richard Payne, 68 days at 6d	34s
Thomas Moore, server, 74½ days at 4d	24s 10d

[*Page total*] – £54 7s 10½d.

[f. 189v] Thomas Bryan, 69 days at 7d	40s 3d
Richard Cooke, server, 55½ days at 4d	18s 6d
John Diggons, 74½ days at 6d	37s 3d
Lewis Richardes, 33½ days at 6d	16s 9d
Anthony Holdernes, 62 days at 7d	36s 2d
John Juell, server, 73½ days at 6d	36s 9d
William Graye, server, 63 days at 2d	10s 6d
Thomas Whomes, 72½ days at 6d	36s 3d
Richard Rooke, 44½ days at 6d	22s 3d
William Evered, server, 44½ days at 4d	14s 10d
William Carro, 75 days at 6d	37s 6d
Thomas Hewes, 65 days at 6d	32s 6d
Richard Addams, 8 days at 8d	5s 4d
John Tyllie, server, 54 days at 6d	27s
Thomas White, server, 19½ days at 4d	6s 6d
William Sybley, server, 19½ days at 4d	6s 6d
Walter Claye, 27 days at 6d	13s 6d
William Pellam, 61 days at 6d	30s 6d
Richard Badcock, 41 days at 6d	20s 6d
Henry Homan, 55 days at 6d	27s 6d
Robert Haman, 61 days at 4d	20s 4d
Robert Hodgekynson, 42½ days at 8d	28s 4d
Thomas Heell, server, 56 days at 3d	14s
John Taddwell, server, 61 days at 3d	15s 3d
Robert Fyssher, 59 days at 5d	24s 7d
John Clarke, 64½ days at 8d	43s
George Graye, server, 73½ days at 4d	24s 6d

Nicholas Johnson, 2 days at 10d	20d
Thomas Johnson, server, 2 days at 4d	8d
Richard Cooke, 3 days at 7d	21d
Ralph Broune, 2 days at 6d	12d
John Golding, 4 days at 8d	2s
Thomas Eatton, server, 3 days at 4d	12d
Henry Harteley, 2 days at 7d	14d
William Androes, server, 43 days at 4d	14s 4d
Robert Wright, server, 60½ days at 6d	30s 3d
Raynold New, server, 71 days at 6d	35s 6d
John Hooper, 48 days at 6d	24s
Robert Smyth, 18 days at 6d	9s
[*Page total*] – £38 9s 2d.	
[f. 190] James Dixson, 17 days at 10d	14s 2d
Richard Ryse, server, 17 days at 8d	11s 4d
Thomas Blosse, 9 days at 8d	6s
Henry Nealle, server, 9 days at 5d	3s 9d
John Winny, 9 days at 8d	6s
John Wythers, server, 9 days at 6d	4s 6d
John Mylles, 2 days at 7d	14d
Robert Archer, server, 2 days at 4d	8d
Robert Hutson, 9 days at 7d	5s 3d
Thomas Wythered, server, 9 days at 4d	3s
Caulkers	
Thomas Bolton, master, 46 days at 10d	38s 4d
William Bolton, server, 37½ days at 6d	18s 9d
John Flower, server, 37½ days at 6d	18s 9d
Robert Brygges, 23 days at 7d	13s 5d
Humphrey Dayll, server, 37½ days at 6d	18s 9d
Robert White, 32½ days at 7d	18s 11½d
Henry Reade, server, 36½ days at 4d	12s 2d
Michael Rowse, 37½ days at 6d	18s 9d
John Stockdayll, 32 days at 7d	18s 8d
John Eastun, 18 days at 6d	9s
Thomas Wynchester, server, 34½ days at 2d	5s 9d
Thomas Coxe, 37½ days at 6d	18s 9d
William Forde, 37½ days at 7d	2s 10½d
Robert Richardes, 14½ days at 7d	8s 5½d
John Castellman, server, 18½ days at 4d	6s 2d
Thomas Pavye, 33½ days at 7d	19s 6½d
Edward Hyllyard, server, 37½ days at 4d	12s 6d

John Hayeward, 8½ days at 7d	4s 11½d
Nicholas Hayewarde, server, 7 days at 5d	2s 11d
William Wood, server, 8½ days at 2d	17d
Gregory Knightlye,[1] 18½ days at 7d	16s 7½d

[*Page total*] – £18 0s 4d.

[f. 190v] William Bastyane, 7½ days at 6d	3s 9d
Arthur Charlles, 7½ days at 4d	2s 6d
John Bote,[2] 34½ days at 6d	17s 3d
Nicholas Archedayll, 45½ days at 6d	22s 9d
William Mundes, 18 days at 8d	12s
William Clappam, server, 18 days at 4d	6s
George Aparke, server, 18 days at 4d	6s
Walter Deane, 18 days at 7d	10s 6d
John Webb, 16 days at 7d	9s 4d
William Baggett, server, 5 days at 4d	20d
Thomas Farnnolde, server, 1 day at 4d	4d
Roger Collyns, 6 days at 6d	3s
William Bulbeck, 6 days at 8d	4s
Edmund Barrett, 5 days at 7d	2s 11d
William Thomas, 5 days at 6d	2s 6d
Richard Eastwood, 5 days at 8d	3s 4d
Cuthbert Lawre, server, 5 days at 6d	2s 6d
Jerome Tayller, server, 5 days at 4d	20d
John Graye, 5 days at 6d	2s 6d
George Browne, 1 day at 7d	7d
Richard Francke, server, 1 day at 3d	3d
Nicholas Claye, 5 days at 7d	2s 11d
William Addams, server, 5 days at 5d	2s 1d
John Sagar, server, 5 days at 5d	2s 1d
John Bunche, 3 days at 8d	2s
William Harber, 3 days at 4d	12d
William Welshe, 3 days at 8d	2s
Thomas Freman, 3 days at 5d	15d
Thomas Wilson, 91 days at 12d	£4 11s
John Hurleston, 91 days at 6d	45s 6d
Thomas Heely, 91 days at 6d	45s 6d
John Bradley, 91 days at 6d	45s 6d

[1]Miswritten 'Kingestlye', suggesting the scribe began to write a form of 'Kingsley'. The correct name is evident from the clearly written entry at f. 128v (above, p. 194).

[2]Very likely the John or James Bote, 'cawker', buried at Deptford 6 Aug. 1593, who in default of heirs bequeathed his house to the parish: Drake, *Hasted's Kent*, p. 51.

John Williamson, 91 days at 3d	22s 9d
Henry Rowse, 91 days at 3d	22s 9d
Thomas Norcott, 13½ days at 7d	7s 10½d
John Rodes, server, 14½ days at 5d	6s 0½d

[*Page total*] – £20 15s 7d.

[f. 191] *Sawyers*

Robert Hartt, master, 91 days at 8d	£3 0s 8d
Ellis Knoswell, 76½ days at 6d	38s 3d
Thomas Miller, 74½ days at 6d	37s 3d
Robert Davys, 74½ days at 6d	37s 3d
John Richardes, 74½ days at 6d	37s 3d
Robert Grene, 74½ days at 6d	37s 3d
Bennet Over, 58½ days at 6d	29s 3d
Robert Turnbull, 58½ days at 6d	29s 3d
Thomas Harbard, 41 days at 6d	20s 6d
Simon Arnolde, 41 days at 6d	20s 6d
William Lynche, 12 days at 6d	6s
Thomas Brome, 12 days at 6d	6s

Oarmakers

William Bexley, master, 31 days at 8d	20s 8d
William Kackett, server, 33 days at 6d	16s 6d
James Rumen, server, 33 days at 6d	16s 6d
Abraham Harman, server, 33 days at 6d	16s 6d
John Androwes, 38 days at 7d	22s 2d
Thomas Mowsse, server, 38 days at 6d	19s
Thomas Curtys, 21 days at 7d	12s 3d
John Peckover, server, 23 days at 6d	11s 6d
John Sellman, 23 days at 6d	11s 6d
John White, 20 days at 7d	11s 8d
Richard Haycock, server, 13 days at 6d	6s 6d
Christopher Ingler, server, 13 days at 6d	6s 6d

[*Page total*] – £26 10s 8d.

[f. 191v] *Smiths*

John Wright, 10 days at 6d	5s
John Tyller, 10 days at 6d	5s
	*[*10s*]

Joiners

William Hardwycke, master, 29 days at 12d	29s
Michael Goodyeare, server, 29 days at 8d	19s 4d
Edward Pursley, server, 29 days at 8d	19s 4d

Peter Geeze, 29 days at 10d	24s 2d
William Hynge, 29 days at 10d	24s 2d
John Hardwycke, 29 days at 10d	24s 2d
Herman Joynnar, 29 days at 10d	24s 2d
Ryce Upjohn, 5 days at 10d	4s 2d
	[£8 8s 6d*]

Victualling. To Thomas Willson of Ratcliff the last day of June for the victualling of 207 of the aforenamed shipwrights, caulkers, sawyers, oarmakers and others, working upon the new building and repairing of Her Grace's two ships called the *Great Bark* and the *Jesus* there by the space of 10,447 days among them all, the Sundays and holy days within the same accounted, begun the first day of April last, and this day ended, which maketh 1,492 weeks 3 days, at 4s 7d every week the man. *Summa* – £341 19s 4d

[*Page total*] – £350 17s 10d.

[f. 192] *Lodging.* To Joan Rocke, Eme Simpson, Joan Brighte, William Alley, Maude Fellon and 16 other persons of Deptford, Greenwich, Rotherhithe and thereabouts the last day of June for the lodging of 171 of the aforenamed shipwrights, caulkers, sawyers, oarmakers, smiths and joiners in 86 featherbeds, working upon the new building and repairing of Her Majesty's said two ships the *Great Bark* and the *Jesus* there, by the space of 1,511 weeks among them all begun the first day of April last and this day ended, at 2d every week the man – £12 11s 10d.

House-carpenters	
John Leache, master, 76 days at 12d	£3 16s
Robert Throughley, server, 52 days at 10d	43s 4d
Thomas Byggen, server, 76 days at 10d	£3 3s 4d
Thomas Awood, 7 days at 10d	5s 10d
Tilers	
John Callawaye, master, 24 days at 12d	24s
Stephen Huggyns, 24 days at 10d	20s
Richard Savage, server, 24 days at 10d	20s
Michael Hutchyns, server, 24 days at 8d	16s

[*Page total*] – £26 0s 4d.*[*Lodging – £12 11s 10d; artificers – £13 8s 6d*]

[f. 192v] *Labourers*

William Alley, master, 20 nights at 4d	6s 8d
Richard Raynsforth, 78 days and nights at 7d	44s 11d

Henry Stevenson, 77 days and nights at 6d	38s 6d
Thomas Thisselton, 83 days and nights at 6d	41s 6d
John Gybson, 54 days at 6d	27s
William Twayttes, 78 days and nights at 6d	39s
John Bastyan, 87 days and nights at 6d	43s 6d
John Addams, 83 days and nights at 6d	41s 6d
James Teeyll, 78 days and nights at 6d	39s
Lawrence Langcaster, 47 days at 6d	23s 6d
William Apprice, 2 days at 6d	12d
Richard Coxe, 37½ days at 6d	18s 9d
John Jyans, 61½ days and nights at 6d	30s 9d
Morgan Apprice, 69 days at 6d	34s 6d
Anthony Westlonde, 71½ days at 6d	35s 9d
John Sturdgeon, 81½ days and nights at 6d	40s 9d
William Sealle, 75 days at 6d	37s 6d
Bernard Nackyll, 53 days at 6d	26s 6d
Thomas Clarke, 9 days at 6d	4s 6d
John Watson, 51½ days at 6d	25s 9d
William Pythen, 84½ days and nights at 6d	42s 3d
Thomas Tressam, 88 days and nights at 6d	44s
William Maddock, 50 days at 6d	25s
Lewis Howell, 6½ days at 6d	3s 3d
John Brace, 79 days at 6d	39s 6d
Hugh Apgullapp, 50 days at 6d	25s
John Raby, 80 days and nights at 6d	40s
John Bussington, 74 days and nights at 6d	37s
John Mansffylde, 49½ days at 6d	24s 9d
Robert Stevens, 70½ days at 6d	35s 3d
Thomas Watson, 38 days at 6d	19s
Henry Dune, 26 days at 6d	13s
Christopher Robynson, 30 days at 6d	15s
William Brock, 71 days at 6d	35s 6d
Thomas Jonnes, 34 days at 6d	17s

[*Page total*] – £50 16s 4d.

[f. 193] William Durrant, 30 days at 6d	15s
Thomas Lawtun, 27 days at 6d	13s 6d
Thomas Hobson, 23½ days at 6d	11s 9d
William Sharpp, 25 days at 6d	12s 6d
John Berde, 34 days at 6d	17s
Richard Shaft, 45 days at 6d	22s 6d
Owen Upjohn, 10½ days and nights at 6d	5s 3d

William Lewys, 8½ days at 6d — 4s 3d
Thomas Mounser, 2 days at 6d — 12d
William Dutton, 24 days at 6d — 12s
John Hayne, 88 days and nights at 6d — 44s
Upp John, 88 days and nights at 6d — 44s
William Barnarde, 88 days and nights at 6d — 44s
Thomas Elkyn, 2 days at 6d — 12d

[£12 7s 9d*]

Watchmen

Nicholas Archedayll, 30 nights at 4d — 10s
William Twayttes, 30 nights at 4d — 10s
John Hurlstone, 30 nights at 4d — 10s
William Currar, 30 nights at 4d — 10s
John Addams, 30 nights at 4d — 10s
Thomas Thisseltun, 30 nights at 4d — 10s
John Sturdgeon, 30 nights at 4d — 10s
William Pattrick, 30 nights at 4d — 10s
Henry Stevenson, 30 nights at 4d — 10s
Anthony Westlonde, 30 nights at 4d — 10s
John Hayen, 30 nights at 4d — 10s
John Jans, 30 nights at 4d — 10s
Thomas Heele, 16 nights at 4d — 5s 4d
John Berde, 16 nights at 4d — 5s 4d
Upp John, 16 nights at 4d — 5s 4d
Richard Shafte, 16 nights at 4d — 5s 4d

[*Page total*] – £19 9s 1d.

[f. 193v] *Ironwork.* To Thomas Willson of Ratcliff, smith, the last day of June for price of 3 thousand 2 hundred 3 quarters 10 pounds weight [*3,678 lbs*] of his own new iron by him made and wrought into spikes of all sorts, clench, rove, overlop nails, bolts with rings and keys, and the same delivered at Deptford into Her Highness's great storehouse there for the use of Her Grace's ships, at 23s 4d every hundredweight – £38 6s 3d; more for 12,950 of 10d nail, at 8s 4d every 1,000 – £5 7s 11d; more for 24,600 of 6d nail, at 5s every 1,000 – £6 3s; more for 12,000 of 4d nail, at 3s 4d every 1,000 – 40s; and more to him for 22,350 of 3d nail, at 2s 6d every 1,000 – 55s 10½d. *Summa* – £54 13s 0½d.

To Thomas Ivey of Limehouse, smith, the same day for price of 3 thousand [*one*] quarter 15 pounds weight [*3,403 lbs*] of his own new iron by him made and wrought into spikes of all sorts, clench, rove, overlop nails, bolts with rings and keys, and the same delivered as aforesaid for the use of Her Majesty's ships, at 23s 4d every hundredweight – £35 8s

11½d; more for the working of [*one*] hundred 7 pounds weight [*119 lbs*] of Her Grace's old iron into like bolts and spikes for the use as aforesaid, at 8s 4d every hundredweight – 8s 11d;[1] more for 7,700 of 10d nail, at 8s 4d every 1,000 – £3 4s 2d; more for 6,700 of 6d nail, at 5s every 1,000 – 33s 6d; more for 8,100 of 4d nail, at 3s 4d every 1,000 – 27s; and more to him for 8,400 of 3d nail, at 2s 6d every 1,000 – 21s. *Summa* – £43 3s 6½d.

To Richard Welles of Greenwich, smith, the same day for price of [*one*] thousand [*one*] hundred 2 quarters weight [*1,288 lbs*] of his own new iron by him wrought into bolts, spikes, clench, rove and overlop nails, and the same delivered as abovesaid for the use of Her Highness's ships, at 23s 4d every hundredweight – £13 8s 4d.

[*Page total*] – £111 4s 11d.*[*With £23 12s 5½d for nails*]

[f. 194] *Ironwork.* To John Sheldon of Rowley,[2] smith, the last day of June for price of 11,300 of 2s nail of him had and the same delivered into Her Majesty's great storehouse at Deptford for the use of Her Grace's ships, at 20s every 1,000 – £10 6s; more for 6,000 of 20d nail, at 16s 8d every 1,000 – £5; more for 3,700 of 10d nail, at 8s 4d every 1,000 – 30s 10d; more for 22,000 of 6d nail, at 5s every 1,000 – £5 10s; more for 18,000 of 4d nail, at 3s 4d every 1,000 – £3; more for 15,700 of 3d nail, at 2s 6d every 1,000 – 39s 3d; and more to him for 5,000 of 2d nail, at 20d every 1,000 – 8s 4d. *Summa* – £28 14s 5d.

To Robert Bradley of Southwark, smith, the same day for price of 5,600 of inch brods by him delivered as aforesaid for the use of Her Highness's ships, at 6d every 100 – 28s; more for 5,600 of brods of inch ½ long, at 8d every 100 – 37s 4d; more for 1,600 brods of 2 inches long, at 10d every 100 – 13s 4d; and more to him for 1,500 of brods of 3 inches long, at 14d every 100 – 17s 6d. *Summa* – £4 16s 2d.

To Peter Whalley of London, ironmonger, the same day for price of 8 iron pots by him delivered there for the use of Her Majesty's ships, at 8s the piece – £3 4s; more for four iron pots, at 6s 8d the piece – 26s 8d; more for one iron pot, price 7s 6d; and more to him for 2½ somes of English nails, at 16s 8d every some – 41s 8d. *Summa* – £6 19s 10d.

To William Pennyfather of London the same day for price of 3 somes of English 2d nails by him delivered as aforesaid for the use of Her Grace's ships, at 16s 8d every some – £2 10s.

[*Page total*] – £43 0s 5d. *[*With £33 6s 1d for nails*]

[1] The calculation gives 106.24999d, which is ¾d below the sum stated (107d).

[2] Rowley Regis in Staffordshire, as evident below (p. 431), though this man is also (p. 200) said to be of the Forest of Dean (in Gloucestershire).

[f. 194v] *Shovels, scoops, bowls, parrels and pulleys.* To John Benbow of London the last day of June for price of 17 dozen of steel shovels of him had and the same delivered into Her Grace's great storehouse at Deptford for the use of Her Majesty's ships, at 8s every dozen – £5 16s; more for 6 dozen of scoops, at 5s every dozen – 30s; more for 13 dozen of great bowls for pitch and rosin, at 10s every dozen – £6 10s; more for 3 parrels of one set, at 12d the piece – 3s; more for 3 parrels of 3 set, at 3s the piece – 9s; more for 4 parrels of 5 set, at 13s 4d the piece – 53s 4d; more for 8 parrels of 4 set, at 10s the piece – £4; more for 10 parrels of 3 set, at 3s 4d the piece – 33s 4d; more for 14 parrels of 2 set, price 16s 8d; more for 2 dozen of great pendant pulleys, at 2s the piece – 48s; more for 4 dozen of pulleys, at 20d the piece – £4; more for 5½ dozen of pulleys, at 16d the piece – £4 8s; more for 5 dozen of pulleys, at 12d the piece – £3; more for 4 dozen of pulleys, at 10d the piece – 40s; more for 9 dozen of pulleys, at 8d the piece – £3 12s; more for 8 dozen and one pulleys, at 6d the piece – 48s 6d; more for 8½ dozen of pulleys, at 4d the piece – 34s; more for 4 dozen of pulleys, at 3d the piece – 12s; and more to him for 4 dozen of pulleys, at 2d the piece – 8s. *Summa* – £49 1s 10d.

Pump-hose, claps and scupper-leathers. To John Harryson of Tower Hill, shoemaker, the same day for price of 5 dozen of great pump-hose by him delivered as aforesaid for the use of Her Highness's ships, at 2s 8d the piece – £8; more for 12 small pump-hose, at 16d the piece – 16s; more for 2½ dozen of great claps, at 16d the piece – 40s; more for 12 small claps, at 8d the piece – 8s; and more to him for 6 dozen of scupper-leathers, at 16d the piece – £4 16s. *Summa* – £16.

[*Page total*] – £65 1s 10d.

[f. 195] *Canvas, pitch, tar, oakum, deal-boards, caulking oil, rosin and divers kinds of cordage, &c.* *[*Cordage – £230 13s 1d*; *pitch, tar and rosin – £140 3s 10d*; *poldavis – £550*; *ironwork – 40s*; *boards – £7 9s 4d*]. To Christopher Draper of London, alderman, the last day of June for price of 3 last of pitch of the great band by him delivered into Her Highness's great storehouse at Deptford for the use of Her Grace's ships, at £4 13s 4d every last – £14; more for 200 coil of white ropes for crane ropes, weighing [*one*] thousand [*one*] hundred [*one*] quarter 23 pounds weight [*1,283 lbs*], at 28s every hundredweight – £16 0s 9d; more for 300 pieces of poldavis canvas, at 36s 8d every piece – £550; more for 28 pieces of tarred ropes weighing 3 thousand 6 hundredweight [*4,032 lbs*], at 21s 4d every hundred[*weight*] – £38 8s; more for 2 sacks with hemp oakum weighing [*one*] thousand [*one*] hundred 2 quarters 14 pounds weight [*1,302 lbs*], at 20s every hundred[*weight*] – £11 12s 6d; more for one dryfat with 69 dozen of white twine, at 7s every dozen – £23 3s; more for a great iron beam, price – 40s; more for 2 hogsheads with caulking oil, at 55s every hogshead – £5 10s; more for [*one*] thousand 3 hundred 21 pounds weight [*1,477 lbs*] of rosin, at 8s every hundred[*weight*] – £5 5s 6d; more for 16 last and one barrel of pitch, at £5 every last – £80 8s 4d; more for 5 last of tar, at £5 every last – £25; more for 1,000 of rowan needles, price – 33s 4d; more for 75 pieces of tarred hawsers weighing 6 thousand 9 hundred 3 quarters weight [*7,812 pounds*], at 21s 4d every hundredweight – £74 8s; more for 203 pieces of small tarred latchet lines weighing 5 thousand 3 hundred 14 pounds weight [*5,950 lbs*], at 28s every hundredweight – £74 7s 6d; and more to him for 128 Norway deal-boards, at 14d every board – £7 9s 4d. *Summa* – £930 6s 3d.

Rafters. To Michael Rozenby of London, merchant, the same day for price of 2 hundred [*240*][1] long rafters for oars of him taken and the same delivered as aforesaid for the use of Her Grace's galleys, of 33 foot long a piece, at £12 10s every hundred after 6 score to the hundred. *Summa* – £25.

[*Page total*] – £955 6s 3d.

[f. 195v] *Deal-boards, pitch, tar, rosin, caulking oil, &c.* *[*Rosin and oil* – (*£19* deleted) *£22*;[2] *deal-boards and spars – £21 1s 8d*; *thrums – 52s 6d*; *masts – £5*] To William Paige of London, merchant, the last day of June for price of one thousandweight of rosin by him delivered into Her Grace's storehouse there for the use of Her Majesty's ships, at 8s every hundred[*weight*] – £4; more for 2 last of pitch, at £5 the last – £10; more for one last of tar, price – £5; more for one hogshead of caulking oil, price – £3; more for 12 spars, at 5d the piece – 5s; more for 12 spars, at 6d the piece – 6s; more for 2 shock of deal-boards, after 60 boards to the shock at 3s 4d the piece – £20; more for 2 hundred one quarter weight [*252 lbs*] of thrums, at 2½d the pound – 52s 6d; more for 6 wainscot boards, at 16d the piece – 8s; more for 2 white boards, price 2s 8d; and more to him for 10 Norway masts of 6, 7, and 8 hands about, at 10s the piece – £5. *Summa* – £50 14s 2d.

Ballast baskets and maunds. To Christian Edes of London, widow, the same day for price of 25 dozen of ballast baskets by her delivered there for the use of the Queen's Majesty's ships, at 22d every dozen – £2 5s 10d; more for 9 dozen and 10 baskets, at 6d the piece – 59s; more for

[1]As shown explicitly below (pp. 302–3), reckoning by long hundred affects the quantity stated as well as the rate, so here the actual supply was 240 items. Further entries make it clear that the word 'long' in the text describes the rafters not the hundreds.

[2]The auditor originally counted the pitch and tar with the rosin (making £19) and then added the oil (£3) to reach the revised sub-total.

8 dozen of middle baskets, at 4d the piece – 32s; more for 3 dozen of 4-eared[1] baskets, at 18d the piece – 54s; more for 2 dozen of great maunds, at 12d the piece – 24s; and more to her for 3 dozen of baskets, at 8d the piece – 24s. *Summa* – £11 18s 10d.

Running glasses. To Richard Stevens of Tower Hill, compass-maker, the same day for price of 4 dozen of running glasses of him had and the same delivered as is aforesaid for the use of Her Grace's ships, at 10s every dozen – £2.

[*Page total*] – £64 13s.

[f. 196] *Hinges, staples, locks and keys, glue and rubbing stones.* To William Hardwicke of London, joiner, the last day of June for certain ironwork of him had for use of the cabin by him set up in Her Grace's ship the *Jesus* there, *viz.* for 6 pair of portal hinges for the doors, at 18d every pair – 9s; more for 17 pair of hinges for settles, at 18d every pair – 25s 6d; more for one pair of cross-hinges, price – 18d; more for 12 bolts with staples, at 6d the piece – 6s; more for 6 locks with keys for settles,[2] at 18d the piece – 9s; more for 6 latches with catches and staples, at 12d the piece – 6s; more for 18 hinges for doors, at 4d the piece – 6s; more for 3 bars of iron for stays with staples, at 16d the piece – 4s; more for a key, price – 8d; more for 24 pounds weight of glue, at 4d the pound – 8s; and more to him for 2 rubbing stones,[3] at 8d the piece – 16d. *Summa* – £3 17s.

Red say and white lockram. To Stephen Andrоes of London, upholsterer, the same day for price of 3 pieces of red say of him had for the making of new flags for the use of Her Grace's ships, at 36s every piece – £5 8s; more for 6½ yards of red say, at 16d the yard – 8s 8d; more for one piece of white lockram, price – £5 10s; more for 6 yards of lockram, at 12d every yard – 6s; more for 10 yards of oleron, at 8d the yard – 6s 8d; more for making of 8 great new flags with the cross of St George, at 2s 4d every flag – 18s 8d; and more to him for making of four small flags, at 16d the piece – 5s 4d. *Summa* – £13 3s 4d.

Bails. To William Scarlett of Paris Garden the same day for price of 3 long bails[4] of him had for the use of Her Grace's galliot, at 2s every bail. *Summa* – 6s.

[*Page total*] – £17 6s 4d.

[1]Meaning four-handled: cf. *OED* 'ear' *sb.*¹. 8.

[2]Here and elsewhere indicating that these benches had cupboards below the seats: cf. *OED* 'settle' *sb.*¹. 3.

[3]Rubstones or whetstones in the general sense.

[4]A *bail* might simply be a cross-bar (the usage which passed into the terminology of cricket), but the meaning here is more likely to be hoops supporting a tilt or canopy: *OED* 'bail' *sb.*². 1.

[f. 196v] *Canvas.* To John Collyns of London, merchant, the last day of June for price of 16 bolts of medrinacks of English making by him delivered into Her Grace's great storehouse at Deptford for the use of Her Majesty's ships, at 35s every bolt. *Summa* – £28.

To Francis Allvaye of London, merchant, the same day for the price of 14 pieces of oleron of English making of him had and the same delivered as aforesaid for the use of Her Grace's ships, at 35s every piece – £24 10s.

Timber and plank oak. To Christopher Nayller of London the same day for price of 10 loads 8 foot of compass and long timber oak of him had and the same delivered there for the use of Her Highness's ships, at 10s every load after 50 foot to the load – £5 0s 8d; more for 5,766 foot of 4-inch plank oak, at 12s every 100 [*foot*] – £34 11s 10d; more for 8,383 foot of 3-inch plank oak, at 10s every 100 foot – £41 18s 2d; more for 1,070 foot of 2-inch plank oak, at 8s every 100 foot – £4 5s 7d. *Summa* – £85 16s 3d.

To John Leache of Deptford the same day for price of 56 loads of compass and long timber oak by him delivered there for the use as aforesaid, at 10s every load after 50 foot to the load – £28; more for 6 loads of ash of talwood mark, after 50 shide to the load at 5s every load with the carriage – 30s; more for felling of 131 loads of shores in Her Grace's wood called West Wood, at 3d every load – 32s 9d; and more to him for four labourers working in the same wood by the space of 39 days among them, at 7d every day – 22s 9d. *Summa* – £32 5s 6d.

[*Page total*] – £170 11s 9d.

[f. 197] *Timber, plank, and, board oak.* To John Dethicke of Colchester, purveyor, the last day of June for price of 92½ loads of compass and long timber oak by him delivered at Deptford for the use of Her Grace's ships, at 10s every load after 50 foot to the load – £46 5s; more for 2,000 foot of 4-inch plank oak, at 10s every 100 [*foot*] – £10; more for 3,050 foot of 3-inch plank oak, at 10s every 100 foot – £15 5s; more for 2,215 foot of 2-inch plank oak, at 8s every 100 foot – £8 17s 2d; and more to him for 2,000 foot of inch board oak, at 5s every 100 [*foot*] – £5. *Summa* – £85 7s 2d.

To John Stebyns of Salcott in Essex the same day for price of 86 loads of compass and long timber oak by him delivered as aforesaid for the use of Her Majesty's ships, at 10s every load – £43; more for 2,000 foot of 4-inch plank oak, at 12s every 100 [*foot*] – £12; more for 1,350 foot of 2-inch plank oak, at 10s every 100 foot – £6 15s; more for 1,200 of 2½ inch plank [*oak*], at 8s every 100 foot – £4 16s; and more to him for 636 foot of inch board oak, at 5s every 100 [*foot*] – £1 11s 9d. *Summa* – £68 2s 9d.

To Henry Layne of Erith the same day for price of 46½ loads of compass and long timber oak of him had and the same delivered as abovesaid for the use of Her Highness's ships, at 10s every load – £23 5s.

To George Brydger the same day for price of 89 loads of compass and long timber oak of him had and the same delivered as aforesaid for the use of Her Grace's ships there, at 10s every load after 50 foot to the load – £44 10s.

[*Page total*] – £221 4s 11d.

[f. 197v] *Plank.* To Matthew Baker of Blackwall the last day of June for price of 1,000 foot of 4-inch plank oak of him had and the same delivered at Deptford for the use of Her Grace's ships there, at 10s every 100 foot, after 5 score to the hundred – £5.

New lead. To John Hemmynge of London, plumber, for price of [*one*] thousand 8 hundred [*one*] quarter 3 pounds [*2,047 lbs*] weight of new lead of him had and the same delivered as aforesaid for the use of Her Highness's ships, at 15s every hundredweight – £13 14s 6d.[1]

Water carriage of provisions. To Vincent Poulle of St Katherine's the same day for service of his hoy of the portage of 40 tuns, with three other his servants, serving Her Highness for the carrying of Her Grace's timber and plank from Woolwich to Deptford by sundry freights and there delivered the same for the use of Her Majesty's ships, by the space of 5 weeks 5 days begun the 8th day of April last and ended the 17th day of May next, at 3s 4d every tun *per mensem* – £9 10s 5d.

To Thomas Grene, master, the same day for the service of his hoy named the *Draggon of London*, of the portage of 50 tuns, serving Her Highness in carrying of divers and sundry provisions from London to Portsmouth and there delivered the same for the use of Her Grace's ships, by the space of 6 weeks begun the first day of April last and ended the 13th day of May then next, at 3s 4d every tun *per mensem* – *Summa* – £12 10s.

[*Page total*] – £40 14s 11d.

[f. 198] *Paper, ink and counters.* To William Prestwood of London, merchant, the last day of June for price of 6 reams of paper royal and 10 quires of him had for the making of pay books for shipwrights, caulkers and others working upon Her Grace's ships at Deptford, Woolwich, Gillingham and Portsmouth, and for the engrossing of the same, at 20s every ream – £6 10s; more for 14½ reams and 3 quires of small paper, at 6s 8d every ream – £4 17s 8d; more for 3 gallons and one pottle of ink, at 5s 4d every gallon – 18s 8d; more for 3 books of paper royal, price –

[1]The calculation gives 3289.8213d, which is about 4¼d below the sum stated (3294d).

15s; and more to him for one pound weight of counters, price – 2s 8d. *Summa* – £13 4s.

Lime and sand. To John Parratt of Deptford, limeman, the same day for price of 8 hundred[*weight*] of lime of him had for the mending and repairing of Her Grace's storehouses there, at 7s every hundred[*weight*] – 56s; and more to him for 7 loads of sand, at 8d every load – 4s 8d. *Summa* – £3 0s 8d.

Tile. To James Brookehowse of Lewisham the same day for price of 8,000 of house tile of him taken for the use as aforesaid, at 12s every 1,000 – £4 16s; and more to him for 60 roof tile, at 2d the piece – 10s. *Summa* – £5 6s.

Reed. To John Ashe of London the same day for price of 1,000 of burning reed by him delivered at Deptford for the needful breaming of Her Highness's ships at their groundings, at 12d every 100 – 10s.

Pumps. To William Bexley the same day for price of 7 long pumps of him had for the use of Her Grace's ships, containing 164 foot at 12d every foot. *Summa* – £8 4s.

[*Page total*] – £30 4s 8d.

[f. 198v] *Netting-, wrain-ropes and oakum.* To William Brooke of Deptford, ropemaker, the last day of June for the workmanship of 2 thousand 6 hundred 2 quarters weight [*2,968 lbs*] of Her Grace's old junks and ropes by him wrought into netting- and wrain-ropes for the use of Her Highness's ships, at 3s 8d every hundredweight – £4 17s 2d.

To Thomas Russell of Ratcliff, ropemaker, the same day for the like workmanship of 9 hundred 3 quarters weight [*1,092 lbs*] of Her Highness's old junks and ropes into netting- and wrain-ropes for the use as aforesaid, at 3s 8d every hundredweight – £1 15s 9d.

To Annes Butler, John Johnson, Thomas Wilson, Edward Cockes and Elizabeth Jarvys the same day for the working and picking of [*one*] thousand [*one*] hundred 3 quarters weight [*1,316 lbs*] of Her Grace's old junks and ropes into oakum for the needful caulking of Her Highness ships at their groundings, at 3s 8d every hundredweight working – £2 3s 1d.

New working of brass. To Robert Hunt of London, founder, the same day for the new working and casting of 2 quarters 13 pounds weight [*69 lbs*] of Her Highness's old brass by him made into cocks and shivers for the use of Her Grace's ships, at 4d every pound weight casting – £1 3s.

Hire of a lighter. To William Provyze of Deptford the same day for the hire of his lighter serving Her Highness in carrying of 22½ loads of shores from Deptford aforesaid to Woolwich and there delivered the same for the use of Her Grace's ships, at 12d every load carrying – £1 2s 6d.

[*Page total*] – £11 1s 6d.

[f. 199] *Sye or hair.* To John Stampp of Brightlingsea the last day of June for price of 45 stone and one quarter [*633½ lbs*][1] of sye or hair of him had and the same delivered at Deptford for the use of Her Grace's ships, at 16d every stone – £3 0s 4d.

A skiff. To William Partridge of Wapping, shipwright, the same day for price of one new skiff by him made and the same delivered for the use of Her Grace's ship called the *Sun*, price – £2 6s 8d.

A new top. To William Carter of Wapping, shipwright, the same day for price of one new top of him had and by him delivered for the use of Her Grace's said ship named the *Sun*, price – 10s.

Raw hide. To Nicholas Chatfeild of London, butcher, the same day for price of one raw hide of him had and the same delivered for the use of Her Grace's ship named the *Falcon*. *Summa* – 10s.

House rent. To Peter Pett of Deptford the same day for one quarter of a year's rent of two cellars of him hired wherein lieth Her Grace's store of rosin for the use of Her Highness's ships; due at this present – £1.

[*Page total*] – £7 7s. [f. 199v *blank*]

[f. 200] *Anno Domini 1563. Anno regni regine Elizabethe quinto*

A payment made the last day of September as well to masters, mariners, keepers of storehouses, docks and timber-yards there wherein lieth Her Grace's store of all manner of provisions needful for the use of her ships, and to shipwrights, caulkers, sawyers, oarmakers and other artificers and labourers for the new building of Her Highness's ship the *Great Bark* and making of four other new galliots there, *viz*. the *Post*, the *Guide*, the *Searcher* and the *Makeshift*;[2] as also to divers persons for sundry kinds of provisions and necessaries by them delivered and the same received into Her Majesty's great storehouse at Deptford Strand for the use of Her Grace's said ships; by one quarter of a year begun the first day of July and this day ended, as followeth:

*[*Keeper of timber-yard*]. To Thomas Marshe, mariner, the last day of September for his wages daily attending and serving Her Highness for the safe-keeping of Her Grace's provisions of divers kinds of stuffs lying in her timber-yards there, and for the rigging and tackling of Her Majesty's ships to the seas, by one whole quarter of a year containing 13

[1]Because, as the calculation demonstrates (633.5 × 16d =724d), this means 45¼ stone not 45 stone + 1 quarter (of cwt).

[2]None of these small vessels saw long service. *Searcher* and *Guide* were sold to London merchants in the following year; *Post* was lost in 1566; and *Makeshift* was simply discarded by 1568: Glasgow, 'List', p. 305.

weeks one day begun the first day of July last and ended as is abovesaid, at 20s every month – £3 5s 8d.

[*Page total*] – £3 5s 8d.

[f. 200v] *[*Shipkeeper*]. To William Rogers, mariner, the last day of September for his wages daily attending and serving Her Majesty in safe-keeping of Her Grace's ship called the *Jesus* there, by the space of 13 months [*recte* weeks] one day begun the first day of October last and ended as is abovesaid, at 20s every month – £13 0s 8d; and more to him for his victuals for like time, at 6s 8d *per mensem* – £4 6s 11d. *Summa* – £17 7s 7d.

*[*Mariners' wages for carrying provisions and coiling up of cables*]. To John Benwell, mariner, the same day for his wages daily attending and serving Her Highness in labouring about the carrying and coiling up of cables, hawsers, warps and other provisions into Her Grace's great storehouse at Deptford and delivering out of the same again to the use of Her Majesty's ships, by one quarter of a year containing 13 weeks one day begun the first day of July last and this day ended, at 13s 4d every month – £2 3s 10d.

To Richard Harwoode, mariner, the same day for his wages daily attending and serving Her Majesty in labouring about the coiling, carriage and delivering of cables, hawsers, warps and other provisions as aforesaid, by like time of 13 weeks one day begun and ended as abovesaid, at 6s 8d *per mensem* – 21s 11d; and more to him for his victuals for like time, at 20d every week – 21s 11d. *Summa* – £2 3s 10d.

To Robert Tasse, mariner, the same day for his wages and victuals daily attending and serving Her Highness in labouring about the like carriage of provisions and coiling up of cables and hawsers into Her Grace's said storehouses there, by the space of 13 weeks one day begun and ended as is abovesaid, at 13s 4d every month – £2 3s 10d.

[*Page total*] – £23 19s 1d.

[f. 201] *[*Mariners' wages for carrying of provisions and coiling up of cables*]. To William Currea and Henry Bareffoote, mariners, the last day of September for their wages and victuals daily attending and serving Her Highness in labouring about the carriage of provisions and coiling of cables and hawsers into Her Grace's great storehouse there, by the space of 13 weeks one day begun the first day of July last and this day ended, at 13s 4d either of them *per mensem*. *Summa* – £4 7s 8d.

To Robert Woode and Richard Tooken, mariners, the same day for their wages and victuals daily attending and serving Her Majesty in labouring about the coiling, carriage and delivering of cables, hawsers and other provisions as aforesaid, by like time of 13 weeks one day begun and ended as is abovesaid, at 13s 4d either of them *per mensem* – £4 7s 8d.

To William Pattricke, mariner, the same day for his wages daily attending and serving Her Highness in labouring about the carrying of provisions and coiling up of cables and hawsers as aforesaid, by like 13 weeks one day begun and ended as abovesaid, at 6s 8d every month – £1 1s 11d.

To John Kynge, mariner, the same day for his wages daily attending and serving Her Majesty in labouring about the coiling, carrying and delivering of provisions as abovesaid, by like time of 13 weeks one day begun and ended as aforesaid, at 6s 8d *per mensem* – £1 1s 11d.

To Thomas Elye, mariner, the same day for his wages daily attending and serving Her Highness in labouring about the carriage of provisions and coiling up of cables and hawsers as is aforesaid, by the space of 6 weeks 5 days within this quarter begun the first day of July last and ended the 16th day of August next, at 6s 8d every month. *Summa* – 11s 2d.

[*Page total*] – £11 10s 4d.

[f. 201v] *[*Clerk*]. To James Gentyll the last day of September for his wages daily attending and serving Her Highness in keeping of the prick and cheque book of masters, mariners and gunners serving in Her Grace's ships upon the river of Thames, by one quarter of a year containing 92 days begun the first day of July last and this day ended, at 8d every day. *Summa* – £3 1s 4d.

*[*Keeper of storehouse*]. To Henry Abraham the same day for his wages daily attending and serving Her Majesty for the safe-keeping of Her Grace's storehouses there wherein lieth Her Highness's store of all kinds of provisions for the use of her ships, by like 92 days begun and ended as aforesaid, at 8d *per diem* – £3 1s 4d.

*[*Purveyor*]. To James Humphrey the same day for his wages daily attending and serving Her Highness for providing of all manner of necessaries for the new building and repairing of Her Majesty's ships by the space of 92 days begun and ended as abovesaid, at 8d *per diem* – £3 1s 4d.

*[*Surveyor*]. To George Wirrall the same day for his wages daily attending and serving Her Highness for the taking surveys of all manner of provisions had of divers persons for the furniture of Her Grace's ships, as well at their settings forth to the seas as also at their comings home again into harbour, by like time of 92 days begun and ended as aforesaid, at 8d every day. *Summa* – £3 1s 4d.

*[*Plug keeper*]. To William Ally, labourer, the same day for his wages daily attending and serving Her Majesty in keeping of the plug and letting forth of the water out of the dock there for the drier keeping of the same,

wherein lieth Her Grace's two ships the *Great Bark* and the *Jesus*, by like 92 days begun and ended as abovesaid, at 8d *per diem* – £3 1s 4d.

[*Page total*] – £15 6s 8d.

[f. 202] *[*Keeper of timber-yard*]. To Thomas Woode, porter, the last day of September for his wages daily attending and serving Her Highness in safe-keeping of Her Grace's timber-yards there wherein lieth her timber, planks, boards, masts and divers other needful things for the use of Her Majesty's ships, by the space of 92 days begun the first day of July last and ended as abovesaid, at 8d every day. *Summa* – £3 1s 4d.

*[*Purveyor*]. To Roger Portar the same day for his wages daily attending and serving Her Highness in providing of timber, planks and boards in divers and sundry places for the use of Her Grace's ships, by like time of 92 days begun and ended as abovesaid, at 8d every day. *Summa* – £3 1s 4d.

*[*Riding charges*]. To John Elmar, messenger, the same day for his wages daily attending and serving Her Highness in carrying of the officers' letters in post to divers and sundry places alongst the sea coast for Her Grace's marine causes, by the like time of 92 days begun and ended as is aforesaid, at 12d *per diem* – £4 12s.

*[*Clerk*]. To Stephen Alexander the same day for his wages daily attending and serving Her Majesty for the writing, making and keeping of the books of report of all such provisions and necessaries as are taken of divers and sundry persons for the use of Her Highness's ships, by one quarter of a year; due at this present – £6 13s 4d.

[*Page total*] – £17 8s.

[f. 202v] *[*Shipwright*]. To Augustino Levello, Venetian shipwright, the last day of September for his wages daily attending and serving Her Highness for the repairing and mending of Her Grace's galleys, by the space of 92 days begun the first day of July last and ended as is abovesaid, at 16d every day. *Summa* – £6 2s 8d.

[*Page total*] – £6 2s 8d.

[f. 203] *Shipwrights*

Edward Bright, master, 92 days at 12d and 14 hours at 2d	£4 14s 4d
Thomas Juell, server, 83 days at 6d and 14 hours at 1d	42s 8d
Daniel Bright, server, 83 days at 6d and 14 hours at 1d	42s 8d
William Foster, server, 83 days at 6d and 14 hours at 1d	42s 8d
John Lestowe, 18 days at 6d and 8 hours at 1d	9s 8d
Matthew Baker, master, 92 days at 12d and 14 hours at 2d	£4 14s 4d

Hugh Blande, server, 83 days at 6d and 14 hours at 1d 42s 8d
Matthew Norton, server, 83 days at 6d and 14 hours at 1d 42s 8d
John Hoole, server, 83 days at 5d and 14 hours at ½d 35s 2d
Philip Garrett, 83 days at 6d and 14 hours at 1d 42s 8d
John Rande, 83 days at 10 and 14 hours at 1½d £3 10s 11d
James Cotes, server, 83 days at 6d and 14 hours at 1d 42s 8d
George Flower, server, 80 days at 6d and 14 hours at 1d 41s 2d
John Ellyson, 69 days at 8d and 14 hours at 1d 47s 2d
John Halle, server, 77 days at 6d and 14 hours at 1d 39s 8d.
John Daulton, 72 days at 7d and 14 hours at 1d 43s 2d
Davy Horne, server, 81 days at 4d and 14 hours at ½d 27s 7d
Michael Too, 80½ days at 7d and 14 hours at 1d 48s 1½d
John Too, server, 80 days at 6d and 14 hours at 1d 41s 2d
Edward Holborne, 80 days at 8d and 14 hours at 1d 54s 6d
Henry Newe, server, 83 days at 5d and 14 hours at ½d 35s 2d
Walter Holborne, 82 days at 8d and 14 hours at 1d 55s 10d
William Whellar, server, 14 days at 5d and 14 hours at ½d 6s 5d
John Brunett, 69 days at 8d and 14 hours at 1d 47s 2d
John Wilkynson, server, 83 days at 4d and 14 hours at ½d 28s 3d
Robert Wright, server, 83 days at 6d and 14 hours at 1d 42s 8d
Raynold Newe, server, 81 days at 6d and 14 hours at 1d 41s 8d
Robert Baker, 17 days at 6d and 14 hours at 1d 9s 8d
Richard Claye, 67 days at 8d and 14 hours at 1d 45s 10d
William Withered, server, 11 days at 4d and 6 hours at ½d 3s 11d
William Spycer, 81 days at 7d and 14 hours at 1d 48s 5d
Thomas Osborne, 81 days at 4d and 14 hours at ½d 27s 7d
[*Page total*] – £66 18s 2½d.

[f. 203v] Robert Waller, 80 days at 2d and 14 hours at ½d 13s 11d
Edward Clarke, 30 days at 7d and 14 hours at 1d 18s 8d
Edward Davy, server, 79 days at 3d and 14 hours at ½d 20s 4d
Henry Greaves, 61½ days at 7d and 14 hours at 1d 37s 0½d
Thomas Bonnam, server, 81 days at 5d and 14 hours at ½d 34s 4d
William Greaves, 81 days at 9d and 14 hours at 1½d £3 2s 6d
Thomas Hewes, server, 81 days at 6d and 14 hours at 1d 41s 8d

Edward Tutmarshe, server, 81 days at 6d and 14 hours at 1d	41s 8d
Richard Johnson, server, 81 days at 6d and 14 hours at 1d	41s 8d
Randall Woode, 35 days at 7d and 8 hours at 1d	22s 1d
Robert Davye, 17 days at 6d and 12 hours at 1d	9s 6d
Henry Freman, 81 days at 6d and 14 hours at 1d	41s 8d
Robert Assehtun, 67 days at 6d and 14 hours at 1d	34s 8d
Davy Baker, 77 days at 6d and 14 hours at 1d	39s 2d
John Myssunton, 81 days at 7d and 14 hours at 1d	48s 5d
James Dyggons, server, 81 days at 5d and 14 hours at ½d	34s 4d
Thomas Tyrrie, 75 days at 7d and 14 hours at 1d	44s 11d
William Greneway, server, 81 days at 6d and 14 hours at 1d	41s 8d
Thomas Harman, 77 days at 7d and 14 hours at 1d	40s 3d
Nicholas Addams, server, 81 days at 3d and 14 hours at ½d	20s 10d
John Pett, 70½ days at 7d and 14 hours at 1d	42s 3½d
Robert Pett, server, 81 days at 5d and 14 hours at ½d	34s 4d
George Upsone, 12 days at 6d and 10 hours at 1d	6s 10d
Henry Upsone, server, 12 days at 4d and 10 hours at ½d	4s 5d
Richard Payne, 74½ days at 8d and 14 hours at 1d	50s 6d
Thomas Moore, server, 80 days at 4d and 14 hours at ½d	27s 3d
Thomas Bryan, 81 days at 7d and 14 hours at 1d	48s 5d
John Dyggons, 17 days at 6d and 12 hours at 1d	9s 6d
Anthony Holdernes, 24 days at 7d and 12 hours at 1d	15s
John Juell, server, 29 days at 6d and 12 hours at 1d	15s 6d
William Graye, server, 28 days at 2d and 12 hours at ½d	4s 8d
Thomas Whomes, 38 days at 6d and 12 hours at 1d	20s
William Carroo, 81 days at 6d and 14 hours at 1d	41s 8d
John Tyllie, server, 19 days at 6d and 14 hours at 1d	10s 8d
William Pellam, 81 days at 6d and 14 hours at 1d	41s 8d
Henry Whoman, 67 days at 6d and 14 hours at 1d	34s 8d
Robert Haman, server, 71 days at 4d and 14 hours at ½d	24s 3d

[*Page total*] – £55 19s 11d.

[f. 204] John Trodewell, server, 81 days at 4d and 14 hours at ½d	27s 7d
Robert Fyssher, server, 62 days at 6d and 14 hours at 1d	32s 2d
William Andrees, server, 81 days at 4d and 14 hours at ½d	27s 7d
John Howper, 80 days at 6d and 14 hours at 1d	41s 2d
Robert Smythe, 72 days at 6d and 14 hours at 1d	37s 2d
Robert Hutson, 81 days at 7d and 14 hours at 1d	48s 5d
Thomas Withered, server, 75 days at 6d and 14 hours at 1d	38s 8d
James Dixson, 81 days at 10d and 14 hours at 1½d	£3 18s 5d
Richard Ryse, 81 days at 8d and 14 hours at 1d	55s 2d
Nicholas Claye, 8 days at 7d	4s 8d
William Addams, server, 8 days at 5d	3s 4d
John Sagear, server, 8 days at 5d	3s 4d
John Bunche, 8 days at 8d	5s 4d
William Harbard, server, 8 days at 4d	2s 8d
Thomas Blosse, 70 days at 8d and 14 hours at 1d	47s
Henry Nealle, server, 81 days at 6d and 14 hours at 1d	41s 8d
John Wynnye, 70 days at 8d and 14 hours at 1d	47s
John Wethers, server, 81 days at 6d and 14 hours at 1d	41s 8d
John Clarke, 80 days at 8d and 14 hours at 1d	54s 6d
George Graye, server, 81 days at 4d and 14 hours at ½d	27s 7d
William Welshe, 10 days at 8d	6s 8d
Thomas Freman, server, 10 days at 5d	4s 2d
Richard Cooke, 17 days at 7d and 12 hours at 1d	11s 11d
John Goldinge, 12 days at 8d	8s
Thomas Cotton, server, 12 days at 4d	4s
Henry Hartely, 78 days at 7d and 14 hours at 1d	46s 8d
Peter Pett, master, 18 days at 12d and 14 hours at 2d	20s 4d
Christopher Sweteman, server, 18 days at 6d and 14 hours at 1d	10s 2d
George Kingeston, server, 40 days at 6d and 14 hours at 1d	21s 2d
Roger Rayner, server, 6 days at 6d	3s
Lawrence Androo, server, 5 days at at 6d	2s 6d
Leonard Cowpar, 19 days at 6d and 12 hours at 1d	10s 6d
Edward Mote, server, 23 days at 2d and 12 hours at ½d	4s 4d
John Mylles, 8 days at 7d and 12 hours at 1d	5s 8d

Robert Archer, server, 8 days at 4d and 12 hours at ½d 3s 2d
William Hartropp, 8 days at 7d and 12 hours at 1d 5s 8d
Richard Badcock, 74 days at 6d and 14 hours at 1d 37s 2d
John Lawson, 4 days at 8d and 8 hours at 1d 3s 4d
Thomas Coxe, 13½ days at 6d and 12 hours at 1d 7s 9d

[*Page total*] – £44 0s 3d.

[f. 204v] Gregory Aldridge, 24 days at 7d and 12 hours at 1d 15s
Richard Davyes, server, 15 days at 2d and 12 hours at ½d 3s
Nicholas Mello, 16 days at 8d and 12 hours at 1d 11s 8d
Richard Wattes, server, 16 days at 4d and 12 hours at ½d 5s 10d
William Grene, server, 16 days at 4d and 12 hours at ½d 5s 10d
John Webb, 29 days at 7d and 12 hours at 1d 17s 11d
William Tyce, server, 29 days at 4d and 12 hours at ½d 10s 2d
Thomas Baker, 46 days at 8d and 14 hours at 1d 31s 10d
Edward Pereson, server, 51 days at 6d and 14 hours at 1d 26s 8d
Roger Worlingtun, 17 days at 7d and 12 hours at 1d 10s 11d
Robert Jonnes, server, 17 days at 3d and 12 hours at ½d 4s 9d
Thomas Norwell, 17 days at 8d and 12 hours at 1d 12s 4d
Edward Soore, server, 14 days at 4d and 10 hours at ½d 5s 1d
Henry Gattes, 68 days at 8d and 14 hours at 1d 46s 6d
William Haywarde, 16½ days at 8d and 12 hours at 1d 11s 8d
Thomas Rossenbye, server, 14 days at 4d and 12 hours at ½d 5s 2d
William Knighte, 17 days at 8d and 12 hours at 1d 12s 4d
John Cossyn, server, 17 days at 4d and 12 hours at ½d 6s 2d
Rowland Shepparde, 16 days at 8d and 12 hours at 1d 11s 8d
Christopher Browne, server, 15 days at 4d and 12 hours at ½d 5s 6d
William Pawson, 16 days at 8d and 12 hours at 1d 11s 8d
John Norfolke, server, 15 days at 4d and 12 hours at ½d 5s 6d
Henry Creswell, server, 16 days at 3d and 12 hours at ½d 4s 6d
Thomas Robynson, 47 days at 8d and 14 hours at 1d 32s 6d

Francis Tythe, 13 days at 8d and 12 hours at 1d	9s 8d
Richard Dodd, server, 16 days at 6d and 12 hours at 1d	9s
John Tythe, server, 16 days at 2d and 12 hours at ½d	3s 2d
Thomas Richardby, 20½ days at 8d and 12 hours at 1d	14s 8d
Richard Benwell, 14 days at 8d and 12 hours at 1d	10s 4d
Thomas Adams, server, 13 days at 4d and 12 hours at ½d	4s 10d
George Aparke, server, 22 days at 2d and 12 hours at ½d	4s 2d
Richard Farrer, 15 days at 7d and 12 hours at 1d	9s 9d
Thomas Deakon, server, 15 days at 6d and 12 hours at 1d	8s 6d
John Hurlley, 14 days at 7d and 12 hours at 1d	9s 2d
Samuel Hurlley, server, 15 days at 2d and 12 hours at ½d	3s
Robert Flowrye, 16 days at 7d and 12 hours at 1d	10s 4d
John Cottycote, server, 16 days at 6d and 12 hours at 1d	9s
Roger Browne, 15 days at 7d and 12 hours at 1d	9s 9d

[*Page total*] – £21 9s 6d.

[f. 205] Robert White, 15 days at 7d and 12 hours at 1d	9s 9d
Henry Reade, server, 15 days at 4d and 12 hours at ½d	5s 6d
Henry Cleave, 13 days at 6d and 12 hours at 1d	7s 6d
Arthur Carr, server, 19 days at 4d and 12 hours at ½d	6s 10d
Thomas Raynoldes, 14 days at 8d and 12 hours at 1d	10s 4d
William Smallewood, 29 days at 7d and 12 hours at 1d	17s 11d
John Hayewarde, 11 days at 8d and 6 hours at 1d	7s 10d
Henry Samon, server, 11 days at 5d and 6 hours at ½d	4s 10d
Anthony Lawrence, 3 days at 10d and 6 hours at 1½d	3s 3d
John Stevenson, server, 3 days at 6d and 6 hours at 1d	2s
Thomas Halle, server, 3 days at 5d and 6 hours at ½d	18d
Robert Fentun, 26 days at 8d and 12 hours at 1d	16s 4d
Henry Ebdyn, server, 26 days at 6d and 12 hours at 1d	14s
Richard Addams, 4 days at 8d and 8 hours at 1d	3s 4d
John Carpenter, server, 4 days at 6d and 8 hours at 1d	2s 8d
John Sybley, server, 4 days at 4d and 8 hours at ½d	20d
John Mylles, 33 days at 7d	19s 3d
Thomas Willson, 92 days at 12d and 14 hours at 2d	£4 14s 4d
John Hurlestone, 92 days at 6d and 14 hours at 1d	47s 2d
Thomas Hellye, 92 days at 6d and 14 hours at 1d	47s 2d
John Bradley, 92 days at 6d and 14 hours at 1d	47s 2d

John Willyamson, 92 days at 3d and 14 hours at ½d	23s 7d
Henry Rowse, 92 days at 3d and 14 hours at ½d	23s 7d
Caulkers	
Thomas Boulttun, master, 11 days at 10d and 12 hours at 1½d	10s 8d
William Bolttun, server, 8 days at 6d and 12 hours at 1d	5s
William Bulbeck, 17 days at 10d and 12 hours at 1½d	15s 8d
William Addamson, server, 62 days at 6d and 12 hours at 1d	32s
William Tubbarde, server, 12 days at 6d and 12 hours at 1d	7s
William Thomas, 3 days at 6d and 6 hours at 1d	2s
Thomas Flemynge, 3 days at 6d and 6 hours at 1d	2s
John Waters, 3 days at 6d and 6 hours at 1d	2s
John Moziar, 5 days at 6d and 6 hours at 1d	3s

[*Page total*] – £24 16s 10d.

[f. 205v] William Mune, 4 days at 8d and 8 hours at 1d	3s 4d
William Trotter, server, 6 days at 4d and 12 hours at ½d	2s 6d
William Foarde, 4 days at 8d and 6 hours at 1d	2s 6d
Robert Langley, 5 days at 6d and 10 hours at 1d	3s 4d
John Stockdayll, 8 days at 7d and 10 hours at 1d	5s 6d
Thomas Norcott, 5 days at 7d and 10 hours at 1d	3s 9d
John Rodes, server, 5 days at 4d and 10 hours at ½d	2s 1d
John Willyams, server, 5 days at 4d and 10 hours at ½d	2s 1d
Nicholas Foxe, 2 days at 7d	14d
George Harryson, 4 days at 7d and 8 hours at 1d	3s
Cornelius Whomes, 3 days at 7d and 6 hours at 1d	2s 4d
William Bastyane, 21 days at 7d and 10 hours at 1d	13s 1d
Edward Bastyane, server, 20 days at 6d and 10 hours at 1d	10s 10d
Richard Bartun, 3 days at 7d and 6 hours at 1d	2s 3d
Walter Claye, 7 days at 6d and 12 hours at 1d	4s 6d
Thomas Clarke, 2 days at 7d and 4 hours at 1d	18d
Robert Edmondes, server, 3 days at 4d and 6 hours at ½d	15d
Gabriel Wright, 4 days at 7d and 8 hours at 1d	3s
Nicholas Archedayll, 81 days at 6d and 14 hours at 1d	41s 8d
Walter Deane, 3 days at 7d and 6 hours at 1d	2s 3d

William Deane, server, 3 days at 3d and 6 hours at ½d	12d
Thomas Clowde, server, 3 days at 3d and 6 hours at ½d	12d
John Webb, 3 days at 7d and 6 hours at 1d	2s 3d
John White, 2 days at 6d and 4 hours at 1d	16d
Henry Baker, 3 days at 6d and 6 hours at 1d	2s
John Haywarde, 2 days at 7d and 4 hours at 1d	18d
Nicholas Haywarde, server, 2 days at 6d and 4 hours at 1d	16d
Richard Clappam, 4 days at 6d and 8 hours at 1d	2s 8d
Roger Collyns, 2 days at 6d and 4 hours at 1d	16d
John Graye, 2 days at 6d and 4 hours at 1d	16d
Lancelot Bytten, 2 days at 6d and 4 hours at 1d	16d
Thomas Wyckars, 2 days at 6d and 4 hours at 1d	16d
John Bote, 2 days at 6d and 4 hours at 1d	16d
Nicholas Cooke, 7 days at 6d and 10 hours at 1d	4s 4d
Richard Rigg, server, 1 day at 4d	4d
Robert Dymmocke, 2 days at 7d and 4 hours at 1d	18d
Roger Lakyn, 3 days at 7d and 6 hours at 1d	2s 3d

[*Page total*] – £7 3s.

[f. 206] Thomas Pavey, 19 days at 7d and 6 hours at 1d	11s 7d
Edward Hylliarde, server, 19 days at 4d and 6 hours at ½d	5s 7d
Peter Hatche, 7 days at 6d and 8 hours at 1d	4s 2d
John Clarke, 2 days at 7d and 4 hours at 1d	18d
Nicholas Jones, 2 days at 6d and 4 hours at 1d	16d
William Hedger, 4 days at 8d and 8 hours at 1d	3s 3d
Robert Thomas, 7 days at 6d and 8 hours at 1d	4s 2d
Richard Daveys, server, [*blank*]	[*blank*]
John Fuller, 11 days at 6d and 12 hours at 1d	6s 6d
John Everyd, 30 days at 6d	15s
Baptist Dyar, 29 days at 6d	14s 6d
John Eastwood, 15 days at 7d	8s 9d
George Farrer, server, 16 days at 4d	5s 4d
Cuthbert Leawes, server, 16 days at 6d	8s
Robert Richardes, 14 days at 7d	8s 2d
William Morrys, server, 10 days at 2d	20d
Sawyers	
Robert Hartt, master, 92 days at 8d and 14 hours at 1d	£3 2s 6d
Ellis Knoswell, 81 days at 6d and 14 hours at 1d	41s 8d
Thomas Myller, 81 days at 6d and 14 hours at 1d	41s 8d

Robert Davyes, 81 days at 6d and 14 hours at 1d	41s 8d
John Richardes, 58 days at 6d and 14 hours at 1d	30s 2d
Robert Grene, 58 days at 6d and 14 hours at 1d	30s 2d.
Bennet Over, 58 days at 6d and 14 hours at 1d	30s 2d
Robert Turnbull, 58 days at 6d and 14 hours at 1d	30s 2d
Simon Arnolde, 81 days at 6d and 14 hours at 1d	41s 8d
Thomas Harbarde, 81 days at 6d and 14 hours at 1d	41s 8d
John Bastyane, 13 days at 6d and 10 hours at 1d	7s 4d
Hugh Mylles, 13 days at 6d and 10 hours at 1d	7s 4d
Davy Evans, 3 days at 6d	18d
Robert Hewes, 3 days at 6d	18d
Roger Welshe, 16 days at 6d and 12 hours at 1d	9s
Richard Mason, 16 days at 6d and 12 hours at 1d	9s

[*Page total*] – £26 7s 9d.

[f. 206v] Thomas Hartt, 9 days at 8d and 6 hours at 1d	6s 6d
Richard Burnett, 13 days at 6d and 12 hours at 1d	7s 6d
John Gryffyn, 13 days at 6d and 12 hours at 1d	7s 6d
William Thomas, 13½ days at 6d and 12 hours at 1d	7s 9d
Robert Wygoode, 13½ days at 6d and 12 hours at 1d	7s 9d
Humphrey Sernnley, 14 days at 6d and 12 hours at 1d	8s
Hugh Edkyn, 14 days at 6d and 12 hours at 1d	8s
Oarmakers	
William Bexley, master, 62 days at 8d	41s 4d
William Kackett, server, 62 days at 6d	31s
James Rumen, server, 62 days at 6d	31s
Abraham Harmon, 62 days at 6d	31s
Henry Coomes, server, 62 days at 4d	20s 8d
John Androes, 67 days at 7d and 18 hours at 1d	20s 7d
Thomas Mowsen, server, 38 days at 6d	19s
John Sutton, server, 67 days at 4d and 18 hours at ½d	23s 1d
Thomas Curtys, 67 days at 7d and 18 hours at 1d	40s 7d
John Peckover, server, 11 days at 6d and 12 hours at 1d	6s 6d
John White, 67 days at 7d and 18 hours at 1d	40s 7d
John Johnson, server, 67 days at 6d and 18 hours at 1d	35s
John Sellman, 8½ days at 6d and 12 hours at 1d	5s 3d
William Pymbill, 67 days at 7d and 18 hours at 1d	40s 7d
John Hayecockes, 12 days at 6d and 12 hours at 1d	7s
Andrew Smythe, server, 16 days at 6d and 12 hours at 1d	9s
William Wynn, 6 days at 6d and 12 hours at 1d	4s

Thomas Pymbill, server, 36 days at 4d	12s
Thomas Morrys, 27 days at 6d	13s 6d

[*Page total*] – £25 4s 8d.

[f. 207] *Victualling.* To Thomas Willson of Ratcliff the last day of September for the victualling of 270 of the aforenamed shipwrights, caulkers, sawyers and oarmakers working upon the new building of Her Highness's ship called the *Great Bark*, and four Her Majesty's galliots there, *viz.* the *Post*, the *Guide*, the *Searcher* and the *Makeshift*, by the space of 11,620 days among them all, the Sundays and holy days within the same accounted, begun the first day of July last and this day ended, which maketh 1,660 weeks, at 4s 7d every week the man. *Summa* – £380 8s 4d.

Lodging. To Ellyn Baker, Joan Rocke, Amy Powell, Alice Borye, Katherine Marshe and 21 other persons of Deptford, Greenwich, Rotherhithe and thereabouts the same day for the lodging of 242 of the aforenamed shipwrights, caulkers, sawyers and oarmakers working upon the new building of the abovesaid ship and galliots there, by the space of 2,160 weeks among them all begun and ended as is aforesaid, at 2d every week the man. *Summa* – £18.

House-carpenters

John Leache, 82 days at 12d and 14 hours at 2d	£4 4s 4d
Thomas Biggen, server, 82 days at 10d and 14 hours at 1½d	£3 10s 1d
Benjamin Leache, server, 64 days at 4d	21s 4d

[*Page total*] – £407 4s 1d.

[f. 207v] *Labourers*

William Allie, master, 20 nights at 4d	6s 8d
Richard Rainsforthe, 100 days and nights at 7d and 14 hours at 1d	59s 6d
Henry Stevenson, 14½ days at 6d	7s 3d
Thomas Thissleton, 102 days and nights at 6d and 14 hours at 1d	52s 2d
William Twayttes, 107 days and nights at 6d and 14 hours at 1d	54s 8d
John Bastyane, 102 days and nights at 6d and 14 hours at 1d	52s 2d
John Addams, 103 days and nights at 6d and 14 hours at 1d	52s 8d
James Tealle, 89 days and nights at 6d and 14 hours at 1d	45s 8d
John Jans, 92 days and nights at 6d and 14 hours at 1d	47s 2d

Morgan Apprice, 21 days at 6d	10s 6d
Anthony Westlande, 96 days and nights at 6d and 14 hours at 1d	49s 2d
John Sturgeon, 26½ days at 6d	13s 3d
William Serrill, 82½ days and nights at 6d and 14 hours at 1d	42s 5d
William Pithen, 96 days and nights at 6d and 14 hours at 1d	49s 2d
Thomas Tressam, 82 days and nights at 6d and 14 hours at 1d	42s 2d
John Brace, 86 days and nights at 6d and 14 hours at 1d	44s 2d
John Rabye, 94 days and nights at 6d and 14 hours at 1d	48s 2d
John Bussynton, 85 days and nights at 6d and 14 hours at 1d	43s 8d
John Mansfelde, 82 days and nights at 6d and 14 hours at 1d	42s 2d
Robert Stevens, 81 days at 6d and 14 hours at 1d	41s 8d
William Brocke, 50 days at 6d	25s
John Haye, 50 days at 6d and 12 hours at 1d	26s
Richard Shafte, 80 days and nights at 6d and 14 hours at 1d	41s 2d
William Dutton, 103 days and nights at 6d and 14 hours at 1d	52s 8d
John Bearde, 81½ days and nights at 6d and 14 hours at 1d	41s 11d
Ambrose Myller, 89 days and nights at 6d and 14 hours at 1d	45s 8d
Thomas Maddocke, 78 days and nights at 6d and 14 hours at 1d	40s 2d
John Powell, 93 days and nights at 6d and 14 hours at 1d	47s 8d
Christopher Mattyson, 12 days at 6d	6s
Thomas Capyas, 49 days and nights at 6d	24s 6d
William Jones, 1 day at 6d	6d
Hugh Graye, 1 day at 6d	6d
George Mathew, 52 days and nights at 6d and 14 hours at 1d	27s 2d
John Parker, 6 days at 6d	3s
Lawrence Langcaster, 39 days and nights at 6d and 14 hours at 1d	20s 8d

Evan Davye, 16 days at 6d	8s
[*Page total*] – £60 15s.	
[f. 208] John Upjohn, 107 days and nights at 6d and 14 hours at 1d	54s 8d
William Foxe, 9 days at 7d	5s 3d
John Kellye, 14 days at 6d	7s
William Barnarde, 80 days at 6d	40s
Watchmen	
Henry Stevenson, 6 nights at 4d	2s
Anthony Westlonde, 30 nights at 4d	10s
John Hayne, 17 nights at 4d	5s 8d
John Jans, 30 nights at 4d	10s
Thomas Heele, 28 nights at 4d	9s 4d
William Brock, 15 nights at 4d	5s
John Uppjohn, 30 nights at 4d	10s
Richard Shafte, 30 nights at 4d	10s
Nicholas Archedayll, 30 nights at 4d	10s
William Twayttes, 30 nights at 4d	10s
John Hurlestone, 30 nights at 4d	10s
William Currar, 30 nights at 4d	10s
John Addams, 30 nights at 4d	10s
Thomas Thissleton, 30 nights at 4d	10s
John Sturgeon, 8 nights at 4d	2s 8d
William Pattrick, 30 nights at 4d	10s
William Dutton, 15 nights at 4d	5s
John Bradley, 23 nights at 4d	7s 8d
John Berde, 17 nights at 4d	5s 8d
John Powell, 13 nights at 4d	4s 4d
[*Page total*] – £13 4s 4d.	

[f. 208v] *Emptions*[1]

Ironwork. To Thomas Willson of Ratcliff, smith, the last day of September for price of 8 thousand 6 hundred 3 quarters 8 pounds weight [*9,724 lbs*] of his own new iron by him made and wrought into all sorts of spikes, clench, rove, overlop nails, ring-bolts, setting bolts, pickaxes and crows of iron, and the same delivered at Deptford into Her Majesty's great storehouse there for the use of Her Grace's ships, at 23s 4d every hundredweight – £101 5s 10d; more for the working of 5 hundred 3 quarters 10 pounds weight [*654 lbs*] of Her Highness's old iron into like

[1]A draft of this section only, and differently ordered survives as BL, Add. MS 78170, section (a), ff. 1–3v. Significant details not carried forward to the final account are noted here; see further Appendix 4 below.

bolts and spikes for the use as aforesaid, at 8s 4d every hundredweight – 49s;[1] more for 37,550 of 10d nail, at 8s 4d every 1,000 – £15 12s 11d; more for 23,650 of 6d nail, at 5s every 1,000 – £5 18s 3d; more for 21,550 of 4d nail, at 3s 4d every 1,000 – £3 12s; more for 17,600 of 3d nail, at 2s 6d every 1,000 – 44s; and more to him for 20,000 of scupper nails, at 4s 4d every 1,000 – £4 6s 8d. *Summa* – £135 8s 8d.

To Richard Welles of Greenwich, smith, the same day for price of 9 hundred 3 quarters 3 pounds weight [*1,095 lbs*] of his own new iron by him made into bolts, spikes, clench, rove and overlop nails, and the same delivered as aforesaid for the use of Her Grace's ships, at 23s 4d every hundredweight – £11 8s 1½d; and more to him for 10 dozen of gimlets, at 3s every dozen – 30s. *Summa* – £12 18s 8d.

To Gilbert Polstead of Greenwich, locksmith, the same day for the price of one new stock lock of him had and by him set up on the Queen's Highness's storehouse door there, and for 2 great keys for locks, price – 3s 4d; more for a new lock with a key set on a chamber door, price – 22d; more for a key for a plate-lock, price – 12d; more for four keys for settles, at 8d the piece – 2s 8d; more for three keys for locks of a press, price – 2s; and more for four keys for hanging locks, price – 2s 8d. *Summa* – 13s 6d.

[*Page total*] – £149 0s 10d *[*Iron with £44 2s 10d for nails – £148 8s 6d*; *locks and keys – 13s 6d*]

[f. 209] To Thomas Ivye of Limehouse, smith, the last day of September for price of 8 thousand 7 hundred 2 quarters one pound weight [*9,801 lbs*] of his own new iron by him made and wrought into spikes of all sorts, clench, rove, overlop nails, setting bolts, ring-bolts, pickaxes and crows of iron, and the same delivered into Her Majesty's great storehouse at Deptford for the use of Her Highness's ships, at 23s 4d every hundredweight – £102 1s 10½d; more for 8 new small anchors for Her Highness's four small galliots the *Guide*, the *Post*, the *Searcher* and the *Makeshift*, weighing [*one*] thousand 3 hundred 14 pounds weight [*1,470 lbs*], at 20s every hundredweight – £13 2s 6d; more for the workmanship of 6 hundred 2 quarters weight [*728 lbs*] of Her Grace's old iron into like bolts and spikes for the use as aforesaid, at 8s 4d every hundredweight – 54s 4d;[2] more for 14,000 of 10d nail, at 8s 4d every 1,000 – £5 16s 8d; more for 14,000 of 6d nail, at 5s every 1,000 – £3 10s; more for 14,000 of 4d nail, at 3s 4d every 1,000 – 46s 8d; and more to him for 14,000 of 3d nail, at 2s 6d every 1,000 – 35s. *Summa* – £131 7s 0½d.

To William Pennyfather of London, ironmonger, the same day for price of 2 somes of English 2d nail of him had for the use of Her Highness's

[1]The calculation gives 583.92854d, which is about 4d below the sum stated (588d). The quantity to yield that figure would be about 658½ lbs, expressed as 5 cwt 3 qrs 14½ lbs.

[2]The calculation gives 650d, which is 2d below the sum stated.

ships, at 14s every some – 28s; more for 3,000 of Flemish 2d nail, at 13d every 1,000 – 3s 3d; more for 1,000 of pump nails, price 14d; more for 1,500 of scupper nail, at 4s 4d the 1,000 – 6s 6d; more for 6 padlocks, at 6d the piece – 3s; more for 6 padlocks, at 4d the piece – 2s; more for 6 somes of English 2d nail, at 15s the some – £4 10s; more for one bag with tack nails, price 13s 4d; more for 12,500 of English 2d nail, at 15d every 1,000 – 17s 7½d; and more to him for 2,500 of Flemish 2d nail, at 14d every 1,000 – 2s 11d. *Summa* – £8 7s 9½d.

[*Page total*] – £139 14s 10d *[*With £21 16s 1½d for nails*]

[f. 209v] *Pulleys, shovels, bowls and scoops.* To John Benbow of London the last day of September for price of 17 dozen of steel shovels of him had and the same delivered into Her Grace's great storehouse at Deptford for the use of Her Majesty's ships, at 8d the piece – £6 16s; more for 12 dozen of scoops, at 5d the piece – £3; more for 66 pulleys, at 6d the piece – 33s; more for 46 pulleys, at 12d the piece – 46s; more for 12 pulleys, at 20d the piece – 20s; more for 33 pulleys, at 2s the piece – £3 6s; more for 10 dozen of great bowls for pitch and rosin, at 10s the dozen – £5; more for 4 dozen [*and*] 2 of pulleys, at 16d the piece – £3 6s 8d; more for 18 pulleys, at 8d the piece – 12s; more for 8 dozen of pulleys, at 4d the piece – 32s; more for a ramhead –16d; more for 2 shivers of wood, price – 8d; more for one great pulley for a tackle, price – 6s 8d; and more to him for [*blank*] great pulleys for tackles, price – 10s. *Summa* – £29 10s 4d.

Pump-hose, claps and scupper-leathers. To John Harryson of Tower Hill, shoemaker, the same day for price of 6 dozen of great pump-hose of 7 inches broad by him delivered as aforesaid for the use of Her Highness's ships, at 2s 8d the piece – £9 12s; more for 5½ dozen of great claps, at 16d the piece – £4 8s; more for 10 dozen of scupper-leathers, at 16d the piece – £8; more for 6 small claps, at 8d the piece – 4s; more for 8 flat pieces of leather and 8 single claps, at 22d the piece – 14s 8d; more for 6 claps with broad necks, at 12d the piece – 6s; and more to him for 2 small scupper-leathers, at 8d the piece – 1s 4d. *Summa* – £23 6s.

Ink, counters and locks. To William Kyrbie of London the same day for price of one gallon 3 quarts and a pint of ink by him delivered to the officers' clerks of Her Grace's Marine Causes for the writing and engrossing of books concerning the same, at 5s 4d every gallon – 9s 4d; more for 4 pounds weight of casting counters, at 2s the pound – 8s; and more for 7 locks for budgets,[1] price – 3s 8d. *Summa* – £1 1s.

[*Page total*] – £53 17s 4d.

[1]Leather pouches. Hence the figurative usage already current 'to open the budget', i.e. to make a disclosure of any kind. Only in the 18th cent., following application of this phrase to the government's economic forecast, did the word acquire its modern and specifically financial meaning.

[f. 210] *Pitch, tar, small masts, caulking oil, deal-boards, sea coal, rafters for oars, &c.* To William Paidge of London, merchant, the last day of September for price of 2 barrels of caulking oil by him delivered into Her Highness's great storehouse at Deptford for the use of Her Grace's ships, at 31s 8d the barrel – £3 3s 4d; more for 30 Dansk deal-boards, at 4s the piece – £6; more for one hundredweight of thrums, at 2½d the pound – 23s 4d; more for 10 chauldrons of sea coal, at 11s 4d every chauldron – £5 13s 4d; more for 6 grindstones, at 4s 6d the piece – 27s; more for 60 spruce deal-boards, at 4s the piece – £12; more for 12 small masts of 4, 7, 8 and 9 hands about, at 13s 4d the mast – £8; more for 25 fir spars, at 4d the piece – 8s 4d; more for 25 round spars, at 6d the piece – 12s 6d; more for one last of tar, price – £5; more for one last of pitch, price – £5; more for 10 masts of 8 hands about, at 13s 4d every mast – £6 13s 4d; more for one shock of deal-boards, at 4s the board – £12; more for 80 pieces of tilt hair, at 11s the piece – £44; more for 60 rafters for oars, after £8 the hundred – £4;[1] and more to him for one hundredweight of thrums, price – 23s 4d. *Summa* – £116 4s 6d.

To John Warner of London, merchant, the same day for price of 30 wainscot boards by him delivered as aforesaid for the use of Her Majesty's ships, at 18d the piece – 45s; more for 2 last of pitch, at £5 the last – £10; more for 2 last of tar, at £5 the last – £10; more for 6 Norway masts of 13 and 14 hands about, at 40s the mast – £12; more for one mast of 18 hands about, price – 50s; more for 2 masts of 10 hands about, at 26s 8d the piece – 53s 4d; more for 14 small masts of 7 hands about, at 10s the piece – £7; more for 150 fir spars, at 4d the piece – 50s; and more to him for 1 hundred 40 [*160*][2] rafters for oars, at £8 every 100 after 6 score to the hundred – £10 13s 4d. *Summa* – £59 11s 8d.

[*Page total*] – £175 16s 2d *[*Oil, pitch and tar – £33 3s 4d*; *boards and spars – £35 15s 10d*; *thrums – 46s 8d*; *sea coal – £5 13s 4d*; *grindstone – 27s*; *masts, rafters and oars – £53 10s*; *tilt hair – £44*]

[f 210v] *Latchet lines, warps, poppet oakum, ratline, rafters for oars, &c.* *[*Cordage – £259 9s 1d*; *rafters for oars – £22 4s*]. To Christopher Draper of London, alderman, the last day of September for price of 376 pieces of tarred latchet line by him delivered into Her Majesty's storehouse at Deptford for the use of Her Highness's ships, weighing 10 thousand [*one*] hundred 21 pounds weight [*11,333 lbs*], at 28s every hundredweight – £141 13s 3d; more for 3 thousand 2 hundred a quarter 4 pounds weight [*3,616 lbs*] of tarred warps of 1½ and 2 inches compass,

[1]As explicit in the next paragraph, this commodity is calculated by long hundred (120) at a unit price of 1s 4d.

[2]MS '*cxl*' here (in line with the calculation by long hundred) standing not for 140 but for 120 + 40, which multiplied by the unit cost is correct for the sum stated.

at 21s 4d every hundredweight – £34 8s 9d; more for 7 white hawsers weighing 16 hundred 24 pounds weight [*1,816 lbs*], at 28s every hundredweight – £22 14s; more for 9 hundred [*one*] quarter 16 pounds weight [*1,052 lbs*] of white poppet oakum, at 20s every hundredweight – £9 7s 10½d; more for 2 hundred 93 [*333*][1] rafters for oars, at 16d the piece after 6 score to the hundred – £22 4s; more for 4 hundred 2 quarters 11 pounds weight [*515 lbs*] of white ratline, at 33s 4d every hundredweight – £7 13s 4d;[2] more for 5,000 of sail needles, at 53s 4d every 1,000 – £8 6s 8d; more for 30 dozen of sail twine, at 6s 8d every dozen – £10; more for 2 grindstones of 3 foot over apiece, at 3s either of them – 6s; more for 21 pieces of small tarred rope weighing 16 hundred 25 pounds weight [*1,817 lbs*], at 23s every hundredweight – £18 13s 2½d;[3] and more to him for 54 sounding lines, at 2s 4d the piece – £6 6s. *Summa* – £281 13s 1d.

Ballast baskets and maunds. To Christian Edes of London, widow, the same day for price of 26½ dozen of middle baskets of her had for the use of Her Grace's ships, at 4s every dozen – £5 6s; more for 19 dozen of ballast baskets, at 22d every dozen – 34s 10d; more for 4 dozen and 9 maunds, at 6s the dozen – 28s 6d; and more to her for 4 yards of white lattice, at 18d every yard – 6s. *Summa* – £8 15s 4d.

Nails. To Peter Whalye of London, ironmonger, the same day for price of 2 somes of English 2d nail by him delivered as aforesaid for the use of Her Majesty's said ships, at 16s 8d the some – £1 13s 4d.

[*Page total*] – £292 1s 9d.

[f. 211] *Rafters for oars.* To William Gyrdellar of London, merchant, the last day of September for price of 4 hundred 60 [*540*][4] rafters for oars of him had for the use of Her Highness's ships, at £9 every hundred after 6 score to the hundred – £40 10s; and more to him for 200 [*and*] 5 score [*340*][5] other rafters at £8 every hundred – £22 13s 4d. *Summa* – £63 3s 4d.

To Richard Howellett of London, merchant, the same day for price of 60 rafters for oars by him delivered for the use as aforesaid, at 16d the piece. *Summa* – £4.

To Edward Kaye of London, merchant, the same day for price of 60 long rafters for oars of him had for the use of Her Grace's ships, at 2s 6d the piece. *Summa* – £7 10s.

[1]MS '*cc.iiij/xx.xiij*' here standing for (120 × 2) + 93, which multiplied by the unit cost is correct for the sum stated.

[2]The calculation gives 1839.2856d, which is about ¾d below the sum stated (1840d).

[3]The calculation gives 4477.6071d, which is about 1d below the sum stated (4778.5d).

[4]MS '*ccccl x*' here standing for (120 × 4) + 60, which multiplied by the unit cost of 1s 6d is correct for the sum stated.

[5]MS '*cc.v/xx*' here standing for (120 × 2) + (5 × 20), which multiplied by the unit cost of 1s 4d is correct for the sum stated.

To John Johnson of London, merchant, the same day for price of 1 hundred 30 [*150*][1] long rafters for oars of him taken for the use of Her Majesty's ships, at £8 every hundred after 6 score to the hundred – £10.

To John Carter of Wapping, shipwright, the same day for price of 12 long oars of him had for the use of Her Highness's ships' boats; by agreement – 18s.

Carved work. To Richard Rowlande of Southwark, carver, the same day for the workmanship and carving of two personages in timber oak by him set up in the head of Her Grace's great new ship at Deptford Strand, for the garnishing and setting forth of the same ship, by agreement – £8 10s; more for carving of 6 heads that bear up the gallery, at 10s the piece – £3; more for making of 2 great heads for the tacks – 25s; more for 42 small heads that stand on the frieze, at 2s the piece – £4 4s; and more to him for carving of 2 cats' heads, at 10s the piece – 20s. *Summa* – £17 19s.

[*Page total*] – £103 10s 4d.

[f. 211v] *Red cloth.* To Thomas Armorar of London, merchant, the last day of September for price of 20½ yards of red broadcloth had of him for the covering of the cabins in Her Grace's four new galliots, *viz.* the *Post*, the *Guide*, the *Searcher* and the *Makeshift*, at 6s 8d every yard – £6 9s 10d; more for 15 yards of red cloth, at 6s 6d every yard – £4 18s 6d; more for 19 yards of red cloth, at 5s 8d every yard – £5 7s 8d; and more to him for 15 yards of red cloth, at 5s 6d every yard – £4 2s 6d. *Summa* – £20 17s 6d.

Sewing of tilts. To Robert Seaton of London, tailor, the same day for making and sewing of 4 tilts of red cloth lined with canvas for the covering of the cabins in Her Highness's said galliots, at 5s the piece. *Summa* – £1.

Canvas. To Edward Halle of London, merchant, the same day for price of 60 bolts of oleron canvas of him had for the use of Her Majesty's ships, at 17s 6d every bolt – £52 10s; more for 2 pieces of white lockram, at £5 10s the piece – £11; more for 762 ells of vitry canvas, at 11d every ell – £41 6s 10d; and more to him for 1,014 ells of canvas, at 8d every ell – £40 9s 4d. *Summa* – £145 6s 2d.

To John Collyns of London, merchant, the same day for price of 26 bolts of medrinacks canvas by him delivered for the use as aforesaid, at 35s every bolt – £45 10s.[2]

Casting of shivers. To Robert Hunte of London, founder, the same day for the workmanship and new casting one hundred 3 quarters weight

[1]MS '*cxxx*' here standing for 120 + 30, which multiplied by the unit cost of 1s 4d is correct for the sum stated.

[2]Draft notes that the merchant's bill was not produced ('*sine bill*"): BL, Add. MS 78170 [item (a)], f. 2.

of Her Highness's old metal into shivers and cocks of brass for the use of Her Majesty's ships, at 4d every pound weight – £3 5s 4d.

[*Page total*] – £215 19s.

[f. 212] *Timber, plank and board oak.* To Christopher Nayller of London, purveyor, the last day of September for price of 5,191 foot of 2-inch plank oak of him had and the same delivered at Deptford for the new building and repairing of Her Grace's ships there, at 8s every 100 foot – £20 15s 2d; more for 14,395 foot of 3-inch plank oak, at 10s every 100 foot – £71 19s 4d; more for 15,281 foot of 4-inch plank oak, at 12s every 100 [*foot*] – £91 13s 9d; more for 2,563 foot of 5-inch plank oak, at 15s every 100 foot – £19 4s 4d; more for 62½ loads 22 foot of timber oak, at 10s every load after 50 foot to the load – £31 9s 4½d; and more to him for 10,880 foot of inch and inch ½ board oak, at 5s every 100 foot – £27 3s 11½d. *Summa* – £262 5s 11d [½d *deleted*].

To John Dethicke of Colchester, purveyor, the same day for price of 12,285 foot of 3-inch plank oak by him provided and the same delivered for the use as aforesaid, at 10s every 100 foot – £61 8s 5¼d; more for 10,340 foot of 4-inch plank oak, at 10s every 100 foot – £51 14s 0¾d; more for 3,159 foot of 2-inch plank oak, at 8s every 100 foot – £12 12s 9d; more for 71 foot of inch ½ board oak, at 5s every 100 foot – 3s 6d, and more to him for 237½ loads of knees and other compass timber oak, at 10s every load after 50 foot to the load – £118 15s. *Summa* – £244 13s 10d.[1]

To Henry Daynes of Inworth in Essex, purveyor, the same day for price of 2,180 foot of 3-inch plank oak of him had for the use of Her Majesty's ships, at 10s every 100 foot – £10 18s 2¾d; more for 1,732 foot of 2-inch plank oak, at 8s every 100 foot – £6 18s 7d; and more to him for 141½ loads 19 foot of timber oak, at 10s every load after 50 foot to the load – £70 18s 9d. *Summa* – £88 15s 6¾d.[2]

[*Page total*] – £595 15s 4d [½d *deleted*].

[f. 212v] *Compass and long timber oak and trenails.* To Henry Lane of Foots Cray the last day of September for price of 167½ loads and 20 foot of timber oak by him delivered at Deptford for the building and repairing of Her Grace's ships there, at 10s every load after 50 foot to the load – £83 17s 1½d; more for 7,000 of trenails of 24 inches long, at 2s every 100 – £7; more for 8,600 of trenails of 16 inches long, at 16d

[1] Draft notes payment made to Richard Dethick: ibid., f.1v. Richard was John Dethick's son, and his original receipt for this sum and another (recorded below, p. 322) is also preserved: BL, Add. MS 78171, f. 39, as more fully detailed in Appendix 4 below.

[2] Draft originally noted no bill delivered; the note was then deleted: BL, Add. MS 78170 [item (a)], f. 1v.

every 100 – £5 14s 8d; more for 10,000 of trenails of 14 inches long, at 14d every 100 – 11s 8d [*recte* £5 16s 8d];[1] more for 4,000 of trenails of 30 inches long, at 2s 6d every 100 – £5; and more to him for 1,000 of trenails of 36 inches long, at 3s every 100 – 30s. *Summa* – £103 13s 5½d.[2]

To John Leach of Deptford Strand the same day for price of 43½ loads 22 foot of hooks, knees and other compass timber oak by him provided and delivered there for the use as aforesaid, at 10s every load after 50 foot to the load – £21 17s 4½d.

To George Bridger, purveyor, the same day for price of 42 loads 13 foot of hooks, knees and other compass timber oak of him had and delivered as abovesaid for the use of Her Highness's ships, at 10s every load. *Summa* – £21 1s 3d.

To Matthew Baker of Blackwall the same day for price of 8 loads of the like knees and compass timber had of him for the use as aforesaid, at 10s every load, *Summa* – £4.

Pumps. To William Bexlye, shipwright, the same day for the price of 9 great pumps of elm timber of him had for the use of Her Majesty's ships, *viz.* one of 22 foot long, one of 23, one of 24, one of 26, one of 17, one of 28, one of 29, and 2 pumps of 30 foot long apiece; all containing in length 229 foot, at 12d every foot. *Summa* – £11 9s.

[*Page total*] – £162 1s 1d.

[f. 213] *New lead and solder.* To John Hemmynge of London, plumber, the last day of September for the price of 26 hundred 3 quarters 4 pounds weight [*3,000 lbs*] of his own new lead had of him for the use of Her Majesty's ships, at 15s every hundredweight – £20 1s 7d;[3] more for 28 scupper pipes of lead for Her Grace's four new galliots, weighing [*one*] hundred 5 pounds weight [*117 lbs*], at 2d every pound – 19s 6d; more for wages of two his men working upon the same galliots by 10 days, at 10d every day – 8s 4d; more for 10½ pounds weight of tin solder, at 8d the pound – 7s; more for 32 sounding leads weighing 3 hundred [*one*] quarter 27 pounds weight [*391 lbs*] every hundred[*weight*] – £3 5s 2d; and more to him for bringing down of the same lead by water to Deptford – 2s 8d. *Summa* – £25 4s 3d.

Ship boats, sye or hair, plank, a copper kettle, &c. To Peter Pett of Deptford the same day for price of 92 stone of sye or hair of him had for the use of Her Grace's ships, at 16d every stone – £6 2s 8d; more for one

[1] 10,000 is likely to have been the correct quantity; the accountant has misread this as 1,000 to give the faulty sub-total, which is carried forward into the sum.

[2] Draft notes payments in part of £24 11s 5d and £40, and in full of £39 2s: BL, Add. MS 78170 [item (a)], f. 1. The halfpenny is overlooked in the margination.

[3] The calculation gives 4821.4284d, which is about 2½d above the sum stated (4819d).

new ship boat, price – £10; more for 4 axes, 4 ginnets and 12 augers by him bought and spent about the working on Her Highness's ships there, by agreement – 20s; more for 1,320 foot of 4-inch plank oak, at 10s every 100 foot – £6 12s 1½d; and more to him for price of one new ship boat for Her Majesty's ship named the *Elizabeth Jonas*; by agreement – £9. *Summa* – £32 14s 9½d.

To George Thornetun of London, merchant, the same day for price of one ship boat of him taken and delivered for the use as aforesaid, by agreement – £5; and more to him for one copper kettle weighing 3 quarters and 20 pounds weight [*104 lbs*], at 10d every pound weight – £4 6s 8d. *Summa* – £9 6s 8d.

Writing paper. To Vincent Gonson of London the same day for price of 11 reams of writing paper by him delivered to the officers' clerks of Her Highness's Marine Causes for the making of muster and prick books for payment made to mariners and gunners serving in Her Grace's ships, at 6s 8d every ream – £3 13s 4d.

[*Page total*] – £70 19s 0½d.

[f. 213v] *Compasses and running glasses.* To Richard Stevens of Tower Hill, compass-maker, the last day of September for price of 5 dozen of compasses of him had for the use of Her Grace's ships, at 32s every dozen – £8; and more to him for 5 dozen of running glasses, at 10s every dozen – 50s. *Summa* – £10 10s.

Water buckets. To John Willyamson of London, cooper, the same day for price of 26½ dozen of wooden water buckets of him taken for the use of Her Majesty's said ships, at 5s every dozen – £6 12s 6d.

Grindstones. To William Thurstone of London the same day for price of three grindstones of 4 foot over apiece by him delivered at Deptford for the use as aforesaid, at 2s 8d the piece – 8s.

Making of flags. To Stephen Androes of London the same day for the making of 6 great new flags with the cross of St George for the use of Her Highness's ships, at 2s the piece – 12s; more for making of 10 small flags, at 16d the piece – 13s 4d; and more to him for thread spent in the sewing of them – 2s 6d. *Summa* – £1 7s 10d.

Red say. To John Sledd of London, mercer, the same day for price of 4 pieces of red say of him taken for the making of flags for the needful use of Her Grace's said ships, at 36s every piece. *Summa* – £7 4s.

Oakum. To Joan Annesley, Amy Powell, Edward Coxe, John Johnson and four other persons of Deptford[1] the same day for the working and

[1]Draft identifies the four others as John Marnelettes, William Foxe, Alice Barnes, and Nicholas Archedaill, and specifies weights picked by and sums paid to all: BL, Add. MS 78170 [item (a)], f. 2v.

picking [*one*] thousand 7 hundred 2 quarters 21 pounds weight [*1,981 lbs*] of the Queen's Majesty's old junks and ropes into oakum for the needful caulking of Her Highness's ships at their groundings, at 3s 8d every hundredweight. *Summa* – £3 4s 11½d.[1]

[*Page total*] – £29 7s 3½d.

[f. 214] *Water carriage of provisions.* To Vincent Poulle of St Katherine's the last day of September for service of his hoy of the portage of 40 tuns, with three other his servants, serving Her Highness for the fetching of Her Grace's timber and planks from Woolwich to Deptford by sundry freights and there delivered the same for the building of Her Majesty's ships, by the space of 3 weeks begun the first day of July last and ended the 21th day of the same, at 3s 4d the tun *per mensem* – £5.

To John Hawkyns, master, the same day for service of his hoy named the *Lambe* of Maldon in Essex serving Her Majesty in carrying of cables, cablets, hawsers, warps, pump-hose, claps, scupper-leathers, hides, sails, oars and divers other provisions from London to the Land's End[2] for the use of Her Grace's ships then at the seas. *Summa* – £1 13s 4d.

Tilt hair. To Thomas Eve of London, merchant, the same day for price of 10 pieces of tilt hair had of him for the covering of Her Grace's four new galliots, *viz.* the *Post*, the *Guide*, the *Searcher* and the *Makeshift*, at 11s every piece. *Summa* – £5 10s.

To Lawrence Searlle of London, merchant, the same day for price of 4 pieces of tilt hair of him had for the use of the same galliots, at 11s every piece – £2 4s.

To Richard Cockes of London, merchant, the same day for price of three pieces of tilt hair of him taken for the use of Her Majesty's said galliots, at 11s every piece – £1 13s.

Ox hides. To Nicholas Chatfylde of London, butcher, the same day for price of 22 ox hides had of him for the use of Her Highness's ships then bound to the seas, at 10s every hide – £11.

[*Page total*] – £27 0s 4d.

[f. 214v] *Netting- and wrain-ropes.* To William Brooke of Deptford ropemaker, the last day of September for the workmanship of 3 thousand [*one*] hundred 14 pounds weight [*3,486 lbs*] of Her Highness's old junks and ropes by him wrought into netting- and wrain-ropes for the use of Her Grace's ships, at 3s 8d every hundredweight. *Summa* – £5 14s 1½d

[1]The calculation gives 778.24991d, which is 1d below the sum stated (779.5d).

[2]A point half a mile south of Warden Point marked as *Sheppey Lands End* on Admiralty charts. See further below, p. 450.

To Thomas Russell of Ratcliff, ropemaker, the same day for the like workmanship of 2 thousand 5 hundred one quarter weight [*2,828 lbs*] of Her Majesty's old junks and ropes in to wrain-ropes and netting for the use as aforesaid, at 3s 8d every hundredweight – £4 12s 8d [*recte* 7d].[1]

House rent. To Peter Pett of Deptford the same day for one quarter of a year's rent of two cellars of him hired wherein lieth Her Grace's store of rosin for the use of Her Majesty's ships, due at this present – £1.

Anchors and cables. To John Bongham of Portsmouth, merchant, the same day for price of 8 great anchors by him delivered into Her Majesty's storehouse at Deptford for the use of Her Grace's ships, weighing 9 thousand 2 hundred one quarter weight [*10,332 lbs*], at 22s every hundredweight – £101 9s 6d; and more to him for price of 6 tarred cables, *viz.* 2 of 13 inches compass, one of 9 inches, 2 of 8 inches and one of 7 inches, all weighing 11 thousand 5 hundredweight [*12,880 lbs*], at 24s every hundredweight – £138. *Summa* – £239 9s 6d.

To James Houmfrey of Southampton, merchant, the same day for price of one great anchor had of him for the use of Her Highness's ships, weighing [*one*] thousand 6 hundred 2 quarters weight [*1,848 lbs*], at 22s every hundredweight. *Summa* – £18 3s.

[*Page total*] – £268 19s 3½d. [f. 215 *blank*]

[f. 216] *Anno Domini 1563. Anno regni regine Elizabethe sexto*

A payment made the last day of December as well to masters, mariners, keepers of storehouses, dock and timber-yards there wherein lieth Her Grace's store of all manner of provisions and necessaries for the use of her ships, and to shipwrights, caulkers, sawyers, house-carpenters and other artificers and labourers for the building of a great new ship late called the *Great Bark*;[2] as also to sundry persons for divers kinds of provisions and needful things of them taken and the same delivered into Her Majesty's storehouse at Deptford Strand for the use of the said ships; by one quarter of a year begun the first day of October last and this day ended, as followeth:[3]

[1] The calculation gives 1111d, which is 1d below the sum stated. Since no loose lbs are involved, the probability is that the Quarter Book scribe has written the final figure as *viijd* instead of *vijd*.

[2] See above, p. 85 & n. 2, and *NEM*, pp. 483–4.

[3] A corrected draft for this Deptford quarter survives as BL, Add MS 78170 [item 1(b)], ff. 4–22v. Significant details not carried through to the final account are noted here. A conspectus of the draft is given in Appendix 4 below.

The George Hoy[1]

Mariners

Thomas Ussher, master, 3 weeks 3 days	17s
John Bennett, master's mate, 3 weeks 3 days	10s
Thomas Elkyn, cook, 3 weeks 3 days	7s 10½d
Henry Burgys, 3 weeks 3 days	5s 8d
John Wylliams, 3 weeks 3 days	5s 8d
Walter Pearce, 3 weeks 3 days	5s 8d
Martin Delanoye, 3 weeks 3 days	5s 8d
Clement Jeslyne, 3 weeks 3 days	5s 8d
[*Gunner*]	
Ralph Kyrbie, master gunner, 3 weeks 3 days	8s 6d

[*Page total*] – £3 11s 8½d.

[f. 216v] *[*Keeper of timber-yard*]. To Thomas Marshe, mariner, the last day of December for his wages daily attending and serving Her Highness for the safe-keeping of Her Grace's provisions of divers kinds of stuffs lying in her timber-yards there, and for the rigging and tackling of Her Majesty's ships to the seas, by one quarter of a year containing 13 weeks one day begun the first day of October last and ended the day first above-written, at 20s every month. *Summa* – £3 5s 4d.

*[*Mariners' wages for carrying of provisions and coiling up of cables*]. To Richard Harwood, mariner, the same day for his wages daily attending and serving Her Majesty in labouring about the carriage of provisions and coiling up of cables into Her Grace's great storehouse there and delivering out of the same again to the use of Her Highness's ships by like time of 13 weeks one day begun and ended as abovesaid, at 6s 8d *per mensem* – 21s 11d; and more for his victuals by like time, at 20d every week – 21s 11d. *Summa* – £2 3s 10d.

To Robert Tasse, mariner, the same day for his wages and victuals daily attending and serving Her Highness in labouring about the like coiling, carrying and delivering of provisions as aforesaid, by like 13 weeks one day begun and ended as abovesaid, at 13s 4d every month – £2 3s 10d.

To Christopher Breachett and William Currea, mariners, the same day for their wages and victuals daily attending and serving Her Majesty in labouring about the carriage in and delivering out of cables, hawsers and other provisions into Her Grace's great storehouse as abovesaid, by the like time of 13 weeks one day begun and ended as aforesaid, at 13s 4d either of them *per mensem* – £4 7s 8d.

[1] In the draft this section occurs at the end of the main gathering, headed: 'The *George Hoy* begun the first day of October last and ended the 24th day of the same next': BL, Add MS 78170 [item (b)], f. 22v.

To Robert Woode and Richard Token, mariners, the same day for their wages and victuals daily attending and serving Her Highness about the carrying of provisions and coiling up of cables and hawsers as aforesaid, by like 13 weeks one day begun and ended as is abovesaid, at 26s 8d between them *per mensem* – £4 7s 8d.

[*Page total*] – £16 8s 4d.

[f. 217] *[*Shipkeeper*]. To Thomas Elye, boatswain, the last day of December for his wages daily attending and serving the Queen's Majesty as well for the safe-keeping of Her Grace's ship called the *Jesus*, as also in labouring about the carrying and coiling up of cables, hawsers and other provisions into Her Grace's great storehouse and delivereing forth of the same again to the use of Her Majesty's ships, by the space of 13 weeks one day begun the first day of October last and this day ended, at 11s 8d every month – £1 18s 4d.

*[*Mariners*]. To John Kynge, mariner, the same day for his wages daily attending and serving Her Majesty in labouring about the carrying of cables, cablets, hawsers, warps and other provisions as aforesaid, by like time of 13 weeks one day begun and ended as is abovesaid, at 6s 8d every month – £1 1s 11d.

To William Pattrycke, mariner, the same day for his wages daily attending and serving Her Highness in labouring about the like carriage of provisions and coiling up of cables as abovesaid, by like 13 weeks one day, at 6s 8d *per mensem* – £1 1s 11d.

*[*Keeper of storehouse*]. To Henry Abraham the same day for his wages daily attending and serving Her Majesty for the safe-keeping of Her Grace's storehouses there wherein lieth Her Highness's provision of all manner of needful things for the use of her ships, by one quarter of a year containing 92 days begun and ended as is above-written, at 8d *per diem*. *Summa* – £3 1s 4d.

*[*Plug keeper*]. To William Allye, labourer, the same day for his wages daily attending and serving Her Highness in keeping of the plug and letting the water forth of the dock there for the drier keeping of the same, wherein lieth two of the Queen's Majesty's ships, that is to say the *Jesus* and one other new ship late called the *Great Bark*, by like time of 92 days begun and ended as aforesaid, at 8d *per diem* – £3 1s 4d.

[*Page total*] – £10 4s 10d.

[f. 217v] *[*Keeper of timber-yard*]. To Thomas Woode, porter, the last day of December for his wages daily attending and serving Her Highness in safe-keeping of Her Grace's timber-yard there wherein lieth her timber, planks, boards, masts and divers other needful things for the use of Her Majesty's ships, by the space of 92 days begun the first day of October last and this day ended, at 8d every day – £3 1s 4d.

*[*Clerk*]. To James Gentyll the same day for his wages daily attending and serving Her Majesty in keeping of the prick and cheque book of masters, mariners and gunners serving in Her Grace's ships upon the river of Thames, by like time of 92 days begun and ended as is abovesaid, at 8d *per diem* – £3 1s 4d.[1]

*[*Purveyor*]. To James Humphrey the same day for his wages daily attending and serving Her Highness in providing of divers and sundry kinds of provisions and necessaries for the use of Her Majesty's ships, by the space of 92 days begun and ended as abovesaid, at 8d *per diem* – £3 1s 4d.

*[*Surveyor*]. To George Wyrrall the same day for his wages daily attending and serving Her Majesty for the taking surveys of all manner of provisions and necessaries as are taken of divers and sundry persons for the furniture of Her Grace's ships, as well at their settings forth to the seas as also at their comings home again into harbour, by the like time of 92 days, begun and ended as aforesaid, at 8d per *diem* – £3 1s 4d.

*[*Purveyor*]. To Roger Porter the same day for his wages daily attending and serving Her Highness in providing of timber, planks and boards, in divers places at sundry times for the building and repairing of Her Majesty's ships, by like time of 92 days begun and ended as abovesaid, at 8d every day – £3 1s 4d.

[*Page total*] – £15 6s 8d.

[f. 218] *[*Riding charges*]. To John Ellmar, messenger, the last day of December for his wages daily attending and serving Her Highness in the carrying of the officers' letters in post to divers and sundry places alongst the sea coast for Her Grace's marine causes, by the space of 92 days begun the first day of October last and ended as abovesaid, at 12d *per diem* – £4 12s.

*[*Shipwright*]. To Augustino Levello, Venetian shipwright, the same day for his wages daily attending and serving Her Majesty for the repairing and mending of Her Grace's galleys, by like time of 92 days begun and ended as is aforesaid, at 16d *per diem* – £6 2s 8d.

*[*Clerk*]. To Stephen Alexander the same day for his wages daily attending and serving Her Highness for the writing, making and keeping of the books of report of all such provisions and necessaries as are taken of divers and sundry persons for the use of Her Grace's ships, by one quarter of a year, due at this present – £6 13s 4d.

[*Page total*] – £17 8s.

[1]Draft notes payment made to servant: ibid., f. 18.

[f. 218v] *Shipwrights*[1]

Edward Brighte, master,[2] 29 days at 12d	29s
John Juell, server, 25 days at 6d	12s 6d
John Leystoo, server, 25 days at 6d	12s 6d
Daniel Bright, server, 25 days at 6d	12s 6d
William Foster, server, 25 days at 6d	12s 6d
Matthew Baker, master,[3] 29 days at 12d	29s
Matthew Norton, server, 25 days at 6d	12s 6d
John Hole, server, 25 days at 5d	10s 5d
Hugh Blande, server, 25 days at 6d	12s 6d
Philip Garrett,[4] 25 days at 6d	12s 6d
William Androes, server, 25 days at 4d	8s 4d
John Rande, 23 days at 10d	19s 2d
James Cotes, server, 25 days at 6d	12s 6d
John Whyte, server, 25 days at 6d	12s 6d
John Ellyson, 25 days at 8d	16s 8d
John Halle, server, 25 days at 6d	12s 6d
John Daulton, 25 days at 7d	14s 7d
Davy Horne, server, 25 days at 4d	8s 4d
Michael Too, 20 days at 7d	11s 8d
John Too, server, 20 days at 6d	10s
Edward Holborne, 20 days at 8d	13s 4d
Henry Newe, server, 20 days at 5d	8s 4d
Walter Holborne, 20 days at 8d	13s 4d
John Brunett,[5] 20 days at 8d	13s 4d
John Wilkynson, server, 20 days at 4d	6s 8d
Robert Wrighte,[6] 20 days at 6d	10s
Reginald Newe, 20 days at 6d	10s
Richard Claye,[7] 20 days at 8d	13s 4d
William Spycer, 20 days at 7d	11s 8d
Thomas Osborne, server, 20 days at 4d	6s 8d
Robert Waller, server, 20 days at 2d	3s 4d
Edward Clarke, 24 days at 7d	14s

[1]Draft begins at this point with the heading: 'A payment made to shipwrights, caulkers, sawyers and others working upon the Queen's Highness's new ship at Deptford Strand, begun the first day of October last and ended the last of December then next', with marginal heading 'The new ship': ibid., f. 5.

[2]Draft brackets Bright with four servers following, and notes all sums paid to Bright: ibid.

[3]Draft brackets Baker with three servers following, and notes all sums paid to Baker: ibid.

[4]Draft brackets this man with next, and notes both sums paid to Christopher Baker: ibid.

[5]Draft marginates '2s 6d': ibid., f. 5v. This indicates conduct money, as specified instances below.

[6]Draft brackets this man with next, and notes both sums paid to Henry Lane: ibid.

[7]Draft marginates '2s 6d': ibid.

Edward Davye, server, 25 days at 3d	6s 3d
John Clarke,[1] 20 days at 8d	13s 4d
George Graye, server, 20 days at 4d	6s 8d
Henry Greaves,[2] 20 days at 7d	11s 8d
Thomas Bonnam, server, 20 days at 5d	8s 4d
[*Page total*] – £22 13s 5d.	
[f. 219] William Greaves, 25 days at 9d	18s 9d
Thomas Hewes, server, 25 days at 6d	12s 6d
Edward Tuttmarshe, server, 25 days at 6d	12s 6d
Richard Johnson, 25 days at 6d	12s 6d
Henry Freman, 20 days at 6d	10s
Robert Ashtonn, 20 days at 6d	10s
Davy Baker, 25 days at 6d	12s 6d
John Myssenton, 20 days at 7d	11s 8d
James Dyggons, server, 25 days at 5d	10s 5d
Thomas Tyrrie,[3] 20 days at 7d	11s 8d
William Greneway,[4] server, 20 days at 6d	10s
William Whellar, server, 25 days at 6d	12s 6d
Thomas Harman,[5] 7 days at 7d	4s 1d
Nicholas Adams, server, 16 days at 3d	4s
John Pett,[6] 25 days at 8d	16s 8d
Robert Pett, server, 25 days at 6d	12s 6d
Thomas Tadwell, server, 2 days at 4d	8d
Thomas Bryan,[7] 20 days at 7d	11s 8d
William Carro, 20 days at 6d	10s
William Pellam, 16 days at 6d	8s
Robert Hamon, server, 3 days at 4d	12d
Robert Fyssher, server,[8] 20 days at 6d	10s
John Howper, 20 days at 6d	10s
Robert Smythe, 20 days at 6d	10s
Thomas Blosse,[9] 20 days at 8d	13s 4d
Henry Nealle, server, 20 days at 6d	10s
John Wynnie, 20 days at 8d	13s 4d
John Weathers, server, 20 days at 6d	10s

[1]Draft brackets this man with next: ibid.
[2]Draft brackets Greaves with three men following: ibid.
[3]Draft marginates '4s' under heading 'conduct' which applies to all such: ibid., f. 6.
[4]*Idem.*
[5]*Idem.*
[6]Draft brackets Pett with server following: ibid.
[7]Draft marginates this man and two following '4s' for conduct: ibid.
[8]Draft notes payment made to Matthew Baker: ibid.
[9]Draft marginates this man and five following '5s' for conduct: ibid.

Robert Uttson, 20 days at 7d	11s 8d.
Thomas Wythered, server, 20 days at 6d	10s
James Dixson,[1] 25 days at 10d	29s 10d
Richard Ryce, 25 days at 8d	16s 8d
Henry Hartely, 20 days at 7d	11s 8d
Richard Badcock,[2] 16 days at 6d	8s
Thomas Robynson, 2 days at 8d	16d
John Everyd,[3] 20 days at 6d	10s
Baptist Dyer,[4] 20 days at 6d	10s
George Kingston,[5] 25 days at 6d	12s 6d
John Francke, 19 days at 7d	11s 1d
Robert Herse, 25 days at 7d	14s 7d
Thomas Willson, 31 days at 12d	31s
John Hurleston, 37 days at 6d	18s 6d
Thomas Heell, 69 days at 6d	34s 6d
John Bradley, 25 days at 6d	12s 6d

[*Page total*] – £26 5s 1d.

[f. 219v] *Caulkers*

William Bulbeck, master, 25 days at 10d	20s 10d
William Adamson, server, 25 days at 6d	12s 6d
William Tubbarde, server, 25 days at 6d	12s 6d
John Eastwoode, 23 days at 7d	13s 5d
George Farrer, server, 25 days at 4d	8s 4d
William Boltton, 14 days at 6d	7s
William Bastyane, 25 days at 7d	14s 7d
Edward Bastyane, server, 16 days at 6d	8s
Cuthbert Leawys, 20 days at 6d	10s
Robert Rychardes, 25 days at 7d	14s 7d
Thomas Pavey, 23 days at 7d	13s 5d
Edward Hylliarde, server, 23 days at 4d	7s 8d
John Stockdayll, 21 days at 7d	12s 3d
John Mozyer, 20 days at 6d	10s
Nicholas Archedayll, 73 days at 6d	36s 6d
Edmund Barrett, 13 days at 7d	7s 7d
George Boatt, server, 13 days at 3d	3s 3d
John Wylliamson,[6] 68 days at 3d	17s

[1]Draft brackets this man with next, and identifies latter as server: ibid.
[2]Draft marginates '4s' for conduct: ibid.
[3]*Idem.*
[4]Likewise: ibid., f. 6v.
[5]Draft identifies as server: ibid.
[6]Draft brackets this man with next, and notes payment made to Thomas Willson: ibid., f. 7.

Henry Rowse, 25 days at 3d	6s 3d
Sawyers	
Robert Hartt, master,[1] 29 days at 8d	19s 4d
Ellis Knoswell, 25 days at 6d	12s 6d
Thomas Myller, 22 days at 6d	11s
Robert Davyes, 22 days at 6d	11s
Simon Arnolde,[2] 20 days at 6d	10s
Thomas Harberde, 20 days at 6d	10s
Gilbert Avys,[3] 10 days at 6d	5s
Thomas Mawpeas, 10 days at 6d	5s

[*Page total*] – £15 19s 6d.

[f. 220]. *Victualling.* To Thomas Willson of Ratcliff the last day of December for the victualling of 108 of the aforenamed shipwrights, caulkers and sawyers working upon the new building of Her Majesty's ship late called the *Great Bark* there, by the space of 2,674 days among them all, Sundays and holy days within the same accounted, begun the first day of October last and ended the day abovesaid, which maketh 382 weeks, at 4s 7d every week the man. *Summa* – £87 10s 10d.[4]

Lodging. To William Awgar, William Allye, William Pattricke and 17 other persons of Deptford, Greenwich, Rotherhithe and thereabouts[5] the same day for the lodging of the aforesaid 108 shipwrights, caulkers and sawyers in 54 featherbeds by the space of 529 weeks among them all, begun and ended as is aforesaid, at 2d every week the man. *Summa* – £4 8s 2d.

[1]Draft brackets this man with the three following, and notes payment made to Robert Hart: ibid., f. 7v.

[2]Draft brackets this man with next: ibid.

[3]Draft brackets this man with next, and notes payment made to Robert Hart: ibid.

[4]Draft has an additional statement headed: 'Charges of victuals provided for the victualling of shipwrights, caulkers and sawyers working at Deptford upon the Queen's Highness's ship there, begun the first day of October last and ended the 29 day of the same', *viz.* William Payntell for 265 loaves of bread, at 12 the dozen – £13 5s; William Hortun for 103 dozen of bread – £5 3s; Richard Duffelde for 6 tuns 3 hogsheads of beer, at 20s the tun – £6 15s; Richard Hyrde for 7 thousand one hundred [*pounds*] weight of beef [*7,100 lbs*], at 14s the hundredweight – £49 14s; Arthur Malby for 3 firkins of butter, at 15s [*the firkin*] – 45s; for 1½ weys 20 lbs of cheese, at 42s 8d the wey; sum – £6 12s 4d. John Callaway for 58 of billet, at 4d the lb – £3 5s 10d. John Vyolett for 51 couple of Holland ling, at 20d the couple – £4 5s 10d [*10d over*]. One peck of mustard seed – 12d. For 3 bushels of bay salt, at 11d the bushel – 2s 9d. Carriage of the victuals by water – 8s 4d. *Sum* – £88 6s 7d: ibid., f. 19. The total of the sums stated is £89 13s 1d.

[5]Draft identifies the other 17 as Alice Greves, Ellen Ellmer, Joan Juell, Katherine Marshe, Elizabeth Fraunces, Alice Newbery, Maud Foxe, Anne Backeler, Annes Hurlestun, Joan Bright, Nicholas Archdeaile, Avys Waters, John Fendell, John Kyng, Alice Bory, Em Sympson and Alice James, and specifies the numbers of men and beds and sums of money in each case: ibid., f. 8.

House-carpenters

John Leache, master,[1] 47 days at 12d	47s
Benjamin Leache, server, 47 days at 4d	15s 8d
Thomas Biggen, server, 47 days at 10d	39s 2d
Thomas Illarrye, 4 days at 10d	3s 4d
Thomas Hylton, 4 days at 10d	3s 4d
Thomas Wood, 4 days at 10d	3s 4d
William Bright, 4 days at 10d	3s 4d

Thatchers

John Fullar, master, 36 days at 12d	36s
Matthew Westerlaye, 36 days at 8d	23s

[*Page total*] – £150 13s 2d.

[f. 220v] *Labourers*

Henry Raynesforthe, master, 82 days at 7d	47s 10d
Thomas Thistellworthe, 82 days at 6d	41s
William Twayttes,[2] 34 days at 6d	17s
John Bastyane, 34 days at 6d	17s
John Adams,[3] 82 days at 6d	41s
James Tealle, 30 days at 6d	15s
John Jans,[4] 33 days at 6d	16s 6d
Morgan Apprice, 30 days at 6d	15s
Anthony Westlonde,[5] 32 days at 6d	16s
William Serryll, 30 days at 6d	15s
William Pythen,[6] 34 days at 6d	17s
Thomas Tressam, 30 days at 6d	15s
John Brace, 30 days at 6d	15s
John Rabye, 26 days at 6d	13s
John Mansfylde, 30 days at 6d	15s
Robert Stevens,[7] 34 days at 6d	17s
Richard Shafte, 34 days at 6d	17s
William Dutton, 30 days at 6d	15s
John Bearde, 30 days at 6d	15s

[1]Draft brackets Leache with two servers following, and indicates all sums paid to Leache: ibid., f. 8v.

[2]Draft gives pay for this man and next as 15s, marginated '2s': ibid. These and similar marginations to this section appear to be corrections rather than indications of conduct money; in all cases the original sum was the commonest one of 15s, suggesting automative scribal error, and the additions bring the sums to the correct figures for the rates cited.

[3]Draft indicates payment made to wife ('*ux*''): ibid.

[4]Draft gives pay as 15s, marginated '18d': ibid.

[5]Draft gives pay as 15s, marginated '12d': ibid.

[6]Draft gives pay as 15s, marginated '2s': ibid., f. 9.

[7]Draft gives pay for this man and next as 15s, marginated '2s': ibid.

Ambrose Myller,[1] 33 days at 6d	16s 6d
Thomas Maddock, 30 days at 6d	15s
John Powell, 82 days at 6d	41s
Thomas Capyas, 30 days at 6d	15s
George Mathew, 82 days at 6d	41s
Lawrence Lancaster, 30 days at 6d	15s
John Upjohn,[2] 72 days at 6d	36s
Evan Davye, 30 days at 6d	15s
John Baillye, 30 days at 6d	15s
William Foxe, 18½ days at 6d	9s 3d
John Arnolde, 3 days at 6d	18d
John Brodehurst, 23 days at 6d	11s 6d
Ralph Courtlonde, 7 days at 6d	3s 6d

[*Page total*] – £30 15s 7d.

[f. 221] *Watchmen*

John Jans, 10 nights at 6d	5s
Anthony Westlonde, 10 nights at 6d	5s
John Bradley, 10 nights at 6d	5s
John Powell, 30 nights at 6d	15s
John Beerde, 11 nights at 6d	5s 6d
Richard Shafte, 11 nights at 6d	5s 6d
Thomas Heell, 16 nights at 6d	8s
Nicholas Archedayll, 30 nights at 6d	15s
John Hurlestone, 12 nights at 6d	6s
William Twayttes, 12 nights at 6d	6s
John Upjohn, 28 nights at 6d	14s
William Currar, 12 nights at 6d	6s
William Dutton, 10 nights at 6d	5s
Thomas Thistellworthe, 30 nights at 6d	15s
John Adams,[3] 30 nights at 6d	15s
William Pattrick, 30 nights at 6d	15s
George Mathew, 20 nights at 6d	10s
William Allye, 20 nights at 6d	10s
John Kynge, 15 nights at 6d	7s 6d
Thomas Elye, 16 nights at 6d	8s
Thomas Marshe, 21 nights at 6d	10s 6d

[*Page total*] – £9 12s.

[1]Draft gives pay as 15s, marginated '18d': ibid.
[2]Draft gives pay as 15s, marginated '21s': ibid.
[3]Draft indicates payment for this man and next made to wife ('*ux*''): ibid., f. 6v.

[f. 221v] *Emptions*

Ironwork. To Thomas Willson of Ratcliff, smith, the last day of December for price of [*one*] thousand 3 hundred one quarter and 20 pounds weight [*1,504 lbs*] of new iron by him wrought into spikes of all sorts, clench, rove, overlop nails, bolts with rings and keys, and the same delivered at Deptford Strand into the Queen's Majesty's great storehouse there for the use of Her Grace's ships, at 23s 4d every hundredweight – £15 13s 4d; more for 5,000 of 2s nail, at 20s every 1,000 – £5; more for 5,500 of 20d nail, at 16s 8d every 1,000 – £4 11s 8d; more for 5,000 of 10d nail, at 8s 4d every 1,000 – 41s 8d; more for 5,000 of 6d nail, at 5s every 1,000 – 25s; more for 5,000 of 4d nail, at 3s 4d every 1,000 – 16s 8d; and more to him for 5,000 of 3d nail, at 2s 6d every 1,000 – 12s 6d. *Summa* – £30 0s 10d.

To Thomas Ivye of Limehouse, smith, the same day for price of 13 hundred one quarter and 3 pounds weight [*1,487 lbs*] of new iron by him made into like bolts, spikes, clench, rove and overlop nails, and the same delivered into Her Highness's said storehouse for the aforesaid use, at 23s 4d every hundredweight – £15 9s 9½d; more for 4,000 of 10d nail, at 8s 4d every 1,000 – 33s 4d; more for 3,000 of 6d nail, at 5s every 1,000 – 15s; more for 2,000 of 4d nail, at 3s 4d the 1,000 – 6s 8d; and more to him for 2,000 of 3d nail, at 2s 6d the 1,000 – 5s. *Summa* – £18 9s 9½d.[1]

To Richard Welles of Greenwich, smith, the same day for the working of 7 hundred 3 quarters 23 [*recte* 28] pounds weight [*891* recte *896 lbs*] of Her Majesty's old iron into bolts and spikes for the use of Her Highness's ships, at 8s 4d every hundredweight working – £3 6s 8¾d;[2] and more to him for the new sharping and righting of 3,500 of Her Grace's old spikes, at 8d every 100 so mended – 23s 4d. *Summa* – £4 10s 0¾d.

To Peter Whalley of London, ironmonger, the same day for price of 4 iron pots of him taken for the use of Her Highness's ships, at 8s every pot. *Summa* – £1 12s.[3]

[*Page total*] – £54 12s 7¼d. *[*With £17 7s 6d for nails*]

[f. 222] *[*Nails*]. To William Pennyfather of London, ironmonger, the last day of December for price of 6,000 of pump nails of him had for the use of the Queen's Highness's ships, at 14d every 1,000 – 7s; more

[1]Draft marginates 'bill lost' (*bis*), but records payments to Ivye ('Ive') and Thomas Jud of £5, £3 9s 9½d and (in full settlement) £10 on 8 May, 9 June and 20 Aug. 1565: ibid., f. 11v.

[2]The calculation gives 795.53367d, which is over 5d below the sum stated (800.75d). The computation would work correctly with an additional 5 lbs, suggesting that the Quarter Book scribe has written the last component as *xxiij* instead of *xxviij*.

[3]Draft notes payment to the merchant's servant 'Dringlone' or 'Dringlove': BL, Add. MS 78170 [item (b)], f. 16v.

for 5,000 of scupper nails, at 4s 4d every 1,000 – 21s 8d; more for one padlock, price – 6d; and more for ½ a some of English 2d nail – 7s 6d. *Summa* – £1 16s 8d.

To Gilbert Mattyse of St Katherine's, smith, the same day for price of 2 grapnels of him taken for the use of Her Grace's brigantines, weighing 3 hundred one quarter and 20 pounds weight [*384 lbs*], at 23s 4d every hundredweight – £3 18s 4d.[1]

To John Preston of St Katherine's, blacksmith, the same day for price of one grapnel had of him had of his own new iron for the use of Her Majesty's galliots, weighing 2 hundred 22 pounds weight [*246 lbs*], at 23s 4d every hundred[*weight*] – £2 11s 3d.

*[*Locks and keys*]. To Gilbert Poulstead of Greenwich, smith, the same day for price of a new key for a great plate-lock for the door in Her Highness's storehouse at Deptford, and for mending of the same lock – 5s; more for a key for a press door, price – 8d; more for mending of a lock – 6d; more for mending of 2 plate-locks – 8d; more for 2 new locks with keys for cupboards in Her Grace's Treasurer's clerks' office there, price – 4s 8d; more for mending of a great key for the office door – 8d; more for 2 pair of portal hinges, at 18d the pair – 3s; more for a spring for a lock – 8d; more for a lock and a key – 2s 6d; and more to him for a new key and for mending of a lock – 12d. *Summa* – 19s 4d.

Shovels, scoops and bowls. To John Benbow of London the same day for price of 6 dozen of steel shovels of him had for the use of Her Grace's ships, at 8s every dozen – 48s; more for 4 dozen of scoops, at 5s every dozen – 20s; and more to him for 2 dozen of great bowls for pitch and rosin, at 10s every dozen – 20s. *Summa* – £4 8s.

[*Page total*] – £13 13s 7d.

[f. 222v] *Deal-boards, small masts, caulking oil and thrums* *[*Boards – £50 0s 8d*; *masts – 10s*; *oil – 21s* (*recte* 21s 8d); *thrums – 11s 8d*]. To John Warner of London, merchant, the last day of December for price of 30 spruce deal-boards of him had for the use of Her Grace's ships, at 3s 4d every board – £5 10s;[2] more for 15 deal-boards, at 4s the piece – £3; more for 60 spruce deal-boards, at 4s 8d the piece – £14; and more to him for 6 small masts, at 20d the piece – 10s. *Summa* – £23.

To Edward Keye of London, merchant, the same day for price of 43 spruce deal-boards had of him for the use as aforesaid, at 5s every board. *Summa* – £10 15s.[3]

[1]The calculation gives 960d, which is 20d above the sum stated; so it is likely that in the original computation the total in pence was mistakenly taken as *ix^{c} xl* instead of *ix^{c} lx*.

[2]Draft notes payment of this much to James Humphrey: BL, Add. MS 78170 [item (b)], f. 13.

[3]Draft notes payment to Thomas Parye: ibid., f. 11.

To William Paidge of London, merchant, the same day for price of 67 spruce deal-boards of him taken for the aforesaid use, at 5s the piece – £16 15s; more for 13 gallons of caulking oil, at 20d every gallon – 21s 8d; and more for ½ hundredweight of thrums, price – 11s 8d. *Summa* – £18 8s 4d.

Canvas and lockram. To John Collyns of London, merchant, the same day for price of 32 bolts of medrinacks canvas taken of him for the making of sails for the use of Her Majesty's ships, at 35s every piece. *Summa* – £56.[1]

To Francis Oldraye of London, merchant, the same day for price of 15 bolts of medrinacks canvas of him had for the aforesaid use, at 35s every piece. *Summa* – £26 5s.

To John Gunnell of London the same day for price of half a piece of white dowlas lockram by him delivered for the making of new flags for the use of Her Highness's ships, by agreement – 48s; and more for 2 yards of medrinacks canvas, price – 2s. *Summa* – £2 10s.

[*Page total*] – £136 8s 4d.

[f. 223] *Cables, cablets, hawsers, warps, latchet and sounding lines, pitch, tar and masts.* To Thomas Allen of London, merchant, the last day of December for price of 36 great tarred cables of Dansk stuff of 9, 10, 11, 12, 13, 14, and 15 inches compass by him delivered at Deptford Strand into the Queen's Majesty's great storehouse there for the use of Her Highness's ships, *poiz.* 76 thousand [*one*] hundred one quarter and 7 pounds weight [*85,267 lbs*]; more for 49 tarred cablets of 7, 7½, and 8 inches compass of like Dansk stuff, *poiz.* 43 thousand 8 hundred 2 quarters 14 pounds weight [*49,126 lbs*]; more for 342 pieces [*of*] tarred hawsers and warps from one inch to 6 inches compass, at 88 thousand 5 hundred 3 quarters and 7 pounds weight [*99,323 lbs*]; more for 119 pieces [*of*] tarred latchet lines and ratline *poiz.* [*one*] thousand 7 hundred one quarter and 7 pounds weight [*1,939 lbs*]; all weighing 210 thousand 4 hundred 7 pounds weight [*235,655 lbs*], at 24s 8d every hundredweight – £2,595 0s 2½d;[2] more for 59 pieces of white lines for sounding lines weighing 5 hundred and one quarter weight [*588 lbs*], at 30s every hundredweight – £7 17s 6d; more for 15 last of tar, at £5 every last – £75; more for 15 last of pitch of the great band, at £5 10s every last – £82 10s; more for 45 masts from 40 to 60 foot long apiece and from 40 to 56 inches compass about at the butt end, at 50s every mast – £112;

[1]Draft notes payments of £16, on 12 May 1564 of £10, and in full settlement of £30: ibid., f. 14.

[2]The calculation gives 622,802.48d, which is here recorded to demonstrate the accuracy of the sum stated (620,802.5d) in this, the single largest transaction recorded in the Quarter Book.

more for 110 masts of 9, 10, and 12 yards long apiece and 25, 27 and 36 inches about at the butt end, at 12s every mast – £66; and more to him for 80 masts of 9 and 10 yards long apiece and 27 and 30 inches compass about at the butt end, at 2s the piece – £8. *Summa* – £2,946 17s 8½d.[1]

To Sir James Croft, knight,[2] the same day for price of 172 coil of tarred hawsers of line stuff[3] of him had and the same delivered into Her Grace's said storehouse at Deptford Strand for the use of Her Majesty's ships, weighing 20 thousand pounds weight [*22,400 lbs*]; more for 30 tarred cablets and 71 coil of tarred latchet lines *poiz*. 13 thousand 6 hundred one quarter and 12 pounds weight [*15,272 lbs*]; all weighing 33 thousand 6 hundred one quarter 12 pounds weight [*37,672 lbs*], at 15s every hundredweight. *Summa* – £252 5s 2d.[4]

[*Page total*] – £3,199 2s 10½d. *[*Cables and tackling – £2,855 2s 10½d; pitch – £157 10s; masts – £186 10s*]

[f. 223v] *Timber and planks.* To John Dethick of Colchester, purveyor, the last day of December for price of 368 foot of 2-inch plank oak by him provided in divers places in Suffolk and delivered at Deptford Strand into Her Highness's timber-yards there for the building and repairing of Her Majesty's ships, at 8s every 100 foot – 29s 6d; more for 1,200 foot of 3-inch plank oak, at 10s every 100 foot – £6; more for 1,561 foot of 4-inch plank oak, at 10s every 100 foot – £7 15s 10½d; and more to him for 77½ loads and 25 foot of timber oak, at 10s every load after 50 foot to the load – £39. *Summa* – £54 5s 4½d.[5]

[1] Draft notes payments by instalment: (1564) 11 Mar. – £500; 28 May – £500; 9 June – £190 2s 6d and £309 17s 6d; 24 Nov. – £200; (1565) 12 Feb. – £100; 7 Feb. (*sic*) – £200; 2 July – £200; 10 July – £200; 21 Aug. (in full settlement save the halfpenny) – £546 17s 8d: BL, Add. MS 78170 [item (b)], f. 17v.

[2] Croft held high office under Edward VI and won Elizabeth's lasting regard by shielding her from implication in Wyatt's rebellion, but his unheroic conduct as governor of Berwick in 1559–60 led to disgrace and debt. He remained a leading figure in his native Herefordshire, and returned to central government as Comptroller of the Household and Privy Councillor in 1570: *Hist. Parl. 1509–58*, i, pp. 724–5; *1558–1603*, i, pp. 672–5. His financial plight in the 1560s was not resolved by land sales, while 'keeping the Countenance of a Gentleman' (R. E. Ham, 'The autobiography of Sir James Croft', *BIHR*, L: (1977), p. 56; that no doubt explains why he was reduced to trading in naval supplies.

[3] MS 'Lynn stuff', understood as 'line' (flax). The writer may have assumed a connection with King's Lynn or possibly Lincoln: cf. 'Lincolnshire cordage' below, p. 525.

[4] The calculation gives 60544.283d, which is about 2¼d above the sum stated (60542d). Possibly the second (and therefore total) quantity should have been ended with *xj* rather than *xij*, giving a total of 37,671 lbs which would yield 60542.676d, but this is still over ½d adrift.

[5] Draft notes payment in full to [Richard] Dethick: BL, Add. MS 78170 [item (b)], f. 12 Richard's receipt for this (omitting the halfpenny) and another sum owed to his father is also preserved: Add. MS 78171 [item 1(f)], f. 39. See above, p. 305 & n. 1, and Appendix 4 below.

To Henry Layne of Bexley, purveyor, the same day for price of 59 loads of hooks, knees and other compass and long timber oak by him delivered for the aforesaid use, at 10s every load. *Summa* – £29 10s.

To Henry Daynes of Inworth, purveyor, the same day for price of 350 [*foot*] of 3-inch plank oak provided by him and delivered as abovesaid for the use of Her Grace's ships, at 10s every 100 foot – 35s; more for 200 foot of 2-inch plank oak, at 8s every 100 foot – 16s; and more to him for 43½ loads of timber oak, at 10s every load after 50 foot to the load – £22 5s. *Summa*- £24 1s 4d.

To John Leache of Deptford, purveyor, the same day for price of 14 loads of timber oak delivered by him there for the use as abovesaid, at 10s every load. *Summa* – £7.

To George Bridger, purveyor, the same day for price of 4 loads of hooks, knees and other compass timber oak of him had for the use of Her Grace's ships, at 10s every load – £2.

To Matthew Baker of Limehouse, shipwright, the same day for price of 613 foot of 3-inch plank oak of him taken and delivered at Deptford for the building of Her Highness's ships there, at 10s every 100 foot – £3 1s 4d.

[*Page total*] – £120 12s 8½d.

[f. 224] *Plank.* To Christopher Nayller of London the last day of December for price of 1,517 foot of 4-inch plank oak by him delivered at Deptford Strand for the building of Her Highness's great new ship there, at 12s every 100 foot – £9 1s 10d; and more to him for 1,657 foot of 3-inch plank oak, at 10s every 100 foot – £8 5s 7d. *Summa* – £17 7s 5d.

Board. To Roger Porter of London the same day for price of 3,400 foot of inch board oak delivered as aforesaid for the abovesaid use, at 5s every 100 foot. *Summa* – £8 10s

Trenails. To Henry Fillyan the same day for price of 10,000 trenails of 24 inches long by him delivered at Deptford for the use of Her Grace's ships there, at 2s every 100 – £10; more for 13,300 of trenails of 18 inches long, at 18d every 100 – £9 19s 6d; and more to him for 12,000 trenails of 14 inches long, at 14d every 100 – £7. *Summa* – £26 19s 6d.

To John Cowper the same day for price of 2,050 trenails of 24 inches long had of him for the aforesaid use, at 2s every 100 – 41s; more for 2,000 trenails of 18 inches long, at 18d every 100 – 30s; and more to him for 1,150 trenails of 14 inches long, at 14d every 100 – 13s 5d. *Summa* - £4 4s 5d.

Painting. To John Lyzarde of London, painter, the same day for the painting and colouring of Her Majesty's great new ship there in colour ed, done in oil; by agreement – £13 6s 8d.

Bails. To Richard Scarllett of Paris Garden the same day for price of 22 bails of him had for the use of Her Highness's four galliots, at 2s the piece. *Summa* – £2 4s.

[*Page total*] – £72 12s.

[f. 224v] *Old junks and ropes wrought into netting and oakum.* To Isaac Mote, Agnes Webb, John Ouneslowe, Agnes Bartlett and 12 other persons of Deptford[1] the last day of December, for price of 3 thousand 2 hundred 7 pounds weight [*3,591 lbs*] of the Queen's Majesty's old junks and ropes wrought be them into oakum for the needful caulking of Her Highness's ships at their groundings, at 3s 8d every hundredweight so working – £5 17s 10d;[2] and more to William Brooke of Deptford, ropemaker, for the working of 4 hundred 14 pounds weight [*462 lbs*] of the like junks into netting- and wrain-ropes for the aforesaid use, at 3s 8d every hundred[*weight*] – 15s 2d.[3] *Summa* – £6 13s.

Lead and solder. To John Hemmynge of London, plumber, the same day for price of 1½ hundred 11 pounds weight [*179 lbs*] of new lead of him had for the use of Her Highness's great new ship there, at 15s the hundredweight – 24s 4d;[4] more for 16 pounds weight of tin solder, at 8d every pound weight – 10s 8d; more for the wages of himself and his man working upon the same ship by the space of 24 days between them, at 10d every day – 20s; and more to him for so much paid for carrying of the said lead and solder from London to Deptford by water – 5s. *Summa* – £3.

Flags. To Stephen Androwes of London, upholsterer, the same day for one piece of red say had of him for the making of flags with the cross of St George for the use of Her Grace's ships, price 36s; more for the making of 8 great new flags, at 2s the piece – 16s; more for the making of 10 smaller flags, at 16d the piece – 13s 4d; and more to him for thread spent in the sewing of the same – 3s. *Summa* – £3 8s 4d.

Yellow rosin. To Thomas Hemmynge of London, merchant, the same day for price of 7 thousand 2 hundred 3 quarters and 4 pounds [*8,152 lbs*]

[1]Draft indicates Mote and Webb as widows, gives the third name as 'Jone Annesley', and identifies the twelve as Laurence Hedd (marginated 'William Cur''), Richard Harwood, Nicholas Archedaill, Joan Kelly, Anthony Westlond, George Bell, John Fellen, John Hurleston, William Ally, John Richardes, Nicholas Starkey and Thomas Willson: BL, Add MS 78170 [item (b)], f. 10.

[2]The calculation gives 1410.7498d, which is 3¼d below the sum stated (1414d). The sum would be almost correct with another 9 lbs; but since *vij* for *xvj* is not an evident scribal error, the fault is likely to be with the original computation.

[3]The calculation gives 181.49998d; which is ½d below the sum stated (182d). In this case a simple 414 lbs (giving a price of 182.16d) may have been used.

[4]The calculation gives 287.67856d, which is about 4¼d below the sum stated (292d). The sum would be almost correct with another 2.5 lbs, but this is not a likely scribal error.

weight of yellow rosin of him had and the same delivered into the Queen's Majesty's great storehouse at Deptford for the use of Her Grace's ships, at 8s every hundredweight – £29 2s 4d.[1]

[*Page total*] – £42 3s 8d.

[f. 225] *Pitch, tar and rosin.* To Richard Morley of Southampton, merchant, the last day of December for price of 3 last and 6 barrels of hard stone pitch of the great band of him had and delivered into Her Highness's great storehouse at Deptford Strand for the use of Her Grace's ships there, at 8s every barrel – £8 4s; more for 6 last and 4 barrels of tar, at £5 every last – £31 5s; and more for 4 hundred pounds weight of yellow rosin, at 8s every hundredweight – 32s. *Summa* – £41 1s.[2]

To Christopher Draper of London, alderman, the same day for price of 5 hundred 6 pounds weight [*566 lbs*] of rosin had of him for the use of Her Majesty's ships, at 8s every hundredweight – 40s 6d;[3] and more to him for 6 barrels of pitch, price – £3. *Summa* – £5 0s 6d.

Paper, ink and counters, &c. To William Prestwoode of London, stationer, the same day for price of 2 reams and 14 quires of paper royal of him had as well for the making of Quarter Books for payments made to masters, mariners, gunners, shipwrights, caulkers and others for keeping Her Highness's ships afloat in harbour and repairing of the same ships, as also for the engrossing of this account, at 20s every ream – 54s; more for 6 quires of demi-paper royal, at 6d the quire – 3s; more for 6 reams and 16 quires of small writing paper, at 6s 8d every ream – 45s 4d; more for one gallon and 3 pints of ink, at 5s 8d every gallon – 6s 4d; more for 2 pounds weight of casting counters, at 2s 6d every pound – 5s; and more to him for dust, wax and quills, by agreement – 6s. *Summa* – £5 19s 8d.

To William Kyrbie of London the same day for price of 3 gallons 2 quarts and one pint of ink by him delivered to the officers' clerks of Her Grace's Marine Causes for the perfecting and engrossing up of books concerning the same, at 5s 8d every gallon – 19s 4d; more for 2 tin

[1]The calculation gives 6987.4281d, which is ½d below the sum stated (6988d). Taking the quantity as a simple 7,279 lbs the computation (6987.84d) would round up correctly; cf. next note. The draft notes payment to 'Nayller' (presumably Christopher, q.v.): BL, Add. MS 78170 [item (b)], f. 18.

[2]Draft notes payment of £21 1s in part and £20 in full settlement: ibid., f. 16.

[3]The calculation gives 485.14282d, which is over ¾d below the sum stated (486d). Taking the quantity as 506 lbs the computation (485.76d) would round up correctly. This entry and the one previously noted suggest the cwt of 100 lbs may have been employed for this particular commodity. The first entry on this folio, being in straight cwts, necessarily agrees by either method; likewise those for rosin on pp. 40 above and below (1st and 2nd), whereas those on pp. 280 and 398 (3rd and 4th) appear to use the otherwise standard cwt of 112 lbs.

standishes,[1] at 2s 6d the piece – 5s; and more to him for one pound weight of counters, wax, quills and dust, by agreement – 6s. *Summa* – £1 10s 4d.[2]

[*Page total*] – £53 11s 6d.

[f. 225v] *Glazing.* To William Byrd of St Katherine's, glazier, the last day of December for price of 3 foot and 3 quarrels of new glass by him set up in the windows about Her Grace's storehouse there, at 6d every foot – 22½d; more for the new leading and closing in of 37 foot of Her Highness's old glass, at 2½d every foot – 8s 2d; more for setting in of 70 quarrels, at 1d the piece – 5s 10d; more for 10 quarrels of glass, price – 10d; and more to him for one quarter of 2d nail, price – 4d. *Summa* – 17s 0½d.

Lighterage. To William Thurston of London, lighterman, the same day as well for the service of his five great lighters of 40 tuns apiece serving Her Majesty for the bringing of Her Grace's provisions of pitch, tar, rosin, cables, hawsers, canvas, and divers other kinds of cordage taken of sundry persons for the use of her ships, from London to Deptford to Her Highness's storehouse there, as also attending upon Her Grace's ships for the having of their apparel and tackle out against their comings on ground to be breamed, caulked, ransacked and tallowed; by the space of 7½ months at several times within the time of this account, at 40s every month – £15; and more to him for wages and victuals of one man attending upon the same lighters by the space of 13 weeks 4 days within the said time, at 3s 4d every week – 45s 3d. *Summa* – £17 5s 3d.[3]

To Henry Brodeleves of London, lighterman, the same day for the hire of his lighter of the portage of 50 tuns serving Her Highness for the fetching of ballast for the ballasting of Her Grace's ships, by the space of 3 weeks at 5s every week. *Summa* – 15s.

Runlet. To John Willyamson of London, cooper, the same day for price of one runlet containing 13 gallons of him had for the putting in of caulking oil for the use of Her Majesty's ships; by agreement – 1s 2d.

[*Page total*] – £18 18s 5½d.

[f. 226] *Hewing and felling of timber oak.* To James Cornyshe of Hull in Yorkshire, master shipwright, the last day of December for wages paid by him to John Downe, Peter Baker, William Lawson, John Corker, James Hodgekynson, Thomas Burlye, Ralph Armytaidge, Richard Hayelles, Ralph Robynson, John Walsey and 12 other shipwrights of Wistow, Cawood, Selby, Brayton and Hull for felling, hewing and squaring of 1,150 trees of

[1] Inkstands.

[2] Draft notes payment to 'John Browen': BL, Add. MS 78170 [item (b)], f. 14.

[3] Draft notes payment of £7 5s 3d in part and £10 in full settlement: ibid., f. 17.

oak in 'Southwoode',[1] Burn park, Stainer park, Temple Hirst park, 'Muskell hagg',[2] Skipwith park and Ryther park within the county of York into 1,420 pieces of timber as floor timbers, futtocks, knees, rails, posts, beams, grains, corner posts and stems for a new ship to be made at Her Majesty's pleasure; by the space of 660 days among them all within the time of this account, at 10d every day the man – £27 10s.

Wharfage. To John Paullmer of Millhall in Kent the same day as well for the hire of his wharf for the laying of Her Highness's provisions of timber, planks and boards thereon, to the number of 687 loads, as also for his attending and safe-keeping thereof there, which said timber, planks and boards was provided in divers and sundry places thereabouts and sent from thence to Deptford Strand for the new building of Her Grace's ships; by the space of 7 years begun the 17th day of July *anno Domini* 1557 and ended the 23th day of June 1563, within the said time; by agreement – £6 13s 4d.

House rent. To Peter Pett of Deptford, master shipwright, the same day for one quarter of a year's rent of two cellars of him hired wherein lieth Her Grace's store of rosin for the use of Her Majesty's ships; due at this present – £1.

[*Page total*] – £35 3s 4d. [f. 226v *blank*]

[f. 227] **Ordinary. Woolwich**:

Anno Domini 1563. Anno regni regine Elizabethe quinto

A payment made the last day of March as well to keepers of storehouses, dock and timber-yards there, and to house-carpenters, sawyers and tilers for new mending and repairing of Her Grace's storehouses, as also to labourers for the unlading and discharging of hoys and other vessels with provisions taken of divers persons for the use of Her Majesty's ships; by one quarter of a year begun the first day of January last and ended as abovesaid, as followeth:[3]

[1] Very likely the two closes called 'Southwoode' in Riccall, mentioned in a 1651 sale deed: East Riding of Yorkshire Archives, Beverley, DDHV/29/36. We are indebted to Miss P. J. Martin of the East Riding Archives Service for this reference.

[2] 'Hagg' (meaning copse) is a common element in the place-names of the area; cf. Moss Hagg, 5 miles west of Selby, though this name is recorded only from 1858: EPNS, *Yorkshire WR*, iv, p. 34. Efforts to locate a place approximating to 'Muskell Hagg' have been unsuccessful, but we are further grateful to Miss Martin for noticing that one of the witnesses to the 'Southwoode' deed cited above was a Nicholas *Maskall*.

[3] A fragment of a draft for this Woolwich quarter survives as BL, Add. MS 78170 [item (c)], f. 23r–v, comprising the payments to storekeepers, an extended version of the payments to sawyers (as noted below), and all elements of the Emptions section except the payment to Dethick.

*[*Keepers of storehouses*]. To Jerome Hewster the last day of March for his wages daily attending and serving Her Highness for the safe-keeping of Her Grace's storehouses there wherein lieth divers and sundry kinds of provisions for the use of Her Majesty's ships, by one quarter of a year containing 90 days begun the first day of January last and this day ended, at 6d *per diem* – £2 5s.

To John Jeckett, porter, the same day for his wages daily attending and serving Her Highness in safe-keeping of Her Grace's timber-yards there wherein lieth her timber, planks and boards for the use of Her Majesty's ships, by like time of 90 days begun and ended as abovesaid, at 6d *per diem* – £2 5s.

[*Page total*] – £4 10s.

[f. 227v] *House-carpenters*

John Leache, master, 6 days at 12d	6s
Thomas Dyckyns, 6 days at 8d	4s
Robert Throughley, 6 days at 9d	4s 6d
Sawyers[1]	
Thomas Phillipps, 2 days at 12d	2s
William Crosse, 2 days at 12d	2s
Tilers	
John Callawaye, master, 20 days at 11d	18s 4d
Stephen Higgyns, 20 days at 10d	16s 8d
Richard Savaidge, 20 days at 10d	16s 8d
Michael Hogesone, 20 days at 8d	13s 4d
Labourers	
John Marshe, 10 days at 8d	6s 8d
John Hilton, 10 days at 8d	6s 8d
Henry Harrys , 6 days at 6d	3s
Charles Deane, 5 days at 6d	2s 6d
Lawrence Chapman, 4 days at 6d	2s
John Carpenter, 6 days at 6d	3s
James Rigwell, 10 days at 6d	5s
Martin Mathew, 18 days at 6d	9s

[*Page total*] – £6 1s 4d. *[*Artificers – £4 3s 6d*; *labourers – 37s 10d*]

[f. 228] John Orton, 8 days at 6d	4s
John Chapman, 6 days at 6d	3s
Thomas Snowe, 10 days at 6d	5s

[1]In the draft this entry follows the format for the officers: 'To Thomas Phillips and William Crosse, sawyers, the same day [i.e. 31 Mar. 1563] for sawing and cutting of timber for the mending of Her Grace's storehouses there, by 2 days at 12d the day a man. *Summa* – 4s.': BL, Add MS 78170 [item (c)], f. 23v.

Robert Wingrose, 3 days at 6d	18d
William Corbye, 2 days at 6d	12d
George Bebster, 6 days at 6d	3s
John Kyent, 10 days at 6d	5s
William Bomer, 6 days at 6d	3s
John Roodes, 20 days at 6d	10s
Robert Tayeller, 6 days at 6d	3s
Henry Burbidge, 6 days at 6d	3s
Thomas Phillypps, 12 days at 6d	6s
William Lyttellwood, 20 days at 6d	10s
John Mathew, 20 days at 6d	10s
Thomas Morrys, 6 days at 6d	3s
John Powell, 4 days at 6d	2s
William Bonnar, 6 days at 6d	3s
John Ellys, 6 days at 6d	3s
John Davy, 6 days at 6d	3s
Richard Thornefall, 12 days at 6d	6s
John Sonmer, 10 days at 6d	5s
John Staples, 10 days at 6d	5s
Thomas Fraunces, 6 days at 6d	3s
Stephen Longokond, 40 days at 6d	20s

[*Page total*] – £6 0s 6d.

[f. 228v] *Emptions*

Timber, plank and trenails. *[*Timber – £128 11s 6d*; *trenails – £21 17s*]. To John Dethick of Colchester, purveyor, the last day of March for price of 221 loads of compass and long timber oak of him had and the same delivered at Woolwich for the use of Her Grace's ships, at 10s every load after 50 foot to the load – £110; more for 1,645 foot of 2-inch plank oak, at 8s every 100 [*foot*] – £6 11s 6d; more for 2,306 foot of 3-inch plank oak, at 10s every 100 [*foot*] – £11 10s; more for 10,000 of trenails of 36 inches long, at 3s every 100 – £15; more for 3,000 of trenails of 30 inches long, at 2s 6d every 100 – £3 15s; more for 3,000 of trenails of 24 inches long, at 2s every 100 – £3; and more to him for 200 of trenails of 12 inches long, at 12d every 100 – 2s. *Summa* – £150 8s 6d.[1]

Ironwork. To Thomas Willson of Ratcliff, smith, the same day for price of [*one*] hundred 2 quarters weight [*137 lbs*] of his own new iron by him wrought into bolts, spikes and nails for the amending and repairing of Her Grace's storehouses there, at 23s 4d every hundredweight – 35s;

[1]Not found in draft. Dethick's account was settled posthumously in June 1564, but this particular sum is not distinguished in the reckoning: see above, p. 305 & n. 1, p. 322 & n. 5, and Appendix 4 below.

more for 1,000 of 10d nails, price – 8s 4d; more for 2,000 of 6d nails, price – 10s; more for 1,000 of 4d nails, price – 3s 4d; and more to him for 1,000 of 3d nails, price 2s 6d. *Summa* – £2 19s 2d.

Lime and brick. To John Parratt of Deptford, limeman, the same day for price of 4 hundred[*weight*] of lime of him had for the needful repairing of the chimneys in Her Grace's victualling houses there, at 7s every hundred[*weight*] – 28s; and more to him for 3,000 of brick, at 11s every 1,000, with the carriage – 33s. *Summa* – £3 1s.

[*Page total*] – £156 8s 8d.

[f. 229] *Burning reed*. To John Martyn, reedman, the last day of March for price of 2,000 of burning reed of him had for the needful breaming of Her Grace's ships, at 10s every 1,000. *Summa* – £1.

To John Byrde the same day for price of 1,300 of burning reed of him had for the use of Her Grace's said ships, at 10s every 1,000 – 13s.

To John Asshe the same day for price of 2,000 of burning reed by him delivered there for the use of Her Majesty's ships, at 10s every 1,000 – £1.

To John Rawllins of Paris Garden for price of 2,000 of burning reed of him had for the use of Her Majesty's said ships, at 12d every 100 – £1.[1]

To Richard Harrys of Paris Garden the same day for price of 900 of burning reed of him had for the use of Her Grace's ships, at 12d every 100 – 9s.

To John Marshall of Erith, reedman, the same day for price of 2,000 of burning reed of him had for the use as aforesaid, at 10s every 1,000 – £1.

To John Mosse of Barking, reedman, the same day for price of 2,000 of burning reed of him had for the use of Her Grace's ships, at 12d every 100 – £1.[2]

[*Page total*] – £6 2s. [f. 229v *blank*]

[f. 230] A payment made the last day of June as well to keepers of storehouses, dock and timber-yards there wherein lieth all manner of provisions for the use of Her Grace's ships, as also to divers persons for necessaries of them had for the repairing of Her Highness's said storehouses there, by one quarter of a year begun the first day of April last and this day ended, as followeth:

*[*Keepers of storehouses, timber-yards, and plug keeper*]. To Jerome Hewster the last day of June for his wages daily attending and serving

[1]Draft indicates payment made to John Hodson; BL, Add. MS 78170 [item (c)], f. 23v.
[2]Draft notres payment to John Jeckett: ibid.

Her Highness in safe-keeping of Her Grace's storehouses there wherein lieth divers kinds of provisions for the use of Her Majesty's ships, by one quarter of a year containing 91 days begun the first day of April last and this day ended, at 6d *per diem* – £2 5s 6d.

To John Jyckett, porter, the same day for his wages daily attending and serving Her Highness in the safe-keeping of Her Grace's timber-yards there wherein lieth her timber, planks and boards for the use of Her Majesty's ships, by like time of 91 days begun and ended as abovesaid, at 6d *per diem* – £2 5s 6d.

To Stephen Longokom, labourer, the same day for his wages daily attending and serving Her Highness in keeping of the plug and letting out of the water in the dock there for the drier keeping of the same, with other needful labour by him done there, by the space of 40 days within this quarter, at 6d *per diem* – £1.

[*Page total*] – £5 11s.

[f. 230v] *Emptions*

House tile. To James Brookehowse of Lewisham the last day of June for price of 3,000 of house tile of him had and the same delivered at Woolwich for the new mending and repairing of Her Grace's storehouses there, at 12s every 1,000 – £1 16s.

[*Page total*] – *Summa predicta*.

[f. 231] A payment made the last day of September as well to keepers of storehouses, dock and timber-yards there wherein lieth divers and sundry kinds of provisions for the use of Her Grace's ships, as also for other needful provisions taken of divers persons for the use of the same ships, by one quarter of a year begun the first day of July last and this day ended, as followeth:

*[*Keepers of storehouses and timber-yards*]. To Jerome Hewster the last day of September for his wages daily attending and serving Her Majesty in safe-keeping of Her Grace's storehouses there wherein lieth divers kinds of provisions for the use of Her Highness's ships, by one quarter of a year containing 92 days begun the first day of July last and this day ended, at 6d *per diem* – £2 6s.

To John Jeckytt, porter, the same day for his wages daily attending and serving Her Highness in safe-keeping of Her Grace's timber-yards there wherein lieth Her Majesty's store of timber, planks and boards for the building and repairing of her ships, by like time of 92 days begun and ended as abovesaid, at 6d *per diem* – £2 6s.

[*Page total*] – £4 12s.

[f. 231v] *Emptions*

Hire of a lighter. To William Provyes of Greenwich the last day of September for the hire of his lighter and service of his men serving Her Highness for the fetching of 22½ loads of Her Grace's shores from Deptford to Woolwich and there delivered the same for the use of Her Majesty's ships, at 12d every load carrying – £1 2s 6d.

[*Page total*] – *Summa predicta.*

[f. 232] *Anno regni regine Elizabethe sexto*

A payment made the last day of December as well to keepers of storehouses, dock and timber-yards there wherein lieth divers kinds of provisions for the use of Her Majesty's ships, as also to labourers and others for new mending and repairing of the dockheads there, and to sundry persons for needful things had of them for the use of the same, by one quarter of a year begun the first day of October last and this day ended, as followeth:

*[*Keeper of storehouses*]. To Jerome Hewstar the last day of December for his wages daily attending and serving Her Highness in safe-keeping of Her Grace's storehouses there wherein lieth divers and sundry needful things for the use of Her Majesty's ships, by one quarter of a year containing 92 days begun the first day of October and ended as abovesaid, at 6d *per diem* – £2 6s.

To John Jeckytt, porter, the same day for his wages daily attending and serving Her Majesty in safe-keeping of Her Highness's dock and timber-yards there wherein lieth Her Grace's store of timber, planks and boards for the use of her ships, by like time of 92 days begun and ended as is aforesaid, at 6d *per diem* – £2 6s.

[£4 12s*]

Labourers

John Hylton, master, 12 days at 8d	8s
Martin Mathew, 11 days at 7d	6s 5d
William Whytbye, 11 days at 7d	6s 5d
William Harryson, 12 days at 6d	6s
John Washe, 12 days at 6d	6s
Robert Phillyppes, 8 days at 6d	4s

[*Page total*] – £6 8s 10d.

[f. 232v] *House-carpenters*

John Leache, master, 6 days at 12d	6s
Thomas Higgons, server, 6 days at 10d	5s

Benjamin Leache, server, 6 days at 4d	2s
	*[*13s*]*

Emptions

Ironwork. To Thomas Willson of Ratcliff, smith, the last day of December for price of 2 quarters and 29 pounds weight [*85 lbs*] of new iron wrought into spikes and dogs of iron for the mending and repairing of the dockhead there, after the rate of 23s 4d every hundredweight – 17s 8½d; more for 300 of nails at 20d every 100 – 5s; more for 500 of nails, at 10d the 100 – 4s 2d; more for 500 of 6d nail, price – 2s 6d; and more to him for 500 of 4d nail, price 20d. *Summa* – £1 11s 0½d.

Marsh earth. To Alice Boughton of Woolwich, widow, the same day for price of 3 lighterfuls of marsh earth had of her for the use of the same dockhead, at 2s 6d every lighterful. *Summa* – 7s 6d.

Lighterage. To John Taster of London, lighterman, the same day for the hire of a lighter which served Her Highness by the space of 2 weeks for the fetching of marsh earth for the use of the said dockhead, at 6s 8d every week – 13s 4d.

[*Page total*] – £3 4s 10½d.

[f. 233] **Ordinary. Gillingham:**

Anno Domini 1563. Anno regni regine Elizabethe quinto

A payment made the last day of March as well to masters, mariners, gunners and others daily attending and serving Her Highness in safe-keeping of Her Grace's ships afloat in harbour and to divers persons for rent of storehouses wherein lieth Her Highness's store for the use of Her Majesty's ships, as also to shipwrights, caulkers, sawyers, smiths and other artificers and workmen for mending and repairing Her Grace's said ships and provisions for the same, for one quarter of a year begun the first day of January last and this day ended, as followeth:

The Elizabeth Jonas

Mariners

John Hurlocke, master, 12 weeks 6 days	£6 8s 7d
John Teigg, boatswain, 12 weeks 6 days	53s 8d
Lancelot Tristram, purser, 12 weeks 6 days	45s
Thomas Waller, cook & steward, 12 weeks 6 days	29s 5½d
Edward Brenden, 12 weeks 6 days	21s 5d
John Collens, 12 weeks 6 days	21s 5d
Richard Brisholde, 12 weeks 6 days	21s 5d
William Kysshan, 12 weeks 6 days	21s 5d

John Pyrton, 5 weeks 3 days	9s
Henry Woode, 12 weeks 6 days	21s 5d
Robert Heallinge, 12 weeks 6 days	21s 5d
John Burnett, 11 weeks	18s 4d
John Blythe, 12 weeks 6 days	21s 5d
William Rumney, 12 weeks 6 days	21s 5d
John Woodroff, 12 weeks 6 days	21s 5d
Roger Reade, 12 weeks 6 days	21s 5d
George Voyse, 12 weeks 6 days	21s 5d
John Apulton, boy, 12 weeks 6 days	10s 8½d
Nicholas Lovett, 12 weeks 6 days	21s 5d
William Symonde, boy, 12 weeks 6 days	10s 8½d
Thomas Searle, 12 weeks 6 days	21s 5d

[*Page total*] – £29 3s 9½d.

[f. 233v] James Robartson, 12 weeks 6 days	21s 5d
John Twyckbearde, 8 weeks 1 day	13s 7d
John Good, 12 weeks 6 days	21s 5d
Thomas Nedam, 8 weeks 6 days	14s 9d
Nicholas Johnson, carpenter, 7 weeks 1 day	29s 9d
John Hitchecock, server, 7 weeks 6 days	11s 11d
Isaac Ashley, server, 5 weeks 4 days	9s 4d
[*Gunner*]	
Lawrence Dilke, master gunner, 12 weeks 6 days	32s 2d
The Triumph	
Mariners	
William Wood, master, 12 weeks 6 days	£6 8s 7d
Thomas Goldstone, boatswain, 12 weeks 6 days	53s 7d
Henry Cooke, purser, 12 weeks 6 days	32s 2d
John Baswell, cook and steward, 12 weeks 6 days	29s 5½d
John Newball, 12 weeks 6 days	21s 5d
Mark Bullen, 12 weeks 6 days	21s 5d
Robert White, 12 weeks 6 days	21s 5d
Peter Trew, 12 weeks 6 days	21s 5d
Thomas Tybboll, 12 weeks 6 days	21s 5d
Robert Keye, 12 weeks 6 days	21s 5d
Thomas Ratlyff, 12 weeks 6 days	21s 5d
Peter Morgan, 7 weeks	11s 8d
John Robson, 12 weeks 6 days	21s 5d
George Mylles, 12 weeks 6 days	21s 5d
Henry Maggett, 12 weeks 6 days	21s 5d
Robert Gyelles, 12 weeks 6 days	21s 5d

John Raggett, 12 weeks 6 days	21s 5d
John Boye, 12 weeks 6 days	21s 5d
Peter Edwardes, 4 weeks 3 days	7s 4d
Edward Wyckes, boy, 12 weeks 6 days	10s 8½d
Henry Morrys, gromet, 12 weeks 6 days	16s 1d
Fabian Bullyn, 12 weeks 6 days	21s 5d
Davy Borrow, 12 weeks 6 days	21s 5d
William Welshe, carpenter, 5 weeks 4 days	23s 2d
Thomas Freman, gromet, 5 weeks 4 days	6s 11d
William Chartram, gromet, 5 weeks 4 days	6s 11d

[*Page total*] – £40 2s 2d.

[f. 234] Ralph Browne, 5 weeks 4 days	16s 1d
Edmund Waller, 5 weeks 4 days	16s 1d
Robert Willett, gromet, 5 weeks 4 days	6s 11d
[*Gunner*]	
Stephen Bull, master gunner, 1 week	2s 6d
The Victory	
Mariners	
William Barnes, master, 12 weeks 6 days	£6 8s 7d
John Light, boatswain, 12 weeks 6 days	53s 7d
Hugh Pope, purser, 12 weeks 6 days	32s 2d
Thomas Gayetes, cook & steward, 12 weeks 6 days	29s 5½d
Adam Puckwell, 12 weeks 6 days	37s 6d
William Persyvall, 12 weeks 6 days	21s 5d
Abel Smythe, 8 weeks 3 days	14s
George Stewarde, 12 weeks 6 days	21s 5d
Peter Hansom, 7 weeks 4 days	12s 8d
Thomas Cossyne, 12 weeks 6 days	21s 5d
Richard Blacke, 10 weeks	16s 8d
Richard Smythe, 2 weeks 3 days	4s
Stephen Justis, 12 weeks 6 days	21s 5d
Ralph Ducke, 9 weeks 3 days	15s 8d
John Grene, 7 weeks 5 days	12s 8d
Arnold Hartt, 12 weeks 6 days	21s 5d.
William Clarke, 2 weeks 3 days	4s
Robert Ussher, gromet, 12 weeks 6 days	16s 1d
Leonard Holte, boy, 12 weeks 6 days	10s 8½d
John Roche, 12 weeks 6 days	21s 5d
Nicholas Claye, carpenter, 5 weeks 4 days	23s 2d
John Claye, gromet, 5 weeks 4 days	6s 11d
John Sager, 5 weeks 4 days	9s 4d

Thomas Hodge, 5 weeks 2 days	8s 9d
William Hodge, gromet, 5 weeks 4 days	6s 11d
Mark Hodge, 5 weeks 2 days	8s 9d
[*Gunner*]	
William Thomas, master gunner, 1 week	2s 6d

[*Page total*] – £31 4s 2d.

[f. 234v] *The Hope*

Mariners	
Robert West, boatswain, 5 weeks 1 day	[*blank*]
Michael Gonson, purser, 12 weeks 6 days	32s 2d
John Mathew, cook and steward, 12 weeks 6 days	29s 5½d
Thomas Starke, 12 weeks 6 days	21s 5d
James Robartson, 12 weeks 6 days	21s 5d
Roger Austen, 12 weeks 6 days	21s 5d
Gregory Stewarde, 12 weeks 6 days	21s 5d
Andrew Streake, 12 weeks 6 days	21s 5d
Andrew Brene, 5 weeks 1 day	8s 7d
Hugh Bowye, 12 weeks 6 days	21s 5d
Henry Burdges, 12 weeks 6 days	21s 5d
John Sustyane, 12 weeks 6 days	21s 5d
John Merrett, 12 weeks 6 days	21s 5d
Richard Abethell, 12 weeks 6 days	21s 5d
William Bateman, gromet, 12 weeks 6 days	16s 1d
John Aboen, boatswain, 6 weeks 6 days	28s 6d
John Newton, boy, 6 weeks 6 days	5s 8½d
Henry Sherwood, carpenter, 5 weeks 4 days	23s 2d
Thomas Platterer, gromet, 5 weeks 4 days	6s 11d
Gunner	
Thomas Dixson, master, 12 weeks 6 days	32s 2d

[*Page total*] – £19 16s 11d.

[f. 235] *The Mary Rose*

Mariners	
William Robynson, boatswain, 12 weeks 6 days	53s 7d
Christopher Davye, purser, 12 weeks 6 days	32s 2d
Roger Cratwaye, cook & steward, 12 weeks 6 days	29s 5½d
Humphrey Stevenson, 12 weeks 6 days	21s 5d
John Cossyn, 12 weeks 6 days	21s 5d
John Drew, 7 weeks 3 days	12s 4d
William Romney, 12 weeks 6 days	21s 5d
William Cocke, 12 weeks 6 days	21s 5d
John Gylbart, 12 weeks 6 days	21s 5d

Thomas Kyngdowne, 12 weeks 6 days	21s 5d
John Welles, gromet, 12 weeks 6 days	16s 1d
Thomas Leonarde, gromet, 12 weeks 6 days	16s 1d
Edward Laughan, boy, 12 weeks 6 days	10s 8½d
Thomas Vaughan, 4 weeks 3 days	7s 4d
Thomas Harrington, 12 weeks 6 days	21s 5d
John Woodcock, 12 weeks 6 days	21s 5d
John Bunche, carpenter, 5 weeks 4 days	23s 2d
William Harbar, gromet, 5 weeks 4 days	6s 11d
John Pulter, server, 5 weeks 4 days	9s 4d
Thomas Butlar, boy, 12 weeks 6 days	10s 8½d
Gunner	
John Butler, master, 3 days	12d

[*Page total*] – £20 0s 2½d.

[f. 235v] *The Lion*

Mariners	
William Hollande, master, 12 weeks 6 days	£5 7s 1½d
William Keyes, boatswain, 5 weeks 1 day	21s 5d
John Butler, purser, 12 weeks 6 days	32s 2d
John Curlle, cook and steward, 12 weeks 6 days	29s 5½d
William Wilkins, 12 weeks 6 days	21s 5d
John Samonde, 12 weeks 6 days	21s 5d
John Russell, 12 weeks 6 days	21s 5d
Robert Goslinge, 12 weeks 6 days	21s 5d
Nicholas Waller, 12 weeks 6 days	21s 5d
William Johnson, 7 weeks 3 days	12s 4d
Silvester Bewell, 12 weeks 6 days	21s 5d
Nicholas Hewes, 12 weeks 6 days	21s 5d
William Charlles, 12 weeks 6 days	21s 5d
Thomas Dayll, 12 weeks 6 days	21s 5d
Thomas Browne, 12 weeks 6 days	21s 5d
Thomas Tayllor, gromet, 7 weeks 3 days	9s 3d
William Richarde, boy, 12 weeks 6 days	10s 8½d
John Kennett, boy, 7 weeks 3 days	6s 1½d
Rowland Derawe, 12 weeks 6 days	21s 5d
Robert Harwoode, boatswain, 6 weeks 3 days	26s 9d
Roger Browne, boy, 6 weeks 3 days	5s 4d
John Harwarde, gromet, 3 weeks 3 days	4s 3d
Gunners	
Edward Tompson, master, 12 weeks 6 days	32s 2d
Peter Arney, server, 12 weeks 6 days	21s 5d

[*Page total*] – £27 14s 1d.

[f. 236] *The Philip and Mary*

Mariners	
John Jones, boatswain, 12 weeks 6 days	53s 7d
John Pursell, purser, [*blank*]	[*blank*]
John Geffery, cook and steward, 12 weeks 6 days	29s 5½d
Francis Williams, 12 weeks 6 days	21s 5d
Gregory Wyckes, 12 weeks 6 days	21s 5d
Thomas Sharpley, 12 weeks 6 days	21s 5d
Zach Swetman, 12 weeks 6 days	21s 5d
Arthur Lyversuche, 12 weeks 6 days	21s 5d
Edward Colson, 12 weeks 6 days	21s 5d
Richard West, 12 weeks 6 days	21s 5d
Thomas James, 12 weeks 6 days	21s 5d
John West, 10 weeks 3 days	17s 4d
John Norrys, 6 weeks 3 days	10s 8d
John Smythe, 9 weeks 2 days	15s 6d
Bartholomew Gayttes, gromet, 12 weeks 6 days	16s 1d
Edward Hawston, gromet, 12 weeks 6 days	16s 1d
Henry Raynsforth, 12 weeks 6 days	21s 5d
Gunner	
Matthew Sharpp, master, 12 weeks 6 days	32s 2d

[*Page total*] – £19 3s 7½d.

[f. 236v] *The Willoughby*

Mariners	
Robert Flynt, boatswain, 12 weeks 6 days	37s 6d
George Halle, purser & steward, 12 weeks 6 days	29s 5½d
Richard Dennes, 12 weeks 6 days	21s 5d
Thomas Durrant, 12 weeks 6 days	21s 5d
Benjamin Flynt, gromet, 12 weeks 6 days	16s 1d
Thomas Wooddrege, 12 weeks 6 days	21s 5d
Richard Babb, 12 weeks 6 days	21s 5d
Richard Flemynge, 10 weeks 2 days	17s 2d
[*Gunners*]	
John Malpas, master gunner, 12 weeks 6 days	32s 2d
John Turnar, server, 12 weeks 6 days	21s 5d

The Tiger

Mariners	
John Aboen, boatswain, 6 weeks	17s 6d
John Hawkins, purser & steward, 12 weeks 6 days	29s 5½d
John Bowye, 12 weeks 6 days	21s 5d
Thomas Butlar, 12 weeks 6 days	21s 5d

Thomas Halle, 12 weeks 6 days	21s 5d
John Newton, boy, 6 weeks	5s
John Beamond, boatswain, 6 weeks 6 days	20s
Matthew Woodstocke, boy, 6 weeks 6 days	5s 8½d
John Johnson, 2 weeks 3 days	4s
[Gunner]	
John Moore, master gunner, 12 weeks 6 days	32s 2d

The Sun

Mariners

Nicholas Starkey, boatswain, 5 weeks 6 days	17s 1d
Francis Burchall, gromet, 5 weeks 6 days	7s 3d
John Lardge, 5 weeks 6 days	9s 9d
[Gunner]	
William Ellys, master gunner, 5 weeks 6 days	14s 7d

[*Page total*] – £23 6s 2½d.

[f. 237] *The Bull*

Mariners

Andrew Walker, boatswain, 12 weeks 6 days	37s 6d
John Willy, purser and steward, 12 weeks 6 days	29s 5½d
Christopher Cowper, 12 weeks 6 days	21s 5d
Edward Thomas, gromet, 12 weeks 6 days	16s 1d
Richard Crannolde, 12 weeks 6 days	21s 5d
Robert Hartely, gromet, 12 weeks 6 days	16s 1d
Henry Tanner, 12 weeks 6 days	21s 5d
Richard Pytman, 12 weeks 6 days	21s 5d
Matthew Robson, 5 weeks 5 days	9s 5d
[Gunner]	
Robert Butlar, master gunner, 3 days	12d

The Falcon

Mariners

Lawrence Cleare, boatswain, 12 weeks 6 days	37s 6d
Henry Baker, purser & steward, 12 weeks 6 days	29s 5½d
Richard Langley, gromet, 12 weeks 6 days	16s 1d
William Warde, 12 weeks 6 days	21s 5d
Richard Bygges, 12 weeks 6 days	21s 5d
[Gunner]	
John Commyn, master gunner, 12 weeks 6 days	32s 2d

The Bright Falcon

Mariners

Robert Blaike, boatswain, 6 weeks 6 days	20s
Edward Tayllor, 12 weeks 6 days	21s 5d

Henry Willyams, 12 weeks 6 days	21s 5d
[*Gunner*]	
John Walker, master gunner, 12 weeks 6 days	32s 2d
The Christopher	
Mariner	
John Worrall, 12 weeks 6 days	21s 5d
[*Page total*] – £23 9s 8d.	

[f. 237v] *The Galley Speedwell*	
Mariners	
Cuthbert Clarke, boatswain, 12 weeks 6 days	53s 7d
Anthony Darnatho, 12 weeks 6 days	21s 5d
William Prince, 12 weeks 6 days	21s 5d
Thomas Purden, 12 weeks 6 days	21s 5d
Thomas Foster, boy, 12 weeks 6 days	10s 8½d
Cornelius Bryan, 4 weeks 3 days	7s 4d
[*Gunner*]	
Maurice Aboen, master gunner 12 weeks 6 days	32s 2d
The Galley Tryright	
Mariners	
Simon Barnsley, boatswain, 12 weeks 6 days	37s 6d
John Godden, purser, 12 weeks 6 days	32s 2d
William Kent, cook and steward, 12 weeks 6 days	29s 5½d
John Tayllor, 12 weeks 6 days	21s 5d
Thomas Bucklande, 2 weeks 3 days	4s
[*Gunner*]	
Thomas Nealle, master gunner, [*blank*]	[*blank*]
The Galley Mermaid	
Mariners	
Henry Pendley, 4 weeks	6s 8d
Henry Fuller, 4 weeks 3 days	7s 4d
Simon Marden, 12 weeks 6 days	21s 5d
George Porter, 12 weeks 6 days	21s 5d
Richard Harman, 12 weeks 6 days	21s 5d
The Mary Grace Hoy	
Mariners	
William Pearson, master, 12 weeks 6 days	53s 7d
John Yonge, 12 weeks 6 days	21s 5d
[*Page total*] – £21 5s 10d.	

[f. 238] *The Rowbarge*	
Mariners	
Robert Blaike, boatswain, 6 weeks	17s 6d

Thomas Whittell, cook and steward, 6 weeks	13s 9d
Andrew Ballerde, boy, 6 weeks	5s
Andrew Roche, 3 weeks 1 day	5s 3d
John Fraunces, 3 weeks 1 day	5s 3d
William Fallett, 6 weeks	10s
Simon Breadstreate, 6 weeks	10s
Thomas Johnson, 6 weeks	10s
William Conney, 6 weeks	10s

Wages of gunners daily attendant in Her Highness's fort at Upnor for the safe-keeping of Her Grace's ships in Gillingham Water.

Thomas Sergaunt, master, 90 days at 16d	£6
Richard Abeseade, 90 days at 12d	£4 10s
Robert Wollgrove, 90 days at 12d	£4 10s
William Bowell, 90 days at 12d	£4 10s
William Chisselton, 90 days at 12d	£4 10s
Randall Stevenson, 90 days at 12d	£4 10s
William Tauton, 90 days at 12d	£4 10s
Robert Halssnoth, 90 days at 12d	£4 10s

[*Page total*] – £41 16s 9d.

[f. 238v] *[*Clerk*]. To Thomas Heynos the last day of March for his wages daily attending and serving Her Highness for the keeping of the book of cheque of masters, mariners and gunners keeping Her Majesty's ships afloat in harbour, as also the prick book of shipwrights and caulkers, by one quarter of a year begun the first day of January last and ended as abovesaid. *Summa* – £5.

*[*Purveyor*]. To Butolph Moungey the same day for his wages daily attending and serving Her Highness in making of provisions of all kind of necessaries for the use of Her Grace's ships, by one like quarter of a year containing 90 days begun and ended as is aforesaid, at 8d *per diem* – £3.

*[*Purveyor*]. To Thomas Baker the same day for his wages daily attending and serving Her Majesty in delivering of all manner of necessary provisions out of Her Grace's storehouses there for the use of Her Highness's ships, by one quarter of a year begun and ended as aforesaid – £2.

[*Page total*] – £10.

[f. 239] *Shipwrights*

Peter Pett, master, 13 days at 12d	13s
Nicholas Johnson, 34 days at 10d	28s 4d
John Hitchecocke, server, 37 days at 4d	12s 4d

Isaac Asheley, server, 47 days at 5d	19s 7d
John Bunche, 47 days at 8d	31s 4d
John Pulter, server, 47 days at 5d	19s 7d
William Harber, server, 47 days at 4d	15s 8d
Henry Sherwood, 47 days at 7d	27s 5d
Thomas Platterar, server, 47 days at 2d	7s 10d
William Welshe, 47 days at 8d	31s 4d
Thomas Freman, server, 47 days at 4d	15s 8d
William Chartram, server, 47 days at 3d	11s 9d
Ralph Browne, 47 days at 7d	27s 5d
Edmund Waller, 32 days at 6d	16s
Robert Willett, server, 47 days at 4d	15s 8d
Nicholas Claye, 47 days at 8d	31s 4d
John Claye, server, 47 days at 4d	15s 8d
John Sager, server, 47 days at 6d	23s 6d
Thomas Hodge, 23 days at 7d	13s 5d
William Hodge, server, 45 days at 4d	15s
Mark Hodge, 46 days at 6d	23s
Gregory Androw, server, 6 days at 6d	3s
Lawrence Androw, server, 6 days at 6d	3s
Christopher Swetman, server, 6 days at 6d	3s
George Kingston, server, 47 days at 5d	19s 7d
Richard Chapman, 27 days at 6d	13s 6d
Thomas Blosse, 27 days at 8d	18s
Henry Neallye, server, 27 days at 4d	9s
John Wynnye, 27 days at 8d	18s
John Wythers, server, 27 days at 6d	13s 6d
Robert Hudson, 24 days at 8d	16s
Richard Gyrdlington, server, 5 days at 5d	2s 1d
Richard Crippes, 52 days at 6d	26s
Thomas Poulter, 51 days at 10d	42s 6d
John Clark, server, 51 days at 4d	17s

[*Page total*] – £30 19s.

[f. 239v] Michael Chamber, 43½ days at 7d	25s 4½d
Roger Raynor, 20 days at 6d	10s
Robert Pakeman, 20 days at 6d	10s
John Mylles, 23 days at 7d	13s 5d
Robert Archer, server, 23 days at 4d	7s 8d
Henry Hartely, 21 days at 7d	12s 3d
Thomas Newbery, 13 days at 7d	7s 7d
Thomas Eaton, server, 13 days at 3d	3s 3d

John Goldinge, 8 days at 8d	5s 4d
William Jenney, server, 13 days at 6d	6s 6d
Richard Bull, 10 days at 6d	5s
George Browne, 9 days at 7d	5s 3d
Richard Francke, server, 9 days at 4d	3s
Richard Daye, 8 days at 8d	5s 4d
William Hartropp, 3 days at 7d	21d
Richard Dennes, server, 46½ days at 4d	15s 6d
George Mathew, 37 days at 6d	18s 6d
Thomas Purden, 21 days at 3d	5s 3d
Roger Awsten, 19 days at 3d	4s 9d
Caulkers	
Robert Bridgges, 18 days and tides at 7d	10s 6d
Humphrey Dayll, server, 18 days and tides at 6d	9s
John Estwood, 12 days and tides at 6d	6s
Roger Lakyn, 18 days and tides at 7d	10s 6d
Henry Aidey, server, 18 days and tides at 2d	3s
William Bastiane, 18 days and tides at 6d	9s
Arthur Carr, server, 18 days and tides at 2d	3s
Michael Rowse, 18 days and tides at 6d	9s
Robert Tapshear, 18 days and tides at 6d	9s
William Thomas, 18 days and tides at 6d	9s
John Stockdayll, 15 days and tides at 6d	7s 6d
Humphrey Lewys, 17 days and tides at 6d	8s 6d
Thomas Winchester, server, 8½ days at 1d	8½d

[*Page total*] [£75 18s 9d *deleted*][1] £13 5s.

[f. 240] *Sawyers*	
William Symonde, 45 days at 6d	22s 6d
William Berryman, 45 days at 6d	22s 6d
Edmund Bell, 10 days at 6d	5s
Robert Taillour, 10 days at 6d	5s
House-carpenters	
Thomas Morton, 29 days at 8d	19s 4d
Francis Colley, 29 days at 8d	19s 4d
Thomas Beckett, 10 days at 6d	5s
John Barnes, server, 10 days at 2d	20d
John Leache, 5 days at 8d	3s 4d
Robert Throughly, server, 5 days at 6d	2s 6d
Thomas Hyggons, 5 days at 5d	2s 1d

[1]Error in anticipation of the next page total.

Victualling. To Thomas Willson of Ratcliff the last day of March for the victualling of 78 of the abovesaid shipwrights, caulkers, sawyers and others working upon the mending and repairing of four Her Highness's ships, *viz.* the *Triumph*, the *Victory*, the *Willoughby* and the *Falcon*, by 2,279 days among them all, Sundays and holy days within the same accounted, which maketh 325 weeks 4 days, at 4s 4d every week the man. *Summa* – £70 10s 6d.

[*Page total*] – £75 18s 9d.

[f. 240v] *Lodging.* To Julyan Guye, Margaret Smythe, Alice Hylles and 16 other persons of Gillingham, Chatham, Rochester, St Margaret's and thereabouts the last of March for the lodging of 78 of the aforenamed shipwrights, caulkers, sawyers and others in 39 featherbeds by the space of 436 weeks among them all, at 2d every week the man. *Summa* – £3 12s 8d.

Labourers

Thomas Tybbolle, 27 days at 3d	6s 9d
Davy Borrow, 27 days at 3d	6s 9d
John Woodstocke, 27 days at 3d	6s 9d
Richard Babb, 27 days at 3d	6s 9d
Richard Pytman, 27 days at 3d	6s 9d
Richard Bigges, 27 days at 3d	6s 9d
William Prince, 27 days at 3d	6s 9d
Simon Marden, 27 days at 3d	6s 9d

[*Page total*] – £6 6s 8d.

[f. 241] *Emptions*

Ironwork [*£35 6s 10½d; nails £9 19s 8d*]. To George Hoope of Chatham, smith, the last day of March for price of [*one*] thousand 9 hundred 2 quarters 5 pounds weight [*2,189 lbs*] of his own new iron by him wrought into bolts, rings, spikes, clench, roves, port-hinges and chains, and the same delivered there for the use of Her Highness's ships at 23s 4d every hundredweight – £22 16s 0½d; more for new working of 531 pounds weight of Her Grace's old iron into like bolts, rings and spikes as aforesaid for the use of her ships, at 9s 4d every hundredweight working – 50s 10d;[1] more for 2,650 of 2s nail, at 20s every 1,000 – 53s; more [*for*] 10,500 of 20d nail, at 16s 8d every 1,000 – £8 15s; more for 16,500 of 10d nail, at 8s 4d every 1,000 – £6 17s 6d; more for 5,500 of 6d nail, a

[1]MS '*D j^qr vj^li*'. The standard calculation (simple because 9s 4d per cwt is 1d per lb) gives 594d, which is 16d below the sum stated (610d). Taking the quantity as 531 lbs gives 594.72d, which suggests that the total is correct, and that the measure is in this case by multiple of pounds. It is, however, possible that the quantity should be 594 lbs ([5 × 112] + 28 + 6), and that the sum has been erroneously supplied by the other reckoning.

5s every 1,000 – 27s 6d; and more to him for 2,000 of 4d nail, at 3s 4d every 1,000 – 6s 8d. *Summa* – £45 6s 6½d.

Nails. To William Pennyfather of London the same day for price of 10,000 of English 2d nail by him delivered there for the use of Her Grace's ships, at 20d every 1,000 – 16s 8d; and more to him for 3,000 of Flemish 3d nail, at 2s 6d every 1,000 – 7s 6d. *Summa* – £1 4s 2d.

Trenails. To John Cowper of Brenchley the same day for price of 10,200 of trenails by him delivered there for the use of Her Majesty's ships, *viz.* for 5,700 of trenails of 24 inches long, at 2s every 100 – £5 14s; more for 2,000 of trenails of 30 inches long, at 2s 6d every 100 – 50s; and more to him for 2,500 of trenails of 20 inches long, at 20d every 100 – 41s 8d. *Summa* – £10 5s 8d.

Netting-ropes and oakum. To William Phedam, Elizabeth Bunche, Julyan Guye and nine other persons of Gillingham, Chatham, Rochester and thereabouts the same day for the working and picking of 4 thousand [*one*] hundred 2 quarters weight [*4,648 lbs*] of Her Majesty's old junks and ropes into oakum for the needful caulking of Her Grace's ships, at 3s 4d every hundredweight working – £6 18s 4d; more to Thomas Hunte for the like working of 2 hundred 2 quarters weight [*280 lbs*] of oakum, at 3s 8d every hundredweight – 9s 2d; and more to him for the working of [*one*] thousand 2 hundred 3 quarters 24 pounds weight [*1,452 lbs*] of the like junks into netting-rope for the use of Her Grace's said ships, at 3s 8d every hundredweight – 47s 3d.[1] *Summa* – £9 14s 9d.

[*Page total*] – £66 11s 1½d.

[f. 241v] *Water carriage of provisions.* To John Sherwoode, master, the last day of March for the service of his hoy named the *John of London* in carrying of divers kinds of provisions, *viz.* 120 boat oars, 2,000 6d nail, 2,000 4d nail, 6 shivers of brass, 4 hundred 2 quarters 14 pounds weight [*518 lbs*] of bright rosin, [*one*] hundredweight of thrums, one last of pitch, 16 small masts, 15 deal-boards, [*one*] hundredweight of twine, 6 coil of ratchet line, 2 dozen of shod shovels, 4 dozen of ballast baskets, 2 hogsheads of train oil and a crane, with divers other kinds of stuffs, from Deptford to Gillingham and there delivered the same for the use of Her Grace's ships. *Summa* – £2 1s 8d.

To John Guye, master, the same day for service of his hoy named the *Nichollas of Chatham* in carrying of divers kinds of stuffs, *viz.* 2 hundredweight of marline, 5 hundredweight of ratline, 5 hundredweight of carvel spikes, 5 hundredweight of overlop nails, 2 tons of Spanish iron, 2,000 foot of inch board, 60 inch ½ boards, 30 2 inch boards, 12 knees

[1] The calculation gives 570.4285d, which is about 3½d above the sum stated (567d).

and divers other needful things for the use of Her Highness's ships, from Deptford to Chatham; by agreement – £1 10s.

To Andrew Bauldewyn, master, the same day for service of his hoy named the *John of Newehide* [New Hythe] in carrying of sundry kinds of stuffs, *viz.* 12 pieces of timber containing 10 ton, 29 2-inch planks, 39 knees great and small containing 8 ton, 8 hundredweight of spikes, bolts, port-hinges, and divers other kinds of provisions, from Woolwich to Gillingham and there delivered the same for the use of Her Majesty's ships; by agreement – £1 6s 8d.

To John Crowxe, master, the same day for service of his ketch in carrying of one last of pitch and one hundredweight of sail twine from London to Gillingham for the use of Her Grace's ships. *Summa* – 10s.

[*Page total*] – £5 8s 4d.

[f. 242] *Water carriage of provisions.* To John Gayttes, master, the last day of March for service of his hoy named the *Julyan of Maydestone* in carrying of 6 cables, 18 hawsers and warps, 60 bolts of poldavis, 2 last of pitch, 3 last of tar, with divers kinds of ironwork and other provisions from Deptford to Gillingham for the needful use of Her Grace's ships there; by agreement – £1 10s.

Rent. To Adam Keller of Chatham the same day for rent of a certain storehouse and ground thereunto belonging wherein lieth Her Grace's provisions for the use of her ships, as cables, cablets, hawsers, warps, canvas, pitch, tar, rosin, ironwork and divers other kinds of stuffs, by one quarter of a year begun the first day of January last and ended as abovesaid – 10s.

To Tomas Wynnall of Chatham the same day for the rent of a certain storehouse wherein lieth Her Highness's store of board, caulking oil, oakum, thrums, pulleys, bowls and divers other kinds of provisions for the use of Her Majesty's ships, by one quarter of a year begun and ended as is aforesaid – 3s 4d.

To Richard Milles of Chatham the same day for rent of a certain storehouse of him hired wherein lieth Her Grace's store of reed for the breaming of Her Highness's ships at their groundings, by one quarter of a year begun and ended as abovesaid – 1s 3d.

Inch board. To Robert Pallmer of Aylesford the same day for price of 800 foot of inch board oak of him had and the same delivered at Chatham for the use of Her Majesty's ships there, at 5s every 100 foot – £2.

[*Page total*] – £4 4s 7d.

[f. 242v] *Brick.* To Thomas Gayton of Snodland the last day of March for price of 2,000 of brick by him delivered there for the use of Her Majesty's ships, at 9s every 1,000. *Summa* – 18s.

Burning reed. To John Fenner and Richard Fenner of New Hythe the same day for price of 7,800 of burning reed by [*them*][1] delivered at Chatham for the needful breaming of Her Grace's ships at their groundings, at 13s 4d every 1,000 – £5 4s; more for 8 bundles of rods and 600 of withies, price 3s 10d; more to them for the laying of 1,750 of reed upon a new shed there for the safe-keeping of Her Highness's ships' tops, galleys' oars and sails, at 12d every 100 laying – 17s 6d. *Summa* – £6 5s 4d.

To Robert Gayttes of Burham Court the same day for price of 1,800 of reed of him taken and the same delivered there for the like use as aforesaid, at 13s 4d every 1,000 – £1 4s.

To Richard Mylles the same day for price of 600 of burning reed by him delivered there for the use of Her Majesty's ships, at 16d every 100 – 8s.

To Robert Curtes the same day for price of 500 of burning reed by him delivered there for the like use as aforesaid, at 16d every hundred – 6s 8d.

*[*Lime – 2s*; *mending of glass windows – 4s 8d*]. To John Hurlocke, master, the same day for price of 6 bushels of lime by him delivered for the mending and repairing of Her Highness's storehouses there, at 4d every bushel – 2s; more for 2 bushels of hair – 8d; and more to him for the mending of the glass windows about Her Grace's storehouses, being broken by a great wind – 4s. *Summa* – 6s 8d.

[*Page total*] – £9 8s 8d.

[f. 243] To Roger Cratwaye of Frindsbury the last day of March for certain stuffs by him brought and consumed in the destroying of rats and mice in Her Grace's ships and storehouses there for the safeguard of Her Highness's sails, canvas and flags; by agreement – 10s.

Hard pitch. To William Gurdellar of London, merchant, the same day for price of one last of hard pitch had of him for the use of the Queen's Majesty's ships; by agreement – £4 13s 4d.

[*Page total*] – £5 3s 4d. [f. 243v *blank*]

[f. 244] A payment made the last day of June as well to masters, mariners, gunners and others daily attending and serving Her Highness in safe-keeping of Her Grace's ships afloat in harbour, and to divers persons for rent of storehouses wherein lieth Her Majesty's store for the use of Her Grace's ships, as also to shipwrights, caulkers, sawyers oarmakers and other artificers and workmen for mending and repairing of Her Highness's ships and provisions for the same; by one quarter of a year begun the first day of April last and this day ended, as followeth:

[1]MS. 'him'.

The Elizabeth Jonas

Mariners

John Hurlocke, master, 13 weeks	£6 10s
John Teigg, boatswain, 13 weeks	54s 2d
[*Lancelot*][1] Tristram, purser, 13 weeks	45s 6d
Thomas Waller, cook and steward, 13 weeks	29s 9½d
Edward Brene, 11 weeks 3 days	19s
John Collens, 8 weeks 3 days	14s
Richard Brissholde, 13 weeks	21s 8d
William Kisshan, 10 weeks 6 days	18s 1d
Henry Woode, 13 weeks	21s 8d
Robert Heallinge, 13 weeks	21s 8d
John Blythe, 13 weeks	21s 8d
William Romney, 13 weeks	21s 8d
John Woodroff, 13 weeks	21s 8d
Roger Reade, 13 weeks	21s 8d
George Voyse, 13 weeks	21s 8d
Nicholas Lovett, 13 weeks	21s 8d
Thomas Searlles, 3 weeks	5s
James Robartson, 3 weeks	5s
John Good, 3 weeks 3 days	5s 8d
Thomas Nedam, 10 weeks 6 days	18s 1d
John Apelton, boy, 13 weeks	10s 10d

[*Page total*] – £27 10s 1½d.

[f. 244v] William Symonde, boy, 13 weeks	10s 10d
John Turnar, boy, 13 weeks	10s 10d
George Stewarde, 6 weeks 3 days	10s 8d
Giles Bevizon, 9 weeks 6 days	16s 5d
[*Gunner*]	
Lawrence Dilke, master gunner, 13 weeks	32s 6d

The Triumph

Mariners

William Woode, master, 13 weeks	£6 10s
Thomas Goldestone, boatswain, 13 weeks	54s 2d
Henry Cooke, purser, 13 weeks	32s 6d
John Baswell, cook and steward, 13 weeks	29s 9½d
John Newball, 13 weeks	21s 8d
Mark Bullen, 13 weeks	21s 8d
Robert White, 10 weeks 6 days	18s 1d
Peter Trew, 13 weeks	21s 8d

[1]MS. 'Lawrence' here but always Lancelot elsewhere: cf. above, p. 333 and other entries

Thomas Tybboll, 13 weeks	21s 8d
Robert Keye, 13 weeks	21s 8d
Thomas Ratlyff, 13 weeks	21s 8d
John Robson, 13 weeks	21s 8d
George Mylles, 13 weeks	21s 8d
Henry Maggett, 13 weeks	21s 8d
Robert Gyelles, 2 weeks	3s 4d
John Raggett, 13 weeks	21s 8d
John Boye, 13 weeks	21s 8d
Fabian Bullen, 13 weeks	21s 8d
Davye Borow, 1 week	20d
Edward Wyckes, boy, 13 weeks	10s 10d
Henry Morrys, gromet, 13 weeks	16s 3d
Thomas Maye, 10 weeks 6 days	18s 1d
Thomas Morrys, 9 weeks 4 days	16s
Thomas Delff, 4 weeks 2 days	7s 2d
[*Gunner*]	
Stephen Bull, master gunner, 13 weeks	32s 6d

[*Page total*] – £35 11s 7½d.

[f. 245] *The Victory*

Mariners

William Barnes, master, 13 weeks	£6 10s
John Light, boatswain, 13 weeks	54s 2d
Hugh Poope, purser, 13 weeks	32s 6d
Thomas Gayttes, cook and steward, 13 weeks	29s 9½d
William Pearcyvall, 13 weeks	21s 8d
Thomas Cossyne, 13 weeks	21s 8d
Stephen Justys, 3 weeks	5s
Arnold Hartt, 3 weeks	5s
John Roche, 13 weeks	21s 8d
Robert Ussher, boy, 13 weeks	10s 10d
Leonard Holt, boy, 13 weeks	10s 10d
Richard Letman, 12 weeks	20s
William Hawkyns, 9 weeks 4 days	16s
Elyarde Carr, 9 weeks 4 days	16s
John Gobye, 9 weeks 4 days	16s
John Poyll, 9 weeks 4 days	16s
Thomas Jonnes, gromet, 4 weeks 2 days	5s 4d
Gunner	
William Thomas, master, 13 weeks	32s 6d

[*Page total*] – £23 4s 11½d.

[f. 245v] *The Hope*

Mariners

John Aboen, boatswain, 13 weeks	54s 2d
Michael Gonson, purser, 13 weeks	32s 6d
John Mathew, cook and steward, 13 weeks	29s 9½d
Thomas [Starke *inserted*], 11 weeks 3 days	19s
James Robartson, 13 weeks	21s 8d
Roger Awsten, 8 weeks 3 days	14s
Gregory Stewarde, 13 weeks	21s 8d
Henry Watson, 13 weeks	21s 8d
Henry Bowye, 13 weeks	21s 8d
Henry Burges, 4 weeks 5 days	7s 10d
John Sustyane, 12 weeks 3 days	20s 8d
John Merrett, 3 weeks 3 days	5s 8d
Richard Abethell, 13 weeks	21s 8d
William Bateman, gromet, 13 weeks	16s 3d
John Lawrence, boy, 13 weeks	10s 10d
Owen Griffyn, 13 weeks	21s 8d
Gunner	
Thomas Dixson, master, 13 weeks	32s 6d

[*Page total*] – £18 14s 2½d.

[f. 246] *The Mary Rose*

Mariners

William Robynson, boatswain, 13 weeks	54s 2d
Christopher Davye, purser, 13 weeks	32s 6d
Roger Cratwaye, cook and steward, 13 weeks	29s 9½d
Humphrey Stevenson, 13 weeks	21s 8d
John Cossyne, 13 weeks	21s 8d
William Romney, 13 weeks	21s 8d
William Cocke, 13 weeks	21s 8d
John Gilbart, 13 weeks	21s 8d
Thomas Harrington, 13 weeks	21s 8d
John Woodcock, 13 weeks	21s 8d
John Welles, gromet, 13 weeks	16s 3d
Thomas Leonarde, gromet, 13 weeks	16s 3d
Edward Laughan, boy, 13 weeks	10s 8d
Thomas Butlar, boy, 13 weeks	10s 8d
Nicholas Bater, 9 weeks 4 days	16s
Gunner	
John Butlar, master, 13 weeks	32s 6d

[*Page total*] – £18 10s 5½d.

[f. 246] *The Lion*

Mariners

William Hollande, master, 13 weeks	£6 10s
Robert Harwoode, boatswain, 13 weeks	54s 2d
John Butler, purser, 13 weeks	32s 6d
John Curlle, cook and steward, 13 weeks	29s 9½d
William Wilkyns, 8 weeks 3 days	14s
John Samonde, 13 weeks	21s 8d
John Russell, 13 weeks	21s 8d
Robert Goslinge, 13 weeks	21s 8d
Nicholas Waller, 13 weeks	21s 8d
Silvester Bewill, 2 weeks 3 days	4s
Nicholas Hewes, 13 weeks	21s 8d
William Charlles, 13 weeks	21s 8d
Thomas Dayll, 13 weeks	21s 8d
Thomas Browne, 13 weeks	21s 8d
Rowland Deraw, 13 weeks	21s 8d
John Harwoode, gromet, 13 weeks	16s 3d
William Richarde, boy, 13 weeks	10s 10d
Roger Browne, boy, 13 weeks	10s 10d
Richard Jonnes, 9 weeks 6 days	16s 5d
William Pyentawyne, 9 weeks 4 days	16s
Gunners	
Edward Tompson, master, 13 weeks	32s 6d
Peter Arney, server, 13 weeks	21s 8d

[*Page total*] – £29 3s 11½d.

[f. 247] *The Philip and Mary*

Mariners

John Jonnes, boatswain, 13 weeks	54s 2d
George Haull, purser, 13 weeks	32s 6d
John Geffery, cook and steward, 13 weeks	29s 9½d
Francis Willyams, 13 weeks	21s 8d
Gregory Wyckes, 13 weeks	21s 8d
Thomas Sharplye, 13 weeks	21s 8d
Zach Sweteman, 13 weeks	21s 8d
Arthur Lyversuche, 13 weeks	21s 8d
Edward Collson, 3 weeks 3 days	5s 8d
Richard West, 13 weeks	21s 8d
Henry Raynsforth, 8 weeks 3 days	14s
Bartholomew Gayttes, gromet, 13 weeks	16s 3d
Edward Hawston, gromet, 13 weeks	16s 3d

James Nicolson, boy, 13 weeks	10s 10d
Thomas James, 13 weeks	21s 8d
Philip Beltt, 8 weeks 4 days	14s 3d
Gunner	
Matthew Sharpp, master, 13 weeks	32s 6d

[*Page total*] – £18 17s 10½d.

[f. 247v] *The Willoughby*

Mariners	
Robert Flynt, boatswain, 13 weeks	37s 11d
Andrew Everington, cook and steward, 8 weeks 4 days	19s 8d
Richard Dennes, 13 weeks	21s 8d
Thomas Durrant, 13 weeks	21s 8d
Thomas Woodrige, 2 weeks 4 days	4s 4d
Richard Babb, 13 weeks	21s 8d
Benjamin Flynt, gromet, 13 weeks	16s 3d
[*Gunners*]	
John Mallpasse, master gunner, 13 weeks	32s 6d
John Turnar, server, 13 weeks	21s 8d

The Bull

Mariners	
Andrew Walker, boatswain, 13 weeks	37s 11d
John Willye, cook and steward, 13 weeks	29s 9½d
Christopher Cowper, 1 week 4 days	2s 8d
Richard Crannolde, 12 weeks	20s
Richard Pytman, 13 weeks	21s 8d
Matthew Robson, 13 weeks	21s 8d
Edward Thomas, gromet, 13 weeks	16s 3d
Robert Hartely, 13 weeks	21s 8d
[*Gunner*]	
Robert Butlar, master gunner, 13 weeks	32s 6d

The Falcon

Mariners	
Lawrence Cleare, boatswain, 8 weeks 3 days	24s 7d
Henry Baker, cook and steward, 8 weeks 3 days	19s 4d
William Warde, 8 weeks 3 days	14s
Richard Bygges, 8 weeks 3 days	14s
Richard Langley, boy, 8 weeks 3 days	7s
[*Gunner*]	
John Commyn, master gunner, 8 weeks 3 days	21s

[*Page total*] – £25 1s 4½d.

[f. 248] *The Tiger*

Mariners

John Beamonde, boatswain, 13 weeks	37s 11d
John Hawkins, cook and steward, 13 weeks	29s 9½d
John Bowye, 13 weeks	21s 8d
Thomas Butlar, 13 weeks	21s 8d
Matthew Woodstock, boy, 13 weeks	10s 10d
Richard Flemynge, 13 weeks	21s 8d
Richard Harman, 13 weeks	21s 8d
[*Gunners*]	
John Moore, master gunner, 13 weeks	32s 6d
Thomas Halle, server, 13 weeks	21s 8d

The Rowbarge

Mariners

Robert Blaike, boatswain, 13 weeks	37s 11d
Thomas Whittell, cook and steward, 13 weeks	29s 9½d
William Fallett, 13 weeks	21s 8d
Simon Breadstreate, 13 weeks	21s 8d
Andrew Ballerde, boy, 13 weeks	10s 10d
Richard Abraham, 8 weeks 4 days	14s 4d
Nicholas Cherrye, 9 weeks 4 days	16s
[*Gunner*]	
John Walker, master gunner, 13 weeks	32s 6d

The Sun

Mariners

Nicholas Starkey, boatswain, 10 weeks 6 days	31s 8d
John Large, 10 weeks 6 days	18s 1d
Francis Birchall, gromet, 10 weeks 6 days	13s 6d
William Clowse, 7 weeks	11s 8d
[*Gunner*]	
William Ellys, master gunner 10 weeks 6 days	27s

[*Page total*] – £25 6s.

[f. 248v] *The Bright Falcon*

Mariners

Nicholas Waters, boatswain, 9 weeks 4 days	27s 11d
Edward Tayllor, 10 weeks	16s 8d
Henry Willyams, 10 weeks 6 days	18s 1d
Thomas Kingdowne, 13 weeks	21s 8d
Ellis Blancke, boy, 9 weeks 4 days	8s
James Smythe, 1 week 3 days	2s 4d

The Galley Speedwell	
Mariners	
Cuthbert Clarke, boatswain, 13 weeks	54s 2d
Anthony Darnatho, 13 weeks	21s 8d
William Prince, 13 weeks	21s 8d
Thomas Purden, 4 weeks 3 days	7s 4d
Cornelius Bryan, 4 weeks 2 days	7s 2d
Thomas Foster, boy, 13 weeks	10s 10d
Leonard Clarke, 4 weeks	6s 8d
[*Gunner*]	
Maurice Aboen, master gunner, 13 weeks	32s 6d
The Galley Tryright	
Mariners	
Simon Barnsley, boatswain, 13 weeks	37s 11d
John Godden, purser, 13 weeks	32s 6d
William Kente, cook and steward, 13 weeks	29s 9½d
John Tayllour, 13 weeks	21s 8d
Patrick Moore, 8 weeks 4 days	14s 4d
[*Gunner*]	
Thomas Nealle, master gunner, 13 weeks	32s 6d
The Mary Grace Hoy	
Mariners	
William Pearson, master, 13 weeks	54s 2d
Richard Boltton, 13 weeks	21s 8d

[*Page total*] – £25 1s 2½d.

[f. 249] *The Galley Mermaid*	
Mariners	
Adam Puckwell, boatswain, 13 weeks	37s 11d
Simon Marden, 13 weeks	21s 8d
George Porter, 1 week 4 days	2s 8d
Thomas Dabnes, 6 weeks 6 days	10s 5d
Robert Puckwell, boy, 6 weeks 6 days	5s 8½d
John Willyams, 1 week 3 days	2s 4d
William Allen, 1 week 3 days	2s 4d

Wages of gunners daily attendant in Her Highness's fort at Upnor for the safe-keeping of Her Grace's ships in Gillingham Water.

Thomas Sergeaunt, master, 91 days at 16d	£6 1s 4d
Richard Abeseade, 91 days at 12d	£4 11s
Robert Woulgrave, 91 days at 12d	£4 11s
William Bowyll, 91 days at 12d	£4 11s
William Chisselton, 91 days at 12d	£4 11s

Randall Stevenson, 91 days at 12d	£4 11d
William Taunton, 91 days at 12d	£4 11s
Robert Halssnoth, 91 days at 12d	£4 11s

[*Page total*] – £42 2s 4½d.

[f. 249v] *[*Clerk*]. To Thomas Heynos the last day of June for his wages daily attending and serving Her Highness for the keeping of the book of cheque of masters, mariners and gunners keeping Her Majesty's ships afloat in harbour, as also the prick book of shipwrights and caulkers, by one quarter of a year begun the first day of April last and ended as abovesaid – £5.

*[*Purveyor*]. To Butolph Moungey the same day for his wages daily attending and serving Her Highness in the making of provisions of all kinds of necessaries for the use of Her Majesty's ships, by one like quarter of a year containing 91 days begun and ended as aforesaid, at 8d *per diem* – £3 0s 8d.

*[*Purveyor or overseer*]. To Thomas Baker the same day for his wages daily attending and serving Her Majesty in delivering of all manner of necessary [*corrected from* necessaries] provisions out of Her Grace's storehouse there for the use of Her Highness's ships, by like 91 days begun and ended as abovesaid, at 8d *per diem* – £3 0s 8d.

[*Page total*] – £11 1s 4d.

[f. 250] *Shipwrights*

Peter Pett, master, 27 days and tides at 12d	27s
Richard Chapman, server, 8 days at 6d	4s
George Kingston, server, 71 days at 5d	29s 7d
Thomas Poulter, 80½ days at 10d	£3 7s 1d
John Clarke, server, 80½ days at 4d	26s 10d
Nicholas Johnson, 73 days at 10d	£3 0s 10d
John Hitchecocke, server, 75½ days at 4d	25s 2d
Isaac Asheley, server, 52 days at 6d	26s
John Bunche, 16 days at 8d	10s 8d
John Pultar, server, 22 days at 6d	11s
William Harbert, server, 16 days at 4d	5s 4d
Henry Sherwood, 80½ days at 7d	46s 11½d
Thomas Platterer, server, 80½ days at 4d	20s 1½d
William Welshe, 71 days at 8d	47s 4d
Thomas Freman, server, 71 days at 5d	29s 7d
William Chartram, server, 76 days at 4d	25s 4d
Ralph Browne, 71 days at 7d	41s 5d
Edmund Waller, 49 days at 6d	24s 6d
Robert Willet, server, 50½ days at 4d	16s 10d

Nicholas Claye, 79 days at 8d	52s 8d
John Claye, server, 84 days at 4d	28s
John Sager, server, 77 days at 6d	38s 6d
Mark Hodge, 66 days at 6d	33s
William Hodge, server, 32 days at 4d	10s 8d
Thomas Blosse, 73 days at 8d	48s 8d
Henry Neally, server, 73 days at 4d	24s 4d
John Wynny, 73 days at 8d	48s 8d
John Wythers, server, 73 days at 6d	36s 6d
Robert Hudson, 68 days at 7d	39s 8d
Richard Cryppes, 60 days at 6d	30s
Michael Chamber, 56 days at 7d	32s 8d
Robert Pakeman, 9 days at 6d	4s 6d
John Milles, 71 days at 7d	41s 5d
Robert Archer, server, 71 days at 4d	23s 8d
Henry Hartely, 73½ days at 7d	42s 10½d
Thomas Newbery, 49½ days at 7d	28s 10½d

[*Page total*] – £55 10s 3d.

[f. 250v] Thomas Eaton, server, 73 days at 3d	18s 3d
John Goldinge, 62½ days at 8d	41s 8d
William Jenney, server, 59½ days at 6d	29s 3d
Richard Bull, 6 days at 6d	3s
George Browne, 66½ days at 7d	38s 3½d
Richard Francke, server, 73½ days at 4d	24s 6d
Richard Daie, 21 days at 8d	14s
William Harttropp, 47 days at 7d	27s 1½d
Thomas Withredge, server, 57 days at 4d	19s
Godfrey Smythe, server, 24½ days at 6d	12s 3d
Griffin Tyther, server, 46 days at 4d	15s 4d
William Adams, 20 days at 6d	10s
Caulkers	
John Bunche, master, 70 days at 10d	58s 4d
William Harber, server, 70 days at 4d	23s 4d
William Elyzon, 61 days at 6d	30s 6d
Samuel Clarke, server, 64 days at 3d	16s
Henry Cleave, 71[½] days at 6d	35s 9d
John Tower, server, 74 days at 4d	24s 8d
Robert Langley, 72½ days at 6d	36s 9d
John Haywarde, 67 days at 7d	39s 1d
Nicholas Haywarde, 67 days at 5d	27s 11d
William Woode, server, 15½ days at 2d	2s 7d

William Bastyane, 47½ days at 6d	23s 9d
Arthur Carr, server, 74 days at 4d	24s 8d
John Clarke, 75½ days at 7d	44s 0½d
William Adamson, 72½ days at 5d	30s 2½d
Richard Cooke, 73½ days at 6d	36s 9d
Thomas Clarke, 71 days at 7d	41s 5d
Robert Edmondes, server, 72½ days at 4d	24s 2d
Robert Tapshier, 26 days at 6d	13s
John Moyssier, 55 days at 6d	27s 6d
Leonard Cowper, 61 days at 7d	35s 7d
Edward Mott, server, 63½ days at 3d	15s 10½d
Thomas Northcott, 36½ days at 7d	21s 3½d
John Arodes, server, 43½ days at 4d	14s 6d
William Raynolde, 63 days at 6d	31s 6d

[*Page total*] – £46 11s 10d.

[f. 251] William Tyte, server, 40 days at 3d	10s
John Wylliams, server, 43 days at 3d	10s 9d
Thomas Boltton, master, 42 days at 10d	35s
William Bolton, server, 42 days at 6d	21s
John Fullar, server, 42 days at 6d	21s
William Munde, 42 days at 8d	28s 4d
William Tratter, server, 42 days at 4d	14s
Walter Deane, 41 days at 7d	23s 11d
George Aparcke, server, 42 days at 3d	10s 6d
William Addeane, server, 42 days at 2d	7s
Robert Bridgges, 15 days at 7d	8s 9d
Humphrey Dayll, server, 39½ days at 6d	19s 9d
Thomas Pavye, 40 days at 7d	23s 4d
Edward Hylliarde, server, 41 days at 4d	13s 8d
Gregory Aldredge, 43 days at 7d	25s 1d
John Stockdayll, 36½ days at 7d	20s 3½d
Michael Rowse, 13½ days at 6d	6s 9d
John Eastwoode, 15 days at 7d	8s 9d
William Collyns, server, 39½ days at 6d	19s 9d
Thomas Wynchester, server, 40½ days at 3d	10s 1½d
Thomas Cockes, 37 days at 6d	18s 6d
John Merrycote, 39½ days at 6d	19s 9d
William Foarde, 24 days at 7d	14s
Robert White, 30½ days at 7d	17s 9½d
Henry Reade, server, 32 days at 4d	10s 8d
George Savidge, 29½ days at 7d	17s 2½d

Nicholas Archedaill, 37 days at 6d	18s 6d
George Mathew, 91 days at 6d	45s 6d
Richard Dennes, 91 days at 3d	22s 9d
Sawyers	
William Symonde, 20 days at 6d	10s
William Beryman, 20 days at 6d	10s
Davy Abedworth, 39 days at 6d	19s 6d
John Rockley, 39 days at 6d	19s 6d
Nicholas Rawborne, 4 days at 6d	2s
Hugh Rawborne, 4 days at 6d	2s
[*Page total*] – £29 6s 5d.	

[f. 251v] Robert Johnson, 23½ days at 6d	11s 9d
Richard Darbye, 23½ days at 6d	11s 9d
Nicholas Gefferye, 38 days at 6d	19s
Richard Garrett, 38 days at 6d	19s
Henry Asheforde, 43 days at 6d	21s 6d
Nicholas Pavy, 43 days at 6d	21s 6d
Oarmakers	
William Bexley, 9 days at 8d	6s
James Rowman, server, 7 days at 6d	3s 6d
Abraham Harman, server, 7 days at 5d	2s 11d
William Kackett, server, 7 days at 6d	3s 6d

Victualling. To Thomas Wilson of Ratcliff the last day of June for the victualling of 115 of the aforenamed shipwrights, caulkers, sawyers, oarmakers and others working upon the repairing and mending of all Her Highness's ships and galleys there, by the space of 7,004 days among them all, Sundays and holy days within the same accounted, begun the first day of April last and this day ended, which maketh 1,000 weeks 4 days, at 4s 5d every week the man. *Summa* – £220 19s.

Lodging. To Julyan Guye, Margaret Smythe, Alice Hilles and divers other persons of Gillingham, Chatham, Rochester and thereabouts the same day for the lodging of 115 of the aforesaid shipwrights, caulkers and others in 63 featherbeds, working upon the repairing and mending of Her Grace's said ships and galleys there, by 865 weeks among them all begun and ended as abovesaid, at 2d every week the man – £8 0s 10d.

[*Page total*] – £235 0s 3d.

[f. 252] *Bricklayers*	
William Phedam, 21 days at 10d	17s 6d
William Daye, server, 16½ days at 7d	9s 7½d
William Beckett, 6 days at 10d	5s

John Tonnge , server, 5 days at 7d 2s 11d

*[*35s 0½d*]

Labourers

Thomas Tybboll, 64 days at 3d	16s
John Woodcocke, 48 days at 3d	12s
Davy Borrow, 7 days at 3d	21d
Richard Babb, 86 days at 3d	28s 2d
Richard Pytman, 48 days at 3d	12s
Richard Bigges, 60 days at 3d	15s
William Prince, 70 days at 3d	17s 6d
Simon Marden, 48 days at 3d	12s
	*[*114s 5d*]

[*Page total*] – £7 9s 5½d.

[f. 252v] *Emptions*

Ironwork. *[*£38 10s 8d*; *nails – £41 10s 10d*] To George Hoope of Chatham, smith, the last day of June for price of 2 thousand 6 hundred 3 quarters 8 pounds weight [*3,004 lbs*] of his own new iron by him wrought into bolts, spikes of all sorts, clench, roves, port-hinges and chains, and the same delivered there for the use of Her Grace's ships, at 23s 4d every hundredweight – £31 5s 10d; more for new working of 3 hundred 14 pounds weight [*350 lbs*] of Her Highness's old iron into like bolts, spikes, clench and roves as aforesaid for the use of her ships, at 1d every pound weight – 29s 2d; more for 4,000 of 2s nail, at 20s every 1,000 – £4; more for 16,000 of 10d nail, at 8s 4d every 1,000 – £6 13s 4d; more for 11,000 of 20d nail, at 16s 8d every 1,000 – £9 3s 4d; and more to him for 25,000 of 6d nail, at 5s every 1,000 – £6 5s. *Summa* – £58 16s 8d.

To Thomas Willson of Ratcliff, smith, the same day for price of 5 hundredweight of spikes and overlop nails by him delivered at Gillingham for the use of Her Majesty's ships there, at 23s 4d every hundredweight – £5 16s 8d; more for 5,000 of 2s nail, at 20s every 1,000 – £5; more for 5,000 of 20d nail, at 16s 8d every 1,000 – £4 3s 4d; more for 5,000 of 10d nail, at 8s 4d every 1,000 – 41s 8d; more for 5,000 of 4d nail, at 3s 4d every 1,000 – 16s 8d; more for 5,000 of 6d nail, at 5s every 1,000 – 25s; more for 5,000 of 3d nail, at 2s 6d every 1,000 – 12s 6d; more for 2,000 of scupper nails, at 5s every 1,000 – 10s; and more to him for 2,000 of clench nail with rove, at 2s every 100 – 20s. *Summa* – £21 5s 10d.

Painting and colouring. To Richard Rogers of Rochester, painter, the same day for the colouring of the *Galley Speedwell*, her masts, yards, oars and pavis all red – 16s; and more to him for the painting of the *Mary Rose* after timber colour, by agreement – £3. *Summa* – £3 16s.

[*Page total*] – £83 18s 6d.

[f. 253] *Water carriage of provisions.* To John Hewet, master, the last day of June for service of his hoy called the *Roose of London* in carrying of divers kinds of provisions, *viz.* 2 last of pitch, 2 last of tar, 3 sacks of white oakum, one sack with thrums, 4,000 foot of inch board, an iron beam, 10 sheets of flat lead, 5 hundred [*weight*] of ratline, 3 dozen of bowls, 2 dozen of scoops, 3 dozen of shovels, 2 hundred[*weight*] of twine, 200 pounds[1] of spikes and overlop nails, 4,000 10d nails, 4,000 6d nails, 2 dozen and 9 pump-hoses, 6 small masts in a raft, with divers other needful things, from Deptford to Gillingham and there delivered the same to the use of Her Grace's ships. *Summa* – £1 15s.

To Henry Kerren, master, the same day for the service of his hoy named the *Unycorne of London* in carrying of one sack of white oakum, 2 copper kettles, one thousandweight of rosin, one last of pitch, 2 last of tar, 6 deal-boards, 4 pitch pots of iron, 20 planks of 2 inches, and one piece of timber oak, from Deptford [*to Gillingham*] and the same delivered there for the use of Her Highness's ships; by agreement – £1 3s 4d.

To Richard Barker, master, the same day for service of his hoy called the *Mary and John of Myllall* [Millhall] in carrying of 5 thousandweight of rosin, 80 deal-boards, 18 loads of timber plank, inch boards and knees, 7 masts in a raft, and divers other needful things for the use of Her Majesty's ships from Woolwich to Gillingham, and there delivered the same; by agreement – £2.

To William Hunt, master, the same day for service of his pinnace in carrying of 2 hogsheads of train oil and 521 pounds weight[2] of rosin from Deptford to Gillingham for the use of Her Grace's ships; by agreement – 10s.

[*Page total*] – £5 8s 4d.

[f. 253v] To William Guye, master, the last day of June for service of his hoy name the *Nichollas of Chatham* in carrying of 3 great masts in a raft from Deptford to Gillingham and there delivered the same to the use of Her Grace's ships the *Elizabeth Jonas* and the *Lion*; by agreement – £1.

To Vincent Poulle, master, the same day for service of his hoy named the *Pelycane of Sainct Katherins* in carrying of divers kinds of provisions, *viz.* 200 galley oars, 2,000 [*foot*] of inch boards, 3 great pumps, 6 shivers with cocks of brass, a new boat for Her Grace's bark the *Sun*, 1,240 foot of squared timber, with divers other needful things for the use of Her Highness's ships, by 2 several times from Deptford and Millhall to Gillingham; by agreement – £2 13s 4d.

[1]So expressed; not clear if 200 lbs or 2 cwt is intended.

[2]Impossible to know if this means 521 lbs or 5 cwt 21 lbs (581 lbs).

To Hugh Edwardes, master, the same day for service of his hoy called the *Jhesus of London* in carrying of 5 thousand 4 hundred 3 quarters 27 pounds weight [*6,159 lbs*] of divers kinds of cordage, 4 bolts of poldavy, 3 compasses, 4 running glasses, 4 pump-hoses, 4 claps, 6 scupper-leathers, 12 pulleys, 18 boat oars and divers other kinds of stuffs from Deptford to Chatham and delivered the same for the use of Her Grace's ships there. *Summa* – £1.

To Andrew Bauldewyn, master, the same day for service of his hoy called the *John of Newehide* [New Hythe] in carrying of 8 hundredweight of rosin and one last of pitch, half a last of tar, 5,000 of 2s nail, 5,000 of 20d nail, 5,000 of 10d nail, 5,000 of 6d nail, 5,000 of 4d nail, 4 tuns of beer, with divers other necessaries for the use of Her Majesty's ships from Deptford to Gillingham and there delivered the same; by agreement – £1 10s.

[*Page total*] – £6 3s 4d.

[f. 254] To Ralph Newman, master, the last day of June for service of his ketch called the *James of Rayneham* in carrying of one thousand[*weight*] of black rosin, 4 hogsheads of beer and other needful things from London to Gillingham for the use of Her Grace's ships there. *Summa* – 13s 4d.

To William Gore, master, the same day for the service of his hoy named the *Katherin of Newhide* [New Hythe] in carrying of one last of tar, 2 last of pitch, one thousandweight of bright rosin, one hogshead of train oil and 2 dozen of spars from London and the same delivered at Gillingham for the use of Her Majesty's ships. *Summa* – 15s.

House rent. To Adam Kellar of Chatham the same day for the rent of a certain storehouse and ground thereunto belonging, wherein lieth Her Grace's provisions for the use of her ships, *viz*. cables, cablets, hawsers, warps, canvas, twine, needles, all kinds of ironwork and divers other kinds of stuffs, by one quarter of a year begun the first day of April last and this day ended – 10s.

To Thomas Wynnall the same day for the hire of a certain storehouse wherein lieth Her Grace's store of pitch, tar, rosin, bowls, scoops, shovels, kettles and divers other needful things for the use of Her Grace's ships, by one quarter of a year begun and ended as aforesaid – 3s 4d.

To Richard Milles of Chatham the same day for rent of a storehouse of him hired wherein lieth Her Grace's store of reed for the breaming of Her Majesty's ships at their groundings, by one quarter of a year begun and ended as abovesaid – 1s 3d.

Elm timber. To Thomas Mourton of Chatham the same day for price of one piece of elm timber containing 22 foot of him had for the use of Her Majesty's ships there, price – 3s 8d.

[*Page total*] – £2 6s 7d.

[f. 254v] *Shores, lime, mapstaves and brick.* To John Hurlocke the last day of June for price of 6 loads of shores by him provided for the shoring of Her Grace's ships at their groundings, at 4s 8d every load – 28s; more for 2 load of ash, price 14s; more for 10 load 10 bushels of lime for the mending of the hearths, backs and furnaces in Her Highness's ships, at 10s every load – 58s 4d [*sic*];[1] more for 2 load of mapstaves, price 8s 8d; and more to him for 2,800 of brick, at 13s 4d every 1,000 with the carriage – 28s 6d; *Summa* – £6 17s 10d

Netting-rope and oakum. To Julian Browne, Anne Harwood, Bennet Roose and five other persons of Gillingham, Chatham, Rochester and thereabouts the same day for working and picking of 2 thousand 2 hundred 2 quarters 7 pounds weight [*2,527 lbs*] of Her Majesty's old junks and ropes into oakum for the needful caulking of Her Grace's ships, at 3s 4d every hundredweight working – £3 15s 3d;[2] and more to Thomas Hunt for the working of 7 hundred 3 quarters 4 pounds weight [*872 lbs*] of the like junks into netting-rope for the use of Her Highness's said ships, at 3s 8d every hundredweight working – 28s 6d.[3] *Summa* – £5 3s 9d.

Empty cask. To Richard Duffelde of St Katherine's the same day for price of 4 tuns of empty beer cask of him had for the use of the Queen's Majesty's ships at their groundings, at 5s every ton – £1.

Stuff for killing of rats. To Roger Cratwaye of Frindsbury the same day for certain stuffs by him bought and consumed in the destroying of rats and mice in all Her Majesty's ships and storehouses there for the safeguard of Her Grace's sails, canvas and flags, for one quarter of a year; by agreement – 10s.

[*Page total*] – £13 11s 7d.

[f. 255] A payment made the last day of September as well to masters, mariners, gunners and others daily attending and serving Her Highness in safe-keeping of Her Grace's ships afloat in harbour and to divers persons for rent of storehouses wherein lieth provisions of sundry needful things for the use of the same ships, as also to shipwrights, sawyers and other artificers and workmen for new making and repairing Her Majesty's said ships, with provisions had for the use of the same; by one quarter of a year begun the first day of July last and this day ended, as followeth:

The Triumph

Mariners

William Wood, master, 2 weeks 3 days	24s 3d

[1] £5 8s 4d is intended, but the price as written is carried forward.

[2] The calculation gives 902.49985d, which is ½d below the sum stated (903d).

[3] The calculation gives 342.57139d, which is ½d above the sum stated (342d).

John Hurlocke, master, 10 weeks 5 days	£5 7s 1d
Thomas Goldestone, boatswain, 13 weeks 1 day	54s 9d
Henry Cooke, purser, 13 weeks 1 day	32s 10d
John Baswell, cook, 13 weeks 1 day	30s 1½d
John Newball, 6 days	17d
Mark Bullyn, 13 weeks 1 day	21s 11d
Peter Trew, 13 weeks 1 day	21s 11d
Thomas Tybboll, 2 weeks 3 days	4s
Robert Keye, 13 weeks 1 day	21s 11d
Thomas Ratlyff, 13 weeks 1 day	21s 11d
John Robson, 7 weeks 3 days	12s 4d
George Mylles, 8 weeks	13s 4d
Henry Maggatt, 7 weeks 4 days	12s 8d
John Raggett, 8 weeks	13s 4d
John Boye, 13 weeks 1 day	21s 11d

[*Page total*] – £20 15s 8½d.

[f. 255v] Fabian Bullyn, 13 weeks 1 day	21s 11d
Thomas Maye, 13 weeks 1 day	21s 11d
Thomas Morrys, 2 weeks 1 day	3s 7d
Thomas Delphe, 2 weeks 1 day	3s 7d
Edward Wyckes, boy, 13 weeks 1 day	10s 11½d
Henry Morrys, boy, 2 weeks 3 days	2s
Thomas Pultar, carpenter, 13 weeks 1 day	54s 9d
John Hitchecock, server, 13 weeks 1 day	21s 11d
Griffin Tether, gromet, 13 weeks 1 day	16s 5d
John Phillipp, 10 weeks 1 day	16s 11d
Peter Dyar, 10 weeks 1 day	16s 11d
Austin Ellyott, 4 weeks 4 days	7s 4d
Henry Launce, 10 weeks 1 day	16s 11d
John Russell, 4 weeks 6 days	8s 1d
Edmund Gybbon, 4 weeks 6 days	8s 1d
William Harrys, 4 weeks 6 days	8s 1d
George Robyns, 4 weeks 6 days	8s 1d
Gunner	
Stephen Bull, master, 13 weeks 1 day	32s 10d

[*Page total*] – £14 3s 0½d.

[f. 256] *The Elizabeth Jonas*

Mariners

John Hurlocke, master, 2 weeks 3 days	24s 3d
John Teigg, boatswain, 2 weeks 3 days	10s 1d
Lancelot Tristram, purser, 2 weeks 3 days	8s 6d

Thomas Waller, cook, 2 weeks 3 days	5s 7d
Richard Brisholde, 2 weeks 3 days	4s
Henry Wood, 2 weeks 3 days	4s
Robert Heallinge, 2 weeks 3 days	4s
John Blythe, 6 days	17d
William Romney, 6 days	17d
John Woodroff, 6 days	17d
Roger Reade, 6 days	17d
Nicholas Lovett, 2 weeks 3 days	4s
John Appulton, boy, 6 days	8½d
John Tornner, boy, 2 weeks 3 days	2s
Peter Jenkyns, 2 weeks 1 day	3s 7d
John Taillour, 2 weeks 3 days	4s
Thomas Haselden, 2 weeks 3 days	4s
John Bell, 1 week 2 days	2s 2d
Lawrence Marybote, 1 week 2 days	2s 2d
John Bunche, carpenter, 1 week 3 days	5s 11d
William Harber, gromet, 1 week 3 days	21d
Gunner	
Lawrence Dilke, master, 2 weeks 3 days	6s

[*Page total*] – £5 2s 4½d.

[f. 256v] *The Victory*

Mariners

William Barnes, master, 2 weeks 3 days	24s 3d
John Light, boatswain, 2 weeks 3 days	10s 1d
Hugh Pope, purser, 2 weeks 3 days	6s
Thomas Gaittes, cook, 2 weeks 3 days	5s 7d
William Parcyvall, 2 weeks 3 days	4s
Thomas Cossyne, 2 weeks 3 days	4s
John Roche, 2 weeks 3 days	4s
Richard Letman, 6 days	17d
William Hawkyns, 2 weeks 3 days	4s
Elyard Carr, 2 weeks 3 days	4s
John Goby, 2 weeks 3 days	4s
John Poyll, 2 weeks 3 days	4s
Thomas Jones, gromet, 6 days	12d
Robert Ussher, boy, 2 weeks 3 days	2s
Leonard Holtt, boy, 2 weeks 3 days	2s
Nicholas Claye, carpenter, 1 week 3 days	5s 11d
John Sager, 1 week 3 days	2s 4d
William Adams, 1 week 3 days	2s 4d

John Claye, gromet, 1 week 3 days 21d
Gunner
William Thomas, master, 2 weeks 3 days 6s
[*Page total*] – £4 18s 8d.

[f. 257] *The Hope*
Mariners
William Hollande, master, 3 weeks 25s
John Abowen, boatswain, 6 weeks 5 days 27s 11d
Michael Gonson, purser, 6 weeks 5 days 16s 8d
John Mathew, cook, 6 weeks 5 days 15s 5d
James Robartes, 6 weeks 5 days 11s 2d
Gregory Stewarde, 6 weeks 5 days 11s 2d
Henry Watson, 6 weeks 5 days 11s 2d
Hugh Boye, 6 days 17d
Richard Abethell, 6 days 17d
Roger Duck, 6 weeks 5 days 11s 2d
John Lawrence, boy, 6 weeks 5 days 5s 7d
Nicholas Batter, 6 days 17d
Nicholas Johnson, carpenter, 6 weeks 5 days 27s 11d
John Longhorne, boy, 6 weeks 5 days 5s 7d
Thomas Johnson, boy, 6 weeks 5 days 5s 7d
Rowland Rawe, 5 weeks 6 days 9s 9d
William Richardes, boy, 5 weeks 6 days 4s 10½d
Richard Hayne, 5 weeks 6 days 9s 9d
John Sennet, gromet, 5 weeks 6 days 7s 4d
William Wilson, gromet, 5 weeks 6 days 7s 4d
Robert Blaike, 5 weeks 6 days 9s 9d
Gunners
Thomas Dixson, master, 6 weeks 5 days 16s 8d
William Bateman, gromet, 6 weeks 5 days 8s 4d
[*Page total*] – £12 12s 4½d.

[f. 257v] *The Mary Rose*
Mariners
William Robynson, boatswain, 13 weeks 1 day 54s 9d
Christopher Davye, purser, 13 weeks 1 day 32s 10d
Roger Cratwaye, cook, 13 weeks 1 day 30s 1½d
Humphrey Stevenson, 13 weeks 1 day 21s 11d
John Cossyne, 13 weeks 1 day 21s 11d
William Romney, 3 weeks 2 days 5s 6d
William Cooke, 3 weeks 2 days 5s 6d
John Gilbart, 6 days 17d

Thomas Harrington, 6 days	17d
John Woodcock, 6 days	17d
John Welles, 8 weeks 5 days	14s 6d
Thomas Leonarde, 4 weeks	6s 8d
Edward Laigghan, boy, 13 weeks 1 day	10s 11½d
Thomas Butlar, boy, 13 weeks 1 day	10s 11½d
John Willyams, 4 weeks 4 days	7s 8d
John Irelonde, [*blank*]	[*blank*]
Paul Hobbard, 3 weeks 5 days	6s 2d
John Checkley, 1 week 3 days	2s 2d
William Hackwell, 3 weeks 5 days	6s 2d
John Edwardes, 3 weeks 5 days	6s 2d
William Beast, 1 week 3 days	2s 2d
John Osborne, 1 week 3 days	2s 2d
William Harvye, 5 weeks 6 days	9s 9d
Ralph Richardes, 5 weeks 6 days	9s 9d
William Marcant, 5 weeks 6 days	9s 9d
John Marcant, 5 weeks 6 days	9s 9d
Richard Love, [*blank*]	[*blank*]
John Robson, 5 weeks 6 days	9s 9d
James Frende, 5 weeks 6 days	9s 9d
Andrew Sampson, 5 weeks 6 days	9s 9d
[*Gunner*]	
John Butlar, master gunner, 13 weeks 1 day	32s 10d

[*Page total*] – £17 13s 7½d.

[f. 258] *The Lion*

Mariners

William Hollande, master, 6 days	7s 2d
Robert Harwood, boatswain, 2 weeks 3 days	10s 1d
John Butlar, purser, 2 weeks 3 days	6s
John Curlle, cook, 2 weeks 3 days	5s 7d
John Samonde, 2 weeks 3 days	4s
John Russell, 2 weeks 3 days	4s
Robert Goslinge, 2 weeks 3 days	4s
Nicholas Waller, 2 weeks 3 days	4s
Nicholas Hewes, 2 weeks 3 days	4s
William Charlles, 2 weeks 3 days	4s
Thomas Dayll, 2 weeks 3 days	4s
Thomas Browne, 2 weeks 3 days	4s
Rowland Rawe, 6 days	17d
Richard Jones, 2 weeks 3 days	4s
William Pynteawyne, 2 weeks 3 days	4s

John Harwarde, gromet, 2 weeks 3 days 3s
William Richardes, boy, 6 days 8½d
Roger Browne, boy, 2 weeks 3 days 2s
Stephen Frende, 1 week 1 day 23d
Henry Sherwood, carpenter, 2 weeks 3 days 10s 1d
Thomas Platterer, gromet, 2 weeks 3 days 3s
Gunners
Edward Tompson, master, 2 weeks 3 days 6s
Peter Arney, 2 weeks 3 days 4s
[*Page total*] – £5 0s 11½d.

[f. 258v] *The Philip and Mary*
Mariners
John Jones, boatswain, 2 weeks 3 days 10s 1d
George Haulle, purser, 2 weeks 3 days 6s
John Geffrey, cook, 2 weeks 3 days 5s 7d
Francis Willyams, 2 weeks 3 days 4s
Gregory Wyckes, 2 weeks 3 days 4s
Thomas Sherpull, 2 weeks 3 days 4s
Zach Sweteman, 2 weeks 3 days 4s
Arthur Lyversoche, 2 weeks 3 days 4s
Richard West, 2 weeks 3 days 4s
Thomas James, 2 weeks 3 days 4s
Philip Beltt, 2 weeks 3 days 4s
Bartholomew Gaittes, gromet, 2 weeks 3 days 3s
Edward Hawston, gromet, 2 weeks 3 days 3s
James Nicollson, boy, 2 weeks 3 days 2s
William Welshe, carpenter, 1 week 4s 2d
Thomas Freman, gromet, 1 week 17d
William Chartram, gromet, 2 weeks 3 days 3s
Gunner
Matthew Sharpp, master, 2 weeks 3 days 6s
[*Page total*] – £3 16s 1d.

[f. 259] *The Willoughby*
Mariners
Robert Flynte, boatswain, 6 days 2s 6d
Andrew Everington, cook, 6 days 2s
Richard Dennys, 6 days 17d
Thomas Durrant, 6 days 17d
Benjamin Flinte, gromet, 6 days 12d
[*Gunner*]
John Malpasse, master gunner, 6 days 2s

The Bull	
Mariners	
Andrew Walker, boatswain, 13 weeks 1 day	38s 4d
John Wyllye, cook, 2 weeks 3 days	5s 7d
Richard Pytman, 13 weeks 1 day	21s 11d
Matthew Robson, cook, 13 weeks 1 day	28s 7d
Robert Harteley, 7 weeks 4 days	12s 8d
Edward Thomas, gromet, 13 weeks 1 day	16s 5d
Richard Babb, 13 weeks 1 day	21s 11d
John Forde, 9 weeks 4 days	16s
Roger Mathew, 3 weeks 3 days	5s 8d
[*Gunner*]	
Robert Butlar, master gunner, 13 weeks 1 day	32s 10d
The Bright Falcon	
Mariners	
Nicholas Waters, boatswain, 13 weeks 1 day	38s 4d
Thomas Kingesdowne, 13 weeks 1 day	21s 11d
Ellis Blancke, boy, 13 weeks 1 day	10s 11½d
Richard Harman, 13 weeks 1 day	21s 11d

[*Page total*] – £15 3s 4½d.

[f. 259v] *The Rowbarge*	
Mariners	
Robert Blaike, boatswain, 6 days	2s 6d
Thomas Whittell, cook, 6 days	2s
William Fallett, 6 days	17d
Simon Breadstreete, 6 days	17d
Richard Abraham, 6 days	17d
Nicholas Cherry, 6 days	17d
Andrew Ballerd, boy, 6 days	8½d
[*Gunner*]	
John Walker, master gunner, 6 days	2s
The Tiger	
Mariners	
John Beamonde, boatswain, 13 weeks 1 day	38s 4d
John Hawkyns, cook, 6 days	2s
John Bowye, 6 days	17d
Thomas Butlar, 7 weeks 4 days	12s 8d
Thomas Haull, 8 weeks 2 days	13s 10d
Richard Fleminge, 8 weeks 1 day	13s 7d
John Geffrey, boy, 13 weeks 1 day	10s 11½d
John Aneell, 10 weeks 1 day	16s 11d
Thomas Dabnyes, 5 weeks 2 days	8s 10d

William Barnes, 3 weeks 2 days 5s 6d
[*Gunner*]
John Moore, master gunner, 13 weeks 1 day 32s 10d

The Serpent
Mariners
John Waters, boatswain, 2 weeks 2 days 5s 3d
John Pylkarton, 7 weeks 2 days 12s 2d
Simon Marden, 7 weeks 2 days 12s 2d
John Hawkyns, 1 week 1 day 23d

[*Page total*] – £10 1s 3d.

[f. 260] *The Galley Speedwell*
Mariners
Cuthbert Clarke, boatswain, 7 weeks 5 days 32s 1d
Giles Bevizon, purser, 7 weeks 5 days 17s 8½d
Anthony Darnatho, 7 weeks 5 days 12s 10d
William Prynce, 2 weeks 3 days 4s
Brian Clarke, boy, 7 weeks 5 days 6s 5d
John Grene, gromet, 5 weeks 2 days 6s 7d
[*Gunner*]
Maurice Abowen, master gunner, 7 weeks 5 days 19s 2d

The Galley Tryright
Mariners
Simon Barnesley, boatswain, 7 weeks 5 days 22s 6d
John Goddyn, purser, 7 weeks 5 days 19s 2d
William Kent, cook, 7 weeks 5 days 17s 8d
Patrick Moore, 2 weeks 3 days 4s
William Waide, 6 days 17d
John Taillor, 5 weeks 2 days 8s 10d
Nicholas Chaunce, gromet, 5 weeks 2 days 6s 7d
[*Gunner*]
Thomas Neall, master gunner, 7 weeks 5 days 19s 2d

The Galley Mermaid
Mariners
Adam Puckwell, boatswain, 2 weeks 3 days 7s 1d
Simon Marden, 2 weeks 3 days 4s
Thomas Dabnes, 2 weeks 3 days 4s
Robert Puckwell, boy, 2 weeks 3 days 2s

The Mary Grace Hoy
Mariners
William Pearson, master, 13 weeks 1 day 54s 9d
Roger Wourrall, 3 weeks 5s

[*Page total*] – £13 14s 10½d.

[f. 260v] *The Guide*

Mariners

John Beckett, boatswain, 7 weeks 6 days	18s
George Emery, 7 weeks 6 days	13s 1d
[*Gunner*]	
Robert Tompson, master gunner, 7 weeks 6 days	19s 8d

The Searcher

Mariners

William Hamblett, boatswain, 2 weeks 2 days	5s 3d
John Pett, 7 weeks 4 days	12s 8d
[*Gunner*]	
Thomas Brewton, master gunner, 7 weeks 4 days	18s 10d

Wages of gunners daily attendant in Her Majesty's fort at Upnor for the safe-keeping of Her Grace's ships in Gillingham Water.

Thomas Sergeaunt, master, 92 days at 16d	£6 2s 8d
Richard Abeseade, 92 days at 12d	£4 12s
Robert Woulgrove, 92 days at 12d	£4 12s
William Bowyll, 92 days at 12d	£4 12s
William Taunton, 92 days at 12d	£4 12s
Robert Haulsnoth, 92 days at 12d	£4 12s
Robert Butler, 92 days at 12d	£4 12s
William Chisselden, 92 days at 12d	£4 12s

[*Page total*] – £42 14s 2d.

[f. 261] *[*Clerk*]. To Thomas Heynos the last day of September for his wages daily attending and serving Her Highness for the keeping of the book of cheque of masters, mariners, gunners and others keeping Her Grace's ships afloat in harbour, as also the prick book of shipwrights and caulkers, by one whole quarter of a year begun the first day of July last and this day ended – £5.

*[*Surveyor*].[1] To Thomas Baker the same day for his wages daily attending and serving Her Majesty in delivering of all manner of necessary wants out of Her Grace's storehouses there to the use of Her Highness's ships, by one like quarter of a year containing 92 days begun and ended as abovesaid, at 8d *per diem* – £3 1s 4d.

*[*Purveyor*]. To Butolph Moungey the same day for his wages daily attending and serving Her Highness for the providing of all manner of

[1]The marginal annotation here clearly distinguishes as 'surveyor' and 'purveyor' offices which had previously both been called 'purveyor' (cf. above, p. 138 and successive occurrences of this section of the Gillingham ordinary). But the job description does not change, and there is no particular reference to the surveying of stores, as applied to the office of surveyor at Deptford (cf. p. 34 and successive occurrences of that section).

needful provisions for the use of Her Majesty's ships, by the space of 19 days within this quarter begun the first day of July last and ended the 19th day of the same, at 8d *per diem* – 12s 8d.

[*Page total*] – £8 14s.

[f. 261v] *Sawyers*

Henry Ashfoard, 11 days at 6d	5s 6d
Edmund Bell, 11 days at 6d	5s 6d

Oarmakers

William Bexley, master, 15 days at 8d	10s
James Rowman, server, 15 days at 6d	7s 6d
Abraham Harman, server, 15 days at 5d	6s 3d
William Kackett, server, 15 days at 6d	7s 6d

Victualling. To John Hurlocke the last day of September for the victualling of the aforenamed six sawyers and oarmakers which wrought there upon the making of oars for the use of Her Highness's ships and galleys, with other needful work by them done, by the space of 88 days among them all, Sundays and holy days accounted in the same, begun the 9th day of July last and ended the 24th day of the same, which maketh 12 weeks 4 days, at 4s 4d every week the man. *Summa* – £2 14s 6d.

Bricklayers

John Callawaye, master, 9 days at 12d	9s
John Huggyns, 9 days at 11d	8s 3d
Stephen Huggins, 9 days at 10d	7s 6d
Richard Savaidge, 9 days at 10d	7s 6d
Lawrence Hartnat, 8 days at 7d	4s 8d
Henry Totenden, 8 days at 7d	4s 8d
Thomas Beden, 8 days at 7d	4s 8d

[*Page total*] – £7 3s. *[*Artificers – £4 8s 6d*; *victualling – 54s 6d*]

[f. 262] *Emptions*

Ironwork. *[*£11 3s 7½d*; *nails – £14 4s 6d*]. To George Hoope of Chatham, smith, the last day of September for price of 8 hundred 3 quarters 11 pounds [*991 lbs*] weight of his own new iron by him wrought into bolts, spikes of all sorts, clench, rove, port-hinges and chains, and the same delivered into Her Grace's storehouses at Gillingham for the use of Her Highness's ships there, at 23s 4d every hundredweight – £10 6s 5½d; more for new working of [*one*] hundred 3 quarters 10 pounds weight [*206 lbs*] of Her Highness's old iron into like bolts and spikes for the use as aforesaid, at 9s 2d the hundred[*weight*] – 17s 2d;[1] more for 7,000 of

[1]The calculation gives 202.32141d, which is about 3½d below the sum stated (206d); this would be correct within ½d for 210 lbs.

4d nail, at 3s 4d every 1,000 – 23s 4d; more for 11,100 of 6d nail, at 5s every 1,000 – 55s 6d; more for 9,000 of 10d nail, at 8s 4d every 1,000 – £3 15s; more for 1,000 of 20d nail – price 16s 8d; more for 5,500 of 2s nail, at 20s every 1,000 – £5 10s; and more to him for 200 of clench nail, at 2s the 100 – 4s. *Summa* – £25 8s 1½d.

Painting. To John Lyzarde of London, painter, the same day for the painting and colouring of 200 oars all red, done with oil, for the use of Her Majesty's galleys at their going to the seas, at 16s the piece. *Summa* – £13 6s 8d.

Glass and solder. To John Teigge of Rochester the same day for price of 111 quarrels of glass by him set up in the cabin of Her Grace's ship called the *Elizabeth Jonas*, at 1d the piece – 9s 3d; more for 2 pounds weight of solder, at 8d the pound – 16d; more for 2 pounds of lead, at 4d the pound – 8d; and more to him for wages of himself and his man working upon the same ship, by 6½ days between them at 10d every day – 5s 5d. *Summa* – 16s 8d.

To Thomas Hendyne of Maidstone the same day for price of 30½ pounds weight of solder had of him for the soldering of the furnaces in Her Grace's ships the *Victory* and the *Philip and Mary*, at 10d every pound – £1 5s 5d.

[*Page total*] – £40 16s 10½d.

[f. 262v] *Water carriage of provisions.* To Vincent Poulle, master, the last day of September for service of his hoy named the *Pellycane of Saincte Katherins* serving Her Highness in carrying of 7 cables of 14, 15, 16, and 17 inches compass, 11 cablets, hawsers and warps of 2, 3, 4, 5, 6, 7 and 8 inches compass, 8 hundredweight of ratline, with divers and sundry other needful provisions, from Deptford to Gillingham and there delivered the same for the use of Her Majesty's ships then bound to the seas; by agreement. *Summa* – £1 15s.

House rent. To Adam Kellar of Chatham the same day for the rent of a storehouse and ground of him hired wherein lieth Her Majesty's store of cables, cablets, hawsers and warps, canvas, sails, ironwork and divers other provisions for the use of Her Grace's ships, by one quarter of a year due at this present – 10s.

To Thomas Winnall of Chatham the same day for the hire of [*a*] certain storehouse wherein lieth Her Highness's store of pitch, tar, rosin and other needful things for the use of her ships, by one quarter of a year, due as is aforesaid – 3s 4d.

To Richard Mylles of Chatham the same day for one quarter of a year's rent of a storehouse hired of him wherein lieth Her Grace's store of reed for the breaming of Her Highness's ships at their groundings – 1s 3d.

To Roger Cratwaye of Frindsbury the same day for certain stuffs by him bought and consumed in the destroying of rats and mice in all Her Grace's ships and storehouses there for the safeguard of Her Highness's sails, canvas and flags, for one whole quarter of a year; by agreement – 10s.

[*Page total*] – £2 19s 7d.

[f. 263] *Inch board.* To Thomas Sergaunt of Frindsbury the last day of September for price of 450 foot of inch board oak of him had and delivered at Gillingham for the use of Her Grace's ships there, at 5s every 100 foot. *Summa* – 17s 6d.

Netting-rope and oakum. To Margaret Blaike, Bennet Roose and Rose Harris of Rochester the same day for the working and picking of [*one*] thousand 2 hundred one quarter 6 pounds weight [*1,378 lbs*] of Her Grace's old junks and ropes into oakum for the needful caulking of Her Highness's ships at their groundings, at 3s 4d every hundredweight working – 41s; and more to Thomas Hunt for the working of [*one*] thousand 2 hundred 17 pounds weight [*1,361 lbs*] of the like junks into netting-rope and oakum for the use of Her Highness's said ships, at 3s 8d every hundredweight working – 44s 6d.[1] *Summa* – £4 5s 6d.

[*Page total*] – £5 3s. [f. 263v *blank*]

[f. 264] *Anno regni regine Elizabethe sexto*

A payment made the last day of December as well to master, mariners, gunners and others daily attending and serving the Queen's Majesty in safe-keeping of Her Grace's ships afloat in harbour and for rent of storehouses wherein lieth divers kinds of provisions for the use of Her Highness's said ships, as also to shipwrights and others for mending and repairing of the same ships, with provisions of divers kinds taken of sundry persons for the use aforesaid; by one quarter of a year begun the first day of October last and this day ended, as followeth:

The Triumph

Mariners

John Hurlocke, master, 13 weeks 1 day	£6 11s 5d
Thomas Goldston, boatswain, 13 weeks 1 day	54s 9d
Henry Cooke, purser, 13 weeks 1 day	32s 10d
John Baswell, cook and steward, 13 weeks 1 day	30s 1½d
Mark Bullyn, 13 weeks 1 day	21s 11d
Peter Trewe, 13 weeks 1 day	21s 11d

[1] The calculation gives 534.67851d, which is about ½d above the sum stated (534d).

Robert Keye, 13 weeks 1 day	21s 11d
Thomas Ratclyff, 13 weeks 1 day	21s 11d
John Boye, 3 weeks	5s
Fabian Bullyn, 13 weeks 1 day	21s 11d
Thomas Maye, 13 weeks 1 day	21s 11d
John Russell, 13 weeks 1 day	21s 11d
Edmund Gybbin, 13 weeks 1 day	21s 11d
William Harrys, 13 weeks 1 day	21s 11d
George Robyns, 13 weeks 1 day	21s 11d
Thomas Mathew, 13 weeks 1 day	21s 11d
Saunder Myller, 13 weeks 1 day	21s 11d
Richard Wygges, 3 weeks 2 days	5s 6d
Edward Wyckes, boy, 13 weeks 1 day	10s 11½d

[*Page total*] – £26 13s 7d.

[f. 264v] John Phillypp, 2 weeks 2 days	3s 10d
Thomas Pultar, carpenter, 13 weeks 1 day	54s 9d
John Hytchecock, server, 13 weeks 1 day	21s 11d
Griffin Tether, gromet, 13 weeks 1 day	16s 5d
Lawrence Tompson, gromet, 3 weeks 1 day	3s 11d
Richard Dyamonde, 10 weeks 6 days	18s 1d
John Awood, 5 weeks 6 days	9s 9d
William Hownsell, 5 weeks 6 days	9s 9d
[*Gunner*]	
Stephen Bull, master gunner, [*blank*]	[*blank*]

The Elizabeth Jonas

Mariners

William Wood, master, 12 weeks 2 days	£6 2s 10d
John Teigg, boatswain, 12 weeks 2 days	51s 2d
Roger Davye, purser, 12 weeks 2 days	43s
Thomas Waller, cook & steward, 12 weeks 2 days	28s 2d
James Morter, 12 weeks 2 days	20s 6d
William Blosse, 12 weeks 2 days	20s 6d
Richard Bartylmew, 12 weeks 2 days	20s 6d
John Abowen, 12 weeks 2 days	20s 6d
John Barwick, 12 weeks 2 days	20s 6d
Brian Baker, 12 weeks 2 days	20s 6d
William Challyner, 12 weeks 2 days	20s 6d
Richard Waddelow, 12 weeks 2 days	20s 6d
Robert Jynner, 12 weeks 2 days	20s 6d
John Coulmerlonde, 12 weeks 2 days	20s 6d
Simon Edwardes, 12 weeks 2 days	20s 6d

William Haydon, 12 weeks 2 days	20s 6d
Robert Moore, 12 weeks 2 days	20s 6d
Thomas Paynter, 12 weeks 2 days	20s 6d
John Barnerde, 12 weeks 2 days	20s 6d
Richard Warren, gromet, 2 weeks 2 days	2s 10d
Henry Perryman, boy, 3 weeks 4 days	3s
Nicholas Johnson, carpenter, 13 weeks 1 day	54s 9d
Thomas Johnson, gromet, 13 weeks 1 day	16s 5d
John Longhorne, gromet, 4 weeks 3 days	5s 6d
Robert Heallinge, 12 weeks 2 days	20s 6d
Henry Morrys, gromet, 12 weeks 2 days	15s 4d
Peter Hacklonde, gromet, 3 weeks 4 days	4s 5d
[*Gunner*]	
Lawrence Dilke, master gunner, 12 weeks 2 days	30s 8d

[*Page total*] – £42 3s 6d.

[f. 265] *The Victory*

Mariners

William Barnes, master, 12 weeks 2 days	£6 2s 10d
John Lighte, boatswain, 12 weeks 2 days	51s 2d
Hugh Pope, purser, 12 weeks 2 days	30s 8d
Thomas Gayttes, cook & steward, 12 weeks 2 days	28s 2d
William Parcyvall, 12 weeks 2 days	20s 6d
William Hawkyns, 12 weeks 2 days	20s 6d
John Robyns, 12 weeks 2 days	20s 6d
Thomas Clarke, 12 weeks 2 days	20s 6d
John Jourdayne, 12 weeks 2 days	20s 6d
Richard Cock, 12 weeks 2 days	20s 6d
John Clarke, 12 weeks 2 days	20s 6d
Richard Brother, 12 weeks 2 days	20s 6d
Thomas Noursse, 12 weeks 2 days	20s 6d
John Lollett, gromet, 4 weeks 3 days	5s 6d
Ralph Leawys, 12 weeks 2 days	20s 6d
Robert Garrett, gromet, 12 weeks 2 days	15s 4d
Christopher Lyvinges, boy, 3 weeks 4 days	3s
Nicholas Claye, carpenter, 12 weeks 2 days	51s 2d
John Claye, gromet, 12 weeks 2 days	15s 4d
John Sager, 10 weeks	16s 8d
Richard Tysson, gromet, 3 weeks 4 days	4s 5d
[*Gunners*]	
William Thomas, master gunner, 12 weeks 2 days	30s 8d
James Saunders, gromet, 4 weeks 3 days	7s 4d

The Mary Rose

Mariners

William Robynson, boatswain, 13 weeks 1 day	54s 9d
Christopher Davye, purser, 13 weeks 1 day	32s 10d
Robert Cratwaye, cook & steward, 13 weeks 1 day	30s 1½d
Humphrey Stevenson, 13 weeks 1 day	21s 11d
John Cossyn, 13 weeks 1 day	21s 11d
William Harvye, 13 weeks 1 day	21s 11d
John Robson, 13 weeks 1 day	21s 11d
James Frende, 13 weeks 1 day	21s 11d
Andrew Sampson, 13 weeks 1 day	21s 11d
William Marcant, 2 weeks 4 days	4s 4d
Edward Laughan, boy, 13 weeks 1 day	10s 11½d

[*Page total*] – £42 11s 9d.

[f. 265v] Thomas Butlar, boy, 4 weeks 3 days	3s 8d
Thomas Stacey, 11 weeks 4 days	19s 4d
Thomas Roger, 4 weeks 3 days	7s 4d
William Armett, 12 weeks 2 days	20s 6d
Richard Yonge, 5 weeks 6 days	9s 9d
Richard Cromer, 5 weeks 6 days	9s 9d
Richard Chapman, [*blank*]	[*blank*]
[*Gunner*]	
John Butlar, master gunner, [*blank*]	[*blank*]

The Hope

Mariners

William Hollande, master, 13 weeks 1 day	£5 9s 5d
John Abowen, boatswain, 13 weeks 1 day	54s 9d
Michael Gonson, purser, 13 weeks 1 day	32s 10d
John Mathew, cook and steward, 13 weeks 1 day	30s 1½d
James Robertes, 13 weeks 1 day	21s 11d
Gregory Stewarde, 13 weeks 1 day	21s 11d
Henry Watson, 13 weeks 1 day	21s 11d
Roger Duck, 3 weeks	5s
Rowland Rawe, 13 weeks 1 day	21s 11d
William Richardes, boy, 13 weeks 1 day	10s 11½d
William Wyllson, gromet, 4 weeks 3 days	5s 6d
John Lawrence, boy, 13 weeks 1 day	10s 11½d
John Sennett, gromet, 4 weeks 3 days	5s 6d
William Bateman, gromet, 4 weeks 3 days	5s 6d
John Bunche, carpenter, 12 weeks 2 days	51s 2d
William Harbert, gromet, 12 weeks 2 days	15s 4d

Richard Bunche, boy, 3 weeks 4 days	3s
John Pyentawyen, 12 weeks 2 days	20s 6d
John Ryder, 12 weeks 2 days	20s 6d
John Landrythe, 9 weeks 6 days	16s 5d
Gunner	
Thomas Dixson, master, 13 weeks 1 day	32s 10d

[*Page total*] – £27 15s 10½d.

[f. 266] *The Philip and Mary*

Mariners	
John Jones, boatswain, 12 weeks 2 days	51s 2d
George Haull, purser, 12 weeks 2 days	30s 8d
John Jeffery, cook and steward, 12 weeks 2 days	28s 2d
Francis Willyams, 12 weeks 2 days	20s 6d
Gregory Wyckes, 12 weeks 2 days	20s 6d
William Hyckes, 5 weeks 6 days	10s 9d
Arthur Lyversuche, 6 weeks	10s 0d
John Haull, 12 weeks 2 days	20s 6d
William Pettyjohn, 12 weeks 2 days	20s 6d
John Rowmett, 12 weeks 2 days	20s 6d
Thomas Kellye, 12 weeks 2 days	20s 6d
John Ryve, 12 weeks 2 days	20s 6d
Bartholomew Gaettes, gromet, 12 weeks 2 days	15s 4d
Edward Hawston, gromet, 3 weeks 4 days	4s 5d
John Nicollson, gromet, 3 weeks 4 days	4s 5d
William Welshe, carpenter, 12 weeks 2 days	51s 2d
Thomas Freman, 12 weeks 2 days	20s 6d
William Chatterham, 3 weeks 5 days	6s
Richard Ryce, [*blank*]	[*blank*]
Thomas Harrington, 5 weeks 6 days	9s 9d
[*Gunner*]	
Matthew Sharpp, master gunner, 12 weeks 2 days	30s 8d

The Lion

Mariners	
Robert Glandfylde, boatswain, 12 weeks 2 days	51s 2d
John Butlar, purser, 12 weeks 2 days	30s 8d
John Curlle, cook and steward, 12 weeks 2 days	28s 2d
John Samonde, 12 weeks 2 days	20s 6d
John Russell, 12 weeks 2 days	20s 6d
William Morrell, 7 weeks 1 day	11s 11d
Richard Cayde, 12 weeks 2 days	20s 6d
Nicholas Woodcock, 12 weeks 2 days	20s 6d

Edmund Foster, 9 weeks 2 days	15s 2d
Thomas Bettson, 12 weeks 2 days	20s 6d
John Rock, 12 weeks 2 days	20s 6d
John Penney, 12 weeks 2 days	20s 6d
[*Page total*] – £34 18s 1d.	
[f. 266v] Lucas Clement, 12 weeks 2 days	20s 6d
Stephen Sangwell, 12 weeks 2 days	20s 6d
Peter Arney, 3 weeks 4 days	6s
Henry Sherwood, carpenter, 12 weeks 2 days	51s 2d
Thomas Platterar, gromet, 12 weeks 2 days	15s 4d
[*Gunner*]	
Edward Tompson, master gunner, 12 weeks 2 days	30s 8d
The Minion	
Mariners	
Robert Rowte, boatswain, 11 weeks	32s 1d
Robert Best, cook and steward, 11 weeks	25s 2½d
Robert Fareley, 2 weeks 2 days	4s 10d
James Hollydaye, 11 weeks	18s 4d
Edward Barker, 11 weeks	18s 4d
John Hore, 11 weeks	18s 4d
James Burnam, 11 weeks	18s 4d
Edward Yowen, 5 weeks 5 days	9s 6d
Matthew Gramite, 11 weeks	18s 4d
John Lasye, 11 weeks	18s 4d
Arculous [*Hercules*] Gulterye, 2 weeks 2 days	3s 10d
John Brownynge, boy, 2 weeks 2 days	23d
Roger Raynerde, 8 weeks 5 days	[*blank*]
George Kyngson, 8 weeks 5 days	[*blank*]
[*Gunner*]	
Robert Butlar, master gunner, 11 weeks	27s 6d
The Bull	
Mariners	
Andrew Walker, boatswain, 5 weeks 1 day	15s
Matthew Robson, cook & steward, 4 weeks 3 days	10s 2d
Richard Babb, 13 weeks 1 day	21s 11d
John Foarde, 4 weeks 3 days	7s 4d
Roger Mathew, 3 weeks	5s
Edward Thomas, boy, 4 weeks 3 days	3s 8d
[*Page total*] – £20 16s 1½d.	

[f. 267] *The Primrose*

Mariners

John Davyes, boatswain, 11 weeks	32s 1d
John Pett, cook and steward, 11 weeks	25s 2½d
Daniel Dyce, 1 week	20d
James Lyell, 11 weeks	18s 4d
Walter Sheple, 11 weeks	18s 4d
Thomas Anye, 8 weeks 2 days	13s 10d
William Odyam, 11 weeks	18s 4d
William Davyes, 2 weeks 2 days	3s 10d
Philip Settell, boy, 2 weeks 2 days	23d
William Sebrey, 11 weeks	18s 4d
Thomas Norwaye, 11 weeks	18s 4d
William Thomas, 11 weeks	18s 4d
James Hedger, 6 weeks 1 day	[*blank*]
[*Gunner*]	
James Longe, master gunner, 11 weeks	27s 6d

The Jennet

Mariners

John Edmondes, boatswain, 12 weeks 1 day	35s 5d
Richard Gurley, purser, 3 weeks 2 days	11s
John Adams, cook and steward, 12 weeks 1 day	27s 10d
William Parrys, 5 weeks 1 day	8s 7d
Richard Bedforde, 12 weeks 1 day	20s 3d
John Jarvys, 6 weeks 3 days	10s 8d
William Bonner, 12 weeks 1 day	20s 3d
John Gouldesmythe, 12 weeks 1 day	20s 3d
Nicholas Safferon, 4 weeks 3 days	7s 4d
Davy Evans, 4 weeks 3 days	7s 4d
John Dyee, 12 weeks 1 day	20s 3d
Hugh Flighte, 12 weeks 1 day	20s 3d
Simon Traves, boy, 3 weeks 3 days	2s 10d
[*Gunner*]	
Richard Haynes, master gunner, 12 weeks 1 day	30s 4d

[*Page total*] – £22 18s 7d.

[f. 267v] *The Tiger*

Mariners

John Beamonde, boatswain, 5 week 5 days	16s 8d
Thomas Dabnys, 5 weeks 1 day	8s 7d
John Geffery, boy, 4 weeks 3 days	3s 8d
William Barnes, 4 weeks 3 days	7s 4d

Richard Perryman, 13 weeks 1 day	21s 11d
[*Gunner*]	
John Moore, master gunner, 5 weeks 2 days	13s 2d
The Bright Falcon	
Mariners	
Nicholas Waters, boatswain, 4 weeks 3 days	12s 11d
Thomas Kingeston, 4 weeks 3 days	7s 4d
Ellis Blanck, gromet, 4 weeks 3 days	5s 6d
The Serpent	
Mariners	
Robert Blaick, boatswain, 4 weeks 3 days	12s 11d
John Hawkyns, 13 weeks 1 day	21s 11d
The Galley Speedwell	
Mariners	
Cuthbert Clarke, boatswain, 13 weeks 1 day	54s 9d
Giles Bevyzon, cook & steward, 13 weeks 1 day	30s 1½d
Anthony Darnatho, 13 weeks 1 day	21s 11d
Brian Clarke, boy, 4 weeks 3 days	3s 8d
Richard Harman, 13 weeks 1 day	21s 11d
John Chamber, 5 weeks 6 days	9s 9d
[*Gunner*]	
Maurice Abowen, master gunner, 13 weeks 1 day	32s 10d
The Mary Grace Hoy	
Mariner	
William Pearson, master, 13 weeks 1 day	54s 9d

[*Page total*] – £18 1s 7½d.

[f. 268] *The Galley Tryright*

Mariners	
Simon Barnesley, boatswain, 2 weeks 6 days	6s 8d
John Goddyn, cook and steward, 13 weeks 1 day	30s 1½d
William Kentt, 13 weeks 1 day	21s 11d
John Taillour, 2 weeks 4 days	4s 6d
Robert Blaick, boatswain, 8 weeks 5 days	25s 5d
George Trowyll, 12 weeks 1 day	20s 3d
Thomas Barne, 12 weeks 1 day	20s 3d
[*Gunner*]	
William Adams, master gunner, 13 weeks 1 day	32s 10d
The Guide	
Mariners	
William Saunders, boatswain, 12 weeks 2 days	35s 10d
Robert Tompson, master gunner, 10 weeks 5 days	26s 8d

The Searcher

Mariner

John Pett, 13 weeks 1 day	21s 11d
[*Gunner*]	
Thomas Brewton, master gunner, 10 weeks 5 days	26s 8d

The George Hoy

Mariners

Thomas Ussher, master, 3 weeks 3 days	17s
John Bennett, boatswain, 3 weeks 3 days	10s
Thomas Elkyn, cook and steward, 3 weeks 3 days	7s 10½d
Henry Burgys, 3 weeks 3 days	5s 8d
Thomas Kyngeston, 8 weeks 5 days	14s 6d
John Wylliams, 3 weeks 3 days	5s 8d
Walter Peace, 3 weeks 3 days	5s 8d
Martin Delanoye, 3 weeks 3 days	5s 8d
Clement Jeslyne, 3 weeks 3 days	5s 8d
Nicholas Waters, boatswain, 8 weeks 5 days	25s 5d
Matthew Robson, cook, 8 weeks 5 days	20s
John Foarde, 8 weeks 5 days	14s 6d
[*Gunner*]	
Ralph Lynche, master gunner, 3 weeks 3 days	8s 6d

[*Page total*] – £21 17s 10d.

[f. 268v] *The Swallow*

Mariners

William Saunders, boatswain, 5 weeks 6 days	17s 1d
John Robertes, [*purser*], 5 weeks 6 days	13s 5d
Davy Gryffith, 5 weeks 6 days	9s 9d
Thomas Wylkins, 5 weeks 6 days	9s 9d
Richard Hewe, 5 weeks 6 days	9s 9d
John Knighte, 5 weeks 6 days	9s 9d
John Baswell, 5 weeks 6 days	9s 9d
Matthew Fyssher, 5 weeks 6 days	9s 9d
Robert Collyns, boy, 5 weeks 6 days	4s 10½d
[*Gunner*]	
Jacob Myller, master gunner, 5 weeks 6 days	14s 8d

The Willoughby

Mariners

Robert Flyntt, boatswain, 5 weeks 6 days	17s 1d
Andrew Everington, cook and steward, 5 weeks 6 days	13s 5d
Richard Dennys, 5 weeks 6 days	9s 9d

William Fytchett, 5 weeks 6 days	9s 9d
John Walker, 3 weeks 2 days	5s 6d
Richard Abraham, 5 weeks 6 days	9s 9d
John Appulton, boy, 5 weeks 6 days	4s 10½d
William Browne, 1 week 2 days	2s 2d
William Brade, 1 week 1 day	23d
[*Gunner*]	
John Malpas, master gunner, 5 weeks 6 days	14s 8d

Wages of gunners daily attendant in the Queen's Majesty's fort at Upnor.

Thomas Sergaunte, master, 92 days at 16d	£6 2s 8d
William Tawnton, 92 days at 12d	£4 12s
Richard Abeseade, 40 days at 12d	40s
Robert Woulgrove, 92 days at 12d	£4 12s
William Bowyll, 92 days at 12d	£4 12s
William Chisselden, 92 days at 12d	£4 12s
Robert Halsnoth, 92 days at 12d	£4 12s
Robert Butler, 92 days at 12d	£4 12s
Anthony Venruther, 52 days at 12d	52s

[*Page total*] – £48 0s 1d.

[f. 269] *[*Clerk*]. To Thomas Heynoes the last day of December for his wages daily attending and serving the Queen's Majesty as well for the keeping of the book of cheque of masters, mariners, gunners and others serving in Her Grace's ships for their safe-keeping in harbour, as also the prick book of shipwrights and caulkers, by one whole quarter of a year, due at this present – £5.

*[*Surveyor*]. To Thomas Baker the same day for his wages daily attending and serving Her Highness in delivery of all manner of needful things out of Her Grace's storehouses there to the use of her ships, by one like quarter of a year, containing 92 days begun the first day of October last and ended as abovesaid, at 8d *per diem*. *Summa* – £3 1s 4d.

Shipwrights	
Peter Pett, master, 92 days at 12d *per diem*	£4 12s
Michael Chamber, 2 days at 7d	14d
Robert Tapshear, 2 days at 6d	12d
Robert Welshe, 1 day at 7d	7d
John Wyllson, 3 days at 6d	18d
Sawyers	
Edmund Bell, 3 days at 6d	18d
Nicholas Hashforth, 3 days at 6d	18d

House-carpenters

Thomas Morton, 2 days at 12d	2s
John Saunders, 2 days at 12d	2s

[*Page total*] – £13 4s 7d. *[*Artificers – £5 3s 3d*; (*surveyor* deleted) *clerk – £5*; *purveyor – 61s 4d*]

[f. 269v] *Emptions*

Ironwork *[*£5 14s 11d*; *nails – £18 11s*]. To George Hoope of Chatham, smith, the last day of December for price of 4 hundred 18 pounds weight [*466 lbs*] of new iron wrought into bolts, spikes, rings and keys had of him for the use of the Queen's Majesty's ships, at 23s 4d every hundredweight – £4 17s 1d; more for the new working of 3 quarters and 22 pounds weight [*106 lbs*] of Her Grace's old iron into like bolts and spikes for the use as aforesaid, at 1d every pound – 8s 10d; more for 1,000 of 2s nail, price – 20s; more for 3,000 of 20d nail, at 16s 8d every 1,000 – 50s; more for 1,000 of 10d nail – 8s 4d; more for 500 of 6d nail, 2s 6d; more for 900 of 4d nail, price – 3s; more for 2 pair of hinges for the *Triumph* her cabin, price – 2s 8d; and more for 12 shaving hooks,[1] at 6d the piece – 6s. *Summa* – £9 18s 5d.

To Thomas Willson of Ratcliff, smith, the same day for price of 5,000 of 2s nail of him had for the use of Her Highness's ships, at 20s every 1,000 – £5; more for 5,500 of 20d nail, at 16s 8d every 1,000 – £4 11s 8d; more for 5,000 of 10d nail, at 8s 4d every 1,000 – 41s 8d; more for 5,000 of 6d nail, at 5s every 1,000 – 25s; more for 5,000 of 4d nail, at 3s 4d every 1,000 – 16s 8d; and more to him for 5,000 of 3d nail, at 2s 6d every 1,000 – 12s 6d. *Summa* – £14 7s 6d.

Painting and colouring. To John Lyzarde of London, painter, the same day for the painting in oil three Her Grace's galleys at Chatham, *viz*. the *Galley Speedwell*, the *Galley Tryright* in colour red and the *Galley Mermaid* in colour black;[2] and more to him for priming and painting the *Victory* her toparmours with the Queen's Majesty's arms in oils; by agreement – £26 13s 4d.

Timber oak. To Henry Layne of Bexley, purveyor, the same day for price of 46 loads 20 foot of oaken timber by him delivered at Gillingham for the building and repairing of Her Grace's ships there, at 9s every load after 50 foot to the load. *Summa* – £20 18s.

[*Page total*] – £71 17s 3d.

[1]More usually 'shave-hook', a plumber's tool with blades (generally triangular) for scraping metal to accept solder: *OED* cites 1485 usage from Oppenheim, *Naval Accounts Hen. VII*, p. 40 (where 'shaffe hokes' is understood more generally as 'hooks with handles or shafts').

[2]The *Mermaid* was indeed also known as the *Black Galley*, originally by way of distinction from the *Galley Subtle* or *Red Galley*: see *NEM*, pp. 496–7.

[f. 270] *Trenails.* To Henry Cowper the last day of December for price of 8,000 trenails of 24 inches long by him delivered at Chatham for the use of Her Grace's ships there, after 5 score to the hundred at 2s every hundred – £8; more for 4,200 of trenails of 20 inches long, at 20d every hundred – £3 10s; more for 5,800 trenails of 18 inches long, at 18d every 100 – £4 7s; more for 5,000 trenails of 14 inches long, at 14d every hundred – 58s 4d; more for 4,600 trenails of 12 inches long, at 12d every hundred – 46s; and more to him for 2,200 of trenails of 10 inches and 10 cast,[1] at 10d every hundred – 18s 4d. *Summa* – £21 19s 8d.

House rent. To Adam Keller of Chatham the same day for one quarter of a year's rent of a storehouse and ground of him hired wherein lieth Her Highness's store of cables, cablets, hawsers, warps, canvas and other needful provisions for the use of her ships, due at this present – 10s; more to Thomas Wynnall for one like quarter's rent of a storehouse hired of him wherein lieth Her Majesty's store of tar, pitch, rosin and other needful things for the aforesaid use, due as abovesaid – 3s 4d; and more to Richard Mylles for the hire of a storehouse wherein lieth Her Grace's store of reed for the breaming of her ships at their grounding, due as aforesaid – 15d. *Summa* – 14s 7d.

Water carriage of provisions. To Vincent Powell, master, the same day for service of his hoy named the *Pellycan of Saincte Katheryns* serving Her Highness in carrying of one last of pitch, one sack of white poppet oakum, 4 pair of screws, 30 planks of 4 inches, 30 planks of 3 inches, 40 planks of 2 inches, 6 great pieces of timber, 500 of inch and featheredge board, and divers other provisions, from Deptford to Chatham and there delivered the same for the use of the Queen's Majesty's ships; by agreement – £1 13s 4d.

Rushes. To Thomas Couller of Gillingham the same day for the price of 150 of rushes of him had for the ridging[2] of the long shed there for the safe-keeping of Her [*Grace's/Highness's*] ships' sails, at 8s per 100 – 12s.

[*Page total*] – £24 19s 7d.

[f. 270v] *Water carriage.* To William Paulmer of Millhall the last day of December for the service of his hoy in carrying of 5,000 of 2s nail, 5,500 2d nail, 5,000 6d nails, 5,000 of 10d nails, 5,000 of 4d nails and 5,000 3d nails from Deptford to Chatham and there delivered the same into Her Grace's storehouse for the use of Her Majesty's ships. *Summa* – 7s.

[1] By estimate.

[2] A thatched roof is secured by a ridge of tightly woven straw or rushes. As with reed, the quantities expressed would be for bundles of a standard size.

Old junks and ropes wrought into netting and oakum. To Margaret Blaicke, Stephen Roose, Henry Cooke, Elizabeth Gonson and six other persons of Gillingham, Chatham, Rochester and thereabouts the same day for the working and picking of 2 thousand 8 hundred and 6 pounds weight [*3,142 lbs*] of the Queen's Majesty's old junks and ropes into oakum for the needful caulking of Her Grace's ships at their groundings, at 3s 4d every hundredweight working – £4 13s 6d; more to Thomas Hunt, ropemaker for the working of [*one*] thousand 5 hundred 2 pounds weight [*1,682 lbs*] of the like ropes and junks into netting-ropes for the use of her ships, at 3s 8d the hundred[*weight*] working – 55s 1½d;[1] and more to him for the picking and working of 9 hundred 10 pounds weight [*1,018 lbs*] of oakum, at 3s 8d every hundredweight – 33s 8d [*recte* 4d].[2] *Summa* – £9 2s 3½d.

Reed. To John Hurlocke of Gillingham the same day for price of 8 bundles of rods by him provided for the use of the long shed there, at 3d the bundle – 2s; more for mapstaves and breaming poles – 20d; more for 2 cop[3] of straw for the breaming of Her Highness's ships – 8d; and more for a hoop for the mending of the *Aid* her maintop, price – 6d. *Summa* – 4s 10d.

To Richard Fenner the same day for price of 900 of burning reed of him had for the breaming of Her Grace's ships at their groundings, at 3s 4d every 100 – £1 10s.

To Edward Yonge of Gillingham the same day for the laying of 150 of rushes upon the long shed there for the ridging of the same, at 10s 8d the 100 – 16s; and more to him for rods, bends and spars by him provided for the use as aforesaid – 3s 4d. *Summa* – 19s 4d.

[*Page total*] – £12 3s 5d [*recte* 2s 5½d].

[f. 271] **Ordinary. Colne**:

Anno Domini 1563. Anno regni regine Elizabethe quinto

A payment made the last day of March as well to keepers of storehouses, dock and timber-yards there wherein lieth Her Highness's store of provisions for the use of Her Grace's ships and to sundry persons for divers kinds of necessaries had for the repairing of the same storehouses, as also for rent of the same; by one quarter of a year begun the first day of January last and this day ended, as followeth:

[1] The calculation gives 660.78564d, which is about 3½d below the sum stated (661.5d); this would be correct with 1,684 lbs.

[2] The calculation gives 399.92852d, which is 4d below the sum stated (404d). Here the probability is that the *viijd* in the rate has been mistakenly repeated as the pence in the total instead of *iiijd*; the figure written is carried forward.

[3] A Kent term for a conical heap of straw or other crop: *OED* 'cop' *sb.*[1] .5.

*[*Storehouse keeper*]. To Edward Lambarde the last day of March for his wages daily attending and serving Her Highness in safe-keeping of Her Grace's storehouses and timber-yards there wherein lieth divers kinds of stuffs pertaining to Her Majesty's ships, by one quarter of a year containing 90 days begun the first day of January last and ended as abovesaid, at 12d *per diem* – £4 10s.

*[*Plug keeper*]. To Thomas Richardson, mariner, the same day for his wages daily attending and serving Her Highness in keeping of the plug for the drier keeping of the dock there wherein lieth Her Grace's ship named the *Trinity Henry*, by like time of 90 days begun and ended as aforesaid, at 6d *per diem* – £2 5s.

[*Page total*] – £6 15s.

[f. 271v] *Emptions*

*[*Shipwright*]. To John Peache, shipwright, the last day of March for the mending of the pump standing in the dock there and for the making of a new box for the use of the same pump; by agreement – 5s.

*[*Iron*]. To William Bewicke, smith, the same day for price of 8 pounds weight of his own new iron, and for the new making of the ironwork belonging to the same pump – 4s 8d; more for a pump staff, one pump-hose with the strops and scupper nails to the same – 3s 8d; and more to him for 7 pounds weight of spikes and small nails, at 3d every pound – 21d. *Summa* – 10s 1d.

*[*Labourers*]. To Robert Consent and three other labourers the same day for their pains taken in lading of the water out of Her Grace's ship the *Trinity Henry* there, with other service done by them within this quarter; by agreement – 10s 6d.

*[*Storehouse rent*]. To William Berryff the same day for one quarter of a year's rent of a certain storehouse and ground of him hired wherein lieth divers and sundry kinds of provisions for the use of Her Majesty's ships, due at this present – 13s 4d.

To Thomas Beryff the same day for one quarter of a year's rent of a certain storehouse and ground of him hired wherein lieth divers kinds of stuffs pertaining to Her Grace's ships, due at this present – 6s 8d.

[*Page total*] – £2 5s 7d.

[f. 272] A payment made the last day of June as well to keepers of storehouses, dock and timber-yards there wherein lieth Her Highness's store of divers kinds of provisions taken of sundry persons for the use of Her Grace's ships, as also for rent of the said storehouses; by one quarter of a year begun the first day of April last and this day ended, as followeth:

*[*Storehouse keeper*]. To Edward Lambarde the last day of June for his wages daily attending and serving Her Highness in safe-keeping of Her Grace's storehouses and timber-yards there wherein lieth divers kinds of provisions for the use of Her Majesty's ships, by one quarter of a year containing 91 days begun the first day of April last and ended as aforesaid, at 12d *per diem* – £4 11s.

*[*Plug keeper*]. To Thomas Richardson, mariner, the same day for his wages daily attending and serving Her Highness in safe-keeping of the plug and letting of the water out of the dock there for the drier keeping of the same wherein lieth Her Grace's ship called the *Trinity Henry*, by like time of 91 days begun and ended as is abovesaid, at 6d *per diem* – £2 5s 6d.

[*Page total*] – £6 16s 6d.

[f. 272v] *Emptions*

*[*Labourers*]. To Robert Consent and three other labourers the last day of June for their pains taken in lading out of the water out of Her Grace's ship called the *Trinity Henry*, by the space of 15 days among them all within this quarter, at 6d *per diem* – 7s 6d.

House rent. To William Berryff the same day for one quarter of a year's rent of a certain storehouse and ground of him hired wherein lieth divers and sundry kinds of provisions for the use of Her Majesty's ships, due at this present – 13s 4d.

To Thomas Berryff the same day for one quarter of a year's rent of a certain storehouse and ground of him hired wherein lieth divers and sundry kinds of stuffs pertaining to Her Grace's ships, due at this present – 6s 8d.

[*Page total*] – £1 7s 6d.

[f. 273] A payment made the last day of September as well to keepers of storehouses, dock and timber-yards there wherein lieth Her Highness's store of divers and sundry kinds of provisions for the use of Her Majesty's ships, as also for rent of the said storehouses; by one quarter of a year begun the first day of July last and this day ended, as followeth:[1]

*[*Storehouse keeper*]. To Edward Lambarde the last day of September for his wages daily attending and serving Her Highness in safe-keeping of Her Grace's storehouses and timber-yards[2] there wherein lieth divers kinds of stuffs pertaining to Her Majesty's ships, by one quarter of a year

[1]The statement from which this entry was composed survives as BL, Add. MS 78171 [item 1(g)], f. 40, printed in full in Appendix 4 below. Significant details not carried forward into the final account are noted here.

[2]Draft specifies 'at Brightlingsea': BL, Add. MS 78171 [item 1(g)], f. 40.

containing 92 days begun the first day of July last and this day ended, at 12d *per diem* – £4 12s.

*[*Plug keeper*]. To Thomas Richardson, mariner, the same day for his wages[1] daily attending and serving Her Majesty in safe-keeping of the plug and letting the water out of the dock there for the drier keeping of the same wherein lieth Her Grace's ship called the *Trinity Henry*; by like time of 92 days begun and ended as is abovesaid, at 6d *per diem*. *Summa* – £2 6s.

[*Page total*] – £6 18s.

[f. 273v] *Emptions*

To Robert Consent and three other labourers the last day of September for their pains taken in lading of the water out of Her Grace's ship called the *Trinity Henry*,[2] with other needful service by them done there within this quarter; by agreement – 7s 4d.

House rent. To William Beryff the same day for one quarter of a year's rent of a certain storehouse and ground[3] of him hired wherein lieth divers and sundry kinds of provisions for the use of Her Majesty's ships, due at this present – 13s 4d.

To Thomas Berryff the same day for one quarter of a year's rent of a certain storehouse and ground[4] of him hired wherein lieth divers needful things pertaining to Her Grace's ships, due at this present – 6s 8d.

[*Page total*] – £1 7s 4d.

[f. 274] *Anno regni regine Elizabethe sexto*

A payment made the last day of December as well to keepers of storehouses, dock and timber-yards there wherein lieth divers kinds of provisions for the use of Her Majesty's ships, as also for rent of the said storehouses; by one quarter of a year begun the first day of October last and this day ended, as followeth:

*[*Storehouse keeper*]. To Edward Lambarde the last day of December for his wages daily attending and serving Her Highness in safe-keeping of Her Grace's storehouses and timber-yards there wherein lieth divers and sundry kinds of things pertaining to Her Majesty's ships, by one

[1]Draft specifies 'shipkeeping wages and victuals': ibid.

[2]Draft describes this as 'having the water out of the dock': ibid.

[3]Draft describes this as 'where the great dock is at Brightlingsea': ibid. This is the only evidence for the site of the main shore installation of the Colne yard.

[4]Draft specifies as 'the slaughter house ("sclarter howse") and ground where the *Salamander*'s dock was': ibid. This is the only evidence of the *Salamander*'s presence and (because there is no further record) presumed end here. Cf. the use of a slaughter-house as a timber store at Deptford: ibid., [item 1 (a)], as noted in Appendix 4 below.

quarter of a year containing 92 days begun the first day of October last and this day ended, at 12d *per diem* – £4 12s.

*[*Plug keeper*]. To Thomas Richardson, mariner, the same day for his wages daily attending and serving Her Majesty in safe-keeping of the plug and letting forth of the water out of the dock there for the drier keeping of the same wherein lieth Her Grace's ship called the *Trinity Henry*, by like time of 92 days begun and ended as is abovesaid, at 6d *per diem*. *Summa* – £2 6s.

[*Page total*] – £6 18s.

[f. 274v] *Emptions*

House rent. To William Berryff the last day of December for one quarter of a year's rent of a certain storehouse and ground of him hired wherein lieth divers kinds of provisions for the use of Her Majesty's ships, due at this present – 13s 4d.

To Thomas Berryff[1] the same day for one quarter of a year's rent of a certain storehouse and ground of him hired wherein lieth sundry things pertaining to Her Highness's ships, due at this present – 6s 8d.

To Robert Consent and three other labourers the same day for their pains taken in lading of water out of Her Grace's ship called the *Trinity Henry* lying in a dock there, with other needful service by them done within this quarter; by agreement – 8s.

[*Page total*] – £1 8s.

[f. 275] **Ordinary. Portsmouth:**

Anno Domini 1563. Anno regni regine Elizabethe quinto

A payment made the last day of March as well to masters, mariners and gunners serving Her Highness in safe-keeping of Her Grace's ships afloat in harbour; and to keepers of storehouses, dock and timber-yards there wherein lieth divers kinds of provisions for the use of her ships; as also to shipwrights, caulkers, sawyers, smiths, joiners and other artificers and labourers for new mending and repairing of Her Grace's said ships, and to divers persons for sundry kinds of provisions of them had towards the same; by one quarter of a year begun the first day of January last and this day ended, as followeth:

The Double Rose

Mariners

William Wilkynson, boatswain, 10 weeks 4 days 24s 2½d

[1] A posthumous reckoning, because Thomas died during this quarter; his will dated 4 Sept. was proved 16 Dec.: PROB 11/46, ff. 312v, 314.

Thomas Marychurche, purser, 10 weeks 4 days	26s 4d
John Foard, 10 weeks 4 days	17s 8d
[*Gunner*]	
Miles Robynson, master gunner, 10 weeks 4 days	26s 4d

[*Page total*] – £4 14s 6½d.

[f. 275v] *The Hart*

Mariners	
William Murrant, master, 12 weeks 6 days	£6 8s 7d
Richard Browne, boatswain, 12 weeks 6 days	37s 6d
Thomas Wilkes, purser, 12 weeks 6 days	32s 2d
John Thompson, steward, 12 weeks 6 days	29s 5½d
Thomas Northway, 12 weeks 6 days	21s 5d
John Twynam, 12 weeks 6 days	21s 5d
John Mappe, 12 weeks 6 days	21s 5d
Thomas Mappe, 12 weeks 6 days	21s 5d
Anthony Addertun, 12 weeks 6 days	21s 5d
Nicholas Waters, 12 weeks 6 days	21s 5d
John Cane, 12 weeks 6 days	21s 5d
John Nichollas, 12 weeks 6 days	21s 5d
Jeffrey Preston, 12 weeks 6 days	21s 5d
William Cotton, 12 weeks 6 days	21s 5d
William Kney, 12 weeks 6 days	21s 5d
John Pattyn, 2 days	6d
Edward Gladdyn, 6 weeks 6 days	11s 5d
Lawrence Browne, 6 weeks 6 days	11s 5d
Arthur Allred, 12 weeks 6 days	21s 5d
Richard Brooke, 2 weeks 4 days	4s 4d
John Lynche, 12 weeks 6 days	21s 5d
Leonard Reigate, 12 weeks 6 days	21s 5d
Gunners	
Robert Thompson, master, 12 weeks 6 days	32s 2d
Christopher Shippe, gromet, 12 weeks 6 days	16s 1d

[*Page total*] – £30 3s 5½d.

[f. 276] *The Swallow*

Mariners	
William Saunders, boatswain, 12 weeks 6 days	37s 6d
John Robertes, purser, 12 weeks 6 days	32s 2d
Davy Gryffyn, cook, 12 weeks 6 days	29s 5½d
Richard Fishebell, 12 weeks 6 days	21s 5d
Matthew Fisher, 12 weeks 6 days	21s 5d
William Harwood, 12 weeks 6 days	21s 5d

Robert Hendyff, 12 weeks 6 days	21s 5d
Thomas Richardes, 12 weeks 6 days	21s 5d
Nicholas Edwardes, 12 weeks 6 days	21s 5d
Richard Myller, 6 weeks 6 days	11s 5d
Richard Tompson, 12 weeks 6 days	21s 5d
Walter Newstub, 12 weeks 6 days	21s 5d
Thomas Wilkins, 12 weeks 6 days	21s 5d
Edward Ewyn, 6 weeks 6 days	11s 5d
William Franck, 12 weeks 6 days	21s 5d
Thomas Burton, 6 weeks 6 days	11s 5d
John Broke, boy, 12 weeks 6 days	10s 8½d
John Haynes, 12 weeks 6 days	21s 5d
Thomas Brokes, 6 weeks 6 days	11s 5d
Thomas Bryan, 12 weeks 6 days	21s 5d
Gunner	
Jacob Myller, master, 12 weeks 6 days	32s 2d

[*Page total*] – £22 4s 7d.

[f. 276v] *The Antelope*

Mariners	
Richard Wright, boatswain, 12 weeks 6 days	37s 7d
Thomas Awstyne, purser, 12 weeks 6 days	32s 2d
John Paullmer, cook, 12 weeks 6 days	29s 5½d
George Lyell, 12 weeks 6 days	21s 5d
James Bull, 12 weeks 6 days	21s 5d
Thomas Webb, 12 weeks 6 days	21s 5d
Robert Lofte, 12 weeks 6 days	21s 5d
Richard Thomas, 12 weeks 6 days	21s 5d
Stephen Robertes, 12 weeks 6 days	21s 5d
Henry Bull, 12 weeks 6 days	21s 5d
William Molle, 12 weeks 6 days	21s 5d
Ralph Dempster, boy, 12 weeks 6 days	10s 8½d
John Bigges, 2 days	6d
Robert Mitchelson, gromet, 12 weeks 6 days	16s 1d
John Bull, 12 weeks 6 days	21s 5d
Walter Prewne, 7 weeks 2 days	12s 2d
Henry Clarke, 12 weeks 1 day	20s 3d
Thomas Farner, 12 weeks 1 day	20s 3d
Gunner	
Roger Bowthe, master, 12 weeks 6 days	32s 2d

[*Page total*] – £20 4s 1d.

[f. 277] *The Jennet*

Mariners

William Gyelles, master, 2 weeks 6 days	19s 1d
Richard Trewe, boatswain, 12 weeks 6 days	37s 6d
William Brooke, purser, 12 weeks 6 days	32s 2d
John Addams, cook, 12 weeks 6 days	29s 5½d
Henry Stapull, 12 weeks 6 days	21s 5d
John Phillipp, 8 weeks 3 days	14s 1d
John Bryan, 12 weeks 6 days	21s 5d
Davy Evans, 12 weeks 6 days	21s 5d
Alexander Golde, boy, 12 weeks 6 days	10s 8½d
William Saunderson, 8 weeks 3 days	14s 1d
John Edmondes, 12 weeks 6 days	21s 5d
Andrew Richbrooke, 6 weeks 6 days	11s 5d
Simon Sanden, 8 weeks 3 days	14s 1d
John Thomas, 6 weeks 6 days	11s 5d
Edward Bollymer, 12 weeks 6 days	21s 5d
William Cartter, 12 weeks 6 days	21s 5d
Richard Barker, 6 weeks 6 days	11s 5d
Edward Stevenson, 12 weeks 6 days	21s 5d
Thomas Shribbe, 12 weeks 6 days	21s 5d
John Saunders, 6 weeks 6 days	11s 5d
Ralph Harwood, 12 weeks 6 days	21s 5d
Nicholas Reade, 2 weeks 3 days	4s 2d
Thomas Drake, 8 weeks 1 day	13s 7d
William Ellyson, carpenter, 3 weeks 2 days	9s 7d
John Evans, 2 weeks	3s 4d
John Gyelles, gromet, 2 weeks 6 days	3s 8d
John Mapp, 4 weeks 3 days	7s 5d
Gunner	
Richard Haynes, master, 12 weeks 6 days	32s 2d

[*Page total*] – £24 3s 5d.

[f. 277v] *The New Bark*

Mariners

William Sampson, master, 12 weeks 6 days	£4 5s 10d
George Braunche, boatswain, 1 week 3 days	4s 2d
Roger Davys, purser, 12 weeks 6 days	32s 2d
Thomas Willson, cook, 12 weeks 6 days	29s 5½d
Cornelius Bryan, 8 weeks 5 days	14s 7d
Thomas Jones, 12 weeks 6 days	21s 5d
Richard Edwardes, 12 weeks 6 days	21s 5d

Clement Jestlyn, 12 weeks 6 days	21s 5d
Robert Marshe, 12 weeks 6 days	21s 5d
Humphrey Dennes, 12 weeks 6 days	21s 5d
William Dawson, 11 weeks 5 days	19s 6d
Edward Prowde, carpenter, 12 weeks 6 days	37s 6d
Gabriel Kyrbye, gromet, 12 weeks 6 days	16s 1d
Robert Sampson, boy, 12 weeks 6 days	10s 8½d
Nicholas Moone, boatswain, 11 weeks 2 days	32s 11d
Thomas Paynter, 11 weeks 2 days	18s 10d
Zach Buggins, gromet, 11 weeks 2 days	14s 1½d
Thomas Howse, 11 weeks 2 days	18s 10d
Henry Harwood, 11 weeks 2 days	18s 10d
Gunner	
John Phillipps, master, 12 weeks 6 days	32s 2d

[*Page total*] – £24 12s 9½d.

[f. 278] *[*Storehouse and timber-yard keepers*]. To John Thomas the last day of March for his wages daily attending and serving Her Highness in safe-keeping of Her Grace's storehouses there wherein lieth divers and sundry kinds of provisions for the use of Her Majesty's ships, by one quarter of a year due at this present – £5.

To John Poell, porter, the same day for his wages daily attending and serving Her Highness in safe-keeping of Her Grace's timber-yards there wherein lieth her timber, plank and board for the use of Her Highness's ships, by 90 days begun the first day of January last and ended as abovesaid, at 6d *per diem* – £2 5s.

To Edward Prestman, labourer, the same day for his wages daily attending and serving Her Highness in keeping of the plug and letting out of the water in the dock there for the drier keeping of the same, by the space of 39 days within this quarter, at 4d *per diem*. *Summa* – 13s.

[*Page total*] – £7 18s.

[f. 278v] *Shipwrights*

Peter Pett, master, 23½ days and tides at 12d	23s 6d
Richard Chapman, server, 19 days at 6d	9s 6d
John Peaze, 78 days and tides at 12d	£3 18s
Thomas Walton, server, 77 days at 4d	25s 8d
Nicholas Gater, 77 days at 6d	38s 6d
Raynold Veazey, 77 days at 6d	38s 6d
John Carpenter, 17 days at 8d	11s 4d
Thomas Chartram, 17 days at 6d	8s 6d
John Herzey, 20 days at 6d	10s
Vincent Newstub, 14 days at 7d	8s 2d

Robert Cotton, 14 days at 5d	5s 10d
John Trenayell, 14 days at 2d	2s 4d
John Barre, 20 days at 6d	10s
William Dallaply, 17 days at 8d	11s 4d
Edmund Forde, server, 17 days at 4d	5s 8d
Thomas Hacker, 17 days at 6d	8s 6d
John Pynnock, 20 days at 7d	11s 8d
John Hiller, 20 days at 6d	10s
Walter Johnson, 20 days at 6d	10s
John Paulmer, 20 days at 6d	10s
Stephen Rogers, 20 days at 8d	13s 4d
Thomas Good, server, 20 days at 4d	6s 8d
Stephen Browne, 13 days at 7d	7s 7d
Richard Goby, server, 14 days at 5d	5s 10d
Robert Blake, 18½ days at 6d	9s 3d
William Louff, server, 18½ days at 5d	7s 8d
John Stokes, 12 days at 8d	8s
William Hareley, 12 days at 6d	6s
James Holcroft, 12 days at 6d	6s
Davy Bigges, 12 days at 8d	8s
William Hurlocke, 12 days at 4d	4s
Thomas Williams, 24 days and tides at 8d	16s
Hugh Goase, 11½ days at 7d	6s 8½d
Maurice Goase, server, 12½ days at 3d	3s 1½d
William Woodman, 50 days at 6d	25s

[*Page total*] – £23 10s 2d.

[f. 279] Philip Payne, 18½ days at 7d	10s 9d
Robert Grig, 12½ days at 6d	6s 3d
Robert Harris, 18 days at 7d	10s 6d
Edward Harse, 9 days at 2d	18d
Thomas Grenelef, 20 days at 7d	11s 8d
Thomas Rogers, server, 21 days at 2d	3s 6d
Richard Willforde, 22 days at 7d	12s 10d
Caulkers	
Thomas Bolton, master, 24 days and tides at 10d	20s
William Bolton, server, 24 days and tides at 6d	12s
Robert Richardes, 17 days at 7d	9s 11d
John Castelman, server, 23½ days and tides at 4d	7s 10d
Robert White, 24 days and tides at 7d	14s
Henry Reade, server, 24 days and tides at 4d	8s
Robert Dymmock, 24 days and tides at 7d	14s

Thomas Cockes, 24 days and tides at 6d	12s
William Browne, 16 days at 6d	8s
Thomas Tanner, 24 days and tides at 6d	12s
Walter Deane, 24 days and tides at 7d	14s
Thomas Clarke, 23 days and tides at 6d	11s 6d
John Millett, 24 days and tides at 6d	12s
John Haywarde, 23½ days and tides at 7d	13s 8½d
William Mune, 23 days and tides at 8d	15s 4d
Thomas Northcott, 19 days and tides at 6d	9s 6d
John Arodes, server, 23 days and tides at 4d	7s 8d
John Webb, 19½ days and tides at 7d	11s 4½d
William Ragget, server, 19½ days and tides at 4d	6s 6d
Richard Chapman, 23 days and tides at 6d	11s 6d
Nicholas Archdaill, 25 days and tides at 6d	12s 6d
Richard Holt, 21 days and tides at 6d	10s 6d
George Mathew, 23 days and tides at 6d	11s 6d
John Bowden, 23 days and tides at 6d	11s 6d
John Atkynson, server, 24 days and tides at 6d	12s
Thomas Mathew, 61½ days and tides at 6d	30s 9d

[*Page total*] – £18 16s 7d.

[f. 279] *Sawyers*

Richard Wilkins, 39½ days at 6d	19s 9d
John Bigbroke, 19½ days at 6d	9s 9d
Nicholas Browne, 20 days at 5d	8s 4d
William Gonshott, 14 days at 6d	7s
William Cowicke, 14 days at 5d	5s 10d

Smiths

Robert Raynolde, 49½ days at 6d	24s 9d
Hugh Gokyn, 52½ days at 6d	26s 3d
John Marshall, 39 days at 6d	19s 6d
Edward Hopper, 20 days at 4d	6s 8d
Richard Welles, 21 days at 8d	14s
Thomas Davye, 21 days at 6d	10s 6d
Thomas Johnson, 21 days at 4d	7s
Thomas Welles, 21 days at 4d	7s

Joiners

George Joynner, 11 days at 8d	7s 4d
Lewis Inglyshe, 11 days at 7d	6s 5d
James Joynner, 11 days at 6d	5s 6d
John Pympon, 11 days at 4d	3s 8d
Michael Barrye, 11 days at 7d	6s 5d

Topmakers

William Bexley, 18 days at 8d	12s
John White, 18 days at 6d	9s
William Kacket, 18 days at 6d	9s
James Romen, 18 days at 6d	9s
Abraham Harmwood, 18 days at 5d	7s 6d

[*Page total*] – £12 2s 2d.

[f. 280] *Victualling.* To John Thomas of Portsmouth the last day of March for the victualling of 83 of the aforenamed shipwrights, caulkers, sawyers, smiths, joiners and topmakers working upon the mending and repairing of Her Grace's ships there by the space of 1,645 days among them all, the Sundays and holy days within the same accounted, begun the first day of January last and this day ended, which maketh 235 weeks, at 4s 1½d every week the man. *Summa* – £48 9s 4½d.

To Eme Prestman the same day for her pains and labour taken in washing of 45 pair of sheets of Her Highness's store wherein lay the said shipwrights, caulkers and others, at 1d every pair washing – 3s 9d.

Labourers

Edward Prestman, 25 days and tides at 8d	16s 8d
Robert Parcivall, 5 days and tides at 6d	12s 6d
William Mylles, 22 days and tides at 6d	11s
Philip Graye, 20½ days at 6d	10s 3d
Knight Marshall, 18 days at 6d	9s
Anthony Tristram, 18 days at 6d	9s
John Sparkes, 5 days at 6d	2s 6d
William Prestman, 26 days at 8d	17s 4d
William Percyvall, 11 days at 6d	5s 6d
Thomas Knight, 8½ days at 6d	4s 3d
	[£4 18s 1d*]

[*Page total*] – £53 11s 2½d.

[f. 280v] *Emptions*

Ironwork. To John Sheldon of Rowley, smith, the last day of March for price of 17,000 of 2s nail by him delivered into Her Grace's storehouse there for the use of Her Highness's ships, at 20s every 1,000 – £17; more for 10,200 of 2d nail, at 16s 8d every 1,000 – £8 10s; more for 17,400 of 10d nail, at 8s 4d every 1,000 – £7 5s; more for 38,500 of 6d nails, at 5s every 1,000 – £9 12s 6d; more for 11,000 of 4d nails, at 3s 4d every 1,000 – 36s 8d; more for 14,500 of 3d nails, at 2s 6d every 1,000 – 36s 3d; and more to him for 24,000 of 2d nails, at 20d every 1,000 – 40s. *Summa* – £48 0s 5d.

To Robert Wheller of Langstone the same day for price of [*one*] thousand 2 hundred [*one*] quarter weight [*1,372 lbs*] of English iron of him had for the use of Her Majesty's ships, at 13s 4d every hundredweight – £8 3s 4d; and more to Richard Welles for bringing of the same from Langstone aforesaid to Portsmouth – 7s 8d. *Summa* – £8 11s.

To Robert Arnolde of Fareham, smith, the same day for price of 3 hundredweight of spikes and overlop nails of him had and the same delivered as aforesaid for the use of Her Grace's ships, at 28s every hundredweight – £4 4s.

To John Hallawaye of Portsmouth the same day for price of 600 of 20d nails by him delivered as abovesaid for the use of Her Highness's ships, at 20d every 100 – 10s; more for 1,500 of 4d nails, at 3s 4d every 1,000 – 5s; more for 500 of 3d nails, price – 15d; and more to him for 3,000 of 2d nails, at 20d every 1,000 – 5s. *Summa* – £1 1s 3d.

To John Robinson of Fareham the same day for price of 800 of 10d nails of him had for the use as aforesaid, at 10d every 100 – 6s 8d; and more to him for 200 of 6d nails, price – 12d. *Summa* – 7s 8d.

[*Page total*] – £62 4s 4d.

[f. 281] *Nails.* To Henry Slatter of Portsmouth the last day of March for price of 1,900 of 10d nails of him had for the use of Her Grace's ships, at 8s 4d every 1,000 – 15s 10d; more for 1,000 of 6d nail, price – 5s; and more to him for 450 of 20d nails, at 20d the 100 – 7s 6d. *Summa* – £1 8s 4d.

New iron. To William Goldstone of London the same day for price of 20 hundred 2 quarters 8 pounds weight [*2,304 lbs*] of English iron by him delivered there for the use of Her Highness's ships, at £12 6s 8d the ton – £12 13s 8d;[1] and more to him for 2 thousand 14 pounds weight [*2,254 lbs*] of Spanish iron, at £13 6s 8d the ton – £13 8s 4d. *Summa* – £26 2s.

Padlocks. To William Pennyfather of London the same day for price of 6 padlocks by him delivered for the use as afore is said, at 6d the piece – 3s; and more to him for 6 other padlocks, at 4d the piece – 2s. *Summa* – 5s.

Pulleys, shovels, scoops and bowls. To John Benbow of London the same day for price of 12 great pulleys of him had for the use of Her Grace's ships, at 20d the piece – 20s; more for 12 pulleys, at 16d the piece – 16s; more for 6 pulleys, at 12d the piece – 6s; more for 12 pulleys, at 8d the piece – 8s; more for 30 pulleys, at 6d the piece – 15s; more for 2 dozen of pulleys, at 4d the piece – 8s; more for 2 dozen of pulleys, at 2d the piece – 4s; more for 4 dozen of steel shovels, at 8s every dozen – £1 12s; more for 2 dozen

[1]The calculation gives 3044.5712d, which is ½d above the sum stated (3044d).

of scoops, at 5s every dozen – 10s; and more to him for 2 dozen of great bowls for pitch and tallow, at 10s every dozen – 20s. *Summa* – £6 19s.

Running glasses. To Richard Stevens of Tower Hill, compass-maker, the same day for price of 5 dozen of running glasses of him had for the use of Her Majesty's ships, at 10s every dozen – £2 10s.

[*Page total*] – £37 4s 4d.

[f. 281v] *Rosin, deal-boards, fir spars and poles, and rafters for oars* *[*Rosin – £55 15s 5d*; *boards and spars – £19 6s 4d; rafters for oars – £7 10s*]. To John Morley of Southampton, merchant, the last day of March for price of 3 thousand 9 hundredweight of yellow rosin by him delivered to Her Grace's storehouse at Portsmouth for the use of Her Highness's ships there, at 7s every hundredweight – £13 13s; and more to him for bringing of the same rosin from Hampton to the dock near Portsmouth – 9d. *Summa* – £13 13s 9d.

To Thomas Turnar of Hampton, merchant, the same day for price of 11 hundredweight of rosin of him had for the use as aforesaid, at 8s every hundred[*weight*] £4 8s; and more to him for the carrying of the same rosin from Hampton to Portsmouth – 18d. *Summa* – £4 9s 6d.

To William Paige of London, merchant, the same day for price of 2 thousand 3 hundred 23 pounds weight [*2,599 lbs*] of rosin of him had for the use of Her Highness's ships, at 7s every hundred[*weight*] – £8 2s 5d;[1] more for 3 shock of deal-boards, after 66 boards to the shock at 16d apiece – £12 8s; and more to him for 2 hundred [*240*] fir spars, after 6 score to the hundred at 4d the piece – £4. *Summa* – £24 10s 5d.

To William Gurdellar of London, merchant, the same day for price of 7 thousand 8 hundred 2 quarters 15 pounds weight [*8,807 lbs*] of yellow rosin of him had for the use of Her Grace's ships, at 7s 6d every hundredweight – £29 9s 9d; more for 50 fir poles, at 14d the piece – 58s 4d; and more to him for 60 long rafters for oars of 19 and 20 foot, at 2s 6d the piece – £7 10s. *Summa* – £39 18s 1d.

Shivers and cocks of brass. To Robert Hunt of London, founder, the same day for price of 4 shivers and 36 cocks of brass of him had for the use of Her Highness's ships there, weighing 2 hundred 19 pounds [*243 lbs*] at 7d every pound weight – £7 1s 9d.

[*Page total*] – £89 13s 6d.

[f. 282] *Pitch, tar, sail needles, and oillet and latchet lines* *[*Cordage – £36 13s 8d*; *pitch and tar – £17 14s 10d*]. To Christopher Draper of London, alderman, the last day of March for price of 5 hundredweight [*560 lbs*] of white twine of him had for the use of Her Grace's ships, at

[1]The calculation gives 1949.25d, which is ¼d above the sum stated (1949d).

7d every pound weight – £16 6s 8d; more for 20 sounding lines, at 2s every line – 40s; more for 30 dozen of sail needles, at 5d every dozen – 12s 6d; more for 31 pieces of oillet line weighing 3 hundred [*one*] quarter 18 pounds [*382 lbs*], at 28s every hundredweight – £4 15s 6d; more for 30 pieces of latchet lines weighing 9 hundred 28 pounds weight [*1,036 lbs*] at 28s every hundred[*weight*] – £12 19s; more for one last of stone pitch, price – £4 13s 4d; and more to him for one last of tar, price – £4 13s 4d. *Summa* – £46 0s 4d.

To Peter Pett and John Thomas the same day for price of 1½ last of pitch of them had for the use of Her Highness's ships, at £4 every last – £6; and more to them for the bringing of the same pitch from Fareham to the dock near Portsmouth – 18d. *Summa* – £6 1s 6d.

To John Warner of London, merchant, the same day for price of 6 barrels of pitch of him had for the use of Her Majesty's ships there; by agreement – £2 6s 8d.

Water buckets. To John Williamson of London, cooper, the same day for price of 4 dozen of water buckets of him had for the use as aforesaid, at 5s every dozen. *Summa* – £1.

Water carriage of provisions. To William Jacklyn, master, the same day for service of his hoy named the *Starr of Lymehowse* serving Her Highness in carrying of 200 bolts of poldavy, [*one*] thousandweight of ratline and marline, 9 hundredweight of spikes and overlop nails, 300 boat oars, 12 thousand [*one*] hundred 2 quarters weight of iron [*13,608 lbs*], 5 thousandweight of rosin, 3 shock of Norway deals, and divers other provisions, from Deptford to Portsmouth and there delivered the same for the use of Her Grace's ships; by agreement – £8.

[*Page total*] – £63 8s 6d.

[f. 282v] *Lanterns*. To John Neave of London the last day of March for price of 10 lanterns of him had for the use of Her Grace's ships there, at 12d the piece – 10s.

Broom. To Nicholas Locke of Chark the same day for price of 2,700 of broom by him delivered at Portsmouth for the use of Her Grace's ships there, at 2s every 100 – £3 14s.

Furze. To Thomas Pyrryn and certain other persons of Portsea, Fratton, Kingston and thereabouts the same day for price of 20 loads of furzes by them delivered there for the use of Her Highness's ships, at 16d every load – £1 6s 8d.

Hoops. To Henry James of Southampton, cooper, the same day for price of 4 dozen of hoops of him had for the use of Her Majesty's ships' tops, at 8s every dozen – 32s; and more to him for the bringing of the same hoops from Hampton to the dock near Portsmouth – 5s 8d. *Summa* – £1 17s 8d.

Elms. To Joan Poundes, widow, the same day for price of 5 elms of her had for the use of Her Grace's ships, by agreement – 16s; more for the felling and squaring of the same elms – 2s; and more for carriage of the said elms from Cosham to the dock near Portsmouth – 6s 3d. *Summa* – £1 4s 3d.

Vitry canvas. To Thomasine Elton of Portsmouth, widow, the same day for price of 19 yards of vitry canvas of her had for the use of Her Grace's ships the *Minion* and the *Primrose*, at 10d every yard. *Summa* – 15s 10d.

Tanned leather and sounding lines. To Ralph Cockes, master of Her Grace's ship the *Primrose* the same day for price of one deep sounding line for the use of the same ship – 5s; and more to him for one back of tanned leather, price – 10s 6d. *Summa* – 15s 6d.

[*Page total*] – £10 3s 11d.

[f. 283] *Compass timber.* To John Peaze of Portsmouth the last day of March for price of 16½ loads and 4 foot of hooks, knees and other compass timber oak of him had and the same delivered for the use of Her Majesty's ships there, at 10s every load after 50 foot to the load. *Summa* – £8 5s 9d.

[*Page total*] – *Summa predicta*. [f. 283v *blank*]

[f. 284] A payment made the last day of June as well to masters, mariners and gunners serving Her Highness in safe-keeping of Her Grace's ships afloat in harbour and to keepers of storehouses, dock and timber-yards there wherein lieth divers kinds of provisions for the use of her ships, as also to shipwrights, sawyers and other artificers and workmen for new mending and repairing of Her Grace's said ships, and to sundry persons for divers kinds of provisions of them had towards the same; by one quarter of a year begun the first day of April last and this day ended, as followeth:

The Hart[1]

Mariners

William Murrant, master, 9 weeks 6 days	£4 2s 6d
Richard Browne, boatswain, 9 weeks 6 days	28s 9d
Thomas Wilkes, purser, 9 weeks 6 days	24s 6d
John Tompson, steward, 9 weeks 6 days	22s 7d
Thomas Northwaye, 9 weeks 6 days	16s 5d
Thomas Mapp, 9 weeks 6 days	16s 5d
Anthony Addertun, 9 weeks 6 days	16s 5d
John Cave, 9 weeks 6 days	16s 5d

[1]Detailed expenses for her docking at Portsmouth this quarter are preserved in BL, Add. MS 78171 [item 1(c)], ff. 19–34. See further Appendix 4 below.

John Nichollas, 9 weeks 6 days	16s 5d
Jeffrey Preston, 9 weeks 6 days	16s 5d
William Cottim, 9 weeks 6 days	16s 5d
John Lynche, 9 weeks 6 days	16s 5d
Leonard Raggett, 9 weeks 6 days	16s 5d
John Heathe, boy, 9 weeks 6 days	8s 2½d

[*Page total*] – £15 14s 3½d.

[f. 284v] John Twynam, 5 weeks 6 days	9s 9d
Arthur Allred, 5 weeks 6 days	9s 9d
William Kneyll, 5 weeks 6 days	9s 9d
[*Gunner*]	
Robert Tompson, master gunner, 9 weeks 6 days	24s 6d
The Antelope	
Mariners	
Richard Wright, boatswain, 9 weeks 6 days	28s 9d
Thomas Awsten, purser, 9 weeks 6 days	24s 6d
John Paulmer, cook, 9 weeks 6 days	22s 7d
George Lyell, 9 weeks 6 days	16s 5d
James Bull, 9 weeks 6 days	16s 5d
Richard Thomas, 9 weeks 6 days	16s 5d
Stephen Robartes, 9 weeks 6 days	16s 5d
Ralph Dempster, boy, 9 weeks 6 days	8s 2½d
Robert Michelson, gromet, 9 weeks 6 days	12s 2d
Walter Prewen, 9 weeks 6 days	16s 5d
Thomas Webb, 5 weeks 6 days	9s 9d
Robert Loft, 5 weeks 6 days	9s 9d
William Mowell, 5 weeks 6 days	9s 9d
John Bull, 5 weeks 6 days	9s 9d
John Lynche, 5 weeks 6 days	9s 9d
Gunner	
Roger Bowth, master, 9 weeks 6 days	24s 6d

[*Page total*] – £15 15s 3½d.

[f. 285] *The Jennet*[1]	
Mariners	
Richard Trewe, boatswain, 9 weeks 6 days	28s 9d
William Brooke, purser, 9 weeks 6 days	24s 6d
John Addams, cook, 9 weeks 6 days	22s 7d
John Bryan, 9 weeks 6 days	16s 5d

[1]Detailed expenses for her docking at Portsmouth this quarter are preserved in BL, Add. MS 78171 [item 1(c)], ff. 19–34. See further Appendix 4 below.

Davy Evans, 9 weeks 6 days	16s 5d
John Edmundes, 9 weeks 6 days	16s 5d
Edward Bullyner, 9 weeks 6 days	16s 5d
Edward Stevenson, 9 weeks 6 days	16s 5d
Ralph Harwood, 9 weeks 6 days	16s 5d
William Carter, 9 weeks 6 days	16s 5d
Thomas Shrybb, 9 weeks 6 days	16s 5d
John Rammore, 2 weeks 3 days	4s
John Mapper, 9 weeks 6 days	16s 5d
Lawrence Thomson, boy, 9 weeks 6 days	8s 2½d
Henry Stable, 9 weeks 6 days	16s 5d
[*Gunner*]	
Richard Haynes, master gunner, 9 weeks 6 days	24s 6d

The Swallow

Mariners

William Saunders, boatswain, 8 weeks 5 days	25s 5d
John Robartes, purser, 8 weeks 5 days	21s 8d
Davy Gryffyn, cook, 8 weeks 5 days	19s 9d
Richard Fishbell, 8 weeks 5 days	14s 6d
William Harwood, 8 weeks 5 days	14s 6d
Thomas Richarde, 8 weeks 5 days	14s 6d
Nicholas Edwardes, 8 weeks 5 days	14s 6d
Walter Newstubb, 8 weeks 5 days	14s 6d
Thomas Wilkyns, 8 weeks 5 days	14s 6d
Robert Collens, boy, 8 weeks 5 days	7s 3d
John Haynes, 8 weeks 5 days	14s 6d
Robert Hendyff, 4 weeks 5 days	7s 11d
Richard Tompson, 4 weeks 5 days	7s 11d
William Francke, 4 weeks 5 days	7s 11d
Thomas Bryan, 4 weeks 5 days	7s 11d
[*Gunner*]	
Jacob Miller, master gunner, 8 week 5 days	21s 8d

[*Page total*] – £25 5s 7½d.

[f. 285v] *The New Bark*

Mariners

William Sampson, master, 13 weeks	£4 6s 8d
Nicholas Moone, boatswain, 13 weeks	37s 11d
Roger Davy, purser, 13 weeks	32s 6d
Thomas Willson, cook, 13 weeks	29s 9d
Robert Marche, 13 weeks	21s 8d
Humphrey Dennes, 13 weeks	21s 8d
Robert Sampson, boy, 13 weeks	10s 10d

Thomas Paynter, 13 weeks	21s 8d
Thomas Howse, 13 weeks	21s 8d
Henry Harwood, 13 weeks	21s 8d
Richard Edwarde, 13 weeks	21s 8d
Thomas Jones, 9 weeks	15s
Zach Buggins, 9 weeks	15s
William Warwicke, 9 weeks	15s
Clement Jeslinge, 9 weeks	15s
[*Gunner*]	
John Phillippes, master gunner, 9 weeks	22s 6d
The Double Rose	
Mariners	
William Wilkynson, boatswain, 9 weeks 6 days	22s 7d
John Foard, 9 weeks 6 days	16s 5d
[*Gunner*]	
Nicholas Robinson, master gunner, 5 weeks 6 days	14s 6d

[*Page total*] – £23 3s 8d.

[f. 286] *The Salamander*	
Mariners	
Robert Glandfelde, boatswain, 4 weeks 2 days	12s 6d
Thomas Norwaye, cook, 4 weeks 2 days	9s 10d
Davy Mortymer, 4 weeks 2 days	7s 2d
John Browninge, 4 weeks 2 days	7s 2d
Richard Pryg, boy, 2 weeks 6 days	2s 3d
The Greyhound Bitch	
Mariners	
Thomas Reade, boatswain, 4 weeks 2 days	12s 6d
Thomas Chestun, 4 weeks 2 days	7s 2d
Rowland Russell, cook, 2 weeks 3 days	5s 6½d
Andrew Maister, boy, 4 weeks 2 days	3s 7d
Robert Ryce, 1 week 6 days	2s 10d
The Three Moons	
Mariners	
Robert Ryce, boatswain, 4 weeks 2 days	12s 6d
William Hannse, 4 weeks 2 days	7s 2d
The Green Dragon	
Mariners	
Thomas Dawson, boatswain, 4 weeks 2 days	12s 6d
Robert Beast, cook, 4 weeks 2 days	9s 10d
William Harwoode, 4 weeks 2 days	7s 2d
John Heathe, boy, 4 weeks 3 days	2s 10d

[*Page total*] – £6 2s 6½d.

[f. 286v] *The Maiden*	
Mariners	
Thomas Gyelles, boatswain, 4 weeks 2 days	9s 10d
Thomas Burnell, 4 weeks 2 days	7s 2d
The Serpent	
Mariners	
Francis Currall, boatswain, 4 weeks 2 days	9s 10d
Robert Tanner, 4 weeks 2 days	7s 2d
The Bear	
Mariners	
Richard Stokes, boatswain, 4 weeks 2 days	9s 10d
John Lytherlande, boy, 4 weeks 2 days	3s 7d
The Raven	
Mariners	
John Bennet, boatswain, 4 weeks 2 days	9s 10d
Thomas Olyver, boy, 4 weeks 2 days	3s 7d
The Red Hart	
Mariners	
William Pallmer, boatswain, 4 weeks 2 days	12s 6d
Thomas Walter, 4 weeks 2 days	7s 2d
Francis Waymouth, 4 weeks 2 days	7s 2d
[*Page total*] – £4 7s 8d.	

[f. 287] *The Bark of Cherbourg*	
Mariners	
Henry Clark, boatswain, 4 weeks 2 days	12s 6d
John Haylles, 4 weeks 2 days	7s 2d
Robert Rutter, 4 weeks 2 days	7s 2d
Richard Whityngton, 4 weeks 2 days	7s 2d
The Flower de Luce	
Mariners	
Thomas Naybour, boatswain, 4 weeks 2 days	9s 10d
Roger Gryffyn, 4 weeks 2 days	7s 2d
The Sparrowhawk	
Mariners	
Thomas Yorke, boatswain, 2 weeks 2 days	5s 3d
Andrew John, 1 week 2 days	2s 2d
The Owlet	
Mariners	
John Leggat, master, 2 weeks 3 days	12s
John Robynson, boatswain, 2 weeks 3 days	5s 7d
John Lewke, boy, 4 weeks 2 days	3s 7d
Roger Harrys, 1 week 5 days	2s 10d

The Gryphon

Mariners

Thomas Galle, boatswain, 4 weeks 2 days	9s 10d
Thomas Bringer, 4 weeks 2 days	7s 2d

[*Page total*] – £4 19s 5d.

[f. 287v] *The Black Bark*

Mariners

James Browne, 4 weeks 2 days	7s 2d
Robert Lawrence, 4 weeks 2 days	7s 2d

The George Hoy

Mariners

Giles Haull, master, 8 weeks 5 days	43s 4d
Thomas Newlande, master's mate, 8 weeks 5 days	20s
John Leache, 8 weeks 5 days	14s 6d
Thomas Elkyn, cook, 8 weeks 5 days	20s
John Quayde, 8 weeks 5 days	14s 6d
Henry Burges, 8 weeks 5 days	14s 6d
John Willyams, 8 weeks 5 days	14s 6d
Simon Halle, 4 weeks 2 days	7s 2d
James Smythe, 8 weeks 5 days	14s 6d
John Halle, boy, 8 weeks 5 days	7s 3d
Robert Garrett, gromet, 8 weeks 5 days	10s 10d
John Bennett, 4 weeks 3 days	7s 4d

[*Page total*] – £10 2s 9d.

[f. 288] *[*Storehouse and timber-yard keeper*]. To John Thomas the ast day of June for his wages daily attending and serving Her Highness n safe-keeping of Her Grace's storehouses there wherein lieth divers and undry kinds of provisions for the use of Her Majesty's ships, by one uarter of a year due at this present. *Summa* – £5.

To Thomas Claye, porter, the same day for his wages daily attending nd serving Her Majesty for the safe-keeping of Her Grace's timber-yards here wherein lieth her timber, planks, boards, masts and all other ecessary provisions for the needful use of Her Grace's ships, by one like uarter of a year containing 91 days begun the first day of April last and his day ended, at 6d *per diem* – £2 5s 6d.

[*Page total*] – £7 5s 6d.

[f. 288v] *Shipwrights*

John Peaze, master, 36½ days and tides at 12d	36s 6d
Nicholas Gattars, 22 days and tides at 6d	11s
Reginald Poole, 34 days and tides at 6d	17s
Thomas Waltun, 32 days and tides at 4d	10s 8d

Vincent Newstub, 28 days and tides at 7d	15s 9d
Robert Cotton, 6 days at 5d	2s 6d
John Trenell, 24 days and tides at 3d	6s
John Carpenter, 34 days and tides at 8d	22s 8d
Edward Hearsey, server, 35 days and tides at 3d	8s 9d
Stephen Rogers, 30 days and tides at 8d	20s
Thomas Good, server, 36 days and tides at 4d	12s
Thomas Greneleff, 35 days and tides at 7d	20s 5d
William Dallopley, 12½ days at 8d	8s 4d
Thomas Hacker, 5 days at 6d	2s 6d
Edward Forte, server, 13½ days at 3d	3s 4½d
John Stockes, 20 days at 8d	13s 4d
William Hurlley, 20 days at 6d	10s
James Holdecrofte, 12 days at 6d	6s
William Arnolde, 13½ days at 2d	2s 3d
John Smalle, 20 days and tides at 6d	10s
Thomas Browne, 12½ days at 6d	6s 3d
Robert Tayller, 13½ days at 6d	6s 9d
William Hewet, 11 days at 4d	3s 8d
Christopher Stevens, 12½ days at 6d	6s 3d
Robert Blayke, 20 days at 7d	11s 8d
Thomas Samboro, 20 days at 5d	8s 4d
William Loffe, 20 days at 5d	8s 4d
John Penyck, 10½ days at 7d	6s 1½d
John Paullmer, 9½ days at 6d	4s 9d
John Hellyar, 9½ days at 6d	4s 9d
John Smyth, 7 days at 8d	4s 8d
Robert Greke, 14 days at 6d	7s
Davy Gryffin, 20 days at 6d	10s
William Jarvys, 20 days at 6d	10s
Thomas Warner, 20½ days at 6d	10s 3d
William Godman, 16½ days at 6d	8s 3d

[*Page total*] – £17 16s 1d.

[f. 289] Davy Bigges, 20½ days at 8d	13s 8d
John Herse, 13½ days at 6d	6s 9d
John Barry, 13½ days at 6d	6s 9d
Nicholas Goddyn, 13½ days at 6d	6s 9d
Sawyers	
Thomas Bearde, 12 days at 6d	6s
Richard Wilkins, 12 days at 5d	5s
John Bydbroke, 20 days at 6d	10s
Thomas Smyth, 20 days at 5d	8s 4d

Smiths

Robert Raynolde, 12 days at 6d	6s
Hugh Coginge, 11 days at 4d	3s 8d

Victualling. To John Thomas the last day of June for the victualling of 44 shipwrights, sawyers and smiths working upon the mending and repairing of 11 Her Grace's ships there by the space of 770 days among them all, Sundays and holy days in the same accounted, begun the first day of April last and this day ended, which maketh 110 weeks at 5s 4d every week the man. *Summa* – £29 6s 8d.

Bricklayers

John Bennet senior, 4 days at 12d	4s
John Bennet junior, 2 days at 8d	16d
John Lea, 2 days at 11d	22d

[*Page total*] – £33 6s 9d *[*Artificers – £4 0s 1d; victuals – £29 6s 8d*].

[f. 289v] *House-carpenters*

John Brocker, 4 days at 10d	3s 4d
Robert Fruiker, 4 days at 10d	3s 4d
Robert Reby, 4 days at 8d	2s 8d
Nicholas Collyns, 4 days at 10d	3s 4d

Labourers

Edward Prestman, master, 28 days at 8d	18s 8d
Thomas Perryn, 11 days at 6d	5s 6d
Nicholas Harwood, 22 days at 6d	11s
Richard Holt, 20 days at 6d	10s
John Perryn, 4 days at 6d	2s
Robert Smythe, 20 days at 6d	10s
William Smythe, 20 days at 6d	10s
Robert Welsman, 20 days at 6d	10s
Philip Gaye, 20 days at 6d	10s
William Pope, 22 days at 6d	11s
John Merrycke, 20 days at 6d	10s
John Rygate, 20 days at 6d	10s
William Bryden, 10 days at 6d	5s
John Fayermaners, 18 days at 6d	9s
John Morrys, 20 days at 6d	10s
Thomas Kynge, 2 days at 6d	12d
Gregory Barkshier, 20 days at 6d	10s
Richard Graye, 18 days at 6d	9s
William Myelles, 18 days at 6d	9s
John Leonard, 6 days at 6d	3s
John Saunders, 12 days at 6d	6s

William Halle, 3 days at 6d	18d
Richard James, 6 days at 6d	3s
Richard Brownynge, 24 days at 6d	12s
Henry Bewen, 9 days at 6d	4s 6d
Morgan Walkyn, 8 days at 6d	4s
William Wheller, 1 day at 6d	6d
William Johnson, 22 days at 6d	11s
William Rayse, 22 days at 6d	11s

[*Page total*] – £12 3s 4d.

[f. 290] *Emptions*

Nails. To Thomas Whomes of Southampton the last day of June fo price of 11,050 of scupper nails by him delivered into Her Highness' storehouse at Portsmouth for the use of Her Grace's ships, at 5s ever 1,000. *Summa* – £2 15s 3d.

To William Robynson of Fareham the same day for price of 2,800 o 10d nails of him had and the same delivered as aforesaid for the use o Her Majesty's ships; by agreement – £1 3s 4d.

Sawing. To William Bearde and Thomas Smythe, sawyers, the sam day for the sawing of 400 foot of 2-inch plank oak for the use of He Highness's ships, at 20d every 100 foot sawing – 6s 8d.

To Richard Wilkins and John Higbrooke [*recte* Bigbrooke], sawyers the same day for their wages and victuals serving Her Highness in sawin and cutting of timber oak and wainscot for the use of Her Grace's ships by the space of 13 days between them both at 20d every day wages an victuals – £1 1s 8d.

Netting-ropes. To Roger Godfrey of Fareham, ropemaker, the sam day for the working of 4 hundred 2 quarters 6 pounds weight [*510 lbs*] o Her Grace's old junks and ropes into netting-ropes for the use of He Highness's ships, at 3s 4d every hundred[*weight*] working – 15s.

Brick. To Thomas Treade the same day for price of 700 of brick of hir had for the use of Her Grace's ships there; price by agreement – 7s 8d.

Canvas. To John Jarvys of Southampton, merchant, the same day fc price of 2 bolts of poldavy of him had and the same delivered as aforesai for the use of Her Grace's ships, at 33s 4d every bolt – £3 6s 8d.

[*Page total*] – £9 16s 3d.

[f. 290v] *Service of hoys and lighters.* To James Machyn, master, th last day of June for service of his hoy named the *Martyn of Colcheste* of the portage of 60 tuns, serving Her Highness in having out and in c the ordnance of Her Grace's ship the *Swallow* at her coming on groun to be new breamed and repaired; by the space of 8 days, by agreemen *Summa* – £3 5s.

To Hans Vauzea, master, the same day for service of his hoy named the *Pellycane of Hollande* serving Her Highness for the having out and in of the ordnance of Her Grace's ships the *New Bark* and the *Phoenix* against their comings on ground to be new breamed and tallowed, being of the portage of 65 tuns; by the space of one week, by agreement – £3 5s.

To John Trodwell of Fareham the same day for the hire of two his lighters serving Her Highness in taking out and in of the ordnance of Her Grace's ship named the *Hart* against the grounding of the same ship; by the space of 8 days, by agreement – £2.

Rosin. To Thomas Fuller the same day for price of 5 hundredweight of rosin of him had and the same delivered at Portsmouth into Her Highness's storehouse there for the use of Her Grace's ships, at 8s every hundredweight. *Summa* – £2.

Broom. To Robert Johnson of Fareham the same day for price of 23 loads of dry broom of him had for the use of Her Grace's ships, at 2s every load – 46s; and more to him for bringing the same broom by water to the dock near Portsmouth – 5s. *Summa* – £2 11s.

[*Page total*] – £13 1s.

[f. 291] *A ship boat.* To Richard Rogers of Rotherhithe the last day of June for price of one ship boat of him had and the same delivered at Portsmouth for the use of Her Highness's ships there; price by agreement – £2 13s 4d.

Ox tallow. To Anthony Brisacke the same day for price of 3 hundred 2 quarters 8 pounds [*400 lbs*] weight of hard ox tallow of him had for the use of Her Grace's ships, at 22s [*recte* 21s 5d] every hundredweight. *Summa* – £3 16s 6d.[1]

Copper nails. To John Awre of Fareham, coppersmith, the same day for price of 25 pounds weight of copper nails of him had for the needful mending of the furnaces and kettles in Her Grace's ships there, and for the amending of 3 Her Grace's kettles; by agreement – £1 10s.

To George Joynner of Southampton the same day for the workmanship, sealing and joining of the cabin in Her Highness's ship the *Aid* with wainscot boards; by agreement – £2 6s 8d.

Carrying of gravel. To John Playeffoote the same day for the hire of his cart and horses serving Her Highness in carrying of gravel for the ballasting of Her Grace's ships, by the space of 4 days at 16d *per diem* – 5s 4d.

Water carriage of provisions. To Andrew Marckes, master, the same day for service of his hoy named the *James of London*, of the portage of

[1]The calculation gives 942.85712d, which is almost 2s 1d above the sum stated (918d); this would be correct at a rate of 21s 5d (257d) per cwt, suggesting a scribal error of *xxij.s* for *xxj.s v.d.*

70 tuns, serving Her Highness in carrying of cables, hawsers, warps and other small cordage, canvas, pitch, tar, oars, pumps, rosin and divers other provisions from London to Portsmouth and there delivered the same for the use of Her Grace's ships, by the space of 4 weeks 3 days beginning the 25th day of May last and ended the 18th day of June next, at 3s 4d every tun *per mensem*. *Summa* – £10.

[*Page total*] – £20 11s 10d.

[f. 291v] To John Startupp of Maidstone in Kent the last day of June for service of his hoy, being of the portage of 50 tuns, serving Her Majesty in carrying of 10 chaldron of sea coal, pitch, tar, oakum, anchors, with divers and sundry other kinds of provisions, from London to Portsmouth and there delivered the same to the use of Her Grace's ships, by the space of 3 weeks 3 days begun the 24th day of May last and ended the 17th day of this present month of June abovesaid, at 3s 4d every tun *per mensem*. *Summa* – £7 2s 9¾d.

Compass timber. To John Peaze of Portsmouth the same day for price of 21 loads 22 foot of hooks, knees and other compass timber oak of him had and the same delivered there for the building and repairing of Her Grace's ships, at 10s every load after 50 foot to the load. *Summa* – £10 14s 5d.

[*Page total*] – £17 17s 2¾d.

[f. 292] A payment made the last day of September as well to masters, mariners and gunners serving Her Highness in safe-keeping of Her Grace's ships afloat in harbour and to keepers of storehouses, dock and timber-yards there wherein lieth provisions of all manner of needful things for the use of her ships; as also to shipwrights, sawyers and other artificers and labourers for new mending and repairing of Her Majesty's said ships with provisions of divers kinds taken of sundry persons for the use of the same; by one quarter of a year begun the first day of July last and this day ended, as followeth:

The New Bark

Mariners

William Sampson, master, 13 weeks 1 day	£4 7s 6d
Nicholas Moone, boatswain, 13 weeks 1 day	38s 4d
Roger Davye, purser, 6 weeks 1 day	15s 4d
William Warwick, cook, 13 weeks 1 day	30s 1½d
Thomas Paynter, 11 weeks 5 days	19s 6d
Thomas Howse, 4 weeks 3 days	7s 4d
Humphrey Dennys, 8 weeks 1 day	13s 7d
Robert Marche, 13 weeks 1 day	21s 11d

Thomas Jones, 8 weeks 1 day 13s 7d
Henry Harwood, 8 weeks 1 day 13s 7d
Clement Jestlyn, 8 weeks 1 day 13s 7d
Zach Buggins, 8 weeks 1 day 13s 7d
Richard Edwardes, 2 weeks 3s 4d
[*Page total*] – £14 11s 3½d.

[f. 292v] Robert Sampson, boy, 13 weeks 1 day 10s 11d
Christopher Tappley, 4 weeks 4 days 7s 8d
John Saye, boy, 9 weeks 4 days 8s
Thomas Wilkes, purser, 7 weeks 17s 6d
Thomas Hodgis, 4 weeks 5 days 7s 10d
William Bitche, 4 weeks 5 days 7s 10d
Thomas Davyes, 4 weeks 5 days 7s 10d
Thomas Teygouse, 2 weeks 3s 4d
Richard Dymock, 4 weeks 5 days 7s 10d
Cornelius Gowston, 4 weeks 5 days 7s 10d
[*Gunnner*]
John Phillipps, master gunner, 13 weeks 1 day 32s 10d
The Salamander
Mariners
Robert Glandfeld, boatswain, 6 weeks 1 day 18s
Thomas Norwaye, cook, 11 weeks 5 days 26s 9d
John Brownynge, 13 weeks 1 day 21s 11d
Davy Mortymar, 13 weeks 1 day 21s 11d
William Saunders, boatswain, 7 weeks 20s 5d
Richard Roche, boy, 7 weeks 5s 10d
The Greyhound Bitch
Mariners
Thomas Reade, boatswain, 13 weeks 1 day 38s 4d
Robert Ryce, 9 weeks 6 days 16s 5d
Richard Golde, 13 weeks 1 day 21s 11d
Anthony Manser, boy, 13 weeks 1 day 10s 11d
Robert Dymmock, gromet, 7 weeks 8s 9d
The Owlet
Mariner
Roger Harrys, 13 weeks 1 day 21s 11d
[*Page total*] – £15 14s 2d.

[f. 293] *The Red Hart*
Mariners
William Paulmer, boatswain, 9 weeks 4 days 27s 11d
Thomas Walter, [*blank*] [*blank*]

Robert Longe, [*blank*]	[*blank*]
Francis Waymouth, 8 weeks 4 days	14s 4d
Richard Gater, 4 weeks 4 days	7s 8d
John Awsten, boatswain, 3 weeks 4 days	10s 5d
The Three Moons	
Mariners	
Robert Ryce, boatswain, 13 weeks 1 day	38s 4d
William Hannes, 6 weeks 5 days	11s 2d
Nicholas Maisters, 7 weeks	11s 8d
The Green Dragon	
Mariners	
Thomas Dawson, boatswain, 9 weeks 3 days	27s 6d
Robert Best, purser, 9 weeks 3 days	22s 3d
William Harwoode, 9 weeks 3 days	15s 8d
John Hathe, boy, 9 weeks 3 days	7s 10d
The Maiden	
Mariners	
Thomas Gyelles, boatswain, 2 weeks	4s 7d
Thomas Burnell, 3 weeks 2 days	5s 6d
John Benfylde, boatswain, 11 weeks 1 day	25s 6d
The Serpent	
Mariners	
Francis Currall, boatswain, 6 weeks 1 day	17s 11d
Robert Tanner, 10 weeks 2 days	17s 2d

[*Page total*] – £12 8s 3d.

[f. 293v] *The Gryphon*	
Mariners	
Thomas Galle, boatswain, 6 weeks 1 day	14s 1d
John Luke, gromet, 13 weeks 1 day	16s 5d
Lewis Edmondes, boatswain, 5 weeks	11s 5d
John Richardes, 5 weeks	8s 4d
John Barnes, 7 weeks 5 days	12s 10d
The Sparrowhawk	
Mariner	
Thomas Yorck, boatswain, 11 weeks 5 days	26s 9d
The Black Bark	
Mariners	
James Browne, 2 weeks	3s 4d
Robert Lawrence, [*blank*]	[*blank*]
Rowland Howlett, 11 weeks 1 day	18s 7d

The Raven
Mariners

John Bennet, boatswain, 13 weeks 1 day	30s 1½d
Walter Pearce, 8 weeks	13s 4d

The Bear
Mariners

Richard Stokes, boatswain, 13 weeks 1 day	30s 1½d
John Richardes, boy, 13 weeks 1 day	10s 11½d

[*Page total*] – £9 3s 1½d.

[f. 294] *The Bark of Cherbourg*

Henry Clarke, boatswain, 8 weeks 6 days	20s 4d
John Haylles, 1 week 3 days	2s 4d
Robert Rutter, 8 weeks 3 days	14s
Richard Whyttington, 10 weeks 3 days	17s 4d

The Flower de Luce
Mariners

Thomas Naybour, boatswain, 13 weeks 1 day	30s 1½d
Roger Gryffine, 13 weeks 1 day	21s 11d
William Parfecte, boy, 13 weeks 1 day	10s 11d

The George Hoy
Mariners

Giles Haull, master, 10 weeks 2 days	51s 4d
Thomas Newlande, master's mate, 8 weeks	18s 4d
Thomas Elkyn, cook, 13 weeks 1 day	30s 1½d
Thomas Geffrey, 13 weeks 1 day	21s 11d
Henry Burgys, 13 weeks 1 day	21s 11d
John Willyams, 13 weeks 1 day	21s 11d
Simon Haull, 8 weeks 1 day	13s 7d
John Halle, boy, 10 weeks 2 days	8s 7d
James Smythe, 3 weeks	5s
Martin Lonye, 4 weeks 5 days	7s 10d
Thomas Ussher, master, 2 weeks 6 days	14s 4d
Clement Jestlyn, 1 week 3 days	2s 4d
[*Gunner*]	
Ralph Kyrbye, master gunner, 10 weeks	25s

[*Page total*] – £16 2s 6d.

[f. 294v] *The Elizabeth Jonas*
Mariners

William Woode, master, 5 weeks 3 days	54s 4d
John Teigg, boatswain, 5 weeks 3 days	22s 7d
Roger Davye, purser, 5 weeks 3 days	13s 6d

Thomas Waller, cook, 5 weeks 3 days	12s 4d
Richard Johnson, 1 week 3 days	2s 2d
William Myll, 3 weeks	5s
Richard Watson, 3 weeks	5s
James Morter, 5 weeks 3 days	9s
Richard Bartilmewe, 5 weeks 3 days	9s
Lawrence Marybote, 5 weeks 3 days	9s
Griffin Jones, 2 weeks 1 day	3s 7d
John Androwes, 5 weeks 3 days	9s
Henry Wood, 5 weeks 3 days	9s
John Abowen, 5 weeks 3 days	9s
William Blosse, 5 weeks 3 days	9s
John Barwicke, 5 weeks 3 days	9s
Anthony Reade, 5 weeks 3 days	9s
Brian Baker, 5 weeks 3 days	9s
Richard Wood, 5 weeks 3 days	9s
Robert Godlye, 5 weeks 3 days	9s
Richard Bowlles, 5 weeks 3 days	9s
John Tayer, 5 weeks 3 days	9s
Robert Moar, 5 weeks 3 days	9s
William Challoner, 5 weeks 3 days	9s
John Bunche, carpenter, 5 weeks 3 days	22s 7d
William Harberde, gromet, 5 weeks 3 days	6s 9d
Richard Bunche, boy, 5 weeks 3 days	4s 6d
Henry Morrys, gromet, 5 weeks 3 days	6s 9d
Richard Warren, gromet, 5 weeks 3 days	6s 9d
Thomas Lorde, 5 weeks 3 days	9s
John Mylner, 5 weeks 3 days	9s
Robert Waddylo, 5 weeks 3 days	9s
Robert Joynar, 5 weeks 3 days	9s
Robert Frost, boy, 5 weeks 3 days	4s 6d
Peter Acklonde, boy, 5 weeks 3 days	4s 6d
William Lynchekyen, 2 weeks	3s 4d

[*Page total*] – £17 8s 2d.

[f. 295] Robert Sampson, 2 weeks	3s 4d
Robert Lyon, 2 weeks	3s 4d
Edward Phillpott, 2 weeks	3s 4d
John Harteley, 2 weeks	3s 4d
John Androwes, 2 weeks	3s 4d
John Clarke, 2 weeks	3s 4d
John Bell, 2 weeks	3s 4d

Richard Matchyne, 2 weeks	3s 4d
John Bayret, 3 weeks 1 day	5s 3d
Christopher Perce, 3 weeks 1 day	5s 3d
William Higon, 3 weeks 1 day	5s 3d
John Tompson, 3 weeks 1 day	5s 3d
George Swan, 3 weeks 1 day	5s 3d
Edward Rowland, 3 weeks 1 day	5s 3d
Thomas White, 3 weeks 1 day	5s 3d
John Blacke, 3 weeks 1 day	5s 3d
John Keche, 3 weeks 1 day	5s 3d
John Comberlonde, 3 weeks 1 day	5s 3d
Robert Stone, 3 weeks 1 day	5s 3d
[*Gunner*]	
Lawrence Dilke, master gunner, 5 weeks 3 days	13s 6d

The Victory

Mariners

William Barnes, master, 5 weeks 3 days	54s 4d
John Light, boatswain, 5 weeks 3 days	22s 7d
Hugh Pope, purser, 5 weeks 3 days	13s 6d
Thomas Gayttes, cook, 5 weeks 3 days	12s 4d
William Addams, 2 weeks 3 days	4s
John Awstyn, 3 weeks 3 days	5s 8d
John Shepard, 5 weeks 3 days	9s
Henry Daeshe, 5 weeks 3 days	9s
John Streater, 5 weeks 3 days	9s
Peter Sheron, 5 weeks 3 days	9s

[*Page total*] – £12 6s 4d.

[f. 295v] William Hobjohn, 5 weeks 3 days	9s
William Parcyvall, 5 weeks 3 days	9s
William Hawkyns, 5 weeks 3 days	9s
Hugh Baldinge, 5 weeks 3 days	9s
Ralph Lewys, gromet, 5 weeks 3 days	6s 9d
Philip Mylles, 5 weeks 3 days	9s
John Robyns, 5 weeks 3 days	9s
Robert Garret, gromet, 5 weeks 3 days	6s 9d
Christopher Lewys, boy, 5 weeks 3 days	4s 6d
Richard Tysen, gromet, 5 weeks 3 days	6s 9d
John Gadde, 5 weeks 3 days	9s
John Taillor, 1 week 5 days	2s 10d
John Lane, 2 weeks 1 day	3s 7d
Henry Browne, 2 weeks 1 day	3s 7d

John Smythe, 2 weeks 1 day	3s 7d
John Gobye, 2 weeks 1 day	3s 7d
Ellyar Karres, 2 weeks 1 day	3s 7d
John Gybes, 2 weeks 1 day	3s 7d
John Gabryell, 2 weeks 1 day	3s 7d
Nicholas Claye, carpenter, 5 weeks 3 days	22s 7d
John Saiger, 5 weeks 3 days	9s
John Claye, gromet, 5 weeks 3 days	6s 9d
William Addams, 5 weeks 3 days	9s
Henry Crotchell, 3 weeks 1 day	5s 3d
John Tabbert, 3 weeks 1 day	5s 3d
John Lange, 3 weeks 1 day	5s 3d
John Coxe, 3 weeks 1 day	5s 3d
Hugh Byllett, 3 weeks 1 day	5s 3d
Richard Cade, 3 weeks 1 day	5s 3d
Edward Crafte, 3 weeks 1 day	5s 3d
John Clarke, 3 weeks 1 day	5s 3d
Thomas Clerk, 3 weeks 1 day	5s 3d
[*Gunners*]	
William Thomas, master gunner, 5 weeks 3 days	13s 6d
James Saunders, 5 weeks 3 days	9s

[*Page total*] – £11 3s 9d.

[f. 296] *The Antelope*

Mariners

Richard Wright, boatswain, 7 weeks	20s 5d
Thomas Awstyn, purser, 7 weeks	17s 6d
Roger Bower, [*blank*][1]	[*blank*]
George Lyell, [*cook*],[2] 7 weeks	16s 1d
Thomas Bridger, 7 weeks	11s 8d
Richard Freeman, 7 weeks	11s 8d
John Segar, 7 weeks	11s 8d
Thomas Ewmes, 7 weeks	11s 8d
Robert Mitchelson, gromet, 7 weeks	8s 9d
William Awstyn, gromet, 7 weeks	8s 9d
William Walter, 2 weeks 1 day	3s 7d
Thomas Webb, 2 weeks 1 day	3s 7d
William Coxson, 2 weeks 1 day	3s 7d
Richard Russell, 2 weeks 1 day	3s 7d
Stephen Robartes, 2 weeks 1 day	3s 7d

[1]Listed as master gunner at end of this section.
[2]Cf. below, p. 424.

Thomas Howne, 2 weeks 1 day	3s 7d
Cedric Lock, 2 weeks 1 day	3s 7d
Anthony Chestar, 2 weeks 1 day	3s 7d
Richard Fayerfont, 4 weeks 5 days	7s 10d
John Roche, 4 weeks 5 days	7s 10d
Dennis Ellyn, 4 weeks 5 days	7s 10d
Walter White, 4 weeks 5 days	7s 10d
Allaine Deonys, 4 weeks 5 days	7s 10d
Roger Mortymer, 4 weeks 5 days	7s 10d
John Herst, 4 weeks 5 days	7s 10d
John Davyes, 4 weeks 5 days	7s 10d
Gunner	
Roger Bower, master, 7 weeks	17s 6d

[*Page total*] – £11 9s.

[f. 296v] *The Aid*

Mariners	
John Vallett, master, 3 weeks 4 days	23s 10d
Paul Saunders, boatswain, 3 weeks 4 days	10s 5d
Edward Cockes, purser, 3 weeks 4 days	8s 10d
Nigel Spark, cook, 3 weeks 4 days	8s 2d
William Collyns, 3 weeks 4 days	6s
Jeffrey Preston, 3 weeks 4 days	6s
Stephen Rochestar, 3 weeks 4 days	6s
John Phyllipps, 3 weeks 4 days	6s
Thomas Payton, 2 weeks 1 day	3s 7d
William Hartt, 2 weeks 1 day	3s 7d
Thomas Williams, 2 weeks 1 day	3s 7d
William Kellye, 2 weeks 1 day	3s 7d
John Spannyarde, 2 weeks 1 day	3s 7d
Christopher Drewe, 2 weeks 1 day	3s 7d
John Jennyns, 2 weeks 1 day	3s 7d
James Robynson, gromet, 3 weeks 4 days	4s 4d
William Wood, boy, 3 weeks 4 days	3s
Robert Sparke, boy, 3 weeks 4 days	3s
Henry Gawgeant, 1 week 2 days	2s 2d
William Willyams, 1 week 2 days	2s 2d
John Androw, 1 week 2 days	2s 2d
Robert Skynnar, 1 week 2 days	2s 2d
Robert Hunt, 1 week 2 days	2s 2d
John Awgar, 1 week 2 days	2s 2d
Robert Collyns, 1 week 2 days	2s 2d

Richard Moore, 1 week 2 days	2s 2d
John Benfylde, 1 week 2 days	2s 2d
John Browne, 1 week 2 days	2s 2d
Stephen Hendye, 1 week 2 days	2s 2d
Richard Bowyer, 1 week 2 days	2s 2d
[*Gunner*]	
Thomas Lysse, master gunner, 3 weeks 4 days	8s 10d

[*Page total*] – £7 5s 6d.

[f. 297] *The Saker*

Mariners	
John Burnam, boatswain, 7 weeks	20s 5d
Thomas Thorney, purser, 7 weeks	17s 7d
John Hodge, cook, 2 weeks 3 days	5s 7d
John Morrys, 7 weeks	11s 8d
John Godfrey, 7 weeks	11s 8d
Richard Burnam, 7 weeks	11s 8d
Thomas Stowill, 7 weeks	11s 8d
Henry Phillyon, gromet, 7 weeks	8s 9d
Simon Edwards, 2 weeks 1 day	3s 7d
John Coo, 3 weeks	5s
[*Gunner*]	
John Hunt, master gunner, 7 weeks	17s 6d

The Sun

Mariners	
Nicholas Starkey, boatswain, 7 weeks	20s 5d
William Clowes, purser, 7 weeks	17s 6d
John Shatham, 7 weeks	11s 8d
John Lardge, 2 weeks 1 day	3s 7d
Francis Birtshall, gromet, 7 weeks	8s 9d
[*Gunner*]	
William Ellys, master gunner, 7 weeks	17s 6d

The Post, and the Makeshift

Mariners	
John Rowse, boatswain, 7 weeks	16s 1d
Robert Brewster, cook, 7 weeks	16s 1d
John Delapoole, 2 weeks 1 day	3s 7d
Peter Haywarde, 7 weeks	11s 8d
Nicholas Tille, boy, 7 weeks	5s 10d

[*Page total*] – £12 17s 8d.

[f. 297v] *The Galley Mermaid*

Mariners

Adam Puckwell, boatswain, 7 weeks	20s 5d
Thomas Cossyne, 2 weeks 1 day	3s 7d
Anthony Aderton, 2 weeks 1 day	3s 7d
Robert Puckwell, boy, 7 weeks	5s 10d
[*Gunner*]	
William Addams, master gunner, 7 weeks	17s 6d

The Galley Eleanor[1]

Mariners

William Spencer, boatswain, 6 weeks 4 days	19s 2d
William Christyane, steward, 6 weeks 4 days	15s 1d
Dennis Davye, 6 weeks 4 days	11s
John Belkey, 6 weeks 4 days	11s
Richard Lawrence, 6 weeks 4 day	11s
Henry Spencer, boy, 6 weeks 4 days	5s 6d
Miles Pepper, purser, 3 weeks 1 day	7s 10d
[*Gunner*]	
John Fayerchielde, master gunner, 6 weeks 4 days	16s 4d

The Double Rose

Mariners

Simon Hall, boatswain, 1 week 3 days	3s 3d
William Mowell, 3 weeks 3 days	5s 8d
Anthony Aderton, 1 week 3 days	2s 4d
[*Gunner*]	
Miles Robinson, master gunner, 3 weeks 3 days	8s 6d

[*Page total*] – £7 7s 7d.

[f. 298] *The Hare*

Mariners

John Aman, boatswain, 2 weeks	4s 7d
Thomas Lane, steward, 2 weeks	4s 7d
William Stacye, 2 weeks	3s 4d
Richard Woodman, 2 weeks	3s 4d
Walter Cherry, boy, 2 weeks	20d
[*Gunner*]	
Nicholas Harde, master gunner, 2 weeks	5s

The Minion

Mariners

Robert Rotte, boatswain, 4 weeks 2 days	12s 6d

[1]The *Eleanor* had been acquired as a pledge from the French Huguenots earlier in the year.

George Hollyns, purser, 3 weeks 1 day	7s 10d
John Tompson, cook, 4 weeks 2 days	9s 10d
John Horre, 4 weeks 2 days	7s 2d
Edward Barker, 4 weeks 2 days	7s 2d
John Derrick, 4 weeks 2 days	7s 2d
John Gybbes, 4 weeks 2 days	7s 2d
John Brownyng, 4 weeks 2 days	7s 2d
Richard Yonge, 4 weeks 2 days	7s 2d
Philip Yeard, 4 weeks 4 days	7s 8d
John Sharpley, 4 weeks 4 days	7s 8d
John Laketon, 4 weeks 4 days	7s 8d
William Payden, 4 weeks 4 days	7s 8d
John Barnes, 3 weeks 1 day	5s 3d
John Tasker, 3 weeks 1 day	5s 3d
Henry Myllar, 3 weeks 1 day	5s 3d
Andrew Borley, 3 weeks 1 day	5s 3d
Thomas Cowper, 3 weeks 1 day	5s 3d

[*Page total*] – £7 12s 7d.

[f. 298v] *The Primrose*

Mariners

John Davyes, boatswain, 4 weeks 2 days	12s 6d
John Pett, purser, 4 weeks 2 days	10s 8d
Robert Farley, cook, 4 weeks 2 days	9s 10d
Peter Shell, 1 week 3 days	2s 4d
Daniel Dyce, 4 weeks 2 days	7s 2d
John Leache, 7 days	20d
John Kowke, [*blank*]	[*blank*]
William Anthony, 4 weeks 2 days	7s 2d
John Jeane, 4 weeks 2 days	7s 2d
Philip Sently, boy, 4 weeks 2 days	3s 7d
Edward Shedell, 4 weeks 4 days	7s 8d
William Hore, 4 weeks 4 days	7s 8d
William Martyn, 4 weeks 4 days	7s 8d
Hugh Davyes, 4 weeks 4 days	7s 8d
Thomas Warraunt, 3 weeks 1 day	5s 3d
Richard Lollett, 3 weeks 1 day	5s 3d
John Twynam, 3 weeks 1 day	5s 3d
Garrett Vanholdernes, [*blank*]	[*blank*]
George Browne, [*blank*]	[*blank*]
William Honntley, [*blank*]	[*blank*]
Thomas Horsley, gromet, [*blank*]	[*blank*]

Gunner

James Longe, master, 4 weeks 2 days	10s 8d

[*Page total*] – £5 19s 2d.

[f. 299] *[*Storehouse keeper and timber-yard*]. To John Thomas the last day of September for his wages daily attending and serving Her Highness in safe-keeping of Her Grace's storehouses there wherein lieth Her Majesty's store of cables, hawsers, warps, pitch, tar, canvas and divers other provisions for the use of her ships; by one quarter of a year, due at this present – £5.

To Thomas Claye, porter, the same day for his wages daily attending and serving Her Majesty in safe-keeping of Her Grace's timber-yards there wherein lieth her planks, masts, timber, boards and other kinds of provisions for the use of Her Highness's ships; by one like quarter containing 92 days begun the first day of July last and this day ended, at 6d *per diem* – £2 6s.

[*Page total*] – £7 6s.

[f. 299v] *Shipwrights*

John Peaze, master, 35 days at 12d	35s
Nicholas Gater, 5 days at 6d	2s 6d
Reginald Vesey, 29½ days at 6d	14s 9d
Thomas Walton, 11 days at 4d	3s 8d
John Stookes, 4 days at 8d	2s 8d
James Holcroft, 4 days at 4d	16d
Vincent Newstub, 4 days at 8d	2s 8d
John Trenaiell, server, 4 days at 3d	12d
	*[*63s 7d*]

Victualling. To the said John Peaze the last day of September for the victualling of himself and two other of the aforenamed shipwrights working upon the mending and repairing of Her Majesty's ships there, by the space of 6 weeks among them all, Sundays and holy days within the same accounted, begun the 27th day of June last and this day ended, at 4s 4d every week the man. *Summa* – £1 6s.

Labourers

Edward Prestman, master, 31½ days at 8d	21s
Philip Gaye, 20 days at 6d	10s
William Mylles, 16 days at 6d	8s
Thomas Balche, 14 days at 6d	7s
William Wary, 4 days at 6d	2s
Robert Walle, 4 days at 6d	2s

John Sparkes, 7 days at 6d	3s 6d
John Rigate, 14 days at 6d	7s
Richard Browning, 31 days at 6d	15s 6d
Thomas Mackrell, 6 days at 6d	3s
John Fayermanners, 3 days at 6d	18d
Thomas Veyll, 2 days at 6d	12d
Richard Browninge junior, 14 days at 4d	4s 8d
	[£4 6s 2d*]*

[*Page total*] – £8 15s 9d.

[f. 300] *Emptions*

Timber, plank and board oak. To Christopher Nayllor of London, purveyor, the last day of September for price of 41 loads of hooks, knees and other compass timber oak of him had and the same delivered at Portsmouth for the building and repairing of Her Highness's ships there, at 10s every load after 50 foot to the load – £20 10s; more for 6,545 foot of inch and inch ½ board oak, at 5s every 100 foot – £16 7s 4d; more for 10,000 [*foot*] of 2-inch plank oak, at 8s every 100 foot – £40; more for 3,608 foot of 3-inch plank oak, at 10s every 100 foot – £18 0s 4d; more for 450 foot of 4-inch plank oak, at 12s every 100 foot – 54s; and more to him for 3 loads of quarters oak, at 16s every load – 48s. *Summa* – £99 19s 8d.

Canvas and rudder irons. To Jeffrey Vaughan the same day for price of 16 bolts of medrinacks canvas of him had and delivered into Her Grace's storehouse there for the use of her ships, at 28s 4d every bolt – £22 13s 4d; and more to him for so much by him paid for certain rudder irons and other ironwork for the use of Her Highness's ship's boat the *Jennet*[1] at her being on the seas – 5s 6d. *Summa* – £22 18s 10d.

Pitch and poppet oakum. To John Browne and Thomas Baker the same day for price of 15 barrels of pitch of the great band of them had and delivered for the use as aforesaid, at 9s every barrel, by agreement – £6 15s; and more to them for 310 pound weight of white poppet oakum, at 13s 4d every hundredweight – 41s 4d. *Summa* – £8 16 4d.

Ink and paper. To John Thomas of Portsmouth the same day for price of 18 quires of writing paper had of him for the making of muster and sea books for masters, mariners and gunners serving in Her Grace's ships there, at 4d every quire, 6s; and more to him for one bottle with ink for like use, price – 8d. *Summa* – 6s 8d.

[*Page total*] – £132 1s 6d.

[f. 300v] *Glazing.* To John Dunynge, glazier, the last day of September for price of 25 foot of glass by him set up in the windows of Her Grace's

[1] *Sc.* 'the boat of Her Highness's ship the *Jennet*'.

storehouse there, at 8d every foot – 20s; more to him for one new casement, price – 2s; and more to him for 28 quarrels of glass by him set into sundry of the said windows, at 1d every quarrel – 2s 4d. *Summa* – £1 4s 4d.

To Edward Barker, glazier, the same day for price of 95 quarrels of glass by him set up in the cabin of Her Majesty's ship the *Elizabeth Jonas* at her going to the seas, at 1d the piece – 7s 11d; and more to him for the glazing of 2 scuttles[1] with other needful work done by him in the same ship, by agreement – 6s. *Summa* – 13s 11d.

New casting of lead. To John Fryar of Southwark, plumber, the same day for the melting and casting of certain Her Highness's old lead into sows and blocks that the same may be the sooner wrought into any other needful things for the use of Her Grace's ships; by agreement – 4s.

To John Raynolde of Titchfield, smith, the same day for price of divers and sundry locks and other ironwork had of him for the use of Her Majesty's ships and storehouses there; by agreement – 10s 6d.

Cutting of timber. To Robert Tompson and one other sawyer the same day for their wages and victuals serving Her Majesty in sawing and cutting of timber, plank, and quarters for the building and repairing of Her Highness's ships there, by the space of 16 days between them both, at 14d every day, wages and victuals. *Summa* – 18s 8d.

[*Page total*] – £3 11s 5d.

[f. 301] *A ship boat.* To John Jackson of Poole the last day of September for price of a small boat of him had for the use of Her Majesty's ship called the *Bark of Boulogne* at the same ship's going to the seas; by agreement – £3 13s 4d.

Small masts. To Robert Harbor of Bursledon the same day for price of 2 small Norway masts of him taken for the use of Her Majesty's ships there, at 30s either of them, by agreement – £3; and more to him for the bringing down of the said masts from Hampton to the dock near Portsmouth – 5s. *Summa* – £3 5s.

Carrying of gravel. To John Ayllen, John Goddyn, Stephen Pirryn and 18 other persons of Portsmouth, Kingston, Portsea, Fratton and thereabouts the same day for the carrying of 124 loads of clay and other marsh earth for the filling up of the dockheads there and repairing of the same docks, at 8d every load. *Summa* – £4 2s 8d.

Pitch, tar and a small cable. To William Barnes the same day for price of one last of tar of the small band by him delivered to the Queen's Majesty's storehouse at Portsmouth for the use of Her Grace's ships, by agreement – £4; more for 5 barrels of pitch of the great band, at 8s the

[1]Scuttles were small openings for ventilation, communication or lighting between decks: *OED* 'scuttle', *sb.*[2].1.

barrel – 40s; and more to him for one tarred cable of 8 inches compass weighing 11 hundred[*weight*], at 18s 6d every hundredweight – £10 3s 6d. *Summa* – £16 3s 6d.

Anchors. To John Bongham of Portsmouth, merchant, the same day for price of 3 great anchors of him had for the use of Her Highness's ships, weighing 3 thousand 8 hundred 8 pounds weight [*4,264 lbs*], at 22s every hundredweight. *Summa* – £41 17s 6d.[1]

[*Page total*] – £69 2s. [f. 301v *blank*]

[f. 302] **Ordinary. Portsmouth:** *Anno regni regine Elizabethe sexto*

A payment made the last day of December as well to masters, mariners and gunners serving Her Highness in safe-keeping of Her Grace's ships afloat in harbour, as also to keepers of storehouses dock and timber-yards there wherein lieth divers kinds of things for the use of her ships, and to shipwrights and other artificers and labourers for new mending and repairing of Her Majesty's said ships, with provisions taken of sundry persons for the use of the same; by one quarter of a year begun the first day of October last and this day ended, as followeth:[2]

The Antelope

Mariners

Richard Wrighte, boatswain, 13 weeks 1 day	38s 4d
Thomas Awstyn, purser, 13 weeks 1 day	32s 10d
George Lyell, cook, 13 weeks 1 day	30s 1d
Thomas Brydger, 13 weeks 1 day	21s 11d
John Seggar, 5 weeks 1 day	8s 7d
Richard Freman, 1 week 4 days	2s 8d
Thomas Evans, 13 weeks 1 day	21s 11d
William Walter, 13 weeks 1 day	21s 11d
Thomas Webb, 13 weeks 1 day	21s 11d
William Coxson, 13 weeks 1 day	21s 11d
Richard Russell, 13 weeks 1 day	21s 11d
Stephen Robert, 11 weeks 4 days	19s 4d
Thomas Hounye, 8 weeks 1 day	13s 7d
Anthony Chestar, 2 weeks 3 days	4s 1d

[*Page total*] – £14 1s.

[1] The calculation gives 10050.856d, which is within 1d of the sum stated (10050d).

[2] A fragment of the draft for this Portsmouth quarter survives as BL, Add. MS 78171 [item 1(b)], ff. 11–18. Significant details not carried forward into the final account are noted here. A brief conspectus of the draft is given in Appendix 4 below.

[f. 302v] Thomas Martyn, 13 weeks 1 day	21s 11d
William Awstyn, gromet, 13 weeks 1 day	16s 5d
Robert Mytchelson, gromet, 13 weeks 1 day	16s 5d
John Lomer, 10 weeks 1 day	16s 11d
Thomas Marchaunt, 3 weeks 4 days	6s
John Hamon, 4 weeks 3 days	7s 4d
John Belkey, 4 weeks 3 days	7s 4d
Lewis Edmondes, 1 week 5 days	2s 10d
Robert Lame, 4 weeks 3 days	7s 4d
George Clement, 3 weeks 2 days	5s 6d
[*Gunner*]	
Roger Bowthe, master gunner, 13 weeks 1 day	32s 10d
The New Bark	
Mariners	
William Sampson, master, 13 weeks 1 day	£4 7s 7d
Nicholas Moone, boatswain, 13 weeks 1 day	38s 4d
Thomas Wilkes, purser, 13 weeks 1 day	32s 10d
William Warwick, cook,[1] 5 weeks 1 day	11s 9d
Robert Mose, 13 weeks 1 day	21s 11d
Thomas Hodges, 13 weeks 1 day	21s 11d
William Riche, 13 weeks 1 day	21s 11d
Thomas Davyes, 13 weeks 1 day	21s 11d
Richard Dymock, 13 weeks 1 day	21s 11d
Cornelius Gowston, 13 weeks 1 day	21s 11d
Anthony Aderton, 13 weeks 1 day	21s 11d
John Gaytt, boy, 13 weeks 1 day	10s 11d
Robert Sampson, boy, 13 weeks 1 day	10s 11d
John Mapp, 10 weeks 5 days	17s 10d
William Mowlde, cook, 4 weeks 3 days	10s 2d
[*Gunner*]	
John Phillippes, master gunner, 13 weeks 1 day	32s 10d
The Post	
Mariners	
John Rowse, boatswain, 13 weeks 1 day	30s 1d
Nicholas Stylle, boy, 13 weeks 1 day	10s 11d

[*Page total*] – £29 8s 5d.

[f. 303] *The Sun*	
Mariners	
Nicholas Starke, boatswain, 13 weeks 1 day	38s 4d
William Clowes, purser, 13 weeks 1 day	32s 10d

[1]Draft marginates 'stay': BL, Add. MS 78171 [item 1(b)], f. 12v.

Francis Burchall, gromet, 13 weeks 1 day 16s 5d
Giles Foster, 13 weeks 1 day 21s 11d
William Thomas, 7 weeks 5 days 12s 10d
William Jones, 6 weeks 4 days 11s
William Gybbins, 4 weeks 6 days 8s 1d
[*Gunner*]
William Ellys, master gunner, 13 weeks 1 day 32s 10d
The Saker
Mariners
John Burnam, boatswain, 13 weeks 1 day 38s 4d
Thomas Thorney, purser, 13 weeks 1 day 32s 10d
John Morrys, cook, 13 weeks 1 day 30s 1d
John Godfrey, 13 weeks 1 day 21s 11d
Richard Burnam, 13 weeks 1 day 21s 11d
Henry Vyllian, gromet, 6 weeks 3 days 8s
Thomas Stowell, boy, 13 weeks 1 day 10s 11d
Richard Machyn, 11 weeks 5 days 19s 7d
John Blacklock, 13 weeks 1 day 21s 11d
John Coo, 10 weeks 1 day 16s 11d
Hugh Jones, 4 weeks 3 days 7s 4d
[*Gunner*]
John Hunt, master gunner, 13 weeks 1 day 32s 10d
The Double Rose
Mariners
Simon Hawell, boatswain, 7 weeks 5 days 17s 8d
William Molde, cook, 7 weeks 5 days 17s 8d
Thomas Chase, boy, 7 weeks 5 days 6s 5d
Robert Smythe, 7 weeks 5 days 12s 10d
[*Page total*] – £24 11s 5d.

[f. 303v] *The Makeshift*
Mariners
Edward Jennyns, 13 weeks 1 day 21s 11d
Peter Haywarde, 4 weeks 3 days 7s 4d
William Jones, 4 weeks 3 days 7s 4d
The Galley Mermaid
Mariners
Adam Puckwell, boatswain, 7 weeks 5 days 22s 6d
Robert Puckwell, boy, 7 weeks 5 days 6s 2d
The Galley Eleanor
Mariners
Robert Spencer, boatswain, 13 weeks 1 day 38s 4d

Miles Peppar, purser, 13 weeks 1 day	32s 10d
William Christyane, steward, 13 weeks 1 day	30s 1d
Dennis Davye, 8 weeks 5 days	14s 6d
John Belkey, 8 weeks 5 days	14s 6d
Richard Lawrence, 13 weeks 1 day	21s 11d
Henry Spencer, boy, 13 weeks 1 day	10s 11d
[*Gunner*]	
John Faierchilde, master gunner, 13 weeks 1 day	32s 10d
The Salamander	
Mariners	
John Brownynge, boatswain, 8 weeks	23s 4d
Thomas Willson, cook,[1] 8 weeks	18s 4d
John Ratter, 8 weeks	13s 4d
Davy Martymer, gromet, 8 weeks	10s
Richard Roche, boy, 4 weeks 3 days	3s 8d
Thomas Marchaunt, 4 weeks 4 days	7s 8d
Lewis Emytt, 4 weeks 4 days	7s 8d
Richard Browninge, 8 weeks	13s 4d

[*Page total*] – £17 18s 6d.

[f. 304] *The Greyhound Bitch*

Mariners	
Thomas Reade, boatswain, 13 weeks 1 day	38s 4d
Richard Golde, 13 weeks 1 day	21s 11d
Anthony Manser, boy, 8 weeks	6s 8d
John Dymmock, gromet, 13 weeks 1 day	16s 5d
Hans Markes, 13 weeks 1 day	21s 11d
Richard Gater, 13 weeks 1 day	21s 11d
Roger Thomas, 4 weeks 2 days	7s 2d
Richard Brownynge, 4 weeks 3 days	7s 4d
Dennis Davye, 4 weeks 3 days	7s 4d
Thomas Bonner, 4 weeks 3 days	7s 4d
Roger Harrys, 4 weeks 3 days	7s 4d
The Three Moons	
Mariners	
Robert Thressher, boatswain, 8 weeks 5 days	25s 5d
Nicholas Maisters, 8 weeks 5 days	14s 6d
Roger Chaundellor, 8 weeks 5 days	14s 6d
Thomas Marller, boy, 8 weeks 5 days	7s 3d
Adam Puckwell, boatswain, 4 weeks 3 days	12s 11d

[1]Draft brackets this man with next, and marginates both 'ending the 25th of November': ibid., f. 14.

Robert Puckwell, boy, 4 weeks 3 days	3s 8d
Robert Smythe, 4 weeks 3 days	7s 4d
William Owsse, 4 weeks 3 days	7s 4d
Simon Allyn, 4 weeks 3 days	7s 4d
Thomas Browne, boy, 4 weeks 3 days	3s 8d
John Beast, 4 weeks 3 days	7s 4d
William Harewood, 4 weeks 3 days	7s 4d
Richard Buckland, cook, 4 weeks 3 days	10s 2d
Rowland Howllett, 4 weeks 3 days	7s 4d
The Sparrowhawk	
Mariners	
Roger Harrys, boatswain, 8 weeks 5 days	20s
Simon Allyn, 8 weeks 5 days	7s 3d
Robert Thressher, boatswain, 4 weeks 3 days	12s 11d

[*Page total*] – £17.

[f. 304v] *The Black Bark*	
Mariners	
Rowland Howllett, boatswain, 8 weeks 5 days	20s
Thomas Browngen, boy, 8 weeks 5 days	7s 3d
Nicholas Masters, 4 weeks 3 days	7s 4d
The Maiden	
Mariners	
John Benffylde, boatswain, 8 weeks	18s 4d
John Watkyns, 8 weeks	13s 4d
The Gryphon	
Mariners	
Lewis Edmondes, boatswain, 8 weeks 5 days	20s
James Richardes, 5 weeks 3 days	9s
John Moore, gromet, 8 weeks 5 days	10s 10d
Robert Lame, 4 weeks 2 days	7s 2d
The Raven	
Mariners	
William Harwood, boatswain, 8 weeks 5 days	20s
John Beast, 8 weeks 5 days	14s 6d
Thomas Marler, boy, 4 weeks 3 days	3s 8d
The Bear	
Mariners	
Richard Bucklande, boatswain, 8 weeks 5 days	20s
Lewis Cornelyas, boy, 8 weeks 5 days	7s 3d
Roger Chaundellor, 4 weeks 3 days	7s 4d

[*Page total*] – £9 6s.

[f. 305] *The Flower de Luce*

Mariners

Thomas Naighbour, boatswain, 3 weeks 6 days	8s 10d
John Lewke, boy, 7 weeks 6 days	6s 5d
Thomas Bonner, 7 weeks 6 days	13s 1d
John Hamon, 4 weeks 2 days	7s 2d

The Hart

Mariners

John Awstyn, boatswain, 13 weeks 1 day	30s 1d
Richard Longe, 13 weeks 1 day	21s 11d
William Davye, gromet, 13 weeks 1 day	16s 5d

[*Page total*] – £5 3s 11d.

[f. 305v] *[*Storehouse keeper*]. To John Thomas senior the last day of December for his wages daily attending and serving the Queen's Majesty in safe-keeping Her Grace's storehouses there wherein lieth divers and sundry kinds of provisions for the use of Her Highness's ships, by one quarter of a year, due at this present – £5.[1]

*[*Clerk*]. To John Thomas junior the same day for his wages daily attending and serving Her Highness, not only for the keeping of the prick and cheque books of masters, mariners and gunners serving in Her Grace's ships within the haven of Portsmouth, but also the book of report of such provisions as are taken of divers persons for the use of the said ships, by one like quarter of a year containing 92 days begun the first day of October last and ended as abovesaid, at 8d *per diem* – £3 1s 4d.

*[*Timber yard keeper*]. To Thomas Claye, porter, the same day for his wages daily attending and serving Her Majesty in safe-keeping of Her Grace's timber-yards there wherein lieth her store of timber, planks, boards, masts, and other needful things for the use of Her Highness's ships, by like time of 92 days begun and ended as is abovesaid, at 6d *per diem* – £2 6s.

*[*Plug keeper*]. To Edward Prestman, labourer, the same day for his wages daily attending and serving Her Highness in keeping of the plug and letting forth of the water out of the dock there for the drier keeping of the same, with other needful service by him done there, by like 92 days begun and ended as aforesaid, at 4d *per diem* – £1 10s 8d.

[*Page total*] – £11 18s.

[f. 306] *Shipwrights*

John Peaze, master, 11 days at 12d	11s

[1]In the draft this entry occurs on an attached sheet, minuted 'enter among the labourers': ibid., f. 16A.

Reginald Veazye, 33 days at 6d	16s 6d
Thomas Wylton server, 10 days at 4d	3s 4d
John West, 11 days at 7d	6s 5d
John Pynnock, 10 days at 7d	5s 10d
Christopher Stevens, 10 days at 6d	5s
Philip Payne, 10 days at 7d	5s 10d
John Paullmer, 10 days at 6d	5s
William Molde, 11 days at 7d	6s 5d
Thomas Davyes, 10 days at 6d	5s
	*[*70s 4d*]

Victualling. To John Thomas of Portsmouth the last day of December for the victualling of the aforesaid 10 shipwrights working upon the repairing and amending of four Her Highness's ships there, *viz*. the *New Bark*, the *Saker*, the *Greyhound Bitch* and the *Three Moons*, by the space of 144 days among them all, the Sundays and holy days within the same accounted, begun the 21th day of October last and ended the 28th day of November next, which maketh 22 weeks 4 days, at 5s 4d every week the man. *Summa* – £6 0s 4d.

[*Page total*] – £9 10s 8d.

[f. 306v] *Labourers*

Robert Veysie, master,[1] 12 days at 8d	8s
Thomas Waltun, 18 days at 6d	9s
Robert Peaze, 4 days at 6d	2s
John Fowlle, 30 days at 6d	15s
William Altam, 30 days at 6d	15s
George Robynson, 30 days at 6d	15s
Robert Mathew, 30 days at 6d	15s
Ralph Warde, 3 days at 6d	18d
John Thressher, 16 days at 6d	8s
William Playefoote, 14 days at 6d	7s
Richard Gaye, 3 days at 6d	18d
John Page, 3 days at 6d	18d
John Morrys, 3 days at 6d	18d
Simon Blackman, 3 days at 6d	18d
William Gyltredge, 2 days at 6d	12d
John Ragett, 3 days at 6d	18d

[1]Draft has this much confused entry: 'To Rainold Vessey, carpenter, for working and caulking aboard the *Saker* to keep her sails dry, and tackle, by the commandment of Mr Morley, beginning the 6th of December and ending the 23 day of the same, which is 16 weeks, at 6d *per diem* – 8s [*marginated*] Enter among the labourers': BL, Add. MS 78171 [item 1(b)], f. 17.

John Pallmer, 14 days at 6d	7s
William Mylles, 13 days at 6d	6s 6d
John Claye, 8 days at 6d	4s
Richard Brownynge, 16 days at 6d	8s

[*Page total*] – £6 9s 6d.

[f. 307] *Emptions*

Timber, plank and board oak. To Christopher Nayller of Southampton the last day of December for price of 11 loads 21½ foot of hooks, knees and other compass timber oak by him delivered at the dock near Portsmouth for the use of the Queen's Majesty's ships, at 10s every load after 50 foot to the load – £5 14s 4½d; more for 3,559 foot of 4-inch plank oak, at 12s every 100 foot – £21 7s 1½d; more for 4,545 foot of 3-inch plank oak, at 10s every 100 foot – £22 18s 9¼d; more for 14,762 foot of 2-inch plank oak, at 8s every 100 foot – £59 5s 11d; and more to him for 26,736 foot of inch and inch ½ board oak, at 5s every 100 foot – £66 16s 10½d. *Summa* – £176 3s 0¾d.[1]

Divers sorts of nails. To John Sheldon of Staffordshire, smith, the same day for price of 3,200 of 2s nail of him had for the use of Her Highness's ships, at 20s every 1,000 – £3 4s; more for 4,300 of 20d nail, at 16s 8d every 1,000 – £3 11s 8d; more for 3,000 of 10d nail, at 8s 4d every 1,000 – 25s; more for 17,300 of 4d nail, at 3s 4d every 1,000 – 57s 8d; more for 34,000 of 3d nail, at 2s 6d every 1,000 – £4 5s; and more to him for 40,200 of 2d nail, at 20d every 1,000 – £3 7s. *Summa* – £18 10s 4d.

Old junks wrought into netting and oakum. To Roger Godfrey of Fareham, ropemaker, the same day for the working of 8 hundred 25 pounds weight [*921 lbs*] of Her Grace's old junks and ropes into netting-ropes for the use of Her Majesty's ships, at 3s 4d every hundred[*weight*] working – £1 7s 6d.[2]

To Roger Harrys of Stoke the same day for the working and picking of [*one*] thousand 6 hundredweight [*1,792 lbs*] of Her Highness's old ropes and junks into oakum for the needful caulking of Her Grace's ships at their groundings, at 3s 4d every hundredweight – 53s 4d; and more to Joan Jackson of Fareham for the working and picking of 8 hundred 3 quarters weight [*980 lbs*] of the like junks and ropes into oakum for the use as aforesaid, at 3s 4d the hundredweight working – 29s 2d. *Summa* – £4 2s 6d.

[*Page total*] – £200 3s [*4*]¾d.

[1]The only entry for this section in the draft, where it is an addendum: ibid.
[2]The calculation gives 328.92851, which is 1d below the sum stated (330d).

[f. 307v] *An anchor.* To Henry Goodman of Hampton, merchant, the last day of December for price of one great anchor of him had for the use of Her Grace's ships, weighing 8 hundred and 13 pounds weight [*909 lbs*]; price by agreement – £8 2s 4d.

Ink and paper. To John Thomas junior the same day for price of 9 quires of writing paper by him bought for the making of muster and prick books for masters, mariners, gunners and others serving in Her Highness's ships, at 4d every quire – 3s; and more for one quart of ink for like use – 14d. *Summa* – 4s 2d.

[*Page total*] – £8 6s 6d.

[f. 308] **Ordinary. Conduct:**

Anno Domini 1562 [1563]. *Anno regni regine Elizabethe quinto*

Conduct money paid to shipwrights, caulkers and others prested to the Queen's Majesty's ships, as followeth :

To Thomas Bryan the first day of February for the conduct of himself and Lewis Richardes and John Deakons, shipwrights, from Bristol to Deptford to the Queen's Majesty's works there, distant 100 miles, at 4s every of them – 12s; more to John Browninge, George Upson, Robert Paddye, Richard Clayes and Robert Baker, shipwrights, for their conduct money from Ipswich to Deptford to the works there, distant 60 miles, at 2s 6d every of them – 12s 6d; and more to Thomas Bolton, William Bolton, John Fowller and 20 other caulkers and shipwrights for their conduct money from London to Chatham for the ransacking and caulking of Her Highness's ships there, distant 24 miles, at 12d every man – 23s. *Summa* – £2 7s 6d.

Anno Domini 1563

To Nicholas Claye, John Adams, John Bunche and John Poulter, shipwrights, the last day of March for their conduct money from Deptford to Chatham to go to the sea in certain Her Grace's ships there,[1] at 12d every of them – 4s; more to John Clark, John Haywarde, William Bastiane and five other caulkers for their conduct money, sent from London to Chatham aforesaid for the like ransacking and caulking of Her Highness's ships, at 12d every of them – 8s. *Summa* – 12s.

[*Page total*] – £2 19s 6d.

[1]Claye went to *Victory* as carpenter, Bunche and Poulter to *Mary Rose* as respectively carpenter and server; all were paid for 5 weeks 4 days up to 31 March (above, pp. 335, 337), showing that they were embarked simultaneously.

[f. 308v] To Nicholas Johnson, Ralph Browne, George Browne and Robert Trashe, carpenters, the last day of March for their conduct money from Deptford to Chatham to serve in certain Her Grace's ships at the seas,[1] distant 24 miles, at 12d every man – 4s; and more to John Leche, carpenter, for the conduct of himself and five other carpenters sent from Deptford to Chatham for the setting up of a crane at the wharf there, distant as aforesaid, at 12d every of them – 6s. *Summa* – 10s.

To John Diggyns, Nicholas Fockes, Thomas Moosen, and 13 other shipwrights and oarmakers the first day of April for their conduct money from Deptford to Chatham, sent thither to be placed in divers Her Highness's ships and galleys at their settings to the sea, at 12d every of them – 16s; more to Thomas Blosse, John Wynney, John Wethers, John Mylles and six other shipwrights for their conduct from Deptford to Chatham to Her Grace's ships there for the perfecting of them in carpentry against their settings to the sea, distant 24 miles, at 12d every man – 10s; more to James Brydger, Roger Mytchell, Thomas Chartram and 21 other shipwrights and caulkers for their conduct from Arundel to Portsmouth, distant 24 miles, at 12d every man – 24s; more to Thomas Rogers, Thomas Ingleaff and seven other shipwrights and caulkers for their conduct from Chichester to Portsmouth, distant 12 miles, at 6d every man – 4s 6d; and more to John Best for the conduct of John Carpenter and five other shipwrights from Lymington and thereabouts to Portsmouth, distant 30 miles, at 12d every man – 6s. *Summa* – £3 0s 6d.

[*Page total*] – £3 10s 6d.

[f. 309] Conduct money paid to shipwrights, caulkers and others discharged from Her Grace's works, as followeth:

To George Upson and Lewis Richardes the last day of March for their conduct money from Deptford from Her Grace's works there to Ipswich from whence they were prested, distant 60 miles, at 2s 6d either of them – 5s; more to Robert Bridges, Humphrey Draike, John Eastwood and seven other shipwrights and caulkers discharged from Her Highness's works at Chatham to London from whence they were prested, distant 24 miles, at 12d every of them – 10s; and more to Nicholas Johnson, John Bunche, William Welshe, Nicholas Claye, John Sacar, Mark Hodges and 49 other shipwrights and caulkers discharged from Her Grace's said works at Chatham to London from whence they were prested, distant as is aforesaid, at 12d every of them, 55s. *Summa* – £3 10s.

[1] Johnson went to *Elizabeth Jonas* as carpenter, R. Browne to *Triumph* as mariner (where named alongside E. Waller, as also in list of Deptford shipwrights for shorter period of same quarter): above, pp. 334, 335, 342.

To John Pynnock the last day of June for conduct of himself, Robert Blaick, Philip Paine and Robert Harris, shipwrights, from Portsmouth to Lymington from whence they were prested, being distant 24 miles, at 12d every of them – 4s; more to John Hillyar, Walter Johnson, John Palmer and three other shipwrights for their conduct from Portsmouth to Southampton from whence they were prested, distant 12 miles, at 6d every man – 3s; more to William Bexley, Edward Hoopar, Thomas Boltton and 27 other shipwrights, caulkers, sawyers, smiths and topmakers for their conduct from Portsmouth to London and thereabouts from whence they were prested, distant 60 miles, at 2s 6d every of them – £3 15s; and more to Thomas Morley for the conduct of Robert Blaick, William Loef, John Palmer, John Heller and John Penock, shipwrights, discharged from Her Highness's said works at Portsmouth to Lymington and thereabouts, distant as abovesaid, at 12d every of them – 5s. *Summa* – £4 7s.

[*Page total*] – £7 17s.

[f. 309v] To Robert Bater the last day of June for the conduct of himself, Robert Davye, Richard Payne, John Diggons, John Twedall, Richard Cooke, Robert Florye, John Collycote and seven other shipwrights, caulkers and oarmakers discharged from Her Highness's works at Deptford to Gillingham, Halstow, Rainham, Faversham, Milton and thereabouts, distant 30 miles. at 12d every man – 15s. more to John Burnett, Richard Claye, Thomas Blosse, Henry Neall, John Wynney, John Wethers, Robert Hutson and Thomas Withered, shipwrights, for the conduct of themselves and six other shipwrights discharged from Her Grace's said works at Deptford to Harwich, Ipswich and thereabouts, distant 60 miles, at 2s 6d every of them – 35s; more to William Pellam, Nicholas Adams, Richard Badcock, Thomas Tyrreas and William Grenewaye, shipwrights, for the conduct of themselves and five other shipwrights discharged from Her Grace's works at Deptford aforesaid to Rye, Appledore, Reading [*Street*] and thereabouts in Kent,[1] distant 54 miles, at 2s every of them – 20s; and more to Thomas Bryan, William Carow, John Evered, Baptist Dyar and Henry Freman, shipwrights, for their conduct, discharged from the said works at Deptford to Bristol and thereabouts, distant 100 miles, at 4s every of them – 20s. *Summa* – £4 10s.

[*Page total*] – £4 10s.

[1]Rye is in Sussex, but the associated places are east of the Rother, in Kent.

[f. 310] **Ordinary. Prests:**

Anno Domini 1562 [1563]. *Anno regni regine Elizabethe quinto*

Money delivered in prest to Edward Baeshe, General Surveyor of Her Grace's victuals for the seas, for the victualling of Her Highness's ships in harbour, as followeth:

To Edward Baeshe, General Surveyor of Her Grace's victuals for the seas, the 4th day of February *anno supradicto*[1] in prest upon the ordinary victualling of masters, mariners and gunners keeping Her Highness's ships afloat in harbour, six hundred pounds – £600.

Anno Domini 1563

To the said Edward Baeshe, General Surveyor of Her Highness's victuals for the seas, the 10th day of April *annis supradictis* in prest upon the ordinary victualling of masters, mariners and gunners keeping Her Highness's ships afloat in harbour, four hundred pounds – £400.

To the same Edward Baeshe, General Surveyor of Her Majesty's said victuals for the seas, the 28th day of May *annis supradictis* in prest upon the ordinary victualling of masters, mariners and gunners keeping Her Grace's ships afloat in harbour, five hundred pounds – £500.

To the aforesaid Edward Baeshe, General Surveyor of Her Grace's victuals for the seas, the 5th day of November *annis supradictis* in prest upon the ordinary victualling of masters, mariners, and gunners keeping Her Majesty's ships afloat in harbour, five hundred pounds – £500.

[*Page total*] – £2,000.

[f. 310v] To Edward Baeshe, General Surveyor of Her Grace's victuals for the seas, the 14th day of December *annis supradictis* in prest upon the ordinary victualling of masters, mariners and gunners keeping Her Majesty's ships afloat in harbour, four hundred pounds – £400.

To the same Edward Baeshe, General Surveyor of Her Majesty's victuals for the seas, the 24th day of December *annis supradictis* in prest upon the ordinary victualling of masters, mariners and gunners keeping Her Highness's ships afloat in harbour, four hundred pounds – £400.

[*Page total*] – £800.

[1] Here the singular wording occurs, but the abbreviated forms occurring elsewhere on this page of the MS are extended to the plural in line with second scribe Alexander's general reference, explicit again in both entries on f. 310v.

[f. 311] **Ordinary. Charges:**

Anno Domini 1563. Anno regni regine Elizabethe sexto

To John Browne the last day of December *annis supradictis* for charges by him sustained in receiving of £9,630 at the Receipt of the Exchequer at the hands of the tellers there at divers times within the time of this account, by virtue of Her Highness's ordinary warrant of £12,000 by the year for the reparation and maintenance of Her Grace's Navy and provisions for the same, at 30s every £1,000, bags, wax, paper, parchment, carriages and suchlike within the same charge accounted – £14 8s.

[*Page total*] – *Summa predicta*. [f. 311v *blank*]

[f. 312] **Extraordinary. Conduct:**

Anno Domini 1563. Anno regni regine Elizabethe quinto

Conduct money paid as well to masters, mariners and gunners as soldiers prested from divers and sundry places by virtue of Her Highness's commission to serve in Her Grace's ships from time to time, as followeth

To Lancelot Tristram the 16th day of May for the conduct of John Moughter, William Speringe, Henry Moughter, William Gent, John Stainer, John Loff, John Cheasman, John Charman, Robert Gent, Richard Whittingham, John Gilbart, Thomas Haywood and 50 other mariners by him prested from Worthing, Kingston, Lancing, Heene, Brighton and thereabouts in Sussex, to Rye to serve Her Highness for the fetching of certain French ships from Newhaven in Normandy to Portsmouth,[1] being distant 36 miles, at 18d every man – £4 13s; more for the conduct of John Pickarden, Jeffrey Hun, Richard Norman, Richard Tomsett and 9 other mariners by him prested from Newhaven and 'Torbaye' in Sussex, being distant 24 miles, at 12d every man – 13s; and more to him for the conduct of Richard Affennyll, William Awborne, John Rowe and 8 other mariners by him prested from Eastbourne in Sussex, distant 12 miles, at 6d every man – 5s 6d. *Summa* – £5 11s 6d.

To John Hewson of Dover the 17th day of May for the conduct of John Maye, Jarmaine Dowes, Nicholas Greye, John Tylman, and 43 other mariners by him prested from Dover, Folkestone, Deal, Walmer, Kingsdown and thereabouts in Kent to Rye for the service aforesaid, distant 24 miles, at 12d every man – 47s; more for the conduct of John Castell, William Treake, William Butcher, Nicholas Benne and 26 other mariners from Hythe and thereabouts to Rye, distant 12 miles, at 6d every

[1]See below, p. 458 & n. 1.

man – 15s; and more for the conduct of Thomas Whelar, Richard Moode, Thomas Pett, Anthony Harrington and 14 other mariners from Sandwich and thereabouts to Rye aforesaid, distant 36 miles, at 18d every man – 27s. *Summa* – £4 9s.

[*Page total*] – £10 0s 6d.

[f. 312v] To Roger Porter the 18th day of May for the conduct of Thomas Davyes, John Bryce, Richard Deane, William Cooke and 13 other mariners by him prested from Lymington, Christchurch and thereabouts in Hampshire and Dorsetshire to serve in Her Grace's ships at Portsmouth, being distant 24 miles, at 12d every man – 17s; more for the conduct of Andrew Vallence, John Hawkyns, James Dover, Henry Venyon and 17 other mariners by him prested from Poole and thereabouts to Portsmouth aforesaid, distant 36 miles, at 18d every man – 31s 6d; more for the conduct of William Marchaunte, Nicholas Tabbott, William Tabott and 22 other mariners by him prested from East Purbeck, West Purbeck and thereabouts, distant 48 miles, at 2s every man – 50s; and more to him for the conduct of John Bigges, Thomas Webbar, Edmund Jordaine, John Ashe, Richard Smythe and 60 other mariners from Weymouth, Melcombe, Langton Herring, Fleet, Chickerell, Wyke Regis, Burton, Abbotsbury and thereabouts in Dorsetshire to Portsmouth, distant 60 miles, at 2s 6d every man – £8 2s 6d. *Summa* – £13 1s.

To Thomas Woodcott of Ratcliff the 24th day of May for the conduct of William Cootes, Dominic Yonge, Richard Trowtinge, Richard Downes, Henry Baker, George Anderson, John Falleck and 30 other mariners by him prested from St Katherine's, Ratcliff, Limehouse, Blackwall and divers other places near unto the river of Thames to Gillingham, distant 24 miles, at 12d every man – 37s; and more to him for the conduct of John Willys, Ralph Turnar, John Coole, Nicholas Bonnar, John Smalle and 42 other mariners by him prested as well from Deptford, Greenwich, Erith, West Ham and thereabouts, as also out of divers ships within the river of Thames, to Portsmouth to serve in Her Grace's ships there, distant 60 miles, at 2s 6d every man – £5 17s 6d. *Summa* – £7 14s 6d.

[*Page total*] – £20 15s 6d.

[f. 313] To John Sluttar of Brighton the 25th day of May for the conduct of Henry Harvye, Serick [*Cedric*] Lock, William Joye, Edmund Beldam and 17 other mariners by him prested from Brighton, Shoreham and thereabouts in Sussex, to Portsmouth to serve in Her Highness's ships there, distant 36 miles, at 18d every man – 31s 6d; and more to him for the conduct of John Androwes, Thomas Robarttes, Robert Stowell and 24 other mariners from Sidlesham, Selsey, Felpham and thereabouts in Sussex to Portsmouth aforesaid, distant 12 miles at 6d every of them – 13s 6d. *Summa* – £2 5s.

To Thomas Woodcott the first day of July for the conduct of John Arche William Allam, Ralph Haull, William Fetchett, John Carter and 233 othe mariners and gunners by him prested from Limehouse, Blackwall, Deptford Barking, Ratcliff, Wapping and divers other places nigh adjoining to th river of Thames to serve in Her Grace's ships at Chatham appointed to th seas, being distant 24 miles, at 12d every man. *Summa* – £11 18s.

To Edward Lambart the 5th day of July for the conduct of Willian Foster, Richard Torkinton, Peter Robson, Thomas Gybson, Rober Gyelles, Richard Constabell and 30 other mariners by him prested fron Wivenhoe, Fingringhoe, St Osyth, Colchester and thereabouts in Esse to Chatham to serve in divers Her Highness's ships appointed to the seas being distant 24 miles, at 12d every man – 36s; more for the conduct o John Slitter, John Dowdaye and 24 other mariners from Salcott, Peldon Tollesbury and thereabouts in Essex to Chatham aforesaid, distant 1 miles, at 6d every man – 13s; and more to him for the conduct of Edmun Locke, William Gielles, John Ellys and 17 other mariners by him preste from Harwich, Woodbridge, Shotley and thereabouts in Essex and Suffol to Chatham to serve in Her Grace's ships there, distant 36 miles, at 18 every man – 30s. *Summa* – £3 19s.

[*Page total*] – £18 2s.

[f. 313v] To James Humphrey the 6th day of July for the conduct o John Harvey, Oliver Pett, John Walton, Richard Rygate, Willian Anderson, John Lyman, George Chettelborrow, George Fenne, Joh Christmas, Richard Crainforth, William Furton, Robert Moar and 56 othe mariners by him prested from Stutton, Holbrook, Erwarton, Harwich Woodbridge, Ufford, Eyke, Sudbourne, Sizewell, Falkenham, Kirton an thereabouts in Suffolk[1] to serve in Her Highness's ships the *Hope*, th *Willoughby* and the *Rowbarge*, then being at Yarmouth, distant 12 miles at 6d every man – 34s; and more to him for the conduct of John Payne Adam Blomfielde, John Myelles, Henry Mynnye, William Newton, Joh Forgan and 18 other mariners by him prested from Sutton, Boyton, Butley Orford, Thorpe and thereabouts in Suffolk to Yarmouth, distant 24 miles at 12d every man – 34s.[2] *Summa* – £2 18s.

To Lancelot Tristram the same day for the conduct of Jeffrey Fraxsor Robert Sutton, John Dowes, Henry Cowper, Thomas Beate, Richar

[1] And (because Harwich is included) Essex.

[2] On 10 Aug. the Privy Council ordered Ralph Chamberlain, commanding these thre ships in the North Sea, to see the *Hope* returned to Gillingham, and while passing the coas of Norfolk and Suffolk to discharge all who could be spared from her and the other tw ships, landing the men as near as possible to the places whence they were first taken, f saving the conduct money payable should they be brought to Gillingham and discharge there: *APC 1558–70*, p. 138. See further below, pp. 460–1, 468–9.

Pissinge and 10 other mariners by him prested from Dover, Kingsdown, Sandwich and thereabouts in Kent to serve in Her Grace's ships at Chatham, distant 36 miles, at 18d every man – 24s; more to him for the conduct of Thomas Parker, John Bayllie, Thomas Houghe, Christopher Parkins, Thomas Homan, William Tompson, George Browne and 25 other mariners by him prested from Deal, St Lawrence in Thanet, St Peters, St John's [*Margate*],[1] and thereabouts in Kent to Chatham, distant 24 miles, at 12d every man – 32s; and more to him for the conduct of Thomas Burr, John Sturgeon and 7 other mariners by him prested from Whitstable and thereabouts in Kent to Chatham aforesaid to be placed in divers Her Highness's ships there appointed to the seas, being distant 12 miles, at 6d every man – 4s 6d. *Summa* – £3 0s 6d.

[*Page total*] – £5 18s 6d.

[f. 314] To Roger Porter the 8th day of July for the conduct of William Garrett, John Skegges, John Knighte, Brian Baker, John Merche and seven other mariners by him prested from Poole in Dorsetshire to Chatham to serve in Her Grace's ships there appointed to the seas, distant 72 miles, at 3s every man – 36s; more for the conduct of Thomas Baker, John Haywarde, Mark Cradler, John Ricarde, Nicholas Strowde, Thomas Bosler, Peter Haywarde, William Harvye, William Lydes, Richard Trewe and 20 other mariners by him prested from East Purbeck, West Purbeck, Weymouth, Portland, Langton, Fleet, Chickerell, Puncknowle and thereabouts in Dorset and Devonshire[2] to Chatham aforesaid, being distant 84 miles, at 3s 6d every man – £5 5s; more to him for the conduct of William Boteswaine, Hugh Bellett, John Ocke, Richard Thistell, John Haywarde, Robert Domy, Richard Kett and 40 other mariners by him prested from Abbotsbury, Burton, Bridport, Symondsbury, Charmouth, Chideock and thereabouts in Devonshire [*recte* Dorset] to Chatham, distant 96 miles, at 4s every man – £9 8s; more to him for the conduct of John James, William Jaye and 18 other mariners by him prested from Seaton, Beer, Sidmouth and thereabouts, distant 120 miles, at 5s every man – £5; more to him for the conduct of Michael Jones, William Gadge, William Vawter, John Crosse and 99 other mariners by him prested from Exmouth, Withycombe Raleigh,[3] Lympstone, Topsham, Dawlish, Powderham and thereabouts to Chatham, distant 132 miles, at 5s 6d every man – £28 7s 6d; more to him for the conduct of John Longe, Gregory Cade, John

[1] St John's or St John the Baptist was the alternative or supplementary name for Margate, the church having this dedication, and in distinction to the adjacent parish of St Peter: Wallenberg, *Place-Names of Kent*, p. 600.

[2] The places specified in this group and the next are all in Dorset; those in the two other groups in this entry are in Devon.

[3] Written as if two places ('Whethycom, Rally').

Rowley, George Backistone and 49 other mariners by him prested from Combeinteignhead, Stokeinteignhead, St Mary Church and thereabouts to Chatham, distant 144 miles, at 6s every man – £15 18s; and more to him for the conduct of John Medam, John Canne, Lawrence Williams, and 61 other mariners by him prested from Paignton, Brixham, Churston Galmpton and thereabouts in Devonshire to Chatham, distant 160 miles at 6s 6d every man – £20 16s. *Summa* – £86 10s 6d.

[*Page total*] – £86 10s 6d.

[f. 314v] To Lancelot Tristram the 10th day of July for the conduct of John Hatley, William Goodson, John Castell, Thomas Atkynson, Robert Clarke, Thomas Tuckar, Henry Readman and 102 other mariners by him prested from Dover, Folkestone, Hythe, Lydd, Rye and thereabouts to Chatham, distant 36 miles, at 18d every man – £8 3s 6d; and more to him for the conduct of Robert Harrys, Henry Martyn, James Bennet, Richard Hemmynge and 21 other mariners by him prested from St Peters, St John' and divers other places in Thanet in Kent to serve in Her Grace's ships at Chatham aforesaid appointed to the sea, distant 24 miles, at 12d every man – 25s. *Summa* – £9 8s 6d.

To William Driver the same day for the conduct of Thomas Cobden Richard Pullman, William Mowes, Thomas Foster, Robert Willys, William Nowell, Hugh Martyn, John Tompson and 195 other mariners by him prested from Shirehampton, Bristol, Leigh, Monmouth, Portbury, Wraxall Wraxall,[1] Carmarthen and thereabouts in Worcestershire and Gloucestershire [*sic*] to serve in Her Grace's ships at Chatham appointed to the seas, distant 120 miles, at 5s every man – £50 15s; more for the conduct of William Bagleye, Richard Shipman, Rosar Nicolles, Francis Hall and 16 other mariners by him prested from Tintern, Trelleck Grange[2] and thereabouts in Gloucestershire [*recte* Monmouthshire] to Chatham, distant 132 miles, at 5s 6d every man – £5 10s; more for the conduct of John Portar, John Davye and 12 other mariners from Newport and thereabouts in Gloucestershire to Chatham, distant 144 miles, at 6s every man – £4 4s; more for the conduct of Richard Browne, George Robyns and seven other mariners from Aust Awre parish and thereabouts in Gloucestershire to Chatham, distant 13[illegible] miles, at 5s 9d every man – 51s 9d; and more to him for the conduct of

[1]MS 'Racksall, Wracksalle'. One of these is Wraxall in north Somerset (5 miles west of Bristol). The other might be Wraxall 5 miles south of Shepton Mallet, also Somerset, though well away from the area suggested; or possibly Wraxall Moor (now lost) in Pucklechurch Glos: cf. EPNS, *Glos*, iii, p. 65.

[2]MS 'Trebles grainge', which must stand for Trelleck Grange three miles west of Tintern though perhaps meaning the parish of Trellech generally.

[3]There is a Newport in Gloucestershire (near Berkeley) but the mileage cited here indicates the larger Newport in Monmouthshire, and this is confirmed by a later entry (p. 462).

Thomas Davyes, Walter Haines, John Therrie and 30 other mariners by him prested from Gloucester, Elmore and thereabouts to Chatham, distant 114 miles, at 4s 9d the man – £7 16s 9d. *Summa* – £70 17s 6d.

[*Page total*] – £80 6s.

[f. 315] To Edward Lambarde the 10th day of July for the conduct of Richard Corkles, Thomas Gybson, John Fordam, John Brome, Matthew Smythe and 70 other mariners by him prested from Wivenhoe, Alresford, Manningtree, St Osyth, East Donyland, Fingringhoe, Colchester, East Mersea, Brightlingsea and thereabouts in Essex to serve in Her Grace's ships at Chatham appointed to the seas, distant 24 miles, at 12d every man – £3 15s; more for the conduct of James Gronell, Odnaye Magna, William Taillor, Davy Lyne and 11 other mariners by him prested from Dovercourt, Harwich and thereabouts in Suffolk [*recte* Essex] to Chatham aforesaid, distant 36 miles, at 18d every man – 22s 6d; and more to him for the conduct of Christopher Catrus, John Chappell, John Fynchen, Thomas Tybbolde, William Morrell and 36 other mariners by him prested from Salcott, Peldon, Barling and thereabouts in Essex to Chatham, distant 12 miles, at 6d every man – 19s 6d. *Summa* – £5 17s.

To Thomas Baker the 13th day of July for the conduct of Roger Raynoldes, John Raynoldes, Peter Annys, William Burnell, John Rowse, Nicholas Somes, George White, John Harbert, Thomas Johnson, Thomas Bromley, Anthony Grove, Thomas Ollyver, William Loggon, John Hutton, Thomas Myllar, John Gybson, John Yewe, John Langley, Thomas Foster, Thomas Bray and 418 other mariners by him prested from divers and sundry places adjoining nigh unto the river of Thames and thereabouts to serve in Her Highness's ships and galleys at Chatham appointed to the seas, distant 24 miles, at 12d every man. *Summa* – £21 18s.

To William Rowes the same day for the conduct of himself, William Shelforde, Robert Richardes and 26 other mariners sent from Chatham to Dover to be placed in her Her Grace's ships there, at 12d every man – 9s.

[*Page total*] – £29 4s.

[f. 315v] To Thomas Baker the 14th day of July for the conduct of Roger Osborne, Thomas Rowff, Bernard Cooke, John Rowff, Robert Pearce, John Godfrey, Nicholas Parrett, Thomas Swingarton and 23 other western bargemen by him prested from Wooburn, Penn, Henley, Marlow and thereabouts alongst the river of Thames to serve in Her Highness's brigantines at Deptford, distant 24 miles, at 12d every man – 31s; and more to him for the conduct of John Pearson, Thomas Sandes, Thomas Merrick and 11 other western bargemen by him prested from Windsor, Egham and thereabouts to Deptford, at 6d every man – 7s. *Summa* – £1 18s.

To John Sluttar of Brighton the 15th day of July for the conduct of Joh Awoode, John Elgate, John Taillor, William Searell and 45 other person by him prested from Brighton and thereabouts in Sussex to serve in He Highness's ships at Chatham appointed to the seas, being distant 36 miles at 18d every man – £3 13s 6d; and more to him for the conduct of Willian Treavett, Robert Dunn, Gregory Thorneton and 47 other mariners by hin prested from Arundel, Worthing, Heene, Sidlesham and thereabouts i Sussex to Chatham aforesaid, distant 48 miles, at 2s every man – £5 *Summa* – £8 13s 6d.

To William Barnes, master, the same day for the conduct of Roge Redheade, Robert Pynson, John Dryver, Robert Pope and 13 othe mariners by him prested from London and thereabouts to serve in He Grace's ships at Chatham, distant 24 miles, at 12d every man – 17s; an more to him for the conduct of John Coxe, Robert Odyn, Edward Randal William Swyfte and 24 other mariners by him prested from Erith Rainham, Dartford and thereabouts in Kent to Chatham aforesaid, bein distant 12 miles, at 6d every man – 14s. *Summa* – £1 11s.

[*Page total*] – £12 2s 6d.

[f. 316] To John Dyett, master, the 15th day of July for the conduct c himself, being commanded from London to Portsmouth to serve in He Grace's ship the *Swallow* – 2s 6d.

To Thomas Claye the 16th day of July for the conduct of Thoma Rogers, Thomas Inglishe, Walter Gare, Hugh Deane, Clement Haull an 10 other mariners by him prested from Chichester and thereabouts to serv in Her Highness's ships the *Antelope* and the *Jennet* at Portsmouth, distar 12 miles, at 6d every man – 7s 6d; and more to him for the conduct o James Bridgar, Robert Mytchell and one other mariner by him preste from Arundel and thereabouts to Portsmouth aforesaid, distant 24 miles at 12d every man – 3s. *Summa* – 10s 6d.

To Henry Tirrell, captain, the same day for the conduct of Hugh Bagnol John Fawkoner, George Phillippes and two others of his retinue, bein commanded from London to Portsmouth to serve in Her Majesty's ship th *Saker* there, distant 60 miles, at 2s 6d every of them. *Summa* – 12s 6d.

To John Commyn, master gunner, the same day for the conduct c Thomas Williams, Nicholas Richardes, Philip Jonnes and eight othe gunners by him prested from London to serve in Her Grace's ship th *Falcon* at Chatham appointed to the seas, distant 24 miles, at 12d ever man – 11s.

To Jacob Myller, master gunner, the same day for the conduct c Thomas Irelande, Peter Nealle, John Hull and 16 other gunners preste by him from London and thereabouts to serve in Her Highness's ship th *Swallow* at Portsmouth, distant 60 miles, at 2s 6d every man – £2 7s 6c

To Jerome Hewstar the same day for the conduct of John Haywarde, Thomas Raynolde and eight other mariners by him prested from Gravesend and thereabouts to Deptford to serve in Her Grace's brigantines there appointed to the seas, distant 24 miles, at 12d every man – 10s.

[*Page total*] – £4 14s.

[f. 316v] To Roger Bowthe, master gunner, the 16th day of July for the conduct of William Pantrie, Robert Harvye, John Parker, Richard Shortbridge and 16 other gunners by him prested from London and thereabouts to Portsmouth to serve in Her Grace's ship the *Antelope* appointed to the seas, distant 60 miles, at 2s 6d every man – £2 10s.

To the said Roger Bowthe the same day for the conduct of John Jobson, Simon Kircke, John Dorrell, John Woodrooff and 16 other gunners by him prested from London to Portsmouth to serve in Her Highness's ship the *Jennet*, distant as aforesaid, at 2s 6d every man – £2 10s.

To Thomas Dixson, master gunner, the same day for the conduct of Andrew Sherwood, Ralph Wilson, John Wynner and 21 other gunners by him prested from London to Chatham to serve in Her Grace's ship the *Hope* there, distant 24 miles, at 12d every man – £1 4s.

To John Malpas, master gunner, the same day for the conduct of John Jonson, Davy Appowell, Jeffrey Cowper and 14 other gunners by him prested from London and thereabouts to Chatham to serve in Her Highness's ship the *Willoughby* there, distant as aforesaid, at 12d every man – 17s.

To Thomas Walker [*recte* John], master gunner, the same day for the conduct of Lawrence Danne, Henry Wilkynson and 10 other gunners by him prested from London and thereabouts to Chatham aforesaid to serve in Her Grace's ship the *Rowbarge*, distant as abovesaid, at 12d every man – 12s.

To Lawrence Dilke, master gunner, the 17th day of July for the conduct of William Edmondes, Roger Goose, Michael Twyesadaie and 32 other gunners by him prested from London and thereabouts to Chatham to serve in Her Highness ship the *Elizabeth Jonas* appointed to the seas, distant 24 miles, at 12d every man – £1 16s.

[*Page total*] – £9 9s.

[f. 317] To Edward Tompson, master gunner, the 17th day of July for the conduct of Robert Wallys, William Sheppard, Richard Hoope, John Chawner, and 26 other gunners by him prested from London to Chatham to serve in Her Grace's ship the *Lion* there appointed to the seas, distant 24 miles, at 12d every man – £1 10s.

To Matthew Sharpe, master gunner, the same day for the conduct of William Williams, William Arnolde, Miles Hudson, John Aborans, John Bowthe and 25 other gunners by him prested from London and thereabouts to Chatham to serve in Her Highness's ship the *Philip and Mary*, being distant as aforesaid, at 12d every man – £1 10s.

To William Thomas, master gunner, the same day for the conduct of Hugh Williams, Matthew Price, William Jonnes and 22 other gunners by him prested from London and thereabouts to Chatham aforesaid to serve in Her Grace's ship called the *Victory*, distant as abovesaid, at 12d every man – £1 5s.

To Thomas Nealle, master gunner, the same day for the conduct of Richard Pynson, Richard Freake, and four other gunners by him prested from London to Chatham to serve in Her Grace's galley the *Tryright* there at 12d every man – 6s.

To Maurice Abowen, master gunner, the same day for the conduct of Richard Barrett, Thomas Parker and four other gunners by him prested from London to Chatham aforesaid to serve in Her Grace's galley the *Speedwell*, being distant 24 miles, at 12d every man – 6s.

To William Adams, master gunner, the same day for the conduct of Thomas Browne, Thomas Warlow, Davy Jonnes and three other gunners by him prested from London and thereabouts to Chatham to serve in Her Grace's galley called the *Mermaid*, appointed to the seas, being distant as aforesaid, at 12d every man – 6s.

[*Page total*] – £5 3s.

[f. 317v] To Thomas Kyrton and Oliver Warbeck, surgeons, the 17th day of July for the conduct of themselves and their two servants, being commanded from London to Portsmouth to serve in Her Highness's ship the *Antelope* and the *Jennet* there, being distant 60 miles, at 2s 6d every man – 10s.

To Thomas Graye of Harwich, master, the same day for the conduct of Edward Harryson, John Raynolde, John Graye and 15 other mariners by him prested from Harwich to Chatham to serve in Her Grace's ships there appointed to the seas, distant 36 miles, at 18d every man – £1 7s.

To William Ellys, master gunner, the same day for the conduct of Thomas Davyes, Edward Hopper and three other gunners by him prested from London to Chatham to serve in Her Majesty's ship called the *Su*... appointed to the seas, distant 24 miles, at 12d every man – 5s.

To John Merrick, Richard Willson, John Hawkes, Richard Woode and nine other surgeons[1] the same day for the conduct of themselves and 1... other their servants, being commanded from London to Chatham to serve in divers Her Grace's ships and galleys there appointed to the seas, distant 24 miles, at 12d every man – £1 6s.

[1]One of them probably the surgeon called Glannsfild, reported (18 July) as having sailed with a convoy to Le Havre: SP 12/29, no. 37 (*CSPD 1547–80*, p. 227).

To William Drury, gentleman, captain, the same day for the conduct of Thomas Brewar, Robert Hickinbotoms, Thomas Hartyll, William Walshe, John Thurlowe, William Sherborne, John Abell, Richard Hollande, Flower Dixe, Ralph Spence, William Shakespeare, Robert Sturgis, John Spendall, John Stephenson, George Lewar, William Bosse, Roger Wonstanley, John Thurgoode, John Cartard, Jeffrey Sparrow and 280 other soldiers called from London and thereabouts to Chatham to serve in Her Highness's ships under him at the seas, distant as abovesaid, at 12d every man – £15.

[*Page total*] – £18 8s.

[f. 318] To James Homes, gentleman, captain, the 17th day of July for the conduct of William Youghyns, Thomas Martyn, Richard Bradmate, John Richardson and 96 other soldiers called from London to Chatham to serve in Her Grace's ships under him at the seas, distant 24 miles, at 12d every man – £5.

To John Clark, Richard Connande, Thomas Trigg, John Pettyto and 18 other soldiers the same day for their conduct, being called from Woking, Godalming and thereabouts in Surrey to Chatham aforesaid to serve in Her Highness's ships there appointed to the seas, being distant 50 miles, at 2s 1d every man – 45s 10d; more to Richard Birde for the conduct of himself, William Pittam, Walter Jaxson and 20 other soldiers called from Copthone, Effingham, Tandridge, Reigate, Brixton, Wallington, and thereabouts in Surrey to serve in Her Grace's said ships as aforesaid, distant 30 miles, at 15d every man – 28s 9d. *Summa* – £3 14s 7d.

To Raynold Jeffery the 19th day of July for the conduct of himself, William Boughton, Robert Ramsey, Thomas Bairley and 23 other soldiers called from Uttlesford, Freshwell, Clavering and thereabouts in Essex to Chatham to serve in Her Grace's ships at the seas, distant 40 miles, at 20d every man – 45s; more for the conduct of Gregory Phebrowne, Thomas Slowman and 4 other soldiers from Witham in Essex to Chatham, distant 28 miles, at 14d every man – 7s; more for the conduct of Richard Barker, Richard Birde, Richard Carter, Thomas Wright and 38 other soldiers called from Ongar, Dunmow, Rochford, Dengie and thereabouts in Essex aforesaid to Chatham, distant 26 miles, at 13d every man – 45s 6d; and more to William Hardinge for the conduct of himself, James Wetherall, Henry Jonnes and 14 other soldiers called from Chelmsford and thereabouts in Essex to Chatham aforesaid to be placed in Her Majesty's ships appointed to the seas, distant 20 miles, at 10d every man – 14s 2d. *Summa* – £5 11s 8d.

[*Page total*] – £14 6s 3d.

[f. 318v] To Nicholas Aldaye the 19th day of July for the conduct of himself and 49 other soldiers called from Horsley in Sussex [*recte* Surrey] to Chatham to serve in Her Grace's ships there appointed to the seas under the conduction of the Lord Clinton, High Admiral of England, 36 miles, at 18d every man – £3 15s.

To Maurice Trought the 20th day of July for the conduct of himself, John Rogers, Richard Ryve, John Phillipp, Robert Honnye, Richard Perryman, Thomas Laye and 220 other mariners commanded from London to Portsmouth to serve in Her Highness's ships there, distant 60 miles, at 2s 6d every man – £28 7s 6d.

To Roger Porter the 25th day of August for the conduct of Anthony Wheaton, John Maxe, William Jaye, John James, Robert Mylles and 15 other mariners by him prested from Seaton, Beer, Sidmouth and thereabouts in Devonshire to Portsmouth for the transportation of certain Her Grace's ships there to Gillingham Water, distant 72 miles,[1] at 3s every man – £3; more for the conduct of William Hewe, Edmund Fortune William Merrymouthe, William Good and 20 other mariners by him prested from Dawlish, Kenton, Cockington and thereabouts to Portsmouth distant 84 miles, at 3s 6d every man – £4 4s; more for the conduct of Roger Martyn, John Pyne, Thomas Burnell, Thomas Tewte and 76 other mariners by him prested from West Teignmouth, East Teignmouth Bishopsteignton and divers other places thereabouts to Portsmouth, distant 96 miles, at 4s every man – £16; and more to him for the conduct of John Cooke and Richard Warren, mariners by him prested from Symondsbury[2] to Portsmouth aforesaid, distant 60 miles, at 2s 6d every man – 5s. *Summa* – £23 9s.

To John Sluttar the same day for the conduct of Nicholas Aldaye Thomas Rogers and two other mariners by him prested from Southampton to serve in Her Grace's ships at Portsmouth, distant 12 miles at 6d every man – 2s.

[*Page total*] – £55 13s 6d.

[f. 319] To Thomas Teigoose the 25th day of August for the conduct of himself, George Swane, John Tompson, Edward Crofte and 69 other mariners commanded from Chatham to Portsmouth for the transportation of certain Her Grace's ships there into Gillingham Water, distant 80 miles at 3s 6d every man. *Summa* – £12 15s 6d.

To Francis Brooke the 6th day of September for the conduct of Robert Pollarde, Stephen Standley, John Jordaine, and seven other mariners by him prested from Poole, Purbeck and Wareham in Dorsetshire to Portsmouth for the transporting of Her Grace's said ships, distant 3[illegible] miles, at 18d every man – 15s; more for the conduct of Peter Sayvie, Pete

[1]See below, p. 471.
[2]In Dorset.

Gower, Henry Bowlinge and 14 other mariners by him prested from East and West Lulworth, Sutton, Melcombe Regis, Fleet, and thereabouts to Portsmouth, distant 48 miles, at 2s every man – 34s; and more to him for the conduct of Robert Wilstone, Richard Tabert, Thomas Wood, James Watson and 22 other mariners by him prested from Abbotsbury, Puncknowle, Burton and thereabouts, distant to Portsmouth 60 miles, at 2s 6d every man – £3 5s. *Summa* – £5 14s.

To John Sluttar of Brighton the 19th day of September for the conduct of William Hame, Richard Goodwyne, John Goodwyne and 18 other mariners by him prested from New Shoreham, Lancing, Worthing and thereabouts in Sussex to Portsmouth for the transporting of Her Highness's ships from there to Gillingham Water, distant 36 miles, at 18d every man – 31s 6d; more for the conduct of Thomas Gillbanck, Thomas Carde, Thomas Ellys and 18 other mariners by him prested from Felpham, Selsey, Itchenor and thereabouts in Sussex to Portsmouth, distant 12 miles, at 6d every man – 10s 6d; and more to him for the conduct of John Jaye and Richard Rigate, mariners by him prested from Climping to Portsmouth, being distant 24 miles, at 12d either of them – 2s. *Summa* – £2 4s.

[*Page total*] – £20 13s 6d.

[f. 319v] To Robert Best the 19th day of September for the conduct of John Edwardes, William Jones, Thomas Felton and 12 other mariners by him prested from Southampton, Hythe, Itchen and thereabouts in Hampshire to Portsmouth, distant 12 miles, at 6d every man – 7s 6d.

To Stephen Bull, master gunner, the same day for the conduct of William Fryvewell, James Saunders, Jeffrey Roode, Henry Smart and 56 other gunners by him prested from London, St Katherine's, Greenwich, Deptford and divers other places thereabouts to Portsmouth to serve in Her Grace's ships there, distant 60 miles, at 2s 6d every man. *Summa* – £7 10s.

To Ralph Cockes, master, the same day for the conduct of Roger Tallyoke, Richard Carpentear, Robert Martyn and 34 other mariners by him prested from the Isle of Wight and thereabouts to Portsmouth to serve in Her Majesty's ships there, distant 24 miles, at 12d every man – £1 17s.

To Mark Bullyn the 28th day of September for the conduct of himself, Thomas Ratclyff, Thomas Maye, John Boyes, and 14 other mariners sent from Chatham to the Gore End with two ship boats for the use of Her Highness's ships the *Minion* and the *Primrose* riding there, distant 24 miles, at 12d every man – 18s.

To Thomas Woodcott the same day for the conduct of James Taillour, John Vaughan, George Fullerton and five other mariners by him prested from London and thereabouts to Portsmouth, distant 60 miles, at 2s 6d every man – £1.

To William Tompson, mariner, the same day for the conduct of himself Robert Graye, William Stafforde, John Clarke and 10 other mariners from Ratcliff and thereabouts to Chatham to serve in one of Her Grace's pinnaces there called the *Sun*, distant 24 miles, at 12d every man – 14s.

[*Page total*] – £12 6s 6d.

[f. 320] To Thomas Fullar of Ipswich the first day of October for the conduct of himself, John Snell, John Bomblett and 11 other mariners from Ipswich aforesaid and thereabouts to Chatham, distant 60 miles, at 2s 6d every man – 35s; more to Andrew Waller, Henry Rainesforde, Richard Crannolde and 4 other mariners for their conduct sent from Chatham to Deptford for the fetching from thence of a boat for the use of Her Grace's ship the *Phoenix*, distant 24 miles, at 12d every man – 7s; more to Robert Keye, John Coossen, William Johnson and 12 other mariners for their conduct from Chatham to Deptford aforesaid for the fetching from thence of Her Highness's bark the *Sun* to harbour amongst the rest of Her Majesty's ships there this winter, at 12d every man – 15s. *Summa* – £2 17s.

To John Robynson of Fareham, master, the same day for the conduct of himself, Richard Taigge, John Plonger, John Thressher and Christopher Beverley, mariners, from Fareham aforesaid and thereabouts to Chatham to serve in the *Black Galley*[1] there, distant 84 miles, at 3s 6d every man – 17s 6d.

Anno regni regine Elizabethe sexto

To Thomas Ricardes the 21th day of November for the conduct of himself Nicholas Edwards, Walter Newstub, Thomas Bryan, Richard Kinge Thomas Greffry, Richard Jacob and 80 other mariners sent from Her Grace's ships the *Swallow* and the *Willoughby* at Chatham to Dover by special order to serve in the *Aid* and other Her Highness's ships on the Narrow Seas;[2] being distant 36 miles, at 18d every man – £6 10s 6d.

[*Page total*] – £10 5s.

[f. 320v] To William Drury, captain, for the conduct of himself, being called from Oxford[3] to Chatham for the taking charge of 300 soldier

[1]The *Mermaid*: cf. above, p. 383 & n. 2.

[2]Edwards, Newstub and Bryan certainly came from *Swallow* (cf. above p. 402); the othe three men named do not appear elsewhere in this account.

[3]Drury, younger son of a Buckinghamshire family, acquired property and status i Oxfordshire by marrying the widow of the Marian minister Lord Williams of Thame: *CP. 1560–3*, pp. 141–2. *Hist. Parl. 1509–58*, ii, pp. 59–60. At Le Havre in July 1563, whe serving as the Lord Admiral's emissary to the Captain-General, he was courteously receive by the Prince de Condé and other Huguenot leaders: SP 12/29, no. 50 (*CSPD 1547–80*, p 229). For career details, see *NEM*, p. 539.

serving Her Highness at the seas in Her Grace's ships the *Elizabeth Jonas* and the *Victory*, being distant 84 miles, at 12d every mile – £3 14s; more for the conduct of his lieutenant from Oxford aforesaid to Chatham, distant as abovesaid, at 6d every mile – 37s; more for the conduct of his ensign bearer by like distance, at 3d every mile – 18s 6d; and more for the conduct of three his sergeants, three drums, one fife and a surgeon from Oxford to Chatham abovesaid, distant as aforesaid, at 1d every of them the mile – 49s 4d; *Summa* – £8 18s 4d.

To Robert Constable, captain, for the conduct of himself being called from Newark upon Trent[1] to Chatham for the taking charge of 200 soldiers serving Her Majesty in the *Lion* and in the *Philip and Mary*, distant 120 miles, at 8d every mile – £4; more for the conduct of his lieutenant, at 4d every mile – 40s; more for the conduct of his ensign bearer, at 2d every mile – 20s; and more for the conduct of two sergeants, two drums, a fife and a surgeon from Newark aforesaid to Chatham, being distant as is abovesaid, at 1d every mile for every of them – £3. *Summa* – £10.

To James Hollmes, captain, for the conduct of himself being called from London to Chatham for the taking charge of 100 soldiers serving Her Highness in the *Philip and Mary* and in the *Lion*, being distant 25 miles, at 4d every mile – 8s 4d; more for the conduct of his lieutenant from London aforesaid to Chatham, distant as abovesaid, at 2d every mile – 4s 2d; and more for the conduct of his ensign bearer, sergeant, drum, fife and surgeon, at 1d every of them for the mile – 10s 5d. *Summa* – £1 2s 11d.

[*Page total*] – £20 1s 3d. [f. 321 *blank*]

[f. 321v] **Coat money:**

Anno Domini 1563. Anno regni regine Elizabethe quinto

To Nicholas Aldaie, servant to the Lord Clinton, High Admiral of England, the 27th day of July for the coat money of himself and 59 others, soldiers, his household servants, appointed to serve in the *Elizabeth Jonas* under the said Lord Admiral, then commanded to the seas for the succours of Newhaven, at 4s for every coat. *Summa* – £12.

To William Drury, captain of 300 soldiers, the same day for the coat money of the said 300 soldiers, appointed to serve Her Highness in the *Elizabeth Jonas*, the *Victory* and other Her Majesty's great ships and galleys appointed to the seas under the conduction of the said Lord Admiral for the purpose aforesaid, at 4s for every coat. *Summa* – £60.

[1]Constable had married the widow of a Newark alderman, and established his residence at a property called the Spittal, a former property of St Leonard's hospital in the town: *Hist. Parl. 1559–1603*, i, p. 642; for further career details see *NEM*, pp. 537–8.

To James Holmes, captain of 100 soldiers, the same day for their coat money appointed to serve in the *Lion*, the *Philip and Mary* and other Her Grace's ships at the seas under the same Lord Admiral for the aforesaid purpose, at 4s for every coat – £20.

[*Page total*] – £92.

[f. 322] **Extraordinary. Charges:**

Anno Domini 1562 [1563]. *Anno regni regine Elizabethe quinto*

To John Ellmer, messenger, the 9th day of January for the hire of three his horses from London to Portsmouth for the carriage of Her Highness's treasure for the payment of captains' diets and wages of masters, mariners and gunners serving Her Majesty in six Her Grace's ships and barks at the seas, at 8s every horse – 24s; more to him for his charges remaining there by the space of 15 days attending the coming of the same ships from Newhaven in Normandy, at 12d every day – 15s; more for the charges of his man attending there by like time, at 6d *per diem* – 7s 6d; more for one journey by him made the 27th day of January with letters from the officers of Her Grace's Marine Causes to Captain Malyn at Dover – 20s; and more to him the 31th day of the same month for one other journey with letters from my Lord Admiral to the aforesaid Malyn at Dover – 20s. *Summa* – £4 6s 6d.

*[*Sea charges*]. To Anthony Robynson of Queenborough the 10th day of January for the hire of three his ketches to attend upon the Queen's Majesty's ships the *Hope*, the *Lion* and the *Swallow* by the space of 2 days for the bouying of the Land's End, the Spaniard and the Last[1] for the surer passing of the ships abovesaid over the Land's End, at 6s 8d every boat – 20s; and more to him for the hire of his ketch in giving attendance upon the *Minion* and the *Primrose* over the Land's End at their last going out of the river of Thames – 6s 8d. *Summa* – £1 6s 8d.

To John West of Dover the same day for his charges in bringing of letters from Captain Malyn there to my Lord Admiral; by agreement – 10s.

[*Page total*] – £6 3s 2d.

[f. 322v] To Rowland Mucklowe the 11th day of January for charges by him sustained about the presting of certain watermen within the river of Thames to serve in two Her Highness's brigantines called the *Wolf* and the *Fox*, travailing about the same by the space of 6 days, at 20d every day, as well boat-hire as other charges in the same accounted – 10s.

[1]The Spaniard bank lies about 3 miles NE of Sheppey Land's End. The Last is further east, a mile north of Reculver.

To Thomas Sallmon of Leigh the same day for charges of himself, two men and the hire of a boat which did pass 160 mariners over the river of Thames from Leigh aforesaid in Essex to All Hallows in Kent, which said 160 mariners was fet [*fetched*] out of Essex and commanded to Chatham in Kent for the manning of Her Grace's ships in the month of August last, which ships did then repair to the seas under the charge of Sir William Woodhouse, knight, at 2d every man. *Summa* – £1 6s 8d.

*[*Dover*]. To John Hewson of Dover the same day for charges by him laid out about the repairing and mending of 3 Her Highness's ships and two Her Grace's brigantines, *viz*. the *Greyhound*, the *Phoenix*, the *Hare*, the *Wolf* and the *Fox*, as well for timber, plank, boards, quarters, masts, oars, clench, rove, rings, spikes, overlop nails, bolts and divers other kinds of ironwork, as also to shipwrights working upon the same – £18 8s 5½d.

*[*A ship boat*]. To Gilles Freman of Leigh the same day for price of one boat by him delivered at Portsmouth for the use of Her Grace's ship the *Bark of Boulogne*, who by tempest of foul weather had lost her boat at the seas; price by agreement – £4.

*[*A mast*] To William Courtney of Dover the same day for price of one mast, containing in length 57 foot and in depth 11 inches, had of him for the use of Her Highness's ship the *Phoenix* for a bowsprit for the same ship, who had broken her bowsprit at the seas; by agreement – £1 6s 8d.

[*Page total*] – £25 11s 9½d.

[f. 323] *[*Clerk* deleted]. To Thomas Baker the 12th day of January for the charges of himself and his horse by the space of 32 days travelling from London to Portsmouth, not only to make survey of all the Queen's Majesty's ships there, but also for the making up and engrossing of the Quarter Books ended the last day of December last, at 2s 6d *per diem* – £4.

*[Nota. *The Lord of Hunsdon is to* (deleted)]. *[Nota. *The Queen's Majesty is to have of the Lord of Hunsdon certain woods in Yorkshire for the use of Her Highness's ships, or else he to repay £1,000 which he hath received in part of payment thereof*]. To Thomas Atkynson of London, scrivener, the 10th day of February for the devising, writing and making of an obligation by commandment of the Lord High Treasurer of England and the officers of Her Grace's Marine Causes between the Queen's Majesty and the Lord of Hunsdon[1] wherein the Lord of Hunsdon standeth bound to Her Highness in £3,000, that Her Grace should either have and

[1]Henry Carey, Lord Hunsdon, was a specially favoured courtier, being the Queen's first cousin: *Hist. Parl. 1509–58*, i. pp. 582–3. Most of his estates were around the Hertfordshire place from which he took his title, but for his Yorkshire interest cf. *CPR 1558–60*, pp. 115–18.

enjoy certain his woods in Yorkshire for the use of Her Majesty's ships or else he to repay again to Her Highness £1,000 by him received in part of payment of the said woods; and also for his travel to the court at three several times for the sealing of the same, by agreement – £1.

To William Charnock of London, scrivener, the same day for the writing of a pair of indentures and two obligations made between the officers of Her Highness's Marine Causes and two other men in Sussex for the sale of certain underwoods there called Strudgwick Wood; by agreement – 6s 8d.

To Butolph Moungey the same day for the charges of himself and his man and their 2 horses travelling from Gillingham to London and from thence to Rye at the commandment of the Lord High Admiral of England for the taking survey of Captain Rybaulde's[1] ship there called the *Rowbarge*; which survey of her and her tackle being had, was by him brought back again to the court, to the said Lord Admiral; by the space of 14 days, at 6s 8d *per diem* – £4 13s 4d.

[*Page total*] – £10.

[f. 323v] *[*Rye. Repairing of ships*]. To Butolph Moungey the 16th day of March for charges by him laid out about the rigging, repairing and mending of Her Highness's ship called the *Rowbarge*, as well for timber, masts, pump-hoses, tallow and ironwork of sundry sorts, as also for shipwrights' wages – £10 11s 7d; more to him for the charges of himself, his man and their 2 horses attending at Rye by the space of 25 days for the bringing of the same ship from thence into Gillingham Water, at 6s 8d *per diem* – £8 6s 8d; and more to him for the charges of himself, his man and their 2 horses by the space of 2 days for the fetching of money for the payment of the same, at 6s 8d *per diem* – 13s 4d. *Summa* – £19 11s 7d.

To William Hollande, master of one of the Queen's Majesty's ships,[2] the same day for the charges of himself and his horse from Portsmouth to London after that he had transported from Deptford to Portsmouth aforesaid one of Her Majesty's ships called the *Aid* to serve on the seas – 13s 4d.

To Peter Pett, one of the Queen's Majesty's master shipwrights, the same day for the charges of himself and his horse, with the hire of the

[1]The Huguenot captain Jean Rybaut, best known for his pioneering settlement of Florida in 1562. On his return later that year he was obliged to seek refuge in England, and would renew his colonial ventures with English support: Williamson, *Hawkins* (1927), pp. 76, 96–7, 115–16. In Edward's reign he had served under English colours, though suspicion of his loyalties led to prolonged imprisonment; in Mary's reign he had assisted the English Protestant exiles in France (cf. *CSPDE*, nos 27, 38, 161, 418, 602; *CSPDM*, nos 348, 427, 486, 621). Now Warwick commended his 'good credit and service'; but by July 1563 his reliability as a collaborator was again being questioned: *CSPF 1563*, nos 534, 973.

[2]The *Lion* (as p. 337).

same, sent to Chatham by the space of 8 days at sundry times for the directing of the shipwrights and caulkers there at the grounding, ransacking and caulking of Her Highness's ships against their equipping to the seas in fashion of war, at 3s 4d *per diem. Summa* – £1 6s 8d.

*[*A new barge*]. To Richard Scarllett of Paris Garden, shipwright, the 17th day of March for price of one new barge by him made for the Lord Bishop of Winchester;[1] and is for the answering of one greater barge had from the said Lord Bishop, the which barge was converted to the shape of a brigantine and sent to Newhaven in Normandy to serve the Queen's Majesty there; by agreement – £22.

[*Page total*] – £43 11s 7d.

[f. 324] To John Browne, John Oliver and four others the 18th day of March for their charges, as well in boat-hire and horse-hire as for meat and drink, by the space of 4 days in going from Deptford to Chatham, tarrying there and returning again from thence for a pay there made to masters, mariners, gunners, boatswains and others keeping Her Grace's ships afloat in Gillingham Water. *Summa* – £1 10s 10d.

To John Ellmar, messenger, the same day for the charges of himself and his horse by 4 several journeys travelling from Deptford to Chatham with letters of advertisements for Her Majesty's sea causes from the Lord Admiral and Vice-Admiral to the officers of Her Grace's ships at their groundings and riggings to the sea in fashion of war, at 6s 8d for every journey – 26s 8d; more to him for the travail of himself and his horse, with the charges of the same, being sent from Deptford and the court at Greenwich with letters from the Lord Admiral, Vice-Admiral and other the officers of Her Grace's Marine Causes to Portsmouth to the captains and others serving Her Highness on the seas, by 15 several times, at 20s for every journey – £15; more for the like travail of himself and horse with their charges, being sent with letters from the said Lord Admiral and Vice-Admiral to Dover to the captains of Her Majesty's ships presently serving on the Narrow Seas, by 2 several times, at 20s either journey – 40s; more for the travail of himself, his man and their horses, with their charges, sent from Deptford to Dover to John Hewson there with money for the presting of mariners within the Five Ports to serve in Her Highness's ships to be put to the seas – 30s; more for his travel and horse, with their charges, sent to Margate in Kent with letters from the officers

[1]Robert Horne, bishop 1561–80; his diocese reached to the Thames, and he had a residence at Southwark, close by Paris Garden. An episcopal barge was not a luxury, but Horne evidently had a grand one, perhaps that which had featured in the funeral of his predecessor Lord Chancellor Gardiner: cf. J.A. Muller, *Stephen Gardiner and the Tudor Reaction* (1926), p. 390.

of Her Grace's ships to the captain of the *Phoenix*[1] for a service by him immediately to be done – 20s; and more to him for the hire of a boat with 4 oars at Margate aforesaid for the setting him aboard of the *Phoenix* with the same letters in Margate Roads – 3s 4d. *Summa* – £21.

[*Page total*] – £22 10s 10d.

[f. 324v] *[*Glass windows*]. To John Basing,[2] captain of Her Highness's ship the *Aid*, the 19th day of March for so much by him paid for the making of the glass windows in the cabin of the same ship for the better transporting of such noble personages as from time to time he transported from Portsmouth to Newhaven in Normandy and [*back*] again – 6s; and more to him for the hire of a boat and two French pilots for the safe mooring of the said ship in an extreme tempest at the Seine head – 12s. *Summa* – 18s.

To Rowland Mucklowe the same day for charges by him sustained at divers and sundry times being sent from London to Gillingham with letters to the officers of Her Highness's Marine Affairs there; by agreement – 13s 4d.

To Griffin Hewson, purser of Her Grace's ship the *Phoenix*, the same day for the charges of himself and his horse, with the hire of the same, sent from Dover to the court at Whitehall with letters from the captain of the same ship, and back again – £1.

To William White for his charges the same day being sent with letters from London to Colchester to George Christmas, Vice-Admiral of Essex,[3] and to Edward Lambert of Brightlingsea for the presting and conducting of mariners out of Essex to serve in the Queen's Majesty's ships at Chatham – 10s.

To John Powell the same day for the charges of himself and his horse, with the hire of the same, in carrying of commission and money from London to Brighton to John Sluttar there for the presting and conducting of mariners out of Sussex to serve in Her Grace's ships at Chatham, appointed to the seas – 15s.

To Michael Gonson the same day for the charges of himself and two men for the safe bringing up of one Andrew Breane, mariner,[4] as a prisoner from Rochester to London, to the officers of Her Highness's Marine Causes there, who was by them committed to the Marshalsea for his offences – 4s.

[*Page total*] – £4 0s 4d.

[1]Thomas Gourlay: cf. below, p. 489.

[2]See *NEM*, p. 530.

[3]Christmas was a prominent figure in Colchester, and had represented the borough in Mary's last parliament: *Hist. Parl. 1509–58*, i, p. 647.

[4]*Alias* Brenne, serving aboard *Hope*; see further below, p. 476.

[f. 325] *[*Caulkers*]. To Thomas Hare, captain of the Queen's Highness's ship the *Phoenix*, the 8th day of April for so much by him paid to certain caulkers working upon the same ship, as also for certain bolts and other ironwork in her consumed, with the repairing of 2 compasses and 3 running glasses during her service on the seas in the month of August last past – 15s 2d.[1]

To Jeffrey Vaughan, being an Assistant of the Admiralty, the 20th day of April for the charges of himself and his horses by 3 sundry journeys travelling from London to Portsmouth and there remaining in the service of the Queen's Majesty for her sea causes by the space of 64 days, at 3s 4d *per diem* – £10 13s 4d; and more to him for the charges of his servant by like time of 64 days, at 8d *per diem* – 42s 8d. *Summa* – £12 16s.

To Griffin Hewson, purser of the *Phoenix*, the first day of May for his charges, as well horse-hire as other ways, travelling from London to Portsmouth with Her Highness's treasure for the payment of wages to masters, mariners and gunners serving Her Majesty in the same ship upon the seas; by agreement – 16s.

To James Humphrey the same day for the lading and carrying down to the wharfs in London, and for boat-hire by him sustained about divers stuffs by him provided in London aforesaid at sundry times within the time of this account, to be sent to Chatham, Portsmouth, Woolwich and Deptford – £1 0s 5d.

To Thomas Distar of the Chancery[2] the same day for the writing, engrossing and sealing with the great seal of 4 commissions for William Holstock, Comptroller of Her Grace's ships, as well for the presting of masters, mariners and gunners, and others, to serve Her Highness by sea, as also for taking of provisions needful for Her Majesty's buildings[3] and setting of her ships to the seas – £1 6s 8d.

To Thomas Apparrey the same day for so much by him paid to James Forman, carter, for carrying from London to Portsmouth a money chest with books in it concerning the payments to the Queen's Majesty's ships there – 3s 8d.

[*Page total*] – £16 17s 11d.

[1]Hare now had another command and *Phoenix* a new captain (below, p. 489); but Hare is here reimbursed for his personal expenditure in the previous year and so is described by the post he then held. See above, pp. 235–6, and *NEM*, pp. 549–50

[2]In fact *John* Dyster, perhaps confused with *Thomas* Lutley, with whom he was jointly appointed clerk of the enrolment of indentures in Chancery in 1558: *CPR 1557–8*, p. 461. *Hist. Parl. 1558–1603*, ii, pp. 72–3; cf. W. J. Jones, *The Elizabethan Court of Chancery* (Oxford, 1967), pp. 131, 163 (where he is called Thomas in the first instance).

[3]Plural as MS; but meaning the building of ships, not shore installations.

[f. 325v] To Lancelot Tristram the 16th day of May for his charges, as well horse-hire as other ways, travelling from Chatham to London and from thence sent to Brighton and so alongst the coast to Rye for the presting of 115 mariners sent from Rye aforesaid to Newhaven in Normandy for the bringing of certain French ships from thence to Portsmouth,[1] being occupied about the same business by the space of 10 days, at 4s *per diem* – 40s; more to him for so much paid to John Sluttar and John Stempe for their pains, costs and horse-hire, travailing about the like presting of mariners in sundry places for the furtherance of the said service – 13s 4d; more paid by him to divers officers, as borsholders, tithingmen[2] and others for the carrying of precepts from place to place alongst the coast, with their pains in the premises – 3s 4d; and more to him for his charges being sent from Rye to Newhaven aforesaid with 300 mariners and there by him delivered unto William Winter, Master of the Queen's Majesty's ordnance for the seas and Surveyor of Her Grace's ships, for the service of Her Highness there, remaining about the same by the space of 13 days, at 2s *per diem* – 26s. *Summa* – £4 2s 8d.

To John Hewson of Dover the 17th day of May for his charges, as well horse-hire as other ways, travelling from Dover aforesaid to Folkestone, Lydd, Hythe, Sandwich, Deal, Walmer, Kingsdown, and divers other places thereabouts in Kent for the presting of mariners sent from thence to Rye for the service aforesaid, being occupied about the same by the space of 7 days, at 3s 4d *per diem* – 23s 4d; and more by him paid for 2 letters of attendance had from Dover castle, at 2s 6d the piece – 5s. *Summa* – £1 8s 4d.

To Thomas Claye the same day for one journey by him made with letters from Portsmouth to the court to bring true advertisement of the state of the *Hart* – 15s; and more to him for the charges of himself and his horse, being commanded to give his attendance at London upon the officers of the Admiralty, by the space of 10 days, at 16d every day – 13s 4d. *Summa* – £1 8s 4d.

[*Page total*] – £6 19s 4d.

[f. 326] To Roger Portar the 18th day of May for the charges of himself and his horse, travelling from London into Hampshire and Dorsetshire about the presting of 128 mariners in sundry places thereabouts to Portsmouth to serve Her Highness at the seas in Her Grace's ship the *Swallow,* travailing about the same by the space of 14 days, at 4s *per diem* – 56s; more for so much by him paid to sundry persons for the carrying of precepts into divers

[1] See below, pp. 458–9.

[2] Variant terms for the local officials also known as headboroughs, equivalent to petty constables.

places for the better furtherance of the said service, for their pains in travailing about the same – 6s 8d; and more paid by him to one other man travailing about the like presting of mariners by the space of 7 days within the same time, at 20d *per diem* – 11s 8d. *Summa* – £3 14s 4d.

To Thomas Woodcott the 24th day of May for his charges, as well boat-hire as other ways, travailing about the presting of 84 mariners from London, Deptford, Greenwich and divers other places alongst the river of Thames to serve in Her Grace's ships at Gillingham and Portsmouth appointed to the seas, being occupied about the same by the space of 10 days, at 2s 4d *per diem* – £1 3s 4d.

To John Sluttar the same day for the charges of himself and his horse travailing about the presting of 50 mariners in divers places in Sussex to serve in Her Highness's ships the *Swallow* and the *Jennet* at the seas, being occupied about the same by the space of 10 days, at 3s *per diem. Summa* – £1 10s.

To Lancelot Tristram the 8th day of June for his charges, as well horse-hire as other ways, travailing about the presting of 30 mariners out of sundry places in Kent to serve in Her Highness's ship the *Sun* at the seas, being occupied about the same by the space of 3 days, at 3s 4d *per diem* – 10s; and more for so much by him paid to Thomas Kinge and Richard Sewell for their charges in travailing and assisting him about the presting of the said mariners and coming with them to Chatham; by agreement – 2s. *Summa* – 12s.

[*Page total*] – £6 19s 8d.

[f. 326v] To John Browne the 10th day of June for the charges of himself, John Ellmar, Thomas Baker, Henry Crayforde, with two other and 8 horses travelling from London to Portsmouth with Her Highness's treasure for the payment of captains' diets, wages of masters, mariners and gunners serving in five Her Grace's ships at the seas, *viz.* the *Aid*, the *Saker*, the *Phoenix*, the *Hare* and the *Bark of Boulogne*, remaining there by the space of 4 days about the same, and for their charges returning to London – £4 13s 4d.

To Lancelot Tristram the same day for one journey by him made from Portsmouth to London, from George Winter, Clerk of Her Highness's ships there, with letters to the officers of Her Grace's Marine Causes; by agreement – 10s.

To Roger Bowthe, master gunner, the same day for his charges as well in boat-hire as other ways, travailing about the presting of divers and sundry gunners within the river of Thames to serve at the seas in Her Highness's ships the *Antelope* and the *Jennet*, being occupied in the same business by the space of 5 days; by agreement – 10s.

To Thomas Woodcott the first day of July for his charges as well boat-hire as other ways, travailing about the presting of 242 mariners out of sundry places nigh unto the river of Thames to serve in divers Her Highness's ships at Chatham appointed to the seas, being occupied about the same by the space of 16 days, at 2s 4d every day – £1 17s 4d.

To William Winter, esquire, Master of the Queen's Majesty's ordnance for the seas and Surveyor of Her Grace's ships, the 5th day of July for the hire of 3 post horses taken up for the riding in post from Portsmouth to the court and so back again, being to and fro 120 miles, at 2d the man for every horse – £3; and more for so much given in reward to guides – 6s 8d. *Summa* – £3 6s 8d.

[*Page total*] – £10 17s 4d.

[f. 327] *[*The charges for fetching the French ships from Newhaven*].[1] To James Humphrey the 5th day of July for the victualling of 300 mariners sent from Rye to Newhaven in Normandy for the fetching from thence 15 sail of French ships and bringing them to Portsmouth, by the space of 10 days – £56 8s; more to him for so much paid to John Cheston, master and owner of the *Prymroose of Ryee*, John Rocker, master and owner of the *Mary Grace of Ryee*, and William Guilforde, master and owner of the *William of Ryee*, and Thomas Breades, master and owner of the *Mary Bennett of Ryee*, for the transporting of 275 of the said mariners in the same four barks from thence to Newhaven,[2] at 16d for every man

[1]On 10 May the Queen had instructed the Lord Admiral to prest 300 men and send them to collect such serviceable French ships as could be found at Le Havre: *CSPF 1563*, no. 728. Warwick welcomed this order because the French were burning their own ships rather than let them fall into English hands. He reported (18 May) that 10 or 12 'fair vessels' were in readiness and a number more could be made so, including 'three handsome pinnaces and shallops … which with a little change might be … a great aid to the galley': ibid., no. 754; cf. no. 800. As shown elsewhere here (pp. 436, 499, 508) the operation was carried out between 19 and 31 May and brought back 15 vessels to Portsmouth, of which 10 are specifically identified (*Flower de Luce*, *Green Dragon*, *Greyhound Bitch*, *Gryphon*, *Owlet*, *Red Hart*, *Salamander*, *Serpent*, *Sparrowhawk*, *Three Moons*); the remaining 5 were *Bark of Cherbourg*, *Bear*, *Black Bark*, *Maiden* and *Raven*, listed with the others at Portsmouth at the end of June (pp. 403–5), by which time a commission had already been issued for their sale (p. 470). *Flower de Luce* was probably the RN ship recently lost; *Salamander* may also have been a recovery (see *NEM*, p. 510). *Green Dragon*, *Owlet*, *Serpent* and *Bark of Cherbourg* must have been sold by the end of 1563, because only the 11 others are listed in the victualling account to 31 December: E 351/2360, m. 2. Any of these ships remaining in English hands may have been returned to their French owners when the peace was signed in April 1564.

[2]On 16 July Sir Francis Knollys, Governor of Portsmouth, recommended retaining the hired Rye merchantmen to serve in place of royal ships, specifically the plague-infected *Saker*: SP 12/29, no. 35 (*CSPD 1547–80*, p. 227). Knollys, whose reports are frequently cited here, was primarily a major figure at court (Privy Councillor and Vice-Chamberlain from 1559, Treasurer of the Household 1570 to his death 1596). At Portsmouth during the Le Havre campaign was the main link between the government and the operational command: *ODNB*. *Hist. Parl. 1509–58*, ii, pp. 479–81; *1558–1603*, ii, pp. 409–14.

by agreement – £18 6s 8d; more to him for so much paid to William Paege for carrying a letter of attendance from Rye to Brighton for the presting of mariners there – 5s; more to him for so much paid to Thomas Aske of London[1] for the exchange of £45 in silver into gold for the expedition of the premises, at 1½d every pound changing – 5s 7½d; more to him for the charges of himself and [*his*] horse, with the hire of the same, as well from London to Rye and presting of mariners thereabouts, as also for the providing of victuals and barks for the abovesaid 300 mariners by the space of 10 days, at 4s every day – 40s; more to him for the charges of John Sluttar, his horse and hire of the same, by the space of 8 days, as well in helping of Lancelot Tristram to prest the same mariners in Sussex as in advertising the officers to London[2] of the proceedings of the premises – 10s 8d; more to him for so much given in rewards to the officers of the town of Rye for their pains taken as well in making proclamations as in gathering the mariners together to be shipped – 6s 8d; more for the charges of himself and [*his*] horse, with the hire of the same, sent from London to Portsmouth and back again for the making out of books for the mustering of the mariners and placing of them into certain Her Highness's ships equipped to the seas, by the space of 21 days, at 2s every day – 42s; and more to him for so much paid for price of 6 quires of small paper and 4 quires of paper royal for the said muster books – 4s. *Summa* – £80 8s 7d.

To Thomas Elye, William Hollande and Christopher Nailler the same day for certain charges by them sustained at divers times in presting of mariners and others to serve in Her Grace's ships – £1 10s.

[*Page total*] – £81 18s 7d.

[f. 327v] To Butolph Moungey the 5th day of July for the charges of himself, his man and their 2 horses, with the hire of the same, sent from Gillingham to Portsmouth and so to Newhaven in Normandy for the transporting of 15 sail of French ships from thence to Portsmouth aforesaid, by the space of 27 days, at 6s 8d every day – £9; more to him for certain charges sustained at Newhaven for carrying from out of the town to the said ships certain their tackling and apparel – 46s 8d; and more to him for certain kettles, pots, tankards, dishes, candles and other necessaries provided for the better bringing away of the same ships – 48s 8d. *Summa* – £13 15s 4d.

To Jeffrey Vaughan the same day for the charges of himself, his man and their 2 horses, with the hire of the same, from London to Portsmouth and from thence sent to Newhaven for the bringing away of the said 15

[1] Cf. *Robert* Aske, a London goldsmith active 1561–83: Heal, *Goldsmiths*, p. 97.
[2] That is, sending notice (*advertisement*) to London, to the officers there.

sail of French ships to Portsmouth, and occupied in the same by the space of 24 days; by agreement – £6 13s 4d.

To Edmund Foster the same day for the like charges of himself, his man and their 2 horses, with the hire of the same, sent from London to Portsmouth and from thence to Newhaven for the bringing from thence 15 sail of French ships to Portsmouth, being occupied about the same by the space of 24 days; by agreement – £6 13s 4d.

To Lancelot Tristram the same day for the charges of himself and his horse, riding into sundry places in Kent for the presting of 60 mariners to serve in Her Grace's ships the *Willoughby* and the *Rowbarge*, appointed to serve in the North Seas, travailing about the same by the space of 8 days, at 3s 4d *per diem* – 26s 8d; more paid by him for a letter of attendance had from Dover castle – 2s 6d; and more paid by him to sundry borsholders for their pains and travail in commanding the mariners to appear before the commission – 2s. *Summa* – £1 11s 2d.

[*Page total*] – £28 13s 2d.

[f. 328] To Edward Lambert the 5th day of July for the charges of himself, his man and their 2 horses riding into sundry places in Essex and Suffolk for the presting of 80 mariners to serve in Her Highness's ships at Chatham appointed to the seas, travailing about the same by the space of 7 days, at 3s every man *per diem* – 42s; more for so much by him paid to Edward Spysall for his pains and horse-hire in carrying of a letter from Brightlingsea to Harwich to Francis Brooke there – 2s; more by him paid to the said Francis Brooke for the pains, costs and charges travailing about the like presting of mariners for the speedier furtherance of the said service – 15s; and more by him paid to John Weolde and three other mariners, with the hire of their boat, in rowing of him from Brightlingsea to Bradwell and back again about Her Majesty's said service; by agreement – 5s. *Summa* – £3 4s.

To James Humphrey the same day for the charges of himself and his horse travelling from London to Suffolk for the presting of 130 mariners to serve in Her Highness's ships the *Hope*, the *Willoughby* and the *Rowbarge* appointed to serve in the North Seas, and for the embarking of the same men at Yarmouth, remaining about the same by the space of 18 days, at 4s *per diem* – £3 12s; more paid by him for the hire of a horse from London to Suffolk aforesaid by like time of 18 days, at 16d *per diem* – 24s; more by him laid out to John Markyn of Walton for the charges of himself and his horse riding between Harwich and Yarmouth alongst the coast of Suffolk to give intelligence of the coming of the said ships for the more speedier calling together and embarking of the same men aboard them – 10s; more paid by him to divers persons for carrying of precepts to sundry towns, as also in rewards to the officers of the said towns in seeking out of mariners which absented themselves from the commission – 7s; and more for so much by him paid to Francis Brooke for his pains and charges about the like presting of mariners by the space of 11 days for the better furtherance of the said service, at 3s *per diem* – 30s. *Summa* – £7 3s.

[*Page total*] – £11 7s.

[f. 328v] To Roger Porter the 8th day of July for the charges of himself, one other and their 2 horses travelling from London into Devonshire for the presting of 239 mariners from there to serve the Queen's Majesty in Her Highness's ships at Chatham appointed to the seas, being occupied about the same by the space of 18 days, at 4s the man per diem – £7 4s; more for so much paid by him to Thomas Claye and one other for their charges and horse-hire travelling into Dorsetshire for the presting of 89 mariners sent to Chatham to serve as aforesaid, by the space of 13 days, at 4s every man per diem – £5 4s; and more for the charges of sundry messengers by him sent with letters to divers justices as well in Dorset as in Devonshire for their aid in the premises – 13s 4d. *Summa* – £13 1s 4d.

To Lancelot Tristram the 10th day of July for the charges of him and his horse, travelling about the presting of 134 mariners out of sundry places in Kent and Sussex to serve in divers Her Grace's ships appointed to the seas, by the space of 8 days, at 3s 4d *per diem* – 36s 8d; more for so much by him paid to John Hewson of Dover for his charges and horse-hire riding into Thanet for the like presting of mariners for the said service – 11s 4d; more by him paid for a letter of attendance had from Dover castle – 2s 6d; more paid to William Browne for his charges riding from Dover alongst the coast to Rye with precepts – 4s 6d; and more to him for the hire of post horses from Dover to London, and also for other charges incident to the premises – 10s. *Summa* – £2 15s.

To John Sluttar of Brighton the same day for the charges of himself and his horse travelling about the presting of 100 mariners from divers places in Sussex to serve in Her Highness's ships at Chatham appointed to the seas, being occupied about the same by the space of 12 days, at 3s *per diem* – 36s; and more to him for the charges of himself and his horse riding from Portsmouth to Southampton for the presting of four pilots for the coast of France, by the space of 2 days, at 3s 4d *per diem* – 6s 8d. *Summa* – £2 2s 8d.

[*Page total*] – £17 19s.

[f. 329] To Edward Lambert of Brightlingsea the 10th day of July for the charges of him and his servant travailing about the presting of 147 mariners from sundry places in Essex and Suffolk to serve in divers Her

Grace's ships at Chatham appointed to the seas, by the space of 4 days, a 3s either of them *per diem* – 24s; more by him laid out in expenses upo the justices at Colchester, with 6s given to the bailly there in riding wit precepts for the furtherance of the said service – 35s; more by him paid t Miles Woodles for riding post with letters to my Lord Admiral and the res of the officers of Her Highness's Marine Causes – 13s 4d; more given b him to one man that daily attended upon the justices, writing of letters an precepts, in reward towards his pains – 6s 8d; more by him paid to tw other men which carried letters and precepts from the Lord Rich and th Lord Darcy[1] to the constables of their hundreds – 4s; and more to the sai Edward Lambert for the charges of himself and his servant, with the hir of a ketch and four men for the bringing of William Hixson fro Brightlingsea abovesaid aboard the *Elizabeth Jonas*, riding by nor' th Minster[2] to William Holstock, Comptroller of Her Majesty's Sea Causes then being there, by agreement – 28s 8d. *Summa* – £5 11s 8d.

To William Driver the same day for the charges of himself and tw others, with their horses, travelling from London to Bristol and from thenc to Newport in Wales for the presting of 329 mariners sent to Chatham t serve in Her Highness's ships appointed to the seas, being occupied abou the same by the space of 17 days, at 4s every man *per diem* – £10 4s; mor by him paid to Davy Gyllen and one other for their charges and horse-hir travelling from Bristol to Gloucester, the Forest of Dean and thereabout for the like presting of mariners, by the space of 5 days, at 4s either of the *per diem* – 40s; and more by him paid to Bartholomew Pointer and Thoma Woode for their travail in presting of mariners aboard of divers ships i Hungroad[3] and thereabouts, by the space of 5 days, at 3s 4d either of the *per diem* – 33s 4d. *Summa* – £13 17s 4d.

[*Page total*] – £19 9s.

[f. 329v] To Thomas Baker the 14th day of July for the charges o himself and his horse travailing about the presting of 181 bargemen out o divers places nigh unto the river of Thames and sent to Deptford for th manning of Her Grace's brigantines there appointed to the seas, bein occupied about the same by the space of 4 days, at 3s 4d every day – 13 4d; more paid by him for the hire of a horse for 4 days travelling in th

[1]Richard, 1st Baron Rich, and John, 2nd Baron Darcy of Chiche, were two of the principa justices of Essex, with their seats at Leighs and St Osyth (*alias* Chiche), respectively. O 30 June the Privy Council had ordered Rich to implement a scheme devised by the Esse justices for raising 1,000 men: SP 12/29, no. 10 (*CSPD 1547–80*, p. 225).

[2]Minster in Sheppey.

[3]The roadstead serving the port of Bristol, at the bend of the Avon two miles south of it entry into the Severn Estuary: EPNS, *Glos*, iii, pp. 131–2 (where the editor surmise derivation from the Middle English *honge* to mean the place where ships rested, or possibl inclined on the mud waiting for the tide – as small craft still do at that point).

same journey – 6s; more paid for boat-hire within the river of Thames at 3 several times, rowing about the presting of bargemen as they came into the river of Thames and went out of the same – 2s 8d; more paid to a tilt-boat[1] at Kingston to row after a barge that came to London, and for ferryage at divers places – 2s 6d; and more by him paid to a guide alongst from Hedsor to Reading, as also to the constables and under officers of the villages for their travail about the said service – 2s 6d. *Summa* – £1 7s.

To Lawrence Dilke, master gunner, the same day for charges by him sustained as well in boat-hire as other ways travailing about the presting of gunners to serve in Her Grace's ships the *Hope*, the *Willoughby* and he *Rowbarge* at their going to the sea; by agreement – 10s.

To Thomas Claye the 15th day of July for the charges of himself and his horse, being sent from London to Portsmouth with letters from the Lord Admiral to John Basing, captain of Her Highness's ship the *Aid*,[2] by agreement – 13s 4d; more to him for one journey by him made the 17th day of August with letters from Portsmouth to London from William Holstock, Comptroller of Her Grace's ships, to the officers of the Admiralty, by agreement – 7s 6d; more for one other journey by him made with letters from the officers of Her Majesty's Sea Causes then at Portsmouth to the Lord Admiral at the court at Windsor – 26s 8d; more to him for the charges of himself and his horse the 6th day of September travelling from Portsmouth to Windsor, the court being there, with letters from William Holstock to the Lord High Admiral of England – 20s; and more to him for one other journey the 27th day of September with letters to the Lord Admiral and the officers of Her Grace's Marine Affairs for bringing advertisement of the arriving of Her Majesty's great ships from Portsmouth – 13s 4d. *Summa* – £4 0s 10d.

[*Page total*] – £5 17s 10d.

[f. 330] *[*Dover. Masts – 66s 8d*; boards and such other timber – £4* <14 corrected to> *4s 10d*; *anchor – 100s 5d*; *broom, oil and tallow – £4 ·s 4d*; *shipwrights* – <43s 1d corrected to> *71s 6d*] To John Hewson of Dover for certain needful things by him provided for Her Highness's ships serving upon the Narrow Seas, and for certain necessary reparations done pon the said ships' boats there, *viz.* first for a flag of St George and 2

[1] A vessel with an awning, commonly used as passenger transport on the Thames.

[2] Basing, who had been captain of and Admiral aboard *Aid* until 31 May, had transferred is command and flag to *Swallow* on 1 June (below, pp. 488, 498). The Lord Admiral eported from the Downs on 26 July that Basing's successor as captain of the *Aid*, John Henshaw, had taken letters from Warwick to the court: SP 12/29, no. 44 (*CSPD 1547–80*, . 228). From Portsmouth on 29 July Sir Francis Knollys transmitted (further) letters from Warwick and Basing, as captain of *Swallow*, to the Privy Council: SP 15/11, no. 104 (*CSPD Addenda 1547–65*, p. 539).

small masts for the *Sun* and the *Searcher* – £3 6s 8d; more for a piece of timber to fish the *Bark of Boulogne*'s mainmast, for sawing of the same, for 12 pounds weight of spikes and 2 quarters of tar – 15s; more for 3 cloveboards, half a 100 of rove and clench, one small knee, one quarter of a 100 of inch board, 20 pounds of pitch, and broom to bream the ship boat with – 11s 7d; more for half a 100 of inch board, 3 cloveboards, half 100 of clench, and certain other ironwork for the *Phoenix*'s boat –18s 3d; more for 3 cloveboards, 3 quarters of rove and clench, a ring-bolt, and for mending the *Aid*'s meat kettle, and for a piece of timber to mend her skiff – 12s 10½d; more for an anchor, an anchorstock, a quarter of trenails for mending the chains, for 2 new chains and for a boat hook and a luff hook for the *Falcon* – £5 0s 5d; more for broom, oil, tallow, thrums, timber and sawing of the same at the grounding of the *Bark of Boulogne*, and for a new main top for her – £4 6s 4d; more for rove, clench, cloveboards, inch board, timber, broom and suchlike for the breaming of the *Falcon*'s boat at another time – 27s 1d; more for the wages and victuals of Robert Ellyson, Hugh Bedoe, Henry Poore, Almaine Drake, shipwrights, and their servants, working upon the foresaid ships and their boats at divers times – 44s 1d; more to the said John Hewson for his charges and hire of a horse from Dover to Deptford for the making up of his account for the premises – 20s; more to the same John Hewson for the charges of himself and his horse, with the hire of the same, travelling to Folkestone and Hythe for the presting of mariners there to serve in her Her Highness's ships then in the Narrow Seas, by the space of 2 days, at 2s *per diem* – 4s and more to him for the taking out of a letter of attendance for the presting of men within the Cinque Ports – 2s 6d. *Summa* – £20 9s 4d.

To Patrick Sealle, Thomas Kyrton and Oliver Warbeck, surgeons, for their charges and hire of a horse among them to carry part of their needful things to Portsmouth – 10s.

[*Page total*] – £20 19s 4d.

[f. 330v] To William Winter, Master of the Queen's Majesty's ordnance for the seas and Surveyor of Her Highness's ships, as well for the hire of 6 horses for himself, his four men and guide, sent in post from the court at Westminster to Portsmouth and from thence to Newhaven in Normandy to the Lord Deputy there, as also for the hire of 6 other horses at his return from thence for himself, his men and guide from Portsmouth to the court at Westminster aforesaid – £6 10s; and more to him for his diets and charges of his men in the same journey by the space of 14 days, at 13s 4d for every day – £9 6s 8d. *Summa* – £15 16s 8d.

To John Hollawey of Portsmouth the 16th day of July for the hire of his bark called the *Mynnyon of Portesmouthe* for the transporting from

Portsmouth aforesaid the abovesaid William Winter to Newhaven, all Her Highness's ships then being there, by agreement – £3 16s 8d.

To Thomas Apparrye the same day for the charges of himself and his horse, with the hire of the same, sent to the court with letters and estimate for money for payment of certain the Queen's Majesty's ships commanded from the seas to be discharged, and tarrying there for answer, by the space of 8 days, at 4s *per diem* – 32s; more for his charges, with the hire of a horse, sent to the court at Windsor with letters and another estimate for money to be obtained for the discharge of the Queen's Highness's great ships, come from Portsmouth and arrived at Chatham, by the space of 4 days, at 4s *per diem* – 16s; and more to him for so much paid to certain mariners of Rye for the lading from out of a cellar there the tackle, sails and apparrelage belonging to the *Greyhound*, lately by misfortune lost there, and for the charges of himself and his horse, with the hire of the same, during the time of lading thereof into a ship of Giles and Robert Graye's – £3 6s 8d. *Summa* – £5 14s 8d.

[*Page total*] – £25 8s.

[f. 331] To John Ellmar, messenger, for the charges of himself and his horse being sent to Chatham with letters as well to the masters of Her Highness's ships there as also to the officers of Her Grace's Marine Causes for the putting of all things in good order, and for the manning of the same ships against the coming of the Lord Admiral thither at his going to the seas with the *Elizabeth Jonas*, the *Victory* and other Her Majesty's great ships, by 5 several journeys within the same time – 33s 4d; more to him for 3 other journeys with letters, the one to Brightlingsea, the other to Portsmouth, and the third with money to Rye, at 20s for every journey – £3; more to him for giving his attendance at Rye by the space of 2 days for the delivery of the said money, by order to the mayor there – 5s; more to him for one journey with letters from the Queen's Majesty to Sir Thomas Cotton, knight, at Oxen Hoath in Kent for his repair to the court to receive Her Highness's instructions to go to the sea withal – 6s 8d; more to him for the charges of himself and his horse, as well for the carrying of letters for Her Highness's sea causes and marine affairs, as also for the charges of his man with the hire of 8 horses and charges of the same, sent to Portsmouth with John Browne, John Powell and 2 others for the carrying of Her Highness's treasure for the payment of captains' diets and wages of masters, mariners and gunners and soldiers discharged out of Her Highness's ships there – £5 11s 8d;[1] more to him for the charges of himself, his man and 6 horses, with the hire of the same, sent

[1]On 2 Aug. Knollys warned that there was no money at Portsmouth to pay the discharged troops: SP 12/29, no. 58 (*CSPD 1547–80*, p. 229).

from London to Portsmouth with money against the coming of the Lord Admiral with Her Highness's ships from Newhaven in Normandy, for the discharge of him and divers others discharged out of Her Grace's ships there – £3 13s 10d; more to him for 3 several journeys by him made with letters from the Lord Admiral and the officers of Her Grace's Marine Causes to Portsmouth to Thomas Morley there, *viz*. the 28th, 29th and 31 of July,[1] at 20s every journey – £3. *Summa* – £17 10s 6d.

[*Page total*] – £17 10s 6d.

[f. 331v] To the aforesaid John Elmar, messenger, for 2 journeys by him made from London to Portsmouth with letters the 5th and 12th day of August from the officers of Her Highness's Marine Causes to Thomas Morley there, at 20s for either journey – 40s; more to him for 3 several journeys with letters the 15th, 18th, and 21th day of August from the officers of Her Grace's said causes to Thomas Heynos at Chatham, at 6s 8d every journey – 20s; more for one journey with letters from Deptford to Portsmouth to George Winter, Clerk of Her Grace's ships – 20s; more to him for the hire of 5 his horses from Deptford to Chatham for the carrying of Her Highness's treasure for the payment of 2 Her Grace's galleys and two brigantines, their companies discharged the 26th day of August, at 5s every horse – 25s; more to him for his charges attending there by 2 days, at 12d *per diem* – 2s; more for his servant attending like time – 12d; and more to him for one other journey with letters from Deptford to Portsmouth the 29th day of August to the said George Winter, Clerk of Her Majesty's ships – 20s. *Summa* – £6 8s.

To Griffin Hewson, purser of Her Grace's ship called the *Phoenix*, the 17th day of July for his charges being sent from London to Portsmouth with letter from the officers of Her Grace's Marine Causes to Thomas Morley, Clerk of Her Highness's storehouses; by agreement – 6s 8d.[2]

To Thomas Jobson, mariner, the same day for his charges sent from London to Dover with letters from the officers of Her Grace's ships to John Hewson there, by agreement – 6s.

[1]Reflecting the intense activity at the end of July when, after attempts to reinforce Le Havre had been thwarted by bad weather, plague and the approach of the French, the operation was aborted and the troops were withdrawn. The terms of surrender were drawn up on 28 July, and were explained in a proclamation of 1 Aug.: *CSPF 1563*, no. 1081. *TRP*, ii, pp. 229–31 (no. 510). See generally SP 12/29, nos 41–58 (*CSPD 1547–80*, pp. 228–9).

[2]Morley's operation at Portsmouth was commended by Knollys (16 July), in seeking for confirmation of his decision to take the victualling of troopships away from Baeshe's hard-pressed agent and make Admiralty staff directly responsible: 'the ready way only of transportation of soldiers over is to have the vessels … under the charge, for victualling and all respects, of the officers of the Admiralty, who are so ready and skilful herein, and namely Mr Morley, Clerk of the Admiralty, that I could not possibly have transported those soldiers with such speed as hath been done if I had not used his service': SP 12/29, no. 35 (*CSPD 1547–80*, p. 227).

To William Dutton the same day for his charges sent from Portsmouth to London with letters from William Holstock, Comptroller of Her Grace's ships, to the officers of the Admiralty – 8s 4d.

To Jerome Hewstar the same day for his charges as well boat-hire as other ways travailing about the presting of mariners to serve in Her Grace's ships, by the space of 3 days, at 2s every day; by agreement – 6s.

[*Page total*] – £7 15s.

[f. 332] *[*Yarmouth. Repairing of ships – £6 13s 4d*; *riding charges – £7* <8s 7d corrected to> *10s*]. To John Goslynge of Yarmouth for so much by him paid to William Garton of the same town for price of [*one*] hundred 3 quarters 21 pounds weight [*217 lbs*] of flat lead, at 12s the hundred[*weight*] – 23s 3d; more for 550 [*foot*] of inch board, at 7s every 100 [*foot*] – 38s 6d; more for 2 small masts and carriage of them to the waterside – 20s 2d; more to him for so much paid to Anthony Lovedaie of Yarmouth aforesaid for 3 pieces of compass and straight timber – 14s; more to him for so much paid to Bennet Kewbett of Yarmouth for 4 ox-hides, at 6s every hide – 24s; more to him for so much paid to Nicholas Fenn of the same town for half 100 of trenails – 10d; more to him for so much paid to Thomas Osborne of Yarmouth, smith, for the new making of 2 bolts and 2 forelocks[1] – 12d; more to him for so much paid for 8 sawed spars – 2s 8d; more to him for the wages and victuals of George Tompson, Edmund Ladd and three other shipwrights by the space of one day in mending the *Mary Willoughby* her boat – 6s 10d; more to him for so much paid to the said William Garton for price of 28 pounds of white oakum – 2s 6d; more to him for so much paid to the said Garton for price of 5 Norway deals, one topmast and 5 fir spars for pumpstaves – 21s 8d; more to the said Goslinge for the charges and travail of Andrew Mytchelson, Thomas Baker and Thomas Pidgyon in presting of mariners upon the coast of Norfolk and Suffolk to serve in the Queen's Majesty's ships upon those seas, by the space of 5 days every of them – 33s 4d; and more to the same Goslinge for the charges of himself and his horse, with the hire of the same, travailing about the presting of mariners at divers towns alongst the coast for the better manning of Her Highness's ships named the *Hope*, the *Rowbarge* and the *Willoughby*, appointed to remain upon that coast for the scouring of those seas of enemies and for the wafting of the Iceland fleet;[2] and for his travail in coming to London for the clearing of his account – £5. *Summa* – £14 8s 9d.

[1]Pins or wedges for securing bolts.

[2]Cf. *CSPF 1563*, no. 1088, reporting (30 July) that two merchantmen had been despatched from King's Lynn to meet and join the Iceland fleet.

To Thomas Woodcott for his boat-hire and travail sustained in presting of certain mariners from out of divers ships in the river of Thames to Portsmouth – 12d.

[*Page total*] – £14 9s 9d.

[f. 332v] To Roger Lappington, gunner, the 18th day of July for his charges in bringing of letters from Portsmouth to London to the officers of Her Highness's Marine Causes there about the Queen's affairs; by agreement – 5s.

To Richard Tolkyn the same day for the charges of himself and his horse, with the hire of the same, riding from London to Portsmouth with letters from the officers of the Admiralty to William Holstock, Comptroller of Her Grace's ships there – 13s 4d.

To William Winter, Master of the Queen's Majesty's ordnance for the seas, the 20th day of July for the hire of 3 post horses taken up for the riding in post from Portsmouth to the court and back again, being to and fro 120 miles, at 2d a mile for every horse – £3; and more for so much by him given in rewards to guides in the same journey – 6s 8d. *Summa* – £3 6s 8d.

To John Browne the 27th day of July for the charges of himself, John Elmar and four others with their 6 horses, travelling from London to Portsmouth with Her Highness's treasure for the payment of captains' diets, wages of masters, mariners, gunners, soldiers and others serving in Her Grace's ships at the seas appointed for the succours of Newhaven – 50s;[1] and more to the said John Browne for the hire of a horse from Portsmouth to London, with his charges by the way, being sent for by the officers of Her Majesty's Marine Causes for the discharge of two Her Highness's galleys and two brigantines, and so returned back again to Portsmouth aforesaid – 30s. *Summa* – £4.

To Thomas Baker the same day for the charges of himself and his horse, travelling from Portsmouth to Reigate, and commanded back again by Benjamin Gonson, Treasurer of Her Grace's Marine Affairs, for a further service by him there to be done – 15s.

[*Page total*] – £9.

[f. 333] To Ralph Chamberlain, captain of the Queen's Majesty's ship the *Hope*, the 20th day of August for so much by him paid to 26 Scottishmen with their 10 cobles[2] or boats in helping to recover and save the ordnance, tackle and apparel of the *Rowbarge*, one of Her Highness's

[1]From Portsmouth on 28 July Knollys reported his decision that no more treasure than absolutely necessary should be shipped to Le Havre, to avoid augmenting the enemy's spoil when the expeditionary force withdrew: SP 12/29, no. 48 (*CSPD 1547–80*, p. 228).

[2]Flat-bottomed fishing boats used in Scotland and on the north-east coast of England.

ships, lost by misfortune in the North Seas, and for helping of the *Hope* and the *Mary Willoughby*, being grounded on the rocks there, at 10s every coble or boat – £5.

To James Humphrey the same day for the charges of himself and his horse, with the hire of the same, for the discharge and setting a-land out of Her Highness's ships that served northwards certain mariners for the wafting and safety of the Iceland fleet this summer, and for sending the *Hope* to Chatham to be discharged; as also for putting the *Mary Willoughby* into order for the wafting of the herring fishing, by the space of 14 days begun the 7th day of August and ended the 20th day of the same, at 4s every day – £2 16s.[1]

To William Pattrick the same day for his charges sent from Deptford with letters to Leigh in Essex to Thomas Salmon of Leigh aforesaid to prepare himself, his ketch and certain others to be ready with the same at the South Foreland to wait upon the Queen's Majesty's great ships at their comings from Portsmouth through the Channel to Chatham, where as the same ships were appointed to harbour – 8s 8d.

To Baptist Dyar, shipwright, the same day for certain charges by him sustained, as well in ironwork, timber and canvas, for repairing and amending of one of Her Majesty's brigantines named the *Searcher*, being spoiled in the Narrow Seas by tempest of foul weather – 15s.

[*Page total*] – £8 19s 8d.

[f. 333v] *[*Portsmouth*]. To William Holstock the 20th day of August for so much by him laid out for the trimming of the great boat and the cock appertaining to Her Highness's ship the *Philip and Mary*, as well for ironwork as broom with other needful things at 2 several times – £1 9s 2d.

To Thomas Baker the same day for his charges, as well horse-hire as boat-hire, travelling from London to Chatham about the placing of 80 mariners and gunners in divers Her Majesty's ships to serve Her Highness at the seas, being occupied about the same by the space of 7 days, at 2s 6d every day – 17s 6d.

To James Gentyll the same day for his charges travelling from Deptford to Chatham and giving his attendance there by the space of 12 days in receiving of mariners and gunners prested from divers places, and for placing them into the *Elizabeth Jonas*, the *Victory*, the *Lion*, the *Philip and Mary* and three galleys equipped to the seas in fashion of war, at 2s 6d for every day – £1 10s.

[1]Cf. Lord Admiral's letter to Cecil of 20 Aug. forwarding reports from Sir Thomas Cotton and Holstock (16 and 17 Aug.) about ships recently damaged by storm: HMC, *Salisbury*, i, p. 279.

To Butolph Moungey the same day for the charges of himself, his man and their horses travelling from Gillingham to Portsmouth, and from thence to Newhaven in Normandy to join with William Winter and Jeffrey Vaughan in commission for certain service by them to be done there,[1] being occupied about the same by the space of 25 days, at 3s 4d every of them by the day – £8 6s 8d.

To Peter Pett, Edmund Bright, master shipwrights, William Barnes, mariner and master of one of the Queen's Majesty's ships,[2] for their horse-hire and charges from London to Portsmouth and [*back*] again, sent thither for the praising[3] of certain French ships of Her Highness's there, being occupied about the same by the space of 8 days, at 30s every of them. *Summa* – £4 10s.

[*Page total*] – £16 13s 4d.

[f. 334] To Thomas Salmon of Leigh in Essex for the charges of himself, two men and one boy, with the hire of his ketch, by the space of 4 days in conveying from Leigh aforesaid to Chatham in Kent to the Queen's Majesty's ships there at their equippings to the seas 186 mariners, at 2d every of them – 31s; and more to him for the hire of two ketches, with the wages of six mariners serving in the same, giving their attendance upon Her Highness's ships through the Swin and amongst the sands until they were clear and past the danger of the said sands at their going to Portsmouth; by agreement – £5. *Summa* – £6 11s 0d.

To Richard Skarlett for his charges travelling upon the Thames in divers places, as well for the presting of shipwrights and sawyers as divers other artificers and workmen commanded to Deptford to Her Grace's works there; by agreement – 6s 8d.

To John White of the Isle of Wight for his charges in conveying from Portsmouth aboard the *Mynnekin*, being at anchor at the East Cow in the Isle of Wight, William Winter, his brother George Winter and their companies to be transported to Newhaven[4] – 3s.

[1]They were appointed on 27 June to negotiate sales to the Queen's own subjects of French ships taken at Le Havre: *CSPF 1563*, no. 949; cf. above, p. 458 & n. 1. Moungey was killed when he accompanied Winter to a conference with Warwick on 19 July (ibid., no. 1024), so this payment dated 20 Aug. was a posthumous settlement. The circumstances of Moungey's death are also reported in the Lord Admiral's despatch of 24 July: SP 12/29, no. 41 (*CSPD 1547–80*, p. 228). The boatswain of *Antelope* is there said to have been killed by the same great piece of ordnance, but it will be seen that Richard Wright continues in pay for this post: cf. above, pp. 401, 416, 424.

[2]The *Victory*: above, p. 415.

[3]I.e. appraising.

[4]William Winter sailed on at 9 a.m. on 27 July aboard *Phoenix*, in company with *Falcon* to assist the evacuation of Le Havre: SP 12/29, no. 45; cf. nos 49, 51 (*CSPD 1547–80*, pp 228–9).

To the widow of John Malyn, late captain of the *Greyhound*,[1] and to John Spritwell of Dover, posted there for the sending of letters at divers times from the captains of the Queen's Majesty's ships serving in the Narrow Seas to the officers of Her Highness's Marine Causes at Deptford – £1 5s.

To Thomas Woode for his travail and charges sent from London to Chatham to Lancelot Tristram with money and commission for the presting of mariners in Kent to serve in divers the Queen's Majesty's ships appointed to the seas – 5s.

[*Page total*] – £8 10s 8d.

[f. 334v] To George Irelande and Ralph Cockes, masters, the 6th day of September for their charges sustained in riding to Portsmouth for the bringing of two Her Grace's ships called the *Minion* and the *Primrose* into Gillingham Water, at 13s 4d either of them – 26s 8d;[2] and more to the said Ralph Cockes for his charges as well boat-hire as other ways in travelling to Southampton, the Isle of Wight and thereabouts for the presting of mariners to transport Her Grace's said ships into Gillingham Water aforesaid, being occupied about the same by 4 days, at 3s 4d *per diem* – 13s 4d. *Summa* – £2.

To John Browne the 15th day of September for the charges of himself, Richard Browninge and one other with their 3 horses riding from Portsmouth to Deptford after that he had made payment to Her Grace's ships there – 21s 8d; and more for so much by him paid for the hire of the said 3 horses from Portsmouth to Deptford aforesaid, at 8s for every horse – 24s. *Summa* – £2 5s 8d.

To John Sluttar of Brighton the 19th day of September for the charges of himself and his horse travelling into sundry places in Sussex for the presting of 52 mariners sent to Portsmouth for the transportation of Her Highness's ships from thence into Gillingham Water, being occupied about the same by the space of 4 days, at 3s 4d *per diem* – 13s 4d; and more for so much by him paid to John Stempe for his pains and charges travailing about the like presting of mariners for the furtherance of the said service by 4 days, at 2s *per diem* – 8s. *Summa* – £1 1s 4d.

[1]It is presumed that the captain died when his ship was driven on to the bar at Rye (above, p. 465; below, p. 481). On 11 Aug. his widow Elizabeth was granted a property in Clerkenwell for 21 years at a rent of £10 10s *per annum*; but this was in reversion to a lease granted in 1538 which would not have fallen in until Lady Day 1579: T. Glasgow jnr, 'John Malen, forgotten hero at Gravelines, 1558', *MM*, LIII (1967), p. 32. *CPR 1560–3*, p. 503.

[2]On the previous day the Lord Admiral had been ordered to remove *Elizabeth Jonas*, *Victory*, *Minion*, *Primrose* and *Philip and Mary* from Portsmouth to Gillingham under the command of Sir Thomas Cotton: HMC, *Salisbury*, pp. 281–2.

To Thomas Wilkes the same day for his pains and charges in carrying of letters from Portsmouth to Deptford to the officers of Her Grace's Marine Causes there – 6s 8d.

[*Page total*] – £5 13s 8d.

[f. 335] To Robert Beast, purser,[1] the 20th day of September for his charges as well horse-hire as other ways in travelling to Southampton and thereabouts for the presting of mariners for the transportation of Her Grace's ships from Portsmouth haven into Gillingham Water; by agreement – 9s 8d,

To Stephen Bull, master gunner, the same day for his charges as well boat-hire as other ways travailing about the presting of gunners from London and thereabouts to serve in Her Grace's great ships at Portsmouth, for the transportation of the same ships from thence into Gillingham Water, being occupied about the same by the space of 3 days, at 3s 4d *per diem* – 10s.

To Roger Porter the same day for the charges of himself, one other and their 2 horses sent from Portsmouth into Devonshire for the presting of 125 mariners from sundry places thereabouts to serve in Her Grace's great ships for the transporting of them from Portsmouth haven into Gillingham Water, travailing about the same by the space of 16 days, at [*each man*] 3s 4d *per diem* – £5 6s 8d; and more for so much by him paid alongst the coast to constables, tithingmen and other officers in divers towns for the carrying of precepts for the furtherance of the said service – 5s 4d. *Summa* – £5 12s.

To Francis Brooke for his charges serving Her Highness under William Holstock, Comptroller of Her Grace's ships, at his being at the seas, as well for the mustering of companies serving in her said ships, as also travailing about other necessary affairs for the same, by the space of 83 days, at 8d for every day – 55s 4d; more for the charges of himself and his horse, with the hire of the same, sent from Portsmouth to Lyme in the West Country for the presting of mariners to serve in Her Majesty's ships for the succours of Newhaven, travailing about the same by the space of 16 days, at 3s 4d every day – 53s 4d; and more to him for so much paid to divers men for the carrying of precepts to sundry towns for the better appearance of mariners at the musters – 3s 4d. *Summa* – £5 12s.

[*Page total*] – £12 3s 8d.

[f. 335v] *[Harwich. Shipwrights. Boards, broom, thrums, pitch Ironwork. Poldavy]* To Edward Lambert of Brightlingsea the 20th day of September for charges by him laid out about the repairing and

[1]Of *Green Dragon*: see above, pp. 412, 447, where the name is *Best*.

amending of two Her Grace's ships and their boats, the *Swallow* and the *Willoughby*, at Harwich, being spoiled by tempest of foul weather at the seas, *viz.* for the wages and victuals of eight shipwrights working upon the said ships by the space of 48 days among them all, at 13d every man *per diem* – 52s; more for price of 21 cloveboards, at 8d the piece – 14s; more for 2 loads of broom, price – 4s; more for price of 11 pounds of thrums, at 4d every pound – 3s 8d; more for 4 barrels of pitch, at 8s every barrel – 32s; more for price of [*one*] hundred one quarter 9 pounds weight [*149 lbs*] of bolts, rings, spikes, overlop nails, clench, rove and other sorts of ironwork for the use of the said ships, at 23s 4d the hundredweight – 31s;[1] more for price of one bolt of poldavy canvas for the mending of the sails of the same ships, by agreement 40s; and more to the said Edward Lambert for the charges of himself, his man and their 2 horses travailing about the providing of the same provisions, by the space of 5 days, at 3s either of them *per diem* – 30s. *Summa* – £10 6s 8d.

To Richard Kynge of Harwich the 23th day of September for the charges of himself and his horse, with the hire of the same, in riding post with letters from Harwich aforesaid to Deptford to the officers of Her Grace's Marine Causes there about Her Highness's affairs, and for his charges being sent back again with answer of the same – 13s 4d.

To Thomas Apparrey, John Elmar and Davy Langford for their boat-hire, horse-hire and other charges sustained at the discharge of the *Galley Speedwell* and the *Galley Tryright* at Chatham, by the space of 4 days in going from Deptford thither and tarrying there in paying the aforesaid galleys, and coming back again – £1 15s 4d.

To Thomas Sabot the 24th day of September for so much by him paid for mending of the rudder iron of one of Her Grace's brigantines called the *Makeshift*,[2] the which was broken at the sea in foul weather – 4s.

[*Page total*] – £12 19s 4d.

[f. 336] To Thomas Baker, servant to William Holstock, Comptroller of Her Highness's ships, for so much by him paid to Roger Parker, Clerk of the Admiralty,[3] for making and writing out of 35 precepts to sundry towns alongst the river of Thames, to the officers there, for the bringing of all able watermen to the musters at Deptford to be placed into Her Majesty's galleys and brigantines at their setting to the sea – 40s; more to him for so much paid to Henry Bullen, Under-marshal of the Admiralty, for his pains and travail to see the said precepts delivered to the officers

[1]The calculation gives 372.5d, which is ½d above the sum stated (372d).

[2]Sabot had commanded the ship from mid-July to mid-August: below, p. 491.

[3]A notary public and later Registrar of the High Court of Admiralty: cf. *CSPD 1547–80*, p. 337; *CPR 1563–6*, no. 2411; *1575–8*, no. 2600.

of the same towns for the better appearances of the said watermen at Deptford – 20s; and more to him for so much paid to Henry Abraham of Deptford for a dinner for the same Roger Parker and others at the general musters there – 26s 8d. *Summa* – £4 6s 8d.[1]

*[*Sea charges*]. To Thomas Salmon of Leigh in Essex for the hire of his crayer with the wages and victuals of himself and seven other mariners attending upon Her Highness's great ships at their coming from Portsmouth amongst the sands, for the avoiding the danger of the same at their comings into Queenborough Water, by the space of 8 days; by agreement – £5.

To John Browne the 6th day of October for the charges of himself, John Elmar, Thomas Apparrey, with two others and 6 horses, travelling from Deptford to Chatham with Her Highness's treasure for the payment of captains' diets, wages of masters, mariners and gunners serving Her Majesty in Her Grace's great ships for the transportation of them from Portsmouth haven into Gillingham Water, remaining about the same by the space of 3 days – £2 3s 4d.

To Richard Crane, vicar of Deptford,[2] toward the relief and succours of himself, his wife, children and household, being restrained from coming out of his house, among others of the parish, by reason of the infection of the plague in his said house there (which I pray God to cease), according to an order long since used in the like time of infection[3] – £1.

[*Page total*] – £12 10s.

[f. 336v] To Thomas Apparrey, as well for his own travail and charges with the hire of his horse and charges of the same, sent to the court at Windsor from Deptford with letters to the Lord Admiral and Sir William Woodhouse, knight, for warrant to be obtained and to be sent to the Lord Treasurer for payment of money for the discharge of certain Her Highness's

[1]Thames watermen had until recently claimed general protection from impressment, alleging theirs to be what would now be called a reserved occupation; but a statute of 1555 laid down penalties for rowers between Gravesend and Windsor who withdrew from the River or hid in 'secret places and out corners' while press commissions were in force: 2 & 3 Ph. & Mar. c. 15, sect. 6.

[2]An error for *Nicholas* Crane, who had been appointed to this Crown living in the previous year. He survived the epidemic only to meet other misfortune, losing his living for nonconformity in 1566 and eventually being imprisoned in Newgate. He died there, of another 'infection', in 1588: *CPR 1560–3*, p. 415. *ODNB*.

[3]The 1563 epidemic of bubonic plague was the worst of the century; the infection had decimated the Le Havre expeditionary force, and was spread by the survivors on their return. The policy of isolating the infected in their houses developed through successive orders from central and local government: J. F. D. Shrewsbury, *A History of Bubonic Plague in the British Isles* (Cambridge, 1971), pp. 20–1. P. Slack, *The Impact of Plague in Tudor and Stuart England* (Oxford, 1985), pp. 201–6. The outbreak at Deptford prevented Gonson from paying ships coming into Gillingham Water, because access to court was prohibited and so he could not apply in person for the cash: HMC, *Salisbury*, i, p. 281.

ships called from the seas, and being returned to the court again for that there was no payment presently to be had, and tarrying there for other letters from the Council to the said Lord Treasurer for the despatch of money for the said payment, by the space of 8 days at 3s 4d for every day – 26s 8d; more to him for certain other charges sustained for himself and his horse, with the hire of the same, sent again from Deptford to the court at Windsor with other letters and estimate, for warrant, and for money to be paid for the discharge of other Her Grace's ships, attending upon the same by the space of 4 days, at 3s 4d every day – 13s 4d; more to him for certain other charges sustained, being sent with letters from the said Lord Treasurer to Sir Richard Sackville, being gone into Sussex[1] before his coming to Sheen – 4s 8d; and more to him for ferryage over the Thames at divers places within the time aforesaid for his horse and himself, and for his boat-hire within the same time – 5s 4d. *Summa* – £2 10s.

*[*Shipkeepers*]. To Thomas Morley for so much paid to Nicholas Moone, Giles Haull and 15 other shipkeepers of Her Highness's ships at Portsmouth for their travail and pains taken in casting, cleansing and laying of floor timber in the *Jennet*'s dock there, by agreement – 22s 8d;[2] and more to him for so much paid to Vincent Newstubb, John Thomas and William Brooke for their charges sustained by the space of 10 days among them all in providing of shores, brick, lime, sand and divers other needful things for Her Majesty's works there – 20s. *Summa* – £2 2s 8d.

To Thomas Bolten, master caulker, for his charges and horse-hire at divers times sent from Deptford to Portsmouth at the grounding of Her Highness's ships there, by the commandment of the officers of Her Grace's said ships – £1 10s.

[*Page total*] – £6 2s 8d.

[f. 337] To Robert Beast for the charges of himself and his horse, with the hire of the same, by the space of 4 days sent to Lymington and thereabouts for the presting of shipwrights to Her Highness's works at Portsmouth, at 3s 4d for every day – 13s 4d; and more to him for his charges by the space of 3 days, sent from Portsmouth to Southampton for the staying of 5 sail of ships to transport soldiers to Newhaven in Normandy, at 12d every day, 3s. *Summa* – 16s 4d.

To Thomas Claye for the charges of himself and his horse, with the hire of the same, sent for London to Portsmouth to Thomas Morley, Keeper of Her Highness's storehouses, presently attending Her Majesty's causes there – 13s 6d; more for the charges of himself, his guide and their 2

[1]Sackville, Privy Councillor and Under-treasurer of the Exchequer, was a leading figure in the county, with his seat at Buckhurst: *Hist. Parl. 1558–1603*, iii, pp. 314–15.

[2]Cf. BL, Add. MS 78171 [item 1(c)], ff. 19–34, as briefly described in Appendix 4 below.

horses riding in post with letters from William Holstock, Comptroller of Her Grace's Marine Causes, then being at Portsmouth, to the court at Windsor, to the Lord Admiral there, and for his charges tarrying for answer of the same – 33s 4d; and more to him for the charges of himself and his horse, with the hire of the same, sent at one other time from Portsmouth with letters to the court at Windsor aforesaid from the same William Holstock to the said Lord Admiral and Sir William Cecil, knight, Principal Secretary – 23s 4d. *Summa* – £3 10s 2d.

To John Henshaw, captain, for his charges and horse-hire riding to and fro from the North Foreland to Dover and so to the ships, for the better despatch of Her Grace's victuals coming from London to be transported to Portsmouth and Newhaven; by agreement – £1.

To Nicholas Starkey, boatswain of the Queen's Majesty's bark called the *Sun*, and William Ellys, master gunner of the same bark, for charges of themselves and hire of their horses, sent by their captain[1] from Hastings to the officers of Her Grace's ships at Deptford for certain necessary wants to be had for the said bark, as well for her rigging as also for the refreshing of munitions – £1 6s 8d.

[*Page total*] – £6 13s 2d.

[f. 337v] To William Streaton, keeper of the Dolphin of Rochester, for charges by him sustained in safe-keeping of one Andrew Brenne, mariner, as a prisoner, who for certain offences by him committed during his service in the Queen's Majesty's ship the *Hope* was after sent up to London to the officers of Her Grace's Marine Causes there, and by them committed to the Marshalsea for his said offences – 3s 7d.

To Lancelot Tristram for charges by him laid out at divers times, as well horse-hire, boat-hire as other ways, travelling about the providing of reed, brick, shores, lime, sand, and divers other kinds of needful things for Her Majesty's works at Gillingham – 16s 8d.

To John Leache of Deptford for the charges of himself [*and*] his horse with the hire of the same, travelling into sundry woods in Kent at divers times for the providing of timber, plank and shores for the needful building of Her Majesty's ships at Deptford aforesaid, by the space of 54 days, at 2s every day – £5 8s.

To Thomas Grene, master of a hoy called the *Dragon of London*, of the portage of 80 tuns, for the hire of his said hoy, wages and victuals of himself and three other mariners for the safe conveying of 148 soldiers with all their armour from Chatham to Queenborough aboard the Queen's Majesty's ship called the *Elizabeth Jonas*, at the going of the same ship to the seas with the Lord High Admiral of England; by agreement – £1 6s.

[1]Peter Paulyn: cf. below, p. 491.

To Stephen Alexander for certain charges by him sustained, as well in boat-hire as other ways, at divers times in going and coming to London for the making perfect of Her Highness's reckonings in the Quarter Books concerning the general pay books pertaining to Her Grace's marine causes, by the space of one whole year begun the first day of January 1562 [*1563*] and ended the last day of December following, 1563 – £4.[1]

[*Page total*] – £11 14s 3d.

[f. 338] To Francis Fullar for the charges of himself and his horse, with the hire of the same, travelling from London to Portsmouth and from thence to Newhaven in Normandy for the transporting from thence into England certain French ships then commanded hither, continuing about the same by the space of 10 days; by agreement – £1 6s 8d.

*[*A ship boat*]. To Thomas Rolff of Rye, shipwright, for price of one cock or boat of him had for the use of the Queen's Majesty's ship called the *Bark of Boulogne*, her own boat being lost by tempest of weather at the sea, price by agreement – £5; and more to him for one anchorstock for the same ship – 2s 6d. *Summa* – £5 2s 6d.

*[*Water carriage*]. To Thomas Mytche of Colchester for the freight of 8 hawsers, 14 bolts of poldavy, 4 dozen of boat oars, 2 hundredweight of spikes and overlop nails, 9 barrels with pitch and tar, and divers other kinds of provisions by him conveyed from the Queen's Majesty's storehouse at Deptford to Harwich for the use of Her Grace's ships the *Swallow* and the *Willoughby* serving on the North Seas; by agreement – £1 10s.

To William Thwayttes, servant to Sir William Woodhouse, knight, for his travail, pains and horse-hire, with the charges thereof, sent from the court at Windsor to Deptford with a privy seal for money for the discharge of certain Her Highness's ships called from the seas, and with a commandment by writing for the sending of 80 mariners to Sir Thomas Cotton in the Narrow Seas for a further strength to Her Grace's ships there – 10s.

To James Humphrey for charges by him sustained, as well for boat-hire as other ways, travailing about the providing of divers and sundry needful provisions for the use of Her Highness's ships, by the space of one whole year begun the first day of October 1562 and ended the last day of September following – £4.

[*Page total*] – £12 9s 2d.

[1] This item was originally entered as a quarterly charge of 20s in the Deptford ordinary, as evident from the draft for the Christmas quarter, where the entry is deleted and marked 'Entered in Extraordinary Charges': BL, Add. MS 78170 [item (b)], f. 10. Cf. above, p. 225 & n. 3 for the similar adjustment in the previous year.

[f. 338v] *[*Water carriage*]. To Nicholas Sallow of Brightlingsea for the hire of his hoy, and wages and victuals of three men and one boy serving Her Highness in carrying of cordage, canvas, pitch, tar and divers other needful things out of Her Grace's great storehouse at Deptford to Queenborough at the going of certain Her Highness's ships to the seas, for 2 several freights; by agreement – £2 6s 8d.

To James Humphrey for the hire of four porters for the carrying down to sundry wharfs in London 1,060[1] rafters for oars, which were taken of divers persons for the use of Her Highness's ships – 7s 6d; more for wharfage of the same rafters at divers wharfs in London – 16d; more for the sending down of 3 grindstones from London to Deptford and for the carriage of the same to the waterside – 9d; more for the carriage of 3 sheets of lead from London to Deptford aforesaid – 4d; and more to him for the hire of divers cars for carrying of 67 deal-boards from the Crutched Friars in London[2] to the Tower wharf, containing 8 loads, at 4d every load – 2s 8d. *Summa* – 12s 7d.

To George Wirrall for his charges, with the hire of his horse and charges of the same, by the space of 37 days, being sent to Harwich, Portsmouth, Dover and Chatham for the surveying of Her Highness's ships at the places aforesaid, as well at their settings forth to the seas as also at their comings home again into harbour, at 3s 4d for every day – £6 3s 4d.

To John Browne for the charges of himself, John Ellmar, Thomas Baker and two others with their horses, travelling as well from Deptford to Chatham with Her Highness's treasure for the payment of the companies serving in Her Grace's two ships northward, the *Swallow* and the *Willoughby*, discharged there, as also from Gillingham to Dover for the making of payment to divers Her Highness's ships serving in the Narrow Seas; being occupied about the same by the space of 7 days – £6 3s 4d.

[*Page total*] – £15 5s 11d.

[f. 339] *[*Dover. Shipwrights and caulkers. Ironwork <inserted – £4> and boards – £4 6½d*] To John Hewson of Dover for certain charges by him there sustained upon divers Her Highness's ships and barks serving upon the Narrow Seas under the charge of Sir Thomas Cotton, knight,

[1]Because this commodity was reckoned by long hundred, the quantity here is probably 1,260.

[2]The precinct of the dissolved priory of Crutched (or crossed) friars, from which the street eastward of Hart Street takes its name; where the Navy had a timber store convenient for onward transmission to the dockyards: Tower wharf is just 500 yards to the south: cf. SP 12/11, no. 3 (*CSPD 1547–80*, p. 148: Winchester to Cecil, 14 Jan. 1560, mentioning in the context of naval victualling that 'the store house at Crosse Friars in London must be had' by arrangement with the Lord Steward). Stow, in a work first published in 1598, describes the priory site as 'now a carpenters yeard': *A Survey of London*, ed. C. L Kingsford (Oxford 1908), i, p. 148.

Admiral there, *viz.* for the grounding, ransacking and caulking of the *Hare*, as well for oakum, pitch, thrums, caulking oil, broom to bream, wood to heat the pitch, and ironwork of divers sorts, as also wages and victuals of Henry Poore, Richard Ellyson, and Edward Erlinge, shipwrights, and their servants, by the space of 3 tides every of them – £3 13s 6d; more to him for certain nails and divers other kinds of ironwork, clove board, inch board, oakum and thrums for repairing of the *Aid* her boat, spoiled by foul weather – 24s 3d; more to him for a piece of timber, a plank and a socket of iron for the renewing of certain capstan bars for the *Falcon* and a thought[1] for her boat, and for the mending of the whip[2] of the same ship for her better steerage – 10s; more to him for price of one piece of timber for the head of the rudder of the *Bark of Boulogne*, and for sawing the same and for certain ironwork, with certain oakum for the same ship's store at her going to the sea – 10s 8d; more to him for oakum, timber, spars, broom, wood, pitch, a pitch kettle, a salt hide, tallow, spikes, nails, rudder irons, thrums and divers other things for the breaming and caulking of the *Phoenix*, being also weather-beaten by tempest – £5 11s 4½d; more to him for 2 pieces of timber, certain oakum and nails for the mending of the stem and wales of the *Aid* her skiff – 4s 3d; more for his charges as well from Dover to Margate as back again for the taking of the musters of all the ships there against their victualling day, being put out of Dover Road by foul weather – 5s 2d; and more to him for the charges of himself and his horse, with the hire of the same, travelling from Dover aforesaid to Deptford and back again for the clearing of his whole year's reckonings for charges by him sustained upon Her Grace's said ships – 24s. *Summa* – £13 3s 2½d.

[*Page total*] – £13 3s 2½d.

[f. 339v] To John Ellmar, messenger, for the charges of himself and his horse, being sent from the Lord Admiral and other the officers of Her Grace's Marine Causes with letters to Portsmouth to William Holstock, Comptroller, by 3 several journeys, at 20s every journey – £3; more for one journey by him made with letters from the Council to Sir William Woodhouse, knight, being in Norfolk[3] – 33s 4d; more for his like charges sent with letters from the officers of the ships at Deptford, as well to the court at Windsor and Horsley to the Lord Admiral and Sir William Woodhouse, as also to Langley and Stanstead to Edward Baeshe[4] and

[1] I.e. thwart (rower's bench); cf. *OED*, 'thoft', 'thought'[2]; 'thwart', *sb.* [2].

[2] I.e. whiptstaff (handle attached to the tiller of small boats): *OED*, 'whip' *sb.* 13.

[3] He lived at Hickling: *Hist. Parl. 1509–58*, i, p. 653.

[4] Baeshe had acquired property at Stanstead Abbots in Hertfordshire in 1559, and set himself up there (being duly lampooned as 'the new made squire of Stanstead' with a nose 'as red as any rose'): *Hist. Parl. 1558–1603*, i, p. 401.

Benjamin Gonson, by 11 several times, at 6s 8d for every journey – £3 13s 4d; more for his charges in carrying of like letters from the aforesaid officers from Deptford to Chatham to William Wood, John Hurlocke and William Barnes, masters of the Queen's Majesty's ships, for divers Her Grace's needful causes at 6 several times, at 6s 8d for every time – 40s; more to him for the charges of himself, his man and 5 horses sent to Chatham with money for the discharge of the *Swallow* and the *Willoughby*, called out of the North Sea to be discharged, and for the hire of the same horses, by the space of 2 days – 28s; more to him for the hire of 6 his horses, as well for carrying of money to pay the ships serving in the Narrow Seas, and for the carrying of certain persons for the safe conveying of the same money thither from Deptford, at 8s every horse – 48s; more to him for certain charges by him sustained as well for the repairing, mending and refreshing of the money saddles, with straps, buckles, girths, peitrels and croups[1] to the same saddles – 16s; more for the wages of himself and his man by the space of 8 days attending upon the payments as well at Chatham for the discharge of the *Swallow* and the *Willoughby*, as also at Dover for payment of the ships serving in the Narrow Seas, at 18d the day between them – 12s and more to the said John Ellmar for the hire of 2 his horses for one journey made by Thomas Morley and his servant from Deptford to Portsmouth for the making of sale of certain French prizes lately fet from Newhaven in Normandy, being occupied about the same by the space of 22 days, by agreement – 44s. *Summa* – £17 14s 8d.

[*Page total*] – £17 14s 8d.

[f. 340] To Thomas Claye for the charges of himself and his horse, with the hire of the same, in riding from Portsmouth to Shoreham, Chichester, Brighton, Southampton and thereabouts to give intelligence unto the country of the sale of the French prizes brought from Newhaven to Portsmouth aforesaid, travelling about the same by the space of 6 days; by agreement – 13s.

To Edward Lambarde of Brightlingsea as well for the charges of himself, his man and their 2 horses in travelling from Brightlingsea aforesaid to Harwich by 3 several times for the delivering of divers kinds of provisions to the *Swallow* and the *Willoughby* at their being there in the North Seas; as also to labourers and others for the helping to deliver the same aboard the said ships' boats – £1 18s 2d.

[1]The peitrel or pectoral is the protective covering for a horse's breast; the croup (meaning primarily the animal's rump) is the covering rear of the saddle: *OED*, 'croup' *sb.*[1]. 2 cites only a 19th-cent. instance of the extended usage.

To George Wirrall for charges by him sustained, as well horse-hire, boat-hire as other ways, travelling at divers times from London to Chatham, Harwich, Dover and Portsmouth for the taking survey of Her Highness's ships at the places aforesaid, not only at their settings forth to the seas but also at their comings home again into harbour, being occupied about the same by the space of 42 days, at 3s *per diem* – *Summa* – £6 6s.

To Rowland Mucklowe for charges sustained in boat-hire and horse-hire travelling from London to Chatham, and so into the Downs, for the conveying of mariners from Chatham aforesaid to Her Grace's ships in the Downs for their better mannings, by the space of 7 days – £1.

*[*The charges of recovering the* Greyhound]. To Butolph Moungey of Gillingham for divers sums of money disbursed by him, as well for lighterage, wharfage, cranage and labourers' wages as also for the charges of himself and his man with their 2 horses, being occupied about the saving and recovering of Her Grace's ordnance, munitions, tackle and apparel which belonged to Her Highness's ship called the *Greyhound*, being lost upon the bar of Rye by tempest of weather – £32.

[*Page total*] – £41 17s 2d.

[f. 340v] To William Wood, one of the chief masters attending Her Highness's ships in harbour, for the charges of himself and his horse, with the hire of the same, by the space of 3 days, being sent for by the officers of Her Highness's ships from Chatham to Deptford for weighty matters concerning Her Grace's said ships – 10s.

To John Hurlocke, master, for the charges of himself, as well boat-hire as horse-hire, travelling from Chatham to London at the commandment of the officers of Her Grace's Marine Causes, and giving attendance there by the space of 3 days; by agreement – 15s; and more to him for the charges of himself, his servant and their 2 horses, in travelling from Chatham aforesaid to the court at Windsor, being sent for by Sir William Woodhouse; as also for 3 other journeys, being sent for from Gillingham to Deptford to the officers of Her Majesty's ships for service by him to be done there – £4 3s 10d. *Summa* – £4 18s 10d.

*[*Storehouse at Rye*]. To Thomas Radforde of Rye, shoemaker, for hire of a storehouse for the safe-keeping of all such cables, hawsers, warps, sails, and other apparel as did lately appertain to the Queen's Majesty's ship called the *Greyhound*, by the space of 24 weeks begun the 29th day of March last past and ended the 12th day of September next, at 2s 6d every week; by agreement – £3.

*[*Cordage*]. To the widow of William Bagge, late of Rye, mariner, for 2 hundredweight ½ [*280 lbs*] of warp and other cordage which her said husband delivered for the use of Her Highness's ship called the

Rowbarge[1] at her equipping to the sea out of the port there, at 22s every hundred[*weight*]; by agreement – £2 15s.

*[*Water carriage*]. To Roger Wattes for the hire of two Gravesend barges, and wages and victuals of eight men serving in them, for the carrying down of 200 fir spars from London to Queenborough for the use of Her Grace's ships at their settings forth to the seas; by agreement – £1.

[*Page total*] – £12 3s 10d.

[f. 341] To Thomas Fullar, master, for the charges of himself and his horse, with the hire of the same, travelling from London to Portsmouth and from thence to Newhaven in Normandy, continuing there by the space of 37 days in rigging, masting and furnishing to the seas certain French ships then appointed into England, beginning his said travel the 3rd day of May last and ended the 8th day of June following; by agreement – £3 6s 8d.

[*Anno regni regis regine Elizabethe sexto*][2]

To John Hewson of Dover the last day of December for his entertainment for his service there, as well for the mustering of the companies of the ships as also for the writing out of warrants from time to time for their re-victuallings, by the space of one whole year begun the first day of January last, 1562 [*1563*], and ended the day aforesaid, at 12d by the day. *Summa* – £18 5s.

To Thomas Baker for the charges of himself and [*his*] horse, with the hire of the same, travelling as well from Deptford to Chatham as also from thence back again, for the perfecting and making up of pay books and other reckonings at the discharge of five Her Grace's ships brought about from Portsmouth haven into Gillingham Water to harbour there, being occupied about the same by the space of 8 days, at 2s 6d every day. *Summa* – £1.

*[*Water carriage*]. To John Clarke, master, for the tunnage of his ship called the *George Bonaventure of Lee* [Leigh], being of the portage of 70 tuns, serving Her Highness by the space of one month in carrying of victuals for 240 men serving in Her Grace's four brigantines the *Post*, the *Guide*, the *Searcher* and the *Makeshift*, at 12d the tun *per mensem*. *Summa* – £3 10s.

[1]Bagge had been the master earlier in the year, so it is likely that he was still so in August when the ship foundered off the coast of Scotland, and there lost his life: cf. above, pp 468–9, below, pp. 483, 487–8.

[2]MS date formula changes in running head to *Anno regni regine Elizabethe quinto & vj^to^* but is editorially adapted and placed before the first entry of the new regnal year, in keeping with the scribe's usual practice.

To Richard Spert, captain, for the charges of himself, his man, his guide and their 3 horses riding post from Aberlady in Scotland to the court at Windsor with letters from Ralph Chamberlain, then Admiral of the North Seas, to the Queen's Majesty's most honourable Privy Council, of the loss of the *Rowbarge* – £8 16s.

[*Page total*] – £34 17s 8d.

[f. 341v] To William Barnes, master, for the charges of himself, his servant and their 2 horses, sent from Chatham to Portsmouth for the sale of certain French prizes lately brought from Newhaven in Normandy thither, being occupied about the same there by the space of 27 days, at 2s 8d for every day – £3 11s 10d.

[*Signatures*][1]

To John Browne the last day of December for charges by him sustained in the receiving of £7,465 11s 2d, as well at the Receipt in Westminster at the hands of the tellers there as also at the hands of others, by several Her Grace's warrants to them directed at divers times within the time of this account for Her Majesty's extraordinary charges by sea, at 30s every £1000, bags, wax, parchment, carriage and suchlike within the said charges accounted – £11 4s.

To Christopher Baker the same day for the charges of himself and his horse, with the hire of the same, by the space of 16 days travelling as well from Deptford to Bristol as back again with letters of importance from the officers of Her Grace's Marine Causes to William Winter, Master of Her Majesty's Ordnance for the Seas, then being there, at 3s 7d every day – £2 13s 4d.

To Richard Wynter, master, the same day for the hire of his hoy, and wages and victuals of his men, serving Her Highness in carrying of ballast aboard the *Victory* for her steadier ballasting; by agreement – £1 6s 8d.

To John Hodges the same day for price of one firkin with tallow by him delivered for the use of Her Majesty's ship the *Saker* at her needful grounding at Portsmouth; by agreement – 5s.

[*Page total*] – £19 0s 10d.

[1]Here and on f. 344v (p. 487 below) the usual signatures of the Holstock and the Winters occur after the first entry as well as at the bottom of the page. These first paragraphs may have been the only entries on the respective pages when originally presented to the officers. The remaining entries are in the same level hand. This would suggest that the signatures were supplied as the account was being compiled, and not in a single operation once the book was finished. Indeed the untiringly regular form of all the signatures seems inconsistent with their having been applied in a single sitting.

[f. 342] **Extraordinary. Prests:**

Anno Domini 1562 [1563]. *Anno regni regine Elizabethe quinto*

Money delivered in prest to Edward Baeshe, General Surveyor of Her Grace's victuals for the seas, as followeth:

To Edward Baeshe, General Surveyor of Her Grace's victuals for the seas, the 21th day of January *annis supradictis* in prest for the victualling of 100 men appointed to pass to Newhaven in two brigantines, the sum of thirty-three pounds six shillings eight pence – £33 6s 8d.

To the same Edward Baeshe, General Surveyor of Her Grace's victuals for the seas, the 5th day of February *annis supradictis* in prest, as well for one month's victuals of 28 days delivered to Her Majesty's ship the *Greyhound* for 120 men begun the 20th day of December last, as also for one other month's victuals to be provided for 430 men serving in several Her Highness's ships, *viz.* the *Aid*, the *Greyhound*, the *Saker*, the *Phoenix*, the *Bark of Boulogne*, the *Hare* and the *Double Rose*, begun the 17th day of January last and to end the 13th day of this present month of February, the sum of three hundred threescore six pounds thirteen shillings four pence – £366 13s 4d.

To the said Edward Baeshe, General Surveyor of Her Highness's victuals for the seas, the 14th day of February *annis supradictis* in prest to be employed in the provision of victuals for one month of 28 days for 410 men serving Her Highness in 6 Her Grace's ships and barks at the seas, begun the 13th day of this present month of February, the sum of two hundred threescore thirteen pounds six shillings eight pence – £273 6s 8d.

[*Page total*] – £673 6s 8d.

[f. 342v] To Edward Baeshe, General Surveyor of Her Grace's victuals for the seas, the 13th day of March *annis supradictis* in prest, as well for one month's victuals of 28 days to be provided for 410 men serving Her Majesty in 6 Her Highness's ships and barks at the seas to begin the 14th day of this present month of March and to end the 10th day of April next, as also for 14 days' victuals delivered at Dover for 100 men serving Her Highness in two of Her Grace's brigantines, begun the 11th day of February last, the sum of three hundred six pounds thirteen shillings four pence – £306 13s 4d.

Anno Domini 1563

To the said Edward Baeshe, General Surveyor of Her Majesty's victuals for the seas, the 4th day of April *annis supradictis* in prest for one month's victuals of 28 days to be provided for 290 men serving Her

Highness in five Her Grace's ships and barks at the seas, to begin the 11th day of this present month of April and to end the 8th day of May next, the sum of one hundred fourscore thirteen pounds six shillings eight pence – £193 6s 8d.

To the aforenamed Edward Baeshe, General Surveyor of Her Highness's victuals for the seas, the 16th day of May *annis supradictis* in prest for one month's victuals of 28 days to be provided for 190 men serving Her Majesty in 5 Her Grace's ships and barks at the seas, begun the 9th day of this present month of May and to end the 5th day of June next, the sum of one hundred fourscore thirteen pounds six shillings eight pence – £193 6s 8d.

[*Page total*] – £693 6s 8d.

[f. 343] To Edward Baeshe, General Surveyor of Her Grace's victuals for the seas, the 19th day of May *annis supradictis* in prest, as well for victualling of 30 mariners and gunners bringing the *Rowbarge* from Rye to Chatham, as also toward the victualling of 300 mariners sent to Newhaven for the bringing from thence certain French ships, the sum of threescore thirteen pounds sixteen shillings – £73 16s.

To the same Edward Baeshe, General Surveyor of Her Majesty's victuals for the seas, the 25th day of May *annis supradictis* in prest, as well for victualling of 180 men to serve in the *Swallow* as also 80 men to serve in the *Falcon*, for one month,[1] the sum of one hundred threescore thirteen pounds six shillings eight pence – £173 6s 8d.

To the aforesaid Edward Baeshe, General Surveyor of Her Highness's victuals for the seas, the first day of June *annis supradictis* in prest to be employed upon the setting forth to the seas of three Her Grace's ships, that is to say the *Antelope*, the *Jennet* and the *Double Rose*, the sum of two hundred threescore pounds – £260.

To the above-named Edward Baeshe, General Surveyor of Her Grace's victuals for the seas, the 27th day of June *annis supradictis* in prest for the victualling of certain ships appointed for Her Highness's service northward, the sum of five hundred and twenty-four pounds – £524.

To the said Edward Baeshe, General Surveyor of Her Majesty's victuals for the seas, the 8th day of July *annis supradictis* in prest to be employed about the charges in conveying out of the river of Gillingham four Her Highness's ships and three her galleys to Portsmouth, the sum of one thousand two hundred threescore six pounds thirteen shillings four pence – £1,266 13s 4d.

[*Page total*] – £2,297 16s.

[1]The same day the Lord Admiral was ordered to set these ships to sea with munitions for Le Havre: *CSPF 1563*, no. 797.

[f. 343v] To Edward Baeshe, General Surveyor of Her Grace's victuals for the seas, the 14th day of July *annis supreadictis* in prest as well for 7 days' rigging victuals for 34 persons, as also for a provision of one month's victuals of 28 days for 240 men to serve in four new galliots, the sum of one hundred threescore five pounds thirteen shillings four pence – £165 13s 4d.

To the said Edward Baeshe, General Surveyor of Her Highness's victuals for the seas, the same day, as, well for the victualling of certain Her Grace's ships at the seas for this month of June, as also for like victualling of 980 men serving in 10 of Her Majesty's ships for the month of July next, the sum of nine hundred threescore fourteen pounds – £974.

To the same Edward Baeshe, General Surveyor of Her Majesty's victuals for the seas, the 20th day of July *annis supradictis* in prest for the victualling of 1,020 men serving Her Highness at the seas in 11 her ships and barks, as well for part of this month of July as for the whole month of August next, the sum of eight hundred sixteen pounds eleven shillings eight pence – £816 11s 8d.

To the aforenamed Edward Baeshe, General Surveyor of Her Grace's victuals for the seas, the same day in prest for the victualling of Her Highness's Navy appointed for Her Majesty's service under the conduction of the Lord High Admiral of England, the sum of one thousand two hundred threescore four pounds sixteen shillings eight pence – £1,264 16s 8d.

[*Page total*] – £3,221 1s 10d.

[f. 344] To Edward Baeshe, General Surveyor of Her Grace's victuals for the seas, the 30th day of July *annis supradictis* in prest for the victualling of 5,200 men serving Her Highness at the seas under the conduction of the Lord High Admiral of England, the sum of three thousand six hundred forty pounds – £3,640.

To the aforesaid Edward Baeshe, General Surveyor of Her Majesty's victuals for the seas, the 5th day of September *annis supradictis* in prest for the victualling of 400 mariners employed presently for the bringing about of six Her Highness's ships into Gillingham Water, *viz*. the *Elizabeth Jonas*, the *Victory*, the *Philip and Mary*, the *Jennet*, the *Minion* and the *Primrose*, the sum of two hundred fourscore ten pounds twelve shillings six pence – £290 12s 6d.

To the same Edward Baeshe, General Surveyor of Her Highness's victuals for the seas, the 21th day of December *annis supredictis* in prest for the victualling of 380 men serving Her Majesty on the Narrow Seas in the *Aid*, the *Falcon*, the *Phoenix*, the *Bark of Boulogne* and the *Hare* under the charge of Sir Thomas Cotton, knight, for one month ended the

28th day of October, the sum of two hundred fifty-three pounds six shillings eight pence – £253 6s 8d.

To the abovesaid Edward Baeshe, General Surveyor of Her Grace's victuals for the seas, the 22th day of December *annis supradictis* in prest for the victualling of 380 men serving Her Highness in the Narrow Seas in the *Aid*, the *Falcon*, the *Phoenix*, the *Bark of Boulogne* and the *Hare* under the charge of Sir Thomas Cotton, knight, for one month begun the 29th day of October last and ended the 25th day of November next, the sum of two hundred fifty-three pounds six shillings eight pence – £253 6s 8d.

[*Page total*] – £4,437 5s 10d.

[f. 344v] To Edward Baeshe, General Surveyor of Her Grace's victuals for the seas, the 23th day of December *annis supradictis* in prest for the victualling of 380 men serving Her Majesty on the Narrow Seas in the *Aid*, the *Falcon*, the *Phoenix*, the *Bark of Boulogne* and the *Hare* under the charge of Sir Thomas Cotton, knight, for one month of 28 days begun the 26th day of November last and to end this 23th day of December,[1] the sum of two hundred fifty-three pounds six shillings eight pence – £253 6s 8d.

[*Signatures*]

To the said Edward Baeshe, General Surveyor of Her Highness's victuals for the seas, the 24th day of December *annis supradictis* in prest towards the victualling of the *Willoughby* with 120 men for 10 weeks 4 days, and the *Swallow* with 180 men for 5 weeks, ended the 28th day of October last, the sum of three hundred fourscore nineteen pounds seven shillings – £399 7s.

[*Page total*] – £652 13s 8d.

[f. 345] **Extraordinary. Sea charges:**

Anno Domini 1562 [1563]. *Anno regni regine Elizabethe quinto*

The Double Rose. To Thomas Perryman, master, the 11th day of January for the wages of himself and 29 other mariners and gunners serving Her Highness in the same ship under him at the seas by the space of one week 4 days begun the first day of January last and ended as abovesaid, at 2s 8d every man – £4; and more for 10 deadshares for like time, at 23d every share – 19s 2d. *Summa* – £4 19s 2d.

The Rowbarge. To William Bagge, master, the 13th day of March for the wages of himself and 32 other mariners and gunners serving in the same ship under him by the space of 3 weeks 3 days begun the 18th day

[1]The only indication of the date (most probably the last of several days) on which this volume was actually written.

of February last and ended as abovesaid, at 5s 8d every man – £9 7s; and more for 14 deadshares for like time, at 4s 3d every share – 59s 6d. *Summa* – £12 6s 6d.

The Greyhound. To John Malyn, captain, the 19th day of March for his diets serving Her Highness as Admiral of Her Grace's ships then presently in the Narrow Seas by the space of 78 days begun the first day of January last and ended as abovesaid, at 5s *per diem* – £19 10s; more for the wages of a master and 119 other mariners and gunners serving Her Majesty in the same ship under him by the space of 2 months 3 weeks one day begun and ended as abovesaid, at 18s 7d every man – £111 10s; more for 20 deadshares divided amongst the master and other officers of the said ship, at 13s 10d every share – £13 16s 8d; more in reward to 4 gunners, at 2s 4d the man – 9s 4d; more in reward to a trumpeter – 23s 2d; and more in reward to a surgeon for like time – 23s 2d. *Summa* – £147 12s 4d.

[*Page total*] – £164 18s.

[f. 345v] *Anno Domini 1563. Anno regni regine Elizabethe quinto*

The Aid. To William Driver, captain, the last day of March for his diets serving Her Highness as Admiral of Her Grace's ships appointed for the scouring of the seas between Newhaven in Normandy and Portsmouth, by the space of 20 days begun the first day of January last and ended the 20th day of the same month, at 6s 8d *per diem* – £6 13s 4d; more for John Basing, captain, for his diets serving Her Majesty in the said ship admiral[1] as aforesaid by the space of 70 days begun the 21th day of January last and ended as abovesaid, at 5s *per diem* – £17 10s; more for the wages of a master and 119 other mariners and gunners serving under them in the same ship by the space of 12 weeks 6 days begun the first day of January last and ended the last day of March following, at 21s 5d every man – £128 10s; more for 20 deadshares by like time, at 16s 1d every share – £16 1s 8d; more in reward to four gunners, at 2s 7d the man – 10s 4d; more in reward to a surgeon – 27s; and more in reward two trumpeters for like time, at 27s either of them – 54s. *Summa* – £173 6s 4d.

The Saker. To John Henshaw, captain, the said last day of March for his diets serving in the same ship by the space of 90 days begun the first day of January last and ended the day abovesaid, at 18d *per diem* – £6 15s; more for the wages of a master and 54 other mariners and gunners serving under him in the said ship by the space of 12 weeks 6 days begun

[1]That is, the ship carrying the Admiral, or 'Admiral-ship', soon commonly abbreviated to 'admiral', as in **22** below.

and ended as aforesaid, at 21s 5d every man – £58 18s 11d; more for 14 deadshares, at 16s 1d every share – £11 5s 2d; more in reward to three gunners, at 2s 7d the man – 7s 9d; more in reward to a trumpeter – 27s; and more in reward to a drum – 10s 8d. *Summa* – £79 4s 6d.

[*Page total*] – £252 10s 10d.

[f. 346] *The Phoenix.* To Thomas Gourlay, captain, the last day of March for his diets serving the Queen's Majesty in the same ship by the space of 90 days begun the first day of January last and ended as abovesaid, at 18d *per diem* – £6 15s; more for the wages of a master and 54 other mariners and gunners serving Her Highness in the said ship under him by the space of 3 months 6 days begun and ended as aforesaid, at 21s 5d every man – £58 18s 11d; more for 14 deadshares, at 16s 1d the share – £11 5s 2d; more in reward to three gunners, at 2s 7d the man – 7s 9d; more in reward to a trumpeter – 27s; and more in reward to a drum – 10s 8d. *Summa* – £79 4s 6d.

The Hare. To Robert Marsh, captain, the last day of March for his diets serving in the said ship by the space of 90 days begun the first day of January last and ended as aforesaid, at 18d *per diem* – £6 15s; more for the wages of a master and 39 other mariners and gunners serving under him in the same ship by the space of 12 weeks 6 days begun and ended as abovesaid, at 21s 5d every man – £42 16s 8d; more for 14 deadshares, at 16s 1d every share – £11 5s 2d; more in reward to three gunners, at 2s 7d the man – 7s 9d; and more in reward to a trumpeter – 27s. *Summa* – £62 11s 7d.

The Bark of Boulogne. To Thomas Hare, captain, the same last day of March for his diets serving in the said ship by the space of 90 days begun the first day of January last and ended as abovesaid, at 18d *per diem* – £6 15s; more for the wages of a master and 49 other mariners and gunners serving in the same ship under him by like time of 12 weeks 6 days begun and ended as aforesaid, at 21s 5d every man – £53 10s 10d; more for 14 deadshares, at 16s 1d the share – £11 5s 2d; more in reward to three gunners, at 2s 7d every man – 7s 9d; more in reward to a trumpeter – 27s; and more in reward to a drum – 10s 8d. *Summa* – £73 16s 5d.

[*Page total*] – £215 12s 6d.

[f. 346v] *The Aid.* To John Basing, captain, the 12th day of August for his diets serving the Queen's Highness in the same ship as Admiral of all Her Grace's ships then present on the seas, by the space of 61 days begun the first day of April last and ended the last day of May following, at 5s *per diem* – £15 5s; more to John Henshaw, captain, for his diets serving Her Majesty in the said ship by the space of 73 days begun the first day of June last and ended the 12th day of August next, at 18d *per diem* – £5 9s 6d; more for the wages of a master and 119 other mariners and gunners serving in the same ship under them by the space of 4 months 4 weeks one day begun the first day of April last and ended the 12th day of August next, at 31s 11d every man – £191 10s; more for 20 deadshares divided amongst the master and other officers in the said ship, at 23s 11d every share – £23 18s 1d; more in reward to four gunners, at 4s every man – 16s; more in reward to two trumpeters, at 39s 10d either of them – £3 19s 8d; and more in reward to a surgeon – 39s 10d. *Summa* – £242 18s 1d.

The Saker. To Henry Tirrell, captain, the said 12th day of August for his diets serving Her Highness in the same ship by the space of 132 days begun the first day of April last and ended the 10th day of August next, at 18d *per diem* – £9 18s; more for the wages of one master and 54 other mariners and gunners serving in the said ship under him by the space of 4 months 3 weeks one day begun the first day of April and ended the 12th day of August following, at 31s 11d every man – £87 15s 5d; more for 14 deadshares, at 23s 11d every share – £16 14s 10d; more in reward to three gunners, at 4s every man – 12s; and more in reward to a trumpeter – 39s 10d. *Summa* – £117 0s 1d.

[*Page total*] – £359 18s 2d.

[f. 347] *The Hare*. To Robert Marsh, captain, the 12th day of August for his diets serving in the same ship by the space of 134 days begun the first day of April last and ended as is aforesaid, at 18d *per diem* – £10 1s; more for the wages of a master and 39 other mariners and gunners serving under him in the same ship by the space of 4 months 3 weeks one day begun and ended as abovesaid, at 31s 11d every man – £63 16s 8d; more for 14 deadshares, at 23s 11d every share – £16 14s 10d; more in reward to three gunners, at 4s the man – 12s; and more in reward to a trumpeter – 39s 10d. *Summa* – £93 4s 4d.

The Double Rose. To Thomas Perryman, master, the same 12th day of August for the wages of himself and 29 other mariners and gunners serving with him in the same ship by the space of 2 months one week 5 days begun the 6th day of June last and ended as abovesaid, at 16s 2d every man – £24 5s; more for 10 deadshares, at 12s 2d every share – £6 1s 8d; and more in reward to two gunners – 4s. *Summa* – £30 10s 8d.

The Antelope. To William Winter, captain, the 12th day of August for his diets serving in the same ship as Admiral of all Her Grace's ships then keeping the Narrow Seas, by the space of 65 days begun the 9th day of June last and ended as aforesaid, at 13s 4d *per diem* – £43 6s 8d; more for the wages of a master and 199 other mariners and gunners serving under him in the said ship by the space of 2 months one week 2 days begun and ended as abovesaid, at 15s 6d every man – £155; more for 20 deadshares, at 11s 5d every share – £11 8s 4d; more in reward to 4 gunners, at 23d every man – 7s 8d; more in reward to three trumpeters, at 19s 4d every man – 58s; more in reward to a drum – 7s 8d; and more in reward to a surgeon – 19s 4d. *Summa* – £214 7s 8d.

[*Page total*] – £338 2s 8d.

[f. 347v] *The Sun.* To Peter Paulyn, captain, the 12th day of August for his diets serving in the same ship by the space of 39 days begun the 5th day of July last and ended the day abovesaid, at 18d *per diem* – 58s 6d; more for the wages of a master and 44 other mariners and gunners serving in the said ship under him by the space of 2 months 2 days begun the 16th day of June last and ended the 12th day of August next, at 13s 10d every man – £31 2s 6d; more for 14 deadshares, at 10s 2d every share – £7 2s 4d; more in reward to three gunners, at 20d every man – 5s; and more in reward to a drummer – 6s 8d. *Summa* – £41 15s.

The Post. To Edward Knight, captain, the said 12th day of August for his diets serving in the same brigantine by the space of 28 days begun the 16th day of July last and ended as aforesaid, at 18d *per diem* – 42s; more for the wages of a master and 39 other mariners, rowers and gunners serving under him in the said brigantine by the space of 4 weeks 6 days begun the 10th day of July and ended the day first above written, at 8s 1d every man – £16 3s 4d; more for 10 deadshares, at 4s 8d every share – 46s 8d; and more in reward to two gunners – 18d. *Summa* – £20 13s 6d.

The Makeshift. To Thomas Sabot, captain, the same day for his diets serving in the said brigantine by the space of 25 days begun the 18th day of July last and ended the 11th day of August next, at 18d *per diem* – 37s 6d; more for the wages of a master and 39 other mariners, gunners and rowers serving in the same brigantine under him by the space of one month 6 days begun the 10th day of July and ended as abovesaid, at 8s 1d every man – £16 3s 4d; more for 10 deadshares, at 4s 8d every share – 46s 8d; and more in reward to two gunners, at 9d either of them – 18d. *Summa* – £20 9s.

[*Page total*] – £82 17s 6d.

[f. 348] *The Elizabeth Jonas.* To the Lord Clinton, High Admiral of England, the 12th day of August for his diets serving the Queen's Majesty in the same ship by the space of 15 days begun the 19th day of July last and ended the 2nd day of August next, at £3 6s 8d *per diem* – £50; more for the wages of a master and 249 other mariners and gunners serving Her Highness under him in the said ship by the space of 3 weeks 5 days begun the 18th day of July and ended the 12th day of August following, at 6s 2d every man – £77 1s 8d; more for 34 deadshares divided amongst the master and the other officers in the same ship, at 4s 8d every share – £7 18s 8d; more in reward to four gunners, at 9d every man – 3s; more in reward to five trumpeters, at 7s 8d every of them – 38s 4d; more in reward to a surgeon – 7s 8d; more in reward to two lodesmen, at 7s 8d either of them – 15s 4d; more to Richard Whitton for his entertainment as captain over 100 arquebusiers in the said ship by the space of 14 days begun the 19th day of July and ended the first day of August next, at 4s *per diem* – 56s; more for the wages over 100 arquebusiers serving under him by like time begun and ended as aforesaid, at 3s 4d every man – £16 13 4d; more for the wages of his lieutenant for like time of 14 days begun and ended as abovesaid, at 2s *per diem* – 28s; more for the wages of one his ensign bearer and one sergeant for like 14 days, at 12d either of them *per diem* – 28s; and more to William Drury, captain, for the wages of 100 soldiers serving Her Majesty in the same ship under him by the space of 15 days begun the 19th day of July last and ended the 2nd day of August next following, at 2s 8d every man – £13 6s 8d. *Summa* – £173 16s 8d.

[*Page total*] – £173 16s 8d.

[f. 348v] *The Victory*. To Clement Paston, captain, the 12th day of August for his diets serving the Queen's Highness in the same ship by the space of 15 days begun the 19th day of July last and ended the 2nd day of August following, at 18d *per diem* – 22s 6d; more for the wages of a master and 199 other mariners and gunners serving Her Majesty in the said ship under him by the space of 3 weeks 5 days begun the 18th day of July last and ended the 12th day of August next, at 6s 2d every man – £61 13s 4d; more for 31 deadshares divided amongst the master and other officers in the same ship, at 4s 8d every share – £7 4s 8d; more in reward to four gunners, at 9d every of them – 3s; more in reward to a trumpeter for like time – 7s 8d; more in reward to a drum – 3s 2d; more in reward to a surgeon – 7s 8d; more to William Drury, captain, for his entertainment as captain over 300 soldiers in the said ship and in the *Elizabeth Jonas* by the space of 15 days begun the 19th day of July last and ended the 2nd day of August next, at 12s *per diem* – £9; more for the wages of his lieutenant for like time of 15 days, at 6s *per diem* – £4 10s; more for the wages of his ensign bearer by like time, at 3s *per diem* – 45s; more for the wages of three sergeants, three drums and one fife by like time of 15 days, at 12d every of them *per diem* – £5 5s; and more to the foresaid William Drury, captain, for the wages of 200 his soldiers serving Her Highness in the same ship by the space of 2 weeks one day begun and ended as is abovesaid, at 2s 8d every man – £26 13s 4d. *Summa* – £118 15s 4d.

[*Page total*] – £118 15s 4d.

[f. 349] *The Galley Mermaid.* To Nicholas Gorges, captain, the 12th day of August for his diets serving in the same galley by the space of 15 days begun the 19th day of July last and ended the 2nd day of August next, at 6s 8d *per diem* – £5; more for the wages of one master and 149 other mariners, gunners and rowers serving in the same galley under him by the space of 3 weeks 5 days begun the 18th day of July last and ended the day abovesaid, at 6s 2d every man – £46 5s; more for 20 deadshares, at 4s 8d every share – £4 13s 4d; more in reward to four gunners, at 9d the man – 3s; more in reward to a drum – 3s 2d; more in reward to a fife – 3s 2d; and more in reward to a surgeon – 7s 8d. *Summa* – £56 15s 4d.

The Hope. To Ralph Chamberlain, captain, the 20th day of August for his diets serving Her Highness in the same ship as Admiral of Her Grace's ships then on the North Seas, by the space of 42 days begun the 10th day of July last and ended as abovesaid, at 10s *per diem* – £21; more for the wages of a master and 259 other mariners and gunners serving in the said ship under him by the space of 6 weeks 3 days begun the 7th day of July last and ended the 20th day of August following, at 10s 8d every man – £138 13s 4d; more for 24 deadshares divided between the master and other officers in the same ship, at 8s every share – £9 12s; more in reward to four gunners, at 16d every man – 5s 4d; more in reward to a surgeon – 13s 5d; more in reward to a trumpeter – 13s 5d; and more in reward to a lodesman – 13s 5d. *Summa* – £171 10s 11d.

[*Page total*] – £228 6s 3d.

[f. 349v] *The Rowbarge.* To Richard Spert, captain, the 20th day of August for his diets serving in the same ship by the space of 45 days begun the 7th day of July last and ended as is aforesaid, at 18d *per diem* – £3 7s 6d; more for the wages of a master and 79 other mariners and gunners serving in the said ship under him by the space of one month 2 weeks 3 days begun and ended as abovesaid, at 10s 8d every man – £42 13s 4d; more for 18 deadshares, at 8s every share – £7 4s; more in reward to four gunners, at 16d every of them – 5s 4d; and more in reward to a surgeon – 13s 5d. *Summa* – £54 3s 7d.

The Galley Tryright. To John Cobham, captain, the 24th day of August for his diets serving in the same galley by the space of 15 days begun the 19th day of July last and ended the 2nd day of August next, at 6s 8d *per diem* – £5; more to Henry Tirrell, captain, for his diets serving in the said galley by the space of 14 days begun the 11th day of August last and ended the 24th day of the same month, at 6s 8d *per diem* – £4 13s 4d; more for the wages of a master and 259 other mariners, gunners and rowers serving under him in the same galley by the space of one month one week 3 days begun the 18th day of July last and ended the 24th day of August following, at 9s every man – £117; more for 20 deadshares, at 6s 9d every share – £6 15s; more in reward to four gunners, at 12d every of them – 4s; more in reward to a surgeon – 11s 4d; more in reward to a trumpeter – 11s 4d; more in reward to a drum – 4s 6d; and more in reward to a fife – 4s 6d. *Summa* – £135 4s.

[*Page total*] – £189 7s 7d.

[f. 350] *The Guide*. To Randall Worsley, captain, the 24th day of August for his diets serving in the same brigantine by the space of 25 days begun the 19th day of July last and ended the 12th day of August next, at 18d *per diem* – 37s 6d; more for the wages of a master and 49 other mariners, gunners and rowers serving under him in the said brigantine by the space of one month 2 weeks 3 days begun the 10th day of July and ended the 23th day of August following, at 10s 8d every man – £25 16s 8d; more in reward to two gunners, at 16d either of them – 2s 8d; and more for 10 deadshares, at 8s every share – £4. *Summa* – £31 16s 10d.

The Galley Speedwell. To Thomas Keys, captain, the said 24th day of August for his diets serving in the same galley by the space of 15 days begun the 19th day of July last and ended the 2nd day of August next, at 6s 8d *per diem* – £5; more to Nicholas Gorges, captain, for his diets serving in the said galley by the space of 15 days begun the 10th day of August last and ended the 24th day of the same month, at 6s 8d *per diem* – £5; more for the wages of a master and 249 other mariners, gunners and rowers serving under them by the space of 5 weeks 3 days begun the 18th day of July last and ended the day abovesaid, at 9s every man – £112 10s; more for 20 deadshares, at 6s 9d every share – £6 15s; more in reward to four gunners, at 12d every of them – 4s; more in reward to a surgeon – 11s 4d; more in reward to a trumpeter – 11s 4d; and more in reward to a drum – 4s 6d. *Summa* – £130 16s 2d.

[*Page total*] – £162 13s.

[f. 350v] *The Searcher*. To Giles Grey, captain, the 26th day of August for his diets serving in the same brigantine by the space of 48 days begun the 10th day of July last and ended as aforesaid, at 18d *per diem* – £3 12s; more for the wages of a master and 49 other mariners, gunners and rowers serving under him in the said galliot by the space of 6 weeks 6 days begun and ended as abovesaid, at 11s 5d every man – £28 10s 10d; more for 10 deadshares, at 8s 6d every share – £4 5s; and more in reward to two gunners, at 18d either of them – 3s. *Summa* – £36 10s 10d.

The Phoenix. To Thomas Gourlay, captain, the last day of August for his diets serving in the same ship by the space of 154 days begun the first day of April last and ended as abovesaid, at 18d *per diem* – £11 9s 6d; more for the wages of a master and 44 other mariners and gunners serving under him in the said ship by the space of 5 months one week, 6 days begun and ended as aforesaid, at 36s 5d every man – £81 18s 9d; more for 14 deadshares, at 27s 4d every share – £19 2s 8d; more in reward to three gunners, at 4s 6d every of them – 13s 6d; more in reward to a trumpeter – 45s 6d; and more in reward to a surgeon – 45s 6d. *Summa* – £117 15s 5d.

The Bark of Boulogne. To Edward Knight, captain, the said last day of August for his diets serving in the same ship by the space of 153 days begun the first day of April last and ended as aforesaid, at 18d *per diem* – £11 9s 6d; more for the wages of a master and 44 other mariners and gunners serving in the same ship under him by the space of 5 months one week 6 days begun and ended as abovesaid, at 36s 5d every man – £81 18s 9d; more for 14 deadshares, at 27s 4d every share – £19 2s 8d; more in reward to three gunners, at 4s 6d the man – 13s 6d; and more in reward to a trumpeter by like time – 45s 6d. *Summa* – £115 9s 11d.

[*Page total*] – £269 16s 2d.

[f. 351] *The Falcon.* To William Spencer, captain, the last day of August for his diets serving in the same ship by the space of 75 days begun the 30th day of May last and ended the 12th day of August next, at 18d *per diem* – £5 12s 6d; more to Robert Marsh, captain, for his diets serving in the said ship by the space of 19 days begun the 13th day of August last and ended the last day of the same month, at 18d *per diem* – 28s 6d; more for the wages of a master and 78 other mariners and gunners serving in the same ship under them by the space of 3 months one week 3 days begun the 30th day of May last and ended the last day of August following, at 22s 4d every man – £88 4s 4d; more for 18 deadshares divided between the master and other officers in the said ship, at 16s 8d every share – £15; more in reward to four gunners, at 2s 8d every of them – 10s 4d; more in reward to a trumpeter – 28s 4d; more in reward to a surgeon – 28s 4d; and more in reward to a lodesman – 28s 4d. *Summa* – £115 0s 8d.

The Double Rose. To Thomas Perryman, master, the 20th day of September for the wages of himself and 23 other mariners and gunners serving in the same pinnace with him by the space of 3 weeks 4 days begun the 27th day of August last and ended the day abovesaid, at 6s every man – £7 4s; more for 10 deadshares by like time, at 4s 6d every share – 42s 6d; and more in reward to two gunners, at 8d either of them – 16d. *Summa* – £9 7s 10d.

[*Page total*] – £124 8s 6d.

[f. 351v] *The Lion.* To John Constable, captain, the 6th day of October for his diets serving the Queen's Majesty in the same ship by the space of 15 days begun the 19th day of July last and ended the 2nd day of August next, at 18d *per diem* – 22s 6d; more to Sir Thomas Cotton, knight, for his diets serving in the said ship as Admiral of Her Highness's ships then in the Narrow Seas, by the space of 28 days begun the 10th day of August last and ended the 6th day of September following, at 10s *per diem* – £14; more to Henry Tirrell, captain, for his diets serving Her Majesty in the same ship by the space of 30 days begun the 7th day of September last and ended the 6th day of October next, at 18d *per diem* – 45s; more for the wages of a master and 239 other mariners and gunners serving in the said ship under them by the space of 2 months 3 weeks 4 days begun the 18th day of July last and ended the 6th day of October following, at 19s 4d every man – £232 13s 4d; more for 24 deadshares divided amongst the master and others the officers in the same ship, at 14s 2d every share – £17; more in reward to four gunners, at 2s 4d every man – 9s 4d; more in reward to a trumpeter – 24s; more in reward to a surgeon – 24s; more in reward to a lodesman – 24s; more in reward to a drum – 9s 8d; more to Robert Constable, captain, for his entertainment as captain over 200 soldiers serving under him in the same ship and in the *Philip and Mary* by the space of 15 days begun the 19th day of July last and ended the 2nd day of August next, at 8s *per diem* – £6; more for the wages of his lieutenant by like time, at 4s *per diem* – £3; more for his ensign bearer by like time, at 2s *per diem* – 30s; more for the wages of two sergeants, two drums, one fife and a surgeon for like 15 days, at 12d every of them *per diem* – £4 10s; and more for the wages of 150 soldiers serving in the said ship under him by like time of 15 days begun and ended as is aforesaid, at 2s 8d every man – £20. *Summa* – £306 11s 10d.

[*Page total*] – £306 11s 10d.

[f. 352] *The Philip and Mary.* To William Holstock, captain, the 6th day of October for his diets serving Her Majesty in the said ship as Vice-Admiral of Her Grace's ships then in the Narrow Seas, by the space of 68 days begun the 30th day of July last and ended as abovesaid, at 6s 8d *per diem* – £22 13s 4d; more for the wages of a master and 239 other mariners and gunners serving under him in the same ship by the space of 2 months 3 weeks 4 days begun the 18th day of July and ended as is aforesaid, at 19s 4d every man – £232 13s 4d; more for 24 deadshares, at 14s 2d every share – £17; more in reward to four gunners, at 2s 7d every man – 9s 4d; more in reward to two trumpeters, at 24s either of them – 48s; more in reward to a surgeon – 24s; more in reward to a drum – 9s 8d; more to James Holmes for his entertainment as captain over 100 soldiers in the said ship by the space of 15 days begun the 19th day of July last and ended the 2nd day of August next, at 4s *per diem* – £3;

more for the wages of his lieutenant by like 15 days, at 2s *per diem* – 30s; more for the wages of his ensign bearer, one sergeant, one drum, one fife and a surgeon by like time, at 12d every of them *per diem* – £3 15s; more to him for the wages of 100 soldiers by like time of 15 days, at 2s 8d every man – £13 6s 8d; and more to Robert Constable, captain, for the wages of 50 his soldiers serving in the same ship by like time of 15 days begun and ended as aforesaid, at 2s 8d every man – £6 13s 4d. *Summa* – £305 2s 8d.

The Elizabeth Jonas. To William Wood, master, the same day for the wages of himself and 199 other mariners and gunners serving under him by the space of 2 weeks 2 days begun the 20th day of September last and ended as abovesaid for the bringing about of the same ship from Portsmouth haven into Gillingham Water, at 3s 10d every man – £38 6s 8d; more for 26 deadshares, at 2s 10d every share – £3 13s 8d; more in reward to four gunners, at 6d every man – 2s; and more in reward to 2 trumpeters – 9s 4d. *Summa* – £42 11s 8d.

[*Page total*] – £347 14s 4d.

[f. 352v] *The Victory.* To Jeffrey Vaughan, captain, the 6th day of October for his diets serving the Queen's Majesty in the same ship by the space of 16 days begun the 20th day of September last and ended as abovesaid, at 18d *per diem* – 24s; more for the wages of a master and 159 other mariners and gunners serving under him for the bringing about of the said ship from Portsmouth haven into Gillingham Water, by the space of 2 weeks 2 days begun and ended as aforesaid, at 3s 10d every man – £30 13s 4d; more for 24 deadshares, at 2s 10d every share – £3 8s; more in reward to four gunners, at 6d every man – 2s; and more in reward to 2 trumpeters – 9s 4d; *Summa* – £35 16s 8d.

The Jennet. To the said Jeffrey Vaughan, captain, the 7th day of October for his diets serving Her Highness in the same ship by the space of 65 days begun the 9th day of June last and ended the 12th day of August next, at 18d *per diem* – £4 17s 6d; more to Randall Worsley, captain, for his diets serving in the same ship by the space of 61 days begun the 13th day of August last and ended the 7th day of October following, at 18d *per diem* – £4 4s; more for the wages of a master and 169 other mariners and gunners serving in the same ship under them by the space of 4 months one week 4 days begun the 9th day of June last and ended the day abovesaid, at 28s 10d every man – £245 1s 8d; more for 20 deadshares, at 21s 7d every share – £21 12s 3d; more in reward to four gunners, at 3s 6d every man – 14s; and more in reward to a surgeon – 36s. *Summa* – £278 5s 5d.

[*Page total*] – £314 2s 1d.

[f. 353] *The Minion.* To George Irelande, master, the 15th day of October for the wages of himself and 64 other mariners and gunners serving Her Highness in transporting of the same ship from Portsmouth haven into Gillingham Water, by the space of 3 weeks 5 days begun the 20th day of September last and ended as is abovesaid, at 6s 2d every man – £20 0s 10d; more for 14 deadshares, at 4s 8d every share – £4 5s 4d; and more in reward to four gunners, at 9d every man – 3s. *Summa* – £23 9s 2d.

The Primrose. To Ralph Cockes, master, the said 15th day of October for the wages of himself and 65 other mariners and gunners serving Her Majesty in bringing about of the said ship from Portsmouth haven into Gillingham Water, by like time of 3 weeks 5 days begun and ended as aforesaid, at 6s 2d every man – £20 7s; more for 14 deadshares, at 4s 8d every share – £3 5s 4d; and more in reward to four gunners – 3s. *Summa* – £23 15s 4d.

The Willoughby. To George Edmunds, captain, the 20th day of November for his diets serving in the same ship on the North Seas by the space of 137 days begun the 7th day of July last and ended the day aforesaid, at 18d *per diem* – £10 5s 6d; more for the wages of one master and 109 other mariners and gunners serving in the said ship under him by the space of 4 months 3 weeks 4 days begun and ended as abovesaid, at 32s 8d every man – £179 13s 4d; more for 18 deadshares, at 24s 6d every share – £22 1s 6d; more in reward to four gunners, at 3s 3d every man – 13s; more in reward to a trumpeter – 40s 8d; more in reward to a surgeon – 40s 8d; and more in reward to a lodesman – 40s 8d. *Summa* – £218 15s 4d.

[*Page total*] – £265 19s 10d.

[f. 353v] *The Swallow.* To John Basing, captain, the 20th day of November for his diets serving the Queen's Majesty in the same ship as Admiral of Her Grace's ships then in the Narrow Seas, by the space of 9 days begun the first day of June last and ended the 9th day of the same, at 5s *per diem* – 45s; more to him for his diets by the space of 64 days begun the 10th day of June last and ended the 12th day of August next, at 18d *per diem* – £4 16s; more to John Henshaw, captain, for his diets serving Her Highness in the said ship by the space of 16 days begun the 13th day of August last and ended the 28th day of the same month, at 18d *per diem* – 24s; more to him for his diets serving in the same ship as Admiral of Her Majesty's ships then on the North Seas, by the space of 84 days begun the 29th day of August last and ended the 20th day of November following, at 5s *per diem* – £21; more for the wages of a master and 159 other mariners and gunners serving in the said ship under them by the space of 6 months 5 days begun the first day of June last and ended the day first above-written, at 41s 2d every man – £329 6s 8d; more for 20 deadshares, at 30s 10d every share – £30 16s 8d; more in reward to four gunners, at 5s 1d every man – 20s 4d; more in reward to a trumpeter – 51s 7d; more in reward to a drum – 20s 5d; more in reward to a surgeon – 51s 7d; and more in reward to a lodesman – 51s 7d. *Summa* – £399 3s 10d.

[*Page total*] – £399 3s 10d.

[f. 354] *The Salamander, the Greyhound Bitch, the Three Moons, the Green Dragon, the Red Hart, the Flower de Luce, the Sparrowhawk, the Owlet, the Gryphon, the Serpent and five other French ships.* To Thomas Woode, Thomas Baker, John Stronge, John Burley, Thomas Fullar, Francis Lynsey, Simon Pendrycas, John Maye, Robert Beaver, Ralph Morrys, Nicholas Wrighte, Michael Cheston and three other masters for the wages of themselves and 275 other mariners and gunners serving the Queen's Highness in the same ships for the bringing of them from Newhaven in Normandy to Portsmouth, by the space of 13 days begun the 19th day of May last and ended the last day of the same month, at 3s 1d every man – £44 14s 2d; and more for 15 deadshares, at 2s 5d every share – 36s 3d. *Summa* – £46 10s 5d.

[*Page total*] *Summa predicta.*

[f. 354v] *Anno regni regine Elizabethe sexto*

The Hare. To Thomas Robins, captain, the last day of December for his diets serving the Queen's Majesty in the same ship by the space of 127 days begun the 27th day of August last and this day ended, at 18d *per diem* – £9 10s 6d; more for the wages of one master and 39 other mariners and gunners serving under him in the same ship by the space of 18 weeks one day begun and ended as abovesaid, at 30s 3d every man – £60 10s; more for 14 deadshares by like time, at 22s 8d every share – £15 17s 4d; and more in reward to three gunners, at 3s 9d the man – 11s 3d. *Summa* – £86 9s 1d.

The Falcon. To Robert Marsh, captain, the same day for his diets serving Her Highness in the same ship by the space of 122 days begun the first day of September last and ended as aforesaid, at 18d *per diem* – £9 3s; more for the wages of one master and 77 other mariners and gunners serving in the said ship under him by the space of 17 weeks 3 days begun and ended as abovesaid, at 29s every man – £113 2s; more for 18 deadshares, at 21s 9d every share – £19 11s 6d; more in reward to four gunners, at 3s 7d every man – 14s 4d; more in reward to a surgeon

– 38s; more in reward to a drum – 14s 5d; and more in reward to a trumpeter – 38s. *Summa* – £147 1s 3d.

The Phoenix. To John Henshaw, captain, the same day for his diets serving Her Majesty in the said ship by like time of 122 days begun and ended as aforesaid, at 18d *per diem* – £9 3s;[1] more for the wages of one master and 59 other mariners and gunners serving under him by like 17 weeks 3 days, at 29s every man – £87; more for 14 deadshares, at 21s 9d every share – £15 4s 6d; more in reward to three gunners, at 3s 7d the man – 10s 9d; more in reward to a surgeon – 38s; more in reward to a trumpeter – 38s; and more in reward to a drum – 14s 5d. *Summa* – £116 8s 8d.

[*Page total*] – £349 19s.

[f. 355] *The Bark of Boulogne*. To Edward Knight, captain, the last day of December for his diets serving Her Highness in the same ship by the space of 122 days begun the first day of September last and this day ended, at 18d *per diem* – £9 3s; more for the wages of a master and 57 other mariners and gunners serving under him in the said ship by the space of 17 weeks 3 days begun and ended as abovesaid, at 29s every man – £84 2s; more for 14 deadshares, at 21s 9d the share – £15 4s 6d; more in reward to three gunners, at 3s 7d every man – 10s 9d; more in reward to a drum – 14s 5d; and more in reward to a trumpeter – 38s. *Summa* – £111 12s 8d.

The Aid. To Sir Thomas Cotton, knight, captain, the same day for his diets serving Her Majesty in the said ship as Admiral of all Her Grace's ships then on the Narrow Seas, by the space of 116 days begun the 7th day of September last and ended as aforesaid, at 13s 4d *per diem* – £77 6s 8d; more for the wages of one master and 139 other mariners, gunners and soldiers serving Her Highness under him in the same ship by 16 weeks 4 days begun and ended as abovesaid, at 27s 8d every man – £193 13s 4d; more for 20 deadshares, at 20s 6d every share – £20 10s; more in reward to 4 gunners, at 3s 4d the man – 13s 4d; more in reward to a surgeon – 34s 6d; more in reward to two trumpeters – £3 9s; more in reward to two lodesmen – £3 9s; and more in reward to a drum and a fife – 27s 4d. *Summa* – £302 3s 2d.

[*Page total*] – £413 15s 10d. [f. 355v *blank*]

[1] This is incompatible with the payment to Henshaw as captain of *Swallow* during a largely overlapping period (*viz*. 13 Aug.–20 Nov.: p. 498), which directly follows his previous command in *Aid* (to 12 Aug.: f. 345v). The Declared Account [**5**, m. 8] confirms Henshaw's captaincy of *Phoenix* and gives no information for *Swallow*.

[f. 356] **Extraordinary. Conduct:**

Anno Domini 1562 [1563]. *Anno regni regine Elizabethe quinto*

Conduct to masters, mariners, gunners, soldiers and others discharged from Her Highness's service to the places from whence they were prested.

The Double Rose. To Thomas Elye, master, the 11th day of January for the conduct of himself, Richard Cloughe, and John Awstyn, mariners, late serving the Queen's Majesty in the same ship and now discharged to the places from whence they were prested, at several distances, after the rate of every 12 miles 6d – 7s 6d.

The Rowbarge. To William Bagg, master, the 13th day of March for the conduct of himself, John Stronge, Thomas Whittell, John Fuglar, Andrew Rotche, Robert Tompson and 26 other mariners and gunners late serving Her Highness in the said ship and now discharged to the places from whence they were prested, being several distances, and after the rate of 6d for every 12 miles – £2 6s 6d.

The Greyhound. To Roger Cowpar the 19th day of March for the conduct of himself, Nicholas Perrye, Stephen Bartlett, William Bartlett, William Harwood, Alexander Grene, William Brayes, Robert Smythe, William Cock and 13 other mariners and gunners late serving Her Highness in the same ship and now discharged to the places from whence they were prested, being several distances, and after the rate of every 12 miles 6d – £3 17s 6d.

Anno Domini 1563

The Aid. To Thomas Willson the last day of March for the conduct of himself, Roger Thatcher, Thomas Ritche, Edmund Mighell, Robert Darbone, John Claye, Robert Brooke, Thomas Harmond, Stephen Graye, Thomas Cautt, William Hatclyff, John Fordam, George Watson, Richard Rawson, William Holtt, Thomas Fuglar, James Shearley and 25 other mariners, gunners and soldiers late serving Her Highness in the said ship and now discharged to the places from whence they were prested, being several distances, and after the rate of every 12 miles 6d – £6 15s.

[*Page total*] – £13 6s 6d.

[f. 356v] *The Saker*. To Thomas Harryson, John Deonys, Francis Waymouthe, Morgan Thomas, Luke Hailles, John Gobye and John Morraunte, mariners, the last day of March for their conduct, late serving the Queen's Majesty in the same ship and now discharged to the places from whence they were prested, being several distances, and after the rate of every 12 miles 6d – 13s 6d.

The Phoenix. To Robert Barley and Robert Massye, mariners, the same day for their conduct, late serving Her Highness in the said ship and now discharged to the places from whence they were prested, according to the distance of miles – 5s.

The Hare. To John Scott the same day for the conduct of himself, Hugh Bowmer and John Saye, mariners, late serving in the same ship[1] and now discharged home to the places from whence they were prested, according to the distance of miles – 9s 6d.

The Bark of Boulogne. To John Moore, John Jenkynson, John Lynsey, Thomas Latche and Nicholas Browne, mariners, the same day for their conduct, late serving Her Majesty in the same ship and now discharged home to the places from whence they were prested, being several distances, after the rate of every 12 miles 6d – 15s.

The Aid. To George Clarke the 12th day of August for the conduct of himself, John Harrys, Cuthbert Wynnye, Thomas Lowman, John Gyll, Walter Symonde, William Tolkyn, William Clarkson, John Willson, William Annderson, John Hammonde, Peter Stone, John Thomas, Hans Pysson, Evan Johnhewys, Richard Barker, Lawrence Browne, John Caumbridge and 33 other mariners and gunners late serving Her Highness in the same ship and now discharged to the places from whence they were prested, being several distances, and after the rate of every 12 miles 6d – £8 13s 6d.

[*Page total*] – £10 16s 6d.

[f. 357] *The Saker*. To Francis Fullar, master, the 12th day of August for the conduct of himself, John Willyngton, Simon Pendrycas, Saunder Gawdye, Francis Courrall, John Gayner, Richard Ruttar, Maurice James, George Duckett, George Prowde and seven other mariners and gunners late serving Her Majesty in the same ship and now discharged home to the places from whence they were prested, being several distances and after the rate of every 12 miles 6d – £3 13s.

The Hare. To Thomas Robynson, master, the same day for the conduct of himself, Richard Scarbroff, John Baesh, Thomas Rowse, Humphrey Duncke, Thomas Dradye, Godfrey Randoll and 10 other mariners and gunners late serving in the said ship and now discharged home to the places from whence they were prested, according to the distances of miles – £2 14s.

The Double Rose. To Thomas Perryman, John Foarde, William Tompson, Robert Treguntus, Thomas Orlarde and eight other mariners and gunners the same day for their conduct, late serving Her Highness in the said ship and now discharged home to the places from whence they

[1]MS 'ships'.

were prested, being several distances, and after the rate of every 12 miles 6d – £1 3s 6d.

The Antelope. To Philip Drewe, Henry Manfylde, William Honnye, Thomas Robartes, John Walter, Richard Thomas, Robert Fuller and 103 other mariners, gunners and soldiers, the same day for their conduct late serving Her Majesty in the same ship and now discharged to the places from whence they were prested, according to the distances of miles, after the rate of 6d for every 12 miles – £18 5s 6d.

The Sun. To William Tompson the same day for the conduct of himself, Francis Leache, Richard Cryppes, and 17 other mariners and gunners late serving in the said ship and now discharged to the places from whence they were prested, according to the distances of miles – £2 15s 6d.

[*Page total*] – £28 11s 6d.

[f. 357v] *The Post*. To Robert Osborne the 12th day of August for the conduct of himself, William Saunders, Ralph Mason, Edward Clarke, William Beaple, John Partridge and seven other mariners and gunners late serving the Queen's Majesty in the said brigantine at the seas and now discharged to the places from whence they were prested, being several distances, after the rate of every 12 miles 6d – £1 9s.

The Elizabeth Jonas. To Robert Typpett the same day for the conduct of himself, William Myll, John Cornelyas, John Dunton, John Haywood, Richard Mase, John Castell, Henry Rayman, Cornelius Hawkyns, Davy Martyn, Cornelius Brene, William Cooke, John Duffyeld, John Rynglande, William Parkyn, William Turner, John Gonbye, Richard Cock, Matthew Dixson, Richard Kynge, Thomas Graunte, William Smyth and 242 other mariners, gunners and soldiers late serving Her Highness in the said ship and now discharged to the places from whence they were prested, being several distances, and after the rate of every 12 miles 6d – £33 2s 10d; more to William Drury, captain, having the charge of 300 soldiers late serving under him in the same ship and in the *Victory*, for the conduct of himself now discharged from Portsmouth to Oxford, distant 74 miles, at 12d every mile – £3 14s; more for the conduct of his lieutenant, like distant, at 6d every mile – 37s; more for the conduct of his ensign bearer, distant as aforesaid, at 3d every mile – 18s 6d; more for the conduct of three sergeants, three drums, a fife and a surgeon, like distant, at 1d every mile the man – 49s 4d; and more to him for the conduct of 100 his soldiers from Portsmouth to London, distant 60 miles, at ½d every mile the man – £12 10s. *Summa* – £54 11s 8d.

The Makeshift. To William Cockes the same day for the conduct of himself, John James, William Maddock, William Cobb and 13 other mariners, gunners and rowers late serving in the said brigantine and now discharged to the places from whence they were prested, being several distances, after the rate of every 12 miles 6d – £2 10s 6d.

[*Page total*] – £58 11s 2d.

[f. 358] *The Victory*. To John Roche the 12th day of August for the conduct of himself, Richard Androw, John Pendryck, Roger Morley, John Mosyar, William Burde, George Highear, John Hudson, Thomas Androwe George Upton, John Breadcake, Richard Lane, Robert Frebarne, Edward Hock, John Dryver, Henry Rawlyns, John Thornborow, Robert Pope Thomas Baytt and 84 other mariners, gunners and soldiers late serving the Queen's Highness in the same ship and now discharged to the places from whence they were prested, being several distances, after the rate of every 12 miles 6d – £22 5s; and more to William Drury, captain, for the conduct of 200 his soldiers which served Her Majesty in the said ship and now discharged as aforesaid from Portsmouth to London, distant 60 miles at ½d every mile the man – £25. *Summa* – £47 5s.

The Galley Mermaid. To Robert Atkyns the same day for the conduc of himself, John Sellman, William Wyne, John Berrye, Peter Webb John Tompson, Robert Bairett, Edmund Bridges, Hugh Kytt, George Roumbolde, John Wyllye, William Clarke and 36 other mariners, gunner and rowers late serving Her Majesty in the said galley and now discharged to the places from whence they were prested, being several distances, and after the rate of every 12 miles 6d – £6 12s 6d.

The Hope. To Ralph Browne the 20th day of August for the conduc of himself, John Archer, Jeffrey Frackson, Robert Sutton, John Dowes John Baillye, Thomas Hoghe, Christopher Graye, Morgan Teigg Matthew Chasser and 157 other mariners and gunners late serving He Highness in the same ship and now discharged to the places from whence they were prested, being several distances, after the rate of ever 12 miles 6d – £10.

The Rowbarge. To Thomas Whittell the same day for the conduct of himself, John Walker, Robert Trasse, Miles Pepper and 37 other mariner and gunners late serving in the same ship and now discharged to the place from whence they were prested, being several distances, after the rat aforesaid – £6 3s.

[*Page total*] – £70 0s 6d.

[f. 358v] *The Galley Tryright*. To Nicholas Fysheborne the 24th da of August for the conduct of himself, Nicholas Frelande, Joh Bagshawe, Richard Cowper, William Nellam, Nicholas Cursell, William Stadder, William Jones, James Rowlson, Robert Taillor and 136 othe mariners, gunners, rowers and soldiers late serving the Queen's Majest in the same galley and now discharged to the places from whence they were prested, being several distances, after the rate of every 12 miles 6d – £12 6s 6d.

The Galley Speedwell. To James Ruddam, Nicholas Foxe, Thomas Ryse, Stephen Jones, William Jones, James Hyll, Hugh Jones, Thomas Jennynges, John Bannock, William Smythe, Davy Hearon, John Morgan, Thomas Goodman, John Haynes, Alexander Meaw, John Osborne, John Fyshwyck, Richard Laike and 168 other mariners, gunners, rowers and soldiers the said 24th day of August for their conduct, late serving Her Highness in the said galley and now discharged home to the places from whence they were prested, being several distances, after the rate of every 12 miles 6d – £16 1s.

The Guide. To William Parcyvall the same day for the conduct of himself, John Godfrey, Thomas Burnam, James Yonge, William Haywarde, Thomas Kydden, Thomas Smythe, John Fullarr, Edward Goldock, Thomas Berryn, Nicholas Jacob and 12 other mariners, gunners and rowers late serving in the said brigantine at the seas and now discharged to the places from whence they were prested, being several distances, and after the rate every 12 miles 6 pence – £2 7s.

The Searcher. To Nicholas Matson the 26th day of August for the conduct of himself, Thomas Sylver, John Pett, Walter Bennett, Morgan Cooke, John Hammonde, William Morrys, John Stacye, Richard Raynoldes, George Turner, William Grene, Richard Walden, Richard Brewton, Humphrey Dellor, William Russell and 35 other mariners, gunners and rowers late serving in the same brigantine and now discharged to the places from whence they were prested, being several distances, after the rate of 6d for every 12 miles – £6 11s 6d.

[*Page total*] – £37 6s.

[f. 359] *The Phoenix.* To Henry Oldernes the last day of August for the conduct of himself, John Grene, John Hasellwood, Henry Hasellwood, William Nealle, John Phillippes, Thomas Laye and nine other mariners and gunners late serving the Queen's Highness in the same ship and now discharged to the places from whence they were prested, being several distances, and after the rate of every 12 miles 6d – £2 8s 6d.

The Bark of Boulogne. To Thomas Hare the same day for the conduct of himself, John Rowlle, John Bateman, William Jennynges, Awstyn Stygons, Richard Moundaye, Peter Stevens, John Lawrence, Richard Gater, John Vynsent, John Myllen, Robert Quycke, and 10 other mariners and gunners late serving Her Majesty in the said ship and now discharged to the places from whence they were prested, being several distances, and after the rate of every 12 miles 6d – £4 3s.

The Falcon. To Nicholas Haye. John Gonson, Jarmayne Dayne, John Fallett, John Merrett, John Preston, Peter Pealle, William Holstock and 11 other mariners and gunners the same day for their conduct, late serving in the said ship and now discharged to the places from whence they were prested, being several distances, and after the rate of every 12 miles 6d – £2 17s 6d.

The Double Rose. To Robert Gere, Simon Halle and Miles Robynson, mariners, the 20th day of September for their conduct late serving in the said pinnace and now discharged to the places from whence they were prested, according to the distance of miles, and after the abovesaid rates – 8s 6d.

The Elizabeth Jonas. To Lawrence Marybote, John Androwes, Anthony Reade, Richard Wood, Robert Godley, John Tayer, Robert Waddylow, John Barrett, Christopher Perrys, William Higgon, George Swan, John Tompson, Thomas White, John Blaick and 151 other mariners and gunners the 6th day of October for their conduct, late serving Her Highness in the same ship and now discharged to the places from whence they were prested, being several distances, and after the rate of every 12 miles 6 pence – £32 9s 6d.

[*Page total*] – £42 7s.

[f. 359v] *The Lion.* To Thomas Graye the 6th day of October for the conduct of himself, Robert Goslinge, Nicholas Water, Nicholas Hewes, Thomas Dayll, Thomas Whytinge, Robert Warden, John Ashley, George Mannors, Adam Wygnor, Robert Mytchell, Richard Dremor, Thomas Sabber, John Harryson, Walter Lambe, Robert Wilkynson, Peter Blancke and 218 other mariners and gunners late serving the Queen's Majesty in the same ship and now discharged to the places from whence they were prested, being several distances, and after the rate of every 12 miles 6d – £36 7s; more to Robert Constable, captain, having the charge of 200 soldiers late serving under him in the said ship and in the *Philip and Mary* and now discharged, for the conduct of himself from Portsmouth to Newark, being distant 120 miles, at 8d every mile – £4; more for the conduct of his lieutenant, like distant, at 4d every mile – 40s; more for the conduct of his ensign bearer, like distant, at 2d every mile – 20s; more for the conduct of two sergeants, two drums, one fife and a surgeon, of like distance, at 1d every mile the man – £3; more for the conduct of 100 his soldiers from Portsmouth to London, distant 60 miles, at ½d every mile the man – £12 10s; and more to James Holmes, captain, for the conduct of 50 soldiers late serving under him in the said ship and now discharged from Portsmouth to London, distant as aforesaid, at 2s 6d every man – £6 5s. *Summa* – £65 2s.

The Victory. To John Shepparde, Henry Dashe, Peter Shearon, Hugh Baldinge, Philip Milles, Henry Cretchell, John Tawborde, John Lange, John Coxe, Hugh Billett, Richard Cade, James Saunders, Robert Pollarde, Stephen Stanley, George Torrye, John Ball, Matthew Ronner, Thomas Baker, Robert Hancock, Nicholas Barefoote, Nicholas Baker, Nicholas Aldernaye, Thomas Webb, Robert Lambe and 114 other mariners and gunners the said 6th day of October for their conduct money, late serving Her Highness in the same ship, and now discharged home to the places from whence they were prested, being several distances, and after the rate of every 12 miles 6 pence – £28 2s 6d.

[*Page total*] – £93 4s 6d.

[f. 360] *The Philip and Mary*. To Zach Swettman, Richard Browne, Thomas Tryttell, John Yonge, William Mytchell, Ralph Smythe, John Payne, James Feardell, Thomas Pacey, Cuthbert Jackson, William Kennett, John Clarke, Fernando Rolphe, Richard Baynam and 144 other mariners and gunners the 6th day of October for their conduct late serving Her Highness in the same ship and now discharged to the places from whence they were prested, being several distances, and after the rate of every 12 miles 6d – £22 10s; more to James Holmes, captain over 100 soldiers late serving Her Majesty in the said ship and in the *Lion*, for the conduct of himself now discharged from Portsmouth to London, being distant 60 miles, at 4d every mile – 20s; more for the conduct of his lieutenant, like distant, at 2d every mile – 10s; more for the conduct of his ensign bearer, sergeant, drum, fife and surgeon, distant as is aforesaid, at 1d the mile every man – 25s; more to him for the conduct of 50 his soldiers from Portsmouth to London aforesaid, at ½d every mile the man – £6 5s; and more to Robert Constable, captain, for the conduct of 100 his soldiers discharged from the same ship to London, at 2s 6d every man – £12 10s. *Summa* – £44.

The Jennet. To Thomas Wood the 7th day of October for the conduct of himself, Richard Trewe, John Bryan, Ralph Harrolde, William Carter, Thomas Shribb, Thomas Wheller, Henry Hudson and 128 other mariners and gunners late serving in the same ship and now discharged to the places from whence they were prested, being several distances, and after the rate of every 12 miles 6d – £19 3s.

The Minion. To George Irelande, master, the 15th day of October for the conduct of himself, John Barnes, John Tasker, Henry Myller, Andrew Burley, Thomas Cowper, William Towe, William Huntley and 37 other mariners and gunners late serving Her Highness in the same ship and now discharged to the places from whence they were prested, being several distances, and after the rate of every 12 miles 6d – £5 12s.

[*Page total*] – £68 15s.

[f. 360v] *The Primrose*. To Ralph Cockes, master, the 15th day of October for the conduct of himself, Thomas Warraunte, John Twynam, William Hewytt, John Beare, John Sprigges, Clement Haull, Robert Jollyff, Traymer Williams, Awdryan Salter, John Locke and 34 other mariners and gunners late serving Her Majesty in the same ship and now discharged to the places from whence they were prested, being several distances, and after the rate of every 12 miles 6d – £7 5s.

The Willoughby. To Thomas Lucas, John Hilles, Richard Torkynton, Peter Robson, Richard Connstable, Edward Crowe, Giles Hewden, John Hawkyns, William Marshall, Richard Woode, Robert Atkynson and 53 other mariners and gunners the 20th day of November for their conduct late serving Her Highness in the said ship and now discharged to the places from whence they were prested, being several distances, and after the rate of every 12 miles 6d – £10 16s 6d.

The Swallow. To John Dyett the said 20th day of November for the conduct of himself, Richard Fishbell, William Harewoode, Thomas Ricardes, Richard Tompson, John Brooke, William Cotten, Francis Whitred and 108 other mariners and gunners late serving in the same ship and now discharged to the places from whence they were prested, being several distances, and after the abovesaid rates – £14 19s 6d.

The Salamander, the Greyhound Bitch, the Three Moons, the Green Dragon, the Red Hart, the Sparrowhawk, the Owlet, and 8 other French ships.[1] To John Justys, Thomas Gibbes, Thomas Pearse, John Castell Thomas Norwaye, Thomas Baker, John Burdgys and 11 other mariners and gunners for their conduct late serving the Queen's Majesty in the same ships for the fetching of them from Newhaven in Normandy to Portsmouth, and now discharged unto the places from whence they were prested, being several distances, and after the rate of every 12 miles 6d – £3 2s.

[*Page total*] – £35 13s.

[f. 361] *Anno regni regine Elizabethe sexto*

The Aid, the Falcon, the Phoenix, the Bark of Boulogne, and the Hare. To John Bell the last day of December for the conduct of himself William Martyn, John Delapoole, William Cowleres, Thomas Gest, Peter Hake, Edward Braye, Jeffrey Nickolles, John Sake, John Graye, John Goodlonde, John Parker, Arthur Alredd, John Tyller, Thomas Atkyns and 63 other mariners and gunners late serving Her Highness in the same ships

[1]The others being *Bark of Cherbourg*, *Bear*, *Black Bark*, *Flower de Luce*, *Gryphon*, *Maiden*, *Raven* and *Serpent*.

at the seas and now discharged home to the places from whence they were prested, being several distances, and after the rate of every 12 miles 6d – £11 18s.

[*Signed*] W. Winter. William Holstock. G. Winter.

[*Page total*] – *Summa predicta*.

III

THE NAVY TREASURER'S DECLARED ACCOUNT FOR 1562–1563

This is the final or returned account for the period covered by the preceding Quarter Book, as presented by Gonson to the Exchequer, and is one in a regular series going back to 1548.[1] It is, however, an exceptional example because it covers the period of the Le Havre operation, and was subject to scrutiny by a commission appointed under the great seal on 5 August 1564 to examine all recent military spending. In addition to the Navy Treasurer's account, the commissioners were required to view those of the late Treasurer of the wars in Normandy, the Surveyor of victuals at Berwick, and the Lieutenant of the Ordnance. Gonson's account incorporates the full text of the commission, and is signed by Lord Treasurer Winchester, Secretary Cecil and the four other commissioners who attended to this part of the investigation. In other respects Gonson's account follows the established format. As is several times explicitly stated, it is based on the Quarter Book, but considerably compresses and often re-assembles its material. It will be seen that the auditors' markings to **4** are sometimes echoed here by the gathering of various items of expenditure under composite headings. The reorganisation can, however, most readily be demonstrated in the *recepta*. As more fully explained in the Introduction to Section II, the corresponding entries in the two accounts have been supplied with identifying symbols: **#A** and **#B** preface ordinary and extraordinary warrants for 1562; **#X** and **#Y** the like for 1563.

While the Quarter Book is a straightforward and comprehensive record of sums received and disbursed, it is the returned account which constitutes the official financial statement of the Treasurer of Marine Causes. In common with most estate and institutional accounts of the period, its purpose is not primarily to show gain or loss, but to clear the accountant of his liabilities. Unpaid credits are therefore counted in with the sums he actually received from the Exchequer and elsewhere to make up the total for which he is responsible. Against this he sets the deficit ('superplusage') on his previous account along with his new disbursements, and carries forward the same old unpaid credits. These sums make up his discharge; and since this is higher than his charge, the account ends again

[1] See full listings in Appendix 1 below.

in 'superplusage'. For the Navy this represents, in modern terms, an overdrawn current account. But the Treasurer has balanced his books by demonstrating that all sums charged against him have been applied to official purposes, and he has thus discharged his personal responsibilities to the Crown.

The account can be summarised thus:

charge	
unpaid credits	£160
receipts: Exchequer	£43,156 8s 8d
sales of Crown lands	£6,000
Court of Wards	£1,385 16s 8d
privy seal loan	£2,008 6s 8d
privy purse	£1,000
sale of *Jerfalcon*	£80
total	£53,790 12s
discharge	
deficit on previous account	£7,728 17s 7½d
payments:	
coats and conduct	£1,294 4s
emptions	£17,726 12s 6d
wages &c.	£16,021 4s 7¾d
rents	£27 5s 7d
carriage	£220 11s 4½d
fetching French ships	£102 18s 5d
recovery of *Greyhound*	£32
riding	£753 2s 3½d
Exchequer fees	£36 13s 4d
to Baeshe for victualling	£19,208 3s 10d
unpaid credits	£160
total	£63,311 13s 7¼d
deficit carried forward	£9,521 1s 7¼d

The manuscript consists of 10 membranes stitched together at the top and formed into a roll, and is written throughout in the hand of a single clerk. In this transcript some headings made redundant by the format of the printed text are omitted. Correspondences between this account and the Quarter Book are so frequent that cross-referencing individual items has not been attempted.

Although this copy of the account is solemnly certified as correct by the examining commissioners, it contains several ellipses where the scribe has omitted elements necessary for the sub-totals given. Conversely in one section consecutive entries are repeated. Fortunately we are able to supply the missing details from the Quarter Book, so that the relevant sections are presented arithmetically correct. Defects of this kind are faults in transcription rather than in the basic accounting. From them it is evident that the parchment E 351 copies were not themselves audited, since the most elementary examination would have revealed the shortcomings. The arithmetic must have been checked on earlier versions, which were then copied to parchment without further scrutiny. For the 1562–63 account there is no paper duplicate in AO; but both versions survive for 1561–62, and from comparison of these it is evident that the E 351 version was compiled directly from the AO. The *recepta* of the second version has no ellipses similar to those in the 1562–63 account, but it incorporates interlined addenda and other corrections in the AO version. In one instance the order of entries is altered in a way which suggests immediate restoration of ellipsed matter.[1] It has not been feasible to make extensive collation of other duplicated versions in the hope of finding defects in E 351s which can be resolved from the corresponding AO 1s; but it seems clear enough that the parchment versions were copied from the paper ones, so that the latter remain useful as counter-checks. The chance survival of a Quarter Book for years where there is no AO version is therefore all the more valuable. Where there is an inconsistency between Quarter Book and Declared Account which cannot be resolved by internal arithmetic or other means, the Quarter Book's detail may be taken as the more reliable. On that basis some adjustments have been made to the text here printed. There are also some errors as to dates and names, and where these can with certainty be corrected by collation with the Quarter Book, the correct data has been supplied. The editorial interpolations are noted in each instance.

[1]AO 1/1682/2, m. 1d *vs* E 351/2198, m. 1d.

5 *Navy Treasurer's Declared Account*

[E 351/2199] *1562–63*

[m. 1d] *The Office of Treasurer of the Marine Causes.* [m. 1] The account of Benjamin Gonson, esquire, Treasurer of the Marine Causes and Affairs, thereunto appointed by letters patents of our late sovereign lord King Edward the Sixth dated the 8th day of July in the third year of His Majesty's reign,[1] to have occupy and enjoy the said office of Treasurer or Treasurership unto the said Benjamin Gonson during his life, with all fees, wages, allowances and pre-eminences thereunto in any wise belonging or hereafter appertaining or due; and further our said late sovereign lord hath given and granted by the said letters patents to the said Benjamin Gonson a certain annuity or yearly fee of 100 marks sterling and for two clerks under him in the said room or office of Treasurer eight pence sterling by the day to either of them, together with the allowances of 6s 8d sterling for every day that the said Benjamin Gonson shall travel and be occupied either by sea or land only for such business as shall be needful and expedient to be overseen or despatched in or concerning the same office of Treasurer, and £8 sterling by the year for his boat-hire; and further [*it*] is granted by the said letters patents that he the same Benjamin Gonson shall have full allowance of and for all and every such sum or sums of money which he by himself or by his deputy or deputies shall disburse, pay, expend or lay out in or abouts the said marine causes and wherewith the same Benjamin shall be in any wise charged for or concerning the same office, he having the hands of two or three of the officers of the said marine causes subscribed to his book or books of account or reckoning of the same testifying the payment or expending thereof; and that the showing of the said letters patents and of the said book or books of account so subscribed as is aforesaid shall be a sufficient warrant unto all and every auditors and other officers and ministers in such behalf authorised and to be authorised to make full and just allowance and discharge of the same; and further that the said Benjamin shall have the costs of his clerks when and as often as he shall send them for the payment or receipt of money for the same marine causes; to have, perceive and enjoy [all and every *inserted*] the foresaid annuity and other the aforesaid sum and sums of money granted in manner and form aforesaid and all other the premises to the said Benjamin Gonson and his assigns during his natural life, of His Majesty's treasure at the Receipt of the Exchequer by the hands of the Treasurer and Chamberlains there for the time being at the feasts of Easter, the Nativity of St John Baptist, St Michael the

[1] *CPR 1549–51*, p. 164. Cf. the renewal to Gonson jointly with Hawkins 1577 [**35**].

Archangel, and the Nativity of Our Lord God, by even portions, as by the said letters patents more at large it doth appear; that is to say as well of all and singular sum and sums of money by him received and had of the Queen's Majesty's treasure as well out of the Receipt of the Exchequer as of the sale of lands and of all and singular sum and sums of money by him received and had out of the Court of Wards and Liveries and out of Her Majesty's privy purse, and also of Sir Edward Rogers, knight, Comptroller of the Queen's most honourable Household of the loan money coming to his hands, as also of the defraying and expending of the same for divers and sundry emptions and provisions provided and bought for the new making and building of two new ships called the *Victory* and the *Triumph* made and finished within the time of this account. and for the repairing and mending of Her Majesty's Navy and for furniture of divers wants of provisions for the said marine affairs, and for the conduct money and wages of shipwrights, caulkers smiths, joiners, bricklayers, sawyers and other artificers and labourers occupied and working in new making, redubbing caulking, ransacking and repairing of Her Highness's said Navy at Deptford Strand, Woolwich, Gillingham, Portsmouth and other places, with the victualling and lodging of the said artificers, and for the wages of mariners and gunners serving in keeping afloat the ships, and in rigging, re-tackling and sewing of sails against the setting forth of the said ships, and for the wages of keepers of storehouses and of clerks of the prick and cheque books, purveyors and overseers and such other ministers, and also for the wages of the Lord Admiral, Vice-Admiral[1] and divers captains, masters, mariners and gunners serving in the Queen's Majesty's Navy appointed to the seas, together with riding and posting charges in and abouts the business and affairs of the said marine causes and divers other costs, charges and expenses incident thereunto as well ordinary as extraordinary, the particulars whereof are contained in a ledger book subscribed on every page with the hands of William Winter, Surveyor, William Holstock, Comptroller and George Winter, Clerk of the said marine causes, according to the tenor of the said letters patents, as by the same book hereupon duly cast, tried, perused and examined may appear.[2] Of all which premises the said Benjamin Gonson, being called before certain commissioners hereafter named, authorised and appointed by Her Majesty's commission to hear and determine the account of the said Benjamin Gonson amongst others, doth yield and make the same his account to Her Majesty's use in manner and form hereafter following for

[1]Only the sea pay of the Lord Admiral and Vice-Admiral (or Lieutenant of the Admiralty) passed through the Treasurer's hands; their ordinary fees and expenses were paid directly from the Exchequer. Cf., *NEM*, pp. 525–6.

[2]The Quarter Book printed above [**4**].

two whole years beginning the first day of January *anno quarto domine regine nostre Elizabethe* and ending the last day of December *anno sexto domine regine predicte*, both days inclusive, the tenor of which said commission hereafter followeth.[1]

ELIZABETH, by the Grace of God, Queen of England, France and Ireland, Defender of the faith, &c., to our right trusty and well beloved cousins and councillors William, Marquess of Winchester, our High Treasurer of England and William, Marquess of Northampton,[2] and to our trusty and well beloved councillors Sir William Cecil, knight, our principal secretary, Sir Ambrose Cave, knight, Chancellor of our Duchy of Lancaster,[3] Sir Richard Sackville, knight, Under-treasurer of our Exchequer,[4] Sir John Mason, knight, Treasurer of our Chamber,[5] and to our trusty and well beloved servants Sir Hugh Paulet, knight,[6] Edward Randolph, esquire, Lieutenant of the Ordnance,[7] Thomas Mildmay, esquire,[8] and Henry Coddenham, esquire, one of our Auditors of the Prests,[9] greeting. Where Benjamin Gonson, esquire, Treasurer of the Admiralty, since the determination of his last account made and determined for one year ended the first day of January in the fourth year of our reign, hath received divers and sundry sums of money of our treasure to be employed for and upon the charge of our said Admiralty within his office; and where Sir Maurice Denys, knight, late Treasurer of

[1]*CPR 1563–6,* no. 929 (pp. 181–2). This was the third and effective issue of the commission. The first (15 May) and second (7 July) did not extend to the Ordnance accounts: ibid., nos 491 (pp. 122–30), 498 (p. 123).

[2]William Parr, brother of Henry VIII's last consort, and therefore Elizabeth I's step-uncle: GEC, *Peerage*, ix, pp. 669–74. *ODNB*.

[3]Privy Councillor, and Chancellor of the Duchy, 1558 to his death in 1568: *ODNB. Hist. Parl. 1509–58*, i, pp. 594–5; *1558–1603*, i, pp. 563–4.

[4]Privy Councillor 1558, Under-treasurer February 1559 to his death in 1566: *ODNB. Hist. Parl. 1509–58*, iii, pp. 246–7; *1558–1603*, iii, pp. 314–15.

[5]Privy Councillor from 1550, and Treasurer from 1558 to his death in 1566: *ODNB. Hist. Parl. 1509–58*, ii, pp. 582–4; *1558–1603*, iii, pp. 29–31.

[6]Winchester's kinsman; Vice-Admiral of Somerset and Dorset since the 1540s; Captain of Jersey from 1550 to his death in 1573; Vice-President of the Council in the Marches of Wales from 1559: *ODNB. Hist. Parl. 1509–58*, iii, pp. 71–2; *1558–1603*, iii, p. 189.

[7]Randolph *alias* Randall held high military command from Philip and Mary, despite involvement in both Wyatt's rebellion and the Dudley conspiracy. On Elizabeth's accession his career promptly advanced. High Marshal of the garrison at Le Havre and second in command to Warwick, in succession to Sir Adrian Poynings (cf. above, p. 221); after the campaign he was appointed Lieutenant of the Ordnance. Killed in action 1566: *ODNB. CSPDM*, nos 131, 161 and *passim*. D. M. Loades, *Two Tudor Conspiracies* (Cambridge, 1965), pp. 207–8 and *passim*.

[8]Auditor of the Court of Augmentations 1536–46, and of the Duchy of Cornwall from 1538, sometime in partnership with his brother Sir Walter (Chancellor of the Exchequer): *ODNB. Hist. Parl. 1509–58*, ii, pp. 600–1; *1558–1603*, iii, p. 51.

[9]Appointed Auditor of Imprests and Foreign Accounts in the Exchequer 19 Jan. 1560, on surrender of a lesser post. Died by 25 Mar. 1570: *CPR 1558–60*, p. 299. Sainty, *Exchequer Officers*, p. 136.

our wars in Normandy, hath received by himself and by his deputy and clerks divers and sundry sums of money of our treasure to be employed about our affairs there committed to his charge; and where also John Abington, esquire,[1] hath likewise received of our treasure divers and sundry sums of money to be by him employed as well for the victualling of our garrison of Berwick during the space that he at any time hath had the charge thereof, as for the victualling of our garrison at Newhaven aforesaid,[2] according to such order as hath been from time to time [m. 1d] to him appointed; and where also William Bromfield, late Lieutenant of our Ordnance in our Tower of London,[3] since the determination of his last account made and determined for three years ended the last day of December in the fourth year of our reign hath received divers and sundry sums of money of our treasure to be employed in our service in and abouts the provision of ordnance, munition and artillery within his office for which they are to render us account; we, trusting in your approved circumspections and wisdoms, have authorised and by these presents do give unto you, ten, nine, eight, seven, six, five or four of you (whereof you our said High Treasurer of England or you William, Marquess of Northampton or you Sir William Cecil our principal secretary to be one) full power and authority from time to time to call before you, ten, nine, eight, seven, six, five or four of you as aforesaid, the said Benjamin Gonson, and to cause him to yield and make before you, ten, nine, eight, seven six, five or four of you as aforesaid, a just true and perfect account of all such sums of money of our treasure as he hath received by any means since the determination of his said last account until the first day of January in the sixth year of our reign; and also to call before you, ten, nine, eight, seven, six, five or four of you as aforesaid, the heirs, executors, administrators deputy or clerks of the said Sir Maurice Denys now deceased,[4] and also the said John Abington; and also the heirs, executors or administrators of the said William Bromfield, and every of them, and to cause them and every of them severally for his or their charge to yield and make before you, ten, nine, eight, seven, six, five or four of you as

[1]Clerk of the Kitchen and, by patent of 12 Jan. 1560, receiver of former Augmentations Office revenues in Kent, Surrey and Sussex (*CPR 1558–60*, p. 250). His principal appointment was as Surveyor-General of Victualling at Berwick (*APC 1558–70*, p. 21 and *passim*). During the Le Havre campaign he assisted Baeshe at Portsmouth; his performance was severely censured by Sir Francis Knollys, though he conceded that Abington 'hath more ado than he can overcome': SP 12/25, nos 28, 33, 36; 12/28, nos 47, 49; 12/29, nos 35 (quotation), 42(ii) (*CSPD 1547–80*, pp. 209, 210, 224, 227, 228).

[2]*Sic*. Not in fact mentioned by name hitherto.

[3]Appointed Lieutenant 4 June 1558. He had died of injuries received at Le Havre, and was succeeded by Randolph: *CPR 1557–8*, p. 302. *ODNB* (Randolph).

[4]He died at Portsmouth on 25 Aug. 1563, seemingly from the bubonic plague spread by troops returning from Le Havre: *Hist. Parl. 1558–1603*, ii, p. 33.

aforesaid, a just true and perfect account to our use of all and singular sums of money of our treasure come to their hands or to the hands of any of them, and of all manner of victuals or other provisions whatsoever it be which they or any of them have had or ought to be charged with to our use, and of the expending defraying and employment of the same in our service within their several charges; wherein our will and pleasure is that you shall use all such ways and means as you shall think best and most convenient for the perfect examination and trial thereof. And we give you, ten, nine, eight, seven, six, five or four of you as is aforesaid by these presents full power and authority to make and give unto the said Benjamin Gonson upon his account allowance, defalcation, deduction and discharge of all such sums of money as he hath paid and debursed for wages and victualling of mariners, artificers workmen and labourers occupied abouts our ships or for emptions and provisions for the same or for any other matter within his charge incident to our marine causes, upon such warrant proof and testimony as you, ten, nine, eight, seven, six, five or four of you as aforesaid, shall think sufficient for the same. And likewise we do give unto you, ten, nine, eight, seven, six, five or four of you as aforesaid by these presents full power and authority to make and give unto the heirs, executors, administrators, deputy or clerks of the said Sir Maurice Denys, or to any of them, upon his or their account to be made before you, ten, nine, eight, seven, six five, or four of you, allowance, defalcation, deduction and discharge of all such sums of money as by the said Sir Maurice Denys or his heirs, executors, administrators, deputy or clerks or any of them have paid for the wages and entertainment of our Lieutenant at Newhaven, or for the wages of any captains, soldiers, officers and ministers serving in the garrison there, and for the entertainment of himself, his clerks, servants and deputies, according to the capitulation to the said Sir Maurice Denys prescribed by our Council, and of any other sum or sums of money which he or they have paid for the wages of any captain or soldier increased to our said garrison after the said capitulation; all the same payments to be affirmed by warrant of our said Lieutenant for the time being or by warrant of the Marshal or Comptroller there being before the arrival of our said Lieutenant there;[1] and of such sums of money as he or they or any of them have paid at Portsmouth, Rye or elsewhere within our realm for the wages and charges

[1]Sir Adrian Poynings was Marshal from the start of the campaign to Nov. 1562, and was succeeded by Edward Randolph; Cuthbert Vaughan served as Comptroller until June 1563: SP 12/24, no. 60; 12/29, no. 40 (list of appointments, ?Sept. 1562, and Knollys to Cecil, 23 July 1563; *CSPD 1547–80*, pp. 207, 228). Cf. SP 12/24, no. 21 (memorandum by Cecil with some previous recommendations, ?Aug. 1562; *CSPD 1547–80*, p. 205). For Poynings see *Hist. Parl. 1558–1603*, iii, pp. 241–2; for Randolph, see above, p. 518 & n. 7.

of any captain or soldier sent thither for our service, and for coat and conduct money, transportation and freight of any captains, soldiers, armour, ordnance and munition for our said service, and of all such sums of money as he or they or any of them have paid and debursed for the charges of fortifications and buildings there upon such proof as you shall think meet for the same; and also of all such sums of money as he or they or any of them have paid and debursed to the said John Abington, appointed General Surveyor of our victuals there, or to any other person or persons, or for any other cause or purpose whatsoever concerning our affairs in Normandy committed to his charge, upon such just matter and proof as to the discretions of you, ten, nine, eight, seven, six, five or four of you as aforesaid, shall be thought good and sufficient for the allowance thereof. And also we give unto you, ten, nine, eight, seven, six, five or four of you, full power and authority by these presents to make and give unto the said John Abington upon his account or accounts to be made before you allowance, defalcation, deduction and discharge of all manner of victuals and other provisions whatsoever which he can justly prove to have delivered at the said town of Newhaven for our garrison there, or to any other place in Normandy, or to our garrison at Berwick, during the time of his service there, or to any other place within this our realm to any person or persons to be employed abouts our service, with all manner of wastes, charges, costs and expenses incident thereunto, the same delivery and charges to be proved by such testimony as in the like cases hath been used or by any other such sufficient proof as you, ten, nine, eight, seven, six, five or four of you shall think meet. And also we give unto you, ten, nine, eight, seven, six, five or four of you as aforesaid, full power and authority by these presents to make and give unto the heirs, executors or administrators of the said William Bromfield allowance, defalcation, deduction and discharge of all such sum and sums of money as he or they or any of them have paid and laid out for any armour, ordnance, munition, artillery or other provision which they or any of them can justly prove to have been bought, provided and delivered into our Tower of London or into any other place to the hands of any person or persons for our service either by sea or land, with all manner costs, charges or expenses incident thereunto. And also our will and pleasure is that you, ten, nine, eight, seven, six, five or four of you, shall give unto the said accountants and to every of them for the costs, charges and expenses of themselves, their deputy, clerks or servants, and for necessaries spent and occupied in their several offices and charges, or for the charges of any other whom you shall employ in the execution of this our commission, such reasonable allowance as you shall think meet, and that you shall do all other thing and things as the nature of these accounts shall require, and after that you have examined, perused and tried the charge and discharge of all and every the said several accounts [of all the premises and *inserted*] every of them in form before declared, and by such other ways and means as to the discretions of you, ten, nine, eight, seven, six, five or four of you shall seem most meet. And that the arrearages and sums of money that shall be found due to us upon and by the determination of the same accounts shall be by the said Benjamin Gonson, the heirs, executors, administrators or deputy of the said Sir Maurice Denys and by the said John Abington and by the heirs, executors or administrators of the said William Bromfield, or their assigns or the assigns of any of them, fully paid and delivered to our use into the Receipt of our Exchequer or to the hands of such person or persons as we shall appoint for the receipt thereof, our will and pleasure is, and we give unto you, ten, nine, eight, seven, six, five or four of you as is aforesaid, by these presents full power and authority to deliver unto the said Benjamin Gonson and to the heirs, executors, administrators, deputy or clerks of the said Sir Maurice Denys and to the heirs, executors or administrators of the said William Bromfield, and also to the said John Abington and to [m. 2] every of them severally, the duplicaments of their accounts in parchment of the premises under the hands and seals of you, ten, nine, eight, seven, six, five or four of you as aforesaid, and under the hands of our auditors of the prests, which duplicaments of accounts so severally delivered to the said accountants we will shall be to the said Benjamin Gonson and to the heirs, executors, administrators, deputy or clerks of the said Sir Maurice Denys and to the heirs, executors, or administrators of the said William Bromfield and to the said John Abington and to every of them and to their heirs, executors, and administrators, and to the heirs, executors and administrators of every of them, as sufficient exoneration, acquittal and discharge against us our heirs and successors for ever, of and for the premises as though the same were sealed under our great seal of England, any law, statute, ordinance or provision heretofore made to the contrary notwithstanding. And furthermore, to the intent we may know and understand how and in what sort and manner our armour, munition, ordnance and artillery which hath been sent unto the said town of Newhaven in Normandy and there committed to the charge and order of the said William Bromfield, Master of the Ordnance there, and also how our armour, munition and ordnance delivered for the furniture of our ships and committed to the charge and order of William Winter, Master of our Ordnance of our ships, is bestowed, and also how and in what manner our emptions and provisions of our store provided and bought for the building and repairing of our ships and committed to the charge and custody of Thomas Morley, keeper of our store, storehouses and store yards appointed for the safe-keeping of the same, is bestowed and employed, our will and pleasure is, and by these presents we give unto you, ten, nine, eight, seven, six, five or four of you as aforesaid, full power and authority to cause the heirs, executors or administrators of the said William Bromfield or any other person or persons whom you shall think meet to call before you, which had the charge or custody of any of our said armour, ordnance, munition or artillery at Newhaven aforesaid, to make before you, ten, nine, eight, seven, six, five or four of you as aforesaid, to our use an account and reckoning of all such armour, munition, ordnance and artillery as hath been sent thither for our service; and also to call before you the said William Winter and to cause him to make before you, ten, nine, eight, seven, six, five or four of you as aforesaid, an account or reckoning of all such ordnance, armour, munition or artillery as he at any time hath had for the service of our ships, or for any other service within his charge on the seas; and likewise to call before you the said Thomas Morley and to cause him to make before you, ten, nine, eight, seven, six, five or four of you as aforesaid an account or reckoning of all our provisions and emptions, as timber, cables, cordage, anchors, canvas, poldavy, masts, pitch, tar, rosin, oil, lead, solder and all other kind of emptions and provisions whatsoever which he at any time hath had in his charge and custody; and of the employing, expending and bestowing of the said armour, ordnance, munition and artillery, and also of the employing, bestowing and expending of the said store, emptions and provisions, and of the wastes and losses of the same in our service, and what and how much thereof doth remain and where and in what place the same doth remain. Wherein our will and pleasure is that you shall use all such ways and means by accounts, declarations, books or otherwise as to the discretions of you, ten, nine, eight, seven, six, five or four of you as aforesaid shall be thought most meet and convenient for the better trial and examination thereof, with all such circumstances as the nature of the same accounts or reckonings shall require. And we do give unto you, ten, nine, eight, seven, six, five or four of you as aforesaid, full power and authority to make and give unto the heirs, executors or administrators of the said William Bromfield, and unto the said William Winter and to every of them, or to any other person or persons whom you shall call to make account before you for our said armour, munition, ordnance and artillery, full allowance, defalcation and discharge of all such armour, ordnance, munition and artillery and other provisions whatsoever as hath by any means been bestowed employed, occupied spent, lost and wasted in our said town of Newhaven in Normandy, or in any other place in Normandy or elsewhere on the other side of the seas, or in any place within this our realm in our service, either by sea or land, upon such proof and testimony as to the discretions of you, ten, nine, eight, seven, six, five or four of you as aforesaid shall be thought meet and sufficient; and likewise to make and give unto the said Thomas Morley allowance, defalcation and discharge of all such kinds of store, emptions and provisions whatsoever as hath been employed, bestowed, expended, lost or wasted in and abouts the building, mending, repairing and furnishing of our ships, or in and abouts any other cause or purpose for our service within his charge, upon such proof and testimony as to the discretions of you, ten, nine, eight, seven, six, five or four of you as aforesaid shall be thought meet and sufficient. And after that you have tried, perused and examined the charge and discharge of the said accounts and reckonings of our said armour, munition, ordnance, artillery, provisions and emptions as aforesaid, and that you, ten, nine, eight, seven, six, five or four of you have thereupon given such order for the safe-keeping of the same or any part thereof so remaining upon the determination of their several accounts, and for the issuing and delivery out again of the same when it shall be needful for our better service therein, as to the discretions of you, ten, nine, eight, seven, six, five or four of you as aforesaid shall be thought most meet and convenient, our will and pleasure is, and we give unto you, ten, nine, eight, seven, six, five or four of you as aforesaid, full power and authority to deliver unto the heirs, executors and administrators of the said William Bromfield or to any other person or persons whom you shall call to account for the armour, munition, ordnance or artillery [sent *inserted*] to Newhaven, and to the said William Winter and to the said Thomas Morley, and to every of them severally, under the hands of you, ten, nine, eight, seven, six, five or four of you as aforesaid, and under the hands of our auditors of our prests, the duplicament of their said accounts, declarations and books to be made and yielded before you, ten, nine, eight, seven, six, five or four of you as aforesaid, containing the charge and discharge and remain of our said armour, ordnance, munition, artillery, store emptions and provisions in manner before rehearsed. Which duplicaments of accounts, declarations or books so severally delivered we will shall be to the heirs, executors and administrators of the said William Bromfield or to any person or persons whom you shall call to account in that behalf and to the said William Winter and to the said Thomas Morley and to every of them, and to their heirs, executors and administrators, and to the heirs executors and administrators of every of them sufficient exoneration and discharge against us, our heirs and successors, of, for and concerning the employing, bestowing and expending of our said armour, ordnance munition, artillery and provisions in our said service, and of, for and concerning the wastes and losses of the same in manner and form aforesaid, and likewise a sufficient declaration whereby may appear wha and how much of our said armour, ordnance, munition, artillery, provisions and emptions ought to remain and be answerable to us upon their said several accounts, declarations, books and reckonings, any law, statute, ordinance, provision or commission heretofore made to the contrary notwithstanding. And these our letters patents or the duplicament of the same shall be as well to you, ten, nine, eight, seven, six, five or four of you our said commissioners as aforesaid, as to the said Benjamin Gonson [m. 2d] and to the heirs, executors, administrators, deputy and clerks of the said Sir Maurice Denys, and to the said John Abington, and to the heirs executors and administrators of the said William Bromfield, and to any other person and persons whom you shall call in that behalf, and to the said William Winter and Thomas Morley and to every of them, sufficient warrant and discharge for and touching the premises and every part thereof. In witness whereof we have caused these our letters of commission to be sealed with our great seal. Witness ourself at Westminster the 5th of August the sixth year of our reign.

That is to say the said accountant is charged with:

Arrearages remaining in the hands of:

The said accountant. None, because he resteth in surplusage upon the determination of his last account[1] the sum [*of*] £7,728 17s 7½d as in the foot of the same appeareth – £0.

Other persons. But he is charged with the arrearages remaining in the hands of Thomas Trollopp of Boston in the county of Lincoln, merchant, and William Browne of Swineshead in the said county, merchant, for so much money delivered unto them by Robert Legge, late Treasurer of the Marine Affairs,[2] in prest and upon bargain of certain cables and other Lincolnshire cordage, and to have the occupying of the same for the space of seven years and then to deliver the value of the same in such kind of cordage and tackle into the Queen's Majesty's storehouse at Deptford Strand, as by one indenture remaining with the officers of the Admiralty appeareth, and there continuing in charge until the said sum of £100 be unto Her Majesty answered as in the foot of his last account appeareth – £100.

Also the said accountant is charged with the arrearages remaining in the hands of Frances Owdrye of Abingdon in the county of Berkshire, poldavy weaver, and William Blacknall of Swallowfield in the same county, yeoman, for so much money by the said accountant delivered to the said Frances by the King and Queen's warrant by way of loan for

[1]E 351/2198.

[2]Comptroller (1544–45) then Treasurer (1546–48); for full career details see *NEM*, p. 557.

certain years upon surety taken for the payment thereof, as in the foot of his last account appeareth – £60.

[*Sum*] – £160.

Money by him received and had of:

[m. 3] *The Treasurer and Chamberlains of the Exchequer*. The said accountant is charged with money by him received and had within the time of this account of the Treasurer and Chamberlains of the Exchequer by the hands of the tellers of the Receipt at divers and several times by virtue of 31 several warrants of privy seal to the said treasurer and chamberlains directed.

By warrant of privy seal dormant dated the 11th day of March *anno primo domine regine* containing the sum of £12,000 to be yearly paid to the said Treasurer of the Marine Causes, *viz*. by the hands of Richard Stoneley, one of the tellers of the Receipt: *xxiiij*^{to} *Martij* 1561 [*1562*] – £500; *xix° die Septembris* 1562 – £500; *v*^{to} *die Novembris* 1562 – £100; *x die Decembris* 1562 – £500; *xviij° eiusdem mensis* – [*£500; 25 December – £1,000; 28 December*][1] – £700; *ultimo eiusdem mensis* – £600; [*sum for 1562 – £4,400* (**#A1**)];[2] *xxiiij*^{to} *Februarij* 1562 [*1563*] – £500; *xxv*^{to} *Maij* 1563 – £500; *xxviij° eiusdem mensis Maij* – £500; *iiij*^{to} *Novembris* – £200; *x° Decembris* [*1563*][3] – £800; *xx° eiusdem mensis Decembris* – £1,000. [*Duplicated matter*].[4] [*sum for 1563 – £3,500* (**#X4**)]. [*Sum*] – £7,900.

By the hands of Thomas Gardener, one other of the tellers of the Receipt: *viij° die Maij* 1562 – £500; *tertio Junij eodem anno* – £300; *xxj° Julii eodem anno* – £100; *xx° Augusti dicto anno* – £1,000; *xxvij° Septembris anno predicto* – £500; *xxvij° Novembris anno predicto* – £400; *iiij*^{to} *Decembris dicto anno* – £100; *xij° eiusdem mensis* – £1,000; *xvij° eiusdem mensis* – £150; *xxviij° eiusdem mensis* – £500; *xxx° eiusdem mensis* – £470; [*sum for 1562 – £5,020* (**#A2**)]; *primo die Februarij* 1562 [*1563*] – £300; *x° die Martij eodem anno* [*– £400; 29 March*][5] – £1,000; [*xxiiij*^{to}][6] *die Maij* 1563 – £230; *xxv*^{to} *die Augusti eodem anno* – £1,000; *iiij*^{to} *die Novembris eodem anno* – £500; *et viij° die Decembris dicto anno* 1563 – £300; [*sum for 1563 – £3,730* (**#X1**)]. [*Sum*] – £8,750.

[1] Ellipse in MS supplied from Quarter Book; the Exchequer scribe's eye skipped from the 18 Dec. date to the 28 Dec. sum.

[2] Inset references preceded by # relate the *recepta* of Declared Account to the equivalent entries in the Quarter Book; see synopsis in Sectional Introduction II, p. 18. These symbols also serve as authority for the editorial supply of ellipsed matter, as at the preceding flag.

[3] MS '1561' in obvious error.

[4] MS repeats in error all six entries for 1563.

[5] Ellipse in MS supplied from Quarter Book.

[6] MS '*xxxiiij*^{to}' in obvious error, corrected from Quarter Book.

By the hands of William Patten, one other of the tellers of the Receipt, *ix° die Novembris* 1562 – £500; *xxviij° Decembris eodem anno* – £540; *xxix° die eiusdem mensis* – £1,140; [*sum for 1562 – £2,180* (**#A3**)]; *iiij^to^ die Novembris* 1563 – £400; et *xiij^tio^ die Decembris eodem anno* – £800; [*sum for 1563 – £1,200* (**#X3**)]. [*Sum*] – £3,380.

And by the hands of Henry Killigrew, one other of the tellers, *xxiiij^to^ Decembris* 1562 – £400 **[#A4]**; *iiij^to^ die Novembris* [*1563*][1] – £500; et *x° Decembris eodem anno* – £700; [*sum for 1563 – £1,200* (**#X2**)]. [*Sum*] – £1,600.

In the whole received within the time of this account by virtue of the said warrant dormant – £21,630 [**#A1–4, X1–14**].[2]

By another warrant of privy seal dated *viij° die Martij*[3] *anno quarto domine regine Elizabethe* by the hands of the said Richard Stoneley *eodem die* – £1,524 7s **[#B3]**.

By another warrant of privy seal dated the 3rd of July *dicto anno quarto domine regine* by the hands of Richard Stoneley *vij° eiusdem mensis* – £66 13s 4d **[#B6]**.

By another warrant of privy seal dated *iiij^to^ die Augusti anno quarto domine regine* by the hands of the said Richard Stoneley *iiij^to^ die Septembris eodem anno* – £140 **[#B8]**.

By another warrant of privy seal dated *iiij^to^ die Septembris anno predicto* by the hands of the said Richard Stoneley *xv^to^ eiusdem mensis* – £113 6s 8d **[#B9]**.

By another warrant of privy seal dated *xv^to^ die Septembris dicto anno quarto domine regine* by the hands of the said Richard Stoneley *xix° eiusdem mensis* – £130 **[#B11]**.

By another warrant of privy seal dated *xiiij^to^ die Octobris dicto anno quarto domine regine* by the hands of the said Richard Stoneley *xvj^to^ eiusdem mensis* – £519. And by the hands of the said Thomas Gardener *dicto xvj^to^ die Octobris* – £208 6s 8d. In all – £727 6s 8d **[#B13]**.

By another warrant of privy seal dated *iij^tio^ die Novembris dicto anno quarto domine regine* by the hands of the said Richard Stoneley *vj^to^ die Novembris eodem anno* – £120 **[#B14]**.

By another warrant of privy seal dated *viij° die Novembris anno quarto domine regine* by the hands of the said Richard Stoneley *xj° die Novembris eodem anno* – £64 **[#B15]**.

[1]MS '1562' in obvious error.

[2]That is to say the combined ordinary receipts of £12,000 for 1562 and £9,630 for 1563, as separately computed in the Quarter Book (cf. the editorially supplied annual totals above, pp. 26, 242).

[3]Quarter Book gives 8 March as receipt date for warrant dated 6 March.

[m. 3d] By another warrant of privy seal dated *xv*^{to}*die Novembris anno quarto predicto domine regine* by the hands of the said Richard Stoneley *xviij° die Novembris eodem anno* – £100; and by the hands of the said Henry Killigrew [*xix°*][1] *die eiusdem mensis* – £246 13s 4d; and by the hands of William Patten *xx° die mensis Novembris predicti* – £40. [*Sum*] – £386 13s 4d **[#B16]**.

By another warrant of privy seal dated *vij° die Septembris anno quinto domine regine Elizabethe* by the hands of the said Richard Stoneley *xvj*^{to} *die Decembris dicto anno quinto* – £200; by the hands of Henry Killigrew *xxvj*^{to} *die eiusdem mensis* – £221 6s 8d; and by the hands of Thomas Gardener *xxvij*^{to} *die eiusdem mensis Decembris* – £100; *in toto* – £521 6s 8d **[#B17]**.

By another warrant of privy seal dated *viij° die Decembris dicto anno quinto domine regine* by the hands of Henry Killigrew aforesaid *xxiiij*^{to} *eiusdem mensis* – £200 **[#B18]**.

By another warrant of privy seal dated *vj*^{to}*die Januarij anno quinto domine regine predicte* by the hands of the aforesaid Henry Killegrew *v*^{to}*die Februarij eodem anno* – £366 13s 4d **[#Y2]**.

By one other warrant of privy seal dated *x° die Maij anno quinto domine regine* by the hands of the aforesaid Richard Stoneley *xj° die Maij eodem anno* – £200 **[#Y6]**.

By one warrant of privy seal dated *x° die Maij anno quinto domine regine* by the hands of the said William Patten *xxiiij*^{to} *die Maij anno predicto* – £800; by the hands of the said Richard Stoneley *eodem die* – £337 16s 8d; and by the hands of the said Thomas Gardener *dicto xxiiij*^{to} *die Maij* – £200; *in toto* – £1,337 16s 8d **[#Y10]**.

By one other warrant of privy seal dated [*30 May*][2] *dicto anno quinto domine regine* by the hands of the said Thomas Gardener *primo Junij anno predicto* – £290 **[#Y11]**.

By another warrant of privy seal dated *viij° die Junij dicto anno quinto domine regine* by the hands of the said Richard Stoneley *xxv*^{to} *eiusdem mensis* – £500; *et xiij*^{tio} *die Julij anno predicto* – £474; *in toto* – £974 **[#Y12]**.

By another warrant of privy seal dated *iiij*^{to} *die Julij anno quinto domine regine predicto* by the hands of the said Henry Killigrew *viij° die Julij dicto anno* – £100; *et xiij*^{tio} *eiusdem mensis* – £190; *in toto* – £290 **[#Y14]**.

By another warrant of privy seal dated *v*^{to} *die Julij dicto anno quinto domine regine* by the hands of the said Thomas Gardener *xiij*^{tio} *die*

[1]MS '*xx°*' but the Quarter Book's date of 19 Nov. is likely to be correct, since otherwise the next entry here would be given as '*eodem die*'.

[2]MS '*ultimo Maij*'. It is likely that it was forgotten May has 31 days, and the Quarter Book date of 30 May is assumed to be correct.

eiusdem mensis – £400; and by the hands of Richard Stoneley aforesaid *xix° eiusdem mensis* – £416 11s 8d; *in toto* – £816 11s 8d **[#Y15]**.

By another warrant of privy seal dated *vij° die Julij dicto anno quinto domine regine* by the hands of William Patten aforesaid *viij° die eiusdem mensis* – £500; and by the hands of the aforesaid Thomas Gardener *eodem die* – £1,500; *in toto* – £2,000 **[#Y16]**.

By another warrant of privy seal dated *xj° die Julij dicto anno quinto regine predicto* by the hands of Henry Killigrew *xiij*^{tio} *eiusdem mensis* – £209 12s 8d **[#Y17]**.

By another warrant of privy seal dated *xiiij*^{to} *die Julij anno quinto predicto* by the hands of the said Richard Stoneley *xv*^{to} *eiusdem mensis* – £378 6s 8d **[#Y18]**.

[m. 4] By another warrant of privy seal dated *xvj*^{to} *die Julij anno quinto supradicto* by the hands of Thomas Gardener aforesaid *xviij° eiusdem mensis* – £1,743 1s 8d; *xix° eiusdem mensis* – £1,264 16s 8d; *xxv*^{to} *Augusti anno predicto* – £500; *xxiiij*^{to} *Octobris anno predicto* – £343 1s 8d; [*sum*] – £3,851; by the hands of Richard Stoneley aforesaid *xxiiij*^{to} *Octobris anno predicto* – £300; and by the hands of Henry Killigrew *eodem die* – £400; and by the hands of the said William Patten the *dicto xxiiij*^{to} *Octobris* – £200; *in toto* – £4,751 **[#Y19]**.

By another warrant of privy seal dated *xvij° die Julij dicto anno quinto domine regine* by the hands of Thomas Gardener aforesaid *xix° Julij dicto anno quinto* – £2,735 3s 4d; and *xxx° die eiusdem mensis* – £904 16s 8d; *in toto*] – £3,640 **[#Y20]**.

By another warrant of privy seal dated *secundo die Septembris anno quinto predicto domine regine* by the hands of the said Richard Stoneley ^{to} *die Septembris dicto anno quinto predicte domine regine* – £240 12s 6d; and by the hands of Thomas Gardener *xxvij° die eiusdem mensis predicto anno* – £240 12s 6d; *in toto* – £481 5s **[#Y22]**.

By one other warrant of privy seal dated *secundo die Octobris dicto anno quinto domine regine* paid by the hands of the said Richard Stoneley ^{to} *die eiusdem mensis* – £170 **[#Y23]**.

By another warrant of privy seal dated *xij° die Octobris predicto anno quinto* by the hands of the said Richard Stoneley *xiij*^{tio} *eiusdem mensis* – £399 7s **[#Y24]**.

By another warrant dated *xij° die Octobris dicto anno* [*quinto*] by the hands of Richard Stoneley aforesaid *xx° Decembris* [*6 Eliz.*][1] – £253 6s d **[#Y26]**.

[1]MS gives 12 Oct. '*dicto anno sexto*' and 20 Dec. '*eodem anno*' but this is a double miscalculation, since regnal year 6 Eliz. began on 17 Nov., and the dates should be as here corrected.

By another warrant of privy seal dated *xxviiij° Octobris dicto anno quinto* by the hands of William Patten aforesaid *xx° Decembris* [*6 Eliz.*][1] – £253 6s 8d **[#Y27]**.

By another warrant of privy seal dated *xvij° die Novembris anno sexto domine regine* by the hands of Henry Killigrew *xxij*^{tio} *die Novembris eodem anno* – £468 2s **[#Y25]**.

By another warrant of privy seal dated *xxiiij*^{to} *die Novembris dicto anno sexto domine regine predicto* by the hands of the above named Richard Stoneley *xx° die Decembris eodem anno* – £253 6s 8d **[#Y28]**.

In all received of the said Treasurer and Chamberlains of the Receipt of the Exchequer of the revenues of the same by the hands of the tellers of the Receipt above-named, as by two several certificates under the hand of Thomas Felton, clerk of the pell, hereupon duly perused and examined may appear – £43,156 8s 8d.

Thomas Gardener, one of the tellers of the Receipt of the Exchequer of the money growing upon the sale of lands. Also the said accountant is charged with money by him likewise received within the time of this account of the abovesaid Thomas Gardener, one of the tellers of the Receipt, of the money growing upon the sale of lands, at two several times, *viz. xxij*^{do} *die Januarij anno quarto domine regine Elizabethe predicte* by a warrant under Her Majesty's signet dated the 21th day of the said month of January, as a parcel of the sum of £8,000 contained in the said warrant – £3,000 **[#B1]**; and the 24th of January aforesaid by another warrant under Her Highness's signet dated the [*23rd*][2] of the same month, as parcel of the sum of £5,000 contained in the said warrant – £3,000 **[#B2]**; in the whole as by a certificate under the hand of the said Thomas Gardener hereupon perused and examined may appear – £6,000.

[m. 4d] *Sir William Damsell, knight, General Receiver of the Court of Wards and Liveries.* Also the said accountant is charged with money by him received within the time of this account of the said Sir William Dansell, knight, General Receiver of the court of Wards and Liveries at sundry times by several warrants to him directed, *viz. xxiij*^{tio} *die Julij anno quarto dicte domine regine* by the Queen's Highness's warrant dated the same day *anno quarto domine regine predicte* – £872 10s **[#B7]**; *ix° die Septembris dicto anno quarto domine regine predicte* by Her Majesty's warrant dated the 7th day of the same month – £326 13s 4d **[#B10]**; and the 5th day of October *dicto anno quarto regine predicte* by Her

[1] MS '*eodem anno*', but again inception of the regnal year has been forgotten.

[2] MS 'xxiiijth' but the Quarter Book gives 23 Jan., which is more likely in itself, and because if both dates were the same '*eodem die*' would have been expected here.

Highness's warrant dated the 2nd day of the same month – £186 13s 4d **[#B12]**; in the whole as by a certificate under the hand of the said Sir William Dansell hereupon perused and examined appeareth – £1,385 16s 8d.

Sir Edward Rogers, knight, General Receiver of the loan money. Also he is charged with money by him received and had at sundry times within this his account of Sir Edward Rogers, knight, Comptroller of the Queen's Majesty's most honourable Household, Receiver-General of the loan money prested to Her Highness upon privy seals by [sundry *inserted*] Her Majesty's warrants under the privy signet to the said Sir Edward Rogers directed, *viz. xxj° die Januarij anno quinto dicte domine regine* by one warrant dated *xviij° eiusdem mensis* – £60 6s 8d **[#Y1]**; *xiiij*^{to} *die Februarij dicto anno quinto* by like warrant dated *v*^{to}*die eiusdem mensis* – £273 6s 8d **[#Y3]**; *xij° die Martij anno quinto predicto* by like warrant dated *viij° eiusdem mensis* – £306 13s 4d **[#Y4]**; *tertio die Aprilis dicto anno quinto regine predicte* by another warrant dated *xxx° die Martij eodem anno* – £193 6s 8d **[#Y5]**; *xiiij*^{to} *die Maij anno predicto* by [*like warrant 8 May – £193 6s 8d* (**#Y7**); *23 May by*][1] another warrant dated *eodem die* – £195 **[#Y8]**; *dicto xxiij*^{tio} *Maij* by like warrant dated *eodem die* – £67 6s 8d **[#Y9]**; *xxvij° die Junij anno quinto regine predicte* by a like warrant dated *xxvj*^{to} *eiusdem mensis* – £619 **[#Y13]**; *et secundo die Septembris predicto anno quinto regine predicte* by a like warrant dated *primo die eiusdem mensis* – £100 **[#Y21]**; in the whole as by the said account of the said Sir Edward Rogers made of the loan money hereupon duly perused conferred and examined may appear – £2,008 6s 8d.

Out of the Queen's Majesty's privy purse. Also the said accountant is charged with money by him received and had of the Queen's Majesty's privy purse the 28th day of September in the fourth year of Her Majesty's reign by the hands of the Right Honourable Sir William Cecil, knight, Her Highness's Principal Secretary, upon the knowledge of the said Sir William Cecil, one of the commissioners of this account had upon the examination of the same, the sum of – £1,000 **[#B5]**.

Francis Lee of Rotherhithe, gunpowder maker. Also the said accountant is charged with money by him received the last day of September *dicto anno quarto domine regine predicte* of Francis Lee of Rotherhithe, gunpowder maker, for the price of one of Her Majesty's ships called the *Jerfalcon* sold to the said Francis Lee by virtue of Her Majesty's warrant under the privy signet dated *xxix° die Junij dicto anno quarto* to the Right Honourable the Lord Clinton and Saye, High Admiral of

[1]Ellipse in MS supplied from Quarter Book; the Exchequer scribe's eye was deceived by the two sums of £193 6s 8d.

England directed, as by a certificate under the hand of the said Francis Lee testifying that he paid for the same the sum of – £80 **[#B4]**.

William Cade, General Receiver of the Duchy of Lancaster:[1] The said accountant is not here charged with any money received out of the court of the Duchy of Lancaster, for that he hath received none of the same revenues within the time of this account, as by a certificate under the hand of William Cade, General Receiver of the said court appeareth – £ *nulla*.

Thomas Stanley, Under-treasurer of the Mint.[2] Neither hath the said accountant received any money within the time of this account of Thomas Stanley, Under-treasurer of the Mint, as by certificate under the hand of the said Under-treasurer appeareth – £ *nulla*.

Thomas Cotton, clerk of the hanaper.[3] Nor yet the said accountant hath received any money within the time of this account of the said Thomas Cotton, clerk of the hanaper, as by certificate under the hand of the said Thomas Cotton appeareth – £ *nulla*.

[m. 5] *Sum total of the charge and receipts aforesaid* – £53,790 12s.

Against the which, the said accountant is allowed for:

Money by the said accountant issued and paid and to be paid for:[4]

The surplusage of the last account. First the said accountant is allowed for money remaining due upon the determination of his last account, for that his payments, provisions and allowances within that time did exceed his receipts, as in the foot of the same account may appear the sum of – £7,728 17s 7½d.

Coat and conduct money. Also the said accountant is allowed for money by him paid as well to divers shipwrights, caulkers, sawyers, carpenters, anchorsmiths, bricklayers, and other artificers and workmen serving and working in the new building, repairing and mending of the Queen's Majesty's ships and storehouses, as also to divers mariners and gunners serving on the sea, prested in divers places of this realm for the

[1]Clerk to the Receiver-General 1541, and subsequently Deputy Receiver; appointed Receiver-General 1558: R. Somerville, *Office-Holders in the Duchy and County Palatine of Lancaster from 1603* (London and Chichester, 1972), p. xix.

[2]London goldsmith, appointed assay-master at Tower I mint 1545; Comptroller there 1552; Under-treasurer 14 July 1561 to death, 1571: *CPR 1560–3*, p. 17. C. E. Challis, 'Mint officials and moneyers of the Tudor period', *British Numismatic Journal*, XLV (1975), p. 68.

[3]Appointed clerk of writs and processes in Star Chamber 2 Feb. 1559, and again (as co-patentee) 31 July 1560; also occurring as deputy clerk of the hanaper (the financial agency of the Chancery) on the pardon roll 15 Jan. 1559: *CPR 1558–60*, pp. 36, 168, 329.

[4]Bracketed heading from m. 8.

said service, *viz.* outwards – £602 8s 10d; homewards – £599 15s 2d; in the whole, as by the said book warranted and subscribed by the said officers of the Admiralty particularly appeareth – £1,202 4s.

Also the said accountant is allowed for money by him paid to Nicholas Alday,[1] servant to the Lord Clinton, High Admiral of England, for the coat money of himself and 59 other soldiers serving in the *Elizabeth Jonas* under the said Lord Admiral – £12; to William Drury for the coat money of 300 soldiers serving in the *Elizabeth Jonas*, the *Victory* and other Her Majesty's great ships and galleys appointed to serve on the seas under the conduction of the said Lord Admiral – £60; and to James Holmes, captain of 100 soldiers appointed to serve in the *Lion* and in the *Philip and Mary* and others – £20; in the whole, at 4s every coat, as by the book of the said officers of the Admiralty appeareth – £92.

[*Sum*] – £1294 4s.

Emptions and provisions, viz.:

[m. 5d] Also the said accountant is allowed for divers kinds of emptions and provisions bought and provided within the time of this account, as well for the new building, mending and repairing of the Queen's Majesty's ships and for the furniture of the same, as for the supplement of the wants in Her Majesty's storehouse there to remain for the service of her Navy and marine causes, part whereof is spent and occupied abouts the furniture of the said ships at divers places hereafter expressed, and the rest remaineth in Her Majesty's storehouses at the same several places, the nature and kinds whereof doth hereafter ensue, *viz.*:

Timber, planks, boards, quarters,[2] *deal, fir, spars, rafters, shores and divers other kinds of wood.* Bought and provided by the said accountant within the time of this account, spent and occupied about the building and repairing of the said ships, and partly remaining in these places following, *viz.* at Deptford Strand – £3,563 7s 2¼d; Woolwich – £789 10s 0¼d; Gillingham – £92 5s 1d; Portsmouth – £521 10s 8¾d; Dover – £26 13s 0d; Rye – £19 11s 7d; Harwich – 14s; and Yarmouth – £6 13s 4d; in the whole – £5,020 5s 9¼d.

Anchors and other ironwork and nails and divers necessaries of brass and copper. Also bought likewise and provided by the said accountant within the time of this account, likewise spent and occupied and partly remaining at these places following, *viz,* at: Deptford Strand – £1,796 3s 3¾d; Woolwich – £8 9s 4½d; Gillingham – £245 8s 3¾d; Portsmouth –

[1] Pardoned by his master's means after involvement in Wyatt's rebellion 1554; implicated in the Dudley conspiracy 1556, but apparently never arrested: *CSPDM*, nos 327, 349–50, 49. Loades, *Tudor Conspiracies*, pp. 190, 229–30.

[2] MS. 'quarterters'.

£264 3s 4d; Colne – 18s 3d; Dover – £9 0s 5d; and Harwich – 31s; in the whole – £2,325 14s.

Cables and hawsers with divers other kind of cordage and tackling. Bought likewise and provided by the said accountant within the time aforesaid and likewise spent and occupied, and partly remaining at these places following, *viz.* at: Deptford Strand – £5,726 19s 6¼d; Gillingham – £4 2s 1d; and Portsmouth – £67 12s 2d; in the whole – £5,798 13s 9¼d.

Canvas and poldavy and other necessaries for sails. Bought and likewise provided by the same accountant within the time aforesaid and likewise spent and occupied, and partly remaining at these places following, *viz.* at: Deptford Strand – £1,222 0s 4½d; Portsmouth – £57 13s 1d; and Harwich – 40s; in the whole – £1,281 13s 5½d.

Masts, oars and rudders. Bought and likewise provided within the time aforesaid by the said accountant and likewise spent and occupied and partly remaining at these places following, *viz.* at: Deptford Strand – £1,431 16s 4d; Portsmouth – £14 11s 8d; and Dover – 66s 8d; in the whole – £1,449 14s 8d.

Pitch, tar and rosin, tallow and oil. Bought and likewise provided by the said accountant within the time of this account and likewise spent and occupied, and partly remaining at these places, *viz.* at: Deptford Strand – £713 3s 3d; Gillingham – £7 9s 4d; Portsmouth – £103 4s 1d; Dover – £4 6s 4d; and Harwich – 32s; in the whole – £829 15s.

[m. 6] *Reed, broom, rushes, fir and straw.* Bought and likewise provided by the said accountant within the time aforesaid, and occupied and spent at these places following; *viz.* at Deptford Strand – £8 11s 4d; Woolwich – £9 7s; Gillingham – £20 17s 2d; Portsmouth – £13 18s 11d; Harwich – 4s; in the whole – £52 18s 5d.

Brick, lime, tile and sand. Bought and likewise provided by the said accountant within the time aforesaid, and occupied and spent at these places following in making and mending of divers furnaces and other necessaries, *viz.* at Deptford Strand – £44 5s 2d; Woolwich – £11 6s 3d; Gillingham – £11 13s 2d; and Portsmouth – 102s 8d; in the whole – £72 7s 3d.

Lead and solder. Bought and provided by the said accountant and spent within the time aforesaid at: Deptford Strand – £92 3s 0¾d; Gillingham – 42s 1d; in the whole – £94 5s 11¾d.

Red say and red cloth. Bought and likewise provided by the said accountant within the time aforesaid for the crosses and coats for soldiers and for tilts for pomps of galleys and for crosses for flags for ship tops, occupied and spent at Deptford Strand – £49 17s 10d.

Barges, ships' boats and skiffs. Bought, provided and made within the time aforesaid for divers purposes hereafter expressed, *viz.* for one bark of 15 tuns to serve for the sounding of the sands at the Thames nouth, bought by agreement – £14; for making of a new barge for the Bishop of Winchester in lieu of a great barge had from him which was converted into a brigantine sent to Newhaven – £22; for three boats for he ship called the *Bark of Boulogne* – £12 15s 10d; for a skiff for the *Sun* - 46s 8d; for a skiff for the *Double Rose* – 38s; and for five other boats nade and provided for certain of the Queen's Majesty's ships – £28 13s d; in the whole – £81 14s 10d.

Ship tops. Bought provided and made within the time aforesaid for he *Victory* and the *Triumph*, and the ship called the *Sun*, at Deptford Strand – £23 10s 6d.

Divers small necessaries. Also the said accountant is allowed for livers and sundry necessaries bought and provided for Her Majesty's ervice abouts the said ships and marine causes spent and occupied within he time of this account, *viz.* for claps, scupper-leathers and pump-hose nd such other stuff – £153 19s; for hair and tilts of hair and sye – £91 8s d; for thrums – £14 19s 4¾d; scoops, bowls, pulleys, parrels, shovels nd other stuff – £157 6s; water buckets, hoops and other coopers' stuff £26 18s 10d; running glasses, compasses and needles – £41 6s 2d; ounding leads – 27s 6d; grinding stones – 68s 4d; locks, keys, bolts and inges £15 19s 8d; cart-[m. 6d] wheels – 12s; baskets and maunds – £47 s 8d; sea coal – £15 16s 10d; glazing of windows – £4 12s 6½d; axes 60s; ballast – 111s; bails – 50s; bear and raw hides – £12 5s 6d; marsh arth – 64s 2d; mapstaves – 11s 8d; billet – 42s 6d; stuff for killing of rats 40s; lanterns – 30s; paper, ink, books, glue and such necessaries – £38 s 6d; and hire of smith's tools – 10s; *viz.* at: Deptford Strand – £607 3s d; Woolwich – £4 5s 2d; Gillingham £7 2s 2d; and Portsmouth £27 10s d; in the whole – £646 1s 0¼d.

All the which emptions and provisions, the several natures and kinds with the particular rates and prices whereof and in the names of the parties f whom the same is provided and bought, together with days and times f the payment and duty thereof, are contained and particularly entered n the said ledger book warranted and subscribed under the hands of the fficers of the Admiralty aforesaid, being hereupon duly collected, erused and examined, amounteth, as by the same book may appear, to he sum of – £17,726 12s 6d.

Wages of artificers, workmen and labourers, with their lodging and victualling, and the wages and entertainment of the Lord Admiral and Vice-Admiral and of divers captains with their retinues serving on the seas for the relief of Newhaven.[1] Also the said accountant is allowed for

[1]Bracketed heading from m. 7d.

money by him debursed and paid as well for the wages of divers artificers workmen and labourers being occupied in the new making, repairing mending and ransacking of the Queen's Majesty's ships, as also for th wages and entertainment of the Lord Admiral and divers captains wit their retinues serving in divers ships under his conduction in He Majesty's service appointed to be done on the seas within the time of thi account, as followeth, *viz.* to:

Shipwrights, caulkers and other artificers. Also allowed to the sai accountant for money by him paid to divers and sundry artificers occupie in and abouts the making, mending and repairing of the Queen's Majesty' ships, as shipwrights, house-carpenters, fellers and hewers of timbe topmakers, sawyers, smiths, joiners and coopers, bricklayers, tilers plumbers and other artificers, at: Deptford Strand – £1,439 5s 2d Woolwich – £11 5s 4d; Gillingham – £254 16s 8½d; Portsmouth – £30 13s 11d; Colne – 22s 6d; Dover – 117s 7d; and Harwich 52s; in the whol – £2,021 13s 2½d.

Shipwrights, mariners and gunners. Also allowed to the sai accountant for money by him likewise paid to divers mariners and gunne serving in the Queen's Majesty's ships for the safe keeping of the sam lying afloat within the time of this account, and labouring in coiling u of cables and in carrying of provisions, at: Deptford Strand – £267 16 3½d; Gillingham – £2,280 19s 2d; Portsmouth – £649 7s 5d; and Coln – £9 2s 6d; in the whole – £3,407 5s 4½d.

Labourers, marshmen and breakers of old docks. Also allowed to th said accountant for money by him likewise debursed and paid within th time aforesaid to divers persons, labourers, marshmen and breakers of ol docks, so being occupied at divers and sundry times, at: Deptford Stran – £357 9s 11d; Woolwich – £73 7s 2d; Gillingham – £10 8s 5d Portsmouth – £52 6s 11d; and Colne – £4 11s 10d.; in the whole – £59 4s 3d.

[m. 7] *Keepers of storehouses, docks and woodyards, and clerks o works.* Also allowed to the said accountant for money by him pai within the time of this account to divers persons having the charge an custody of storehouses, timber-yards and docks for the safe-keeping a well of the provisions as of the ships and for watching of the same, [an to clerks for keeping *inserted*] the prick and cheque books of the wage at: Deptford Strand – £247 1s 9d; Woolwich – £37 10s; Gillingham – £4 1s 6d; Portsmouth – £70 11s; and Colne – £45 12s 6d; in the whole – £44 16s 9d.

Purveyors and overseers of workmen and labourers. Also allowed t the said accountant for money by him likewise paid within the tim aforesaid to divers persons being appointed as well to provide victuals and to give attendance for the uttering and serving of the same to the artificers and workmen as being occupied abouts purveying and providing of the said provisions, and overseeing of the said artificers, workmen and labourers, *viz.* at Deptford Strand – £57 19s 4d; and at Gillingham – £38; in the whole – £95 19s 4d.

Victualling and lodging of the artificers and workmen aforesaid. Also allowed to the said accountant for money by him paid as well for the victualling of the said shipwrights and other artificers and workmen during the time that they served in the said works, besides their said wages – £2,309 15s 5d; and also for the lodging of the same workmen at divers and sundry places, and for divers necessities incident to the same at sundry times within the space of this account – £96 3s 4d; *viz.* at: Deptford Strand – £1,701 19s 9½d; Gillingham – £345 1s; Portsmouth – £357 16s 5½d; Dover – 21s 6d; in the whole, as by the said ledger book subscribed and warranted as aforesaid – £2,405 18s 9d.

Workmanship in the making and sealing of cabins. Also the said accountant is allowed for money by him paid by a bargain in great for the workmanship, sealing and finishing of two cabins set up in Her Highness's new ships called the *Victory* and the *Triumph*, and for making of new cupboards, besides forms, stools and trestles and other joined work made and finished at Deptford Strand – £70; and for the making of a new cabin in the ship called the *Aid* at Portsmouth – 46s 8d; in the whole, as by the said ledger book warranted and subscribed by the said officers of the Admiralty appeareth – £72 6s 8d.

Workmanship in the carving of personages in timber and carving and painting of arms for ships and galleys. Also the said accountant is allowed for money by him likewise paid to divers artificers and workmen for carving of personages in timber, being set up in Her Majesty's new ships, and for carving of arms for like purpose, and for painting and colouring of ships and galleys, and for making and sewing of flags and tilts and such other, at: Deptford Strand – £77 1s 8d; Gillingham – £43 16s; and Portsmouth – 16s; in the whole, as by the said ledger book warranted and subscribed as aforesaid more at large appeareth – £121 13s 8d.

[m. 7d] *Working of old ropes and junks into oakum.* Also allowed to the said accountant for money by him paid to divers ropemakers for workmanship of certain old ropes and junks into oakum, netting and wrain ropes occupied for caulking and for other necessary service abouts the ships, *viz.* at: Deptford-Strand – £85 5s 10¾d; Gillingham – £94 3s 11d; Portsmouth – £10 19s 4d; in the whole, as by the said ledger book warranted and subscribed as aforesaid particularly appeareth – £190 9s 1¾d.

Entertainment of the Lord Admiral and Vice-Admiral and divers captains with their retinues serving on the seas. Also the said accountant is allowed for money by him paid and debursed within the time of this account to the Lord Clinton, High Admiral of England, for his entertainment after the rate of 66s 8d *per diem*, and to Sir William Woodhouse, Vice-Admiral of England, for his entertainment after 20s *per diem*; and to certain other appointed Vice-Admirals at certain times of the fleets being abroad in divers places on the seas, after several rates *per diem*, *viz.* 13s 4d, 10s, 8s, 6s 8d and 5s, and to divers captains after 18d *per diem*; to divers masters, officers, mariners and gunners after 6s 8d *per mensem*; and also for the wages and entertainment of divers lieutenants, officers of bands and soldiers serving under the said captains, with deadshares to officers of the ships, and rewards to trumpeters, gunners and drums after divers and sundry rates, the charges whereof for every retinue serving in the several ships following hereafter doth ensue, *viz.* to the said Lord Admiral and his retinue serving in the ship called the *Elizabeth Jonas* in the months of July and August 1563 – £173 16s 8d; to William Wood, master, and to divers mariners and gunners serving in the same ship in the months of September and October 1563 – £42 11s 8d; to Sir William Woodhouse, Vice-Admiral of England, with his retinue serving in the ship called the *Hope* in August and September 1562 – £174 14s 6d; and to Ralph Chamberlain, serving as Admiral of the North Seas in the same ship, with his retinue, in the months of July and August 1563 – £171 10s 11d; to William Holstock, captain of the ship called the *Lion*, serving as Vice-Admiral of the fleet in August and September 1562 for him and his retinue – £149 8s 5d; to Sir Thomas Cotton, Admiral of the Narrow Seas and to John Constable, Henry Tirrell and Robert Constable captains, with their retinues, serving in the *Lion* aforesaid in July and August 1563 – £306 11s 10d; to George Beeston serving as Admiral in the ship called the *Hart* with his retinue in September and October 1562 – £211 6s to Thomas Jones, captain of the *Swallow*, for him and his retinue serving in August, September and October 1562 – £163 3s; to John Basing, captain of the same ship, for him and his retinue serving as Admiral of the Narrow Seas in June 1563 – £399 3s 10d; to John Malyn, captain of the *Willoughby* with his retinue, [m. 8] serving as Admiral of two ships appointed for wafting over of Her Grace's munition and artillery into Ireland and to apprehend certain pirates in the same coast in August, September and October 1562 – £133 11s 2d; and to George Edmunds and his retinue serving in the same ship in the months of July, August, September, October and November 1563 – £218 15s 4d; to William Barnes, captain of the *Victory*, for him and his retinue in October and November [*1562*][1] – £2

[1]MS. '1563', cf. above, p. 235, where Barnes is also more accurately called 'master'.

11s; to [-] Clement Paston[1] and William [*Drury*],[2] captains of the same ship, with their retinue, in July and August 1563 – £118 15s 4d; and to Jeffrey Vaughan, captain of the same ship, with his retinue, in September and October 1563 – £35 16s 8d; to William Wood, captain of the *Triumph*, for him and his retinue in October and November [*1562*][3] – £41 14s 10d;[4] to William Driver, captain of the *New Bark*, with his retinue, serving in October and November aforesaid[5] – £154 17s 4d; to John Henshaw, captain of the *Saker*, with his retinue, serving in September, October, November, December, January, February and March 1562[*–3*] – £172 8s 6d; and to Henry Tirrell with his retinue serving in the same ship in April, May, June, July and August 1563 – £117 0s 1d; to Thomas Hare, captain of the *Phoenix*, with his retinue, serving in June, July, August, September, October, November and December 1562 – £132 13s 8d; and to Thomas Gourlay with his retinue serving as captain of the same ship at divers times in the months of January, February, March, April, May, June, July and August 1563 – £196 19s 11d; and to John Henshaw, captain of the same ship, with his retinue in the months of September, October, November and December 1563 – £116 8s 8d; to Robert Marsh, captain of the *Hare*, with his retinue, serving in August, September, October, November, December, January, February and March 1562[*–3*], and in April, May, June, July and August 1563 – £241 4s 11d; and to Thomas Robins with his retinue serving in the same ship in August, September, October, November and December 1563 – £86 10s 1d; to Thomas Elye, captain of the pinnace called the *Double Rose*, with his retinue, in the months of October, November and December [*1562*][6] – £38 4s 6d; and to Thomas Perryman, shipmaster, serving in the same ship with his retinue in the months of January 1562 [*1563*] and June, July, August and September 1563 – £44 17s 8d; to Sir Thomas Cotton, Admiral of the Narrow Seas, and to William Driver, serving as Admiral, and to [*John*][7] Basing and John Henshaw, captains of the *Aid*, with their retinues, serving at divers times in the months of December, January, February and March 1562[*–3*], and in April, May, September, October, November and December 1563 – £779 14s 5d; to Thomas Gourlay, captain of the *Bark of Boulogne*, and his retinue, serving in the month of December 1562 – £21 0s 6d; to

[1]MS. 'Sir Clement', but this man was not knighted: cf. above, p. 492, where he is described correctly.

[2]MS. 'Dryver' in error for the next but one entry: cf. above, ibid. Vaughan was the captain in command of the ship; Paston and Drury were additional military commanders aboard.

[3]MS. '1563', but cf. above, pp. 234–5.

[4]Quarter Book (as above) ends this sum with 9d.

[5]I.e. 1562, as above, p. 235, further demonstrating that '1563' is an error in the previous entry.

[6]MS. '1563', but cf. above, p. 236. The error is from repetition of the previous entry.

[7]MS. 'Robert' in error; cf. above, p. 488.

Thomas Hare, [m. 8d] captain of the same ship, with his retinue, serving in the months of January, February, and March 1563 – £73 16s 5d; and to Edward Knight, captain of the same ship, with his retinue, serving in the month[*s*] of June, July, August, September, October, November and December 1563 – £227 2s 7d; to William Barnes, captain of the *Antelope*, with his retinue, serving in the month of December 1562 – £26 11s 8d; and to William Winter serving in the same ship as Admiral of the Narrow Seas, with his retinue, in the months of June, July and August 1563 – £214 7s 8d; to John Vallet, captain of the *Jennet*, and his retinue, serving in the month of December 1562 – £28 1s; and to Jeffrey Vaughan, captain of the same ship, with his retinue, in June, July and August 1563 – £278 5s 5d; to John Malyn, serving in the *Greyhound* as Admiral of the Narrow Seas in the months of December, January, February and March 1562[–*3*], with his retinue – £183 2s 8d; to William Bagge, master of the *Rowbarge*, with his retinue, serving in the months of February and March 1562 [*1563*] – £12 6s 6d; and to Richard Spert, captain of the same, with his retinue, serving in July and August 1563 – £54 3s 7d; to Peter Paulyn, captain of the *Sun* and his retinue, serving in the months of July and August aforesaid – £41 15s; to Edward Knight, captain of the brigantine called the *Post*, with his retinue, in the months of July and August aforesaid – £20 13s 6¼d; to Thomas Sabot, captain of the *Makeshift*, with his retinue, serving in the same months of July and August – £20 9s; to Nicholas Gorges, captain of the *Galley Mermaid*, and his retinue, serving in July and August aforesaid – £56 15s 4d; to John Cobham and Henry Tirrell, captains of the *Galley Tryright*, with their retinues, serving in July and August aforesaid – £135 4s; to Randall Worsley, captain of the brigantine called the *Guide*, with his retinue, serving in the months of July and August aforesaid – £31 16s 10d to Thomas Keys, captain of the *Galley Speedwell*,[1] and his retinue, serving in July and August aforesaid – £130 16s 2d; to Giles Grey, captain of the *Searcher*, and his retinue, serving in July and August aforesaid – £36 5s 10d; to William Spencer and Robert Marsh, captains of the brigantine called the *Falcon,* and their retinues, serving in the months of May, June, July, August, September, October, November and December 1563 – £262 1s 11d; to William Holstock, Admiral of the Narrow Seas, serving in the ship called the *Philip and Mary*, and to James Holmes, captain, with their retinues, serving in the months of July and August 1563 – £305 2s 8d; to George Ireland, captain of the *Minion*, and his retinue, serving in the months of September and October 1563 – £23 9s 2d; to Ralph Coxe, [m. 9] captain of the *Primrose*, and his retinue, serving in September and October aforesaid – £23 15s 4d; to Thomas Salmon of Leigh in Essex,

[1]MS 'Spepewell'. For Keys see *NEM*, p. 556.

for the hire of his crayer and for the wages of himself and seven mariners attending upon the great ships at their coming from Portsmouth for sounding of the sands for danger to the ships – 100s; and to John Bowrley, a reward for conveying over the Lord of Warwick – 20s; and also for a French pilot serving in the *New Bark* upon the coast of France – 60s; amounting in the whole as by the said ledger book containing the number of the said captains and their several retinues of mariners, soldiers and gunners with their particular rates and terms of service warranted and subscribed under the hands of the said officers of the Admiralty more at large may appear – £6,664 17s 6¼d.

In all the wages aforesaid as by the said ledger book warranted and subscribed by the said officers of the Admiralty containing the names of the said artificers, workmen and labourers, and also the names of the said captains serving on the seas and their several numbers and retinues with the particular rates of their wages and times of the same, hereupon duly perused and examined may appear more at large, the sum of – £16,021 4s 7¾d.

The charges in fetching 15 sail of French ships from Newhaven in Normandy to Portsmouth. Also the said accountant is allowed for money by him paid and debursed to Thomas Wood, Thomas Baker, John Stronge, John Barley, Thomas Fuller, Francis Lindsey, Simon Pendricas, John May, Robert Beaver, Ralph Morrice, Nicholas Wright, Michael Cheston and [*three*][1] other masters for the wages of themselves and certain mariners and gunners serving for the bringing of 15 sail of French ships from Newhaven to Portsmouth, *viz.* the *Salamander*, the *Greyhound*, the *Three Moons*, the *Green Dragon*, the *Red Hart*, the *Flower de Luce*, the *Sparrowhawk*, the *Owlet*, the *Gryphon*, the *Serpent* and five other French ships[2] – £46 10s 5d; and for the victualling of the said mariners being sent from Rye for the same purpose – £56 8s; in the whole as by the said ledger book warranted and subscribed by the said officers of the Admiralty particularly appeareth – £102 18s 5d.

The charges in recovering the ship called the Greyhound *lost upon the bar of Rye.* Also the said accountant is allowed for money paid to Butolph Moungey of Gillingham for so much money by him laid out for lighterage, wharfage, cranage and labourers' wages, and for the charges of the said Butolph and his man, being occupied about the saving and recovering of the ordnance, munition, tackle and apparel which belonged to Her Majesty's ship called the *Greyhound* lost upon the bar of Rye by

[1]MS 'iiij', a clear error; cf. the equivalent entry in the Quarter Book (above, p. 499) where the correct figure is given.

[2]The others being *Bark of Cherbourg*, *Bear*, *Black Bark*, *Maiden* and *Raven*.

tempest of weather, as by the said ledger book avouched by the officers of the Admiralty as aforesaid appeareth – £32.

Rents of storehouses and timber yards. Also allowed to the said accountant for money by him paid within the time of this account for the rents and hire of storehouses and timber-yards for the stowage and safe-keeping of the said provisions, *viz.* at: Deptford Strand – £8; Gillingham – £8 5s 7d; Colne – £8; and Rye – 60s; as by the said ledger book particularly appeareth – £27 5s 7d.

Riding and posting charges about the marine causes with other costs and expenses. Also allowed to the said accountant for money by him paid and debursed as well for the riding charges and horse-hire of divers messengers and posts sent abroad in carrying of letters to divers places on the sea coasts for the necessary affairs of the marine causes as occasion from time to time did require, as also for the charges and horse-hire of divers persons sent abroad into sundry places of this realm for presting and mustering of shipwrights, caulkers and other artificers retained to serve and work on the building, mending and repairing of Her Majesty's ships, and for the presting and mustering of mariners to serve in the said ships, and for mustering of the mariners upon their discharge out of service; with the charge of boat-hire for presting of mariners upon the river of Thames, with divers other costs, charges and expenses incident to the said marine causes, as by the said ledger book warranted and subscribed by the said officers of the Admiralty in two titles of extraordinary charges hereupon perused and examined doth particularly appear, the sum of – £695 10s 3½d.

[m. 9d] Also allowed to the said accountant for the portage of £38,400 by him received and had out of the Receipt of the Exchequer within the time of this account by the hands of the tellers there; *viz.* for the charges of carriage and for bags, paper, parchment, ink, and other such necessities after the rate of 30s for every £,1000, as by the said ledger book warranted and subscribed as aforesaid appeareth – £57 12s.

[*Sum*] – £753 2s 3½d.

Carriage of the said provisions. Also allowed to the said accountant for money by him paid as well for the freight and hire of divers hoys crayers and lighters for sundry carriages by water, as also for the carriage of divers parcels of the said provisions to and from sundry places by land *viz.* at Deptford Strand – £101 5s 10d; Woolwich – £8 0s 6d; Gillingham – £50 16s 4d; and Portsmouth – £61 9s 8d; in the whole as by the said ledger book warranted and subscribed by the officers of the Admiralty above named particularly appeareth – £220 11s 4½d.

Ordinary allowances by order of the court. Also allowed to the said accountant for money paid to Thomas Pymme, esquire, one of the barons of the Exchequer, at 66s 8d *per annum*, as the like allowance is made to Edward Saxilby, late one of the barons of the said court,[1] as in the precedent account appeareth, *viz*. for the said two years – £6 13s 4d.

Also allowed to the said accountant for money by him paid to the two auditors [*infilled space*] of the prests by order of the Lord Treasurer, Chancellor and Under-treasurer of the Exchequer, in consideration of necessities employed yearly in their offices and of other charges incident to the same, at £10 *per annum*, as in the precedent account appeareth, *viz*. for the said two years – £20.

Also allowed to the said accountant for his charges and his clerks during the time of making out and declaring this his account, by discretion of the Lord Treasurer, Chancellor and Under-treasurer, as in the former account appeareth – £10.

[*Sum*] – £36 13s 4d.

Money paid and advanced in prest to:

Edward Baeshe, esquire, General Surveyor of the victuals for the seas, to be by him employed in the victualling of Her Majesty's ships at sundry times within the space of this account, *viz. secundo die Martij anno quarto domine regine Elizabethe* – £500; *xiij^{tio} Aprilis eodem anno* – £200; *v^{to} die Junij eodem anno quarto* – £300; *viij° die Julij dicto anno quarto domine regine* – £36; *xxiiij^{to} die Julij predicto* – £660; *quinto die Septembris anno predicto predicte domine regine* – £140; *xvj^{to} die Septembris eodem anno* – £113 6s 8d; *xx° die eiusdem mensis* – £500; *eodem die et anno* – £130; *sexto die Octobris dicto anno quarto* – £186 13s 4d; *xvj^{to} die eiusdem mensis* – £60; *septimo die Novembris dicto anno quarto* – £120; *x° die eiusdem mensis* – £500; *xxj° die Novembris anno quinto domine regine* – £386 13s 4d; *xxvij° die eiusdem mensis* – £400; *xv^{to} die Decembris dicto anno quinto* – £200; *xxj° die Januarii dicto anno quinto domine regine predicte* – £33 6s 8d; *iiij^{to} die Februarii predicto anno quinto domine regine predicte* – £600; *v^{to} die Februarii eodem anno* – £366 13s 4d; *xiiij^{to} die eiusdem mensis* – £273 6s 8d; *xiij^{tio} die Martij dicto anno quinto regine predicte* – £306 13s 4d; *iiij^{to} die Aprilis eodem anno* – £193 6s 8d; *x° die eiusdem mensis* – £400; *xvj^{to} die Maij predicto anno quinto domine regine predicte* – £193 6s 8d; *xix° die eiusdem mensis* – £73 16s; *xxv^{to} die eiusdem mensis* – £173 6s 8d; *xxviij° die eiusdem mensis* – £500; *primo die Junij predicto anno quinto domine regine* – £260; *xxvij° die eiusdem mensis* – £524; *viij° die Julij dicto anno quinto*

[1] Saxilby *alias* Saxby, advanced to the bench of the Exchequer 28 Nov. 1549, reappointed by Mary and, on 1 Feb. 1559, by Elizabeth. He died by 30 Sept. 1562, when Pymme succeeded him: *CPR 1548–9*, p. 248; *1558–60*, p. 56; *1560–3*, p. 248. E. Foss, *Biographia Juridica. A Biographical Dictionary of the Judges of England … 1066–1870* (1870), pp. 543, 588.

domine regine – £1,266 13s 4d; *xiiij* *to* *die eiusdem mensis* – £974; *eisdem die et anno* – £165 13s 4d; *xx*° *die Julij dicto anno quinto* – £816 11s 8d; *eisdem die et anno* – £1,264 16s 8d; 30 *die eiusdem mensis* – £3,640; *quinto die Septembris predicto anno quinto* – £290 12s 6d; *quinto die Novembris eodem anno* – £500; *xiiij* *to* *die Decembris anno sexto dicte domine regine* – £400; *xxj*° *die eiusdem mensis* – £253 6s 8d; *xxij**do* *eiusdem mensis* – £253 6s 8d; *xxiij**tio* *eiusdem mensis* – £253 6s 8d; *xxiiij* *to* *die eiusdem mensis* – £399 7s; *et xxiiij* *to* *die mensis Decembris dicto anno sexto domine regine predicte* – £399 7s; in all as by 43 several indentures of the dates aforesaid subscribed and sealed by the said Edward Baeshe and also by the account of the same Edward Baeshe hereupon perused, conferred and examined may appear, amounting to the sum of – £19,208 3s 10d.

[m. 10] *Sum total of the payments and allowances aforesaid, viz.*:

The superplusage of the last account – £7,728 17s 7½d.

Coat and conduct money – £1,294 4s.

Emptions and provisions: Deptford Strand – £15,352 10s 5½d; Woolwich – £822 17s 9¾d; Gillingham – £392 19s 4¾d; Rye – £19 11s 7d; Dover – £43 7s 3d; Harwich – £6 1s; Colne – 18s 3d; Portsmouth – £1,081 13s 5d; Yarmouth – £6 13s 4d. [*Sum*] – £17,726 12s 6d.

Wages and entertainment of artificers and workmen with their victuals: Deptford Strand – £4,406 6s 5½d; Woolwich – £122 2s 6d; Gillingham – £3,309 6s 8½d; Portsmouth – £1,448 11s 0½d; Dover – £6 19s 1d; Colne – £60 9s 4d; Harwich – 52s. [*Sum*] – £9,356 7s 1½d.

The Lord Admiral and Vice-Admiral and of divers captains soldiers and mariners serving on the seas – £6,664 17s 6¼d.

[*Sum of wages &c.*] – £16,021 4s 7¾d.

Rents of storehouses and timber yards: Deptford Strand – £8; Gillingham – £8 5s 7d; Rye – 60s; Colne – £8. [*Sum*] – £27 5s 7d.

Carriage of provisions and wharfage: Deptford Strand – £100 4s 10d; Woolwich – £8 0s 6d; Gillingham – £50 16s 4d; Portsmouth – £61 9s 8¼d. [*Sum*] – £220 11s 4½d.

The charges in fetching of 15 sail of French ships from Newhaven in Normandy to Portsmouth – £102 18s 5d.

The charges in recovery of ordnance, munition, tackle and apparel belonging to the ship called the *Greyhound* lost upon the bar of Rye – £32.

Riding and posting charges, with other costs about the sea causes – £753 2s 3½d.

Allowances ordinary by order of the court – £36 13s 4d.

Money advanced in prest to Edward Baeshe, General Surveyor of the victuals for the seas – £19,208 3s 10d.

[*Total discharged*] – £63,151 13s 7¼d.

Money depending upon:[1]

Thomas Trolloppe of Boston in the county of Lincoln, merchant, and William Browne of Swineshead in the same county, merchant, for so much money above-charged which was delivered to them by Robert Legge, late Treasurer of the marine affairs, in prest upon a bargain of certain cables and other Lincolnshire cordage to have the occupying of the same money for the space of seven years and then to deliver the value thereof into the Queen's Majesty's storehouse at Deptford Strand in such kind of cordage as is mentioned in a pair of indentures of the 22th day of November in the second year of the reign of the late King Edward the [*Sixth*] [*1548*] made between the said Robert Legge and other the officers of the Admiralty on the one party and the said Thomas Trollopp and William Browne on the other party and remaining with the said officers, which [m. 10d] said Thomas Trolloppe and William Browne stand bound by obligation remaining with this accountant for the performance thereof, dated the said 22th day of November *anno secundo nuper regis Edwardi sexti*, and have yet brought in no cordage and therefore here depending – £100.

Francis Owdrye of Abingdon in the county of Berkshire, poldavy weaver, and William Blacknall of Swallowfield in the same county, yeoman, for so much money by the said accountant delivered to the said Francis which he received by virtue of the Queen's Majesty's warrant to the Treasurer and Chamberlains of the Exchequer bearing date at Greenwich the 4th day of May *annis quarto et quinto nuper regis et regine Philippi et Marie* [*1558*] by way of loan for certain years upon sureties taken for the repayment thereof at five payments within six years, *viz.* at Michaelmas 1559 – £20, at Michaelmas 1560 – £20, at the same feast 1561 – £20, at the same feast 1562 – £20, and at Michaelmas 1563 – £20; for the payment whereof the said Francis Owdrye and William Blacknall stand bound to this accountant in the sum of £200 by obligation dated *xiiij*[to] *die Maij dictis annis quarto et quinto Philippi et Marie* remaining with the said accountant, of which said sum of £100 the first two payments are paid to the hands of this accountant and by him answered in his account *de anno tertio domine regine* – £40, and so is yet behind unpaid by the said Francis Owdrye the sum of – £60. [*Sum*] – £160.[2]

[1]Outstanding debts to the Navy, which the accountant sets against the charge for which he is liable.

[2]That is, the amount of the surety (£200), which is forfeit because repayments have fallen into arrears, less the two repayments of £20 each which had actually been made.

And so the said accountant is in surplusage upon the determination of this his account – £9,521 1s 7¼d.

[*Signed*] Winchester, W. Cecil, R. [Sackv]ille, Edward Randolph, Tho. Mildmay, A. Cave.

Examinatur per nos Iohannem Hamby,[1] *Henricum Coddenham, auditores.*

[1]John Hamby, an Auditor of Imprests in the Exchequer, appointed 1560 alongside Coddenham, and serving to his death in 1573: Sainty, *Exchequer Officers*, p. 136.

IV

EXTRACTS FROM
JAMES HUMPHREY'S BOOK OF FORMS, 1568

James Humphrey of Ipswich was a junior clerk in the naval administration, and features most prominently here as a recruiting agent for mariners from East Anglia [**4**, *passim*]. The first two letters below show him operating at Aldeburgh and at Holbrook on the Stour estuary. It is likely that he was the man of this name who was a freeman of Ipswich, though he may have come to rest, like many other naval officials, in Deptford church.[1] He also had a private trade in naval supplies, and is sometimes described as a purveyor.

The volume from which the following extracts are taken is a miscellany of models, forms and calculations, composed in 1568, and which Humphrey doubtless used as a working manual. It passed to James, Duke of York and Lord High Admiral, who in February 1666 lent it to the Navy Board 'to read and deliver to him back again'. In 1669 Pepys had some selections transcribed and bound.[2] This copy survives as Rawlinson MS C. 846 in the Bodleian Library. At some later point he acquired Humphrey's original volume, which he incorporated into his library (now PL 1266), presumably at the same time relegating the 1669 copy to the secondary collection which passed in due course to the Bodleian. It is impossible to say whether Pepys ever had legitimate title to the original.[3]

Five items from the Humphrey's collection were printed, from the Rawlinson copies, in *British Naval Documents*. For completeness sake

[1]For the sources for these speculations, see the entry in *NEM*, p. 554.

[2]Pepys, *Diary*, vii, p. 50 (21 Feb. 1666); ix, p. 501 (29 March 1669). Pepys's title to his extracts admirably summarises the whole: 'Memorandum that the original manuscript out of which the following collection is extracted seems to be designed for a book of rates, as containing not only divers historical informations but many forms of instructions, warrants, bills, tables of calculations, estimates and methods of proceedings both ancient and modern relating to the naval force and service of England, and digested to the year 1568, by one James Humfrey, who by several particulars in the said book appeares to have been some purveyor or clerk in the Office of the Navy at that day': Bodl. MS Rawlinson C. 846, f. 5.

[3]The full contents of PL 1266 are listed in *Cat. PL*, pp. 6–8. In most cases the originals from which Humphrey made his copies cannot now be traced. It should, however, be pointed out that the important naval memoranda of March 1559 analysed by Glasgow, 'Maturing', pp. 12–14 from Pepys's Rawlinson copy (C. 846, no. 4, ff. 46–61), themselves copied from PL 1266, pp. 108–23) are derived from the original 'Book of Sea Causes' among the State Papers (above, p. xxii & n. 1). These documents have since been printed from the SP originals in *BND*, pp. 62–70, and are therefore not included here.

these appear again here, (apart from the first, which dates from Edward VI's reign)[1] though from the earlier and more authoritative texts in the Pepys Library. To these are added such other items from PL 1266 as are relevant to the theme of this volume. The documents are interesting mainly for the way in which they demonstrate different aspects of Admiralty practice.

Items **6–10** relate to the recruitment and discharge of mariners. They present a coherent sequence of paperwork, though the examples are from different times and places. When the fleet was to be manned, commissioners were appointed, usually to cover each of the shires to be mustered. One or more Admiralty officers and their servants would be named to each commission, and Humphrey writes the first letter not only as clerk but also as commissioner, instructing the local officers to muster all the seamen within their jurisdiction at a given day and time. The locality is not specified, and may have been the next stop on Humphrey's itinerary rather than the place from which he dated his letter. Nor is the actual place of assembly mentioned because it would have been known to all concerned. When the muster had been held and the men selected, a second letter then instructed the same officials to ensure that the named men (eight in this case) were each supplied with conduct money, and despatched to join the fleet. The conduct money was reimbursed – in time. There seems to have been no anxiety that the men so recruited would take the conduct money and abscond, probably because they were well known in their communities and would have nowhere else to go. The men themselves then received letters of instruction, specifying the place and day at which they should report for duty, which raises the interesting question of how many ordinary seamen would have been sufficiently literate to read them. Perhaps the Admiralty clerk did not consider that to be his business, but the fact that these letters were issued at all creates a supposition that most were expected to be able to read.[2] Items **9** and **10** bear the names of the Winter brothers, much more senior officers than Humphrey, and are individual letters of discharge, the first 'invalided out', the second normal. Whether such letters were standard,

[1]Bodl. MS Rawlinson C. 846, ff. 135–7, printed as *BND*, no 60 (on pp. 98–9). The Bodleian and *BND* references for items here printed from PL 1266 are shown in first footnotes to each entry below.

[2]Levels of literacy in Elizabethan England are still much debated. In the early seventeenth century the proportion of those below the gentry and merchant classes able to write their names varied from 25 per cent to 50 per cent according to locality. Reading was regarded as a separate skill, and somewhat more widespread. Cf. D. Cressy, *Literacy and the Social Order: Reading and Writing in Tudor and Stuart England* (Cambridge, 1980), esp. table 6.6 on p. 132, which in a ranking of illiteracy by trades between 1580 and 1700 places mariners at 46%. No comparative figures are available for the mid-sixteenth century, but it would be surprising if more than a third of ordinary mariners could have read the instructions here mentioned.

or issued only in exceptional circumstances, is not known, but it would be surprising if William Winter signed the scores of discharges which sickness prompted from the fleet on any major operation, or that George could have signed the thousands of normal dismissals. To some extent, therefore, these samples may be exceptional. The normal practice was probably that captains or pursers would have been responsible for such notes, the main purpose of which was to save the discharged man from arrest or harassment as a vagrant on his way home. The fact that the letter in respect of Thomas Woodles [**10**] refers to his wages and conduct money having been paid means that it was not intended to be used as a licence to beg, as was sometimes conceded if the discharged men were unable or unwilling to wait for pay.

Three items relate to the passage of ships rather than men, and each represents a different type of discharge. The first [**11**] is of a foreign hulk, which had probably been requisitioned when it found itself in the wrong place at the wrong time, and was intended as a protection against officious privateers. The second [**12**] contains no suggestion of service to the Crown, but is simply a passport designed to enable an Irish crayer trading to Bristol to get home without interference. Realistically such passports can only have been respected by port officials and royal ships.[1] The third piece in this group [**13**] is as much an explanation as a safe-conduct, issued in respect of a London ship which had been engaged in supplying the English forces at Leith in the summer of 1560. It purports to guarantee safe passage home, but also offers (no doubt to the owners) an explanation as to why two of her original crew of nine are not returning with her. This passport was issued by Holstock while commanding afloat (as the Principal Officers of Elizabeth's Navy commonly did when needed, and as their successors would sometimes continue to do for a century more). It is therefore an ad hoc operational order, but one which Humphrey uses to illustrate another standard administrative process.

Much of Humphrey's compendium consists of tables for calculating rates of pay, travelling expenses and prices of commodities. Two items have been selected which relate to other parts of the present collection. Although Humphrey's manuscript was written a decade into Elizabeth's reign and is principally a guide to practice then current, some of his examples are taken from the reigns of Edward VI and Mary. The first five items in **14** appear to use actual travel allowances claimed by the Navy Officers between June and September 1552, though the regularity of the figures suggests they may be models. It will be seen that the Vice-Admiral,

[1]There would have been no licensed privateers operating at this time, because there was no war, and such a protection would not have deterred pirates.

Treasurer and Clerk each claim the allowance for every one of the 96 days of account, and the Comptroller and Surveyor likewise for 92 of the 96. The payment was a flat rate payable for every day spent away from base, not merely a maximum against which specific expenses could be charged.[1] Nevertheless it is unlikely to have been triggered so extensively. The sixth item shows the Comptroller's regular allowances. A table of the fees and allowances established by patent for all the Principal Officers is given in *NEM* (pp. 525–6).

The table of wages [**15**] is of special importance as an early model for the graded and compound pay scale which is illustrated in a more developed form from 1587 [**22**]. Humphrey's table is not a new establishment, but represents the *status quo* in 1568. It is consistent with a simpler table of monthly wages drawn up a decade earlier, during Queen Mary's war.[2] The basic mariner's wage had been set at 6s 8d per month at the end of Henry VIII's reign, and it is likely that all the gradations shown by Humphrey are of the same vintage. Although we have ourselves used his table to interpret other data,[3] and it will be found consistent with many of the wage rates shown in the Quarter Book [**4**], it is still a primitive instrument and must be read with caution. It does, however, indicate how the basic daily rate was rounded downwards for fractions of a week (a mariner on 3d a day gets only 8d for three days, and so on).

PL 1266 is a small octavo volume of 426 pages, written throughout in a sixteenth-century italic hand, presumably that of Humphrey himself.[4] The whole collection is dated 1568. The selections are printed as they occur in the manuscript, because Humphrey's sequence was thematic not chronological. The individual details, though not without interest, are incidental to the formulaic purpose of the collection. Significant variations in the Bodleian copies as printed in *British Naval Documents* are noted.

[1]Each officer's allowances were paid quarterly by specific warrant to the Exchequer, as may be demonstrated from one instance: on 11 March 1559 a privy seal warrant authorised the payment to Gonson of his daily travel allowance for 87 days between 29 Sept. and 24 Dec. 1558 (97 days inclusive): E 404/111, no. 4.

[2]*NEM*, pp. 452–3. The 1558 table gives a flat rate of 31s 8d per month for masters, irrespective of the size of the ship, but for all other categories represented in both tables, the rates are identical.

[3]Below, p. 563 & n. 3.

[4]The Bodleian MS is mostly written in careful imitation of this original hand; the list of contents and some other matters are supplied in Pepys's clerk's normal writing.

6 *Writ for recruitment of seamen*

[PL 1266, p. 171][1] *20 March 1568*

A precept to be sent to the constables or any other the Queen's Majesty's officers for giving warning to all mariners and seafaring [*men*] within their precinct to appear before Her Highness's commissioners by a hour appointed.

After my hearty commendations, this[2] shall be to desire you, as also in the Queen's Majesty's name to[3] charge and command you that forthwith upon the sight hereof, [*you*] do charge all mariners and seafaring men within your precinct and liberty to appear before me tomorrow by 7 of the clock before noon to view and take up (the muster seen) such men as shall be thought meet for Her [*Highness's*] service presently to be done, as you and every of you and them tomorrow shall understand according to a commission unto me given. And then[4] you and every of the said seafaring men fail not to be there, for the better advancement of Her Grace's service, wherein you shall show yourselves obedient subjects, and as you and every of them will avoid Her Highness's indignation and displeasure at your peril. From Holbrook, the 20 day of March *anno* 1567 [*1568*].

Your loving friend, James Humphrey.

7 *Order for payment of conduct money to recruits*

[PL 1266, p. 172][5] *12 March 1568*

A bill to be sent to the constables or any officers for the sending away of such mariners as be prested for the service of the Queen's Majesty.

After my most hearty commendations, these shall be to charge, as also in the Queen's Majesty's name to command you upon the sight hereof, to charge and set forth the eight men hereunder written, as you tender the advancement and furtherance of Her Highness's service presently to be done, and that you do command them to be at Chatham in Kent on Saturday next,[6] and there to present themselves before the officers of Her

[1]Copy in Bodl. MS Rawlinson C. 846, p. 113.

[2]So MS here and elsewhere, though it may represent 'these' (*sc*. 'these letters). The Bodleian copy follows these usages and the other quirks noted below.

[3]MS here and elsewhere 'do'.

[4]So MS, but 'that' would be expected.

[5]Copy in Bodl. MS Rawlinson C. 846, p. 114. Printed *BND*, no. 63 (pp. 101–2), interpolating editorial heading, and omitting MS heading, greeting, valediction and names.

[6]The next Saturday was the following day, so 20 March must be intended.

Highness's ships, who will place them as it shall seem good to the same officers, as according to a bill of their names and charge which you shall receive by this bearer, as also 4s for every of them, prest and conduct money of the said eight mariners whose names be hereunder written. And fail you not this to do as you and every of them will avoid Her Grace's displeasure, at your extreme perils. Written at Aldeburgh the 12 day of March *anno* 1567 [*1568*].

Your friend, James Humphrey.

William Compas. Thomas Toote. Robert Flicke.[1] John Meatime. William Connar. Edward Briall. John Bentune. Robert Woolgrove.

8 *Order for recruits to report for duty*

[PL 1266, p. 173][2] *25 March 1568*

A bill to be given unto those mariners that be prested, whither they shall repair and before whom they must make their appearance to be placed.

These shall be to require, and also in the Queen's Majesty's name to charge and command all you whose names be here under-written that you do immediately repair to Chatham in Kent, where as Her Highness's ships now be, and there to present yourselves before the officers of Her Highness's ships, who will place you as it shall seem good unto them; and that you be there by the first day of April then next [*following*] without any further delay. And not to fail, as you and every of you will answer to the contrary at your uttermost perils. Written at Ipswich the 25 day of March 1567 [*1568*].[3]

Your friend, [*blank*].

Thomas Sturgen. Robert Hyll. John Haulle. James Pecocke. John Tawbot. Robert Davie. John Grimble.

[1]Presumably the future Portuguese merchant and member of the Drapers' company, who was commodore of the London squadron aboard *Merchant Royal* in the 1587 Cadiz expedition: Corbett, *Spanish War*, pp. xviii–xix & n. 1, 105, 159. Wernham, *Expedition*, pp. xix, 114 (evidence of association with Suffolk and Norfolk), 327–8.

[2]Copy in Bodl. MS Rawlinson C. 846, p. 115. Printed *BND*, no. 64 (p. 102), interpolating editorial heading, and omitting MS heading, dating clause, valediction and names.

[3]Assuming that these entries are in true sequence, the year of grace should have changed to 1568 on 25 March. The Bodl. copy is dated 20 March; this has no independent authority, but may indicate that the copyist suspected error in the original (also evident in setting **6** ahead of **7**).

9 *Pass for a seaman discharged as sick*

[PL 1266, p. 174][1] *10 June 1566*

A passport for the discharge of a mariner out of service, being sick, not able to serve.

Forasmuch as this bearer hereof, William Patche of Essex, mariner, who hath served the Queen's Majesty in Her Highness's ship named the *Philip and Mary*, and hath served from the 18 day of April to the last of May next, and is now discharged from the same service, being sick and not able longer to serve, I William Winter, esquire, Master of Her Grace's Ordnance for the seas and Surveyor of Her Highness's Marine Causes, do license the said William Patche to pass to his dwelling place in Essex aforesaid. Therefore this shall be to require all you to whom these presents shall come to suffer him quietly to pass by you without any of your lets or trouble in the same. In witness whereof I have firmed this passport with my hand the 10 day of June *anno* 1566.
W. Winter.

To all mayors, sheriffs, bailiffs, constables and all other the Queen's Majesty's officers and loving subjects to whom these presents shall come.

10 *Passport for a seaman discharged at any time*

[PL 1266, p. 175][2] *18 June 1566*

A passport needful for every mariner discharged from the Queen's Majesty's ships out of service at any time.

Forasmuch as this bearer Thomas Woodles, mariner, who hath served the Queen's Majesty in Her Grace's ship named the *Great Bark* is now discharged from the same service, and he is paid his wages for the time that he hath served, as also his conduct money to his habitation, according to the distance of miles; wherefore this shall be to desire and require all you to whom these presents shall come quietly to permit the forenamed Thomas Woodles to pass by you home to his habitation into the town of Ipswich in Suffolk without any of your lets or trouble in the premises. In witness whereof I George Winter, Clerk of Her Highness's Ships, have caused this passport to be made and put to my firm[3] the 18 day of June *anno* 1566.
G. Winter.

[1]PL 1266, p. 174; copy in Bodl. MS Rawlinson C. 846, p. 116.
[2]Copy in Bodl. MS Rawlinson C. 846, p. 117.
[3]MS. 'putto my firme' (*sc.* put to it my signature as affirmation).

To all mayors, sheriffs, bailiffs, constables and all other the Queen's Majesty's officers and loving subjects to whom these presents shall come.

11 *Pass for discharge of a merchantman from the Queen's service*

[PL 1266, p. 176][1] *17 March 1564*

A passport for the discharge of hulks as other strangers' ships when they are discharged out of the Queen's Highness's service.

Be it known unto all men by these presents that this Kyrson Sulsune, master and owner of an hulk named the *David of Lubicke* hath served the Queen's Majesty in Her Highness's wars at the seas this present summer, and is now discharged from the same service by the Lord High Admiral of England. Wherefore this shall be to desire and require all you to whom these presents shall come quietly to permit the said Kyrson Sulsune with his hulk to pass by you without any of your lets or hindrance in this behalf, as you will answer to the contrary at your perils. From Portsmouth the 17 day of March *anno Domini* 1563 [*1564*].

12 *Pass for a merchantman previously detained*

[PL 1266, p. 177][2] *1 August 1566*

A passport for a certain crayer of Carrickfergus in Ireland stayed at Bristol and afterwards discharged.

This shall be to desire and also require all you to whom these presents shall come that whereas the *Katheren of Watterforde*, a crayer of burthen of 16 tuns, Nicholas Kennet master of the same crayer and four mariners with him, and Thomas White and four other merchants in them, is licensed to depart from this port of Bristol directly to the Queen's city of Waterford in Ireland for and in certain considerations, wherefore this shall be to desire all you to whom these presents shall come to permit and suffer them quietly to pass by you home to their dwelling to the city of Waterford aforesaid, without any of your lets or hindrances in the premises. In witness whereof I William Winter, esquire, Master of the Queen's

[1]Copy in Bodl. MS Rawlinson C. 846, p. 118. The latter is supplemented by a note in the copyist's normal hand: 'Memorandum that the rate at which all English ships, barks, crayers and hoys were about this time taken up to serve the King or Queen's Highness was (as the same author's collection says) after 12d for every tun by the month (of 28 days) according to their respective burthens, and 16d per tun for strangers' ships, as Venetians; as also hulks serving the King or Queen's Majesties for their Highness's affairs'.

[2]Copy in Bodl. MS Rawlinson C. 846, p. 119.

Ordnance for the seas and Surveyor of Her Grace's Navy, have caused this passport to be made and put to my hand. At Bristol the first day of August 1566.

W. Winter.

To the Queen's Majesty's customers, comptrollers, searchers and other Her Highness's officers to whom these presents shall come.

13 *Order for detention of a merchantman*

[PL 1266, p. 178][1] *11 June 1560*

A bill for the discharge of a ship out of Scotland named the *Annegallant of London.*

This bearer Thomas Clarke, master of the *Anne Gallant of London*, is now discharged this present 11 day of June 1560 of her freight or lading, which lading is 31 tuns of beer, and maketh here in full beer delivered 27 tuns 2½ hogsheads,[2] and the same ship hath in her appointed for her safe bringing home seven men and a boy; and the rest of her men, which is two, be here stayed to serve the Queen's Majesty in Her Highness's ships now present here.[3] Written at Leith in Scotland aboard Her [*Highness's*] ship named the *Swallow* the day and year abovesaid.

By me W.H. [*William Holstock*]

14 *Orders for making warrants for payments to the Admiralty officers*

[PL 1266, pp. 181–2][4] [*Undated*]

The order for the making of warrants for the officers of the Queen's Majesty's Marine Causes, to be delivered to my Lord Keeper of the Great Seal for the giving out of liberates into the Exchequer for the payment of the same.

[1]Copy in Bodl. MS Rawlinson C. 846, p. 120. Printed *BND*, no. 62 (p. 101).

[2]*BND* gives '2 pipes and a half', misinterpreting the abbreviation for hogsheads (*hh*).

[3]This was the campaign in support of the Lords of the Congregation against the Queen Mother, Mary of Guise. Holstock was captain of *Swallow* throughout. Off Huntly on 19 Aug. he fought and captured the *John* of Leith, inbound from France with wine and salt, and took her in to Tynemouth. The owners' petition for recovery was passed to Elizabeth by the Scots Queen: *CSP Scot.* i, pp. 293, 294, 306, 308, 554 (no. 1022: petition), 557 (no. 1024: Mary's letter, 4 Oct.).

[4]Copy in Bodl. MS Rawlinson C. 846, p. 123.

Vice-Admiral. Memorandum that Sir William Woodhouse, knight, Lieutenant of the Admiralty, asketh allowance for his travelling as well by sea as by land by the space of 96 days begun the 25 day of June and ended the 28 of September next *anno* 1552, at 10s the day – £48.

Treasurer. Item Benjamin Gonson, Treasurer of the Queen's Highness's Marine Causes, asketh allowance for his travelling as well by sea as by land by the space of 96 days begun the 25 day of June and ended the 28 of September, at 6s 8d *per diem* – £32.

Comptroller. Item William Broke, Comptroller of the Queen's Majesty's ships, asketh allowance for his travelling as well by sea as by land by the space of 96 days begun the 25 day of June and ended the 28 day of September next 1552, at 4s *per diem* – £18 8s.

Surveyor. Item William Winter, Surveyor of the Queen's Majesty's Marine Causes, asketh allowance for his travelling as well by sea as by land by the space of 96 days begun the 25 day of June last and ended the 28 of September next, at 4s the day – £18 8s.

Clerk. Item Richard Howlett, Clerk of the Queen's Majesty's ships, asketh allowance for his travelling as well by sea as by land by the space of 96 days begun the 25 day of June and ended the 28 of September, as 3s 4d *per diem* – £16.

The Comptroller. In diets by the quarter – £18 8s. In fee by the quarter – £12 10s. Two clerks by the quarter – £6 1s 8d. In boat-hire – £2. [*Sum*] – £38 19s 8d.

15 *Rates of wages*

[PL 1266, pp. 189–91][1] [*Undated*]

Rates of men's wages serving at the seas in the King or Queen's Majesty's ships, barks, galleys and pinnaces as followeth:

	Day	*Weeks*	*Months*
A master of the greatest ship, his wages	17d	10s	40s
A master of a lesser ship, his wages	11½d	6s 8d	26s 8d
A master of a smaller charge, his wages	9d	5s 3d	21s
A pilot of a great ship's [*wages*]	7d	4s 2d	16s 8d

[1]Copy in Bodl. MS Rawlinson C. 846, pp. 127–9.

A lodesman			
A quartermaster			
A master mate			
A master carpenter			
A boatswain			
A purser	5d	2s 11d	11s 8d
A steward			
A cook			
A yeoman of the sheets			
A yeoman of the halyards			
A yeoman of the jeers			
A yeoman of the hawsers			
A quartermaster's mate			
A carpenter's mate			
A boatswain's mate	4d	2s 3½d	9s 2d
A steward's mate			
A cook's mate			
A coxswain			
A master gunner	4½d	2s 6d	10s
A drummer			
A surgeon	6½d	3s 9d	15s
A trumpeter			
A master gunner's mate	3¾d	22½d	7s 6d
A quartermaster gunner			
A mariner	3d	20d	6s 8d
A gromet	2d	15d	5s
A boy	1½d	10d	3s 4d
A master of a great ship	17d	10s	40s
A lodesman of a great ship	7d	4s 2d	16s 8d
A master's mate of a great ship	5½d	3s 4d	13s 4d
A boatswain of a great ship	7d	4s 2d	16s 8d
A carpenter of a great ship	7d	4s 2d	16s 8d
A purser	6d	3s 6d	14s

Payment of mariner's wages	3 days 8d
	4 days 11d
	5 days 14d
	6 days 17d

V

PAPERS RELATING TO WAGES AND WAGE RATES

In this section are gathered a few papers which supplement the formal accounts, and illustrate aspects of the financial administration from different angles. The government needed more immediate information about naval costs, regularly updated, especially when an operation was impending or in progress. For this purpose the Navy Treasurer sent the Privy Council monthly estimates for sea wages, of which two examples from the time of the Le Havre campaign are here printed [**16, 17**].[1] The format is deliberately concise – much like the 'half-sheet of paper' which was all Churchill wanted to see from his advisers. In order to simplify the projection of wage costs, the complex structure outlined in Humphrey's table [**15**] was reduced to an average rate of 9s 4d per man per month of 28 days, which is 4d a day, inclusive of 'dead shares' and rewards. This did not represent anyone's specific pay, but was what Hawkins calls 'the medium of all servitors' [**20**], based on the numbers of ordinary seamen at 3d per day and officers of various grades at higher rates, each of whom might in reality serve only for some part of the period of account. This shorthand reckoning had long been the practice, and the figure of 9s 4d per man/month had stood since Mary's reign.[2] Such calculation can never have been more than approximate, and like all military budgeting would have assumed maximum complements, with some margin beyond that. Nevertheless our own rudimentary calculation, using the models printed here, suggests that the medium was realistic.[3]

[1] See examples of equivalent estimates from the Victualler: **24–6** below.

[2] Oppenheim, *History*, p. 113. In Henry VIII's last year the 'medium' was 8s per man per month, though this excluded captains: ibid., p. 76 & n. 1 (from SP 1/215, ff. 43–45v [*LP*, xx, I, no. 363], a set of calculations for a notional 100 men in times of flesh and fish, 9 March 1546).

[3] Taking as example the estimate for the *New Bark* from **17**, the basic calculation (120 men including captain serving 4 Aug.–30 Nov., i.e. 119 days inclusive) is correct: 4d × 120 × 119 = £238. Assuming the number of petty officers usual in 1562 for a ship of 120 men to have been equivalent to the establishment of 1587 [**22** (on p. 579)], Humphrey's table [**15**] supplies for them the daily rates current in 1562: captain – 18d, master – 11½d, his mate – 5d, pilot – 7d, boatswain – 5d, his mate – 4d, four quartermasters at 5d each – 1s 8d, their four mates at 4d each – 1s 4d; carpenter – 5d, his mate – 4d, purser – 5d, steward – 5d, his mate – 4d, cook – 5d, his mate – 4d, trumpeter – 6½d, master gunner – 4½d, his mate – 3½d, four quartermaster gunners at 3¾d each – 1s 3d; thus 28 officers, leaving 92 ship's company, of whom assume 84 seamen at 3d, 4 gromets at 2d and 4 boys at 1½d: the total

Even these monthly estimates demonstrate the huge discrepancy between the cost of maintaining the Navy and that of actually using it. The annual ordinary budget supposedly provided what would later be called the fleet in being. The highest level of the ordinary during Elizabeth's reign was the £12,000 set in 1559; yet that exact sum could be spent in sending just six ships to sea for four months' active service.[1] Naval expenses for the Le Havre campaign amounted to about one-seventh of the total identifiable military cost of around £200,000.[2] That outlay could only be met by massive borrowing, including the loans from individuals secured on privy seal warrants and £10,000 from the City of London [**4** (p. 243)], from which the Navy received directly £2,008 6s 8d [**4** (pp. 242 × 248; **5** (p. 531)]. Repayment of these debts forced the Crown to sell lands with a rental income which would have paid the naval ordinary for a year.[3]

The Queen had nevertheless managed to find £1,000 in her privy purse which she lent to the Navy in the early months of the Le Havre operation [**4** (p. 27)]. This sum had originally been paid over informally, but was retrospectively converted into a privy seal loan. This detail emerges from a further set of estimates sent to the Council in the year 1564–65 [**18**]. These papers have been included because the copies in Pepys's collection enable part of the fire-damaged Cotton originals to be reconstructed.

In the case of **19**, Pepys has transmitted the copy of a paper whose original can no longer be found. This is a defence of Hawkins's first 'bargain', by comparing the ordinary and extraordinary charges between 1579 and 1584. It is closely related to a letter written to Burghley in April

in daily rates is 414.25d, so the average is *3.45d*. The Quarter Book gives the actual earning of those aboard the *New Bark* [**4** (p. 235)] for 82 days inclusive (10 Sept.–30 Nov. 1562), being the latter 82 of the 119 days covered by the estimate of 30 Nov. [**17**]. The total charge is £154 17s 4d, which includes £17 11s 4d in deadshares and specified rewards, and a higher rate to Capt. Driver while serving as Admiral during 50 of the 82 days. With these extra the medium is 3.77d. Recomputing Driver's pay to the standard for a captain for the whole period reduces the medium to *3.46d.*

[1]PL 2875, p. 58 (*Cat. PL*, p. 127), an estimate of 1572 for setting eight ships and six pinnaces to sea 'in warlike manner', at a total cost of £40,000.

[2]Dietz (*Engl. Pub. Finance 1558–1641*, pp. 11–12) gives figures based on the Declared Accounts of the various treasurers at war and the Navy Treasurer [**5**], which add up as follows: army – £179,981; navy – £28,800; total – £196,781. He specifically excludes from the naval costs the building of *Victory* and *Triumph* and repairs to other ships. Hammer (*Elizabeth's Wars*, p. 67) sets the cost of Le Havre at £250,000, excluding borrowing of £42,000; the basic figure rounds up the £246,380 given in a brief summary of military spending for the whole reign drawn up after Elizabeth's death (SP 12/287, no. 59; *CSPD 1601–3*, p. 304), which Dietz (p. 12 n. 11) noted as less reliable than the figures he extrapolated from the contemporary accounts.

[3]Hammer, *Elizabeth's Wars*, p. 67, calculating rental values from R. Hoyle (ed.), *The Estates of the English Crown, 1558–1640* (Cambridge, 1992), editor's introduction, table 1.2 on p. 16.

1585, and so was probably drawn up by Hawkins about the same time in response to the commission of enquiry. It purports to show a saving of £4,000 a year, but should be regarded as optimistic.[1] His Declared Account for 1578, for example, shows a total expenditure not of £10,200 but of £14,956.[2] For 1582, however, the figure was down to £8,639.[3] How the reduction was achieved is not apparent, although it may have been by placing more work out on a contract basis, since contractors were not required to account. Hawkins would be exonerated from charges of malpractice, and a new bargain was drawn up in 1585 but the arrangements soon became inadequate with the approach and outbreak of the war. In 1588 almost £91,000 was spent on the Navy,[4] and even in a less momentous year of war (1592) the total annual expenditure was over £28,000.[5]

One element in this increase was the general pay rise awarded to seamen in 1586, the first for forty years. Discussion of this topic has been unnecessarily complicated through the misinterpretation of a pay scale dated January 1582. This forms part of a quarto booklet in the State Papers which also contains calculations for victualling, tonnage, manning levels and cordage. The whole document has been satisfactorily printed before,[6] and does not need to be repeated here. It does, however, require further analysis. It is headed:

> January *anno* 1581 [*1582*]. The wages for the officers of the Queen's ships at sea determined by the Officers of the Navy, which are not to be exceeded, *viz.*

Oppenheim supposed this to mean that the rates which followed were being newly raised at this date and by virtue of this document. He also understood it to mark the end of the old system of deadshares and rewards, instituting in its place a fixed monthly payment according to the size of the ship.[7] This interpretation has passed into later works.[8] Corbett, whose

[1]Dr Adams (in 'Hawkins bargains') suggests £3,000 as a more realistic figure.
[2]E 351/2214. The full figure is £14,956 17s 6½d.
[3]E 351/2218. Ordinary payments: £4,015 6s 10d; extraordinary: £4,624 7s 11¼d; total: £8,639 14s 9¼d.
[4]E 351/2225. Ordinary payments: £2,283 1s 11½d; extraordinary: £88,530 13s 7¼d; total: £90,813 15s 6¾d.
[5]E 351/2229. Ordinary payments: £5,554 16s 7½d; extraordinary: £22,956 1s 7d; other items: £75 1s 1d; total: £28,585 19s 3½d.
[6]SP 12/142, no. 19 (*CSPD 1581–90*, p. 44), printed Corbett, *Spanish War*, pp. 258–68.
[7]*History*, p. 152.
[8]Loades, *Tudor Navy*, p. 200 & n. 3, follows Oppenheim in referring to a 1582 pay rise. Rodger, *Safeguard*, pp. 500–501, prints the rates from the 1582 document from Corbett, and then those established in 1626, with the clear implication the one endured until replaced by the other.

examination of the whole issue of pay at this period remains the most thorough, had difficulty with Oppenheim's claim that the deadshares and rewards ceased 'except as a form of expression' after 1582, since they were demonstrably being paid five years later. Indeed he was suspicious of the whole suggestion of novelty: 'whatever was the intention of the Admiralty officers … they did not abide by it'; '… the scale of 1582 can never have been adhered to very strictly'.[1] This in any case seemed at odds with the clear evidence for a general pay rise in 1586. Corbett was in fact doing his best to disagree with Oppenheim, but was hamstrung by accepting Oppenheim's assumption that the 1582 document (which Corbett was himself printing) proclaims a new scale. Yet it does nothing of the kind. *Wages … determined by the Officers of the Navy* means only that they are the wages in current use, and January 1582 is no more than the date at which this particular statement of them was compiled. This is manifest from the other sections of the booklet: the calculations for victualling, transport, manning, cordage and so forth. Such things were not suddenly invented at this particular moment in time. The document is in fact a compendium or book of forms, much like James Humphrey's of 1568. It is written throughout in a single hand, and is not especially neat, suggesting a desk-top aid rather than a formal submission. Corbett (p. 258 n. 1) thought he detected the hand of Sir John Hawkins in its interlinear annotations, and that is very likely; but he did not recognise the main scribe. This was almost certainly William Borough, who was advanced to the joint Clerkship of the Ships by patent of 24 March 1582.[2] It is reasonable to assume that he took up his duties some while before that formality, and that the booklet dated January was compiled by way of familiarising himself with his new responsibilities.

This re-evaluation of the 1582 document has important implications for its tonnage calculation, which (again mostly because of Oppenheim) has commonly been ascribed to Matthew Baker.[3] These aspects of the matter are to be treated in the 'Fragments' volume to which they are more relevant. The present purpose is merely to set the pay scale of 1587 [**22**], here printed for the first time, in its proper sequence. To this end, though we have not felt it necessary to reprint the 1582 rates, we have repeated the two principal evidences for the pay rise actually granted in 1586, the

[1]Corbett, *Spanish War*, pp. 297–91; quotations from pp. 289, 291.

[2]*CPR 1580–2*, no. 1407. Two holograph papers by Borough, though more carefully written, may be cited in support of his authorship of the 1582 booklet: SP 12/240, no. 40, SP 12/243, no. 110 (*CSPD 1591–4*, pp. 111, 301), an estimate of 10 Oct. 1591, and the calculation of tonnage ascribed to 1592.

[3]Oppenheim, *History*, p. 132, printing the tonnage section of SP 12/152, no. 19 with the comment: 'In 1582 a rule was devised which remained in use for nearly half an century and was said to have been due to Matthew Baker'. No part of this statement can now be accepted.

esults of which are shown in the scale of the following year. The sequence s very straightforward. In the last days of 1585 Hawkins sent Burghley proposal for an all-round increase in wages [**20**]. In order to add ersuasive strength to his argument, Hawkins also proposed a reduction n manning levels, which were probably fixed by custom rather than by eed. Burghley gave the matter close attention, annotating one copy of Hawkins's original submission. His acceptance of its proposals is shown n a further paper, *c.* June 1586, in which the effects of the new scale are worked out in the case of one particular ship, the *Lion* [**21**]. Finally a full view of the new rates can now be seen from the 1587 scale [**22**]. The ource is another piece preserved bv Pepys, in this case the original copy. Iere, not in the 1582 booklet, are the wages of the men who fought the Armada and during the rest of the Spanish war. The layout of the locument shows that ships were not yet rated by armament, but grouped y the numbers of men they carried. Their pay increase was timely in view f inflation, and may have eased recruiting problems to some extent. Iowever, theoretical rates were less important than prompt and full ayment, and in that respect the Navy Board's record continued to be atchy.

With the new pay structure in place, the administration then called for ncrease in the general funding of the Navy. The last document in this ection [**23**] derives from the commissions established in 1585 to nvestigate the much maligned 'bargains'. The first part corresponds fairly losely with **20**, but it then goes on to outline some of the abuses which ave followed, and recommends a return to what might be called a flexible' ordinary. By this system any amount which the Treasurer spent ver and above his ordinary would be automatically paid out of the Exchequer without any further specific warrant. This suggestion was rounded on the precedent of the 1565 victualling contract [**28**]. In the ontext it was a revolutionary proposal and was never implemented, robably because of Elizabeth's desire to retain full control over financial isbursements. Extraordinary warrants continued to be used to supplement he ordinary – and the 'quieter times' hoped for were not to arrive in the Queen's lifetime.

16 *Estimate for monthly sea wages*

[SP 12/25, no. 13 (*CSPD 1547–80*, p. 208)][1] *14 October 156*

The 14th day of October *anno regni regine Elizabethe quarto.*

An estimate of the charges of four Her Majesty's ships to be discharged having in them 460 men, for wages and conduct and for one month's victuals of 100, as followeth:

Men. The *Hart* – 200. The *Swallow* – 160.

First for the diets of captains and wages of 360 masters, mariners and gunners serving in the same ships by the space of 2 months 2 weeks days begun the 4th day of August last and to end the 16th day of thi present month of October, at 9s 4d every man the month of 28 days; diets deadshares and rewards in the same accounted – £444.

Item for the conduct of 300 of the said men to be discharged to th places from whence they were prested – £75.

Summa – £519.

Men. The *Willoughby* – 100.

Item for the diets of one captain and wages of 100 mariners and gunner serving in the same ship by the space of 2 months 2 weeks 4 days begu the 4th day of August last and to end the 16th day of this present, at 9s 4 every man the month of 28 days; diets, deadshares and rewards in th same accounted – £123 6s 8d.

Item for the conduct of the said 100 men to be discharged to the place from whence they were prested – £25.

Item for one month's victuals of the said 100 men over and besides weeks' victuals at her going forth to the seas – £60.

Summa – £208 6s 8d.

Summa totalis – £727 6s 8d.

17 *Estimate for monthly sea wages*

[SP 12/25, no. 66 (*CSPD 1547–80*, p. 212)][2] *30 November 156*

The last day of November 1562 *anno regni regine Elizabethe quinto.*

An estimate for the diets of captains and wages of masters, mariner and gunners serving in Her Highness's ships and barks as followeth:

[1]Mis-dated November in the Calendar. Cf. above, p. 228, where the payment to th *Willoughby* is recorded, and pp. 166, 186–7, for payments to standing crew for these thre ships from 1 Oct.

[2]Cf. above, p. 224, for related payments to four of these ships.

The *New Bark* – 120 men. First to William Driver, captain, for his diets, nd for the wages of 119 masters, mariners and gunners serving Her Iighness in the same ship under him by the space of 4 months one week egun the 4th day of August last and ended the last day of November ollowing, at 9s 4d every man the month of 28 days; diets, deadshares and ewards in the same accounted – £238.

The *Phoenix* – 40 [*men*]. Item to Thomas Hare, captain, for his diets, nd for the wages of 39 masters, mariners and gunners serving in the same hip under him by like time begun and ended as abovesaid, at 9s 4d every nan the month; diets, deadshares and rewards in the same accounted – 79 6s 8d.

The *Saker* – 50 [*men*]. Item to John Henshaw, captain, for his diets, and or the wages of 49 masters, mariners and gunners serving in the same hip under him by like time begun and ended as abovesaid, at 9s 4d every nan the month; diets, deadshares and rewards in the same accounted – 99 3s 4d.

The *Hare* – 40 [*men*]. Item to [*Robert*][1] Marsh, captain, for his diets, nd for the wages of 39 masters, mariners and gunners serving in the same hip under him by like time begun and ended as abovesaid, at 9s 4d every nan the month; diets, deadshares and rewards in the same accounted – 79 6s 8d.

The *Double Rose* – 30 [*men*]. Item for the wages of Thomas Elye, naster, and 29 mariners and gunners serving in the same pinnace under im by the space of 6 weeks 2 days begun the 11th day of October last nd ended the last day of November as abovesaid, at 9s 4d every man the nonth; deadshares and rewards in the same accounted – £25 10s.

Summa totalis – £521 6s 8d.

18 *Four statements of naval charges presented to the Privy Council*

BL, Cotton MS Otho E. IX, ff. 120–4][2] *1564–65*

Headings lost. No. 3 is clearly a draft of no. 1]

tem 1] [f. 120] […] who[le char]ge […] with[in] […] one whole year is day end[ed] […] received within the said time […] [app]eareth.

First, for the debt due upon the determination of his account the last ay of December 1564 – £640.

[1]MS 'Thomas' in error (probably by anticipation of next entry); cf. name as correctly ven in the Quarter Book (above, p. 236).

[2]With *lacunae* supplied from PL 2876, pp. 176–8 (copy of latter part of fourth item).

Item, for so much borrowed of Her Majesty, to be repaid as by the privy seal thereof appeareth – £1,000.[1]

Item, for 12 months' ordinary for keeping Her Highness's ships in harbour, begun the first day of January 1564 [*so MS*] and ended the las day of December as abovesaid, according to Her Grace's warrant o £6,000 by the year, and £334 18s for every month – £4,018 [19s].

Item for the diets of Anthony Jenkynson, late captain of the *Aid*, anc for wages and conduct of 94 mariners and gunners serving under him in the same ship – £138 5s 5[½]d.

Summa – £5,797 4s 5½d.

Received by the said Benjamin Gonson by your Lordships' orders, o Richard Stoneley, esquire – £100.

Received more by your Lordships' like orders given the 2nd day o November, of the four tellers – £500.

Received more by your Lordships' like orders given the 12th day o the same month, of the said Richard Stoneley – £233 9s 7[½]d.

Received more by your Lordships' like orders given the 19th day o the same month, of Thomas Gardener, esquire – £100.

Received more by your Lordships' like orders given the 26th day o the same month, of Henry Killigrew, esquire – £100.

Received more by your Lordships' like orders given the 3rd day o December, of the aforesaid Thomas Gardener – £200.

Received more by your Lordships' like orders given the 13th day o the same month, of the aforesaid Henry Killigrew – £200.

Received more by your Lordships' like orders given the 24th day o the same month, of the aforesaid Thomas Gardener – £100.

Summa – £1,533 9s 7½d.

Remaineth owing the last day of December aforesaid – £4,263 14s 10c

[*item 2*] [f. 121] The state of the […] marine causes within [the charg of] Benjamin Gonson, for […] due since the last day of […] until thi present last day [of December] *annis supradictis.*

For wages, victuals and lodging, as well of shipwrights, caulkers an other artificers, with divers kinds of provisions, as also for wages c masters, mariners and gunners serving in Her Highness's ships for thei safe-keeping afloat in Gillingham Water, by the space of 9 whole month begun the first day of January 1565 [*so MS*] and ended as abovesaid, a £333 6s 8d for every month, after the rate of £4,000 *per annum*, as by He Majesty's ordinary warrant appeareth – £3,000.

[1]See next note.

Received of the four tellers at divers times, as by the particulars appeareth – £533 6s [8d].

And so remaineth at this day to pay – £2,466 13[s 4d].

Besides which sum of £2,466 13s 4d due the abovesaid last day of September last – £333 6s 8d to be paid monthly for the ordinary doth grow, which for 3 months to end the last day of December amounted to – £1,000.

Beseeching your honours also to apperceive that I do owe Her Highness for money borrowed our of her privy purse in September in the fourth year of Her Majesty's reign,[1] for the which I have Her Grace's privy seal dated at Greenwich the 17th day of July in the 5th year of her said reign [*1563*], as by the same privy seal appeareth – £1,000.

[*Signed*] Benjamin Gonson.

[*item 3*] [f. 122] […] for her agr[…]

First, for the debt due upon the determination of his account the last day of December 1564, besides £2,729 14s 7d received since – [£640].

Item, for so much borrowed of Her Majesty, to be repaid as by the privy seal thereof more plainly appeareth – £1,000.

Item, for 9 months' ordinary begun the first day of January last and ended the last day of September following, after £333 6s 8d for every month – £3,000.

Summa – £4,640.

Memorandum that in the aforesaid debt is nothing ment[ioned] the wages of one captain and 100 me[n] under him in the *Aid*, who be owning 2 mon[ths'] wages ended the 15th of this present; by estim[ation] – £93 6s 8d.

[*Signed*] Benjamin Gonson.

[*item 4*] [ff. 123–4] *The Queen's Majesty's ships. Men.* The *Triumph* – 'xx …'.[2] The *White Bear* – 21. The *Elizabeth Jonas* – 21. The *Victory* – 18. The *Mary Rose* – 13. The *Hope* – 13. The *Philip and Mary* – 13. The *Lion* – 13. The *Jesus* – 13. The *Minion* – 10. The *Primrose* – 10. The *Antelope* – 10. The *Jennet* – 10. The *Swallow* – 10. The *New Bark* – 7. The *Aid* – 7. The *Willoughby* – 7. The *Falcon* – 3. The *Phoenix* – 3. The *Saker* – 3. The *Bark of Boulogne* – 3. The *Hare* – 3. The *Sun* – 3. The *George* – 3. The *Galley Speedwell* – 3. The *Galley Tryright* – 3. The *Galley Eleanor* – 3. The *Makeshift* – 1. The *Post* – 1. [*Sum*] – 259.

[1] 28 Sept. 1562, as more fully recorded in the Quarter Book (above, p. 27 & n. 2).

[2] Loss of text before means that it is not certain what number above 20 was written. This list has been adapted from a tabular structure, and the column heading 'men' is given here in the first instance only.

[An[1] estimate of the ordinary charges within the charge or office o Benjamin Gonson, Treasurer of Her Majesty's Marine Causes, for the safe-keeping of Her [Highness's said ships in] harbour and for diver [kinds of provision needf]ul for the same, as also for other [charge incident] thereunto, for one month of 28 days [hereafter more] at larg appearing:

Masters. First for the wages of four masters attending upon the sam ships for like time, at 40s every of them – £8.

Boatswains. Item for the wages of 12 boatswains serving in 12 of th same ships for like time, at [14s] 8d every of them – £10; item for th wages of 12 other boatswains serving in 12 other of the same ships [for like time, at 11s 8d every of them – £7. [*Sum*] – £17.

Master gunners. Item for the wages of 23 master gunners attendin upon [23] of the same ships for like times, at 10s every of them – £11 10s

Pursers. Item for the wages of one purser serving in one of the sai ships for like time at 6d every day – 14s; item for the wages of three othe pursers serving in three other of the said ships for like time, at 10s ever of them – 30s. [*Sum*] – £2 4s.

Stewards and cooks. Item for the wages of 16 other persons servin as stewards and cooks in 16 of the same ships for like time, at 9s 2d ever of them – £7 6s 8d.

Mariners. Item for the wages of 150 mariners serving in the aforesai ships for like time, at 6s 8d every of them – £53 6s 8d.

Shipwrights, carpenters and sawyers. Item for the wages of thre master shipwrights attending upon the said ships for like time, at 28s ever of them – £4 4s; item for the wages of 33 other shipwrights, caulkers an sawyers attending upon the said ships for like time, at 18s 8d every o them – £30 16s; item for the victualling and lodging of the said 3 shipwrights, caulkers and sawyers for like time, at 17s every of them – £3 12s. [*Sum*] – £65 12s.

[*Wages.* Item for] the wages of A[ugustino Levello, Venetia ship]wright, for like time, at [16d every day – £12 17s 4d].

[*The*] *Castle* [*of*] *Upnor.* Item for the wages of one master gunne daily attending in the castle at Upnor for like time, at 16d every day – [£ 17s 4d]; item for the wages of seven other gunners also attending ther for like time, at 28s every of them – £9 16s. [*Sum*] – £11 13s 4d.

Provisions of divers kinds. Item for provisions of divers kinds, *vi* ironwork, timber, plank, board, trenails, pitch, tar, rosin, pulleys, parrel shivers of brass, caulking oil, burning reed, &c., employed upon He Majesty's ships for like time – £106.

[1]PL text begins here.

Cordage. Item for provisions of cable, cablets, hawsers, warps and sundry other kinds of cordage for like time – £135 7s 8d.

Charges incident to the premises. Item for water carriages, land carriages, lighterage, house rent, watchmen's wages, labourers' wages, clerks' wages, keepers' of storehouses and timber-yards wages, and riding charges for like time – £33 0s 9½d.

Sum total – £452 15s 5½d.

[*Signed*] Benjamin Gonson. W. Winter. William Holstock.
G. Winter.

19 *Comparison of the ordinary and extraordinary charges before and after 1579*

[PL 2875, p. 60 (*Cat. PL*, p. 127)][1] [c. *April 1585*]

A parallel of the charge ordinary and extraordinary before the year 1579 and that of the 5 years following in relation to the Navy.

[*Left hand column*] A note of the charge ordinary and extraordinary before the year 1579 as they fell but yearly for these natures following:

First the ordinary was yearly – £5,714.

The provisions of cordage, canvas and such likes that was spent at the seas and supplied again by warrant was yearly – £2,000.

The extra building of ships and repairing in dry dock and otherwise was yearly near about – £2,500.

So as one year's charge was – £10,200.

Amounts unto for 5 years – £51,000.[2]

With all this expense the Navy was never bettered nor the remain of provisions increased, but only grew poor and poorer.

[*Right hand column*] A note of what charges have grown in these 5 years from Christmas *anno* 1579 to Christmas 1584 since the alteration in the Office:

First the ordinary has been yearly £4,000, which is for these 5 years – £20,000.

[1]Copied by one of Pepys's clerks from the State Papers, but the original is no longer extant there. Cf. a list of ship repairs and other works done between Michaelmas 1579 and Christmas 1584: ibid., pp. 117–19 (*Cat. PL*, p. 128; *FAES* II. 10), also from an untraced original, but closely related to data supplied by Hawkins to Burghley 8 April 1585: SP 2/178, no. 12 (*CSPD 1581–90*, p. 236), printed in Williamson, *Hawkins* (1927), pp. 57–9.

[2]Miswritten '510000:00' for '51000:0:00' (the colons separating pounds/shillings/pence).

The charge of reparations extra in this time has been near about – £8,000.

The provisions of cordage, canvas, anchors and other provisions spent at the sea, and also laid up in store, within the said time is near about – £11,200.

The new building of wharves, storehouses, smiths' forges and transportations within this time is near about – £1,200.

Summa – £40,400.

So as the whole charge for the same natures amounting in 5 years to £40,400 is yearly near about – £8,100.

[*Below both columns*] The charge besides this is increased in provisions of cordage, canvas, anchors, shivers of brass, pulleys, new building of houses and wharves for the furtherance of service (which is extant in the Office) to the value of £10,000, which for these 5 years does make an increase of £2,000 yearly; and the same being taken out of the whole charge of £8,100 yearly aforesaid, it does plainly appear that in this time of 5 years there is not spent above £6,100 yearly, which said sum being deducted out of the great charge before (on the first side written) of £10,214 yearly, the charge does fall out less now than in former time – £4,000 yearly.

20 *Proposed increase of seamen's wages; enclosed with a letter from Hawkins to Burghley*

[SP 12/185, nos 33, 33(ii) (*CSPD 1581–90*, p. 293)][1] *28 December 158[5]*

My duty in humble manner remembered unto your good Lordship.

I do send herewith the book which your Lordship commanded me to make [*not printed here*], the substance whereof your Lordship may briefly see in the latter end of the book, and so by the paging see the charge particularly, either for the whole Navy for 3 months with all their company, or else for 3 months for their transportation to Portsmouth with a third part of their numbers.

I do also send your Lordship a note to show how fit and commodiou[s] it would be to augment the sailors' wages, which no doubt would greatl[y]

[1]No. 33 is the letter and no. 33(ii) its second enclosure. There are two other attached copies of the latter: no. 33(iii), which carries some marginalia by Burghley, and no. 33(iv). PL 2875, p. 62 is a copy of the last of these. The second enclosure was first printed in Laughton, *Armada*, ii, pp. 352–3; the letter and both enclosures are in Corbett, *Spanish War*, pp. 269–82.

strengthen [the *deleted*] and benefit the service and nothing at all increase the charge. Your Lordship may with honour and safety prefer it.

I have received two letters for wheat to be had out of Kent and a letter for elms from Reading, for which I humbly thank your good Lordship, and I humbly take my leave. From London, the 28th of December 1585.

Your honourable Lordship's ever most bounden, John Hawkins.

The 28th of December 1585. A note to show the commodity that would grow to Her Majesty and country by increasing the wages of the servitors by sea in Her Highness's ships.

First, if it might please Her Majesty to allow for the medium of all servitors an increase of 4s 8d every man by the month, it would fall out to be unto every man (one with the other) 6d by the day. So as the common man that had but 6s 8d by the month shall have 10s, and so every officer will be increased after that rate a third part more in his wages.

By this mean Her Majesty's ships would be furnished with able men, such as can make shift for themselves, keep themselves clean [*MS* 'clere' *but the other copies* 'cleane'] without vermin and noisomeness which breedeth sickness and mortality. All which would be avoided.

The ships would be able to continue longer in the service that they should be appointed unto, and would be able to carry victuals for a longer time.

There is no captain or master exercised in service but would undertake with more courage any enterprise with 250 able men than with 300 of tag and rag, and assure himself of better success.

The wages being so small causeth the best men to run away, to bribe and make mean to be cleared from the service, and insufficient, unable and unskilful persons supply the place, which discourageth the captains, masters and men that know what service requireth.

If it shall please Her Majesty to yield unto this increase, Her Highness's service would be far safer and much better, and yet the charge nothing increased, as for example:

The charge of the *Lion* for one month's wages and victuals of 300 men after the old rate of 23s 4d per man doth amount to £350.

The same ship being now furnished with 250 able men after the new rate of 28s wages and victuals for every man *per mensem*, will amount unto (even as before) monthly £350.

So as all the commodities are obtained without any increase of charge to Her Majesty.

The sailors also (in consideration of Her Majesty's gracious liberality) shall be bound for to bring into the said service every man his sword and dagger.

21 *Acceptance of new wage rates, annotated by Burghley*

[SP 12/186, no. 43 (*CSPD 1581–90*, p. 304)][1] [c. *June 1586*

Officers usually in her Majesty's ships, as for example the *Lion*.

1. The captain hath sometime 20s a day, sometime 26s 8d a day according to the greatness of his charge.

2. The master hath 6s 8d by the month and 7 deadshares, being 5s every share, which maketh in all 41s 8d *per mensem*.

3. The master's mate hath 6s 8d and 4 deadshares, which is 26s 8d *per mensem*.

4. In this ship is allowed 2 mates.

5. The pilot hath *[6s 8d and in reward 8s 4d] –15s *per mensem*.

6. The boatswain hath 6s 8d and 2 deadshares, which is 16s 8d *per mensem*.

7. The mate hath 6s 8d and one deadshare, which is 11s 8d.

8. The boatswain hath 2 mates.

9, 10, 11, 12. Four quartermasters have apiece 11s 8d *per mensem*.

13, 14, 15, 16. The four mates have 6s 8d apiece *per mensem* and half a deadshare, which is 2s 6d, and maketh in all 9s 2d for apiece *per mensem*.

17. The steward *[hath 6s 8d and 5s] – 11s 8d.

18. His mate *[6s 8d and 2s 6d] – 9s 2d.

19. The cook *[likewise[2]] – 11s 8d.

20. His mate *[likewise] – 9s 2d.

21. Yeoman of the halyards } * [likewise] – 11s 8d.
21. Yeoman of the jeer } – 11s 8d.

*[Yeoman of the sheets – 11s 8d.]

23. The surgeon *per mensem* – 15s *[as the pilot hath].

24. The purser *per mensem* – 11s 8d *[*ut supra*].

25, 26, 27, 28. Four trumpeters *per mensem* – 15s apiece *[*ut supra* as the pilot].

29. A drummer per *mensem* – 11s 8d.

30. A fife *per mensem* – 11s 8d.

31. The master gunner *per mensem* *[11s 8d and 3s 4d in reward] – 10s [*recte* 15s].

32. His mate *per mensem* – 7s 6d *[in reward but 10d].

33, 34, 35, 36. Four quartermaster's mates – 7s 6d *[in reward but 10d].

37. A swabber [*inserted* or ('*vel*') sweeper] – 11s 8d *[*ut supra*].

[1]Burghley supplied the matter here preceded by *, and the marginal numbers. Printed Corbett, *Spanish War*, pp. 285–6, with (pp. 286–91) useful commentary. Loades, *Tudor Navy*, p. 200 & n. 3, wrongly assigns this pay rise to 1582.

[2]I.e. the cook like the steward, the cook's mate like the steward's mate; the 'likewise' does not always refer to the immediately preceding entry.

*[37 officers. All these are to have a third part more as the mariners shall have. Mariners and soldiers have had but 6s 8d and now are to have 10s.]

22 *Rates of wages*

[Bodl. MS Rawlinson A. 171, ff. 310–13 (*Cat. Rawl.*, col. 152)][1] *December 1587*

[f. 310] December *anno* 1587. The rates of wages of all officers in every of Her Majesty's ships.

The Lord Admiral hath for his diet every day – £3 6s 8d. All other Admirals and Vice-Admirals are to be paid by warrant from the Lord Admiral by his discretion.

Men. The *Elizabeth Jonas* – 500. The *Triumph* – 500. The *Bear* – 500. The *Victory* – 400. The *Ark* – 400.

Wages.

The master *per mensem* – £3 2s 6d; [*week*] 15s 7½d; [*day*] 2s 2¾d. Two mates, each at – £1 10s. A pilot – £1 10s; [*week*] 7s 6d; [*day*] 12¾d. A boatswain – £1 10s. Two mates, each at – 17s 6d; [*week*] 4s 4½d; [*day*] 7½d. Four quartermasters, each at – £1 5s. Four quarter [masters'] mates, each at – 17s 6d. Four yeoman of: the jeer, the halyards, the sheets, the tacks; each at – 17s 6d. A master carpenter – £1 5s; [*week*] 6s 3d; [*day*] 10¾d. Two mates to use both axe and mallet – 17s 6d. If any more caulkers or carpenters be appointed, to have each *per mensem* – 13s 9d; [*day*] 3s 5¼d; [*day*] 5¾d. A purser – £1; [*week*] 5s; [*day*] – 8½d. A steward – 17s 6d. Two mates – 13s 9d. A cook – 17s 6d. Two mates – 13s 9d. A surgeon – £1. Two servants in common pay. Four trumpeters, each at – £1. A drum, a fife; each at – 15s; [*week*] 3s 9d; [*day*] 6½d. A coxswain – 17s 6d. His mate – 13s 9d. A skiffswain – 17s 6d. His mate – 13s 9d. Two swabbers, each at – 13s 9d. An armourer – 18s 8d; [*week*] 4s 8d; [*day*] 8d. A gunmaker – 18s 8d.

A master gunner *per mensem* – 15s. Two mates, each at – 11s 3d; [*week*] 2s 9¾d; [*day*] 4¾d. Four quarter gunners, each at – 11s 3d. Four quarter gunners' mates, each at – 11s 3d. Yeoman of the powder room – 11s 3d.

[1]The original has three columns for monthly, weekly and daily pay; the two latter are only partially completed, to which no significance should be attached. The tabular structure is replaced here by a run-on treatment which omits repeated matter and superfluous numerals. The sums are for the month except as shown.

[f. 310v] *Men.* The *Mary Rose* – 250. The *Bonaventure* – 250. The *Lion* – 250. The *Hope* – 250. The *Nonpareil* – 250. The *Revenge* – 250. The *Vanguard* – 250. The *Rainbow* – 250.

Wages.

A master *per mensem* – £3; [*week*] – 15s; [*day*] 2s 1¾d. Two mates, each at – £1 5s. A pilot – £1 5s; [*week*] – 6s 3d; [*day*] 10¾d. A boatswain – £1 5s. Two mates, each at – 17s 6d; [*week*] 4s 4½d; [*day*] 7½. Four quartermasters, each at – 17s 6d. Four quartermasters' mates, each at – 13s 9d; [*week*] 3s 5¼d; [*day*] 5¾d. Four yeomen of: the jeer, the halyards, the sheets; each – 14s; [*week*] 3s 6d; [*day*] 6d. A master carpenter – £1 5s. His mate, a caulker – 17s 6d. If any more carpenters or caulkers be appointed, each to have – 13s 9d. A purser – 16s 8d; [*week*] 4s 2d; [*day*] 7⅐d. A steward – 17s 6d. One mate – 13s 9d. A cook – 17s 6d. One mate – 13s 9d. A surgeon – £1; [*week*] 5s; [*day*] 8½d. A servant and gromet in common pay. Three trumpeters, each at – £1. If an admiral,[1] four trumpeters. A drum, a fife; each at – £1 5s; [*week*] 3s 9d; [*day*] 6½d. A coxswain – 17s 6d. His mate – 13s 9d. A swabber – 13s 9d. His mate – 11s 3d; [*week*] 2s 9¾d; [*day*] 4¾d. An armourer – 18s 8s. A gunmaker – 18s 8d; [*week*] 4s 8d; [*day*] 8d.

A master gunner *per mensem* – 15s. Two mates, each at – 11s 3d. Four quarter gunners, each at – 11s 3d. Four quarter gunners' mates, each at – 11s 3d. Yeoman of the powder room – 11s 3d.

[f. 311] *Men.* The *Dreadnought* – 200. The *Swiftsure* – 180. The *Antelope* – 170. The *Swallow* – 160. The *Foresight* – 160.

Wages.

A master *per mensem* – £2 10s; [*week*] 12s 6d; [*day*] 23½d. One mate – £1 5s. A pilot – £1 5s; [*week*] 6s 3d; [*day*] 10¾d. A boatswain – 17s 6d. One mate – 13s 9d. Four quartermasters, each at – 17s 6d; [*week*] 4s 4½d; [*day*] 7½d. Four quartermasters' mates, each at – 13s 9d. Two yeomen of: the jeer and halyards; the sheets and tacks: each at – 14s; [*week*] 3s 6d; [*day*] 6d. A master carpenter – 17s 6d. His mate, a caulker – 13s 9d; [*week*] 3s 5¼d; [*day*] 5¾d. If any more caulkers or carpenters be appointed, each to have *per mensem* – 13s 4d. A purser – 13s 4d. A steward – 17s 6d. One mate – 13s 9d. A cook – 17s 6d. One mate – 13s 9d. A surgeon – £1; [*week*] 5s; [*day*] 8½d. One servant in common pay. A trumpeter – £1. If an admiral three trumpeters. A drum, a fife, each at – 15s; [*week*] 3s 9d; [*day*] 6½d. A coxswain – 17s 6d. His mate – 13s 9d

[1]Meaning an Admiral's command, or (as later termed) flagship; in the 1560s the usage was still 'ship admiral' (cf. above, p. 488), and the contraction by which the ship becomes the personification of the flag officer was an innovation, for which *OED* cites the earliest usage from 1588.

A swabber – 13s 9d. His mate – 11s 3d; [*week*] 2s 9¾d; [*day*] 4¼d. An armourer – 18s 8d; [*week*] 4s 8d; [*day*] 8d.

A master gunner *per mensem* – 15s. Two mates, each at – 11s 3d. Four quarter gunners – 11s 3d. Yeoman of the powder room – 11s 3d.

[f. 311v] *Men.* The *Aid* – 120. The *Bull* – 100. The *Tiger* – 100.

Wages.

A master per *mensem* – £2 5s; [*week*] 11s 3d; [*day*] 19¼d. One mate – £1. A pilot – £1; [*week*] 5s; [*day*] 8½d. A boatswain – 17s 6d. One mate – 13s 9d. Four quarter masters, each at – 17s 6d; [*week*] 4s 4½d; [*day*] 7½d. Four quarter[masters'] mates, each at – 13s 9d. A master carpenter –17s 6d. His mate, a caulker – 13s 9d; [*week*] 3s 5¼d; [*day*] 5¾d. A purser – 13s 4d. A steward – 17s 6d. One mate – 13s 9d. A cook – 17s 6d. One mate – 13s 9d. A surgeon – £1. A trumpeter – £1. If an admiral three trumpeters. A drum, a fife; each at – 15s; [*week*] 3s 9d; [*day*] 6½d. A swabber – 13s 9d. An armourer – 18s 8d; [*week*] 4s 8d; [*day*] 8d.

A master gunner *per mensem* – 15s. One mate – 11s 3d; [*week*] 2s 9¾d; [*day*] 4¾d. Four quarter gunners – 11s 3d. Yeoman of the powder room – 11s 3d.

[f. 312] *Men.* The *Scout* – 70. The *Handmaid* – 70. The *Tremontaine* – 70. The *Achates* – 60.

Wages.

A master *per mensem* – £2; [*week*] 10s; [*day*] 17d. One mate – £1. A pilot – £1; [*week*] 5s; [*day*] 8½d. A boatswain – 17s 6d. One mate – 13s 9d. Four quartermasters, each at – 17s 6d; [*week*] 4s 4½d; [*day*] 7½d. A master carpenter – 17s 6d. His mate, a caulker – 13s 9d; [*week*] 3s 5¼d; [*day*] 5¾d. A purser – 13s 4d; [*week*] 3s 4d; [*day*] 5¾d. A steward – 17s 6d. A cook – 17s 6d. A surgeon – £1. A trumpeter – £1. A swabber – 13s 9d.

A master gunner *per mensem* – 15s; [*week*] 3s 9d; [*day*] 6½d. One mate – 11s 3d; [*week*] 2s 9¾d; [*day*] 4¾d. Four quarter gunners, each at – 11s 3d.

[f. 312v] *Men.* The *Marline* – 35. The *Charles* – 40. The *Moon* – 40. The *Advice* – 40. The *Makeshift* – 40. The *Spy* – 40. The *Sun* – 30.

Wages.

A master *per mensem* – £1 7s; [*week*] 6s 9d; [*day*] 11½d. One mate – 17s 6d. A boatswain – 17s 6d; [*week*] 4s 4½d; [*day*] 7½d. Two quartermasters, each at – 17s 6d. A purser – 13s 4d; [*week*] 3s 4d; [*day*] 5¾d. One to be both cook and steward – 13s 9d; [*week*] 3s 5¼d; [*day*] 5¾d. A carpenter – 17s 6d. A trumpeter – £1; [*week*] 5s; [*day*] 8½d.

A master gunner *per mensem* – 15s; [*week*] 3s 9d; [*day*] 6½d. One mate – 11s 3d; [*week*] 2s 9¾d; [*day*] 4¾d.

Men. The *Cygnet* – 16. Ketches and small barks – 8.
[*Wages*].
A master *per mensem* – £1. One mate – 17s 6d. A boatswain – 13s 9d. One for cook and steward – 13s 9d.

A gunner – 13s 4d [*so altered, and added*] for the *Cygnet*, 11s 3d for ketches.

[f. 313] Every common man's wages – 10s; [*week*] 2s 6d; [*day*] 4¼d. A gromet's wages – 7s 6d; [*week*] 1s 10½d; [*day*] 3¼d. A boy's wages – 5s; [*week*]; 1s 3d; day – 2⅐d.

[*Here signed, as at the foot of each preceding page*]: W. Winter, John Hawkins, W. Borough.

A preacher with the Lord Admiral – £3. Preachers with other noblemen – £2. A preacher with Sir Robert Southwell – £2.[1]

Determined by the Lord Admiral and [con]firmed by Sir W.W. 12 March 1587 [*1588*] aboard the *Ark* at Margate.[2]

23 *Summary of arrangements for the ordinary and extraordinary, with proposal for increase*

[SP 12/202, no. 35 (*CSPD 1581–90*, p. 417)][3] *27 June 1587*

The state and manner how Her Majesty's ships have been continued and ordered since the eleventh year of Her Majesty's reign, *viz.*:

[1]Cf. a paper sent from Hawkins to Burghley 12 Sept. 1588 asking for increase of pay for certain categories, including preachers: one at £3 (*Ark*), five at £2 (*Elizabeth Jonas*, *Bear*, *Rainbow*, *Lion*, *Revenge*): SP 12/216, no. 18(i), printed in Laughton, *Armada*, ii, p. 231. These were the commands of, respectively, the Lord Admiral, Sir Robert Southwell, Lord Sheffield, Lord Henry Seymour, Lord Thomas Howard, and the Vice-Admiral (Drake). Southwell was the Lord Admiral's son-in-law, and was given exalted status on that account: cf. Laughton, i, p. 24 and R. W. Kenny, *Elizabeth's Admiral: The Political Career of Charles Howard, Earl of Nottingham 1536–1624* (Baltimore and London, 1970), pp. 93, 143. The only peer commanding in 1588 who is not assigned a preacher was the Earl of Cumberland in *Elizabeth Bonaventure*. The chaplains' historian was puzzled by the allocation of preachers in the September 1588 list, noting that none was assigned to the largest ship, *Triumph* (Frobisher): G. C. Taylor, *The Sea Chaplains: A History of the Chaplains of the Royal Navy* (Oxford, 1978), p. 45. The March regulation shows that the social rank of the captains, not the size of the ship, was the determining factor.

[2]The Lord Admiral's presence with the fleet in Margate Road from 10 March is recorded in despatches: Laughton, *Armada*, i, pp. 105, 108

[3]See Glasgow, 'Maturing', p. 18 n. 1, and Loades, *Tudor Navy*, p. 183 n. 4.

How it was in time past. First there was allowed and paid by warrant dormant – £5,714 yearly. For which sum there was performed these things following:

The wages of the shipkeepers.

The ransacking and keeping of the ships in harbour till they come to be new built or dry docked.

The grounding of the said ships as was fit for them, and as their time came about to continue them in harbour, some in three years, some in two years, and others of the lesser sort once a year. For this service aforesaid all kind of ironwork and stuff was provided.

The mooring of the ships in harbour.

The wages of the gunners in Upnor Castle.

The wages of clerks, &c., keepers of the plugs at Chatham, Deptford, Woolwich and Portsmouth.

The fees of shipwrights, porters, messengers and suchlike.

The rent for storehouses.

Fees for keeping of houses at Woolwich and Portsmouth.

Repairing of houses at Deptford, Woolwich, Chatham and Portsmouth.

The watch at Chatham and Deptford.

All this aforesaid hath been borne upon the old ordinary warrant abovesaid of £5,714 yearly.

There was also besides this (*communibus annis*) an extraordinary charge which passed by warrant from Her Majesty for the new building and repairing of ships in dry docks, to the sum of – £2,500 yearly.[1]

So that, this whole charge for the purposes aforesaid, from the year of *anno* 1568 unto the year of *anno* 1579 was – £8,214 yearly.

How it is now. Then followed the agreement with John Hawkins in *anno* 1579. And since that time the ordinary abovesaid, and the extraordinary charge of repairing and new reforming of the ships in dry docks hath been maintained only upon the charge of the first ordinary warrant of £5,714 yearly.

How it is now greatly increased, for which it is fit an ordinary be considered of for their maintenance.

The sea service by mean of this troublesome time doth greatly increase charge and business, so as it is impossible for any one man to answer the office of Treasurer and to take this care.

Sir William Winter and the rest of the Officers of the Navy, having substantially considered with my Lord Admiral, do and will endeavour

[1]Cf. SP 12/48, no. 63 (*CSPD 1547–80*, p. 324): Lord Treasurer and Sir Walter Mildmay to Cecil, 23 Dec. 1568 (reporting repair of four great ships that year, the cost of which was to be repaid to Gonson on presentation of his warrant).

themselves and are most desirous to ease Her Majesty's charge, and to do it in such sort as the Navy and provisions thereunto belonging be surely and sufficiently provided for all service; and withal to take such substantial care as Her Majesty be not overcharged, whereby Her Highness shall be encouraged to continue and maintain the said Navy in forcible and ready order for the defence of Her Majesty and our country.

How it may be. Therefore my opinion is as followeth:

That it may please Her Majesty to appoint certain of her Council and some others to join with my Lord Admiral in commission to see how this charge may be settled, and a new warrant dormant made for such a sum as should be by them determined.

In the end of which warrant there would be such a clause made as was in the last bargain with Mr Baeshe,[1] that what charge should exceed above the warrant dormant (and reason showed under the hands of the Lord Admiral and three or two of the Officers to the Lord Treasurer) that th[en] thereupon at the year's end such overplus should be paid to the Treasurer of the Navy without any other warrant to be provided from Her Majesty for the same.

And for that divers disorders have been in the carpentry, the provisions appertaining to the rigging, and the powder and furniture of artillery had out of the Tower, where by great purloining and waste of the provisions appertaining to those matters aforesaid Her Majesty hath been greatly burdened and overcharged. This in duty, if it may stand with the consideration and liking of the commissioners, that during these times of service I think it would be meet there were a provost marshal [*these words underlined and repeated in margin by annotator*] attendant upon the Lord Admiral and Officers of the Navy to do such present execution aboard the ships upon [*blot*] offenders as should be appointed and adjudged by the said Lord Admiral and the Officers of the Navy according to the quality of the o[ff]ence committed.

When it shall please God to send a quieter time, then the said commissioners may have order to compound a certainty of Her Majesty's charge of all manner of expense belonging to the Navy, and so divide it to the charge of few or such number of persons as shall be by them thought meet for Her Highness's profit and safety.

[*Annotated*] 27 June 1587.

[1]The 1565 contract [**28**].

VI

THE NAVY VICTUALLER'S 1565 CONTRACT AND RELATED PAPERS

At the beginning of Elizabeth's reign this essential service was under the control of Edward Baeshe, who had been appointed General Surveyor of Victuals for the Seas on 18 June 1550.[1] At first his accounts were rendered irregularly, but in accordance with the Privy Council ruling of 1557 they became annual or 'as often besides' as required by the Council. In fact there is then a gap in the extant sequence, which resumes in 1561.[2] As part of the general investigation of military spending after the Le Havre fiasco, Baeshe's accounts from 1 January 1562 were examined by special commissioners appointed under the great seal on 1 May 1564.[3] Meanwhile a new patent had been issued in 1563 to Baeshe in partnership with John Elliot.[4] Then with the 1565 bargain printed here [**28**], victualling was placed on a contract basis, and the new procedures by which Baeshe alone was accountable to the Exchequer were defined.[5] Thereafter the Declared Accounts survive in full.[6] For just one calendar year we also have a set of his Quarter Books on which, as with those of the Treasurer, the annual accounts are based.[7] A large amount of supporting material is to be found

[1]*CPR 1549–51*, p. 309. Baeshe previously shared the office with Richard Wattes; their Declared Account for 1 July 1547–28 June 1550 is the first extant in the series: E 351/2353 (printed *NEM*, pp. 171–236). The first Declared Account wholly in Baeshe's name runs from 28 June 1550 to 29 Sept. 1552: E 351/2355 (*NEM*, pp. 245–68). For his successive patents and other biographical details, see *NEM*, pp. 526–8; for a general listing of his accounts, see Appendix 1 below.

[2]*NEM*, p. 310.

[3]*CPR 1563–6*, p. 121 (no. 492); the commission was headed by the Earl of Arundel, Lord Steward, and included the Earl of Pembroke, Lord Robert Dudley (created Earl of Leicester while the commission was at work) and Sir Walter Mildmay. The account which the commission inspected is E 351/2360 (31 Dec. 1561–31 Dec. 1563). Cf. above, pp. 517–18 & n. 1 (similar investigation of Gonson's accounts).

[4]*CPR 1563–6*, p. 487.

[5]In this 16th-century usage 'bargain' means simply 'agreement', without the modern implication of cheapness. Pepys's copy uses the term 'contract' which had by then become established.

[6]E 351/2362 (1 Jan.–31 Dec. 1565) *et seq.*

[7]BL, Harleian MS 167, ff. 1–38v, containing the four Quarter Books for the calendar year 1 Jan. to 31 Dec. 1563, with some supplementary material. Though having the appearance of drafts, these are actually contemporary rough copies. This is clear because, except for a few sections in which the page structure of the original is retained, the *summa pagine* occurs randomly; likewise the signatures (of Woodhouse and Holstock), which are themselves

among the State Papers and elsewhere. Reconstructing Baeshe's operation ought therefore to be fairly straightforward, but there are inevitably some residual mysteries.

By about 1560 he had been provided with a headquarters on Tower Hill and a number of storehouses at Ratcliff, St Katherine's and Rochester, all at considerable expense.[1] Before the bargain, he received most of his money from Gonson as it was required. Four samples are given [**24–7**] of the brief statements he submitted to the Privy Council, requesting ad hoc warrants for the month ahead.[2] After 1565 he was provided with his ordinary in regular tranches directly from the Exchequer, and paid the bills as they came in from the various agents who were working on his behalf (and at his appointment) in the different localities. The earlier hand-to-mouth procedure was scrapped, partly because it was unpredictable, and partly because it was thought to be unnecessarily expensive, and this indenture or contract was agreed in its place. In spite of its precise-seeming language, it is full of holes and ambiguities. The bases are the daily 'allowance' for each man, and the rates of 4½d per man/day in harbour and 5d at sea. This represented a significant reduction on the previously prevailing rates, which helps to explain why the contract was insisted upon, and why it was to be complained against so vigorously.[3] The base rates determined what Baeshe was expected to provide, and how much he would be allowed to do so. He was allowed to indent for this money in advance, but it was provided only on the basis of the agreed ordinary. Perhaps it was felt

representational, i.e. copies with some suggestion of a displayed signature, but manifestly written by the same hand as the rest of the text, and with no intention to deceive. They are therefore compositionally the reverse of the preliminary versions of the Treasurer's Quarter Books preserved in the Evelyn MSS (for which see Appendix 4). For the most part Baeshe's papers give simply the dates and numbers of men for which ships were victualled; commodities, quantities and prices are not itemised, though cash totals are given at the foot of each original page, and at the end. Special payments are mentioned for victuals provided at Le Havre between April and June (f. 20v) and, singularly, for the building of 'a cage or pryson house' at Tower Hill (f. 21), presumably for Baeshe's livestock; the Declared Account adds that this was made by the Lord Treasurer's order: E 351/2360, m. 6.

[1] Details in Oppenheim, *History*, p. 140, citing Baeshe's accounts, and noting that the St Katherine's storehouse was hired from the compiler of the Anthony Roll 'who seems to have taken great interest in naval matters'.

[2] Such estimates must have been sent regularly, but **24** and **25** from 1562 are the only examples for the period surviving in the State Papers. From the following year, **26** and **27** were retained in Cecil's private archive, which also contains other estimates dated 4 and 1[illegible] Oct. 1563: HMC, *Salisbury*, i, p. 283, nos 937, 939. No significance attaches to the archival descent. The warrants requested by Baeshe can be traced to the issues listed in the Quarter Book 4 by means of the references prefaced by the # symbol.

[3] Cf. the contracted sea rate of 5d a day, which amounts to 11s 8d per man for a month of 28 days, with the 13s 4d for the same in the estimate for December 1562 [**25**], which represents a daily rate per man of 5.7d.

that he had been feeding too many extraneous mouths. Although it is not specified, there is a distinction built into this agreement between ordinary and extraordinary provisioning. The specified ordinary allowance of £1,981 4s (paid as £165 2s monthly) represented a minimum commitment which did not vary from year to year. Even this was a reduction of about 25 per cent on the equivalent Baeshe had received in 1562 and 1563.[1] How this was calculated or projected, we do not know. Operational victualling costs, exceptional for 1563, meant the actual sums passing through Baeshe's hands were much higher. Under the contract these were to be covered by extraordinary warrants, as before, only now the payments would be based upon authorised numbers, not upon Baeshe's estimates. At the same time, the General Surveyor was required to assume responsibility for the maintenance of storehouses in every port, and to pay rents for them. The standby provision for 1,000 men, originally stipulated in 1557,[2] was retained.

It was superficially a most unattractive bargain, because the rates were not generous and there was little flexibility. Presumably, although this is not stated, an equivalent of the 'dead pay' was allowed, and the numbers budgeted for were inflated by an agreed percentage to provide the General Surveyor with a profit margin.[3] Nevertheless at the end of the financial year any deficit ('surplusage') on his account was underwritten by the Exchequer without further warrant. Although it is not stated in the contract, Baeshe retained the £50 annual fee derived from his 1563 patent.[4] The only sweeteners which the contract added were an interest-free 'float' of £500, and licence to import salt and other commodities in exchange for export of ox-hides resulting from the slaughter process; customs were payable on the hides, but by implication the imports were duty-free.

Because of the increasing cost of Baeshe's supplies and other complicating factors the terms contracted in 1565 soon became unrealistic, and in response to his repeated representations of the fact some allowances were made. A further £1,000 was loaned to him in 1569 for general

[1]The ordinary prests for 1562 and 1563 total respectively £2,400 and £2,800, paid irregularly but in round £100s: above, pp. 206, 435.

[2]*BND*, p. 71.

[3]This is a grey area, but one of the principal incentives to enter into a contract was the opportunity to make a secure profit, and this could only be done by adjusting either the rates or the numbers. The rates were only adjusted twice during Baeshe's incumbency, so the conclusion should probably be that it was the numbers which were regularly inflated, following calculations which are now obscure.

[4]As with all Navy Office appointments conferred by patent, this fee was payable directly from the Exchequer, and so does not feature in Baeshe's own accounts; the fee was perpetuated when the patent was renewed in 1582: *CPR 1582–3*, no. 433.

purposes.[1] More specifically, in 1573 he obtained a privy seal warrant adjusting the terms of his original bargain by raising the daily allowances to 5½d per man in harbour and 6d at sea [**29**]. Even so, there was still not a great deal of margin, as a paper of the following year demonstrates [**30**]. The actual deployment it anticipates was to be of no great moment, and much of its content is general complaint: nothing is to be had without ready money, his allowance will cover barely half the cost of what he is committed to provide, and he is expected to pay for the casks he needs. Nevertheless the paper illuminates a number of ways in which Baeshe operated. Firstly, he specifies that he needs the money in advance, according to the numbers projected and the duration of the service. Secondly, he was provided with letters from the Privy Council authorising purveyance, which would have specified the quantity of each main provision that he was to be allowed to purchase from each shire. The Council office maintained its own record, enabling central government to know just how much could be asked of particular localities. Indeed the quota system which we know was operating by 1587 was probably in place much earlier.[2] Unfortunately, the staple which Baeshe had been able to create at Portsmouth turned into another deficit when his storehouse burned down in 1576.

His loan was eventually extended to £2,000, and he sought leave to pay off £1,500 in annual instalments of £100 while he lived, leaving the original £500 debt to his successor.[3] That successor was designated in 1582, when a new patent was issued to Baeshe in association with James

[1]So Oppenheim (*History*, p. 141), without source, and his data in this matter are flawed but Baeshe's loan had certainly been raised to £2,000 by 1576 (cf. below, n. 3). The Crown might have felt generous in 1569 following the seizure of treasure being shipped to the Spanish government in the Netherlands; but although Baeshe was initially an indirect beneficiary of this action, in the long term he suffered from the resulting stoppage in trade (cf. below, p. 602 & n. 3).

[2]*BND*, pp. 109–12. Cf. Council orders of 15 Nov. 1573 (to the Commissioners for victuals in Somerset to allow Peter Rowte, Baeshe's deputy, to ship 500 qrs of wheat to Rochester); 1 Feb. 1574 (to the Lord President of the North to allow Baeshe's servant Dennis Robinson to bring 100 qrs of wheat and 300 qrs malt and barley out of Yorkshire); 18/19 Sept. 1576 (to Lord Cobham to arrange collection of 300 qrs of wheat and 400 qrs of barley from specific hundreds in Kent): *APC 1571–5*, pp. 141, 184; *1575–7*, p. 205.

[3]SP 12/110, no. 37 (*CSPD 1581–90*, p. 534). This undated suit from Baeshe to the Queen was calendared under 1576 because of its reference to the Portsmouth fire, the date of which (4 Aug. 1576, supplied from SP 12/108, no. 70) was pencilled on to the MS by the editor. This is consistent with **31**, which shows that by 1586 Baeshe's debt had been reduced to £1,000 (of which half was the original £500, repayable within six months of his death or retirement, and the other half would be the residue of the additional £1,500 after ten annual repayments of £100). On the other hand, Baeshe refers specifically to the *16* years of his bargain, which would place the petition in 1581, and would mean his repayments had been more substantial. Oppenheim's commentary (*History*, pp. 141–2) follows the calendar as to date, but is defective as to the sums involved and the manuscript reference.

Quarles, the Clerk of the Queen's Kitchen.[1] But that did not affect Baeshe's contractual obligations or his current deficit. By 1586, despite having reduced his loan as proposed, Baeshe was so deep in trouble that asked to dissolve the bargain on the six-months notice he was entitled to give. In his representation to Lord Admiral Howard [**31**], accompanied by a letter to Secretary Walsingham [**32**], he cites specific and substantial rises in commodity prices, and claims that so far from being able to pay off his remaining £1,000 debt, an equivalent sum would be lost to him by supplying that summer's operations. His masters were not deaf to his pleas, though they had not responded to his every appeal. So this time the rates were increased again to 6d in harbour and 6½d at sea.[2] But by now and after forty years of service Baeshe had had enough, and must genuinely have wanted to retire and enjoy the victuals in his own larder. That would normally have been possible by arrangement with his co-patentee; in this case there was still the contract, and from this no release came; Baeshe had in fact made himself indispensable,[3] and was to continue in post for the remaining ten months of his life.

Oppenheim supposed that during his forty years Baeshe 'had never been charged with dishonesty and died poor'.[4] A rather different picture is given by the anonymous author of a verse tirade against him which survives in a manuscript at Arundel Castle.[5] The writer was undoubtedly motivated by private grudges including designs on Baeshe's wife, and most of his outpourings can be dismissed as malevolent gossip. The business through which Baeshe had climbed to the ranks of the gentry made him a simple target ('Duke of Albeif … and Marques of the Marybones / Countie of Calvs heads … and vicownt Neats tongs': ll. 29–31), and accusations of gluttony, alcoholic excess and sexual depravity could be embroidered easily enough. Yet like all such squibs, it must have had some circumstantial basis or else it would have been pointless. The poem refers to John Elliot, Baeshe's colleague in the victualling patent of 1563, and the man with whom he accounted to the end of 1564. The bargain of April 1565 then put everything in Baeshe's hands, which seems

[1]*CPR 1582–3*, no 433 (patent of 27 Nov. 1582), where Quarles is identified as an officer in the Household. His particular position was noted by Oppenheim (*History*, p. 142 n. 3), from BL, Lansdowne MS 62, no. 55 (f. 132 now f. 131), a memorandum of Household appointments dated 4 May 1590.

[2]And by a further halfpenny in each category the following year: Oppenheim, *History*, p. 142.

[3]For the government's reluctance to release Baeshe from his contract at such a critical moment see B. Pearce, 'Elizabethan food policy and the armed forces', *EcHR*, [1st ser.] xii (1942), pp. 40–1.

[4]Ibid., p. 143.

[5]R. Hughey (ed.), *The Arundel Harington Manuscript of Tudor Poetry* (Columbus, Ohio, 1969), i, pp. 225–33; ii, pp. 293–301.

consistent with the poem's suggestion that Baeshe, having 'gan to disdaine / the name of Purveyor' somehow elbowed his partner out of the business ('gaue poore Elliott such a trip') and turned himself into a 'Noble Synior' once he was in sole control (ll. 68–9, 77–81). Likely as not Baeshe was simply the more vigorous and competent administrator, and merited the high responsibility with which he was so long entrusted.

24 *Report by Baeshe to the Privy Council*

[SP 12/25, no. 48 (*CSPD 1547–80*, p. 211)][1] *11 November 1562*

xj° Novembris 1562. The victualling for the seas.

Portsmouth. The *New Bark* – 120. The *Saker* – 50. The *Hare* – 30. The *Phoenix* – 40. [*Total*] – 240 men. These ships shall end their victualling the 21 of this present.

If it is your Lordships' pleasure to have these ships further victualled, then there must be a warrant for £160 for a month to begin the 22 of November and ending the 19 of December next.[2]

Gillingham. The *Jennet* – 80. The *Antelope* – 80. The *Greyhound* – 60. The new ship – 60. The *Bark of Boulogne* – 30. [*Total*] – 310 men. These ships are appointed to be transported from Gillingham to Portsmouth.[3]

The victualling and necessaries for these five ships for the month of 28 days cometh to – £206 13s 4d.

Summa totalis – £366 13s 4d.

The *Phoenix* – 40 men. She was victualled at Portsmouth for 3 weeks without warrant begun the first of November. *Summa* – £20.

Totalis – £386 13s 4d.

25 *Report by Baeshe to the Council*

[SP 12/26, no. 3 (*CSPD 1547–80*, p. 212)] *5 December 1562*

Quinto Decembris 1562. The victualling for the seas.

The *New Bark* – 120 men. The *Saker* – 50. The *Phoenix* – 40. The *Hare* – 30. The *Bark of Boulogne* – 30. The *Double Rose* – 30. [*Total*] – 300 men.

Memorandum in the stead of the *New Bark* the *Aid* is appointed with the same men.[4] These ships end their victualling the 19th of this present month of December. The charges of the victualling of the said ships for one month of 28 days after the rate of 13s 4d the man *per mensem*, per estimation – £200.

Memorandum. Your Lordships' pleasure to be known whether the said ships shall have another month's victuals to begin the 20th of the month

[1]Cf. above, p. 228.

[2]This was duly covered by a warrant of 15 Nov.: above, p. 30, entry **#B16**.

[3]Cf. the warrant for wages for this operation: ibid., entry **#B15**. As noted to the next entry, the new ship was the *Aid*.

[4]The *Aid* was newly arrived from Gillingham following her launch at Deptford on 6 Oct., and *New Bark*'s captain, William Driver, took command: above, p. 308 & n. 1, 235, 236.

and to end the 16th of January next; and then the warrant is to be had for the said £200.[1]

26 *Report by Baeshe to the Privy Council*

[Hatfield House, Cecil Papers 154/36 (HMC, *Salisbury*, i, p. 283, no. 940)] *24 October 1563*

xxiiij[to] *Octobris 1563.* The victualling of the Queen's Majesty's ships.

A report made by Edward Baeshe, General Surveyor of the victuals for the seas, touching the debt due within his office for the victualling of the Queen's Majesty's ships in all places.

[*Margin*: The warrant dormant remaineth in the Exchequer in the name of Benjamin Gonson, Treasurer of the Admiralty]. There is owing upon the ordinary warrant of £12,000 by year (after the yearly allotment of £3,000 for the victualling of the Queen's ships in harbour) for 3 quarters of a year ending at Michaelmas last 1563, *ultra* £1,600 by him already received of Mr Gonson – £650.

More for the said victualling for the full month of October – £250.

There is due upon a warrant for the victualling of the Queen's Majesty's ships serving upon the Narrow Seas under the charge of Sir Thomas Cotton for one month of 28 days begun the first of October and ending the 28th of the same – £253 6s 8d.[2]

[*Margin*: There lacketh a warrant]. Memorandum, for a warrant for £253 6s 8d for the like victualling for one other month to begin the 29th of October.[3]

There is also due upon a warrant to Sir Thomas Woodhouse for the victualling of the *Swallow* and the *Willoughby* to end the 28th of this present October – £399 7s.[4]

Memorandum to have the Lords' letters to call home the said ships or else order for the longer continuing of them in victualling.

Totalis – £1,552 13s 8d.

[1]Supplied by warrant of 8 Dec.: above, p. 31, entry **#B18**.
[2]Second warrant of 12 Oct.: above, p. 250, entry **#Y26**.
[3]Supplied by warrant of 28 Oct.: ibid., entry **#Y27**.
[4]First warrant of 12 Oct.: above, p. 249, entry **#Y24**.

27 *Report by Baeshe to the Privy Council*

[Hatfield House, Cecil Papers 154/43 (HMC, *Salisbury*, i, p. 285, no. 947)] *17 December 1563*

xvij° Decembris 1563. The victualling of the Queen's Majesty's ships under the charge of Edward Baeshe.

Ships in the Narrow Seas under the charge of Sir Thomas Cotton. The *Aid* – 140 men; the *Falcon* – 80; the *Phoneix* – 60; the *Bark of Boulogne* – 60; the *Hare* – 40; [total] 380 men, whose victualling shall end the 23th of this present month.

To know your Lordships' pleasure whether the said ships shall have another month's victuals to begin the 24th of this present; and then it is necessary to have a warrant for – £253 6s 8d.

Money already due.

Harbour victualling. There is due upon the ordinary warrant of £12,000 by year for the victualling in harbour, wherein is appointed £300 by year for the victualling, of which remaineth unpaid for the year to end the last of December 1563 – £900.

The victualling at the seas. There remaineth due upon a privy seal for one month's victuals begun the first of October and ending the 28th of the same – £253 6s 8d.[1] Also due upon another privy seal for the like victualling for a month begun the 29th of October and ending the 25th of November last – £253 6s 8d.[2] Also due upon a privy seal for the like victualling for a month begun the 26th of November and ending the 23th of December – £253 6s 8d.[3]

The privy seal not yet out. More, a privy seal for a month's victualling to be provided, to begin the 24th of December and to end the 20th of January next – £253 6s 8d.

Totalis – £1,913 6s 8d.

It may please your good Lordships to appoint order for some money for the poor men against Christmas, wherein I do now crave your honourable letter to the Lord Treasurer to have at the least £500, parcel of the harbour charge.

Mr Gonson. To have your Lordships' like order for money for the discharge of the superfluous number of shipkeepers, which for lack of a pay do consume victuals and run [*continue*] in daily wages. *Summa* for them is – £800.

[1]Second warrant of 12 Oct.: above, p. 250, entry **#Y26**.
[2]Warrant of 28 Oct.: ibid., entry **#Y27**.
[3]Warrant of 24 Nov.: ibid., entry **#Y28**.

28 *Baeshe's contract for victualling*

[BL, Cotton MS Otho E. IX, ff. 99–102v, 116–19][1] *13 April 1565*

[*Pepys's title*: Victualling contract. 1564. *Anno Eliz.* 7. The indenture of covenants between Her Majesty and Edward Baeshe, General Surveyor of her victuals for the seas relating to the victualling of her Navy, 13 April 1564.[2]]

This indenture made between the most high and mighty princess Elizabeth, by [the] grace of God, Queen of England, France and Ireland, Defender of the Faith, &c., on the one part, and Edward Baeshe, esquire, General Surveyor of Her Majesty's victuals for the seas and marine affairs on the other part, witnesses that Her Highness, for the well and assured furniture of her Navy, and for the ease and commodity of her subjects in excluding of all purveyors for the sea causes by virtue of commission, hath commanded certain of Her Majesty's officers to have conference with the said Edward Baeshe concerning the victualling of Her Majesty's ships by a price certain, the said Edward Baeshe bearing all charges, whereupon the said Edward Baeshe, in consideration of divers respects, articles and agreements contained in this indenture, hath taken upon him that he by himself, his ministers, deputies and assigns, shall well [and suffici]ently serve the victuall[ing of all] such mariners and soldiers [as] from time to time shall be appointed not only to serve in any of Her Highness's own ships and vessels, as well at the seas as for the safe-keeping of them in harbour, but also in any other ship or vessel called or appointed to serve Her Majesty from time to time.

The order of which victualling shall be made or performed as in this present indenture is expressed. First every man to have for his allowance by the day one pound of biscuit, one gallon of beer and 2 pounds of beef which shall be for the Sundays, Mondays, Tuesdays and Thursdays; and for Wednesdays, Fridays and Saturdays every man to have by the day one quarter of a stockfish, half a quarter of a pound of butter, and a quarter of a pound of cheese, saving for the Fridays to have the quantity of the fish butter and cheese but for one meal, or else instead of stockfish [such

[1]With *lacunae* supplied from PL 2876, pp. 161–8; errors in the Pepys copy are noted only in matters of substance, and marginal headings in the original, repeated in the copy, are omitted. The contract was drawn up by Sir Walter Mildmay, who passed the draft to Cecil on 7 April: SP 12/36, no. 33 (*CSPD 1547–80*, p. 250). The draft, or another copy, was subsequently adapted to serve as the model for the contract with James Quarles, who took over when Baeshe died in 1587: SP 15/12, no. 53 (*CSPD Addenda 1547–65*, p. 563).

[2]The year date is a copyist's error: 13 April in Elizabeth's 7th year is 1565 by old and modern reckoning alike.

quantity of other fish or] herrings as the time of [the] year seemeth countervailing the said proportion of stockfish, and in such order and manner as of old time it hath been used and accustomed.

All which said victualling, as well for harbour as for the seas, shall be used and delivered by the said E.B.[1] in such sort and manner and in such good and seasonable victuals as hath been of old time used, and shall be by the head officers of the Admiralty approved and allowed.

Also the pursers to be paid by the said E.B. for necessaries, as wood, candle, dishes, cans and lanterns, *viz.* in time of service by the seas 4d for every man by the month, and 2s to every ship for lading charges, and for harbour 8d for every man's necessaries by the month, the payment to be made according as he hath warrant to victual, or else the said E.B. delivering sufficient necessaries of all [kind]s to the pursers, [he may det]ain the necessary money himself.

Item, the said E.B. shall victual as well in harbour as to the seas so many men as from time to time shall be particularly expressed in any warrant to be subscribed by the Lord Admiral or by two of the head officers of the Marine Affairs for the time, to be limited in the same warrant; which victuals the said E.B. of good and seasonable meat and drink shall deliver to the pursers, that is to say when the ships inlie in Thames at the storehouse at Ratcliff, and when the ships shall lie at Chatham and Gllingham at the storehouse at Rochester, and when the ships shall lie at Portsmouth and in the Narrow Seas at the storehouse at Dover, the same to be delivered at the wharf at the waterside.

Always provided that the ship boats do come for their victuals according to such order as hath been accustomed.

Also it is [a]greed that neither [the said E.]B. nor his deputies or assigns shall take any provision of victuals by virtue of commission unless he be commanded to victual upon the seas above 2,000 men upon the sudden. In all which said services he shall have the aid of Her Majesty's commission to be made forth according to the laws of this realm, with promise that the provision shall be made by agreement with the parties.

Also the said E.B. doth covenant and agree to have a store or staple of victuals to serve 1,000 men for one month of 28 days, to be delivered upon 14 days' warning, part at London, part at Portsmouth and part at Dover.

Item it is agreed that the said E.B. at his charges shall pay yearly the rents of the storehouses at Ratcliff and Rochester, and also pay all purveyors' and clerks' wages and all other charges ordinary and extraordinary touching the victualling with cake and biscuit bags.

[1]The Cotton text uses this abbreviation as followed here.

[And if] any provision of victuals [be sent b]y order of the Lord Admiral or other the head officers of the Marine Affairs further than the wharf and quays after the fleet or ships serving on the seas, then the Queen's Majesty to bear the charges of transportation and adventure.

Item the said E.B. shall bring monthly or quarterly the warrants for his said victualling to two of the head officers of the Marine Affairs, and they to make up his reckonings for the victualling of the number of men in every ship according as is expressed in the said warrants, and there to subscribe his books; whereupon he shall have his due allowance in the Exchequer upon his account, and the Queen's Majesty for her part is pleased and contented and doth also grant that the said E.B. shall have due allowance and payment for the victualling of every man so victualled as aforesaid, *viz.* for every man in [harb]our 4[½d the day, and] for the sea 5d the day; w[hich said vict]ualling and allowance shall be month[ly] or quarterly from time to time contained in one or more particular books which Her Highness's pleasure is shall be subscribed by two of the head officers of the Marine Affairs as is aforesaid. Whereupon the said E.B shall yearly in Hilary term exhibit his account into Her Highness's court of Exchequer at Westminster, where Her Highness's pleasure is that he shall have his accounts to pass in due form without further controlment having his books so subscribed from year to year as is aforesaid, and the duplicament of the account to be a sufficient discharge to the said E.B against the Queen's Majesty, her heirs and successors.

Also Her Highness is pleased and contented that there shall be a warrant of privy seal directed to the Treasurer and Chamberlains of the Exchequer not only to content and pay from time to time [yearly in] prest [to the said E.B. the] sum of £1,981 4s, the same to be [paid] monthly £165 2s[1] for the whole year, amounting to the said sum of £1,981 [4s], but also to deliver to the said E.B. in prest the sum of £500 to remain with him to amplify his store until it shall please Her Highness to revoke this bargain upon which revocation within 6 months then next following the said E.B shall satisfy unto the Queen's Highness the said prest of £500.

And as Her Highness's pleasure is upon the determination of every year's account he shall pay unto the Receipt at Westminster all such sum of money as shall fall out due upon him, so also Her Highness is pleased and contented that if upon any such account there shall remain any surplusage to the said E.B., that then the said Lord Treasurer, Chancellor and Under-Treasurer of [the][2] Exchequer for the time being shall and may give order that the said surplusage may be paid and answered to the said

[1]MS. '£165 ijs'; Pepys's copyist misread 'ij' as '11' and failed to check the arithmetic: one twelfth of £1,981 4s is £165 2s.

[2]MS. 'this'.

[E.B. and his assigns with]out any further warrant [in that] behalf. Also the Queen's M[ajesty] is pleased and contented that the said E.B., his deputies and assigns, shall have the use and occupying of all Her Majesty's brewhouses, mills, garners and storehouses, as well at the Tower-Hill[1] as at Dover, Portchester Castle and Portsmouth, with all the grounds, profits and commodities to them or any of them belonging or appertaining, paying such rents as for the same hath been heretofore paid and due to Her Majesty and not otherwise. And the said E.B. at his costs and charges to keep all reparations of them and to discharge Her Majesty of all and every fee and fees, allowance or allowances, incident for the keeping of them. Also the Queen's Majesty is pleased and contented and also doth grant that when any victualling shall be to the seas, that at the beginning of every month the said E.B. shall have his warrant and a full prest of [money according] to the [number of men that] shall be appointed to his victualling, and so it shall be continued with him from month to month so long as the service shall endure.

And be it remembered that if upon any victualling, as well to the seas as in harbour, any victuals shall be saved, the said E.B. shall join with the rest of the officers of the Admiralty to abate so much victuals upon the next victualling as hath been accustomed; which abatement shall be contained in his quarter-books so as Her Highness may take the benefit thereof, whereunto the said E.B. doth promise to put his helping hand and all that he may for the Queen's Majesty's profit and good service.

Also the Queen's Majesty is pleased and contented that in case the said E.B. by order of the Lord Admiral or other the officers of the Marine Affairs shall provide for the sea causes any mass of beer or other provisions which shall not be expended by the sudden discharge of the mariners, [that then the loss of such vict]uals, if any be, to be borne by [Her] Highness upon the good testimonial of two of the head officers by their subscription to his books mentioning the said loss, whereupon he shall have due allowance upon his account.

Always provided that the said victuals whereof the loss shall grow be not under the victualling of 1,000 men to the sea at one time. And if it shall be thought meet upon good testimonial of the officers that any part of the victuals provided whereof loss might grow cannot conveniently in reasonable time be expended in harbour or otherwise sold without loss, then it shall and may be lawful to the Lord Treasurer of England for the time being to license the same to be transported beyond the seas, there to be sold and uttered for the better saving of the Queen's Majesty from loss.

[1]MS. 'Towell Hill' in obvious error.

Also the Queen's Majesty's pleasure is that the [officers] of the Marine Affairs do give from time to time strait charge to the pursers and stewards to preserve the cask and biscuit bags, and to render back the same so nigh as they can, having reasonable allowance by the said E.B. for water cask and 4d for the drawage of every tun of cask as they now have.

Also the Queen's Majesty is pleased and contented and also doth grant for her heirs and successors that it may and shall be lawful to the said E.B., his deputies and assigns, during the time of his bargain to transport yearly out of this realm for his benefit, any law or statute to the contrary notwithstanding, the hides of so many oxen as he shall slaughter for the victualling aforesaid and not otherwise, so as with the only sale of the said hides beyond the seas the said E.B., his deputies or assigns, may bring and return into England both cask, clapboard, hoops, salt, canvas and other necessaries, and thereby may be the better able to serve and per[form the] covenants made with Her Highness, w[hereof] part of the hides to be transported out of the port of the city of London, part at Rochester, part at Dover and part at Portsmouth, according to the place of the slaughter.

Always provided that the said E.B., his deputies and assigns, shall answer and pay to Her Highness's customers at the said ports all such customs for the said hides as heretofore hath been accustomed or is due for the same, and shall have a testimony to the Treasurer from one or two of the head officers of the Marine Affairs witnessing that the said hides were of the oxen slaughtered for the service aforesaid. Also it is agreed that the said bargain, covenants, articles and agreements to have beginning from the last day of December last past and so to continue during the Queen's Majesty's pleasure. Always provided that when it shall please Her Majesty to revoke this bargain, that then the said E.[B]. to have half a yea[r's war]ning, and then to serve as heretofore he hath been accustomed by virtue of Her Highness's commission or otherwise as to Her Majesty shall seem good. Also the Queen's Majesty is pleased and contented that the said E.B. shall have, continue and enjoy during his life the name, place and office of General Surveyor of her victuals for her ships, according to Her Highness's letters patents,[1] and to have the fees, diets and allowances during his said life from time to time as is contained in the said letters patents, in such sort and manner as he now hath the same out of the Receipt of the Exchequer, this bargain notwithstanding. Also it is further agreed that when it shall please Her Majesty to lessen the number of men in harbour for the keeping of Her Highness's ships, then upon the determination of every year's account of the said E.B. this pres [*of*] £1,981 4s may at the pleasure of Her Majesty be shortened [accord]ing

[1]Of 30 Oct. 1563: *CPR 1560–3*, p. 487.

to the number [of the] men so taken away or lessened. In witness whereof Her Majesty, for the performance of her part of the articles, covenants and agreements in this indenture, the great seal of England hath caused to be thereunto put, and the said E.B. for the like performance of his part hath subscribed his name and set his seal. Dated the 13th [year *deleted*] of April in the 7th year of the reign of our said most gracious sovereign Lady.

29 *Privy seal warrant adjusting terms of the 1565 contract*

[SP 12/191, no. 28(ii), second item *17 July 1573*
(*CSPD 1581–90*, p. 341)][1]

Elizabeth, by the Grace of God, Queen of England, France and Ireland, Defender of the Faith, &c., to the Treasurer and Chamberlains of the Exchequer that now be or hereafter shall be, to the Barons and all other officers of our said Exchequer for the time being, and to every of them, greeting. Whereas our servant Edward Baeshe, General Surveyor of our victuals for the sea causes, hath bargained with us to serve the victualling our ships after certain rates and prices and under certain agreements, covenants and conditions, as by one indenture made between us on the one party and the said Ed. Baeshe on the other party, sealed with our great seal of England[2] appeareth at large, which bargain he hath continued these 8 years ending the last day of December then last past as by his several accounts appeareth, by which bargain he is bound and so doth victual our ships in harbour after the rate of 4½d the man *per diem* and our ships being in service on the seas after the rate of 5d the man *per diem*, and forasmuch as he hath of long time complained unto us and our Privy Council[3] as well for divers losses by him sustained by reason of the last stay of intercourse with the Low Countries,[4] as also

[1]A copy enclosed with Baeshe's submissions of 1586 [**31–2**]; the first part of no. 28(ii) is a rehearsal of the terms of the 1565 contract [**28**], at the foot of which is minuted 'The last increase of rates granted unto the said Edward Baeshe by Her Majesty is severally set out in the page next following', i.e. the document presented here.

[2]The contract of 1565 [**28**].

[3]Unrecorded in the State Papers and the Privy Council registers.

[4]Following upon Elizabeth's seizure of £85,000 being sent to pay the Spanish army in the Netherlands, after the treasure ships had sheltered at Plymouth and Southampton in November 1568. Retaliation and counter-retaliation swiftly closed trade between England and the Spanish dominions, which had barely recovered from the previous embargoes of 1563–64. This second *intercursus interruptus* lasted over four years, and a limited re-opening of the ports had only recently been agreed at the time of this warrant. Cf. R. B. Wernham, *Before the Armada: The Growth of English Foreign Policy, 1485–1588* (1966), pp. 296–302, 327. As Baeshe himself later made explicit [**31**], it was the resulting loss of his perquisite in exporting ox hides which hurt him most.

by reason of the great dearth and increase of prices of victuals[1] which he is not able to serve at those rates and prices without extreme loss and undoing, we therefore of our mere motion and especial grace are pleased and contented and do grant that you allow unto the said Edward Baeshe in and upon every his accounts yearly and from henceforth to be declared until we shall revoke this our grant upon the amendment of our prices in cheapness which hereafter may by God's his goodness happen, for every man that is or shall be victualled in harbour from the feast of the Annunciation of Our Lady last past 5½d the day and for every man that he shall victual unto the seas 6d by the day if the number shall exceed 200 and not otherwise; [*margin*: in harbour at 5½d the man *per diem*, at the seas 6d the man *per diem*], the same to be contained in the yearly or quarterly books subscribed by the officers of the Marine Affairs as hath been accustomed, whereunto these presents shall be sufficient warrant unto our said officers of our Marine Affairs without any other warrant to them to be delivered for the same, whereupon you are yearly to pass his account in due form and in such order, manner and form as heretofore hath been used and accustomed, giving unto the said Ed Baeshe the said allowances according to this our grant and pleasure signified by these presents, and these our letters shall be your sufficient warrant and discharge in this behalf. Given under our privy seal at Croydon the 17th of July 1573 in the 15 year of our reign, as in the same privy seal amongst other things therein contained more at large in doth and may appear.

[*Certification as copy*] 22 July 1586. *Examinatur per Barth Dodington.*[2]

30 *Estimate for victualling*

[SP 12/95, no. 81 (*CSPD 1547–80*, p. 477)][3] *20 April 157-*

[f. 181] The victualling of the Queen's Majesty's ships under the charge of Edward Baeshe.

The 20th day of April 1574.

An estimate of the charges to be sustained at Her [*word repeated*] Highness's pleasure to the victualling for 24 of Her Grace's ships and

[1]The politically induced depression in English trade was only one factor here. In 157- grain prices throughout western Europe rose to a peak unprecedented and not reached again for a decade: cf. indices in J. Thirsk (ed.), *The Agrarian History of England and Wales*, iv *1500–1640* (Cambridge, 1967), pp. 819–20, 853–4, and below, p. 603 n. 1.

[2]One of the Queen's auditors (so described 1589): *CSPD 1581–90*, p. 613.

[3]Copy (as two items) in PL 2875, pp. 71, 72 (*Cat. PL*, p. 127).

barks to be put to the seas in warlike manner according to their several numbers set down by the officers, *viz.*[1]

1,000 men 14 days. First for the victuals for a 1,000 men 14 days appointed for the rigging of the ships after the rate of 6d the man *per diem* according to the bargain – £350.

6,200 men 1 month. Item for the victualling of 6,200 men in all the ships for their sea service for one month of 28 days after the rate of 6d the man by the day – £4,240.

Transportation of victuals. The charges of a number of ships and hoys to transport the victuals to shipboard, by estimation for the whole month's victualling – £200.

Sum – £4,790.

Verte fol. ['Turn the page'].

[f. 181v] 20 April 1574. Remembrances for Edward Baeshe touching the victualling of 6,200 men at the seas.

To know for how many months the provision shall be made for the numbers, and the place of the staple, and the beginning of the victualling.

If the provision shall be for 3 months it is necessary that I have for two months in hand, or if it be for two months, then that I may have for 6 weeks in hand.

Also, I am to have by my bargain commissioners of provisions when the numbers appointed for the sea service shall exceed 3,000 men, wherein I would be loath to deal if Her Majesty might be otherwise served.

I am to have presently by the Lords [*of the Council*] letters to divers shires that the commissioners there may suffer me and my deputies to provide and lade such proportions as shall be appointed in the said letters, and that they will give aid to my deputies, and appoint how the provisions may be delivered from those that may best spare the same, and ready money to be paid at reasonable [rate *deleted*] prices.[2]

Because in this dear year I shall not be able to victual according to the bargain, that I may have your favourable report to Her Majesty for recompense upon just proof made of the loss.

[1]These ships patrolled the Channel while musters were taken on land. Further details are in SP 12/95, no. 88; 12/96, pp. 281, 288, 316 and *passim*, 12/97, nos 3, 4, 11; 12/115, no. (*CSPD 1547–80*, pp. 477, 479, 480, 481, 553).

[2]On 1 May the Council issued seven letters for purveyance of grain and victuals to enable Baeshe to establish a staple at Portsmouth, 'according to the minute and rates remayning in the Chest', i.e. the Council's archive: *APC 1571–5*, p. 232. The store was destroyed in a fire at the yard on 4 Aug. 1576, and Baeshe lost £240 worth of stock: SP 12/108, no 70; SP 12/110, no. 37 (*CSPD 1547–80*, pp. 526–7, 534: Thomas Thorney reporting the disaster in detail to Baeshe, 8 Aug.; statement by Baeshe of his loss, n.d.).

Memorandum, in this dear year there is nothing to be had without ready money.

Besides my proportion for the Queen's Majesty's ships I am to have a supply in store for the victuals.

It shall justly appear that having wheat at 30s the quarter with all charges, malt at 2s the quarter, beef at 2d the pound (besides cask and salt), stockfish at £15 the last, butter at 4d the pound, cheese at 2d the pound, necessaries at one farthing the man *per diem*, that a man's victuals by the day is 8d at the least for the harbour victualling.

Memorandum, the [housing *deleted*] houses at Portsmouth, and the great numbers of cask, clapboard and other necessary things of no small charge which I am to bear by my hard bargain.

31 *Report by Baeshe to the Lord Admiral*

[SP 12/191, no. 28(i) (*CSPD 1581–90*, p. 341)][1] *23 July 1586*

The 23th of July 1586. To the Right Honourable the Lord Howard, Lord High Admiral of England.

A declaration by Edward Baeshe, General Surveyor of Her Highness's Victuals for the Sea Causes.

First I have served Her Majesty's father, her brother, her sister and herself in the said office by the space of 40 years past, whereof for the space of 19 years I did serve by sundry commissions of purveying and 21 years the residue by bargain made with Her Majesty.[2] [*Margin*: How I came into the bargain Sir William Winter is able to report.] Which bargain for 8 years thereof I did serve the victualling in harbour at 4½d the man *per diem* and for the seas at 5d the man *per diem*, in respect I had a licence to transport over the seas into the Low Countries a number of hides and corn, and also my remain of victuals from time to time, and to bring necessary provisions from thence. And (my Lord) by the space of 4 years there was a restraint of traffic thither, so as there grew a loss unto me to the sum of £2,800,[3] whereupon I did deliver back my licence. And then it pleased Her Majesty to increase to me 1d for the victualling of every man *per diem* [**29**], and to deliver me in prest £500 to be paid upon the dissolving of my bargain or within one year after, and so I have now 5½d the man *per diem* in harbour and 6d the man for the seas. And for that rate

[1]Originally enclosed with following document.

[2]Above [**28**].

[3]See above, p. 599 n. 4. Baeshe previously claimed his loss to be £500 *per annum* (SP 12/110, no. 37), but since the stoppage lasted well into a fifth year, the total here is reasonably consistent with his earlier reckoning.

I am to discharge Her Majesty of all other charges incident to the victualling, *viz.* purveyors' and clerks' wages, hire of storehouses and reparations of them, wastes, spoils and decays of victuals, and the losses growing by the purveyors, and a number of other charges. And touching the daily allowances of a man *per diem*, the same is well known to your Lordship, together with the goodness of my victuals.

Item, by my bargain it is mentioned that either Her Majesty or else I, upon 6 months' warning, should be at liberty to revocate the bargain, whereof for many years past I have been very desirous for my part to be discharged, considering the enhancing in prices of all victuals,[1] *viz.* wheat from 12s or 13s 4d the quarter to 33s 4d the quarter, malt from 8s the dearest to 18s and 20s the quarter, beef from 1d the pound to 2¼d and more, stockfish from £9 the 1,000 to £16 and £20 the 1,000, butter from 33s 4d the bushel to £3 and £4 the bushel, cheese from 20s the wey to 40s and 50s the wey, hops from 13s 4d the 100 to 53s 4d the 100, and bay-salt from 26s 8d the wey to £5 6s 8d the wey, and necessaries to the pursers from 8d the man to 12d the man, beside the wages of all labourers.

Item, now upon the great dearth and scarcity of victuals I have signified to my Lord Treasurer and to your Lordship the 7th of May last that I am not able any longer to continue my bargain,[2] but in most humble manner do desire to be discharged thereof according to the bargain at the end of the 6 months which will be the 7th of November next, being heartily sorry that any hindrance should grow to Her Majesty in case I shall not be able to perform to serve at the said rates.

Item, by a just rate which I have delivered to your Lordship and to my Lord Treasurer shall plainly appear that the now setting forth to the seas of the 1,000 men in four of Her Majesty's great ships for 3 months will be to my loss of £534, beside a loss of £588 more in the victualling of the galley, the *Bull*, and the other Her Majesty's pinnaces now at the seas with

[1] 1586 was another year of exceptionally high grain prices across western Europe, and Baeshe's authoritative figures are consistent with data extrapolated from a wide range of other sources against a base of *100* for the years 1450–99. Wheat prices in England, which had peaked in 1573 at *427* and fallen back to around *300* in the early 1580s, rose again to *427* in 1585 and *626* in 1586. The average for all grain rose from around *400* in the early 1580s to *684* in 1586. The price of oxen rose above *400* on the index for the first time in 1585 (*434* from around *350* in the early 1580s), and there was a similar increase in the price of all cattle. Butter was up to *330* in 1586 from around *250* in the previous decade, and likewise cheese to *265* from around *200*: Thirsk, *Agrarian History*, pp. 818, 826, 842 (where the figures will be seen more fully than can be presented here).

[2] The actual report is dated 6 May: SP 12/189, no. 8 (*CSPD 1581–90*, pp. 325–6). If Baeshe's recollection is correct, it was sent with a covering letter of the following day, no longer extant.

500 men in them,[1] to end at the feast of St Michael next, beside that victualling in harbour as upon just examination it will appear whereby my prest money of £1,000 which I do owe unto Her Majesty (to be repaid *viz.* £500 thereof within 6 months after the dissolving of my bargain, and the other £500 within one year after) is consumed and spent. And so I must be driven to make provision for Her Majesty's satisfaction accordingly unless it shall please Her Majesty of her great clemency to have consideration thereof for that hitherto I have had no recompense or reward of service, or other increase other than such as is before declared. I trust it shall appear by my bargain that I have saved Her Majesty £1,000 yearly beside the great benefit to the whole realm in excluding of purveying of victuals by commission.

Item, I am now an old man and not able to travel in body as I have done heretofore, offering nevertheless to the uttermost of my power to serve Her Highness as I shall be commanded, and yet withal I am heartily sorry that the realm should be eftsoons troubled with purveyors within my charge, for whereas (in my time) I have spent so many oxen at a victualling to the seas at one time as Her Majesty's most honourable Household doth spend in a year, I have had no part thereof by commission of purveying. Most humbly beseeching Her most royal Majesty by your good Lordship's means to receive this my humble petition in good part and [to] commit this my humble suit to the Lord Treasurer and to your Lordship or to any other to whom Her Majesty shall think good, that they may faithfully report unto Her Highness the just cause of my complaint and not a[ny] longer to require my service otherwise than in such sort as I shall not consume myself and in the end to leave Her service undone.

Item, it is to be considered that in the beginning of May last I had order [for] money for the victualling of the said four ships, and then all victuals was at an exceeding dear price and scarcity, notwithstanding I was driven to make a great part of my provision, and have kept the same till now, to an exceeding great loss, because I would not be without when the service should be required.

[1]Cf. Navy officers to Burghley, 24 May, reporting that the whole of £1,000 which Burghley had provided for setting out four great ships had been swallowed up in a single contract for cordage; Hawkins to Burghley, 25 May, with charges for *Bonavolia* (ex-*Eleanor* the only surviving galley), *Makeshift (II)* and *Spy* for three months, and *Bull* and *Cygnet* for two: SP 12/189, nos 40, 40(i), 41 (*CSPD 1581–90*, p. 329).

32 *Baeshe to Sir Francis Walsingham,*[1] *enclosing the above*

[SP 12/191, no. 28 (*CSPD 1581–90*, p. 341)] *24 July 1586*

Right Honourable: I do understand by my Lord Admiral that he hath acquainted you with my most humble suit to the Queen's Majesty, which is to be discharged of my hard bargain at the end of 6 months, unless I may be otherwise so considered by Her Highness, that I may be able to continue without an utter spoil and ruin to myself. And Sir, being on Saturday last[2] with His Lordship and with the rest of my fellows at Deptford, I did deliver to him a declaration which he promised me to read to Her Majesty, the copy whereof His Lordship thought meet I should present to Your Honour with my humble suit that it may please Your Honour at your convenient leisure to peruse the same and to give me your furtherance to Her Majesty as occasion shall command. And like as Her Majesty shall find me most willing and ready to serve, so without her gracious consideration towards me I cannot perform my bargain. And Sir, I do mean at Her Majesty's coming to Windsor and at his Lordship's return from the ships[3] to repair to the court to deliver to Her Majesty my most humble suit. Thus I do most humbly beseech the Almighty to bless Your Honour with long life, good health and many happy days. Written at London the 24th of July 1586.

Your Honour's most humble to command, Edward Baeshe.

[1]Walsingham was Principal Secretary and Privy Councillor 1573–90: *ODNB*. *Hist. Parl. 1558–1603*, iii, pp. 571–4.

[2]The previous day (23 July).

[3]A routine visit, as the Lord Admiral had no sea command this year: cf. Kenny, *Elizabeth's Admiral*, p. 119.

VII

PAPERS RELATING TO SIR JOHN HAWKINS AS TREASURER OF THE NAVY

John Hawkins was a central figure in the story of the Elizabethan Navy.[1] It was his slaving and piratical expeditions in the 1560s which first engaged the Queen's support and complicity. He enjoyed high favour at court, and it was through him that Francis Drake (with whom he fell out in his later years) became 'the Queen's pirate'.[2] The letter which he wrote to the Queen on his return to England in September 1565 [**33**] neatly expresses his self confidence, both as adventurer and courtier. Relations with Spain were at a low ebb in 1570, following Hawkins's debacle at San Juan de Ulúa and the diversion of Alba's payships in 1568, which had provoked the suspension of trade with the Low Countries. Alba had toyed with the idea of assisting the northern rebels in 1569. In the following year Pope Pius V had excommunicated Elizabeth, and was looking hopefully towards Philip II to carry out the sentence.[3] However, the countries were not at war, and the coup which Hawkins is suggesting to Leicester in the second of his letters here [**34**] would have been an act of piracy on a grand scale. The 'extreme injuries' referred to were mainly Hawkins's own losses,[4] because, although the Merchant Adventurers had suffered from the interruption of trade, they had managed to shift their mart to Emden, which was not under Alba's control.[5] The reception of his suggestion seems to have been less than enthusiastic. His projection of the value of the fleet, at 'sixty hundred thousand pounds' (i.e., £6 million) is sceptically scaled down to £600,000 in a marginal note. Although the former estimate may have been nearer the mark, it would have been a big exaggeration.[6] A second note deflates the estimate of losses sustained to no more than £200,000; in other words nowhere near justifying such a massive seizure. Whoever was responsible

[1]Treasurer of the Navy 1577–95. For principal biographical and bibliographical details, see *NEM*, pp. 550–51.

[2]Kelsey appears to have invented this apt description with the title of his 1998 biography of Drake, which reminds us, among other things, of just how irascible both men were.

[3]Philip had consistently advised against this step, and was not at all willing to play his allotted role: H. Kamen, *Philip of Spain* (1997), pp. 132–4.

[4]Cf. also the hardships suffered by Baeshe [**29**], above p. 599 & n. 4.

[5]W. MacCaffrey, *The Shaping of the Elizabethan Regime* (1969), p. 194.

[6]It is likely that the value of the entire *flota* at this point would have been about 6 million ducats, or £2,000,000.

for the annotations, 'Her Highnesses free consent' was clearly no forthcoming, because nothing came of the suggestion and, given the stat of international relations at the time, that is not surprising.

Hawkins's credit was in no way diminished by this failure, although i was recognised both by the Queen and Cecil (and probably by Leiceste as well) that he needed a curb rather than a spur. When his father-in-law Benjamin Gonson, was anxious to stand down as Treasurer of the Nav in 1577, Hawkins was the obvious man to succeed him. Gonson ha served continuously since 1549, and must have been approachin seventy.[1] In the autumn of 1577 he surrendered his letters patent, an received instead a new appointment jointly with Hawkins [**35**]. Why th change was made in this way is not apparent. Gonson was old and in poo health. He clearly had no intention of continuing his duties, and died soo after. In the circumstance his inclusion in the grant was a mere gesture but whether it was a gesture to him or to Hawkins's opponents an doubters we do not know.

The long dreaded war finally arrived in 1585, but it spluttered into lif without any formal declaration. Knowing that Elizabeth's negotiation with the Dutch were advancing, in May Philip arrested all English ship in Spanish harbours, and confiscated their cargoes. If this was intende to intimidate the Queen, it had the opposite effect. The treaty of Nonsuch agreed on 10 August and concluded on the 20th, committed Elizabeth t the military support of the rebels in specific terms. The Queen als authorised Drake's expedition in retaliation for the seizures, but al without the 'defiance' which had been customary upon such breakdowns. It appears that the English Council was already fearing a pre-emptiv strike in March [**36**], when it took the exceptional step of ordering th senior officers of the Admiralty to assume personal responsibility fo security at Gillingham. They are to 'lie at the ships', each for a month a a time on a rotating basis. It was probably sabotage rather than a large scale attack which was feared, because there would have been little tha a senior officer could do if he had been attacked in force.[3] However, if th shipkeepers really were negligent, or absent from their posts, then an number of ships could have been fired by a few committed saboteurs, an a tightening of control (which is what these instructions intend) woul have been an appropriate response.

Hawkins's surviving correspondence is extensive, and only a fe examples are presented here. Letters **33** and **34**, although outside th

[1]Benjamin's date of birth is not known, but is thought to have been about 1510: *ODN*

[2]G. Parker and C. Martin, *The Spanish Armada* (1988), pp. 100–1.

[3]The obvious step to protect against an attack in force would have been to strengthen th fort at Upnor, guarding the anchorage, but that was not done.

general scope of this collection, are included chiefly because they represent a further line of archival descent from the Earl of Leicester's servant Sir Richard Browne via Evelyn to Pepys.[1] Although their substance has been published before,[2] they are printed here in full for the first time.

[1]These two Hawkins MSS belong to a collection of 'several letters of the old Lord of Leicesters in Queen Elizabeth's time' which Evelyn first showed to Pepys in November 1665: Pepys, *Diary*, vi, p. 308. All the Leicester papers, with other MSS acquired by Evelyn, were loaned to Pepys on 6 Dec. 1681. Evelyn invited Pepys to 'take your owne time in returning them', and in fact they were never returned: G. de la Bédoyère (ed.), *Particular Friends: The Correspondence of Samuel Pepys and John Evelyn* (Woodbridge, 1997), pp. 125–7. The papers may still have been at Sayes Court, Deptford, when Evelyn acquired the lease of this property, previously occupied by his wife's family. See table below, p. 659.

[2]The papers received from Evelyn were bound up in three volumes to which Pepys gave the title of 'State Papers' (PL 2502–4); these were calendared by E. K. Purnell for the Historical Manuscripts Commission with the misleadingly comprehensive title of *Report on the Pepys Manuscripts, preserved at Magdalene College, Cambridge* (1911). The two Hawkins letters (pp. 65–6 and 174–5) are printed verbatim but with omissions.

33 *John Hawkins to the Queen*

[PL 2502, pp. 427–8 (HMC, *Pepys*, pp. 65–6)][1] *20 September 1565*

Pleaseth it Your Majesty to be informed that the 20th day of September I arrived in a port of Cornwall called Padstow, with Your Majesty's ship the *Jesus*, in good safety. Thanks be to God, our voyage being reasonably well accomplished according to our pretence.

Your Majesty's commandment at my departing from Your Grace at Enfield I have accomplished, so as I doubt not but it shall be found honourable to Your Highness, for I have always been a help to all Spaniards and Portingals that have come in my way, without any force or prejudice by me offered to any of them, although many times in this trade they have been under my power.

I have also discovered the coast of Florida in those parts, where there is thought to be any great wealth. And because I will not be tedious to Your Highness I have declared the commodities of it to Mr Winter, who will show my Lord Robert of it at large.

Thus as my most bounden duty is, I rest, praying to Almighty God for the preservation of Your Majesty in most prosperous estate.

From Padstow the 20th day of September 1565.

Your Majesty's most humble and obedient servant, John Hawkins.

34 *Proposal from Hawkins to Leicester*

[PL 2503, pp. 371–2 (HMC, *Pepys*, pp. 173–4)][2] *4 June 1570*

The Indies fleet cometh to the Azores in the midst of August and brings with them in gold, silver and jewels to the value of twenty millions of ducats, which is in our English money sixty hundred thousand pounds [*Margin*: £600,000].

This whole fleet (with God's grace) shall be intercepted and taken within these 3 months for the extreme injuries offered unto this realm, which wrongs being satisfied with the costs, the great mass shall be at the courtesy of the Queen's Highness to restore or keep. [*Margin*: The third part that is taken shall satisfy the losses].

To which enterprise John Hawkins shall furnish 10 ships in warlike manner at his own costs and charges.

To which enterprise also it is required that the Right Honourable the Earl of Leicester (with his friends) shall obtain and borrow of Her

[1]The Calendar prints the text *in extenso* save the valediction. See J. A. Williamson, *Hawkins of Plymouth* (1949), p. 87.

[2]The Calendar prints the text *in extenso* save first sentence and valediction.

Highness two ships furnished with ordnance, powder and munition, to say, the *Bonaventure* and the *Bull.*

Also toward the furniture of the ten ships of John Hawkins it is needful to have 2 last of powder and 200 calivers complete, for which powder and calivers there shall be good payment satisfied into the Tower.

There is nothing more needed toward this enterprise but Her Highness's free consent, and so God preserve her long. The 4th of June 1570.

John Hawkins.

35 *Patent for Gonson and Hawkins as joint-Treasurers of the Navy*

[C 66/1172, mm. 2–3 *18 November 1577*
(*CPR 1575–8*, p. 518, no. 3573)][1]

Elizabeth, by the grace of God [Queen of England, France and Ireland, Defender of the Faith] &c. [to all to whom all these presents shall come] greeting. Whether as our dearest brother of most famous memory Edward the sixth, late King of England, by his letters patent under his great seal of England bearing date at Westminster the 8th day of July the third year of his reign[2] did give and grant unto our trusty and wellbeloved servant Benjamin Gonson the room and office of Treasurer of his Marine Causes, to have, occupy and enjoy the said office of Treasurer or treasurership unto the same Benjamin Gonson during his life, with all fees, wages and pre-eminences thereunto in any wise belonging or afterward to appertain or to be due; whereas also our said brother of his ample grace did give and grant for him, his heirs and successors unto the said Benjamin Gonson a certain annuity or yearly fee of 100 marks sterling, and for two clerks under him in the said room or office of Treasurer 8d sterling by the day to either of them together, with the allowance of 6s 8d for every day that the said Benjamin Gonson should travel or be occupied either by sea or land for such business as were needful and expedient to be overseen or despatched in any concerning the same office of Treasurer, and £8 sterling by the year for his boat-hire; and where also our said dearest brother, for him, his heirs and successors, did grant unto the said Benjamin Gonson that he the said Benjamin Gonson should have full allowances of and for all and every such sum and sums of money which he the said Benjamin

[1] Copy in BL, Cotton MS. Otho E. IX, ff. 125–128v, itself copied in PL 2876, pp. 181–5. These copies derive from the sealed instrument and supply some routine formulae abbreviated on the patent roll, here extended in square brackets. Titles, *lacunae* and other variants and corruptions in the copies are not noticed. Editorial interpolations are as usual italic within further brackets.

[2] *CPR 1549–51*, p. 164.

by himself or by his deputy or deputies should disburse, pay, expend or lay out in or about the said marine causes and wherewith the said Benjamin should be in any wise charged for or concerning the same office, he having the hands of two or three of the officers of his [*His Majesty's*] said marine causes subscribed to his book and books of account or reckonings of the same, testifying the payment or expending thereof, and that the showing of his said letters patents and of the said book and books of account so subscribed as aforesaid should be a sufficient warrant to all and every his [*H.M.'s*] auditors and other officers and ministers in such behalf authorized to make full and just allowance and discharge of the same; and where also our said brother did grant unto the said Benjamin that he the said Benjamin should have the costs of his clerks when and as often as he should send them for the payment or receipt of his money for the same marine causes to have, perceive and enjoy all and every the aforesaid annuity and other the aforesaid sum and sums of money granted in manner and form aforesaid, and all other the premises to the same Benjamin Gonson and his assigns during his natural life, of the Receipt of the Exchequer by the hands of the Treasurer and Chamberlains there for the time being, at the feast of Easter, the Nativity of St John Baptist, St Michael the Archangel and the Nativity of Our Lord God, by even portions, as by the said letters patents more at large doth and may appear, which said letters patents the said Benjamin Gonson hath surrendered up in our Chancery to be cancelled, and there remain cancelled as we be credibly informed, by reason whereof the said office and other the premises are come into our hands and remain in our disposition to that intent that we should grant our letters patents of the same office and other the premises to the said Benjamin Gonson and to our wellbeloved servant John Hawkins, esq., or to the longer liver of them, in manner and form following. Know ye therefore that we, of our especial grace, certain knowledge and mere motion, as well in consideration of the said surrender as also for the good, faithful and acceptable service unto us done by our said servants Benjamin Gonson and John Hawkins, are contented and pleased, and by these presents for us, our heirs and successors, do give and grant unto the said Benjamin Gonson and John Hawkins, and to the longer liver of them, the room or office of Treasurer of our Marine Causes, and the said Benjamin Gonson and John Hawkins, and the longer liver of them, we do constitute, ordain and appoint by these presents Treasurer of our Marine Causes, to have, occupy and enjoy the said office of Treasurer or treasurership unto the said Benjamin Gonson and John Hawkins, and to the longer liver of them during the natural life of them and of the longer liver of them, with all fees and wages, allowances and pre-eminences thereunto in any wise belonging or hereafter to appertain or be due. And further, of our more ample grace, we have given and granted, and by these presents do give and grant unto the said Benjamin Gonson and John Hawkins and to the longer liver of them a certain annuity [*inserted* and] yearly fee of 100 marks sterling, and for two clerks under them or the longer liver of them in the said room or office of Treasurer 8d sterling by the day to either of them, together with the allowances of 6s 8d sterling for every day that the said Benjamin Gonson and John Hawkins, or the longer liver of them, shall travel and be occupied either by sea or land for such business as shall be needful and expedient to be overseen or despatched in or concerning the same office of Treasurer, and £8 sterling by the year for their boat-hire. And further we will and grant by these presents, for us, our heirs and successors, to the said Benjamin Gonson and John Hawkins, and the longer liver of them, that the same Benjamin Gonson and John Hawkins, and the longer liver of them, shall have full allowance of and for all and every such sum or sums of money which they the said Benjamin Gonson and John Hawkins, and the longer liver of them, by themselves or by the longer liver of them, or by their deputy or deputies, shall disburse, pay and expend or lay out in or about our marine causes, and wherewith the said Benjamin Gonson and John Hawkins, or the longer liver of them, shall be in any wise charged for or concerning the same office, they or the longer liver of them having the hands of two or three of our officers of our said marine causes subscribed to their book and books of account or reckonings of the same testifying the payment or expenditure thereof, and that the showing of these our letters patents, and of the said book or books of account so subscribed as is aforesaid shall be a sufficient warrant to all and every our auditors and other officers and ministers in such behalf authorized to make full and just allowance and discharge of the same. And further we will and grant by these presents, for us and our heirs and successors, to the said Benjamin Gonson and John Hawkins, and to the longer liver of them, that they the said Benjamin and John, and the longer liver of them, shall have the costs of their clerks when and as often as they shall send them for the payment or receipt of our money for our said marine causes. To have, perceive and enjoy all and every the aforesaid annuity and other the aforesaid sum and sums of money granted in manner and form aforesaid, and all other the premises to the same Benjamin Gonson and John Hawkins, and to the longer liver of them, and to the assigns of them, and the longer liver of them, during their natural lives, of our treasure at the receipt of our Exchequer by the hands of our Treasurer and Chamberlains there for the time being, at the feast of Easter, the Nativity of St John Baptist, St Michael the Archangel and the Nativity of Our Lord God, by even portions. [*Be it noted*] that express mention [of the yearly <*sic*> or certainty of the premises or any of them, or any other gift or grant by us or any of our progenitors to the foresaid Benjamin Gonson and John Hawkins, or to either of them, before this time made, in these presents is not made, or any act, statute, ordinance, provision, proclamation or restraint to the contrary heretofore had, made, ordained or provided, or any other thing, cause or matter whatsoever notwithstanding]. In witness whereof [we <*have*> caused these our letters to be made patents. Witness ourselves at Westminster the 18th day of November [in the 20th year of our reign]. *Per breve de privato sigillo.*

36 *Direction from the Privy Council for the Navy officers to take personal watch aboard the Queen's ships*

[SP 12/177, no. 32 (*CSPD 1581–90*, p. 232)][1] *22 March 1585*

After our hearty commendations. Whereas Her Majesty is advertised that some practice and device is taken in hand to burn and destroy the Navy, we have thought good to signify unto you that Her Majesty's pleasure is that one of you, the four Principal Officers, do monthly lie at the ships to see the performance of those things which we have devised to prevent the mischief intended. And further, Her Majesty is given to understand that the shipkeepers which Her Majesty doth maintain in wages and victuals are many of them insufficient, and that divers of the best sort give bad attendance upon the service. Therefore, these shall be to require you in Her Majesty's name and specially to charge you and every of you that the place may be furnished with able and sufficient men as near as it may be, and to charge all sorts of shipkeepers whatsoever that receive wages and victuals [*sc. that they*] do lie aboard continually upon pain of [*blank*] unless for some urgent cause the officers shall give leave to any person by writing so to be absent. Whereof fail you not, as you tender Her Majesty's displeasure &c.

[*Filing endorsement*]: Copy of a letter to the officers of the Navy for defence of the same, 22th March 1584 [*1585*].

[1]Copy in PL 2875, p. 61 (*Cat. PL*, p. 127), reproducing the *lacunae* of the original.

VIII

EDWARD FENTON'S NOTEBOOK AND OTHER PAPERS RELATING TO THE EXPEDITION OF 1590

Captain Edward Fenton is chiefly remembered as commander of a notoriously futile and ill-executed expedition to the South Atlantic in 1582–83. Fenton himself seems to have been promoted above his competence, and soon lost control. He turned with particular anger and eventually violence against his Lieutenant-General, the younger William Hawkins (Sir John's nephew). It was an episode which Hakluyt thought best forgotten, since he drastically edited his only narrative of it (by Fenton's Vice-Admiral, Luke Ward) for the standard edition of *Principall Navigations.* When Fenton's own journal of the voyage at last found an editor, it would be given a title which enduringly associates *Fenton* with *troublesome.*

Fenton was shunned on his return. But he was an intelligent and cultivated man with friends at court, and he managed to survive his disgrace. Like many another he redeemed himself by war service, and commanded *Mary Rose* in 1588. Significantly he retained the regard of Sir John Hawkins. They were connected by marriage, since Fenton's wife Thomasine and Katherine, Lady Hawkins, were sisters – the daughters and co-heiresses of the previous Navy Treasurer Benjamin Gonson.[1] So it was quite natural that when Hawkins, busy at the end of Armada year, wanted to delegate his routine work, he asked the Queen to appoint Fenton. He was duly named deputy Treasurer for the year 1 January to 31 December 1589.[2] The account book here printed [**37**] shows Fenton exercising this charge during that year and the next. The extension of Fenton's deputyship into 1590 is not formally recorded, but Hawkins's absence at sea for much of that year adequately accounts for it. Nevertheless, though Hawkins attempted to resign the Treasurership on at least three occasions between 1590 and 1594, there was no suggestion that Fenton would be the appropriate successor.[3]

[1]For further details of Fenton's career, see *NEM*, pp. 541–2. He is sometimes loosely called Hawkins's brother-in-law.

[2]SP 12/219, nos 28, 29 (*CSPD 1581–90*, p. 565): petition of Hawkins, 14 Dec., and warrant appointing Fenton deputy Treasurer, n.d.; printed in Laughton, *Armada*, ii, pp. 306–9.

[3]Williamson, *Hawkins* (1927), pp. 466–8, using SP 12/231, no. 83; 12/242, no. 79; 12/247, no. 27 (*CSPD 1581–90*, p. 660; *1590–4*, pp. 244, 419): Hawkins to Burghley, 16 April 1590, 3 July 1592 and [blank] Feb. 1594; the first printed in Oppenheim, *History*, pp. 147–8, the two others by Williamson, *loc. cit.*

This is a personal aide-memoire, not a formal account. It shows sums received from Exchequer, and the expenses which Navy Treasury's could set against that income by way of discharging its liability. Within its limited compass it reflects a considerable range of naval activity in the early years of the Spanish war. The Armada itself is recalled with a payment for bringing the most celebrated trophy of victory into the Thames. The major expedition of the following year, fully documented in one of the Society's previous volumes,[1] is also still being paid for here, as the returned ships are taken back into the charge of the administrators. Meanwhile a major shipbuilding programme was in hand, with the master shipwrights Baker, Pett and Chapman each having a great ship on the stocks, and smaller ones besides.

Most notably there are payments for the further ventures into the Atlantic which were mounted in 1590. In September 1589, before the return of the unsuccessful Drake/Norris expedition, Frobisher took a squadron of royal ships to the Portuguese coast, while the Earl of Cumberland commanded a larger force of his own off the Azores. Frobisher had some success (and might have achieved more had he worked in tandem with Cumberland). This encouraged Hawkins to press a scheme of his own for rotating squadrons to maintain a longer-term blockade. A first detachment of six ships was being prepared in the winter of 1589/90 [**39**]. At the same time Elizabeth had sent an expeditionary force to support the French Huguenot leader Henri IV in establishing his right to succeed the assassinated Henri III; in response the French Catholic League had appealed to Philip II for assistance. The English government, fearful of massive Spanish intervention in Brittany, decided in February to halt the naval expedition [**41**]. Hawkins was dismayed, not least because his own preparations were wasted [**42**]; but with English troops on the ground in northern France, the government was certainly right to question the wisdom of committing a large part of the Navy to a speculative mission elsewhere.

By early summer perspectives had altered, and a two-part naval operation was despatched. Frobisher went to the Azores to intercept what treasure might come his way; while Hawkins was to keep to the Spanish coast, with one eye for the troopships going to Brittany. Neither part of the 1590 expedition achieved any notable military or financial success, but the effort was far from wasted. The voyages were, as Michael Oppenheim put it, not an obvious success 'to those who measured the fortune of a cruise by the amount of plunder brought back', but had some

[1] R. B. Wernham (ed.), *The Expedition of Sir John Norris and Sir Francis Drake to Spain and Portugal, 1589* (NRS, Vol. 127, 1988).

useful part in weakening Spanish military operations in northern Europe.[1] They demonstrated that England was capable of keeping squadrons at sea away from home waters for prolonged periods. Hawkins recognised this, consoling himself that although denied a great victory, he had been 'very well provided, both of shipping, victual, furniture, and a quiet and sufficient company' [**45**].[2]

That was not quite truthful, because there was as ever an insufficiency of money, and Hawkins was busy for several months in recovering his costs [**46–50**]. Frobisher's squadron was restricted by a victualling provision for four months, at 6d a man per day. Hawkins made his own arrangements, and allowed his men an extra 2d a day. He also wrote into his contract a clause for reimbursement at the higher rate for six months if the expedition should be postponed, and the delay in February enabled him to claim on that basis. Six months at the 8d rate amounted to precisely twice four months at 6d. In all he claimed to have laid out £7,504 on provisions alone, and half of this was still owing to him in the following year [**50**]. There was a side issue resulting from an act of piracy by the returning ships, compounded by the efforts of Hawkins and his son to obstruct recovery of the goods seized [**45, 48**].

These pieces further illustrate the long-term service which Hawkins performed as Treasurer, as he gathered together papers dating back eleven years [**38**]. In February 1590, just before the expedition was stalled, he solicited a new warrant dormant, raising the ordinary by over £3,000 to reflect increasing costs which included the building of seven new ships and twenty smaller craft. In discounting one expense for his own project from the costings, he carefully observed the principle that the ordinary did not cover operations, but no doubt also meant to forestall any accusation of special pleading [**40**]. The Council endorsed his proposal to the penny, and the increase to £8,973 was authorised in March [**43**].

The grinding business of auditing the accounts is highlighted in a passage omitted from the previous printing of the document, presumably because it was considered too dull [**44**]. Actually the detail is an instructive one in the context of the present volume, and helps to explain

[1]M. Oppenheim (ed.), *The Naval Tracts of Sir William Monson* (NRS, Vols 22, 23, 43 & 47, 1902–14), i, p. 251, repr. in Williamson, *Hawkins* (1927), p. 461.

[2]See generally Monson, *Tracts*, i, pp. 240–52 (incl. command list at p. 242); Williamson, *Hawkins* (1927), pp. 450–61, and State Papers there cited (many of which are printed below); H. A. Lloyd, 'Sir John Hawkins' instructions, 1590', *BIHR*, XLICV (1971), pp. 125–8; the instructions themselves are now also printed in HMC, *Bath*, V, pp. 253–4. R. B. Wernham, *After the Armada: England and the Struggle for Western Europe, 1588–1595* (Oxford, 1984), pp. 236, 241–5; Loades, *Tudor Navy*, pp. 259–60; J. McDermott, *Martin Frobisher: Elizabethan Privateer* (2001), pp. 378–88; Hammer, *Elizabeth's Wars*, pp. 162–4; Kelsey, *Hawkins*, pp. 234–41.

why even one of the Elizabethan Navy's greatest servants eventually tired of its administration.

Fenton's manuscript, now PL 513, is a small paper booklet, 4.4 × 6.1 ins in limp leather covers, written throughout in the same hand which is undoubtedly Fenton's own.[1] It must certainly have come to Pepys by descent from Thomasine Fenton. After Fenton's death without issue (1603), his widow married Christopher Browne, grandfather of Evelyn's wife Mary.[2] A more substantial collection of Fenton's papers was given by Evelyn to Pepys on 6 December 1681, by way of substitute for the Drake journal which Pepys actually wanted.[3] The volume Evelyn did provide included the journal of Fenton's voyage as Lieutenant-General to Frobisher in 1578, and that of the expedition of 1582–83 under his own command.[4] All this material has now been printed by the Hakluyt Society.[5] Transmission of the smaller Fenton manuscript cannot be located with such precision, but there can be no doubt that it was along the same Fenton–Browne–Evelyn channel, adding a further strand to the archival descent already represented here.[6] The notebook is published here for the first time and, as far as the surviving material allows, is collated with the original warrants in the Public Records.[7] The supplementary documents come from the State Papers, of which only extracts have previously been printed.

[1]Cf. SP 12/118, no. 40 (holograph letter from Fenton to Walsingham, 25 Nov. 1577).

[2]Fenton was buried at Deptford on 31 Aug. 1603; his widow remarried there on 30 July 1604: Drake, *Hasted's Kent*, pp. 38, 41.

[3]J. R. Tanner (ed.), *Private Correspondence and Miscellaneous Papers of Samuel Pepys, 1679–1703*, (1936), II, pp. 17–18; also in *Part. Friends*, p. 125.

[4]PL 2133 (*Cat. PL*, p. 31).

[5]E. G. R. Taylor (ed.), *The Troublesome Voyage of Captain Edward Fenton, 1582–1583* (Hakluyt Soc., 2nd ser. CXIII, 1959 for 1957), pp. 49, 83–149, 297–8. J. McDermott (ed.), *The Third Voyage of Martin Frobisher to Baffin Island, 1578* (Hakluyt Soc., 3rd ser. VI, 2001), pp. 64–9, 137–76.

[6]Above, pp. 21, 611.

[7]All from the Exchequer files, E 404/128–9. There is nothing relevant in the Privy Seal Office file for the period (PSO 2/20).

37 *Notebook of Edward Fenton, Deputy to Sir John Hawkins as Treasurer of the Navy*

[PL 513 (*Cat. PL*, p.2)] *1588–91*

[*first leaf, in same hand as text*] Edward Fenton's book 1590.

Anno 1590. The agreement for the building of three great ships, four lesser and six great longboats, viz.

Merhonour. To Matthew Baker for building the great ship at Woolwich – £3,600.
Quittance. Answer. More to him for the building of two lesser ships – £1,400.
More to him for building two great longboats – £200.
[*Sum*] – £5,200.

Defiance. To Peter Pett for building a great ship in her Majesty's yard at Deptford Strand – £3,000
Advantage. More for building of an crompster[1] – £600.
More for building of two longboats – £200.
[*Sum*] – £3,800

The *Garland.* To Richard Chapman for building a great ship in his own dock at Deptford[2] – £3,200
The *Crane.* More to him for a lesser ship – £700.
More for two longboats – £200.

The division of the warrant granted 14 December 1588

For payment of debts in *anno* 1587 – £8,921 8s 8d.
For debts in *anno* 1588 – £3,343 2s 10d.
For new building and repairing of the *Bear*, the *Mary Rose*, the *Hope* and the *Bonaventure* – £6,000.
[*Sum*] – £18,264 11s 6d.
Received for repairing the four ships in dry dock – £4,500.
More for the new buildings – £1,000.
More for provisions to be made by Mr Allen[3] – £500.
More for debts in *anno* 1587 and 1588 – £12,262 18s 1d.
Fully paid – £18,262 18s 1d.

[1] *OED* 'crumster', a kind of galley or hoy (from Dutch *krom*, crooked).
[2] One of the Queen's master-shipwrights, by patent of 1587; builder of the first *Ark Royal* (as *Ark Ralegh*): Oppenheim, *History*, pp. 121, 152.
[3] See above, p. 74 n. 1.

A warrant granted the 16th of January 1588 [1589] *for pay of Her Majesty's ships and others serving in the Narrow Seas.*[1]

Received of Mr Stoneley 20 January 1588 [*1589*] for the overplus of the ordinary Christmas quarter 1588 and guarding the River – £1,940 17s 4d.

Of Mr Killigrew 27 February for sea store – £300.

Of Mr [Freke *deleted*] Taylor 10 April 1590 for a pay in the Narrow Seas – £2,054.

Of Mr Freke 5 May 1589 for the *Vanguard*, *Swallow* and *Tiger* – £1,033.

Of Mr Taylor 12 May 1589 for bringing about of Don Pedro's ship[2] and the *Lion* – £406.

Of Mr Killigrew 9 July 1589 for a pay on the Narrow Seas – £1,192.

Of Mr Taylor 14 September for the *Vanguard* – £349 3s.

Of Mr Killigrew 20 October 1589 for the Narrow Seas – £1,747 10s.

Of Mr Freke 29 December for the pay of the *Vanguard* and *Rainbow* – £1,106 5s.

Of Mr Killigrew 17 February 1589 [*1590*] for the pay of the *Vanguard* and *Moon* – £483 5s.

Of Mr Freke 26 February 1589 [*1590*] for the pay of the *Tremontaine* and *Rainbow* – £358 15s.

[1]Stoneley (above, p. 23 n. 2), Killigrew (p. 25 n. 2), Robert Freke and Robert Taylor were the four tellers of the Exchequer. Freke was appointed by patent 8 May 1571, and served to his death 8 Oct. 1592; Taylor was appointed 7 May 1571, and surrendered by 28 May 1603: *CPR 1569–72*, nos 1350, 2421. Sainty, *Exchequer Officers*, p. 233 (correcting *CPR* date for Taylor's patent). While Stoneley and Killigrew enjoyed life tenure, Freke and Taylor were appointed merely 'during good behaviour', a precaution introduced following discovery of massive defaults by Stoneley himself and his former colleagues (cf. above, p. 24 n. 3).

[2]*Nuestra Señora del Rosario*, commanded by Don Pedro de Valdés, vice-flagship of the Andalusian squadron, and at 1,150 *toneladas* the fourth-largest ship in the Armada fleet, had famously and controversially surrendered to Drake off Plymouth on 1 Aug. 1588. She had been taken into Sir John Gilbert's custody at Dartmouth where her ordnance and other contents were inventoried and in part removed. In May 1589, the Privy Council ordered her to be transferred to William Hawkins and brought into the Thames; this warrant covers that operation, including £190 13s 3d paid to the 121 men involved in preparing and sailing her to Chatham. Later in 1589 she was moved to dry dock at Deptford, and in 1618 she was scuttled as a breakwater at Chatham: P. Martin, *Spanish Armada Prisoners: the Story of the* Nuestra Señora del Rosario *and her crew, and of other Prisoners in England, 1587–97* (Exeter Maritime Studies, 1: Exeter, 1988), pp. 36–7. The present entry adds to the extensive documentary evidence assembled in Martin's monograph. It may also be mentioned that there is also in the Pepys Library the manuscript 'Libro de cargos' of 1587 (PL 2269: *Cat. PL*, pp. 55–7), which inventories provisions for Don Pedro's squadron. This was probably acquired by Pepys during his visit to Spain in 1683–84; we are obliged to Dr R. Luckett for suggesting this as a more likely provenance for the MS than its actually being aboard the *Rosario* when captured.

Anno 1590. Of Mr Freke 6 April 1590 for the pay of the *Antelope* and setting forth of the *Vanguard* – £663 15s.

Of Mr Killigrew 24 April 1590 for the discharge of the *Charles* and *Scout* – £337.

Of Mr Stoneley 24 July 1590 for pay of the *Vanguard*, the *Tremontaine* and the *Moon* on the Narrow Seas – £870 5s.

Of Mr Stoneley 21 September 1590 for the discharge of the *Vanguard* – £563 15s.

Of Mr Killigrew 11 October 1590 for the discharge of the *Tremontaine* and the *Spy* – £225 2s 2d.

Of Mr Killigrew 11 January 1590 [*1591*] as well for the pay of the *Moon* as discharge of the *Answer* &c. – £554 18s 6d.

Of Mr Stoneley 22 January 1590 [*1591*] for the discharge of the *Advantage* and the *Black Dog* – £500 2s 6d.

A warrant granted the 29 of May 1589[1]

For the new buildings – £6,000.

For repairing the four ships – £1,500.

For provisions of sundry sorts – £3,000.

Fully paid – £105,000.

A warrant granted the 21th of July 1589,[2] viz.

For setting to the seas of the *Lion*, the *Elizabeth Bonaventure*, under the charge of Sir Martin Frobisher – £1,531.

[1]E 404/128, bundle 31 Eliz. I. The 'new buildings' were the three great ships mentioned above (*Merhonour*, *Defiance* and *Garland*), those repaired were *White Bear*, *Hope*, *Elizabeth Bonaventure* and *Mary Rose*, and the provisions included cordage, canvas, anchors and masts, part of which had already been supplied.

[2]Ibid. (another item). Frobisher was sent to intercept treasure ships off the Portuguese coast, supplementing the larger but less official operation led by Cumberland. The warrant authorised a total of £2,954 to set three warships and one pinnace to sea for three months: £1,322 to Quarles for victualling and £1,632 to Hawkins for wages of the 620 men. Frobisher's commission (30 Aug.) gave him command of the Queen's *Lion*, *Elizabeth Bonaventure*, *Advice* and *Sun*, and Hawkins's privateer *Repentance*: SP 12/225, no. 74 (*CSPD 1581–90*, p. 614); cf. SP 12/225, nos 32–4 (*CSPD 1581–90*, p. 610: memoranda by Lord Admiral and Burghley, 19 July). In the event *Sun* was omitted and the squadron comprised the three warships and pinnace which the warrant of 21 July allowed; by that authority £1,300 1s 8d was eventually paid for 12 months' wages for 620 men aboard those four vessels: E 351/2226, m. 19d. Though Frobisher lost the best of his prizes on the way home, the advantage of deploying two squadrons was demonstrated, and the strategy was repeated the next year: McDermott, *Frobisher*, pp. 378–80; also pp. 372–4 concerning the Breton ship *Gerosme* of Paimpol, taken by *Lion*.

18 July 1589. A letter from the council for eight hoys sent to Ostend[1] – £97 8s.

A warrant granted the 15th of August 1589

For transporting the *Revenge*, the *Nonpareil*, the *Dreadnought* &c. from Plymouth serving in the Portugal voyage – £500.[2]

The division of the warrant of the 28th of November 1589,[3] viz.

For the new buildings – £6,100.
For repairing the four ships – £2,047 3s 4d.
For provision of canvas, cordage &c. – £5,844 7s 7d.
[*Sum*] – £13,991 10s 11d.
Whereof,
Received for the new buildings – £4,000.
More for repairing the four ships – £2,047 3s 4d.
[*Margin*: Note Mr Allen £1000]. More for provisions of canvas, cordage &c. at sundry times – £4,000.
For the new buildings 18 April 1590 – £1,000.
Of Mr Stoneley 11 June 1590 for the new buildings in full of £6100 – £1,100.
Of Mr Stoneley 3 October 1590 for cordage had of James Lawrence and John Borne – £170 2s 10d.
Of Mr Freke 17 December 1590 for provisions in full of this warrant – £1,674 4s 9d.
Fully paid – £13,991 10s 11d.

A warrant granted 4 February 1589 [1590][4]

[1]*APC 1588–9*, p. 369 (Privy Council to the Lord Treasurer authorising payment of this sum to Hawkins, 10 July). Cf. Wernham, *Expedition*, p. 205

[2]The ships of the Drake/Norris expedition. The returning fleet had been scattered by weather; Norris arrived back in Plymouth on 2 or 3 July to find Drake already there. On 1[illegible] July the Privy Council instructed the Admiralty officers John Thomas and Christopher Baker to take the Queen's ships back into their charge: *APC 1588–9*, pp. 394–6. Wernham, *Expedition*, pp. lv, 199, 207, 281.

[3]E 404/129, bundle 32 Eliz. I. In the same terms as the warrant of 29 May (above, p. 62[illegible] & n. 1), recording that total costs under the three heads now stood at £29,491 10s 10d, of which £15,500 had already been discharged, and authorising payment of the residual £13,99[illegible] 10s *10d* to Hawkins.

[4]E 404/129, bundle 32 Eliz. In addition to the £2,435 4s allowed for Hawkins's expedition the warrant provided £3,033 10s for Sir Robert Constable, Lieutenant of the Ordnance, to furnish the new ships with brass ordnance; part of this was to be had from various coastal forts, and new iron ordnance was to be sent to the forts instead. Because large sums had been assigned for the shipbuilding and other extraordinary naval charges, as well as for troops in Ireland and the Low Countries, the Lord Treasurer was authorised to pay this warrant from sale of lands.

For provisions to serve the six ships which were appointed under the charge of Sir John Hawkins, knight[1] – £2,435 4s.

Whereof, received of the same [*margin*: resteth £435 4s.] – £2,000.

The division of the warrant granted 19 February 1589 [1590][2]

For provision of hemp to make cordage by Mr Allen – £1,000.

For a provision of canvas to furnish the whole Navy – £2,176 5s.

For a provision to furnish the seven new ships – £7,262 4s.

For 100 bolts of medrinacks to furnish the *Victory* – £125.

For 10 new boats and 10 new pinnaces – £390.

For provisions of masts and yards to furnish the Navy, and making of them – £1,200.

[*Sum*] – £12,153 9s.

For the overplus of the ordinary of Michaelmas and Christmas quarters 1589 – £1,698 14s 6d.

For timber and plank – £400.

For a supply of great anchors – £350.

For a provision of sea store for the whole Navy – £1,220.

For debts owing to Mr Stookes – £200;[3] and the Muscovia company – £990.[4]

[*Sum*] – £1,190.

For a provision to remain in store – £4,000.

[*Sum*] – £8,858 14s 6d. [*Carried forward*] – £12,153 9s.

Totalis – £21,012 3s 6d.

Whereof,

[1]Hawkins had been preparing to return to the Azores since September 1589, and six ships were being prepared at Chatham by December that year. The preparations were halted on 3 Feb. because of the government's concern about Spanish designs on Brittany: Williamson, *Hawkins* (1927), pp. 455–6, based on material from the State Papers, most of which is collected below.

[2]E 404/129, bundle 32 Eliz I. Hawkins, Palmer and the younger Gonson had submitted an estimate of £17,012 3s 6d for the new shipbuilding and setting the rest of the Navy to sea (including debts already incurred). The warrant authorised payment of this sum and an additional £4,000 for future needs, making the total of £21,012 3s 6d given here.

[3]Possibly Henry Storcke, Hanseatic merchant in London (occ. *CPR 1578–80*, nos 1144, 731).

[4]Representing cordage delivered on credit, the sum for which rose to £1,558 0s 3d by 30 June, and was settled in December: SP 12/232, nos 70–71; 12/234, no. 60, cited in T. S. Willan, *The Early History of the Russia Company, 1553–1603* (Manchester, 1956), p. 185, noting that this was a regular and substantial transaction, and quoting from M. Wretts-Smith, 'The English in Russia during the second half of the sixteenth century', *TRHS*, 4th ser. III (1920), p. 95: 'The fleet that defeated the Spanish Armada was largely rigged with Russian cordage and cables'.

Received of Mr Stoneley 4 March 1589 [*1590*] for furnishing the 7 new ships – £2,000; for provision of sail canvas – £1,000; and provision of masts – £200.

[*Sum*] – £3,200.

Of Mr Killigrew 5 March for the discharge of the overplus of the ordinary in Michaelmas and Christmas quarters 1589 – £1,698 14s 6d; and for the discharge of timber and plank – £400. [*Sum*] – £2,098 14s 6d.

To be borne of the warrant of 18 May 1590.

Of Mr Freke 23 March 1590 for presting mariners for which there wa no warrant – £1,158 15s.

Of Mr Stoneley 25 April 1590 for the same purpose – £500.

More of Mr Stoneley 25 April 1590 for provisions – £500.

More of Mr Killigrew 23 July 1590 for provisions – £2,584 13s 4d.

More of Mr Taylor 17 December 1590 for payment of debts for provision – £2,000.

More of Mr Taylor 21 December 1590 for payment of debts for provision – £1,000.

The warrant dormant granted 13 March 1589 [1590][1]

For the ordinary in harbour – £8,973 12s.

Per mensem – £747 16s.

For 3 months – £2,243 8s.

The division of the warrant granted 18 May 1590

For 3 months' pay of 2,570 men – £7,196.

For conduct in discharge of 2,000 men – £750.

For wages and conduct in discharge of 1,000 men at Chatham – £700.

For prest and conduct of 2,600 mariners for this service – £1,658 15s.

Fully paid – £10,304 15s.

Whereof,

Received of Mr Freke 20 May 1590 for one month's wages for 2,570 me – £1799.

More the same day of Mr Stoneley for wages and conduct in discharg of 1,000 men at Chatham – £700.

[1]Printed as **43** below, where the annual total has an additional 10d.

More of Mr Freke 25 May 1590 for the relief of the companies serving under Sir John Hawkins and Sir Martin Frobisher[1] – £600.

[*Sum*] – £3,099.

More of Mr Killigrew 7 October 1590 towards the pay of Sir Martin Frobisher's companies – £1,000.

More of Mr Freke 14 October 1590 towards the pay and conduct in discharge of Sir Martin Frobisher's companies – £500.

More the 21th of October 1590, *viz.* of Mr Freke £600, of Mr Stoneley £400, and of Mr Killigrew £400, towards the payment of certain the companies of Sir Martin Frobisher – £1,400.

More of Mr Killigrew 3 November 1590 for the payment of 90 men serving in the *Foresight* under the charge of Sir John Hawkins discharged at Portsmouth,[2] *viz.* for wages £378, and for conduct in discharge £22 10s; total – £400 10s.

Of Mr Killigrew 9 November 1590 for discharge of the *Hope* at Chatham serving under the charge of Sir John Hawkins[3] – £1,165.

[*Sum*] – £4,465.10.0

More of Mr Taylor 19 November 1590 for money disbursed by the captains serving under Sir Martin Frobisher for men discharged by them at Plymouth[4] – £872 4s 2d.

More of Mr Killigrew 20 November 1590 in part of payment of £372 15s. for discharge of 70 men serving in the *Foresight* under Sir John Hawkins southward [*margin*: £163 9s 2d] – £209 5s 10d.

A warrant granted 28 July 1590 for the pay of the surplusage of Lady and Midsummer quarters 1590.

Received of Mr Stoneley 14 August 1590 in full thereof – £2,921 6s 4d.

[1]A revised version of Hawkins's stalled scheme now went ahead. Frobisher, flying his flag in *Revenge*, would take a squadron of seven to the Azores, while Hawkins in *Mary Rose*, with *Hope*, *Nonpareil* (in place of the *Ark*), *Swiftsure*, *Foresight* and *Rainbow*, would go no further than the Spanish coast, in case the threat to Brittany was resumed. The captains were paid from 25 May, and the fleets sailed soon afterwards: Willamson, *Hawkins* (1927), p. 58, following details in Monson, *Tracts*, i, p. 242, derived from the Treasurer's Declared Accounts.

[2]Hawkins was recalled at the end of October when there were renewed fears of Spanish intervention in Brittany: Williamson, *Hawkins* (1927), p. 460.

[3]Capt. George Fenner in the *Hope* was Hawkins's Vice-Admiral.

[4]Frobisher's squadron had returned to Plymouth by 9 Sept.: McDermott, *Frobisher*, p. 2.

The names of Her Majesty's ships	*Their tonnage*	*Their numbers of men in harbour*	*Their numbers at sea*	*Mariners*	*Gunners*	*Soldiers*
The *Triumph*	1000	30	500	340	40	120
The *Elizabeth Jonas*	900	30	500	340	40	120
The *White Bear*	900	30	500	340	40	120
The *Merhonour*	900	30	500	340	40	120
The *Victory*	800	17	400	268	32	100
The *Ark Raleigh*	800	17	400	268	32	100
The *Mary Rose*	600	12	250	150	30	70
The *Hope*	600	12	250	150	30	70
The *Elizabeth Bonaventure*	600	12	250	150	30	70
The *Golden Lion*	600	12	250	150	30	70
The *Garland*	500	12	250	150	30	70
The *Revenge*	500	12	250	150	30	70
The *Nonpareil*	500	12	250	150	30	70
The *Defiance*	500	12	250	150	30	70
The *Vanguard*	500	12	250	150	30	70
The *Rainbow*	500	12	250	150	30	70
The *Galley Bonavolia*	100	4	250	230	8	12
The *Dreadnought*	400	10	200	140	20	50
The *Swiftsure*	360	10	180	140	20	40
The *Antelope*	340	9	160	140	16	30
The *Swallow*	300	9	160	140	16	30
The *Foresight*	300	9	160	140	16	30
The *Aid*	240	6	120	88	12	22
The *Crane*	160	6	100	76	12	12
The *Advantage*	160	6	100	76	12	12
The *Answer*	160	6	100	76	12	12
The *Quittance*	160	6	100	76	12	12
The *Bull*	160	6	100	76	12	12
The *Tiger*	160	6	100	76	12	12
The *Tremontaine*	130	6	70	52	8	10
The *Scout*	120	5	70	52	8	10
The *Achates*	100	4	60	42	8	10
The *Popinjay*	100	3	60	42	8	10
The *Charles*	70	4	40	30	4	[illegible]
The *Moon*	60	4	40	30	4	[illegible]

'he names of Her 1ajesty's ships	*Their tonnage*	*Their numbers of men in harbour*	*Their numbers at sea*	*Mariners*	*Gunners*	*Soldiers*
'he *Spy*	60	4	40	30	4	6
'he *Advice*	60	4	40	30	4	6
'he *Marline*	40	4	35	27	4	4
'he *Sun*	30	3	30	25	3	2
'he *Cygnet*	20	2	20	16	2	2
'he *Frigate*	20	2	35			
'he *George*	100	10				
'he *Jennet*	200	2				
'he *Primrose*	60	6				
long boats	6	6	180			
Jpnor Castle gunners	9					

um:	*Of the tonnage*	*In harbour*	*At Sea*	*Mariners*	*Gunners*	*Soldiers*
	23705	441	7830	5231	760	1738

38 *Hawkins to Burghley*

;P 12/226, no. 30 (*CSPD 1581–90*, p. 616)][1] *12 September 1589*

Iy bounden duty in humble manner remembered unto your good ordship. I have now gathered together my receipts and payments for 11 ears ended the last of December 1588, which note I send your Lordship erewith. If it may please your good Lordship to give order to clear this ırplusage as in noted in the foot of this declaration, I shall ever be bound pray for your Lordship, I shall be able to clear the office with credit, ıd I shall go forward the better with ability and courage to furnish this ıterprise I have in hand, which shall be a rare example of order and enefit for Her Majesty's service.

[1]See Williamson, *Hawkins* (1927), pp. 465–6.

I do also send herewith a declaration how the money received this yea of *anno* 1589 is expended and more, for as long as I have whereof mysel I can hardly forbear to satisfy the exclamation of poor men.

I hope within 8 or 10 days to be able to wait upon your Lordship, tha I may at large declare the manner of my proceeding, which your Lordshi will easily conceive to be substantially done, and with easy charge although many make mountains of molehills.[1] Thus humbly praying you good Lordship to take some honourable and favourable care of me, humbly take my leave. From Deptford, the 12th of September 1589.

Your honourable Lordship's humbly bounden, John Hawkins.

39 *Estimate for setting out six ships*

[SP 12/230, no. 35 (*CSPD 1581–90*, p. 644)][2] [*January 159*

Ark Raleigh, Mary Rose Nonpareil, Rainbow, Swiftsure, Foresight

An estimate of sea store, the waste and wea of tackle and apparel of the said six ships nominated in the margin, *viz*.:

	Number	£	*s*
Cable and hawsers	Of 7 inches, 6 pieces, 42 cwt	42	0
	Of 6 inches, 11 pieces, 70 [*c*]wt	70	0
	Of 5 inches, 12 pieces, 60 [*cwt*]	60	0
	Of 4 inches, 12 pieces, 48 [*cwt*]	48	0
	Of 3 inches, 10 pieces, 15 [*cwt*]	15	0
	Of 2 inches, 18 pieces, 27 [*cwt*]	27	0
	Of one inch, 18 pieces, 18 [*cwt*]	18	0
Ratline, marline, lines &c.	Ratline, 6¼ cwt at 24s per cwt	7	10
	Marline, 4 cwt 12 lb weight at 28s per cwt	5	15
	Lines, 26 at 2s the piece	2	12
Sail canvas	medrinacks canvas, 170 pieces at 25s the piece	211	10
	Dansk poldavy, 46 pieces at 22s per piece	50	12

[1]The 'mountain out of the molehill' expression was seemingly coined in Nicholas Uda translation of the *Paraphrases of Erasmus* (1548), and was given further currency by t 1570 edition of John Foxe's *Acts and Monuments*: F. P. Wilson (rev.), *The Oxford Dictiona of English Proverbs* (3rd edn, Oxford, 1970), p. 547.

[2]Cf. SP 12/229, nos 2, 3, 28 (*CSPD*, pp. 632, 634).

Sundry necessaries for sea store	Item, small sea store for the said 6 ships, *viz.* flags, ensigns, pennants, lead lines, sounding leads, dipsea[1] lines, bolts, spikes, nails of all sorts, rough and clench, gromets, shackles, ring-bolts, fids, fid hooks, fid hammers, port hooks, port-hinges, can hooks, luff hooks, tacks, rings, oakum, pitch, tar, rosin, bowls, buckets, shovels, scoops, ballast baskets, compasses, running glasses, double plates, fishes for masts, &c., at £60 the ship, one with the other	360	0	0
Waste and wear of tackle, powder&c.	For the waste and wear of ground tackle, sails, cordage, ransacking of the ships, loss of boats and suchlike, which may be per estimation	2,000	0	0
	For the waste of powder, shot, munition and furniture out of the Tower, which may be per estimation	1,200	0	0
Summa totalis		4,117	19	0

40 *Estimate from the Navy Board to Burghley, with application for increase in the ordinary*

SP 12/230, no. 66 (*CSPD 1581–90*, p. 648)][2] *9 February 1590*

The 9th of February *anno* 1589 [*1590*]. A note of such provisions as shall be necessary to furnish the seven new ships[3] and all the rest of Her Majesty['s] Navy for setting forth to the seas in warlike manner, *viz.*

[1]So MS; often elsewhere 'dipsy' or 'dipsie' by false association with 'dip', but actually meaning 'deep sea', though in fact used in coastal waters. A sounding line of about 150 fathoms with a scoop to collect gravel: Smith, *Sea Grammar*, p. 55.

[2]Here omitting some figures repeated in the margin of the MS. Cf. **37** under 19 Feb. above, p. 627).

[3]That is the three great ships (*Merhonour*, *Defiance*, *Garland*) and four lesser (*Quittance*, *Answer*, *Advantage*, *Crane*), as explained at the start of Fenton's book.

Hemp. A note to Mr Allen under our hands for £1,000 to be delivered him in prest to provide hemp to make cordage for supply of such wants as shall be needful to set forth and furnish Her Majesty's Navy to the seas in warlike manner – £1,000.

The seven new ships. A provision to furnish the seven new ships, as by the note of particulars [*Marked* 'B'] – £7,262 4s.

Sail canvas. Item for a provision of canvas to furnish the whole Navy (those six ships appointed to the seas of Sir John Hawkins excepted) amount[eth] to 1,741 bolts of medrinacks, accounting the same at 25s the bolt. *Summa* [*Marked*: 'C'] – £2,176 5s.

Boats and pinnaces. Item for 10 new boats and 10 new pinnaces to furnish the Navy, accounting each boat at £30 the piece amounteth [*to*] £300. And more for the pinnaces at £9 the piece, amounteth to £90 *Summa* – £390.

Masts and yards. For a provision of masts to furnish the Navy with new masts and yards needful, by estimation £1,000. And more for making of great masts for the *Bear*, the *Victory*, the *Revenge* &c. *Summa* – £1,200.

Overplus of the ordinary. For the overplus of the ordinary, Michaelmas and Christmas quarters *anno* 1589 – £1,698 14s 6d.

Timber and plank. More for timber and plank owing for by the Officers over and besides, to the sum of – £400.

Great anchors. For a supply of great anchors for the whole Navy – £350.

Sea store. Item for a provision for sea store for 12 great ships, at £60 the ship – £720; and more for the sea store of 14 of the lesser ships, with the galley, at £30 the ship – £420; and more for seven pinnaces and the *George* hoy at £10 the piece – £80. *Summa* – £1,220.

Debts of the Office. The debts of the Office for which there is no warrant. To Mr Stoakes for cordage – £200; to the Muscovia company – £990. [*Sum*] – £1,190.

Summa totalis – £17,012 3s.

£4,000 for store. Memorandum, the provision and charge heretofore set down or such[like *deleted*] as be requisite to furnish the whole Navy to the seas in warlike manner [*is*] without consideration of any remain to supply such wants as may happen in service; wherefore we think it very convenient that over and besides the former sums there may be allowed the sum of £4,000 to provide cordage, canvas and suchlike necessaries provisions [*sic*] to remain in store.

More ordinary. Item it is very necessary that the new ordinary be considered of and concluded, that a new warrant dormant be made whereby the allowance may be delivered into the Office accordingly; otherwise the Office will fall continually into new debts.

May it please your good Lordship, we think it very necessary that warrants be procured for the sums above specified, which notwithstanding your Lordship may issue and dispose of the money from time to time as the necessity of the service shall require.

[*Signed*] John Hawkins, Henry Palmer,[1] B. Gonson.[2]

41 *Privy Council agenda paper, minuted with the decision to halt Hawkins's expedition*

[SP 12/230, no. 80 (*CSPD 1581–90*, p. 648)][3] *23 February 1590*

A memorial for the Navy.

Whether all the ships shall be removed at one time to Portsmouth, or part of them; and if part of them, then to consider when they shall be removed, and with what number of mariners and with what proportion of victuals.

Minuted: So many as can be put in a readiness to go directly to the seas with 3 months' victual, and such new ships as cannot be put in a readiness to follow afterwards.

When the victuallers shall begin to provide and prepare his [*sic*] victuals, whether for the whole Navy or for part, and for what time.

Minuted: To provide victuals out of hand for the whole Navy, consisting of 10,000 men.

Whether it be convenient that Sir John Hawkins shall proceed in his voyage.

Minuted: Thought unmeet for him to go.

Letters to be written to the States to set out such ships as are agreed on by treaty.[4]

Margin: Ordered so.

[1]Sir Henry Palmer, appointed Surveyor of the Navy 11 July 1589, following the death of Sir William Winter. For Palmer's career details, see *NEM*, p. 560.

[2]Benjamin Gonson jnr, son of the former Treasurer, and himself Clerk of the Ships 1588–1600; for further career details, see *NEM*, pp. 546–7.

[3]See Williamson, *Hawkins* (1927), p. 455.

[4]Article 25 of the treaty of Nonsuch (Aug. 1585), by which Elizabeth had taken the United Provinces under her protection, required the States-General to match any fleet which the Royal Navy put to sea against a Spanish fleet entering the Channel, the combined force to be under the command of the English Admiral: J. Dumont (Baron de Carlscroon), *Corps Universel Diplomatique* (Amsterdam, 1726–31), vi, I, p. 455. Wernham, *Before the Armada*, p. 371. In February the Prince of Orange had responded to the Queen's demand for details of vessels the Dutch could supply. In a letter dated Feb. but endorsed 6 March the Queen announced that she had fitted out certain ships, and called on the States to honour the treaty by supplying an equivalent force for three months: *L&ISPF*, i, pp. 211–12.

To appoint and look to the ordnance, and to see the carriages fetched for the same.

Minuted: A master of the ordnance to be appointed.[1]

42 *Hawkins to Burghley*

[SP 12/231, no. 2 (*CSPD 1581–90*, p. 651)][2] *1 March 1590*

The book of the whole army. My most honourable good Lord, I do herewith send the book which I showed your Lordship firmed by the Officers.

The ordinary warrant dormant: £8,973 12s 10d; monthly £747 16s. I do also send your Lordship a form of the warrant for the new warrant dormant, which your Lordship may allow or alter at your pleasure. Upon the backside whereof I have noted the true monthly charge, which was mistaken yesterday, for that we accounted after 13 months, and it is paid by order from your Lordship out of the Exchequer after 12 months to the year.

The overthrow of the journey. I am many ways burdened and brought behind-hand, and especially by the overthrow of this journey, which I had with great care and cost brought to pass, hoping as your Lordship did see an orderly and a sparing beginning, so if it had pleased God that it should have proceeded, there should have been seen, with God's favour, a rare example of government, wherein matter of great moment might have been performed; but seeing it is thus, I can but say, the will of God be done.

His demands. I am many ways to be an humble suitor to your good Lordship to look favourably to me, else I shall be utterly cast down for many things are now out of my hands wherein I have stretched my ability and many of my friends, and especially this late journey intended the remain of the warrant of the 27 of March 1588 – £2,147 10s; the consideration for my ship the *Repentance* – £714;[3] my portion with

[1]An operational appointment. The office of Master of Naval Ordnance had lapsed with the death of Sir William Winter in Feb. 1589: see *NEM*, p. 572 n. 1.

[2]Headings minuted in another hand. For content, see Williamson, *Hawkins* (1927), p. 456.

[3]Hawkins's privateer, so named by Lady Hawkins; renamed *Dainty* at the Queen's request (allegedly because the original name was inappropriate to so graceful a vessel): Kelsey, *Hawkins*, pp. 240, 242. As *Repentance* she had served with the squadron of royal ships sent south under Frobisher's command in autumn 1589, and Hawkins was seeking reimbursement for stores provided and damage sustained in an action off Sagres Point; he had written to Burghley to this effect a few days earlier: SP 12/230, no. 92 (*CSPD 1581–90*, p. 649: letter of 25 Feb.); an enclosure more precisely naming the sum owed as £714 5s (the owner's seventh of the third part, for shipping, of goods valued at £15,000) has been misplaced under Feb. 1589: SP 12/222, no. 96 (*CSPD*, p. 581). Cf. **37** above, **45** below, Monson, *Tracts*, i, pp. 238–9, and McDermott, *Frobisher*, p. 378 (though n. 26 leads to incorrect reference on p. 475).

Sir Francis Drake, which Her Majesty promised me long since, being – £7,000.

His request. All which I thought should seem by me small matters in comparison of that which God would have blessed me with if I had proceeded; but now being out of hope that ever I shall perform any royal thing, I do put on a mean mind, and humbly pray your Lordship to be good lord to me; to whom only I will be beholding [*beholden*], and will be disposed of and all that I have by your Lordship, and ever thankful; and so leave to trouble your Lordship. From London, the first of March 1589 [*1590*].

Your Lordship's ever bounden, John Hawkins.

43 *Privy seal warrant authorising a new and increased ordinary*

[SP 15/13, no. 132 *13 March 1590*
(*CSPD Addenda 1580–1625*, pp. 304–5)][1]

Elizabeth &c., to the Treasurer and Chamberlains of our Exchequer, greeting. Whereas with the advice of our Council, whereof our Admiral was one, we did heretofore assent to the augmentation of a charge for the keeping of our ships in harbour, the book of which augmentation was subscribed with the hands of certain of our Privy Council to whom the same cause was committed to be considered, and thereupon did address our warrants for the payment of £5,714 2s 2d yearly or from time to time monthly by equal parts to Benjamin Gonson our late servant and Treasurer of our Marine Causes, as well for the keeping and repairing of our ships in harbour as for other charges incident to the same;[2] forasmuch as upon conference which we have caused our Privy Council, amongst whom our Admiral was one, to be lately had with our Officers of our Marine Causes, we find that by reason our Navy is greatly increased by the making of sundry new ships and pinnaces more than ever heretofore have been, our charges also for keeping of our said ships and other vessels in harbour is increased by the sum of £3,259 2s 2d yearly, as by a book thereof made

[1]See Williamson, *Hawkins* (1927), p. 465.

[2]The warrant by which the ordinary was originally fixed at £5,714 2s 2d *per annum* has not been traced; it reverted to this figure after the period of the Hawkins bargains (1579–87), when it had been at its lowest level of £4,000 [**19**]. A new warrant was drawn up on 12 Nov. 1588, raising the ordinary from £5,714 2s 2d to £7,268 0s 6d *wef* 1 Jan. 1589: SP 12/218, no. 16 (*CSPD 1581–90*, p. 558); but since the present document takes no account of that rise, it must have been rescinded. The 1590 warrant was specifically replaced by another, calendared conjecturally under January 1599, which took the sum to exactly £11,000: 12/270, no. 26 (*CSPD 1598–1601*, p. 157). Cf. Oppenheim, *History*, pp. 160–3, where additional fluctuations in the ordinary are noted; but this 1590 warrant extant in the SP Addenda was overlooked, and therefore no uncertainty was detected about the 1588 version.

by our said Officers containing the particular charges of the same plainly appeareth, we have thought meet that the said former warrant of £5,714 2s 2d by the year shall cease, and so do will [*word repeated*] and command you to take order therein accordingly, and that of such our treasure as is or hereafter shall be in the receipt of our said Exchequer you shall yearly and from time to time monthly after the last day of December last past deliver and pay or cause to be delivered [*and*] paid in prest monthly by equal portions to our servant Sir John Hawkins, knight, or to his sufficient deputy, or to the Treasurer of our Navy for the time being, the sum of £8,973 12s 10d[1] for the keeping and repairing of our said ships and other vessels in harbour, the money already received since the first of January last upon the old warrant of £5,714 2s 2d being deducted, and also so much money to be deducted out of the foresaid sum as you our Treasurer of England shall by good information understand not to be chargeable until our new ships shall be finished and brought in order to be kept in harbour with their number [*of men*] to them limited, and except also to be from time to time paid such sums of money as ought not to be in charge for the harbour wages of any of our said ships serving on the seas and being otherwise in pay for their said service; willing and commanding also that if any of our said ships and vessels be repaired in dry dock, and that the surplusage of this warrant at the year's end will not bear out the said charge, that then upon a certificate thereof made and delivered unto our High Treasurer of England for the time being, avouched under the hands of the Lord Admiral and the Officers of our Marine Causes for the time being, you shall deliver and pay or cause to be delivered and paid to Sir John Hawkins, knight, or his sufficient deputy, or to the Treasurer of the Navy then being, such sum or sums of money as by the said certificate shall be found due, without any further warrant to be had or procured from us unto you for the same. And these our letters shall be your sufficient warrant and discharge in this behalf. Given under our privy seal at our manor of Greenwich the 13th day of March in the 32th year of our reign.

Ex[*aminatur*] *per* Vin. Skinner.[2]

[1]It will be readily seen that the old ordinary plus the increased annual charge actually amounts to these pounds and 4s 4d, and 8s 5d has been added to achieve the new figure.

[2]Sir Vincent Skinner (Kt 1603) was Burghley's private secretary by 1575/6 to 1593; writer of tallies and auditor of the Receipt of the Exchequer 1593–1609: Sainty, *Exchequer Officers*, p. 207. *Hist. Parl. 1558–1603*, iii, pp. 390–1.

44 *Hawkins to Burghley*

[SP 12/231, no. 83 (*CSPD 1581–90*, p. 651)][1] *16 April 1590*

My bounden duty in humble manner remembered unto your good Lordship. I do perceive Her Majesty is not well satisfied concerning the employments of the great sums of money that have been received into the Office of the Navy, although your honour did very honourably both take pain and care to see the strict and orderly course that is used in the Office, and thereupon deliver your mind plainly to Her Majesty as your Lordship found it, for which I shall ever acknowledge myself dutifully bound to honour and serve your Lordship to the uttermost of my ability. And whereas Her Highness's pleasure is to be further satisfied in mine accounts, there hath nothing been more desired nor could be more welcome or acceptable to me, and when it shall be Her Majesty's pleasure to nominate the persons that I shall attend upon, I will briefly show the state of every year's account sufficiently avouched by books to the last day of December 1588, which is 11 years, *whereof 5 years are passed by duplicaments before your Lordship, three years are passed by like duplicaments firmed by Sir Walter Mildmay and the Barons of the Exchequer by your Lordship's order; two years' books are yet with the auditors, and the last book is in my hand, firmed by the Officers, ready to be delivered to the auditors, upon the finishing of the other two books already in their hands.* If any worldly thing that I possess could free me of this mistrust and importable care and toil, I would most willingly depart with it, for as the case standeth I think there is no man living that that so careful, so miserable, so unfortunate and so dangerous a life; only I see your Lordship with care and truth doth search into the true order, the sufficiency and validity of the course that is carried in the Office, which otherwise I would even plainly give over my place and submit myself to Her Majesty's mercy, though I lived in prison all the days of my life. The matters in the Office grow infinite and chargeable beyond all measure and such as hardly any man can give a reason of the innumerable businesses that daily grow; yet the mistrust is more troublesome and grievous than all the rest, for with the answering of the one and toil of the other there is hardly any time left to serve God or to satisfy man. The greater sort that serve in this Office be grown so proud, obstinate and insolent, nothing can satisfy them,[2] and the common sort very disobedient, so as a man that

[1]Printed (in original spelling) in Oppenheim, *History*, pp. 147–8, intentionally omitting the central part here italicised, and the valediction. Cf. Williamson, *Hawkins* (1927), p. 466.

[2]Oppenheim, *History* (p. 147 n. 3), identifies this as a probable reference to William Borough.

must answer the immoderate desire of all these were better to choose to die than to live. The painful place which your Lordship doth hold and the immoderate demands that comes before you having with the favour of Her Majesty the help of an absolute power to bind and loose may easily demonstrate the burden that so mean a man as I am doth bear (which must pass everything by petition and mistrust) to satisfy the multitude of demands that are in this Office, and although they be many and as well satisfied as in any office in all England, yet few are contented, but go away with grudging and murmur. It were a great vanity for me to commend mine own service, neither do I go about to accumulate to myself any commendation for that I thought I never performed my duty sufficiently, but if the estate of the Office be considered what it was when I came into it and what it is now, there will be found great odds wherein I have travailed as carefully as I could and as my credit could obtain mean to reduce the state of the [Office *deleted*] ships and their furniture into good and perfect order. In recompense whereof my only desire is that it may please Her Majesty some course may be taken wherein Her Majesty may be satisfied that a plain and honest course hath been taken and carried in the Office, and then to dispose of my place to whom it shall please Her Highness, and I shall be ready to serve Her Majesty in any other way that I shall be appointed wherein my skill or ability will extend. And so I humbly take my leave. From Deptford the 16 of April 1590.

Your Lordship's ever bounden, John Hawkins.

45 *Hawkins to Burghley*

[SP 12/233, no. 118 (*CSPD 1581–90*, p. 695)][1] *31 October 1590*

My bounden duty in humble manner remembered unto your good Lordship. I did refrain to write to your Lordship for that I ever hoped upon some notable thing to come into our hands; but thus it hath pleased God to deal with us that we met with nothing whereby I should have occasion to have advertised your Lordship as I desired, and thus God's infallible word is performed, in that the Holy Ghost said Paul doth plant, Apollo doth water, but God giveth the increase.[2] For I may boldly say unto your Lordship I was very well provided both of shipping, victual, furniture and a quiet and sufficient company; but seeing this hath been the good pleasure of God, I do content myself and hold all to come for the best.

[1]See Williamson, *Hawkins* (1927), pp. 460–1, quoting the Queen's reaction: 'God's death This fool went out a soldier and is come in a divine' (also given in Monson, *Tracts*, i, p. 25[?] n. 28).

[2]1 Corinthians 3: 6, 7.

I do send your Lordship a copy of the letter I sent to my Lord Admiral, to the end your Lordship may see the circumstance of matters past and to be necessarily done for the ordering of Her Majesty's ships, and especially for their abode here this winter, that will be very profitable to Her Majesty, ease much charge, and aptest for service as the time requireth; which advice I give simply for Her Majesty's better service, without respect of anything else, notwithstanding I refer me to the better judgement of your Lordship and others who know what may fit better as service may come on. In the mean time I will order them ready to stay or come away as I shall be commanded.

If I might entreat your Lordship, I would gladly bring the cochineal and the hangings of leather to London myself, of which there shall not be diminished one grain or one piece. If it be ordered that the ships come about, I will bring it in the ships; if I come by land, then I will bring it with me in good order, and then according to the equity of the matter your Lordship may restore or detain at your good pleasure.[1]

My charge was very great at my departing from hence, for I provided very substantially and was forced to gage some things here, and I have very great need of money. Your Lordship may consider, by the order that shall be determined, what money will be requisite for me, to whose honourable consideration I shall always refer me; and although God hath thus dealt with me, yet I hope your Lordship will not think but I have done my endeavour.

The pursuivant[2] that was sent down about the cochineal hath been very earnest to have the possession of it, and now perceiving that I was arrived, he hastened the sending away of it; and seeing it was here and the time cut short, I presumed to stay it till your Lordship's pleasure were returned by this messenger, for so I saw it was your Lordship's pleasure in a letter that Sir John Gilbert[3] send me at this instant from the lords of Her

[1]As they returned towards Plymouth in June the Hawkins and Frobisher ships had stopped a number of friendly Dutch merchantmen and seized goods (including silver, cochineal and ginger) worth 100,000 florins. Following protests from the States-General and the States of Zeeland, the Privy Council ordered restitution, but meanwhile Hawkins and his son Richard appear to have colluded in mixing the cochineal with low-grade substitutes in order to pocket a quantity of the better sort: *L&ASPF 1590–1*, nos 199–200. *APC 1590–1*, pp. 81–3 (Council's stinging letter to Hawkins, warrant to their officer to arrest other suspects, and letter to Drake and others to assist the investigation, all 20 Nov.). Kelsey, *Hawkins*, p. 240.

[2]David Atkinson, messenger of the Chamber. His report from Plymouth of 21 Nov. (which cannot have been received in London before issue of the Council's orders of the previous day) describes the adulteration of 40 bags of cochineal, the refusal of Richard Hawkins to return some of the goods, and the forcible seizure by Sir John of what was being returned to London: SP 12/234, no. 2 (*CSPD 1581–90*, p. 696). Following receipt of the Council's instructions, Hawkins subsequently restored this to the local authorities [**48**].

[3]One of the Deputy Lieutenants of Devon.

Majesty's Council that the goods should remain till express order came from their Honours.

I do send your Lordship a copy of the note of the goods which I lef here with the Mayor, the Customer and Humphrey Fones[1] with order tc them that it might remain till your Honour's pleasure were known. Anc thus with continual prayer to God for your Lordship's happiness I humbly take my leave. From Plymouth the last of October 1590.

Your honourable Lordship's humbly bounden, John Hawkins.

46 *Estimate for victuals for Hawkins's voyage*

[SP 12/234, no. 9 (*CSPD 1581–90*, p. 697)] *7 November 159(*

The 7th November 1590. An estimate of the charge for 2 month's victual for 1,340 men serving at the seas in six Her Majesty's ships specified ir the margin under the charge of Sir John Hawkins, knight, upon the coas and islands of Spain and Portugal, *viz.*:

[*Margin*]	*men*
The *Mary Rose*	250
The *Hope*	250
The *Nonpareil*	250
The *Rainbow*	250
The *Swiftsure*	180
The *Foresight*	160
	1,340

For the victualling of 1,340 men serving at the seas in the ships abov specified under charge of Sir John Hawkins, knight, for 2 months of 28 day to the month, to be accounted from the ending of their victuals they carrie from Chatham with them, which was the 13th of September last, and to enc the 8th of this [*word repeated*] month of [September *deleted*] Novembe after the rate of 6d per day for every man, amounteth [*to*] – £1,876.

Item, for the victuals of 930 men (the companies of the *Mary Rose*, th *Nonpareil*, the *Rainbow* and the *Swiftsure* now at Plymouth) for 6 days to begin the 9th of this month and to end the 14th of the same, at wha time we account the one half of their companies may be discharged, at 6 every man *per diem*, amounteth [*to*] – £139 10s.

[1] Walter Peperell was the incumbent Mayor. Humphrey Fownes *alias* Founes had held th office in 1588–89; he was a wine merchant, and from 1580–99 the civic official responsib for regulation of the wine trade. We are indebted to Miss A. Morgan, Plymouth Cit Archivist, for these details.

More for the victuals of 465 men one month of 28 days (half the companies of the said four ships) to bring them from Plymouth to Chatham, at 14s per man, amounteth – £325 10s.

Summa – £2,341.

[*Signed*] Henry Palmer, W. Borough, B. Gonson.

47 *Estimate for paying off half Hawkins's men*

[SP 12/234, no. 10 (*CSPD 1581–90*, p. 697)] *7 November 1590*

The 7th November 1590. An estimate of the charge for a pay to be made at Plymouth for discharging half the companies of four Her Majesty's ships lately arrived there, which served in a voyage to the southwards under charge of Sir John Hawkins, knight, *viz*.:

	The whole company	*The half number*
	men	*men*
The *Mary Rose*	250	125
The *Nonpareil*	250	125
The *Rainbow*	250	125
The *Swiftsure*	180	90
	930	465

Wages. For the wages of 465 men to be discharged out of the ships above specified, for 7 months (of 28 days to the month) and 12 days begun the 21th April 1590 and to end the 14th of this month November, after the rate of 14s each man per month, diets, shares and rewards in the same accounted, amounteth [*to*] – £2,418.

Conduct. Item for the conduct in discharge of the said 465 men, supposing the same number to be most of them of Devonshire and Cornwall, after the rate of 2s per man – £46 10s.

Summa – £2,464 10s. [*Signed*] W. Borough, B. Gonson.

Imprests to be abated. There is to be abated out of the sum of £2,464 10s above specified for one month's imprest delivered the said company before they went forth, at 14s per man, the sum – £325 10s.

And so, there resteth to be allowed for the discharge of the said number of 465 men the sum of – £2,139.

[*Signed*] W. Borough, B. Gonson.

48 *Hawkins to Burghley*

[SP 12/234, no. 49 (*CSPD 1581–90*, p. 702)][1] *8 December 1590*

My bounden duty humbly remembered unto your good Lordship. We arrived by Dover with four of Her Majesty's good ships and the *Daynty*[2] in good safety, God be thanked, the 8th day of December, and mind to ply into Chatham with all speed possible. I have written from hence to Mr Fenton and the Officers to attend upon your Lordship with an estimate of the wages of the company now to be discharged, which is hath their numbers, which I could not diminish, considering the winter time.

The prize at Dartmouth is discharged there, and a perfect inventory sent unto your Lordship of all that was found in her by the Customer or Collector Mr Blackaller,[3] to which inventory both he and I have subscribed; and lest the same may not come so soon to your Lordship's hands by land as now by me, I have sent your Lordship a copy of it word for word.

I have delivered the cochineal to those your Lordship and the rest of the lords wrote for; even at my being under sail I gave order for it. The ryals of plate and the matters of worth I have here with me in the *Mary Rose*, which I will bring to your Lordship; so have I other things wherein your Lordship shall see I have diminished nothing. And so praying to God for your Lordship's health and prosperity, I humbly take my leave. From the *Mary Rose* near Dover, the 8th of December 1590.

Your honourable Lordship's ever bounden, John Hawkins.

49 *Summary of expenses of Hawkins's expedition*

[SP 12/234, no. 51 (*CSPD 1581–90*, p. 702] *10 December 1590*

10 December 1590. A brief estimate of the charge of a voyage made by Sir John Hawkins, knight, with six of Her Majesty's ships to the southwards, *viz.*:

	men
The *Mary Rose*	250
The *Hope*	250
The *Nonpareil*	250

[1]See Williamson, *Hawkins* (1927), p. 459.
[2]Hawkins's ship, ex-*Repentance*; see **42**.
[3]Christopher Blackaller of Dartmouth, who d. by Feb. 1592: PROB 11/79, f. 135r–v. C[f.] *CSPD 1591–4*, p. 462; *CPR 35 Eliz. I*, no. 149.

The *Rainbow*	250
The *Swiftsure*	180
The *Foresight*	160
	1,340

For wages and conduct in discharge of the men serving in the same ships – £6,760 5s.
More for victualling of the same companies – £6,083 5s.
More for sea store outerbound – £310 14s.
Totalis – £13,514 4s.

50 *Expenses claimed by Hawkins for victualling of his expedition*

[SP 12/239, no. 108 (*CSPD 1591–4*, p. 78)][1] [c. *July 1591*]

Reasons to show that I should receive present payment for the victual prepared by me for the fleet serving under my charge at the Isles of the Azores in *anno* 1590.

First, I was appointed to provide victual for that fleet by Her Majesty's consent, which was performed for 6 months, with condition by Her Highness's promise that if the enterprise were stayed, then Her Majesty would repay unto me the whole charge of that provision.

When the charge was fully performed by me and the ships ready victualled, it was Her Highness's pleasure to stay the journey, whereupon Her Highness gave order that I should be satisfied for the victual so by me provided.

The charge of the said victual for 1,340 men for 6 months after the rate of 8d for every man by the day, by reason the victual was choice and the cask dear, did amount unto the sum of – £7,504.

Whereof, there was assigned by my Lord Treasurer to be paid unto me by Mr Quarles[2] for 4 months' victual for the said number of £1,340 men after the rate of 6d every man *per diem* the sum of – £3,752.

[1]See Williamson, *Hawkins* (1927), p. 458.

[2]James Quarles, Clerk of the Queen's Kitchen, appointed Surveyor-General of Naval Victualling jointly with Baeshe by patent 27 Nov. 1582: *CPR 1582–3*, no. 433; Oppenheim, *History*, p. 142 & n. 3, citing BL, Lansdowne MS 62, f. 132. He took over as Surveyor on Baeshe's death in May 1587, and the victualling accounts in his name run from 1 July that year to 31 Dec. 1593. Those for 1594 and 1595 were tendered by his executrix (see Appendix 1 below), but he certainly lived until 1595, being reappointed to the commission of the peace in Essex and Herts. in July, and resigning his patent 7 Nov., a renewal being issued the following day to him jointly with Marmaduke Darrell: *CPR 1594–5*, nos 541, 746, 753, 1035.

And so, there remaineth to be paid unto me for 2 months' victual after the rate of 6d by the day – £1,876.

And more, there is to be paid unto me for the increase of 2d by the day for the whole 6 months – £1,876.

And so the whole amounteth to the sum of £3,752.

Of which sum I do most humbly desire payment as by Her Majesty's gracious order and promise was always appointed.

[*Signed*] John Hawkins.

For money disbursed for sundry emptions for the better furnishing of Her Highness's said ships before their going forth and after their return in the West Country, as is entered upon the books of *anno* 1590, for which there was no warrant granted by Her Majesty, the sum of – £572 8s.

For wages paid to the companies of the said ships, by means of their long stay at the seas, for which there was no warrant granted by Her Majesty, the sum of – £1,775 13s.

[*sub-total*] – £2,349 1s.

For sea victuals, as appeareth on the other side [*above*] £3,752.

Totalis – £6,101 1s.

[*Signed*] John Hawkins.

Appendix 1

LISTS OF ACCOUNTS: TREASURER OF THE NAVY AND THE SURVEYOR-GENERAL OF VICTUALLING FOR THE NAVY TO 1603

The main sets of Declared Accounts are in E 351 (Exchequer, Declared Accounts in Rolls); they are handsomely written and on parchment. The versions in AO 1 (Auditors of the Imprest and Commissioners of Audit, ditto) are paper duplicates, sometimes with slight variations in stated terminal dates as shown here. These lists omit some supplementary accounts for parts of years or particular operations which are numbered within the sequences of the main annual series.

Treasurer of the Navy: Quarter Books

Bodleian ref. MS Rawlinson	*Accountant*	*Years*	*Corresponding Declared Account*
A. 200	Benjamin Gonson	1562–3 [**4**]	E 351/2199
A. 201	Gonson	1570	E 351/2206
A. 202	Gonson	1574	E 351/2210
A. 203	John Hawkins	1578	E 351/2214
A. 206	Fulke Grevill	1600	E 351/2238

Treasurer of the Navy: Declared Accounts

PRO reference	*Accountant(s)*	*Term*
E 351/2888	Robert Legge	25 Dec. 1546–25 Dec. 1547 [*NEM*, I.80]
E 351/2194	Benjamin Gonson	29 Sept. 1548–24 Oct. 1551 [*NEM*, I.81]
E 351/2195	Gonson	29 Sept. 1554–25 Dec. 1555 [*NEM*, I.89]
E 351/2196	Gonson	25 Dec. 1555–25 Dec. 1556 [*NEM*, II.90]
E 351/2197	Gonson	1 Jan. 1559–31 Dec. 1560
AO 1/1682/1	~	~
AO 1/1784/297	~	~
E 351/2198	Gonson	1 Jan. 1561–1 Jan. 1562
AO 1/1682/2	~	~
E 351/2199	Gonson	1 Jan. 1562–31 Dec. 1563 [**5**]
E 351/2200	Gonson	1 Jan. 1564–31 Dec. 1564

E 351/2201	Gonson	1 Jan. 1565–31 Dec. 1565
AO 1/1682/3	~	~
E 351/2202	Gonson	1 Jan. 1566–31 Dec. 1566
E 351/2203	Gonson	1 Jan. 1567–31 Dec. 1567
AO 1/1682/4	~	~
E 351/2204	Gonson	1 Jan. 1568–31 Dec. 1568
E 351/2205	Gonson	1 Jan. 1569–31 Dec. 1569
AO 1/1682/5	~	~
E 351/2206	Gonson	1 Jan. 1570–31 Dec. 1570
AO 1/1682/6	~	~
E 351/2207	Gonson	1 Jan. 1571–31 Dec. 1571
E 351/2208	Gonson	1 Jan. 1572–31 Dec. 1572
AO 1/1682/7	~	~
E 351/2209	Gonson	1 Jan. 1573–31 Dec. 1573
AO 1/1683/8	~	~
E 351/2210	Gonson	1 Jan. 1574–31 Dec. 1574
AO 1/1683/9	~	~
E 351/2211	Gonson	1 Jan. 1575–31 Dec. 1575
AO 1/1683/10	~	~
E 351/2212	Gonson *per* R. Paterson & his wife	1 Jan. 1576–31 Dec. 1576
AO 1/1683/11	~	~
E 351/2213	Gonson	1 Jan. 1577–31 Dec. 1577
AO 1/1683/12	~	~
E 351/2214	John Hawkins	1 Jan. 1578–31 Dec. 1578
AO 1/1684/13	~	~
E 351/2215	Hawkins	1 Jan. 1579–31 Dec. 1579
AO 1/1684/14	~	~
E 351/2216	Hawkins	1 Jan. 1580–31 Dec. 1580
AO 1/1684/15	~	~
E 351/2217	Hawkins	1 Jan. 1581–31 Dec. 1581
AO 1/1684/16	~	~
E 351/2218	Hawkins	1 Jan. 1582–31 Dec. 1582
AO 1/1684/17	~	~
E 351/2219	Hawkins	1 Jan. 1583–31 Dec. 1583
AO 1/1685/18	~	~
E 351/2220	Hawkins	1 Jan. 1584–31 Dec. 1584
AO 1/1685/19	~	~
E 351/2221	Hawkins	1 Jan. 1585–31 Dec. 1585
AO 1/1685/20	~	~
E 351/2223	Hawkins	1 Jan. 1586–31 Dec. 1586
AO 1/1685/21	~	~
E 351/2224	Sir J. Hawkins *per* executrix	1 Jan. 1587–31 Dec. 1587
AO 1/1685/22	~	~
E 351/2225	Sir J. Hawkins *per* executrix	1 Jan. 1588–31 Dec. 1588
AO 1/1686/23	~	~
E 351/2226	Sir J. Hawkins *per* executrix	1 Jan. 1589–31 Dec. 1589
AO 1/1686/24	~	~
E 351/2227	Sir J. Hawkins *per* executrix	1 Jan. 1590–31 Dec. 1590
AO 1/1686/25	~	~

E 351/2228	Sir J. Hawkins *per* executrix	1 Jan. 1591–31 Dec. 1591
AO 1/1687/26	~	~
E 351/2229	Sir J. Hawkins *per* executrix	1 Jan. 1592–31 Dec. 1592
AO 1/1687/27	~	~
E 351/2230	Sir J. Hawkins *per* executrix	1 Jan. 1593–31 Dec. 1593
AO 1/1687/28	~	~
E 351/2231	Sir J. Hawkins *per* executrix	1 Jan. 1594–31 Dec. 1594
AO 1/1688/29	~	~
E 351/2232	Sir J. Hawkins *per* executrix	1 Jan. 1595–24 Apr. 1596
AO 1/1688/31	*Sir J. H. & Sir Francis Drake* per *H.'s executrix*	~
E 351/2233	Hawkins & Drake *per* executors	1 Jan. 1595–1 Mar. 1596
AO 1/1688/30	~	*1 Jan. 1595–31 Dec. 1595*
E 351/2234	R. Langforde	6 May 1596–31 Dec. 1596
AO 1/1689/32	~	~
E 351/2235	Langforde	1 Jan. 1597–31 Dec. 1597
AO 1/1689/33	~	~
E 351/2236	Langforde	1 Jan. 1598–31 Dec. 1598
AO 1/1689/34	~	~
E 351/2237	Fulke Grevill	1 Jan. 1599–31 Dec. 1599
AO 1/1690/35	~	~
E 351/2238	Grevill	1 Jan. 1600–31 Dec. 1600
AO 1/1690/36	~	~
E 351/2239	Grevill	1 Jan. 1601–31 Dec. 1601
AO 1/1690/37	~	~
E 351/2240	Sir F. Grevill	1 Jan. 1602–31 Dec. 1602
AO 1/1691/38	~	~
E 351/2241	Grevill	1 Jan. 1603–31 Dec. 1603
AO 1/1691/39	~	*28 June 1602–3 Jan. 1604*

Surveyor-General of Victualling: Quarter Books

BL reference	*Accountant*	*Year*	*Corresponding Declared Account*
Harleian MS 167 ff. 1–38v	Edward Baeshe	1563	E 351/2360

Surveyor-General of Victualling: Declared Accounts

PRO reference	*Accountant(s)*	*Term*
E 351/2353	Edward Baeshe & Richard Wattes	1 July 1547–28 June 1550 [*NEM*, I.85]
E 351/2354	Wattes	8 Sept. 1548–28 June 1550 [*NEM*, I.86]
E 351/2355	Baeshe	28 June 1550–29 Sept. 1552 [*NEM*, I.87]

E 351/2356	Baeshe	29 Sept. 1552–1 Jan. 1555 [*NEM*, II.92]
E 351/2357	Baeshe	1 Jan. 1555–31 Dec. 1556 [*NEM*, II.93]
E 351/2358	Baeshe	1 Jan. 1559–1 Jan. 1561
AO 1/1784/298	~	*1 Jan. 1559–31 Dec. 1560*
E 351/2359	Baeshe	1 Jan. 1561–31 Dec. 1561
AO 1/1784/299	~	~
E 351/2360	Baeshe	31 Dec. 1561–31 Dec. 1563
AO 1/1748/300	~	*1 Jan. 1562–31 Dec. 1563*
E 351/2361	Baeshe & John Elliott	31 Dec. 1563–31 Dec. 1564
E 351/2362	Baeshe	1 Jan. 1565–31 Dec. 1565
E 351/2363	Baeshe	1 Jan. 1566–31 Dec. 1566
E 351/2364	Baeshe	1 Jan. 1567–31 Dec. 1567
E 351/2365	Baeshe	1 Jan. 1568–31 Dec. 1568
E 351/2366	Baeshe	1 Jan. 1569–31 Dec. 1569
AO 1/1785/304	~	~
E 351/2367	Baeshe	1 Jan. 1570–31 Dec. 1570
AO 1/1785/305	~	~
E 351/2368	Baeshe	1 Jan. 1571–31 Dec. 1571
AO 1/1785/306	~	~
E 351/2369	Baeshe	1 Jan. 1572–31 Dec. 1572
E 351/2370	Baeshe	1 Jan. 1573–31 Dec. 1573
AO 1/1785/307	~	~
E 351/2371	Baeshe	1 Jan. 1574–31 Dec. 1574
AO 1/1785/308	~	~
E 351/2372	Baeshe	1 Jan. 1575–31 Dec. 1575
AO 1/1786/309	~	~
E 351/2373	Baeshe	1 Jan. 1576–31 Dec. 1576
AO 1/1786/310	~	~
E 351/2374	Baeshe	1 Jan. 1577–31 Dec. 1577
AO 1/1786/311	~	~
E 351/2375	Baeshe	1 Jan. 1578–31 Dec. 1578
AO 1/1786/313	~	~
E 351/2376	Baeshe	1 Jan. 1579–31 Dec. 1579
AO 1/1786/314	~	~
E 351/2377	Baeshe	1 Jan. 1580–31 Dec. 1580
AO 1/1787/315	~	~
E 351/2378	Baeshe	1 Jan. 1581–31 Dec. 1581
AO 1/1787/317	~	~
E 351/2379	Baeshe	1 Jan. 1582–31 Dec. 1582
AO 1/1787/318	~	~
E 351/2380	Baeshe	1 Jan. 1583–31 Dec. 1583
AO 1/1787/319	~	~
E 351/2381	Baeshe	1 Jan. 1584–31 Dec. 1584
AO 1/1787/320	~	~
E 351/2382	Baeshe	1 Jan. 1585–31 Dec. 1585
AO 1/1787/321	~	~
E 351/2383	Baeshe	1 Jan. 1586–31 Dec. 1586
AO 1/1788/322	~	~

E 351/2384	Baeshe *per* executrix	1 Jan. 1587–30 June 1587
AO 1/1788/322A	~	~
E 351/2385	James Quarles	1 July 1587–31 Dec. 1587
AO 1/1788/323	~	~
E 351/2386	Quarles	1 Jan. 1588–31 Dec. 1588
AO 1/1788/325	~	~
E 351/2387	Quarles	1 Jan. 1589–31 Dec. 1589
AO 1/1789/326	~	~
E 351/2388	Quarles	1 Jan. 1590–31 Dec. 1590
AO 1/1789/327	~	~
E 351/2389	Quarles	1 Jan. 1591–31 Dec. 1591
AO 1/1789/328	~	~
E 351/2390	Quarles	1 Jan. 1592–31 Dec. 1592
AO 1/1789/330	~	~
E 351/2391	Quarles	1 Jan. 1593–31 Dec. 1593
AO 1/1790/331	~	~
E 351/2392	Quarles *per* executrix	1 Jan. 1594–31 Dec. 1594
AO 1/1790/332	~	~
E 351/2393	Quarles *per* executrix & Marmaduke Darell	1 Jan. 1595–31 Dec. 1595
AO 1/1790/333	~	~
E 351/2394	Quarles *per* ex. & Darell	1 Jan. 1596–31 Dec. 1596
AO 1/1790/334	~	~
E 351/2396	Quarles *per* ex. & Darell	1 Jan. 1597–31 Dec. 1597
AO 1/1791/337	~	~
E 351/2397	Quarles *per* ex. & Darell	1 Jan. 1598–31 Dec. 1598
AO 1/1792/339	~	~
E 351/2398	Quarles *per* ex. & Darell	1 Jan. 1599–31 Dec. 1599
AO 1/1792/340	~	~
E 351/2399	Darell	1 Jan. 1600–31 Dec. 1600
AO 1/1792/341	~	~
E 351/2400	Sir M. Darell	1 Jan. 1601–31 Dec. 1601
AO 1/1792/342	~	~
E 351/2401	Darell	1 Jan. 1602–31 Dec. 1602
AO 1/1792/343	~	~
E 351/2402	Darell	1 Jan. 1603–31 Dec. 1603
AO 1/1793/344	~	~

Appendix 2

GLOSSARY

This list is meant for quick reference, and includes technical terms and some obsolete words of general application. Terms appearing once only are mostly dealt with at that point. This is not a general dictionary, but has application only to the present volume. Since its purpose is to help the reader rather than highlight the editors' ignorance, uncertain terms are not included. This applies both to words which could not be interpreted (and therefore printed within inverted commas in the text), and to items described in commonplace words but the precise application of which cannot be stated. The definitions derive chiefly from *OED* and Captain John Smith's *Sea Grammar* in the edition by K. Goell (1970), assisted by previous NRS volumes and the glossary in Professor Rodger's *Safeguard of the Sea*. D. King, J. B. Hattendorf and J. Worth Estes, *A Sea of Words: A Lexicon and Companion for Patrick O'Brian's Seafaring Tales* (New York, 1995) is also useful, though its definitions reflect eighteenth-century usages which were sometimes different from those of the sixteenth.

Admiral. Sometimes used for a ship commanded by an Admiral.
advertisement. News, notice.
arrearages. Arrears.
Augmentations (court of). Government department which between 1536 and 1554 administered the properties of the dissolved monasteries and confiscations from the church; its residual functions were absorbed by the Exchequer.

band (of pitch, tar). A form of 'bond', meaning thickness, hence binding quality.
bay salt. Sea salt.
billet. Cut of firewood.
block. Pulley.
bonaventure (in full, bonaventure mizzen). Aftermost mast of a four-masted ship.
bowsprit. Spar extending from *stem*.
brigantine. Small oared warship.
brod. Round-headed nail.

cablet. Small cable.
caliver. Hand gun.
can hook. Rope or chain forming sling for cask.
chaldron. Cauldron, used as measure, *viz.* 32 bushels (4 quarters).
clap. Leather flange.
clench (nail). A form of 'clinch', having the point driven back into the material through which it has passed, forming a double-headed clamp, or hammered into a *rove*. In shipbuilding, used to fasten the overlapping planks or strakes in the construction of the hull (hence 'clinker-built').
cloveboard. A form of 'clapboard', i.e. a small size of split oak.
cock of brass. Socket of *block* or *shiver*.
conduct (of troops). Marshalling from place of recruitment to point of assembly, and home again. **Conduct money** was paid to the men per mile travelled.
crayer. Small merchantman.
crow. Crowbar.
customer. Customs collector.

Dansk. (1) Danish. (2) Of Danzig (Gdansk), hence generally of Baltic goods, and so often indistinguishable from meaning (1).
deadshare. Supplementary payment or *reward.* Originally the actual pay due to men killed, taken by their officers as a perquisite, but having become a fixed bonus on a graduated scale payable to all officers and (eventually) crew.
deal. (1, and usually here) Sawn plank of fir or pine, hence **deal-boards** (2) Fir or pine wood itself.
device. Scheme, scheming.
diet. Provision of food and drink, or cash in lieu.
dowlas. Coarse linen, named from the place now Plougastel-Daoulas in Brittany, immediately south of Brest.
duplicament. Duplicate.

ell (measure). 45 inches; derived from length of a man's arm.
emptions. Purchases.
entertainment. Maintenance, in cash or kind (not show).
extraordinary (of funding). Whatever was not provided for by the *ordinary*, such as operational cost (no suggestion of oddity or unacceptable excess).

fid. Conical pin of hard wood used to splice rope.
firkin. Small cask, generally a quarter of a barrel or half a *kilderkin* (here often used as unit of measure rather than actual cask).

furniture. Supplies of any kind.

galliot. Small galley.
garnet. Clamp attached to lines for hauling cargo &c.
gun stone. Stone shot.

hogshead. Large cask, used as measure varying for particular commodities.
hoy. Small single-masted vessel.
hulk. Large vessel, descended from the medieval cog (not later meaning of dismasted and redundant vessel).

joined (of furniture). Made by joiner (better crafted than work of mere carpenter).
junk. Old rope.

keel. Lowermost longitudinal timber of ship.
knee. Right-angled timber bracing deck to hull, a fundamental component of ship construction.

last. Measure of capacity, varying by commodity and locality. For pitch and tar usually 2 barrels.
latchet, latchet line. Loop of cord for attaching additional canvas to catch wind.
lath. Small strip of wood.
lead line. Sounding line.
leech (elsewhere **leach**). Border of sail, hence **leech hooks** for attaching to line.
livery (arrows). Military issue.
luff hook. For attaching a **luff** (a tackle composed of a double and single block) to a strong point.

mapstave (variant of mopstave). Pole with *thrums* attached for sweeping or mopping.
marline. Light line of two strands.
marsh earth. Soil dug away to form and seal pond for docking ships, the activity of **marshmen**.
maund. Wicker basket.
medrinacks. Type of canvas, perhaps named from Medernach in Luxembourg.
mizzen. Aftermost mast of a ship, save where there was a fourth, *bonaventure* mizzen.

Narrow Seas. English Channel.

oleron. Canvas, named from the island Oléron on the Atlantic coast of France, north of La Rochelle.

ordinary (of funding). The fixed sum from which regular and anticipated expenses were met; so by extension the sums thus disbursed. Anything beyond was *extraordinary*.

overlop nail. A form of *clench*.

parcel. Item (not package).

parrel. Band of rope, chain, or iron collar by which middle of yard is fastened to mast.

pavis. Arrangement of shields on ship's side, originally defensive but becoming ornamental.

pinnace. (1) Small warship. (2) Great warship's boat. (3) Small vessel or tender of any kind.

pipe. Large cask, generally 4 barrels or 2 *hogsheads* (often used here as unit of measure rather than actual cask).

poiz. Abbreviation for 'poise' (weight).

polancre (pulley). Heavy lifting tackle.

poldavy. Coarse canvas, named from Pouldavid, west of Douranenez in Brittany.

portage. Burthen.

Portingal. Portuguese (ship).

practice. Scheme, plot.

prest. Sum of money advanced for public service.

Principal Secretary. Originally and still notionally the monarch's personal secretary, but developing into the 'Secretary of State' (as the term became settled in the seventeenth century). Usually two incumbents, though from 1558 to 1572 Sir William Cecil was sole Secretary and the Queen's first minister. The qualification 'principal' was in distinction to the Latin and French secretaries, who were never more than translators and draftsmen.

privy seal. Used to authenticate a large variety of official business not requiring the formality of letters patent under the great seal; the usual means by which the Crown authorised payments out of the Exchequer and itself triggered by the *signet*.

purveyor. Crown official procuring goods for public service by compulsory purchase at flat rate below market price; the system known as **purveyance** (though this word is also used in the general sense of conveyance).

quarter (measure). 28 pounds, i.e. a quarter of a hundredweight.

rafter. Straight timber from which oars were made.
ramhead. Stout timber forming the securing upper half of the foreyard or mainyard halyard tackle, the 'knight' forming the lower half.
ransack. Search and clean thoroughly (always here in this simple original sense).
ratline. Small line fastened to shrouds, serving as foot-holds.
redub. Repair.
reward. Bonus (not necessarily for exceptional service).
ring-bolt. Bolt with an eye at one end, to which a ring is attached. For securing ordnance and other uses.
River, the. The Thames.
road. Anchorage.
rod. Here always a natural straight shoot of wood.
rosin. Resin, specifically in solid form after distillation, and used as a preservative.
rouse. Cure with salt, hence **rouser**.
rove. Washer into which the point of *clench* nail is burred, i.e. hammered back, to form a rivet.
rowbarge. Here one of the small oared vessels built for Henry VIII in 1545/6, most of them sold in Edward VI's reign and replaced by pinnaces with the same names.
running glass. Hour glass.

sales. Sale of Crown lands/goods.
say. Fine serge.
scupper. Opening on ship's side at deck level, allowing water to drain away, so **scupper-leathers**.
server. Artisan's mate or assistant; see above, p. 20.
service. Military duty.
shide. Piece of wood split from another. As a quantity, half a cubic foot.
shipkeeper. Official in charge of laid-up ship(s).
shiver. Grooved wheel of a pulley, itself secured with a *cock*.
shore. Prop or strut, specifically one used to support ships being built or repaired.
signet. Notionally the monarch's personal seal, applied in the office of the Principal Secretaries, and used for letters and other documents requiring immediate despatch.
skiff. Ship's boat.
sledge. Sledgehammer.
sow (of lead). Block or ingot, of no fixed weight.

stem. Large upright timber forming central support at bow.
stockfish. Cod cured by exposure, but then needing to be beaten o mashed.
stocklock. Lock in wooden case.
stranger. Foreigner.
superplusage, surplusage (in account). Deficit.

tacks. Tackle.
talwood. Firewood, usually as cut to convenient size.
teller. Accounting clerk (as still current in banking); here always one o the four such on the establishment of the Exchequer of Receipt.
thrum. Strand of wool or cloth gathered to make mop heads, as i *mapstaves*.
tile pin. Wooden peg securing tile to framework of roof.
tilt. Awning or canopy, sometimes of hair cloth; hence **tilt hair**.
topgallant. Extension above topmast.
tops (of ship). Specifically the fighting tops (platforms atop mast); bu also used to enumerate the masts themselves, giving general indicatio of a ship's size.
travail/travel. The two words have a common etymology, and cannot b distinguished from the original spelling. Here 'travel' has been printe where the modern meaning of the term predominates.
treasure. Within the documents always meaning simply cash.
trenail. Wooden nail.
tunnage (as expense). Hire charge based on cargo capacity.

Vice-Admiral. (1) Chief agent of the Admiralty Court in each county; member of the local aristocracy or gentry, not a seaman. (2) Secon highest member of the Council for Marine Causes, also calle Lieutenant of the Admiralty (see above, p. xxiv). (3) Deputy to Lor Admiral afloat, or the like to any designated Admiral. (The term Admiral and Vice-Admiral were as yet used interchangeably since an 'Admiral' was himself considered the deputy of the Lord Admiral.)
victualler. (1) Man supplying victuals. (2) Ship carrying them.
vitry. Canvas, named from Vitré in Brittany.

waft/wafting. Convoy.
Wards and Liveries (court of). Government department handling certai of the Crown's feudal rights and revenues.
wey (of cheese). Standard measure, given in one source (1542) as 22 lbs.

Appendix 3

MANUSCRIPT DESCENTS

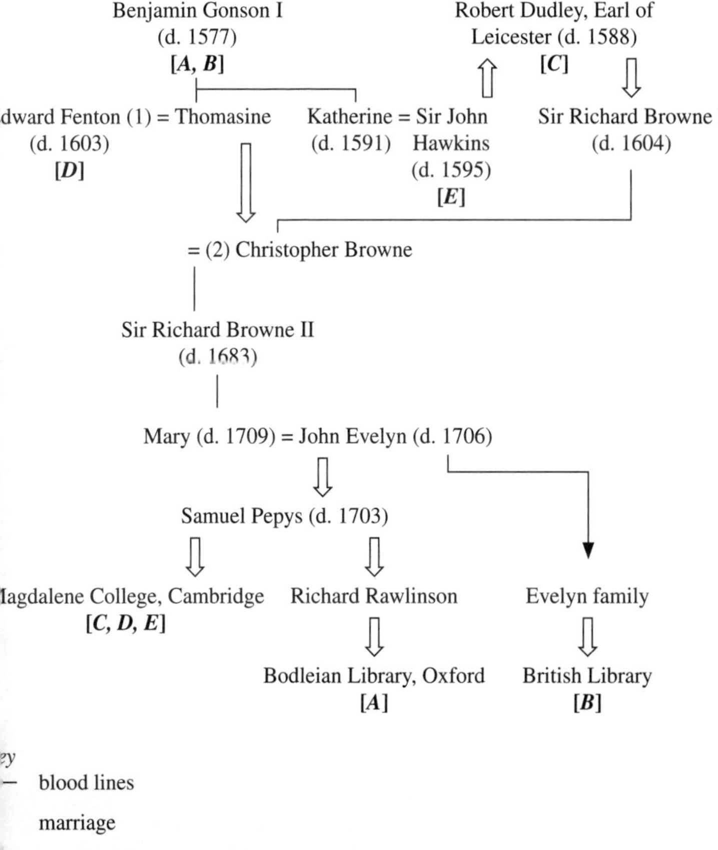

Key

— blood lines

marriage

further transmission of MSS

[A] Navy Treasurer's Quarter Books, including **4** above
[B] Draft sections of Quarter Books, etc. described in Appendix 4
[C] Leicester papers, eventually becoming Pepys's 'State Papers'
[D] Fenton's notebook as Deputy Treasurer, **37** above, and other papers
[E] Letters to Leicester, descending with [*C*], including **33–4** above

Details of individual transmissions are given above, pp. 21, 349, 611, 622, 661.

Appendix 4

DESCRIPTION OF BRITISH LIBRARY, ADD. MSS 78169–78171

'hese papers are principally drafts and other matter used in compiling the 562–3 Quarter Book. As mentioned above (p. 21 and Appendix 3), they orm part of the material which Mary Evelyn inherited from her Gonson ncestors; they remained among the Evelyn family papers after the)uarter Book itself had been given to Pepys. Following acquisition of the omplete Evelyn archive by the British Library, a descriptive list was ompiled for eventual publication, now available in the Library and via he online catalogue. We are grateful to the British Library Board and to)r F. Harris for permission to use the Library catalogue entry as the basis or this appendix. The original descriptions were the work of Mr H. Celliher, to whom we are also indebted. The BL format has been largely eshaped to serve the needs of the present volume. Spelling has been nodernised and other adjustments have been made to conform to our onventions. Minor diplomatic details have been omitted, and Gonson's rivate papers are treated more briefly. At the time of writing the papers emain in loose sections; it is intended that they should be bound with a onsecutive foliation for each numbered volume, and that foliation is nticipated here; but in order to preserve a record of the component ructure, the individual fragments are here distinguished by item numbers nd letters, which will not be marked on the documents.[1] We have added full transcript of one short item by way of general illustration of the rocess through which drafts and fragments were absorbed into the nished Quarter Book. The chosen example nevertheless shows that seful scraps of additional information can sometimes be found where nese working papers happen to survive.

L Add. MS 78169. Evelyn Papers, vol. II (formerly Evelyn MS 68)

enjamin Gonson's draft Quarter Book for Deptford yard for the fourth Christmas) quarter of 1562 (1 Oct.–31 Dec.) [*as finalised in* **4**, ff. 42–57 above, pp. 79–106)].

[1]The BL's provisional catalogue currently distinguishes the elements of Add. MS 78171 items 1 (a)–(g) and 2; in the description below, this format is also applied to Add. MS 3170.

[ff. 1–6] Payments for ships' companies (*Sun* … *Aid*) and dockyard officers, (Marshe … Saunder) [**4**, ff. 42–45v (pp. 80–6)]

[f. 7] New heading [*omitted in* **4** *but reproduced in annotation above*]

[ff. 7–10v] Payments to workforce (shipwrights … victualling) [**4**, ff. 46–48v (pp. 86–91)]

[f. 11] Lodging [*naming all lodging keepers, with numbers of men, beds and days; only summarised in* **4**, f. 48v (p. 92)]

[ff. 11v–13v] Payments to workforce (house-carpenters … watchmen) [**4**, ff. 49–50v (pp. 92–6)]

[ff. 14–22v] Emptions [*elements, differently ordered, of section finalised in* **4**, ff. 51–7 (pp. 96–106)] [f. 23 *blank*]

[f. 24v] Victualling [*itemising commodities, only summarised in* **4**, f. 48v (p. 91)]

[Found as single sewn gathering. Formally written, with marginal addenda in the hand of Stephen Alexander, mostly recording discharge of sums, many indicating the payment to masters of their servers' wages along with their own. Latest dated annotation refers to a partial payment made 2 October 1563: above, p. 85 n. 3. At the foot of each page is a note of audit according to the abacus (auditors' use).]

BL Add. MS 78170. Evelyn Papers, vol. III (formerly Evelyn MS 69)

(a) Fragments of Gonson's draft Quarter Book for Deptford yard for the third (Michaelmas) quarter of 1563 (1 July–30 Sept.) [*the whole finalised as* **4**, ff. 200–214v]

[ff. 1–3v] Emptions [*elements, differently ordered, of section finalised in* **4**, ff 208v–214v (pp. 285–309); *including complete listing of oakum pickers summarised in* **4**, f. 213v (pp. 307–8)].

[Found as a loose leaf and a loose bifolium. Each page signed by William Holstock and George Winter]

(b) Draft of Gonson's Quarter Book for Deptford yard for the fourth (Christmas) quarter of 1563 (1 Oct.–31 Dec.) [*finalised as* **4**, ff. 216–2… (pp. 309–27)]

[f. 4] Cover with title.

[f. 5] Heading [*omitted* **4**, f. 218v; *reproduced in annotation above*]

[ff. 5–7v] Payments to workforce (shipwrights … victualling) [*as* **4**, ff. 218v–219v (pp. 313–16)]

[f. 8] Lodging [*naming all lodging keepers, with numbers of men, beds and days named; only summarised in* **4**, f. 220 (p. 316)] [ff. 8v–9v] Payments to workforce (house-carpenters … watchmen [*as* 4, ff. 220–21 (pp. 317–18)]

[ff. 10–17] Emptions [*partial and differently ordered draft for* **4**, ff. 221v–226 (pp. 319–27), *with several entries marked as paid in instalments*] [ff. 17v–18v *blank*]

[f. 19] Victualling [*itemising commodities, for which only summary in* 4, f. 220 (p. 316)] [f. 19v *blank*]

[ff. 20–22v] Heading, and payments to officers (Marshe … Alexander) *as* **4**, ff. 216–18 (pp. 309–12)]

[f. 22v] New heading [*omitted in* **4**], and payments to mariners of *George* [**4**, f. 216 (p. 310)]

Found as single sewn gathering. Original and marginalia as Add. 78169. Latest dated annotation refers to a partial payment made 21 August 1565: above, p. 322 & n. 1. Each page signed by William Holstock and George Winter]

c) Fragment of Gonson's draft Quarter Book for Woolwich yard for the first (Lady Day) quarter of 1563 (1 Jan.–31 Mar.) [*the whole finalised as* **4**, ff. 227–9 (pp. 327–30)]

[f. 23r–v] Payments to officers [as **4**, f. 227 (p. 328)] and Emptions [*all but one of elements finalised in* **4**, ff. 228v–229 (pp. 329–30); *with another not carried in final account*]

Found as loose leaf. Signed by Holstock and George Winter]

BL Add. MS 78171. Evelyn Papers, vol. IV

[1] Further drafts and supplementary papers relating to Benjamin Gonson's official accounts, 1562–64 (from Evelyn MSS 68, 69 and 283)

a) Bills for timber delivered to Deptford in Midsummer and Christmas quarters 1562 [*relating to entries in* **4**, ff. 23v–24, 53r–v (pp. 53–5, 100)]

[ff. 1–2] Midsummer quarter 1562. Charges for carrying timber of Bamford, Bridger and Leche for shores out of West Wood, 30 June 1562. 66 loads of Bamford's timber from Rushmore ('Russehmun') Hill to Deptford – £8 17s 4d. Shores for Deptford and Woolwich of Leche, from West Wood – £5 9s 8d. Richard Gyldun for felling 94 loads of shores in West Wood – 27s 6d. Queen's timber from Fickleshole: carriage – £6 10s 1d; sawyers – 10s 8d [**4**, ff. 23v–24 (pp. 53–5)].[1]

[1]Only the last two figures can be identified in the relevant quarter's account, but Bamford is there paid a much larger sum for 66½ loads of timber, and Gyldun (otherwise Golden) is paid a smaller amount for loading carts in West Wood.

Minuted: *per* S. Alexander.

Midsummer quarter 1562. Bridger's timber from Cudham ('Cowdam') to Deptford – £5.

Thomas Burde for lading carts at Cudham ('Cawdam') – 4s 6d [**4**, f. 24 (p. 55); at 'Prebill Hill']

Richard Basset for loading carts at Fickleshole – 6s.

Christmas quarter 1562. To Bridger 28 October for timber from 'Prebilhill' to Deptford – £3 4s, and from 'Fysshers oke' to Deptford – £ 6s 4d. [*Sum*] – £5 1s 4d.

Minuted: *per* S. Alexander.

Total – £38 7s 6d.

Paid to Leche 30 October 1562 in part payment of this bill – £20.

[Found as separate bifolium loose in Add. MS 78169. Mostly crossed through]

[ff. 3–10] Payments by John Leche of Deptford, carpenter, 8 Nov. 1562 to sundry persons for carrying the Queen's timber provided by Henry Bamford, George Bridger, Henry Awstyn and Leche himself, purveyors from divers woods in Kent, and delivered at Deptford for building and repairing the Queen's ships.

Carriage of Bamford's timber – £8 13s 9d

Debts owing by Bamford to divers persons – £4 6s 8d

Carriage of Bridger's timber – £7 17s 7d

Carriage of the Queen's timber from Fickleshole – £7 18s 11½d; marked as entered in Christmas quarter 1562 [*summarised in* **4**, f. 53 (p. 100)]

Carriage of the Queen's shores out of West Wood to Deptford 1562 – 46s 5d; carriage of shores out of West Wood to the slaughter house[1] at Deptford, for Woolwich, by Leche – £3 4s 2d; both marked as entered in Christmas quarter 1562 [*combined and summarised ibid*. Each page of this section signed by George Winter]

Carriage of Awystn's timber out of Eltham – 10s 3d; marked as entered in Deptford 1562 [*summarised ibid.*]

Sum total – £13 19s 10d. *With other calculations.*

[Found as single sewn gathering loose in Add. MS 78169]

[1]Cf. item 1(g) below. This term could mean a fortification: *OED* 'slaughter-house', citing Edward VI in his journal as the first instance of a rare usage (30 July 1552: W. K. Jordan (ed.), *The Chronicle and Political Papers of King Edward VI* (Ithaca NY, 1966), 138 & n. 127). But there is no evidence for bulwarks defending the yards, and such structures could scarcely have stored ships' timbers; the Brightlingsea reference is in any case to hired premises. We must accept the odd coincidence that in both places a slaughter-house, in the usual sense (and not necessarily related to naval purposes), was sometimes used for wood or other dockyard stores.

b) Fragment of Gonson's draft Quarter Book for Portsmouth yard for he fourth or Christmas quarter 1563 (1 Oct.–31 Dec.) [*as finalised in* **4**, f. 302–307v (pp. 424–32)]

[ff. 11–18] All payments to ships' companies and workforce (*Antelope* .. labourers). Emptions (first element only) [*as rearranged in* **4**, ff. 302–7 pp. 424–31)]

Each page signed by Holstock and George Winter. Some marginal notes or rearrangement of entries, as. 'Enter among the labourers'; one such n a separate slip (f. 16A) pasted in, also signed by Holstock]

c) Account book of Thomas Morley for works at Portsmouth 1563

Charges sustained as well in grounding of the Queen's Majesty's ships t Portsmouth dock, as also in perfecting of the *Jennet*'s dock for the ringing in of the *Hart*; which charges began and money defrayed since pril last, 1563, and included in Midsummer quarter ending the 5 of June cf. **4**, ff. 284, 285, 336v (above, pp. 400–2, 475)].

Statement of the final account, with Morley's autograph note of receipt, November 1563

Inserted papers (*found loose*):

Owing to Robert Haselet and Edmund Clerk of Bursledon ('Bursseldon') or the freight of 18,350 of talwood brought from Curbridge ('Kirbridg') the dock, as appearing by books delivered to [Richard] Howlett, at 2s d the 1,0000 – £2 6s 10d, certified *per me* John Thomas.

Minuted: 12 August 1563. William Winter.

Owing to the bearer Hugh Bruer of Bursledon ('Burselldine') for the eight of 8, 10, or 12 thousand tall wood from Curbridge ('Cyrbryge') the dock near Portsmouth two years past, as appearing by bill of arriage delivered to Howlett at his last being at Portsmouth. Written 19 pril 1561, and witnessed as a true copy of a bill of John Thomas for ugh Bower [*with signatures of others*].

Minuted: 12 August 1563. Mr Morley, I pray you pay this poor man. V. Winter.[1]

ound as single sewn gathering, incompletely foliated. Partly deleted by rossing through, and bearing occasional marginal notes in another hand]

[1]Richard Howlett was succeeded as Clerk of the Ships by George Winter on 10 Oct. 1560. either payment is mentioned in the 1562–63 Quarter Book.

(d) Fragment relating to next item

Pen trials, including 'Thomas Wilson for victualling' several times.

[Found as single leaf loose in Add. MS 78170. In same hand as **(e)**]

(e) Summary of bills from Thomas Wilson, ironmonger; heade 'Thomas Willson his reckoning, to end the last of December 1562, fo victuals' [*in fact summarising bills for ironwork except as here noted i this synopsis*]:

Deptford, 31 March, ironwork – £10 6s 1d [above, p. 39]; 30 June – £4 0s 1½d, £2 4s 2d [pp. 46–7, 50]; 30 September [*victualling*] – £295 12 1d [p. 67]; 31 December [*victualling*] – £229 10s 4d [p. 91]. Gillingham 30 June – £18 5s 4d [pp. 139–40]; 30 September – £7 15s 2d [p. 155] Deptford, 30 September – £91 0s 7d [p. 72]; 31 December – £193 7s 9 [p. 101 (where £183 7s 10d)]. Gillingham, 30 September – £10 3s 4d [p 156]. [*Sum*] – £83 11s 1d.

Some additional calculations

[Found as single leaf loose in Add. MS 78170]

(f) Retrospective settlement of the account of the Colchester purveyo John Dethick, 1563

Receipt by Richard Dethick for payment by Gonson of his father Joh Dethicke's reckoning made 15 June 1564 for work done in Michaelma and Christmas quarters 1563.

Marginated: These two bills may be sent up by the next messenger fo the discharge of these two sums.

First due to him in Michaelmas quarter 1563 for provisions – £244 1 10d [above, p. 305; in Add. MS 78170 marked as paid to Richard Dethick

More to him in Christmas quarter 1563 for like – £54 5s 4d [above, p 322, where 4½d; and in Add. MS 78170, f. 12, marked as paid to Richar Dethick]

[*Sum*] – £298 19s 2d.

Paid to him at various times [*sums itemised*] – £212 4s 6d.

Resteth to clear his reckoning – £86 14s 8d, which sum Richard Dethic has received the day abovesaid from Benjamin Gonson. *Per me* Richar Dethick.

[Found as single leaf loose in Add. MS 78170]

(g) Charges to be entered in Quarter Book for Colne yard for the third or Michaelmas quarter 1563 (1 July–30 Sept) [*components finalised in* **4**, f. 273 (above, pp. 387–8); *here fully transcribed*][1]

1563. To Edward Lambard for his wages at 12d the day in keeping of the storehouses and timber-yard at Brightlingsea, begun the first day of July and ended the last day of September, which is 92 days – £4 12s.

To Thomas Richardson for his shipkeeping wages and victuals in keeping of the *Trinity Harry*, at 6d the day, begun and ended as before written, which is 92 days – £2 6s.

To Robert Consent with three other labourers besides the shipkeeper n having the water out of the dock at divers times in this quarter – 7s 4d.

To William Beryff of Brightlingsea for the rent of the storehouses and ground where the great dock is at Brightlingsea for this quarter – 13s 4d.

To Thomas Berryff of Brightlingsea for the rent of the slaughter-house 'sclarter howse')[2] and ground where the *Salamander*'s dock was for this quarter – 6s 8d.

[*Sum*] – £8 5s 4d.

[*Minuted*] Entered in Colne in Michaelmas quarter 1563. *Per* S. Alexander.

[*Endorsed*] A copy of the Quarter Book for the charges at Colne begun the first day of July and ended the last of September.

Found as single leaf in Evelyn papers, exact location not recorded by BL. nformally written, and probably sent up from the yard]

2] Gonson family estate and business papers, 1572–7 (formerly Evelyn MS 290; found with Add. MS 78244)

These relate partly to the manor of Fritwell, Oxon, formerly granted to William Gonson in 1530, descending through his son Christopher (d. 553) to his grandson Benjamin (d. 25 June 1576), and of which the Earl of Rutland was lord: see *VCH Oxon*. vi, p. 138. Benjamin (III) of Fritwell was thus the nephew of Benjamin (I), Navy Treasurer (d. 1577), and first ousin of Benjamin (II), of Great Baddow, Clerk of the Ships (d. 1600). *Papers more fully described in BL catalogue*]

[1]This draft is of special interest because it confirms that Stephen Alexander was the scribe f the latter part of the 1562–63 Quarter Book (cf. above, p. 21 & n. 2). It adds to our nowledge of the small establishment known as Colne, showing that this was located not eside but within Brightlingsea (cf. above, p. 175 n. 2). It also provides the last known eference to the *Salamander*. The low level of activity in the Colne yard suggests that her areer ended there.

[2]The final version of this gives the usual formula: 'a certain storehouse and ground'.

(a) Receipts from named tenants in Fritwell and Somerton, Oxon. 24 October 1572. Signed by Benjamin (I) and Sir John Hawkins. With a contemporary copy.

(b) Receipt by Roger Wood, servant of the Earl of Rutland, to Benjamin (I) and Hawkins for 200 marks in full payment for the earl's lease of the manor of Fritwell: Rolls Chapel, 29 September 1573.

(c) Memorandum by Thomas Ellus of an agreement between Benjamin (I) and [Edmund] Hopcroft for the purchase by Hopcroft of two tenements in Fritwell, with one close in the occupation of Benjamin (III) of Fritwell, n.d. [*c.* 1573].

(d) Letter of Benjamin (III) to Benjamin (I), relating to his outstanding debt, 8 April 1575.

(e) Letter of [? Florence] Harle to [Benjamin (II)] following the death of his cousin and the writer's son-in-law Benjamin (III), relating to the debt inherited by his widowed daughter: Duddington, 27 June 1576.

(f) Letter of John Edmondes to Benjamin (II) at Great Baddow relating to money owed to the writer's sister[-in-law], Gonson's kinswoman: Tower Street, 21 August 1577.

(g) Six letters, &c., in Spanish, relating to shipping business, most dated 2 December 1549.

LIST OF SOURCES

Fuller details, including references to any other MS copies and previous printings, will be found in the first footnotes of entries.

Section I: First Naval Business in the State Papers

No.	Document	Date	Reference
1	List of ships	20 Feb 1559	SP 12/2, no. 30
2	Ordinances for Admiralty officers	*c.* 1560	SP 12/15, no. 4

Section II: The Navy Treasurer's Quarter Book for 1562–1563

No.	Document	Date	Reference
3	Privy Seal warrant	28 Oct 1563	E 404/115, bundle 5 Eliz. I
4	Quarter Book	1562–3	Bodl. MS Rawlinson A. 200

Section III: The Navy Treasurer's Declared Account for 1562–1563

No.	Document	Date	Reference
5	Declared Account	1562–3	E 351/2199

Section IV: Extracts from James Humphrey's Book of Forms, 1568

No.	Document	Date	Reference
6	Writ for recruitment of seamen	20 Mar 1568	PL 1266, p. 171
7	Order for conduct money	12 Mar 1568	PL 1266, p. 172
8	Order for recruits to report	25 Mar 1568	PL 1266, p. 173
9	Pass for a seaman discharged	10 Jun 1566	PL 1266, p. 174
10	Passport for a seaman discharged	18 Jun 1566	PL 1266, p. 175
11	Pass for discharge of merchantman	17 Mar 1564	PL 1266, p. 176
12	Pass for merchantman detained	1 Aug 1566	PL 1266, p. 177
13	Order for detention of merchantman	11 Jun 1560	PL 1266, p. 178
14	Orders for warrants for payments to Admiralty officers	[undated]	PL 1266, pp. 181–2
15	Rates of wages	[undated]	PL 1266, pp. 189–91

Section V: Papers relating to Wages and Wage Rates

No.	Document	Date	Reference
16	Estimate for monthy sea wages	14 Oct 1562	SP 12/25, no. 13
17	Estimate for monthy sea wages	30 Nov 1562	SP 12/25, no. 66
18	Naval charges	1564–65	BL, Cotton MS. Otho E. IX, ff. 120–4
19	Comparison of ordinary and extraordinary charges	*c.* Apr 1585	PL 2875, p. 60

20	Proposed increase of wages	28 Dec 1585	SP 12/185, nos 33, 33(ii)
21	Acceptance of new wage rates	*c*. June 1586	SP 12/186, no. 43
22	Rates of wages	Dec 1587	Bodl., MS Rawlinson A. 171, ff. 310–13
23	Summary of ordinary and extraordinary	27 June 1587	SP 12/202, no. 35

Section VI: The Navy Victualler's 1565 Contract and related papers

24	Report by Baeshe to Privy Council	11 Nov 1562	SP 12/25, no. 48
25	Report by Baeshe to Privy Council	5 Dec 1562	SP 12/26, no. 3
26	Report by Baeshe to Privy Council	24 Oct 1563	Hatfield House, Cecil Papers 154/36
27	Report by Baeshe to Privy Council	17 Dec 1563	Hatfield House, Cecil Papers 154/43
28	Baeshe's contract	13 Apr 1565	BL, Cotton MS. Otho E IX, ff. 99–102v, 116–19
29	Adjustment of contract	17 July 1573	SP 12/191, no. 28(ii)
30	Estimate for victualling	20 April 1574	SP 12/95, no. 81
31	Report by Baeshe to Lord Admiral	23 July 1586	SP 12/191, no. 28(i)
32	Baeshe to Walsingham	24 July 1586	SP 12/191, no. 28

Section VII: Papers relating to Sir John Hawkins as Treasurer of the Navy

33	Hawkins to Queen	20 Sep 1565	PL 2502, pp. 427–8
34	Hawkins to Leicester	4 June 1570	PL 2503, pp. 371–2
35	Patent for Gonson and Hawkins	18 Nov 1577	C 66/1172, mm. 2–3
36	Privy Council to Navy officers	22 Mar 1585	SP 12/177, no. 32

Section VIII: Edward Fenton's Notebook and other papers relating to the Expedition of 1590

37	Notebook of Edward Fenton	1588–91	PL 513
38	Hawkins to Burghley	12 Sep 1589	SP 12/226, no. 30
39	Estimate for setting out ships	Jan 1590	SP 12/230, no. 35
40	Estimate from Navy Board	9 Feb 1590	SP 12/ 230, no. 66
41	Privy Council agenda	23 Feb 1590	SP 12/230 no. 80
42	Hawkins to Burghley	1 Mar 1590	SP 12/231, no. 2
43	Warrant for increased ordinary	13 Mar 1590	SP 15/13, no. 132
44	Hawkins to Burghley	16 April 1590	SP 12/231, no. 83
45	Hawkins to Burghley	31 Oct 1590	SP 12/233, no. 118
46	Estimate for victuals	7 Nov 1590	SP 12/234, no. 9
47	Estimate for paying off men	7 Nov 1590	SP 12/234, no. 10
48	Hawkins to Burghley	8 Dec 1590	SP 12/234, no. 49
49	Summary of expenses	10 Dec 1590	SP 12/234, no. 51
50	Expenses claimed by Hawkins	*c*. July 1591	SP 12/239, no. 108

INDEX

Roman abbreviations are used for the dockyards and other principal locations:

B	Bristol
C	Chatham
Co	Colne (Brightlingsea)
D	Deptford
Dv	Dover
H	Harwich
G	Gillingham
L	London
P	Portsmouth
R	Rye
T	Thames
U	Upnor
W	Woolwich
Y	Great Yarmouth

Within parentheses these letters show association with a yard (as of merchants serving in oods) rather than actual employment there. The symbol > is used in conjunction with these bbreviations and other place names to indicate movement. The destination is not always he place at which men were subsequently listed for payment. The term ‘conductor’ is pplied to all involved in recruiting, mustering and conducting seamen, soldiers and ockyard workers. ‘Proxy’ here means those receiving money on behalf of others. Longer ntries reflect the successive postings given in the Quarter Book, the arrangement of which s not wholly chronological. In order to distinguish or combine index entries for individual ames, the days of paid work in each quarter have been compared. This sometimes stablishes separate identities; but rather more often it suggests that men were shifted from ob to job and from place to place. Very often a group of men would move together, and ockyard workers regularly transferred to and from ships. The frequency with which unusual ames reappear in differing employments encourages the presumption of similiar mobility mong the rest.

alic upper-case abbreviations are used for names of royal ships:

D	*Aid*
N	*Antelope*
B	*Bark of Boulogne*
C	*Bark of Cherbourg*
E	*Bear*
F	*Bright Falcon*
G	*Brigantine*
K	*Black Bark*
L	*Bull*
R	*Christopher*
R	*Double Rose*
J	*Elizabeth Jonas*
L	*Flower de Luce*
N	*Falcon*
B	*Great Bark*
C	*Greyhound Bitch*
D	*Green Dragon*
E	*George Hoy*
GH	*Greyhound*
GL	*Galley Eleanor*
GM	*Galley Mermaid/Black Galley*
GP	*Gryphon*
GS	*Galley Speedwell*
GT	*Galley Tryright*
GU	*Guide*
HP	*Hope*
HR	*Hare*
HT	*Hart*
JL	*Jesus (of Lübeck)*
JT	*Jennet*
LN	*(Golden) Lion*
MD	*Maiden*
MG	*Mary Grace hoy*
MK	*Makeshift I*
MN	*Minion*
MR	*Mary Rose*

MW *Mary Willoughby*
NB *New Bark*
OW *Owlet*
PM *Philip and Mary* later *Nonpareil*
PR *Primrose I*
PT *Post*
PX *Phoenix*
RH *Red Hart*
RV *Raven*
RW *Rowbarge*
SH *Sparrowhawk*
SK *Saker*
SM *Salamander*
SN *Sun*
SP *Serpent*
SR *Searcher*
SW *Swallow*
TG *Tiger*
TM *Three Moons*
TP *Triumph*
VY *Victory*

FrP one or more of the French prizes taken at Le Havre, *viz.*: *BC, BE, BK, FL, GC, GD*, *GP, MD, OW, RH, RV, SH, SM, SP, TM*

dist. distinguished from
~ indicates repetition of preceding term
□ indicates new sub-entry

Offices and functions of the naval administration are treated under *Admiralty*. Most othe[r] subjects are grouped as: *animals*; *cloth*; *commodities and matter* (not covered by othe[r] groupings); *crimes and disorders*; *dockyards*; *dues*; *furniture/fittings*; *occupations*; *official[s]* (other than naval); *ordnance*; *seals*; *seamen*; *services*; *ships*; *soldiers*; *timber*; *tools*; *victualling*; *victuals*; *weather*; *weights and measures*.

For reasons of economy imposed by the Society, the index could not be completed to th[e] format of the companion volume.

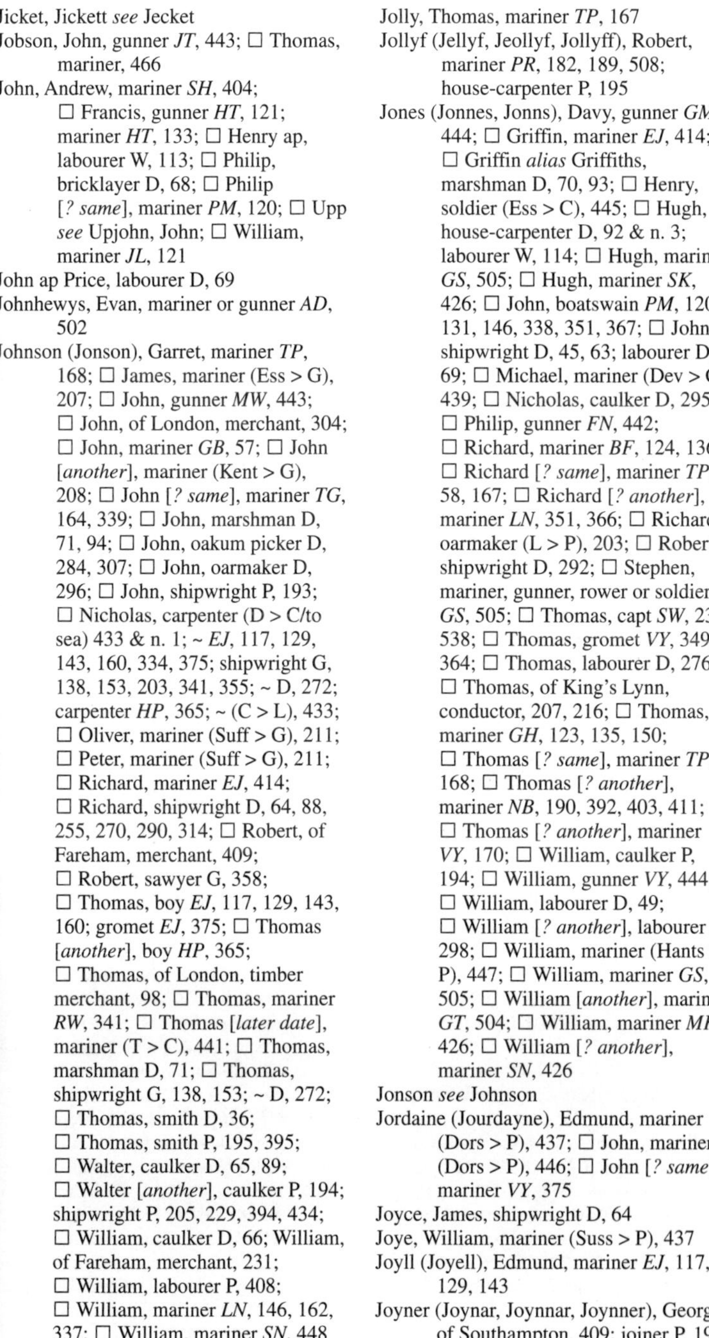

NAVY RECORDS SOCIETY
(FOUNDED 1893)

The Navy Records Society was established for the purpose of printing unpublished manuscripts and rare works of naval interest. Membership of the Society is open to all who are interested in naval history, and any person wishing to become a member should either complete the online application form on the Society's website, www.navyrecords.org.uk, or apply to the Hon. Secretary, Robin Brodhurst, The Mill, Stanford Dingley, Reading, RG7 6LS, United Kingdom, email address robinbrodhurst@gmail.com. The annual subscription is £40, which entitles the member to receive one free copy of each work issued by the Society in that year, and to buy earlier issues at reduced prices.

A list of works, available to members only, is shown below; very few copies are left of those marked with an asterisk. Volumes out of print are indicated by **OP**. Prices for works in print are available on application to Mrs Annette Gould, 8 Hawthorn Way, Lindford, Hampshire, GU35 0RB, United Kingdom, to whom all enquiries concerning works in print should be sent. Those marked 'TS', 'SP' and 'A' are published for the Society by Temple Smith, Scolar Press and Ashgate, and are available to non-members from Ashgate Publishing Limited, Wey Court East, Union Road, Farnham, Surrey, GU9 7PT, United Kingdom. Those marked 'A & U' are published by George Allen & Unwin, and are available to non-members only through bookshops.

Vol. 1. *State papers relating to the Defeat of the Spanish Armada, Anno 1588*, Vol. I, ed. Professor J. K. Laughton. TS.

Vol. 2. *State papers relating to the Defeat of the Spanish Armada, Anno 1588*, Vol. II, ed. Professor J. K. Laughton. TS.

Vol. 3. *Letters of Lord Hood, 1781–1783*, ed. D. Hannay. **OP**.

Vol. 4. *Index to James's Naval History*, by C. G. Toogood, ed. by the Hon. T. A. Brassey. **OP**.

Vol. 5. *Life of Captain Stephen Martin, 1666–1740*, ed. Sir Clements R. Markham. **OP**.

Vol. 6. *Journal of Rear Admiral Bartholomew James, 1752–1828*, ed. Professor J. K. Laughton & Cdr. J. Y. F. Sullivan. **OP**.

Vol. 7. *Hollond's Discourses of the Navy, 1638 and 1659*, ed. J. R. Tanner. **OP**.

Vol. 8. *Naval Accounts and Inventories in the Reign of Henry VII*, ed. M. Oppenheim. **OP**.

Vol. 9. *Journal of Sir George Rooke*, ed. O. Browning. **OP**.

Vol. 10. *Letters and Papers relating to the War with France 1512–1513*, ed. M. Alfred Spont. **OP**.

Vol. 11. *Papers relating to the Spanish War 1585–1587*, ed. Julian S. Corbett. TS.

Vol. 12. *Journals and Letters of Admiral of the Fleet Sir Thomas Byam Martin, 1773–1854*, Vol. II (see No. 24), ed. Admiral Sir R. Vesey Hamilton. **OP**.

Vol. 13. *Papers relating to the First Dutch War, 1652–1654*, Vol. I, ed. Dr S. R. Gardiner. **OP**.

Vol. 14. *Papers relating to the Blockade of Brest, 1803–1805*, Vol. I, ed. J. Leyland. **OP**.

Vol. 15. *History of the Russian Fleet during the Reign of Peter the Great, by a Contemporary Englishman*, ed. Admiral Sir Cyprian Bridge. **OP**.

Vol. 16. *Logs of the Great Sea Fights, 1794–1805*, Vol. I, ed. Vice Admiral Sir T. Sturges Jackson. **OP**.

Vol. 17. *Papers relating to the First Dutch War, 1652–1654*, Vol. II, ed. Dr S. R. Gardiner. **OP**.

Vol. 18. *Logs of the Great Sea Fights*, Vol. II, ed. Vice Admiral Sir T. Sturges Jackson.

Vol. 19. *Journals and Letters of Admiral of the Fleet Sir Thomas Byam Martin*, Vol. II (see No. 24), ed. Admiral Sir R. Vesey Hamilton. **OP**.

Vol. 20. *The Naval Miscellany*, Vol. I, ed. Professor J. K. Laughton.

Vol. 21. *Papers relating to the Blockade of Brest, 1803–1805*, Vol. II, ed. J. Leyland. **OP**.

Vol. 22. *The Naval Tracts of Sir William Monson*, Vol. I, ed. M. Oppenheim. **OP**.

Vol. 23. *The Naval Tracts of Sir William Monson*, Vol. II, ed. M. Oppenheim. **OP**.

Vol. 24. *The Journals and Letters of Admiral of the Fleet Sir Thomas Byam Martin*, Vol. I, ed. Admiral Sir R. Vesey Hamilton.

Vol. 25. *Nelson and the Neapolitan Jacobins*, ed. H. C. Gutteridge. **OP**.

Vol. 26. *A Descriptive Catalogue of the Naval MSS in the Pepysian Library*, Vol. I, ed. J. R. Tanner. **OP**.

Vol. 27. *A Descriptive Catalogue of the Naval MSS in the Pepysian Library*, Vol. II, ed. J. R. Tanner. **OP**.

Vol. 28. *The Correspondence of Admiral John Markham, 1801–1807*, ed. Sir Clements R. Markham. **OP**.

Vol. 29. *Fighting Instructions, 1530–1816*, ed. Julian S. Corbett. **OP**.

Vol. 30. *Papers relating to the First Dutch War, 1652–1654*, Vol. III, ed. Dr S. R. Gardiner & C. T. Atkinson. **OP**.

Vol. 31. *The Recollections of Commander James Anthony Gardner, 1775–1814*, ed. Admiral Sir R. Vesey Hamilton & Professor J. K. Laughton.

Vol. 32. *Letters and Papers of Charles, Lord Barham, 1758–1813*, ed. Professor Sir John Laughton.

Vol. 33. *Naval Songs and Ballads*, ed. Professor C. H. Firth. **OP**.

Vol. 34. *Views of the Battles of the Third Dutch War*, ed. by Julian S. Corbett. **OP**.

Vol. 35. *Signals and Instructions, 1776–1794*, ed. Julian S. Corbett. **OP**.

Vol. 36. *A Descriptive Catalogue of the Naval MSS in the Pepysian Library*, Vol. III, ed. J. R. Tanner. **OP**.

Vol. 37. *Papers relating to the First Dutch War, 1652–1654*, Vol. IV, ed. C. T. Atkinson. **OP**.

Vol. 38. *Letters and Papers of Charles, Lord Barham, 1758–1813*, Vol. II, ed. Professor Sir John Laughton. **OP**.

Vol. 39. *Letters and Papers of Charles, Lord Barham, 1758–1813*, Vol. III, ed. Professor Sir John Laughton. **OP**.

Vol. 40. *The Naval Miscellany*, Vol. II, ed. Professor Sir John Laughton.

*Vol. 41. *Papers relating to the First Dutch War, 1652–1654*, Vol. V, ed. C. T. Atkinson.

Vol. 42. *Papers relating to the Loss of Minorca in 1756*, ed. Captain H. W. Richmond, R.N. **OP**.

*Vol. 43. *The Naval Tracts of Sir William Monson*, Vol. III, ed. M. Oppenheim.

Vol. 44. *The Old Scots Navy 1689–1710*, ed. James Grant. **OP**.

Vol. 45. *The Naval Tracts of Sir William Monson*, Vol. IV, ed. M. Oppenheim.

Vol. 46. *The Private Papers of George, 2nd Earl Spencer*, Vol. I, ed. Julian S. Corbett. **OP**.

Vol. 47. *The Naval Tracts of Sir William Monson*, Vol. V, ed. M. Oppenheim.

Vol. 48. *The Private Papers of George, 2nd Earl Spencer*, Vol. II, ed. Julian S. Corbett. **OP**.

Vol. 49. *Documents relating to Law and Custom of the Sea*, Vol. I, ed. R. G. Marsden. **OP**.

*Vol. 50. *Documents relating to Law and Custom of the Sea*, Vol. II, ed. R. G. Marsden.

Vol. 51. *Autobiography of Phineas Pett*, ed. W. G. Perrin. **OP**.

Vol. 52. *The Life of Admiral Sir John Leake*, Vol. I, ed. Geoffrey Callender.

Vol. 53. *The Life of Admiral Sir John Leake*, Vol. II, ed. Geoffrey Callender.

Vol. 54. *The Life and Works of Sir Henry Mainwaring*, Vol. I, ed. G. E. Manwaring.

Vol. 55. *The Letters of Lord St Vincent, 1801–1804*, Vol. I, ed. D. B. Smith. **OP**.

Vol. 56. *The Life and Works of Sir Henry Mainwaring*, Vol. II, ed. G. E. Manwaring & W. G. Perrin. **OP**.

Vol. 57. *A Descriptive Catalogue of the Naval MSS in the Pepysian Library*, Vol. IV, ed. Dr J. R. Tanner. **OP**.

Vol. 58. *The Private Papers of George, 2nd Earl Spencer*, Vol. III, ed. Rear Admiral H. W. Richmond. **OP**.

Vol. 59. *The Private Papers of George, 2nd Earl Spencer*, Vol. IV, ed. Rear Admiral H. W. Richmond. **OP**.

Vol. 60. *Samuel Pepys's Naval Minutes*, ed. Dr J. R. Tanner.

Vol. 61. *The Letters of Lord St Vincent, 1801–1804*, Vol. II, ed. D. B. Smith. **OP**.

Vol. 62. *Letters and Papers of Admiral Viscount Keith*, Vol. I, ed. W. G. Perrin. **OP**.

Vol. 63. *The Naval Miscellany*, Vol. III, ed. W. G. Perrin. **OP**.

Vol. 64. *The Journal of the 1st Earl of Sandwich*, ed. R. C. Anderson. **OP**.

*Vol. 65. *Boteler's Dialogues*, ed. W. G. Perrin.

Vol. 66. *Papers relating to the First Dutch War, 1652–1654*, Vol. VI (with index), ed. C. T. Atkinson.

*Vol. 67. *The Byng Papers*, Vol. I, ed. W. C. B. Tunstall.

*Vol. 68. *The Byng Papers*, Vol. II, ed. W. C. B. Tunstall.

Vol. 69. *The Private Papers of John, Earl of Sandwich*, Vol. I, ed. G. R. Barnes & Lt. Cdr. J. H. Owen, R.N. Corrigenda to *Papers relating to the First Dutch War, 1652–1654, Vols I–VI*, ed. Captain A. C. Dewar, R.N. **OP**.

Vol. 70. *The Byng Papers*, Vol. III, ed. W. C. B. Tunstall.

Vol. 71. *The Private Papers of John, Earl of Sandwich*, Vol. II, ed. G. R. Barnes & Lt. Cdr. J. H. Owen, R.N. **OP**.

Vol. 72. *Piracy in the Levant, 1827–1828*, ed. Lt. Cdr. C. G. Pitcairn Jones, R.N. **OP**.

Vol. 73. *The Tangier Papers of Samuel Pepys*, ed. Edwin Chappell.

Vol. 74. *The Tomlinson Papers*, ed. J. G. Bullocke.
Vol. 75. *The Private Papers of John, Earl of Sandwich*, Vol. III, ed. G. R. Barnes & Cdr. J. H. Owen, R.N. **OP**.
Vol. 76. *The Letters of Robert Blake*, ed. the Rev. J. R. Powell. **OP**.
*Vol. 77. *Letters and Papers of Admiral the Hon. Samuel Barrington*, Vol. I, ed. D. Bonner-Smith.
Vol. 78. *The Private Papers of John, Earl of Sandwich*, Vol. IV, ed. G. R. Barnes & Cdr. J. H. Owen, R.N. **OP**.
*Vol. 79. *The Journals of Sir Thomas Allin, 1660–1678*, Vol. I *1660–1666*, ed. R. C. Anderson.
Vol. 80. *The Journals of Sir Thomas Allin, 1660–1678*, Vol. II *1667–1678*, ed. R. C. Anderson.
Vol. 81. *Letters and Papers of Admiral the Hon. Samuel Barrington*, Vol. II, ed. D. Bonner-Smith. **OP**.
Vol. 82. *Captain Boteler's Recollections, 1808–1830*, ed. D. Bonner-Smith. **OP**.
Vol. 83. *Russian War, 1854. Baltic and Black Sea: Official Correspondence*, ed. D. Bonner-Smith & Captain A. C. Dewar, R.N. **OP**.
Vol. 84. *Russian War, 1855. Baltic: Official Correspondence*, ed. D. Bonner-Smith. **OP**.
Vol. 85. *Russian War, 1855. Black Sea: Official Correspondence*, ed. Captain A.C. Dewar, R.N. **OP**.
Vol. 86. *Journals and Narratives of the Third Dutch War*, ed. R. C. Anderson. **OP**.
Vol. 87. *The Naval Brigades in the Indian Mutiny, 1857–1858*, ed. Cdr. W. B. Rowbotham, R.N. **OP**.
Vol. 88. *Patee Byng's Journal*, ed. J. L. Cranmer-Byng. **OP**.
*Vol. 89. *The Sergison Papers, 1688–1702*, ed. Cdr. R. D. Merriman, R.I.N.
Vol. 90. *The Keith Papers*, Vol. II, ed. Christopher Lloyd. **OP**.
Vol. 91. *Five Naval Journals, 1789–1817*, ed. Rear Admiral H. G. Thursfield. **OP**.
Vol. 92. *The Naval Miscellany*, Vol. IV, ed. Christopher Lloyd. **OP**.
Vol. 93. *Sir William Dillon's Narrative of Professional Adventures, 1790–1839*, Vol. I *1790–1802*, ed. Professor Michael Lewis. **OP**.
Vol. 94. *The Walker Expedition to Quebec, 1711*, ed. Professor Gerald S. Graham. **OP**.
Vol. 95. *The Second China War, 1856–1860*, ed. D. Bonner-Smith & E. W. R. Lumby. **OP**.
Vol. 96. *The Keith Papers, 1803–1815*, Vol. III, ed. Professor Christopher Lloyd.

Vol. 97. *Sir William Dillon's Narrative of Professional Adventures, 1790–1839*, Vol. II *1802–1839*, ed. Professor Michael Lewis. **OP**.

Vol. 98. *The Private Correspondence of Admiral Lord Collingwood*, ed. Professor Edward Hughes. **OP**.

Vol. 99. *The Vernon Papers, 1739–1745*, ed. B. McL. Ranft. **OP**.

Vol. 100. *Nelson's Letters to his Wife and Other Documents*, ed. Lt. Cdr. G. P. B. Naish, R.N.V.R.

Vol. 101. *A Memoir of James Trevenen, 1760–1790*, ed. Professor Christopher Lloyd & R. C. Anderson. **OP**.

Vol. 102. *The Papers of Admiral Sir John Fisher*, Vol. I, ed. Lt. Cdr. P. K. Kemp, R.N. **OP**.

Vol. 103. *Queen Anne's Navy*, ed. Cdr. R. D. Merriman, R.I.N. **OP**.

Vol. 104. *The Navy and South America, 1807–1823*, ed. Professor Gerald S. Graham & Professor R. A. Humphreys.

Vol. 105. *Documents relating to the Civil War, 1642–1648*, ed. The Rev. J. R. Powell & E. K. Timings. **OP**.

Vol. 106. *The Papers of Admiral Sir John Fisher*, Vol. II, ed. Lt. Cdr. P. K. Kemp, R.N. **OP**.

Vol. 107. *The Health of Seamen*, ed. Professor Christopher Lloyd.

Vol. 108. *The Jellicoe Papers*, Vol. I *1893–1916*, ed. A. Temple Patterson.

Vol. 109. *Documents relating to Anson's Voyage round the World, 1740–1744*, ed. Glyndwr Williams. **OP**.

Vol. 110. *The Saumarez Papers: The Baltic, 1808–1812*, ed. A. N. Ryan. **OP**.

Vol. 111. *The Jellicoe Papers*, Vol. II *1916–1925*, ed. Professor A. Temple Patterson.

Vol. 112. *The Rupert and Monck Letterbook, 1666*, ed. The Rev. J. R. Powell & E. K. Timings. **OP** (damaged stock available).

Vol. 113. *Documents relating to the Royal Naval Air Service*, Vol. I (1908–1918), ed. Captain S. W. Roskill, R.N. **OP** (damaged stock available).

*Vol. 114. *The Siege and Capture of Havana, 1762*, ed. Professor David Syrett. **OP** (damaged stock available).

Vol. 115. *Policy and Operations in the Mediterranean, 1912–1914*, ed E. W. R. Lumby. **OP**.

Vol. 116. *The Jacobean Commissions of Enquiry, 1608 and 1618*, ed. A. P. McGowan.

Vol. 117. *The Keyes Papers*, Vol. I *1914–1918*, ed. Professor Paul Halpern.

Vol. 118. *The Royal Navy and North America: The Warren Papers, 1736–1752*, ed. Julian Gwyn. **OP**.

Vol. 119. *The Manning of the Royal Navy: Selected Public Pamphlets, 1693–1873*, ed. Professor John Bromley.

Vol. 120. *Naval Administration, 1715–1750*, ed. Professor D. A. Baugh.

Vol. 121. *The Keyes Papers*, Vol. II *1919–1938*, ed. Professor Paul Halpern.

Vol. 122. *The Keyes Papers*, Vol. III *1939–1945*, ed. Professor Paul Halpern.

Vol. 123. *The Navy of the Lancastrian Kings: Accounts and Inventories of William Soper, Keeper of the King's Ships, 1422–1427*, ed. Susan Rose.

Vol. 124. *The Pollen Papers: the Privately Circulated Printed Works of Arthur Hungerford Pollen, 1901–1916*, ed. Professor Jon T. Sumida. A. & U.

Vol. 125. *The Naval Miscellany*, Vol. V, ed. Dr N. A. M. Rodger. A & U.

Vol. 126. *The Royal Navy in the Mediterranean, 1915–1918*, ed. Professor Paul Halpern. TS.

Vol. 127. *The Expedition of Sir John Norris and Sir Francis Drake to Spain and Portugal, 1589*, ed. Professor R. B. Wernham. TS.

Vol. 128. *The Beatty Papers*, Vol. I *1902–1918*, ed. Professor B. McL. Ranft. SP.

Vol. 129. *The Hawke Papers: A Selection, 1743–1771*, ed. Dr R. F. Mackay. SP.

Vol. 130. *Anglo-American Naval Relations, 1917–1919*, ed. Michael Simpson. SP.

Vol. 131. *British Naval Documents, 1204–1960*, ed. Professor John B. Hattendorf, Roger Knight, Alan Pearsall, Dr Nicholas Rodger & Professor Geoffrey Till. SP.

Vol. 132. *The Beatty Papers*, Vol. II *1916–1927*, ed. Professor B. McL. Ranft. SP

Vol. 133. *Samuel Pepys and the Second Dutch War*, transcribed by Professor William Matthews & Charles Knighton; ed. Robert Latham. SP.

Vol. 134. *The Somerville Papers*, ed. Michael Simpson, with the assistance of John Somerville. SP.

Vol. 135. *The Royal Navy in the River Plate, 1806–1807*, ed. John D. Grainger. SP.

Vol. 136. *The Collective Naval Defence of the Empire, 1900–1940*, ed. Nicholas Tracy. A.

Vol. 137. *The Defeat of the Enemy Attack on Shipping, 1939–1945*, ed. Professor Eric Grove. A.

Vol. 138. *Shipboard Life and Organisation, 1731–1815*, ed. Brian Lavery. A.

Vol. 139. *The Battle of the Atlantic and Signals Intelligence: U-boat Situations and Trends, 1941–1945*, ed. Professor David Syrett. A.
Vol. 140. *The Cunningham Papers*, Vol. I: *The Mediterranean Fleet, 1939–1942*, ed. Michael Simpson. A.
Vol. 141. *The Channel Fleet and the Blockade of Brest, 1793–1801*, ed. Roger Morriss. A.
Vol. 142. *The Submarine Service, 1900–1918*, ed. Nicholas Lambert. A.
Vol. 143. *Letters and Papers of Professor Sir John Knox Laughton (1830–1915)*, ed. Professor Andrew Lambert. A.
Vol. 144. *The Battle of the Atlantic and Signals Intelligence: U-Boat Tracking Papers 1941–1947*, ed. Professor David Syrett. A.
Vol. 145. *The Maritime Blockade of Germany in the Great War: The Northern Patrol, 1914–1918*, ed. John D. Grainger. A.
Vol. 146. *The Naval Miscellany*, Vol. VI, ed. Michael Duffy. A.
Vol. 147. *The Milne Papers*, Vol. I *1820–1859*, ed. Professor John Beeler. A.
Vol. 148. *The Rodney Papers*, Vol. I *1742–1763*, ed. Professor David Syrett. A.
Vol. 149. *Sea Power and the Control of Trade. Belligerent Rights from the Russian War to the Beira Patrol, 1854–1970*, ed. Nicholas Tracy. A.
Vol. 150. *The Cunningham Papers*, Vol. II: *The Triumph of Allied Sea Power 1942–1946*, ed. Michael Simpson. A.
Vol. 151. *The Rodney Papers*, Vol. II *1763–1780*, ed. Professor David Syrett. A.
Vol. 152. *Naval Intelligence from Germany: The Reports of the British Naval Attachés in Berlin, 1906–1914*, ed. Matthew S. Seligmann. A.
Vol. 153. *The Naval Miscellany*, Vol. VII, ed. Susan Rose. A.
Vol. 154. *The Chatham Dockyard, 1815–1865*, ed. Philip MacDougall. A.
Vol. 155. *Naval Courts Martial, 1793–1815*, ed. John D. Byrn. A.
Vol. 156. *Anglo-American Naval Relations, 1919–1939*, ed. Michael Simpson. A.
Vol. 157. *The Navy of Edward VI and Mary I*, ed. C. S. Knighton & Professor David Loades. A.
Vol. 158. *The Mediterranean Fleet, 1919–1929*, ed. Paul Halpern. A.
Vol. 159. *The Fleet Air Arm in the Second World War*, ed. Ben Jones. A

Occasional Publications:

Vol. 1. *The Commissioned Sea Officers of the Royal Navy, 1660–1815*, ed. Professor David Syrett & Professor R. L. DiNardo. SP.

Vol. 2. *The Anthony Roll of Henry VIII's Navy*, ed. C. S. Knighton & Professor D. M. Loades. A.